LARGEST ISLAND/
Most Northerly Land p.61
Northernmost Volcano p.56
Longest Fjord p.59
Oldest Rock p.60

Largest Area
below Sea Level p.61
Largest Lake p.64
•Largest Swamp p.61

•Biggest Larva Flow p.55

Largest Bay p.59

Tallest
Stalagmite p.62
Deepest Cave p.62

Highest Mountain p.62
Greatest Plateau p.62
Highest Lake p.64

•Greatest Tide p.60

Largest Stalactite p.61•

Greatest Mountain Range p.62•

Most Southerly
Arctic Iceberg p.60

•Deepest Depression
p.61

Highest Waterfall
p.63

LARGEST DESERT
p.64

•Largest
Peninsula
p.61

Greatest River
and Estuary p.63
Longest Tributary/
Longest Sub-Tributary p.63
Largest Freshwater Island p.61
Greatest River Basin p.63

Longest River
p.63

Largest Delta p.63

•Greatest Waterfall p.63

Highest Navigable Lake p.64

Deepest
Gorge p.65

•Most Northerly Antarctic Iceberg p.60

Highest Volcano/
Highest Dormant Volcano/
Highest Active Volcano p.55

•Remotest Inhabited Island p.61

•Remotest Island p.61

•Greatest Current p.59

Southernmost Volcano p.56
Deepest Depression p.61

GUINNESS BOOKS

Guinness Superlatives Ltd., 2 Cecil Court, London Road, Enfield, Middlesex

TITLE PAGE ILLUSTRATION: THE ROYAL MARINES FREE FALL PARACHUTE TEAM WITH A NEW
BRITISH AND EUROPEAN STACKING RECORD OF 17. SEE P. 191

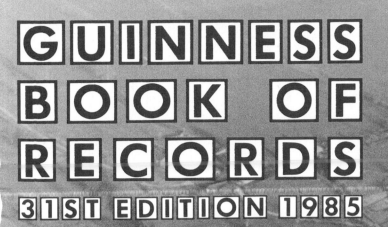

GUINNESS BOOK OF RECORDS
31ST EDITION 1985

Editor and Compiler
NORRIS D. McWHIRTER
(with the late A. ROSS McWHIRTER from 1955 to 1975)

Assistant General Editor
MOIRA F. STOWE

Art Editor
DAVID ROBERTS

Correspondence Editor
COLIN SMITH

Sports Editor
PETER J. MATTHEWS

Assistant Sports Editor
JULIAN FARINO

British Library Cataloguing in Publication Data

Guinness book of records.—31
  1. Curiosities and wonders—Periodicals
032′.02   AG240

ISBN 0–85112–419–4

Standard Book Number ISBN: 0 85112 419 4
Standard Book Number ISBN: 0–85112 420 8 (*Australian Edition*)

Printed in England. Produced by William Clowes Limited, Beccles, Suffolk.
Printed by Jarrold Printing, Norwich, Norfolk.
Litho origination by East Anglian Engraving, Norwich, Norfolk.

hernia operation. His height progressed as follows:

Age in Years	Height		Weight lb	Weight kg	Age in Years	Height		Weight lb	Weight kg
5	5′ 4″	*163 cm*	105	*48*	15	7′ 8″	*234 cm*	355	*161*
8	6′ 0″	*183 cm*	169	*77*	16	7′ 10½″	*240 cm*	374	*170*
9	6′ 2½″	*189 cm*	180	*82*	17	8′ 0½″	*245 cm*	315[1]	*143*
10	6′ 5″	*196 cm*	210	*95*	18	8′ 3½″	*253 cm*	—	—
11	6′ 7″	*200 cm*	—	—	19	8′ 5½″	*258 cm*	480	*218*
12	6′ 10½″	*210 cm*	—	—	20	8′ 6¾″	*261 cm*	—	—
13	7′ 1¾″	*218 cm*	255	*116*	21	8′ 8¼″	*265 cm*	491	*223*
14	7′ 5″	*226 cm*	301	*137*	22.4[2]	8′ 11″	*272 cm*	439	*199*

[1] *Following severe influenza and infection of the foot.*
[2] *Wadlow was still growing during his terminal illness.*

Dr C. M. Charles, Associate Professor of Anatomy at Washington University's School of Medicine in St Louis, Missouri and Dr Cyril MacBryde measured Robert Wadlow at 272 cm *8 ft 11.1 in* in St Louis on 27 June 1940. Wadlow died 18 days later in a hotel, at 1.30 a.m. on 15 July 1940, in Manistee, Michigan as a result of cellulitis (inflammation of cellular tissue) of the right ankle aggravated by a brace, which had been poorly fitted only a week earlier.

He was buried in Oakwood Cemetery, Alton, Illinois in a coffin measuring 10 ft 9 in *328 cm* in length, 32 in *81 cm* wide and 30 in *76 cm* deep. His greatest recorded weight was 35 st 1 lb *222,71 kg*, on his 21st birthday. He weighed 31 st 5 lb *199 kg* at the time of his death. His shoes were size 37AA (18½ in *47 cm* long) and his hands measured 12¾ in *32,5 cm* from the wrist to the tip of the middle finger (*cf.* the depth of this page at 11 in *27,9 cm*). He wore a size 25 ring.

His arm span was 9 ft 5¾ in *288 cm* and his peak daily consumption attained 8000 calories. At the age of 9 he was able to carry his father, Harold F. Wadlow (d. Sept 1967) later Mayor of Alton, who stood 5 ft 11 in *182 cm* and weighed 170 lb *72 kg*, up the stairs of the family home. His last words were 'The doctor says I won't get home for the . . . celebrations' (a reference to his paternal grandparents golden wedding).

GIANT LEAGUE

The only other men for whom heights of 8 ft *244 cm* or more have been reliably reported are the ten listed below. In seven cases, gigantism was followed by acromegaly, a disorder which causes an enlargement of the nose, lips, tongue, lower jaw, hands and feet, due to renewed activity by an already swollen pituitary gland, which is located at the base of the brain.

John F. Carroll (1932–69) of Buffalo, New York State, USA (1) 8 ft 7¾ in *263,5 cm.*

John William Rogan (1871–1905), a Negro of Gallatin, Tennessee, USA (2) 8 ft 6 in *259,1 cm.*

Don Koehler (1925–81) of Denton, Montana, USA (4) 8 ft 2 in *248,9 cm*, latterly lived in Chicago.

Bernard Coyne (1897–1921) of Anthon, Iowa USA (5) 8 ft 2 in *248,9 cm.*

Väinö Myllyrinne (1909–63) of Helsinki, Finland (6) 8 ft 1.2 in *247 cm.*

Patrick Cotter O'Brien (1760–1806) of Kinsale, County Cork, Ireland (7) 8 ft 1 in *246 cm.*

'Constantine' (1872–1902) of Reutlingen, West Germany (8) 8 ft 0.8 in *245,8 cm.*

Gabriel Estevao Monjane (b. 1944–*fl.* 1984) of Monjacaze, Mozambique (9) *c.* 8 ft 0¾ in *245,7 cm.*

Sulaimān 'Ali Nashnush (b. 1943–*fl.* 1984) of Tripoli, Libya (10) 8 ft 0.4 in *245 cm.*

(1) *Severe kypho-scoliosis (two dimensional spinal curvature). The figure represents his height with assumed normal spinal curvature, calculated from a standing height of 8 ft 0 in* 244 cm, *measured on 14 Oct 1959. His standing height was 7 ft 8¼ in* 234 cm *shortly before his death.*
(2) *Measured in a sitting position. Unable to stand owing to ankylosis (stiffening of the joints through the formation of adhesions) of the knees and hips. Weighed only 175 lb* 79 kg.
(3) *Started growing abnormally at the age of 12. Has been credited with heights up to 8 ft 6 in* 259 cm.
(4) *Spinal curvature reduced his standing height to c. 7 ft 10 in* 238,4 cm. *Abnormal growth started at the age of 10. He had a twin sister who is 5 ft 9 in* 175 cm *tall. His father was 6 ft 2 in* 187 cm *and his mother 5 ft 10 in* 177 cm.
(5) *Eunuchoidal giant (Daddy long-legs syndrome). Rejected by Army in 1918 when 7 ft 9 in* 236 cm. *Still growing at time of death.*
(6) *Stood 7 ft 3½ in* 222 cm *at the age of 21 years. Experienced a second phase of growth in his late thirties and may have stood 8 ft 3 in* 251 cm *at one time.*
(7) *Revised height based on skeletal remeasurement in 1975.*
(8) *Eunuchoidal. Height estimated, as both legs were amputated after they turned gangrenous. He claimed a height of 8 ft 6 in* 259 cm.
(9) *Eunuchoidal. Measured 7 ft 5 in* 226 cm *at the age of 16 and 7 ft 10 in* 238,7 cm *in Dec 1965. Latest measurement taken in May 1967. Has not been anthropometrically assessed since joining a Portuguese circus (billed height 265 cm* 8 ft 8⅓ in).
(10) *Operation to correct abnormal growth successfully carried out in Rome in 1960.*

A table of the tallest giants of all-time in the 31 countries with men taller than 7 ft 4 in *223,5 cm* was listed in the 15th edition of the *Guinness Book of Records* (1968) at page 9.

Muhammad Aalam Channa (b. Sehwan, 1956), who works as an attendant at the shrine of Lal Shahbaz Qalandar in Pakistan assumed the role of the world's tallest man in 1981 with the death of Don Koehler (see above). A height of 8 ft 2¾ in *251 cm* attributed to him by news agencies and the international press was proved in 1984 to be exaggerated by 4.5 in *15 cm.* The tallest living humans are thus Monjane and Nashnush (see above).

England

The tallest Englishman ever recorded was William Bradley (1787–1820), born in Market Weighton, Humberside. He stood 7 ft 9 in *236 cm.* John Middleton (1578–1623), the famous Childe of Hale, from near Liverpool, was credited with a height of 9 ft 3 in *282 cm* but a life-size impression of his right hand (length 11½ in *29,2 cm, cf.* Wadlow's 12¾ in *32,4 cm*) painted on a panel in Brasenose College, Oxford indicates his true stature was nearer 7 ft 8 in *233,3 cm.* James Toller (1795–1819) of St Neots, Cambridgeshire was alleged to be 8 ft 6 in *259 cm* but was actually 7 ft 6 in *229 cm.* Albert Brough (1871–1919), a publican of Nottingham, reached a height of 7 ft 7½ in *232 cm.* Frederick Kempster (1889–1918) of Bayswater, London, was reported to have measured 8 ft 4½ in *255 cm* at the time of his death, but photographic evidence suggests that his height was 7 ft 8½ in *235 cm.*

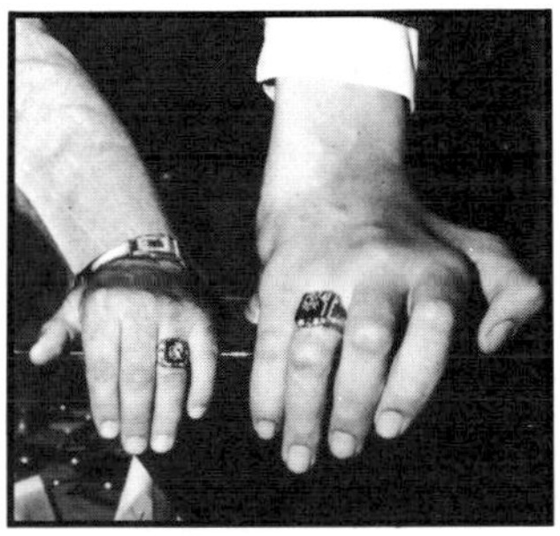

above: **The largest hand in the world surmounted by the world's largest ring (size 25) both belonging to Robert Wadlow.** (*Robert K Graul, Alton Telegraph*)

right: **The long and the short of it. Robert Wadlow, (8 ft 11.1 in *272 cm*) alongside Pauline Musters, (23.2 in *59 cm*) (see also p. 6).**

He measured 234 cm *7 ft 8.1 in* in 1913. Henry Daglish, who stood 7 ft 7 in *231 cm* died in Upper Stratton, Wiltshire, on 16 March 1951, aged 25. The much-publicised Edward (Ted) Evans (1924–58) of Englefield Green, Surrey, was reputed to be 9 ft 3 in *282 cm* but actually stood 7 ft 8½ in *235 cm*. The tallest fully mobile man now living in Great Britain is Christopher Paul Greener (b. New Brighton, Merseyside, 21 Nov 1943) of Hayes, Kent, who measures 7 ft 6¼ in *229 cm* (weight 26 st *165 kg*). Terence Keenan (b. 1942) of Rock Ferry, Merseyside measured 7 ft 6 in *229 cm* in 1968, but is confined to a wheelchair owing to a leg condition. His abnormal growth began at the age of 17 when he was only 5 ft 4 in *163 cm* tall.

Scotland

The tallest Scotsman, and the tallest recorded 'true' (non-pathological) giant, was Angus Macaskill (1825–63), born on the island of Berneray, in the Sound of Harris, in the Western Isles. He stood 7 ft 9 in *236 cm* and died in St Anns', on Cape Breton Island, Nova Scotia, Canada. Lambert Quételet (1796–1874), a Belgian anthropometrist, considered that a Scotsman named MacQuail, known as 'the Scotch Giant', stood 8 ft 3 in *251 cm*. He served in the famous regiment of giants of Frederick William I (1688–1740), King of Prussia. His skeleton, now in the Staatliche Museum zu Berlin, East Germany, measures 220 cm *7 ft 2.6 in*. Sam McDonald (1762–1802) of Lairg in Sutherland, was reputed to be 8 ft *244 cm* tall but actually stood 6 ft 10 in *208 cm*. William Olding (b. 1914–*fl.* 1942) of Glasgow measured 7 ft 6½ in *230 cm* (weight 366 lb *166 kg*). The tallest Scotsman now living is George Gracie (b. 1938) of Forth, Strathclyde. He stands 7 ft 3 in *221 cm* and weighs 28 st *178 kg*. His brother Hugh (b. 1941) is 7 ft 0½ in *215 cm*.

Wales

The tallest Welshman on record was William Evans (1599–1634) of Monmouthshire, who was porter to King James I. He stood 7 ft 6 in *228,2 cm*.

Ireland

The tallest Irishman was the 8 ft 1 in *246 cm* tall Patrick Cotter O'Brien (1760–1806), born in Kinsale, County Cork. He died at Hotwells, Bristol (See Table p. 5).

Twins

The tallest twins (identical) ever recorded were the Knipe brothers (b. 1761–*fl.* 1780) of Magherafelt, near Londonderry, Northern Ireland, who both measured 7 ft 2 in *218,4 cm*. The world's tallest living twins (also identical) are Dan and Doug Busch (b. 12 Aug 1961) of Flagstaff, Arizona, USA who both measure 6 ft 11 in *210,8 cm*. Britain's tallest twins are Jonathan and Mark Carratt (b. 11 June 1955) of Maltby, South Yorkshire who are 6 ft 8 in *203,2 cm* and 6 ft 9 in *205,7 cm* respectively. David and John Moore (b. 29 Mar 1963) of Erith, Kent both measure 6 ft 8¼ in *203,6 cm*.

TALLEST GIANTESSES

World *All-time*

Giantesses are rarer than giants but their heights are still spectacular. The tallest woman in history was the acromegalic giantess Zeng Jinlian (pronounced San Chung Lin) (b. 26 June 1964) of Yujiang village in the Bright Moon Commune, Hunan Province, central China, who was 247 cm *8 ft 1 in* when she died on 13 Feb 1982. She began to grow abnormally from the age of 4 months and stood 156 cm *5 ft 1½ in* before her 4th birthday and 217 cm *7 ft 1½ in* when she was 13. Her hands measured 25,5 cm *10 in* and her feet 35,5 cm *14 in* in length. She suffered from both scoliosis and diabetes. Her parents are 163 cm *5 ft 4½ in* and 156 cm *5 ft 1½ in* while her brother was 158 cm *5 ft 2½ in* aged 18.

United Kingdom

The tallest woman in British medical history has been Jane ('Ginny') Bunford, born on 26 July 1895 at Bartley Green, Northfield, West Midlands, England. Her abnormal growth started at the age of 11 following a head injury, and on her 13th birthday she measured 6 ft 6 in *198 cm*. Shortly before her death on 1 April 1922 she stood 7 ft 7 in *231 cm* tall, but she had severe kyphoscoliosis and would have measured about 7 ft 11 in *241 cm* with assumed normal spinal curvature. Her skeleton, now preserved in the Anatomical Museum in the Medical School at Birmingham University, has a mounted height of 7 ft 4 in *223,5 cm*.

Living

The tallest living woman is Sandy Allen (b. 18 June 1955, Chicago) of Niagara Falls, Ontario, Canada. On 14 July 1977 she underwent a pituitary gland operation, which inhibited further growth at 7 ft 7¼ in *231,7 cm*. A 6½ lb *2,91 kg* baby, her acromegalic growth began soon after birth. She now weighs 33 st *209,5 kg* and takes a size 16EEE American shoe (=14½ UK or 50PP Continental).

Tallest Couple

Anna Hanen Swan (1846–88) of Nova Scotia, Canada, was billed at 8 ft 1 in *246 cm* but actually measured 7 ft 5½ in *227 cm*. In London on 17 June 1871 she married Martin van Buren Bates (1845–1919) of Whitesburg, Letcher County, Kentucky, USA, who stood 7 ft 2½ in *220 cm* making them the tallest married couple on record.

SHORTEST DWARFS

The strictures which apply to giants apply equally to dwarfs, except that exaggeration gives way to understatement. In the same way as 9 ft *274 cm* may be regarded as the limit towards which the tallest giants tend, so 23 in *58 cm* must be regarded as the limit towards which the shortest mature dwarfs tend (*cf.* the average length of new-born babies is 18–20 in *46–50 cm*). In the case of child dwarfs their *ages* are often enhanced by their agents or managers.

There are many forms of human dwarfism, but those suffering from ateleiosis (midgets) are generally the shortest. They have essentially normal proportions but suffer from growth hormone deficiency. Such dwarfs tended to be even shorter at a time when human stature was generally shorter due to lower nutritional standards.

World *All-time*

The shortest mature human of whom there is independent evidence was Pauline Musters ('Princess Pauline'), a Dutch midget. She was born at Ossendrecht, on 26 Feb 1876 and measured 30 cm *12 in* at birth. At the age of 9 she was 55 cm *21.65 in* tall and weighed only 1,5 kg *3 lb 5 oz*. She died, at the age of 19, of pneumonia, with meningitis, her heart weakened from alcoholic excesses, on 1 Mar 1895 in New York City, NY, USA. Although she was billed at 48 cm *19 in*, she had earlier been medically measured to be 59 cm *23.2 in* tall. A *post mortem* examination showed her to be exactly 61 cm *24 in* (there was some elongation after death). Her mature weight varied from 3,4–4 kg *7½–9 lb* and her 'vital statistics' were 47–48–43 cm *18½–19–17 in*, which suggests she was overweight.

In 1938 a height of 19 in *48 cm* was attributed to Paul Del Rio (b. Madrid, Spain, 1920) by *Life Magazine* when he visited Hollywood, but the fact that his presence created no great impression among other dwarfs in the film capital and that he weighed as much as 12 lb *5,4 kg* suggests that he was closer to 26 in *66 cm* tall.

In 1979 a height of 50 cm *19.68 in* and a weight of 4 lb 6 oz *1,98 kg* were reported for a nine-year-old Greek girl named Stamatoula being cared for at the Lyrion Convent, Athens. The child, believed to be the survivor of twins, is suffering from Seckel's 'bird-face' syndrome and growth had allegedly ceased, but in a similar case from Corsica the girl eventually reached a height of 34 in *86,3 cm* and a weight of 26 lb *11,8 kg*.

Male All-time

The shortest recorded adult male dwarf was Calvin Phillips, born on 14 Jan 1791 in Bridgewater, Massachusetts, USA. He weighed 2 lb *907 g* at birth and stopped growing at the age of 5. When he was 19 he measured 26½ in *67 cm* tall and weighed 12 lb *5,4 kg* with his clothes on. He died two years later, in April 1812, from progeria, a rare disorder characterised by dwarfism and premature senility.

Living

The world's shortest known mobile living adult human is Antonio Ferreira (b. 1943), a rachitic dwarf of Arcozelo, Portugal who measures 75 cm *29½ in*. He is a professional drummer. In July 1982 an unconfirmed height of 28 in *71 cm* was reported for a chicken farmer named Ghucam Ahmed Dar living near Srinagar in Kashmir, India.

United Kingdom

The shortest mature human ever recorded in Britain was Miss

Joyce Carpenter (b. 21 Dec 1929), a rachitic dwarf of Charford, Hereford and Worcester, who stood 29 in *74 cm* tall and weighed 30 lb *13,60 kg*. She died on 7 Aug 1973 aged 43. Hopkins Hopkins (1737–54) of Llantrisant, Mid Glamorgan was 31 in *79 cm*. Hopkins, who died from progeria weighed 19 lb *8,62 kg* at the age of 7 and 13 lb *6 kg* at the time of his death. There are an estimated 2000 people of severely restricted growth, (i.e. under 4 ft 8 in *142 cm*), living in Britain today.

The shortest adult living in Britain is Michael Henbury-Ballan (b. 26 Nov 1938) of Bassett, Southampton, who is 37 in *91 cm* tall and weighs 5½ st *35 kg*. A 5 lb 14 oz *2,66 kg* baby, he stopped growing at the age of 13 years. His fraternal twin brother Malcolm is 5 ft 9 in *175 cm* tall and weighs 11 st 7 lb *73 kg*.

Twins shortest

The shortest twins ever recorded were the primordial dwarfs Matjus and Bela Matina (b. 1903–fl. 1935) of Budapest, Hungary who later became naturalized Americans. They both measured 30 in *76 cm*. The world's shortest living twins are John and Greg Rice (b. 1952) of Palm Beach, Florida, USA who both measure 34 in *86,3 cm*.

Oldest

There are only two centenarian dwarfs on record. The older is Hungarian-born Miss Susanna Bokoyni ('Princess Susanna') of Newton, New Jersey, USA who celebrated her 104th birthday on 6 Apr 1983. She is 3 ft 4 in *101 cm* tall and weighs 37 lb *16,78 kg*. The other was Miss Anne Clowes of Matlock, Derbyshire, who died on 5 Aug 1784 aged 103 years. She was 3 ft 9 in *114 cm* tall and weighed 48 lb *21,7 kg*.

Most variable stature

Adam Rainer, born in Graz, Austria, in 1899, measured 118 cm *3 ft 10.45 in* at the age of 21. But then he suddenly started growing at a rapid rate, and by 1931 he had reached 218 cm *7 ft 1¾ in*. He became so weak as a result that he was bed-ridden for the rest of his life. He died on 4 March 1950 aged 51. He measured 234 cm *7 ft 8 in* and was the only person in medical history to have been both a dwarf and a giant.

TRIBES

Tallest

The tallest major tribe in the world is the Tutsi (also known as Watussi) (pop. *c.* 10,000), Nilotic herdsmen of Rwanda and Burundi, Central Africa where the average adult height (males) is more than 6 ft *183 cm*. The Tehuelches of Patagonia, long regarded as of gigantic stature (*i.e.* 7–8 ft *213–244 cm*), have in fact an average height (males) of 5 ft 10 in *178 cm*. The Montenegrins of Yugoslavia, with a male average of 5 ft 10 in *178 cm* (in the town of Trebinje the average height is 6 ft *183 cm*), compare with the men of Sutherland, at 5 ft 9½ in *176,5 cm*. In 1912 the average height of the men living in Balmaclellan, in the Kircudbright district of Dumfries and Galloway was reported to be 5 ft 10.4 in *179 cm*.

Shortest

The smallest pygmies are the Mbuti, with an average height of 4 ft 6 in *137 cm* for men and 4 ft 5 in *135 cm* for women, with some groups averaging only 4 ft 4 in *132 cm* for men and 4 ft 1 in *124 cm* for women. They live in the forests near the river Ituri in Zaïre, Africa.

WEIGHT

Heaviest men *World*

The heaviest human in recorded medical history was Jon Brower Minnoch (b. 29 Sept 1941) of Bainbridge Island, Washington, USA, who was carried on planking by a rescue team into the University Hospital, Seattle in March 1978. Dr. Robert Schwartz, the endocrinological consultant, estimated, by extrapolating his intake and elmination rates, that he was 'probably more' than 1400 lb *635 kg* (100 st). His highest actually recorded bodyweight was 975 lb *442 kg* in September 1976. To roll him over in his hospital bed it took 13 attendants. After nearly 2 years on a 1200 calorie per day diet he was discharged at 476 lb *216 kg* (34 st). He had to be readmitted in October 1981 having reportedly gained 200 lb *91 kg* (over 14 st) in 7 days. He died *c.* 10 Sept 1983. This former taxi-cab driver stood 6 ft 1 in *1,85 m* tall. He was 400 lb *180 kg* in 1963, and 700 lb *315 kg* in 1966.

The oldest dwarf on record, Hungarian-born Susanna Bokoyni, who celebrated her 105th birthday on 6 Apr 1984.

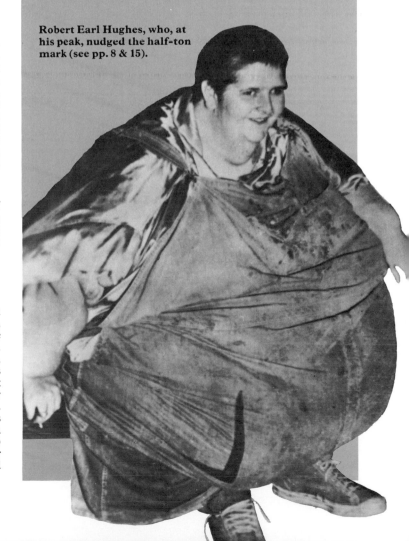

Robert Earl Hughes, who, at his peak, nudged the half-ton mark (see pp. 8 & 15).

The only others for whom weights of more than 60 st (840 lb) *381 kg* have been reported are the 8 listed below:				
	lb	st	lb	kg
Michael Walker *né* Francis Lang (b. 1934) USA (6 ft 2 in *188 cm*)[1]	est. 1187	84	11	538
Robert Earl Hughes (1926–58) USA (6 ft 0½ in *184 cm*)	1069	76	5	485
Mills Darden (1798–1857) USA (7 ft 6 in *229 cm*)	1020	72	12	463
John Hanson Craig (1856–94) USA (6 ft 5 in *195 cm*)[2]	907	64	11	............*411*
Arthur Knorr (1914–60) USA (6 ft 1 in *185 cm*)[3]	900	64	4	408
Albert Pernitsch (b. 1956) of Graz, Austria....................	878	67	10	398
Toubi (b. 1946) Cameroon	857½	61	3½	389
T. J. Albert (b. 1957) St. Albans, W. Virginia, USA[4]....................	856	61	2	388
T. A. Valenzuela (1895–1937) Mexico (5 ft 11 in *180 cm*)	850	60	10	386

[1] *Reduced to 369 lb 167 kg by Feb. 1980. Peak weight was only estimated in 1971.*
[2] *Won $1000 in a 'Bonny Baby' contest in New York City in 1858.*
[3] *Gained 300 lb 136 kg in the last 6 months of his life.*
[4] *A French press report attributed a weight of 470 kg 1036 lb to him in 1979.*

Great Britain

The heaviest recorded man in Great Britain was Peter Yarnall of East Ham, London, who died on 30 March 1984 aged 34 years. He was 5 ft 10 in *177,8 cm* tall and weighed 59 st *374 kg*. His coffin measured 7 ft 4 in *2,23 m* in length, 4 ft *1,21 m* across and had a depth of 2 ft 9 in *83,8 cm*.

Britain's heaviest man is the 6 ft 11 in *210,8 cm* tall professional wrestler Luke McMasters ('Giant Haystacks') (b. Camberwell, London 1946) of Manchester. A 14 lb *6,35 kg* baby he weighed 25 st *158,7 kg* at the age of 18 years and 32 st *203 kg* when he was 25. His weight now fluctuates between 41 st *260 kg* and 43 st *273 kg* but he once tipped the scales at 50 st *317 kg*.

Ireland

The heaviest Irishman is reputed to have been Roger Byrne, who was buried in Rosenallis, County Laoighis (Leix), on 14 Mar 1804. He died in his 54th year and his coffin and its contents weighed 52 st *330 kg*. Another Irish heavyweight was Lovelace Love (1731–66), born in Brook Hill, County Mayo. He weighed 'upward of 40 st *254 kg*' at the time of his death.

Heaviest women *World*

The heaviest woman ever recorded was the late Mrs Percy Pearl Washington, 46 who died in hospital in Milwaukee, on 9 Oct 1972. The hospital scales registered only up to 800 lb (57 st 2 lb) *362,8 kg* but she was believed to weigh about 880 lb (62 st 12 lb) *399,1 kg*. The previous feminine weight record had been set 84 years earlier at 850 lb (60 st 10 lb) *386 kg* although a wholly unsubstantiated report exists of a woman Mrs Ida Maitland (1898–1932) of Springfield, Mississippi, USA, who reputedly weighed 65 st 1 lb (911 lb) *413,2 kg*.

A more reliable and better documented case was that of Mrs Flora Mae Jackson (*née* King), a 5 ft 9 in *175 cm* Negress born in 1930 at Shuqualak, Mississippi, USA. She weighed 10 lb *4,5 kg* at birth, 19 st 1 lb (267 lb) *121 kg* at the age of 11, 44 st 5 lb (621 lb) *282 kg* at 25 and 60 st (840 lb) *381 kg* shortly before her death in Meridian, Mississippi, on 9 Dec 1965. She was known in show business as 'Baby Flo'.

Great Britain and Ireland

The heaviest woman ever recorded in Great Britain was a patient admitted to the Royal Free Hospital in Hampstead, London in *c.* 1975. After her death the intrigued undertaker took the hearse over a weighbridge, loaded and unloaded, so revealing, after making an allowance for the coffin, a weight of 46 stone *292 kg*.

Heaviest twins

The heaviest twins in the world were Billy Leon (1946–79) and Benny Loyd (b. 7 Dec 1946) McCrary *alias* McGuire of Hendersonville, North Carolina, USA, who in November 1978 were weighed at 743 lb *337 kg* (Billy) and 723 lb *328 kg* (Benny) and had 84 in *213 cm* waists. As professional tag wrestling performers they were *billed* at weights up to 770 lb *349 kg*. Billy died at Niagara Falls, Ontario, Canada on 13 July 1979 after a mini-motorcycle accident.

Lightest World

The lightest adult human on record was Lucia Zarate (b. San Carlos, Mexico 2 Jan 1863, d. October 1889), an emaciated Mexican ateleiotic dwarf of 26½ in *67 cm*, who weighed 2,125 kg *4.7 lb* at the age of 17. She 'fattened up' to 13 lb *5,9 kg* by her 20th birthday. At birth she weighed 2½ lb *1,1 kg*. The lightest adult ever recorded in the United Kingdom was Hopkins Hopkins (Shortest dwarfs, see pp. 6–7).

The thinnest recorded adults of normal height are those suffering from Simmonds' Disease (Hypophyseal cachexia). Losses up to 65 per cent of the original body-weight have been recorded in females, with a 'low' of 3 st 3 lb *20 kg* in the case of Emma Shaller (b. St Louis, Missouri 8 July 1868, d. 4 Oct 1890), who stood 5 ft 2 in *157 cm*. Edward C. Hagner (1892–1962), *alias* Eddie Masher (USA) is alleged to have weighed only 3 st 6 lb *22 kg* at a height of 5 ft 7 in *170 cm*. He was also known as 'the Skeleton Dude'. In August 1825 the biceps measurement of Claude-Ambroise Seurat (b. 10 Apr 1797, d. 6 Apr 1826) of Troyes, France was 4 in *10 cm* and the distance between his back and his chest was less than 3 in *8 cm*. According to one report he stood 5 ft 7½ in *171 cm* and weighed 5 st 8 lb *35 kg*, but in another account was described as 5 ft 4 in *163 cm* and only 2 st 8 lb *16 kg*. It was recorded that the American exhibitionist Rosa Lee Plemons (b. 1873) weighed 27 lb *12 kg* at the age of 18.

In July 1977 the death was reported of an 83 year old woman in Mexborough, South Yorkshire who scaled only 2 st 5 lb *15 kg* (height not recorded).

Lightest Great Britain

Robert Thorn (b. 1842) of March, Cambridgeshire weighed 49 lb *22 kg* at the age of 32. He was 4 ft 6 in *137 cm* tall and had a 27 in *68 cm* chest (expanded) and 4½ in *11 cm* biceps.

Slimming

The greatest recorded slimming feat was that of William J. Cobb (b. 1926), *alias* 'Happy Humphrey', a professional wrestler of Macon, Georgia, USA. It was reported in July 1965 that he had reduced from 57 st 4 lb *364 kg* to 16 st 8 lb *105 kg*, a loss of 40 st 10 lb *259 kg* in 3 years. His waist measurement declined from 101 to 44 in *257 to 112 cm*. In October 1973 it was reported that 'Happy' was back to his normal weight of 46½ st or 650 lb *295 kg*. By July 1979 Jon Brower Minnoch (1941–83) (see p. 7) had reduced to 476 lb *216 kg* (34 st); if his estimated peak weight was authentic, this indicated a weight loss of 924 lb *419 kg* (66 st) in 16 months.

The US circus fat lady Mrs Celesta Geyer (b. 1901), *alias* Dolly Dimples, reduced from 553 lb *251 kg* to 152 lb *69 kg* in 1950–51, a loss of 401 lb *182 kg* in 14 months. Her vital statistics diminished *pari passu* from 79–84–84 in *200–213–213 cm* to a *svelte* 34–28–36 in *86–71–91 cm*. Her book 'How I lost 400 lbs' was not a best-seller because of the difficulty of would-be readers identifying themselves with the dress-making and other problems of losing more than 28 st *178 kg* when 4 ft 11 in *150 cm* tall. In December 1967 she was reportedly down to 7 st 12 lb *50 kg*. The speed record for slimming was established by Paul M. Kimelman, 21, of Pittsburgh, Pennsylvania, USA, who from 25 Dec 1966 to August 1967 went on a crash diet of 300–600 calories per day to reduce from 487 lb (34 st 11 lb) *215,9 kg* to 130 lb (9 st 4 lb) *59 kg*—a total loss of 357 lb (25 st 7 lb) *156,9 kg*. He has now stabilised at 175 lb (12 st 7 lb) *79 kg*. In February 1951 Mrs Gertrude Levandowski (b. 1893) of Burnips, Michigan, USA successfully underwent a protracted operation for the removal of a cyst which subsequently reduced her weight from 44 st *280 kg* to 22 st *140 kg* (See also p. 21).

Claude Halls (b. 1937) of Sible Hedingham, Essex reduced from 33 st 6¾ lb *212,6 kg* to 12 st 10 lb *80,7 kg*—a loss of 20 st 10¾ lb *131,8 kg*—in the 14 months January 1974 to March 1975. In the first 7 days with Weight Watchers he lost 5 st 7 lb *35 kg*.

The feminine Weight Watchers champion in Britain was Mrs Dolly Wager (b. 1933) of Charlton, London, who, between September 1971 and 22 May 1973 reduced from 31 st 7 lb *197 kg* to 11 st *69,8 kg* so losing 20 st 7 lb *130 kg*.

Weight gaining

The reported record for gaining weight was set by Jon Minnoch (see p. 7 and above) when in October 1981 he was readmitted to University Hospital, Seattle, Washington State, USA having re-gained 200 lb *91 kg* in 7 days. Miss Doris James of San Francisco, California, USA is alleged to have gained 23 st 3 lb *147 kg* in the 12 months before her death in August 1965, aged 38, at a weight of 48 st 3 lb *306 kg*. She was only 5 ft 2 in *157 cm* tall.

Greatest differential
The greatest weight differential recorded for a married couple is 65 st 12 lb *419 kg* in the case of Mills Darden (72 st 12 lb *463 kg*—see p. 8) and his wife Mary (7 st *44,5 kg*). Despite her diminutiveness, however, Mrs Darden bore her husband 3 (perhaps 5) children before her death in 1837. The UK record is held by Luke McMasters (see p. 8) and his 7½ st *47,6 kg* wife Rita, where their weight differential was at times 42½ st *270 kg*. They have three sons.

2. ORIGINS

EARLIEST MAN

SCALE OF TIME
If the age of the Earth-Moon system (latest estimate 4450 million years) is likened to a single year, Hominids appeared on the scene at about 4.15 p.m. on 31 December, Britain's earliest known inhabitants arrived at about 11.10 p.m., the Christian era began about 14 seconds before midnight and the life span of a 119-year-old person (pp. 10 & 11) would be about three-quarters of a second. Present calculations indicate that the Sun's increased heat, as it becomes a 'red giant' will make life insupportable on Earth in about 10,000 million years. Meanwhile there may well be colder epicycles. The period of 1000 million years is sometimes referred to as an aeon.

Man (Homo sapiens) is a species in the sub-family Homininae of the family Hominidae of the super-family Hominoidea of the sub-order Simiae (or Anthropoidea) of the order Primates of the infra-class Eutheria of the sub-class Theria of the class Mammalia of the sub-phylum Vertebrata (Craniata) of the phylum Chordata of the sub-kingdom Metazoa of the animal kingdom.

Earliest *Primate*
The first primates appeared in the Palaeocene epoch about 69,000,000 years ago. The earliest members of the sub-order Anthropoidea are known from both Africa and South America in the early Oligocene, 34–30 million years ago, when the two infra orders, Platyrrhini and Catarrhini from the New and Old Worlds respectively were already distinct.

Earliest *Hominid*
Characteristics typical of the Hominidae such as the large brain and bipedal locomotion do not appear until much later. The earliest undoubted hominid relic found is an Australopithecine jaw bone with two molars 2 in *5 cm* in length found by Kiptalam Chepboi near Lake Baringo, Kenya in Feb 1984 and dated at 4 million years by associated fossils and 5.6–5.4 million years by rock correlation by K-Ar dating.

The most complete of the earliest hominid skeletons is that of 'Lucy' (forty per cent complete) found by Dr Donald C. Johanson and T. Gray at Locality 162 by the Awash river, Hadar, in the Afar region of Ethiopia on 30 Nov 1974. She is about 3 million years old, was 3½ ft *106 cm* tall.

Parallel tracks of hominid footprints extending over 80 ft *25 m* were discovered at Laetoli, Tanzania in 1978, first by Paul Abell, in volcanic ash dating to 3.5 million years ago. The height of the smallest of the seemingly 3 individuals was estimated to be 4 ft 7 in *120 cm*.

Earliest Genus *Homo*
The earliest species of the genus *Homo* is *Homo habilis* or 'Handy Man' named by Dr Louis Leakey in 1964. The greatest age attributed to fossils of this genus is for the skull KNM-ER (Kenya National Museum-East Rudolf) 1470 discovered in 1972 by Bernard Ngeneo at Koobi Fora by Lake Turkana, North Kenya. It is dated to 1.9 million years old and was reconstructed by Mrs Meave Leakey.

The earliest stone tools are between 2 and 2.4 million years old. They have been excavated from two sites in Ethiopia, one at the Omo Valley and the other at Hadar.

Evidence for the earliest man made structure was found in an excavation at Olduvai Gorge by Dr Mary Leakey in 1960. A concentration of stones arranged in a circle appears to have been used to anchor the supports of a hut or wind break 1.8 million years ago.

Earliest *Homo Erectus*
The earliest *Homo erectus* (upright man), the species directly ancestral to *Homo sapiens*, was discovered by Bernard Ngeneo

The oldest human relic yet found. Piece of jaw bone which pushes our ancestry back 5,000,000 years or 200,000 generations. *See Earliest Hominid, left. (Andrew Hill)*

at Koobi Fora, North Kenya. It is also the most complete skull known of this species and is about 1.5 million years old.

Earliest *Homo sapiens*
Many fossil skulls showing characteristics typical of *Homo sapiens* but retaining primitive features associated with *Homo erectus* are known. These early *Homo sapiens* fossils have been recovered from sites in both Africa and Europe and are between 100,000 and 140,000 years old.

Great Britain
The earliest evidence for the presence of hominids in Great Britain dates from the time of the Cromerian interglacial (425,000–500,000 BC). Five worked flint artefacts of this period were found in deposits of this interglacial in a quarry near Westbury-sub-Mendip, Somerset, and described in 1975 by Michael J. Bishop. The oldest human remains ever found in Britain are pieces of a brain case from a specimen of *Homo sapiens*, recovered in June 1935 and March 1936 by Dr Alvan T. Marston from the Boyn Hill terrace in the Barnfield Pit, near Swanscombe, northern Kent. The remains were associated with a middle Acheulian tool culture and probably date to the Holsteinian interglacial (230,000 BC). A hominid tooth, mandible fragment and vertebra were found in Pontnewydd Cave, Lower Elwy Valley, North Wales in October 1980. They were dated by the Thorium/Uranium method to between 175,000 and 200,000 BC.

3. LONGEVITY

No single subject is more obscured by vanity, deceit, falsehood and deliberate fraud than the extremes of human longevity. Extreme claims are generally made on behalf of the very aged rather than *by* them.

Many hundreds of claims throughout history have been made for persons living well into their second century and some, insulting to the intelligence, for people living even into their third. Centenarians surviving beyond their 113th year are in fact of the extremest rarity and the present absolute proven limit of human longevity does not yet admit of anyone living to celebrate any birthday after their 119th.

In the 30 year period 1950–1979 the deaths of 6 men and 10 women were recorded in England and Wales aged 110, 111 and in one case 112 (see Table). The 1971 Census showed 65 citizens of 108 and over. The odds of surviving from one birthday to the next are only worse than 50–50 after a 105th birthday.

World's oldest ever human holds court with children born long after he was 110.

AUTHENTIC NATIONAL LONGEVITY RECORDS

Country	Years	Days	Person	Born		Died	
Japan	119	—	Shigechiyo Izumi	29 June	1865	fl. 29 June	1984
United States[1]	113	273	Fannie Thomas	24 Apr	1867	22 Jan	1981
Canada[2]	113	124	Pierre Joubert	15 July	1701	16 Nov	1814
Spain[3]	112	228	Josefa Salas Mateo	14 July	1860	27 Feb	1973
France	112	66	Augustine Teissier (Sister Julia)	2 Jan	1869	9 Mar	1981
United Kingdom[4]	112	39	Alice Stevenson	10 July	1861	18 Aug	1973
Morocco	>112		El Hadj Mohammed el Mokri (Grand Vizier)		1844	16 Sept	1957
Poland	112	+	Roswlia Mielczarak (Mrs)		1868	7 Jan	1981
Ireland	111	327	The Hon. Katherine Plunket	22 Nov	1820	14 Oct	1932
Australia	111	235	Jane Piercy (Mrs)	2 Sept	1869	3 May	1981
South Africa[5]	111	151	Johanna Booyson	17 Jan	1857	16 June	1968
Czechoslovakia	111	+	Marie Bernatkova	22 Oct	1857	fl. Oct	1968
Channel Islands (Guernsey)	110	321	Margaret Ann Neve (*née* Harvey)	18 May	1792	4 April	1903
Northern Ireland	110	234	Elizabeth Watkins (Mrs)	10 Mar	1863	31 Oct	1973
Yugoslavia	110	150+	Demitrius Philipovitch	9 Mar	1818	fl. Aug	1928
Netherlands[6]	110	141	Gerada Hurenkamp-Bosgoed	5 Jan	1870	25 May	1980
Greece[7]	110	+	Lambrini Tsiatoura (Mrs)		1870	19 Feb	1981
USSR[8]	110	+	Khasako Dzugayev	7 Aug	1860	fl. Aug	1970
Sweden	109	353	Anna Julia Karlsson (*née* Mauritsdottir)	11 April	1872	30 Mar	1982
Norway	109	208	Marie Olsen (Mrs)	1 May	1850	24 Nov	1959
Tasmania (State of)	109	179	Mary Ann Crow (Mrs)	2 Feb	1836	31 July	1945
Italy	109	179	Rosalia Spoto	25 Aug	1847	20 Feb	1957
Scotland	109	14	Rachel MacArthur (Mrs)	26 Nov	1827	10 Dec	1936
Belgium	108	327	Mathilda Vertommen-Hellemans	12 Aug	1868	4 July	1977
Germany[9]	108	128	Luise Schwarz	27 Sept	1849	2 Feb	1958
Iceland	108	45	Halldóra Bjarndóttir	14 Oct	1873	28 Nov	1981
Portugal[10]	108	+	Maria Luisa Jorge	7 June	1859	fl. July	1967
Finland	109	182	Andrei Akaki Kuznetsoff	17 Oct	1873	fl. 17 Apr	1983
Malaysia	106	+	Hassan Bin Yusoff	14 Aug	1865	fl. Jan	1972
Luxembourg	105	228	Nicolas Wiscourt	31 Dec	1872	17 Aug	1978

[1] *Ex-slave Mrs Martha Graham died at Fayetteville, North Carolina on 25 June 1959 reputedly aged 117 or 118. Census researches by Eckler show that she was seemingly born in Dec 1844 and hence aged 114 years 6 months. Mrs Rena Glover Brailsford died in Summerton, South Carolina, USA on 6 Dec 1977 reputedly aged 118 years. Mrs Rosario Reina Vasquez who died in California on 2 Sept 1980 was reputedly born in Sonora, Mexico on 3 June 1866, which would make her 114 years 93 days. The 1900 US Federal Census for Crawfish Springs Militia District of Walker County, Georgia, records an age of 77 for a Mark Thrash. If the Mark Thrash (reputedly born in Georgia in December 1822) who died near Chattanooga, Tennessee on 17 Dec 1943 was he, and the age attributed was accurate, then he would have survived for 121 years.*

[2] *Mrs Ellen Carroll died in North River, Newfoundland, Canada on 8 Dec 1943, reputedly aged 115 years 49 days. Research is underway on the Ontario 1881 Census records on the claim of David Trumble to have been b. 15 Dec 1867.*

[3] *Snr Benita Medrana of Avila died on 28 Jan 1979 allegedly aged 114 years 335 days.*

[4] *London-born Miss Isabella Shepheard was allegedly 115 years old when she died at St Asaph, Clwyd, North Wales, on 20 Nov 1948, but her actual age was believed to have been 109 years 90 days. Charles Alfred Nunez Arnold died in Liverpool on 15 Nov 1941 reputedly aged 112 years 66 days based on a baptismal claim (London, 10 Sept 1829). Mrs Elizabeth Cornish (née Veale) who was buried at Stratton, Cornwall on 10 Mar 1691/2 was reputedly baptized on 16 Oct 1578, 113 years 4 months earlier.*

[5] *Mrs Susan Johanna Deporter of Port Elizabeth, South Africa, was reputedly 114 years old when she died on 4 Aug 1954. Mrs Sarah Lawrence, Cape Town, South Africa was reputedly 112 on 3 June 1968.*

[6] *Thomas Peters was recorded to have been born on 6 Apr 1745 in Leeuwarden and died aged 111 years 354 days on 26 Mar 1857 in Arnhem.*

[7] *The claim that Liakon Efdokia died 17 Jan 1982 aged 118 years 13 days is not substantiated by the censuses of 1971 or 1981. Birth registration before 1920 was fragmentary.*

[8] *There are allegedly 21,700 centenarians in USSR (cf. 7000 in USA). Of these 21,000 are ascribed to the Georgian SSR i.e. one in every 232. In July 1962 it was reported that 128, mostly male, were in the one village of Medini.*

[9] *West Germany: An unnamed female died in 1979 aged 112 years and an unnamed male died, aged also 112 years in 1969. The Austrian record is 108 years (female d. 1975) and the Swiss record is also 108 years (female d. 1967).*

[10] *Senhora Jesuina da Conceicao of Lisbon was reputedly 113 years old when she died on 10 June 1965.*

Note: *fl* is the abbreviation for *floruit*, Latin for he (or she) was living at the relevant date.

The height of credulity was reached on 5 May 1933, when a news agency solemnly filed a story from China with a Peking date-line that Li Chung-yun, the 'oldest man on Earth', born in 1680, had just died aged 256 years (*sic*). It was solemnly announced on 29 July 1982 that one of China's 5,000,000 census enumerators had unearthed in the Guangxi Region, Lan Buping, whose birthdate was entered as 13 Apr 1848. The French anthropologist Jean Rauch recorded in 1969 the death of Anai Dollo of the Auris sub-group of the Dogon people in the village of Bongo in Mali at the reputed age of 122. The tribe's oral tradition was that he had participated in their most sacred rite (held strictly at 60 year intervals) three times—as a baby in 1847, in 1907 and in 1967. The most extreme case of longevity recently claimed in the USSR has been 168 years for Shirali 'Baba' Mislimov of Barzavu, Azerbaijan, who died on 2 Sept 1973 and was reputedly born on 26 Mar 1805. No interview of this man was ever permitted to any Western journalist or scientist. He was said to have celebrated the 100th birthday of his third wife Hartun, in 1966, and that of one of his grandchildren in August 1973. It was reported in 1954 that in the Abkhasian Republic of Georgia, USSR, where aged citizens are invested with an almost saint-like status, 2.58 per cent of the population was aged over 90—24 times the proportion in the USA.

Official Soviet insistence in 1961 on the unrivalled longevity of the country's citizenry is curious in view of the fact that the 592 persons in their unique 'over 120' category must have spent at least the first 78 years of their prolonged lives under Tsarism.

Dr Zhores A. Medvedev, the expelled Soviet gerontologist, in Washington DC, on 30 Apr 1974 referring to USSR claims stated 'The whole phenomenon looks like a falsification' adding 'He [Stalin] liked the idea that [other] Georgians lived to be a 100 or more.' 'Local officials tried hard to find more and more cases for Stalin.' He points out (a) the *average* life-span in the regions claiming the highest incidence of centenarians is lower than the USSR average and (b) that, contrary to the rest of the world the incidence of centenarians claimed in the Caucasus had declined rapidly from 8000 in 1950 to 4500 in 1970. Dr Medvedev, in December 1977, put the *proven* limit in the USSR as low as 108 years.

It was announced in February 1984 that the 1982 Census in China revealed only 3765 centenarians of whom two thirds were women. In the US the mid-1983 figure was 32,000. Birth and death registration however became complete only in 1933 and was only 30.9 per cent by 1915.

Oldest authentic centenarian *World*

The greatest *authenticated* age to which any human has ever lived is a unique 119th birthday in the case of Shigechiyo Izumi of Asan on Tokunoshima an island 820 miles *1320 km* SW of Tokyo, Japan. He was born where he lives on 29 June 1865 and recorded as a 6-year-old in Japan's first census of 1871. He watches television and says the best way to a long life is 'not to worry' and to leave things to 'God, the Sun, and Buddha'. He was visited by the Editor on 3 Apr 1980. The word 'anamelanism' has been suggested as a name for the unexplained phenomenon of his white hair returning to black at his temples.

Oldest authentic centenarian *Great Britain*

The United Kingdom has an estimated population of some 4000 centenarians of whom only 22 per cent are male. The only UK citizens with birth and death certificates more than 112 years apart have been Miss Alice Stevenson (1861–1973) and Miss Janetta Jane Thomas (1869–1982). The latter was born at Llantrisant, Glamorgan on 2 Dec 1869 and died on 5 Jan 1982 aged 112 years 35 days or 4 days short of Miss Stevenson (see Table, page 10). Britain's oldest proven man has been John Mosley Turner (b. 15 June 1856), who died on 22 Mar 1968 aged 111 years 281 days. In April 1706 a John Bailes was buried at All Saints Church, Northampton, having apparently been baptised on 20 Aug 1592. If these two John Bailes were the same person, he would have been 113 years 8 months. The oldest living person born in Britain is Mrs Anna Williams (b. 2 June 1873) of Tuxedo Old People's Home, Swansea, Glamorgan, who reached 111 years in 1984.

The first recorded case in the UK of three siblings being centenarians occurred on 26 Nov 1982 when Miss Frances Adams M.Sc became 100. Her brother was Dr John Andrew Adams (1867–1967) and her sister Dr Elizabeth Hart (*née* Adams) (1876–1977). The family came from Omagh, Co Tyrone, Northern Ireland.

Oldest Quadruplets

The world's oldest quads are the Ottman quads of Munich, West Germany—Adolf; Anne-Marie; Emma and Elisabeth. They celebrated their 72nd birthday on 5 May 1984.

above: From left, Dr Elizabeth Hart, Dr John Adams, and Miss Frances Adams who are the first trio of centenarian siblings to be recorded in the UK.

left: Identical twin sisters Mildred Widman Philippi and Mary Widman Franzini of St. Louis, Missouri, USA who celebrated their 102nd birthday in June 1982.

Oldest Triplets

The longest-lived triplets on record were Faith, Hope and Charity Caughlin born at Marlboro, Massachusetts, USA on 27 Mar 1868. The first to die was Mrs (Ellen) Hope Daniels aged 93 on 2 Mar 1962.

Oldest twins *World and Great Britain*

The oldest recorded twins were Eli and John Phipps (b. 14 Feb 1803, Affinghton, Virginia, USA). Eli died at Hennessey, Oklahoma on 23 Feb 1911 aged 108 years 9 days on which day John was still living in Shenandoah, Iowa. The chances of identical twins both reaching 100 are said to be one in 700 million. On 17 June 1982, identical twin sisters, Mildred Widman Philippi and Mary Widman Franzini of St. Louis, Missouri, USA celebrated their 102nd birthday. The oldest twins on record in Great Britain have been the Bean twins Robert, of Birkenhead, Merseyside and Mary (later Mrs Simpson) of Etton, Cambridgeshire who celebrated their 100th birthday on 19 Oct 1973. Robert died before the end of 1973.

Most reigns

The greatest number of reigns during which any English subject could have lived is ten. A person born on the day (11 April) that Henry VI was deposed in 1471 had to live to only the comparatively modest age of 87 years 7 months and 6 days to see the accession of Elizabeth I on 17 Nov 1558. Such a

The Ottman quadruplets of Munich, West Germany who celebrated their 72nd birthday in May 1984.

person could have been Thomas Carn of London, reputedly born in 1471 and died 28 Jan 1578 in his 107th year.

Last 18th-century link

The last Briton with 18th-century paternity was Miss Alice J. Grigg of Belvedere, Kent (d. 28 Apr 1970) whose father William was born on 26 Oct 1799.

Oldest Mummy

Mummification (from the Persian word *măm*, wax) dates from 2600 BC or the 4th dynasty of the Egyptian pharaohs. The oldest surviving mummy is of *Wati*, a court musician of *c.* 2400 BC from the tomb of Nefer in Saqqâra, Egypt found in 1944.

4. REPRODUCTIVITY

MOTHERHOOD

Most children *World*

The greatest officially recorded number of children produced by a mother is 69 by the first of the two wives of Feodor Vassilyev (b. 1707–fl. 1782), a peasant from Shuya, 150 miles *241 km* east of Moscow. In 27 confinements she gave birth to 16 pairs of twins, 7 sets of triplets and 4 sets of quadruplets. The case was reported by the Monastery of Nikolskiy on 27 Feb 1782 to Moscow. At least 67 survived infancy. Empress Ekaterina II (The Great) (1762–96) was reputed to have evinced interest. The children, of whom almost all survived to their majority, were born in the period *c.* 1725–65.

Currently the world's most prolific mother is reported to be Leontina Albina (*née* Espinosa) (b. 1925) of San Antonio, Chile, who was reported pregnant in November 1980 having already produced 54 children. Her husband Gerardo Secunda Albina (variously Alvina) (b. 1921) states that he was married in Argentina in 1943 and they had 5 sets of triplets (all boys) before coming to Chile. 'Only' 40 (24 boys and 16 girls) survive. Eleven were lost in an earthquake thus indicating the truth about the many other children born earlier than those born in Chile.

Great Britain

The British record is seemingly held by Elizabeth, wife of John Mott married in 1676 of Monks Kirby, Warwickshire, who produced 42 live-born children. She died in 1720, 44 years

later. According to an inscription on a gravestone in Conway Church cemetery, Gwynedd, North Wales, Nicholas Hookes (d. 27 Mar 1637) was the 41st child of his mother Alice Hookes, but further details are lacking. It has not been possible to corroborate or refute this report. Mrs Elizabeth Greenhille (d. 1681) of Abbot's Langley, Hertfordshire is alleged to have produced 39 children (32 daughters, 7 sons) in a record 38 confinements. Her son Thomas was author of 'Art of Embalming' (1705).

Great Britain's champion mothers of today are believed to be Mrs Margaret McNaught (b. 1923), of Balsall Heath, Birmingham (12 boys and 10 girls, all single births) and Mrs Mabel Constable (b. 1920), of Long Itchington, Warwickshire who also has had 22 children including a set of triplets and two sets of twins.

Oldest mother *World*

Medical literature contains extreme but unauthenticated cases of septuagenarian mothers, such as Mrs Ellen Ellis, aged 72, of Four Crosses, Clwyd, who allegedly produced a still-born 13th child on 15 May 1776 in her 46th year of marriage. Many very late maternities will be cover-ups for illegitimate grandchildren. The oldest recorded mother for whom the evidence satisfied medical verification was Mrs Ruth Alice Kistler (*née* Taylor), formerly Mrs Shepard (1899–1982), of Portland, Oregon, USA. A birth certificate indicates that she gave birth to a daughter, Suzan, at Glendale, near Los Angeles, California, on 18 Oct 1956, when her age was 57 years 129 days. After her death a person purporting to be a relative alleged for an unknown motive that Mrs Kistler had 'changed the birth date'.

Great Britain

The oldest British mother reliably recorded is Mrs Winifred Wilson (*née* Stanley) of Eccles, Greater Manchester. She was born in Wolverhampton on 11 Nov 1881 or 1882 and had her tenth child, a daughter Shirley, on 14 Nov 1936, when aged 54 or 55 years and 3 days. She died aged 91 or 92 in January 1974. At Southampton, on 10 Feb 1916, Mrs Elizabeth Pearce gave birth to a son when aged 54 years 40 days. According to a report in *The Lancet* (1867) a woman aged 62 gave birth to triplets. She had previously had 10 children.

Ireland

The oldest Irish mother recorded was Mrs Mary Higgins of Cork, County Cork (b. 7 Jan 1876) who gave birth to a daughter, Patricia, on 17 Mar 1931 when aged 55 years 69 days.

Descendants

In polygamous countries, the number of a person's descendants can become incalculable. The last Sharifian Emperor of Morocco, Moulay Ismail (1672–1727), known as 'The Blood-thirsty', was reputed to have fathered a total of 548 sons and 340 daughters.

Capt Wilson Kettle (b. 1860) of Grand Bay, Port aux Basques, Newfoundland, Canada, died on 25 Jan 1963, aged 102, leaving 11 children by two wives, 65 grandchildren, 201 great-grandchildren and 305 great-great-grandchildren, a total of 582 living descendants. Mrs Johanna Booyson (see page 10), of Belfast, Transvaal, was estimated to have 600 living descendants in South Africa in January 1968.

Mrs Sarah Crawshaw (d. 25 Dec 1844) left 397 descendants according to her gravestone in Stones Church, Ripponden, Halifax, West Yorkshire.

Multiple great-grandparents

The report in 1983 that Jane Kau Pung (1877–1982) had left 4 great-great-great-great-grandchildren has proved to be incorrect. She in fact proved to be one of many cases of great-great-great-grandparents. Of these cases the youngest person to learn that their great-granddaughter had become a grandmother was Mrs Ann V. Weirick (1888–1978) of Paxtonville, Pennsylvania, USA, who received news of her great-great-great-grandson Matthew Stork (b. 9 Sept 1976) when aged only 88. She died on 6 Jan 1978. Britain's youngest 3 greats grandmother is Mrs Violet Lewis (b. June 1885) of Southampton.

Most living ascendants

Jesse Jones Werkmeister (b. 27 Oct 1979) of Tilden Nebraska, USA, had a full set of grandparents and great-grandparents and four great-great-grandparents, making 18 direct ascendants. This was equalled on 21 Oct 1980 on the birth of Kendel Shenner, at Big Beaver, Saskatchewan, Canada.

MULTIPLE BIRTHS

Lightest twins

The lightest recorded birthweight for a pair of surviving twins has been 2 lb 3 oz *992 g* in the case of Mary 16 oz *453 g* and Margaret 19 oz *538 g* born to Mrs Florence Stimson, Queens Road, Old Fletton, Peterborough, England, delivered by Dr Macaulay on 16 Aug 1931. Margaret is now Mrs M. J. Hurst.

'Siamese' twins

Conjoined twins derived the name 'Siamese' from the celebrated Chang and Eng Bunker (known in Thailand as Chan and In) born at Meklong, on 11 May 1811 of Chinese parents. They were joined by a cartilaginous band at the chest and married in April 1843 the Misses Sarah and Adelaide Yates of Wilkes County, North Carolina, USA and fathered ten and twelve children respectively. They died within three hours of each other on 17 Jan 1874, aged 62. The only known British example to reach maturity were the pygopagus twins Daisy and Violet Hilton born in Brighton, Sussex, on 5 Feb 1908, who were joined at the buttocks. They died in Charlotte, North Carolina, USA, on 5 Jan 1969, aged 60 from Hong Kong flu. The earliest successful separation of Siamese twins was performed on xiphopagus girls joined at the sternum at Mt Sinai Hospital, Cleveland, Ohio by Dr Jac S. Geller on 14 Dec 1952.

The rarest form of conjoined twins is Dicephales tetrabrachius dipus (two heads, four arms and two legs) of which only three examples are known today. They are the pair Masha and Dasha born in the USSR on 4 Jan 1950, an unnamed pair separated in a 10-hour operation in Washington, DC, USA on 23 June 1977, and Fonda Michelle and Shannon Elaine Beaver of Forest City, North Carolina, USA born on 9 Feb 1980. The only known British example were the 'Scottish brothers', who were born near Glasgow in 1490. They were brought to the Court of King James IV of Scotland in 1491, and lived under the king's patronage for the rest of his reign. They died in 1518 aged 28 years, one brother succumbing five days before the other, who 'moaned piteously as he crept about the castle gardens, carrying with him the dead body of the brother from whom only death could separate him and to whom death would again join him'.

Leontina Albina of San Antonio, Chile; who built her unrivalled family of 54 children with 5 sets of triplets before she was 22.

MULTIPLE BIRTHS

	World	United Kingdom
HIGHEST NUMBER REPORTED AT SINGLE BIRTH	10 (decaplets) (2 male, 8 female) Bacacay, Brazil, 22 Apr 1946 (also report from Spain, 1924 and China, 12 May 1936)	
HIGHEST NUMBER MEDICALLY RECORDED[1]	9 (nonuplets) (5 male, 4 female) to Mrs Geraldine Brodrick at Royal Hospital, Sydney, Australia on 13 June 1971. 2 males stillborn. Richard (12 oz *340 g*) survived 6 days 9 (all died) to patient at University of Pennsylvania, Philadelphia 29 May 1972 9 (all died) reported from Bagerhat, Bangladesh, *c.* 11 May 1977 to 30-year-old mother	6 (sextuplets) (all female) to Mrs Janet Walton (b. 1952) at Liverpool Maternity Hospital on 18 Nov 1983. All survive. 6 (2 male, 4 female) to Mrs Sheila Ann Thorns (*née* Manning) at New Birmingham Maternity Hospital on 2 Oct 1968. Three survive. 6 (1 male, 5 female) to Mrs Rosemary Letts (*née* Egerton) at University College Hospital, Greater London, on 15 Dec 1969. One boy and 4 girls survive
HIGHEST NUMBER SURVIVING[2]	6 out of 6 (3 males, 3 females) to Mrs Susan Jane Rosenkowitz (*née* Scoones) (b. Colombo, Sri Lanka, 28 Oct 1947) at Mowbray, Cape Town, South Africa on 11 Jan 1974. In order of birth they were: David, Nicolette, Jason, Emma, Grant and Elizabeth. They totalled 24 lb 1 oz *10,915 kg* 6 out of 6 (4 males, 2 females) to Mrs Rosanna Giannini (b. 1952) at Careggi Hospital, Florence, Italy on 11 Jan 1980. They are Francesco, Fabrizio, Giorgio Roberto, Letizia and Linda 6 out of 6 (all female) see also above right: Mrs Janet Walton	6 out of 6 (see above)

	Heaviest (World and UK)	*Most Sets* (World and UK)
QUINTUPLETS *World*	25 lb *11,35 kg* Mrs Lui Saulien, Chekiang, China, 7 June 1953 25 lb *11,35 kg* Mrs Kamalammal, Pondicherry, India, 30 Dec 1956	No recorded case of more than a single set
QUADRUPLETS *World*	10,35 kg *22 lb 13 oz* Mrs Ayako Takeda, Tsuchihashi Maternity Hospital, Kagoshima, Japan, 4 Oct 1978 (4 girls)	4 Mde Feodor Vassilyev, Shuya, Russia (d. *ante* 1770)
TRIPLETS[3] *World* *UK*	26 lb 6 oz *11,96 kg* (unconfirmed) Iranian case (2 male, 1 female) 18 Mar 1968 24 lb 0 oz *10,886 kg* Mrs Mary McDermott, of Bearpark, Co Durham, 18 Nov 1914	15 Maddalena Granata (1839–*fl.* 1886)
TWINS *World* *UK*	27 lb 12 oz *12,590 kg* (surviving) Mrs J. P. Haskin, Fort Smith, Arkansas, USA, 20 Feb 1924 The 35 lb 8 oz, *16,1 kg* reported in *The Lancet* from Derbyshire, England, on 6 Dec 1884 for the Warren Case (2 males liveborn) is believed to have been a misprint for 25 lb 8 oz *11,6 kg*	16 Mde Vassilyev (see above). *Note also* Mrs Barbara Zulu of Barbeton, South Africa bore 3 sets of girls and 3 mixed sets in 7 years (1967–73) 15 Mrs Mary Jonas of Chester (d. 4 Dec 1899)—all sets were boy and girl

[1] Mrs Edith Bonham (d. 1469) of Wishford Magna, Wiltshire reportedly had septuplets.
[2] The South African press were unable to verify the birth of 5 babies to Mrs Charmaine Craig (*née* Peterson) in Cape Town on 16 Oct 1980 and a sixth on 8 Nov. The reported names were Frank, Salome, John, Andrew, William and belatedly Deborah.
[3] Mrs Anna Steynvaait of Johannesburg, South Africa produced 2 sets within 10 months in 1960.

The oldest surviving unseparated twins are the craniopagus pair Yvonne and Yvette Jones (b. 1949) of Los Angeles, California, USA whose heads are fused together at the crown. They have turned down an operation to separate them.

Most twins *Geographically*
In Chungchon, South Korea it was reported in September 1981 that there was unaccountably 38 pairs in only 275 families—the highest ever recorded ratio.

Marian Taggart (née Chapman) who blossomed from being the world's tiniest recorded baby of only 10 oz *283 g*. She had been born 6 weeks premature at South Shields, Tyne and Wear on 5 June 1938. (*H. R. Taggart*)

Fastest triplet birth
The fastest recorded natural birth of triplets has been 2 minutes in the case of Mrs James E. Duck of Memphis, Tennessee (Bradley, Christopher and Carmon) on 21 Mar 1977.

Quindecaplets
It was announced by Dr Gennaro Montanino of Rome that he had removed the foetuses of 10 girls and 5 boys from the womb of a 35-year-old housewife on 22 July 1971. A fertility drug was responsible for this unique and unsurpassed instance of quindecaplets.

Longest and shortest pregnancy
Claims up to 413 days have been widely reported but accurate data are bedevilled by the increasing use of oral contraceptive pills which is a cause of amenorrhoea. *The US Medical Investigator* of 27 Dec 1884 reported a case of 15 months 20 days and the *Histoire de l'Academie* of 1751 the most extreme case of 36 months. In the pre-pill era English law has accepted pregnancies with extremes of 174 days (*Clark* v. *Clark*, 1939) and 349 days (*Hadlum* v. *Hadlum*, 1949). Ernestine Hudgins was born weighing 17 oz *482 g* 18 weeks premature in San Diego, California, USA on 8 Feb 1983.

BABIES
Heaviest *World*
The heaviest viable babies on record, of normal parentage, were boys of 22 lb 8 oz *10,2 kg* born to Sig Carmelina Fedele of Aversa, Italy in September 1955 and by caesarian section to Mrs Christina Samane at Sipetu Hospital, Transkei, South Africa on 24 May 1982. By February 1983 the latter's weight had increased to 53 lb *24 kg* (height 3 ft 6 in *56,5 cm*). Mrs Anna Bates *née* Swan (1846–88), the 7 ft 5½ in *227 cm* Canadian giantess (see also p. 6), gave birth to a boy weighing 23 lb 12 oz *10,77 kg* (length 30 in *76 cm*) at her home in Seville, Ohio, USA on 19 Jan 1879, but the baby died less than 24 hours later. Her first child, an 18 lb *8,16 kg* girl (length 24 in *61 cm*) was still-born when she was delivered in 1872. On 9 Jan 1891 Mrs Florentin Ortega of Buenos Aires, Argentina produced a still-born boy weighing 25 lb *11,3 kg*. In May 1939 a deformed baby weighing 29 lb 4 oz *13,26 kg* was born in a hospital at Effingham, Illinois, USA, but died two hours later.

Heaviest *United Kingdom*

The greatest recorded live birth weight in the United Kingdom is 21 lb *9,53 kg* for a child born on Christmas Day, 1852. It was reported in a letter to the *British Medical Journal* (1 Feb 1879) from a doctor in Torpoint, Cornwall. The only other reported birth weight in excess of 20 lb *9,07 kg* is 20 lb 2 oz *9,13 kg* for a boy born to a 33-year-old schoolmistress in Crewe, Cheshire, on 12 Nov 1884 with a 14½ in *36,8 cm* chest.

Most bouncing baby

The most bouncing baby on record was probably James Weir (1819–1821) who, according to his headstone in Cambushne-than, Old Parish Cemetery, Wishaw, Strathclyde, Scotland was 8 st or 112 lb *50,8 kg* at 13 months, 3 ft 4 in *1,01 m* in height and 39 in *99 cm* in girth. Therese Parentean, who died in Rouyn, Quebec, Canada on 11 May 1936 aged 9 years, weighed 24 st 4 lb *154 kg*. (*cf.* 27 st *171 kg* for Robert Earl Hughes at the age of ten [see table p. 8 and Chest measurements p. 15]).

Lightest

The lowest birth weight recorded for a surviving infant, of which there is definite evidence, is 10 oz *283 g* in the case of Mrs Marian Taggart *née* Chapman (b. 5 June 1938, d. 31 May 1983) who was born six weeks premature in South Shields, Tyne and Wear. She was born unattended (length 12¼ in *31 cm*) and was nursed by Dr D. A. Shearer, who fed her hourly for the first 30 hours with brandy, glucose and water through a fountain-pen filler. At three weeks she weighed 1 lb 13 oz *821 g* and by her first birthday 13 lb 14 oz *6,29 kg*. Her weight on her 21st birthday was 7 st 8 lb *48,08 kg*. The smallest viable baby reported from the United States has been Jacqueline Benson born at Palatine, Illinois, on 20 Feb 1936, weighing 12 oz *340 g*.

A weight of 8 oz *227 g* was reported on 20 Mar 1938 for a baby born prematurely to Mrs John Womack, after she had been knocked down by a lorry in East St Louis, Illinois, USA. The baby was taken alive to St Mary's Hospital, but died a few hours later. On 23 Feb 1952 it was reported that a 6 oz *170 g* baby only 6½ in *17 cm* long lived for 12 hours in a hospital in Indianapolis, Indiana, USA. A twin was still-born.

Coincident birthdates

The only verified example of a family producing five single children with coincident birthdays is that of Catherine (1952); Carol (1953); Charles (1956); Claudia (1961) and Cecilia (1966), born to Ralph and Carolyn Cummins of Clintwood, Virginia, USA, all on 20 February. The random odds against five single siblings sharing a birthdate are one in 17,797,577,730—almost 4 times the world's population.

The three children of the Henriksen family of Andenes, Norway, Heidi (b. 1960); Olav (b. 1964) and Lief-Martin (b. 1968) all celebrate their birthday infrequently, because these all fall on Leap Day – February 29. Ralph Bertram Williams was born on 4 July 1982 in Wilmington, North Carolina, USA. His father, grandfather and, in 1876, his great-grandfather were also born on 4 July.

Most southerly birth

Emilio Marcos Palma (Argentina) born 7 Jan 1978 at the Sargento Cabral Base, Antarctica is the only infant who can claim to be the first born on any continent.

Test tube baby *Earliest*

Louise Brown (5 lb 12 oz *2,6 kg*) was delivered by Caesarian section from Lesley Brown, 31, in Oldham General Hospital, Lancashire, at 11.47 p.m. on 25 July 1978. She was externally conceived on 10 Nov 1977.

5. PHYSIOLOGY AND ANATOMY

Hydrogen (63 per cent) and oxygen (25.5 per cent) constitute the commonest of the 24 elements in the human body. In 1972 four more trace elements were added—fluorine, silicon, tin and vanadium. The 'essentiality' of nickel has not yet been finally pronounced upon.

BONES

Longest

Excluding a variable number of sesamoids, there are 206 bones in the human body. The thigh bone or *femur* is the longest. It constitutes usually 27½ per cent of a person's stature, and may be expected to be 19¾ in *50 cm* long in a 6 ft *183 cm*-tall man. The longest recorded bone was the femur of the German giant Constantine, who died in Mons, Belgium, on 30 Mar 1902, aged 30 (see p. 5). It measured 76 cm *29.9 in*. The femur of Robert Wadlow, the tallest man ever recorded, measured an estimated 29½ in *75 cm*.

Smallest

The *stapes* or stirrup bone, one of the three auditory ossicles in the middle ear, is the smallest human bone, measuring from 2,6 to 3,4 mm *0.10 to 0.17 in* in length and weighing from 2,0 to 4,3 mg *0.03 to 0.065 g*.

MUSCLES

Largest

Muscles normally account for 40 per cent of the body weight and the bulkiest of the 639 muscles in the human body is the *gluteus maximus* or buttock muscle, which extends the thigh.

Smallest

The smallest muscle is the *stapedius*, which controls the *stapes* (see above), an auditory ossicle in the middle ear, and which is less than 1/20th of an inch *0,127 cm* long.

Smallest waists

Queen Catherine de Medici (1519–89) decreed a waist measurement of 13 in *33 cm* for ladies of the French Court. This was at a time when females were more diminutive. The smallest recorded waist among women of normal stature in the 20th century is a reputed 13 in *33 cm* in the case of the French actress Mlle Polaire (1881–1939) and Mrs Ethel Granger (1905–82) of Peterborough who reduced from a natural 22 in *56 cm* over the period 1929–39.

Largest chest measurements

The largest chest measurements are among endomorphs (those with a tendency towards globularity). In the extreme case of Hughes (see table p. 8) this was reportedly 124 in *315 cm*, but in the light of his known height and weight a figure of 104 in *264 cm* would be more supportable. George Macaree (formerly Britain's heaviest man) has a chest measurement of 75 in *190,5 cm* (waist 70 in *177,8 cm*), at a bodyweight of 31 st *196,8 kg* (height 5 ft 10 in *177,8 cm*) and Luke McMasters (see p. 8) has a chest measurement of 73 in *185,4 cm* (waist 68 in *172,7 cm*). Among muscular subjects (mesomorphs) of normal height *expanded* chest measurements above 56 in *142 cm* are extremely rare. Vasili Alexeyev (b. 1942), the 6 ft 1¼ in *186 cm* Russian super-heavyweight weight-lifting champion, had a 60½ in *153,6 cm* chest at his top weight of 350 lb *158,7 kg*. Arnold Schwarzenneger (b. 1948) of Graz, Austria, the 6 ft 1 in *185 cm* former Mr Universe and 'the most perfectly developed man in the history of the world', had a chest measurement of 57 in *145 cm* (bicep 22 in *55,8 cm*) at his best bodyweight of 235 lb *107 kg*. The American power lifter Gary Aprahamian, (b. 2 Feb 1962) the first to achieve a cold (not pumped) bicep measurement over 25 in *63,5 cm* with 25⅜ in *64,4 cm* has a normal chest measurement of 61 in *155 cm*.

Longest necks

The maximum measured extension of the neck by the successive fitting of copper coils, as practised by the Padaung or Kareni people of Burma, is 15¾ in *40 cm*.

BRAIN AND BRAIN POWER

Largest

The brain of an average adult male (*i.e.* 20–55 years) weighs 1424 g *3 lb 2.2 oz*, decreasing gradually to 1395 g *3 lb 1.1 oz* with advancing age. The heaviest non-diseased brain on record was that of Ivan Sergeyvich Turgenev (1818–83), the Russian author. His brain weighed 2012 g *4 lb 6.9 oz*.

Human brains are getting heavier. Examination of post-mortem records shows that the average male brain weight has increased from 1372 g *3 lb 0.4 oz* in 1860 to 1424 g *3 lb 2.2 oz* today. Women's brains have also put on weight, from 1242 g *2 lb 11.8 oz* to 1265 g *2 lb 12.6 oz* and in recent years have been growing almost as fast as men's.

Smallest

The lightest 'normal' or non-atrophied brain on record was

one weighing 1096 g *2 lb 6.7 oz* reported by Dr P. Davis and Prof E. Wright of King's College Hospital, London in 1977. It belonged to a 31 year old woman.

Highest IQ

Intelligence quotients or IQ's comprise the subject's mental age divided by his chronological or actual age multiplied by 100 such that an 8 year old more gifted than an average 16 year old would have an IQ of $\frac{16}{8} \times 100 = 200$. The highest childhood score has been achieved by Marilyn Mach vos Savant of St. Louis, Missouri, USA who as a 10 year old achieved a ceiling score for 23 year olds thus giving her an IQ of 230.

In adult High IQ clubs admission requirements are not on IQ points but are gauged in percentiles. An IQ exhibited by 1 person in 10,000 for instance coincides with 158 on the Stanford-Binet scale but 187 on the Cattell scale. The most elite ultra High IQ Society is the Mega Society with less than 20 members with percentiles of 99.99999 or 1 in a million. The topmost scorer in the Mega admission test, devised by its founder Ronald K. Hoeflin, has been Jeff Warol of San Diego, California with a raw score of 43 out of 48.

The highest IQ published for a national population is 115 for the Japanese born in 1960–61. At least 10 per cent of their whole population has an IQ > 130.

Human computer

The fastest extraction of a 13th root from a 100 digit number is in 1 min 28.8 sec by Willem Klein (b. 1912, Netherlands) on 7 Apr 1981 at the National Laboratory for High Energy Physics (KEK), Tsukuba, Japan. Mrs Shakuntala Devi of India demonstrated the multiplication of two 13-digit numbers 7,686,369,774,870 × 2,465,099,745,779 picked at random by the Computer Department of Imperial College, London on 18 June 1980, in 28 sec. Her correct answer was 18,947,668,177,995,426,462,773,730.

Some experts on calculating prodigies refuse to give credence to the above—largely on the grounds that it is so vastly superior to the calculating feats of any other invigilated prodigy.

Human memory

Bhandanta Vicitsara recited 16,000 pages of Bhuddist canonical texts in Rangoon, Burma in May 1974. Rare instances of eidetic memory—the ability to re-project and hence 'visually' recall material—are known to science.

The greatest number of places of π

All India Radio broadcast in its *Weekly Roundup* on 5 July 1981 part of a recording made earlier that day of Rajan Srinivasen Mahadevan, 23, in the process of reciting 'pi' from memory (in English) to 31,811 places in 3 hr 49 min (incl. 26 min of breaks) at the Lion Seva Mandir, Mangalore. His rate was 156.7 digits per minute. Mr Mahadevan has explained to the Editor that he learns each digit separately and acquires a 'feeling', when he is able to recall the number at will. The British record is 20,013 by Creighton Carvello on 27 June 1980 in 9 hr 10 min at the Saltscar Comprehensive School, Redcar, Cleveland, England. Note: It is only the *approximation* of π at $^{22}/_7$ which recurs after its sixth decimal place and can, of course, be recited *ad nauseam*. The true value is a string of random numbers fiendishly difficult to memorise. The average ability for memorizing random numbers is barely more than 7.

HANDS, FEET AND HAIR

Touch sensitivity

The extreme sensitivity of the fingers is such that a vibration with a movement of 0.02 of a micron can be detected.

Most fingers and toes

At an inquest held on a baby at Shoreditch, East London on 16 Sept 1921 it was reported that the boy had 14 fingers and 15 toes.

Least toes

The 'lobster claw syndrome' exhibited by the two-toed Doma tribe of the Zambesi valley, Zimbabwe and the Kalanga tribe of the eastern Kalahari desert, Botswana is hereditary *via* a single mutated gene.

Longest finger nails

The longest finger nails ever reported are those of Shridhar Chillal, (b. 1937) of Poona, India. The aggregate measurement, on 1 Apr 1984, was 135 in *343 cm* for the 5 nails on his left hand (thumb 32½ in *82,5 cm*). He last cut his nails in 1952.

Longest hair

Swami Pandarasannadhi, the head of the Tirudaduturai monastery, Tanjore district, Madras, India was reported in 1949 to have hair 26 ft *7,93 m* in length. From photographs it appears that he was afflicted with the disease Plica caudiformis, in which the hair becomes matted and crusted as a result of neglect. The length of hair of Miss Skuldfrid Sjorgren (b. Stockholm) was reported from Toronto, Canada in 1927 to have reached twice her height at 10 ft 6 in *3,20 m*.

Longest beard

The longest beard preserved was that of Hans N. Langseth (b. 1846 near Eidsroll, Norway) which measured 17½ ft *5,33 m* at the time of his burial at Kensett, Iowa in 1927 after 15 years residence in the United States. The beard was presented to the Smithsonian Institution, Washington, DC in 1967. Richard Latter (b. Pembury, Kent, 1831) of Tunbridge Wells, Kent, who died in 1914 aged 83, reputedly had a beard 16 ft *4,87 m* long but contemporary independent corroboration is lacking and photographic evidence indicates this figure was exaggerated. The beard of the bearded lady Janice Deveree (b. Bracken Co., Kentucky, USA, 1842) was measured at 14 in *36 cm* in 1884. The beard of Mlle Helene Antonia of Liège, Belgium, a 17th century exhibitionist was said to have reached her hips.

Longest moustache

The longest moustache on record was that of Masuriya Din (b. 1908), a Brahmin of the Partabgarh district in Uttar Pradesh, India. It grew to an extended span of 8 ft 6 in *2,59 m* between 1949 and 1962. Karna Ram Bheel (b. 1928) was granted permission by a New Delhi prison governor in February 1979 to keep his 7 ft 10 in *238 cm* moustache grown since 1949 during his life sentence. Birger Pellas (b. 21 Sept 1934) of Malmö, Sweden has a 2,216 m *7 ft 3¾ in* moustache grown since 1973. The longest moustache in Great Britain is that of Mr John Roy (b. 14 Jan 1910), of Weeley, near Clacton, Essex. It attained a peak span of 68½ in *174 cm* between 1939 and when measured on the BBC TV 'Nationwide' programme on 2 Apr 1976.

DENTITION

Earliest

The first deciduous or milk teeth normally appear in infants at 5–8 months, these being the mandibular and maxillary first incisors. There are many records of children born with teeth, the most distinguished example being Prince Louis Dieudonné, later Louis XIV of France, who was born with two teeth on 5 Sept 1638. Molars usually appear at 24 months, but in Pindborg's case published in Denmark in 1970, a 6-week premature baby was documented with 8 natal teeth of which 4 were in the molar region.

Most

Cases of the growth in late life of a third set of teeth have been recorded several times. A reference to a case in France of a fourth dentition, known as Lison's case, was published in 1896. A triple row of teeth was noted in 1680 by Albertus Hellwigius.

Most dedicated dentist

Brother Giovanni Battista Orsenigo of the Ospedale Fatebenefratelli, Rome, Italy, a religious dentist, conserved all the teeth he extracted in three enormous cases during the time he exercised his profession from 1868 to 1904. In 1903 the number was counted and found to be 2,000,744 teeth.

Most valuable tooth

In 1816 a tooth belonging to Sir Isaac Newton (1643–1727) was sold in London for £730. It was purchased by a nobleman who had it set in a ring which he wore constantly.

OPTICS

Smallest visible object

The resolving power of the human eye is 0.0003 of a radian or an arc of one minute ($\frac{1}{60}$th of a degree), which corresponds to 100 microns at 10 in. A micron is a thousandth of a millimetre, hence 100 microns is 0.003937, or less than four thousandths, of an inch. The human eye can, however, detect a bright light source shining through an aperture only 3 to 4 microns across. In October 1972 the University of Stuttgart, W. Germany reported that their student Veronica Seider (b. 1951) possessed a visual acuity 20 times better than average. She could identify people at a distance of more than a mile *1,6 km*. The Russians are reputedly working on a new type of lens implant which will give the wearer super-human sight.

Colour sensitivity
The unaided human eye, under the best possible viewing conditions, comparing large areas of colour, in good illumination, using both eyes, can distinguish 10,000,000 different colour surfaces. The most accurate photo-electric spectrophotometers possess a precision probably only 40 per cent as good as this. About 7.5 per cent of men and 0.1 per cent of women are colour blind. The most extreme form, monochromatic vision, is very rare. The highest recorded rate of red-green colour blindness is in Czechoslovakia and the lowest rate among Fijians and Brazilian Indians.

VOICE

Highest and lowest
The highest and lowest recorded notes attained by the human voice before this century were a staccato E in *alt altissimo* (e[iv]) by Ellen Beach Yaw (US) (1869–1947) in Carnegie Hall, NYC, USA, on 19 Jan 1896, and an A$_1$ (55 cycles per sec) by Kasper Foster (1617–73). Madeleine Marie Robin (1918–60) the French operatic coloratura could produce and sustain the B above high C in the Lucia mad scene in *Lucia di Lammermoor*. Since 1950 singers have achieved high and low notes far beyond the hitherto accepted extremes. However, notes at the bass and treble extremities of the register tend to lack harmonics and are of little musical value. Frl Marita Gunther, trained by Alfred Wolfsohn, has covered the range of the piano from the lowest note, A$_{\parallel}$ to c^{v}. Of this range of $7\frac{1}{4}$ octaves, six octaves are considered to be of musical value. Mr Roy Hart, also trained by Wolfsohn, has reached notes below the range of the piano. Barry Girard of Canton, Ohio in May 1975 reached the e (4340 Hz) above the piano's top note. The highest note put into song is G^{iv} first occurring in *Popoli di Tessaglia* by Mozart. The lowest vocal note in the classical repetoire is in Mozart's *Il Seraglio* by Osmin who descends to low D (73.4 cps). J. D. Sumner of Nashville, Tennessee in his album *Blessed Assurance* reaches the C below low C (32.7 cps). Stefan Zucker sang A in *alt altissimo* for 3.8 sec in the tenor role of Salvini in the première of Bellini's *Adelson e Salvini* in NYC, USA on 12 Sept 1972.

Greatest range
The normal intelligible outdoor range of the male human voice in still air is 200 yd *180 m*. The *silbo*, the whistled language of the Spanish-speaking Canary Island of La Gomera, is intelligible across the valleys, under ideal conditions, at five miles *8 km*. There is a recorded case, under freak acoustic conditions, of the human voice being detectable at a distance of $10\frac{1}{2}$ miles *17 km* across still water at night. It was said that Mills Darden (see table page 8) could be heard 6 miles *9 km* away when he bellowed at the top of his voice.

Because of their more optimal frequency, female screams register higher readings on decibel meters than male bellows. The annual World Shouting Championship record is 111.9 dBA by Anthony Fieldhouse on 12 Sept 1982 at Scarborough. The highest scientifically measured emission has been one of 120 dBA on a Bruel & Kjaer Precision Sound Level Meter by the screaming Susan Birmingham at Hong Kong Island School on 6 Mar 1982.

Lowest detectable sound
The intensity of noise or sound is measured in terms of pressure. The pressure of the quietest sound that can be detected by a person of normal hearing at the most sensitive frequency of *c.* 2750 Hz is 2×10^{-5} pascal. One tenth of the logarithm to this standard provides a unit termed a decibel (dBA). Prolonged noise above 150 decibels will cause immediate permanent deafness while above 192 dBA a fatal over-pressure shock wave can be formed. A noise of 30 decibels is negligible.

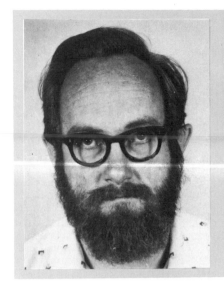

One of the highest scoring members of the Mega Society, Christopher Harding of Rockhampton, Queensland, Australia, who scored 197 on the Binet scale (see Highest IQ, p. 16).

Highest detectable pitch
The upper limit of hearing by the human ear has long been regarded as 20,000 Hz (cycles per sec), although children with asthma can often detect a sound of 30,000 cycles per sec. It was announced in February 1964 that experiments in the USSR had conclusively proved that oscillations as high as 200,000 cycles per sec can be heard if the oscillator is pressed against the skull.

Fastest talker
Few people are able to speak *articulately* at a sustained speed above 300 words per min. The fastest broadcaster has been regarded as Gerry Wilmot (b. Victoria, BC, Canada, 6 Oct 1914) the ice hockey commentator in the post-World War II period. Raymond Glendenning (1907–74), the BBC horseracing commentator, once spoke 176 words in 30 sec while commentating on a greyhound race. In public life the highest speed recorded is a 327 words per min burst in a speech made in December 1961 by John Fitzgerald Kennedy (1917–63), then President of the United States. Tapes of attempts to recite Hamlet's 262-word Soliloquy in under 24 sec (655 w.p.m.) have proved unintelligible. Results of tests by a radio station on John Moschitta (USA) in March 1983 indicate intelligibility at a rate of 534 in 58 sec or 552 words per min.

BLOOD

Blood groups
The preponderance of one blood group varies greatly from one locality to another. On a world basis Group O is the most common (46 per cent), but in some areas, for example Norway, Group A predominates.

The full description of the commonest sub-group in Britain is O MsNs, P+, Rr, Lu(a−), K−, Le(a−b+), Fy(a+b+), Jk(a+b+), which occurs in one in every 270 people.

The rarest blood group on the ABO system, one of 14 systems, is AB, which occurs in less than 3 per cent of persons in the British Isles. The rarest type in the world is a type of Bombay blood (sub-type A-h) found so far only in a Czechoslovak nurse in 1961 and in a brother (Rh positive) and sister (Rh negative) named Jalbert in Massachusetts, USA reported in February 1968. The American male has started a blood bank for himself.

Richest natural resources
Joe Thomas of Detroit, Michigan, USA was reported in August 1970 to have the highest known count of Anti-Lewis B, the rare blood antibody. A US biological supply firm pays him $1500 per quart *1,13 l*. The Internal Revenue regard this income as a taxable liquid asset.

Champion plasmapheresis blood donor
Since 1966 Allen Doster, a self-employed beautician, has (to 1 Jan 1983) donated 1508 US pints at Roswell Park Memorial Institute, New York, USA as a plasmapheresis donor. The

present-day normal limit on donations is 5 pints per annum. A 50-year-old haemophiliac Warren C. Jyrich required 2400 donor units *1080 l* of blood when undergoing open heart surgery at the Michael Reese Hospital, Chicago, USA in December 1970.

Largest vein
The largest vein in the human body is the *inferior vena cava*, which returns most of the blood from the body below the level of the heart.

Most alcoholic subject
California University Medical School, Los Angeles reported in December 1982 the case of a confused 24 year old female, who was shown to have a blood alcohol level of 1510 mg per 100 ml—nearly 19 times the UK driving limit and triple the normally lethal limit. After two days she discharged herself.

The United Kingdom's legal limit for motorists is 80 mg of alcohol per 100 ml of blood. The hitherto recorded highest figure in medical literature of 656 mg per 100 ml was submerged when the late Samuel Riley (b. 1922) of Sefton Park, Merseyside, was found by a disbelieving pathologist to have a level of 1220 mg on 28 Mar 1979. He had expired in his flat and had been an inspector at the plant of a well-known motor manufacturer.

BODY TEMPERATURE

Highest body temperature
Willie Jones, a 52 year old black, was admitted to Grady Memorial Hospital, Atlanta, Georgia on 10 July 1980 with heat stroke on a day when the temperature reached 90° F *32,2° C* with 44% humidity. His temperature was found to be 46,5° C *115.7° F*. After 24 days he was discharged 'at prior baseline status'.

Lowest body temperature
There are two recorded cases of patients surviving body temperatures as low as 60.8° F *16,0° C*. Dorothy Mae Stevens, (1929–74) was found in an alley in Chicago, Illinois on 1 Feb 1951 and Vickie Mary Davis aged 2 years 1 month in an unheated house in Marshalltown, Iowa on 21 Jan 1956, both with this temperature. People may die of hypothermia with body temperatures of 95.0° F *35,0° C*.

ILLNESS AND DISEASE

Commonest disease
The commonest non-contagious disease in the world is periodontal disease, such as gingivitus, which afflicts some 80 per cent of the US population. In Great Britain 13 per cent of people have lost all their teeth before they are 21 years old. During their lifetime few completely escape its effects. Infestation with pinworm (*Enterobius vermicularis*) approaches 100 per cent in some areas of the world.

The commonest contagious disease in the world is coryza (acute nasopharyngitis) or the common cold. Only 872,000 working days were reportedly lost as a result of this illness in Great Britain between mid-1981 and mid-1982, since absences of less than three days were not reported. The greatest reported loss of working time in Britain is from neurotic disorders, which accounted for 27,384,700, or 7.59 per cent, of the total of 361,015,100 days lost from mid 1982 to mid 1983.

The most resistant recorded case to being infected at the Medical Research Council Common Cold Unit, Salisbury, Wiltshire is J. Brophy, who has had one mild reaction in 24 visits.

Rarest disease
Medical literature periodically records hitherto undescribed diseases. A disease as yet undescribed but predicted by a Norwegian doctor is podocytoma of the kidney—a tumour of the epithelial cells lining the glomerulus of the kidney. The last case of endemic Smallpox was recorded in Ali Maow Maalin in Merka, Somalia on 26 Oct 1977.

Kuru, or laughing sickness, afflicts only the Fore tribe of eastern New Guinea and is 100 per cent fatal. This was formally attributed to the cannibalistic practice of eating human brains. The rarest fatal diseases in England and Wales have been those from which the last deaths (all males) were all recorded more than 40 years ago—yellow fever (1930), cholera nostras (1928) and bubonic plague (1926).

Most infectious disease
The most infectious of all diseases is the pneumonic form of plague, which also has a mortality rate of about 99.99 per cent. This is matched by rabies and AIDS (Auto-immune deficiency syndrome). Leprosy, transmissible by coughing, sneezing or spitting, is the most bacilliferous of communicable diseases. The bacillus is *Mycobacterium leprae* discovered by G. H. A. Hansen (Norway) (1841–1912) in 1871.

Highest mortality
Rabies in humans has been regarded as uniformly fatal when associated with the hydrophobia symptom. A 25-year-old woman Candida de Sousa Barbosa of Rio de Janeiro, Brazil, after surgery by Dr Max Karpin, was believed to be the first ever survivor of the disease in November 1968, though some sources give priority to Matthew Winkler, 6, who, on 10 Oct 1970, was bitten by a rabid bat.

Leading cause of death
The leading cause of death in industrialised countries is arteriosclerosis (thickening of the arterial wall) which underlies much coronary and cerebrovascular disease.

Most notorious carrier
The most publicized of all typhoid carriers has been Mary Mallon, known as Typhoid Mary, of New York City, NY, USA. She was the source of nine outbreaks, notably that of 1903. She was placed under permanent detention from 1915 until her death in 1938. A still anonymous dairy farmer from Camden, N.Y. was the source of 409 cases (40 fatal) in August 1909.

Parkinson's disease
The most protracted case of Parkinson's disease (named after Dr James Parkinson's essay of 1817) for which the earliest treatments were not published until 1946, is 56 years in the case of Frederick G. Humphries of Croydon, Greater London whose symptoms became detectable in 1923.

MEDICAL EXTREMES

Heart stoppage
The longest recorded heart stoppage is a minimum of 3 hr 32 min in the case of Miss Jean Jawbone, 20, who was revived by a team of 26, using peritoneal dialysis, in Winnipeg Medical Centre, Manitoba, Canada on 19 Jan 1977. A 'Mammalian diving reflex' can be triggered in humans falling into water cooler than 70° F *21° C*. In February 1974 Vegard Slettmoen, 5, fell through the ice on the river Nitselv, Norway. He was found 40 min later *2,5 m 8 ft* down but was revived in Akershus Central Hospital without brain-damage.

The longest recorded interval in a *post mortem* birth was one of 84 days in the case of a baby girl delivered on 5 July 1983 from a clinically dead woman in Roanoke, Virginia, who had been kept on life support since suffering a seizure in April.

Pulse rates
A normal adult pulse rate is 70–72 beats per min at rest for males and 78–82 for females. Rates increase to 200 or more during violent exercise and drop to as low as 12 in the extreme cases of Dorothy Mae Stevens (see Lowest body temperature, p. 18), and Jean Hilliard (b. 1962) of Fosston, Minnesota, USA on 20 Dec 1980.

Longest coma
The longest recorded coma was that undergone by Elaine Esposito (b. 3 Dec 1934) of Tarpon Springs, Florida, USA. She never stirred since an appendicectomy on 6 Aug 1941, when she was 6, in Chicago, Illinois, USA, and she died on 25 Nov 1978 aged 43 years 357 days, having been in a coma for 37 years 111 days.

Longest dream
Dreaming sleep is characterised by rapid eye movements known as REM. The longest recorded period of REM is one of 2 hr 23 min on 15 Feb 1967 at the department of Psychology, University of Illinois, Chicago on Bill Carskadon, who had had his previous sleep interrupted.

Largest stone
The largest stone or vesical calculus reported in medical

literature was one of 13 lb 14 oz *6,29 kg* removed from an 80-year-old woman by Dr Humphrey Arthure at Charing Cross Hospital, London, on 29 Dec 1952.

Longest in iron lung

The longest recorded survival by an 'iron lung' patient is that of Mrs Laurel Nisbet (b. 17 Nov 1912) of La Crescenta, California, USA. She has been in an iron lung continuously since 25 June 1948. The longest survival in an 'iron lung' in Britain has been 30 years by Denis Atkin in Lodge Moor Hospital, Sheffield, South Yorkshire. Mr John Prestwich (b. 1938) of Kings Langley, Hertfordshire has been dependent on a negative pressure respirator since 24 Nov 1955. Paul Bates of Horsham, West Sussex, was harnessed to a mechanical positive pressure respirator on 13 Aug 1954. He has received an estimated 213,312,128 respirations into his lungs *via* his trachea up to 1 May 1983.

Fastest nerve impulses

The results of experiments published in 1966 have shown that the fastest messages transmitted by the human nervous system travel as fast as 180 mph *288 km/h*. With advancing age impulses are carried 15 per cent more slowly.

Fastest reactions

The fastest recorded reaction times recorded for sprinters at the 1980 Olympic Games were 120/1000ths of a second for Romy Müller (GDR) in the women's 200 metre semi-final and 124/1000ths for Wilbert Greaves (GB) in the 110 m hurdles heats. These compare with 11/1000ths for the cockroach *Periplaneta americana*.

Hiccoughing

The longest recorded attack of hiccoughs or singultus is that afflicting Charles Osborne (b. 1894) of Anthon, Iowa, USA, from 1922 to date. He contracted it when slaughtering a hog and has hiccoughed about 430 million times in the interim period. He has been unable to find a cure, but has led a reasonably normal life in which he has had two wives and fathered eight children. He does admit, however, that he cannot keep in his false teeth.

Sneezing

The most chronic sneezing fit ever recorded is that of Donna Griffiths (b. 1969) of Pershore, Hereford & Worcester. She started sneezing on 13 Jan 1981 and surpassed the previous duration record of 194 days on 27 July 1981. She sneezed an estimated million times in the first 365 days. She achieved her first sneeze-free day on 16 Sept 1983—the 978th day. The highest speed at which expelled particles have ever been measured to travel is 103.6 mph *167 km/h*.

Snoring *Loudest*

The highest measured sound level recorded by any chronic snorer is 87.5 decibels at Hever Castle, Kent in the early hours of 28 June 1984. Melvyn Switzer of Hampshire was 1 ft *30 cm* from the meter. His wife Julie is deaf in one ear.

Yawning

In Lee's case, reported in 1888, a 15-year-old female patient yawned continuously for a period of 5 weeks.

Sleeplessness

Researches indicate that on the Circadian cycle for the majority peak efficiency is attained between 8 and 9 p.m. and the low point comes at 4 a.m. The longest recorded period for which a person has voluntarily gone without sleep is 449 hr (18 days 17 hr) by Mrs Maureen Weston of Peterborough, Cambridgeshire in a rocking chair marathon on 14 Apr–2 May 1977. Though she tended to hallucinate toward the end of this surely ill-advised test, she surprisingly suffered no lasting ill-effects. Victims of the very rare condition chronic colestites (total insomnia) have been known to go without definable sleep for many years. An example has been Jesus de Frutos (b. 1925) of Segovia, Spain who claims only to have dozed since 1954.

Motionlessness

The longest that anyone has continuously remained motionless is 10 hr 58 min by William A. Fuqua of Corpus Christi, Texas before a crowd of 4000 in Glendale Gallery and Mall, California, USA from 6 am to 4.58 pm on 13 May 1984. After a 4 min break he remained motionless for a further 62 min. Perry Nichol (b. 1956) at the WEA building, Adelaide, South

Australia remained motionless for 10 hr 31 min on 9 July 1983. The longest recorded case of involuntarily being made to stand to attention was when Staff Sgt Samuel B. Moody USAF, was so punished in Narumi prison camp, Nagoya, Japan for 53 hr in the spring of 1945. He survived to write *Reprieve from Hell*.

Most voracious fire eaters

Reg Morris blew a flame from his mouth to a distance of 27 ft *8,23 m* igniting a bonfire, at The Castle Working Men's Club, Brownhills, Walsall, West Midlands on 5 Nov 1983. On 5 Dec 1983 he extinguished 8393 torches of flame successively in his mouth in 2 hr at the 'Wheel Inn', Brownhills, W. Midlands. On 13 Feb 1982 at the 'Six Bells' Stoke Poges, Bucks, Jean Leggett set a female record of 6607.

Human salamanders

The highest dry-air temperature endured by naked men in the US Air Force experiments in 1960 was 400° F *204,4° C* and for heavily clothed men 500° F *260° C*. Steaks require only 325° F *162,8° C*. Temperatures of 140° C *284° F* have been found quite bearable in *Sauna* baths.

The highest temperature recorded by pyrometer for the coals in any fire walk was 1494° F *812° C* for a walk by 'Komar' (Vernon E. Craig) of Wooster, Ohio at the International Festival of Yoga and Esoteric Sciences, Maidenhead, England on 14 Aug 1976.

Thirty five people from the Sawau tribe on the island of Beqa in the Fijian group participated in a firewalk with the temperature over 1000° F *537° C* on 18 May 1982.

Swallowing

The worst reported case of compulsive swallowing was an insane female Mrs H. aged 42, who complained of a 'slight abdominal pain'. She proved to have 2533 objects, including 947 bent pins, in her stomach. These were removed by Drs Chalk and Foucar in June 1927 at the Ontario Hospital,

Fire-eater Reg Morris of Walsall, West Midlands, who extinguished 8393 torches of flame in 2 hours on 5 Dec 1983. (*Eddie Brown, Express and Star*)

Canada. The heaviest object extracted from a human stomach has been a 5 lb 3 oz *2,53 kg* ball of hair in Swain's case from a 20-year-old female compulsive swallower in the South Devon and East Cornwall Hospital, England on 30 Mar 1895.

Sword

Edward Benjamin 'Count Desmond' (b. 1941 of Binghamton, NY, USA) swallowed thirteen 23 in *58,4 cm* long blades to below his xiphisternum and injured himself in the process. *This category has now been retired and no further claims will be entertained.*

Fasting

Most humans experience considerable discomfort after an abstinence from food for even 12 hr but this often passes off after 24–48 hr. Records claimed unless there is unremitting medical surveillance are inadmissible. The longest period for which anyone has gone without solid food is 382 days by Angus Barbieri (b. 1940) of Tayport, Fife, who lived on tea, coffee, water, soda water and vitamins in Maryfield Hospital, Dundee, Angus, from June 1965 to July 1966. His weight declined from 33 st 10 lb *214,1 kg* to 12 st 10 lb *87,4 kg*.

Hunger strike

The longest recorded hunger strike was one of 94 days by John and Peter Crowley, Thomas Donovan, Michael Burke, Michael O'Reilly, Christopher Upton, John Power, Joseph Kenny and Seán Hennessy in Cork Prison, Ireland, from 11 Aug to 12 Nov 1920. These nine survivors from 12 prisoners owed their lives to expert medical attention and an appeal by the nationalist leader Arthur Griffith (1872–1922). The longest recorded hunger strike in a British gaol is 385 days from 28 June 1972 to 18 July 1973 by Denis Galer Goodwin in Wakefield Prison, West Yorkshire protesting his innocence of a rape charge. He was fed by tube orally.

The longest recorded case of survival without food *and* water is 18 days by Andreas Mihavecz, 18, of Bregenz, Austria who was put into a holding cell on 1 Apr 1979 in a local government building in Höchst, Austria but was totally forgotten by the police. On 18 Apr 1979 he was discovered close to death having had neither food nor water. He had been a passenger in a crashed car.

David Purley GM, the racing driver who survived a crash at Silverstone in July 1977 in which he decelerated from 108 mph to zero in 26 inches *66 cm*, thereby experiencing a g force of 179.8. Momentarily, he thus weighed more than an African elephant. (*Sun*)

Underwater

The world record for voluntarily staying underwater is 13 min 42.5 sec by Robert Foster, aged 32, an electronics technician of Richmond, California, who stayed under 10 ft *3,05 m* of water in the swimming pool of the Bermuda Palms Motel at San Rafael, California, USA, on 15 Mar 1959. He hyperventilated with oxygen for 30 min before his descent.

g forces

The acceleration g, due to gravity, is 32 ft 1.05 in per sec per sec *978,02 cm/sec²* at sea-level at the Equator. A *sustained* acceleration of 25 g was withstood in a dry capsule during astronautic research by Dr Carter Collins of California, USA. The highest g value endured on a water-braked rocket sled is 82.6 g for 0.04 of a sec by Eli L. Beeding Jr. at Holloman Air Force Base, New Mexico, USA, on 16 May 1958. He was put in hospital for 3 days. A man who fell off a 185 ft *56,39 m* cliff (before 1963) has survived a *momentary* g of 209 in decelerating from 68 mph *109 km/h* to stationary in 0.015 of a sec.

The racing driver David Purley GM survived a deceleration from 108 mph *173 km/h* to zero in 26 in *66 cm* in a crash at Silverstone on 13 July 1977 which involved a force of 179.8 g. He suffered 29 fractures, 3 dislocations and 6 heart stoppages.

A land diver of Pentecost Island, New Hebrides dived from a platform 81 ft 3 in *24,76 m* high with liana vines attached to his ankles on 15 May 1982. The body speed was 50 ft *15,24 m* per sec 34 mph *54 km/h*. The jerk transmitted a momentary g force in excess of 110.

Electric shock *Highest voltage*

The worst reported shock received from a power line was one of 230,000 volts by Brian Latasa, 17, on the tower of ultra-high-voltage in Griffith Park, Los Angeles on 9 Nov 1967. People insulated from the ground can have 'bare hand' contact with impunity working on power system voltages up to 765,000 volts in the USA and 400,000 volts in the UK. Laboratory work in France involves voltages up to 5 million volts while an aircraft in a thunder cloud may attain 30 million volts relative to the earth.

Isolation

The longest recorded period for which any volunteer has been able to withstand total deprivation of all sensory stimulation (sight, hearing and touch) is 92 hr, recorded in 1962 at Lancaster Moor Hospital, Lancashire.

The farthest that any human has been isolated from all other humans has been the lone pilots of lunar command modules when antipodal to their Apollo missions, two lunar explorers 2200 miles *3540 km* distant.

Pill-taking

The highest recorded total of pills swallowed by a patient is 414,134 between 9 June 1967 and 1 Jan 1983 by C. H. A. Kilner (b. 1926) of Bindura, Zimbabwe, following a successful operation to remove a cancerous pancreas on 26 May 1966.

Most injections

The diabetic Mrs Evelyn Ruth Winder (b. 1921) of Invercargill, New Zealand gave an estimated 56,380 insulin injections to herself over 52 years to May 1984.

Most tattoos

The seeming ultimate in being tattooed is represented by Wilfred Hardy of Huthwaite, Nottinghamshire, England. Not content with a perilous approach to within 4 per cent of totality, he has been tattooed on the inside of his cheek, his tongue, gums and eyebrows. Walter Stiglitz of North Plainfield, New Jersey, USA in March 1984 claimed 5457 separate tattoos by six artists. Britain's most decorated woman is Rusty Field (b. 1944) of Aldershot, Hampshire, who after 12 years under the needle of Mr Skuse, has come within 15 per cent of totality. He stated he always had designs on her.

OPERATIONS

Longest

The most protracted reported operation, for surgical as opposed to medical control purposes, has been one of 96 hr performed on Mrs Gertrude Levandowski (see also p. 8) during the period 4–8 Feb 1951. The patient suffered from a weak heart and the surgeons had to exercise the utmost caution during the operation. The 'slowest' operation on record is one on the feet of Mrs Doreen Scott of Derby, England on 20 Nov 1981. She had been waiting since 10 March 1952.

Most

Padmabhushan Dr M. C. Modi, a pioneer of mass eye surgery in India since 1943 has performed 833 cataract operations in a single working day.

Oldest subject

The greatest recorded age at which a person has been subjected to an operation is 111 years 105 days in the case of James Henry Brett, Jr (b. 25 July 1849, d. 10 Feb 1961) of Houston, Texas, USA. He underwent a hip operation on 7 Nov 1960. The oldest age established in Britain was the case of Miss Mary Wright (b. 28 Feb 1862) who died during a thigh operation at Boston, Lincolnshire on 22 Apr 1971 aged 109 years 53 days.

Heart transplant *Earliest and longest surviving*

The first human heart transplant operation was performed on Louis Washkansky, aged 55, at the Groote Schuur Hospital, Cape Town, South Africa, between 1.00 a.m. and 6 a.m., on 3 Dec 1967, by a team of 30 headed by Prof. Christiaan Neethling Barnard (b. Beaufort West, South Africa, 8 Oct 1922). The donor was Miss Denise Ann Darvall, aged 25. Washkansky died on 21 Dec 1967. The longest surviving heart transplantee has been Emmanuel Vitra, of Marseilles (b. 1921) France who received the heart of a 20 year old man on 28 Nov 1968 and entered the 16th year of his new life in 1983. Britain's longest-surviving heart transplant patient is Mr Keith Castle (b. 1927) of Battersea, London who received his new heart on 18 Aug 1979 at Papworth Hospital, Cambridge.

Artificial heart

On 1–2 Dec 1982 at the Utah Medical Center, Salt Lake City, Utah, USA, Dr Barney B. Clark, 61 of Des Moines, Wisconsin, USA received an artificial heart. The surgeon was Dr William C. De Vries. The heart was a Jarvik Mark 7 designed by Dr Robert K. Jarvik. Dr Clark died on 23 Mar 1983, 112 days later.

Earliest kidney transplant

R. H. Lawler (b. 1895) (USA) performed the first homo transplantation of the kidney in the human in 1950. The longest survival, as between identical twins, has been 20 years.

Earliest appendicectomy

The earliest recorded successful appendix operation was performed in 1736 by Claudius Amyand (1680–1740). He was Serjeant Surgeon to King George II (reigned 1727–60).

Earliest anaesthesia

The earliest recorded operation under general anaesthesia was for the removal of a cyst from the neck of James Venable by Dr Crawford Williamson Long (1815–78), using diethyl ether $(C_2H_5)_2O$, in Jefferson, Georgia, USA, on 30 Mar 1842. The earliest amputation under an anaesthetic in Great Britain was by Dr William Scott and Dr James McLauchlan at the Dumfries and Galloway Infirmary, Scotland on 19 Dec 1846.

Most durable cancer patient

The most extreme recorded case of survival from diagnosed cancer is that of Mrs Winona Mildred Melick (*née* Douglass) (b. 22 Oct 1876) of Long Beach, California. She had four cancer operations in 1918, 1933, 1966 and 1968 but died from pneumonia on 28 Dec 1981, 67 days after her 105th birthday.

Laryngectomy

On 24 July 1924 John I. Poole of Plymouth, Devon after diagnosis of carcinoma, then aged 33 underwent total laryngectomy in Edinburgh. He died on 19 June 1979 after surviving nearly 55 years as a 'neck-breather'. Mr F. B. Harvey of Plymouth, Devon has been a neck-breather since 1929.

Fastest amputation

The shortest time recorded for a leg amputation in the pre-anaesthetic era was 13–15 sec by Napoleon's chief surgeon Dominique Larrey. There could have been no ligation.

Largest Tumour

The largest tumour ever recorded was Spohn's case of an ovarian cyst weighing 328 lb *148,7 kg* from a woman in Texas, USA in 1905. She recovered fully. The most extreme case reported in Britain was of a cyst weighing 298 lb *135 kg* removed from a woman in England in 1846. The patient did not survive.

After nearly 30 years on the waiting list, Mrs Doreen Scott of Derby finally received an operation on her feet on 20 Nov 1981. (*Cumbrian Newspapers Ltd*)

Surgical instruments

The largest surgical instruments are robot retractors used in abdominal surgery introduced by Abbey Surgical Instruments of Chingford, Essex in 1968 and weighing 11 lb *5 kg*. Some bronchoscopic forceps measure 60 cm *23½ in* in length. The smallest are Elliot's eye trephine, which has a blade 0.078 in *0,20 cm* in diameter and 'straight' stapes picks with a needle-type tip or blade of 0,3 mm *0.013 in* long.

PSYCHIC FORCES

Extra-sensory perception

The two most extreme published examples of ESP in scientific literature have been those of the Reiss case of a 26 year old female at Hunter College, New York State, USA in 1936 and of Pavel Stepánek (Czechoslovakia) in 1967–68. The importance which might be attached to their cases was diminished by subsequent developments. The Reiss subject refused to undergo any further tests under stricter conditions. When Stepánek was retested at Edinburgh University with plastic cards he 'failed to display any clairvoyant ability'. Much smaller departures from the laws of probability have however been displayed in less extreme cases carried out under strict conditions.

Most durable ghosts

Ghosts are not immortal and, according to the *Gazetteer of British Ghosts*, seem to deteriorate after 400 years. The most outstanding exception to their normal 'half-life' would be the ghosts of Roman soldiers thrice reported still marching through the cellars of the Treasurer's House, York Minister after nearly 19 centuries. The book's author, Peter Underwood, states that Britain has more reported ghosts per square mile than any other country with Borley Rectory near Long Melford, Suffolk the site of unrivalled activity between 1863 and its destruction by fire in 1939. Andrew M. Green, author of *Ghost Hunting, A Practical Guide* claims to possess the only known letter from a *poltergeist*.

Chapter 2

THE LIVING WORLD

The only species of living animal able to munch 20 feet *6,09 m* above the ground, the giraffe from Africa. (*Biofotos*)

ANIMAL KINGDOM GENERAL RECORDS

Note—Guinness Superlatives Ltd has published a specialist volume entitled *The Guinness Book of Animal Facts and Feats* (3rd Edition) by Gerald L. Wood (price £8.95). This work treats the dimensions and performances of the Classes of the Animal Kingdom in greater detail, giving also the sources and authorities for much of the material in this chapter.

Largest and heaviest

The largest and heaviest animal in the world is the female Blue or Sulphur-bottom whale (*Balaenoptera musculus*), also called Sibbald's rorqual (see table). The longest specimen ever recorded was a female landed at the Compania Argentina de Pesca, Grytviken, South Georgia some time in the period 1904–20 which measured 107 Norwegian fot 33,58 m *110 ft 2½ in* in length. A nursing cow whale may generate up to 1300 lb *590 kg* of milk per day. The tongue and heart of the 190 tonne *187 ton* female (see table) taken by the *Slava* whaling fleet in the Southern Ocean on 20 Mar 1947 weighed 4.22 tons *4,29 tonnes* and 1540 lb *698,5 kg* respectively.

The low frequency pulses made by blue whales when communicating with each other have been measured up to 188 dB making them the loudest sounds emitted by any living source. They have been detected 850 km *530 miles* away.

Heaviest brain

The Sperm whale (*Physeter macrocephalus*) has the heaviest brain of any living animal. The brain of a 49 ft *14,93 m* bull processed in the Japanese factory ship *Nissin Maru No. 1* in the Antarctic on 11 Dec 1949 weighed 9,2 kg *20.24 lb* compared with 6,9 kg *15.38 lb* for a 90 ft *27 m* Blue whale. The heaviest brain recorded for an elephant was an exceptional 16.5 lb *7,5 kg* in the case of a 1.94 ton *1957 kg* Asiatic cow. The brain of the adult bull African elephant is normally 9¼–12 lb *4,2–5,4 kg*.

Largest eye

The giant squid (*Architeuthis* sp.) has the largest eye of any living animal. The ocular diameter may exceed 38 cm *15 in* (*cf.* 30 cm *11.81 in* for a 33⅓ long-playing record).

Largest egg

The largest egg laid by any known animal was that of the Elephant bird (*Aepyornis maximus*) which lived in southern Madagascar until *c*. AD 900. One example preserved in the British Museum (Natural History) measures 85,6 cm *33.7 in* round the long axis with a circumference of 72,3 cm *28.5 in*, giving a capacity of 8,88 litres *2.35 gal* or equivalent to 180–185 hen's eggs. It weighed about 27 lb *12,2 kg*.

The largest egg of any living animal is that of the Whale shark (*Rhincodon typus*). One egg case measuring 12 in by 5.5 in by 3.5 in *30 × 14 × 9 cm* was picked up on 29 June 1953 at a depth of 31 fathoms (186 ft *56,6 m*) in the Gulf of Mexico 130 miles *209 km* south of Port Isabel, Texas, USA. The egg contained a perfect embryo of a Whale shark 13.78 in *35 cm* long.

Longest gestation

The viviparous Alpine black salamander (*Salamandra atra*) has a gestation period of up to 38 months at altitudes above

1400 m *4600 ft* in the Swiss Alps, but this drops to 24–26 months at lower altitudes.

Fastest and slowest growth

The fastest growth in the Animal Kingdom is that of the Blue whale calf (see table and p. 22). A barely visible ovum weighing a fraction of a milligramme (*0.000035 oz*) grows to a weight of *c.* 26 tons *26 tonnes* in 22¾ months, made up of 10¾ months gestation and the first 12 months of life. This is equivalent to an increase of 30,000 million-fold. The slowest growth is that of the deep sea clam *Tindaria callistiformis* of the North Atlantic, which takes *c.* 100 years to reach a length of 8 mm *0.31 in.*

Highest Altitude

The highest altitude attained by any non-human animal is by turtles aboard the USSR Zond 5 in circumlunar flight. In April 1967 NASA reported that bacteria had been discovered at an altitude of 135,000 ft (25.56 miles) *41 100 m.*

Greatest size difference between sexes (Dimorphism)

The largest female marine worms of the species *Bonellia viridis* are at least 100 million times heavier than the smallest males. The female is up to 100 cm *39.3 in* long against the miserable 1,0 mm *0.04 in* of the male.

Highest g force

The highest force encountered in nature is the 400 g *averaged* by the Click beetle *Athous haemorrhoidalis* (a common British species) when 'jack-knifing' into the air to escape predators. One example measuring 12 mm *0.47 in* in length and weighing 40 mg *0.00014 oz* which jumped to a height of 30 cm *11¾ in* was calculated to have 'endured' a peak brain deceleration of 2300 g at the end of the movement.

Internal temperatures

The highest average mammalian blood temperature is that of the Domestic goat (*Capra hircus*) with 103.8° F *39,9° C.* That of the dromedary *Camelus dromedarius* reaches 41° C *105.8° F* at the end of a hot day. The lowest mammalian blood temperature is that of the Spiny anteater (Echidna), (*Tachyglossus aculeatus*), a monotreme found in Australia and New Guinea, with a normal range of 72°–87° F *22,2°–24,4° C.* The ice worm of Alaska has an internal temperature of − 10° C *14° F.*

Most prodigious eater

The most phenomenal eating machine in nature is the larva of the Polyphemus moth (*Antheraea polyphemus*) of North America which, in the first 48 hours of its life, consumes an amount equal to 86,000 times its own birthweight. In human terms, this would be equivalent to a 7 lb *3,17 kg* baby taking in 269 tons *273 tonnes* of nourishment!

Most valuable furs

The highest-priced animal pelts are those of the Sea otter (*Enhydra lutris*), also known as the Kamchatka beaver, which fetched up to $2700 (*then £675*) before their 55-year-long protection started in 1912. The protection ended in 1967, and at the first legal auction of Sea otter pelts at Seattle, Washington, USA on 31 Jan 1968, Neiman-Marcus, the famous Dallas department store, paid $9200 (*then £3832*) for four pelts from Alaska. In 1983 the most expensive full fur coat in New York City was $100,000 (*£67,000*) (Russian lynx) manufactured by Ben Kahn and Maximilian.

Heaviest ambergris

The heaviest piece of ambergris (a fatty deposit in the intestine of the Sperm whale) on record was a 1003 lb *455 kg* lump recovered from a Sperm whale (*Physeter macrocephalus*) caught off Tasmania on 24 Dec 1912. It was later sold in London for £23,000 equivalent in 1984 to more than £500,000.

Most valuable

The most valuable animals in cash terms are thoroughbred racehorses. It was announced in October 1980 that *Easy Jet* (see Chap. XII Horseracing) had been syndicated for $30 million (*£14.2 million*). The most valuable zoo exhibit is the Giant panda (*Ailuropoda melanoleuca*), 'Chu-Lin' (b. Sept 1982) of Madrid Zoo, Spain, the only panda cub in Europe has been valued at more than £1 million. The most valuable marine exhibits are 'Orky' and 'Corky', the worlds only captive breeding pair of killer whales (*Orcinus orca*) at Marineland, Palos Verdes, Los Angeles. In 1983 they were valued at $2,000,000 (*then £1,290,000*).

Newest Phylum

The 35th and only second new Phylum since 1900 was added to tuxonomy in 1982 with the confirmation of the minute *Loricifera* found by R. M. Kristensen (Denmark).

1. MAMMALS (*Mammalia*)

Largest and heaviest *British waters*

The largest Blue whale ever recorded in the waters of Great Britain was probably an 88 ft *26,8 m* specimen killed near the Bunaveneader station in Harris in the Western Isles, Scotland in 1904. In Dec 1851 the carcase of a blue whale measuring 94 ft 9 in *28,87 m* in length (girth 42 ft *13,7 m*) was brought into Bantry harbour, Co. Cork, Ireland after it had been found floating dead in the sea. A specimen stranded on the west coast of Lewis, Western Isles, Scotland in *c.* 1870 was credited with a length of 105 ft *32 m* but the carcase was cut up by the local people before the length could be verified. The length was probably exaggerated or taken along the curve of the body instead of in a straight line from the tip of the snout to the notch in the flukes. Four Blue whales have been stranded on British coasts since 1913, at least two of them after being harpooned by whalers. The last occurrence (*c.* 60 ft *18 m*) was at Wick, Highland, Scotland on 15 Oct 1923.

Blue whales inhabit the colder seas and migrate to warmer waters in the winter for breeding. Observations made in the Antarctic in 1947–8 showed that a Blue whale can maintain a speed of 20 knots (23 mph *37 km/h*) for 10 min when frightened. It has been calculated that a 90 ft *27 m* Blue whale travelling at 20 knots *37 km/h* would develop 520 hp *527 cv*. Newborn calves measure 6,5–8,6 m *21 ft 3½ in–28 ft 6 in* in length and weigh up to 3000 kg *2.95 tons.*

It has been estimated that there were about 13,000 Blue whales living throughout the oceans in 1984. This compares with a peak estimate of 220,000 in the past. The species has been protected *de jure* since 1967, although non-member countries of the International Whaling Commission. *e.g.* Panama and Taiwan, are not bound by this agreement. A world-wide ban on commercial whaling is due to come into effect in 1986.

Deepest dive

The greatest *recorded* depth to which a whale has dived is 620 fathoms (3720 ft *1134 m*) by a 47 ft *14,32 m* bull Sperm whale (*Physeter macrocephalus*) found with its jaw entangled with a submarine cable running between Santa Elena, Ecuador and Chorillos, Peru, on 14 Oct 1955. At this depth the whale withstood a pressure of 1680 lb/in² *118 kg.f/cm²* of body surface. On 25 Aug 1969 another bull Sperm whale was killed 100 miles *160 km* south of Durban after it had surfaced from a dive lasting 1 hr 52 min, and inside its stomach were found two small sharks which had been swallowed about an hour earlier. These were later identified as *Scymnodon* sp., a species found only on the sea floor. At this point from land the depth of water is in excess of 1646 fathoms (10,476 ft *3193 m*) for a radius of 30–40 miles *48–64 km*, which now suggests that the Sperm whale sometimes descends to a depth of over 10,000 ft *3000 m* when seeking food.

Largest on land *World*

(*See also table*) The largest living land animal is the African bush elephant (*Loxodonta africana*). The average adult bull stands 10 ft 6 in *3,2 m* at the shoulder and weighs 5.6 tons *5,7 tonnes*. The largest specimen ever recorded, and the largest land animal of modern times, was a bull shot 25 miles *40 km* north-northeast of Mucusso, southern Angola on 7 Nov 1974. Lying on its side this elephant measured 13 ft 8 in *4,16 m* in a projected line from the highest point of the shoulder to the base of the forefoot, indicating that its standing height must have been about 13 ft *3,96 m*. Other measurements included an overall length of 35 ft *10,67 m* (tip of extended trunk to tip of extended tail) and a forefoot circumference of 5 ft 11 in *1,80 m*. The weight was computed to be 26,998 lb (12.05 tons, *12,24 tonnes*) (see also Shooting, Ch. 12).

Largest on land *Britain*

The largest wild mammal in the British Isles is the Red deer (*Cervus elaphus*). A full-grown stag stands 3 ft 8 in *1,11 m* at the shoulder and weighs 230–250 lb *104–113 kg*. The heaviest ever recorded was probably a stag killed at Glenfiddich, Banff, Scotland in 1831, which weighed 525 lb *238 kg*. The heaviest park Red deer on record was a stag weighing 476 lb *215 kg* (height at shoulder 4 ft 6 in *1,37 m*) killed at Woburn, Bedfordshire in 1836. The so-called wild pony (*Equus caballus*) may weigh up to 700 lb *320 kg* but there are no truly feral populations living today.

Smallest *Land*

(*See also table*) The endangered Kitti's hog-nosed bat (*Craseonycteris thonglongyai*) or Bumblebee bat, is now restricted to one cave near the forestry station at Ban Sai Yoke on the Kwae Noi River, Kanchanaburi, Thailand. Mature specimens (both sexes) have a wing span of c. 160 mm *6.29 in* and weigh 1,75–2 g *0.062–0.071 oz*. The smallest mammal found in the British Isles is the European pygmy shrew (*Sorex minutus*). Mature specimens have a head and body length of 43–64 mm *1.69–2.5 in*, a tail length of 31–46 mm *1.22–1.81 in* and weigh between 2,4 and 6,1 g *0.084 and 0.213 oz*.

Smallest *Marine*

The smallest totally marine mammal in terms of weight is probably Commerson's dolphin (*Cephalorhynchus commersoni*) also known as Le Jacobite, which is found in the waters off the southern tip of South America. In one series of six adult specimens the weights ranged from 23 kg *50.7 lb* to 35 kg *77.1 lb*. The Sea otter (*Enhydra lutris*) of the north Pacific is of comparable size (55–81.4 lb *25–38,5 kg*), but this species sometimes comes ashore during storms.

Rarest

A number of mammals are known only from a single (holotype) specimen. An example is Garrido's hutia (*Capromys garridoi*) known only from a single specimen collected on the islet of Cayo Maja, off southern Cuba in April 1967. In 1979 zoologists uncovered the first evidence that the Bali leopard (*Panthera pardus balica*) still existed on the island. On 19 Jan 1984 the Wild Life Service in Tasmania announced that a Tasmanian wolf had been sighted in October 1982.

Britain's rarest native mammal is the Large mouse-eared bat (*Myotis myotis*) (see p. 27).

Fastest *World*

(*See also table*) The fastest of all land animals over a short distance (*i.e.* up to 600 yd *549 m*) is the Cheetah or Hunting leopard (*Acinonyx jubatus*) of the open plains of East Africa, Iran, Turkmenia and Afghanistan, with a probable maximum speed of 60–63 mph *96–101 km/h* over suitably level ground. Speeds of 71, 84 and even 90 mph, *114, 135 and 145 km/h* have been claimed for this animal, but these figures must be considered exaggerated. Tests in London in 1937 showed that on an oval greyhound track over 345 yd *316 m* a female cheetah's average speed over three runs was 43.4 mph *69,8 km/h* (*cf.* 43.26 mph *69,6 km/h* for the fastest racehorse), but this specimen was not running flat out and had great difficulty negotiating the bends. The fastest land animal over a sustained distance (*i.e.* 1000 yd *914 m* or more) is the Pronghorn antelope (*Antilocapra americana*) of the western United States. Specimens have been observed to travel at 35 mph for 4 miles *56 km/h for 6 km*, at 42 mph for 1 mile *67 km/h for 1,6 km* and 55 mph for half a mile *88,5 km/h for 0,8 km*.

Speed champions of the animal kingdom, the Cheetah, which can reach 60–63 mph *96–101 km/h* and the Pronghorn antelope which can maintain 55 mph *88,5 km/h* for half a mile and 35 mph *56 km/h* for 4 miles *6 km*.
(*Pat Gibbon*)

	SUPERLATIVES OF THE	
	Largest/Heaviest	**Longest/Tallest**
WHOLE ANIMAL KINGDOM	190 tonnes Blue Whale (*Balaenoptera musculus*); female 27,6 m *90½ ft* long caught by Soviet ship *Slava* in Antarctica, 1947	180 ft *55 m* Bootlace worm (*Lineus longissimus*); St Andrews, Fife, Scotland, 1864
MAMMALS	Land Mammal: est. 12,24 tonnes African bush elephant (*Loxodonta africana*) Angola, 1974	20 ft *6,09 m* Giraffe (*Giraffa camelopardalis tippelskirchi*) from Kenya. 'George' d. Chester Zoo, 22 July 1969
BIRDS	345 lb *156,5 kg* Ostrich (*Struthio c. camelus*). Up to 9 ft *2,7 m* tall North Africa	Largest wing span 11 ft 11 in *3,63 m* Wandering albatross (*Diomedea exulans*) Tasman Sea, 18 Sept 1965
REPTILES	> 2 tonnes, Luzon, 1823; 28 ft 4 in *8,63 m* Norman River, Australia, July 1957, Salt-water crocodile (*Crocodylus porosus*)	10 m *32 ft 9 in* Reticulated python (*Python reticulatus*) Celebes, 1912
SNAKES	Nearly 500 lb *227 kg* Anaconda (*Eunectes murinus*) girth 44 in *111 cm*, length 27 ft 9 in *8,45 m* Brazil, c. 1960	(See above) Of venomous species 18 ft 9 in *5,71 m* King Cobra (*Ophiophagus hannah*) or Hamadryad, Malaya 1937 (d. London Zoo)
AMPHIBIANS	143 lb *65 kg* Chinese giant salamander (*Andrias davidianus*) Hunan Province	5 ft 11 in *180 cm* length of above specimen
FISHES	42.4 tons *43 tonnes* Whale shark (*Rhincodon typus*) Koh Chik, Gulf of Siam 1919. Length 60¾ ft *18,5 m*	(Of freshwater fish) 416 lb *189 kg* Nile perch (*Lates niloticus*) (length 6 ft *1,8 m*), Lake Victoria, Sept 1978.
SPIDERS	'Nearly 3 oz *85 g*' *Lasiodora klugi*; Manaos, Brazil 1945	10.6 in *270 mm* legspan. *Lasiodora sp.*; Puraque, W. Brazil 1973
CRUSTACEANS	44 lb 6 oz *20,14 kg* North Atlantic lobster (*Homarus americanus*) overall length 3½ ft *1,06 m* Nova Scotia, 11 Feb 1977	> 12 ft *3,65 m* claw span Giant Spider Crab (*Macrocheira kaempferi*) Eastern Japan
INSECTS	3.5 oz *100 g* Goliath beetle (*Goliathus giganteus*) equatorial Africa	13 in *330 mm* female Giant stick insect (*Pharnacia serratipes*) Indonesia
MOLLUSCS	2 tons/*tonnes* Atlantic giant squid (*Architeuthis dux*) Thimble Tickle Bay, Newfoundland, 2 Nov 1878	57 ft *17,37 m* giant squid (*Architeuthis longimanus*) Tentacle 49 ft *14,93 m*, New Zealand, 1887

Fastest *Britain*

The fastest British land mammal over a sustained distance is the Roe deer (*Capreolus capreolus*), which can cruise at 25–30 mph *40–48 km/h* for more than 20 miles *32 km*, with occasional bursts of up to 40 mph *64 km/h*. On 19 Oct 1970 a frightened runaway Red deer (*Cervus elaphus*) registered a speed of 42 mph *67,5 km/h* on a police radar trap as it charged through a street in Stalybridge, Greater Manchester.

Slowest and sleepiest

The slowest moving land mammal is the Ai or Three-toed sloth (*Bradypus tridactylus*) of tropical America. The average ground speed is 6–8 ft *1,83–2,44 m* a minute (0.068–0.098 mph *0,109–0,158 km/h*), but in the trees it can 'accelerate' to 15 ft *4,57 m* a minute (0.17 mph *0,272 km/h*) (*cf.* these figures with the 0.03 mph *0,05 km/h* of the common garden snail and the

ANIMAL KINGDOM

Smallest/Lightest	Fastest	Longest Lived	Commonest	Rarest
0.008 in *0,2 mm* long Hairy-winged beetles (family *Ptiliidae*) and battledore-wing fairy flies (family *Myrmaridae*)	350 km/h *217 mph* Peregrine falcon (*Falco peregrinus*) during stoop. Germany 1963–7	*c.* 220 years Ocean quahog (*Arctica islandica*). Example with 220 annual growth rings reported from mid-Atlantic, 1982	Nematode sea worms. Est. population 4×10^{25} *cf.* Est. total of all living things on Earth of 3×10^{33}	A member of species known only from a single specimen or holotype.
0.062–0.071 oz *1,75–2,0 g* Kitti's hog-nosed bat (*Craseonycteris thonglongyai*), Thailand	60–63 mph *96–101 km/h* Cheetah (*Acionyx jubatus*)	119 years Man, (see p 11) *Homo sapiens* 1865–*fl.* 1984	House mouse (*Mus musculus*): distribution embraces all continents	Single Tasmanian wolf or thylacine (*Thyalacine cynocephalus*) positively identified after a 21 year void, Tasmania, July 1982 by a wildlife ranger. Last captured specimen d. 7 Sept. 1936.
0.056 oz *1,6 g* male Bee humming-bird (*Mellisuga helenae*) Cuba, Caribbean Overall length 57 mm 2¼ in	*Level flight: 106.2 mph 171 km/h* White throated spinetail swift (*Hirundapus caudacutus*) USSR, 1942	72+ years male Andean Condor (*Vultur gryphus*) Moscow Zoo, *fl.* 1892–1964	In the wild: 10,000 million Red-billed quelea (*Quelea quelea*) sub-Saharan Africa	Yellow-fronted bowerbird (*Amblyornis flavifrons*) one male sighting from 1895 to 1981
0.7 in 18 mm Gecko (*Sphaerodactylus parthenopion* British Virgin Islands, 1964	On land: 18 mph *29 km/h* Six-lined racerunner (*Cnemidophorus sexlineatus*) South Carolina, 1941	Record was under continuous observation 116+ years *Testudo graeca* Paignton, Devon, d. 1957	Sea snake (*Astrotia stokesii*) found *en masse* from Arabia sea to south western Pacific	Holotype—Dwarf chameleon (*Evoluticanda tuberculata*), Madagascar
4.7 in *11,9 cm* Thread snake (*Leptotyphlops bilineata*), West Indies	7 mph *11 km/h* Black mamba (*Dendroaspis polylepsis*) Tanzania April 1906	40 years 3 months, Common Boa (*Boa c. constrictor*) named 'Popeye', Philadelphia Zoo, USA, d. April 1977	(see above) In May 1929 a coiled mass of these sea snakes in the Malacca Straits measured 60 miles *96 km*	Keel-scaled boa (*Casarea dussumieri*) of Round Island, western Indian Ocean has total population of 75.
8,5–12,4 mm *0.33–0.48 in* Arrow-poison frog (*Sminthillus limbatus*) Cuba	*c.* 18 mph *29 km/h* take-off speed by champions in frog leaping contests	*c.* 55 years Japanese giant salamander (*Andrias japonicus*) 1826–1881, Amsterdam Zoo, Netherlands	Marine toad (*Bufo marinus*) world-wide distribution. Female may ovulate 35,000 eggs in a year	Israel painted frog (*Discoglossus nigriventer*) Lake Huleh—5 since 1940
0.00014 oz *4 mg* Dwarf pygmy goby (*Pandaka pygmaea*) Luzon, Philippines. Males 7,5–9,9 mm *0.28–0.38* long. Up to 7150 per oz.	47.8 mph *77 km/h* Wahoo (*Acanthocybium solandri*)	82 years Lake sturgeon (*Acipenser fulvescens*) based on annuli; Lake Winnebago, Wisconsin, USA, 1951–54	Deep-sea bristlemouth (*Cyclothone elongata*) 3 in *76 mm* long; world-wide	Holotypes (see above)
0.016 in *0,43 mm* male *Patu maiplesi*, Western Samoa, 1956	1.17 mph *1,88 km/h* female *Tegenaria gigantea*	*c.* 28 years female *Mygalomorphae* (tarantula) Mexico *c.* 1923–1951	Crab spiders (family *Thomisidae*) are common with worldwide distribution	Trapdoor spider (genus *I inhistius*) south-east Asia
0.01 in *0,25 mm*, water flea (genus *Alonella*) northern Europe	18 mph *28 km/h* Lobsters *H. vulgaris* and *Polinurus vulgaris* when leaping backwards	*c.* 50 years North American lobster (see left)	>500 million tonnes krill (*Euphausia superba*) of the southern oceans. A 10 million tonne swarm was tracked in March 1981	Holotypes (see above)
See above: Smallest in Whole Animal Kingdom	36 mph *58 km/h* Deer bot-fly (*Cephenemyia pratti*)	>30 years Splendour beetles (*Buprestidae*) in larval stage	Springtails (Order Collembola) attain densities of 5000 per ft^2 or 54 000/m^2	(Butterfly) Only 2 specimens of the Eight spotted skipper (*Dalla octomaculata*) of Costa Rica, found since 1900. Many holotypes exist
0.02 in *0,5 mm* diameter univalve shell *Ammonicera rota*; British waters	(Of snails) 55 yd *50,3 m* per hour Common garden snail *Helix aspersa cf.* Some species 23 in *58 cm* per hour	See above: Longest lived Whole Animal Kingdom	Sea hare (*Tethys californicus*) can lay a million eggs in a day	Prices up to $12,000 have been offered by conchologists for examples of *Conus cypraea*

0.17 mph *0,27 km/h* of the giant tortoise). The slowest swimming marine mammal is the Sea Otter (*Enhydra lutris*) which has a top speed of *c.* 6 mph *9,6 km/h*. Some armadillos and opossums sleep more than two thirds of their life.

Longest lived

No other mammal can match the extreme proven 119 years attained by Man (*Homo sapiens*) (see pp. 10 and 11). It is probable that the closest approach is made by the Asiatic elephant (*Elephas maximus*). The greatest age that has been verified with absolute certainty is 78 years in the case of a cow named 'Modoc', who died at Santa Clara, California, USA on 17 July 1975. She was imported into the USA from Germany in 1898 at the age of two. The longest lived marine mammal is Baird's beaked whale (*Berardius bairdii*) which has a maximum life-span of *c.* 70 years.

Highest living

The highest living wild mammal in the world is probably the Yak (*Bos grunniens*), of Tibet and the Szechwanese Alps, China, which occasionally climbs to an altitude of 20,000 ft *6100 m* when foraging. There are also reliable records of the Woolly hare (*Lepus oiostolus*) and the Woolly wolf (*Canis lupus chanco*) being seen at 19,800 ft *6035 m* and 19,000 ft *5790 m* respectively on the Tibetan Plateau.

Largest herds

The largest herds on record were those of the Springbok (*Antidorcas marsupialis*) during migration across the plains of the western parts of southern Africa in the 19th century. In 1849 John (later Sir John) Fraser observed a *trekbokken* that took three days to pass through the settlement of Beaufort West, Cape Province. Another herd seen moving near Nels

The largest cat in captivity, the Litigon (a cross between an Indian Lion and a Tigon) which weighs c. 800 lb *363 kg* and stands 4 ft 4 in *1,32 m* at the shoulder. (*Calcutta Zoo*)

Poortje, Cape Province in 1888 was estimated to contain 100,000,000 head, although 10,000,000 is probably a more realistic figure. A herd estimated to be 15 miles *24 km* wide and more than 100 miles *160 km* long was reported from Karree Kloof, Orange River, South Africa in July 1896.

The largest concentration of wild mammals found living anywhere in the world today is that of the Brazilian free-tailed Bat (*Tadarida brasiliensis*) in Bracken Cave, San Antonio, Texas, USA, where up to twenty million animals assemble after migration.

Longest and shortest gestation periods

The longest of all mammalian gestation periods is that of the Asiatic elephant (*Elephas maximus*), with an average of 609 days or just over 20 months and a maximum of 760 days—more than two and half times that of a human. By 1981 only *c.* 35,000 survived. The gestation period of the American opossum (*Didelphis marsupialis*), also called the Virginian opossum, is normally 12–13 days but may be as short as 8 days.

The gestation periods of the rare Water opossum or Yapok (*Chironectes minimus*) of Central and northern South America (average 12–13 days) and the Eastern native cat (*Dasyurus viverrinus*) of Australia (average 12 days) may also be as short as 8 days.

Largest litter

The greatest number of young born to a *wild* mammal at a single birth is 31 (30 of which survived) in the case of the Tailless tenrec (*Tenrec ecaudatus*) found in Madagascar and the Comoro Islands. The normal litter size is 12–15, although females can suckle up to 24.

Youngest breeder

The Streaked tenrec (*Hemicentetes semispinosus*) of Madagascar is weaned after only 5 days, and females are capable of breeding 3–4 weeks after birth.

CARNIVORES

Largest Land *World*

The largest living terrestrial carnivore is the Kodiak bear (*Ursus arctos middendorffi*), which is found on Kodiak Island and the adjacent Afognak and Shuyak islands in the Gulf of Alaska, USA. The average adult male has a nose to tail length of 8 ft *2,4 m* (tail about 4 in *10 cm*), stands 52 in *132 cm* at the shoulder and weighs between 1050 and 1175 lb *476–533 kg*. In 1894 a weight of 1656 lb *751 kg* was recorded for a male shot at English Bay, Kodiak Island, whose *stretched* skin measured 13 ft 6 in *4,11 m* from the tip of the nose to the root of the tail.

This weight was exceeded by a 'cage-fat' male in the Cheyenne Mountain Zoological Park, Colorado Springs, Colorado, USA which scaled 1670 lb *757 kg* at the time of its death on 22 Sept 1955. In 1981 an unconfirmed weight of over 2000 lb *907 kg* was reported for an Alaskan brown bear on exhibition at the Space Farms Zoological Park at Beemerville, New Jersey, USA.

Weights in excess of 1600 lb *725 kg* have also been reported for the Polar bear (*Ursus maritimus*), but the average adult male weighs 850–900 lb *386–408 kg* and measures 7¾ ft *2,4 m* nose to tail. In 1960 a Polar bear allegedly weighing 2210 lb *1002 kg* before skinning was shot at the polar entrance to Kotzebue Sound, north-west Alaska. The mounted specimen has a standing height of 11 ft 1¼ in *3,38 m*.

Largest Land *Britain*

The largest land carnivore found in Britain is the Badger (*Meles meles*). The average adult boar (sows are slightly smaller) measures 3 ft *90 cm* in length—including a 4 in *10 cm* tail—and weighs 27 lb *12,3 kg* in the early spring and 32 lb *14,5 kg* at the end of the summer when it is in 'grease'. In December 1952 a boar weighing exactly 60 lb *27,2 kg* was killed near Rotherham, South Yorkshire.

Largest Marine

The largest toothed mammal ever recorded is the Sperm whale (*Physeter macrocephalus*), also called the cachalot. The average adult bull measures 47 ft *14,3 m* in length and weighs about 33 tons *33,5 tonnes*. The largest accurately measured specimen on record was a 67 ft 11 in *20,7 m* bull captured off the Kurile Islands, north-west Pacific, by a USSR whaling fleet in the summer of 1950. Twelve cachalots have been stranded on British coasts since 1913. The largest, a bull measuring 61 ft 5 in *19 m*, was washed ashore at Birchington, Kent on 18 Oct 1914. Another bull estimated at 65 ft *19,8 m* but badly decomposed was stranded at Ferryloughan, Co. Galway, Ireland on 2 Jan 1952.

Smallest

The smallest living member of the Order Carnivora is the Least weasel (*Mustela rixosa*), also called the Dwarf weasel, which is circumpolar in distribution. Four races are recognised, the smallest of which is *M. r. pygmaea* of Siberia. Mature specimens have an overall length of 177–207 mm *6.96–8.14 in* and weigh between 35 and 70 g *1¼–2½ oz*.

Largest feline

The largest member of the cat family (Felidae) is the long-furred Siberian tiger (*Panthera tigris altaica*), also called the Amur or Manchurian tiger. Adult males average 10 ft 4 in *3,15 m* in length (nose to tip of extended tail), stand 39–42 in *99–107 cm* at the shoulder and weigh about 585 lb *265 kg*. In 1950 a male weighing 384 kg *846.5 lb* was shot in the Sikhote Alin Mts, Maritime Territory, USSR. In November 1967 David H. Hasinger of Philadelphia, USA shot an outsized Indian tiger (*Panthera tigris tigris*) in northern Uttar Pradesh which measured 10 ft 7 in *3,22 m* between pegs (11 ft 1 in *3,37 m* over the curves) and weighed 857 lb *388,7 kg* (*cf.* 9 ft 3 in *2,82 m* and 420 lb *190 kg* for average adult male). It is now on display in the US Museum of Natural History, Smithsonian Institution, Washington, DC.

The largest 'Big Cat' presently in captivity is an adult male Litigon (an Indian lion/Tigon cross) named 'Cubanacan' at Alipore Zoological Gardens, Calcutta, India, who is believed to weigh at least 800 lb *363 kg*. This animal stands 52 in *1,32 m* at the shoulder (*cf.* 44 in *1,11 m* for the lion 'Simba') and measures a record 11 ft 6 in *2,5 m* in total length.

The average adult African lion (*Panthera leo*) measures 9 ft *2,7 m* overall, stands 36–38 in *91–97 cm* at the shoulder and weighs 400–410 lb *181–185 kg*. The heaviest wild specimen on record was one weighing 690 lb *313 kg* shot by Mr Lennox Anderson just outside Hectorspruit in the eastern Transvaal, South Africa in 1936. In July 1970 a weight of 826 lb *375 kg* was reported for a black-maned lion named 'Simba' (b. Dublin Zoo, 1959) at Colchester Zoo, Essex. He died on 16 Jan 1973 at Knaresborough Zoo, North Yorkshire, where his stuffed body is currently on display.

Smallest feline

The smallest member of the cat family is the Rusty-spotted cat

(*Felis rubiginosa*) of southern India and Sri Lanka. The average adult male has an overall length of 25–28 in *64–71 cm* (tail 9–10 in *23–25 cm*) and weighs about 3 lb *1,35 kg.*

PINNIPEDS (Seals, Sea-lions and Walruses)

Largest *World*
The largest of the 32 known species of pinniped is the Southern elephant seal (*Mirounga leonina*), which inhabits the sub-Antarctic islands. Adult bulls average 16¼ ft *5 m* in length (tip of inflated snout to the extremities of the outstretched tail flippers), 12 ft *3,7 m* in maximum bodily girth and weigh about 5000 lb (2.18 tons *2268 kg*). The largest accurately measured specimen on record was a bull killed in Possession Bay, South Georgia on 28 Feb 1913 which measured 21 ft 4 in *6,5 m* after flensing (original length about 22½ ft *6,85 m*) and probably weighed at least 4 tons/tonnes. There are old records of bulls measuring 25–30 ft *7,62–9,14 m* and even 35 ft *10,66 m* but these figures must be considered exaggerated.

Largest *British*
The largest pinniped among British fauna is the Grey seal (*Halichoerus grypus*), also called the Atlantic seal. In one sample taken during the breeding season at the Farne Islands, Northumberland the heaviest (a male) weighed 310 kg *683¼ lb* (length from nose to tip of flippers 2,45 m *8 ft 0½ in.*)

Smallest *World*
The smallest pinnipeds are the Ringed seal (*Phoca hispida*) of the Arctic and the closely-related Baikal seal (*P. sibirica*) of Lake Baikal and the Caspian seal (*P. caspica*) of the Caspian Sea, USSR. Adult specimens (males) measure up to 5 ft 6 in *1,67 m* in length and reach a maximum weight of 280 lb *127 kg.* Females are about two-thirds this size.

Smallest *British*
Britain's smallest pinniped is the Common seal (*Phoca vitulina*). Adult males measure 1,5–1,85 m *4 ft 11 in–6 ft 0¼ in* in length and weigh up to 105 kg *231 lb.* Females are four-fifths this size.

Most abundant
The most abundant species of pinniped is the Crabeater seal (*Lobodon carcinophagus*) of Antarctica. In 1978 the total population was believed to be nearly 15,000,000.

Rarest
The last reliable sighting of the Caribbean or West Indian monk seal (*Monachus tropicalis*) was on Serranilla Bank off the coast of Mexico's Yucatan peninsula in 1952. In 1974 two seals were sighted near Cay Verde and Cay Burro, SE Bahamas, but a 1980 expedition found nothing. It has been suggested that they may have been escaped California sea-lions which have been recorded in the Gulf of Mexico on several occasions.

Fastest and deepest
The highest swimming speed recorded for a pinniped is 25 mph *40 km/h* for a Californian sea lion (*Zalophus californianus*). The deepest dive recorded for a pinniped is 600 m *1968 ft* for a bull Weddell seal (*Leptonychotes weddelli*) in McMurdo Sound, Antarctica in March 1966. At this depth the seal withstood a pressure of 875 lb/in² *6033 kPa* of body area. The exceptionally large eyes of the Southern elephant seal (*Mirounga leonina*), point to a deep-diving ability, and unconfirmed measurements down to 2000 ft *609 m* have been claimed.

Longest lived
A female Grey seal (*Halichoerus grypus*) shot at Shunni Wick in the Shetland Islands on 23 Apr 1969 was believed to be 'at least 46 years old' based on a count of dental annuli.

BATS

Largest *World*
The only flying mammals are bats (order Chiroptera), of which there are about 1000 living species. That with the greatest wing span is the Bismarck flying fox (*Pteropus neohibernicus*) of the Bismarck Archipelago and New Guinea. One specimen preserved in the American Museum of Natural History has a wing spread of 165 cm *5 ft 5 in* but some unmeasured bats probably reach 183 cm *6 ft.*

Largest *Britain*
The largest bat found in Britain (15 species) is the very rare large mouse-eared bat (*Myotis myotis*). Mature specimens have a wing span of 355–450 mm *13.97–17.71 in* and weigh up to 45 g *1.58 oz* females).

Smallest *World*
For details of Kitti's hog-nosed bat see p. 24 and 25.

Smallest *Britain*
The smallest native British bat is the Pipistrelle (*Pipistrellus pipistrellus*). Mature specimens have a wing span of 190–250 mm *7.48–9.84 in* and weigh between 3 and 8 g *0.1–0.28 oz.*

Rarest *World*
At least three species of bat are known only from the single or type specimen. They are: the Small-toothed fruit bat (*Neopteryx frosti*) from Tamalanti, West Celebes (1938/39); *Paracoelops megalotis* from Vinh, Vietnam (1945); and *Latidens salimalii* from the High Wavy Mountains, southern India (1948).

Rarest *Britain*
The rarest bat on the British list is now the Large mouse-eared bat (*Myotis myotis*) of Southern England. In 1982 only two males were known to survive.

Fastest
Because of the great practical difficulties few data on bat speeds have been published. The greatest velocity attributed to a bat is 32 mph *51 km/h* in the case of a Brazilian free-tailed bat (*Tadarida brasiliensis*), but this may have been wind-assisted. In one American experiment using an artificial mine tunnel and 17 different kinds of bat, only four of them managed to exceed 13 mph *20,8 km/h* in level flight.

Longest lived
The greatest age reliably reported for a bat is 31 years 5 months for an Indian flying fox (*Pteropus giganteus*) which died at London Zoo on 11 Jan 1979.

Highest detectable pitch
Because of their ultrasonic echolocation bats have the most acute hearing of any terrestrial animal. Vampire bats (*Desmodontidae*) and fruit bats (*Pteropodidae*) can hear frequencies as high as 150 kHz (*cf.* 20 kHz for the adult human limit but 153 kHz for the Bottle-nosed dolphin (*Tursiopis truncatus*)).

An adult bull Southern Elephant Seal, of the sub-Antarctic the largest known pinniped which can weigh up to 4 tons and measure over 22 ft *6,7 m* in length.

PRIMATES

Largest

The largest living primate is the Mountain gorilla (*Gorilla gorilla beringei*) of the volcanic mountain ranges of W Rwanda, SW Uganda and E Zaire. The average adult male stands 5 ft 9 in *1,75 m* tall (including crest) and weighs about 430 lb *195 kg*. The greatest height (top of crest to heel) recorded for a gorilla is 195 cm *6 ft 4¾ in* for a male collected by a German expedition at Alimbongo, N Kivu on 16 May 1938.

The heaviest gorilla ever kept in captivity was a male of the mountain race named 'N'gagi', who died in San Diego Zoo, California, USA on 12 January 1944 aged 18 years. He scaled 683 lb *310 kg* at his heaviest in 1943, and weighed 636 lb *288 kg* at the time of his death. He was 5 ft 7¾ in *1,72 m* tall and boasted a record chest measurement of 78 in *198 cm*. The heaviest gorilla living in captivity today is a Western lowland (*Gorilla g. gorilla*) male called 'Zaak', who was received at Kobe Oji Zoo, Japan in December 1962. He tipped the scales at 628 lb *285 kg* in June 1976, but has not been weighed since.

Smallest

The smallest known primate is the rare Pen-tailed shrew (*Ptilocercus lowii*) of Malaysia, Sumatra and Borneo. Adult specimens have a total length of 230–330 mm *9–13 in* (head and body 100–140 mm *3.93–5.51 in*, tail 130–190 mm *5.1–7.5 in*) and weigh 35–50 g *1.23–1.76 oz*. The Pygmy marmoset (*Cebuella pygmae*) of the Upper Amazon Basin and the Lesser mouse-lemur (*Microcebus murinus*) of Madagascar are also of comparable length but heavier, adults weighing 50–75 g *1.76–2.64 oz* and 45–80 g *1.58–2.82 oz* respectively.

Rarest

The rarest primate is the hairy-eared dwarf lemur (*Allocebus trichotis*) of Madagascar which, until fairly recently, was known only from the holotype specimen and three skins. In 1966, however, a live example was found on the east coast near Mananara.

Longest lived

The greatest irrefutable age reported for a non-human primate is *c.* 59 years in the case of a male Orang-utan (*Pongo pygmaeus*) named 'Guas', who died in Philadelphia Zoological Garden, Pennsylvania, USA on 9 Feb 1977. When he was received on 1 May 1931 he was at least 13 years of age. The world's oldest living primate is a male Chimpanzee (*Pan troglodytes*) named 'Jimmy' at Seneca Zoo, Rochester, N.Y., USA, who was still alive in March 1984 aged 53 years 9 months. The famous Western Lowland gorilla 'Massa' (b. July 1931) was still alive in March 1984 aged 52 years 8 months.

Strength

In 1924 'Boma', a 165 lb *74,80 kg* male chimpanzee at Bronx Zoo, New York, NY, USA recorded a right-handed pull (feet braced) of 847 lb *384 kg* on a dynamometer (*cf.* 210 lb *95 kg* for a man of the same weight). On another occasion an adult female chimpanzee named 'Suzette' (estimated weight 135 lb *61 kg*) at the same zoo registered a right-handed pull of 1260 lb *572 kg* while in a rage. A record from the USA of a 100 lb *45 kg* chimpanzee achieving a two-handed dead lift of 600 lb *272 kg* with ease suggests that a male gorilla could with training raise 1800 lb *816 kg*.

MONKEYS

Largest

The only species of monkey reliably credited with weights of more than 100 lb *45 kg* is the Mandrill (*Mandrillus sphinx*) of equatorial West Africa. The greatest reliable weight recorded is 119 lb *54 kg* for a male but an unconfirmed weight of 130 lb *59 kg* has been reported. (Adult females are about half the size of males).

Smallest

The smallest known monkey is the Pygmy marmoset (*Cebuella pygmaea*) of the Upper Amazon Basin (see Primate Smallest).

Oldest

The world's oldest living monkey is a male White-throated capuchin (*Cebus capucinus*) called 'Bobo' owned by Dr

Two aged members of the Primate order: *top* 'Massa', the famous Western Lowland gorilla aged 52 years and 8 months (*Terrence McBride*), and *above* 'Bobo' the oldest living monkey who was 48 years old in 1983. (*Reginald L. Dean*)

Raymond T. Bartus of the American Cyanamid Company in Pearl River, NY, USA, which celebrated his 48th birthday in 1983.

Rarest

The rarest living monkey is the Golden lion tamarin (*Leontopithecus rosalia*) of south-east Brazil. In 1980 there were less than 100 of these animals left, all of them in the São João basin in the State of Rio de Janeiro, and the species could well be extinct in the wild by 1985–90.

Mammals

RODENTS

Largest

The world's largest rodent is the Capybara (*Hydrochoerus hydrochaeris*), also called the Carpincho or Water hog, which is found in tropical South America. Mature specimens have a head and body length of 3¼–4½ ft *0,99–1,4 m* and weigh up to 250 lb *113 kg* (cage-fat specimen). Britain's largest rodent is now the Coypu (*Myocastor coypus*) also known as the Nutria, which was introduced from Argentina by East Anglian fur-breeders in 1929. Three years later, the first escapes were recorded and by 1960 at least 200,000 coypus were living in East Anglia. About 80 per cent were killed by the winter of 1963 and a government campaign of extermination has reduced the population to *c.* 4000 animals and a target date of 1990 has been set for the complete eradication of the species in Britain. Adult males measure 30–36 in *76–91 cm* in length (including short tail) and weigh up to 28 lb *13 kg* in the wild state (40 lb *18 kg* in captivity).

Smallest

The smallest known rodent is the Northern Pygmy mouse (*Baiomys taylori*) of central Mexico and southern Arizona and Texas, USA, which measures up to 109 mm *4.3 in* in total length and weighs 7–8 g *0.24–0.28 oz*. Britain's smallest rodent is the Old World harvest mouse (*Micromys minutus*), which measures up to 135 mm *5.3 in* in total length and weighs 7–10 g *0.24–0.35 oz*.

Rarest

The rarest rodent in the world is probably the Little earth hutia (*Capromys sanfelipensis*) of Juan Garcia Cay, an islet off southern Cuba. It has not been recorded since its discovery in 1970.

Longest lived

The greatest reliable age reported for a rodent is 27 years 3 months for a Sumatran crested porcupine (*Hystrix brachyura*) which died in National Zoological Park, Washington DC, USA, on 12 Jan 1965.

Fastest breeder

The female Meadow vole (*Microtus agrestis*) found in Britain, can reproduce from the age of 25 days and have up to 17 litters of 6–8 young in a year.

INSECTIVORES

Largest

The largest insectivore is the Moon rat (*Echinosorex gymnurus*), also known as Raffles' gymnure, which is found in Burma, Thailand, Malaysia, Sumatra and Borneo. Mature specimens have a head and body length of 265–445 mm *10.43–17.52 in*, a tail measuring 200–210 mm *7.87–8.26 in* and weigh up to 1400 g *3.08 lb*. Although the much larger Anteaters (family Tachyglossidae and Myrmecophagidae) feed on termites and other soft-bodied insects they are not insectivores, but belong to the orders Monotremata and Edentata, ('without teeth').

Smallest

The smallest insectivore is Savi's white-toothed pygmy shrew (*Suncus etruscus*), also called the Etruscan shrew, which is found along the coast of the northern Mediterranean and southwards to Cape Province, South Africa. Mature specimens have a head and body length of 36–52 mm *1.32–2.04 in*, a tail length of 24–29 mm *0.94–1.14 in* and weigh between 1,5 and 2,5 g *0.052* and *0.09 oz*.

Longest lived

The greatest reliable age recorded for an insectivore is 16+ years for a Lesser hedgehog-tenrec (*Echinops telfairi*), which was born in Amsterdam Zoo, Netherlands in 1966 and was later sent to Jersey Zoo. It was still alive in March 1984.

ANTELOPES

Largest

The largest of all antelopes is the rare Giant eland (*Tragelaphus derbianus*), of West and Central Africa, which may surpass 2000 lb *907 kg*. The Common eland (*T. oryx*) of East and South Africa has the same shoulder height of up to 5 ft 10 in *1,78 m* but is not quite so massive, although there is one record of a 5 ft 5 in *1,65 m* bull shot in Nyasaland (now Malawi) in *c.* 1937 which weighed 2078 lb *943 kg*.

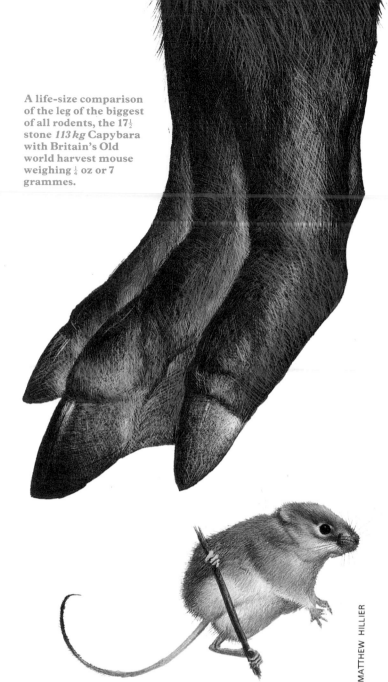

A life-size comparison of the leg of the biggest of all rodents, the 17½ stone *113 kg* Capybara with Britain's Old world harvest mouse weighing ¼ oz or 7 grammes.

MATTHEW HILLIER

Smallest

The smallest known antelope is the Royal antelope (*Neotragus pygmaeus*) of West Africa. Mature specimens measure 10–12 in *25–31 cm* at the shoulder and weigh only 7–8 lb *3–3,6 kg* which is the size of a large Brown hare (*Lepus europaeus*). Salt's dik-dik (*Madoqua saltina*) of NE Ethiopia and Somalia weighs only 5–6 lb *2,2–2,7 kg* when adult, but this species stands about 14 in *35,5 cm* at the withers.

Rarest

The rarest antelope is the Arabian oryx (*Oryx leucoryx*) which has not been reported in the wild since 1972 when 3 were killed and 4 others captured on the Jiddat-al Harasis plateau, South Oman. On 31 Jan 1982 ten specimens, nine of them born and bred at San Diego Zoo, California, USA, were released into the open desert in South Oman under the protection of a nomadic tribe.

Oldest

The greatest reliable age recorded for an antelope is 25 years 4 months for an Addax (*Addax nasomaculatus*) which died in Brookfield Zoo, Chicago, Illinois, USA on 15 Oct 1960.

DEER

Largest

The largest deer is the Alaskan moose (*Alces alces gigas*). Adult bulls average 6 ft *1,83 m* at the shoulder and weigh *c.* 1100 lb *500 kg*. A bull standing 7 ft 8 in *2,34 m* between pegs and weighing an estimated 1800 lb *816 kg* was shot on the Yukon River in the Yukon Territory, Canada in September 1897. Unconfirmed measurements up to 8 ft 6 in *2,59 m* at the shoulder and estimated weights up to 2600 lb *1180 kg* have been claimed. The record antler span is 78½ in *199 cm*.

Smallest
The smallest true deer (family Cervidae) is the Northern pudu (*Pudu mephistophiles*) of Ecuador and Colombia. Mature specimens measure 13–14 in *33–35 cm* at the shoulder and weigh 16–18 lb *7,2–8,1 kg*. The smallest ruminant is the Lesser Malay chevrotain (*Tragulus javanicus*) of SE Asia, Sumatra and Borneo. Adult specimens measure 8–10 in *20–25 cm* at the shoulder and weigh 6–7 lb, *2,7–3,2 kg*.

Rarest
The rarest deer in the world is Fea's muntjac (*Muntiacus feae*), which until recently, was known only from two specimens collected on the borders of S Burma and W Thailand. In December 1977 a female was received at Bangkok Zoo.

Oldest
The greatest reliable age recorded for a deer is 26 years 8 months for a Red deer (*Cervus elaphus scoticus*) which died in Milwaukee Zoo, Wisconsin, USA on 28 June 1954.

MARSUPIALS

Largest
The largest of all marsupials is the Red kangaroo (*Macropus rufus*) of central, southern and eastern Australia. Adult males stand up to 7 feet *2,13 m* tall, weigh up to 175 lb *79 kg* and measure up to 9 ft 6 in *2,9 m* along the curves of the body.

Smallest
The smallest known marsupial is the very rare Ingram's planigale (*Planigale ingrami* = *P. subtilissima*), a flat-skulled mouse found only in north-west Australia. Adult males have a head and body length of 45 mm *1.77 in*, a tail length of 50 mm *2 in* and weigh about 4 g *0.14 oz*.

Longest lived
The greatest reliable age recorded for a marsupial is 26 years 0 months 22 days for a Common Wombat (*Vombatus ursinus*) which died in London Zoo on 20 Apr 1906.

Fastest speed, highest and longest jumps
The highest speed recorded for a marsupial is 40 mph *64 km/h* for a young female eastern grey kangaroo (*Macropus giganteus*). The greatest height cleared by a hunted kangaroo is 10 ft 6 in *3,20 m* over a pile of timber and during the course of a chase in January 1951 a female Red kangaroo (*Macropus rufus*) made a series of bounds which included one of 42 ft *12,80 m*. There is also an unconfirmed report of an eastern grey kangaroo jumping nearly 13,5 m *44 ft 8½ in* on the flat.

TUSKS

Longest
The longest recorded elephant tusks (excluding prehistoric examples) are a pair from Zaïre preserved in the National Collection of Heads and Horns kept by the New York Zoological Society in Bronx Park, New York City, NY, USA. The right tusk measures 11 ft 5½ in *3,49 m* along the outside curve and the left 11 ft *3,35 m*. Their combined weight is 293 lb *133 kg*. A single tusk of 11 ft 6 in *3,5 m* has been reported. Ivory rose from $2.30 to $34/lb in 1970–80.

Heaviest
The heaviest recorded tusks are a pair in the British Museum (Natural History) which were collected from an aged bull shot by an Arab with a muzzle-loading gun at the foot of Mt. Kilimanjaro, Kenya in 1897. They originally weighed 240 lb *109 kg* (length 10 ft 2½ in *3,11 m*) and 225 lb *102 kg* (length 10 ft 5½ in *3,18 m*) respectively, giving a total weight of 465 lb *211 kg*, but their combined weight today is 440½ lb *200 kg*.

The greatest weight ever recorded for an elephant tusk is 117 kg *258 lb* for a specimen collected in Benin, West Africa and exhibited at the Paris Exposition in 1900.

HORNS

Longest
The longest horns grown by any living animal are those of the Water buffalo (*Bubalus arnee* = *B. bubalis*) of India. One huge bull shot in 1955 had horns measuring 13 ft 11 in *4,24 m* from tip to tip along the outside curve across the forehead. The longest single horn on record was one measuring 81¼ in *206 cm* on the outside curve found on a specimen of domestic Ankole cattle (Bos taurus) near Lake Ngami, Botswana. The largest spread recorded for a Texas longhorn steer is 9 ft 9 in *2,97 m*.

Longest *Rhinoceros*
The longest recorded anterior horn for a rhinoceros is one of 62¼ in *158 cm* found on a female southern race White rhinoceros (*Ceratotherium simum simum*) shot in South Africa in *c.* 1848. The posterior horn measured 22¼ in *57 cm*. There is also an unconfirmed record of an anterior horn measuring 81 in *206 cm*.

HORSES AND PONIES
The world's horse population is estimated to be 75,000,000.

Largest
The largest horse ever recorded was a 19.2 hand (6 ft 6 in *1,98 m*) pure-bred Belgian stallion named 'Brooklyn Supreme' (1928–48) owned by C. G. Good of Ogden, Iowa, USA which weighed 3200 lb 1.42 tons *1,44 tonnes* at his heaviest in 1938 and had a chest girth of 102 in *259 cm*.

In April 1973 the Belgian mare 'Wilma du Bos' (foaled 15 July 1966), owned by Mrs Virgie Arden of Reno, Nevada, USA was reported to weigh slightly in excess of 3200 lb *1451 kg* when in foal and being shipped from Antwerp. The normal weight of this 18.2-hand *1,88 m* mare is about 2400 lb *1088 kg*. The British weight record is held by the 17.2-hand (5 ft 10 in *1,78 m*) Shire stallion 'Honest Tom 5123' (foaled in 1884), owned by James Forshaw of Littleport, Cambridgeshire, which scaled 2912 lb *1325 kg* in 1891. This poundage may have been exceeded by another huge Shire stallion named 'Great Britain 978', bred by Henry Bultitaft of Ely, Cambridgeshire in 1876, but no weight details are available. In 1888 this horse was sold to Phineas T. Barnum, the American showman, for exhibition purposes.

The heaviest horse living in Britain today is the 17.2 hands (5 ft 10 in *1,78 m*) champion Percheron stallion 'Pinchbeck Union Crest' (foaled 27 Jan 1964), owned by Mr. George Sneath of Pinchbeck, Spalding, Lincs., which weighs 23½ cwt *1194 kg*.

Tallest
The tallest horse documented was the Percheron-Shire cross 'Firpon' (foaled 1959), owned by Julio Falabella which stood 21.1 hands (7 ft 1 in *2,16 m*) and weighed 2976 lb *1350 kg*. He died on the Recco de Roca Ranch near Buenos Aires, Argentina on 14 Mar 1972. A height of 21.1 hands was also claimed for the Clydesdale gelding 'Big Jim' (foaled 1950) bred by Lyall M. Anderson of West Broomley, Montrose, Scotland. He died in St Louis, Missouri in 1957. A claim for 21.2 hands (7 ft 2 in *2,18 m*) was made in 1908 for a horse named 'Morocco' weighing 2835 lb *1286 kg* in Allentown, Pennsylvania, USA.

Smallest
The smallest breed of horse (*sic*) is the Falabella of Argentina which was developed over a period of 70 years by crossing and recrossing a small group of undersized horses originally discovered in the southern part of the country. Adult specimens stand less than 7.2 hands *76 cm* and average 80–100 lb *36–45 kg*. The smallest mature horse bred by Julio Falabella of Recco de Roca before he died in 1981 was a mare which stood 3.3 hands *38 cm* and weighed 26¼ lb *11,9 kg*. 'Smidget', (b. 1979) owned by Ron Boeger of Happy Day ranch, Durham, California, USA, measures 21 in *53,34 cm* or '5 hands one' at the shoulder and weighs 75 lb *34,02 kg*.

Oldest
The greatest reliable age recorded for a horse is 62 years in the case of 'Old Billy' (foaled 1760), believed to be a cross between a Cleveland and Eastern blood, who was bred by Mr Edward Robinson of Wild Grave Farm in Woolston, Lancashire. In 1762 or 1763 he was sold to the Mersey and Irwell Navigation Company and remained with them in a working capacity (*i.e.* marshalling and towing barges) until 1819 when he was retired to a farm at Latchford, near Warrington, where he died on 27 Nov 1822. The skull of this horse is preserved in the Manchester

AUSTRALIAN WORLD ANIMAL RECORDS

WEDGE TAILED EAGLE
which has the largest wing span of any living eagle at 9 ft 4 in 2,84 m.

TASMANIAN WOLF (THYLACINE)
*world's rarest mammal. Single specimen identified
in July 1982 after 21 year void.*

SPINY ANTEATER (ECHIDNA)
*which has the lowest mammalian blood temperature
of 72°–87° F 22,2°–24,4° C.*

SALT-WATER CROCODILE
world's largest reptile. Weight can reach 2 tonnes.

MATTHEW HILLIER

Museum, and his stuffed head is now on display in the Bedford Museum. The greatest reliable age recorded for a pony is 54 years for a stallion owned by a farmer in Central France which was still alive in 1919. The greatest age recorded for a thoroughbred racehorse is 42 years in the case of the bay gelding 'Tango Duke' (foaled 1935), owned by Mrs Carmen J. Koper of Barongarook, Victoria, Australia. The horse died on 25 Jan 1978.

Strongest *draught*

The greatest load ever hauled by a pair of draught-horses was 48 short tons *43,5 tonnes* (= 50 pine logs or 36,055 board-feet of timber) on a special sledge litter *pulled across snow* for a distance of 275 yd *251 m* at the Nester Estate, Ewen, Ontanagon County, Michigan, USA on 26 Feb 1893. The two horses, both Clydesdales, had a combined weight of 3500 lb *1587 kg*. On 4 Sept 1924 a pair of Shire geldings owned by Liverpool Corporation registered a much more impressive *maximum* pull equivalent to a starting load of 50 tons *51 tonnes* on a dynamometer at the British Empire Exhibition at Wembley, London.

DOGS

Guinness Superlatives has published a more specialist book *The Guinness Book of Pet Records* (£7.95) by Gerald L. Wood.

UK dog population 5,542,000 (1982 estimate) compared with 46,000,000 for the USA).

Largest

The heaviest breed of domestic dog (*Canis familiaris*) is the St Bernard. The heaviest recorded example is 'Benedictine Schwarzwald Hof', owned by Thomas and Ann Irwin of Grand Rapids, Michigan, USA. He was whelped on 17 Dec 1970 and weighed 21 st 11 lb *138,34 kg* in May 1978, (height at shoulder 39 in *99 cm*). He has not been weighed since. The heaviest dog ever recorded in Britain is 'Heidan Dark Blue' (whelped 23 Apr 1978) also called 'Jason', a St Bernard owned by Nicol Plummer of Skeffington, Leics. In December 1981 he reached a peak 21 st 10¾ lb *138,23 kg* (shoulder height 34 in *86,3 cm*) but by January 1983 he was down to 15 st *95,25 kg* after being put on a diet and shortly before his death on 4 Nov 1983 he scaled 14 st 10 lb *93,4 kg*.

Tallest

The tallest breeds of dog are the Great Dane and the Irish wolfhound, both of which can exceed 39 in *99 cm* at the shoulder. In the case of the Great Dane the extreme recorded example is 'Shamgret Danzas' (whelped in 1975), owned by Mr and Mrs Peter Comley of Milton Keynes, Bucks. He stands 41½ in *105,4 cm* and has weighed up to 17 st *108 kg*. The Irish Wolfhound 'Broadbridge Michael' (1920–29), owned by Mrs Mary Beynon of Sutton-at-Hone, Kent, stood 39½ in *100,3 cm* at the age of 2 years.

Smallest

The world's smallest breeds of dog are the Yorkshire terrier, the Chihuahua and the Toy poodle, *miniature* versions of which have been known to weigh less than 16 oz *453 g* when adult. In April 1971 a weight of 10 oz *283 g* was reliably reported for a fully-grown Yorkshire terrier called 'Sylvia' (shoulder height 3½ in *89 mm*) owned by Mrs Connie Hutchins of Walthamstow, Greater London.

Oldest

Authentic records of dogs living over 20 years are rare, but even 34 years has been accepted by one authority. The greatest reliable age recorded for a dog is 29 years 5 months for a Queensland 'heeler' named 'Bluey', owned by Mr Les Hall of Rochester, Victoria, Australia. The dog was obtained as a puppy in 1910 and worked among cattle and sheep for nearly 20 years. He was put to sleep on 14 Nov 1939. The British record is 27 years 313 days for a Welsh collie named 'Taffy' owned by Mrs Evelyn Brown of Forge Farm, West Bromwich, W. Midlands. He was whelped on 2 Apr 1952 and was put to sleep on 9 Feb 1980.

Strength and endurance

The greatest load ever shifted by a dog was 6400½ lb *2905 kg* of railroad steel pulled by a 176 lb *80 kg* St Bernard named 'Ryettes Brandy Bear' at Bothell, Washington, USA on 21 July 1978. The 4-year-old dog, owned by Douglas Alexander of Monroe, Washington, pulled the weight on a four-wheeled carrier across a concrete surface for a distance of 15 ft *4,57 m* in less than 90 sec. The strongest dog in the world in terms of most proportionate weight hauled is 'Barbara-Allen's Dark Hans', a 97 lb *44 kg* Newfoundland, who pulled 5045½ lb *2289 kg* (= 52 lb *23,5 kg* per lb *0,45 kg* body weight) across a cement surface at Bothell on 20 July 1979. The dog, owned by Miss Terri Dickinson of Kenmore, Washington, was only 12 months old when he made the attempt. The record time for the annual 1049 mile *1688 km* sled race from Anchorage to Nome, Alaska (inaugurated 1973) is 12 days 7 hr 45 min by Rick Swenson's team of dogs in the 1981 race.

Rarest

The world's rarest breed of dog is the Tahltan bear dog, which was formerly used by the Tahltan Indians of western Canada for hunting big game. Only two examples of this hound still survive, both of them spayed bitches, which means the Tahltan will soon become extinct. The last known dog, 'Iskut' owned by Mrs Winnie Acheson of Atlin, British Columbia died on 20 Apr 1982 aged 15 years. One of the bitches lives in Atlin, the other at Carcross, 60 miles *96 km* further north.

Guide dog

The longest period of *active service* reported for a guide dog is 13 years 2 months in the case of a Labrador-retriever bitch named 'Polly' (whelped 10 Oct 1956), owned by Miss Rose Resnick of San Rafael, California, USA. The dog was put to sleep on 15 Dec 1971.

Largest litter

The largest recorded litter of puppies is one of 23 thrown on 19 June 1944 by 'Lena', a foxhound bitch owned by Commander W. N. Ely of Ambler, Pennsylvania, USA. On 6–7 Feb 1975 'Careless Ann', a St Bernard, owned by Robert and Alice Rodden of Lebanon, Missouri, USA also produced a litter of 23, 14 of which survived. The British record is held by 'Settrina Baroness Medina', (d. 1983) an Irish Red Setter owned by Mgr M. J. Buckley, Director of the Wood Hall Centre, Wetherby, West Yorkshire. The bitch gave birth to 22 puppies, 15 of which survived, on 10 Jan 1974.

Most prolific

The greatest sire of all time was the champion greyhound 'Low Pressure', nicknamed 'Timmy', whelped in September 1957 and owned by Mrs Bruna Amhurst of Regent's Park, London. From December 1961 until his death on 27 Nov 1969 he fathered 2414 registered puppies, with at least 600 others unregistered.

Most valuable

On 12 Oct 1983 it was reported that a genetic coyote-beagle cross killed at Storrs, Connecticut, USA had a value of $340,000 (then £225,000) in the ensuing litigation.

Highest and longest jump

The canine 'high jump' record for a leap and a scramble over a smooth wooden wall (without any ribs or other aids) is held by a German shepherd dog named 'Max of Pangoula', who scaled an 11 ft 5⅛ in *3,48 m* wall, at Chikurubi prison's dog training school near Harare, Zimbabwe on 18 Mar 1980. His trainer was Chief Prison Officer Alec Mann. 'Young Sabre', another German shepherd dog, handled by Cpl David Smith scaled a ribbed wall with regulation shallow slats to a height of 11 ft 8 in *3,55 m* at RAF Newton, Nottinghamshire on 17 July 1981. The longest recorded canine long jump was one of 30 ft *9,14 m* by a greyhound named 'Bang' made in jumping a gate in coursing a hare at Brecon Lodge, Gloucestershire in 1849.

Ratting

The greatest ratter of all time was Mr James Searle's bull terrier bitch 'Jenny Lind', who killed 500 rats in 1 hr 30 min at 'The Beehive', Old Crosshall Street, Liverpool on 12 July 1853. Another bull terrier named 'Jacko' owned by Mr Jemmy Shaw, was credited with killing 1000 rats in 1 hr 40 min, but the feat was performed over a period of ten weeks in batches of 100 at a time. The last 100 were accounted for in 5 min 28 sec in London on 1 May 1862.

Tracking

The greatest tracking feat on record was performed by a Dobermann Pinscher named 'Sauer', trained by Detective-Sergeant Herbert Kruger. In 1925 he tracked a stock-thief 100 miles *160 km* across the Great Karroo, South Africa by scent alone. In 1923 a collie dog named 'Bobbie', lost by his owners

Mammals

while they were on holiday in Wolcott, Indiana, USA, turned up at the family home in Silverton, Oregon 6 months later, after covering a distance of some 2000 miles *3200 km*. The dog, later identified by householders who had looked over him along the route, had apparently travelled back through the states of Illinois, Iowa, Nebraska and Colorado, before crossing the Rocky Mountains in the depths of winter.

Top show dog
The greatest number of 'Best-in-Show' awards won by any dog in all-breed shows is the 140 compiled between May 1977 and mid-1980 by the Standard poodle bitch 'Ch. Lou-Gins Kiss Me Kate' (whelped 23 May 1976) owned by Mr and Mrs Jack Phelan of Manhattan, Illinois, USA.

Top trainer
The most successful dog trainer in the world is Mrs Barbara Woodhouse of Rickmansworth, Hertfordshire, who has trained 17,393 dogs to obey the basic commands during the period 1951 to 19 Apr 1984. The fastest dog trainer is Mr Armand Rabuttinio of Aston, Pennsylvania, USA. His highest total for a single day (9 am–6 pm) is 132 dogs at a training marathon held at Upland, Pennsylvania on 12 June 1982.

Police Dogs
The world's top police dog is 'Trep' of Dade County Crime Force, Florida, USA with $63 million (*then £36 million*) worth of narcotics sniffed out. Demonstrating at a school with 10 hidden packets, Trep once found 11. 'Sergeant Blitz', a drug-sniffing police dog in Savannah, Georgia, USA was the subject of a $10,000 (*£5250*) 'contract' in January 1977. 'General', a US Army dog 'arrested' 220 narcotics offenders in the period April 1974–March 1976.

Greatest dog funeral
The greatest dog funeral on record was for the mongrel dog 'Lazaras' belonging to the eccentric Emperor Norton I of the United States, Protector of Mexico, held in San Francisco, in 1862 which was attended by an estimated 10,000 people.

CATS (*UK cat population 4,897,000 (1982 estimate) compared with 42,000,000 for the USA*)

Heaviest
The heaviest domestic cat (*Felis domesticus*) on record is a seven year old neutered male tabby named 'Himmy' owned by Thomas Vyse of Redlynch, Cairns, Queensland Australia. On 23 June 1982 he weighed, *20,7 kg* 45 lb 10 oz (neck 15 in *38,1 cm*, waist 32 in *81,28 cm*, length 38 in *96,52 cm*). The heaviest cat ever recorded in Britain is a ten-year-old male tabby called 'Poppa' owned by Miss Gwladys Cooper of Newport, Gwent, S. Wales. He recorded a weight of 44 lb *19,95 kg* in May 1983.

LARGEST PET LITTERS

Animal/Breed	Date	No.	Owner
CAT *Burmese/Siamese*	7.8.1970	15*	Mrs Valerie Gane, Church Westcote, Kingham, Oxfordshire.
DOG *Foxhound*	19.6.1944	23	Cdr W. N. Ely, Ambler, Pennsylvania, USA.
DOG *St Bernard*	6/7.2.1975	23	R. and A. Rodden, Lebanon, Missouri, USA.
RABBIT *New Zealand White*	1978	24	Joseph Filek, Sydney, Cape Breton, Nova Scotia, Canada.
GUINEA PIG	1972	12	Laboratory Specimen.
HAMSTER *Golden Hamster*	28.2.1974	26†	L. and S. Miller, Baton Rouge, Louisiana, USA.
MOUSE *House Mouse*	12.2.1982	34‡	Marion Ogilvie, Blackpool, Lancs.
GERBIL	5.1983	14	Sharon Kirkman, Bulwell, Nottingham.
GERBIL	1960's	15§	George Meares, genetecist-owner gerbil breeding farm, St Petersburg, Florida, USA.

* 4 still born   † 18 killed by mother   ‡ 33 survived   § Uses special food formula

Towser, who has caught over 23,000 mice whilst prowling the Glenturret Distillery near Crieff in Tayside, Scotland.

Smallest
The smallest breed of domestic cat is the Singapura or 'Drain Cat' of Singapore. Adult males average 6 lb *2,72 kg* in weight and adult females 4 lb *1,81 kg*. A male Siamese cross named 'Ebony-Eb-Honey Cat' owned by Miss Angelina Johnston of Boise, Idaho, USA tipped the scales at only 1 lb 12 oz *0,79 kg* in February 1984 when aged 23 months.

Oldest
Cats are generally longer-lived than dogs. Information on this subject is often obscured by two or more cats bearing the same nickname in succession. The oldest cat ever recorded was probably the tabby 'Puss', owned by Mrs T. Holway of Clayhidon, Devon who celebrated his 36th birthday on 28 Nov 1939 and died the next day. A more recent and better-documented case was that of the female tabby 'Ma', owned by Mrs Alice St George Moore of Drewsteignton, Devon. This cat was put to sleep on 5 Nov 1957 aged 34.

Largest kindle
The largest litter ever recorded was one of 19 kittens (4 stillborn) delivered by Caesarean section to 'Tarawood Antigone', a 4-year-old brown Burmese, on 7 Aug 1970. Her owner, Mrs Valerie Gane of Church Westcote, Kingham, Oxfordshire, said the result was a mis-mating with a half-Siamese. Of the 15 survivors, 14 were males and one female.

The largest live litter (all of which survived) was one of 14 kittens born in December 1974 to a Persian cat named 'Bluebell', owned by Mrs Elenore Dawson of Wellington, Cape Province, South Africa.

Most prolific
A cat named 'Dusty', aged 17, living in Bonham, Texas, USA, gave birth to her 420th kitten on 12 June 1952. A 21-year-old cat 'Tippy' living in Kingston-upon-Hull, Humberside gave birth to her 343rd kitten in June 1933.

Richest and most valuable
When Mrs Grace Alma Patterson of Joplin, Missouri, USA died in January 1978 she left her entire estate worth $250,000 (*then £131,000*) to her 18 lb *8,16 kg* white alley cat 'Charlie Chan'. When the cat dies the estate, which includes a three-bedroom house, a 7 acre *2,9 ha* pet cemetery and a collection of valuable antiques, will be auctioned off and the proceeds donated to local and national humane societies. In 1967 Miss Elspeth Sellar of Grafham, Surrey turned down an offer of 2000 guineas (*£2100*) from an American breeder for her champion copper-eyed white Persian tom 'Coylum Marcus' (b. 28 Mar 1965) who died on 14 Apr 1978.

Best climber
On 28 Feb 1980 a female cat climbed 70 ft *21,3 m* up the sheer pebble-dash outside wall of a five-storey block of flats in Bradford, Yorkshire and took refuge in a roof space. It had been frightened by a dog.

Mousing Champion
The greatest mouser on record is a female tortoiseshell named

CAGED PET LONGEVITY
The greatest recorded ages for commonly kept pets

Animal/Species	Name, Owner etc.	Years	Months
RABBIT *European* ....fl. August 1977		18*	—
GUINEA PIG ....*Snowball* Died: 14 Feb 1979 (owner, M. A. Wall) Bingham, Notts.		14	10½
GERBIL ....*Sahara fl.* 1981, (owner, Aaron Milstone) Lathrap Village, Mich, USA.		8+	
MOUSE ....*Dixie* Died: 25 April 1981 (owner, A. Newton) Sheffield, S Yorkshire.		6	6
RAT ....Died: *c.* 1924 Philadelphia, Pennsylvania, USA.		5	8

> * 18 years also reported for a doe still living in 1947.
> Note: A report of 10 years 2 months for a hamster has been published but details are lacking.

'Towser' (b. 21 Apr 1963) owned by Glenturret Distillery Ltd near Crieff, Tayside, Scotland who notched up her 23,029th kill on 25 Apr 1984. She averages 3 mice per day.

RABBITS

Largest
The largest breed of domestic rabbit (*Oryctolagus cuniculus*) is the Flemish Giant. Adults weigh 7–8,5 kg *15.4–18.7 lb* (average toe to toe length when fully stretched 36 in *91 cm*), but weights up to 25 lb *11,3 kg* have been reliably reported for this breed. The largest British breed is the Giant Rabbit (British). Adults regularly weigh 12–15 lb *5,4–6,8 kg*, and examples over 20 lb *9 kg* have been recorded. In April 1980 a five month old French lop doe weighing 12 kg *26.45 lb* was exhibited at the Reus Fair, NE Spain.

The heaviest recorded wild rabbit (av. weight 3½ lb *1,58 kg*) is one of 8 lb 4 oz *3,74 kg*, killed by Norman Wilkie of Markinch, Fife, Scotland while ferreting on 20 Nov 1982.

Smallest
The smallest breeds of domestic rabbit are the Netherland dwarf and the Polish, both of which have a weight range of 2–2½ lb *0,9–1,13 kg* when fully grown.

Most prolific
The most prolific domestic breeds are the New Zealand white and the Californian. Does produce 5–6 litters a year, each containing 8–12 young (*cf.* five litters and three to seven young for the wild rabbit).

HARES

Largest
In November 1956 a Brown hare (*Lepus europaeus*) weighing 15 lb 1 oz *6,83 kg* was shot near Welford, Northamptonshire. The average adult weight is 8 lb *3,62 kg*

2. BIRDS (*Aves*)

Largest *Ratite*
The largest living bird is the North African ostrich (*Struthio camelus camelus*), which is found in reduced numbers south of the Atlas Mountains from Upper Senegal and Niger across to the Sudan and central Ethiopia (*see Table*).

Largest *Carinate*
The heaviest flying bird or carinate is the Kori bustard or Paauw (*Otis kori*) of East and South Africa. Weights up to 40 lb *18 kg* have been reliably reported for cock birds shot in South Africa. The Mute swan (*Cygnus olor*), which is resident in Britain, can also reach 40 lb *18 kg* on occasion, and there is a record from Poland of a cob weighing 22,5 kg *49.5 lb* which could not fly. The heaviest bird of prey is the Andean condor (*Vultur gryphus*), adult males averaging 20–25 lb *9,09–11,3 kg*. A weight of 31 lb *14,1 kg* has been claimed for a California condor (*Gymnogyps californianus*) (average weight 20 lb *9 kg*) now preserved in the California Academy of Sciences, Los Angeles.

Largest wing span
The Wandering albatross (*Diomedea exulans*) of the southern oceans has the largest wing span of any living bird (*see Table*). The only other bird reliably credited with a wingspread in excess of 11 ft *3,35 m* is the vulture-like Marabou stork (*Leptoptilus crumeniferus*) of Africa. In the 1930s an extreme measurement of 13 ft 4 in *4,06 m* was reported for a male shot in Central Africa, but this species rarely exceeds 9 ft *2,43 m*.

Smallest *World*
The smallest bird in the world in the male Bee hummingbird (*Mellisuga helenae*) of Cuba and the Isle of Pines (*see Table*). The smallest bird of prey is the 35 g *1.23 g* White-fronted falconet (*Microhierax latifrons*) of NW Borneo which is sparrow-sized. The smallest sea bird is the Least storm petrel (*Halocyptena microsoma*), which breeds on many of the small islands in the Gulf of California, NW Mexico. Adult specimens average 140 mm *5½ in* in total length.

Smallest *Great Britain*
The smallest regularly-breeding British bird is the Goldcrest (*Regulus regulus*), also known as the Golden crested wren or Kinglet. Adult specimens measure 90 mm *3.5 in* total length and weigh between 3,8 and 4,5 g *0.108 and 0.127 oz*.

Most abundant *Wild*
The most abundant species of wild bird is the Red-billed quelea (*Quelea quelea*) (*see Table*). The most abundant sea bird is probably Wilson's storm-petrel (*Oceanites oceanicus*) of the Antarctic. No population estimates have been published, but the number must run into hundreds of millions. Britain's most abundant sea-bird is the Common guillemot (*Uria aalge*) with an estimated 577,000 breeding pairs in 1969–70.

Most abundant *Domestic*
The most abundant species of domesticated bird is the Chicken, the domesticated form of the wild Red jungle fowl (*Gallus gallus*) of south-east Asia. In 1974 there were believed to be about 4,000,000,000 in the world, or about one chicken for every member of the human race. The fowl stock in Britain was estimated at 130,000,000 in 1972, producing 270,000,000 chicks annually.

Most abundant *Great Britain*
The commonest nesting birds found in Great Britain are the Blackbird (*Turdus merula*), the House sparrow (*Passer domesticus*), the Starling (*Sturnus vulgaris*), the chaffinch (*Fringilla coelebs*), the blue tit (*Parus caeruleus*) and the Dunnock or Hedge sparrow (*Prunella modularis*), all of which have a peak breeding population in excess of 5 million pairs. Between 1964 and 1974 the population of the Wren (*Troglodytes troglodytes*) increased tenfold after a series of mild winters, and at the end of this period there were an estimated 10 million pairs. This bird, however, is severely affected by very cold weather and suffers heavy losses during bad winters. It was estimated in 1967 that 250,000 pigeon fanciers owned an average of 40 racing pigeons per loft, making a population of *c.* 10 million in Great Britain.

Rarest *World*
Because of the practical difficulties involved in assessing bird populations in the wild, it is virtually impossible to establish the identity of the world's rarest living bird (*see Table*). Contenders are the Ooaa (*Moho braccatus*) of Kauai, Hawaiian Islands, of which only a single pair survived in 1980 and the Bishop's ooaa (*Moho bishopi*), another species of Hawaiian honeyeater last sighted in 1904 on Molokai, which was rediscovered on nearby Maui in 1982.

Rarest *Great Britain*
According to the British Ornithologists' Union there are more than 40 species of birds which have been recorded only once in the British Isles—most of them since the end of the Second World War in 1945. That which has not recurred for the longest period is the Black-capped petrel (*Pterodroma hasitata*), of the West Indies. A specimen was caught alive on a heath at Southacre, near Swaffham, Norfolk in March or April 1850. On 28–29 May 1979 an Aleutian tern (*Sterna aleutica*) was sighted on the Farne Islands, Northumberland. This bird breeds on the coasts of Alaska and eastern Siberia, and until then had never been recorded outside the N. Pacific. The most tenuously established British bird is the Snowy owl (*Nyctea*

scandiaca). During the period 1967–75 one pair bred regularly on Fetlar, Shetland Isles and reared a total of 21 young, but soon afterwards the old male took off for an unknown destination, having driven off all the young males, and left the females without a mate. On 19–22 April 1979 an adult male was seen on Fair Isle some 80 miles *129 km* further south, but it did not find its way to Fetlar. The white-tailed Sea Eagle (*Haliaeetus albicilla*) was re-introduced from Norway to Rhum, West Scotland in 1975.

Fastest and slowest flying
The fastest flying bird in level flight is the White-throated spine-tailed swift (*Hirundapus caudacutus*) (*see Table*). The slowest flying bird is the American woodcock (*Scolopax minor*), which has been timed at 5 mph *8 km/h* without sinking.

The bird which presents the hunter with the greatest difficulty is the Red-breasted merganser (*Mergus serrator*). On 29 May 1960 a specimen flushed from the Kukpuk River, Cape Thompson, northern Alaska, USA by a light aircraft recorded an air speed of 80 mph *128 km/h* in level flight for nearly 13 sec before turning aside.

Fastest and slowest wing beat
The fastest recorded wing beat of any bird is that of the Horned sungem (*Heliactin cornuta*) of tropical South America with a rate of 90 beats a second. Large vultures (Vulturidae) sometimes exhibit a flapping rate as low as one beat per sec, and condors can cruise on air currents for up to 60 miles *96 km* without beating their wings once.

Longest lived
The greatest irrefutable age reported for any bird is 72+ years (*see Table*). The British record is 68+ years in the case of a female European eagle-owl (*Bubo bubo*) which was still alive in 1899. Other records which are regarded as *probably* reliable include 73 years (1818–91) for a Greater sulphur-crested cockatoo (*Cacatua galerita*); 72 years (1797–1869) for an African grey parrot (*Psittacus erithacus*); 70 years (1770–1840) for a Mute swan (*Cygnus olor*) and 69 years for a raven (*Corvus corax*). In 1972 a Southern ostrich (*Struthio camelus australis*) aged 62 years and 3 months was killed in the Ostrich Abattoir at Oudtshoorn, Cape Province, South Africa. 'Jimmy', a red and green Amazon parrot owned by Mrs Bella Ludford of Liverpool, England was allegedly hatched in captivity on 3 Dec 1870 and lived 104 years in his original brass cage dying on 5 Jan 1975. On 28 Oct 1982 the death was reported of London zoo's famous Greater sulphur crested cockatoo 'Cocky' after spending 57 years in the parrot house. He was already a mature bird when he was acquired by a Mr R. Stevens at the turn of the century, and was probably at least 40 years of age when he was presented to the zoo in 1925.

Eggs *Largest*
The largest egg produced by any living bird is that of the ostrich (*Struthio camelus*). The average example measures 6–8 in *15–20 cm* in length, 4–6 in *10–15 cm* in diameter and weighs 3.63–3.88 lb *1,65–1,78 kg* (equal to the volume of two dozen hen's eggs). It requires about 40 min for boiling. The shell though $\frac{1}{16}$ in *1,5 mm* thick can support the weight of a 20 st *127 kg* man. The largest egg laid by any bird on the British list is that of the Mute swan (*Cygnus olor*), which measures 4.3–4.9 in *109–124 mm* in length and between 2.8 and 3.1 in *71–78,5 mm* in diameter. The weight is 12–13 oz *340–368 g*.

Eggs *Smallest*
The smallest egg laid by any bird is that of the Vervain hummingbird (*Mellisuga minima*) of Jamaica. Two specimens measuring less than 10 mm *0.39 in* in length weighed 0,365 g *0.0128 oz* and 0,375 g *0.0132 oz* respectively (*cf* 0,5 g *0.017 oz* for the Bee hummingbird). The smallest egg laid by a bird on the British list is that of the Goldcrest (*Regulus regulus*), which measures 12,2–14,5 mm *0.48–0.57 in* in length and between 9,4 and 9,9 mm *0.37 and 0.39 in* in diameter with a weight of 0,6 g *0.021 oz*. Eggs emitted from the oviduct before maturity, known as 'sports', are not reckoned to be of significance in discussion of relative sizes.

The egg of the Goldcrest, the smallest laid by a British bird.

Incubation *Longest and shortest*
The longest normal incubation period is that of the Wandering albatross (*Diomedea exulans*), with a normal range of 75–82 days. There is a case of an egg of the Mallee fowl (*Leipoa ocellata*) of Australia taking 90 days to hatch against its normal incubation of 62 days. The shortest incubation period is the 10 days of the Great spotted woodpecker (*Dendrocopus major*) and the Blackbilled cuckoo (*Coccyzus erythropthalmus*). The idlest of cock species include hummingbirds (family Trochilidae), Eider duck (*Somateria mollissima*) and Golden pheasant (*Chrysolophus pictus*) among whom the hen bird does 100 per cent of the incubation, whereas the female Common kiwi (*Apteryx australis*) leaves this to the male for 75–80 days.

Longest flights
The greatest distance covered by a ringed bird is 14,000 miles *22 530 km* by an Arctic tern (*Sterna paradisea*), which was banded as a nestling on 5 July 1955 in the Kandalaksha Sanctuary on the White Sea coast and was captured alive by a fisherman 8 miles *13 km* south of Fremantle, Western Australia on 16 May 1956. The bird had flown south via the Atlantic Ocean and then circled Africa before crossing the Indian Ocean. It did not survive to make the return journey.

Highest flying
The highest acceptable altitude recorded for a bird is 27,000 ft *8230 m* for 30 Whooper swans (*Cygnus cygnus*) flying in from Iceland to Northern Ireland. They were spotted by an airline pilot over the Outer Hebrides on 9 Dec 1967, and the height was also confirmed by air traffic control in Northern Ireland after the swans had been picked up on radar.

Most airborne
The most aerial of all birds is the Sooty tern (*Sterna fuscata*) which, after leaving the nesting grounds, remains continuously aloft for 3 or 4 years before returning to the breeding grounds. The most aerial land bird is the Common swift (*Apus apus*) which remains 'airborne' for 2–3 years until it is mature enough to breed.

Fastest swimmer
The fastest swimming bird is the Gentoo penguin (*Pygoscelis papua*) which has a maximum burst speed of *c.* 17 mph *27,4 km/h*. The deepest diving bird is the Emperor penguin (*Aptenodytes forsteri*) of the Antarctic which can reach a depth of 265 m *870 ft* and remain submerged for up to 18 min.

Most acute vision
Birds of prey (Falconiformes) have the keenest eyesight in the avian world, and their visual acuity is at least 8–10 times stronger than that of human vision. The Golden eagle (*Aquila chrysaetos*) can detect an 18 in *46 cm* long hare at a range of 2 miles *3,2 km* in good light and against a contrasting background, and a Peregrine falcon (*Falco peregrinus*) can spot a pigeon at a range of over 5 miles *8 km*.

Highest g force
Recent American scientific experiments have revealed that the beak of the Red-headed woodpecker (*Melanerpes erythrocephalus*) hits the bark of a tree with an impact velocity of 13 mph *20,9 km/h*. This means that when the head snaps back the brain is subject to a deceleration of about 10 g.

Feathers *Longest*
The longest feathers grown by any bird are those of the Phoenix fowl or Onagadori (a strain of red junglefowl *Gallus gallus*) which has been bred in south-western Japan since the mid 17th century. In 1972 a tail covert measuring 10,6 m *34 ft 9¼ in* was reported for a rooster owned by Masasha Kubota of Kochi, Shikoku. The two central pairs of tail feathers of Reeve's pheasant (*Syrmaticus reevesi*) of central and northern China can exceed 8 ft *2,43 m*.

Feathers *Most*
In a series of 'feather counts' on various species of bird a Whistling swan (*Cygnus columbianus*) was found to have 25,216 feathers, 20,177 of which were on the head and neck. The ruby-throated hummingbird (*Archilochus colubris*) has only 940.

Earliest and latest cuckoo
It is unlikely that the Cuckoo (*Culculus canorus*) has ever been *heard and seen* in Britain earlier than 2 Mar, on which date one

The Peregrine Falcon and the White throated spinetail swift—the fastest flyers in the Animal Kingdom (see table pp. 24 and 25).

MATTHEW HILLIER

was observed under acceptable conditions by Mr William A. Haynes of Trinder Road, Wantage, Oxfordshire in 1972. The two latest dates are 16 Dec 1912 at Anstey's Cove, Torquay, Devon and 26 Dec 1897 or 1898 in Cheshire.

Champion bird-spotter

The world's leading bird-spotter or 'twitcher' is Norman Chesterfield (b. 8 Mar 1913) of Wheatley, Ontario, Canada. By 5 Apr 1984 he had logged 6000 of the 8733 known species. The British life list record is 450 by Ron Johns and the British year list record is 330 by Stephen Webb of Chelmsford, Essex in 1980. The latter left his wife in the middle of their wedding anniversary dinner to chase a Forster's tern in Cornwall.

Nests *Largest*

The largest bird's nest on record is one 9½ ft *2,9 m* wide and 20 ft *6 m* deep built by a pair of Bald eagles (*Haliaeetus leucocephalus*) and possibly their successors near St Petersburg, Florida, USA reported in 1963 and estimated to weigh more than 2 tons/*tonnes*. The Golden eagle (*Aquila chrysaetos*) also constructs huge nests, and one 15 ft *4,57 m* deep was reported from Scotland in 1954. It had been in use for 45 years. The incubation mounds built by the Mallee fowl (*Leipoa ocellata*) of Australia are much larger, having been measured up to 15 ft *4,57 m* in height and 35 ft *10,6 m* across. The nest site may involve the mounding of matter weighing 300 tonnes *295 tons.*

DOMESTICATED BIRDS

Chicken *Heaviest*

The heaviest breed of chicken is one called the White Sully developed by Mr Grant Sullens of West Point, California, USA over a period of 7 years. One monstrous rooster named 'Weirdo' reportedly weighed 22 lb *10 kg* in January 1973, and was so ferocious that he had already killed two cats and crippled a dog which came too close. The heaviest British breed is the Dorking, with roosters weighing up to 14 lb *6,36 kg*.

Chicken flying *for distance*

The record distance flown by a chicken is 310 ft 6 in *94,64 m*

by *Shorisha* owned by Morimitzu Meura at Hammatzu, Japan on 8 Mar 1981. Hens are better fliers than cocks.

Turkey *Heaviest*

The greatest dressed weight recorded for a turkey (*Meleagris gallapavo*) is 78 lb 14¾ oz *35,8 kg* for a stag reared by Dale Turkeys of Caynham, Shropshire. It won the annual 'heaviest turkey' competition in London on 15 Dec 1982. Turkeys were introduced into Britain *via* Spain from Mexico in 1549.

Most expensive

The highest price reached at auction (auctioneer Michael Nicholson) for a turkey was the £3000 paid by Alan Dann of Dewhurst, the butcher chain for the 78 lb 14¾ oz *35,8 kg* stag (see above) aboard HMS Wellington at Temple Embankment, London on 15 Dec 1982.

Longest lived

The longest lived domesticated bird (excluding the ostrich) is the domestic goose (*Anser anser domesticus*) which normally lives about 25 years. On 16 Dec 1976 a gander named 'George' owned by Mrs Florence Hull of Thornton, Lancashire, died aged 49 years 8 months. He was hatched out in April 1927. The longest lived small cagebird is the canary (*Serinus canaria*). The oldest example on record was a 34-year-old cock bird named 'Joey' owned by Mrs K. Ross of Hull. The bird was purchased in Calabar, Nigeria in 1941 and died on 8 Apr 1975. The oldest budgerigar (*Melopsittacus undulatus*) was a hen bird named 'Charlie' owned by Miss J. Dinsey of Stonebridge, London. She died on 20 June 1977 aged 29 years 2 months.

Most talkative

The world's most talkative bird is a male African grey parrot (*Psittacus erythacus*) named 'Prudle', owned by Mrs Lyn Logue of Golders Green, London, which won the 'Best talking parrot-like bird' title at the National Cage and Aviary Bird Show held in London each December for 12 consecutive years (1965–76). Prudle, who has a vocabulary of nearly 800 words, was taken from a nest at Jinja, Uganda in 1958. He retired undefeated.

3. REPTILES (Reptilia)

(Crocodiles, snakes, turtles, tortoises and lizards.)

Largest and heaviest

The largest reptile in the world is the Estuarine or Salt-water crocodile (*Crocodylus porosus*) of south-east Asia, northern Australia, New Guinea, the Malay archipelago and the Solomon Islands (*see Table*).

Smallest

The smallest known species of reptile is believed to be *Sphaerodactylus parthenopion*, a tiny gecko found only on the island of Virgin Gorda, one of the British Virgin Islands, in the West Indies (*see Table*). It is possible that another gecko, *Sphaerodactylus elasmorhynchus*, may be even smaller. The only known specimen was an apparently mature female with a snout-vent length of 17 mm *0.67 in* and a tail the same measurement found on 15 March 1966 among the roots of a tree in the western part of the Massif de la Hotte in Haiti.

The smallest reptile found in Britain is the Viviparous or Common lizard (*Lacerta vivipara*). Adult specimens have an overall length of 118–178 mm *4.64–7.01 in* and weigh 8–15 g *0.28–0.53 oz*.

Fastest

The highest speed measured for any reptile on land is 18 mph *29 km/h* for a Six-lined racerunner (*Cnemidophorus sexlineatus*) (*see Table*). The highest speed claimed for any reptile in water is 22 mph *35 km/h* by a frightened Pacific leatherback turtle (see below).

Lizards *Largest*

The largest of all lizards is the Komodo monitor or Ora (*Varanus komodoensis*), a dragonlike reptile found on the Indonesian islands of Komodo, Rintja, Padar and Flores. Adult males average 225 cm *7 ft 5 in* in length and weigh about 59 kg *130 lb*. Lengths up to 30 ft *9,14 m* (*sic*) have been claimed for this species, but the largest specimen to be accurately measured was a male presented to an American zoologist in 1928 by the Sultan of Bima which taped 3,05 m *10 ft 0.8 in*. In 1937 this animal was put on display in St Louis Zoological Gardens, Missouri, USA for a short period. It then measured 10 ft 2 in *3,10 m* in length and weighed 365 lb *166 kg*. The longest lizard in the world is the slender Salvadori monitor (*Varanus salvadori*) of New Guinea which has been reliably measured up to 15 ft 7 in *4,75 m*.

Lizards *Oldest*

The greatest age recorded for a lizard is more than 54 years for a male Slow worm (*Anguis fragilis*) kept in the Zoological Museum in Copenhagen, Denmark from 1892 until 1946.

Chelonians *Largest*

The largest living chelonian is the Pacific leatherback turtle (*Dermochelys coriacea schlegelii*). The average adult measures 6–7 ft *1,83–2,13 m* in overall length (length of carapace 4–5 ft *122–152 cm*) and weighs up to 1000 lb *453 kg*. The greatest weight reliably recorded is 1908 lb *865 kg* for a male captured off Monterey, California, USA on 29 Aug 1961 measuring 8 ft 4 in *2,54 m* overall. The largest chelonian found in British waters is the Atlantic leatherback turtle (*Dermochelys coriacea coriacea*). A male which drowned off Crail, Fifeshire, Scotland measured 6 ft 4 in *1,93 m* in total length and weighed 772 lb *350 kg*.

The largest living tortoise is *Geochelone gigantea* of the Indian Ocean islands of Aldabra, Mauritius, and the Seychelles (introduced 1874). Adult males in the wild can exceed 450 lb *200 kg* but much heavier specimens have been recorded. A male named 'Marmaduke' received at London Zoo in 1951 recorded a peak weight of 616 lb *279 kg* before his death on 27 Jan 1963.

Chelonians *Longest lived*

The greatest authentic age recorded for a tortoise is 152+ years for a male Marion's tortoise (*Testudo sumeirii*) brought from the Seychelles to Mauritius in 1766 by the Chevalier de Fresne, who presented it to the Port Louis army garrison. This specimen (it went blind in 1908) was accidentally killed in 1918. When the famous Royal Tongan tortoise 'Tu'malilia' (believed to be a specimen of *Testudo radiata*) died on 19 May

1966 it was reputed to be over 200 years old, having been presented to the then King of Tonga by Captain James Cook (1728–79) on 22 Oct 1773, but this record may well have been conflated between two (or more) overlapping residents. The greatest proven age of a continuously observed tortoise is 116 + years for a Mediterranean spur-thighed tortoise (*Testudo graeca*) (*see Table*).

Chelonians *Slowest moving*

In a recent 'speed' test carried out in the Seychelles a male giant tortoise (*Geochelone gigantea*) could only cover 5 yd *4,57 m* in 43.5 sec (0.23 mph *0,37 km/h*) despite the enticement of a female tortoise. The National Tortoise Championship record is 18 ft *5,48 m* up a 1.12 gradient in 43.7 sec by 'Charlie' at Tickhill, South Yorkshire on 2 July 1977.

SNAKES

Longest *World*

The longest of all snakes (average adult length) is the Reticulated python (*Python reticulatus*) of south-east Asia, Indonesia and the Philippines (*see Table*).

Longest *In captivity*

The longest (and heaviest) snake ever held in captivity was a female reticulated python (*Python reticulatus*) named 'Colossus' who died in Highland Park Zoo, Pennsylvania, USA on 15 Apr 1963. She measured 28 ft 6 in *8,68 m* in length, and scaled 320 lb *145 kg* at her heaviest. Another female reticulated python 'Cassius', owned by Mr. Adrian Nyoka of Knaresborough Zoo, North Yorkshire measured about 25 ft 6 in *7,77 m* at the time of her death on 3 Apr 1980. She yielded a 29 ft *8,84 m* skin.

Longest *British*

The longest snake found in Britian is the Grass snake (*Natrix natrix*), which is found throughout southern England, parts of Wales and in Dumfries and Galloway, Scotland. Adult males average 660 mm *26 in* in length and adult females 760 mm *29.92 in*. The longest accurately measured specimen was probably a female killed in South Wales in 1887 which measured 1775 mm *5 ft 10 in*.

Shortest

The shortest known snake is the thread snake *Leptotyphlops bilineata*, which is found on the islands of Martinique, Barbados and St Lucia in the West Indies (*see Table*). The shortest venomous snake is the Spotted dwarf adder (*Bitis paucisquamata*) of Little Namaqualand, South West Africa, with adults averaging 9 in *228 mm* in length.

Heaviest

The heaviest snake is the Anaconda (*Eunectes murinus*) (*see Table*). The heaviest venomous snake is the Eastern diamondback rattlesnake (*Crotalus adamanteus*) of the south-eastern United States. One specimen measuring 7 ft 9 in *2,36 m* in length weighed 34 lb *15 kg*. Less reliable lengths up to 8 ft 9 in *2,66 m* and weights up to 40 lb *18 kg* have been reported. In February 1973 a posthumous weight of 28 lb *12,75 kg* was reported for a 14 ft 5 in *4,39 m* long King cobra (*Ophiophagus hannah*) at New York Zoological Park (Bronx Zoo).

Venomous *Longest and Shortest*

The longest venomous snake in the world is the King cobra (*Ophiophagus hannah*) (*see Table*).

Oldest

The greatest irrefutable age recorded for a snake is 40 years 3 months and 14 days for a male Common boa (*Boa constrictor constrictor*) (*see Table*).

Fastest moving

The fastest moving land snake is probably the slender Black mamba (*Dendroaspis polylepis*) (*see Table*). A speed of 15 mph *24 km/h* may be possible for short bursts over level ground. The British grass snake (*Natrix natrix*) has a maximum speed of 4.2 mph *6,8 km/h*.

Most venomous

The world's most venomous snake is the sea snake *Hydrophis belcheri* which has a venom one hundred times as toxic as that of the Australian taipan (*Oxyuranus scutellatus*). The snake abounds round Ashmore Reef in the Timor Sea, off the coast of North West Australia. The most venomous land snake is the Small scaled or Western taipan (*Oxyuranus microlepidotus*) of the Diamantina River and Cooper's Creek drainage bases in

Channel County, Queensland which has a venom nine times as toxic as that of the Tiger snake (*Notechis scutatus*) of South Australia and Tasmania. One specimen yielded 110 mg *0.00385 oz* of venom after milking, a quantity sufficient to kill 125,000 mice. It is estimated that between 30,000 and 40,000 people (excluding Chinese and Russians) die from snakebite each year, 75 per cent of them in densely populated India. Burma has the highest mortality rate with 15.4 deaths per 100,000 population per annum.

Most venomous *Britain*

The only venomous snake in Britain is the adder (*Vipera berus*). Since 1890 ten people have died after being bitten by this snake, including six children. The most recently recorded death was on 1 July 1975 when a 5-year-old was bitten at Callander, Central Scotland and died 44 hr later. The longest-recorded specimen was a female measuring 43½ in *110,5 cm* which was killed by Graham Perkins of Paradise Farm, Pontrilas, Hereford and Worcester in August 1977.

Rarest

The rarest snake in the world is the keel-scaled boa (*see Table*). Britain's rarest snake is the Smooth snake (*Coronella austriaca*) of Southern England, which has a total population of less than 2000.

Longest fangs

The longest fangs of any snake are those of the Gaboon viper (*Bitis gabonica*) of tropical Africa. In a 6 ft *1,83 m* long specimen they measured 50 mm *1.96 in*. On 12 Feb 1963 a Gaboon viper bit itself to death in the Philadelphia Zoological Gardens, Philadelphia, Pennsylvania, USA. Keepers found the dead snake with its fangs deeply embedded in its own back.

4. AMPHIBIANS *(Amphibia)*

Largest *World*

The largest species of amphibian is the Chinese giant salamander (*Andrias davidianus*), which lives in the cold mountain streams and marshy areas of north-eastern, central and southern China (*see Table*).

Largest *Britain*

The heaviest British amphibian is the Common toad (*Bufo bufo*) of which a female has been weighed at 118 g *4.16 oz*.

The longest is the Warty or Great crested newt (*Triturus cristatus*). One female specimen collected at Hampton, Greater London measured 162 mm *6.37 in* in total length.

Smallest *World and Britain*

The smallest species of amphibian is the frog *Sminthillus limbatus*, found only in Cuba (*see Table*). The smallest amphibian found in Britain is the Palmate newt (*Triturus helveticus*). Adult specimens measure 7,5–9,2 cm *2.95–3.62 in* in total length and weigh up to 2,39 g *0.083 oz*. The Natterjack or Running toad (*Bufo calamita*) has a maximum snout-vent length of only 80 mm *3.14 in* (female) but it is a bulkier animal.

Longest lived

The greatest authentic recorded for an amphibian is 55 years for a Japanese giant salamander (*Andrias japonicus*) (*see Table*).

Rarest *World and Britain*

The rarest amphibian in the world is the Israel painted frog (*Discoglossus nigriventer*) (*see Table*). Britains rarest amphibian is the Natterjack toad (see above). In 1983 the total population was estimated at 20,000, a third of them living among the sand dunes between Southport and Liverpool.

Highest and lowest

The greatest altitude at which an amphibian has been found is 8000 m *26,246 ft* for a Common toad (*Bufo vulgaris*) collected in the Himalayas. This species has also been found at a depth of 340 m *1115 ft* in a coal mine.

Most poisonous

The most active known poison is the batrachotoxin derived from the skin secretions of the Golden dart-poison frog (*Phyllobates terribilis*) of western Colombia, South America, which is at least 20 times more toxic than that of any other known dart-poison frog. An average adult specimen contains enough poison (1100 micrograms *0.038 oz*) to kill 2200 people.

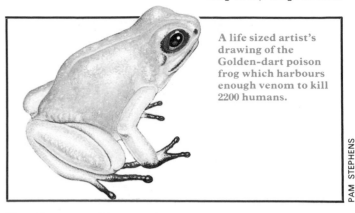

A life sized artist's drawing of the Golden-dart poison frog which harbours enough venom to kill 2200 humans.

PAM STEPHENS

Newt *Largest world*

The largest newt in the world is the Pleurodele or Ribbed newt (*Pleurodeles waltl*), which is found in Morocco and on the Iberian Peninsula. Specimens measuring up to 40 cm *15.74 in* in total length and weighing over 1 lb *450 g* have been reliably reported.

Newt *Smallest world*

The smallest newt in the world is believed to be the Striped newt (*Notophthalmus perstriatus*) of the south-eastern United States. Adult specimens average 51 mm *2.01 in* in total length.

Frog *Largest World*

The largest known frog is the rare Goliath frog (*Rana goliath*) of Cameroun and Equatorial Guinea. A female weighing 3306 g *7 lb 4.5 oz* was caught in the River Mbia, Equatorial Guinea on 23 Aug 1960. It had a snout–vent length of 34 cm *13.38 in* and measured 81,5 cm *32.08 in* overall with legs extended.

Frog *Largest Britain*

The largest frog found in Britain is the *introduced* Marsh frog (*Rana r. ridibunda*). Adult males have been measured up to 96 mm *3.77 in* snout to vent, and adult females up to 133 mm *5.25 in*, the weight ranging from 60 to 95 g *1.7–3 oz*.

Longest jump

(*Competition Frog Jumps are invariably triple jumps*). The record for three consecutive leaps is 10,3 m *33 ft 5¼ in* by a female South African sharp-nosed frog (*Rana oxyrhyncha*) named 'Santjie' at a frog Derby held at Lurula Natal Spa, Paulpietersburg, Natal on 21 May 1977. In May 1976 at the annual Calaveras Jumping Jubilee at Angels Camp, California, USA e. Davey Croakett owned by Dennis Matasci made a leap of 20 ft 3 in *6,17 m*.

Tree frog *Largest*

The largest species of tree frog is *Hyla vasta*, found only on the island of Hispaniola (Haiti and the Dominican Republic) in the West Indies. The average snout–vent length is about 9 cm *3.54 in* but a female collected from the San Juan River, Dominican Republic, in March 1928 measured 14,3 cm *5.63 in*.

Tree frog *Smallest*

The smallest tree frog in the world is the Least tree frog (*Hyla ocularis*), found in the south-eastern United States. It has a maximum snout–vent length of 15,8 mm *0.62 in*.

Toad *Largest World*

The most massive toad in the world is probably the Marine toad (*Bufo marinus*) of tropical South America. An enormous female collected on 24 Nov 1965 at Miraflores Vaupes, Colombia and later exhibited in the Reptile House at Bronx Zoo, New York City, USA had a snout–vent length of 23,8 cm *9.37 in* and weighed 1302 g *2 lb 11¼ oz* at the time of its death in 1967.

Toad *Largest Britain*

The largest toad and heaviest amphibian found in Britain is the Common toad (*Bufo bufo*). An outsized female collected in Kent with a snout–vent length of 99 mm *3.89 in* weighed 118 g *4.16 oz*.

Toad *Smallest World*

The smallest toad in the world is the sub-species *Bufo taitanus beiranus*, first discovered in *c.* 1906 near Beira, Mozambique, East Africa. Adult specimens have a maximum recorded snout–vent length of 24 mm *0.94 in*.

5. FISHES (*Agnatha, Gnathostomata*)

Largest marine *World*

The largest fish in the world is the rare plankton-feeding Whale shark (*Rhincodon typus*), which is found in the warmer areas of the Atlantic, Pacific and Indian Oceans. It is not, however, the largest marine animal, since it is smaller than the larger species of whales (mammals) (*see Table*). The largest carnivorous fish (excluding plankton eaters) is the comparatively rare Great white shark (*Carcharodon carcharias*), also called the 'Man eater', which ranges from the tropics to temperate zone waters. Adult specimens (females are larger than males) average 14–15 ft *4,3–4,6 m* in length and generally scale between 1150–1700 lb *522–771 kg* but larger individuals have been recorded. In June 1930 a female measuring 37 ft *11,27 m* in length was reportedly trapped in a herring weir at White Head Island, New Brunswick, Canada but this measurement is unconfirmed. A 21 ft *6,4 m* female caught off Castillo de Cojimar, Cuba in May 1945 weighed 7302 lb *3312 kg*.

The longest of the bony or 'true' fishes (Pisces) is the Oarfish (*Regalecus glesne*), also called the 'King of the Herrings', which has a worldwide distribution. In *c.* 1885 a 25 ft *7,6 m* long example weighing 600 lb *272 kg* was caught by fishermen off Pemaquid Point, Maine, USA. Another oarfish, seen swimming off Asbury Park, New Jersey by a team of scientists from the Sandy Hook Marine Laboratory on 18 July 1963, was estimated to measure 50 ft *15,2 m* in length. The heaviest bony fish in the world is the Ocean sunfish (*Mola mola*), which is found in all tropical, sub-tropical and temperate waters. On 18 Sept 1908 a huge specimen was accidentally struck by the SS *Fiona* off Bird Island about 40 miles *65 km* from Sydney, New South Wales, Australia and towed to Port Jackson. It measured 14 ft *4,26 m* between the anal and dorsal fins and weighed 4927 lb *2235 kg*.

Britain

The largest fish ever recorded in the waters of the British Isles was a 36 ft 6 in *11,12 m* Basking shark (*Cetorhinus maximus*) washed ashore at Brighton, East Sussex in 1806. It weighed an estimated 8 tons/*tonnes*. The largest bony fish found in British waters is the Ocean sunfish (*Mola mola*). A specimen weighing 800 lb *363 kg* stranded near Montrose, Scotland on 14 Dec 1960 was sent to the Marine Research Institute in Aberdeen.

Largest Freshwater *World*

The largest fish which spends its whole life in fresh or brackish water is the rare Pa beuk or Pla buk (*Pangasianodon gigas*) (*see Table*). This size *was* exceeded by the European catfish or Wels (*Silurus glanis*) in earlier times (in the 19th century lengths up to 15 ft *4,57 m* and weights up to 720 lb *336,3 kg* were reported for Russian specimens), but today anything over 6 ft *1,83 m* and 200 lb *91 kg* is considered large. The Arapaima (*Arapaima glans*), also called the Pirarucu, found in the Amazon and other South American rivers and often claimed to be the largest freshwater fish, averaged 6½ ft *2 m* and 150 lb *68 kg*. The largest 'authentically recorded' measured 8 ft 1½ in *2,48 m* in length and weighed 325 lb *147 kg*. It was caught in the Rio Negro, Brazil in 1836. In September 1978, a Nile perch (*Lates niloticus*) weighing 416 lb *188,6 kg* was netted in the eastern part of Lake Victoria, Kenya.

Largest Freshwater *Britain*

The largest fish ever caught in a British river was a Common sturgeon (*Acipenser sturio*) weighing 507½ lb *230 kg* and measuring 9 ft *2,74 m*, which was accidentally netted in the Severn at Lydney, Gloucestershire on 1 June 1937. Larger specimens have been taken at sea—notably one weighing 700 lb *317 kg* and 10 ft 5 in *3,18 m* long netted by the trawler *Ben Urie* off Orkney and landed at Aberdeen on 18 Oct 1956.

Smallest

The shortest and lightest freshwater fish is the Dwarf pygmy goby (*Pandaka pygmaea*) (*see table*). The shortest recorded marine fish—and the shortest known vertebrate—is the dwarf goby *Trimmatom nanus* of the Chagos Archipelago, central Indian Ocean. In one series of 92 specimens collected by the 1978–9 Joint Services Chagos Research Expedition of the British Armed Forces the adult males averaged 8,6 mm *0.338 in* in length and the adult females 8,9 mm *0.35 in*. The lightest of all vertebrates and the smallest catch possible for any fisherman

FRESHWATER FISH RECORDS

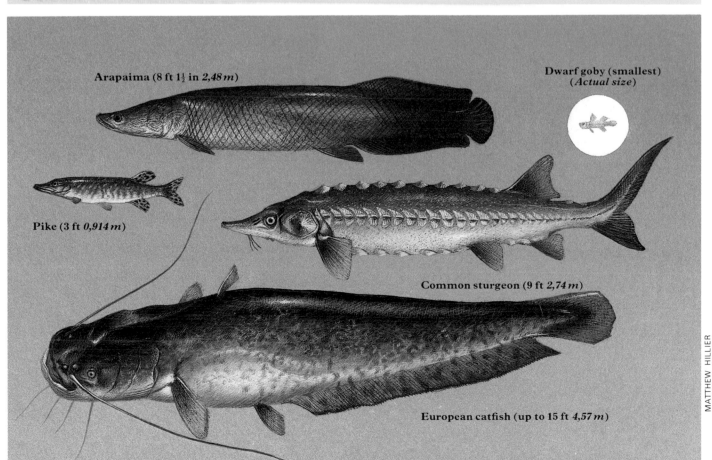

Arapaima (8 ft 1½ in *2,48 m*)

Dwarf goby (smallest) (*Actual size*)

Pike (3 ft *0,914 m*)

Common sturgeon (9 ft *2,74 m*)

European catfish (up to 15 ft *4,57 m*)

MATTHEW HILLIER

is the dwarf goby (*Schindleria praematurus*) from Samoa which measures 12–19 mm *0.47–0.74 in*. Mature specimens have been known to weigh only 2 mg, which is equivalent to *17,750 to the oz*. The smallest British marine fish is Guillet's goby (*Lebutus guilleti*) which does not exceed 24 mm *0.94 in*. It has been recorded from the English Channel, the west coast of Ireland and the Irish Sea. The smallest known shark is the Long-faced dwarf shark (*Squaliolus laticaudus*) of the western Pacific which does not exceed 150 mm *5.9 in*.

The world's smallest commercial fish is the now endangered Sinarapan (*Mistichthys luzonensis*), a goby found only in Lake Buhi, Luzon. Adult males measure 10–13 mm *0.39–0.51 in* in length, and a dried 1 lb *454 g* fish cake contains about 70,000 of them!

Fastest

The cosmopolitan sailfish (*Istiophorus platypterus*) is generally considered to be the fastest species of fish, although the practical difficulties of measurement make data extremely difficult to secure. A figure of 68.1 mph *109,7 km/h* (100 yd *91 m* in 3 sec) has been cited for one off Florida, USA. The swordfish (*Xiphias gladius*) has also been credited with very high speeds, but the evidence is based mainly on bills that have been found deeply embedded in ships' timbers. A speed of 50 knots (57.6 mph *92,7 km/h*) has been calculated from a penetration of 22 in *56 cm* by a bill into a piece of timber, but 30–35 knots (35–40 mph *56–64 km/h*) is the most conceded by some experts. A Wahoo (*Acanthocybium solandri*), 1,1 m *43 in* in length is capable of attaining a speed of 77 km/h *47.8 mph* (*see Table*).

Longest lived

Aquaria are of too recent origin to be able to establish with certainty which species of fish can be regarded as being the longest lived. Early indications are, however, that it is the Lake sturgeon (*Acipenser fulvescens*) of North America (*see Table*). In July 1974 a growth ring count of 228 years (*sic*) was reported for a female Koi fish, a form of fancy carp, named 'Hanako' living in a pond in Higashi Shirakawa, Gifu Prefecture, Japan, but the greatest authoritatively accepted age for this species is 'more than 50 years'. In 1948 the death was reported of an 88-year-old female European eel (*Anguilla anguilla*) named 'Putte' in the aquarium at Halsingborg Museum, southern Sweden. She was allegedly born in the Sargasso Sea, North Atlantic in 1860, and was caught in a river as a three year old elver.

Oldest goldfish

Goldfish (*Carassius auratus*) have been reported to live for over 40 years in China. The British record is held by a specimen named 'Fred' owned by Mr A. R. Wilson of Worthing, Sussex, which died on 1 Aug 1980, aged 41 years.

Shortest lived

The shortest-lived fishes are probably certain species of the sub-order Cyprinodontei (killifish) found in Africa and South America which normally live about eight months.

Most abundant

The most abundant species of fish in the world is probably the 3 in *76 mm* long deep-sea bristlemouth *Cyclothone elongata* which has a worldwide distribution.

Deepest

The greatest depth from which a fish has been recovered is 8300 m *27,230 ft* in the Puerto Rico Trench (27,488 ft *8366 m*) in the Atlantic by Dr Gilbert L. Voss of the US research vessel *John Elliott* who took a 6½ in *16,5 cm* long *Bassogigas profundissimus* in April 1970. It was only the fifth such brotulid ever caught. Dr Jacques Picard and Lieutenant Don Walsh, US Navy, reported they saw a sole-like fish about 1 ft *33 cm* long (tentatively identified as *Chascanopsetta lugubris*) from the bathyscaphe *Trieste* at a depth of 35,802 ft *10 912 m* in the Challenger Deep (Marianas Trench) in the western Pacific on 24 Jan 1960. This sighting, however, has been questioned by some authorities, who still regard the brotulids of the genus *Bassogigas* as the deepest-living vertebrates.

Most and least eggs

The Ocean sunfish (*Mola mola*) produces up to 300,000,000 eggs, each of them measuring about 0.05 in *1,3 mm* in diameter. The egg yield of the tooth carp *Jordanella floridae* of Florida, USA is only *c.* 20 over a period of several days.

Most Valuable

The world's most valuable fish is the Russian sturgeon (*Huso huso*). One 2706 lb *1227 kg* female caught in the Tikhaya Sosna River in 1924 yielded 541 lb *245 kg* of best quality caviare.

Dr Takayaki Hosogi, the owner of a 7 year old 35 in *89 cm* long fancy carp called 'Fujitavo', which won the All-Japan Koi Championship on 1 Mar 1982, has since refused an offer of £69,400 for this specimen.

Most venomous

The most venomous fish in the world are the Stonefish (*Synanceidae*) of the tropical waters of the Indo-Pacific, and in particular *Synanceja horrida* which has the largest venom glands of any known fish. Direct contact with the spines of its fins, which contain a strong neurotoxic poison, often proves fatal.

Most electric

The most powerful electric fish is the Electric eel (*Electrophorus electricus*), which is found in the rivers of Brazil, Colombia, Venezuela and Peru. An average sized specimen can discharge 400 volts at 1 ampere, but measurements up to 650 volts have been recorded.

6. STARFISHES (*Asteroidea*)

Largest

The largest of the 1600 known species of starfish in terms of total arm span is the very fragile bisingid *Midgardia xandaros*. A specimen collected by the Texas A & M University research vessel *Alaminos* in the southern part of the Gulf of Mexico in the late summer of 1968, measured 1380 mm *54.33 in* tip to tip, but the diameter of its disc was only 26 mm *1.02 in*. Its dry weight was 70 g *2.46 oz*. The heaviest species of starfish is the five-armed *Thromidia catalai* of the Western Pacific. One specimen collected off Ilot Amedee, New Caledonia on 14 Sept 1969 and later deposited in Noumea Aquarium weighed an estimated 6 kg *13.2 lb* (total arm span 630 mm *24.8 in*). The largest starfish found in British waters is the Spiny starfish (*Marthasterias glacialis*). In January 1979 Jonathon MacNeil of the Isle of Barra, Western Isles, found a specimen on the beach which originally spanned 30 in *76,2 cm*.

Smallest

The smallest known starfish is *Asterina phylactica*, found in the Adriatic and the Mediterranean as well as waters off south-western Britain, which is not known to exceed 15 mm *0.58 in* in diameter.

Deepest

The greatest depth from which a starfish has been recovered is 7584 m *24,881 ft* for a specimen of *Porcellanaster ivanovi* collected by the USSR research ship *Vityaz* in the Marianas Trench, in the West Pacific *c.* 1962.

7. ARACHNIDS (*Arachnida*)

SPIDERS (order Araneae)

Largest *World*

The world's largest known spiders in terms of leg-span are the bulky theraphosid spiders of the genera *Lasiodora* and *Grammostola* of Brazil, and *Theraphosa* of NE South America, all of which have been credited with leg spans in excess of 10 in *250 mm* (*see Table*).

Largest *Britain*

Of the 617 known British species of spider covering an estimated population of over 500,000,000,000, the Cardinal spider (*Tegenaria gigantea*) of Southern England has the greatest leg span. On 24 Sept 1983 Mr Craig Stangroom of Little Odell, Bedfordshire collected an outsized female in his garden which had a span of at least 143 mm *5.63 in*. The well-known 'Daddy Longlegs' spider (*Pholcus phalangioides*) rarely exceeds 3 in *75 mm* in leg span, but one out-sized specimen collected in England measured 6 in *15,2 cm* across. The heaviest spider found in Britain is the orb weaver *Araneus quadratus*. On 10 Sept 1979 a female weighing 2,25 g *0.079 oz* was collected at Lavington, Sussex by J. R. Parker.

Smallest *World and Britain*

The smallest known spider is *Patu marplesi* (family Symphytognathidae) of Western Samoa (*see Table*).

Britain's smallest spider is the rare but widely distributed *Theonoe minutissima*. Adult specimens of both sexes have a body length of 1,25 mm *0.048 in.*

Rarest

The most elusive of all spiders are the rare trapdoor spiders of the genus *Liphistius*, which are found in south-east Asia (*see Table*). The most elusive spiders in Britain are the four species which are known only from the holotype specimen. These are the jumping spiders *Salticus mutabilis* (1 male Bloxworth, Dorset, 1860) and *Heliophanus melinus* (1 female Bloxworth, 1870); the crab spider *Philodromus buxi* (1 female Bloxworth pre-1879); and the cobweb spider *Robertus insignis* (1 male Norwich, 1906).

Commonest *World and Britain*

For world's commonest see Table. The commonest spider in Britain is *Araneus diadematus*, which has been recorded from all but four counties of Great Britain and Ireland.

Fastest

The highest speed recorded for a spider on a level surface is by *Tegenaria gigantea* (*see Table*). This is 33 times her body length per sec compared with the human record of 5½ times.

Longest lived

The longest lived of all spiders are the primitive *Mygalomorphae* (tarantulas and allied species) (*see Table*). The longest-lived British spider is probably the purse web spider (*Atypus affinis*). One specimen was kept in a greenhouse for nine years.

Largest and smallest webs

The largest webs are the aerial ones spun by the tropical orb weavers of the genus *Nephila*, which have been measured up to 18 ft 9¾ in *573 cm* in circumference. The smallest webs are spun by spiders like *Glyphesis cottonae*, etc. which are about the size of a postage stamp.

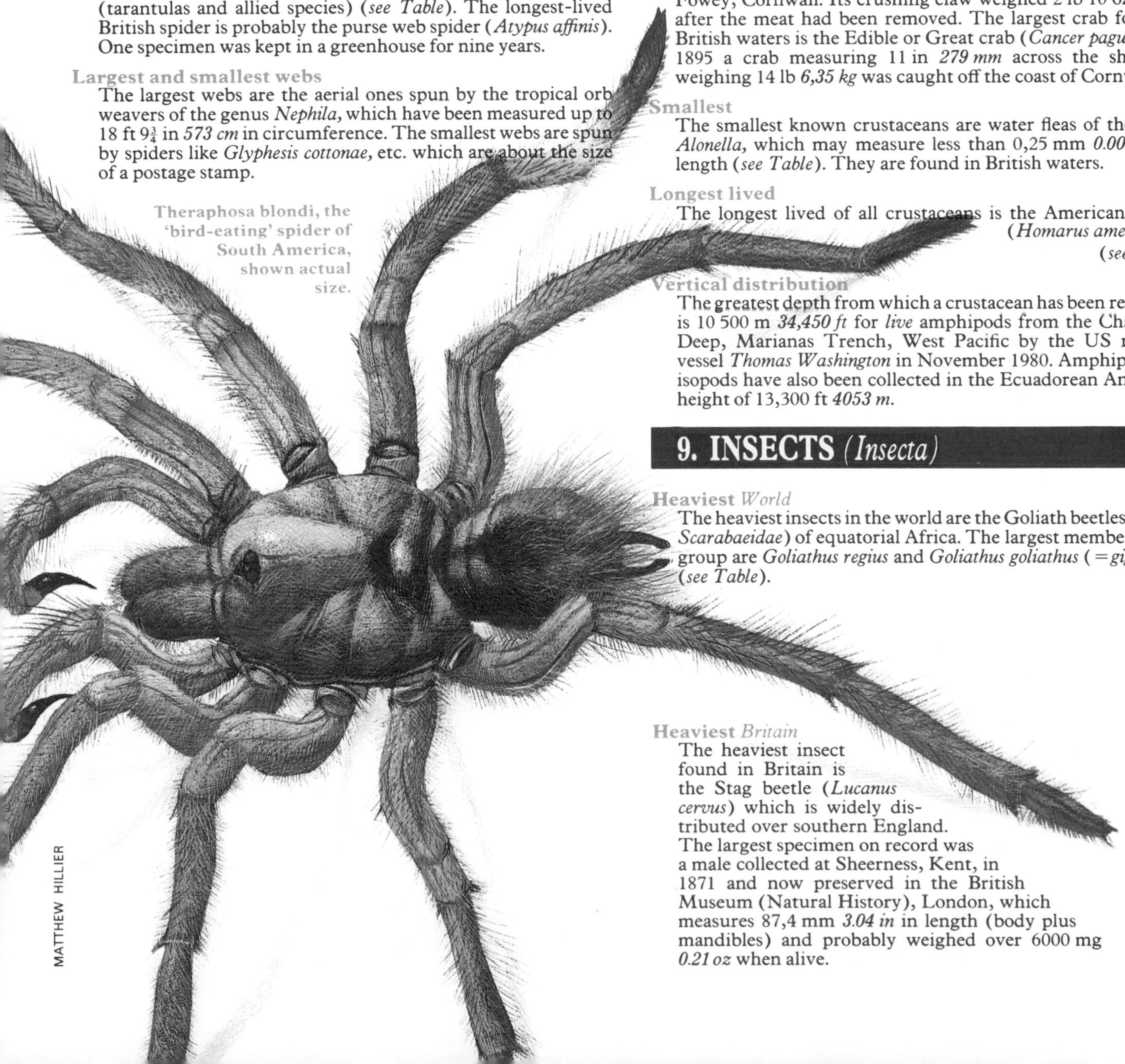

Theraphosa blondi, the 'bird-eating' spider of South America, shown actual size.

Most venomous

The most venomous spiders in the world are the Brazilian wandering spiders of the genus Phoneutria, and particularly *P. fera*, which has the most active neurotoxic venom of any living spider. These large and highly aggressive creatures frequently enter human dwellings and hide in clothing or shoes. When disturbed they bite furiously several times, and hundreds of accidents involving these species are reported annually. Fortunately an effective antivenin is available, and when deaths do occur they are usually children under the age of seven.

8. CRUSTACEANS (*Crustacea*)

(Crabs, lobsters, shrimps, prawns, crayfish, barnacles, water fleas, fish lice, woodlice, sandhoppers, krill, etc.)

Largest *World*

The largest of all crustaceans (although not the heaviest) is the sanschouo or giant spider crab (*Macrocheira kaempferi*), also called the stilt crab, which is found in deep waters off the south-eastern coast of Japan (*see Table*).

Largest *Britain*

The largest crustacean found in British waters is the Common or European lobster (*Homarus vulgaris*), which averages 2–3 lb *900–1360 g*. In June 1931 an outsized specimen weighing 20¼ lb *5,80 kg* and measuring 4 ft 1½ in *1,26 m* in total length, was caught in a caisson during the construction of No. 3 jetty at Fowey, Cornwall. Its crushing claw weighed 2 lb 10 oz *1188 g* after the meat had been removed. The largest crab found in British waters is the Edible or Great crab (*Cancer pagurus*). In 1895 a crab measuring 11 in *279 mm* across the shell and weighing 14 lb *6,35 kg* was caught off the coast of Cornwall.

Smallest

The smallest known crustaceans are water fleas of the genus *Alonella*, which may measure less than 0,25 mm *0.0098 in* in length (*see Table*). They are found in British waters.

Longest lived

The longest lived of all crustaceans is the American lobster (*Homarus americanus*) (*see Table*).

Vertical distribution

The greatest depth from which a crustacean has been recovered is 10 500 m *34,450 ft* for *live* amphipods from the Challenger Deep, Marianas Trench, West Pacific by the US research vessel *Thomas Washington* in November 1980. Amphipods and isopods have also been collected in the Ecuadorean Andes at a height of 13,300 ft *4053 m*.

9. INSECTS (*Insecta*)

Heaviest *World*

The heaviest insects in the world are the Goliath beetles (family *Scarabaeidae*) of equatorial Africa. The largest members of the group are *Goliathus regius* and *Goliathus goliathus* (=*giganteus*) (*see Table*).

Heaviest *Britain*

The heaviest insect found in Britain is the Stag beetle (*Lucanus cervus*) which is widely distributed over southern England. The largest specimen on record was a male collected at Sheerness, Kent, in 1871 and now preserved in the British Museum (Natural History), London, which measures 87,4 mm *3.04 in* in length (body plus mandibles) and probably weighed over 6000 mg *0.21 oz* when alive.

BUTTERFLIES AND MOTHS (order Lepidoptera)

Largest *World*

The largest known butterfly is the protected Queen Alexandra's birdwing (*Ornithoptera alexandrae*) which is restricted to the Popondetta Plain in Papua New Guinea. Females may have a wing span exceeding 280 mm *11.02 in* and weigh over 5 g *0.176 oz*. The largest moth in the world (although not the heaviest) is the Hercules moth (*Cosdinoscera hercules*) of tropical Australia and New Guinea. A wing area of up to 40.8 in² *263,2 cm²* and a wing span of 280 mm *11 in* have been recorded. In 1948 an unconfirmed measurement of 360 mm *14.17 in* was reported for a female captured near the post office at the coastal town of Innisfail, Queensland, Australia. The rare Owlet moth (*Thysania agrippina*) of Brazil has been measured up to 300 mm *11.81 in* wing span, and the Philippine atlas moth (*Attacus crameri caesar*) up to 280 mm *11.02 in*, but both these species are lighter than *C. hercules*.

Largest *Britain*

The largest (but not the heaviest) of the 21,000 species of insect found in Britain is the very rare Death's head hawkmoth (*Acherontia atropos*). One female found dead in a garden at Tiverton, Devon, in 1931 had a wing span of 5.75 in *145 mm* and weighed nearly 3 g *0.10 oz*. The largest butterfly found in Britain is the Monarch butterfly (*Danaus plexippus*), also called the Milkweed or Black-veined brown butterfly, a rare vagrant which breeds in the southern United States and Central America. It has a wing span of up to 5 in *127 mm* and weighs about 1 g *0.04 oz*. The largest *native* butterfly is the Swallowtail (*Papilio machaon brittannicus*), females of which have a wing span up to 100 mm *3.93 in*. This species is now confined to a few fens in Suffolk, Cambridgeshire and the Norfolk Broads.

Smallest *World and Britain*

The smallest of the 140,000 known species of Lepidoptera are the moths *Johanssonia acetosea* found in Britain, and *Stigmella ridiculosa* from the Canary Islands, which have a wing span of *c.* 2 mm *0.08 in* with a similar body length. The world's smallest known butterfly is the Dwarf blue (*Brephidium barberae*) of South Africa. It has a wing span of 14 mm *0.55 in*. The smallest butterfly found in Britain is the Small blue (*Cupido minimus*), which has a wing span of 19–25 mm *0.75–1.0 in*.

Rarest

The rarest British butterfly (59 species) is the Chequered Skipper (*Carterocephalus palaemon*) now confined to a single site near Fort William, Inverness, Scotland. The Heath Fritillary *Melitaea athalia* is now confined to three sites in Kent and Cornwall. The Large blue (*Maculinea arion*) was officially declared extinct in 1979. Since its demise this butterfly has reportedly been seen in various parts of Britain. These sightings may have been examples of the very similar Holly Blue (*Celastrina argiolus*) or the Chalk Hill blue (*Lysandra coridon*).

Most acute sense of smell

The most acute sense of smell exhibited in nature is that of the male Emperor moth (*Eudia pavonia*) which, according to German experiments in 1961, can detect the sex attractant of the virgin female at the almost unbelievable range of 11 km *6.8 miles* upwind. This scent has been identified as one of the higher alcohols ($C_{16}H_{29}OH$), of which the female carries less than 0,0001 mg.

Longest

The longest insect in the world is the giant stick-insect *Pharnacia serratipes* of Indonesia (*see Table*). The longest known beetles (excluding antennae) are the Hercules beetles (*Dynastes hercules* and *D. neptunus*) of Central and South America, which have been measured up to 190 mm *7.48 in* and 180 mm *7.08 in* respectively. More than half the length however, is taken up by the prothoracic horn.

Smallest *World*

The smallest insects recorded so far are the 'Hairy-winged' beetles of the family *Ptiliidae* (= *Trichopterygidae*) and the 'battledore-wing fairy flies' (parasitic wasps) of the family *Myrmaridae* (*see Table*). They are smaller than some of the protozoa (single-celled animals). The male bloodsucking banded louse *Enderleinellus zonatus*, ungorged, and the parasitic wasp (*Caraphractus cinctus*) may each weigh as little as 0,005 mg, or *5,670,000 to an oz*. The eggs of the latter each weigh 0,0002 mg, *or 141,750,000 to an oz*.

Commonest

The most numerous of all insects are Springtails (Order Collembola), which have a wide geographical range (*see Table*).

Fastest flying

Experiments have proved that the widely publicised claim by an American entomologist in 1926 that the Deer bot-fly *Cephenemyia pratti* could attain a speed of 818 mph *1316 km/h* (*sic*) was wildly exaggerated. If true it would have generated a supersonic 'pop'! Acceptable modern experiments have now established that the highest maintainable airspeed of any insect, including the Deer bot-fly, is 24 mph *39 km/h*, rising to a maximum of 36 mph *58 km/h* for short bursts (*see Table*).

Longest lived

The longest-lived insects are the Splendour beetles (*Buprestidae*) (*see Table*).

Loudest

The loudest of all insects is the male cicada (family Cicadidae). At 7400 pulses/min its tymbal organs produce a noise (officially described by the United States Department of Agriculture as 'Tsh-ee-EEEE-e-ou') detectable more than a quarter of a mile *400 m* distant. The only British species is the very rare Mountain cicada (*Cicadetta montana*), which is confined to the New Forest area in Hampshire.

Southernmost

The farthest south at which any insect has been found is 77° S (900 miles *1450 km* from the South Pole) in the case of a springtail (order Collembola).

Largest locust swarm

The greatest swarm of Desert locusts (*Schistocera gregaria*) ever recorded was one covering an estimated 2000 miles² *5180 km²* observed crossing the Red Sea in 1889. Such a swarm must have contained about 250,000,000,000 insects weighing about 500,000 tons *508 000 tonnes*.

Fastest wing beat

The fastest wing beat of any insect under natural conditions is 62,760 a min by a tiny midge of the genus *Forcipomyia*. In experiments with truncated wings at a temperature of 37° C *98.6° F* the rate increased to 133,080 beats/min. The muscular contraction–expansion cycle in 0.00045 or 1/2218th of a sec, further represents the fastest muscle movement ever measured.

Slowest wing beat

The slowest wing beat of any insect is 300 a min by the swallowtail butterfly (*Papilio machaon*). Most butterflies beat their wings at a rate of 460–636 a min.

Hive record

The greatest reported amount of wild honey ever extracted from a single hive is 549 lb *249,02 kg* recorded by A. D. Wilkes of Cairns, Queensland, Australia in the 11 months Feb–Dec 1983.

Dragonflies *Largest*

The largest dragonfly in the world is *Megaloprepus caeruleata* of Central and South America, which has been measured up to 191 mm *7.52 in* across the wings and 120 mm *4.72 in* in body length. The largest dragonfly found in Britain is *Anax imperator*, which has a wing span measurement of up to 106 mm *4.17 in*. The smallest British dragonfly is *Lestes dryas*, which has a wing span of 20–25 mm *0.78–0.98 in*.

Flea *Largest*

The largest known flea is *Hystrichopsylla schefferi schefferi*, which was described from a single specimen taken from the nest of a Mountain beaver (*Aplodontia rufa*) at Puyallup, Washington, USA in 1913. Females measure up to 8 mm *0.31 in* in length which is the diameter of a pencil. The largest flea (61 species) found in Britain is the Mole and Vole flea (*H. talpae*), females of which have been measured up to 6 mm *0.23 in*.

Flea *Longest jump*

The champion jumper among fleas is the common flea (*Pulex irritans*). In one American experiment carried out in 1910 a specimen allowed to leap at will performed a long jump of 13 in *330 mm* and a high jump of 7¾ in *197 mm*. In jumping 130 times its own height a flea subjects itself to a force of 200 g. Siphonapterologists recognise 1830 varieties.

10. CENTIPEDES (*Chilopoda*)

Longest

The longest known species of centipede is a large variant of the widely distributed *Scolopendra morsitans*, found on the Andaman Islands, Bay of Bengal. Specimens have been measured up to 13 in *330 mm* in length and 1½ in *38 mm* in breadth. The longest centipede found in Britain is *Haplophilus subterraneus*, which measures up to 70 mm *2.75 in* in length and 1,4 mm *0.05 in* across the body, but on 1 Nov 1973 Mr Ian Howgate claims to have seen a thin amber-coloured specimen in St Albans, Herts, measuring at least 4½ in *114 mm*.

Shortest

The shortest recorded centipede is an unidentified species which measures only 5 mm *0.19 in*. The shortest centipede found in Britain is *Lithobius dubosequi*, which measures up to 9,5 mm *0.374 in* in length and 1,1 mm *0.043 in* across the body.

Most legs

The centipede with the greatest number of legs is *Himantarum gabrielis* of southern Europe which has 171–177 pairs when adult.

Fastest

The fastest centipede is probably *Scutigera coleoptrata* of southern Europe which can travel at 1.1 mph *1,8 km/h*.

11. MILLIPEDES (*Diplopoda*)

Longest

The longest known species of millipede are *Graphidostreptus gigas* of Africa and *Scaphistostreptus seychellarum* of the Seychelles in the Indian Ocean, both of which have been measured up to 280 mm *11.02 in* in length and 20 mm *0.78 in* in diameter. The longest millipede found in Britain is *Cylindroiulus londinensis* which measures up to 50 mm *1.96 in*.

Shortest

The shortest millipede in the world is the British species *Polyxenus lagurus*, which measures 2,1–4,0 mm *0.082–0.15 in*.

Most legs

The greatest number of legs reported for a millipede is 355 pairs (710 legs) for an unidentified South African species.

12. SEGMENTED WORMS (*Annelida*)

Longest

The longest known species of giant earthworm is *Microchaetus rappi* (= *M. microchaetus*) of South Africa. An average-sized specimen measures 136 cm *4 ft 6 in* in length (65 cm *25½ in* when contracted), but much larger examples have been reliably reported. In *c.* 1937 a giant earthworm measuring 22 ft *6,70 m* in length when naturally extended and 20 mm *0.78 in* in diameter was collected in the Transvaal, and in November 1967 another specimen measuring 11 ft *3,35 m* in length and 21 ft *6,40 m* when naturally extended was found reaching over the national road (width 6 m *19 ft 8⅓ in*) near Debe Nek, eastern Cape Province. The longest segmented worm found in Britain is the King rag worm (*Nereis virens*). On 19 Oct 1975 a specimen measuring 44 in *111,7 cm* when fully extended was collected by Mr James Sawyer in Hauxley Bay, Northumberland. On 5 Nov 1982 the mutilated body of an earthworm measuring 5 ft 1 in *155 cm* in length was found at Herne Bay, Kent, but was discarded before it could be identified.

Shortest

The shortest known segmented worm is *Chaetogaster annandalei*, which measures less than 0,5 mm *0.019 in* in length.

13. MOLLUSCS (*Mollusca*)

(Squids, octopuses, shellfish, snails, etc.)

Largest squid

The largest known invertebrate is the Atlantic giant squid

The 5 ft 1 in *155 cm* earthworm found at Herne Bay, Kent, in November 1982. (*Arnold Bosworth*)

Architeuthis dux (*see Table*). The largest squid ever recorded in British waters was an *Architeuthis monachus* found at the head of Whalefirth Voe, Shetland on 2 Oct 1959 which measured 24 ft *7,31 m* in total length.

Largest octopus

The largest octopus known to science is *Octopus apollyon* of the coastal waters of the North Pacific which regularly exceeds 12 ft *3,7 m* in radial spread and 55 lb *25 kg* in weight. One huge individual caught single-handed by skin-diver Donald E. Hagen in Lower Hoods Canal, Puget Sound, Washington, USA on 18 Feb 1973 had a relaxed radial spread of 23 ft *7,01 m* and weighed 118 lb 10 oz *53,8 kg*. In November 1896 the remains of an unknown animal weighing an estimated 6–7 tons/*tonnes* were found on a beach near St Augustine, Florida, USA. Tissue samples were later sent to the US National Museum in Washington, DC, and in 1970 they were *positively* identified as belonging to a giant form of octopus (*Octopus giganteus*). Some experts, however, do not agree with this assessment because there was no evidence of tentacles or a beak and believe the decomposing carcase was more probably that of a large whale or shark. The largest octopus found in British waters is the Common octopus (*Octopus vulgaris*). It may span 7 ft *2,13 m* and weigh more than 10 lb *4,5 kg*.

Longest lived mollusc

The longest lived mollusc is the Ocean Quahog (*Artica islandica*) (*see Table*).

SHELLS

Largest

The largest of all existing bivalve shells is the marine Giant clam *Tridacna gigas*, which is found on the Indo-Pacific coral reefs. A specimen measuring 110 cm *43.3 in* across and weighing 292 kg *643.7 lb* (over a quarter of a ton) was collected near Irimote Island, Okinawa, Japan, and announced on 19 May 1983. It is now preserved in the local botanical garden. Another lighter specimen was measured to be 137 cm *53.9 in* overall. The largest bivalve shell found in British waters is the Fan mussel (*Pinna fragilis*). One specimen found at Tor Bay, Devon measured 37 cm *14.56 in* in length and 20 cm *7.87 in* in breadth at the hind end.

Smallest

The smallest shell is the univalve *Ammonicera rota*, which measures 0,5 mm *0.02 in* in diameter (*see Table*). The smallest bivalve shell also found in British waters is the coinshell *Neolepton sykesi*, which has an average length of 1,2 mm *0.047 in*. This species is only known from a few examples collected off Guernsey, Channel Islands and West Ireland.

Most Expensive Shell

For details of most expensive shell see table.

GASTROPODS

Largest

The largest known gastropod is the Trumpet or Baler conch (*Syrinx aruanus*) of Australia. One outsized specimen collected off Western Australia in 1979 and now owned by Don Pisor (who bought it from a fisherman in Kaoh-siung, Taiwan in November 1979) of San Diego, California, USA measures 77,2 cm *30.39 in* in length and has a maximum girth of 101 cm *39.76 in*. It weighed nearly 40 lb *18,14 kg* when alive.

The largest known land gastropod is the African giant snail (*Achatina* sp.). An outsized specimen 'Gee Geronimo' found by Christopher Hudson (1955–79) of Hove, E. Sussex, measured 15½ in *39,3 cm* from snout to tail, (shell length 10¾ in *27,3 cm*) in December 1978 and weighed exactly 2 lb *900 g*. The snail was collected in Sierra Leone in June 1976 where shell lengths up to 14 in *35,5 cm* have been reliably reported.

The largest land snail found in Britain is the Roman or Edible snail (*Helix pomatia*), which measures up to 4 in *10 cm* in overall length and weighs up to 3 oz *85 g*. The smallest British land snail is *Punctum pygmaeum*, which has a shell measuring 0.023–0.035 in *0,6–0,9 mm* by 0.047–0.059 in, *1,2–1,5 mm*.

Speed

The fastest-moving species of land snail is probably the common garden snail (*Helix aspersa*) (*see Table*).

14. RIBBON WORMS (*Nemertina*)

Longest

The longest of the 550 recorded species of ribbon worms, also called nemertines (or nemerteans), is the 'Boot-lace worm' (*Lineus longissimus*), which is found in the shallow waters of the North Sea (*see Table*).

15. JELLYFISHES (*Scyphozoa*)

Largest and smallest

The largest jellyfish is the Arctic giant jellyfish (*Cyanea capillata arctica*) of the north-western Atlantic. One specimen washed up in Massachusetts Bay had a bell diameter of 7 ft 6 in *2,28 m* and tentacles stretching 120 ft *36,5 m*. The largest cnidarian found in British waters is the rare 'Lion's mane' jellyfish (*Cyanea capillata*), also known as the Common sea blubber. One specimen measured at St Andrew's Marine Laboratory, Fife, Scotland had a bell diameter of 91 cm *35.8 in* and tentacles stretching over 13,7 m *45 ft*. Some true jellyfishes have a bell diameter of less than 20 mm *0.78 in*.

Most venomous

The most venomous cnidarian is the Australian sea wasp (*Chironex fleckeri*) which carries a cardio-toxic venom similar in strength to that found in the Asiatic cobra. These box jellyfish have caused the deaths of 66 people off the coast of Queensland, Australia since 1880. Victims die within 1–3 min if medical aid is not available. A most effective defence is women's panty hose, outsize versions of which are now worn by Queensland lifesavers at surf carnivals.

16. SPONGES (*Porifera*)

Largest

The largest known sponge is the barrel-shaped Loggerhead sponge (*Spheciospongia vesparium*) of the West Indies and the waters off Florida, USA. Single individuals measure up to 3 ft 6 in *105 cm* in height and 3 ft *91 cm* in diameter. Neptune's cup or goblet (*Poterion patera*) of Indonesia grows to 4 ft *120 cm* in height, but it is a less bulky animal. In 1909 a Wool sponge (*Hippospongia canaliculata*) measuring 6 ft *183 cm* in circumference was collected off the Bahama Islands. When first taken from the water it weighed between 80 and 90 lb *36 and 41 kg* but after it had been dried and relieved of all excrescences it scaled 12 lb *5,44 kg* (this sponge is now preserved in the US National Museum, Washington, DC, USA).

Smallest

The smallest known sponge is the widely distributed *Leucoso-lenia blanca*, which measures 3 mm *0.11 in* in height when fully grown.

Deepest

Sponges have been recovered from depths of up to 18,500 ft *5637 m*.

Coral

The world's largest reported coral is a stony colony of *Galaxea fascicularis* found on 7 Aug 1982 by Dr Shohei Shirai.

17. EXTINCT ANIMALS

Longest *World*

The longest dinosaur so far recorded is Diplodocus ('double-beam'), an attenuated titanosaurid which ranged over Western North America about 150 million years ago. A composite reconstruction in the Carnegie Museum of Natural History in Pittsburgh, Pennsylvania measures 87 ft 6 in *26,6 m* in total length—head and neck 22 ft *6,7 m*; body 15 ft *4,5 m*; tail 50 ft 6 in *15,4 m*—and has a mounted height of 11 ft 9 in *3,5 m* at the pelvis (the highest point on the body).

Longest *Britain*

In 1975 an amateur fossil-hunter working on the cliff-face near Brighstone, Isle of Wight, uncovered an unusual 228 mm *9 in* long bone which was later identified as the haemal arch (a bone running beneath the vertebrae of the tail) of a Diplodocus-type sauropod.

Heaviest *World*

The heaviest land vertebrates of all time were the massive brachiosaurids ('arm lizards') of the Late Jurassic (135–165 million years ago) of East Africa, the Sahara, Portugal and the south-western USA. A complete skeleton excavated by a German expedition at the famous Tendaguru site, southern Tanganyika (Tanzania) between 1909 and 1911 and now mounted in the Humboldt Museum für Naturkunde, East Berlin measures 74 ft 6 in *22,7 m* in total length (height at shoulder 21 ft *6,4 m*) and has a raised head height of 39 ft *11,8 m*. *Brachiosaurus brancai*, as it was named, weighed a computed 78,26 tonnes *77 tons* in life, but the museum also possesses bones from other individuals collected at the same site which are up to one-third as big again.

In the summer of 1972 the remains of another enormous brachiosaurid new to science, were discovered in the Dry Mesa Quarry on the Uncompahgre Plateau, western Colorado, USA. From the evidence of the bones already collected, including 8 ft *2,43 m* long matching shoulder blades, 'Supersaurus', as it has been nicknamed, is about 22 per cent larger than Brachiosaurus: this presupposes an overall length of *c*. 90 ft *27,4 m*, a shoulder height of 26 ft *7,9 m* and a raised head height of nearly 50 ft *15,2 m* if it is built on the same anatomical lines. The weight of such an animal, based on the cube of the fossil dimensions, would be *c*. 140 tonnes *138 tons*. In 1979 another shoulder blade measuring 8 ft 10 in *2,69 m* in length was discovered in the same quarry.

Heaviest *Britain*

Britain's heaviest land vertebrate was the sauropod *Cetiosauriscus oxoniensis* ('whale lizard'), which roamed across southern England about 150 million years ago. It measured up to 68 ft 6 in *20,88 m* in total length and probably weighed at least 30 tons/*tonnes*.

Largest land predator

The largest of the flesh-eating dinosaurs was probably the 6¾ tons/*tonnes* Tyrannosaurus rex ('king tyrant lizard') which stalked over what are now the states of Montana and Wyoming in the USA about 75,000,000 years ago. No complete single skeleton of this dinosaur has ever been discovered, but a composite individual has a bipedal height of 18 ft *5,5 m*. It has been estimated that the overall length was about 40 ft *12,0 m*. *Tarbosaurus efremovi* ('alarming lizard'), its Mongolian counterpart, measured up to 46 ft *14 m* in length but had a longer tail and was less heavily built. In 1934 the skeleton of a huge *Antrodemus* (= Allosaurus) with a much heavier body in proportion to its height than the tyrannosaurids was excavated near Kenton, Oklahoma, USA. This carnosaur had a bipedal height of 16 ft *4,87 m* and measured 42 ft *12,8 m* in overall length.

EARLIEST OF THEIR TYPES

Type	Scientific name and year of discovery	Location	Estimated years before present
Ape	Unnamed species (May 1979)	Padaung Hills, Burma	40,000,000
Primate	Tarsier-like	Indonesia	70,000,000
	Lemur	Madagascar	70,000,000
Social insect	*Sphecomyrma freyi* (1967)	New Jersey, USA	110,000,000
Bird	*Archaeopteryx lithographica* (1861)	Bavaria, W. Germany	190,000,000
Mammal	*Megazostrodon* (1966)	Thaba-ea-Litau, Lesotho	190,000,000
Reptiles	*Hylonomus, Archerpeton, Protoclepsybrops Romericus*	all in Nova Scotia	290,000,000
Amphibian	*Ichthyostega* (first quadruped)	Greenland	350,000,000
Spider	*Palaeostenzia crassipes*	Tayside, Scotland	370,000,000
Insect	*Rhyniella procursor*	Tayside, Scotland	370,000,000
Vertebrates (Fish scales)	*Anatolepis*	Crook County, Wyoming, USA	510,000,000
Crustacean	*Karagassiema* (12 legged)	Sayan Mts, USSR	c. 650,000,000
Metazoans	Bore hole tracks	Zambia	1,000,000,000
Eukaryotes	(c. Sept 1983)	Tianjin, China	1,800,000,000
Microfossils	Carbonaceous microspheroids	'North Pole', Western Australia	3,500,000,000

Note: Free Oxygen began forming in the Earth's atmosphere about 2300 million years ago.

Most brainless
Stegosaurus ('plated reptile'), which measured up to 30 ft *9 m* in total length had a walnut-sized brain weighing only 2½ oz *70g*, which represented 0.004 of 1 per cent of its computed body weight of 1¾ tons/*tonnes*. (*cf.* 0.074 of 1 per cent for an elephant and 1.88 per cent for a human). It roamed widely across the Northern Hemisphere about 150,000,000 years ago.

Largest dinosaur eggs
The largest known dinosaur eggs are those of *Hypselosaurus priscus*, ('high ridge lizard'), a 40 ft *12,19 m* long titanosaurid which lived about 80,000,000 years ago. Some examples found in the valley of the Durance near Aix-en-Provence, southern France in October 1961 would have had, uncrushed, a length of 12 in *300 mm* and a diameter of 10 in *255 mm* (capacity 5.8 pints *3,3 l*).

Largest flying creature
The largest flying creature is the pterosaur *Quetzalcoatlus northropi* which glided over what is now the state of Texas, USA about 65 million years ago. Partial remains discovered in Big Bend National Park, West Texas in 1971 indicate that this reptile must have had a wing span of 11–12 m *36–39 ft* and weighed about 190 lb *86 kg*.

Largest marine reptile
The largest marine reptile ever recorded was *Stretosaurus macromerus*, a short-necked pliosaur from the Kimmeridge Clay of Stretham, Cambridgeshire and Oxfordshire. A mandible found at Cumnor, Oxfordshire and now in the University Museum, Oxford has a restored length of over 3 m *9 ft 10 in* and must have belonged to a reptile measuring at least 46 ft *14 m* in total length. *Kronosaurus queenslandicus*, another pliosaur, was also of comparable size, and a complete skeleton in the Museum of Comparative Zoology at Harvard University, Cambridge, Massachusetts, USA measures 42 ft *12,8 m* in total length.

Largest crocodile
The largest known crocodile was *Deinosuchus riograndensis*, which lived in the lakes and swamps of what is now the state of Texas, USA about 75,000,000 years ago. Fragmentary remains discovered in Big Bend National Park, West Texas, indicate a hypothetical length of 16 m *52 ft 6 in*, compared with the 12–14 m *39.3–45.9 ft* of the *Sarcosuchus imperator* of Niger. The huge gavial *Rhamphosuchus*, which lived in what is now northern India about 2,000,000 years ago, was even longer reaching 60 ft *18,3 m*, but it was not so heavily built.

Largest chelonians
The largest prehistoric chelonian was *Stupendemys geographicus*, a pelomedusid turtle which lived about 5,000,000 years ago. Fossil remains discovered by Harvard University palaeontologists in Northern Venezuela in 1972 indicate that this turtle had a carapace (shell) measuring 218–230 cm *7 ft 2 in–7 ft 6½ in* in mid-line length and measured 3 m *9 ft 10 in* in overall length. It had a computed weight of 4500 lb *2041 kg* in life.

Largest tortoise
The largest prehistoric tortoise was probably *Geochelone* (= *Colossochelys*) *atlas*, which lived in what is now northern India, Burma, Java, the Celebes and Timor about 2 million years ago. In 1923 the fossil remains of a specimen with a carapace 5 ft 11 in *180 cm* long (7 ft 4 in *223 cm* over the curve) and 2 ft 11 in *89 cm* high were discovered near Chandigarh in the Siwalik Hills. This animal had a total length of 8 ft *2,44 m* and is computed to have weighed 2100 lb *852 kg* when it was alive. Recently the fossil remains of other giant tortoises (*Geochelone*) have been found in Florida and Texas, USA.

Longest snake
The longest prehistoric snake was the python-like *Gigantophis garstini*, which inhabited what is now Egypt about 55,000,000 years ago. Parts of a spinal column and a small piece of jaw discovered at Fayum in the Western Desert indicate a length of *c.* 37 ft *11 m*. Another fossil giant snake, *Madtsoia bai* from Patagonia, S. America, measured *c.* 10 m *33 ft* in length, comparable with the longest constrictors living today.

Largest amphibian
The largest amphibian ever recorded was the gharial-like *Prionosuchus plummeri* which lived 230,000,000 years ago. In 1972 the fragmented remains of a specimen measuring an estimated 9 m *30 ft* in life, were discovered in North Brazil.

Largest fish
No prehistoric fish larger than living species has yet been discovered. The claim that the Great shark (*Carcharodon megalodon*), which abounded in Miocene seas some 15,000,000 years ago, measured 80 ft *24 m* in length, based on ratios from fossil teeth has now been shown to be in error. The modern estimate is that this shark did not exceed 43 ft *13,1 m*.

Stegosaurus, which has earned the title of the most brainless dinosaur had only a 2½ oz *70 g* brain to control its 1¾ ton body. (*Pat Gibbon*)

Largest insect

The largest prehistoric insect was the dragonfly *Meganeura monyi*, which lived about 280,000,000 years ago. Fossil remains (*i.e.* impressions of wings) discovered at Commentry, central France, indicate a wing expanse of up to 70 cm *27.5 in.*

Britain's largest dragonfly was *Typus* sp. (family *Meganeuridae*), which is only known from a wing impression found on a lump of coal in Bolsover colliery, Derbyshire in July 1978. It had an estimated wing span of 50–60 cm *19.68–23.62 in* and lived about 300,000,000 years ago, making it the oldest flying creature so far recorded.

Most southerly

The most southerly creature yet found is a freshwater salamander-like amphibian *Labyrinthodont*, represented by a 2½ in *63,5 mm* piece of jawbone found near Beardmore Glacier Antarctica, 325 miles *532 km* from the South Pole, dating from the early Jurassic of 200,000,000 years ago. This discovery was made in December 1967.

Largest bird

The largest prehistoric bird was the flightless *Dromornis stirtoni*, a huge emu-like creature which lived in central Australia 11,000,000 years ago. Fossil leg bones found near Alice Springs in 1974 indicate that the bird must have stood *c.* 10 ft *3 m* in height and weighed *c.* 1100 lb *500 kg*. The giant moa *Dinornis maximus* of New Zealand was even taller, attaining a maximum height of 12 ft *3,6 m* but it only weighed about 500 lb *227 kg*.

The largest known flying bird was the giant teraton *Argentavis magnificens* which lived in Argentina about 6 million years ago. Fossil remains discovered at a site 100 miles *160 km* west of Buenos Aires in 1979 indicate that this gigantic vulture had a wing span of 7,0–7,6 m *23–25 ft* and weighed about 120 kg *265 lb.*

Largest mammals

The largest land mammal ever recorded was *Baluchitherium* (= Indricotherium, Pristinotherium and Benaratherium), a long-necked hornless rhinoceros which roamed across western Asia and Europe (Yugoslavia) about 35 million years ago. A restoration in the American Museum of Natural History, New York measures 17 ft 9 in *5,41 m* to the top of the shoulder hump and 37 ft *11,27 m* in total length, and this particular specimen must have weighed about 20 tonnes/tons in the flesh. The bones of this gigantic browser were first discovered in the Bugti Hills in east Baluchistan, Pakistan in 1907–08.

The largest marine mammal was the serpentine *Basilosaurus* (*Zeuglodon*) *cetoides*, which swam in the seas over what are now the American states of Arkansas and Alabama 50 million years ago. It measured up to 70 ft *21,3 m* in length.

Largest mammoth

The largest prehistoric elephant was the Steppe mammoth *Mammuthus* (*Parelephas*) *trogontherii*, which roamed over what is now central Europe a million years ago. A fragmentary skeleton found in Mosbach, West Germany indicates a shoulder height of 4,5 m *14 ft 9 in.*

Tusks *Longest*

The longest tusks of any prehistoric animal were those of the straight-tusked elephant *Palaeoloxodom antiquus germanicus*, which lived in northern Germany about 300,000 years ago. The average length in adult bulls was 5 m *16 ft 5 in.* A single tusk of a woolly mammoth (*Mammuthus primigenius*) preserved in the Franzens Museum at Brno, Czechoslovakia measures 5,02 m *16 ft 5½ in* along the outside curve. In *c.* August 1933, a single tusk of an Imperial mammoth (*Mammuthus imperator*) measuring 16 + ft *4,87 + m* (anterior end missing) was unearthed near Post, Gorza County, Texas, USA. In 1934 this tusk was presented to the American Museum of Natural History in New York City, NY, USA.

Tusks *Heaviest*

The heaviest single fossil tusk on record is one weighing 150 kg *330 lb* with a maximum circumference of 35 in *89 cm* now preserved in the Museo Civico di Storia Naturale, Milan, Italy. The specimen (in two pieces) measures 11 ft 9 in *3,58 m* in length.

The heaviest recorded fossil tusks are a pair belonging to a 13 ft 4 in *4,06 m* tall Columbian mammoth (*Mammuthus columbi*) in the State Museum, Lincoln, Nebraska, USA which have a combined weight of 498 lb *226 kg* and measure 13 ft 9 in *4,21 m* and 13 ft 7 in *4,14 m* respectively. They were found near Campbell, Nebraska in April 1915.

Antlers *Greatest Span*

The prehistoric Giant deer (*Megaceros giganteus*), which lived in northern Europe and northern Asia as recently as 8000 BC, had the longest horns of any known animal. One specimen recovered from an Irish bog had greatly palmated antlers measuring 14 ft *4,3 m* across.

PLANT KINGDOM (*Plantea*)

PLANTS

The medicinal value of plants was known to Neanderthal man *c.* 60,000 BC. The world's oldest garden has yet to be identified but is probably that of a Chinese temple. The world's oldest Botanical Garden is that at Pisa dating from 1543. Britain's oldest is the Botanic Garden, Oxford founded as a Physic Garden in 1621.

Oldest Living Thing

'King Clone', the oldest known clone of the creosote plant (*Larrea tridentata*) found in south west California, was estimated in February 1980 by Prof. Frank C. Vasek to be 11,700 years old. It is possible that crustose lichens in excess of 500 mm *19.6 in* in diameter may be as old. In 1981 it was estimated that Antarctic lichens of more than 100 mm *3.9 in* in diameter are at least 10,000 years old.

Rarest

Plants thought to be extinct are rediscovered each year and there are thus many plants of which specimens are known in but a single locality. The small pink blossoms of *Presidio manzanita* survive in a single specimen reported in June 1978 at an undisclosed site in California. *Pennantia baylisiana*, a tree found in 1945 on Three Kings Island, off New Zealand, only exists as a female and cannot fruit. In May 1983 it was reported that there was a sole surviving specimen of the lady's slipper orchid (*Cypripedium calceolus*). *Sporastatia cinerea*, a new genus of alpine lichen for Britain was found in Choire Garbh snowfield in the Cairngorm Scotland in 1982.

Northernmost

The yellow poppy (*Papaver radicatum*) and the Arctic willow (*Salix arctica*) survive, the latter in an extremely stunted form, on the northernmost land (83° N).

Southernmost

Lichens resembling *Rhinodina frigida* have been found in Moraine Canyon in 86° 09′ S 157° 30′ W in 1971 and in the Horlick Mountain area, Antarctica in 86° 09′ S 131° 14′ W in 1965. The southernmost recorded flowering plant is the Antarctic Hair Grass (*Deschampsia antarctica*) which was found in latitude 68° 21′ S on Refuge Island, Antarctica on 11 Mar 1981.

Highest

The greatest certain altitude at which any flowering plants have been found is 21,000 ft *6400 m* on Kamet (25,447 ft *7756 m*) by N. D. Jayal in 1955. They were *Ermania himalayensis* and *Ranunculus lobatus*.

Roots

The greatest reported depth to which roots have penetrated is a calculated 400 ft *120 m* in the case of a wild fig tree at Echo Caves, near Ohrigstad, East Transvaal, South Africa. An elm tree root of at least 360 ft *110 m* was reported from Auchencraig, Largs, Strathclyde *c.* 1950. A single winter rye plant (*Secale cereale*) has been shown to produce 387 miles *622,8 km* of roots in 1.83 ft³ *0,051 m³* of earth.

Worst weeds

The most intransigent weed is the mat-forming water weed *Salvinia auriculata*, found in Africa. It was detected on the filling of Kariba Lake in May 1959 and within 11 months had choked an area of 77 miles² *199 km²* rising by 1963 to 387 miles² *1002 km²*. The world's worst land weeds are regarded as purple nut sedge, Bermuda grass, barnyard grass, jungle-rice, goose grass, Johnson grass, Guinea grass, cogon grass and lantana. The most damaging and widespread cereal weeds in Britain are the wild oats *Avena fatua* and *A. ludoviciana*. Their seeds

The world's southernmost flowering plant, Antarctic Hair Grass, which has been found on Refuge Island, Antarctica, in Latitude 68° 21′ S. (*Dr. R. I. Lewis Smith*)

can withstand temperatures of 240° F *115,6° C* for 15 min and remain viable.

Most spreading plant

The greatest area covered by a single clonal growth is that of the wild box huckleberry (*Gaylussacia brachyera*), a mat-forming evergreen shrub first reported in 1796. A colony covering 8 acres, *3,2 hectares* was discovered in 1845 near New Bloomfield, Pennsylvania. Another colony, covering about 100 acres, was 'discovered' on 18 July 1920 near the Juniata River, Pennsylvania. It has been estimated that this colony began 13,000 years ago.

Longest Philodendron

A Philodendron, 569 ft *173,4 m* in length grows in the home of Mr M. J. Linhart in Thornton, Leicestershire.

Longest Passion Plant

In November 1974 a Passion plant, fed by a hormone by Dennis and Patti Carlson, was reported to have grown to a length of 600 ft *182 m* at Blaine, Minnesota, USA.

Largest aspidistra

The aspidistra (*Aspidistra elatior*) was introduced to Britain as a parlour palm from Japan and China in 1822. The biggest aspidistra in Britain is one 50 in *127 cm* tall with more than 500 leaves spanning 5 ft *1,52 m* grown by Gertie James in Staveley, Chesterfield.

Earliest flower

The oldest fossil of a flowering plant with palm-like imprints was found in Colorado, USA, in 1953 and dated about 65,000,000 years old.

Largest cactus

The largest of all cacti is the saguaro (*Cereus giganteus* or *Carnegiea gigantea*), found in Arizona, south-eastern California, USA and Sonora, Mexico. The green fluted column is surmounted by candelabra-like branches rising to a height of 16 m *52 ft 6 in* in the case of a specimen measured on the boundary of the Saguaro National Monument, Arizona. They have waxy white blooms which are followed by edible crimson fruit. An armless cactus 78 ft *24 m* in height was measured in April 1978 by Hube Yates in Cave Creek, Arizona.

Longest seaweed

Claims made that the seaweed off Tierra del Fuego, South America, grows to 600 ft *182,5 m* and even to 1000 ft-*305 m* in length have gained currency. More recent and more reliable records indicate that the longest species of seaweed is the Pacific giant kelp (*Macrocystis pyrifera*), which does not exceed 196 ft *60 m* in length. It can grow 45 cm *18 in* in a day. The longest of the 700 species of British seaweed is the brown seaweed *Chorda filum* which grows up to a length of 20 ft *6,10 m*. The Japanese *Sargassum muticum* introduced *c.* 1970 can grow to 30 ft *9,0 m*.

Mosses

The smallest of mosses is the pygmy moss (*Ephemerum*) and the longest is the brook moss (*Fontinalis*), which forms streamers up to 3 ft *91 cm* long in flowing water.

Largest vines

The largest recorded grape vine was one planted in 1842 at Carpinteria, California, USA. By 1900 it was yielding more than 9 tons/*tonnes* of grapes in some years, and averaging 7 tons/*tonnes* per year. It died in 1920. Britain's largest vine (1898–1964) was at Kippen, Stirling with a girth, measured in 1956, of 5 ft *1,52 m*. England's largest vine is the Great Vine, planted in 1768 at Hampton Court, Greater London. Its girth is 85 in *215,9 cm* with branches up to 114 ft *34,7 m* long and an average yield of 703 lb *318,8 kg*. In 1983 Mr L. Stringer of Dartford, Kent obtained a yield of 1015½ lb *460,6 kg* from a 4 year old vine.

Most northerly and southerly vineyards

A vineyard at Sabile, Latvia, USSR is just north of Lat. 57° N. The most northerly commercial vineyard in Britain is that at Renishaw hall, Derbyshire with 2600 vines. It lies in Lat. 53° 18′ N. The most southerly commercial vineyard is operated by Moorilla Estates Pty Ltd at Berridale, Tasmania in Lat. 42° 47′ S.

BLOOMS AND FLOWERS

Largest bloom *World*

The mottled orange-brown and white parasitic stinking corpse lily (*Rafflesia arnoldii*) has the largest of all blooms. These attach themselves to the cissus vines of the jungle in south-east Asia and measure up to 3 ft *91 cm* across and ¾ inch *1,9 cm* thick, and attain a weight of 15 lb *7 kg*. The spathe and spadix of the less massive green and purple flower of *Amorphophallus titanum* of Sumatra may attain a length of more than 1,5 m *5 ft*.

The largest known inflorescence is that of *Puya raimondii*, a rare Bolivian plant with an erect panicle (diameter 8 ft *2,4 m*) which emerges to a height of 35 ft *10,7 m*. Each of these bears up to 8000 white blooms (see also Slowest-flowering plant p. 48). The flower-spike of an agave was in 1974 measured to be 52 ft *15,8 m* long in Berkeley, California.

The world's largest blossoming plant is the giant Chinese

The Meikleour beech hedge in Perthshire—the tallest in the world. Some of its trees now exceed 120 ft *36,5 m*.

HEDGES

Tallest hedge *World*

The world's tallest hedge is the Meikleour beech hedge in Perthshire, Scotland. It was planted in 1746 and has now attained a trimmed height of 85 ft *26 m*. It is 600 yd *550 m* long. Some of its trees now exceed 120 ft *36,5 m*.

Tallest hedge *Yew*

The tallest yew hedge in the world is in Earl Bathurst's Park, Cirencester, Gloucestershire. It was planted in 1720, runs for 170 yd *155 m*, reaches 36 ft *11 m*, is 15 ft *4,5 m* thick at its base and takes 20 man-days to trim.

Tallest hedge *Box*

The tallest box hedge is 35 ft *10,7 m* in height at Birr Castle, Offaly, Ireland dating from the 18th century.

wisteria at Sierra Madre, California, USA. It was planted in 1892 and now has branches 500 ft *152 m* long. It covers nearly an acre, weighs 225 tons *228 tonnes* and has an estimated 1,500,000 blossoms during its blossoming period of five weeks, when up to 30,000 people pay admission to visit it.

Largest bloom *Great Britain*

The largest bloom of any indigenous British flowering plant is that of the wild white water lily (*Nymphaea alba*), which measures 6 in *15 cm* across. Other species bear much larger inflorescences.

Smallest flowering plant

The floating flowering aquatic duckweed *Wolffia angusta* of Australia described in 1980 is only 0,6 mm $\frac{1}{42}$ *of an inch* in length and 0.33 mm $\frac{1}{85}$ *of an inch* in width. It weighs about 0,00015 g *1/190,000 of an oz*. The smallest land plant regularly flowering in Britain is the chaffweed (*Cetunculus minimus*), a single seed of which weighs 0,00003 of a gramme.

It takes 5000 wolffia plants, the world's smallest flowering plants, to fill an ordinary thimble. (*Wayne P Armstrong*)

Plant Kingdom

Smallest plant

The smallest 'plant' is a uni-cellular alga and is listed under Protista smallest (see p. 52).

Most valuable

The Burpee Co $10,000 prize offered in 1954 for the first all-white marigold was won on 12 Aug 1975 by Alice Vonk of Sully, Iowa, USA.

Fastest growth

The case of a *Hesperogucca whipplei* of the family Liliaceae growing 12 ft *3,65 m* in 14 days was reported from Tresco Abbey, Isles of Scilly in July 1978.

Slowest flowering plant

The slowest flowering of all plants is the rare *Puyu raimondii*, the largest of all herbs, discovered in Bolivia in 1870. The panicle emerges after about 150 years of the plant's life. It then dies. (See also above under Largest blooms.) Some agaves, erroneously called Century plants, first flower after 40 years.

Largest wreath

The largest wreath constructed was the wreath built by The Gothenburg Florists at Liseberg Amusement Park, Sweden, completed on 4 Sept 1982. It measured 20,83 m *68 ft 4 in* in diameter and weighed 1980 kg (*1.95 tons*).

Longest daisy chain

The longest daisy chain, made in 7 hr, was one of 4529 ft 6 in *1380,5 m* at the Museum of Childhood, Sudbury, Derbyshire on 6 June 1981. The team is limited to 16.

Orchid *Largest and Tallest*

The largest of all orchids is *Grammatophyllum speciosum*, native to Malaysia. Specimens have been recorded up to 25 ft *7,62 m* in height. The largest orchid flower is that of *Phragmipedium caudatum*, found in tropical areas of America. Its petals are up to 18 in *46 cm* long, giving it a maximum outstretched diameter of 3 ft *91 cm*. The flower is, however, much less bulky than that of the stinking corpse lily (see above). The tallest free-standing orchid is *Grammatophyllum speciosum* (see above). *Galeola foliata* may attain 49 ft *15 m* on decaying rainforest trees in Queensland, Australia.

The first flowering in Britain of *Grammatophyllum wallisii* from Mindanao, Philippines at Burnham Nurseries, Kingsteignton, Devon in 1982 produced 557 flowers.

Orchid *Smallest*

The smallest orchid is *Platystele Jungermannoides*, found in Central America. Its flowers are 1 mm *0.04 in* across.

Orchid *Highest priced*

The highest price ever paid for an orchid is 1150 guineas (£1,207.50), paid by Baron Schröder to Sanders of St Albans for an *Odontoglossum crispum* (variety *pittianum*) at an auction by Protheroe & Morris of Bow Lane, London, on 22 Mar 1906. A Cymbidium orchid called Rosanna Pinkie was sold in the United States for $4500 (*then £1600*) in 1952.

Largest rhododendron

The largest species of rhododendron is the scarlet *Rhododendron arboreum*, examples of which reach a height of 60 ft *18,25 m* at Mangalbarė, Nepal. The cross-section of the trunk of a *Rhododendron giganteum*, reputedly 90 ft *27,43 m* high from Yunnan, China is preserved at Inverewe Garden, Highland. The largest in the United Kingdom is one 25 ft *7,60 m* tall and 272 ft *82,90 m* in circumference at Government House, Hillsborough, Co. Down. A specimen 35 ft *10,65 m* high and 3 ft 3 in *99 cm* in circumference has been measured at Trego-than, Truro, Cornwall.

Largest rose tree

A 'Lady Banks' rose tree at Tombstone, Arizona, USA, has a

trunk 40 in *101 cm* thick, stands 9 ft *2,74 m* high and covers an area of 5380 ft² *499 m²* supported by 68 posts and several thousand feet of piping. This enables 150 people to be seated under the arbour. The cutting came from Scotland in 1884.

FRUITS AND VEGETABLES

Most and least nutritive

An analysis of the 38 commonly eaten raw (as opposed to dried) fruits shows that the one with the highest calorific value is avocado (*Persea americana*), with 741 calories per edible pound or *163 cals per 100 gr*. That with the lowest value is cucumber with 73 calories per pound *16 cals per 100 gr*. Avocados probably originated in Central and South America and contain also vitamins A, C, and E and 2.2 per cent protein.

Melon

A watermelon weighing 200 lb *90,7 kg* was reported by Grace's Garden in April 1980. The growers were Ivan and Lloyd Bright of Hope, Arkansas, USA.

Pineapple *Largest*

A pineapple weighing 17 lb *7,71 kg* was picked by H. Retief in Malinda, Kenya in December 1978. Pineapples up to 13 kg *28.6 lb* were reported in 1978 from Tarauaca, Brazil.

Potato

A record display of 252 varieties of potato (*Solanum tuberosum*) was mounted at the Royal Horticultural Show in Westminster, London by Donald MacLean on 9–10 Oct 1979.

RECORD DIMENSIONS AND WEIGHTS FOR FRUIT VEGETABLES AND FLOWERS GROWN IN THE UNITED KINGDOM

Many data subsequent to 1958 come from the annual *Garden News* and Phostrogen Ltd. Giant Vegetable and Fruit Contest and the Super Sunflower Contest.

APPLE	3 lb 1 oz	*1,357 kg*	V. Loveridge	Ross-on-Wye, Hereford and Worcester	1965
ARTICHOKE	8 lb	*3,625 kg*	A. R. Lawson	Tollerton, North Yorkshire	1964
BEETROOT	29 lb	*13,154 kg*	F. A. Pulley	Maidstone, Kent	1964
BROAD BEAN	$23\frac{3}{8}$ in	*59,3 cm*	T. Currie	Jedburgh, Borders	1963
	$23\frac{3}{8}$ in	*59,3 cm*	Mrs M. Adrian	Irvine, Ayrshire	1982
BROCCOLI	28 lb $14\frac{3}{4}$ oz	*13,100 kg*	J. T. Cooke	Funtington, W. Sussex	1964
BRUSSELS SPROUT[1]	16 lb 1 oz	*7,285 kg*	E. E. Jenkins	Shipston-on-Stour, Warwickshire	1974
CABBAGE[2]	114 lb 3 oz	*51,8 kg*	P. G. Barton	Cleckheaton, W. Yorkshire	1977
CARROT[3]	8 lb 4 oz	*3,74 kg*	E. Stone	East Woodyates, Wiltshire	1983
CAULIFLOWER	52 lb $11\frac{1}{2}$ oz	*23,900 kg*	J. T. Cooke	Funtington, W. Sussex	1966
CELERY	35 lb	*15,875 kg*	C. Bowcock	Willaston, Merseyside	1973
CUCUMBER[4]	11 lb 15 oz (indoor)	*5,414 kg*	K. Lloyd	Kidwelly, Dyfed	1983
	8 lb 4 oz (outdoor)	*3,740 kg*	C. Bowcock	Willaston, Merseyside	1973
DAHLIA[5]	10 ft 3 in	*3,12 m*	Mrs M. Henderson	Bromley, Kent	1983
DWARF BEAN	$17\frac{1}{2}$ in	*43,4 cm*	C. Bowcock	Willaston, Merseyside	1973
GLADIOLUS	8 ft $4\frac{1}{2}$ in	*2,55 m*	A. Breed	Melrose, Roxburghshire	1981
GOOSEBERRY	2.06 oz	*58,5 g*	A. Dingle	Macclesfield, Cheshire	1978
GOURD	196 lb	*88,900 kg*	J. Leathes	Herringfleet Hall, Suffolk	1846
GRAPEFRUIT*	3 lb 8 oz	*1,585 kg*	A. J. Frost	Willington, Bedfordshire	1977
HOLLYHOCK	24 ft 3 in	*7,39 m*	W. P. Walshe	Eastbourne, E. Sussex	1961
KALE[6]	12 ft tall	*3,65 m*	B. T. Newton	Mullion, Cornwall	1950
LEEK	9 lb $5\frac{1}{2}$ oz	*4,235 kg*	C. Bowcock	Willaston, Merseyside	1973
LEEK, POT	107.88 in³	*1768 cm³*	R. S. Bell	Ashington, Northumberland	1982
LEMON[7]	4 lb	*1,81 kg*	V. Waldron	Didcot, Oxfordshire	1982
LETTUCE	25 lb	*11,335 kg*	C. Bowcock	Willaston, Merseyside	1974
LUPIN*	6 ft $0\frac{1}{2}$ in	*1,84 m*	J. Lawlor	New Malden, Surrey	1971
MANGOLD	$54\frac{1}{2}$ lb	*24,720 kg*	P. F. Scott	Sutton, Humberside	1971
MARROW	105 lb 8 oz	*47,85 kg*	D. C. Payne	Tewkesbury, Glos.	1982
MUSHROOM[8]	54 in circum.	*1,37 m*	—	Hasketon, Suffolk	1957
ONION[9]	7 lb 6 oz	*3,345 kg*	S. C. Hill	Galashiels, Selkirk	1981
PARSNIP[10]	10 lb $0\frac{1}{2}$ oz	*4,776 kg*	C. Moore	Peacehaven, E. Sussex	1980
PEAPOD	$10\frac{1}{8}$ in	*25,7 cm*	T. Currie	Jedburgh, Borders	1964
PEAR[11]	2 lb $10\frac{1}{2}$ oz	*1,200 kg*	Mrs. K. Loines	Hythe, Hampshire	1973
PETUNIA*	8 ft 4 in	*2,53 m*	G. A. Warner	Dunfermline, Fife	1978
POTATO[12]	7 lb 1 oz	*3,200 kg*	J. H. East	Spalding, Lincolnshire	1963
	7 lb 1 oz	*3,200 kg*	J. P. Busby	Atherstone, Warwickshire	1982
PUMPKIN[13]	402 lb	*182,34 kg*	R. Marshall	Coventry, Warwickshire	1982
RADISH[14]	17 lb	*7,711 kg*	K. Ayliffe	Brecon, Powys	1976
RED CABBAGE	42 lb	*19,05 kg*	R. Straw	Staveley, Derbyshire	1925
RHUBARB	5 lb 11 oz	*2,579 kg*	A. C. Setterfield	Englefield, Berkshire	1978
RUNNER BEAN	39 in long	*99 cm*	Mrs. E. Huxley	Churton, Cheshire	1976
SAVOY CABBAGE	38 lb 8 oz	*17,450 kg*	W. H. Neil	Retford, Nottinghamshire	1966
SHALLOT*	2 lb 12 oz (47 bulbs)	*1,245 kg*	M. Silverstoff	Falmouth, Cornwall	1977
STRAWBERRY	8.17 oz	*231 g*	G. Anderson	Folkestone, Kent	1983
SUGAR BEET[15]	28 lb	*12,7 kg*	W. Featherby	Everingham, Humberside	1977
SUNFLOWER[16]	23 ft $6\frac{1}{2}$ in tall	*7,17 m*	F. Kelland	Exeter, Devon	1976
SWEDE	48 lb 12 oz	*22,11 kg*	A. Foster	Alnwick, Northumberland	1980
TOMATO[17]	4 lb 5 oz	*1,956 kg*	R. A. Butcher	Stockbridge, Hants	1983
TOMATO PLANT	45 ft $9\frac{1}{2}$ in (length)	*13,96 m*	Chosen Hill School	Gloucester, Glos.	1981
TOMATO TRUSS	20 lb 4 oz	*9,175 kg*	C. Bowcock	Willaston, Merseyside	1973
TURNIP[18]	35 lb 4 oz	*15,975 kg*	C. W. Butler	Nafferton, Humberside	1972

1 *A Brussels Sprout plant measuring 11 ft 8 in* 3,55 m *was grown by Ralph G. Sadler of Watchbury Farm, Barford, Warwickshire on 6 July 1978.*

2 *The Swalwell, County Durham Red Cabbage of 1865 grown by William Collingwood (d. 8 Oct 1867) reputedly weighed 123 lb* 55,7 kg *and was 259 in* 6,57 m *in circumference.*

3 *A specimen of 7 kg* 15 lb 7 oz *was grown by Miss I. G. Scott of Nelson, New Zealand in October 1978.*

4 *A 17 lb 4 oz* 7,82 kg *example was grown by Nadine Williams of Knott, Texas, USA in 1982. A Vietnamese variety 6 ft* 1,83 m *long was reported by L. Szabo of Debrecen, Hungary in September 1976.*

5 *A 16 ft 5 in* 5,0 m *dahlia was grown by Sam and Pat Barnes of Chattahoochee, Florida, USA in 1982.*

6 *F. Doven of Mt Lawley, Australia grew a kale measuring 4,16 m* 13 ft $7\frac{1}{2}$ in *in 1982.*

7 *An 8 lb 2 oz* 3,68 kg *lemon with a $29\frac{1}{2}$ in* 74,9 cm *girth was grown by Dyan Joy Rokusek of Santa Barbara, California, USA in August 1982.*

8 *Same size reported by J. Coombes at Mark, Somerset on 28 July 1965. In September 1968 one weighing 18 lb 10 oz* 8,425 kg *was reported from Whidbey I. Washington, USA. A specimen of the edible* Termitomyces titanicus *found near Kitwe, Zambia on 18 Dec 1978 measured 26 in* 63 cm *in diameter and weighed 5.5 lb* 2,5 kg.

9 *An onion of $7\frac{1}{2}$ lb* 3,4 kg *was grown by Nelson W. Hope of Cardiff, California in 1965 with a girth of 26 in* 66 cm. *Its original gross weight was reputedly 8 lb* 3,62 kg.

10 *One 60 in* 152 cm *long was reported by M. Zaninovich of Waneroo W. Australia.*

11 *A specimen weighing 1,405 kg* 3.09 lb *was harvested on 10 May 1979 at Messrs K. & R. Yeomans, Arding, Armidale, NSW, Australia.*

12 *One weighing 18 lb 4 oz* 8,275 kg *reported dug up by Thomas Siddal in his garden in Chester on 17 Feb 1795. A yield of 515 lb* 233,5 kg *from a $2\frac{1}{2}$ lb parent seed by Bowcock planted in April 1977. Six tubers weighing 54 lb 8 oz* 24,72 kg *by Alan Nunn of Rhodes, Greater Manchester were reported on 18 Sept 1949.*

13 *A squash (Cucurbita moschata) of 513 lb* 232,69 kg *was grown by Harold Fulp, Jr., at Ninevah, Indiana, USA in 1977. A pumpkin (*C. maxima*) of $493\frac{1}{2}$ lb* 223,8 kg *was grown by Howard Dill of Windsor, Nova Scotia, Canada in October 1981.*

14 *A radish of 25 lb* 11,34 kg *was grown by Glen Tucker of Stanbury, South Australia in August 1974 and by Herbert Breslow of Ruskin, Florida, USA in 1977.*

15 *One weighing $45\frac{1}{2}$ lb* 20,63 kg *was grown by R. Meyer of Brawley, California in 1974.*

16 *A sunflower of 7,38 m* 24 ft $2\frac{1}{2}$ in *was grown by Martien Heijms of Oirschot, The Netherlands in 1983.*

17 *Grace's Gardens reported a 6 lb 8 oz* 2,94 kg *tomato grown by Clarence Daily of Monona, Wisconsin in 1977.*

18 *A 73 lb* 33,1 kg *turnip was reported in Dec. 1768 and one of 51 lb* 23,1 kg *from Alaska in 1981.*

* *Not in official contest.*

The heaviest orange ever reported is one weighing 5 lb 8 oz 2,50 kg *exhibited in Nelspruit, South Africa on 19 June 1981. It was the size of a human head but was stolen.*

Two giants of the vegetable world *top*: the 105 lb 8 oz *47,85 kg* marrow grown by D. C. Payne of Tewkesbury, England, and *above*: R. Marshall of Coventry with his 402 lb *182,34 kg* pumpkin. (*Garden News*)

FERNS

Largest

The largest of all the more than 6000 species of fern is the tree fern (*Alsophila excelsa*) of Norfolk Island, in the South Pacific, which attains a height of up to 60 ft *18,28 m*.

Smallest

The world's smallest ferns are *Hecistopteris pumila*, found in Central America, and *Azolla caroliniana*, which is native to the United States.

GRASSES

Commonest and fastest growing

The world's commonest grass is *Cynodon dactylon* or Bermuda grass. The 'Callie' hybrid, selected in 1966, grows as much as 6 in *15,2 cm* a day and stolons reach 18 ft *5,5 m* in length. The tallest of the 160 grasses found in Great Britain is the common reed (*Phragmites communis*), which reaches a height of 9 ft 9 in *2,97 m*.

Shortest

The shortest grass native to Great Britain is the very rare sand bent (*Mibora minima*) from Anglesey, Gwynedd which has a maximum growing height of under 6 in *15 cm*.

LEAVES

Largest *World*

The largest leaves of any plant belong to the raffia palm (*Raphia raffia*) of the Mascarene Islands, in the Indian Ocean and the Amazonian bamboo palm (*R. toedigera*) of South America, whose leaf blades may measure up to 65 ft *19,81 m* in length with petioles up to 13 ft *3,96 m*.

The largest undivided leaf is that of *Alocasia macrorrhiza*, found in Sabah, East Malaysia. One found in 1966 was 9 ft 11 in *3,02 m* long and 6 ft 3½ in *1,92 m* wide, with a unilateral area of 34.2 ft² *3,17 m²*.

Largest *Great Britain*

The largest leaves to be found in outdoor plants in Great Britain are those of *Gunnera manicata* from Brazil with leaves 6–10 ft *1,82–3,04 m* across on prickly stems 5–8 ft *1,52–2,43 m* long.

Fourteen-leafed clover

A fourteen-leafed white clover (*Trifolium repens*) was found by Randy Farland near Sioux Falls, South Dakota, USA on 16 June 1975.

SEEDS

Largest

The largest seed in the world is that of the double coconut or Coco de Mer (*Lodoicea seychellarum*), the single-seeded fruit of which may weigh 40 lb *18 kg*. This grows only in the Seychelles, in the Indian Ocean.

Smallest

The smallest seeds are those of *Epiphytic* orchids, at 35,000,000 to the oz (*cf.* grass pollens at up to 6,000,000,000 grains/oz). A single plant of the American ragweed can generate 8,000,000,000 pollen grains in five hours.

Most viable

The most protracted claim for the viability of seeds is that made for the Arctic lupin (*Lupinus arcticus*) found in frozen silt at Miller Creek in the Yukon, Canada in July 1954 by Harold Schmidt. The seeds were germinated in 1966 and were dated by the radiocarbon method of associated material to at least 8000 BC and more probably to 13,000 BC.

Most conquering conker

The highest recorded battle honours for an untreated conker (fruit of the Common horse-chestnut or *Aesculus hippocastanum*) is a 'five thousander plus', which won the BBC Conker Conquest in 1954. A professor of botany has however opined that this heroic specimen might well have been a 'ringer', probably an ivory or tagua nut (*Phytelephas macrocarpa*).

TREES AND WOOD

Most massive tree

The most massive living thing on Earth is the biggest known Giant Sequoia (*Sequoiadendron giganteum*) named the 'General Sherman', standing 272.4 ft *83,02 m* tall, in the Sequoia National Park, California, USA. It has a true girth of 79.8 ft *24,32 m* (1980) (at 5 ft *1,52 m* above the ground). The 'General Sherman' has been estimated to contain the equivalent of 600,120 board feet of timber, sufficient to make 5,000,000,000 matches. The foliage is blue-green, and the red-brown tan bark may be up to 24 in *61 cm* thick in parts. Estimates (1981) place its weight, including its root system, at 6000 long tons *6100 tonnes*. The largest known petrified tree is one of this species with a 295 ft *89,9 m* trunk near Coaldale, Nevada, USA.

The seed of a 'big tree' weighs only 1/6000th of an oz *4,7 mg*. Its growth at maturity may therefore represent an increase in weight of 1,300,000 million-fold.

The tree canopy covering the greatest area is the great Banyan

Plant Kingdom

Ficus bengalensis in the Indian Botanical Garden, Calcutta with some 1000 subsidiary trunks formed from aerial roots. It covers overall some 4 acres *1,6 ha* and is believed to date from *c.* 1770.

Greatest girth *World*

El Arbol del Tule, in the state of Oaxaca, in Mexico is a 135 ft *41 m* tall Montezuma cypress (*Taxodium mucronatum*) with a girth of 117.6 ft *35,8 m* at a height of 5 ft *1,52 m* above the ground in 1982. A figure of 167 ft *51 m* in circumference was reported for the pollarded European chestnut (*Castanea sativa*) known as the 'Tree of the 100 Horses' (Castagno di Cento Cavalli) on Mount Etna, Sicily, Italy in 1972 and measurements up to 180 ft *54,5 m* have been attributed to Baobab trees (*Adansonia digilata*).

Greatest girth *Britain*

The tree of greatest girth in Britain is a sweet ('Spanish') chestnut (*Castanea sativa*) in the grounds of Canford School, Nr. Wimborne, Dorset, with a bole 43 ft 9 in *13,33 m* in circumference. The largest-girthed living British oak is one at Bowthorpe Farm near Bourne, south Lincolnshire, measured in September 1973 to be 39 ft 1 in *11,91 m*. The largest 'maiden' (i.e. not pollarded) oak is the Majesty Oak at Fredville Park, near Nonington, Kent, with a girth of 38 ft 1 in *11,60 m* (1973).

Fastest growing

Discounting bamboo, which is not botanically classified as a tree, but as a woody grass, the fastest rate of growth recorded is 35 ft 3 in *10,74 m* in 13 months by an *Albizzia falcata* planted on 17 June 1974 in Sabah, Malaysia. The youngest recorded age for a tree to reach 100 ft *30,48 m* is 64 months for one of the species planted on 24 Feb 1975, also in Sabah.

Slowest growing

The speed of growth of trees depends largely upon conditions, although some species, such as box and yew, are always slow-growing. The extreme is represented by a specimen of Sitka spruce which required 98 years to grow to 11 in *28 cm* tall with a diameter of less than 1 in *2,5 cm* on the Arctic tree-line. The growing of miniature trees or *bonsai* is an oriental cult mentioned as early as *c.* 1320.

Tallest *World All-Time and currently*

The tallest tree ever measured by any governmental forester was recently re-discovered in a report by William Ferguson, Inspector of Victoria State Forests. He reported in February 1872 a fallen Mountain ash (*Eucalyptus regnans*) 18 ft *5,48 m* in diameter at 5 ft *1,52 m* above ground level and 435 ft *132,5 m* in length. The closest measured rivals to this champion have been:

ft	m	Species	Location	Date
415	126.5	Lynn Valley Douglas fir	*Pseudotsuga menziesii*	British Columbia, Canada	1902
393	119.7	The Mineral Douglas fir	*Pseudotsuga menziesii*	Washington State, USA	1930
380	115.8	Nisqually fir	*Pseudotsuga menziesii*	Nisqually River, Washington State	1899
375	114.3	Cornthwaite Mountain ash	*Eucalyptus regnans*	Thorpdale, Victoria Australia	1880
*367.8	112.1	'Tallest Tree', Redwood Creek	*Sequoia sempervirens*	Humboldt County, California, USA	1963
367.6	112	a Coast redwood	*Sequoia sempervirens*	Guerneville, California, USA	1873

* Tallest standing tree in the world. Crown dying back. Height last re-estimated at 362 ft *110,3 m* in 1972.

Currently the tallest standing broadleaf tree is a Mountain ash in the Styx Valley, Tasmania at 325 ft *99 m*.

Research into a Douglas Fir with a claimed height of 417 ft *127,1 m* and with a butt diameter of 25 ft *7,62 m* supposedly felled by George Cary in Lynn Valley (see above) has been shown by Dr A. C. Carder to have been a hoax perpetrated *c.* 1922 by the Vancouver branch of a lumberman's club to impress their parent club in Seattle, Washington. Their photographic 'evidence' was later proved to be of an outsize but lesser Douglas fir felled in Kerrisdale in 1896.

Tallest *Great Britain*

The tallest trees in Great Britain are a Grand fir (*Abies grandis*) at Strone, Cairndow, Strathclyde, and Douglas firs at The Hermitage, Perth, at Moniac Glen, Inverness, and by the River Findhorn in Nairn; and a Sitka spruce (*Picea suchensis*) at the same place. All were 197 ft *60 m* in 1983. The tallest in England is a Douglas fir (*Pseudotsuga taxifolia*) measured at 174 ft *53,0 m* at Broadwood, Dunster, Somerset. The tallest

measured in Northern Ireland is a Giant Sequoia (*Sequoiadendron giganteum*), measured in 1983 to be 164 ft *50 m* tall at Caledon Castle, County Tyrone. The tallest in Wales is a Grand Fir (*Abies grandis*) at Leighton Park, Powys (pl. 1886) measured in 1982 to be 190 ft *58 m*.

Tallest *Ireland*

The tallest tree in Ireland is a Sitka spruce (*Picea sitchensis*) 166 ft *50,59 m* tall at Curraghmore, Waterford, measured in March 1974.

Tallest Christmas Tree

The world's tallest cut Christmas tree was a 221 ft *67,36 m* tall Douglas fir (*Pseudotsuga taxifolia*) erected at Northgate Shopping Center, Seattle, Washington in December 1950. The tallest Christmas tree erected in Britain was the 85 ft 3¼ in *25,98 m* long spruce from Norway erected for the Canterbury Cathedral appeal on the South Bank, London on 20 Nov 1975.

Oldest tree *World*

The oldest recorded tree was a bristlecone pine (*Pinus longaeva*) designated WPN-114, which grew at 10,750 ft *3275 m* above sea-level on the north-east face of the Wheeler Ridge on the Sierra Nevada, California, USA. During studies in 1963 and 1964 it was found to be about 4900 years old but was cut down with a chain saw. The oldest known *living* tree is the bristlecone pine named *Methuselah* at 10,000 ft *3050 m* in the California side of the White Mountains confirmed as 4600 years old. In March 1974 it was reported that this tree had produced 48 live seedlings. Dendrochronologists estimate the *potential* life-span of a bristlecone pine at nearly 5500 years, but that of a California Big Tree (*Sequoia giganteum*) at perhaps 6000 years. No single cell lives more than 30 years. A report in March 1976 stated that some enormous specimens of Japanese cedar (*Cryptomeria japonica*) had been dated by carbon-14 to 5200 BC.

Oldest tree *Great Britain*

Of all British trees that with the longest life is the yew (*Taxus baccata*), for which a maximum age well in excess of 1000 years is usually conceded. The oldest known is the Fortingall Yew near Aberfeldy, Tayside, part of which still grows. In 1777 this tree was over 50 ft *15,24 m* in girth and it cannot be much less than 2500 years old today. The 1500 years attributed by the Royal Archeological Society to the Eastham yew in Wirral is possible but many are very much bigger and older.

Earliest species

The earliest species of tree still surviving is the maiden-hair tree (*Ginkgo biloba*) of Chekiang, China, which first appeared about 160,000,000 years ago, during the Jurassic era. It was 'rediscovered' by Kaempfer (Netherlands) in 1690 and reached England *c.* 1754. It has been grown in Japan since *c.* 1100 where it was known as *ginkyō* ('silver apricot') and is now known as *icho*.

Most leaves

Little work has been done on the laborious task of establishing which species has most leaves. A large oak has perhaps 250,000 but a Cypress may have some 45–50 million leaf scales.

Remotest

The tree remotest from any other tree is believed to be one at an oasis in the Ténéré Desert, Niger Republic. In February 1960 it survived being rammed by a lorry driven by a Frenchman. There were no other trees within 50 km *31 miles*. The tree was transplanted and it is now in the Museum at Niamey, Niger.

Most expensive

The highest price ever paid for a tree is $51,000 (*then £18,214*) for a single Starkspur Golden Delicious apple tree from near Yakima, Washington, USA, bought by a nursery in Missouri in 1959.

Largest forest *World*

The largest afforested areas in the world are the vast coniferous forests of the northern USSR, lying mainly between latitude 55° N, and the Arctic Circle. The total wooded area amounts to 2,700,000,000 acres *1100 million ha* (25 per cent of the world's forests), of which 38 per cent is Siberian larch. The USSR is 34 per cent afforested.

Largest forest *Great Britain*

The largest forest in England is Kielder Forest (72,336 acres

29 273 ha), in Northumberland. The largest forest in Wales is the Coed Morgannwg (Forest of Glamorgan) (42,555 acres *17 221 ha*). Scotland's most extensive forest is the Glen Trool Forest (51,376 acres *20 791 ha*) in Kirkcudbrightshire. The United Kingdom is 7 per cent afforested.

Longest Avenue of Trees

The longest avenue of trees has been the now partly felled private avenue of 1750 beeches in Savernake Forest near Marlborough, Wiltshire. It measured 3.25 miles *5,23 km.*

Wood *Heaviest*

The heaviest of all woods is black ironwood (*Olea laurifolia*), also called South African ironwood, with a specific gravity of up to 1.49, and weighing up to 93 lb/ft³ *1490 kg/m³*. The heaviest British wood is boxwood (*Buxus sempervirens*) with an extreme of 64 lb/ft³ *1025 kg/m³*.

Wood *Lightest*

The lightest wood is *Aeschynomene hispida*, found in Cuba, which has a specific gravity of 0.044 and a weight of only 2¾ lb/ft³ *44 kg/m³*. The wood of the balsa tree (*Ochroma pyramidale*) is of very variable density—between 2½ and 24 lb/ft³ *40 and 384 kg/m³*. The density of cork is 15 lb/ft³ *240 kg/m³*.

Bamboo *Tallest*

The tallest recorded bamboo was a Thorny bamboo culm (*Bambusa arundinacea*) felled at Pattazhi, Travancore, Southern India, in November 1904 measuring 121½ ft *37,03 m.*

Bamboo *Fastest growing*

Some species of the 45 genera of bamboo have attained growth rates of up to 36 in *91 cm* per day (0.00002 mph *0,00003 km/h*), on their way to reaching a height of 100 ft *30 m* in less than three months.

TALLEST TREES IN THE BRITISH ISLES
By species

		ft	m
ALDER (Italian)	Westonbirt, Gloucester	98	30
ALDER (Common)	Ashburnham Park, East Sussex	105	32
ASH	Old Roar Ghyll, St. Leonards, East Sussex	135	41
BEECH	Beaufront Castle, Northumberland	144	44
BEECH (Copper)	Chart Park Golf Course, Dorking, Surrey	121	37
BIRCH (Silver)	Woburn Sands, Bedfordshire	97	29
CEDAR (Blue Atlas)	Brockhampton Pk, Hereford & Worcs	125	38
CEDAR (of Lebanon)	Leaton Knolls, Shropshire	140	42
CHESTNUT (Horse)	Ashford Chase, Hampshire	130	39
CHESTNUT (Sweet)	Godinton Park, Kent	122	37
CYPRESS (Lawson)	Endsleigh, Devon	133	40
CYPRESS (Leyland)	Bicton, Devon	118	36
CYPRESS (Monterey)	Bicton, Devon	124	38
DOUGLAS FIR	The Hermitage, Perth, Tayside	197	60
ELM (Wych)[1] (Huntingdon)	Howlett's Park Zoo, Kent	132	40
ELM (Wych)[1] (Smooth Leaf)	North Inch, Perth, Tayside	132	40
EUCALYPTUS (Blue Gum)	Glencormack, Co. Wicklow	144	44
GRAND FIR	Strone, Cairndow, Strathclyde	197	60
GINKGO	Linton Park (Maidstone), Kent	93	28
HEMLOCK (Western)	Murthly Castle, Tayside	170	52
HOLLY	Ashburnham Park, East Sussex	80	24
HORNBEAM	Wrest Park, Bedfordshire	105	32
LARCH (European)	Glenlee, Dumfries & Galloway	150	46
LARCH (Japanese)	Blair Castle, Tayside	123	37
LIME	Duncombe Park, North Yorkshire	150	45
METASEQUOIA	Savill Garden, Berkshire	80	24
MONKEY PUZZLE	Lochnaw, Dumfries & Galloway	95	29
OAK (Common)	Leeds Castle, Kent	135	41
OAK (Sessile)	Whitfield Ho., Hereford & Worcs	140	42
OAK (Red)	Cowdray Park, West Sussex	115	35
PEAR	Borde Hill, West Sussex	64	19
PINE (Corsican)	Stanage Park, Powys	144	44
PLANE	Bryanston, Dorset	156	48
POPLAR (Black Italian)	Fairlawne, Kent	150	46
POPLAR (Lombardy)	Marble Hill, Twickenham, G. London	130	39
REDWOOD (Coast)	Bodnant, Gwynedd	148	45
SILVER FIR	Benmore, Strathclyde	158	48
SPRUCE (Sitka)	River Findhorn, Nairn	197	60
SYCAMORE	Drumlanrig Castle, Dumfries & Galloway	112	34
TULIP-TREE	Taplow House, Buckinghamshire	120	36
WALNUT	Gayhurst, Newport Pagnell, Buckinghamshire	80	24
WALNUT (Black)	Bisham Abbey, Buckinghamshire	118	36
WELLINGTONIA	Castle Leod, Easter Ross, Highland	165	50
WILLOW (Weeping)	Ashford Chase, Hampshire	79	24
WINGNUT (Caucasian)	Abbotsbury, Dorset	115	35
YEW	Close Walks, Midhurst, West Sussex	95	29

[1] *It was estimated in 1980 that more than 17 million of the 23 million elms in southern England had since 1968 been killed by the fungus that causes Dutch elm disease* Ceratocystis ulmi.

KINGDOM PROTISTA

PROTISTA

Protista were first discovered in 1676 by Antonie van Leeuwenhoek of Delft (1632–1723), a Dutch microscopist. Among Protista are characteristics common to both plants and animals. The more plant-like are termed Protophyta (protophytes), including unicellular algae, and the more animal-like are placed in the phylum Protozoa (protozoans), including amoeba and flagellates.

Largest

The largest protozoans in terms of volume, which are known to have existed were calcareous foraminifera (Foraminiferida) belonging to the genus *Nummulites*, a species of which, in the Middle Eocene rocks of Turkey, attained 22 cm *8.6 in* in diameter. The largest existing protozoan, a species of the fan-shaped *Stannophyllum* (Xenophyophorida), can exceed this in length (25 cm *9.8 in* has been recorded) but not in volume.

Smallest

The smallest of all protophytes is the marine microflagellate alga *Micromonas pusilla*, with a diameter of less than 2 microns or micrometres $(2 \times 10^{-6}$ m) or *0.00008 in.*

Fastest moving

The protozoan *Monas stigmatica* has been measured to move a distance equivalent to 40 times its own length in a second. No human can cover even seven times his own length in a second.

Fastest reproduction

The protozoan *Glaucoma*, which reproduces by binary fission, divides as frequently as every three hours. Thus in the course of a day it could become a 'six greats grandparent' and the progenitor of 510 descendants.

KINGDOM FUNGI

Largest

Jenny Pearson-Smith, 10 of Khimera Farm, Hawkinge, Kent found a puff ball (*Lycoperdon gigantea*) 72½ in *184 cm* in circumference and 18 lb 6½ oz *8,34 kg* in weight in October 1983. A 72 lb *32,6 kg* example of the edible mushroom (*Polyporus frondosus*) was reported by Joseph Opple near Solon, Ohio in September 1976.

The largest officially recorded tree fungus was a specimen of *Oxyporus* (*Fomes*) *nobilissimus*, measuring 56 in *142 cm* by 37 in *94 cm* and weighing at least 300 lb *136 kg* found by J. Hisey in Washington State, USA, in 1946. The largest recorded in the United Kingdom is an ash fungus (*Fomes fraxineus*) measuring 50 in by 15 in *127 cm* by *38 cm* wide, found by the forester A. D. C. LeSueur on a tree at Waddesdon, Buckinghamshire, in 1954.

Most poisonous toadstool

The yellowish-olive death cap (*Amanita phalloides*) is regarded as the world's most poisonous fungus. It is found in England. From six to fifteen hours after tasting, the effects are vomiting, delirium, collapse and death. Among its victims was Cardinal Giulio de' Medici, Pope Clement VII (b. 1478) on 25 Sept 1534.

The Registrar General's Report states that between 1920 and 1950 there were 39 fatalities from fungus poisoning in the United Kingdom. As the poisonous types are mostly *Amanita* varieties, it is reasonable to assume that the deaths were predominantly due to *Amanita phalloides*. The most recent fatality was probably in 1960.

Aeroflora

Fungi were once classified in the subkingdom Protophyta of the Kingdom Protista. The highest total fungal spore count was 161,037 per m³ near Cardiff on 21 July 1971. A plant tree pollen count of 2160 per m³ was recorded near London on 9 May 1971. The lowest counts of airborne allergens are nil. The highest recorded grass pollen count in Britain was one of 2824 per m³ recorded at Aberystwyth on 29 June 1961.

KINGDOM PROCARYOTA

Earliest life form

In June 1980 Prof J. William Schopf announced the discovery of 5 microbial life forms in rock dated to 3500 million years old in the 'North Pole' region of northern Western Australia.

The earliest life-form reported from Britain is *Kakabekia barghoorniana*, a microorganism similar in form to an orange slice, found near Harlech, Gwynedd, Wales in 1964 and dated to 2000 million years ago.

BACTERIA

Antonie van Leeuwenhoek (1632–1723) was the first to observe bacteria in 1675. The largest of the bacteria is the sulphur bacterium *Beggiatoa mirabilis*, which is from 16 to 45 microns in width and which may form filaments several millimetres long.

The bacteria *Thermoactinomyces vulgaris* have been found alive in cores of mud taken from the bottom of Windermere, Cumbria, England which have been dated to 1500 years before the present.

Smallest free-living entity

The smallest of all free-living organisms are pleuro-pneumonia-like organisms (PPLO) of the *Mycoplasma*. One of these, *Mycoplasma laidlawii*, first discovered in sewage in 1936, has a diameter during its early existence of only 100 millimicrons, or 0.000004 in. Examples of the strain known as H.39 have a maximum diameter of 300 millimicrons and weigh an estimated 1.0×10^{-16} gramme. Thus a 190 tonne Blue whale would weigh 1.9×10^{24} or 1.9 quadrillion times as much.

Highest

In April 1967 the US National Aeronautics and Space Administration reported that bacteria had been recently discovered at an altitude of 135,000 ft (25.56 miles) *41 100 m*.

Longest lived

The oldest deposits from which living bacteria are claimed to have been extracted are salt layers near Irkutsk, USSR, dating from about 600,000,000 years ago. The discovery was not accepted internationally. The US Dry Valley Drilling Project in Antarctica claimed resuscitated rod-shaped bacteria from caves up to a million years old.

Fastest

The rod-shaped bacillus *Bdellovibrio bacteriovorus*, by means of a polar flagellum rotating 100 times/sec, can move 50 times its own length of 2 μm per second. This would be the equivalent of a human sprinter reaching 200 mph *320 km/h* or swimmer crossing the Channel in 6 min.

Toughest

The bacterium *Micrococcus radiodurans* can withstand atomic radiation of 6.5 million röntgens or 10,000 times that fatal to the average man. In March 1983 John Barras (University of Oregon, USA) reported bacteria from sulfurous sea bed vents thriving at 306°C *583°F* in the East Pacific Rise at Lat. 21°N.

VIRUSES

Largest

Dmitriy Ivanovsky (1864–1920) first reported filterable objects in 1892 byt Martinus Willem Beijerink (1851–1931) first confirmed the nature of viruses in 1898. These are now defined as aggregates of two of more types of chemical (including either DNA or RNA) which are infectious and potentially pathogenic. The longest known is the rod-shaped *Citrus tristeza* virus with particles measuring 200×10 nm (1 nanometer = 1×10^{-9} m).

Smallest

The smallest known viruses are the nucleoprotein plant viruses such as the satellite of tobacco *necrosis virus* with spherical particles 17 nm in diameter. A putative new infectious submicroscopic organism but without nucleic acid, named a 'prion', was announced from the University of California in February 1982. Viroids (RNA cores without protein coating) are much smaller than viruses. They were discovered by Theodor O. Diener (USA) in February 1972.

PARKS, ZOOS, OCEANARIA AND AQUARIA

PARKS

Largest *World*

The world's largest park is the Wood Buffalo National Park in Alberta, Canada (established 1922), which has an area of 11,172,000 acres (17,560 miles² *45 480 km²*).

Largest *Britain*

The largest National Park in Great Britain is the Lake District National Park which has an area of 866 miles² *2240 km²*. The largest private park in the United Kingdom is Woburn Park (3000 acres *1200 ha*), near Woburn Abbey, the seat of the Dukes of Bedford.

ZOOS

Largest game reserve

It has been estimated that throughout the world there are some 500 zoos with an estimated annual attendance of 330,000,000. The largest zoological reserve in the world has been the Etosha Reserve, Namibia established in 1907 with an area which grew to 38,427 miles² *99 525 km²*.

Oldest

The earliest known collection of animals was that set up by Shulgi, a 3rd dynasty ruler of Ur in 2094–2097 BC at Puzurish in south-east Iraq. The oldest known zoo is that at Schönbrunn, Vienna, Austria, built in 1752 by the Holy Roman Emperor Franz I for his wife Maria Theresa. The oldest existing privately owned zoo in the world is that of the Zoological Society of London, founded in 1826. Its collection, housed partly in Regent's Park, London (36 acres *14,5 ha*) and partly at Whipsnade Park, Bedfordshire (541 acres *219 ha*) (opened 23 May 1931), is the most comprehensive in the United Kingdom. The stocktaking on 1 Jan 1984 accounted for a total of 11,435 specimens. These comprised 2848 mammals, 2141 birds, 506 reptiles and amphibians, an estimated total of 1870 fish and an estimated total of 4070 invertebrates. Locusts, ants and bees are excluded from these figures. The record annual attendances are 3,031,571 in 1950 for Regent's Park and 756,758 in 1961 for Whipsnade.

OCEANARIA

Earliest and largest

The world's first oceanarium is Marineland of Florida, opened in 1938 at a site 18 miles *29 km* south of St Augustine, Florida, USA. Up to 5,800,000 gal *26,3 million litres* of sea-water are pumped daily through two major tanks, one rectangular (100 ft *30,48 m* long by 40 ft *12,19 m* wide by 18 ft *5,48 m* deep) containing 375,000 gal *1,7 million litres*, and one circular (233 ft *71 m* in circumference and 12 ft *3,65 m* deep) containing 330,000 gal *1,5 million litres*. The tanks are seascaped, including coral reefs and even a shipwreck. The salt water tank at Hanna-Barbera's Marineland, located at Palos Verdes, California, USA is 251½ ft *76,65 m* in circumference and 22 ft *6,7 m* deep, with a capacity of 530,000 gal *2,4 million litres*. The total capacity of this whole oceanarium is 2,080,000 gal *9,4 million litres*. Their killer whale 'Orky' at 14,000 lb *6350 kg* is the largest in captivity.

AQUARIA

Largest aquarium

The world's largest aquarium, as opposed to fish farm, is the John G. Shedd Aquarium at 12th Street and Lake Shore Drive, Chicago, Illinois, USA, completed in November 1929 at a cost of $3,250,000 (then £668,725). The total capacity of its display tanks is 375,000 gal *1,7 million litres* with reservoir tanks holding 1,665,000 gal *7,5 million litres*. Exhibited 5500 specimens from 350 species. Most of these specimens are collected by the Aquarium collecting boat based in Miami, Florida, and are shipped by air to Chicago. The record attendances are 78,658 in a day on 21 May 1931, and 4,689,730 visitors in the single year of 1931.

Chapter 3

THE NATURAL WORLD

The world's highest waterfalls, the Angel Falls of Venezuela (see p. 63). (*David F Hoy*)

THE EARTH

The Earth is not a true sphere, but flattened at the poles and hence an oblate. The polar diameter of the Earth (7899.806 miles *12 713,505 km*) is 26.575 miles *42,769 km* less than the equatorial diameter (7926.381 miles *12 756,274 km*). The Earth has a pear shaped asymmetry with the north polar radius being 148 ft *45 m* longer than the south polar radius. There is also a slight ellipticity of the equator since its long axis (about longitude 37° W) is 522 ft *159 m* greater than the short axis. The greatest departures from the reference ellipsoid are a protuberance of 240 ft *73 m* in the area of Papua New Guinea and a depression of 344 ft *105 m* south of Sri Lanka, in the Indian Ocean.

The greatest circumference of the Earth, at the equator, is 24,901.46 miles *40 075,02 km*, compared with 24,859.73 miles *40 007,86 km* at the meridian. The area of the surface is estimated to be 196,937,400 miles² *510 065 600 km²*. The period of axial rotation, *i.e.* the true sidereal day, is 23 hr 56 min 4.0996 sec, mean time.

The mass of the Earth was first assessed by Dr Nevil Maskelyne (1732–1811) in Perthshire, Scotland in 1774. The modern value is 5,880,000,000,000,000,000,000,000 tons *5,974 × 10²¹ tonnes* and its density is 5.515 times that of water. The volume is an estimated 259,875,300,000 miles³ *1 083 207 000 000 km³*. The Earth picks up cosmic dust but estimates vary widely with 30,000 tons/*tonnes* a year being the upper limit. Modern theory is that the Earth has an outer shell or lithosphere 50 miles *80 km* thick, then an outer and inner rock layer or mantle extending 1745 miles *2809 km* deep, beneath which there is an iron rich core of radius 2164 miles *3482 km*. If the iron rich core theory is correct, iron would be the most abundant element in the Earth. At the centre of the core the estimated density is 13.09 g/cm³; the temperature 4500° C and the pressure 23,600 tons f/in² or 364 GPa.

1. NATURAL PHENOMENA

EARTHQUAKES

(Note: Seismologists record all dates with the year *first*, based not on local time but on Greenwich Mean Time).

Greatest *World*

It is estimated that each year there are some 500,000 detectable seismic or micro-seismic disturbances of which 100,000 can be felt and 1000 cause damage. The deepest recorded hypocentres are of 720 km *447 miles* in Indonesia in 1933, 1934 and 1943.

An inherent limitation in the widely used Gutenberg–Richter scale (published in 1954) precludes its usefulness when extended to the relative strengths of the strongest earthquakes ever recorded. Its use of surface-wave magnitudes, based on amplitudes of waves of a period of 20 sec, results in the 'damping' of any increase in amplitude where fault ruptures break over a length much above 60 km *37 miles*. These however provenly may reach a length of 800 to 1000 km *500–620 miles*. This 'overload' or 'saturation effect' has resulted in the adoption since 1977 of the Kanamori scale for comparing the most massive earthquakes. Magnitudes are there defined in terms of energy release using the concept of the seismic moment, devised by K-Aki in 1966. Thus the most massive instrumentally recorded earthquake has been the cataclysmic Lebu shock south of Concepción, Chile on 1960 May 22 estimated at 10^{26} ergs. While this uniquely rates a magnitude of 9.5 on the Kanamori scale, it ranks in only equal 4th place (with the 1922 Chilean earthquake) at Magnitude 8.3 on the Gutenberg–Richter scale. For the removal of doubt the progressive records on the two scales are shown in the table below.

PROGRESSIVE LIST OF THE WORLD'S STRONGEST INSTRUMENTALLY RECORDED EARTHQUAKES

Kanamori Scale Magnitudes M_s	Gutenberg–Richter Scale Magnitude M_w	Where $M_s = \frac{2}{3}(\log_{10}E - 11.8)$ and $M_w = \frac{2}{3}[\log_{10}(2E \times 10^4) - 10.7]$ Where E = energy released in dyne/cm	
8.8	8.6	Colombia coast	1906 Jan 31
(8.6)	8.6	Assam, India	1950 Aug 15
9.0	(8½)	Kamchatka, USSR	1952 Nov 4
9.1	(8.3)	Andreanof, Aleutian Is., USA	1957 Mar 9
9.5	(8.3)	Lebu, Chile	1960 May 22

Worst death roll *World*

The greatest loss of life occurred in the earthquake (*ti chen*) in the Shensi, Shansi and Honan provinces of China, of 1556 Feb 2, (new style) (Jan 23 os) when an estimated 830,000 people were killed. The highest death roll in modern times has been in the Tangshan 'quake (Mag. 8.2) in Eastern China on 1976 July 27 (local time was 3 a.m. July 28). A first figure published on 4 Jan 1977 revealed 655,237 killed, later adjusted to 750,000. On 22 Nov 1979 the New China News Agency unaccountably reduced the death toll to 242,000. The site of the city was still a prohibited area 5½ years later in Jan 1982. The greatest material damage was in the 'quake on the Kwanto plain, Japan, of 1923 Sept 1 (Mag. 8.2, epicentre in Lat. 35° 15′ N, Long. 139° 30′ E). In Sagami Bay the sea-bottom in one area sank 400 m *1310 ft*. The official total of persons killed and missing in the *Shinsai* or great 'quake and the resultant fires was 142,807. In Tōkyō and Yokohama 575,000 dwellings were destroyed. The cost of the damage was estimated at £1000 million (now more than £4000 million). It has however been estimated that a 7.5 magnitude shock (G-R scale) 30 miles *48 km* north of Los Angeles would result in damage estimated at $70,000 million.

Worst death roll *Great Britain and Ireland*

The East Anglian or Colchester earthquake of 1884 Apr 22 (9.18 a.m.) (epicentres Lat. 51° 48′ N, Long. 0° 53′ E, and Lat. 51° 51′ N, Long. 0° 55′ E) caused damage estimated at £10,000 to 1200 buildings, and according to *The Great English Earthquake* by Peter Haining, the death of at least 3 and possibly 5 people. Langenhoe Church was wrecked. Windows and doors were rattled over an area of 53,000 miles² *137 250 km²* and the shock was felt in Exeter and Ostend, Belgium. It has been estimated to have been of magnitude 5.2 on the Richter scale. The highest instrumentally measured magnitude is 6.0 for the Dogger Bank event of 7 June 1931. The strongest Scottish tremor occurred at Inverness at 10.45 p.m. on 1816 Aug 13, and was felt over an area of 50,000 miles² *130 000 km²*. The strongest Welsh tremor occurred in Swansea at 9.45 a.m. on 1906 June 27 (epicentre Lat. 51° 38′ N, Long. 4° W). It was felt over an area of 37,800 miles² *97 900 km²*. No earthquake with its epicentre in Ireland has ever been instrumentally measured, though the effects of remoter shocks have been felt. However, there was a shock in 1734 August which damaged 100 dwellings and five churches.

VOLCANOES

The total number of known active volcanoes in the world is 850 of which many are submarine. The greatest active concentration is in Indonesia, where 77 of its 167 volcanoes have erupted within historic times. The name volcano derives from the now dormant Vulcano Island (from the God of fire Vulcanus) in the Aeolian group in the Mediterranean.

Greatest eruption

The total volume of matter discharged in the eruption of Tambora, a volcano on the island of Sumbawa, in Indonesia, 5–7 Apr 1815, was 150–180 km³. The energy of this 1395 mph *2215 km/h* eruption, which lowered the height of the island by 4100 ft *1250 m* from 13,450 ft to 9350 ft *2850 m*, was 8.4×10^{26} ergs. A crater seven miles *11 km* in diameter was formed. Some 90,000 were killed or died of famine. This compares with a probable 60–65 km³ ejected by Santorini and 20 km³ ejected by Krakatoa (see Greatest explosion). The internal pressure at Tambora has been estimated at 3270 kg/cm² or 20.76 tons/in².

The ejecta in the Taupo eruption in New Zealand *c.* AD 130 has been estimated at 30,000 million tonnes/*tons* of pumice moving at one time at 400 mph *700 km/h*. It flattened 16 000 km² *6180 miles²* (over 26 times the devastated area of Mt. St. Helens). Less than 20 per cent of the 14×10^9 tonnes of pumice ejected in this most violent of all documented volcanic events fell within 200 km *125 miles* of the vent.

Longest lava flow

The longest lava flow in historic times, known as *pahoehoe* (twisted cord-like solidifications), is that from the eruption of Laki in 1783 in south-east Iceland which flowed 65–70 km *40.5–43.5 miles*. The largest known pre-historic flow is the Roza basalt flow in North America *c.* 15 million years ago, which had an unsurpassed length (480 km *300 miles*), area (40 000 km² *15,400 miles²*) and volume (1250 km³ *300 miles³*).

Greatest explosion

The greatest explosion (possibly since Santorini in the Aegean Sea 1626 ± 1 BC) occurred at *c.* 10 a.m. (local time), or 3.00 a.m. GMT, on 27 Aug 1883, with an eruption of Krakatoa, an island (then 18 miles² *47 km²*) in the Sunda Strait, between Sumatra and Java, in Indonesia. A total of 163 villages were wiped out, and 36,380 people killed by the wave it caused. Rocks were thrown 34 miles *55 km* high and dust fell 3313 miles *5330 km* away 10 days later. The explosion was recorded four hours later on the island of Rodrigues, 2968 miles *4776 km* away, as 'the roar of heavy guns' and was heard over 1/13th part of the surface of the globe. This explosion has been estimated to have had about 26 times the power of the greatest H-bomb test detonation but was still only a fifth part of the Santorini cataclysm.

Highest *Extinct*

The highest extinct volcano in the world is Cerro Aconcagua (stone sentinel) (22,834 ft *6960 m*) on the Argentine side of the Andes. It was first climbed on 14 Jan 1897 by Mathias Zurbriggen and was the highest summit climbed anywhere until 12 June 1907.

Highest *Dormant*

The highest dormant volcano is Volcán Llullaillaco (22,057 ft *6723 m*), on the frontier between Chile and Argentina.

Highest *Active*

The highest volcano regarded as active is Volcán Antofalla (6450 m *21,162 ft*), in Argentina, though a more definite claim is made for Volcán Guayatiri or Guallatiri (19,882 ft *6060 m*), in Chile, which erupted in 1959.

Northernmost and southernmost

The northernmost volcano is Beeren Berg (7470 ft *2276 m*) on the island of Jan Mayen (71° 05′ N) in the Greenland Sea. It erupted on 20 Sept 1970 and the island's 39 inhabitants (all male) had to be evacuated. It was possibly discovered by Henry Hudson in 1607 or 1608, but definitely visited by Jan Jacobsz May (Netherlands) in 1614. It was annexed by Norway on 8 May 1929. The Ostenso seamount (5825 ft *1775 m*) 346 miles *556 km* from the North Pole in Lat. 85° 10′ N, Long. 133° W was volcanic. The most southerly known active volcano is Mount Erebus (12,450 ft *3795 m*) on Ross Island (77° 35′ S), in Antarctica. It was discovered on 28 Jan 1841 by the expedition of Captain (later Rear-Admiral Sir) James Clark Ross, RN (1800–62), and first climbed at 10 a.m. on 10 Mar 1908 by a British party of five, led by Professor (later Lieut.-Col. Sir) Tannatt William Edgeworth David (1858–1934).

Largest crater

The world's largest *caldera* or volcano crater is that of Toba, north central Sumatra, Indonesia covering 685 miles² *1775 km²*.

GEYSERS

Tallest World

The Waimangu (Maori, *black water*) geyser, in New Zealand, erupted to a height in excess of 1500 ft *457 m* in 1904, but has not been active since it erupted violently at 6.20 a.m. on 1 Apr 1917 and killed 4 people. Currently the world's tallest active geyser is the US National Parks' Service Steamboat Geyser, in Yellowstone National Park, which from 1962 to 1969 erupted with intervals ranging from 5 days to 10 months to a height of 250–380 ft *76–115 m*. The greatest measured water discharge has been 825,000 gal *37 850 hl* by the Giant Geyser, also in Yellowstone National Park, Wyoming, which has been dormant since 1955. The *Geysir* ('gusher') near Mount Hekla in south-central Iceland, from which all others have been named, spurts, on occasions, to 180 ft *55 m*, while the adjacent Strokkur, reactivated by drilling in 1963, spurts at 10–15 min intervals.

2. WEATHER

Guinness Superlatives Ltd. have published a more specialist volume entitled the *Guinness Book of Weather Facts and Feats* (2nd Edition) by Ingrid Holford (Price £8.95).

The meteorological records given below necessarily relate largely to the last 140–160 years, since data before that time are both sparse and often unreliable. Reliable registering thermometers were introduced as recently as *c.* 1820. The longest continuous observations have been maintained at the Radcliffe Observatory, Oxford since 1815 though discontinuous records have enabled the Chinese to assert that 903 BC was a very bad winter.

Palaeo-entomological evidence is that there was a southern European climate in England *c.* 90,000 BC, while in *c.* 6000 BC the mean summer temperature reached 67° F *19,4° C*, or 6 deg F *3,3 deg C* higher than the present. It is believed that 1.2 million years ago the world's air temperature averaged 95° F *35° C*. The earliest authentic recording of British weather relates to the period 26 Aug–17 Sept 55 BC. The earliest reliably known hot summer was in AD 664 during our driest-ever century and the earliest known severe winter was that of AD 763–4. In 1683–4 there was frost in London from November to April. Frosts were recorded during August in the period 1668–89.

Most equable temperature

The location with the most equable recorded temperature over a short period is Garapan, on Saipan, in the Mariana Islands, Pacific Ocean. During the nine years from 1927 to 1935, inclusive, the lowest temperature recorded was 19,6° C *67.3° F* on 30 Jan 1934 and the highest was 31,4° C *88.5° F* on 9 Sept 1931, giving an extreme range of 11,8 deg C *21.2 deg F*. Between 1911 and 1966 the Brazilian off-shore island of Fernando de Noronha had a minimum temperature of 18,6° C *65.5° F* on 17 Nov 1913 and a maximum of 32,0° C *89.6° F* on 2 Mar 1965, an extreme range of 13,4 deg C *24.1 deg F*.

Greatest temperature ranges

The greatest recorded temperature ranges in the world are around the Siberian 'cold pole' in the eastern USSR.

PROGRESSIVE RECORDINGS OF EXTREME HIGH TEMPERATURES WORLD WIDE

127.4° F	53,0° C	Ouargla, Algeria	27 Aug	1884
130° F	54,4° C	Amos, California, USA	17 Aug	1885
130° F	54,4° C	Mammoth Tank, California, USA	17 Aug	1885
134° F	56,7° C	Death Valley, California, USA	10 July	1913
136.4° F	58,0° C	Al'Aziziyah (el-Azizia), Libya*	13 Sept	1922

* Obtained by the US National Geographical Society but not officially recognised by the Libyan Ministry of Communications.

A reading of 140° F 60° C at Delta, Mexico, in August 1953 is not now accepted because of over-exposure to roof radiation. The official Mexican record of 136.4° F 58,0° C at San Luis, Sonora on 11 Aug 1933 is not internationally accepted.

A freak heat flash reported from Coimbra, Portugal, in September 1933 said to have caused the temperature to rise to 70° C 158° F for 120 sec is apocryphal.

PROGRESSIVE RECORDINGS OF EXTREME LOW TEMPERATURES WORLD WIDE

−73° F	−58,3° C	Floeberg Bay, Ellesmere I., Canada		1852
−90.4° F	−68° C	Verkhoyansk, Siberia, USSR	3 Jan	1885
−90.4° F	−68° C	Verkhoyansk, Siberia, USSR	5 & 7 Feb	1892
−90.4° F	−68° C	Oymyakon, Siberia, USSR	6 Feb	1933
−100.4° F	−73,5° C	South Pole, Antarctica	11 May	1957
−102.1° F	−74,5° C	South Pole, Antarctica	17 Sept	1957
−109.1° F	−78,34° C	Sovietskaya, Antarctica	2 May	1958
−113.3° F	−80,7° C	Vostok, Antarctica	15 June	1958
−114.1° F	−81,2° C	Sovietskaya, Antarctica	19 June	1958
−117.4° F	−83,0° C	Sovietskaya, Antarctica	25 June	1958
−122.4° F	−85,7° C	Vostok, Antarctica	7–8 Aug	1958
−124.1° F	−86,7° C	Sovietskaya, Antarctica	9 Aug	1958
−125.3° F	−87,4° C	Vostok, Antarctica	25 Aug	1958
−126.9° F	−88,3° C	Vostok, Antarctica	24 Aug	1960
−128.6° F	−89,2° C	Vostok, Antactica	21 July	1983

Temperatures in Verkhoyansk (67° 33′ N, 133° 23′ E) have ranged 192 deg F *106,7 deg C* from −94° F −*70° C* (unofficial) to 98° F *36,7° C*. The greatest temperature variation recorded in a day is 100 deg F *55,5 deg C* (a fall from 44° F *6,7° C* to −56° F −*48,8° C*) at Browning, Montana, USA, on 23–24 Jan 1916. The most freakish rise was 49 deg F *27,2 deg C* in 2 min at Spearfish, South Dakota, from −4° F −*20° C* at 7.30 a.m. to 45° F *7,2° C* at 7.32 a.m. on 22 Jan 1943. The British record is 29 deg C *52.2 deg F* (−7° C *19.4° F* to 22° C *71.6° F*) at Tummel Bridge, Tayside on 9 May 1978.

Longest freeze

The longest recorded unremitting freeze in the British Isles was one of 34 days at Moor House, Cumbria, from 23 Dec 1962 to 25 Jan 1963. This was almost certainly exceeded at the neighbouring Great Dun Fell, where the screen temperature never rose above freezing during the whole of January 1963. Less rigorous early data includes a frost from 5 Dec 1607 to 14 Feb 1608 and a 91-day frost on Dartmoor, Devon in 1854–5. No temperature lower than 34° F *1° C* has ever been recorded on Bishop Rock, Isles of Scilly.

Upper atmosphere

The lowest temperature ever recorded in the atmosphere is −143° C −*225.4° F* at an altitude of about 50–60 miles *80,5–96,5 km*, during noctilucent cloud research above Kronogård, Sweden, from 27 July to 7 Aug 1963. A jet stream moving at 408 mph *656 km/h* at 154,200 ft *47 000 m* (29.2 miles *46 km*) was recorded by Skua rocket above South Uist, Outer Hebrides, Scotland on 13 Dec 1967.

Thickest Ice

The greatest recorded thickness of ice is 2.97 miles (15,670 ft) *4776 m* measured by radio echo soundings from a U.S. Antarctic Research aircraft at 69° 9′ 38″ S 135° 20′ 25″ E 400 km *250 miles* from the coast in Wilkes Land on 4 Jan 1975.

Deepest Permafrost

The deepest recorded permafrost is more than 4500 ft *1370 m* reported from the upper reaches of the Viluy River, Siberia, USSR in February 1982.

Most recent White Christmas and Frost Fair

London has experienced seven 'White' or snowing Christmas Days since 1900. These have been 1906, 1917 (slight), 1923 (slight), 1927, 1938 (slight) and 1970. These were more frequent in the 19th century and even more so before the change of the calendar, which, by removing 3–13 Sept brought forward all dates subsequent to 2 Sept 1752 by 11 days. The last of the nine recorded Frost Fairs held on the Thames since 1564/65 was from December 1813 to 26 Jan 1814.

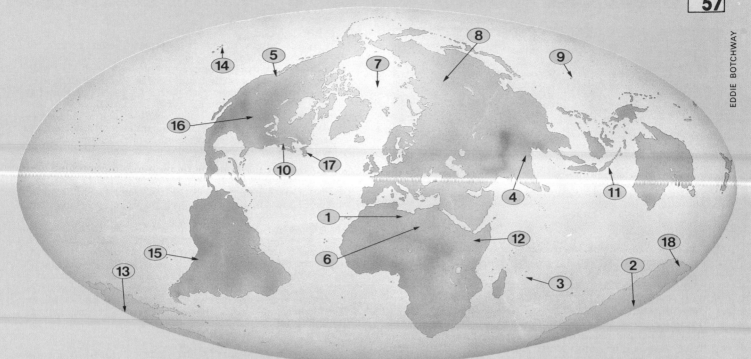

EDDIE BOTCHWAY

WEATHER RECORDS

1. HIGHEST SHADE TEMPERATURE: *World* 136.4° F *58° C* al'Azīzīyah, Libya, (alt. 367 ft *111 m*) 13.9.1922 *UK & Ireland* 98.2° F *36,77° C* Raunds, Northants; Epsom, Surrey and Canterbury, Kent 9.8.1911**(a)**

2. LOWEST SCREEN TEMPERATURE: *World* − 128.6° F *−89,2° C* Vostok, Antarctica, 21.7.1983 **(b).** *UK & Ireland* −17° F *−27,2° C* 11.2.1895 and −27,2° C *−17° F* 10.1.1982 both at Braemar, Grampian, Scotland **(c)**

3. GREATEST RAINFALL (24 hours): *World* 73.62 in *1870 mm*, Cilaos, La Réunion, Indian Ocean, 15–16.3.1952 **(d)** *UK & Ireland* 11.00 in *279 mm*, Martinstown, Dorset, 18–19.7.1955

4. GREATEST RAINFALL (Calendar Month): *World* 366.14 in *9299 mm*, Cherrapunji, Meghalaya, India, July 1861 *UK & Ireland* 56.54 in *1436 mm*, Llyn Llydau, Snowdon, Gwynedd, October 1909

4. GREATEST RAINFALL (12 months): *World* 1041.78 in *26 461 mm*, Cherrapunji, Meghalaya, 1.8.1860–31.7.1861 *UK & Ireland* 257.0 in *6527 mm*, Sprinkling Tarn, Cumbria, in 1954 **(e)**

4. WETTEST PLACE (Annual mean): *World* Cherrapunji, India (alt. 4308 ft *1313 m*) 451.8 in *11477,4 mm* (av. 1851–1960). In 1948 621 in *15 773 mm* UK & Ireland Styhead Tarn (1600 ft *487 m*), Cumbria, 172.9 in *4391 mm*

5. GREATEST SNOWFALL (f) (12 months): *World* 1224.5 in *31 102 mm*, Paradise, Mt Rainier, Washington, USA 19.2.1971 to 18.2.1972 *UK & Ireland* 60 in *1524 mm* Upper Teesdale and Denbighshire Hills, Clwyd, Wales, 1947

6. MAXIMUM SUNSHINE: (g) *World* >97 per cent (over 4300 hours), eastern Sahara, annual average *UK & Ireland* 78.3 per cent (382 hours) Pendennis Castle, Falmouth, Cornwall, June 1925

7. MINIMUM SUNSHINE: *World* Nil at North Pole— for winter stretches of 186 days *UK & Ireland* Nil in a month at Westminster, London, in December 1890 **(h)**

8. BAROMETRIC PRESSURE (Highest): *World* 1083.8 mb. (*32.00 in*), Agata, Siberia, USSR (alt. 862 ft *262 m*), 31.12.1968. *UK & Ireland* 1054.7 mb. (*31.15 in*), Aberdeen, 31.1.1902

9. BAROMETRIC PRESSURE (Lowest): **(j)** *World* 870 mb (*25.69 in*), 300 miles *482 km* west of Guam,

Pacific Ocean, in Lat. 16°44′ N, Long. 137°46′ E. 12.10.1979 *UK & Ireland* 925.5 mb (*27.33 in*), Ochtertyre, near Crieff, Tayside, 26.1.1884

10. HIGHEST SURFACE WIND-SPEED: (k) *World* 231 mph *371 km/h*, Mt. Washington (6288 ft *1916 m*), New Hampshire, USA 12.4.1934 *UK & Ireland* 144 mph *231 km/h* (125 knots), Coire Cas ski lift (3525 ft *1074 m*), Cairn Gorm, Highland, 6.3.1967 **(l)**

11. THUNDER-DAYS (Year): **(m)** *World* 322 days, Bogor (formerly Buitenzorg), Java, Indonesia (average, 1916–19) *UK & Ireland* 38 days, Stonyhurst, Lancashire, 1912 and Huddersfield, West Yorkshire, 1967

12. HOTTEST PLACE (Annual mean): **(n)** *World* Dallol, Ethiopia, 94° F *34,4° C* (1960–66) *UK & Ireland* Penzance, Cornwall, and Isles of Scilly, both 52.7° F *11,5° C*, average 1931–60

13. COLDEST PLACE (Extrapolated annual mean): *World* Polus Nedostupnosti, Pole of Cold (78° S., 96° E.), Antarctica, −72° F *−57,8° C* Coldest measured mean: − 70° F *−56,6° C* Plateau Station, Antarctica *UK & Ireland* Braemar, Aberdeenshire 6,35° C 43.43° F (1959–1981)

14. MOST RAINY DAYS (Year): *World* Mt. Wai-'ale-'ale (5148 ft *1569 m*), Kauai, Hawaii, up to 350 per annum *UK & Ireland* Ballynahinch, Galway, 309 days in 1923

15. DRIEST PLACE (Annual mean): *World* Nil—in the Desierto de Atacama, near Calama, Chile *UK & Ireland* Great Wakering, Essex, 19.2 in *487 mm* (1916–50) **(o)**

15. LONGEST DROUGHT: *World* c. 400 years to 1971 Desierto de Atacama, Chile *UK & Ireland* 73 days Mile End, Greater London, 4.3 to 15.5.1893 **(p)**

16. HEAVIEST HAILSTONES: (q) *World* 1.67 lb *750 g* (7½ in *19 cm* diameter, 17½ in *44,45 cm* circumference), Coffeyville, Kansas, USA 3.9.1970 *UK and Ireland* 5 oz *141 g*, Horsham, West Sussex, 5.9.1958

17. LONGEST SEA LEVEL FOGS (Visibility less than 1000 yd *914,4 m*): *World* Fogs persist for weeks on the Grand Banks, Newfoundland, and the average is more than 120 days per year **(r)** *UK & Ireland* London duration record was 26.11 to 1.12.1948 and 5.12 to 9.12.1952 (both 4 days 18 hours)

18. WINDIEST PLACE: *World* The Commonwealth Bay, George V Coast, Antarctica, where gales reach 200 mph *320 km/h UK & Ireland* Tiree, Strathclyde (89 ft *27 m*); annual average 17.4 mph *28 km/h*. Fair Isle (1974–78) returned 20.6 mph *33,1 km/h*

Footnotes
(a) The 100.5° F *38,6° C* reported from Tonbridge, Kent was a non-standard exposure and is estimated to be equivalent of 97–98° F *36–36,7° C*
(b) Vostok is 11,220 ft *3419 m* above sea-level. The coldest permanently inhabited place is the Siberian village of Oymyakon (pop. 600) (63° 16′ N., 143° 15′ E.), (2300 ft *700 m*) in the USSR where the temperature reached − 96° F *− 71,1° C* in 1964.
(c) The − 23° F *−30,5° C* at Blackadder, Borders, on 4 Dec 1879, and the −20° F *−28,9° C* at Grantown-on-Spey on 24 Feb 1955, were not standard exposures. The lowest official temperature in England is − 15° F *− 26,1° C* at Newport, Shropshire on 10 Jan 1982. The lowest maximum temperature for a day was − 19,1° C *− 2.3° F* at Braemar on 10 Jan 1982.
(d) This is equal to 7435 tons *7554 tonnes* of rain per acre. Elevation 1200 m *3937 ft*.
(e) The record for Ireland is 145.4 in *3921 mm* near Derriana Lough, County Kerry in 1948.
(f) The record for a single snow storm is 189 in *4800 mm* at Mt. Shasta, Ski Bowl, California, and for 24 hr, 76 in *1930 mm* at Silver Lake, Colorado, USA on 14–15 April 1921. The greatest depth of snow on the ground was 27 ft 7 in *8407 mm* at Helen Lake, Mount Lassen in April 1983. London's earliest recorded snow was on 25 Sept 1885, on the latest on 27 May 1821. Less reliable reports suggest snow on 12 Sept 1658 (Old Style) and on 12 June 1791.
(g) St Petersburg, Florida, USA, recorded 768 consecutive sunny days from 9 Feb 1967 to 17 March 1969.
(h) The south-eastern end of the village of Lochranza, Isle of Arran, Strathclyde is in shadow of mountains from 18 Nov to 8 Feb each winter.
(j) The USS *Repose*, a hospital ship, recorded 25.55 in *856 mb* in the eye of a typhoon in 25° 35′ N 128° 20′ E off Okinawa on 16 Sept 1945.
(k) The highest speed yet measured in a tornado is 280 mph *450 km/h* at Wichita Falls, Texas, USA on 2 Apr 1958.
(l) The figure of 177.2 mph *285,2 km/h* at RAF Saxa Vord, Unst, in the Shetlands, Scotland, on 16 Feb 1962, was not recorded with standard equipment. There were gales of great severity on 15 Jan 1362 and 26 Nov 1703.
(m) Between Lat. 35° N and 35° S. there are some 3200 thunderstorms each 12 night-time hours, some of which can be heard at a range of 18 miles *29 km*.
(n) In Death Valley, California, USA, maximum temperatures of over 120° F *48,9° C* were recorded on 43 consecutive days—6 July to 17 Aug 1917. At Marble Bar, Western Australia (maximum 121° F *49,4° C*) 160 consecutive days with maximum temperatures of over 100° F *37,8° C* were recorded—31 Oct 1923 to 7 Apr 1924. At Wyndham, Western Australia, the temperature reached 90° F *32,2° C* or more on 333 days in 1946.
(o) The lowest rainfall recorded in a single year was 9.29 in *23,6 cm* at one station in Margate, Kent in 1921.
(p) The longest drought in Scotland was one of 38 days at Port William, Dumfries & Galloway on 3 Apr to 10 May 1938.
(q) Much heavier hailstones are sometimes reported. These are usually not single but coalesced stones. An ice block of 1–2 kg *35–70 oz.* was reputed at Withington, Manchester on 2 Apr 1973. The *Canton Evening News* reported on 14 Apr 1981 5 killed and 225 injured by a hailstorm with stones weighing up to 30 lb *13,6 kg* (sic).
(r) Lower visibilities occur at higher altitudes. Ben Nevis is reputedly in cloud 300 days per year.

Bill Burrell, who reported $-15°F$ *$-26,1°C$* from Newport in Shropshire on 10 Jan 1982—the lowest ever recorded in England.

Most intense rainfall

Difficulties attend rainfall readings for very short periods but the figure of 1.50 in *38,1 mm* in 1 min at Barst, Guadeloupe on 26 Nov 1970, is regarded as the most intense recorded in modern times. The cloudburst of 'near 2 ft *609 mm* in less than a quarter of half an hour' at Oxford on the afternoon of 31 May (Old Style) 1682 is regarded as unacademically recorded. The most intense rainfall in Britain recorded to modern standards has been 2.0 in *51 mm* in 12 min at Wisbech, Cambridgeshire on 28 June 1970.

Falsest St. Swithin's Days

The legend that the weather on St. Swithin's Day, celebrated on 15 July (Old and New Style) since AD 1912, determines the rainfall for the next 40 days is one which has long persisted. There was a brilliant 13½ hr sunshine in London on 15 July 1924, but 30 of the next 40 days were wet. On 15 July 1913 there was a 15-hr downpour, yet it rained on only 9 of the subsequent 40 days in London.

Best and worst British summers

According to Prof. Gordon Manley's survey over the period 1728–1978 the best (*i.e.* driest and hottest) British summer was that of 1976 and the worst (*i.e.* wettest and coldest) that of 1879. Temperatures of >32° C (89.8° F) were recorded on 13 consecutive days (25 June–7 July 1976) within Great Britain including 7 such consecutive days in Cheltenham (1–7 July), where 35,9° C *96.6° F* was reached on 3 July. In 1983 there were 40 days >80°F *26,6° C* in Britain between 3 July–31 Aug including 17 consecutively (3–19 July). London experienced its hottest month (July) since records began in 1840.

Humidity and discomfort

Human comfort or discomfort depends not merely on temperature but on the combination of temperature, humidity, radiation and wind-speed. The United States Weather Bureau uses a Temperature-Humidity Index, which equals two-fifths of the sum of the dry and wet bulb thermometer readings plus 15. A THI of 98.2 has been twice recorded in Death Valley, California—on 27 July 1966 (119° F and 31 per cent) and on 12 Aug 1970 (117° F and 37 per cent). A person driving at 45 mph *72 km/h* in a car without a windscreen in a temperature of −45° F *−42,7° C* would, by the chill factor, experience the equivalent of −125° F *−87,2° C*, *i.e.* within 3.5 deg F *2,0 deg C* of the world record.

Largest mirage

The largest mirage on record was that sighted in the Arctic at 83° N 103° W by Donald B. MacMillan in 1913. This type of mirage known as the Fata Morgana appeared as the same 'Hills, valleys, snow-capped peaks extending through at least 120 degrees of the horizon' that Peary had misidentified as Crocker Land 6 years earlier. On 17 July 1939 a mirage of Snaefells Jokull (4715 ft *1437 m*) on Iceland was seen from the sea at a distance of 335–350 miles *539–563 km*.

Longest Lasting Rainbow

A rainbow lasting over 3 hours was reported from the coastal border of Gwynedd and Clwyd, North Wales on 14 Aug 1979.

Lightning

The visible length of lightning strokes varies greatly. In mountainous regions, when clouds are very low, the flash may be less than 300 ft *91 m* long. In flat country with very high clouds, a cloud-to-earth flash may measure 4 miles *6 km* though in the most extreme cases such flashes have been measured at 20 miles *32 km*. The intensely bright central core of the lightning channel is extremely narrow. Some authorities suggest that its diameter is as little as half an inch *1,27 cm*. This core is surrounded by a 'corona envelope' (glow discharge) which may measure 10–20 ft *3–6 m* in diameter.

The speed of a lightning discharge varies from 100 to 1000 miles/sec *160–1600 km/sec* for the downward leader track, and reaches up to 87,000 miles/sec *140 000 km/sec* (nearly half the speed of light) for the powerful return stroke. In Britain there is an average of 6 strikes/mile[2] per annum or 3,7 per km[2] and an average of 4200 per annum over Greater London alone. Every few million strokes there is a giant discharge, in which the cloud-to-earth and the return lightning strokes flash from and to the top of the thunder clouds. In these 'positive giants' energy of up to 3000 million joules (3×10^{16} ergs) is sometimes recorded. The temperature reaches about 30,000° C, which is more than five times greater than that of the surface of the Sun. A theory that lightning was triggered by cosmic rays was published in 1977.

Highest waterspout

The highest waterspout of which there is a reliable record was one observed on 16 May 1898 off Eden, New South Wales, Australia. A theodolite reading from the shore gave its height as 5014 ft *1528 m*. It was about 10 ft *3 m* in diameter. The Spithead waterspout off Ryde, Isle of Wight on 21 Aug 1878 was measured by sextant to be 'about a mile' or *600 m* in height. A waterspout moved around Torbay, Devon on 17 Sept 1969 which, according to press estimates, was 1000 ft *300 m* in height.

Cloud extremes

The highest standard cloud form is cirrus, averaging 27,000 ft *8250 m* and above, but the rare nacreous or mother-of-pearl formation sometimes reaches nearly 80,000 ft *24 000 m* (see also Noctilucent clouds, Chapter 4). The lowest is stratus, below 3500 ft *1066 m*. The cloud form with the greatest vertical range is cumulo-nimbus, which has been observed to reach a height of nearly 68,000 ft *20 000 m* in the tropics.

Tornadoes (see also Accidents and Disasters Chap XI)

Britain's strongest tornado was at Southsea, Portsmouth on 14 Dec 1810 (Force 8 on the Meaden-TORRO scale). The Newmarket tornado (Force 6) of 3 Jan 1978 caused property damage estimated at up to £1,000,000. On 23 Nov 1981, 58 tornadoes were reported in one day from Anglesey to Eastern England.

3. STRUCTURE AND DIMENSIONS

OCEANS

Largest

The area of the Earth covered by sea is estimated to be 139,670,000 miles[2] *361 740 000 km²* or 70.92 per cent of the total surface. The mean depth of the hydrosphere was once estimated to be 12,450 ft *3795 m*, but recent surveys suggest a lower estimate, of 11,660 ft *3554 m*. The total weight of the water is estimated to be 1.3×10^{18} tons, or 0.022 per cent of the Earth's total weight. The volume of the oceans is estimated to be 308,400,000 miles[3] *1 285 600 000 km³* compared with only 8,400,000 miles[3] *35 000 000 km³* of fresh water.

The largest ocean in the world is the Pacific. Excluding adjacent seas, it represents 45.8 per cent of the world's oceans and covers 64,186,300 miles[2] *166 240 000 km²* in area. The average depth is 13,740 ft *4188 m*. The shortest navigable trans-Pacific distance from Guayaquil, Ecuador to Bangkok, Thailand is 10,905 miles *17 550 km*.

Deepest *World*

The deepest part of the ocean was first pin-pointed in 1951 by HM Survey Ship *Challenger* in the Marianas Trench in the Pacific Ocean. The depth was measured by sounding and by echo-sounder and published as 5960 fathoms (35,760 ft

10 900 m). Subsequent visits to this same Challenger Deep have resulted in slightly deeper measurements, now refined to 5968 fathoms (35,808 ft *10 914 m*) or 6.78 miles *10,91 km* published by the US Defense Mapping Agency in 1983. On 23 Jan 1960 the US Navy bathyscaphe *Trieste* descended to the bottom there but the depth calibrations (made for fresh rather than salt water) yielded a figure within one fathom or 6 ft *1,8 m* of the above figure. A metal object, say a pound ball of steel, dropped into water above this trench would take nearly 64 min to fall to the sea-bed 6.78 miles *10,91 km* below, where hydrostatic pressure is over 18,000 lb/in² *1250 bars*. The average depth of the Pacific Ocean is 13,740 ft *4188 m*.

Deepest British waters
The deepest point in the territorial waters of the United Kingdom is an areas 6 cables (*1100 m*) off the island of Raasay, Highland, in the Inner Sound at Lat. 57° 30′ 33″ N, Long. 5° 57′ 27″ W. A depth of 1038 ft (173 fathoms, *316 m*) was found in December 1959 by HMS *Yarnton* (Lt-Cdr A. C. F. David, RN.)

Largest sea
The largest of the world's seas is the South China Sea, with an area of 1,148,500 miles² *2 974 600 km²*. The Malayan Sea, comprising the waters between the Indian Ocean and the South Pacific, south of the Chinese mainland covering 3,144,000 miles² *8 142 900 km²* is not now an entity accepted by the International Hydrographic Bureau.

Largest gulf
The largest gulf in the world is the Gulf of Mexico, with an area of 580,000 miles² *1 500 000 km²* and a shoreline of 3100 miles *4990 km* from Cape Sable, Florida, USA, to Cabo Catoche, Mexico.

Largest bay
The largest bay in the world measured by shore-line length is Hudson Bay, northern Canada, with a shoreline of 7623 miles *12 268 km* and with an area of 317,500 miles² *822 300 km²*. The area of the Bay of Bengal is however 839,000 miles² *2 172 000 km²*. Great Britain's largest bay is Cardigan Bay which has a 140 mile *225 km* long shoreline and measures 72 miles *116 km* across from the Lleyn Peninsula, Gwynedd to St David's Head, Dyfed in Wales.

Longest fjords and sea lochs *World*
The world's longest fjord is the Nordvest Fjord arm of the Scoresby Sund in eastern Greenland, which extends inland 195 miles *313 km* from the sea. The longest of Norwegian fjords is the Sogne Fjord, which extends 183 km *113.7 miles* inland from Sygnefest to the head of the Lusterfjord arm at Skjolden. It averages barely 4,75 km *3 miles* in width and has a deepest point of 1245 m *4085 ft*. If measured from Huglo along the Bømlafjord to the head of the Sørfjord arm at Odda, Hardangerfjorden can also be said to extend 183 km *113.7 miles*. The longest Danish fjord is Limfjorden (100 miles *160 km* long).

Longest sea loch *Great Britain*
Scotland's longest sea loch is Loch Fyne, which extends 42 miles *67,5 km* inland into Strathclyde (formerly Argyllshire.)

Highest seamount
The highest known submarine mountain, or seamount, is one discovered in 1953 near the Tonga Trench, between Samoa and New Zealand. It rises 28,500 ft *8690 m* from the sea bed, with its summit 1200 ft *365 m* below the surface.

Remotest spot from land
The world's most distant point from land is a spot in the South Pacific, approximately 48° 30′ S, 125° 30′ W, which is about 1660 miles *2670 km* from the nearest points of land, namely Pitcairn Island, Ducie Island and Cape Dart, Antarctica. Centred on this spot, therefore, is a circle of water with an area of about 8,657,000 miles² *22 421 500 km²*—about 7000 miles² *18 000 km²* larger than the USSR, the world's largest country (see Chapter 11).

Most southerly
The most southerly part of the oceans is 85° 34′ S, 154° W, at the snout of the Robert Scott Glacier, 305 miles *490 km* from the South Pole.

Longest voyage
The longest possible great circle sea voyage is one of 19,860

miles *31 960 km* from a point 150 miles *240 km* west of Karachi, Pakistan to a point 200 miles *320 km* north of Uka' Kamchatka *via* the Mozambique Channel, Drake Passage and Bering Sea.

Sea temperature
The temperature of the water at the surface of the sea varies from −2° C *28.5° F* in the White Sea to 35,6° C *96° F* in the shallow areas of the Persian Gulf in summer. Ice-focused solar rays have been known to heat lake water to nearly 80° F *26,8° C*. The normal Red Sea temperature is 22° C *71.6° F*. The highest temperature recorded in the ocean is 662° F *350° C*, measured by the research submersible *Alvin* at Lat. 21° N on the East Pacific Rise in November 1979, emanating from a sea-floor geothermal spring at a depth of 2600 m *8530 ft*.

STRAITS

Longest
The longest straits in the world are the Tatarskiy Proliv or Tartar Straits between Sakhalin Island and the USSR mainland running from the Sea of Japan to Sakhalinsky Zaliv. This distance is 800 km *497 miles*—thus marginally longer than the Malacca Straits.

Broadest
The broadest named straits in the world are the Davis Straits between Greenland and Baffin Island with a minimum width of 210 miles *338 km*. The Drake Passage between the Diego Ramirez Islands, Chile and the South Shetland Islands is 710 miles *1140 km* across.

Narrowest
The narrowest navigable straits are those between the Aegean island of Euboea and the mainland of Greece. The gap is only 45 yd *40 m* wide at Khalkis. The Seil Sound, Strathclyde, Scotland, narrows to a point only 20 ft *6 m* wide where the Clachan bridge joins the island of Seil to the mainland and is thus said by the islanders to span the Atlantic.

WAVES

Highest
The highest officially recorded sea wave was measured by Lt Frederic Margraff USN from the USS *Ramapo* proceeding from Manila, Philippines, to San Diego, California, USA, on the night of 6–7 Feb 1933, during a 68-knot (78.3 mph *126 km/h*) hurricane. The wave was calculated to be 112 ft *34 m* from trough to crest. The highest instrumentally measured wave was one 86 ft *26,2 m* high, recorded by the British ship *Weather Reporter*, in the North Atlantic on 30 Dec 1972 in Lat. 59° N, Long. 19° W. It has been calculated on the statistics of the Stationary Random Theory that one wave in more than 300,000 may exceed the average by a factor of 4.

On 9 July 1958 a landslip caused a 100 mph *160 km/h* wave to wash 1740 ft *530 m* high along the fjord-like Lituya Bay, Alaska, USA.

Highest seismic wave
The highest estimated height of a *tsunami* (often wrongly called a tidal wave) was one of 85 m *278 ft*, which appeared off Ishigaki Island, Ryukyu Chain on 24 Apr 1971. It tossed a 750 ton block of coral more than 2,5 km *1.3 miles*. *Tsunami* (a Japanese word meaning *nami*, a wave; *tsu*, overflowing) have been observed to travel at 490 mph *790 km/h*.

CURRENTS

Greatest
The greatest current in the oceans of the world is the Antarctic Circumpolar Current or West Wind Drift Current which was measured in 1969 in the Drake Passage between South America and Antarctica to be flowing at a rate of 9500 million ft³ *270 000 000 m³* per sec—nearly treble that of the Gulf Stream. Its width ranges from 185 to 1240 miles *300–2000 km* and has a proven surface flow rate of $\frac{4}{10}$ of a knot *0,75 km/h*.

Strongest
The world's strongest currents are the Nakwakto Rapids, Slingsby Channel, British Columbia, Canada (Lat. 51° 05′ N, Long. 127° 30′ W) where the flow rate may reach 16.0 knots *29,6 km/h*. The fastest current in British territorial waters is 10.7 knots *19,8 km/h* in the Pentland Firth between the Orkney Islands and Caithness.

GREATEST TIDES

Extreme tides are due to lunar and solar gravitational forces affected by their perigee, perihelion and syzygies. Barometric and wind effects can superimpose an added 'surge' element. Coastal and sea-floor configurations can accentuate these forces. The normal interval between tides is 12 hr 25 min.

World

The greatest tides in the world occur in the Bay of Fundy, which divides the peninsula of Nova Scotia, Canada, from the United States' north-easternmost state of Maine and the Canadian province of New Brunswick. Burncoat Head in the Minas Basin, Nova Scotia, has the greatest mean spring range with 47.5 ft *14,50 m* and an extreme range of 53.5 ft *16,30 m*. Tahiti experiences virtually no tide.

Great Britain

The place with the greatest mean spring range in Great Britain is Beachley, on the Severn, with a range of 40.7 ft *12,40 m*, compared with the British Isles' average of 15 ft *4,57 m*. Prior to 1933 tides as high as 28.9 ft *8,80 m* above and 22.3 ft *6.80 m* below datum (total range 51.2 ft *15,60 m*) were recorded at Avonmouth though an extreme range of 52.2 ft *15,90 m* for Beachley was officially accepted. In 1883 a freak tide of greater range was reported from Chepstow, Gwent.

ICEBERGS

Largest and Tallest

The largest iceberg on record was an Antarctic tabular 'berg of over 12,000 miles² *31 000 km²* (208 miles *335 km* long and 60 miles *97 km* wide and thus larger than Belgium) sighted 150 miles *240 km* west of Scott Island, in the South Pacific Ocean, by the USS *Glacier* on 12 Nov 1956. The 200 ft *61 m* thick Arctic ice island T.1 (140 miles² *360 km²*) (discovered in 1946) was tracked for 17 years. The tallest iceberg measured was one of 550 ft *167 m* reported off western Greenland by the US icebreaker *East Wind* in 1958.

Most southerly Arctic

The most southerly Arctic iceberg was sighted in the Atlantic by a USN weather patrol in Lat. 28° 44′ N, Long. 48° 42′ W in April 1935. The southernmost iceberg reported in British home waters was one sighted 60 miles *96 km* from Smith's Knoll, on the Dogger Bank, in the North Sea.

Most northerly Antarctic

The most northerly Antarctic iceberg was a remnant sighted in the Atlantic by the ship *Dochra* in Lat. 26° 30′ S, Long. 25° 40′ W, on 30 Apr 1894.

The tallest iceberg ever sighted was photographed from the deck of the US Icebreaker *East Wind* in 1958. (*Official US Coast Guard photo*)

LAND

There is satisfactory evidence that at one time the Earth's land surface comprised a single primeval continent of 80 million miles² *2 × 10⁸ km²*, now termed Pangaea, and that this split about 190 million years ago, during the Jurassic period, into two super-continents, termed Laurasia (Eurasia, Greenland and Northern America) and Gondwanaland (Africa. Arabia, India, South America, Oceania and Antarctica) and named after Gondwana, India, which itself split 120 million years ago. The South Pole was apparently in the area of the Sahara as recently as the Ordovician period of *c.* 450 million years ago.

ROCKS

The age of the Earth is generally considered to be within the range of 4550 ± 50 million years, by analogy with directly measured ages of meteorites and of the moon. However, no rocks of this great age have yet been found on the Earth since geological processes have presumably destroyed them.

Oldest *World*

The greatest reported age for any scientifically dated rock is 3800 ± 100 million years for granite gneiss rock found near Granite Falls in the Minnesota river valley, USA as measured by the lead-isotope and rubidium-uranium methods by the US Geological Survey and announced on 26 Jan 1975. These metamorphic samples compare with the Amîtsoq gneiss from Godthaab, Greenland unreservedly accepted to be between 3700 and 3750 million years. Zirconium silicate crystals from Mt Narrayer, Australia were dated to 4200 million years (1983).

Oldest *Great Britain*

The original volcanic products from which were formed the gneiss and granulite rocks of the Scourian complex in the north west Highlands and the Western Isles were crystallized 2800 million years ago.

Largest

The largest isolated monolith in the world is the 1237 ft *377 m* high Mount Augustus (3627 ft *1105 m* above sea-level), discovered on 3 June 1858, 200 miles *320 km* east of Carnarvon, Western Australia. It is an upfaulted monoclinal gritty conglomerate 5 miles *8 km* long and 2 miles *3 km* across and thus twice the size of the celebrated monolithic arkose Ayer's Rock (1100 ft *335 m*), 250 miles *400 km* south-west of Alice Springs, in Northern Territory, Australia. It was estimated in 1940 that La Gran Piedra, a volcanic plug in the Sierra Maestra, Cuba weighs 61,355 tons/*tonnes*.

CONTINENTS

Largest

Only 29.08 per cent, or an estimated 57,270,000 miles² *148 328 000 km²* of the Earth's surface is land, with a mean height of 2480 ft *756 m* above sea-level. The Eurasian land mass is the largest, with an area (including islands) of 20,733,000 miles² *53 698 000 km²*. The Afro-Eurasian land mass, separated artificially only by the Suez Canal covers an area of 32,233,000 miles² *83 483 000 km²* or 56.2% of the Earth's landmass.

Smallest

The smallest is the Australian mainland, with an area of 2,941,526 miles² *7 618 493 km²*, which, together with Tasmania, New Zealand, New Guinea and the Pacific Islands, is described sometimes as Oceania.

Land remotest from the sea *World*

There is an as yet unpinpointed spot in the Dzoosotoyn Elisen (desert), northern Xinjiang Uygur Zizhiqu (Sin Kiang), China's most north westerly province, that is more than 1500 miles *2400 km* from the open sea in any direction. The nearest large city to this point is Urümqi (Urümchi) to its south.

Land remotest from the sea *Great Britain*

The point furthest from the sea in Great Britain is a point near Meriden, West Midlands, England, which is 72½ miles *117 km* equidistant from the Severn Bridge, the Dee and Mersey estuaries and the Welland estuary in the Wash. The equivalent point in Scotland is in the Forest of Atholl, north-west Tayside 40½ miles *65 km* equidistant from the head of Loch Leven, Inverness Firth and the Firth of Tay.

Peninsula

The world's largest peninsula is Arabia, with an area of about 1,250,000 miles² *3 250 000 km²*.

ISLANDS

Largest *World*

Discounting Australia, which is usually regarded as a continental land mass, the largest island in the world is Greenland (renamed Kalaatdlit Nunaat 1 May 1979), with an area of about 840,000 miles² *0 175 000 km²*. There is evidence that Greenland is in fact several islands overlaid by an ice cap without which it would have an area of 650,000 miles² *1 680 000 km²*.

Largest *Great Britain*

The mainland of Great Britain (Scotland, England and Wales) is the eighth largest in the world, with an area of 84,186 miles² *218 041 km²*. It stretches 603½ miles *971 km* from Dunnet Head in the north to Lizard Point in the south and 287½ miles *463 km* across from Porthaflod, Dyfed to Lowestoft, Suffolk. The island of Ireland (32,594 miles² *84 418 km²*) is the 20th largest in the world.

Freshwater

The largest island surrounded by fresh water is the Ilha de Marajó (18,500 miles² *48 000 km²*), in the mouth of the River Amazon, Brazil. The world's largest inland island (*i.e.* land surrounded by rivers) is Ilha do Bananal, Brazil (7000 miles² *18 130 km²*). The largest island in a lake is Manitoulin Island (1068 miles² *2766 km²*) in the Canadian (Ontario) section of Lake Huron. The largest lake island in Great Britain is Inchmurrin in Loch Lomond, Strathclyde/Central, Scotland with an area of 284 acres *115 ha*.

Remotest *World uninhabited*

The remotest island in the world is Bouvet Øya (formerly Liverpool Island), discovered in the South Atlantic by J. B. C. Bouvet de Lozier on 1 Jan 1739, and first landed on by Capt. George Norris on 16 Dec 1825. Its position is 54° 26′ S, 3° 24′ E. This uninhabited Norwegian dependency is about 1050 miles *1700 km* from the nearest land—the uninhabited Queen Maud Land coast of eastern Antarctica.

Remotest *World inhabited*

The remotest inhabited island in the world is Tristan da Cunha, discovered in the South Atlantic by Tristão da Cunha, a Portuguese admiral, in March 1506. It has an area of 38 miles² *98 km²* (habitable area 12 miles² *31 km²*) and was annexed by the United Kingdom on 14 Aug 1816. After evacuation in 1961 (due to volcanic activity, 198 islanders returned in November 1963. The nearest inhabited land is the island of St Helena, 1320 miles *2120 km* to the north-east. The nearest continent, Africa is 1700 miles *2735 km* away.

Remotest *Great Britain*

The remotest of the British islets is Rockall 191 miles *307 km* west of St Kilda, Western Isles. This 70 ft *21 m* high rock measuring 83 ft *25 m* across was not formally annexed until 18 Sept 1955. The remotest British island which has ever been inhabited is North Rona which is 44 miles *70,8 km* from the next nearest land at Cape Wrath and the Butt of Lewis. It was evacuated *c.* 1844. Muckle Flugga, off Unst, in the Shetlands, is the northernmost inhabited with a population of 3 (1971) and is in a latitude north of southern Greenland. Just to the north of it is the rock of Out Stack in Lat. 60° 51′ 35.7″ N.

Highest Rock Pinnacle

The world's highest rock pinnacle is Ball's Pyramid near Lord Howe Island, Pacific which is 1843 ft *561 m* high, but has a base axis of only 200 m *220 yd*. It was first scaled in 1965.

Northernmost land

On 26 July 1978 Uffe Petersen of the Danish Geodetic Institute observed the islet of OOdaq Ø 30 m *100 ft* across, 1,36 km *1478 yd* north of Kaffeklubben Ø off Pearyland, Greenland in Lat. 83° 40′ 32.5″ N, Long. 30° 40′ 10.1″ W. The island is 706,4 km *438.9 miles* from the North Pole.

Southernmost land

The South Pole, unlike the North Pole, is on land. The Amundsen-Scott South Polar station was built there at an altitude of 9370 ft *2855 m* in 1957. It is drifting bodily with the ice cap 27–30 ft *8–9 m* per annum in the direction 43° W and was replaced by a new structure in 1975.

Greatest archipelago

The world's greatest archipelago is the 3500 mile *5600 km* long crescent of more than 13,000 islands which forms Indonesia.

Newest

The world's newest island, Lateiki Island which appeared after a volcanic eruption was annexed by Tonga in June 1979.

Largest atoll

The largest atoll in the world is Kwajalein in the Marshall Islands, in the central Pacific Ocean. Its slender 176 mile *283 km* long coral reef encloses a lagoon of 1100 miles² *2850 km²* The atoll with the largest land area is Christmas Atoll, in the Line Islands, in the central Pacific Ocean. It has an area of 248 miles² *642 km²* of which 125 miles² *323 km²* is land. Its principal settlement, London, is only 2½ miles *4,0 km* distant from Paris.

Longest reef

The longest reef is the Great Barrier Reef off Queensland, north-eastern Australia, which is 1260 statute miles *2027 km* in length. Between 1959 and 1971 a large section between Cooktown and Townsville was destroyed by the proliferation of the Crown of Thorns starfish (*Acanthaster planci*).

DEPRESSIONS

Deepest *World*

The deepest depression so far discovered is the bed rock in the Bentley sub-glacial trench, Antarctica at 2538 m *8326 ft* below sea level. The greatest submarine depression is a large area of the floor of the north-west Pacific which has an average depth of 15,000 ft *4570 m*. The deepest exposed depression on land is the shore surrounding the Dead Sea, 1291 ft *393 m* below sea-level. The deepest point on the bed of this saltiest of all lakes is 336 m *1102 ft* below sea level. The deepest part of the bed of Lake Baykal in Siberia, USSR, is 4872 ft *1484 m* below sea-level.

Deepest *Great Britain*

The lowest lying area in Great Britain is in the Holme Fen area of the Great Ouse, in Cambridgeshire, at 9 ft *2,75 m* below sea-level. The deepest depression in England is the bed of part of Windermere, 94 ft *28,65 m* below sea-level, and in Scotland the bed of Loch Morar, Highland 987 ft *300,8 m* below sea-level.

Largest

The largest exposed depression in the world is the Caspian Sea basin in the Azerbaydzhani, Russian, Kazakh and Turkmen Republics of the USSR and northern Iran (Persia). It is more than 200,000 miles² *518 000 km²* of which 143,550 miles² *371 800 km²* is lake area. The preponderant land area of the depression is the Prikaspiyskaya Nizmennost', lying around the northern third of the lake and stretching inland for a distance of up to 280 miles *450 km*.

CAVES

Longest

The most extensive cave system in the world is that under the Mammoth Cave National Park, Kentucky, USA first discovered in 1799. On 9 Sept 1972 an exploration group led by Dr John P. Wilcox completed a connection, pioneered by Mrs Patricia Crowther on 30 Aug between the Flint Ridge Cave system and the Mammoth Cave system, so making a combined system with a total mapped passageway length which is now over 474 km *294.5 miles*. The longest cave system in Great Britain is the Ease Gill system which now has 47,9 km *29.8 miles* of explored passage.

Largest cavern

The world's largest cave chamber is the Sarawak Chamber, Lubang Nasib Bagus, in the Gunung Mulu National Park, Sarawak discovered and surveyed by the 1980 British–Malaysian Mulu Expedition. Its length is 700 m *2300 ft*; and its average width is 300 m *980 ft* and it is nowhere less than 70 m *230 ft* high. It would be large enough to garage 7500 buses.

Longest stalactite

The longest known stalactite in the world is a wall-supported column extending 195 ft *59 m* from roof to floor in the Cueva de Nerja, near Málaga, Spain. Probably the longest free-hanging stalactite is one of 7 m *23 ft* in the Poll an Ionain cave in County Clare, Ireland. The tallest cave column is the 106 ft *32,3 m* tall Bicentennial Column in Ogle Cave in Carlsbad Caverns National Park, New Mexico, USA.

Tallest stalagmite

The tallest known stalagmite in the world is La Grande Stalagmite in the Aven Armand cave, Lozère, France, which has attained a height of 98 ft *29 m* from the cave floor. It was found in September 1897.

DEEPEST CAVES BY COUNTRIES
These depths are subject to continuous revisions.

Depth			
m	Ft		
1535	*5036*	Réseau de Foillis (Gouffre Jean Bernard)	France
1402	*4600*	Snieznaja Piezcziera	USSR
1338	*4390*	Puerta de Illamina	Spain
1246	*4088*	Sistema Huautla	Mexico
1219	*3999*	Schwensystem	Austria
1215	*3986*	Corchia Fighera System	Italy
975	*3199*	Anou Ifflis	Algeria
878	*2880*	Holloch	Switzerland
768	*2520*	Jaskinia Sniezna	Poland
765	*2510*	Brezno pri Gamsovo Glavici	Yugoslavia
751	*2464*	Ghar Parau, Zagros	Iran
308	*1010*	Ogof Ffynnon Ddu	Wales
214	*702*	Giant's Hole System	England
179	*587*	Reyfad Pot	N Ireland
140	*459*	Carrowmore Cavern	Rep. of Ireland

MOUNTAINS

The *Guinness Book of Mountains and Mountaineering Facts and Feats* by Edward Pyatt (£8.95) was published in May 1980.

Highest *World*

An eastern Himalayan peak of 29,028 ft *8848 m* above sea-level on the Tibet–Nepal border (in an area first designated Chu-mu-lang-ma on a map of 1717) was discovered to be the world's highest mountain in 1852 by the Survey Department of the Government of India, from theodolite readings taken in 1849 and 1850. In 1860 its height was computed to be 29,002 ft *8840 m*. On 25 July 1973 the Chinese announced a height of 8848,1 m or *29,029 ft 3 in*. In practice the altitude can only be justified as 29,028 ft ± 25 feet or a mean *8848 m*. The 5½ mile *8,85 km* high peak was named Mount Everest after Col. Sir George Everest, CB. (1790–1866), formerly Surveyor-General of India. Other names for Everest are: Sagarmatha (Nepalese), Qomolongma (Chinese) and Mi-ti Gu-ti Cha-pu Long-na (Tibetan). After a total loss of 11 lives since the first reconnaissance in 1921, Everest was finally conquered at 11.30 a.m. on 29 May 1953. (For details of ascents, see under Mountaineering in Chapter 12.) The mountain whose summit is farthest from the Earth's centre is the Andean peak of Chimborazo (20,561 ft *6267 m*), 98 miles *158 km* south of the equator in Ecuador, South America. Its summit is 7057 ft *2150 m* further from the Earth's centre than the summit of Mt Everest. The highest mountain on the equator is Volcán Cayambe (19,285 ft *5878 m*), Ecuador, in Long. 77° 58′ W. A mountaineer atop the summit would be moving at 1671 km/h *1038 mph* relative to the Earth's centre due to the Earth's rotation.

Highest *Insular*

The highest insular mountain in the world is the unsurveyed Ngga Pulu formerly Mount Sukarno, formerly Carstensz Pyramide in Irian Jaya, Indonesia, once Netherlands New Guinea. According to cross-checked altimeter estimates, it is 16,500 ft *5030 m* high.

Steepest Slope

Mount Rakaposhi (25,498 ft *7772 m*) rises 5,99 vertical kilometers *19,652 ft* from the Hunza Valley, Pakistan in 10 horizontal kilometres *32,808 ft* with an overall gradient of 31°.

Highest *UK and Ireland*

A list of the highest points in the 72 geographical divisions of the United Kingdom and the 26 counties of the Republic of Ireland was given on page 63 of the 23rd (1977) Edition.

The highest mountain in the United Kingdom is Ben Nevis (4406 ft *1343 m* excluding the 12 ft *3,65 m* cairn), 4¼ miles *6,85 km* south-east of Fort William, Highland, Scotland. It was climbed before 1720 but though acclaimed the highest in 1790 was not confirmed to be higher than Ben Macdhui (4300 ft *1310 m*) until 1847. In 1834 Ben Macdhui and Ben Nevis (Gaelic, *Beinn Nibheis*) (first reference, 1778) were respectively quoted as 4570 ft *1393 m* and 4370 ft *1332 m*. The highest mountain in England is Scafell Pike (3210 ft *978 m*) in Cumbria; in Wales is Snowdon (*Yr Wyddfa*) (3560 ft *1085 m*) in Gwynedd; and in the island of Ireland is Carrauntual (3414 ft *1041 m*) in County Kerry.

There is some evidence that, before being ground down by the ice-cap, mountains in the Loch Bà area of the Isle of Mull, Strathclyde were 15,000 ft *4575 m* above sea-level.

Highest *Peaks over 3000 ft 915 m*

There are 577 peaks over 3000 ft *915 m* in the whole British Isles and 165 peaks and 136 tops in Scotland higher than England's highest point, Scafell Pike. The highest mountain off the mainland is Sgùrr Alasdair (3309 ft *1008 m*) on Skye named after Alexander (Gaelic, *Alasdair*) Nicolson, who made the first ascent in 1873.

Highest unclimbed

The highest unclimbed mountain is now only the 31st highest—Zemu Gap Peak (25,526 ft *7780 m*) in the Sikkim Himalaya.

Largest

The world's tallest mountain measured from its submarine base (3280 fathoms *6000 m*) in the Hawaiian Trough to peak is Mauna Kea (Mountain White) on the island of Hawaii, with a combined height of 33,476 ft *10 203 m* of which 13,796 ft *4205 m* are above sea-level. Another mountain whose dimensions, but not height, exceed those of Mount Everest is the volcanic Hawaiian peak of Mauna Loa (Mountain Long) at 13,680 ft *4170 m*. The axes of its elliptical base, 16,322 ft *4975 m* below sea-level, have been estimated at 74 miles *119 m* and 53 miles *85 km*. It should be noted that Cerro Aconcagua (22,834 ft *6960 m*) is more than 38,800 ft *11 826 m* above the 16,000 ft *4875 m* deep Pacific abyssal plain or 42,834 ft *13 055 m* above the Peru-Chile Trench which is 180 miles *290 km* distant in the South Pacific.

Greatest ranges

The world's greatest land mountain range is the Himalaya-Karakoram, which contains 96 of the world's 109 peaks of over 24,000 ft *7315 m*. Himalaya derives from the sanskrit *him*, snow; *alaya*, home. The greatest of all mountain ranges is, however, the submarine Indian/East Pacific Oceans Cordillera extending 19,200 miles *30 900 km* from the Gulf of Aden to the Gulf of California by way of the seabed between Australia and Antarctica with an average height of 8000 ft *2430 km* above the base ocean depth.

Longest lines of sight

Vatnajökull (6952 ft *2118 m*), Iceland has been seen by refracted light from the Faeroe Islands 340 miles *550 km* distant. In Alaska Mt McKinley (20,320 ft *6193 m*) has been sighted from Mt Sanford (16,237 ft *4949 m*) from a distance of 230 miles *370 km*. McKinley, so named in 1896, was called Denali (Great One) in the Athabascan language.

Greatest plateau

The most extensive high plateau in the world is the Tibetan Plateau in Central Asia. The average altitude is 16,000 ft *4875 m* and the area is 77,000 miles² *200 000 km²*.

Sheerest wall

The 3200 ft *975 m* wide northwest face of Half Dome, Yosemite, California, USA is 2200 ft *670 m* high but nowhere departs more than 7 degrees from the vertical. It was first climbed (Class VI) in 5 days in July 1957 by Royal Robbins, Jerry Gallwas and Mike Sherrick.

Highest halites

Along the northern shores of the Gulf of Mexico for 725 miles *1160 km* there exists 330 subterranean 'mountains' of salt, some of which rise more than 60,000 ft *18 300 m* from bed rock and appear as the low salt domes first discovered in 1862.

Lowest hill

The official map of Seria, Brunei shows an artificial hillock named Bukit Thompson by the 13th hole on the Panaga Golf Course at 15 ft *4,5 m*.

WATERFALLS

Highest

The highest waterfall (as opposed to vaporized 'Bridal Veil') in the world is the Salto Angel in Venezuela, on a branch of the River Carrao, an upper tributary of the Caroni with a total drop of 3212 ft *979 m*—the longest single drop is 2648 ft *807 m*. They were named for the United States pilot James (Jimmy) Angel (died 8 Dec 1956), who had crashed nearby on 9 Oct 1937. The falls, known by the Indians as Cherun-Meru, were first reported by Ernesto Sanchez La Cruz in 1910.

Highest *United Kingdom*

The tallest waterfall in the United Kingdom is Eas a'Chùal Aluinn, from Glas Bheinn (2541 ft *774 m*), Highland, Scotland, with a drop of 658 ft *200 m*. England's highest fall above ground is Caldron (or Cauldron) Snout, on the Tees, with a fall of 200 ft *60 m* in 450 ft *135 m* of cataracts, but no sheer leap. It is on the border of Durham and Cumbria. The cascade in the Gaping Gill Cave descends 365 ft *111 m*. The highest Welsh waterfall is the Pistyll-y-Llyn on the Powys-Dyfed border which exceeds 300 ft *90 m* in descent.

Highest *Ireland*

The highest falls in Ireland are the Powerscourt Falls (350 ft *106 m*), on the River Dargle, County Wicklow.

Greatest

On the basis of the average annual flow, the greatest waterfalls in the world are the Boyoma (formerly Stanley) Falls in Zaïre with 600,000 cusec *17 000 m³/sec*. The peak flow of the Guaíra (Salto das Sete Quedas) on the Alto Paraná river between Brazil and Paraguay at times attained a peak flow rate of 1,750,000 cusec *50 000 m³/sec*. The completion of the Itaipu dam in 1982 ended this claim to fame.

It has been calculated that, when some 5,500,000 years ago the Mediterranean basins began to be filled from the Atlantic through the Straits of Gibraltar, a waterfall 26 times greater than the Guaíra and perhaps 800 m *2625 ft* high was formed.

Widest

The widest waterfalls in the world are the Khône Falls (50–70 ft *15–21 m* high) in Laos, with a width of 6.7 miles *10,8 km* and a flood flow of 1,500,000 cusec *42 500 m³/sec*.

RIVERS

Longest *World*

The two longest rivers in the world are the Amazon (*Amazonas*), flowing into the South Atlantic, and the Nile (*Bahr-el-Nil*) flowing into the Mediterranean. Which is the longer is more a matter of definition than simple measurement.

The true source of the Amazon was discovered in 1953 to be a stream named Huarco, rising near the summit of Cerro Huagra (17,188 ft *5238 m*) in Peru. This stream progressively becomes the Toro then the Santiago then the Apurimac, which in turn is known as the Ene and then the Tambo before its confluence with the Amazon prime tributary the Ucayali. The length of the Amazon from this source to the South Atlantic *via* the Canal do Norte was measured in 1969 to be 4007 miles *6448 km* (usually quoted to the rounded off figure of 4000 miles *6437 km*).

If, however, a vessel navigating down the river turns to the south of Ilha de Marajó through the straits of Breves and Boiuci into the Pará, the total length of the water-course becomes 4195 miles 6750 km. *The Pará is* not *however a tributary of the Amazon, being hydrologically part of the basin of the Tocantins.*

The length of the Nile watercourse, as surveyed by M. Devroey (Belgium) before the loss of a few miles of meanders due to the formation of Lake Nasser, behind the Aswan High Dam, was 4145 miles *6670 km*. This course is the hydrologically acceptable one from the source in Burundi of the Luvironza branch of the Kagera feeder of the Victoria Nyanza *via* the White Nile (*Bahrel-Jebel*) to the delta.

Longest *Great Britain*

The longest river in Great Britain is the Severn, which empties into the Bristol Channel and is 220 miles *354 km* long. Its basin extends over 4409 miles² *11 419 km²*. It rises in north-western Powys and flows through Shropshire, Hereford and Worcester, Gloucestershire and Avon and has a record 17 tributaries. The

A stretch of the 4145 mile *6670 km* long River Nile taken below the First Cataract. (*David Cadisch*)

longest river *wholly* in England is the Thames, which is 215 miles, *346 km* long to the Nore. Its remotest source is at Seven Springs, Gloucestershire, whence the River Churn joins the other head waters. The source of the Thames proper is Trewsbury Mead, Coates, Cirencester, Gloucestershire. The basin measures 3841 miles² *9948 km²*. The Yorkshire Ouse's 11 tributaries aggregate 629 miles *1012 km*.

The longest river wholly in Wales is the Usk, with a length of 65 miles *104,5 km*. It rises on the border of Dyfed and Powys and flows out via Gwent into the Severn Estuary. The longest river in Scotland is the Tay, with Dundee, Tayside, on the shore of the estuary. It is 117 miles *188 km* long from the source of its remotest head-stream, the River Tummel, Tayside and has the greatest volume of any river in Great Britain, with a flow of up to 49,000 cusecs *1387 m³* per sec. Of Scottish rivers the Tweed and the Clyde have most tributaries with 11 each.

Longest *Ireland*

The longest river in Ireland is the Shannon, which is longer than any river in Great Britain. It rises 258 ft *78,6 m* above sea-level, in County Cavan, and flows through a series of loughs to Limerick. It is 240 miles *386 km* long, including the 56 mile *90 km* long estuary to Loop Head. The basin area is 6060 miles² *15 695 km²*.

Shortest river

The world's shortest named river is the D River, Lincoln City, Oregon, USA which connects Devil's Lake to the Pacific Ocean and is 440 ft *134 m* long at low tide.

Largest basin and longest tributary

The largest river basin in the world is that drained by the Amazon (4007 miles *6448 km*). It covers about 2,720,000 miles² *7 045 000 km²*. It has about 15,000 tributaries and subtributaries, of which four are more than 1000 miles *1609 km* long. These include the Madeira, the longest of all tributaries, with a length of 2100 miles *3380 km*, which is surpassed by only 14 rivers in the whole world.

Longest sub-tributary

The longest sub-tributary is the Pilcomayo (1000 miles *1609 km* long) in South America. It is a tributary of the Paraguay (1500 miles *2415 km* long), which is itself a tributary of the Paraná (2500 miles *4025 km*).

Longest estuary

The world's longest estuary is that of the often frozen Ob', in the northern USSR, at 550 miles *885 km*. It is up to 50 miles *80 km* wide.

Largest delta

The world's largest delta is that created by the Ganga (Ganges) and Brahmaputra in Bangla Desh (formerly East Pakistan) and West Bengal, India. It covers an area of 30,000 miles² *75 000 km²*.

Greatest flow

The greatest flow of any river in the world is that of the Amazon, which discharges an average of 4,200,000 cusec *120 000 m³/sec* into the Atlantic Ocean, rising to more than

7,000,000 cusec *200 000 m³/sec* in full flood. The lowest 900 miles *1450 km* of the Amazon average 300 ft *90 m* in depth.

Submarine river

In 1952 a submarine river 250 miles *400 km* wide, known as the Cromwell current, was discovered flowing eastward 300 ft *90 m* below the surface of the Pacific for 3500 miles *5625 km* along the equator. Its volume is 1000 times that of the Mississippi.

Subterranean river

In August 1958 a crypto-river was tracked by radio isotopes flowing under the Nile with 6 times its mean annual flow or 500,000 million m³ *20 million million ft³*.

Largest swamp

The world's largest tract of swamp is in the basin of the Pripet or Pripyat River—a tributary of the Dnieper in the USSR. These swamps cover an estimated area of 18,125 miles² *46 950 km²*.

RIVER BORES

World

The bore on the Ch'ient'ang'kian (Hang-chou-fe) in eastern China is the most remarkable of the 60 in the world. At spring tides the wave attains a height of up to 25 ft *7,5 m* and a speed of 13–15 knots *24–27 km/h*. It is heard advancing at a range of 14 miles *22 km*. The annual downstream flood wave on the Mekong sometimes reaches a height of 46 ft *14 m*. The greatest volume of any tidal bore is that of the Canal do Norte (10 miles *16 km* wide) in the mouth of the Amazon.

Great Britain

The most notable of the 8 river bores in the United Kingdom is that on the Severn, which attained a measured height of 9¼ ft *2,8 m* on 15 Oct 1966 downstream of Stonebench, and a speed of 13 mph *20 km/h*. It travels from Framilode towards Gloucester.

LAKES AND INLAND SEAS

Largest *World*

The largest inland sea or lake in the world is the Kaspiskoye More (Caspian Sea) in the southern USSR and Iran (Persia). It is 760 miles *1225 km* long and its total area is 139,000 miles² *360 700 km²*. Of the total area some 55,280 miles² *143 200 km²* (38.6 per cent) is in Iran, where it is named the Darya-ye-Khazar. Its maximum depth is 1025 m *3360 ft* and its surface is 28,5 m *93 ft* below sea-level. Its estimated volume is 21,500 miles³ *89 600 km³* of saline water. Its surface has varied between 32 m *105 ft* (11th century) and 22 m *72 ft* (early 19th century) below sea level. The USSR Government plan to reverse the flow of the upper Pechora River from flowing north to the Barents Sea by blasting a 70 mile *112 km* long canal with nuclear explosives into the south-flowing Kolva river so that *via* the Kama and Volga rivers the Caspian will be replenished.

Lake in a lake

The largest lake in a lake is Manitou Lake (41.09 miles² *106,42 km²*) on the world's largest lake island Manitoulin Island (1068 miles² *2766 km²*) in the Canadian part of Lake Huron. It contains itself a number of islands.

Underground lake

Reputedly the world's largest underground lake is the Lost Sea 300 ft *91 m* subterranean in the Craighead Caverns, Sweetwater, Tennessee, USA measuring 4½ acres *1,8 ha* and discovered in 1905.

Freshwater lake *World*

The freshwater lake with the greatest surface area is Lake Superior, one of the Great Lakes of North America. The total area is 31,800 miles² *82 350 km²* of which 20,700 miles² *53 600 km²* are in Minnesota, Wisconsin and Michigan, USA and 11,100 miles² *27 750 km²* in Ontario, Canada. It is 600 ft *182 m* above sea-level. The freshwater lake with the greatest volume is Baykal (see p. 61 and right) with an estimated volume of 5520 miles³ *23 000 km³*.

Freshwater lake *United Kingdom*

The largest lake in the United Kingdom is Lough Neagh (48 ft *14,60 m* above sea-level) in Northern Ireland. It is 18 miles *28,9 km* long and 11 miles *17,7 km* wide and has an area of 147.39 miles² *381,73 km²*. Its extreme depth is 102 ft *31 m*.

Freshwater lakes or lochs *Great Britain*

The largest lake in Great Britain, and the largest inland loch in Scotland is Loch Lomond (23 ft *7,0 m* above sea-level), which is 22.64 miles *36,44 km* long and has a surface area of 27.45 miles² *70,04 km²*. It is situated in the Strathclyde and Central regions and its greatest depth is 623 ft *190 m*. The lake or loch with the greatest volume is however Loch Ness with 262,845,000,000 ft³ *7 443 000 000 m³*. The longest lake or loch is Loch Ness which measures 24.23 miles *38,99 km*. The three arms of the Y-shaped Loch Awe aggregate, however, 25.47 miles *40,99 km*. The largest lake in England is Windermere, in the county of Cumbria. It is 10½ miles *17 km* long and has a surface area of 5.69 miles² *14,74 km²*. Its greatest depth is 219 ft *66,75 m* in the northern half. The largest *natural* lake in Wales is Llyn Tegid, with an area of 1.69 miles² *4,38 km²*, although it should be noted that the largest lake in Wales is that formed by the reservoir at Lake Vyrnwy, where the total surface area is 1120 acres *453,25 ha*.

Freshwater lakes or loughs *Republic of Ireland*

The largest lough in the Republic of Ireland is Lough Corrib in the counties of Mayo and Galway. It measures 27 miles *43,5 km* in length and is 7 miles *11,25 km* across at its widest point with a total surface area of 41,616 acres (65.0 miles² *168 km²*).

Largest Lagoon

The largest lagoon in the world is Lagoa dos Patos in southernmost Brazil. It is 158 miles *254 km* long and extends over 4110 miles² *10 645 km²*.

Deepest *World*

The deepest lake in the world is Ozero (Lake) Baykal in central Siberia, USSR. It is 385 miles *620 km* long and between 20 and 46 miles *32–74 km* wide. In 1957 the lake's Olkhon Crevice was measured to be 1940 m *6365 ft* deep and hence 1485 m *4872 ft* below sea-level (see pp. 61 and left).

Deepest *Great Britain*

The deepest lake in Great Britain is the 10.30 mile *16,57 km* long Loch Morar, in Highland. Its surface is 30 ft *9 m* above sea-level and its extreme depth 1017 ft *310 m*. England's deepest lake is Wast Water (258 ft *78 m*), in Cumbria. The lake with the greatest mean depth is Loch Ness with *c.* 426 ft *130 m*.

Highest *World*

The highest steam-navigated lake in the world is Lago Titicaca (maximum depth 1214 ft *370 m*), with an area of about 3200 miles² *8285 km²* (1850 miles² *4790 km²* in Peru, 1350 miles² *3495 km²* in Bolivia), in South America. It is 130 miles *209 km* long and is situated at 12,506 ft *3811 m* above sea-level. There is an unnamed glacial lake near Everest at 19,300 ft *5880 m*. Tibet's largest lake Nam Tso of 722 miles² *1956 km²* is at 15,060 ft *4578 m*.

Highest *United Kingdom*

The highest lake in the United Kingdom is the 1.9 acre *0,76 ha* Lochan Buidhe at 3600 ft *1097 m* above sea-level in the Cairngorm Mountains, Scotland. England's highest is Broad Crag Tarn (2746 ft *837 m* above sea-level) on Scafell Pike, Cumbria and the highest named freshwater in Wales is The Frogs Pool, a tarn near the summit of Carnedd Llywelyn, Gwynedd at *c.* 2725 ft *830 m*.

Desert *Largest*

Nearly an eighth of the world's land surface is arid with a rainfall of less than 25 cm *9.8 in* per annum. The Sahara in N. Africa is the largest in the world. At its greatest length it is 3200 miles *5150 km* from east to west. From north to south it is between 800 and 1400 miles *1275 and 2250 km*. The area covered by the desert is about 3,250,000 miles² *8 400 000 km²*. The land level varies from 436 ft *132 m* below sea-level in the Qattâra Depression, Egypt, to the mountain Emi Koussi (11,204 ft *3415 m*) in Chad. The diurnal temperature range in the western Sahara may be more than 80° F or *45° C*.

Sand dunes

The world's highest measured sand dunes are those in the Saharan sand sea of Isaouane-n-Tifernine of east central Algeria in Lat. 26° 42′ N, Long. 6° 43′ E. They have a wave-length of near 3 miles *5 km* and attain a height of 1410 ft *430 m*.

Gorge *Largest*

The largest land gorge in the world is the Grand Canyon on the Colorado River in north-central Arizona, USA. It extends

Great Britain's longest (24.23 miles) and most voluminous lake—Loch Ness of monstrous fame. (*Heather Angel*)

from Marble Gorge to the Grand Wash Cliffs, over a distance of 217 miles *349 km*. It varies in width from 4 to 13 miles *6–20 km* and is some 5300 ft *1615 m* deep. The submarine Labrador Basin canyon is *c.* 2150 miles *3440 km* long.

Gorge *Deepest*
The deepest canyon is El Cañón de Colca, Peru reported in 1929 which is 3223 m *10,574 ft* deep. It was first traversed by a University of Kracow kayak team on 12 May–14 June 1981. A stretch of the Kali River in central Nepal flows 18,000 ft *5485 m* below its flanking summits of the Dhaulagiri and Annapurna groups. The deepest submarine canyon yet discovered is one 25 miles *40 km* south of Esperance, Western Australia, which is 6000 ft *1800 m* deep and 20 miles *32 km* wide.

Cliffs *Highest*
The highest sea cliffs yet pinpointed anywhere in the world are those on the north coast of east Moloka'i, Hawaii near Umilehi Point, which descend 3300 ft *1005 m* to the sea at an average gradient of >55°. The west face of Thor Peak, Baffin Island, Canada allowed an abseiling or rappelling record of 3250 ft *990 m* by Steve Holmes (USA) in July 1982. The highest cliffs in North West Europe are those on the north coast of Achill Island, in County Mayo, Ireland, which are 2192 ft *668 m* sheer above the sea at Croaghan. The highest cliffs in the United Kingdom are the 1300 ft *396 m* Conachair cliffs on St Kilda, Western Isles (1397 ft *425 m*). The highest sheer sea cliffs on the mainland of Great Britain are at Clo Mor, 3 miles *4,8 km* south-east of Cape Wrath, Highland, Scotland which drop 921 ft *280,7 m*. England's highest cliff (gradient >45°) is Great Hangman Hill, near Combe Martin, in North Devon, which descends from 1043 ft *318 m* to the sea in 984 ft *300 m*, the last 700 ft *213 m* of which is sheer.

Natural arch *Longest*
The longest natural arch in the world is the Landscape Arch in the Arches National Park, 25 miles *40 km* north of Moab, Utah, USA. This natural sandstone arch spans 291 ft *88 m* and is set about 100 ft *30 m* above the canyon floor. In one place erosion has narrowed its section to 6 ft *1,82 m*. Larger, however, is the Rainbow Bridge, Utah discovered on 14 Aug 1909 with a span of 278 ft *84,7 m* but more than 22 ft *6,7 m* wide.

Natural bridge *Highest*
The highest natural arch is the sandstone arch 25 miles *40 km* WNW of K'ashih, Sinkiang, China, estimated in 1947 to be nearly 1000 ft *312 m* tall with a span of about 150 ft *45 m*.

Longest glaciers
It is estimated that 6,020,000 miles² *15 600 000 km²*, or about 10.4 per cent of the Earth's land surface, is permanently glaciated. The world's longest known glacier is the Lambert Glacier, discovered by an Australian aircraft crew in Australian Antarctic Territory in 1956–7. It is up to 40 miles *64 km* wide and, with its upper section, known as the Mellor Glacier, it measures at least 250 miles *402 km* in length. With the Fisher Glacier limb, the Lambert forms a continuous ice passage about 320 miles *514 km* long. The longest Himalayan glacier is the Siachen (47 miles *75,6 km*) in the Karakoram range, though the Hispar and Biafo combine to form an ice passage 76 miles *122 km* long. The fastest moving major glacier is the Quarayaq in Greenland which flows 20–24 m *65–80 ft* per day.

Greatest avalanches
The greatest natural avalanches, though rarely observed, occur in the Himalaya but no estimates of their volume had been published. It was estimated that 3,500,000 m³ *120 000 000 ft³* of snow fell in an avalanche in the Italian Alps in 1885. The 250 mph *400 km/h* avalanche triggered by the Mount St. Helens eruption in Washington, USA on 18 May 1979 was estimated to measure 2800 million m³ *96,000 million ft³* (see also Disasters, Chapter 11).

Chapter 4

THE UNIVERSE AND SPACE

The universe is the entirety of space, matter and anti-matter. An appreciation of its magnitude is best grasped by working outward from the Earth, through the Solar System and our own Milky Way Galaxy, to the remotest extragalactic nebulae and quasars.

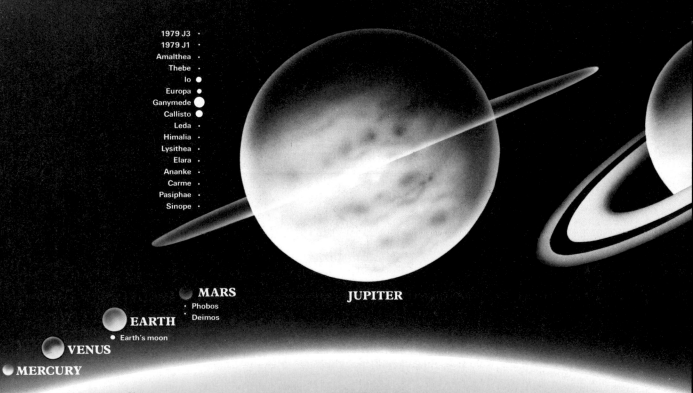

1979 J3
1979 J1
Amalthea
Thebe
Io
Europa
Ganymede
Callisto
Leda
Himalia
Lysithea
Elara
Ananke
Carme
Pasiphae
Sinope

JUPITER

MARS
Phobos
Deimos

EARTH
Earth's moon

VENUS

MERCURY

THE SUN

The Guinness Book of Astronomy Facts and Feats (2nd Edition) by Patrick Moore was published in June 1983 price £9.95.

LIGHT-YEAR—that distance travelled by light (speed 186,282.397 miles/sec *299 792,458 km/s⁻¹* or 670,616,629.2 mph *1 079 258 848,8 km/h⁻¹ in vacuo*) in one tropical year (365.24219878 mean solar days at January 0,12 hours Ephemeris time in AD 1900) and is 5,878,499,814,000 miles *9 460 528 405 000 km*. The unit was first used in March 1888 and fixed at this constant in October 1983.

MAGNITUDE—a measure of stellar brightness such that the light of a star of any magnitude bears a ratio of 2.511886 to that of a star of the next magnitude. Thus a fifth magnitude star is 2.511886 times as bright, while one of the first magnitude is exactly 100 (or 2.511886⁵) times as bright, as a sixth magnitude star. In the case of such exceptionally bright bodies as the Sun, Venus, the Moon (magnitude −12.71) or the Sun (magnitude −26.78), the magnitude is expressed as a minus quantity.

PROPER MOTION—that component of a star's motion in space which, at right angles to the line of sight, constitutes an apparent change of position of the star in the celestial sphere.

METEOROIDS

Meteor shower

Meteoroids are of cometary or asteroidal origin. A meteor is the light phenomenon caused by the entry of a meteoroid into the Earth's atmosphere. The greatest meteor 'shower' on record occurred on the night of 16–17 Nov 1966, when the Leonid meteors (which recur every 33¼ years) were visible between western North America and eastern USSR. It was calculated that meteors passed over Arizona, USA, at a rate of 2300 per min for a period of 20 min from 5 a.m. on 17 Nov 1966.

METEORITES

Oldest

It was reported in August 1978 that dust grains in the Murchison meteorite which fell in Australia in September 1969 pre-date the formation of the Solar System 4600 million years ago.

Largest *World*

When a meteoroid penetrates to the Earth's surface, the remnant is described as a meteorite. This occurs about 150 times per year over the whole land surface of the Earth. Although the chances of being struck are deemed negligible, the most anxious time of day for meteorophobes is 3 p.m. The largest known meteorite is one found in 1920 at Hoba West, near Grootfontein in south-west Africa. This is a block 9 ft *2,75 m* long by 8 ft *2,43 m* broad, estimated to be 132,000 lb (59 tons/*tonnes*). The largest meteorite exhibited by any museum is the 'Tent' meteorite, weighing 68,085 lb (30.39 tons *30 882 kg*) found in 1897 near Cape York, on the west coast of Greenland, by the expedition of Commander (later Rear-Admiral) Robert Edwin Peary (1856–1920). It was known to the Eskimos as the Abnighito and is now exhibited in the Hayden Planetarium in New York City, NY, USA. The largest piece of stony meteorite recovered is a piece of 1770 kg *3902 lb* part of a 4 tonne shower which struck Jilin (formerly Kirin), China on 8 Mar 1976. The oldest dated meteorites are from the Allende fall in Chihuahua, Mexico on 8 Feb 1969 dating back to 4610 million years.

There was a mysterious explosion of 12½ megatons in Lat. 60° 55′ N, Long. 101° 57′ E, in the basin of the Podkamennaya Tunguska river, 40 miles north of Vanavar, in Siberia, USSR, at 00 hrs 17 min 11 sec UT on 30 June 1908. The cause was variously attributed to a meteorite (1927), a comet (1930), a nuclear explosion (1961) and to anti-matter (1965). This devastated an area of about 1500 miles² *3885 km²* and the shock was felt as far as 1000 km (more than *600 miles*) away. The theory is now favoured that this was the terminal flare of stony

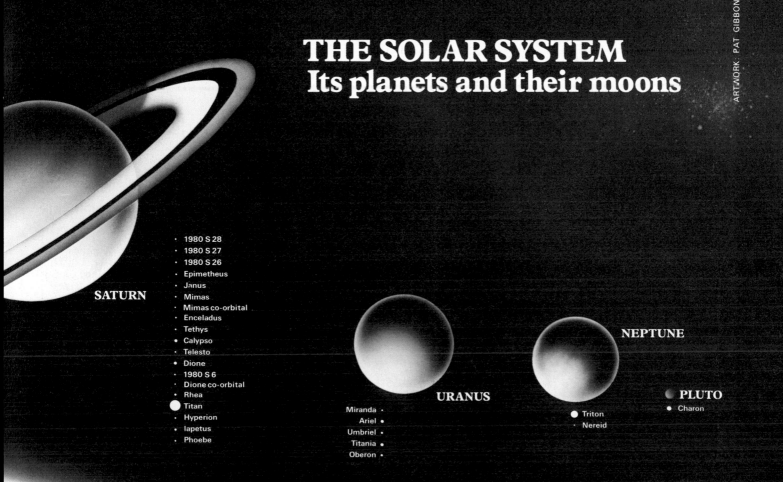

THE SOLAR SYSTEM
Its planets and their moons

ARTWORK: PAT GIBBON

SATURN
- 1980 S 28
- 1980 S 27
- 1980 S 26
- Epimetheus
- Janus
- Mimas
- Mimas co-orbital
- Enceladus
- Tethys
- Calypso
- Telesto
- Dione
- 1980 S 6
- Dione co-orbital
- Rhea
- Titan
- Hyperion
- Iapetus
- Phoebe

URANUS
- Miranda
- Ariel
- Umbriel
- Titania
- Oberon

NEPTUNE
- Triton
- Nereid

PLUTO
- Charon

debris from a comet, possibly Encké's comet, at altitude of only 6 km *or less than 20,000 ft*. A similar event may have occurred over the Isle of Axeholm, Lincolnshire a few thousand years before. A stony meteorite with a diameter of 10 km *6.2 miles* striking the Earth at 25 km/sec *55,925 mph* would generate an explosive energy equivalent to 100 million megatons. Such events should not be expected to recur more than once in 75 million years.

Largest *United Kingdom and Ireland*

The heaviest of the 22 meteorites known to have fallen on the British Isles since 1623 was one weighing at least 102 lb *46,25 kg* (largest piece 17 lb 6 oz *7,88 kg*), which fell at 4.12 p.m. on 24 Dec 1965 at Barwell, Leicestershire. Scotland's largest recorded meteorite fell in Strathmore, Tayside on 3 Dec 1917. It weighed 22¼ lb *10,09 kg* and was the largest of four stones totalling 29 lb 6 oz *13,324 kg*. The largest recorded meteorite to fall in Ireland was the Limerick Stone of 65 lb *29,5 kg*, part of a shower weighing more than 106 lb *48 kg* which fell near Adare County Limerick, on 10 Sept 1813. The larger of the two recorded meteorites to land in Wales was one weighing 28 oz *794 g* of which a piece weighing 25½ oz *723 g* went through the roof of the Prince Llewellyn Hotel in Beddgelert, Gwynedd, shortly before 3.15 a.m. on 21 Sept 1949. Debris from the Bovedy Fall in N. Ireland in 1969 spread over 50 miles *80 km*.

Largest craters

It has been estimated that some 2000 asteroid-Earth collisions have occurred in the last 600 million years. A total of 102 collision sites or astroblemes have been recognized. A crater 150 miles *241 km* in diameter and ½ mile *805 m* deep has been postulated in Wilkes Land, Antarctica since 1962. It would be caused by a 13,000 million ton meteorite striking at 44,000 mph *70 811 km/h*. USSR scientists reported in December 1970 an astrobleme with a 60 mile *95 km* diameter and a maximum depth of 1300 ft *400 m* in the basin of the River Popigai. There is a possible crater-like formation or astrobleme 275 miles *442,5 km* in diameter on the eastern shore of the Hudson Bay, Canada, where the Nastapoka Islands are just off the coast.

The largest proven crater is the Coon Butte or Barringer crater, discovered in 1891 near Canyon Diablo, Winslow, northern Arizona, USA. It is 4150 ft *1265 m* in diameter and now about 575 ft *175 m* deep, with a parapet rising 130–155 ft *40–48 m* above the surrounding plain. It has been estimated that an iron-nickel mass with a diameter of 200–260 ft *61–79 m* and weighing about 2,000,000 tons/*tonnes* gouged this crater in *c.* 25,000 BC. Evidence was published in 1963 discounting a meteoric origin for the crypto-volcanic Vredefort Ring (diameter 26 miles *41,8 km*), to the south-west of Johannesburg, South Africa, but this has now been re-asserted. The New Quebec (formerly the Chubb) 'Crater', first sighted on 20 June 1943 in northern Ungava, Canada, is 1325 ft *404 m* deep and measures 6.8 miles *10,9 km* round its rim.

Fireball *Brightest*

The brightest fireball ever photographically recorded was by Dr Zdenek Ceplecha over Sumava, Czechoslovakia on 4 Dec 1974 with a momentary magnitude of −22 or 10,000 times brighter than a full Moon.

Tektites

The largest tektite of which details have been published has been of 3,2 kg *7.04 lb* found in 1932 at Muong Nong, Saravane Province, Laos and now in the Paris Museum.

AURORAE

Most frequent

Polar lights, known since 1560 as Aurora Borealis or Northern Lights in the northern hemisphere and since 1773 as Aurora Australis in the southern hemisphere, are caused by electrical solar discharges in the upper atmosphere and occur most frequently in high latitudes. Aurorae are visible at some time on *every* clear dark night in the polar areas within 20 degrees of the magnetic poles. The extreme height of aurorae has been measured at 1000 miles *620 miles*, while the lowest may descend to 45 miles *72,5 km*. Reliable figures exist only from 1952, since when the record high and low number of nights of auroral displays in Shetland (geomagnetic Lat. 63°) has been 203 (1957) and 58 (1965). The most recent great display in north-west Europe was that of 4–5 Sept 1958.

Lowest latitudes

Extreme cases of displays in very low latitudes are Cuzco, Peru (2 Aug 1744); Honolulu, Hawaii (1 Sept 1859) and questionably Singapore (25 Sept 1909).

Noctilucent clouds

Regular observations in Western Europe date only from 1964, which when the record high and low number of nights on which these phenomena (at heights of *c.* 52 miles *85 km*) have been observed have been 41 (1974) and 15 (1970).

THE MOON

The Earth's closest neighbour in space and only natural satellite is the Moon, at a mean distance of 238,855 statute miles *384 400 km* centre-to-centre or 233,812 miles *376 284 km* surface to surface. In the present century the closest approach (smallest perigee) was 216,398 miles *348 259 km* surface-to-surface or 221,441 miles *356 375 km* centre-to-centre on 4 January 1912, and the farthest distance (largest apogee) was 247,675 miles *398 598 km* surface-to-surface or 252,718 miles *406 711 km* centre-to-centre on 2 March 1984. The moon was only a few Earth radii distant during the 'Gerstenkorn period' 3900 million years ago. It has a diameter of 2159.3 miles *3475,0 km* and has a mass of 7.23×10^{19} tons *$7,35 \times 10^{19}$ tonnes* with a mean density of 3.342. The average orbital speed is 2287 mph *3680 km/h*. The first direct hit on the Moon was achieved at 2 min 24 sec after midnight (Moscow time) on 14 Sept 1959, by the Soviet space probe *Luna II* near the *Mare Serenitatis*. The first photographic images of the hidden side were collected by the USSR's *Luna III* from 6.30 a.m. on 7 Oct 1959, from a range of up to 43,750 miles *70 400 km* and transmitted to the Earth from a distance of 470 000 km *292,000 miles*. The oldest of the moon material brought back to Earth by the *Apollo* programme crews has been soil dated to 4720 million years.

'Blue moon'

Owing to sulphur particles in the upper atmosphere from a forest fire covering 250,000 acres *100 000 ha* between Mile 103 and Mile 119 on the Alaska Highway in northern British Columbia, Canada. the Moon took on a bluish colour, as seen from Great Britain, on the night of 26 Sept 1950. The Moon also appeared green after the Krakatoa eruption of 27 Aug 1883 (see p. 55) and in Stockholm for 3 min on 17 Jan 1884.

Crater *Largest and Deepest*

Only 59 per cent of the Moon's surface is directly visible from the Earth because it is in 'captured rotation', *i.e.* the period of rotation is equal to the period of orbit. The largest wholly visible crater is the walled plain Bailly, towards the Moon's South Pole, which is 183 miles *295 km* across, with walls rising to 14,000 ft *4250 m*. The Orientale Basin, partly on the averted side, measures more than 600 miles *965 km* in diameter. The deepest crater is the Newton crater, with a floor estimated to be between 23,000 and 29,000 ft *7000–8850 m* below its rim and 14,000 ft *2250 m* below the level of the plain outside. The brightest directly visible spot on the Moon is *Aristarchus*.

Highest mountains

In the absence of a sea level, lunar altitudes are measured relative to an adopted reference sphere of radius 1738,000 km or *1079.943 miles*. Thus the greatest elevation attained on this basis by any of the 12 US astronauts has been 7830 m *25,688 ft* on the Descartes Highlands by Capt. John Watts Young USN and Major Charles M. Duke Jr on 27 Apr 1972.

Temperature extremes

When the Sun is overhead the temperature on the lunar equator reaches 243°F *117,2°C* (31 deg F *17,2 deg C* above the boiling point of water). By sunset the temperature is 58°F *14,4°C* but after nightfall it sinks to −261°F *−162,7°C*.

THE SUN

Distance extremes

The Earth's 66,620 mph *107 220 km/h* orbit of 584,017,800 miles *939 885 500 km* around the Sun is elliptical, hence our distance from the Sun varies. The orbital speed varies between 65,520 mph *105 450 km/h* (minimum) and 67,750 mph *109 030 km/h*. The average distance of the Sun is 1.000 000 230 astronomical units or 92,955,829 miles *149 597 906 km*.

The closest approach (perihelion) is 91,402,000 miles *147 097 000 km* and the farthest departure (aphelion) is 94,510,000 miles *152 099 000 km*. The Solar System is revolving around the centre of the Milky Way once in each 225,000,000 years, at a speed of 481,000 mph *774 000 km/h* and has a velocity of 42,500 mph *68 400 km/h* relative to stars in our immediate region such as Vega, towards which it is moving.

Temperature and dimensions

The Sun has an internal temperature of about 16 000 000 K, a core pressure of 500,000,000 tons/in^2 *7,7 PPa* and uses up 4,000,000 tons/*tonnes* of hydrogen per sec, thus providing a luminosity of 3×10^{27} candlepower, with an intensity of 1,500,000 candles/in^2 *1 530 000 candelas*. The Sun has the stellar classification of a 'yellow dwarf' and, although its density is only 1.407 times that of water, its mass is 332,946 times as much as that of the Earth. It has a mean diameter of 865,270 miles *1 392 520 km*. The Sun with a mass of 1.958×10^{27} tons *1,989 $\times 10^{27}$ tonnes* represents more than 99 per cent of the total mass of the Solar System but will exhaust its energy in 10,000 million years.

Sun-spots *Largest*

To be visible to the *protected* naked eye, a Sun-spot must cover about one two-thousandth part of the Sun's disc and thus have an area of about 500,000,000 miles^2 *1300 million km^2*. The largest Sun-spot occurred in the Sun's southern hemisphere on 8 Apr 1947. Its area was about 7000 million miles^2 *18 000 million km^2* with an extreme longitude of 187,000 miles *300 000 km* and an extreme latitude of 90,000 miles *145 000 km*. Sun-spots appear darker because they are more than 1500 deg C cooler than the rest of the Sun's surface temperature of 5525° C. The largest observed solar prominence was one protruding 365,000 miles *588 000 km*, photographed on 19 Dec 1973 during the 3rd and final manned Skylab mission.

Most frequent

In October 1957 a smoothed Sun-spot count showed 263, the highest recorded index since records started in 1755 (*cf.* previous record of 239 in May 1778). In 1943 one Sun-spot lasted for 200 days from June to December.

ECLIPSES

Earliest recorded

For the Middle East, lunar eclipses have been extrapolated to 3450 BC and solar ones to 4200 BC. No centre of the path of totality for a solar eclipse crossed London for the 575 years from 20 Mar 1140 to 3 May 1715. On 14 June 2151 at 18.25 GMT the eclipse will be 99 per cent total in central London but total in Sheffield and Norfolk. The most recent occasion when a line of totality of a solar eclipse crossed Great Britain was on 29 June 1927 for 24.5 sec at 6.23 a.m. at West Hartlepool, Cleveland and the next instance will clip the coast at St Just, Cornwall at 10.10 a.m. on Wednesday 11 Aug 1999. On 30 June 1954 a total eclipse was witnessed from Unst, Shetland Islands but the centre of the path of totality was to the north.

Longest duration

The maximum *possible* duration of an eclipse of the Sun is 7 min 31 sec. The longest actually *measured* was on 20 June 1955 (7 min 8 sec), seen from the Philippines. One of 7 min 29 sec should occur in mid-Atlantic on 16 July 2186, which will then be the longest for 1469 years. The longest possible in the British Isles is 5½ min. That of 15 June 885 lasted nearly 5 min, as will that of 20 July 2381 in the Border area. Durations can be extended by observers being airborne as on 30 June 1973 when an eclipse was 'extended' to 72 min aboard *Concorde*. An annular eclipse may last for 12 min 24 sec. The longest totality of any lunar eclipse is 104 min. This has occurred many times.

Most and least frequent

The highest number of eclipses possible in a year is seven, as in 1935, when there were five solar and two lunar eclipses; or four solar and three lunar eclipses, as occurred in 1982. The lowest possible number in a year is two, both of which must be solar, as in 1944 and 1969.

COMETS

Earliest recorded

The earliest records of comets date from the 7th century BC. The speeds of the estimated 2,000,000 comets vary from 700 mph *1125 km/h* in outer space to 1,250,000 mph *2 000 000 km/h* when near the Sun. The successive appearances of Halley's Comet have been traced back to 467 BC. It was first depicted in the Nuremberg Chronicle of AD 684. The first prediction of its return by Edmund Halley (1656–1742) proved true on Christmas Day 1758, 16 years after his death. Its next perihelion should be at 9.3 (*viz.* at 7 a.m. on the 9th) February 1986, 75.81 years after the last, which was on 19 Apr 1910. The 33rd sighting occurred on 16 Oct 1982 at a magnitude of 24.2 by David C. Jewitt and G. Edmond Danielson using the 200 inch *508 cm* Hale telescope at Palomar Observatory, California.

Closest approach

On 1 July 1770, Lexell's Comet, travelling at a speed of 23.9 miles/sec *38,5 km/sec* (relative to the Sun), came within 745,000 miles *1 200 000 km* of the Earth. However, the Earth is believed to have passed through the tail of Halley's Comet, most recently on 19 May 1910.

Largest

Comets are so tenuous that it has been estimated that even the head of one rarely contains solid matter much more than *c.* 1 km *0.6 miles* in diameter. Tails, as in the case of the brightest of all, the Great Comet of 1843, may trail for 205,000,000 miles *330 million km*. The head of Holmes Comet of 1892 once measured 1,500,000 miles *2 400 000 km* in diameter. Comet Bennett which appeared in January 1970 was found to be enveloped in a hydrogen cloud measuring some 8,000,000 miles *12 750 000 km* in length.

Shortest period

Of all the recorded periodic comets (these are members of the Solar System), the one which most frequently returns is Encke's Comet, first identified in 1786. Its period of 1206 days (3.3 years) is the shortest established. Not one of its 51 returns (including 1977) has been missed by astronomers. Now increasingly faint, it is expected to 'die' by February 1994. The most frequently observed comets are Schwassmann–Wachmann I, Kopff and Oterma which can be observed every year between Mars and Jupiter.

Longest period

At the other extreme is Delavan's Comet of 1914, whose path was not accurately determined. It is not expected to return for perhaps 24 million years.

PLANETS

Largest

Planets (including the Earth) are bodies within the Solar System and which revolve round the Sun in definite orbits. Jupiter, with an equatorial diameter of 88,846 miles *142 984 km*

The USSR postage stamp which depicts the orbit of *Sputnik 1*, launched in October 1957 (see p. 74). (*Novosti*)

An artist's impression of how the asteroid *Ceres* would look if it departed from its present orbit between Mars and Jupiter, and got to within 800 miles *1290 km* of the Earth. It was first spotted on the first day of the 19th century.

ARTWORK: PAUL DOHERTY

and a polar diameter of 83,082 miles *133 708 km* is the largest of the nine major planets, with a mass 317.83 times, and a volume 1321.4 times that of the Earth. It also has the shortest period of rotation resulting in a Jovian day of only 9 hr 50 min 30.003 sec in the equatorial zone.

Smallest and coldest
The smallest and coldest planet is Pluto, with its partner Charon, announced on 22 June 1978 which have an estimated surface temperature of −360° F *−220° C* (100 deg F *53 deg C* above absolute zero). Their mean distance from the Sun is 3,674,488,000 miles *5 913 514 000 km* and their period of revolution is 248.54 years. The diameter is *c.* 3000 km *1880 miles* and the mass is about 1/500th of that of the Earth. Pluto was first recorded by Clyde William Tombaugh (b. 4 Feb 1906) at Lowell Observatory, Flagstaff, Arizona, USA, on 18 Feb 1930 from photographs taken on 23 and 29 Jan and announced on 13 Mar. Because of its orbital eccentricity Pluto moved closer to the Sun than Neptune between 23 Jan 1979 and 15 Mar 1999.

A mini-planet of diameter 1.2 miles *1,9 km* was announced in Nov 1983. This body orbiting inside Mercury was detected by IRAS (Infra-red Astronomical Satellite)) but may be only a cometary cadaver.

Fastest
Mercury, which orbits the Sun at an average distance of 35,983,100 miles *57 909 200 km*, has a period of revolution of 87.9686 days, so giving the highest average speed in orbit of 107,030 mph *172 248 km/h*.

Hottest
For Venus a surface temperature of 462° C *864° F* has been estimated from measurements made from the USSR *Venera* and US Pioneer Cytherean surface probes. Venus has a canyon 4 miles *6,4 km* deep and 250 miles *402 km* long 1000 miles *1609 km* south of Venusian equator.

Nearest
The fellow planet closest to the Earth is Venus, which is, at times, about 25,700,000 miles *41 360 000 km* inside the Earth's orbit, compared with Mars's closest approach of 34,600,000 miles *55 680 000 km* outside the Earth's orbit. Mars, known since 1965 to be cratered, has temperatures ranging from 85° F *29,4° C* to −190° F *−123° C*.

Surface features
By far the highest and most spectacular is Olympus Mons (formerly Nix Olympica) in the Tharsis region of Mars with a diameter of 500–600 km *310–370 miles* and a height of 26 ± 3 km *75,450–95,150 ft* above the surrounding plain.

Brightest and faintest
Viewed from the Earth, by far the brightest of the five planets visible to the naked eye (Uranus at magnitude 5.5 is only marginally visible) is Venus, with a maximum magnitude of −4.4. The faintest is Pluto, with magnitude of 15.0.

Densest and least dense
Earth is the densest planet with an average figure of 5.515 times that of water, whilst Saturn has an average density only about one-eighth of this value or 0.687 times that of water.

Conjunctions
The most dramatic recorded conjunction (coming together) of the other seven principal members of the Solar System (Sun, Moon, Mercury, Venus, Mars, Jupiter and Saturn) occurred on 5 Feb 1962, when 16° covered all seven during an eclipse in the Pacific area. It is possible that the seven-fold conjunction of September 1186 spanned only 12°. The next notable conjunction will take place on 5 May 2000.

SATELLITES

Most
Of the nine major planets, all but Venus and Mercury have satellites. The planet with the most is Saturn with at least 21 satellites. The Earth and Pluto are the only planets with a single satellite. The distance from their parent planets varies from the 5827 miles *9378 km* of *Phobos* from the centre of Mars to the 14,730,000 miles *23 705 000 km* of Jupiter's outer satellite *Sinope* (Jupiter IX). The Solar System has a total of at least 48 satellites.

Largest and smallest
The largest and heaviest satellite is *Ganymede* (Jupiter III), which is 2.02 times heavier than our own Moon and has a diameter of 3270 miles *5262 km*. The smallest satellite is *Leda* (Jupiter XIII) with a diameter of less than 9 miles *15 km*.

Largest asteroids
In the belt which lies between Mars and Jupiter, there are some 45,000 (only just over 3000 numbered to March 1984) minor planets or asteroids which are, for the most part, too small to yield to diameter measurement. The largest and first discovered (by G. Piazzi at Palermo, Sicily on 1 Jan 1801) of these is *Ceres*, with a diameter of 637 miles *1025 km*. The only

PROGRESSIVE RECORDS OF THE MOST DISTANT MEASURED HEAVENLY BODIES

The possible existence of galaxies external to our own Milky Way system was mooted in 1789 by Sir William Herschel (1738–1822). These extra-galactic nebulae were first termed 'island universes'. Sir John Herschel (1792–1871) opined as early as 1835 that some might be more than 250,000,000,000 million miles distant. The first direct measurement of any body outside our Solar System was in 1838. Distances in the table below are based on a Hubble ratio of 60 km/s/Mpc and assume that the edge of the observable Universe is at a distance of 16,300 million light years. The launch of the Space Telescope in 1985 may produce a new champion with an even higher speed of recession and z value.

Estimated Distance in Light Years[1]	Object	Method	Astronomers	Observatory	Date
nearly 11 (now 11.08)	61 Cygni	Parallax	F. Bessel	Königsberg, Germany	1838
> 20 (now 26)	Vega	Parallax	F. G. W. Struve	Dorpat (now Tartu), Estonia	1840
n 300	Limit	Parallax			by 1900
750,000 (now 2.12 m)[2]	Galaxy M31	Cepheid variable	E. P. Hubble	Mt. Wilson, Cal., USA	1923
900,000 (now 2.12 m)[2]	Galaxy M31	Cepheid variable	E. P. Hubble	Mt. Wilson, Cal., USA	1924

Millions of Light Years	Recession Speed % of c	Object	Red shift[3]	Astronomers	Observatory	Date
250	1.5	Ursa Major Galaxy		E. P. Hubble	Mt. Wilson, Cal., USA	by 1934[4]
> 350	> 2.1			M. L. Humason	Palomar, Cal., USA	1949
> 1600	> 10			M. L. Humason	Palomar, Cal., USA	1954
5300	32.6	Cluster 1448	0.403		Palomar, Cal., USA	1956
5900	36.2	3C 295 in Boötes	0.461	R. Minkowski	Palomar, Cal., USA	June 1960
6700	41.0	QSO 3C 147	0.545	M. Schmidt & T. A. Matthews	Palomar, Cal., USA	Feb 1964[5]
13,100	80.1	QSO 3C 9	2.01	M. Schmidt	Palomar, Cal., USA	April 1965
c. 13,200	81.3	QSO 0106 × 01	2.11	E. M. Burbridge et al.	Palomar, Cal., USA	Dec 1965
13,300	81.4	QSO 1116 + 12	2.12	C. R. Lynds & A. N. Stockton	Steward, Ariz., USA	March 1966
				M. Schmidt	Palomar, Cal., USA	March 1966
13,400	82.4	QSO Pks 0237–23	2.22	H. C. Arp et al.	Palomar, Cal., USA	Dec 1966
13,600	83.7	QSO 4C 25.05	2.36	E. T. Olsen & M. Schmidt	Palomar, Cal., USA	Dec 1967
14,300	87.5	QSO 4C 05.34	2.00	Π. Lynds & D. Willo	Kitt Peak, Arizona, USA	March 1970
14,700	90.2	QSO OH 471	3.40	R. F. Carswell & P. A. Strittmatter	Steward, Ariz., USA	March 1973
14,800	90.7	QSO OQ 172	3.53	E. J. Wampler et al.	Lick, Cal., USA	May 1973
14,900	91.6	QSO Pks 2000–330	3.78	B. A. Peterson et al.	Siding Spring, NSW, Australia	April 1982

Note: c is the notation for the speed of light. (see p. 67).   [1] Term first utilised in March 1888.   [2] Re-estimate by G. de Vancouleurs in May 1977.   [3] Discovered by Vesto Slipher from Flagstaff, Arizona, USA 1920. Redshift, denoted by z, is the measure of the speed of recession indicated by the ratio resulting from the subtraction of the rest wavelength of an emission line from the observed wavelength divided by the rest wavelength.   [4] In this year Hubble opined that the observable horizon would be 3000 m light-years.   [5] Then said that QSO 3C2 and 286 might be more distant—claimed by Dr Shklovsky (USSR) to be receding at 0.55 c (modern value 0.546 c) in Dec. 1963. 3C2 later confirmed to be receding at 0.612 c.

one visible to the naked eye is asteroid 4 *Vesta* (diameter 345 miles *555 km*) discovered on 29 Mar 1807 by Dr Heinrich Wilhelm Olbers (1758–1840), a German amateur astronomer. The closest measured approach to the Earth by an asteroid was 485,000 miles *780 000 km* in the case of *Hermes* on 30 Oct 1937 (asteroid now lost). The most distant detected is 2060 *Chiron*, found between Saturn and Uranus on 18–19 Oct 1977, by Charles T. Kowal from the Hale Observatory, California, USA.

STARS

Largest and most massive

The most massive known star is the faint-blue R 136a, 179,000 light years distant in the Tarantula Nebula (or 30 Doradus), an appendage of the Lesser Magellanic Cloud and assessed in February 1983 to have a mass 2100 times greater than our own Sun and a diameter 50 times greater. However, Betelgeux (top left star of Orion) has a diameter of > 400 million km *250 million miles* or over 300 times greater than the Sun. In 1978 it was found to be surrounded by a tenuous 'shell' of potassium 1.6×10^{12} km or 11 000 astronomical units in diameter. The light from Betelgeux left it in AD 1460.

Smallest and lightest

A mass of 0.014 that of the Sun is estimated for the very faint star RG 0058.8-2807 which was discovered by I. Neill Reid and Gerard Gilmore using the U.K. Schmidt telescope and was announced in April 1983. The white dwarf star L362-81 has an estimated diameter of 3500 miles *5600 km* or only 0.0040 that of the Sun.

Brightest

Sirius A (*Alpha Canis Majoris*), also known as the Dog Star, is apparently the brightest star of the 5776 stars of naked eye visibility in the heavens, with an apparent magnitude of −1.46. It is in the constellation *Canis Major* and is visible in the winter months of the northern hemisphere, being due south at midnight on the last day of the year. The Sirius system is 8.64 light-years distant and has a luminosity 26 times as much as that of the Sun. It has a diameter of 1,450,000 miles *2,33 million km* and a mass of 4.20×10^{27} tons *$4,26 \times 10^{27}$ tonnes*. The faint white dwarf companion Sirius B has a diameter of only 6000 miles *10 000 km* but is 350,000 times heavier than the Earth.

Farthest

The Solar System, with its Sun's nine principal planets, 48 satellites, asteroids and comets was estimated in 1982 to be 28,000 light-years from the centre of the lens-shaped Milky Way galaxy (diameter 70,000 light-years) so that the most distant stars in our galaxy are estimated to be 63,000 light-years distant.

Nearest

Excepting the special case of our own Sun (*q.v.* above) the nearest star is the very faint *Proxima Centauri*, which is 4.22 light-years (24,800,000,000,000 miles *$4,00 \times 10^{13}$ km*) away. The nearest star visible to the naked eye is the southern hemisphere star *Alpha Centauri*, or *Rigel Kentaurus* (4.35 light-years), with a magnitude of −0.29. By AD 11,800 the nearest star will be Barnard's Star (see below under Stellar Planets) at a distance of 3.85 light years.

Most and least luminous

If all the stars could be viewed at the same distance the most luminous would be R136a (see Most Massive Star) which has a total luminosity 60 million times greater than that of the Sun and an absolute visual magnitude of about −9.0 so that this star is visually 320,000 times brighter than the Sun. The variable η Carinae in c. 1840 was perhaps visually 4 million times more luminous than the Sun. The faintest star detected is the recently discovered RG 0058.8–2807 (see Lightest Star) which has a total luminosity only 0.00021 that of the Sun and an absolute visual magnitude of 20.2 so that the visual brightness is less than one millionth that of the Sun.

Brightest supernova

Supernovae, or temporary 'stars' which flare and then fade, occur perhaps five times in 1000 years in our galaxy. The brightest 'star' ever seen by historic man is believed to be the supernova SN 1006 in April 1006 near *Beta Lupi* which flared for 2 years and attained a magnitude of −9 to −10. It is now believed to be the radio source G.327.6 + 14.5 nearly 3000 light-years distant.

Constellations

The largest of the 89 constellations is *Hydra* (the Sea Serpent), which covers 1,302.844 deg^2 or 6.3 per cent of the hemisphere and contains at least 68 stars visible to the naked eye (to 5.5 mag.). The constellation *Centaurus* (Centaur), ranking ninth in area embraces however at least 94 such stars. The smallest constellation is *Crux Australis* (Southern Cross) with an area of 68.477 deg^2 compared with the 41,252.96 deg^2 of the whole sky.

Longest name

The longest name for any star is *Shurnarkabtishashutu*, the Arabic for 'under the southern horn of the bull'.

Black Holes

The first tentative identification of a Black Hole was announced in December 1972 in the binary-star X-ray source Cygnus X-1. The best candidate is now LMC X-3 of 10 solar masses and 180,000 light-years distant reported in Jan 1983. The critical size has been estimated to be as low as a diameter of 3.67 miles *5,90 km*. In early 1978 supermassive Black Holes were suggested with a mass of 100 million suns or 2×10^{35} tonnes.

THE UNIVERSE

Outside the Milky Way galaxy, which is part of the so-called Local Group of galaxies moving toward the Virgo cluster 50 million light-years distant, at a speed estimated to be between 200 and 500 km/sec *450,000 and 1,100,000 mph*, there exist 10,000 million other galaxies. The largest discrete object in the Universe is the filament of galaxies comprising the Lynx-Ursa Major and the Pisces-Perseus Superclusters 700 million light-years in length. They were shown to be connected in Oct 1982 by Riccardo Giovanelli and Martha Hayes, working at Arecibo, Puerto Rico.

Farthest visible object

The remotest heavenly body visible with the *naked eye* is the Great Galaxy in *Andromeda* (Mag. 3.47), known as Messier 31. This is a rotating nebula in spiral form, and its distance from the Earth is about 2,120,000 light-years, or about 12,500,000,000,000,000,000 miles *20×10^{18} km* and is moving towards us. It is just possible however that, under ideal seeing conditions, Messier 33, the Spiral in Triangulum (Mag. 5.79), can be glimpsed by the naked eye of keen-sighted people at a distance of 2,360,000 light years.

Quasars

In November 1962 the existence of quasi-stellar radio sources ('quasars' or QSO's) was established by Maarten Schmidt with 3C-273 with a red shift of z = 0.158. Quasars have immensely high luminosity for bodies so distant and of such small diameter. It was announced in May 1983 that the quasar S5 0014 + 81 had a visual luminosity 1.1×10^{15} times greater than that of the Sun. The first double quasar (0957 + 56) among 1500 known quasars, was announced in May 1980.

Pulsars

The earliest observation of a pulsating radio source or 'pulsar' CP 1919 by Dr Jocelyn Bell Burnell was announced from the Mullard Radio Astronomy Observatory, Cambridgeshire, England, on 29 Feb 1968. The fastest spinning, and most accurate stellar clock, is pulsar 1937 + 214 which is in the region of the minor constellation Vulpecula (The Fox) 16,000 light years distant. It has a pulse period of 1.557806449 millisec and the amazingly slow spin-down rate of only 1×10^{-19} sec/sec.

Remotest object

Both the interpretation of the very large redshifts exhibited by quasars and the estimation of equivalent distances remain controversial. The record redshift of z = 3.78 for quasar PKS 2000-330 (see Table page 71) has been interpreted as indicating proximity to the 'observable horizon' at 16,300 million light years, which is 96,000,000,000,000,000,000,000,000 miles *$1,54 \times 10^{23}$ km*. It was announced in April 1983 that the most distant known galaxy, which is associated with the radio source 3C 324, has a redshift of 1.21. The 3 K background radiation or primordial hiss discovered in 1965 by Arno Penzias and Robert Wilson of Bell Laboratories appears to be moving at a velocity of 99.9998 per cent c.

Age of the Universe

For the age of the Universe a value of 15 ± 3 aeons or gigayears (an aeon or gigayear being 1000 million years) is obtained from cosmochronology and nucleochronology. Based on the presently accepted Friedman models of the Universe with zero cosmological constant then the equivalent Hubble ratio is about 60 km/s/Mpc which compares to the most likely experimental value of 100 km/s/Mpc. In 1973 an *ex nihilo* creation was postulated by Edward P. Tryon (US). An inflationary model now rivals the 'Big Bang' theory of creation. This concept involves a phase transition when the temperature was 10^{27} K.

ROCKETRY AND MISSILES

Earliest uses

War rockets, propelled by a charcoal-saltpetre-sulphur gunpowder, were described by Tseng Kung Liang of China in 1042. These early rockets became known in Europe by 1258. The pioneer of military rocketry in Britain was Col. Sir William Congreve, Bt., MP (1772–1828), Comptroller of the Royal Laboratory, Woolwich, Greater London and Inspector of Military Machines, whose 'six-pound *2,72 kg* rocket' was developed to a range of 2000 yd *1825m* by 1805 and first used by the Royal Navy against Boulogne, France on 8 Oct 1806.

The first launching of a liquid-fuelled rocket (patented 14 July 1914) was by Dr Robert Hutchings Goddard (1882–1945) of the United States, at Auburn, Massachusetts, USA, on 16 Mar 1926, when his rocket reached an altitude of 41 ft *12,5 m* and travelled a distance of 184 ft *56 m*. The USSR's earliest rocket was the semi-liquid fuelled GIRD-IX tested on 17 Aug 1933.

Longest ranges

On 16 Mar 1962, Nikita Khrushchyov, then Prime Minister of the USSR, claimed in Moscow that the USSR possessed a 'global rocket' with a range of 30 000 km (*about 19,000 miles*) *i.e.* more than the Earth's semi-circumference and therefore capable of hitting any target from either direction.

Most powerful *World*

It has been suggested that the USSR lunar booster which blew up at Tyuratam in the summer (? July) of 1969 had a thrust of 10–14 million lb *4,5–6,35 million kg*. There is some evidence of the launch of a USSR 'G' class lunar booster, larger than the US Saturn V, on 11 May 1973.

PROGRESSIVE ROCKET ALTITUDE RECORDS

Height in miles	Height in km	Rocket	Place	Launch	Date
0.71	*1,14*	A 3 in *7,62 cm* rocket	near London, England	April	1750
1.24	*2*	Reinhold Tiling[1] (Germany) solid fuel rocket	Osnabruck, Germany	April	1931
3.1	*5*	GIRD-X liquid fuel (USSR)	USSR	25 Nov	1933
8.1	*13*	USSR 'Stratosphere' rocket	USSR		1935
52.46	*84.42*	A.4 rocket (Germany)[2]	Peenemünde, Germany	3 Oct	1942
c. 85	*c. 136*	A.4 rocket (Germany)[2]	Heidelager, Poland	early	1944
118	*190*	A.4 rocket (Germany)[2]	Heidelager, Poland	mid	1944
244	*392,6*	V-2/W.A.C. Corporal (2-stage) Bumper No. 5 (USA)	White Sands, NM, USA	24 Feb	1949
318	*512*	Geophysical rocket V-5-V (USSR)	Tyuratam, USSR		1950–52
682	*1097*	Jupiter C (USA)	Cape Canaveral, Florida, USA	20 Sept	1956
>800	*>1300*	ICBM test flight R-7 (USSR)	Tyuratam, USSR	Aug	1957
>2700	*>4345*	Farside No. 5 (4-stage) (USA)	Eniwetok Atoll	20 Oct	1957
70,700	*113 770*	Pioneer 1-B Lunar Probe (USA)	Cape Canaveral, Florida, USA	11 Oct	1958
215,300,000*	*346 480 000*	Luna 1 or Mechta (USSR)	Tyuratam, USSR	2 Jan	1959
242,000,000*	*389 450 000*	Mars 1 (USSR)	USSR	1 Nov	1962
2,845,000,000[3]	*4 580 000 000*	Pioneer 10 (USA) (see page 73)	Kennedy Space Center, Cape Canaveral, Florida, USA	2 Mar	1972

* Apogee in solar orbit. [1] There is some evidence that Tiling may shortly after have reached 9500 m (5.90 miles) with a solid fuel rocket at Wangerooge, East Friesian Islands, W. Germany. [2] The A4 was latterly referred to as the V2 rocket, a code for second revenge weapon (vergeltungswaffe) following upon the V1 'flying bomb'. [3] This distance was attained at 1.30 a.m. on 13 June 1983 when Pioneer 10 crossed the orbit of Neptune. In Oct 1986 it will cross Pluto's mean orbit so leaving the Solar System. It will cross the furthest extension of Pluto's orbit in April 1989 and will continue at 49 000 km/h 30,450 mph towards the edge of the heliosphere (solar magetosphere) and the heliopause (zone of 'solar wind'). In AD 34 593 it will make its nearest approach to the 12th nearest star Ross 248, 10.3 light-years distant. However before AD 1990 Voyager I travelling faster will surpass Pioneer 10 in remoteness from Earth.

The most powerful rocket that has been publicised is the Saturn V, used for the Project Apollo and Skylab programmes on which development began in January 1962, at the John F. Kennedy Space Center, Merritt Island, Florida, USA. The rocket is 363 ft 8 in *110,85 m* tall, with a payload of 74 783 kg *73.60 tons* in the case of *Skylab I*, and gulps 13.4 tons *13,6 tonnes* of propellant per sec for 2½ min (2010 tons *2042 tonnes*). Stage I (S-IC) is 138 ft *42,06 m* tall and is powered by five Rocketdyne F-1 engines, using liquid oxygen (LOX) and kerosene, each delivering 1,514,000 lb *686 680 kg* thrust. Stage II (S-II) is powered by five LOX and liquid hydrogen Rocketdyne J-2 engines with a total thrust of 1,141,453 lb *517 759 kg* while Stage III (designated S-IVB) is powered by a single 228,290 lb *103 550 kg* thrust J-2 engine. The whole assembly generates 175,600,000 hp and weighs up to 7,600,000 lb (3393 tons *3447 tonnes*) fully loaded in the case of *Apollo 17*. It was first launched on 9 Nov 1967, from Cape Canaveral (then Kennedy), Florida.

Highest Pay Load

Skylab I, (launched on 14 May 1973) fell to Earth on its 34,981 st orbit over the Western Australian coast at 16.32 GMT on 11 July 1979. Large pieces of *Skylab I* were found 12 km *7.45 miles* south of Rawlinna and sold to a Hong Kong syndicate. The piece which most worried keraunothnetophobes was a 5175 lb *2347 kg* airlock shroud.

Highest velocity

The first space vehicle to achieve the Third Cosmic velocity sufficient to break out of the Solar System was *Pioneeer 10* (see table p. 72).The Atlas SLV-3C launcher with a modified Centaur D second stage and a Thiokol Te-364-4 third stage left the Earth at an unprecedented 32,114 mph *51 682 km/h* on 2 Mar 1972. The highest recorded velocity of any space vehicle has been 240 000 km/h *149,125 mph* in the case of the US-German solar probe *Helios B* launched on 15 Jan 1976.

Ion rockets

Speeds of up to 100,000 mph *160 000 km/h* are envisaged for rockets powered by an ion discharge. An ion thruster has been maintained for 9715 hours (404 days 19 hrs) at the Lewis Research Center in Cleveland, Ohio, USA. Ion rockets were first used in flight by NASA's SERT I rocket launched on 20 July 1964.

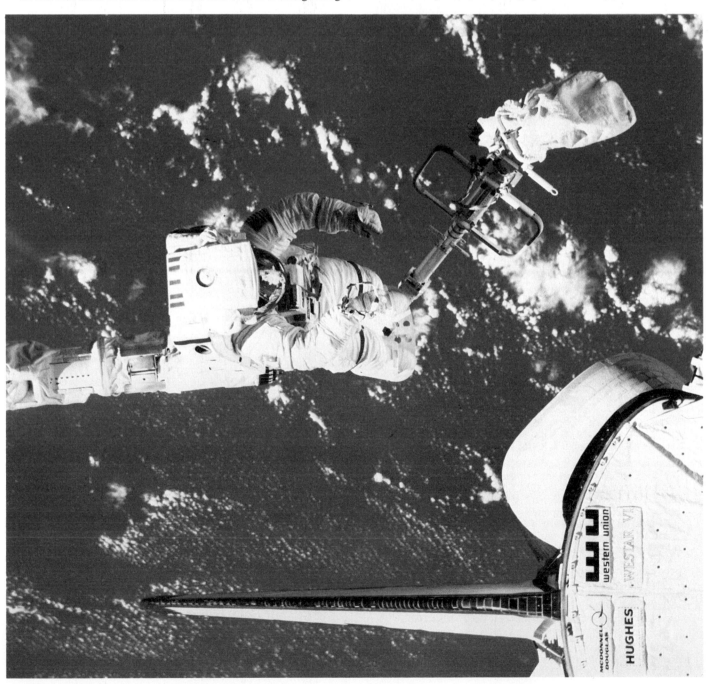

Captain Bruce McCandless USN floating untethered, in his Manned Manoeuvring Unit above Hawaii for a space 'first' on 7 Feb 1984 (see p. 74). (*Daily Telegraph Colour Library*)

Yuriy Gagarin who completed the first manned space flight aboard *Vostok 1* on 12 Apr 1961. (*Novosti*)

Lt.Col. Aleksey A Leonov, the first person to venture outside a space capsule on 18 Mar 1965. (*Novosti*)

The first woman to orbit the Earth, Valentina Tereshkova, who completed 48 orbits on 16–19 June 1963. (*Novosti*)

SPACE FLIGHT

The physical laws controlling the flight of artificial satellites were first propounded by Sir Isaac Newton (1642–1727) in his *Philosophiae Naturalis Principia Mathematica* ('Mathematical Principles of Natural Philosophy'), begun in March 1686 and first published in the summer of 1687. The first artificial satellite was successfully put into orbit at an altitude of 142/588 miles *228,5/946 km* and a velocity of more than 17,750 mph *28 565 km/h* from Tyuratam, a site located 170 miles *275 km* east of the Aral Sea on the night of 4 Oct 1957. This spherical satellite *Sputnik* ('Fellow Traveller') *1*, officially designated 'Satellite 1957 Alpha 2', weighed 83,6 kg *184.3 lb*, with a diameter of 58 cm *22.8 in*, and its lifetime is believed to have been 92 days, ending on 4 Jan 1958. It was designed under the direction of Dr Sergey Pavlovich Korolyov (1907–66).

Earliest successful manned satellite
The first successful manned space flight began at 9.07 a.m. (Moscow time), or 6.07 a.m. GMT, on 12 Apr 1961. Cosmonaut Flight Major (later Colonel) Yuriy Alekseyevich Gagarin (born 9 Mar 1934) completed a single orbit of the Earth in 89.34 min in the 4.65 ton *4,72 tonnes* space vehicle *Vostok* ('East') 1. The take-off was from Tyuratam in Kazakhstan, and the landing was 108 min later near the village of Smelovka, near Engels, in the Saratov region of the USSR. The maximum speed was 17,560 mph *28 260 km/h* and the maximum altitude 327 km *203.2 miles* in a flight of 40 868,6 km *25,394.5 miles*. Major Gagarin, invested a Hero of the Soviet Union and awarded the Order of Lenin and the Gold Star Medal, was killed in a jet plane crash near Moscow on 27 Mar 1968.

First woman in space
The first woman to orbit the Earth was Junior Lieutenant (now Lt-Col) Valentina Vladimirovna Tereshkova, now Nikolayev (b. 6 Mar 1937), who was launched in *Vostok 6* from Tyuratam, USSR, at 9.30 a.m. GMT on 16 June 1963, and landed at 8.16 a.m. on 19 June, after a flight of 2 days 22 hr 42 min, during which she completed over 48 orbits (1,225,000 miles *1 971 000 km*) and passed momentarily within 3 miles *48 km* of *Vostok 5*. Svetlana Savitskaya (USSR) became the second woman in space on 19 Aug 1982 and Dr Sally K. Ride (US) the third on 18–24 June 1973.

First in flight fatality
Col. Vladimir Mikhailovich Komarov (b. 16 Mar 1927) was launched in *Soyuz* ('Union') 1 at 00.35 a.m. GMT on 23 Apr 1967. The spacecraft was in orbit for about 25½ hr but he impacted on the final descent due to parachute failure and was the first man undisputedly known to have died during space flight.

First 'walk' in space
Lt-Col Aleksey A. Leonov from *Voskhod 2* was the first to engage in 'extra vehicular activity' on 18 Mar 1965. Capt Bruce McCandless II USN, 46 from the space shuttle *Challenger* was the first to engage in untethered EVA, at an altitude of 164 miles *264 km* above Hawaii, on 7 Feb 1984. His MMU (Manned Maneuvering Unit) back-pack cost $15 million to develop.

Longest manned space flight
The longest time spent in space is 211.37 days, by Anatoly Berezovoi and Valentin Lebedev on board the Salyut-Soyuz research station *Salyut 7*. They were launched on 13 May 1982 in Soyuz T5 and landed at 10.03 p.m. Moscow time on 10 Dec 1982, 190 km *118 miles* east of Dzhezkazgan. They travelled 141 million km *87.6 million miles*. Valeriy Ryumin holds the aggregate duration record at 362 days in 3 flights.

Astronaut *Oldest and youngest*
The oldest of the 127 people of 12 nationalities in space has been Dr William Thornton (US) aged 54 years 4 months while on the Space Shuttle mission ST5 8 aboard the *Challenger* in Aug–Sept 1983. The youngest has been Major (later Col) Gherman Stepanovich Titov (b. 11 Sept 1935), who was aged 25 years 329 days when launched in *Vostok 2* on 6 Aug 1961. The only 5-time space man has been Capt John W. Young, USN.

Duration record on the Moon
The crew of *Apollo 17* collected a record 253 lb *114,8 kg* of rock and soil during their 22 hr 5 min 'extra-vehicular activity'. They were Capt Eugene A. Cernan, USN (b. Chicago, 14 Mar 1934) and Dr Harrison H. (Jack) Schmitt (b. Santa Rosa, New Mexico, 3 July 1935) who became the 12th man on the moon. The crew were on the lunar surface for 74 hr 59½ min during this longest of lunar missions which took 12 days 13 hr 51 min on 7–19 Dec 1972.

First extra-terrestrial vehicle
The first wheeled vehicle landed on the Moon was *Lunakhod I* which began its Earth-controlled travels on 17 Nov 1970. It moved a total of 10,54 km *6.54 miles* on gradients up to 30° in the Mare Imbrium and did not become non-functioning until 4 Oct 1971. The lunar speed and distance record was set by the *Apollo 16* Rover with 11.2 mph *18 km/h* downhill and 22.4 miles *33,8 km*.

Closest approach to the Sun
The research spacecraft *Helios B* approached within 27 million miles *43,4 million km* of the Sun, carrying both US and West German instrumentation on 16 Apr 1976.

Largest space object
The heaviest object orbited is the Saturn V third stage with *Apollo 15* (space craft) which, prior to trans-lunar injection in parking orbit weighed 140 512 kg *138.29 tons*. The 442 lb *200 kg* US RAE (radio astronomy explorer) B or *Explorer 49* launched on 10 June 1973 has, however, antennae, 1500 ft 415 m from tip to tip.

Most expensive project
The total cost of the US manned space programme up to and including the lunar mission of *Apollo 17* has been estimated to be $25,541,400,000 (then £9,823,150,000). The first 15 years of the USSR space programme from 1958 to September 1973 has been estimated to have cost $45,000 million. The cost of the NASA Shuttle programme was $9.9 billion (£4350 million) to the launch of *Columbia* on 12 Apr 1981.

Chapter 5

THE SCIENTIFIC WORLD

All known matter in, on and beyond the Earth is made up of chemical elements. It is estimated that there are 10^{87} electrons in the known universe. The total of naturally-occurring elements so far detected is 94, comprising, at ordinary temperatures, two liquids, 11 gases and 81 solids. The so-called 'fourth state' of matter is plasma, when negatively charged electrons and positively-charged ions are in flux.

1. THE 108 ELEMENTS

There are 94 known naturally-occurring elements comprising, at ordinary temperatures, two liquids, 11 gases, 72 metals and 9 other solids. To date the discovery of a further 14 transuranic elements (Elements 95 to 107, and 109) has been claimed of which 8 are undisputed.

Category	Name	Symbol	Discovery of Element	Record
Commonest (lithosphere)	Oxygen	O	1771 Scheele (Germany-Sweden)	46.60% by weight
Commonest (atmosphere)	Nitrogen	N	1772 Rutherford (GB)	78.09% by volume
Commonest (extra-terrestrial)	Hydrogen	H	1776 Cavendish (GB)	90% of all matter
Rarest (of the 94)	Astatine	At	1940 Corson (US) *et al.*	1/100th oz *0.35 g* in Earth's crust
Lightest	Hydrogen	H	1776 Cavendish (GB)	0.005612 lb/ft³ *0,00008989 g/cm³*
Lightest (Metal)	Lithium	Li	1817 Arfwedson (Sweden)	33.30 lb/ft³ *0.5334 g/cm³*
Densest	Osmium	Os	1804 Tennant (GB)	1410 lb/ft³ *22.59 g/cm³*
Heaviest (Gas)	Radon	Rn	1900 Dorn (Germany)	*0.6274 lb/ft³ 0.01005 g/cm³* at 0° C
Newest[1]	Unnilennium	Une	1982 G. Munzenberg *et al.* W. Germany	Highest atomic number (element 109)
Purest	Helium	^{4}He	1868 Lockyer (GB) and Jannsen (France)	2 parts in 10^{15} (1978)
Hardest	Carbon	C	— prehistoric	Diamond allotrope, Knoop value 8400
Most Expensive	Californium	Cf	1950 Seaborg (US) *et al.*	Sold in 1970 for $10 per µg
Most Stable[2]	Tellurium	^{128}Te	1782 von Reichenstein (Austria)	Half-life of 1.5×10^{24} years
Least Stable	Lithium (isotope 5)	Li 5	1817 Arfwedson (Sweden)	Lifetime of 4.4×10^{-22} sec.
Most Isotopes	Caesium	Cs	1860 Bunsen & Kirchoff (Germ.)	36
	Xenon	Xe	1898 Ramsay and Travers (GB)	36
Least Isotopes	Hydrogen	H	1776 Cavendish (GB)	3 (confirmed)
Most Ductile	Gold	Au	*ante* 3000 BC	1 oz drawn to 43 miles *1 g/2.4 km*
Highest Tensile Strength	Boron	B	1808 Gay-Lussac and Thenard (France)	3.9×10^6 lb f/in² *26.8 GPa*
Lowest Melting/Boiling Point (non-metallic)[3]	Helium	^{4}He	1895 Ramsay (GB)	−272.375° C under pressure *(2532 kPa)* and −268.928° C
Lowest Melting/Boiling Point (metallic)	Mercury	Hg	— protohistoric	−38.836° C/356.66° C
Highest Melting/Boiling Point (non-metallic)	Carbon (carbyne 6)	C	prehistoric[4]	3530° C/3870° C
Highest Melting/Boiling Point (metallic)[4]	Tungsten	W	1783 J. J. & F. d'Elhuyar (Spain)	3422° C and 5730° C
Largest Expansion (negative)	Plutonium	Pu	1940 Seaborg (US) *et al.*	-5.8×10^{-5} cm/cm/deg C between 450–480° C (Delta prime allotrope disc. 1953)
Lowest Expansion (positive)	Carbon (diamond)	C	— prehistoric	1.0×10^{-6} cm/cm/deg C (at 20° C)
Highest Expansion (metal)	Caesium	Cs	1860 Bunsen & Kirchoff (Germ.)	9.7×10^{-5} cm/cm/deg C (at 20° C)
Highest Expansion (solid)	Neon	Ne	1898 Ramsay and Travers (GB)	1.94×10^{-3} cm/cm/deg C at −248.59° C
Most Toxic	Radium	^{224}Ra	1898 The Curies and Bemont (France)	Naturally occurring isotope 17,000 × more toxic than plutonium 239

[1] *Provisional IUPAC name. Unniloctium (Uno) or Element 108 has not yet been discovered. A single atom of Une (Element 109) was created by bombardment of bismuth by iron ions at the GSI laboratory, Dormstadt, W. Germany by Dr Peter Armbruster on 29 Aug 1982.*

[2] *Double beta decay estimate. Alpha particle record is Samarium 148 at 8×10^{15} years and Beta particle record is Cadmium 113 at 9×10^{15} years.*

[3] *Monatomic hydrogen H is expected to be a non-liquifiable superfluid gas.*

[4] *The carbyne forms of carbon were discovered by A. E. Goresy and G. Donnay (USA) and A. M. Sladkov and Yu. P. Koudrayatsev (USSR) in 1968.*

Lightest and heaviest sub-nuclear particles

By April 1982 the existence of 25 'stable' particles, 44 meson resonance multiplets, 58 baryon resonance multiplets, and 3 dibaryon resonance multiplets was accepted, representing the possible eventual discovery of 243 particles and an equal number of anti-particles. The heaviest 'stable' particle fully accepted is the charmed lambda baryon, symbol Λ_c^+, of mass 2282 MeV and lifetime 1×10^{-13} sec. The heaviest particle known is the upsilon triple prime meson, symbol Y''', of mass 10570 MeV and lifetime 5×10^{-23} sec, which consists of a bottom or beauty quark and its anti-quark, and which was first identified in April 1980 by two groups using the Cornell electron storage ring facilities at Cornell University, Ithaca, New York, USA. Sub-atomic concepts require that the masses of the graviton, photon, and neutrino should all be zero. Based on the sensitivities of various cosmological theories, upper limits for the masses of these particles are 7.6×10^{-67} g for the graviton; 3.0×10^{-53} g for the photon and 1.4×10^{-32} g for the neutrino (*cf.* 9.10953×10^{-28} g for the mass of an electron.)

Newest particles

It was announced in August 1983 at CERN, Geneva, Switzerland, that by using the CERN 540 GeV Super Proton Synchrotron proton-antiproton beam collider, evidence had been obtained for the two charged intermediate vector mesons, the W^+ and W^- (mass 80.9 ± 1.5 GeV), and their neutral

CHEMICAL COMPOUNDS

It has been estimated that there are 4,040,000 described chemical compounds of which 63,000 are (1978) in common use.

Most Refractory	Tantalum Carbide $TaC_{0.88}$	Melts at 3990 deg C
Most Refractory (plastics)	Modified polymides	900° F *482° C* for short periods
Lowest Expansion	Invar metal (Ni-Fe alloy with C and Mn)	1.3×10^{-7} cm/cm/deg C at 20° C
Highest Tensile Strength	Sapphire whisker Al_2O_3	6×10^6 lb/in² *42,7 GPa*
Highest Tensile Strength (plastics)	Polyvinyl alcoholic fibres	1.4×10^5 lbf/in² *1,03 GPa*
Most Magnetic	Cobalt-copper-samarium Co_3Cu_2Sm	10,500 oersted coercive force
Least Magnetic alloy	Copper nickel alloy CuNi	963 parts Cu to 37 parts Ni
Most Pungent	Vanillaldehyde	Detectable at 2×10^{-8} mg/litre
Sweetest[1]	Talin from arils of katemfe (Thaumatococcus daniellii) discovered in W. Africa	6150 × as sweet as 1% sucrose
Bitterest	Denatonium saccharide	3000 × as bitter as quinine sulphate
Most Acidic[2]	Perchloric acid ($HClO_4$)	pH value of normal solution tends to 0.
Most Alkaline	Caustic soda (NaOH) and potash (KOH) and tetramethylammonium hydroxide ($N(CH_3)_4OH$)	pH value of normal solution is 14.
Highest Specific Impulse	Hydrogen with liquid fluorine	447 lb f/sec/lb *4382 N/sec/kg*
Most Poisonous	Thiopentone (a barbiturate)	Intracardiac injection will kill in 1 to 2 sec
Highest Ductility in tension (max. superplasticity)	Pb38 Sn62	$49\frac{1}{2}$ times pre-stressed length by Ahmed and Langdon, Univ. of S. California, 1977

[1] *Found in 1839, reported in 1852 but the protein thaumatin not isolated until 1972.*
[2] *The most powerful acid, assessed on its power as a hydrogen-ion donor, is a solution of antimony pentafluoride in fluorosulphonic acid—$SbF_5 + FSO_3H$. Concentrated hydrochloric acid HCL, an aqueous solution has a pH value tending to −1.*

counterpart, the Z^0 (mass 95.6 $\pm$ 1.4 GeV). These transmit the weak force between the most fundamental particles, the quarks and the leptons and are known as 'weakons'. The earliest evidences for W^+ and W^- came on 20 Jan 1983 and for Z^0 in May 1983.

Most and Least stable

In 1982 the proton was measured to be stable against decay with a lifetime in excess of 8×10^{30} years, although theoretical predictions based on the 'grand unified theory' suggest that the lifetime may be less than 1×10^{34} years. The least stable or shortest lived particles are the five baryon resonances N (2220), N (2600), N (3030), Δ (2850) and Δ (3230), all 1.6×10^{-24} sec.

Substance smelliest

The most evil smelling substance, of the 17,000 smells so far classified, must be a matter of opinion but ethyl mercaptan (C_2H_5SH) and butyl seleno-mercaptan (C_4H_9SeH), are powerful claimants, each with a smell reminiscent of a combination of rotting cabbage, garlic, onions and sewer gas.

Most expensive perfume

The retail prices of the most expensive perfumes tend to be fixed at public relations rather than economic levels. The most expensive fragrant ingredient in perfume is pure French middle note jasmine essence at £2900 per kg or £82.20p per oz. The key ingredient is muscone, a macrocyclic ketone, from natural musk oil which in 1980 sold for £15,000 per kg or £425 per oz.

Most potent poison

The rickettsial disease, Q-fever can be instituted by a *single* organism but is only fatal in 1 in 1000 cases. About 10 organisms of *Francisella tularenesis* (formerly *Pasteurella tularenesis*) can institute tularaemia variously called alkali disease, Francis disease or deerfly fever, and this is fatal in upwards of 10 cases in 1000.

Most powerful nerve gas

VX, 300 times more toxic than phosgene ($COCl_2$) used in World War I, was developed at the Chemical Defence Experimental Establishment, Porton Down, Wiltshire in 1952. Patents were applied for in 1962 and published in February 1974 showing it to be Ethyl S-2-diisopropylamino-ethylmethylphosphonothiolate. The lethal dosage is 10 mg-minute/m³ airborne or 0,3 mg orally.

Most absorbent substance

The US Department of Agriculture Research Service announced on 18 Aug 1974 that 'H-span' or Super Slurper composed of one half starch derivative and one fourth each of acrylamide and acrylic acid can, when treated with iron, retain water 1300 times its own weight.

Finest powder

The ultimate in fine powder is solid helium which was first postulated to be a monatomic powder as early as 1964.

2. DRINK AND DRUGS

As from 1 Jan 1981 the strength of spirits has been expressed only in terms of percentage volume of alcohol at 20° C. Absolute or '100% vol' alcohol was formerly expressed to be 75.35 degrees over proof or 75.35° OP. In the USA proof is double the actual percentage of alcohol by volume at 60° F *15,6° C* such that absolute alcohol is 200 per cent proof spirit. 'Hangovers' are said to be aggravated by the presence of such toxic congenerics as amyl alcohol ($C_5H_{11}OH$).

Most alcoholic

During independence (1918–40) the Estonian Liquor Monopoly marketed 98 per cent potato alcohol (196 proof US). In 31 US states *Everclear* 190 proof or 95% vol alcohol, is marketed by the American Distilling Co 'primarily as a base for home-made cordials'. Royal Navy rum, introduced in 1655, was 40° OP (79% vol) before 1948, but was reduced to 4.5° UP (under proof) or 46% vol, before its abolition on 31 July 1970. Full strength Pusser's naval rum was again sold by E. D. & F. Man from 1984.

Oldest wine

The oldest datable wine has been an amphora salvaged and drank by Capt. Jacques Cousteau from the wreck of a Greek trader sunk in the Mediterranean *c* 230 BC. A wine jar recovered in Rome has been found to bear the label 'Q. Lutatio C. Mario Cos' meaning that it was produced in the consulship of Q. Lutatius and C. Marius *i.e.* in 102 BC. A bottle of 1748 Rudesheimer Rosewein was auctioned at Christie's, London for £260 on 6 Dec 1979.

Beer *Strongest world*

The strongest beer as measured by original gravity is the German EKU Kulminatur Urtyp hell 28 with 1131.7° and 13.52% alcohol by volume. The world's most alcoholic beer is Samichlaus Bier brewed by Brauerei Hürlimann of Zürich, Switzerland. It is 13.70 per cent alcohol by volume at 20° C with an original gravity of 1117.8°.

Beer *Strongest Great Britain*

The strongest regularly brewed beer in Britain is Thomas Hardy's brewed by Eldridge Pope & Co at their Dorchester Brewery, Dorset. It has an alcoholic content of 12.48 per cent by volume at 60° F and an original gravity of 1125.8°.

Beer *Weakest*

The weakest liquid ever marketed as beer was a sweet Ersatz beer which was brewed in Germany by Sunner, Colne-Kalk, in 1918. It had an original gravity of 1000.96° and a strength 1/30th that of the weakest beer now obtainable in the U.K.

Most expensive wine

Record prices paid for single bottles *usually* arise when two or more self-promoters are seeking publicity. They bear little relation to the market value. The highest price paid for any bottle (meaning a container as opposed to a measure) of wine is $31,000 (*then £13,140*) for a bottle of 1822 Château Lafite, bought by John Grisanti at the Heublein auction in San Francisco, USA on 28 May 1980 conducted by Michael Broadbent of Christie's. The US record is $2000 (*then £1000*) a bottle ($24,000 (*then £12,000*) for a case) of Napamedoc Cabernet, vintage 1979, by the Robert Mondavi Winery on 21 June 1981.

Greatest wine auction and wine tasting

The largest single sale of wine was conducted by Christie's of King Street, St James's, London on 10–11 July 1974 at Quaglino's Ballroom, London when 2325 lots comprising

The smallest bottle of spirits, a mean 1,3 millilitres which is sold for 33p.

432,000 bottles realised £962,190. The largest ever reported wine-tasting was that staged by the Wine Institute at St Francis Hotel, San Francisco, California on 17 July 1980 with 125 pourers, 90 openers and a consumption of 3000 bottles.

Most expensive liqueurs

The most expensive liqueur in France is *Eau de vie de pêche* at 190 F (*now £17.00*) for a 75 cl bottle at Fauchon in Paris. Remy Martin's Louis XIII cognac retails at £380 a bottle.

Most expensive spirits

The most expensive bottle of spirits at auction is £780 for a magnum of *Grande Armée Fine Champagne Cognac, 1811* at Christie's Geneva on 13 Nov 1978. *Cognac Chatereau la faut* (1865) retails for 2800 F (*now £255*) a bottle at Fauchon. In Britain *Hennessy Private Reserve Grande Champagne* retails for £120 (including VAT) for a standard bottle.

Largest bottles

The largest bottle normally used in the wine and spirit trade is the Jeroboam (equal to 4 bottles of champagne or, rarely, of brandy and from 5 to 6½ bottles of claret according to whether blown or moulded) and the Double Magnum (equal, since *c.* 1934 to 4 bottles of claret or, more rarely, red Burgundy). A complete set of Champagne bottles would consist of a ¼ bottle, through the ½ bottle, bottle, magnum, Jeroboam, Rehoboam, Methuselah, Salmanazer and Balthazar, to the Nebuchadnezzar, which has a capacity of 16 litres *28.14 pt*, and is equivalent to 20 bottles. In May 1958 a 5 ft *152 cm* tall sherry bottle with a capacity of 20½ Imperial gal *93,19 litres* was blown in Stoke-on-Trent, Staffordshire. This bottle, with the capacity of 131 normal bottles, was named an 'Adelaide'.

Smallest bottles

The smallest and meanest bottles of liquor now sold are White Horse bottles of Scotch whisky containing 1,3 millilitres or *22 minims* at 33p a bottle or £2.16 per 'case' of 12.

Largest collections

The largest reported collection of unduplicated miniature bottles is one of 22,109 by April 1984 owned by David L. Maund of Upham, Hampshire.

The largest reported collection of distilled spirits or liqueurs in any bar is 1406 unduplicated labels collected by Ian Boasman at Bistro French, Avenham Street, Preston, Lancashire audited in May 1984.

The world's greatest collection of whisky bottles is one of 3100 unduplicated labels assembled by Sgn Edward Giaccone at his Whiskyteca, Salo, Lake Garda, Italy.

Champagne cork flight

The longest distance for a champagne cork to fly from an untreated and unheated bottle 4 ft *1,22 m* from level ground is 105 ft 9 in *32,23 m* by Peter Kirby at Idlewild Park, Reno, Nevada, USA on 4 July 1981.

Most powerful drugs

The most powerful commonly available drug is d-Lysergic Acid Diethylamide tartrate (LSD-25, $C_{20}H_{25}N_3O$) first produced in 1938 for common cold research and as a hallucinogen by Dr Albert Hoffman (Swiss) on 16–19 Apr 1943. The most potent analgesic drug is the morphine-like R33799 confirmed in 1978 to have almost 12,000 times the potency of morphine. Interferon was reported available for $10 US per millionth of a microgramme.

Most lethal man-made chemical

TCDD (2,3,7,8-tetrachlorodibenzo-p-dioxin) utilized in herbicides, discovered in 1872, is said to be 150,000 times more deadly than cyanide at 3.1×10^{-9} moles/kg.

Most prescribed drug

The top-selling prescription drug in the world is the anti-ulcer drug Tagamet marketed by Smithkline-Beckman of Philadelphia, USA. The sales in 1981 were estimated at $800 million. The most prescribed drug in the United Kingdom is the tranquillizer Valium with over 1 million users.

3. PHOTOGRAPHY

CAMERAS

Earliest

The earliest veiled reference to a photograph on glass taken in a camera was in a letter from Joseph Nicéphore Niepce (1765–1833), a French physician and scientist dated 19 July 1822. It was a photograph of a copper engraving of Pope Pius VII taken at Gras, near Chalon-sur-Saône. The earliest photograph taken in England was one of a diamond-paned window in Laycock (or Lacock) Abbey, Wiltshire, taken in August 1835 by William Henry Fox Talbot, MP (1800–77), the inventor of the negative-positive process. The negative of this was donated to the Science Museum, London in 1937 by his granddaughter Matilda. The world's earliest aerial photograph was taken in 1858 by Gaspard Félix Tournachon (1820–1910), *alias* Nadar, from a balloon near Villacoublay, on the outskirts of Paris, France.

Largest

The largest camera ever built is the 27 ton/*tonne* Rolls Royce camera built for Product Support (Graphics) Ltd, of Derby, England completed in 1959. It measures 8 ft 10 in *2,69 m* high, 8 ft 3 in *2,51 m* wide and 35 ft *10,66 m* in length. The lens is a 63″ f 15 Cooke Apochromatic. Its value after improvements in 1971 was in excess of £100,000.

Smallest

Apart from cameras built for intra-cardiac surgery and espionage, the smallest camera that has been marketed is the circular Japanese 'Petal' camera with a diameter of 1.14 in *2,9 cm* and a thickness of 0.65 in *1,65 cm*. It has a focal length of 12 mm *0.47 in*. The BBC TV programme *Record Breakers* showed prints from this camera on 3 Dec 1974.

Fastest

In 1972 Prof. Basof of the USSR Academy of Sciences published a paper describing an experimental camera with a time resolution of 5×10^{-13} sec or ½ picosec. The fastest production camera in the world is the Imacon 675 manufactured by John Hadland (PI) Ltd of Bovingdon, Hertfordshire which is capable of taking pictures at a *rate* of 600 million per sec. Uses include laser, ballistic, detonic, plasma and corona research.

Most expensive camera

The most expensive complete range of camera equipment in the world is that of Nikon of Tokyo, Japan, who marketed in October 1983 their complete range of 14 cameras with 75 lenses and 457 accessories for £113,780 excluding VAT. The highest auction price for an antique camera is £21,000 for a J. B. Dancer stereo camera, patented in 1856 and sold at Christie's, South Kensington on 12 Oct 1977.

4. TELESCOPES

Earliest

Although there is evidence that early Arabian scientists understood something of the magnifying power of lenses, their first use to form a telescope has been attributed to Roger Bacon (*c.* 1214–92) in England. The prototype of modern refracting telescopes was that completed by Johannes Lippershey for the Netherlands government on 2 Oct 1608.

Part of the largest scientific instrument in the world. The $78 million VLA radio telescope in New Mexico, USA. Here 7 mobile dishes are lit by a rainbow – there are another 20 deployed over 39 miles *62,7 km* of rail. (*Douglas W. Johnson/Science Photo Library*)

Largest *Reflector World*

The largest telescope in the world is the alt-azimuth mounted 6 m *236.2 in* telescope sited on Mount Semirodriki, near Zelenchukskaya in the Caucasus Mountains, USSR, at an altitude of 6830 ft *2080 m*. Work on the mirror, weighing 70 tons/*tonnes* was not completed until the summer of 1974. Regular observations were begun on 7 Feb 1976 after 16 years work. The weight of the 42 m *138 ft* high assembly is 840 tonnes *827 tons*. Being the most powerful of all telescopes its range, which includes the location of objects down to the 25th magnitude, represents the limits of the observable Universe. Its light-gathering power would enable it to detect the light from a candle at a distance of 15,000 miles *24 000 km*.

A design for a 500 ton 10 metre *393.7 inch* reflector comprising 36 independently controlled fitting hexagonal mirrors was adopted in Oct 1980. If sited on Mauna Kea, Hawaii it would be expected to cost $50 million and be completed by 1989. The design of a 25 m *984 in* composite hexagonal reflector was announced by the USSR in August 1979.

Note: The attachment of an electronic charge-coupled device (CCD) increases the 'light-grasp' of a telescope by a factor up to 100 fold. Thus a 200 in *508 cm* telescope achieves the light gathering capacity of a 1000 inch *25,4 m* telescope.

Largest *Reflector Great Britain*

The largest British (and European) reflector is the Isaac Newton 100 in *254 cm* reflector formerly installed (1969–78) at the Royal Greenwich Observatory, Herstmonceux Castle, East Sussex. It was built in Newcastle upon Tyne, Tyne and Wear, weighs 92 tons *93,5 tonnes*, cost £641,000 and was inaugurated on 1 Dec 1967. It has been dismantled and re-erected on the 2423 m *7949 ft* high Roque de los Muchachos, La Palma, Canary Islands and became operational in February 1984. It is hoped that the William Herschel 4,2 m *167.3 in* reflector will also become operational at this new Northern Hemisphere Observatory in 1988.

Largest *Refractor*

The largest refracting (*i.e.* magnification by lenses) telescope in the world is the 62 ft *18,90 m* long 40 in *101,6 cm* telescope completed in 1897 at the Yerkes Observatory, Williams Bay, Wisconsin, and belonging to the University of Chicago, Illinois, USA. In 1900 a 125 cm *49.2 in* refractor 54,85 m *180 ft* in length was built for the Paris Exposition but its optical performance was too poor to justify attempts to use it. The largest in the British Isles is the 28 in *71,1 cm* at the Royal Greenwich Observatory (then in London) completed in 1894.

Radio *Largest steerable dish*

Radio waves of extra-terrestrial origin were first detected by Karl Jansky of Bell Telephone Laboratories, Holmdel, New Jersey, USA using a 100 ft *30,48 m* long shortwave rotatable antenna in 1932. The world's largest trainable dish-type radio telescope is the 100 m *328 ft* diameter, 3000 ton *3048 tonnes* assembly at the Max Planck Institute for Radio Astronomy of Bonn in the Effelsberger Valley, W. Germany; it became operative in May 1971. The cost of the installation begun in November 1967 was 36,920,000 DM (*then £6,150,000*).

Radio *Largest Dish*

The world's largest dish radio telescope is the partially-steerable ionospheric assembly built over a natural bowl at Arecibo, Puerto Rico, completed in November 1963 at a cost of about $9,000,000 (*then £3.75 million*). The dish has a diameter of 1000 ft *304,8 m* and covers 18½ acres *7,82 ha*. Its sensitivity was raised by a factor of 1000 and its range to the edge of the observable Universe at some 15,000 million light-years by the fitting of new aluminium plates at a cost of $8.8 million. Rededication was on 16 Nov 1974. The RATAN-600 radio telescope completed in the Northern Caucasus, USSR in 1976 has 895 metal mirror panels mounted in a circle 576 m *1890 ft* across.

Radio *Largest World*

The world's largest radio telescopic installation is the US National Science Foundation VLA (Very Large Array). It is Y-shaped with each arm 13 miles *20,9 km* long with 27 mobile antennae (each of 25 cm *82 ft* diameter) on rails. It is 50 miles *80 km* west of Socorro in the Plains of San Augustin, New Mexico, and was dedicated on 10 Oct 1980 at a cost of $78 million (*now £41 million*).

A computer-linked very long base-line array of 25 m *82 ft* radio telescopes stretched over 4200 km *2600 miles* on Latitude 49.3° N has been planned by the Canadian Astronomical Society.

Radio *Largest Great Britain*
The British Science Research Council 5 km radio telescope at Lord's Bridge, Cambridgeshire to be operated by the Mullard Radio Astronomy Observatory of Cambridge University will utilise eight mobile 42 ft *12,80 m* rail-borne computer-controlled dish aerials, which will be equivalent to a single steerable dish 5 km *3 miles 188 yd* in diameter. The project cost more than £2,100,000 and was completed in 1973.

Solar
The world's largest solar telescope is the 480 ft *146,30 m* long McMath telescope at Kitt Peak National Observatory near Tucson, Arizona, USA. It has a focal length of 300 ft *91,44 m* and an 80 in *2,03 m* heliostat mirror. It was completed in 1962 and produces an image measuring 33 in *83,8 cm* in diameter.

Observatory *Highest*
The highest altitude observatory in the world is the University of Denver's High Altitude Observatory at an altitude of 14,100 ft *4297 m*, opened in 1973. The principal instrument is a 24 in *60,48 cm* Ealing Beck reflecting telescope.

Observatory *Oldest*
The oldest astronomical observatory building extant in the world is 'Tower of the Winds' used by Andronichus of Cyrrhos in Athens, Greece *c.* 70 BC, and equipped with sundials and clepsydra.

Planetaria *World*
The ancestor of the planetarium is the rotatable Gottorp Globe, built by Andreas Busch in Denmark between 1654 and 1664 to the orders of Olearius, court mathematician to Duke Frederick III of Holstein. It is 34.6 ft *10,54 m* in circumference, weighs nearly 3½ tons/*tonnes* and is now preserved in Leningrad, USSR. The stars were painted on the inside. The earliest optical installation was not until 1923 in the Deutsches Museum, Munich, by Zeiss of Jena, Germany. The world's largest planetarium is in Moscow, USSR, and has a diameter of 82½ ft *25,15 m*.

Planetaria *Great Britain*
The United Kingdom's first planetarium was opened at Madame Tussaud's, Marylebone Road, London, on 19 Mar 1958. Accurate images of 8900 stars (some below naked eye magnitude) are able to be projected on the 70 ft *21,33 m* high copper dome.

Space Telescope
The first space observatory was the Orbiting Solar observatory 0504 launched on 18 Oct 1967. The largest will be the NASA Space Telescope of 10,9 tonnes *10.7 tons* and 13 m *42 ft 7 in* in overall length with a 94 inch *240 cm* reflector to be launched to 600 km *370 miles* altitude in 1985.

5. NUMEROLOGY

In dealing with large numbers, scientists use the notation of 10 raised to various powers to eliminate a profusion of noughts. For example, 19,160,000,000,000 miles would be written 1.916×10^{13} miles. Similarly, a very small number, for example 0,0000154324 of a gramme, would be written $1,5432 \times 10^{-5}$. Of the prefixes used before numbers the smallest is 'atto-' from the Danish atten for 18, indicating a trillionth part (10^{-18}) of the unit, and the highest is 'exa' (Greek, hexa, six), symbol E, indicating six groups of 3 zeros 10^{18} or a trillion (UK) or a quintillion (US) fold.

Highest numbers
The highest lexicographically accepted named number in the system of successive powers of ten is the centillion, first recorded in 1852. It is the hundredth power of a million, or one followed by 600 noughts. The highest named number outside the decimal notation is the Buddhist *asankhyeya*, which is equal to 10^{140}.

The number 10^{100} is designated a Googol. The term was devised by Dr Edward Kasner (US) (d. 1955). Ten raised to the power of a Googol is described as a Googolplex. Some conception of the magnitude of such numbers can be gained when it is said

that the number of electrons in some models of the observable Universe does not exceed 10^{87}.

The highest number ever used in a mathematical proof is a bounding value published in 1977 and known as Graham's number. It concerns bichromatic hypercubes and is inexpressible without the special 'arrow' notation, devised by Knuth in 1976, extended to 64 layers.

Prime numbers
A prime number is any positive integer (excluding 1) having no integral factors other than itself and unity, *e.g.* 2, 3, 5, 7 or 11. The lowest prime number is thus 2. The highest known prime number is $2^{132,049} - 1$, discovered on 23 Sept 1983 on a Cray One computer, at the University of California's Lawrence Livermore Laboratory, by David Slowinski. The number contains 39,751 digits. The lowest non-prime or composite number is 4.

Perfect numbers
A number is said to be perfect if it is equal to the sum of its divisors other than itself, *e.g.* $1 + 2 + 4 + 7 + 14 = 28$. The lowest perfect number is 6 ($1 + 2 + 3$). The highest known and the 29th so far discovered, is $(2^{132,049} - 1) \times 2^{132,048}$. It is a consequence of the highest known prime (see above).

Most innumerate
The most innumerate people are the Nambiquara of the north west Matto Grosso of Brazil who lack any system of numbers. They do however have a verb which means 'they are two alike'.

Most accurate and most inaccurate version of 'pi'
The greatest number of decimal places to which *pi* (π) has been calculated is 8,388,608 or 2^{23} by Yasumasu Kanada and Yoshiaki Tamura (Japan) in 6.8 hr on a HITAC M280H in Feb 1983. The published value to two million places, in what has been described as the world's most boring 800 page publication, was 3.141592653589793 ... (omitting the next 1,999,975 places)... 1457297909. In 1897 the General Assembly of Indiana enacted in House Bill No. 246 that *pi* was *de jure* 4.

Earliest measures
The earliest known measure of weight is the *beqa* of the Amratian period of Egyptian civilisation *c.* 3800 BC found at Naqada, Egypt. The weights are cylindrical with rounded ends from 188,7 to 211,2 g *6.65–7.45 oz*. The unit of length used by the megalithic tomb-builders in Britain *c.* 3500 BC appears to have been 2.72 ± 0.003 ft *82,90 cm ± 0.09 cm*. This was deduced by Prof. Alexander Thom (b. 1894) in 1966.

Time measure *Longest*
The longest measure of time is the *kalpa* in Hindu chronology. It is equivalent to 4320 million years. In astronomy a cosmic year is the period of rotation of the sun around the centre of the Milky Way galaxy, *i.e.* about 225 million years. In the Late Cretaceous Period of *c.* 85 million years ago the Earth rotated faster so resulting in 370.3 days per year while in Cambrian times some 600 million years ago there is evidence that the year contained 425 days.

Time measure *Shortest*
Owing to variations in the length of a day, which is estimated to be increasing irregularly at the average rate of about a milli-second per century due to the Moon's tidal drag, the second has been redefined. Instead of being 1/86,400th part of a mean solar day, it has, since 1960, been reckoned as 1/31,556,925,9747th part of the solar (or tropical) year at AD 1900, January 0. 12 hr, Ephemeris time. In 1958 the second of Ephemeris time was computed to be equivalent to 9,192,631,770 ± 20 cycles of the radiation corresponding to the transition of a caesium 133 atom when unperturbed by exterior fields. The greatest diurnal change recorded has been 10 milliseconds on 8 Aug 1972 due to the most violent solar storm recorded in 370 years of observations. A pulse of laser light lasting only 30 femto-seconds (3×10^{-14} of a second) was generated by Charles V. Shank at Bell Laboratories, Holmdel, NJ, USA in April 1982. It was 9 micrometres long *i.e.* 14 wave-lengths.

The accuracy of the caesium beam frequency standard approaches 8 parts in 10^{14} compared to 2 parts in 10^{13} for the methane-stabilised helium-neon laser and 6 parts in 10^{13} for the hydrogen maser.

6. GEMS AND OTHER PRECIOUS MATERIALS

PRECIOUS STONE RECORDS

Note: The carat was standardised at 205 mg in 1877. The metric carat of 200 mg was introduced in 1914.

Largest	Largest Cut Stone	Other records
Diamond (first recorded in India c. 300 BC recognized as pure crystallised carbon in 1796) 3106 metric carats (over 1¼ lb)—*The Cullinan,* found by Mr Gray on 25 Jan 1905 in the Premier Mine, Pretoria, South Africa. The first synthetic diamonds were produced by Prof H. T. Hall at the General Electric Research Laboratories, USA on 16 Dec 1954. In Feb 1984 a Tass report from Leningrad, USSR announced that the Institute of High Frequency Currents had produced an artificial diamond weighing 4½ lb *2,04 kg.*	530.2 metric carats of 74 facets. Cleaved from *The Cullinan* in 1908, by Jak Asscher of Amsterdam and polished by Henri Koe known as *The Star of Africa* or Cullinan I and now in the Royal Sceptre. The Cullinan II is of 317.40 carats. Third on the list of the 55 diamonds of more than 100 ct is the Great Mogul of 280 old carats lost in the sack of Delhi in 1739 and arguably the most valuable object ever lost.	Diamond is the *hardest* known naturally-occurring substance, with 5 times the indentation hardness of the next hardest mineral, corundum (Al_2O_3). The peak hardness value on the Knoop scale is 8400 compared with an average diamond of 7000. The rarest colour for diamond is blood red. The largest example is a flawless 5.05 ct stone found in Lichtenburg, S. Africa in 1927 and now in a private collection in the U.S. The diamond per carat record price of $113,000 was set by the 41.3 ct 'Polar Star' bought in Geneva for $4.6 million (*then £1.95 million*) on 21 Nov 1980.
Emerald (green beryl) [$Be_3Al_2(SiO_3)_6$]	86,136 carat natural beryl Gleim emerald. Found in Carnaiba, Brazil, Aug 1974. Carved by Richard Chan (Hong Kong). Appraised at $1,292,000 (*£718,000*) in 1982.	$520,000 (then £305,000) paid for an 18.35 ct gem emerald ring sold at Sotheby Parke Bernet, New York, in Apr 1977.
Sapphire (corundum any colour but red) (Al_2O_3) 2302 carat stone found at Anakie, Queensland, Australia, in c. 1935, now a 1318 carat head of President Abraham Lincoln (1809–65).	1444 carat black star stone carved from 2097 carats in 1953–5 into a bust of General Dwight David Eisenhower (1890–1969).	*Note:* both the sapphire busts are in the custody of the Kazanjian Foundation of Los Angeles, California, USA. Auction record for a single stone was set by a step-cut sapphire of 66.03 carats at £579,300 from the Rockefeller collection at Sotheby's Zurich on 8 May 1980.
Ruby (red corundum) (Al_2O_3) 3421 carat broken stone reported found in July 1961 (largest piece 750 carats).	1184 carat natural gem stone of Burmese origin. The largest star ruby is the 138.72 carat Rosser Reeves stone at the Smithsonian Institution.	Since 1955 rubies have been the world's most precious gem attaining a price of up to £4000 per carat by 1969. A world record carat price of $100,639 (*then £46,600*) was set at Christie's sale in Geneva in November 1979 for a 4.12 carat caspian-shaped ruby. The ability to make corundum prisms for laser technology up to over 12 in *30 cm* in length seems to have little bearing on the market for natural gems.

RECORDS FOR OTHER PRECIOUS MATERIALS

Largest
PEARL
(Molluscan consecretion)
14 lb 1 oz *6,37 kg* 9½ in *24 cm* long by 5½ in *14 cm* in diameter—*Pearl of Laotze*
Found: At Palawan, Philippines, 7 May 1934 in shell of giant clam.
Present location: The property of Wilburn Dowell Cobb from 1936 until his death, it was valued at $4,080,000 in July 1971. On 15 May 1980 it was bought at auction in San Francisco by Peter Hoffman, a jeweller of Beverley Hills, California for $200,000 (*then £85,000*). An appraisal for the new owner Gina Diane Barbish in May 1982 by the San Francisco Gem Laboratory suggested a value of $32,640,000.

OPAL
(SiO_2nH_2O)
220 troy oz (yellow-orange).
Found: Coober Pedy, South Australia.
Present location: The Olympic Australis (17,700 carats) found in Aug 1956 owned by Altmann & Cherny Pty Ltd is on public display in Melbourne and is valued at $1.8 million (US). An opal containing much 'potch' (colourless material) named the Desert Flame was found at Andamooka, South Australia. The 34,215 carat mass first reported in Sept 1969 was broken up and auctioned off on 29 Aug 1978.

ROCK CRYSTAL (QUARTZ)
SiO_2
Ball: 106¾ lb *40,48 kg* 12⅞ in *32,7 cm* diameter, the *Warner* sphere
Found: Burma, (originally a 1000 lb *450 kg* piece).
Present location: US National Museum, in Washington, DC.

TOPAZ
$Al_2SiO_4(F,OH)_2$
'Brazilian Princess' 21,325 carat 221 facets.
Found: Light blue: from Brazil.
Present location: Exhibited by Smithsonian Institution, November 1978. Valued at $1,066,350 or $50 per carat. Cut from a 79 lb *35,8 kg* crystal. World's largest facetted stone.

AMBER
(Coniferous fossil resin)
33 lb 10 oz *15.25 kg.*
Found: Reputedly from Burma acquired in 1860.
Present location: Bought by John Charles Bowing (d. 1893) for £300 in Canton, China. Natural History Museum, London, since 1940.

NEPHRITE JADE
$Ca_2(Mg, Fe)_5(Si_4O_{11})_2(OH)_2$
Boulder of 143 tons/*tonnes* and 21,300 ft³ *603 m³*
Found: In China. Reported 17 Sept 1978.

Present location: Jadeite $Na_2O.Al_2O_3 4SiO_2$ can be almost any colour excepting red or blue. The largest known example has been a block weighing 33 tons from Burma.

MARBLE
(*Metamorphosed* $CaCO_3$)
90 tons/*tonnes* (single slab)
Found: Quarried at Yule, Colorado, USA.
Present location: A piece of over 45 tons/*tonnes* was dressed from this slab for the coping stone of the Tomb of the Unknown Soldier in Arlington National Cemetery, Virginia, USA.

NUGGETS—GOLD (Au)
7560 oz (472½ lb *214,32 kg*) (reef gold) *Holtermann Nugget*
Found: Beyers & Holtermann Star of Hope Gold Mining Co., Hill End, NSW, Australia, 19 Oct 1872.
Present location: The Holtermann nugget contained some 220 lb *99.8 kg* of gold in a 630 lb *285,7 kg* slab of slate. The purest large nugget was the *Welcome Stranger*, found at Moliagul, Victoria, Australia, which yielded 2248 troy oz *69,92 kg* of pure gold from 2280¼ oz *70,92 kg.*

SILVER (AG)
2750 lb troy *Found:* Sonora, Mexico.
Present location: Appropriated by the Spanish Government before 1821.

OTHER GEM RECORDS:
Largest Crystal of Gem Quality
A 520,000 carat (2 cwt 5 lb *103,8 kg*) aquamarine, [$Be_3Al_2(SiO_3)_6$] found near Marambaia, Brazil in 1910. Yielded over 200,000 carats of gem quality cut stones.

Rarest Gem Mineral
Painite ($CaZrB(Al_9O_{18})$) discovered by A C D Pain near Ohngaing, Mogok, Burma in 1951. Deep red crystals of 1.31 and 2.12 gm are in the British Museum (Natural History).

Densest Gem Mineral
Stibiotantalite [$(SbO)_2(Ta,Nb)_2O_6$] a rare brownish-yellow mineral found in San Diego County, California, has a density of 7.46. The alloy platiniridium has a density of 22.0.

Smallest Brilliant Cut Diamond
A 57 facet diamond of 0.0012 of a carat (0.24 milligrams) by A. Van Moppes & Zoon (Diamant) BV of Amsterdam certified on 26 Jan 1949.

Largest Crystal
A 380 000 kg *187 tons* beryl ($Be_3Al_2Si_6O_{18}$) measuring 18 m *59 ft* long and 3,5 m *11½ ft* in diameter was recorded at Malakialina, Malagasy in 1976.

Newest Gemstones
Tanzanite was discovered in Tanzania in 1969. It reached $1200 (*then £670*) per carat in 1977. The deep purple Royal Lavalite found in Hotazel, South Africa by Randy Polk of Phoenix, Arizona reached $1300 (*then £840*) per carat in 1982.

The *Olympic Australis* opal of 17,700 carats appraised at £1,285,000.

SCIENTIFIC WORLD

7. PHYSICAL EXTREMES (Terrestrial)

The Princeton Large Torus which in May 1980 produced a temperature of 82 million degrees C, the highest sustained figure ever produced.

Temperature Highest

The highest man-made temperatures yet attained are those produced in the centre of a thermonuclear fusion bomb, which are of the order of 300,000,000 – 400,000,000° C. Of controllable temperatures, the highest effective laboratory figure reported is 82 million degrees C at the Princeton Plasma Physics Laboratory, USA in the fusion research PLT (Princeton Large Torus) in May 1980. A figure of 3000 million °C was reportedly achieved in the USSR with Ogra injection-mirror equipment in c. 1962.

Temperature Lowest

The lowest temperature reached is 5×10^{-8} Kelvins above absolute zero attained in a two stage nuclear demagnetization cryostat at the Helsinki University of Technology, Otaniemi, Finland by the team of Prof. Olli V. Loúnasmaa (b. 1920) and announced in March 1979. Absolute or thermodynamic temperatures are defined in terms of ratios rather than as differences reckoned from the unattainable absolute zero, which on the Kelvin scale is $-273,15°$ C or $-459.67°$ F. Thus the lowest temperature ever attained is 1 in 5.5×10^9 of the melting point of ice (0° C or 273.15 K or 32° F). Tokyo University's Institute of Solid State Physics announced on 15 Feb 1983 that a team led by Prof. Kazuo Ono had attained a temperature within 0.00003 of a degree of absolute zero at which molecular motion ceases.

Highest pressures

The highest sustained laboratory pressures yet reported are of 1.72 mega bars (11,000 tons force/in² *160 GPa*) achieved in the giant hydraulic diamond-faced press at the Carnegie Institution's Geophysical Laboratory, Washington DC reported in June 1978. This laboratory announced solid hydrogen achieved at 57 kilobars pressure on 2 Mar 1979. If created, metallic hydrogen is expected to be silvery white but soft with a density of 1.1 g/cm³. The pressure required for the transition is estimated by H. K. Mao and P. M. Bell to be 1 Megabar at 25°C. Using dynamic methods and impact speeds of up to 18,000 mph *29 000 km/h*, momentary pressures of 75,000,000 atmospheres (490,000 tons/in² *7000 GPa*) were reported from the United States in 1958.

Highest velocity

The highest velocity at which any solid visible object has been projected is 150 km/sec *335,000 mph* in the case of a plastic disc at the Naval Research Laboratory, Washington DC, reported in August 1980.

Finest balance

The most accurate balance in the world is the Sartorius Model 4108 manufactured in Göttingen, W. Germany, which can weigh objects of up to 0,5 g to an accuracy of 0,01 μg or 0,00000001 g which is equivalent to little more than one sixtieth of the weight of the ink on this full stop .

Largest bubble chamber

The largest bubble chamber in the world is the $7 million (*then £2.5 million*) installation completed in October 1973 at Weston, Illinois. It is 15 ft *4,57 m* in diameter and contains 7259 gal *33 000 litres* of liquid hydrogen at a temperature of $-247°$C with a super conductivity magnet of 30,000 gauss.

Fastest centrifuge

Ultra-centrifuges were invented by Theodor Svedberg (b. 30 Aug 1884) (Sweden) in 1923. The highest man-made rotary speed ever achieved and the fastest speed of any earth-bound object is 4500 mph *7250 km/h* by a swirling tapered 6 in *15,2 cm* carbon fibre rod in a vacuum at Birmingham University, England reported on 24 Jan 1975.

Finest cut

The $13 million Large Optics Diamond Turning Machine at the Lawrence Livermore National Laboratory, California was reported in June 1983 to be able to sever a human hair 3000 times lengthwise.

Longest echo

The longest recorded echo in any building in Great Britain is one of 15 sec following the closing of the door of the Chapel of the Mausoleum, Hamilton, Strathclyde built in 1840–55.

Most powerful electric current

The most powerful electric current generated is that from the Zeus capacitor at the Los Alamos Scientific Laboratory, New Mexico, USA. If fired simultaneously the 4032 capacitors would produce for a few microseconds twice as much current as that generated elsewhere on Earth.

Hottest Flame

The hottest flame that can be produced is from carbon subnitride (C_4N_2) which at one atmosphere pressure is calculated to reach 5261 K.

Highest Measured Frequency

The highest frequency ever directly measured is a visible yellow light at $5.20206528 \times 10^{14}$ hertz (c. 520 terahertz or million million cycles per second) in February 1979 by the US National Bureau of Standards Boulder Laboratories and the National Research Council Laboratory in Ottawa, Canada.

Lowest friction

The lowest coefficient of static and dynamic friction of any solid is 0.02, in the case of polytetrafluoroethylene ($[C_2F_4]_n$), called PTFE—equivalent to wet ice on wet ice. It was first manufactured in quantity by E. I. du Pont de Nemours & Co Inc in 1943, and is marketed from the USA as Teflon. In the United Kingdom it is marketed by ICI as Fluon. In the centrifuge at the University of Virginia a 30 lb *13,60 kg* rotor magnetically supported has been spun at 1000 rev/sec in a vacuum of 10^{-6} mm of mercury pressure. It loses only one revolution per second per day, thus spinning for years.

Smallest hole

A hole of 40 Å (4×10^{-9} mm) was shown visually using a JEM 100C electron microscope and Quantel Electronics devices at the Dept. of Metallurgy, Oxford on 28 Oct. 1979. To find such a hole is equivalent to finding a pinhead in a haystack with sides of 1.2 miles *1,93 km*. An electron microscope beam on a sample of sodium beta-alumina at the University of Illinois, USA, in May 1983 accidentally bored a hole 2×10^{-9} mm in diameter.

Most powerful laser beams

The first illumination of another celestial body was achieved on 9 May 1962, when a beam of light was successfully reflected from the Moon by the use of a maser (microwave amplification by stimulated emission of radiation) or laser (light amplification by stimulated emission of radiation) attached to a 48 in *121,9 cm* telescope at Massachusetts Institute of Technology, Cambridge, Massachusetts, USA. The spot was estimated to be 4 miles *6,4 km* in diameter on the Moon. The device was propounded in 1958 by Dr Charles Hard Townes (born 1915) of the USA. A maser light flash is focused into liquid nitrogen-cooled ruby crystal. Its chromium atoms are excited to a high energy state in which they emit a red light which is allowed to escape only in the direction desired. Such a flash for 1/5000th of a second can bore a hole through a diamond by vaporization at 10,000°C, produced by 2×10^{23} photons. The 'Shiva' laser was reported at the Lawrence Livermore Laboratory, California to be concentrating 2.6×10^{13} watts into a pinhead-sized target for 9.5×10^{-11} in a test on 18 May 1978.

Brightest light

The brightest steady artificial light sources are 'laser' beams with an intensity exceeding the Sun's 1,500,000 candles/in² 232

500 candelas/cm² by a factor of well in excess of 1000. In May 1969 the USSR Academy of Sciences announced blast waves travelling through a luminous plasma of inert gases heated to 90,000 K. The flare-up for up to 3 micro-seconds shone at 50,000 times the brightness of the Sun *viz.* 75,000 million candles/in² *11 625 million candelas/cm².* Of continuously burning sources, the most powerful is a 200 kW high-pressure xenon arc lamp of 600,000 candle-power, reported from the USSR in 1965.

The synchrotron radiation from a 4 × 0.5 in *100 × 2,5 mm* slit in the SPEAR high energy physics plant at the end of the 2 mile *3,2 km* long Stanford Linear Accelerator, California, USA has been described as the world's most powerful light beam.

The most powerful searchlight ever developed was one produced during the 1939–45 war by the General Electric Company Ltd at the Hirst Research Centre in Wembley, Greater London. It had a consumption of 600 kW and gave an arc luminance of 300,000 candles/in² *46 500 candelas/cm²* and a maximum beam intensity of 2,700,000,000 candles from its parabolic mirror (diameter 10 ft *3,04 m*).

Most durable light

The average bulb lasts for 750–1000 hr. There is some evidence that a carbon filament bulb burning in the Fire Department, Livermore, south Alameda County, California has been burning since 1901.

Heaviest magnet

The heaviest magnet in the world is one measuring 60 m *196 ft* in diameter, with a weight of 36,000 tons/*tonnes* for the 10 GeV synchrophasotron in the Joint Institute for Nuclear Research at Dubna, near Moscow, USSR. Intermagnetics General Corporation announced in 1975 plans for a 180 kG vanadium-gallium magnet.

Magnetic fields *Strongest and weakest*

The strongest magnetic field strength achieved has been one of 301 kilogauss *30,1 teslas* at the Francis Bitter National Magnet Laboratory at Massachusetts Institute of Technology, by Mathias J. Leupold and Robert J. Weggel, announced in July 1977. The outer magnet is of super-conducting niobium-titanium.

The weakest magnetic field measured is one of 8×10^{-11} gauss in the heavily shielded room at the Francis Bitter National Magnet Laboratory, Cambridge, Massachusetts, USA. It is used for research by Dr David Cohen into the very weak magnetic field generated in the heart and brain.

Most powerful microscope

The world's most powerful microscope was announced by Dr Lawrence Bartell and Charles Ritz of the University of Michigan in July 1974 with an image magnification of 260 million fold. It uses an optical laser to decode holograms produced with 40 KeV radiation and has produced photographs of electron clouds of atoms of neon and argon. In Sept 1983 the Japanese National Optical Centre announced their ARM (Atomic Resolution Microscope) as the world's most powerful. The lightest high power microscope in the world is the 1200 × McArthur Microscope made in Cambridge, England and weighing 9 oz *255 g*.

Dr. Albert Crewe (b. 1927 in U.K.) of the University of Chicago is projecting a scanning electron microscope by 1986 capable of seeing between atoms.

Loudest noise

The loudest noise created in a laboratory is 210 decibels or 400,000 acoustic watts reported by NASA from a 48 ft *14,63 m* steel and concrete horn at Huntsville, Alabama, USA in October 1965. Holes can be bored in solid material by this means.

Highest note

The highest note yet attained is one of 60,000 megahertz (60 GHz) (60,000 million vibrations/sec), generated by a 'laser' beam striking a sapphire crystal at the Massachusetts Institute of Technology in Cambridge, Massachusetts, USA, in September 1964.

Most powerful particle accelerator

The 2 kilometre *6562 ft* diameter proton synchrotron at the Fermi National Accelerator Laboratory east of Batavia, Illinois, USA is the highest energy 'atom-smasher' in the world. On 14 May 1976 an energy of 500 billion (5×10^{11}) electron volts was attained. Work on doubling the energy to nearly 1 Tera electron volts or 1000 GeV by 1985 was begun in July 1979. On 15 Aug 1983 0.7 TeV was achieved. This involves 1000 super-conducting magnets maintained at a temperature of $-452°$ F *$-268,8°$ C* by means of the world's largest 4500 litre *990 gal* per hour helium liquefying plant which began operating on 18 Apr 1980.

The aim of CERN (*Conseil Européan pour la Recherche*) to collide beams of protons and antiprotons in their Super Proton Synchroton (SPS) near Geneva, Switzerland at 270 GeV × 2 = 540 GeV was achieved at 4.55 a.m. on 10 July 1981. This was the equivalent of striking a fixed target with protons at 150 TeV or 150 000 GeV.

The US Department of Energy set up a study for a $5 billion Super Superconductivity Collider (SSC) 1995 with two 20 TeV proton and antiproton colliding beams on 16 Aug 1983. If 8 tesla magnets were used the diameter would be 19,6 km *12.1 miles* but with 3 tesla magnets this would be 52,3 km *32.5 miles.*

Quietest place

The 'dead room', measuring 35 ft by 28 ft *10,67 × 8,50 m* in the Bell Telephone System laboratory at Murray Hill, New Jersey, USA, is the most anechoic room in the world, eliminating 99.98 per cent of reflected sound.

Sharpest objects and Smallest Tubes

The sharpest objects yet made are glass micropipette tubes used in intracellular work on living cells. Techniques developed and applied by Prof Kenneth T. Brown and Dale G. Flaming of the Department of Physiology, University of California, San Francisco achieved by 1977 bevelled tips with an outer diameter of 0.02 μm and 0.01 μm inner diameter. The latter is smaller than the smallest known nickel tubing by a factor of 340 and is 6500 times thinner than human hair.

Highest vacuum

The highest (or 'hardest') vacuums obtained in scientific research are of the order of 10^{-14} torr at the IBM Thomas J. Watson Research Center, Yorktown Heights, New York, USA in October 1976 in a cryogenic system with temperatures down to $-269°$C $-452°$F. This is equivalent to depopulating (baseball-sized) molecules from 1 metre apart to 80 km apart or from 1 yard to 50 miles.

Lowest viscosity

The California Institute of Technology, USA announced on 1 Dec 1957 that there was no measurable viscosity, *i.e.* perfect flow, in liquid helium II, which exists only at temperatures close to absolute zero ($-273,15°$C or $-459.67°$F).

Highest voltage

The highest potential difference ever obtained in a laboratory has been 32 ± 1.5 million volts by the National Electrostatics Corporation at Oak Ridge, Tennessee, USA on 17 May 1979.

Largest wind tunnel *World*

The world's largest wind tunnel is a low-speed tunnel with a 40 × 80 ft *12,19 × 24,38 m* test section built in 1944 at the Ames Research Center, Moffett Field, California, USA. The tunnel encloses 800 tons/*tonnes* of air and cost approximately $7,000,000 (*then £1,735,000*). The maximum volume of air that can be moved is 60,000,000 ft³ *1 700 000 m³* per min. On 30 July 1974 NASA announced an intention to increase it in size to 80 × 120 ft *24,38 × 36,57 m* for 345 mph speeds with a 135,000 hp *136 900 cv* system. The most powerful is the 216,000 hp *219 000 cv* installation at the Arnold Engineering Test Center at Tullahoma, Tennessee, USA opened in September 1956. The highest Mach number attained with air is Mach 27 at the works of the Boeing Company in Seattle, Washington State, USA. For periods of micro-seconds, shock Mach numbers of the order of 30 (22,830 mph *36 735 km/h*) have been attained in impulse tubes at Cornell University, Ithaca, New York State, USA.

Largest wind tunnel *Great Britain*

The most powerful wind tunnel in the United Kingdom is the intermittent compressed air type installation at the BAC plant at Warton, Lancashire which can be run at Mach 4, which is equivalent to 3044 mph *4898 km/h* at sea level.

Chapter 6

THE ARTS AND ENTERTAINMENTS

A panel from the multi-panelled *The Life of Christ* by Jackson Bailey. It covers an area of 11,000 ft² *1022 m²*.

1. PAINTING

Guinness Superlatives has published a more specialist book *Guinness Book of Art Facts and Feats* (£6.95) by John FitzMaurice Mills.

Earliest *World*

Evidence of Palaeolithic art was first found in 1834 in the cave of Chaffaud near Sévigné, Vienne, France by Brouillet with an engraving of two deer on a piece of flat bone from the cave, now dated to *c* 20,000 BC. It was not published until 1861 by Edouard Lartet (1801–71). The oldest known dated examples come from La Ferrassie, near Les Eyzies in the Périgord, France, in layers dated to *c* 25,000 BC. Blocks of stone were found with engraved animals and female symbols; some of the blocks also had symbols painted in red ochre. Pieces of ochre with ground facets have been found at Lake Mungo, NSW in a context *ante* 30,000 BC but there is no evidence whether these were used for body-painting or art.

Largest World *All time*

Panorama of the Mississippi, completed by John Banvard (1815–

91) in 1846, showing the river for 1200 miles *1930 km* in a strip probably 5000 ft *1525 m* long and 12 ft *3,65 m* wide, was the largest painting in the world, with an area of more than 1.3 acres *0,52 ha*. The painting is believed to have been destroyed when the rolls of canvas, stored in a barn at Cold Spring Harbor, Long Island, New York State, USA, caught fire shortly before Banvard's death on 16 May 1891.

Existing

A larger painting now only partially in existence is *The Battle of Gettysburg*, completed in 1883, after 2½ years of work, by Paul Philippoteaux (France) and 16 assistants. The painting was 410 ft *125 m* long, 70 ft *21,3 m* high and weighed 5.36 tons *5,45 tonnes*. It depicts the climax of the Battle of Gettysburg, in southern Pennsylvania, USA, on 3 July 1863. In 1964 the painting was bought by Joe King of Winston-Salem, North Carolina, USA after being stored by E. W. McConnell in a Chicago warehouse since 1933. In 1964, owing to deterioration, the sky was trimmed down so decreasing the area. Jackson Bailey's *Life of Christ* exhibited by Religious Art Institute of

HIGHEST PRICE PAINTINGS—Progressive Records

Price	Equivalent 1984 Value	Painter, title, sold by and sold to	Date
£6500	£238,700	Antonio Correggio's *The Magdalen Reading* (in fact spurious) to Elector Friedrich Augustus II of Saxony.	1746
£8500	£286,650	Raphael's *The Sistine Madonna* (1513–14) from Piacenza to Elector Friedrich Augustus II of Saxony.	1759
£16,000	£325,240	Van Eycks' *Adoration of the Lamb*, 6 outer panels of Ghent altarpiece by Edward Solby to the Government of Prussia.	1821
£24,600*	£733,200	Murillo's *The Immaculate Conception* by estate of Marshal Soult to the Louvre (against Czar Nicholas I) in Paris.	1852
£70,000	£3,230,000	Raphael's *Ansidei Madonna* (1506) from Perugia by the 8th Duke of Marlborough to the National Gallery.	1885
£100,000	£4,680,000	Raphael's *The Colonna Altarpiece* (1503–05) from Perugia by Seldemeyer to J. Pierpont Morgan.	1901
£102,880	£3,675,000	Van Dyck's *Elena Grimaldi-Cattaneo* (portrait) by Knoedler to Peter Widener (1834–1915).	1906
£102,880	£2,756,500	Rembrandt's *The Mill* by 6th Marquess of Lansdowne to Peter Widener.	1911
£116,500	£3,484,000	Raphael's smaller *Panshanger Madonna* by Joseph (later Baron) Duveen (1869–1939) to Peter Widener.	1913
£310,400	£9,225,000	Leonardo da Vinci's *Benois Madonna* (c. 1477) to Czar Nicholas II in Paris.	1914
£821,429*	£5,985,000	Rembrandt's *Aristotle Contemplating the Bust of Homer* by estate of Mr and Mrs Alfred W. Erickson to New York Metropolitan Museum of Art.	1961
£1,785,714	£9,687,500	Leonardo da Vinci's *Ginevra de' Benci* (c. 1475) by Prince Franz Josef II of Liechtenstein to National Gallery of Art, Washington DC, USA.	1967
£2,310,000*	£10,447,500	Velázquez's *Portrait of Juan de Pareja* by the Earl of Radnor to the Wildenstein Gallery, New York.	1970
£2,729,000*	£3,760,000	Turner's *Juliet and Her Nurse* by Trustees of Whitney Museum, New York to undisclosed bidder at Park Bernet, New York.	1980

* Indicates price at auction, otherwise prices were by private treaty.

America Inc. of Atlanta, Georgia comprises 50 panels 11 × 20 ft *3,35 × 6,09 m* and was completed in 1968–70 with an area of 11,000 ft² *1022 m²*.

'Old Master'

The largest 'Old Master' is *Il Paradiso*, painted on canvas between 1587 and 1590 by Jacopo Robusti, *alias* Tintoretto (1518–94), and his son Domenico (1565–1637) on the east wall of the Sala del Maggior Consiglio in the Palazzo Ducale (Doge's Palace) in Venice, Italy. The work is 22 m *72 ft 2 in* long and 7 m *22 ft 11½ in* high and contains some 350 human figures or heads.

Largest *Great Britain*

The largest painting in Great Britain is the giant oval *Triumph of Peace and Liberty* by Sir James Thornhill (1676–1734), on the ceiling of the Painted Hall in the Royal Naval College, Greenwich. It measures 106 ft *32,3 m* by 51 ft *15,4 m* and took 20 years (1707–1727) to complete.

A painting 6050 ft² *562 m²* in area and weighing more than a ton was painted for the 4th European Youth Games under the direction of David A. Judge and to the design of Norman G. Warner in Colchester, Essex between 29 Oct 1975 and 24 May 1976 by 365 people.

Picasso's *Self Portrait: Yo Picasso* which broke the auction record for a 20th century painting in May 1981 when it sold for $5.3 million (*then £2,950,000*) at Sotheby's, New York City.

World's largest Poster

The largest recorded poster was one measuring 200 ft by 100 ft *60,9 × 30,4 m* erected on the Thames Embankment, London on 26 Sept. 1983 by The Hutton Company for their client 'The Reader's Digest'. The 20 sections of white terylene supported PVC totalled 20,000 ft² *1858 m²* in area.

Most valuable

The 'Mona Lisa' (*La Gioconda*) by Leonardo da Vinci (1452–1519) in the Louvre, Paris, was assessed for insurance purposes at the highest ever figure of $100,000,000 (*then £35.7 million*) for its move for exhibition in Washington, DC, and New York City, NY, USA, from 14 Dec 1962 to 12 Mar 1963. However, insurance was not concluded because the cost of the closest security precautions was less than that of the premiums. It was painted in *c.* 1503–7 and measures 77 × 53 cm *30.5 × 20.9 in.* It is believed to portray either Mona (short for Madonna) Lisa Gherardini, the wife of Francesco del Giocondo of Florence, or Constanza d'Avalos, coincidentally nicknamed La Gioconda, mistress of Guiliano de Medici. Francis I, King of France, bought the painting for his bathroom in 1517 for 4000 gold florins or 92 oz *15,30 kg* of gold worth some £220,000 (mid-1984). Dr Pulitzer claims the Louvre have a painting of Constanza by Leonardo while his Swiss syndicate have the Mona Lisa proper in London first bought from Florence by William Blaker.

HIGHEST PRICE

Auction price *World*

The highest price ever bid in a public auction for any painting is $6,400,000 (*then £2,689,076*) for *Juliet and Her Nurse* painted by Joseph Mallord William Turner (1775–1851) of London when in Venice, Italy in 1836 and sold on 30 May 1980 at Sotheby Parke Bernet's, New York City, to an undisclosed collector possibly a 'woman in white' from Argentina. The painting had been sold by the Whitney Museum in New York and is 3 ft × 4 ft *91 × 122 cm.*

Private Treaty

It was announced on 12 Nov 1980 that the National Gallery, London had acquired Albrecht Altdorfer's *Christ Taking Leave of His Mother*, valued by Christie's at 'about £6 million', from the trustees of the Wernher collection at Luton Hoo, Bedfordshire.

By A Woman Artist

The highest price ever paid for a painting by a female artist is $1,100,000 (*then £705,000*), at Christie's, New York on 17 May 1983, for *Reading Le Figaro* by Mary Cassatt (b. Pennsylvania, USA, 1844–d. 1926). She worked mainly from Paris.

Abstract

The auction record for an abstract painting is £1,512,000 for *Composition with Red, Blue and Yellow* painted in 1930 by Piet Mondrian (1872–1944) at Christies, London on 27 June 1983. The purchaser was Shigeki Kameyama.

Miniature portrait

The highest price ever paid for a portrait miniature is the £75,000 given by an anonymous buyer at a sale held by Sotheby's, London on 24 Mar 1980 for a miniature of Jane

Broughton, aged 21, painted on vellum by Nicholas Hilliard (1547–1619) in 1574. The painted surface measures 1.65 in *42 mm* in diameter.

Modern painting

The record for a 20th century painting was set at $5.3 million (*then £2,950,000*) at Sotheby Parke Bernet, New York City on 21 May 1981 by Picasso's 1901 *Self Portrait: Yo Picasso* sold to an anonymous dealer. The 19th century record is $3,740,000 (*then £2,413,000*) for *L'Attente* by Degas sold at Sotheby Parke Bernet, New York City, on 18 May 1983.

Living artist *World*

The highest price at auction for a work by a then living artist is £961,200 for a painting of July 1945 by the late Joan Miró (Spain) at Christie's, London on 27 June 1983. It was the property of Mr & Mrs Armand P. Bartos. The $1,950,000 paid for the two canvasses *Two Brothers* (1905) and *Seated Harlequin* (1922) by Pablo Diego José Francisco de Paula Juan Nepomuceno Crispín Crispiano de la Santisima Trinidad Ruiz y Picasso (1881–1973) of Spain, bought by the Basle City Government from the Staechelin Foundation in Dec 1967 were more expensive if inflation is allowed for.

British and Irish

The highest price for any painting by a living United Kingdom born artist is $350,000 (*then £167,000*) for the painting *Triptych* (in memory of George Dyer) by Francis Bacon (b. Dublin, Ireland, 1909, then part of the United Kingdom) sold on 18 May 1981 at Christie's, New York City, USA.

Drawing

The highest price ever attached to any drawing is £804,361 for the cartoon *The Virgin and Child with St John the Baptist and St Anne*, measuring 54½ in × 39¼ in *137 × 100 cm*, drawn in Milan, probably in 1499–1500, by Leonardo da Vinci (1452–1519) of Italy, retained by the National Gallery, London in 1962. Three United States bids of over $4,000,000 (*then £1,428,570*) were reputed to have been made for the cartoon.

MOST PROLIFIC

Painter

Picasso was the most prolific of all painters in a career which lasted 78 years. It has been estimated that Picasso produced about 13,500 paintings or designs, 100,000 prints or engravings, 34,000 book illustrations and 300 sculptures or ceramics. His life-time *oeuvre* has been valued at £500 million. Morris Katz (b. 1932) of Greenwich Village, New York City is the most prolific painter of saleable portraits in the world. His sales total as of 21 April 1982 was 110,600. Described as the 'King of Schlock Art', he sells his paintings 'cheap and often'.

Portraitist

John A. Wismont Jr. (b. New York City, 20 Sept 1941), formerly of Disneyland, Anaheim, California, painted 45,423 water colour paintings by 1978 including 9853 in 1976.

Most repetitious painter

Antonio Bin of Paris has painted the *Mona Lisa* on some 300 occasions. These sell for up to £1000 apiece.

Oldest and youngest RA

The oldest ever Royal Academician has been (Thomas) Sidney Cooper CVO, who died on 8 Feb 1902 aged 98 yr 136 days, having exhibited 266 paintings over the record span of 69 consecutive years (1833–1902). The youngest ever RA has been Mary Moser (1744–1819) (later Mrs Hugh Lloyd), who was elected on the foundation of the Royal Academy in 1768 when aged 24.

Youngest exhibitor

The youngest ever exhibitor at the Royal Academy of Arts Annual Summer Exhibition has been Lewis Melville 'Gino' Lyons (b. 30 Apr 1962). His *Trees and Monkeys* was painted on 4 June 1965, submitted on 17 Mar 1967 and exhibited to the public on 29 Apr 1967.

Largest galleries

The world's largest art gallery is the Winter Palace and the neighbouring Hermitage in Leningrad, USSR. One has to walk 15 miles *24 km* to visit each of the 322 galleries, which house nearly 3,000,000 works of art and objects of archaeological interest. The world's largest modern art museum is the Georges Pompidou National Centre for Art and Culture, Beauborg,

Mary Cassatt (1844–1926), whose *Reading Le Figaro* was auctioned for $1,100,000 (*then £705,000*) at Christie's—the highest price ever for a female artist.

opened in Paris in 1977 with 17 700 m² *183,000 ft²* of floor space. The most heavily endowed is the J Paul Getty Museum, Malibu, California with an initial £700,000,000 in Jan 1974 and now £60 million p.a. for acquisitions. It has 38 galleries.

Finest brush

The finest standard brush sold is the 000 in Series 7 by Winsor and Newton known as a 'triple goose'. It is made of 150–200 Kolinsky sable hairs weighing 15 mg *0.000529 oz*.

MURALS

Earliest

The earliest known murals on man-made walls are the clay relief leopards at Çatal Hüyük in southern Anatolia, Turkey, discovered by James Malaart at level VII in 1961 and dating from *c.* 6200 BC.

Largest

The world's largest 'mural' was unveiled in 44 colours on the 30 storey Villa Regina condominium, Biscayne Bay, Miami, Florida on 14 Mar 1984 covering 300,000 ft² *27 870 m²*. The design of the 23 storey Vegas World hotel calls for definite murals with an area of 57,000 ft² *5295 m²*.

Largest mosaic

The world's largest mosaic is on the walls of the central library of the Universidad Nacional Autónoma de Mexico, Mexico City. There are four walls, the two largest measuring 12,949 ft² *1203 m²* each representing the pre-Hispanic past. The largest Roman mosaic in Britain is the Woodchester Pavement, Gloucestershire of *c.* AD 325, excavated in 1793, now recovered with protective earth. It measures 47 ft *14,3 m* square comprising 1½ million tesserae. A brilliant total reconstruction was carried out by Robert and John Woodward in 1973–1982.

MUSEUMS

Oldest

The oldest museum in the world is the Ashmolean Museum in

Oxford built in 1679–83. Since 1924 it has housed an exhibition of historic scientific instruments.

Largest

The largest museum in the world is the American Museum of Natural History on 77th to 81st Streets and Central Park West, New York City, NY, USA. Founded in 1874, it comprises 19 interconnected buildings with 23 acres *9 ha* of floor space. The largest museum in the United Kingdom is the British Museum (founded in 1753), which was opened to the public in 1759. The main building in Bloomsbury, London, was built in 1823 and has a total floor area of 17.57 acres *7,11 ha*. Britains' most visited museum is The Science Museum, Kensington with 4,553,550 attendances in 1982. The world's largest complex of museums is the Smithsonian Institution comprising 13 museums with 5600 employees and 24 million visitors in 1983.

'WORK OF ART'

Largest

The largest work of art ever perpetrated was the wrapping in 1983 of 11 islands in Biscayne Bay, Florida, USA in flamingo pink plastic tutus by Christo's 6,500,000 ft² *603 000 m²* work entitled 'Surrounded Islands'.

2. SCULPTURE

Earliest *World*

A piece of ox rib found in 1973 at Pech de l'Aze, Dordogne, France in an early Middle Palaeolithic layer of the Riss glaciation *c.* 105,000 BC has several engraved lines on one side, thought to be possibly intentional. A churinga or curved ivory

Korczak Ziólkowski (1908–82), who devoted his life to rock blasting a face at Mt Rushmore, South Dakota, USA, into the world's largest projected sculpturing entitled 'Crazy Horse'.

plaque rubbed with red ochre from the Middle Palaeolithic Mousterian site at Tata, Hungary has been dated to 100,000 BC by the thorium/uranium method. The earliest known example of sculpture is a 2½ in *6,3 cm* long figure of a horse carved from mammoth ivory dated to *c.* 28,000 BC and found in the Vogelherd cave in south-west Germany.

Great Britain

The earliest example of an engraving found in Britain is of a horse's head on a piece of rib-bone from Robin Hood Cave, Creswell Crag, Derbyshire. It dates from the Upper Palaeolithic period (*c.* 15,000 to 10,000 BC). The earliest Scottish rock carving from Lagalochan, Strathclyde dates from *c.* 3000 BC.

Most expensive *World and Ancient*

The highest price ever paid for a sculpture is $3,900,000 (*then* £2,400,000) paid by private treaty in London in early 1977 by J. Paul Getty's Museum in California for the 4th century BC bronze statue of a youth attributed to the school of Lysippus. It was found by fishermen on the seabed off Faro, Italy in 1963.

Living sculptor

The highest price paid for the work of a living sculptor is the $1,265,000 (*then* £702,780) given at Sotheby Parke Bernet, New York on 21 May 1982 for the 75 in *190,5 cm* long elmwood *Reclining figure* by Henry Moore, OM, CH, (b. Castleford, West Yorkshire, 30 July 1898).

Largest

The world's largest sculptures are the mounted figures of Jefferson Davis (1808–89), Gen Robert Edward Lee (1807–70) and Gen Thomas Jonathan ('Stonewall') Jackson (1824–63), covering 1.33 acres *0,5 ha* on the face of Stone Mountain, near Atlanta, Georgia. They are 90 ft *27,4 m* high. Roy Faulkner was on the mountain face for 8 years 174 days with a thermo-jet torch working with the sculptor Walker Kirtland Hancock and other helpers from 12 Sept 1963 to 3 Mar 1972. If completed the world's largest sculpture will be that of the Indian chief Tashunca-Uitco (*c.* 1849–77), known as Crazy Horse, of the Oglala tribe of the Dakota or Nadowessioux (Sioux) group. The sculpture was begun on 3 June 1948 near Mount Rushmore, South Dakota, USA. A projected 563 ft *171,6 m* high and 641 ft *195 m* long, it was the uncompleted life work of one man, Korczak Ziólkowski (1908–82). The horse's nostril is 50 ft *15,2 m* deep and 35 ft *10,7 m* in diameter. In 1983 another 200,000 tons of granite blasted off the mountain face brought the total to 7.6 million tons.

Ground figures

In the Nazca Desert, 300 km *185 miles* south of Lima, Peru there are straight lines (one more than 7 miles *11,2 km* long), geometric shapes and shapes of plants and animals drawn on the ground sometime between 100 BC and AD 600 for an uncertain but probably religious, astronomical, or even economic, purpose by a not precisely identified civilization. They were first detected from the air in *c.* 1928 and have also been described as the world's longest works of art.

Hill figures

In August 1968, a 330 ft *100 m* tall figure was found on a hill above Tarapacá, Chile.

The largest human hill carving in Britain is the 'Long Man' of Wilmington, East Sussex, 226 ft *68 m* in length. The oldest of all White Horses in Britain is the Uffington White Horse in Oxfordshire, dating from the late Iron Age (*c.* 150 BC) and measuring 374 ft *114 m* from nose to tail and 120 ft *36 m* high.

Most massive mobile

The most massive mobile is *White Cascade* weighing 8 tons/ *tonnes* and measuring 100 ft *30,48 m* from top to bottom installed on 24–25 May 1976 at the Federal Reserve Bank of Philadelphia, Pennsylvania, USA. It was designed by Alexander Calder (1898–1976), whose first mobiles were exhibited in Paris in 1932 and whose *Big Crinkley* sold for a record £555,572 at Sotheby's, New York on 10 May 1984.

3. LANGUAGE & LITERATURE

Earliest

A linguistic mutation is believed to have been the social tool which enabled hunters to become the earliest fast-learning and talkative modern humans *c.* 45,000 BC emerging from the area of Iran. The earliest written language discovered is on Yangshao culture pottery from Paa-t'o, near Xi'an (Sian) in the Shanxi (Shensi) province of China bearing proto-characters for the numbers 5, 7 and 8 and dated to 5000–4000 BC. The earliest dated tablets are from Nippur, southern Iraq from a level equivalent to Uruk V/VI and dated in 1979 to *c.* 3400 BC. Tokens or tallies from Tepe Asiab and Ganji-I-Dareh Tepe in Iran have however been dated to 8500 BC.

Oldest
The written language with the longest continuous history is Chinese extending over more than 6000 years from the Yangshao culture (see above) to the present day.

Oldest words in English
It was first suggested in 1979 that languages ancestral to English and to Latvian (both Indo-European) split *c.* 3500 BC. Research shortly to be published will indicate some words of a pre-Indo-European substrate survive in English—apple (apal), bad (bad), gold (gol) and tin (tin).

Commonest language
Today's world total of languages and dialects still spoken is about 5000 of which some 845 come from India. The language spoken by more people than any other is Northern Chinese, or Mandarin, by an estimated 68 per cent of the population, hence 695 million people in 1983. The so-called national language (*Guóyǔ*) is a standardised form of Northern Chinese (*Běifānghuà*) as spoken in the Peking area. This was alphabetised into *zhùyīn fúhào* of 37 letters in 1913 by Wa Chih-hui (1865–1953). In 1958 the *pinyin* system, which is a phonetic pronunciation guide, was introduced. The next most commonly spoken language and the most widespread is English, by an estimated 400,000,000 in mid-1981. English is spoken by 10 per cent or more of the population in 45 sovereign countries.

In Great Britain and Ireland there are six indigenous tongues: English, Cornish, Scots Gaelic, Welsh, Irish Gaelic, and Romany (Gipsy). Of these English is, of course, predominant. Mr Edward (Ned) Maddrell (1877–1974) of Glen Chass, Port St Mary, Isle of Man, died as the last islander whose professed tongue was Manx. Cornish, now happily saved, came within an ace of extinction. A dictionary was published in 1887, four years before the death of the then last fluent speaker John Davey. In the Channel Islands, apart from Jersey and Guernsey *normand*, there survive words of Sarkese or *Sèrtchais* in which the Parable of the Sower, as recited by some fishermen, was noted and published by Prince Louis Lucien Bonaparte (1813–91) in 1862.

Most complex
The following extremes of complexity have been noted: Chippewa, the North American Indian language of Minnesota, USA, has the most verb forms with up to 6000; Tillamook, the North American Indian language of Oregon, USA, has the most prefixes with 30; Tabassaran, a language in Daghestan, USSR, uses the most noun cases with 35, while Eskimaus use 63 forms of the present tense and simple nouns have as many as 252 inflections. In Chinese the 40 volume *Chung-wén Tà Tz'u-tién* dictionary lists 49,905 characters. The fourth tone of 'i' has 84 meanings, varying as widely as 'dress', 'hiccough' and 'licentious'. The written language provides 92 different characters of 'i⁴'. The most complex written character in Chinese is that representing *xiè* consisting of 64 strokes meaning 'talkative'. The most complex in current use is *yù* with 32 strokes meaning to urge or implore.

Most and least irregular verbs
Esperanto was first published by its inventor Dr Ludwig Zamenhof (1859–1917) of Warsaw in 1887 without irregular verbs and is now estimated (by text book sales) to have a million speakers. The even earlier interlanguage Volapük, invented by Johann Martin Schleyer (1831–1912), also has absolutely regular configuration. Standard Swahili though designed to be strictly regular has 3 irregular imperatives. According to *The Morphology and Syntax of Present-day English* by Prof. Olu Tomori, English has 283 irregular verbs of which 30 are merely formed with prefixes.

Rarest and commonest sounds
The rarest speech sound is probably the sound written ř in

Wa Chih-hui (1865–1953) who formulated in 1913, *zhùyīn fúhào*, the Northern Chinese world's most used alphabet of 37 letters. *below:* The earliest known writings of the—the 7000 year old Chinese markings now decoded to mean the numbers 'five', 'seven', and 'eight'.

Czech which occurs in very few languages and is the last sound mastered by Czech children. In the southern Bushman language !xo there is a click articulated with both lips, which is written ⊙. The *l* sound in the Arabic word *Allah*, in some contexts, is pronounced uniquely in that language. The commonest sound is the vowel *a* (as in the English father); no language is known to be without it.

Literature, smallest
The *Great Soviet Encyclopaedia* states that only one word of Khazar survives—*oqurüm*, meaning 'I have read'.

Vocabulary
The English language contains about 490,000 words plus another 300,000 technical terms, the most in any language, but it is doubtful if any individual uses more than 60,000. Those in Great Britain who have undergone a full 16 years of education use perhaps 5000 words in speech and up to 10,000 words in written communications. The membership of the International Society for Philosophical Enquiry (no admission for IQ's below 148) have an average vocabulary of 36,250 words.

Greatest linguist
If the yardstick of ability to speak with fluency and reasonable accuracy is adhered to, it is doubtful whether any human could maintain fluency in more than 20–25 languages concurrently or achieve fluency in more than 40 in a lifetime.

The most multi-lingual living person in the world is Georges Henri Schmidt (b. Strasbourg, France, 28 Dec 1914), the Chief of the UN Terminology Section in 1965–71. The 1975 edition of *Who's Who in the United Nations*, listed 'only' 19 languages because he was then unable to find time to 'revive' his former fluency in 12 others. Britain's greatest linguist is George Campbell (b. 9 Aug 1912), who is retired from the BBC Overseas Service where he *worked* with 54 languages.

Historically the greatest linguists have been proclaimed as Cardinal Mezzofanti (1774–1849) (fluent in 26 or 27), Professor Rask (1787–1832), Sir John Bowring (1792–1872) and Dr Harold Williams of New Zealand (1876–1928), who had been fluent in 28 languages.

ALPHABET

Earliest
The development of the use of an alphabet in place of pictograms occurred in the Sinaitic world between 1700 and 1500 BC. This western Semitic language developed the consonantal system based on phonetic and syllabic principles. The oldest letter is 'O', unchanged in shape since its adoption in the Phoenician alphabet *c.* 1300 BC. The newest letters added to the English alphabet, are 'j' and 'v' which are of post-Shakespearean use *c.* 1630. Formerly they were used only as variants of 'i' and 'u'. There are 65 alphabets now in use.

Longest and shortest
The language with most letters is Cambodian with 72 (including useless ones) and Rotokas in central Bougainville Island has least with 11 (just a, b, e, g, i, k, o, p, ř, t and u).

Most and least consonants and vowels
The language with most distinct consonantal sounds is that of

George Campbell, Britain's greatest linguist who worked with 54 languages during his time with the BBC Overseas Service.

the Ubykhs in the Caucasus, with 80–85, and that with least is Rotokas, which has only 6 consonants. The language with the most vowels is Sedang, a central Vietnamese language with 55 distinguishable vowel sounds and that with the least is the Caucasian language Abkhazian with two such. The record in written English for consecutive vowels is 6 in the musical term *euouae*. The Estonian word jäääärne, meaning the edge of the ice, has the same 4 consecutively. Voiauai, a language in Pará State, Brazil consists solely of 7 vowels. The English word 'latchstring' has 6 consecutive letters which are consonants, but the German word *Angstschweiss* has 8.

Largest letters

The largest permanent letters in the world are the giant 600 ft *183 m* letters spelling READYMIX on the ground in the Nullarbor near East Balladonia, Western Australia. This was constructed in December 1971.

Smallest Letters

The 16 letters MOLECULAR DEVICES have been etched into a salt crystal by an electron beam so that the strokes were only 2 to 3 nm (10^{-9}) wide—the width of 20 hydrogen atoms. This was done by Michael Isaacson at Cornell University, Ithaca, NY, USA in February 1982.

WORDS

Longest words *World*

The longest word ever to appear in literature occurs in *The Ecclesiazusae*, a comedy by Aristophanes (448–380 BC). In the Greek it is 170 letters long but transliterates into 182 letters in English, thus : lopadotemachoselachogaleokranioleipsanodrim-hypotrimmatosilphioparaomelitokatakechymenokichlepikoss-yphophattoperisteralektryonoptekephalliokigklopeleiolagoiosi-raiobaphetraganopterygon. The term describes a fricassee of 17 sweet and sour ingredients including mullet, brains, honey, vinegar, pickles, marrow and ouzo (a Greek drink laced with anisette).

A compound word of 195 sanskrit characters (which transliter-ates into 428 letters in the Roman alphabet) describing the region near Kanci, Tamil Nadu, India appears in a 16th century work by Tirumalāmbā, queen of Vijayanagara.

English

The longest word in the Oxford English Dictionary is floccipaucinihilipilification (alternatively spelt in hyphenated form with 'n' in seventh place), with 29 letters, meaning 'the action of estimating as worthless', first used in 1741, and later by Sir Walter Scott (1771–1832). Webster's Third International Dictionary lists among its 450,000 entries : pneumonoultramicroscopicsilicovolcanoconiosises (47 letters) the plural of a lung disease contracted by some miners.

The nonce word used by Dr Edward Strother (1675–1737) to describe the spa waters at Bristol was aequeosalinocal-calinoceraceoaluminosocupreovitriolic of 52 letters.

The longest regularly formed English word is praeterjtranssubstantiationalistically (37 letters), used by Mark McShane in his novel *Untimely Ripped*, published in 1963. The medical term hepaticocholangiocholecystenterostomies (39 letters) refers to the surgical creations of new communications between gallbladders and hepatic ducts and between intestines and gallbladders. The longest words in common use are disproportionableness and incomprehensibilities (21 letters). Interdenominationalism (22 letters) is found in Webster's Dictionary and hence perhaps interdenominationalistically (28 letters) is permissible. H W Jones of Altrincham, Cheshire has compiled 8700 lesser words from its 28 letters.

Longest palindromes

The longest known palindromic word is *saippuakivikauppias* (19 letters), the Finnish word for a dealer in lye (*i.e.* caustic soda). The longest in the English language is *redivider* (9 letters). The nine-letter word, *Malayalam*, is a proper noun given to the language of the Malayali people in Kerala, southern India while *Kanakanak* near Dillingham, Alaska is a 9 lettered palindromic place-name. The contrived chemical term *detartrated* has 11 letters. Some baptismal fonts in Greece and Turkey bear the circular 25 letter inscription NIΨON AN-OMHMATA MH MONAN OΨIN meaning 'wash (my) sins not only (my) face'. This appears at St Mary's Church, Nottingham, St Paul's, Woldingham, Surrey and other churches. The longest palindromic composition devised is one of 65,000 words completed by Edward Benbow of Bewdley, Hereford & Worcs. in Jan 1983. It begins 'Rae hits Eb, sire . . . .' and hence predictably ends '. . . . Beer is best, I hear . . . .'

Longest scientific name

The systematic name for deoxyribonucleicacid of the human mitochondria, contains 16,569 nucleotide residues and is thus *c.* 207,000 letters long. It was published in key form in *Nature* on 9 Apr 1981.

Longest anagrams

The longest non-scientific English words which can form anagrams are the 18-letter transpositions 'conservationalists' and 'conversationalists'. The longest scientific transposals are cholecystoduodenostomy/duodenocholecystostomy and hy-dropneumopericardium/pneumohydropericardium each of 22 letters.

In his research into anagrams A. J. Capper has found only one 4 letter word with 13 and one 5 letter word with 28 anagrams—these are 'aber' and 'aster'.

Longest abbreviation

The longest known abbreviation is S.K.O.M.K.H.P.K.J.C.D.P.W.B., the initials of the Syarikat Kerjasama Orang-orang Melayu Kerajaan Hilir Perak Kerana Jimat Cermat Dan Pinjam-meminjam Wang Berhad. This is the Malay name for The Cooperative Company of the Lower State of Perak Govern-ment's Malay People for Money Savings and Loans Ltd., in Teluk Anson, Perak, West Malaysia (formerly Malaya). The abbreviation for this abbreviation is Skomk. The 55-letter full name of Los Angeles (El Pueblo de Nuestra Señora la Reina de los Angeles de Porciuncula) is abbreviated to LA or 3.63 per cent of its length.

Longest Acronym

The longest acronym is NIIOMTPLABOPARMBETZHELBETRABS-BOMONIMONKONOTDTEKHSTROMONT with 56 letters (54 in cyrillic) in the *Concise Dictionary of Soviet Terminology* meaning : The laboratory for shuttering, reinforcement, concrete and ferroconcrete operations for composite-mono-lithic and monolithic constructions of the Department of the Technology of Building—assembly operations the Scientific Research Institute of the Organisation for building mechani-sation and technical aid of the Academy of Building and Architecture of the USSR.

Commonest words and letters

In written English the most frequently used words are in order : the, of, and, to, a, in, that, is, I, it, for *and* as. The most used in conversation is I. The commonest letter is 'e' and the commonest initial letter is 'T'.

WORLD'S LONGEST WORDS

Japanese[1]	Chi-n-chi-ku-ri-n (12 letters) —a very short person (slang)	Icelandic	Hæstaréttarmálaflutningsmaður (29 letters) —supreme court barrister
Spanish	Suberextraordinarisimo (22 letters) —extraordinary	Russian	ryentgyenoelyektrokardiografichyeskogo (33 Cyrillic letters, transliterating as 38) —of the radioelectrocardiographic.
French	Anticonstitutionnellement (25 letters) —anticonstitutionally. Anthropoclimatologiquement[2] (26 letters) —anthropoclimatologically	Hungarian	Megszentségtelenithetetlenségeskedéseitekért (44 letters) —for your unprofaneable actions.
		Turkish[5]	Cekoslovakyalilastiramadiklarimizdanmiymissiniz (47 letters) —'are you not of that group of persons that we were said to be unable to Czechoslovakianise?
Croatian	Prijestolonasijednikovica (25 letters) —wife of an heir apparent.	Dutch	Kindercarnavalsoptochtvoorbereidingswerkzaamheden (49 letters) —preparation activities for a children's carnival procession
Italian	Precipitevolissimevolmente (26 letters) —as fast as possible.	Mohawk[3]	tkanuhstasrihsranuhwe'tsraaksahsrakaratattsrayeri' (50 letters) —the praising of the evil of the liking of the finding of the house is right.
Portuguese	inconstitucionalissimamente (27 letters) —with the highest degree of unconstitutionality.		
German[4,5]	Donaudampfschiffahrtselectrizitaetenhauptbetriebswerkbauunterbeamtengesellschaft (81 letters) —The club for subordinate officials of the head office management of the Danube steamboat electrical services (Name of a pre-war club in Vienna).		
Swedish[5]	Spårvagnsaktiebolagsskensmutsskjutarefackföreningspersonalbeklädnadsmagasinsförrådsförvaltaren (94 letters) —Manager of the depot for the supply of uniforms to the personnel of the track cleaners' union of the tramway company.		

[1] Patent applications sometimes harbour long compound 'words'. An extreme example is one of 13 kana which transliterates to the 40 letter Kyūkitsürohekimenfuchakunenryōsekisanryō meaning 'the accumulated amount of fuel condensed on the wall face of the air intake passage'.

[2] Not accepted by *savants* to be an acceptable French word.

[3] Lengthy concatenations are a feature of Mohawk. Above is an example.

[4] The longest dictionary word in every day usage is Kraftfahrzeugreparaturwerkstätten (33 letters or 34 if the ä is written as ae) meaning motor vehicle repair shops (or service garages).

[5] Agglutinative words not found in standard dictionaries.

Most meanings

The most over-worked word in English is the word *set* which has 58 noun uses, 126 verbal uses and 10 as a participial adjective.

Most succinct word

The most challenging word for any lexicographer to define briefly is the Fuegian (southernmost Argentina and Chile) word 'mamihlapinatapai' meaning 'looking at each other hoping that either will offer to do something which both parties desire but are unwilling to do'.

Most synonyms

The condition of being inebriated has more synonyms than any other condition or object. Delacourt Press of New York City, USA has published a selection of 1224 from 2241 compiled by Paul Dickson of Garrett Park, Maryland, USA.

Most homophones

The most homophonous sounds in English are *air* and *sol* which, according to the researches of Dora Newhouse of Los Angeles, both have 38 homophones. The homonym with most variant spellings is *Air* with Aire, are, Ayer, Ayr, Ayre, err, e'er, ere, eyre and heir.

Most accents

Accents were introduced in French in the reign of Louis XIII (1601–43). The word with most accents is *hétérogénéité*, meaning heterogeneity. An atoll in the Pacific Ocean 320 miles *516 km* east-south-east of Tahiti is named Héréhérétué. An example of a Hungarian word with 6 accents is újjáépítésére meaning 'for its reconstruction'.

Shortest holoalphabetic sentence

The contrived headline describing the escape from shipboard confinement of a wryneck bird from the valley kibbutz (designated by the Hebrew letter qoph) might read 'Cwm kvutza qoph jynx fled brigs' representing the ultimate in 26 letter sentences containing all 26 letters. This was devised by Greg and Peter Maggs of Urbana, Illinois, USA with the aid of 3 computers.

PERSONAL NAMES

Earliest

The earliest personal name which has survived is seemingly that of a predynastic king of Upper Egypt *ante* 3050 BC, who is indicated by the hieroglyphic sign for a scorpion. It has been suggested that the name should be read as Sekhen. The earliest known name of any resident of Britain is Divitiacus, King of the Suessiones, the Gaulish ruler of the Kent area *c.* 100 BC under the name Prydhain. Scotland, unlike England, was never fully conquered by the Roman occupiers (AD 43–410). Calgācus (b. *c.* AD 40), who led the final resistance in Scotland was the earliest native whose name has been recorded.

Longest pedigree

The only non-Royal English pedigree that can with certainty show a clear pre-Conquest descent is that of the Arden family. Shakespeare's mother was a Mary Arden. It is claimed on behalf of the Clan Mackay that their clan can be traced to Loarn, the Irish invader of south west Pictland, now Argyll, *c.* AD 501.

Longest single name

The longest Christian or given name on record is one of 622 letters given by Mr Scott Roaul Sör-Lökken of Missoula, Montana, USA to his daughter Miss S. Ellen Georgianna Sör Lökken (b. 1979). The 'S' stands for a 598 letter name designed to throw a monkey wrench into the computers of federal bureaucracy. She is known as 'Snow Owl' for short or 'Oli' for shorter.

Longest surname *World*

The longest name used by anyone is Adolph Blaine Charles David Earl Frederick Gerald Hubert Irvin John Kenneth Lloyd Martin Nero Oliver Paul Quincy Randolph Sherman Thomas Uncas Victor William Xerxes Yancy Zeus Wolfeschlegelsteinhausenbergerdorff, Senior, who was born at Bergedorf, near Hamburg, Germany, on 29 Feb 1904. On printed forms he uses only his eighth and second Christian names and the first 35 letters of his surname. The full version of the name of 590 letters appeared in the 12th edition of *The Guinness Book of Records*. He now lives in Philadelphia, Pennsylvania, USA, and has shortened his surname to Mr Wolfe + 585, Senior.

United Kingdom

The longest surname in the United Kingdom was the six-barrelled one borne by the late Major L.S.D.O.F. (Leone Sextus Denys Oswolf Fraudatifilius) Tollemache-Tollemache-de Orellana-Plantagenet-Tollemache-Tollemache, who was born on 12 June 1884 and died of pneumonia in France on 20 Feb 1917. Of non-repetitious surnames, the last example of a five-barrelled one was that of the Lady Caroline Jemima Temple-Nugent-Chandos-Brydges-Grenville (1858–1946). The longest single English surname is Featherstonehaugh (17 letters), correctly pronounced on occasions (but improbably

Lady Home of the Hirsel who, despite being married to the same man, had to change her name 4 times.

on the correct occasion) Featherstonehaw or Festonhaw or Fessonhay or Freestonhugh or Feerstonhaw or Fanshaw.

Scotland

In Scotland the surname nin (feminine of mac) Achinmacdholicachinskerray (29 letters) was recorded in an 18th century parish register.

Most Christian names

The great-great-grandson of Carlos III of Spain, Don Alfonso de Borbón y Borbón (1866–1934) had 94 Christian names of which several were lengthened by hyphenation.

Shortest

The commonest single-letter surname is O, prevalent in Korea, but with 52 examples in US phone books (1973–81) and 12 in Belgium. This name causes most distress to those concerned with the prevention of cruelty to computers. Every other letter, except Q, has been traced in US phone books (used as a surname) by A. Ross Eckler. There are two one-lettered Burmese names E (calm), pronounced aye and U (egg), pronounced Oo. U *before* the name means 'uncle'. There exist among the 47,000,000 names on the Dept. of Health & Social Security index 6 examples of a one-lettered surname. Their identity has not been disclosed, but they are 'A', 'B', 'J', 'N', 'O' and 'X'. Two-letter British surnames include By and On and have recently been joined by Oy, Za and others. The Christian name 'A' has been used for 5 generations in the Lincoln Taber family of Fingringhoe, Essex.

Commonest family name *World*

The commonest family name in the world is the Chinese name Chang which is borne, according to estimates, by between 9.7 and 12.1 per cent of the Chinese population, so indicating even on the lower estimate that there are at least some 104 million Changs—more than the entire population of all but 7 of the 168 other sovereign countries of the world.

English

The commonest surname in the English-speaking world is Smith. The most recent published count showed 659,050 nationally insured Smiths in Great Britain, of whom 10,102 were plain John Smith and another 19,502 were John (plus one or more given names) Smith. Including uninsured persons there were over 800,000 Smiths in England and Wales alone, of whom 81,493 were called A. Smith. There were an estimated 2,382,509 Smiths in the USA in 1973.

'Macs'

There are, however, estimated to be 1,600,000 persons in Britain with M', Mc or Mac (Gaelic genitive of 'son') as part of their surnames. The commonest of these is Macdonald which accounts for about 55,000 of the Scottish population.

Commonest Christian name

From the latest available full year (1982) birth registrations for England and Wales at the General Register Office at St Catherine's House, Kingsway, London, the most favoured first forename choice of parents from the classless 1.44% sample of the 9021 entries bearing the (easily) commonest surname of Smith are boys Christopher, well ahead of Andrew, Matthew, Paul and Michael, and girls Sarah, just ahead of Rebecca and Emma, followed by Gemma and Laura. This survey was carried out by C. V. Appleton. From 1196 to at least 1925 William and John were first and second.

Most versions

Mr Edward A. Nedelcov of Regina, Saskatchewan, Canada has collected 924 versions of the spelling of his family name since January 1960. Mzilikazi of Zululand (b. *c.* 1795) had his name chronicled in 325 spellings, according to researches by Dr R. Kent Rasmussen.

Most Changed

Excluding members of the royal family the living monogamous woman who has most times changed her name is Lady Home of the Hirsel formerly Lady Douglass-Home; Countess of Home; Lady Dunglass and originally Miss Elizabeth Alington.

Most contrived name

In the United States the determination to derive commercial or other benefit from being the last listing in the local telephone book has resulted in self-given names, starting with up to 9 z's—an extreme example being Zachary Zzzzzzzzzra in the San Francisco book. The U.K. record for terminality at Zz demonstrates admirable British restraint. The alpha and omega of Britain's 82 directories are Mrs Maude E. Aab of Hull, Humberside and Mr P. B. Zzytt of Wells, Somerset. In 1929 the Registrar-General recorded the death of a Jokine Zzuppichine of Liverpool aged 68.

PLACE-NAMES

Earliest

The world's earliest place names are pre-Sumerian but have not yet been deciphered. The earliest recorded British place-name is Belerion, the Penwith peninsula of Cornwall, referred to as such by Pytheas of Massilia in *c.* 308 BC. The name Salakee on St Mary's, Isles of Scilly is however arguably of a pre Indo-European substrate meaning *tin island.* There are reasons to contend that Leicester (Roman, Ligora Castrum) contains an element reflecting its founding by the Western Mediterranean navigators, the Ligurians, as early as *c.* 1200 BC. The earliest distinctive name for what is now Great Britain was Albion by Himilco *c.* 500 BC. The oldest name among England's 46 counties is Kent, first mentioned in its Roman form of Cantium (from the Celtic *canto,* meaning a rim, *i.e.* a coastal district) from the same circumnavigation by Pytheas. The earliest mention of England is the form *Angelcymn,* which appeared in the Anglo-Saxon Chronicle in AD. 880.

Longest *World*

The official name for Bangkok, the capital city of Thailand, is Krungtep Mahanakhon. The full name is however: Krungthep Mahanakhon Bovorn Ratanakosin Mahintharayutthaya Mahadilokpop Noparatratchathani Burirom Udomratchanivetmahasathan Amornpiman Avatarnsathit Sakkathattiyavisnukarmprasit (167 letters) which in its most scholarly transliteration emerges with 175 letters. The longest place-name now in use in the world is Taumatawhakatangihangakoauauotamatea(turipukakapikimaungahoronuku)pokaiwhenuakitanatahu, the unofficial 85-letter version of the name of a hill (1002 ft *305 m* above sea-level) in the Southern Hawke's Bay district of North Island, New Zealand. This Maori name means 'the hill whereon was played the flute of Tamatea, circumnavigator of lands, for his lady love'. The official version has 57 letters (1 to 36 and 65 to 85). Ijouaououene, a mountain in Morocco, has 8 consecutive vowel letters as rendered by the French.

Great Britain

The longest place-name in the United Kingdom is the concocted 58-letter name Llanfairpwllgwyngyllgogerychwyrndrobwllllantysiliogogogoch, which is translated: 'St Mary's Church by the pool of the white hazel trees, near the rapid

whirlpool, by the red cave of the Church of St Tysilio'. This is the name used for the reopened (April 1973) village railway station in Anglesey, Gwynedd, Wales, but the *official* name consists of only the first 20 letters of what the Welsh would regard as a 51 letter word since 'll' and 'ch' may be regarded as one. The longest Welsh place-names listed in the Ordnance Survey Gazetteer are Lower Llanfihangel-y-Creuddyn (26 letters), a village near Aberystwyth, Dyfed, and Llansantffraid Cwmdeuddwr (24 letters), Powys.

England
The longest single-word (unhyphenated) place-name in England is Blakehopeburnhaugh, a hamlet between Byrness and Rochester in Northumberland, of 18 letters. The nearby Cottonshopeburnfoot (19 letters) is locally rendered as one word though not by the Ordnance Survey. The hyphenated Sutton-under-Whitestonecliffe, North Yorkshire has 27 letters on the Ordnance Survey but with the insertion of 'the' and the dropping of the final 'e' 29 letters in the Post Office List. The longest parish name is Saint Mary le More and All Hallows with Saint Leonard and Saint Peter, Wallingford (68 letters) in Oxfordshire formed on 5 Apr 1971.

Scotland
The longest single-word place-name in Scotland is Coignafeuinternich in Inverness-shire. Kirkcudbrightshire (also 18 letters) became merged into Dumfries and Galloway on 16 May 1975. A 12-acre *5 ha* loch 9 miles *14 km* west of Stornoway on Lewis, Western Isles is named Loch Airidh Mhic Fhionnlaidh Dhuibh (31 letters).

Ireland
The longest place-name in Ireland is Muckanaghederdauhaulia (22 letters), 4 miles *6 km* from Costello in Camus Bay, County Galway. The name means 'soft place between two seas'.

Shortest
The shortest place names in the world are the French village of Y (population 143), so named since 1241, the Danish village Å on the island Fyn, the Norwegian village of Å (pronounced 'Aw'), the Swedish place Å in Vikholandet, U in the Caroline Islands, Pacific Ocean; and the Japanese town of Sosei which is alternatively called Aioi or O. There was once a '6' in West Virginia, USA. The shortest place-names in Great Britain are the two-lettered places of Ae (population 199 in 1961) Dumfries and Galloway; Oa on the island of Islay, Strathclyde and Bu on Wyre, Orkney Islands. In the Shetland Islands there are skerries called Ve and two stacks called Aa. The island of Iona was originally I. The River E flows into the southern end of Loch Mhór, Invernessshire, and O Brook flows on Dartmoor, Devon. The shortest place-name in Ireland is Ta (or Lady's Island) Lough, a sea-inlet on the coast of County Wexford. Tievelough, in County Donegal, is also called Ea.

Most spellings
The spelling of the Dutch town of Leeuwarden has been recorded in 225 versions since AD 1046. The Cambridgeshire village of Gamlingay is recorded in 110 other spellings since the Gamelinge or Gamelingei of the Doomsday Book in 1086.

PRINTED TEXTS AND BOOKS
Oldest printed
The oldest surviving printed work is a Korean scroll or *sutra* from wooden printing blocks found in the foundations of the Pulguk Sa pagoda, Kyongju, Korea, on 14 Oct 1966. It has been dated no later than AD 704. It was claimed in November 1973 that a 28-page book of Tang dynasty poems at Yonsei University, Korea was printed from metal type *c.* 1160.

Oldest mechanically printed
It is widely accepted that the earliest mechanically printed full length book was the 42-line Gutenberg Bible, printed at Mainz, Germany, in *c.* 1454 by Johann Henne zum Gensfleisch zur Laden, called 'zu Gutenberg' (*c.* 1398–*c.* 1468). Work on water marks published in 1967 indicates a copy of a surviving printed 'Donatus' Latin grammar was made from paper in *c.* 1450. The earliest exactly dated printed work is the Psalter completed on 14 Aug 1457 by Johann Fust (*c.* 1400–66) and Peter Schöffer (1425–1502), who had been Gutenberg's chief assistant. The earliest printing by William Caxton (*c.* 1422–1491) though undated would appear to be *The Recuyel of the Historyes of Troye* in late 1473 to spring 1474.

Largest *Book*
The largest book in the world is the *Super Book* measuring 9 ft × 10 ft 2⅛ in *2,74 × 3,07 m* weighing 557 lb *252,6 kg* consisting of 300 pages published in Denver, Colorado, USA in 1976.

Publication
The largest publication in the world is the 1112 volume set of *British Parliamentary Papers* published by the Irish University Press in 1968–72. A complete set weighs 3¼ tons *3,3 tonnes*, costs £32,804 and would take 6 years to read at 10 hours per day. The production involved the death of 34,000 Indian goats, and the use of £15,000 worth of gold ingots. The total print is 500 sets.

Dictionary
Deutches Wörterbuch started by Jacob and Wilhelm Grimm in 1854 was completed in 34,519 pages and 33 volumes in 1971. Today's price is DM5456.97 (*now* £1428). The largest English language dictionary is the 12-volume Royal quarto *The Oxford English Dictionary* of 15,487 pages published between 1884 and 1928 with a first supplement of 963 pages in 1933. Of the 4-volume supplement, edited by R. W. Burchfield, the final (Se-Z) volume and the Bibliography are due to appear in 1985. The work contains 414,825 words, 1,827,306 illustrative quotations and reputedly 227,779,589 letters and figures, 63.8 times more than the Bible. The greatest outside contributor has been Marghanita Laski with 175,000 quotations since 1958.

The New Grove Dictionary of Music and Musicians (Editor: Stanley Sadie) published in 20 volumes by Macmillan's in February 1981 contains over 22 million words and 4500 illustrations and is the largest specialist dictionary yet published.

Smallest book
The smallest marketed bound printed book with cursive material is one of 20 pages measuring 1,4 × 1,4 mm $\frac{1}{18}$ × $\frac{1}{18}$ *in*, comprising the children's story 'Ari' (the ant) made by Asao Hoshio in Tokyo, Japan and published in 200 copies in June 1980. Toppan Printing Co of Tokyo, Japan also published a bound edition of 'The Lord's Prayer' with letters 70 microns high and measuring 1,4 mm square on 2 Apr 1981.

Longest novel
The longest important novel ever published is *Les hommes de bonne volonté* by Louis Henri Jean Farigoule (b. 26 Aug 1885), *alius* Jules Romains, of France, in 27 volumes in 1932–46. The English version *Men of Good Will* was published in 14 volumes in 1933–46 as a 'novel-cycle'. The 4959 page edition published by Peter Davies Ltd has an estimated 2,070,000 words excluding a 100 page index. The novel *Tokuga-Wa Ieyasu* by Sohachi Yamaoka has been serialised in Japanese daily newspapers since 1951. Now completed it will require nearly 40 volumes in book form.

Encyclopaedias *Earliest*
The earliest known encyclopaedia was compiled by Speusippus (*post* 408–*c.* 338 BC) a nephew of Plato, in Athens *c.* 370 BC. The earliest encyclopaedia compiled by a Briton was *Liber exerptionum* by the Scottish monk Richard (d. 1173) at St Victor's Abbey, Paris *c.* 1140.

Largest
The largest encyclopaedia is *La Enciclopedia Universal Ilustrada Europeo-Americana* (J. Espasa & Sons, Madrid and Barcelona) totalling 105,000 pages and an annual supplement since 1935 comprising 165,200,000 words. The number of volumes in the set in August 1983 was 104, and the price is $2325 (£1660).

Most comprehensive
The most comprehensive English language encyclopaedia is the *Encyclopaedia Britannica*, first published in Edinburgh, Scotland, in December 1768–1771. A group of booksellers in the United States acquired reprint rights in 1898 and completed ownership in 1899. In 1943 the *Britannica* was given to the University of Chicago, Illinois, USA. The current 30-volume 15th edition contains 33,141 pages and 43,000,000 words from 4277 contributors. It is now edited in Chicago and in London.

Longest index
The Tenth Collective Index of *Chemical Abstracts* completed in June 1983 contains 23,948,253 entries in 131,445 pages and 75 volumes, and weighs 380 lb *172,3 kg*.

The world's longest index, that of the *Chemical Abstracts*, comprising 75 volumes standing 14½ ft *4,4 m* high, and weighing 380 lb *172,3 kg*.

Maps *Oldest*

The oldest known map of any kind is a clay tablet depicting the river Euphrates flowing through northern Mesopotamia, Iraq, dated *c.* 3800 BC. The earliest surviving product of English map-making is the Anglo Saxon *mappa mundi*, known as the Cottonian manuscript from the late 10th century. The earliest printed map in the world is one of western China dated to 1115. The earliest printed map of Britain was Ptolemy's outline printed in Bologna, Italy in 1477.

Most expensive work of art

The highest price paid for any book or any work of art was £8,140,000 for the 226 leaf *The Gospel Book of Henry the Lion, Duke of Saxony* at Sotheby's, London on 6 Dec. 1983. The book, 13½ × 10 in *34,3 × 25,4 cm*, was illuminated by the monk Herimann in *c.* 1170 at Helmershansen Abbey with 41 full page illustrations, and was bought by Hans Kraus for the Hermann Abs consortium.

Printed Book

The highest price ever paid for a printed book is $2,400,000 (*then £1,265,000*) for one of the only 21 complete known copies of the Gutenberg Bible, printed in Mainz, W. Germany in *c.* 1454. It was bought from the Carl and Lily Pforzheimer Foundation by Texas University in a sale arranged by Quaritch of London in New York on 9 June 1978.

Broadsheet

The highest price ever paid for a broadsheet has been $412,500 (*then £264,500*) for one of the 22 known copies of *The Declaration of Independence*, printed in Philadelphia in 1776 by Samuel T. Freeman & Co, and sold to the Chapin Library, Williams College, Williamstown, Massachusetts, USA at Christie's, New York City on 22 Apr 1983.

Manuscripts

The highest price ever paid for a complete manuscript is £2.2 million by Armand Hammer at Christie's, London on 12 Dec 1980 for Leonardo da Vinci's 36-page Codex Leicester illustrated manuscript on cosmology compiled in *c.* 1507. It was sold by the trustees of the Holkham estate.

The auction record for a musical manuscript is £330,000 for *The Rite of Spring* by Igor F. Stravinsky (1882–1971), by Otto Haas for the Paul Sacher Collection in Basel, Switzerland at Sotheby's, London on 11 Nov 1982.

Atlas

The highest price paid for an atlas is £340,000 for a Gerardus Mercator atlas of *c.* 1571 of Europe, sold at Sotheby's, London, on 13 Mar 1979.

BIBLE

Oldest

The oldest leather and papyrus Dead Sea Scrolls were discovered in Cave 4 near Qumran in 1952. They comprise fragments of Exodus and Samuel I dating to *c.* 225–200 BC. The oldest known bible is the *Codex Vaticanus* written in Greek *ante* AD 350 and preserved in the Vatican Museum, Rome. The earliest complete Bible *printed* in English was one edited by Miles Coverdale, Bishop of Exeter (*c.* 1488–1569), while living in Antwerp, and printed in 1535. William Tyndale's New Testament in English had, however, been printed in Cologne and in Worms, Germany in 1525 while John Wycliffe's first manuscript translation dates from 1382.

Longest and shortest books

The longest book in the Authorized version of the Bible is the Book of Psalms, while the longest book including prose is the Book of the Prophet Isaiah, with 66 chapters. The shortest is the Third Epistle of John, with 294 words in 14 verses. The Second Epistle of John has only 13 verses but 298 words.

Longest and shortest psalm and verse

Of the 150 Psalms, the longest is the 119th, with 176 verses, and the shortest is the 117th, with two verses. The shortest verse in the Authorised Version (King James) of the Bible is verse 35 of Chapter XI of the Gospel according to St. John, consisting of the two words 'Jesus wept'. The longest is verse 9 of Chapter VIII of the Book of Esther, which extends to a 90-word description of the Persian empire.

Total letters and words, longest name

The total number of letters in the Bible is 3,566,480. The total number of words depends on the method of counting hyphenated words, but is usually given as between 773,692 and 773,746. The word 'and' according to Colin McKay Wilson of the Salvation Army appears 46,227 times. The longest personal name in the Bible is the 18 letter Maher-shalal-hash-baz, the symbolic name of the second son of Isaiah (Isaiah, Chapter VIII, verses 1 and 3). The caption of Psalm 22, however, contains a Hebrew title sometimes rendered Al-'Ayyeleth Hash-Shahar (20 letters).

DIARIES AND LETTERS

Longest diary

The diary of Edward Robb Ellis (b. 1911) of New York City begun in 1927 is estimated after 55 years to run to 15 million words. The diary of T. C. Baskerville of Chorlton-cum-Hardy, Manchester, maintained since 1939 comprises an estimated 5,000,000 words. Col Ernest Loftus CBE of Harare, Zimbabwe began his daily diary on 4 May 1896 at the age of 12 and has thus completed 88 years.

Letters Longest

The longest personal letter based on a word count is one of 1,401,000 words written in 44 months between 1 Oct 1978 and 31 May 1982 by Bruce Anders during US Naval Service, to Cathleen L. Howald of Fairbanks, Alaska, USA.

To an editor *Longest*

The Upper Dauphin Sentinel of Pennsylvania, USA published a letter of 25,513 words over 8 issues from August to November 1979, written by John Sultzbaugh of Lykens, Pennsylvania.

Most

David Green of Castle Morris, Dyfed has had 99 letters published in the main correspondence section of *The Times* by August 1983.

Shortest

The shortest correspondence on record was that between Victor Marie Hugo (1802–85) and his publisher Hurst and Blackett in 1862. The author was on holiday and anxious to know how his new novel *Les Misérables* was selling. He wrote '?'. The reply was '!'.

The shortest letter to the London *Times* was a two word answer by J. F. Q. Switzer on 18 Dec 1979 to an enquiry as to why Sir Barnes Wallis used bouncing bombs instead of torpedoes to breach the Mohne Dam, Germany. It read, 'Sir, Torpedo ncts'.

Most personal mail

The highest confirmed mail received by any private citizen in a year is 900,000 letters by the baseball star Hank Aaron reported by the US Postal Department in June 1974. About a third were letters of hate engendered by his bettering of 'Babe' Ruth's career record for 'home runs' set in 1927. (See Chap. 12.)

Pen pals most durable

The longest sustained correspondence on record is one of 75 years from 11 Nov 1904 between Mrs Ida McDougall of Tasmania, Australia and Miss R. Norton of Sevenoaks, Kent until Mrs McDougall's death on 24 Dec 1979.

Birthday card—most parsimonious

Mrs Amelia Finch (b. 18 Apr 1912) of Lakehurst, New Jersey, USA and Mr Paul E. Warburgh (b. 1 Feb 1902) of Huntington, New York have been exchanging the same card since 1 Feb 1927.

Christmas cards

The greatest number of personal Christmas cards sent out is believed to be 62,824 by Mrs Werner Erhard of San Francisco, California in December 1975. Many must have been to unilateral acquaintances. The earliest known Christmas card was sent out by Sir Henry Cole (1808–82) in 1843 but did not become an annual ritual until 1862.

AUTOGRAPHS AND SIGNATURES

Earliest

The earliest surviving examples of an auto-graph are those made by scribes on cuneiform clay tablets from Tell Abu Şalābīkh, Iraq dated to the early Dynastic III A *c.* 2600 BC. A

The world's oldest autograph—that of the Sumerian scribe, Adu, on a clay tablet made in Iraq *c.* 2600 BC (*Oriental Institute, University of Chicago*).

scribe named 'a-du' has added 'dub-sar' after his name thus translated 'Adu, scribe'. The earliest surviving signature on a papyrus is that of the scribe Amen-'aa dated to the Egyptian middle kingdom which began in *c.* 2130 BC and which is in the Leningrad Museum, USSR. A signum exists for William I (the Conqueror) *c.* 1070. The earliest English sovereign whose handwriting is known to have survived is Edward III (1327–77). The earliest full signature extant is that of Richard II (dated 26 July 1386).

The world's oldest autograph made on papyrus written by the Egyptian scribe Amen'aa some 500 years later than Adu's cuneiform tablet shown above. It is in the Leningrad Museum, USSR. (*Dr Ragab's Papyrus Institute*).

The most expensive work of art ever, *The Gospel Book of Henry the Lion, Duke of Saxony* which realised £8,140,000 on 6 Dec 1983 at Sotheby's, London.

The Magna Carta does not bear even the mark of King John (reigned 1199–1216), but carries only his seal affixed on 19 June 1215.

Most expensive

The highest price ever paid on the open market for a single autograph letter signed is $100,000 (*then* £45,500), paid on 18 Oct 1979 at a Charles Hamilton auction in New York City for a brief receipt signed by the Gloucestershire-born Button Gwinnett (1732–77), one of the 56 signatories of the United States' Declaration of Independence of 1776.

The highest price paid for a signed autograph letter of a living person is $12,500 (*then* £5430) at the Hamilton Galleries on 22 Jan 1981 for a letter from President Ronald Reagan praising Frank Sinatra.

A record $4250 (*then* £2500) was paid at a Hamilton sale on 12 Aug 1982 by Barry D Hoffman for the signed portrait of Al Capone (1899–1947).

Most valuable

Only one example of the signature of Christopher Marlowe (1564–93) is known. It is in the Kent County Archives on a Will of 1583. It is estimated that a seventh Shakespearean signature would realise at least £1 million at auction.

AUTHORS

Most prolific

The most prolific writer for whom a word count has been published was Charles Hamilton, *alias* Frank Richards (1875–1961), the Englishman who created Billy Bunter. At his height in 1908 he wrote the whole of the boys' comics *Gem* (founded 1907) and *Magnet* (1908–40) and most of two others, totalling 80,000 words a week. His lifetime output has been put at 100,000,000 words. He enjoyed the advantages of the use of electric light rather than candlelight and of being unmarried. The champion of the goose quill era was Józef Ignacy Kraszewski (1812–87) of Poland who produced more than 600 volumes of novels and historical works.

Soho Tokutomi (1863–1957) wrote the history *Kinsei Nippon Kokuminshi* in 100 volumes of 429,425 pages and 19,452,952 letters in 35 years.

Most novels

The greatest number of novels published by an authoress is 904 by Kathleen Lindsay (Mrs Mary Faulkner) (1903–73) of Somerset West, Cape Province, South Africa. She wrote under two other married names and 8 pen names. Baboorao Arnalkar (b. 9 June 1907) of Maharashtra State, India between 1936 and 1984 has published 1092 short mystery stories in book form and several non-fiction books.

After receiving a probable record 743 rejection slips the British novelist John Creasey MBE (1908–73), under his own name and 25 *noms de plume* had 564 books totalling more than 40,000,000 words published from 1932 to his death on 9 June 1973. The British authoress with the greatest total of full-length titles is Miss Ursula Harvey Bloom (b. Chelmsford, Essex 1892) (Mrs A. C. G. Robinson, formerly Mrs Denham-Cookes), who reached 500 by December 1975, starting in 1924 with *The Great Beginning* and including the best sellers *The Ring Tree* (novel) and *The Rose of Norfolk* (non-fiction). Enid Mary Blyton (1898–1968) (Mrs Darrell Waters) completed 600 titles of children's stories, many of them brief, with 59 in the single year 1955. She was translated into a record 128 languages.

Most text books

Britain's most successful writer of text books is the ex-schoolmaster Ronald Ridout (b. 23 July 1916) who between 1948 and April 1984 had 468 titles published with sales of 81,710,000. His *The First English Workbook* has sold 5,004,000.

The annual aggregate sales of all titles by Louis Alexander of Haslemere, Surrey, reached 4,573,000 in the year 1977.

Highest paid

In 1958 Mrs Deborah Schneider of Minneapolis, Minnesota, USA, wrote 25 words to complete a sentence in a competition for the best blurb for Plymouth cars. She won from about 1,400,000 entrants the prize of $500 (*then* £178) every month for life. On normal life expectations she would have collected $12,000 (£4285) per word. No known anthology includes Mrs Schneider's deathless prose but it is in her deed box at her bank 'Only to be opened after death'. She passed $6000 a word by 1983.

Greatest Advance

The greatest advances paid for any book is an amount in excess of £3 million for Frederick Forsyth's seventh novel *The Fourth Protocol*.

Top selling

It was announced on 13 Mar 1953 that 672,058,000 copies of the works of Generalissimo Stalin (born Yózef Vissarionovich Dzhugashvili) (1879–1953), had been sold or distributed in 101 languages.

The all-time estimate of book sales by Erle Stanley Gardner (1889–1970) (US) to 1 Jan 1984 were 317,076,968 copies in 37 languages. The top selling authoress has been Dame Agatha Christie (*née* Miller) (later Lady Mallowan) (1890–1976) whose 87 crime novels sold an estimated 300,000,000 in 103 languages. *Sleeping Murder* was published posthumously in 1977. Currently the top-selling authoress is Barbara Cartland (Mrs McCorquodale) with global sales of 370,000,000 for 373 titles in 17 languages. In 1977, 1980 and 1981 she published 24 titles in the calendar year.

Longest Biography

The longest biography in publishing history is that of Sir Winston Churchill by his son Randolph (4832 pages) and Martin Gilbert (12,480 pages) to date comprising some 7,620,000 words.

Most rejections

The greatest recorded number of publisher's rejections for a manuscript is 190 for his 130,000 word manuscript *World Government Crusade* written in 1966 by Gilbert Young (b. 1906) of Bath, England. The record for rejections before publication (and wide acclaim) is 69 from 55 publishers by Prof. Steven Goldberg's *The Inevitability of Patriarchy*.

Oldest authoress

The oldest authoress in the world was Mrs Alice Pollock (*née* Wykeham-Martin) (1868–1971), of Haslemere, Surrey, whose book *Portrait of My Victorian Youth* (Johnson Publications) was published in March 1971 when she was aged 102 years 8 months.

Literary luncheons

Literary luncheons were inaugurated by Christina Foyle (Mrs Ronald Batty) in October 1930 at the Old Holborn Restaurant, London. Attendances reached over 1500 at the Grosvenor House, Park Lane, London at lunches for Mistinguett (1873–1956) and Dr Edvard Benes (1884–1948) in 1938.

Longest literary gestation

The standard German dictionary *Deutsches Wörterbuch*, begun by the brothers Grimm in 1854, was finished in 1971. *Acta Sanctorum* begun by Jean Bolland in 1643, arranged according to saints' days, reached the month of November in 1925 and an introduction for December was published in 1940.

Poet Laureate *Youngest and oldest*

The youngest Poet Laureate was Laurence Eusden (1688–1730), who received the bays on 24 Dec 1718 at the age of 30 years and 3 months. The greatest age at which a poet has succeeded is 73 in the case of William Wordsworth (1770–1850) on 6 Apr 1843. The longest lived Laureate was John Masefield, OM, who died on 12 May 1967, aged 88 years 345 days. The longest which any poet has worn the laurel is 41 years 322 days, in the case of Alfred (later the 1st Lord) Tennyson (1809–92), who was appointed on 19 Nov 1850 and died in office on 6 Oct 1892.

Longest poem

The lengthiest poem ever published has been the Kirghiz folk epic *Manas*, which appeared in printed form in 1958 but which has never been translated into English. It runs to 'more than 500,000 lines'. Short translated passages appear in *The Elek Book of Oriental Verse*.

The longest poem ever written in the English language is one on the life of King Alfred by John Fitchett (1766–1838) of Liverpool which ran to 129,807 lines and took 40 years to write. His editor Robert Riscoe added the concluding 2585 lines.

Roger Brien's (b. Montreal, 1910) *Prométhée—dialogue des vivants et des morts* runs to 456,047 lines written in 1964–81. Brien has written another 497,000 lines of French poetry in over 90 published works.

Most successful

The most translated poem is believed to be *If* by Joseph Rudyard Kipling (1865–1936), first published in 1910. It was put into 27 languages and according to Kipling 'anthologized to weariness'.

HIGHEST PRINTINGS

World

The world's most widely distributed book is the Bible, portions of which have been translated into 1785 languages. This compares with 222 languages by Lenin. It has been estimated that between 1815 and 1975 some 2,500,000,000 copies were printed of which 1,500,000,000 were handled by Bible Societies. The total distribution of complete Bibles by the United Bible Societies (covering 150 countries) in the year ending 31 Oct 1983 was 11,211,617.

It has been reported that 800,000,000 copies of the red-covered booklet *Quotations from the Works of Mao Tse-tung* were sold or distributed between June 1966, when possession became virtually mandatory in China, and September 1971 when their promoter Marshal Lin Piao died in an air crash.

It is believed that in the USA Van Antwerp Bragg and Co. printed some 60 million copies of the 1879 edition of *The McGuffey Reader*, compiled by Henry Vail in the pre-copyright era for distribution to public schools.

The total disposal through non-commercial channels by Jehovah's Witnesses of the 192 page hard bound book *The Truth That Leads to Eternal Life* published by the Watchtower Bible and Tract Society of Brooklyn, New York, on 8 May 1968, reached 105,250,000 in 115 languages by May 1984.

BEST SELLERS

The world's all-time best *selling* copyright book is the *Guinness Book of Records* first published from 107 Fleet Street, London EC4 in September 1955 by the Guinness Brewery to settle arguments in Britain's 81,400 pubs and edited by Norris Dewar McWhirter (b. 12 Aug 1925) and his twin brother Alan Ross McWhirter (k. 27 Nov 1975). Its cumulative sale in 24 languages to mid-1984 was in excess of 49 million copies and increasing by some 50,000 per week.

Best Seller Lists

The *Sunday Times* best seller list (which excludes books published annually) was first published on 14 Apr 1974. *The Country Diary of an Edwardian Lady* (publisher Michael Joseph) held No 1 position for 59 consecutive weeks up to the paper's 10 month closure which started on 30 Nov 1978. Its global sales in 13 languages reached 2,233,006 copies by 13 May 1983.

Fiction

The novel with the highest sales has been *Valley of the Dolls* (first published March 1966) by Jacqueline Susann (Mrs Irving Mansfield) (1921–74) with a world-wide total of 27,956,000 to 1 May 1984. In the first 6 months Bantam sold 6.8 million. In the United Kingdom the highest print order has been 3,000,000 by Penguin Books Ltd. for their paperback edition of *Lady Chatterley's Lover*, by D. H. (David Herbert) Lawrence (1885–1930). The total sales to May 1984 were 4,600,000. Alistair Stuart MacLean (b. Scotland, April 1922) between 1955 and 1982 wrote 26 books of which the sales of 18 have exceeded a million copies and 13 have been filmed. *The Cruel Sea* by Nicholas Monsarrat (1910–79) published in 1951 by Cassell, reached sales of 1,200,000 in its *original* edition.

Fastest Publisher

The fastest time in which a book has been published is less than 24 hours from receipt of final manuscript to finished copies, in the case of John Lisners' *The House of Horrors* a 223 page paperback on the North London mass murderer Dennis Nilsen sentenced to life imprisonment at 4.23 pm on 4 Nov 1983.

Slowest seller

The accolade for the world's slowest selling book (known in US publishing as sloow-sellers) probably belongs to David

Molly Weir of Pinner, Middlesex, the most prolific autobiographical writer. In 13 years (1970–83) she wrote 7 books on her life experiences.

Wilkins's Translation of the New Testament from Coptic into Latin published by Oxford University Press in 1716 in 500 copies. Selling an average of one each 139 days, it remained in print for 191 years.

PUBLISHERS AND PRINTERS

Oldest Publisher

The Oxford University Press's first publication is dated 1468 though probably not issued until *c.* 1478.

Prolific Publisher

In terms of new titles per annum Britain's most prolific publisher in 1983 was Cambridge University Press with 771. The UK published a record 51,071 book titles in 1983 of which a record 12,091 were reprints.

Largest Printer *World*

The largest printers in the world are R. R. Donnelley & Sons Co. of Chicago, Illinois, USA. The company, founded in 1864, has plants in 15 main centres, turning out $1,500,000,000 (£1070 million) worth of work per year. More than 116,000 tons of inks and 1,375,000 tons of paper and board are consumed every year.

The largest printer under one roof is the United States Government Printing Office (founded 1860) in Washington, DC, USA. The Superintendent of Documents sells over $50 million (£27.7 million) worth of US governmental publications every year and maintains an inventory of over 16,000 titles in print.

Print order

The initial print order for the 53rd Automobile Association Members' Handbook (1984–5) was 4,800,000 copies. The total print since 1908 has been 86,700,000. It is currently printed by web offset by Petty & Sons of Leeds.

The aggregate print of The Highway Code (instituted 1931) reached 90,000,000 after 50 years in mid-1981).

LIBRARIES

Largest *World*

The largest library in the world is the United States Library of Congress (founded on 24 Apr 1800), on Capitol Hill, Washington, DC. By 1982 it contained 79,762,191 items, including 19,721,066 volumes and pamphlets. The buildings contain 64.6 acres *26.14 ha* of floor space and contain 532 miles *856 km* of shelving. The James Madison Memorial Extension was dedicated in April 1980 and has 34.5 acres *14 ha* of floor space.

The largest non-statutory library in the world is the New York Public Library (founded 1895) on Fifth Avenue with a floor space of 525,276 ft² *48 800 m²* and 88 miles *141,6 km* of shelving. Its collection including 82 branch libraries embraces 9,049,612 volumes, 12,850,854 manuscripts and 354,288 maps.

The greatest personal library ever amassed was that of Sir Thomas Phillipps. Dispersal began in 1886. The residue was bought largely unseen by the brothers Lionel Robinson CBE MC and Philip Robinson for £100,000. Sales began on 1 July 1946.

Great Britain

The largest library in the United Kingdom is the British Library, dispersed among 19 buildings in London and a 60 acre *24,3 ha* site at Boston Spa, West Yorkshire, with a total staff of over 2000. The British Library Reference Division contains over 11,330,000 volumes. Stock increases involve over 4 miles *6,43 km* of added material annually. The British Library's Newspaper Library at Colindale, North London, opened in 1932, has 550,000 volumes and parcels and 177,500 reels of microfilm comprising 70,000 different titles on 22 miles *35,4 km* of shelving. The British Library Lending Division in West Yorkshire (shelf capacity 96 miles *154,5 km*) runs the largest library inter-lending operation in the world; it handles annually nearly 3 million requests from libraries (UK and overseas) for items they do not hold in stock. The British Library National Sound Archive holds 500,000 discs and 35,000 hours of recorded tape. The largest public library in the United Kingdom is the extended Mitchell Library, North Street, Glasgow with a floor area of 510,000 ft² *47 380 m²* or 11.7 acres *4,7 ha* and an ultimate capacity for 4,000,000 volumes. The earliest public library in Scotland is in Kirkwall, Orkney, founded in 1683.

Overdue books

The most overdue book taken out by a known borrower was one reported on 7 Dec 1968, checked out in 1823 from the University of Cincinnati Medical Library on Febrile Diseases (London, 1805 by Dr J. Currie). This was returned by the borrower's great-grandson Richard Dodd. The fine calculated to be $2264 (*then £1102 10s*) was waived.

PERIODICALS

Oldest *World*

The oldest continuing periodical in the world is *Philosophical Transactions of the Royal Society*, published in London, which first appeared on 6 Mar 1665.

Great Britain

The bi-monthly *The Gospel Magazine* has been published since 1766. Curtis's *Botanical Magazine* has been in continuous publication since 1 Feb 1787, as several 'parts' a year forming a series of continuously numbered volumes. Britain's oldest weekly periodical is *Lancet* first published in 1823. The *Scots Magazine* began publication in 1739 and ran till 1826, and with three breaks has been produced continuously since 1924.

Largest circulations *World*

The largest circulation of any weekly periodical is that of *TV Guide* (USA) which in 1974 became the first magazine in history to sell a billion (1000 million) copies in a year. The weekly average for July–December 1983 was 17,066,126. In its 40 basic international editions *The Reader's Digest* (established February 1922) circulates 30,727,000 copies monthly in 17 languages, including a United States edition of more than 17,750,000 copies and a United Kingdom edition (established 1939) of 1,495,253 copies (av. January–December 1983).

Parade, the syndicated Sunday newspaper colour magazine, is distributed with 132 newspapers every Sunday. The current circulation is 24,234,121 (April 1984). Britain's highest circulation Sunday colour supplement is the *News of the World's SunDay* at 4,037,873 (1984). (See also p. 97).

Great Britain

The highest circulation of any periodical in Great Britain is that of the *Radio Times* (instituted on 28 Sept 1923). The average weekly sale for July–December 1983 was 3,204,087 copies with a readership of 9,037,000. The highest sale of any issue was 9,778,062 copies for the Christmas issue of 1955. *TV Times* averaged sales of 3,109,059 in the period July–Dec 1983 with an estimated readership of 8,889,000 (July–Dec 1983).

Annual

Old Moore's Almanack has been published annually since 1697, when it first appeared as a broadsheet, by Dr Francis Moore (1657–1715) of Southwark, London to advertise his 'physiks'. The annual sale certified by its publishers W. Foulsham & Co. Ltd of Slough, England is 1 million copies and its aggregate sale is estimated to be in excess of 108 million.

CROSSWORDS

First

The earliest known crossword was a 9 by 9 Double Diamond published in *St Nicholas* for September 1875 in New York City, USA. This was discovered by Dr Kenneth Miller of Newcastle upon Tyne, England inventor of the colour crossword in 1983. The first crossword published in a British newspaper was one furnished by C. W. Shepherd in the *Sunday Express* of 2 Nov 1924. However a 25 letter acrostic of Roman provenance was discovered on a wall in Cirencester, England in 1868.

Largest

The world's largest published crossword has been one compiled by Robert Trucot of Québec, Canada. It contained 12,489 clues across and 13,125 down and covered 38.28 ft² *3,55 m²*.

Fastest and slowest solution

The fastest recorded time for completing *The Times* crossword under test conditions is 3 min 45.0 sec by Roy Dean, 43 of Bromley, Greater London in the BBC 'Today' radio studio on 19 Dec 1970. Dr John Sykes won the *Times* championship 4 times (1972–5). In May 1966 *The Times* of London received an announcement from a Fijian woman that she had just succeeded in completing their crossword No. 673 in the issue of 4 Apr 1932.

Most durable compilers

Adrian Bell (1901–1980) of Barsham, Suffolk contributed a record 4520 crosswords to *The Times* from 2 Jan 1930 until his death. R. J. Baddock of Plymouth (b. 30 Oct 1894) has been a regular contributor to national newspapers since 13 Aug 1926. The most prolific compiler is Roger F. Squires of Ironbridge, Shropshire, who compiles 33 published puzzles single-handedly each week. His total output to August 1984 was over 23,000.

ADVERTISING RATES

The highest ever price for a single page has been $280,940 (£200,670) for a four-colour back cover in *Parade* (circulation 24.2 million per week) in April 1984 (see above). The record for a four colour inside page is $255,400 (£182,430) in *Parade* (in April 1984). The advertising revenue from the November 1982 US edition of *Readers Digest* was a peak $14,716,551 (*then £9,495,000*).

The highest expenditure ever incurred on a single advertisement in a periodical is $3,200,000 (£1,600,000) by Gulf and Western Industries on 5 Feb 1979 for insertions in *Time* Magazine (US and selected overseas editions). The British record is some £100,000 for a 20-page colour supplement by Woolworths in *The Radio Times* of 16 Nov 1972. The colour rate for a single page in *The Radio Times* is £20,000, and £44,550 for a centre spread in April 1984. The world's highest newspaper advertising rate is 37,350,000 Yen (£117,823) for a full page in the morning edition and 30,825,000 Yen (£97,240) for the evening edition of the *Yomiuri Shimbun* of Tokyo (April 1984). The highest rate in Britain is a full page in *The News of the World* at £43,344 (March 1984).

World's Oldest Existing Newspaper

The oldest existing newspaper in the world is the Swedish official journal *Post och Inrikes Tidningar*, founded in 1645. It is published by the Royal Swedish Academy of Letters.

The oldest existing commercial newspaper is the *Haarlems Dagblad/Oprechte Haarlemsche Courant*, published in Haarlem, in the Netherlands.

The *Courant* was first issued as the *Weeckelycke Courante van Europa* on 8 Jan 1656 and a copy of issue No. 1 survives.

UNITED KINGDOM

The newspaper with the earliest origins in the United Kingdom is *Berrow's Worcester Journal* (originally the *Worcester Post Man*), published in Worcester.

It was traditionally founded in 1690 and has appeared weekly since June 1709. No complete file exists.

The Northampton Mercury (now *Mercury and Herald*) was first published on 2 May 1720. A complete file showing continuous publication exists in the town's central library.

The *London Gazette* (originally the *Oxford Gazette*) was first published on 16 Nov 1665. The oldest Sunday newspaper in the United Kingdom is *The Observer*, first issued on 4 Dec 1791.

Largest and smallest

The most massive single issue of a newspaper was the 7½ lb *3,40 kg New York Times* of Sunday 17 Oct 1965. It comprised 15 sections with a total of 946 pages, including about 1,200,000 lines of advertising.

The largest page size ever used has been 51 in × 35 in *130 cm × 89 cm* for *The Constellation*, printed in 1859 by George Roberts as part of the Fourth of July celebrations in New York City, NY, USA.

The *Worcestershire Chronicle* was the largest British newspaper.

A surviving issue of 16 Feb 1859 measures 32¼ in × 22½ in *82 cm × 57 cm*.

The smallest original page size has been 3 × 3¾ in *7,6 × 9,5 cm* of the *Daily Banner* (25 cents per month) of Roseberg, Oregon, USA, issues of which, dated 1 and 2 Feb 1876, survive. The *Answers to Correspondents* published by Messrs Carr & Co, Paternoster Square, London in 1888 was 3½ × 4½ in *9 × 11 cm*.

Roger F. Squires of Telford, crossword editor of The Birmingham Post whose lifetime output of solvable puzzles in 1984 surpassed the 23,000 mark.

Longest Editorship

Sir Etienne Dupuch OBE of Nassau, Bahamas, editor of the *Tribune* since 1 Apr 1919 entered his 66th year in the chair on 1 Apr 1984. The longest editorship of any United Kingdom national newspaper has been more than 59 years by C. P. Scott (1846–1932) of the (then *Manchester*) *Guardian*, who was appointed aged 25 in 1877 and died on 1 Jan 1932.

Most Syndicated Cartoonist

Ranan R. Lurie (b. 26 May 1932) of the Asahi Shimbun is the most widely syndicated political cartoonist in the world. His work is published in 51 countries in 400 newspapers with a combined circulation of 62 million copies.

LONGEST LIVED STRIP

The most durable newspaper comic strip has been the Katzenjammer Kids (Hans and Fritz) created by Rudolph Dirks and first published in the *New York Journal* on 12 Dec 1897 and perpetuated by his son John.

The earliest strip was The Yellow Kid, which first appeared in the New York *Journal* on 18 Oct 1896. The most widely syndicated is *Blondie* (originated in 1930) appearing in 1800 newspapers in 55 countries, in 15 languages with a readership of an estimated 150 million daily.

BRITAIN'S MOST EXPENSIVE PAPER

Britain's most expensive paper is *The Sunday Times* at 45p (or 9s 0d in the money prior to 15 Feb 1971), or 60 per cent higher than the price of the original 1955 fully bound edition of this publication.

MOST

The United States had 1711 English-language daily newspapers at 1 Feb 1983 with a combined net paid circulation of 62,487,177 copies per day.

The peak year for US newspapers was 1910, when there were 2202.

The leading newspaper readers in the world are the people of Sweden, where 554 newspapers were sold for each 1000 compared with the UK figure of 410.

Most Durable Feature

The longest lasting feature in the British national press from one pen was *Your Stars* by Edward Lyndoe. It ran from Oct 1933 to 1982 in *The Sunday People*. Frank Lowe has contributed a weekly natural history column to the *Bolton Evening News* every week since 4 Feb 1926. Albert E. Pool (b. 1909) has been a part-time journalist for the *Lincolnshire and South Humberside* (formerly *The Hull*) *Times* since March 1923.

C. P. Scott, who was editor of The Guardian for 59 years. (*Radio Times Hulton Picture Library*)

MOST MISPRINTS

The record for misprints in *The Times* was set on 22 Aug 1978 when on page 19 there were 97 in 5½ single column inches. The passage concerned 'Pop' (Pope) Paul VI.

Most Durable Advertiser

The Jos Neel Co, a clothing store in Macon, Georgia, USA (founded 1880) has run an 'ad' in the *Macon Telegraph* every day in the upper left corner of page 2 since 22 Feb 1889 or 34,092 times to May 1984.

CIRCULATION FIGURES.

Earliest 1,000,000
The first newspaper to achieve a circulation of 1,000,000 was *Le Petit Journal*, published in Paris, France, which reached this figure in 1886, when selling at 5 centimes. The *Daily Mail* first reached a million on 2 Mar 1900.

Highest World
The highest circulation for any newspaper in the world is that for the *Yomiuri Shimbun* (founded 1874) of Japan which attained a figure of 13,791,370 copies on 1 April 1984. This is achieved by totalling the figures for editions published in various centres with a morning figure of 8,940,155 and an evening figure of 4,851,215. It reaches 38 per cent of Japan's 34 million households. It has a staff of 3060 and 436 bureaux.

Great Britain
The highest circulation of any single newspaper in Britain is that of the Sunday newspaper *The News of the World*, printed in Bouverie Street, London. Single issues have attained a sale of 9,000,000 copies with an estimated readership of more than 19,000,000. The paper first appeared on 1 Oct 1843, and surpassed the million mark in 1905. The latest sales figure is 4,037,873 copies per issue (average for 1 July 1983 to 31 Dec 1983), with an estimated readership of 10,939,000.

The highest net sale of any daily newspaper in the United Kingdom is that of *The Sun*, founded in London in 1964. The latest sales figure is 4,127,578 (1 July 1983–31 Dec 1983), with an estimated readership of 12,410,000.

Most read
The national newspaper which achieves the closest to a saturation circulation is *The Sunday Post*, established in Glasgow in 1914. In 1983 its estimated readership in Scotland of 2,696,000 represented 66 per cent of the entire population aged 15 and over. The *Arran Banner* (founded March 1974) has a readership of 97+ per cent on Britain's seventh largest off-shore island.

4. MUSIC

The Guinness Book of Music (2nd edition) (price £8.95), by Robert and Celia Dearling with Brian Rust was published in Spring 1981 and contains more detailed treatment of musical facts and superlatives.

Origins

Whistles and flutes made from perforated phalange bones have been found at Upper Palaeolithic sites of the Aurignacian period (*c.* 25,000–22,000 BC) *e.g.* at Istallóskö, Hungary and in Molodova, USSR. The world's earliest surviving musical notation dates from *c.* 1800 BC. A heptatonic scale deciphered from a clay tablet by Dr Duchesne-Guillemin in 1966–7 was found at a site in Nippur, Sumer, now Iraq. An Assyrian love song also *c.* 1800 BC to an Ugaritic god from a tablet of notation and lyric was reconstructed for an 11 string lyre at the University of California, Berkeley on 6 Mar 1974. Musical history is, however, able to be traced back to the 3rd millennium BC, when the yellow bell (*huang chung*) had a recognised standard musical tone in Chinese temple music.

INSTRUMENTS

Piano *Earliest*

The earliest pianoforte in existence is one built in Florence, Italy, in 1720 by Bartolommeo Cristofori (1655–1731) of Padua, and now preserved in the Metropolitan Museum of Art, New York City.

Piano *Grandest*

The grandest grand piano built was one of 1¼ tons/*tonnes* 11 ft 8 in *3,55 m* in length made by Chas. H. Challen & Son Ltd of London in 1935. The longest bass string measured 9 ft 11 in *3,02 m* with a tensile of 30 tons/*tonnes*.

Piano *Most Expensive*

The highest price ever paid for a piano is $390,000 (*then £177,273*) at Sotheby Parke Bernet, New York City on 26 Mar 1980 for a Steinway grand of *c.* 1888 sold by the Martin Beck Theatre and bought by a non-pianist.

Organ largest *World*

The largest and loudest musical instrument ever constructed is the now only partially functional Auditorium Organ in Atlantic City, New Jersey, USA. Completed in 1930, this heroic instrument had two consoles (one with seven manuals and another movable one with five), 1477 stop controls and 33,112 pipes ranging in tone from $\frac{3}{16}$ of an inch *4,7 mm* to the 64 ft *19 m* tone. It had the volume of 25 brass bands, with a range of seven octaves. The world's largest fully functional organ is the six manual 30,067 pipe Grand Court Organ installed in the Wanamaker Store, Philadelphia, Pennsylvania, USA in 1911 and enlarged between then and 1930. It has a 64 ft *19,5 m* tone gravissima pipe. The world's largest church organ is that in Passau Cathedral, Germany. It was completed in 1928 by D. F. Steinmeyer & Co. It was built with 16,000 pipes and five manuals. The world's most powerful electronic organ is the 5000 watt Royal V. Rogers organ, designed by Virgil Fox with 465 speakers installed by Orient Shoji Co in Chuo-ku, Tokyo, Japan in June 1983. The chapel organ at West Point US Military Academy, NY has, since 1911, been expanded from 2406 to 18,200 pipes.

Great Britain

The largest organ in Great Britain is that completed in Liverpool Anglican Cathedral on 18 Oct 1926, with two five-manual consoles of which only one is now in use, and 9704 speaking pipes (originally 10,936) ranging from tones ¾ in to 32 ft *1,9 cm to 9,75 m.*

Musicians *Most Durable*

Elsie Maude Stanley Hall (1877–1976) gave piano recitals for 90 years giving her final concert in Rustenburg. Transvaal, South Africa aged 97. Charles Bridgeman (1779–1873) of All Saints Parish Church, Hertford, England, who was appointed organist in 1792, was still playing 81 years later in 1873. The nongenarian Norwegian pianist Reidar Thommesen (b. 7 June 1889) is still playing over 30 hours a week in theatre cafés.

Loudest organ stop

The loudest organ stop in the world is the Ophicleide stop of the Grand Great in the Solo Organ in the Atlantic City Auditorium (see above). It is operated by a pressure of 100 in

254 cm of water (3½ lb/in² *24 kPa*) and has a pure trumpet note of ear-splitting volume, more than six times the volume of the loudest locomotive whistles.

Brass instrument *Largest*

The largest recorded brass instrument is a tuba standing 7½ ft *2,28 m* tall, with 39 ft *11,8 m* of tubing and a bell 3 ft 4 in *1 m* across. This contrabass tuba was constructed for a world tour by the band of John Philip Sousa (1854–1932), the United States composer, in *c.* 1896–8, and is still in use. This instrument is now owned by a circus promoter in South Africa.

Horns *Longest Alphorn*

The longest alphorn is one of 17,98 m *59 ft* built from a spruce log by Herr Stocker in Switzerland in 1976. It was demonstrated by Herr Lamy for David Frost on 28 June 1981.

Stringed instrument *Largest*

The largest movable stringed instrument ever constructed was a pantaleon with 270 strings stretched over 50 ft² *4,6 m²* used by George Noel in 1767. The greatest number of musicians required to operate a single instrument was the six required to play the gigantic orchestrion, known as the Apollonican, built in 1816 and played until 1840.

Guitar *Largest and Most Expensive*

The largest and presumably also the loudest playable guitar in the world is one 10 ft 1 in *3,07 m* tall, and in excess of 300 lb *136 kg* in weight, built by Sparkling Ragtime Productions of San Francisco, and the Guild of American Luthiers, Tacoma, Washington, USA in December 1980. The most expensive standard sized guitar is the German chittara battente by Jacob Stadler, dated 1624, which was sold for £10,500 at Christie's, London on 12 June 1974.

Double bass *Largest and Most player*

The largest double bass ever constructed was one 14 ft *4,26 m* tall, built in 1924 in Ironia, New Jersey, USA by Arthur K. Ferris, allegedly on orders from the Archangel Gabriel. It weighed 11.6 cwt. *590 kg* with a sound box 8 ft *2,43 m* across, and had leathern strings totalling 104 ft *31,7 m.* Its low notes could be felt rather than heard. On 25 Oct 1981 5 members of 'Bass Ten' from Bournemouth, Dorset bowed and 5-fingered a double bass simultaneously in a rendition of Monti's *Czardas.*

'Cello *Most valuable*

The highest ever auction price for a violoncello is £145,000 at Sotheby's, London on 8 Nov 1978 for a Stradivari made in Cremona, Italy in 1710.

Violin *Most valuable*

The highest ever price paid at auction for a violin is $290,000 (*then £145,000*) for the 'Huberman' *ex* Kreisler Stradivari dated 1733 at Sotheby's, London on 3 May 1979. Some 700 of the 1116 violins by Stradivarius (1644–1737) have survived. His Alarol violin was confirmed by Jacques Francais to have been sold by private treaty by W. E. Hill for $1.2 million (*then £600,000*) to a Singaporean.

Violinist *Underwater*

The pioneer violinist to surmount the problems of playing the violin underwater was Mark Gottlieb. Submerged in Evergreen State College swimming bath in Olympia, Washington, USA in March 1975 he gave a submarine rendition of Handel's Water Music. His most intractable problem was his underwater *détaché.* On 7 Oct 1979 the first underwater quartet performed in the *Challenge the Guinness* TV show on Channel 7 in Tokyo, Japan.

Most durable fiddlers

Rolland S. Tapley retired as a violinist from the Boston Symphony Orchestra after playing for a reputedly unrivalled 58 years from February 1920 to 27 Aug 1978. Otto E. Funk, 62, walked 4165 miles *6702 km* from New York City to San Francisco, California playing his Hopf violin every step of the way westward. He arrived on 16 June 1929 after 183 days on the road.

Drum *Largest*

The largest drum ever constructed was one 12 ft *3,65 m* in diameter weighing 600 lb *272 kg* for the Boston World Peace Jubilee of 1872.

Highest and lowest notes

The extremes of orchestral instruments (excluding the organ)

Ten time champions, the 34 men behind the Shotts & Dykehead Caledonian Pipe Band. (*Owens of Wishaw*)

range between a handbell tuned to g^v (6272 cycles/sec) and the sub-contrabass clarinet, which can reach C_{11} or 16.4 cycles/sec. The highest note on a standard pianoforte is c^v (4186 cycles/sec), which is also the violinist's limit. In 1873 a sub double bassoon able to reach $B_{111}\#$ or 14.6 cycles/sec was constructed but no surviving specimen is known. The extremes for the organ are g^{vi} (the sixth G above middle C) (12,544 cycles/sec) and C_{111} (8.12 cycles/sec) obtainable from $\frac{3}{4}$ in *1,9 cm* and 64 ft *19 m* pipes respectively.

Easiest and most difficult instruments

The American Music Conference announced in September 1977 that the easiest instrument is the ukulele, and the most difficult are the French horn and the oboe, which latter has been described as 'the ill woodwind that no-one blows good'.

ORCHESTRAS

Largest *Orchestra*

The most massive orchestra ever assembled was one of 20,100 at the Ullevaal Stadium, Oslo, of Norges Musikkorps Forbund bands from all Norway on 28 June 1964. On 17 June 1872, Johann Strauss the younger (1825–99) conducted an orchestra of 987 pieces supported by a choir of 20,000, at the World Peace Jubilee in Boston, Massachusetts, USA. The number of first violinists was 400.

Marching band

The largest marching band on record was one of 2560 musicians in the official State Parade for the Merdeka celebrations in Kuala Lumpur, Malaysia on 31 Aug 1982. The whole parade numbered 25,000. The longest recorded musical march is one of 61 km *37.9 miles* from Lillehammer to Hamar, Norway in 15 hours when, on 10 May 1980, 26 of 35 members of the Trondheim Brass Band survived the playing of 135 marches.

Most Durable

The Cork Symphony Orchestra has performed under the baton of Dr Aloys Fleischmann for 50 seasons (1935–84).

Most successful bands

Most British Open Brass band Championship titles (inst. 1853) have been won by the Black Dyke Mills Band which has won 22 times from 1862 to 1974 including three consecutive wins in 1972–4. The most successful pipe band is the Shotts & Dykehead Caledonian Pipe Band with their 10th world title in August 1980.

Greatest attendance *Classical*

The greatest attendance at any classical concert has been 400,000 for the Boston Pops Orchestra, conducted by Arthur Fiedler (1895–1979) at the Hatch Memorial Shell, Boston, Massachusetts, USA on 4 July 1976. At the 1978 concert the 83-year-old conductor was presented with a testimonial bearing a record 500,000 signatures.

Pop Festival

The greatest claimed attendance at a Pop Festival has been 600,000 for the 'Summer Jam' at Watkins Glen, New York, USA, on Sunday 29 July 1973 of whom about 150,000 actually paid. There were 12 'sound towers'. The attendance at the third Pop Festival at East Afton Farm, Freshwater, Isle of Wight, England on 30 Aug 1970 was claimed by its promoters, Fiery Creations, to be 400,000.

Single Performer

The largest paying audience ever attracted by a solo performer is an estimated 175,000 in the Maracaña Stadium, Rio de Janeiro, Brazil to hear Frank Sinatra (b. 1915) on 26 Jan 1980. Elton John entertained an estimated 400,000 in Central Park, New York City, USA at a free concert in the summer of 1980.

Greatest Choir

Excluding 'sing alongs' by stadium crowds, the greatest choir is one of 60,000 which sang in unison as a finale of a choral contest among 160,000 participants in Breslau, Germany on 2 Aug 1937.

COMPOSERS

Most prolific

The most prolific composer of all time was probably Georg Philipp Telemann (1681–1767) of Germany. He composed 12 complete sets of services (one cantata every Sunday) for a year, 78 services for special occasions, 40 operas, 600 to 700 orchestral suites, 44 Passions, plus concertos and chamber music. The most prolific symphonist was Johann Melchior Molter (*c.* 1695–1765) of Germany who wrote 169. Joseph Haydn (1732–1809) of Austria wrote 108 numbered symphonies some of which are regularly played today.

Most rapid

Among composers of the classical period the most prolific was Wolfgang Amadeus Mozart (1756–91) of Austria, who wrote *c.* 1000 operas, operettas, symphonies, violin sonatas, divertimenti, serenades, motets, concertos for piano and many other instruments, string quartets, other chamber music, masses and litanies, of which only 70 were published before he died aged 35. His opera *The Clemency of Titus* (1791) was written in 18 days and three symphonic masterpieces, *Symphony No. 39 in E flat major*, *Symphony in G minor* and the *Jupiter Symphony in C*, were reputedly written in the space of 42 days in 1788. His overture *Don Giovanni* was written in full score at one sitting in Prague in 1787 and finished on the day of its opening performance.

Longest symphony

The longest of all single classical symphonies is the orchestral symphony No. 3 in D minor by Gustav Mahler (1860–1911) of Austria. This work, composed in 1896, requires a contralto, a womens' and boys' choir in addition to a full orchestra. A full performance requires 1 hr 40 min, of which the first movement alone takes between 30 and 36 min. The Symphony No. 2 (the Gothic, or No. 1), composed in 1919–22 by Havergal Brian

(1876–1972) was played by over 800 performers (4 brass bands) in the Victoria Hall, Hanley, Staffordshire on 21 May 1978 (conductor Trevor Stokes). A recent broadcast required 1 hr 45½ min. Brian wrote an even vaster work based on Shelley's 'Prometheus Unbound' lasting 4 hr 11 min but the full score has been missing since 1961. The symphony *Victory at Sea* written by Richard Rodgers and arranged by Robert Russell Bennett for NBC TV in 1952 lasted for 13 hr.

Longest piano composition

The longest continuous non-repetitious piano piece ever published has been 'The Well-Tuned Piano' by La Monte Young first presented by the Dia Art Foundation at the Concert Hall, Harrison St, New York City on 28 Feb 1980. The piece lasted 4 hr 12 min 10 sec. *Symphonic Variations,* composed by Kaikhosru Shapurji Sorabji (b. 1892) into 500 pages of close manuscript in 3 volumes in the 1930's, would last for 6 hours at the prescribed tempo.

Longest silence

The longest interval between the known composition of a major composer, and its performance in the manner intended, is from 3 Mar 1791 until 9 Oct 1982 (over 191 years), in the case of Mozart's *Organ Piece for a Clock*, a fugue fantasy in F minor (K 608), arranged by the organ builders Wm Hill & Son and Norman & Beard Ltd at Glyndebourne, East Sussex.

HIGHEST PAID MUSICIANS

Pianist

Wladziu Valentino Liberace (b. West Allis, Wisconsin, USA, 16 May 1917) has earned each 26 week season with a peak of $138,000 (*then £49,285*) for a single night's performance at Madison Square Garden, New York City, USA in 1954. The highest paid classical concert pianist was Ignace Jan Paderewski (1860–1941), Prime Minister of Poland (1919–20), who accumulated a fortune estimated at $5,000,000, of which $500,000 (*then £110,000*) was earned in a single season in 1922–23. The *nouveau riche* wife of a US industrialist once required him to play in her house behind a curtain. For concerts Artur Rubinstein (1887–1982), between 1937 and 1976, commanded 70 per cent of the gross.

Greatest Span

Sergei Vassilievitch Rachmaninov (1873–1943) had a span of 12 white notes and could play a left hand chord of C, E♭, G, C, G.

Singer *Most Successful*

Of great fortunes earned by singers, the highest on record are those of Enrico Caruso (1873–1921), the Italian tenor, whose estate was about $9,000,000 (*then £1,875,000*) and the Italian-Spanish coloratura soprano Amelita Galli-Curci (1889–1963), who received about $3,000,000 (£750,000). In 1850, up to $653 was paid for a single seat at the concerts given in the United States by Johanna ('Jenny') Maria Lind, later Mrs Otto Goldschmidt (1820–87), the 'Swedish Nightingale'. She had a range from g to e‴ of which the middle register is still regarded as unrivalled. The tenor Count John Francis McCormack (1884–1945) of Ireland gave up to 10 concerts to capacity audiences in a single season in New York City.

David Bowie drew a fee of $1.5 million (*then £960,000*) for a single show at the US Festival in Glen Helen Regional Park, San Bernardino County, California on 26 May 1983. The 4 man Van Halen rock band attracted a matching fee.

Worst

While no agreement exists as to the identity of history's greatest singer, there is unanimity on the worst. The excursions of the soprano Florence Foster Jenkins (1868–1944) into lieder and even high coloratura culminated on 25 Oct 1944 in her sell-out concert at the Carnegie Hall, New York, USA. The diva's (already high) high F was said to have been made higher in 1943 by a crash in a taxi. It is one of the tragedies of musicology that Madame Jenkins' *Clavelitos*, accompanied by Cosme McMoon, was never recorded for posterity. Her latter day amateur rival has been Mrs Hazel Saunders of Clent, Hereford & Worcester.

OPERA

Longest

The longest of commonly performed operas is *Die Meistersinger*

von Nürnberg by Wilhelm Richard Wagner (1813–83) of Germany. A normal uncut performance of this opera as performed by the Sadler's Wells company between 24 Aug and 19 Sept 1968 entailed 5 hr 15 min of music. *The Heretics* by Gabriel von Wayditch (1888–1969) a Hungarian-American, is orchestrated for 110 pieces and lasts 8½ hr.

Shortest

The shortest opera published was *The Deliverance of Theseus* by Darius Milhaud (b. September 1892) first performed in 1928 which lasts for 7 min 27 sec.

Aria

The longest single aria, in the sense of an operatic solo, is Brünnhilde's immolation scene in Wagner's *Gotterdammerung*. A well-known recording of this has been precisely timed at 14 min 46 sec.

Opera houses *Largest*

The largest opera house in the world is the Metropolitan Opera House, Lincoln Center, New York City, NY, USA, completed in September 1966 at a cost of $45,700,000 (*then £16,320,000*). It has a capacity of 3800 seats in an auditorium 451 ft *137 m* deep. The stage is 234 ft *71 m* wide and 146 ft *44,5 m* deep. The tallest opera house is one housed in a 42-storey building on Wacker Drive in Chicago, Illinois, USA.

Most tiers

The Teatro della Scala (La Scala) in Milan, Italy, shares with the Bolshoi Theatre in Moscow, USSR, the distinction of having the greatest number of tiers. Each has six, with the topmost being nicknamed the *Galiorka* by Russians.

Opera singers *Youngest and Oldest*

The youngest opera singer in the world has been Jeanette Gloria La Bianca, born in Buffalo, New York on 12 May 1934, who sang Rosina in *The Barber of Seville* at the Teatro dell'Opera, Rome, on 8 May 1950 aged 15 years 361 days, having appeared as Gilda in *Rigoletto* at Velletri 45 days earlier. Ginetta La Bianca was taught by Lucia Carlino and managed by Angelo Carlino. The tenor Giovanni Martinelli sang Emperor Altoum in *Turandot* in Seattle, Washington, USA on 4 Feb 1967 when aged 81.

Danshi Toyotake (b. 1 Aug 1891) has been singing *Gidayu* for 84 years.

Longest encore

The longest operatic encore, listed in the *Concise Oxford Dictionary of Opera*, was of the entire opera Cimarosa's' *Il Matrimonio Segreto* at its première in 1792. This was at the command of the Austro-Hungarian Emperor Leopold II (1790–92).

It was reported on 5 July 1983 that Placido Domingo received 83 curtain calls and was applauded for 1 hr 30 min after singing the lead in Puccini's *La Boheme* at the State Opera House in Vienna, Austria.

SONG

Oldest

The oldest known song is the *shaduf* chant, which has been sung since time immemorial by irrigation workers on the man-powered pivoted-rod bucket raisers of the Nile water mills (or *saqiyas*) in Egypt. The oldest known harmonized music performed today is the English song *Sumer is icumen in* which dates from c. 1240.

National anthems

The oldest national anthem is the *Kimigayo* of Japan, in which the words date from the 9th century. The anthem of Greece constitutes the first four verses of the Solomos poem, which has 158 stanzas. The shortest anthems are those of Japan, Jordan and San Marino, each with only four lines. Of the 23 wordless national anthems the oldest is that of Spain dating from 1770.

Longest rendering

'God Save the King' was played non-stop 16 or 17 times by a German military band on the platform of Rathenau Railway Station, Brandenburg, on the morning of 9 Feb 1909. The reason was that King Edward VII was struggling inside the train with the uniform of a German Field-Marshal before he could emerge.

Top songs of all time

The most frequently sung songs in English are *Happy Birthday to You* (based on the original *Good morning to all*), by Mildred and Pat?? Hill of New York (published in 1935 and in copyright until 2010); *For He's a Jolly Good Fellow* (originally the French *Malbrouk*), known at least as early as 1781, and *Auld Lang Syne* (originally the Strathspey *I fee'd a Lad at Michaelmass*), some words of which were written by Robert Burns (1759–96). *Happy Birthday* was sung in space by the Apollo IX astronauts on 8 Mar 1969.

Top selling sheet music

Sales of three non-copyright pieces are known to have exceeded 20,000,000 namely *The Old Folks at Home* by Stephen Foster (1855), *Listen to the Mocking Bird* (1855) and *The Blue Danube* (1867). Of copyright material the two topsellers are *Let Me Call You Sweetheart* (1910, by Whitson and Friedman) and *Till We Meet Again* (1918, by Egan and Whiting) each with some 6,000,000 by 1967. Other huge sellers have been *St Louis Blues, Stardust* and *Tea for Two*.

Most successful songwriter

In terms of sales of single records, the most successful of all song writers has been Paul McCartney (see also Gramophone, p. 105) formerly of the Beatles and now of Wings. Between 196? and ?an 1978 he wrote jointly or solo 43 songs which sold a million or more.

Eurovision Contest

In the ?9 contests since 1956 Luxembourg has won outright 5 times (1961–65–72–73–83). France has won 4 outright (1958–60–6?–77) and shared 1 (1969). The UK won in 1967 (Sandie Shaw, *Puppet On A String*), 1976 (Brotherhood of Man, *Save Your Kisses For Me*), 1981 (Bucks Fizz, *Making Your Mind Up*) and shared in 1969 (Lulu, *Boom, Bang-a-Bang*). Norway twice scored zero with Jahn Teigan and *Mil etter mil* (1980) and Finn Kalvik and *Aldri i livet* (1981).

HYMNS

Earliest

There are more than 950,000 Christian hymns in existence. The music and parts of the text of a hymn in the *Oxyrhynchus Papyri* from the 2nd century are the earliest known hymnody. The earliest exactly datable hymn is the *Heyr Himna Smiður* (*Hear the maker of heaven*) from 1208 by the Icelandic bard and chieftain Kolbeinn Tumason (1173–1208).

Longest and shortest

The longest hymn is *Hora novissima tempora pessima sunt; vigilemus* by Bernard of Cluny (12th century), which runs to 2966 lines. In English the longest is *The Sands of Time are sinking* by Mrs Anne Ross Cousin, *née* Cundell (1824–1906), which is in full 152 lines, though only 32 lines in the Methodist Hymn Book. The shortest hymn is the single verse in Long Metre *Be Present at our Table Lord*, anon., but attributed to 'J. Leland'.

Most prolific hymnists

Mrs Frances (Fanny) Jane Van Alstyne *née* Crosby (1820–1915) (USA) wrote 8500 hymns although she had been blinded at the age of 6 weeks. She is reputed to have knocked off one hymn in 15 min. Charles Wesley (1707–88) wrote about 6000 hymns. In the seventh (1950) edition of *Hymns Ancient and Modern* the works of John Mason Neale (1818–66) appear 56 times.

BELLS

Oldest *World*

The oldest bell in the world is the tintinnabulum found in the Baby?? Palace of Nimrod in 1849 by Mr (later Sir) Austen Henry ??rd (1817–94) dating from *c.* 1100 BC. The oldest known tower bell is one in Pisa, Italy dated MCVI (1106).

Great Britain

The fragile hand bell known as the Black or Iron Bell of St. Patrick is dated *c.* AD 450. The oldest tower bell in Great Britain is one of 1 cwt *50 kg* at St Botolph, Hardham, Sussex still in use but dated *ante* 1100. The oldest inscribed bell is the Gargate bell at Caversfield church, Oxfordshire and is dated *c.* 1200–1210. The oldest *dated* bell in England is one hanging in Lissett church, near Bridlington, Humberside discovered in October 1972 to bear the date MCCLIIII (1254).

above: The 93 year old Danshi Toyotake (left) who has been singing *Gidayu* since 1899. She can still do it because she did it yesterday.

below: David Bowie (born David Robert Jones in London on 8 Jan 1947) who attracted history's highest ever fee of $1.5 million for a single show in California on the 'Serious Moonlight Tour' in May 1983. (*Pictorial Press*)

Heaviest *World*

The heaviest bell in the world is the Tsar Kolokol, cast on 25 Nov 1735 in Moscow, USSR. It weighs 193 tons *196 tonnes*, measures 5,9 m *19 ft 4¼ in* diameter and 5,87 m *19 ft 3 in* high, and its greatest thickness is 24 in *60 cm*. The bell is cracked, and a fragment, weighing about 11 tons/*tonnes* was broken from it. The bell has stood, unrung, on a platform in the Kremlin, in Moscow, since 1836.

The heaviest bell in use is the Mingun bell, weighing 55,555 viss or *90.52 tons* with a diameter of 16 ft 8½ in *5,09 m* at the lip, in Mandalay, Burma, which is struck by a teak boom from the outside. It was cast at Mingun late in the reign of King Bodawpaya (1782–1819). The heaviest swinging bell in the world is the Petersglocke in the South-West tower of Cologne Cathedral, Germany, cast in 1923 with a diameter of 3,40 m *11 ft 1¾ in* weighing 25,4 tonnes *25.0 tons*.

Great Britain

The heaviest bell hung in Great Britain is 'Great Paul' in the south-west tower of St Paul's Cathedral, London, cast in 1881. It weighs 16 tons 14 cwt 2 qrs 19 lb net *17 002 kg* and has a diameter of 9 ft 6½ in *2,90 m* and sounds note E-flat. 'Big Ben', the hour bell in the clock tower of the House of Commons, was cast in 1858 and weighs 13 tons 10 cwt 3 qrs 15 lb *13 761 kg*. It is the most broadcast bell in the world and is note E.

Ringing Peals

A ringing peal is defined as a diatonic 'ring' of five or more bells hung for full-circle change ringing. Of 5500 rings so hung only 70 are outside the United Kingdom and Ireland. The heaviest ring in the world is that of 13 bells cast in 1938–39 for the Anglican Cathedral, Liverpool. The total bell weight is 16½ tons *16,76 tonnes* of which Emmanuel, the tenor bell note A, weighs 82 cwt 11 lb *4170,8 kg*.

Carillon *Largest*

The largest carillon (minimum of 23 bells) in the world is the Laura Spelman Rockefeller Memorial carillon in Riverside Church, New York City, USA with 74 bells weighing 102 tons. The bourdon, giving the note lower C, weighs 40,926 lb *18 563 kg*. This 18.27 ton bell, cast in England, with a diameter of 10 ft 2 in *3,09 cm* is the largest *tuned* bell in the world.

Heaviest

The heaviest carillon in Great Britain is in St Nicholas Church, Aberdeen, Scotland. It consists of 48 bells, the total weight of which is 25 tons 8 cwt 2 qrs 13 lb *25 838 kg*. The bourdon bell weighs 4 tons 9 cwt 3 qrs 26 lb *4571 kg* and is the note G-sharp.

Bell ringing

Eight bells have been rung to their full 'extent' (40,320 unrepeated changes of Plain Bob Major) only once without relays. This took place in a bell foundry at Loughborough, Leicestershire, beginning at 6.52 a.m. on 27 July 1963 and ending at 12.50 a.m. on 28 July, after 17 hr 58 min. The peal was composed by Kenneth Lewis of Altrincham, Greater Manchester, and the eight ringers were conducted by Robert B. Smith, aged 25, of Marple, Greater Manchester. Theoretically it would take 37 years 355 days to ring 12 bells (maximus) to their full extent of 479,001,600 changes. The greatest number of peals (minimum of 5040 changes, all in tower bells) rung in a year is 209 by Mark William Marshall of Ashford, Kent in 1973. The late George E. Fearn rang 2666 peals from 1928 to May 1974. Matthew Lakin (1801–1899) was a regular bell-ringer at Tetney Church near Grimsby for 84 years.

5. THEATRE

Guinness Superlatives has published a more specialist book *The Guinness Book of Theatre Facts and Feats* by Michael Billington, priced £8.95.

Origins

Theatre in Europe has its origins in Greek drama performed in honour of a god, usually Dionysus. The earliest amphitheatres date from the 5th century BC and the largest of all known is one at Megalopolis in central Greece, where the auditorium reached a height of 75 ft *23 m* and had a capacity of 17,000. The first stone-built theatre in Rome erected in 55 BC could accommodate 40,000 spectators.

Oldest *World*

The oldest indoor theatre in the world is the Teatro Olimpico in Vicenza, Italy. Designed in the Roman style by Andrea di Pietro, *alias* Palladio (1508–80), it was begun three months before his death and finished by his pupil Vicenzo Scamozzi (1552–1616) in 1583. It is preserved today in its original form.

Great Britain

The earliest London theatre was James Burbage's 'The Theatre', built in 1576 near Finsbury Fields, London. The oldest theatre still in use in Great Britain is The Royal, Bristol. The foundation stone was laid on 30 Nov 1764, and the theatre was opened on 30 May 1766 with a 'Concert of Music and a Specimen of Rhetorick'. The City Varieties Music Hall, Leeds was a singing room in 1762 and so claims to outdate the Theatre Royal. Actors were legally rogues and vagabonds until the passing of the Vagrancy Act in 1824. The oldest amateur dramatic society is the Old Stagers inaugurated in Canterbury, Kent in 1841. They have performed in every year except the years of World War I and II.

Largest *World*

The world's largest building used for theatre is the National People's Congress Building (*Ren min da hui tang*) on the west side of Tian an men Square, Peking, China. It was completed in 1959 and covers an area of 12.9 acres *5,2 ha*. The theatre seats 10,000 and is occasionally used as such as in 1964 for the play 'The East is Red'. The highest capacity purpose-built theatre is the Perth Entertainment Centre, Western Australia completed at a cost of $A 8.3 million (*then £4.2 million*) in November 1976 with 8003 seats. The stage area is 12,000 ft² *1148 m²*.

Great Britain

The highest capacity theatre is the Odeon, Hammersmith, Greater London, with 3483 seats. The largest theatre stage in Great Britain is the Opera House in Blackpool, Lancashire. It was re-built in July 1939 and has seats for 2975 people. Behind the 45 ft *14 m* wide proscenium arch, the stage is 110 ft *33 m* high, 60 ft *18 m* deep and 100 ft *30 m* wide, and there is dressing room accommodation for 200 artistes.

Britain's largest open air theatre is at Scarborough, North Yorkshire opened in 1932 with a seating capacity of 7000 plus standing room for 9000 and a 182 ft *55 m* long stage.

Smallest

The smallest regularly operated professional theatre in the world is the Piccolo in Juliusstrasse, Hamburg, West Germany. It was founded in 1970 and has a maximum capacity of 30 seats.

Largest amphitheatre

The largest amphitheatre ever built is the Flavian amphitheatre or Colosseum of Rome, Italy, completed in AD 80. Covering 5 acres *2 ha* and with a capacity of 87,000, it has a maximum length of 612 ft *187 m* and maximum width of 515 ft *175 m*.

Largest stage

The largest stage in the world is in the Ziegfeld Room Reno, Nevada with 176 ft *53,6 m* passerelle, three main lifts each capable of raising 1200 show girls (64¼ tons *65,3 tonnes*), two 62½ ft *19,1 m* circumference turntables and 800 spotlights.

Longest runs

The longest continuous run of any show in the world is *The Mousetrap* by Dame Agatha Mary Clarissa Christie, DBE (*née* Miller, later Lady Mallowan) (1890–1976). This thriller opened on 25 Nov 1952, at the Ambassadors Theatre (capacity 453) and moved after 8862 performances 'down the road' to St Martin's Theatre on 25 Mar 1974. The 30th Anniversary performance on 25 Nov 1982 was the 12,481st. The Vicksburg Theatre Guild of Vicksburg, Mississippi, USA have been playing the melodrama *Gold in the Hills*, by J. Frank Davis discontinuously but every season since 1936.

Revue

The greatest number of performances of any theatrical presentation is 42,921 (to January 1984) in the case of *The Golden Horseshoe Revue*—a show staged at Disneyland Park, Anaheim, California, USA. The show was first put on on 16 July 1955 and has been seen by 16 million people. The three main performers Fulton Burley, Dick Hardwick and Betty Taylor play as many as five houses a day in a routine lasting 45 min.

Broadway

The long-run record for any Broadway show was set on 29 Sept 1983 with the 3389th performance of *Chorus Line*. It opened on 25 July 1975 and had been seen by an estimated 22,300,000 people with a box office receipt of $260 million. The off-Broadway musical show *The Fantasticks* by Tom Jones and Harvey Schmidt achieved its 9987th performance as it entered its 25th year at the Sullivan Street Playhouse, Greenwich Village, New York City on 3 May 1984. It has been played in a record 8681 productions in 67 countries.

Musical shows

The longest-running musical show ever performed in Britain was *The Black and White Minstrel Show* later *Magic of the Minstrels*. The aggregate but discontinuous number of performances was 6464 with a total attendance of 7,794,552. The show opened at the Victoria Palace, London on 25 May 1962 and closed on 4 Nov 1972. It re-opened for a season in June 1973 at the New Victoria and finally closed on 8 Dec 1973.

Jesus Christ Superstar, which opened at Palace Theatre, London on 8 Aug 1972, closed on 23 Aug 1980 after 3357 performances having played to 2 million people with box office receipts of £7 million. By 1984 it had been produced in 37 other countries.

Shortest runs *World*

The shortest run on record was that of *The Intimate Revue* at the Duchess Theatre, London, on 11 Mar 1930. Anything which could go wrong did. With scene changes taking up to 20 min apiece, the management scrapped seven scenes to get the finale on before midnight. The run was described as 'half a performance'.

Broadway

The opening and closing nights of many Broadway shows have coincided. Spectacular failures are known as 'turkeys' of which

Barry Manilow (born Barry Mann in Brooklyn, New York on 17 June 1946) who sold out his 1983 Broadway concert in a record 4 hours. (*London Features International*)

Jack Howarth MBE (1896–1984) whose 76 years as an actor culminated in his portrayal of *Coronation Street's* Albert Tatlock. (*Granada TV*)

there were 11 in 1978–79. *Frankenstein*, which opened and closed on Broadway on 4 Jan 1981, lost an estimated $2 million but *A Doll's Life* (23–26 Sept 1982) lost close to $4 million.

Concert

The fastest sell-out in Broadway history occurred when seats for 'Barry Manilow In Concert' for 12 nights (21 Feb–5 Mar 1983) was sold out for $782,160 (*then £500,000*) in 4 hours at the 1983 seat Uris Theatre.

Lowest attendance

The ultimate in low attendances was recorded in December 1983 when the comedy *Bag* in Grantham, Lincolnshire opened to a nil attendance.

Youngest Broadway producer

Margo Feiden (Margo Eden) (b. New York, 2 Dec 1944) produced the musical *Peter Pan*, which opened on 3 Apr 1961 when she was 16 years 5 months old. She wrote *Out Brief Candle*, which opened on 18 Aug 1962. She is now a leading art dealer.

One-man shows

The longest run of one-man shows is 849 by Victor Borge (b. Copenhagen, 3 Jan 1909) in his *Comedy in Music* from 2 Oct 1953 to 21 Jan 1956 at the Golden Theater, Broadway, New York City. The world aggregate record for one-man shows is 1700 performances of *Brief Lives* by Roy Dotrice (b. Guernsey, 26 May 1923) including 400 straight at the Mayfair Theatre, London ending on 20 July 1974. He was on stage for more than $2\frac{1}{2}$ hr per performance of this 17th century monologue and required 3 hr for make up and 1 hr for removal of make-up so aggregating 40 weeks in the chair.

Most durable actors and actresses

Kanmi Fujiyama (b. 1929) played the lead role in 10,288 performances by the comedy company Sochiku Shikigeki from Nov 1966 to June 1983. Dame Anna Neagle, DBE (b. 20 Oct 1904) played the lead role in *Charlie Girl* at the Adelphi Theatre, London for 2062 of 2202 performances between 15 Dec 1965 and 27 Mar 1971. She played the role a further 327 times in 327 performances in Australasia. Frances Etheridge has played Lizzie, the housekeeper, in *Gold in the Hills* (see Longest Runs) more than 660 times over a span of 47 years since 1936. Jack Howarth MBE (1896–1984) was an actor on the stage and in television for 76 years from 1907 until his last appearance after 23 years as Albert Tatlock in *Coronation Street* on 25 Jan 1984.

Most roles

The greatest recorded number of theatrical, film and television roles is 2357 from 1951 to May 1984 by Jan Leighton (US).

Longest play

The longest recorded theatrical production has been *The Warp* by Neil Oram directed by Ken Campbell, a 10 part play cycle played at the Institute of Contemporary Art, The Mall, London, on 18–20 Jan 1979. Russell Denton was on stage for all but 5 min of the 18 hr 5 min. The three intermissions totalled 3 hr 10 min.

Shakespeare

The first all-amateur company to have staged all 37 of Shakespeare's plays was The Southsea Shakespeare Actors, Hampshire, England (founded 1947) in October 1966 when, under their amateur director, K. Edmonds Gateley MBE, they presented *Cymbeline*. The longest is *Hamlet* with 4042 lines and 29,551 words. Of Shakespeare's 1277 speaking parts the longest is Hamlet with 11,610 words.

Longest chorus line

The longest chorus line in performing history were up to 120 in some of the early Ziegfeld's Follies. In the finale of *Chorus Line* on the night of 29 Sept 1983 when it broke the record as the longest-running Broadway show ever, 332 top-hatted 'strutters' performed on the stage.

Cabaret

The highest paid entertainer is Wayne Newton (b. 1942) who is paid up to $250,000 (*now £113,650*) per performance in Las Vegas hotels by the Summa Corporation.

Ice shows

Holiday on Ice Production Inc, founded by Morris Chalfen in 1945, stages the world's most costly live entertainment with up to seven productions playing simultaneously in several of 75 countries drawing 20,000,000 spectators paying $40 million (*£22.2 million*) in a year. The total skating and other staff exceeds 900. The most prolific producer of Ice Shows was Gerald Palmer (1908–83) with 137 since 1945 including 34 consecutive shows at Empire Pool, Wembley, London with attendances up to 850,000. Hazel Wendy Jolly (b. 1933) has appeared in the Wembley Winter Pantomime for 27 years.

Most ardent theatregoers

Dr H. Howard Hughes (b. 1902) Professor Emeritus of Texas Wesleyan College, Fort Worth, Texas, has attended 5512 shows in the period 1956–83. Britain's leading 'first nighter' Edward Sutro MC (1900–78) saw 3000 first night productions in 1916–56 and possibly more than 5000 in his 60 years of theatre-going. The highest precisely recorded number of theatre attendances in Britain is 3596 shows in 31 years from 28 Mar 1953 to 28 Mar 1984 by John Iles of Salisbury, Wiltshire. He estimates he has travelled 144,749 miles *232 938 km* and seen 178,134 performers in 9416 hours (over 56 weeks) inside theatres. The world's largest arts festival is the annual Edinburgh Festival Fringe (instituted in 1959). In 1983, 454 groups gave 6886 performances of 875 shows between 21 Aug and 10 Sept.

Fashion shows

The most prolific producer and most durable commentator of fashion shows is Adalene Ross of San Francisco, California with totals over 4698 in both categories to mid-1984.

Professional wrestling

The professional wrestler who has received most for a single bout has been Kanii Antonio Inoki of Japan on 26 Jun 1976.

He received $2 million for the drawn wrestler v boxer bout against Muhammad Ali in the Budokan Arena, Tokyo. Lou Thesz has won 7 of the world's many 'world' titles. 'Fabulous' Moolah has won major US women's alliance titles every year since 1956. The heaviest ever wrestler has been William J. Cobb of Macon, Georgia, USA (b. 1926), who was billed in 1962 as the 802 lb *363 kg* (57 st 4 lb) 'Happy' Humphrey. Ed 'Strangler' Lewis (1890–1966) *né* Robert H. Friedrich, fought 6200 bouts in 44 years losing only 33 matches. He won world titles in 1921, 1922, 1928 and 1931–32. See also Ch 12 Heaviest Sportsmen.

6. GRAMOPHONE

Guinness Superlatives has published more specialist books: *The Guinness Book of British Hit Singles (4th edition)* (£5.95 paperback), *The Guinness Book of 500 Number One Hits* (£5.95 paperback), *The Guinness Book of British Hit Albums* (£5.95 paperback), *Hits of the 70's* (£6.50 hardback), *Hits of the 60's* (£5.95 paperback) and *The Guinness Hits Challenge* (£3.95 paperback) all by Tim & Jo Rice, Paul Gambaccini and Mike Read. *The Billboard Book of US Top 40 Hits* by Joel Whitburn is priced £8.95 (paperback), and *The Guinness Book of Recorded Sound* by Robert and Celia Dearling with Brian Rust is priced £9.95 (hardback).

Origins

The gramophone (phonograph) was first *conceived* by Charles Cros (1842–88) a French poet and scientist, who described his idea in sealed papers deposited in the French Academy of Sciences on 30 Apr 1877. However the realisation of a practical device was first *achieved* by Thomas Alva Edison (1847–1931) of the USA. The first successful machine was constructed by his mechanic, John Kruesi on 4–6 Dec 1877, demonstrated on 7 Dec and patented on 19 Feb 1878.

Earliest Recordings

The earliest birthdate of anyone whose voice is recorded is Alfred, first Baron Tennyson (1809–1892). The earliest singer was Peter Schram, the Danish baritone of whom a cylinder was made in Don Giovanni on his 70th birthday on 5 Sept 1889.

Tape Recording

Magnetic recording was invented by Valdemar Poulsen (1869–1942) of Denmark with his steel wire Telegraphone in 1898. Fritz Pfleumer (German patent 500900) introduced tape in 1928. Tapes were first used at the Blattner Studios, Elstree, Hertfordshire in 1929. Plastic tapes were devised by BASF of Germany in 1932–35, but were not marketed until 1950 by Recording Associates of New York. In April 1983 Olympic Optical Industry Co. of Japan marketed a micro-cassette recorder 10,7 × 5,1 × 1,4 cm *4.2 × 2 × 0.55 in* weighing 125 g *4.4 oz*.

Most record players

The country with the greatest number of record players is the United States, with a total in excess of 75,000,000. A total of more than half a billion dollars (*now £225 million*) is spent annually on 500,000 juke boxes in the United States. In the US retail sales of discs and tapes reached $4100 million (*then £1440 million*) in 1978 which included sales of 273 million stereo LPs and 190 million singles and 127.8 million stereo tapes. In Sweden disc and tape sales were a record $17.92 (*£9.95*) per head in 1976.

Oldest records

The BBC record library contains over 1,000,000 records, including 5250 with no known matrix. The oldest records in the library are white wax cylinders dating from 1888. The earliest commercial disc recording was manufactured in 1895.

Smallest record

The smallest functional gramophone record is one 1⅜ in *3,5 cm* in diameter of 'God Save the King' of which 250 were made by HMV Record Co in 1924.

Phonographic Identification

Dr Arthur B. Lintgen (b. 1932) of Rydal, Pennsylvania, USA has a seemingly unique ability to identify the music on phonograph records purely by visual inspection without hearing a note.

Earliest jazz records

The earliest jazz record made was *Indiana* and *The Dark Town Strutters Ball*, recorded for the Columbia label in New York City, NY, USA, on or about 30 Jan 1917, by the Original Dixieland Jazz Band, led by Dominick (Nick) James La Rocca (1889–1961). This was released on 31 May 1917. The first jazz record to be released was the ODJB's *Livery Stable Blues* (recorded 24 Feb), backed by *The Dixie Jass Band One-Step* (recorded 26 Feb), released by Victor on 7 Mar 1917.

Most successful solo recording artist

On 9 June 1960 the Hollywood Chamber of Commerce presented Harry Lillis (*alias* Bing) Crosby, Jr (1904–77) with a platinum disc to commemorate the alleged sale of 200,000,000 records from the 2600 singles and 125 albums he had recorded. On 15 Sept 1970 he received a second platinum disc when Decca claimed a sale of 300,650,000 discs. No independently audited figures of his global life time sales from his royalty reports have ever been published and experts regard figures so high as this before the industry became highly developed as exaggerated.

Similarly no independently audited figures have been published for Elvis Aron Presley (1935–77). In view of Presley's worldwide tally of over 170 major hits on singles and over 80 top-selling albums from 1956 continuing after his death, it may be assumed that it was he who must have succeeded Crosby as the top-selling solo artist of all-time. CBS Records reported in August 1983 that sales of albums by Julio Iglesias (b. 1943) in 6 languages had surpassed 100,000,000.

Most successful group

The singers with the greatest sales of any group have been the Beatles. This group from Liverpool, Merseyside, comprised George Harrison, MBE (b. 25 Feb 1943), John Ono (formerly John Winston) Lennon, MBE (b. 9 Oct 1940–k. 8 Dec 1980), James Paul McCartney, MBE (b. 18 June 1942) and Richard Starkey, MBE *alias* Ringo Starr (b. 7 July 1940). The all-time Beatles sales by May 1984 have been estimated by EMI at over 1000 million discs and tapes.

All 4 ex-Beatles sold many million further records as solo artists. Since their break-up in 1970, it is estimated that the most successful group in the world in terms of record sales is the Swedish foursome ABBA (Agnetha Faltskog, Anni-Frid Lyngstad, Bjorn Ulvaeus and Benny Andersson) with a total of 210 million discs and tapes by April 1984.

Golden discs *Earliest*

The earliest recorded piece eventually to aggregate a total sale of a million copies were performances by Enrico Caruso (b. Naples, Italy, 1873, and d. 2 Aug 1921) of the aria *Vesti la giubba* (*On with the Motley*) from the opera *I Pagliacci* by Ruggiero Leoncavallo (1858–1919), the earliest version of which was recorded with piano on 12 Nov 1902. The first single recording to surpass the million mark was Alma Gluck's *Carry me back to old Virginny* on the Red Seal Victor label on the 12-inch *30,48 cm* single faced (later backed) record 74420. The first actual golden disc was one sprayed by RCA Victor for the US trombonist and band-leader Alton 'Glenn' Miller (1904–44) for his *Chattanooga Choo Choo* on 10 Feb 1942.

Most

The only *audited* measure of million-selling singles and 500,000 selling albums within the United States, is certification by the Recording Industry Association of America introduced 14 Mar 1958. Out of the 2342 RIAA gold record awards made to 1 Jan 1984, the most have gone to The Beatles with 43 (plus one with Billy Preston) as a group. McCartney has 20 more awards outside the group and with Wings (including one with Stevie Wonder and one with Michael Jackson). The most awards to an individual is 45 to Elvis Presley (1935–77) spanning 1958 to 1 Jan 1984. Globally however Presley's total of million-selling singles has been authoritatively put at 'approaching 80'.

Most recorded song

Three songs have each been recorded over 1000 times—*Yesterday* written by Paul McCartney and John Lennon (see above) with 1186 versions between 1965 and 1 Jan 1973; *Tie A Yellow Ribbon Round the old Oak Tree* written by Irwin Levine and L. Russell Brown with more than 1000 from 1973 to 1 Jan 1979; and *My Way* written by Paul Anka (b. Ottawa, 30 July 1941) and recorded in numerous versions since Sinatra's 1968 hit recording.

Most recordings

Miss Lata Mangeshker (b. 1928) between 1948 and 1974 has reportedly recorded not less than 25,000 solo, duet and chorus backed songs in 20 Indian languages. She frequently had 5 sessions in a day and has 'backed' 1800 films to 1974.

Michael Joseph Jackson whose album *Thriller* released in Dec 1982 became, by April 1984, the first ever to surpass the 35 million mark in sales. (*London Features International*)

Mohammed Rafi (d. 1 Aug 1980) claimed to have recorded 28,000 songs in 11 Indian languages between 1944 and 1980.

Biggest sellers *Singles*

The greatest seller of any gramophone record to date is *White Christmas* by Irving Berlin (b. Israel Bailin, at Tyumen, Russia, 11 May 1888) with 25,000,000 for the Crosby single (recorded 29 May 1942) and more than 100,000,000 in other versions. The highest claim for any 'pop' record is an unaudited 25,000,000 for *Rock Around the Clock*, copyrighted in 1953 by James E. Myers under the name Jimmy DeKnight and the late Max C. Freedmann and recorded on 12 Apr 1954 by Bill Haley (1927–1981) and the Comets. The top-selling British record of all-time is *I Want to Hold Your Hand* by the Beatles, released in 1963, with world sales of over 13,000,000. The first single to sell over 2,000,000 copies in Great Britain was *Mull of Kintyre*, released in November 1977, by Wings, a group which includes Paul McCartney (see Beatles above), Linda McCartney (b. New York 24 Sept 1942) and Denny Laine (b. Jersey 29 Oct 1944). It was written by McCartney and Laine.

Albums

The best selling album of all time is *Thriller* by Michael Joseph Jackson (b. Gary, Indiana, 29 Aug 1958) with global sales in excess of 35 million copies by April 1984. The best selling album by British performers is considered to be *Dark Side Of The Moon* recorded by Pink Floyd (Dave Gilmour, Nick Mason, Roger Waters, and Rick Wright), in June 1972–January 1973 in London, with sales of over 17 million by April 1984.

The charts—*US Singles*

Singles record charts were first published by *Billboard* on 20 July 1940 when the No. 1 was *I'll Never Smile Again* by Tommy Dorsey (b. 19 Nov 1905, d. 26 Nov 1956). Three discs have stayed top for a record 13 consecutive weeks—*Frenesi* by Artie Shaw from December 1940; *I've Heard that Song Before* by Harry James from February 1943 and *Goodnight Irene* by

Gordon Jenkins and the Weavers from August 1950. *Tainted Love* by Soft Cell stayed on the chart for 43 consecutive weeks from January 1982. The Beatles have had most No. 1 records (20) and Elvis Presley has had most hit singles on Billboard's Hot 100—97 from 1956 to May 1984.

US Albums

Billboard first published an album chart on 15 Mar 1945 when the No. 1 was *King Cole Trio* featuring Nat 'King' Cole (b. 17 Mar 1919, d. 15 Feb 1965). *South Pacific* was No. 1 for 69 weeks (non-consecutive) from May 1949. *Dark Side of The Moon* by Pink Floyd (see above) enjoyed its 520th week on the *Billboard* charts in May 1984. The Beatles had most No. 1's (15) and Presley most hit albums (81 from 1956 to May 1984).

UK Singles

Singles record charts were first published in Britain on 14 Nov 1952 by *New Musical Express. I Believe* by Frankie Laine (b. 30 Mar 1913) held No. 1 position for 18 weeks (non-consecutive) from April 1953, with *Rose Marie* by Slim Whitman (b. 20 Jan 1924) the consecutive record holder with 11 weeks from July 1955. The longest stay has been the 122 weeks of *My Way* by Francis Albert Sinatra (b. 12 Dec 1917) in 9 separate runs from 2 Apr 1969 into 1972. The record for an uninterrupted stay is 56 weeks for Engelbert Humperdinck's *Release Me* from 26 Jan 1967. The Beatles and Presley hold the record for most No. 1 hits with 17 each, with Presley having an overall record of 104 hits in the UK singles chart from 1956 to May 1984.

UK Albums

The first British album chart was published on 8 Nov 1958 by *Melody Maker*. The first No. 1 LP was the film soundtrack *South Pacific* which held the position for a record 70 consecutive weeks and eventually accumulated a record 115 weeks at No. 1. The album with the most total weeks on chart was the soundtrack to *The Sound of Music* with 381 weeks. The Beatles have had most No. 1 albums—12; and Elvis Presley the most hit albums—86.

Fastest selling LPs

The fastest selling record of all time is *John Fitzgerald Kennedy—A Memorial Album* (Premium Albums), recorded on 22 Nov 1963, the day of Mr Kennedy's assassination, which sold 4,000,000 copies at 99 cents (*then 35 p*) in six days (7–12 Dec 1963), thus ironically beating the previous speed record set by the satirical LP *The First Family* in 1962–3. The fastest selling British record is the Beatles' double album *The Beatles* (Apple) with 'nearly 2 million' in its first week in November 1968.

Richard Clayderman (b. Philippe Pages, 1954) of France is reputed to have sold 25 million LP's in the 3 years to Jan 1983 for which he collected 127 gold and 23 platinum records.

Advance sales

The greatest advance sale was 2,100,000 for *Can't Buy Me Love* by the Beatles, released in the United States on 16 Mar 1964. The Beatles also equalled their British record of 1,000,000 advance sales, set by *I Want to Hold Your Hand* (Parlophone transferred to Apple, Aug 1968) on 29 Nov 1963, with this same record on 20 Mar 1964. The UK record for advance sales of an LP is 1,000,000 for the Epic album *Super Trouper* by ABBA released in November 1980.

Loudest *Pop Group*

The amplification at *The Who* concert at Charlton Athletic Football Ground, London on 31 May 1976 provided by a Tasco PA System had a total power of 76,000 watts from eighty 800 W Crown DC 300 A Amplifiers and twenty 600 W Phase Linear 200's. The readings at 50 m *164 ft* from the front of the sound system were 120 db. *Exposure to such noise levels is known to cause PSH—Permanent Shift of Hearing or partial deafness.*

Grammy Awards

The record number of Grammy awards in a year is 8 by Michael Joseph Jackson in 1984 (see also *US Albums*). The all-time record is 23 by Sir Georg Solti KBE.

7. CINEMA

Guinness Superlatives has published a more specialist book *Guinness Book of Film Facts and Feats* by Patrick Robertson, priced £8.95.

FILMS

Origins

The earliest motion pictures ever taken were by Louis Aimé Augustin Le Prince (1842–1890). He was attested to have

Allan Dwan (*above* and *left*) of Canada, the most prolific film director in history with his pith helmet and megaphone. Douglas Fairbanks leans against the tripod. The film being shot was the 1922 version of *Robin Hood*. (*Ronald Grant*)

achieved dim moving outlines on a whitewashed wall at the Institute for the Deaf, Washington Heights, New York, USA as early as 1885–87. The earliest surviving film (sensitized 2⅛ in *53,9 mm* wide paper roll) is from his camera, patented in Britain on 16 Nov 1888, taken in early October 1888 of the garden of his father-in-law, Joseph Whitley in Rounday, Leeds, South Yorkshire at 10 to 12 frames per second. The first commercial presentation of *motion pictures* was at Holland Bros' Kinetoscope Parlour at 1155 Broadway, New York City on 14 April 1894. Viewers could see 5 films for 25 cents or 10 for 50 cents from a double row of Kinetoscopes developed by William Kennedy Laurie Dickson (1860–1935) assistant to Thomas Alva Edison (1847–1931) in 1889–91. The earliest publicly presented film on a *screen* was *La Sortie de Ouvriers de l'Usine Lumière* probably shot in August or September 1894 in Lyon, France. It was exhibited at 44 Rue de Rennes, Paris on 22 Mar 1895 by the Lumière Brothers, Auguste Marie Louis Nicholas (1862–1954) and Louis Jean (1864–1948).

Earliest 'Talkie'

The earliest sound-on-film motion picture was achieved by Eugene Augustin Lauste (b. Paris 17 Jan 1857) who patented his process on 11 Aug 1906 and produced a workable system using a string galvanometer in 1910 at Benedict Road, Stockwell, London. The earliest public presentation of sound on film was by the Tri-ergon process at the Alhambra cinema, Berlin, Germany on 17 Sept 1922.

Most expensive film

The highest ever budgeted film has been *Star Trek* which received its world première in Washington D.C. on 6 Dec 1979. Paramount Studios stated that the cost of this space epic directed by Robert Wise and produced by Gene Roddenberry, was $46 million (*then £21 million*). A figure of $60 million has been attributed to *Superman II* but never substantiated.

Least expensive film

Cecil Hepworth's highly successful release of 1905 *Rescued by Rover* cost £7 13s 9d (*then $37.40*).

Most expensive film rights

The highest price ever paid for film rights is $9,500,000 (*then £4,950,000*) announced on 20 Jan 1978 by Columbia for *Annie*, the Broadway Musical by Charles Strouse starring Andrea McCardle, Dorothy Loudon and Reid Shelton.

Longest film

The longest film ever premièred was the 48 hr long *The Longest Most Meaningless Movie in the World* in 1970. It was British made and later heavily cut to 90 min.

Highest box office gross

The box office gross championship for films is highly vulnerable to inflated ticket prices. Calculations based on the 1983 value of the dollar shows that *Gone With the Wind* with Clark Gable (1901–1960) and Vivien Leigh (1913–1967) released in 1939 is unsurpassed at $312 million. The highest numerical (as opposed to value) dollar champion is Steven Spielberg's *ET: The Extra-Terrestrial*, released on 11 June 1982, and which by 2 Jan 1983 had grossed $322 million (*then £208 million*). On 29 May 1983 *The Return of the Jedi* (20th Century Fox) grossed $8,440,105 (*£5,445,200*) for a single day record, and a record $6,219,929 (*£4,013,000*) for its opening day on 25 May.

Largest loss

It was reported on 20 Nov 1980 that United Artists had withdrawn *Heaven's Gate* because its total cost including distribution and studio overheads had reached $57,000,000.

Highest earnings *By an actor*

The highest rate of pay in cinema history was set by Marlon Brando (b. 3 Apr 1924) for his brief part in *Superman*. He reportedly received $3,700,000 (*then £1,850,000*) and a further $15 million (*then £7.5 million*) after suing for a contracted share of box office royalties. In July 1980 it was reported that Burt Reynolds (b. 11 Feb 1936) received $238,095 per day from 20th Century-Fox for his part in *Cannonball Run*. The highest straight payment for a role has been $12 million (*£7,742,000*) by Sylvester Stallone in *Over the Top* reported in September 1983.

By a Stuntman

Dar Robinson was paid $100,000 (*then £45,500*) for the 1100 ft *335 m* leap from the CN Tower, Toronto in Nov 1979 for *High Point*. His parachute opened at only 300 ft *91 m* above the ground.

Longest Series

Japan's *Tora-San* films have now stretched from *Tora-San I* in August 1968 to *Tora-San XXXII* in 1983 with Kiyoshi Atsumi (b. 1929) starring in each for Shochiku Co.

Character most portrayed

The character most frequently recurring on the screen is Sherlock Holmes, created by Sir Arthur Conan Doyle (1859–1930). Sixty-one actors portrayed him in 175 films between 1900 and 1980.

Largest studios

The largest complex of film studios in the world are those at Universal City, L.A., California. The Back Lot contains 561 buildings and there are 34 sound stages on the 420 acre *170 ha* site.

Most Prolific Director

Allan Dwan (1885–1981) the Canadian born pioneer directed, from 1909 to the early 'sixties, more than 400 films.

Oscars *Most*

Walter (Walt) Elias Disney (1901–66) won more 'Oscars'— the awards of the United States Academy of Motion Picture Arts and Sciences, instituted on 16 May 1929 for 1927–8—than any other person. The physical count comprises 20 statuettes, and nine other plaques and certificates including posthumous awards. The only person to win four Oscars in a starring rôle has been Miss Katharine Hepburn, formerly Mrs Ludlow Ogden Smith (b. Hartford, Conn., 9 Nov 1909) in *Morning Glory* (1932–3), *Guess Who's Coming to Dinner* (1967), *The Lion in Winter* (1968) and *On Golden Pond* (1981). She was 12 times nominated. Only 4 actors have won two Oscars in starring rôles—Frederic March (1897–1975) in 1931/32 and 1946, Spencer Tracy in 1937 and 1938, Gary Cooper in 1941 and 1952, and Marlon Brando in 1954 and 1972. Edith Head (Mrs Wiard B. Ihnen) (d. 1981) won 8 individual awards for costume design. Oscars are named after Mr Oscar Pierce of Texas, USA. The films with most awards have been *Ben Hur* (1959) with 11, followed by *Gone With the Wind* (1939) with 10 and *West Side Story* (1961) with 10. The film with the highest number of nominations was *All About Eve* (1950) with 14. It won six. The youngest ever winner was Shirley Temple (b. 24 Apr 1928) aged 5 with her honorary Oscar, and the oldest George Burns, (b. 20 Jan 1896) aged 80 for *The Sunshine Boys* in 1976.

Japan's best known face—that of Kiyoshi Atsumi who has starred in *Tora San* for more than 15 years.

Rita Moreno whose trophies include all 4 of the major show business awards—Oscars (motion pictures, founded in 1928), Tony (theatre, 1947), Emmy (TV, 1948) and Grammy (recording, 1957).

Versatility showbusiness awards

The only 3 performers to have won Oscars, Emmy, Tony and Grammy awards have been Helen Hayes (b. 1900) in 1932–1976; Richard Rodgers (1902–1979), composer of musicals and Rita Moreno (b. 1931) in 1961–1977. Barbra Streisand (b. 24 Apr 1942 in Brooklyn, NY) received Oscar, Grammy and Emmy awards in addition to a special 'Star of the Decade' Tony award.

CINEMAS

Earliest

The earliest structure designed and exclusively used for exhibiting projected films is believed to be one erected at the Atlanta Show, Georgia USA in October 1895 to exhibit C. F. Jenkins' phantoscope. The earliest cinema constructed in Great Britain was built without permission at Olympia, London, to house the 'Theatregraph' promoted by Robert William Paul (1869–1943). This was completed by 16 Apr 1896.

Largest *World*

The largest cinema in the world is the Radio City Music Hall, New York City, opened on 27 Dec 1932 with 5945 (now 5882) seats. The Roxy, opened in New York City on 11 March 1927 had 6214 (later 5869) seats but was closed on 29 Mar 1960. Cineplex, opened at the Toronto Eaton Centre, Canada on 19 Apr 1979 has 18 separate theatres with an aggregate capacity of 1700.

Great Britain

Great Britain's largest cinema is the Odeon Theatre, Ham-mersmith, Greater London, with 3483 seats. The Playhouse, Glasgow had 4235 seats.

Drive-In

The world's largest drive-in cinema is Loew's Open Air at Lynn, Mass., USA with a capacity of 5000 cars. The earliest, at Wilson Boulevard, Camden, New Jersey opened on 6 June 1933.

Most cinemas

Sam Marino has more cinemas per total population than any other country in the world, with 1 cinema for every 1512 inhabitants. Saudi Arabia (population 8.4 million) has no cinemas. Ascension Island has a record 733 cinema seats for a population of 971 (31 Dec 1981).

Highest cinema going

The people of the Philippines (population 48.4 million) go to the cinema more often than those of any other country in the world with an average of 19.06 attendances per person per annum (1979–80). The Soviet Union claims to have most cinemas in the world, with 163,400 in 1974, but this includes buildings merely equipped with even 16 mm projectors. The USA has 16,965 actual cinemas (1979). The number of cinemas in the UK reached a peak 4714 in 1944 declining to 695 with 1301 screens by 1 Apr 1984. The average weekly admissions has declined from 33,420,000 in 1944 to 1,376,470 by September 1983.

Biggest screen

The permanently installed cinema screen with the largest area is one of 96 ft × 70 ft 6 in *29,26 × 21,48 m* installed in the Imax Theatre, Taman Mini Park, Jakarta, Indonesia opened in March 1984. It was made by Harkness Screens Ltd at Boreham Wood, Herts. A temporary screen 297 ft × 33 ft *90,5 × 10 m* was used at the 1937 Paris Exposition.

Most films seen

Albert E. Van Schmus (b. 1921) saw 16,945 films in 32 years (1949–1982) as a rater for Motion Picture Association of America Inc.

8. RADIO BROADCASTING

Origins

The earliest description of a radio transmission system was written by Dr Mahlon Loomis (USA) (b. Fulton County, NY, 21 July 1826) on 21 July 1864 and demonstrated between two kites more than 14 miles *22 km* apart at Bear's Den, Loudoun County, Virginia in October 1866. He received US patent No. 129,971 entitled Improvement in Telegraphing on 20 July 1872. He died in 1886.

Earliest patent

The first patent for a system of communication by means of electro-magnetic waves, numbered No. 12039, was granted on 2 June 1896 to the Italian-Irish Marchese Guglielmo Marconi, GCVO (Hon) (1874–1937). A public demonstration of wireless transmission of speech was, however, given in the town square of Murray, Kentucky, USA in 1892 by Nathan B. Stubblefield. He died destitute on 28 March 1928. The first permanent wireless installation was at The Needles on the Isle of Wight, by Marconi's Wireless Telegraph Co., Ltd., in November 1896.

Earliest broadcast *World*

The world's first advertised broadcast was made on 24 Dec 1906 by the Canadian born Prof Reginald Aubrey Fessenden (1868–1932) from the 420 ft *128 m* mast of the National Electric Signalling Company at Brant Rock, Massachusetts, USA. The transmission included Handel's *Largo*. Fessenden had achieved the broadcast of speech as early as November 1900 but this was highly distorted.

Great Britain

The first experimental broadcasting transmitter in Great Britain was set up at the Marconi Works in Chelmsford, Essex, in December 1919, and broadcast a news service in February 1920. The earliest regular broadcast was made from the Marconi transmitter '2MT' at Writtle, Essex, on 14 Feb 1922.

Transatlantic transmissions

The earliest transatlantic wireless signals (the letter S in Morse

Code) were received by Marconi, George Stephen Kemp and Percy Paget from a 10 kW station at Poldhu, Cornwall, at Signal Hill, St John's, Newfoundland, Canada, at 12.30 p.m. on 12 Dec 1901. Human speech was first heard across the Atlantic in November 1915 when a transmission from the US Navy station at Arlington, Virginia was received by US radio-telephone engineers on the Eiffel Tower.

Earliest radio-microphones

The radio-microphone, which was in essence also the first 'bug', was devised by Reg Moores (GB) in 1947 and first used on 76 MHz in the ice show *Aladdin* at Brighton Sports Stadium, East Sussex in September 1949.

Longest BBC national broadcast

The longest BBC national broadcast was the reporting of the Coronation of Queen Elizabeth II on 2 June 1953. It began at 10.15 a.m. and finished at 5.30 p.m., after 7 hr 15 min.

Longest continuous broadcast *World*

The longest continuous broadcast (excluding disc-jockeying) has been one of 484 hr (20 days 4 hr) by Larry Norton of WGRQ FM Buffalo, New York, USA on 19 Mar–8 Apr 1981. *No further claims for the above category will be entertained.* Radio Telefís Éireann transmitted an unedited reading of *Ulysses* by James Joyce (1882–1941) for 29 hr 38 min 47 sec on 16–17 July 1982.

Local and Hospital radio

The longest local radio transmission has been 84 hr by Robert W. Morgan of Community Radio Station WKRC, Co. Kildare, Ireland on 8–11 Jan 1982. Brian Sheard completed 208 hr 15 min of broadcasting on Manchester Hospital Radio on 15–23 Feb 1980.

Topmost Prize

Mary Buchanan, 15, on WKRQ, Cincinnati, USA won a prize of $25,000 for 40 years (viz $1 million) on 21 Nov 1980.

Brain of Britain Quiz

The youngest person to become 'Brain of Britain' on BBC radio was Anthony Carr, 16, of Anglesey in 1956. The oldest contestant has been the author and translator Hugh Merrick (d. 1981) in his 80th year in August 1977. The record score is 35 by the 1981 winner Peter Barlow of Richmond, Surrey.

Most durable programmes *BBC*

The longest running BBC radio series is *The Week's Good Cause* beginning on 24 Jan 1926. The St Francis Leprosy Guild appeal by Cardinal Basil Hume of 27 Jan 1980 raised a record £89,221. The longest running record programme is *Desert Island Discs* which began on 29 Jan 1942 and on which programme only one guest, Arthur Askey CBE, (1900–82) had been stranded a fourth time (on the 1572nd show on 20 Dec 1980). The *Desert Island* programme has been presented since its inception by Roy Plomley, OBE who devised the idea. The longest running solo radio feature is *Letter from America* by (Alfred) Alistair Cooke, Hon KBE (b. Salford 20 Nov 1908), first broadcast on 24 Mar 1946. The longest running radio serial is *The Archers* which was created by Godfrey Baseley and was first broadcast on 29 May 1950. Up to May 1984 the signature tune *Barwick Green* had been played over 35,390 times. The only one of 367 roles which has been played without interruption from the start has been that of Philip Archer by Norman Painting OBE (b. Leamington Spa, 23 Apr 1924).

Most Heard Broadcaster

Larry King has broadcast on network for 27½ hours a week since 30 Jan 1978 from Washington DC on Mutual Broadcasting Systems to all 50 States (now on 272 Stations).

Earliest antipodal reception

Frank Henry Alfred Walker (b. 11 Nov 1904) on the night of 12 Nov 1924 received on his home-made 2 valve receiver on 75 metres, signals from Marconi's yacht *Electra* (call sign ICCM) in Australian waters at Crown Farm, Cuttimore Lane, Walton-on-Thames, Surrey, England.

Most assiduous Radio Ham

Richard C. Spenceley (d. 30 July 1982) of KV4AA at St Thomas, Virgin Islands built his contacts (QSO's) to a record level of 48,100 in 365 days in 1978.

Most stations

The country with the greatest number of radio broadcasting

The late Richard C. Spenceley of the Virgin Islands, who achieved 48,100 amateur radio contacts in the single year of 1978.

stations is the United States, where there were 9317 authorised broadcast stations in Feb 1982 of which 4641 were AM (Amplitude modulation) and 4676 FM (Frequency modulation).

Highest listening

The peak recorded listenership on BBC Radio was 30,000,000 adults on 6 June 1950 for the boxing fight between Lee Savold (US) and Bruce Woodcock (GB) (b. Doncaster, S. Yorks, 1921).

Highest response

The highest recorded response from a radio show occurred on 27 Nov 1974 when on a 5 hr talk show on WCAU, Philadelphia, USA, Howard Sheldon, the astrologist registered a call count of 388,299 calls on the 'Bill Corsair Show'.

Smallest Set

The Toshiba AM-FM 302 launched in January 1983 measures 4.9 × 3.5 × 2.2 in *12,4 × 8,9 × 5,6 cm* and weighs 3 oz *85 g*.

9. TELEVISION

Guinness Superlatives have published *The Guinness Book of TV Facts and Feats* by Kenneth Passingham (price £9.95).

Invention

The invention of television, the instantaneous viewing of distant objects by electrical transmissions, was not an act but a process of successive and inter-dependent discoveries. The first commercial cathode ray tube was introduced in 1897 by Karl Ferdinand Braun (1850–1918), but was not linked to 'electric vision' until 1907 by Prof. Boris Rosing (disappeared 1918) of Russia in St Petersburg (now Leningrad). A. A. Campbell Swinton FRS (1863–1930) published the fundamentals of television transmission on 18 June 1908 in a brief letter to *Nature* entitled 'Distant Electric Vision'. The earliest public demonstration of television was given on 27 Jan 1926 by John Logie Baird (1888–1946) of Scotland, using a development of the mechanical scanning system patented by Paul Nipkow on 6 Jan 1884. He had achieved the transmission of a Maltese Cross over 10 ft *3,05 m* at 8, Queen's Arcade, Hastings, East Sussex by February 1924 and the first facial image (of William Taynton, 15) at 23, Frith Street on 30 Oct 1925. Taynton had to be bribed with 2s 6d. A patent application for the Iconoscope had been filed on 29 Dec 1923 by Dr Vladimir Kosma Zworykin (1889–1982). It was not issued until 20 Dec 1938. Kenjiro Takayanagi (b. 20 Jan. 1889) succeeded in transmitting a 40-line electronic picture on 25 Dec 1926 with a Braun cathode-ray tube and a Nipkow disc at Hamamatsu Technical College, Japan. Baird launched his first television 'service' via a BBC transmitter on 30 Sept 1929 and marketed the first sets, The Baird Televisions, at £26.25 in May 1930. Public transmissions on 30 lines were made from 22 Aug 1932 until 11 Sept 1935.

Earliest service

The world's first high definition (*i.e.* 405 lines) television broadcasting service was opened from Alexandra Palace, Haringey, Greater London, on 2 Nov 1936, when there were about 100 sets in the United Kingdom. The Chief Engineer was Mr Douglas Birkinshaw. A television station in Berlin, Germany, made a low definition (180 line) transmission from 22 Mar 1935. The transmitter burnt out in Aug 1935.

Transatlantic transmission

The earliest transatlantic transmission by satellite was achieved at 1 a.m. on 11 July 1962, *via* the active satellite *Telstar 1* from Andover, Maine, USA, to Pleumeur Bodou, France. The picture was of Mr Frederick R. Kappell, chairman of the American Telephone and Telegraph Company, which owned the satellite. The first 'live' broadcast was made on 23 July 1962 and the first woman to appear was the *haute couturière*, Ginette Spanier, directrice of Balmain, the next day. On 9 Feb 1928 the image of J. L. Baird (see above) and of a Mrs Howe was transmitted from Station 2 KZ at Coulsdon, Surrey, England to Station 2 CVJ, Hartsdale, NY, USA.

Longest telecast

The longest pre-scheduled telecast on record was a continuous transmission for 163 hr 18 min by GTV 9 of Melbourne, Australia covering the Apollo XI moon mission on 19–26 July 1969. The longest continuous TV transmission under a single director was the Avro Television Production *Open het Dorp* transmitted in the Netherlands on 26–27 Nov 1962 for 23 hr 20 min under the direction of Theo Ordeman.

Video-tape recording *Earliest*

Alexander M. Poniatoff first demonstrated video-tape recording known as Ampex (his initials plus 'ex' for excellence) in 1956. The earliest demonstration of a home video recorder was on 24 June 1963 at the BBC News Studio at Alexandra Palace, London of the Telcan developed by Norman Rutherford and Michael Turner of the Nottingham Electronic Valve Co.

Most durable shows *World*

The world's most durable TV show is NBC's *Meet the Press* first transmitted on 6 Nov 1947 and weekly since 12 Sept 1948, originated by Lawrence E. Spivak, who appeared weekly as either moderator or panel member until 1975. On 11 Dec 1980 Mike Douglas presented the 4754th version of his show started in 1960.

Great Britain

Andy Pandy was first transmitted on 11 July 1950 but consisted of repeats of a cycle of 26 shows until 1970. *Come Dancing* was first transmitted on 29 Sept 1950 but is seasonal. *Sooty* was first presented on BBC by its devisor Harry Corbett (born 1918) from 1952 to 1967 and is continued by his son Matthew on ITV. *The Good Old Days* light entertainment ran from 20 July 1953 to 31 Dec 1983. Barney Colehan produced all 244 programmes. The *BBC News* was inaugurated in vision on 5 July 1954. Richard Baker OBE read the news from 1954 to Christmas 1982. Of current affairs programmes the weekly BBC *Panorama* was first transmitted on 11 Nov 1953 but has summer breaks, whereas Granada's *What The Papers Say* has been transmitted weekly since 5 Nov 1956. The monthly *Sky at Night* has been presented by Patrick Moore OBE without a break or a miss since 26 Apr 1957. The longest serving TV quizmaster is Bamber Gascoigne of Granada's *University Challenge* which has run since 21 Sept 1962. The longest running domestic drama serial is Granada's *Coronation Street* which has run twice weekly since 9 Dec 1960.

Most sets

The US had, by January 1984, 84.8 million TV households, with 32.2 million on Cable TV, 17.8 million on Pay TV and 25 million on Subscription satellite TV, with 3.4 million having video disc or video cassette. The number of homes with colour sets was 71,400,000 (88%) by January 1982. The number of licences current in the United Kingdom was 18,631,753 on 1 Apr 1984 of which 15,370,481 (82.5 per cent) were for colour sets. Black and white licences became less commonplace than colour in 1976.

TV Watching

In July 1978 it was estimated that the *average* American child by his or her 18th birthday has watched 710 solid days (17,040 hours) of TV, seen more than 350,600 commercials and more than 15,000 TV murders. In 1983 it was estimated that the US national average watching per household reached a record 7 hr 2 min per day in 83.3 million TV households. There are 571 TV sets per 1000 people in the USA compared with 348 in Sweden and 330 in Britain.

Greatest audience

The greatest projected number of viewers worldwide for a televised event is 2500 million for the live and recorded transmissions of the XXIIIrd Olympic Games in Los Angeles, California from 27 July to 13 Aug 1984. The American Broadcasting Co airing schedule comprised 187½ hours of coverage on 56 cameras.

The programme which attracted the highest ever viewership was the *Goodbye, Farewell and Amen* final episode of M*A*S*H (the acronym for Mobile Army Surgical Hospital 4077) transmitted by CBS on 28 Feb 1983 to 60.3 per cent of all households in the United States. It was estimated that some 125 million people tuned in, taking a 77 per cent share of all viewing. The UK record is 39 million for the wedding of TRH the Prince and Princess of Wales in London on 29 July 1981.

The engineer John Logie Baird (1888–1946) who pioneered television in 1924–1926. The world's potential audience has grown from his selling a few sets in May 1930 to over 2000 million in 1984. He is buried in Helensburgh, Scotland where his father was the minister.

Most expensive production
The Winds of War, a seven part Paramount World War II saga, aired by ABC was the most expensive ever TV production costing $42 million over 14 months shooting. The final episode on 13 Feb 1983 attracted a rating of 41.0 per cent (% of total number of viewers), and a share of 56 per cent (% of total sets turned on that were tuned in).

Largest contracts *World*
The highest rate for any TV contract ever signed was one for $7 million (*then £3,100,000*) for 7 hours of transmission by Marie Osmond by NBC announced on 9 Mar 1981. The figure includes talent and production costs.

Currently television's highest-paid performer is John William Carson (b. 23 Oct 1925), the host of *The Tonight Show*. His current NBC contract reportedly calls for annual payment of $5,000,000 (*now £2,275,000*) for his one hour evening show aired four times weekly. The highest-paid current affairs or news performer is Dan Rather of CBS who reportedly signed an $8 million (*then £4.7 million*) contract for five years from 1982.

Great Britain
The largest contract in British television was one of a reported £9,000,000, inclusive of production expenses, signed by Tom Jones (b. Thomas Jones Woodward, 7 June 1940) of Treforest, Mid Glamorgan, Wales in June 1968 with ABC-TV of the United States and ATV in London for 17 one-hour shows per annum from January 1969 to January 1974.

Highest paid TV Performer
Carroll O'Connor, star of *Archie Bunker's Place*, receives $275,000 (*£182,500*) for each of 22 episodes in the 1982/83 season totalling $6,050,000 (*£4 million*). Peter Falk (b. 16 Sept 1927), the disarmingly persistent detective *Columbo*, was paid from $300,000 to $350,000 for a single episode of his series of six. Singer Kenny Rogers was reported in February 1983 to have been paid $2 million (*then £1,280,000*) for a single taping of a concert for HBO (Home Box Office) TV Channel.

Largest TV prizes *World*
On 24 July 1975 WABC-TV, New York City transmitted the first televised Grand Tier draw of the State Lottery in which the winner took the grand prize of $1,000,000 (*now £454,545*). This was however taxable.

Most successful appeals
The Jerry Lewis Labor Day Telethon on 4 Sept 1979 raised $31,103,787 (*then £14,138,000*) in pledges for the Muscular Dystrophy Association. The East African Emergency Appeal broadcast on BBC TV by Sue Lawley on 19 June 1980, reached £5,591,643 in donations (excluding government grant), banked when it closed on 3 Apr 1981 for the five distributing charities.

Biggest sale
The greatest number of episodes of any TV programme ever sold has been 1144 episodes of 'Coronation Street' by Granada Television to CBKST Saskatoon, Saskatchewan, Canada, on 31 May 1971. This constituted 20 days 15 hr 44 min continuous viewing. A further 728 episodes (Jan 1974–Jan 1981) were sold to CBC in August 1982.

Most prolific scriptwriter
The most prolific television writer in the world is the Rt Hon Lord Willis known as Ted Willis (b. 13 Jan 1918), who in the period 1949–84 has created 29 series, including the first seven years and 2,250,000 words of *Dixon of Dock Green* which ran from 1955 to 1976, 27 stage plays and 28 feature films. He had 22 plays produced. His total output since 1942 can be estimated at 17,750,000 words.

'Mastermind' Records
The BBC TV series began on 11 Sept 1972 producing a record 38 points by Miss Margaret Harris (on 'Life and work of Cecil Rhodes') in 1984 final. Sir David Hunt KCMG, OBE won the 'Mastermind Champions' contest on 3 May 1982.

TV Producer
The most prolific TV producer in the world is Aaron Spelling (b. 1928) who, in 25 years from 1956 to 1981, produced 1435 TV episodes totalling 1457½ hours of air time. His output included *Starsky and Hutch* (89 episodes) and *Charlie's Angels* (109 episodes).

Bamber Gascoigne who has served as quizmaster on *University Challenge* since 1962. (*Granada TV*)

Highest TV advertising rates
The highest TV advertising rate has been $450,000 per ½ min (*then £10,000 per sec*) for CBS network prime time during the transmission of the final episode of M*A*S*H on 28 Feb 1983 (see above). The series of 252 episodes over 104 hours started on 17 Sept 1972 and won 14 out of 19 Emmys. In Great Britain the peak time weekday 60 sec spot rate (5.40–10.40 p.m.) for Thames Television is £36,260 + VAT (April 1984).

Most takes
The highest number of 'takes' for a TV commercial is 28 in 1973 by Pat Coombs, the comedienne, who has supported Dick Emery on BBC TV. Her explanation was 'Everytime we came to the punch line I just could not remember the name of the product'.

Commercial records
In 1977 James Coburn of Beverly Hills, California was reputed to have been paid $500,000 (*then £250,000*) for uttering two words on a series of Schlitz beer commercials. The words 'Schlitz Light' were thus at a quarter of a million dollars per syllable. Brooke Shields (b. 31 May 1965) was reportedly paid $250,000 (*then £125,000*) for one minute of film by a Japanese TV commercial film maker in 1979. Faye Dunaway was reported in May 1979 to have been paid $900,000 (*then £450,000*) for uttering 6 words for a Japanese department store TV Commercial. Britain's most durable TV Commercial has been the Brooke Bond chimpanzee commercial first transmitted on 21 Nov 1971 and 1687 more times to October 1979.

World's Smallest Sets
The Seiko TV-Wrist Watch launched on 23 Dec 1982 in Japan has a 1.2 in *30,5 mm* screen and weighs only 80 g *2.8 oz*. Together with the receiver unit and the headphone set the entire black and white system, costing 108,000 Yen (*then £260*), weighs only 320 g *11,3 oz*. The smallest single-piece TV set is the Casio-Keisanki TV-10 weighing 338 g *11.9 oz* with a 2.7 in *6,85 cm* screen launched in Tokyo in July 1983. The smallest colour TV set is the Matsushita Electric Industry Co 1.34 lb *607 g* 'Color-Solo' television with dimensions of 11 × 3,8 × 18 cm *4.3 × 1.5 × 7.0 in* and a 1.5 in *381 mm* screen which can also serve as a portable video monitor. It was displayed in Chicago in June 1983.

Highest Definition
A TV system with a 1125 line definition was demonstrated by NHK (Nippon Hoso Kyokai) built by Hitachi and Sony at Brighton, Sussex on 19 Sept 1982.

Chapter 7

THE WORLDS STRUCTURES

The world's tallest obelisk seen through the world's tallest columns at the Temple of Karnak, Egypt, which took 1700 years to build. (*David Cadisch*)

EARLIEST STRUCTURES

World

The earliest known human structure is a rough circle of loosely piled lava blocks found on the lowest cultural level at the Lower Palaeolithic site at Olduvai Gorge in Tanzania excavated by the Leakeys' (see p. 9) in 1960. The structure was associated with artifacts and bones and may represent a work-floor, dating to *c.* 1,800,000 BC. The earliest evidence of *buildings* yet discovered is that of 21 huts with hearths or pebble-lined pits and delimited by stake holes found in October 1965 at the Terra Amata site in Nice, France thought to belong to the Acheulian culture of *c.* 400,000 years ago. Excavation carried out between 28 June and 5 July 1966 revealed one hut with palisaded walls with axes of 49 ft *15 m* and 20 ft *6 m*. The oldest free standing structures in the world are now believed to be the megalithic temples at Mgarr and Skorba in Malta and Ggantija in Gozo dating from *c.* 3250 BC. The remains of a stone tower 20 ft *6,1 m* high originally built into the walls of Jericho has been excavated and is dated to 5000 BC. The foundations of the walls have been dated to as early as 8350 BC.

Great Britain

Twelve small stone clusters, associated with broken bones and charcoal in stratum C of the early palaeolithic site at Hoxne, Suffolk may be regarded as Britain's earliest structures dated *c.* 250,000 BC. Remains of the earliest dated stone shelter and cooking pit were discovered in 1967 at Culver Well, Isle of Portland, Dorset (Mesolithic, 5200 BC ± 135). On the Isle of Jura, Strathclyde, Scotland a hearth consisting of three linked stone circles has been dated to the Mesolithic period 6013 ± 200 BC. The only original piece of Roman building from the 1st century AD surviving is the bottom 14 ft *4,25 m* of the Dover beacon.

Ireland

The earliest known evidence of human occupation in Ireland dates from the Mesolithic period *c.* 7500 at the Carrowmore site in County Sligo. Ireland became enisled or separated from Great Britain *c.* 9050 BC. Nearby megalithic burials dated to 3800 ± 80 BC are the earliest in Europe.

1. BUILDINGS FOR WORKING

LARGEST BUILDINGS

Industrial

The largest industrial plant in the world is the Nizhniy Tagil Railroad Car and Tank Plant, 85 miles *136 km* northwest of Sverdlovsk, USSR which has 827 000 m² or 204.3 acres of floor space. It has an annual capacity to produce 2500 T-72 tanks.

Commercial *World*

The greatest ground area covered by any building in the world under one roof is the auction building of the Co-operative VBA (Verenigde Bloemenveilingen Aalsmeer), which measures 808,75 × 375 m *884.4 × 410.1 yds* with a floor surface of 303,282 m² *74.94 acres*. The first section of this site of the world's largest flower auction at Aalsmeer, Netherlands was completed in February 1972. The building with the largest cubic capacity in the world is the Boeing Company's main assembly plant at Everett, Washington State, USA completed in 1968 with a capacity of 200 million ft³ *5,6 million m³*.

Great Britain

The largest building in Britain is the Ford Parts Center at Daventry, Northamptonshire, which measures 1,978 × 780 ft *602 × 237 m* and 1.6 million ft² or 36.7 acres *14,86 ha*. It was opened on 6 Sept 1972 at a cost of nearly £8 million. It employs 1600 people and is fitted with 14,000 fluorescent lights.

Largest Construction Project

The Madinat Al-Jubail Al-Sinaiyah project in Saudi Arabia (1976–1996) covering 230,412.8 acres *932,43 km²* is the largest in history. The work force on the city and industrial port complex is increasing to a peak of 33,187 from the mid-1982 figure of 17,200. The total earth moving and dredging volume will reach 345 million m³ or *0.82 of a cubic mile*.

Scientific

The most capacious scientific building in the world is the Vehicle Assembly Building (VAB) at Complex 39, the selected site for the final assembly and launching of the Apollo moon spacecraft on the Saturn V rocket, at the John F. Kennedy Space Center (KSC) on Merritt Island, Cape Canaveral, Florida, USA. It is a steel-framed building measuring 716 ft *218 m* in length, 518 ft *158 m* in width and 525 ft *160 m* high. The building contains four bays, each with its own door 460 ft *140 m* high. Construction began in April 1963 by the Ursum Consortium. Its floor area is 343,500 ft² (7.87 acres *3,18 ha*) and its capacity is 129,482,000 ft³ *3 666 500 m³*. The building was 'topped out' on 14 Apr 1965 at a cost of $108,700,000 (*then £38.8 million*).

Administrative

The largest ground area covered by any office building is that of the Pentagon, in Arlington, Virginia, USA. Built to house the US Defense Department's offices it was completed on 15 Jan 1943 and cost an estimated $83,000,000 (*then £20,595,000*). Each of the outermost sides of the Pentagon is 921 ft *281 m* long and the perimeter of the building is about 1500 yd *1370 m*. The five storeys of the building enclose a floor area of 6,500,000 ft² *604 000 m²* (149.2 acres *60,3 ha*). During the day 29,000 people work in the building. The telephone system of the building has over 44,000 telephones connected by 160,000 miles *257 500 km* of cable and its 220 staff handle 280,000 calls a day. Two restaurants, six cafeterias and ten snack bars and a staff of 675 form the catering department of the building. The corridors measure 17 miles *27 km* in length and there are 7748 windows to be cleaned.

Office

The largest office buildings with the largest rentable space in the world are The World Trade Center in New York City, USA with a total of 4,370,000 ft² *406 000 m²* (100.32 acres *40,6 ha*) in each of the twin towers of which the taller Tower Two (formerly B) is 1362 ft 3¼ in *415,22 m*. The tip of the TV antenna on Tower One is 1710 ft *521,2 m* above street level.

Single office *Great Britain*

The largest single office in the United Kingdom is that of West Midlands Gas at Solihull, West Midlands, built by Spooners (Hull) Ltd in 1962. It now measures 753 ft by 160 ft *230 by 49 m* (2.77 acres *1,12 ha*) in one open plan room accommodating 2170 clerical and managerial workers.

TALLEST BUILDINGS

World

The tallest office building in the world is the Sears Tower, the national headquarters of Sears, Roebuck & Co. in Wacker Drive, Chicago, Illinois with 110 storeys rising to 1454 ft *443 m* and begun in August 1970. Its gross area is 4,400,000 ft² (101.0 acres *40,8 ha*). It was 'topped out' on 4 May 1973. It surpassed the World Trade Center in New York City in height at 2.35 p.m. on 6 Mar 1973 with the first steel column reaching to the 104th storey. The addition of two TV antennae brought the total height to 1559 ft *475,18 m*. The building's population is 16,700 served by 103 elevators and 18 escalators. It has 16,000 windows. Tentative plans for a 169 storey 2300 ft *701 m* tall building, projected to cost $1250 million, for the Chicago Loop, Illinois, USA were published on 27 Oct 1981.

An artist's impression of the Madinat Al-Jubail project in Saudi Arabia, the world's largest construction project.

Great Britain

The tallest office block in Britain and the tallest cantilevered building in the world is the £72 million National Westminster tower block in Bishopsgate, City of London completed in 1979. It has 49 storeys and 3 basement levels, serviced by 21 lifts, and is 600 ft 4 in *183 m* tall. The gross floor area is 636,373 ft² *59,121 m²* (14.6 acres *5,9 ha*).

HABITATIONS

Greatest altitude

The highest inhabited buildings in the world are those in the Indian–Tibet border fort of Bāsisi at *c.* 19,700 ft *5988 m*. In April 1961, however, a 3-room dwelling was discovered at 21,650 ft *6600 m* on Cerro Llullaillaco (22,058 ft *6723 m*), on the Argentine–Chile border, believed to date from the late pre-Columbian period *c.* 1480. A settlement on the T'e-li-mo trail in southern Tibet is at an apparent altitude of 19,800 ft *6019 m*.

Northernmost

The most northerly habitation in the world is the Danish Scientific station set up in 1952 in Pearyland, northern Greenland (Kalaalit Nunaat), over 900 miles *1450 km* north of the Arctic Circle. Eskimo hearths dated to before 1000 BC were discovered in Pearyland in 1969. Polar Eskimos were discovered in Inglefield Land, NW Greenland in 1818. The USSR's drifting research station 'North Pole 15', passed within 1¼ miles *2,8 km* of the North Pole in December 1967. The most northerly continuously inhabited place is the Canadian Department of National Defence outpost at Alert on Ellesmere Island, Northwest Territories in Lat. 82° 30′ N, Long. 62° W, set up in 1950.

Southernmost

The most southerly permanent human habitation is the United States' Scott–Amundsen South Polar Station (see Chapter X) completed in 1957 and replaced in 1975.

EMBASSIES AND CIVIC BUILDINGS

Largest

The largest embassy in the world is the USSR embassy on Bei Xiao Jie, Peking, China, in the north-eastern corner of the Northern walled city. The whole 45 acre *18,2 ha* area of the old Orthodox Church mission (established 1728), now known as the *Bei guan*, was handed over to the USSR in 1949. The largest in Great Britain is the United States of America Embassy in Grosvenor Square, London. The Chancery Building, completed in 1960, alone has 600 rooms for a staff of 700 on seven floors with a usable floor area of 255,000 ft² (5.85 acres *2,37 ha*).

Great Britain

The oldest municipal building in Britain is the Exeter Guildhall first referred to in a deed of 1160. The Tudor front was added in 1593.

EXHIBITION CENTRES

Largest *Great Britain*

Britain's largest exhibition centre is the National Exhibition

Centre, Birmingham opened in February 1976. Five halls which inter-connect cover 87 180 m² *938,397 ft²* or 21.54 acres with a volume of 1 168 466 m³ or *41.26 million ft³*.

INDUSTRIAL STRUCTURES

Tallest chimneys *World*

The world's tallest chimney is the $5.5 million International Nickel Company's stack 1245 ft 8 in *379,6 m* tall at Copper Cliff, Sudbury, Ontario, Canada, completed in 1970. It was built by Canadian Kellogg Ltd., in 60 days and the diameter tapers from 116.4 ft *35,4 m* at the base to 51.8 ft *15,8 m* at the top. It weighs 38,390 tons *39 006 tonnes* and became operational in 1971. The world's most massive chimney is one of 1148 ft *350 m* at Puentes, Spain, built by M. W. Kellogg Co. It contains 20,600 yd³ *15 750 m³* of concrete and 2.9 million lb *1315 tonnes* of steel and has an internal volume of 6.7 million ft³ *189 720 m³*. Europe's tallest chimney serves the Zasavje thermo-power plant in Trboulje, Yugoslavia completed to 350 metres *1181 ft* on 1 June 1976.

Great Britain

The tallest chimney in Great Britain is one of 850 ft *259 m* at Drax Power Station, North Yorkshire, begun in 1966 and topped out on 16 May 1969. It has an untapered diameter of 87 ft 9 in *26 m* and has the greatest capacity of any chimney. The architects were Clifford Tee & Gale of London. The oldest known industrial chimney in Britain is the Stone Edge Chimney, near Chesterfield, Derbyshire built to a height of 55 ft *16,76 m ante* 1771.

Cooling towers

The largest cooling tower in the world is that adjacent to the nuclear power plant at Uentrop, W. Germany which is 590 ft *179,8 m* tall. It was completed in 1976. The largest in the United Kingdom of the Ferrybridge and Didcot type measure 375 ft *114 m* tall and 300 ft *91 m* across the base.

HANGARS

Largest *World*

Hangar 375 ('Big Texas') at Kelly Air Force Base, San Antonio, Texas, USA completed on 15 Feb 1956. It has 4 doors each 250 ft *76,2 m* wide and 60 ft *18,28 m* high weighing 598 tons/*608 tonnes*. The high bay area measures 2000 × 300 × 90 ft *609,6 × 91,4 × 27,4 m* and is surrounded by a 44 acre *17,8 ha* concrete apron. Delta Air Lines' jet base on a 140 acre *56,6 ha* site at Hartsfield International Airport, Atlanta, Georgia, has 36 acres *14,5 ha* under roof.

Great Britain

The largest hangar building in the United Kingdom is the Britannia Assembly Hall at the former Bristol Aeroplane Company's works at Filton, Avon, now part of British Aerospace. The overall width of the Hall is 1054 ft *321 m* and the overall depth of the centre bay is 420 ft *128 m*. It encloses a floor area of 7½ acres *3,0 ha*. The cubic capacity of the Hall is 33,000,000 ft³ *934 000 m³*. The building was begun in April 1946 and completed by September 1949.

GARAGES

Largest *World*

The world's largest parking garage is at O'Hare Airport, Chicago, Illinois with 6 levels and a capacity for 9250 cars. It is operated by Allright Auto Parks Inc, the world's largest parking company.

Great Britain

Great Britain's highest capacity underground car park is that under the Victoria Centre, Nottingham with a capacity of 1650 cars, opened in June 1972.

Private

The largest private garage ever built was one for 100 cars at the Long Island, New York mansion of William Kissam Vanderbilt (1849–1920).

Parking lot

The parking lots at Giants Stadium, East Rutherford, New Jersey, USA have a capacity for 26,000 automobiles and 500 buses. The largest parking area in Great Britain is that for 15,000 cars and 200 coaches at the National Exhibition Centre, Birmingham (see pp. 113–114).

Filling stations

Little America, west of Cheyenne, Wyoming, USA, at the junction of Interstate Routes 80 and 25 claims to be the world's biggest gas station with 52 diesel and gas pumps—none self-service. The highest in the world is at Leh, Ladakh, India at 3658 m *12,001 ft* operated by Indiaoil. The largest filling station of the 36,000 in the United Kingdom is the Esso service area on the M4 at Leigh Delamere, Wiltshire, opened on 3 Jan 1972. It has 48 petrol and diesel pumps and extends over 43 acres *17,4 ha*.

GLASSHOUSE

Largest *Great Britain*

The largest glasshouse in the United Kingdom is one covering 22.5 acres *9,10 ha* owned by Van Heyningen Bros. at Waterham, Herne Bay, Kent completed in October 1982. The crop of 160,000 tomato plants is under 1155 tons of glass.

GRAIN ELEVATOR

Largest

The world's largest single-unit grain elevator is that operated by the C-G-F-Grain Company at Wichita, Kansas, USA. Consisting of a triple row of storage tanks, 123 on each side of the central loading tower or 'head house', the unit is 2,717 ft *828 m* long and 100 ft *30 m* wide. Each tank is 120 ft *37 m* high, with an inside diameter of 30 ft *9 m* giving a total storage capacity of 20,000,000 bushels *7,3 million hl* of wheat. The largest collection of elevators in the world are the 23 at City of Thunder Bay, Ontario, Canada, on Lake Superior with a total capacity of 103.9 million bushels *37,4 million hl*.

SEWAGE WORKS

Largest *World*

The largest single full treatment sewage works in the world is the West-Southwest Treatment Plant, opened in 1940 on a site of 501 acres *203 ha* in Chicago, Illinois, USA. It serves an area containing 2,940,000 people. It treated an average of 835,000,000 US gal *3160 million litres* of wastes per day in 1973. The capacity of its sedimentation and aeration tanks is 1 280 000 m³ *1.6 million yd³*.

Great Britain

The largest full treatment works in Britain and probably in Europe is the GLC Beckton Works which serves a 2,966,000 population and handles a daily flow of 207 million gal *941 million litres* in a tank capacity of 757,000 ft³ *21 400 m³*.

WOODEN BUILDING

Largest

The world's largest buildings in timber are the two US Navy airship hangers built in 1942–3 at Tillamook, Oregon. Now used by the Louisiana-Pacific Corporation as a saw mill they measure 1000 ft long, 170 ft high at the crown and 296 ft wide at the base (*304,8 m × 51,8 m × 90,22 m*) and are worth $6 million (*now £2.7 million*).

AIR-SUPPORTED BUILDING

Largest

The world's largest air-supported roof is that of the 80,600 capacity octagonal Pontiac Silverdome Stadium, Michigan, USA measuring 522 ft *159 m* in width and 722 ft *220 m* in length. The air pressure is 5 lb/in² *34,4 kPa* supporting the 10 acre *4 ha* translucent 'Fiberglas' roofing. The structural engineers were Geiger-Berger Associates of New York City. The largest standard size air hall is one 860 ft *262 m* long, 140 ft *42,6 m* wide and 65 ft *19,8 m* high, at Lima, Ohio, USA, made by Irvin Industries of Stamford, Connecticut, USA.

2. BUILDINGS FOR LIVING

WOODEN BUILDINGS

Oldest

The oldest extant wooden buildings in the world are those comprising the Pagoda, Chumanar gate and the Temple of Horyu (Horyu-ji), at Nara, Japan, dating from *c.* AD 670 and completed in 715. The nearby Daibutsuden, built in 1704–11, once measured 285.4 ft long, 167.3 ft wide and 153.3 ft tall *87 × 51 × 46,75 m*. The present dimensions are 188 × 165.3 × 159.4 ft *57,3 × 50,4 × 48,6 m*.

CASTLES

Earliest *World*
The oldest castle in the world is that at Gomdan, in the Yemen, which originally had 20 storeys and dates from before AD 100.

Great Britain
The oldest stone castle extant in Great Britain is Richmond Castle, Yorkshire, built in *c.* 1075. Iron Age relics from the first century BC or AD have been found in the lower levels of the Dover Castle site.

Ireland
The oldest Irish castle is Ferrycarrig near Wexford dating from *c.* 1180. The oldest castle in Northern Ireland is Carrickfergus Castle, County Antrim, Northern Ireland, which dates from before 1210.

Largest *World, UK and Ireland*
The largest inhabited castle in the world is the Royal residence of Windsor Castle at New Windsor, Berkshire. It is primarily of 12th century construction and is in the form of a waisted parallelogram 1890 ft by 540 ft *576 by 164 m*. The total area of Dover Castle however covers 34 acres *13,75 ha* with a width of 1100 ft *335,2 m* and a curtain wall of 1800 ft *550 m* or if underground works are taken in, 2300 ft *700 m*. The overall dimensions of Carisbrooke Castle (450 ft by 360 ft *110 by 137 m*), Isle of Wight, if its earthworks are included, are 1350 ft by 825 ft *411 m by 251 m*. The largest castle in Scotland is Edinburgh Castle with a major axis of 1320 ft *402 m* and measuring 3360 ft *1025 m* along its perimeter wall including the Esplanade. The most capacious of all Irish castles is Carrickfergus (see above) but that with the most extensive fortifications is Trim Castle, County Meath, built in *c.* 1205 with a curtain wall 1455 ft *443 m* long.

Forts *Largest*
The largest ancient castle in the world is Hradčany Castle, Prague, Czechoslovakia originating in the 9th century. It is a very oblong irregular polygon with an axis of 570 m *1870 ft* and an average traverse diameter of 128 m *420 ft* with a surface area of 7,28 ha *18 acres*. Fort George, Ardersier, Scotland built in 1748–69 measures 2100 ft *640 m* in length and has an average width of 620 ft *189 m*. The total site covers 42½ acres *17,2 ha*.

Thickest walls
Urnammu's city walls at Ur (now Muqayyar), destroyed by the Elamites in 2006 BC were 27 m *88⅓ ft* thick. The walls of the Great Tower or Donjon of Flint Castle, built in 1277–80 are 23 ft *7,01 m* thick. The largest Norman keep in Britain is that of Colchester Castle measuring 152½ ft *46 m* by 111½ ft *34 m*.

PALACES

Largest *World*
The largest palace in the world is the Imperial Palace (*Gu gong*) in the centre of Peking (*Bei jing*, the northern capital), China, which covers a rectangle 1050 yd by 820 yd *960 by 750 m*, an area of 177.9 acres *72 ha*. The outline survives from the construction of the third Ming Emperor, Yung lo of 1402–24, but due to constant re-arrangements most of the intramural buildings are 18th century. These consist of 5 halls and 17 palaces of which the last occupied by the last Empress was the Palace of Accumulated Elegance (*Chu xia gong*) until 1924.

The Palace of Versailles, 23 km *14 miles* southwest of Paris has a facade with 375 windows, 634 yards *580 m* in length. The building, completed in 1682 for Louis XIV occupied more than 30,000 workmen under Jules Hardouin-Mansert.

Residential
The largest residential palace in the world is the Vatican Palace, in the Vatican City, an enclave in Rome, Italy. Covering an area of 13½ acres *5,5 ha* it has 1400 rooms, chapels and halls, of which the oldest date from the 15th century.

Great Britain
The largest palace in the United Kingdom in Royal use is Buckingham Palace, London, so named after its site, bought in 1703 by John Sheffield, the 1st Duke of Buckingham and

The throne room of the 1788 room palace of the world's richest man the Sultan of Brunei. The chandeliers are the world's largest. (*Terry Fincher Photographers International*)

Normanby (1648–1721). Buckingham House was reconstructed in the Palladian style between 1835 and 1836, following the design of John Nash (1752–1835). The 610 ft *186 m* long East Front was built in 1846 and refaced in 1912. The Palace, which stands in 39 acres *15,8 ha* of garden, has 600 rooms including a ballroom 111 ft *34 m* long.

The largest ever Royal palace has been Hampton Court Palace, Greater London, acquired by Henry VIII from Cardinal Wolsey in 1525 and greatly enlarged by the King and later by William III, Anne and George I, whose son George II was its last resident monarch. It covers 4 acres *1,6 ha* of a 669 acre *270,7 ha* site.

Largest moat
The world's largest moats are those which surround the Imperial Palace in Peking (see above). From plans drawn by French sources it appears to measure 54 yd *49 m* wide and have a total length of 3600 yd *3290 m*. The city's moats total in all 23½ miles *38 km*.

FLATS

Largest
The largest blocks of private flats in Britain are the Barbican Estate, London, EC2 with 2011 flats on a 40 acre *16 ha* site with covered parking space for 2000 cars. The architects were Chamberlain, Powell and Bon.

Tallest *World*
The tallest block of flats in the world are Lake Point Towers of 70 storeys, and 645 ft *197 m* in Chicago, Illinois, USA.

Great Britain
The tallest residential block in Great Britain is the Shakespeare Tower in the Barbican in the City of London, which has 116 flats on 44 storeys and rises to a height of 419 ft 2½ in *127,77 m* above the street. The first of the three Barbican towers was 'topped out' in May 1971.

Most Expensive
The highest price quoted for any apartment is the penthouse of Trump Tower at 5th Avenue and 56th Street, New York City quoted in April 1983 at $10 million (£*7,150,000*).

HOTELS

Largest *World*
The hotel with most rooms in the world is the 12 storey Hotel Rossiya in Moscow, USSR, with 3200 rooms providing accomodation for 6,000 guests, opened in 1967. It would thus

require more than 8½ years to spend one night in each room. In addition there is a 21 storey 'Presidential' tower in the central courtyard. The hotel employs about 3000 people, and has 93 lifts. The ballroom is reputed to be the world's largest. Muscovites are not permitted as residents while foreigners are charged 16 times more than the very low rate charged to USSR officials. The Izmailovo Hotel complex, opened in July 1980 for the XXIInd Olympic Games in Moscow, was designed to accommodate 9500 people.

The largest commercial hotel building in the world is The Waldorf Astoria, on Park Avenue, New York City, NY, USA. It occupies a complete block of 81,337 ft² (*1,87 acres 0,75 ha*) and reaches a maximum height of 625 ft 7 in *191 m*. The Waldorf Astoria has 47 storeys and 1852 guest rooms and maintains the largest hotel radio receiving system in the world. The Waldorf can accommodate 10,000 people at one time and has a staff of 1700. The restaurants have catered for parties up to 6000 at a time. The coffee-maker's daily output reaches 1000 US gal *3785 litres*. The electricity bill is $2,000,000 each year. The hotel has housed 6 Heads of States simultaneously. It was opened on 1 Oct 1931.

The Las Vegas Hilton, Nevada, USA built in 1974–81 has 3174 rooms, 12 international restaurants and a staff of 3600. It has a 10 acre *2,47 ha* rooftop recreation deck and 125,000 ft² *11 600 m²* of convention space.

Great Britain

The greatest sleeping capacity of any hotel in Great Britain is 1859 in the London Forum Hotel, Cromwell Road, London SW7 with a staff of 419. It was opened in 1973. The Regent Palace Hotel, Piccadilly Circus, London, opened 20 May 1915, has however 225 more rooms totalling 1140. The largest hotel is the Grosvenor House Hotel, Park Lane, London, which was opened in 1929. It is of 8 storeys covering 2½ acres *1 ha* and caters for more than 100,000 visitors per year in 470 rooms. The Great Room is the largest hotel room measuring 181 ft by 131 ft *55 by 40 m* with a height of 23 ft *7 m*. Banquets for 1500 are frequently handled.

Tallest

The tallest hotel in the world, measured from the street level of its main entrance to the top, is the 723 ft *220,3 m* tall 70 storey Peachtree Center Plaza, Atlanta, Georgia, USA. The $50 million 1100 room hotel is operated by western International Hotels and owned by Portman Properties. Their Detroit Plaza measuring from the rear entrance level is however 748 ft *227,9 m* tall. Britain's tallest hotel is the 27 storey 380 ft *132,24 m* tall London Forum Hotel (see above).

The ground was broken in June 1980 for the building of the £100 million Raffles City project in Singapore. The central tower of 71 storeys will be 230 metres *754 ft 7 ins* tall.

Largest Lobby

The world's largest hotel lobby is that of The Grand Hotel, Taipei, Taiwan completed on 10 Oct 1973. It measures 47 × 35 m *154 × 114 ft* and is 9,6 m *31½ ft* high.

Most expensive

The world's costliest hotel accommodation was the Royale Suite in the Nova Park Elysées, Rue François, Paris at $5500 (£3525) per day. It has 8 rooms, 7 bathrooms, 3 terraces and a conference room covering 431,5 m² *4644 ft²*.

The most expensive hotel suite in Britain is the Royal Suite on the 8th floor of the Hotel Inter-Continental, London W1, at £632.50 (incl. VAT) (May 1984).

Spas

The largest spa in the world measured by number of available hotel rooms is Vichy, Allier, France, with 14,000 rooms. Spas are named after the watering place in the Liège province of Belgium where hydropathy was developed from 1626. The highest French spa is Baréges, Hautes-Pyrénées, at 4068 ft *1240 m* above sea level.

HOUSING

Largest estate

The largest housing estate in the United Kingdom is the 1670-acre *675 ha* Becontree Estate, on a site of 3000 acres *1214 ha* in Barking and Redbridge, Greater London, built between 1921 and 1929. The total number of homes is 26,822, with an estimated population of nearly 90,000.

New towns

Of the 23 new towns being built in Great Britain that with the largest eventual planned population is Milton Keynes, Buckinghamshire, with a projected 250,000 for 1992.

Largest house *World*

The largest private house in the world is the 250-room Biltmore House in Asheville, North Carolina, USA. It is owned by George and William Cecil, grandsons of George Washington Vanderbilt II (1862–1914). The house was built between 1890 and 1895 in an estate of 119,000 acres *48 160 ha*, at a cost of $4,100,000 (now £1,708,333) and now valued at $55,000,000 with 12,000 acres *4856 ha*. The most expensive private house ever built is The Hearst Ranch at San Simeon, California, USA. It was built in 1922–39 for William Randolph Hearst (1863–1951), at a total cost of more than $30,000,000 (*then £6,120,000*). It has more than 100 rooms, a 104 ft *32 m* long heated swimming pool, an 83 ft *25 m* long assembly hall and a garage for 25 limousines. The house required 60 servants to maintain it.

The Hotel Nova Park Elysées in Paris which in 1983 was proclaimed to have the world's most expensive suite—the Royale Suite at $5500 a night.

Great Britain

The largest house in Great Britain was Wentworth Woodhouse, near Rotherham, South Yorkshire, formerly the seat of the Earls Fitzwilliam and now a teachers' training college. The main part of the house, built over 300 years ago, has more than 240 rooms with over 1000 windows, and its principal façade is 600 ft *183 m* long. The Royal residence, Sandringham House, Norfolk, has been reported to have had 365 rooms before the demolition of 73 surplus rooms in 1975. The largest house in Ireland is Castletown in County Kildare, owned by the Hon. Desmond Guinness and is the headquarters of the Irish Georgian Society. Scotland's largest house is Hopetoun House, West Lothian, built between 1696 and 1756 with a west façade 675 ft *206 m* long.

Smallest

The smallest house in Britain is the 19th century fisherman's cottage at 22 High Street, Conwy, Gwynedd. It has a 72 in *182 cm* frontage, is 122 in *309 cm* high and has two tiny rooms and a staircase. The house with the narrowest known frontage is the 58 inches *1,47 m* of 21, Manor Road, Kingston, Portsmouth. It was built over a footpath.

The naval veteran of the Battle of Jutland (1916) Alexander Wortley (1900–80) lived his last 20 years in a green painted box in the garden of David Moreau in Langley Park, Buckinghamshire. It measured 5 × 4 × 3 ft *1,5 × 1,2 × 0,91 m* with an extension for his feet—small enough as he said to 'keep women out'. He paid no rent, rates or taxes and did not believe in insurance, pensions or governments.

Most expensive *Houses*

The most expensive private house is The Kenstead Hall with the adjoining Beechwood property in The Bishop's Avenue, Hampstead, London, residence of the late king of Saudi Arabia. It was put on the market for £16 million in August 1982.

Oldest

The oldest house in Britain is Eastry Court near Sandwich, Kent dating from AD 603. Some of the original timbers and stone infill still survives behind its present Georgian façade.

Stately home most visited

The most visited stately home in the United Kingdom in 1983 was Warwick Castle, near Stratford-on-Avon with 512,000 visitors.

Barracks

The oldest purpose built barracks in the world are believed to be Collins Barracks, formerly the Royal Barracks, Dublin, Ireland, completed in 1704 and still in use.

3. BUILDINGS FOR ENTERTAINMENT

STADIUM

Largest *World*

The world's largest stadium is the open Strahov Stadium in Praha (Prague), Czechoslovakia. It was completed in 1934 and can accommodate 240,000 spectators for mass displays of up to 40,000 Sokol gymnasts.

Football

The largest football stadium in the world is the Maracaña Municipal Stadium in Rio de Janeiro, Brazil, where the football ground has a normal capacity of 205,000, of whom 155,000 may be seated. A crowd of 199,854 was accommodated for the World Cup final between Brazil and Uruguay on 16 July 1950. A dry moat, 7 ft *2,13 m* wide and more than 5 ft *1,5 m* deep, protects players from spectators and *vice versa*. Britain's most capacious football stadium is Hampden Park, Glasgow opened on 31 Oct 1903 and once surveyed to accommodate 184,000 compared with an attendance of 149,547 on 17 Apr 1937 and the present licensed limit of 74,400.

Covered

The Azteca Stadium, Mexico City, Mexico, opened in 1968, has a capacity of 107,000 of whom nearly all are under cover. The largest covered stadium in Britain is the Empire Stadium Wembley, Brent, Greater London, opened in April 1923. It was the scene of the 1948 Olympic Games and the final of the 1966 World Cup. In 1962–3 the capacity under cover was increased to 100,000 of whom 45,000 may be seated. The original cost was £1,250,000.

Largest roof

The transparent acryl glass 'tent' roof over the Munich Olympic Stadium, W. Germany measures 914,940 ft² (21.0 acres *8,5 ha*) in area resting on a steel net supported by masts. The roof of longest span in the world is the 680 ft *207,2 m* diameter of the Louisiana Superdome (see below). The major axis of the elliptical Texas Stadium completed in 1971 at Irving, Texas is however 240 m *787 ft 4 in.*

Indoor

The world's largest indoor stadium is the 13 acre *5,26 ha* $173 million (then £75 million) 273 ft *83,2 m* tall Superdome in New Orleans, Louisiana, USA, completed in May 1975. Its maximum seating capacity for conventions is 97,365 or 76,791 for football. Box suites rent for $35,000 excluding the price of admission. A gondola with six 312 in *7,92 m* TV screens produces instant replay.

Ballroom

The dance floor used for championships at Earl's Court Exhibition Hall, Kensington, London extends 256 ft *78 m* in length.

Amusement resort

The world's largest amusement resort is Disney World in 27,443 acres *11 105 ha* of Orange and Osceola counties, 20 miles *32 km* south west of Orlando in central Florida, USA. It was opened on 1 Oct 1971. This $400 million investment attracted a peak 13,221,000 visitors in 1981. The most attended resort in the world is Disneyland, Anaheim, California (opened 1955) where the total number of visitors reached 233,949,291 to 21 Apr 1984. The greatest attendance in a day was 82,516 on 16 Aug 1969 and the annual peak 11,522,000 in 1980/81.

The $900 million Epcot Center (Experimental Prototype Community of Tomorrow) near Orlando, Florida, was opened in Oct 1982.

Largest pleasure beach

The largest pleasure beach in the world is Virginia Beach, Virginia, USA. It has 28 miles *45 km* of beach front on the Atlantic and 10 miles *16 km* of estuary frontage. The area embraces 255 miles² *600 km²* and 134 hotels and motels.

Piers *Earliest longest and most*

A pleasure pier was completed at Great Yarmouth, Norfolk in 1808 but was washed away in 1953. The Old Pier, Weymouth, Dorset dates back to 1812. The longest pleasure pier in the world is Southend Pier at Southend-on-Sea in Essex. It is 1.34 miles *2,15 km* in length. It was first opened in August 1889 with final extensions made in 1929. In 1949–50 the pier had 5,750,000 visitors. The pier railway was closed in October 1978.

The resort with most piers is Atlantic City, New Jersey, USA with 6 pre-war and 5 currently. In Britain only Blackpool has three—North, Central and South.

Earliest fair

The earliest major international fair was the Great Exhibition of 1851 in the Crystal Palace, Hyde Park, City of Westminster, Greater London which in 141 days attracted 6,039,195 admissions.

Largest fair

The largest ever International Fair site was that for the St Louis, Missouri, Louisiana Purchase Exposition which covered 1271.76 acres *514,66 ha*. It also staged the 1904 Olympic Games and drew an attendance of 19,694,855.

Record fair attendance

The record attendance for any fair was 64,218,770 for Expo 70 held on an 815 acre *330 ha* site at Osaka, Japan from March to 13 Sept 1970. It made a profit of 19,439,402,017 yen (*then £22.6 million*).

Big wheel

The original Ferris Wheel, named after its constructor, George W. Ferris (1859–96), was erected in 1893 at the Midway, Chicago, Illinois, at a cost of $385,000 (*then £79,218*). It was 250 ft *76 m* in diameter, 790 ft *240 m* in circumference, weighed 1070 tons *1087 tonnes* and carried 36 cars each seating 60

people, making a total of 2160 passengers. The structure was removed in 1904 to St Louis, Missouri, and was eventually sold as scrap for $1800 (*then £370*). In 1897 a Ferris Wheel with a diameter of 300 ft *91 m* was erected for the Earl's Court Exhibition, London. It had ten 1st-class and 30 2nd-class cars. The largest wheel now operating is 'The Rainbow' at Mitsui Greenland Park, Arao City, Kumamoto, Japan with a height of 70 m *229 ft 8 in*. It has 36 cars and was completed in March 1983.

Fastest and Longest switchbacks

The maximum speeds claimed for switchbacks, scenic railways or roller coasters have in the past been exaggerated for commercial reasons. The twin track triple helix American Eagle at Marriott's Great America, Gurnee, Illinois opened on 23 May 1981 has a vertical drop of 147.4 ft *44,92 m* on which a speed of 66.31 mph *106,73 km/h* is reached. The longest roller coaster in the world is *The Beast* at Kings Island near Cincinnati, Ohio, USA. Scientific tests at the base of its 141 ft *42,98 m* high drop returned a speed of 64.77 mph *104,23 km/h* on 5 Apr 1980. The run of 7400 ft or 1.40 miles *2,25 km* incorporates 800 ft *243,8 m* of tunnels and a 540 degree banked helix. The tallest is the Moonsault Scramble at the Fujikyu Highland Park, nr. Kawaguchi Lake, Japan opened on 24 June 1983. It is 75 m *246 ft* tall (with a speed of 105 km/h *65.2 mph*).

Longest slide

The longest slide in the world is at the Bromley Alpine Slide on Route 11 in Peru, Vermont, USA. This has a length of 4600 ft *1402 m* (0.87 mile) and a vertical drop of 820 ft *250 m*.

Restaurants

The earliest restaurant, so described, was opened by M. Boulanger in Rue des Paulies, Paris in 1765. The highest restaurant in the world is at the Chacaltaya ski resort, Bolivia at 5340 m *17,519 ft*. The highest in Great Britain is the Ptarmigan Observation Restaurant at 3650 ft *1112 m* above sea-level on Cairngorm (4084 ft *1244 m*) near Aviemore, Highland, Scotland.

Harem Largest

The world's most capacious harem is the Winter Harem of the Grand Seraglio at Topaki, Istanbul, Turkey completed in 1589 with 400 rooms. By the time of the deposing of Abdul Hamid II in 1909 the number of *carge* (those who serve) had dwindled from 1200 to 370 odalisques with 127 eunuchs.

Night club Oldest

The earliest night club (*boite de nuit*) was 'Le Bal des Anglais' at 6 Rue des Anglais, Paris, 5e France. It was founded in 1843 but closed *c.* 1960.

Largest

The largest night club in the world is Gilley's Club (formerly Shelly's) built in 1955 and extended in 1971 on Spencer Highway, Houston, Texas, USA with a seating capacity of 6000 under one roof covering 4 acres *1,6 ha*. In the more classical sense the largest night club in the world is 'The Mikado' in the Akasaka district of Tōkyō, Japan, with a seating capacity of 2000. It is 'manned' by 1250 hostesses. Binoculars are essential to an appreciation of the floor show.

Lowest

The lowest night club is the 'Minus 206' in Tiberias, Israel on the shores of the Sea of Galilee. It is 206 m *676 ft* below sea-level. An alternative candidate is 'Outer Limits', opposite the Cow Palace, San Francisco, California which was raided for the 151st time on 1 Aug 1971. It has been called 'The Most Busted Joint' and 'The Slowest to Get the Message'.

PUBLIC HOUSES

Oldest

There are various claimants to the title of the United Kingdom's oldest inn. A foremost claimant is 'The Fighting Cocks', St Albans, Hertfordshire (an 11th century structure on an 8th century site). The timber frame of The Royalist Hotel, Digbeth Street, Stow-on-the-Wold, Gloucestershire has been dated to 1000 years before the present. It was the inn 'The Eagle and the Child' in the 13th century and known to exist in AD 947. An origin as early as AD 560 has been claimed for 'Ye Olde Ferry Boat Inn' at Holywell, Cambridgeshire. There is some evidence that it antedates the local church, built in 980, but the earliest documents are not dated earlier than 1100. There is evidence that the 'Bingley Arms', Bardsey, near Leeds, West Yorkshire, restored and extended in 1738, existed as the 'Priest's Inn' according to Bardsey Church records dated 905.

The oldest pub in Ireland is Grace Neill's Bar, Donaghadee, County Down built in 1611. An inn stood on the site of the Brazen Head Inn, Lower Bridge Street, Dublin since the late 12th century. The present structure dates from 1668.

Largest *World*

The largest beer-selling establishment in the world is the Mathäser, Bayerstrasse 5, München (Munich), West Germany, where the daily sale reaches 84,470 pts *48 000 litres*. It was established in 1829, was demolished in World War II and re-built by 1955 and now seats 5500 people. The through-put at the Dube beer halls in the Bantu township of Soweto, Johannesburg, South Africa may, however, be higher on some Saturdays when the average consumption of 6000 gal (48,000 pts *27 280 litres*) is far exceeded.

Great Britain

The largest public house in Great Britain is the Courage House, Downham Tavern, Downham Way, Bromley, Kent built in 1930. Two large bars (counter length 45 ft *13,7 m*) accommodate 1000 customers with 18–20 staff.

Smallest

The smallest pub in Great Britain is the 17th century 'The Nutshell', Bury St Edmunds, Suffolk with maximum dimensions of 15 ft 10 in by 7 ft 6 in *4,82 × 2,28 m* or 118.74 ft² *11,03 m²*. The bar room in the Earl Grey, Quenington, Gloucestershire measures 116.37 ft² *10,81 m²*.

Longest bars *World*

The world's longest permanent bar is the 340 ft *103,6 m* long bar in Lulu's Roadhouse, Kitchener, Ontario, Canada opened on 3 Apr 1984. The famous Working Men's Club bar at Mildura, Victoria, Australia has a counter 298 ft *90,8 m* in length, served by 27 pumps. Temporary bars have been erected of greater length. The Bar at Erickson's on Burnside Street, Portland, Oregon, in its heyday (1883–1920) possessed a bar which ran continuously around and across the main saloon measuring 684 ft *208,48 m*. The chief bouncer Edward 'Spider' Johnson had a chief assistant named 'Jumbo' Reilly who weighed 23 stone and was said to resemble 'an ill-natured orang-utan'. Beer was 5 cents for 16 fluid ounces.

United Kingdom and Ireland

The longest bar in the United Kingdom with beer pumps is the Long Bar at The Cornwall Coliseum Auditorium at Carlyon Bay, St. Austell, Cornwall measuring 104 ft 4 in *31,8 m* and having 34 dispensers (beer and lager). The longest bar in a pub is of 71 ft 11 in *21,92 m* with 29 dispensers in 'The Mount Pleasant Inn', Repton, Derbyshire. The Grand Stand Bar at Galway Racecourse, Ireland completed in 1955, measures 210 ft *64 m*.

An old picture of Britain's highest pub, 'The Cat and Fiddle' which still serves drinks all the year round at 1690 ft *515 m* above sea level in Derbyshire.

Longest tenure

There are no collated records on licensees but the 'Glan-y-Afon Inn', Milwr near Holywell, North Wales had a 418 year long (1559–1977) run within a family which ended with the retirement of Mrs Mary Evans.

Longest name

The pub with the longest name is the 40 letter 'The Ferret and Firkin in the Balloon up the Creek', in Lots Road, Chelsea, London.

Shortest name

The public house in the United Kingdom with the shortest name was the 'X' at Westcott, Cullompton, Devon but in October 1983 the name was changed to the 'Merry Harriers'.

Commonest name

The commonest pub name in Britain is 'Red Lion' of which there are probably about 630. John A. Blackwell of Poole, Dorset has spotted over 5000 different pub names. Gordon Wright of Wollaton, Nottinghamshire has recorded 16,840 differently named pubs in a collection of 'inn-signia' begun in 1914 by the late James Leaver of Ruislip, Middlesex.

Highest

The highest public house in the United Kingdom is the 'Tan Hill Inn' in North Yorkshire. It is 1732 ft *528 m* above sea-level, on the moorland road between Reeth, North Yorkshire and Brough, Cumbria. The highest pub open the year round is the 'Cat and Fiddle' in Cheshire, near Buxton, Derbyshire at 1690 ft *515 m*. The White Lady Restaurant, 2550 ft *777 m* up on Cairngorm (4084 ft *1244 m*) near Aviemore, Highland, Scotland is the highest licensed restaurant.

Most visits

Stanley House of Totterdown, Bristol has visited 3298 differently named pubs in Britain by way of public transport only to 1 May 1982. Jimmy Young GM BEM, of Better Pubs Ltd claims to have visited 23,338 different pubs.

4. TOWERS AND MASTS

TALLEST STRUCTURES

World

The tallest structure in the world is the guyed Warszawa Radio mast at Konstantynow near Gabin and Płock 60 miles *96 km* north-west of the capital of Poland. It is 646,38 m *2120 ft 8 in* tall or more than four tenths of a mile. The mast was completed on 18 July 1974 and put into operation on 22 July 1974. It was designed by Jan Polak and weighs 550 tons/*tonnes*. The mast is so high that anyone falling off the top would reach their terminal velocity and hence cease to be accelerating before hitting the ground. Work was begun in July 1970 on this tubular steel construction, with its 15 steel guy ropes. It recaptured for Europe a record held in the USA since the Chrysler Building surpassed the Eiffel Tower in 1929.

A PROGRESSIVE RECORD OF THE WORLD'S TALLEST STRUCTURES

Height in ft	m	Structure	Location	Material	Building or Completion Dates
204	62	Djoser step pyramid (earliest Pyramid)	Saqqâra, Egypt	Tura limestone casing	c. 2650 BC
300.8	91,7	Pyramid of Meidum	Meidum, Egypt	Tura limestone casing	c. 2600 BC
331.6	101,1	Snefru Bent pyramid	Dahshûr, Egypt	Tura limestone casing	c. 2600 BC
342	104	Snefru North Stone pyramid	Dahshûr, Egypt	Tura limestone casing	c. 2600 BC
480.9[1]	146,5	Great Pyramid of Cheops (Khufu)	El Gizeh, Egypt	Tura limestone casing	c. 2580 BC
525[2]	160	Lincoln Cathedral, Central Tower	Lincoln, England	lead sheathed wood	c. 1307–1548
489[3]	149	St Paul's Cathedral spire	City of London, England	lead sheathed wood	1315–1561
465	141	Minster of Notre Dame	Strasbourg, France	Vosges sandstone	1420–1439
502[4]	153	St Pierre de Beauvais spire	Beauvais, France	lead sheathed wood	–1568
475	144	St Nicholas Church	Hamburg, Germany	stone and iron	1846–1847
485	147	Rouen Cathedral spire	Rouen, France	cast iron	1823–1876
513	156	Köln Cathedral spires	Cologne, W. Germany	stone	–1880
555[5]	169	Washington Monument	Washington, DC, USA	stone	1848–1884
985.9[6]	300,5	Eiffel Tower	Paris, France	iron	1887–1889
1046	318	Chrysler Building	New York City, USA	steel and concrete	1929–1930
1250[7]	381	Empire State Building	New York City, USA	steel and concrete	1929–1930
1572	479	KWTV Television Mast	Oklahoma City, USA	steel	Nov 1954
1610[8]	490	KSWS Television Mast	Roswell, New Mexico, USA	steel	Dec 1956
1619	493	WGAN Television Mast	Portland, Maine, USA	steel	Sept 1959
1676	510	KFVS Television Mast	Cape Girardeau, Missouri, USA	steel	June 1960
1749	533	WTVM & WRBL Television Mast	Columbus, Georgia, USA	steel	May 1962
1749	533	WBIR-TV Mast	Knoxville, Tennessee, USA	steel	Sept 1963
2063	628	KTHI-TV Mast	Fargo, North Dakota, USA	steel	Nov 1963
2120.6	646,38	Warszawa Radio Mast (see p. 119)	Płock, Poland	galvanised steel	22 July 1974

[1] *Original height. With loss of pyramidion (topmost stone) height now 449 ft 6 in 137 m.*
[2] *Fell in a storm.*
[3] *Struck by lightning and destroyed 4 June 1561.*
[4] *Fell April 1573, shortly after completion.*
[5] *Sinking at a rate of 0.0047 ft per annum or 5 in 12,7 cm since 1884.*
[6] *Original height. With addition of TV antenna in 1957, now 1052 ft 320,75 m.*
[7] *Original height. With addition of TV tower on 1 May 1951, now 1427 ft 449 m. Exterior is clad in limestone from the Empire Quarry, Indiana.*
[8] *Fell in gale in 1960.*

Great Britain

The tallest structure in the United Kingdom is the Independent Broadcasting Authority's mast at Belmont, north of Horncastle, Lincolnshire completed in 1965 to a height of 1265 ft *385 m* with 7 ft *2,13 m* added by meteorological equipment installed in September 1967. It serves Yorkshire TV and weighs 210 tons.

PROGRESSIVE LIST OF HIGHEST STRUCTURES IN GREAT BRITAIN

Feet	Metres		
404	123	Salisbury Cathedral Spire	c. 1305–
525	160	Lincoln Cathedral	1307–1548
489	149	St Paul's Cathedral, London	1315–1561
518.7	158,1	Blackpool Tower, Lancashire	1894–
562	171,29	New Brighton Tower, Merseyside	1898–1919
820	250	GPO Radio Masts, Rugby	1925–
1000*	304,8	ITA Mast, Mendlesham, Suffolk	July 1959
1265	385	IBA Mast, Emley Moor, Yorkshire	1965–1969†
1265	385	IBA Mast, Belmont	1965–
1272	387,1	IBA Mast, Belmont	Sept. 1967

* *ITA masts of the same height followed at Lichfield, Staffordshire; Black Hill, Strathclyde; Caldbeck, Cumbria; and Durris, Grampian.*
† *Severely damaged by icing and replaced.*

TALLEST TOWERS

World

The tallest self-supporting tower (as opposed to a guyed mast) in the world is the $44 million CN Tower in Metro Centre, Toronto, Canada, which rises to 1822 ft 1 in *555,33 m*. Excavation began on 12 Feb 1973 for the 130,000 ton/*tonne* structure of reinforced, post-tensioned concrete topped out on 2 Apr 1975. The 416-seat restaurant revolves in the Sky Pod at 1140 ft *347,5 m* from which the visibility extends to hills 74½ miles *120 km* distant. Lightning strikes the top about 200 times (30 storms) per annum.

The tallest tower built before the era of television masts is the Eiffel Tower, in Paris, France, designed by Alexandre Gustav Eiffel (1832–1923) for the Paris exhibition and completed on 31 Mar 1889. It was 300,51 m *985 ft 11 in* tall, now extended by a TV antenna to 320,75 m *1052 ft 4 in* and weighs 7340 tonnes *7224 tons*. The maximum sway in high winds is 12,7 cm *5 in*. The whole iron edifice which has 1792 steps, took 2 years, 2 months and 2 days to build and cost 7,799,401 francs 31 centimes.

Great Britain

The tallest self-supported tower in Great Britain is the 1080 ft *329,18 m* tall Independent Broadcasting Authority transmitter at Emley Moor, West Yorkshire, completed in September 1971. The structure, which cost £900,000, has an enclosed room at the 865 ft *263,65 m* level and weighs with its foundations more than 15,000 tons/*tonnes*. The tallest tower of the pre-television era was the New Brighton Tower of 562 ft *171,29 m* built on Merseyside in 1897–1900 and dismantled in 1919–21.

5. BRIDGES

Oldest *World*

Arch construction was understood by the Sumerians as early as 3200 BC and a reference exists to a Nile bridge in 2650 BC. The oldest surviving datable bridge in the world is the slab stone single arch bridge over the River Meles in Smyrna (now Izmir), Turkey, which dates from *c.* 850 BC.

Great Britain

The clapper bridges of Dartmoor and Exmoor (*e.g.* the Tarr Steps over the River Barle, Exmoor, Somerset) are thought to be of prehistoric types although none of the existing examples can be certainly dated. They are made of large slabs of stone placed over boulders. The Romans built stone bridges in England and remains of these have been found at Corbridge (Roman, Corstopitum), Northumberland dating to the 2nd century AD; Chesters, Northumberland and Willowford, Cumbria. Remains of a very early wooden bridge have been found at Aldwinkle, Northamptonshire.

LONGEST

Cable suspension *World*

The world's longest bridge span is the main span of the Humber Estuary Bridge, England at 4626 ft *1410 m*. Work began on 27 July 1972, after a decision announced on 22 Jan 1966. The towers are 162,5 m *533 ft 1⅝ in* tall from datum and are 1⅜ in *36 mm* out of parallel, to allow for the curvature of the Earth. Including the Hessle and the Barton side spans, the bridge stretches 2220 m or 1.37 miles. The bridge was structurally completed on 18 July 1980 at a cost of £96 million and was opened by HM the Queen on 17 July 1981. Tolls, ranging between £1 for cars and £7.50 for heavy vehicles, operative from 4 May 1981, are the highest in Britain.

The Mackinac Straits Bridge between Mackinaw City and St Ignace, Michigan, USA, is the longest suspension bridge in the world measured between anchorages (1.58 miles *2543 m*) and has an overall length, including viaducts of the bridge proper measured between abutment bearings, of 3.63 miles *5853,79 m*. It was opened in November 1957 (dedicated 28

The world's longest bridge span across the Humber Estuary, England. It took 8 years to complete. (*Freeman Fox Ltd*)

June 1958) at a cost of $100 million (*then £35,700,000*) and has a main span of 3800 ft *1158 m*.

The double-deck road-rail Akashi-Kaikyo bridge linking Honshū and Shikoku, Japan is planned to be completed in 1988. The main span will be 5840 ft *1780 m* in length with an overall suspended length with side spans totalling 11,680 ft *3560 m*. Work began on the approaches in October 1978 and the eventual cost is expected to exceed 1000 billion (10^{12}) yen.

Plans for a Messina Bridge linking Sicily with the Italian mainland are dependent upon EEC budgets. One preliminary study calls for towers 1000 ft *304,8 m* tall and a span of 3000 m *9842 ft* or 1.86 miles. The escalating cost of such a project was estimated by 1983 already to have passed the £2000 million mark.

Cantilever *World*

The Quebec Bridge (Pont de Québec) over the St Lawrence River in Canada has the longest cantilever truss span of any in the world—1800 ft *549 m* between the piers and 3239 ft *987 m* overall. It carries a railway track and 2 carriageways. Begun in 1899, it was finally opened to traffic on 3 Dec 1917 at a cost of 87 lives, and $Can.22,500,000 (*then £4,623,000*).

Great Britain

The longest cantilever bridge in Great Britain is the Forth Bridge. Its two main spans are 1710 ft *521 m* long. It carries a double railway track over the Firth of Forth 156 ft *47,5 m* above the water level. Work commenced in November 1882 and the first test trains crossed on 22 Jan 1890 after an expenditure of £3 million. It was officially opened on 4 Mar 1890. Of the 4500 workers who built it, 57 were killed in various accidents.

Steel arch *World*

The longest steel arch bridge in the world is the New River Gorge bridge, near Fayetteville, West Virginia, USA, completed in 1977 with a span of 1700 ft *518,2 m*.

Great Britain

The longest steel arch bridge in Great Britain is the Runcorn–Widnes bridge, Cheshire opened on 21 July 1961. It has a span of 1082 ft *329,8 m*.

Floating bridge

The longest floating bridge in the world is the Second Lake Washington Bridge, Seattle, Washington State, USA. Its total length is 12,596 ft *3839 m* and its floating section measures 7518 ft *2291 m* (1.42 miles *2,29 km*). It was built at a total cost of $15,000,000 (*then £5,357,000*) and completed in August 1963.

Covered bridge

The longest covered bridge in the world is that at Hartland, New Brunswick, Canada measuring 1282 ft *390,8 m* overall, completed in 1899.

Railway bridge

The longest railway bridge in the world is the Huey P. Long Bridge, Metairie, Louisiana, USA with a railway section 22,996 ft *7009 m* (4.35 miles *7 km*) long. It was completed on 16 Dec 1935 with a longest span of 790 ft *241 m*. The Yangtse River Bridge, completed in 1968 in Nanking, China is the world's longest combined highway and railway bridge. The rail deck is 6772 m *4.20 miles* and the road deck is 4589 m *2.85 miles*.

Great Britain

The longest railway bridge in Britain is the second Tay Bridge (11,653 ft *3552 m*), Tayside, Scotland opened on 20 June 1887. Of the 85 spans, 74 (length 10,289 ft *3136 m*) are over the waterway. The 878 brick arches of the London Bridge to Deptford Creek viaduct built in 1836 extend for 3¾ miles *6,0 km*.

Longest bridging

The world's longest bridging is the Second Lake Pontchartrain Causeway, completed on 23 Mar 1969, joining Lewisburg and Metairie, Louisiana, USA. It has a length of 126,055 ft *38 422 m* (23.87 miles). It cost $29,900,000 (*then £12.45 million*) and is 228 ft *69 m* longer than the adjoining First Causeway completed in 1956. The longest railway viaduct in the world is the rockfilled Great Salt Lake Railroad Trestle, carrying the Southern Pacific Railroad 11.85 miles *19 km* across the Great Salt Lake, Utah, USA. It was opened as a pile and trestle bridge on 8 Mar 1904, but converted to rock fill in 1955–60.

The longest stone arch bridging in the world is the 3810 ft *1161 m* long Rockville Bridge north of Harrisburg, Pennsylvania, USA, with 48 spans containing 196,000 tons/*tonnes* of stone and completed in 1901.

Widest bridge

The world's widest long-span bridge is the 1650 ft *502,9 m* span Sydney Harbour Bridge, Australia (160 ft *48,8 m* wide). It carries two electric overhead railway tracks, 8 lanes of roadway and a cycle and footway. It was officially opened on 19 Mar 1932. The Crawford Street Bridge in Providence, Rhode Island, USA, has a width of 1147 ft *350 m*. The River Roch is bridged for a distance of 1460 ft *445 m* where the culvert passes through the centre of Rochdale, Greater Manchester and this is sometimes claimed to be a breadth.

HIGHEST

World

The highest bridge in the world is the bridge over the Royal Gorge of the Arkansas River in Colorado, USA. It is 1053 ft *321 m* above the water level. It is a suspension bridge with a main span of 880 ft *268 m* and was constructed in 6 months, ending on 6 Dec 1929. The highest railway bridge in the world

The world's highest bridge across the Royal Gorge 1053 ft *321 m* above the Arkansas River in Colorado, USA.

is the single track span at Fades, outside Clermont-Ferrand, France. It was built in 1901–9 with a span of 472 ft *144 m* and is 435 ft *132,5 m* above the River Sioule.

Great Britain

The highest railway bridge in Great Britain is the Ballochmyle viaduct over the River Ayr, Strathclyde built 169 ft *51,5 m* over the river bed in 1846–8 with the then world's longest masonry arch span of 181 ft *55,16 m*.

AQUEDUCTS

World longest *Ancient*

The greatest of ancient aqueducts was the Aqueduct of Carthage in Tunisia, which ran 87.6 miles *141 km* from the springs of Zaghouan to Djebel Djougar. It was built by the Romans during the reign of Publius Aelius Hadrianus (AD 117–38). By 1895, 344 arches still survived. Its original capacity has been calculated at 7,000,000 gal *31,8 million litres* per day. The triple-tiered aqueduct Pont du Gard, built in AD 19 near Nîmes, France, is 160 ft *48 m* high. The tallest of the 14 arches of Aguas Livres Aqueduct, built in Lisbon, Portugal, in 1784 is 213 ft 3 in *65 m*.

World longest *Modern*

The world's longest aqueduct, in the modern sense of a water conduit, as opposed to an irrigation canal, is the California State Water Project aqueduct, completed in 1974, to a length of 826 miles *1329 km* of which 385 miles *619 km* is canalised.

Great Britain *Longest*

The longest bridged aqueduct in Britain is the Pont Cysylltau in Clwyd on the Frankton to Llantisilio branch of the Shropshire Union Canal. It is 1007 ft *307 m* long, has 19 arches up to 121 ft *36 m* high above low water on the Dee. It was designed by Thomas Telford (1757–1834) of Scotland, and was opened for use in 1805.

6. CANALS

Earliest *World*

Relics of the oldest canals in the world, dated by archaeologists *c.* 4000 BC, were discovered near Mandali, Iraq early in 1968.

Earliest *Great Britain*

The earliest canals in Britain were first cut by the Romans. In the Midlands the 11 mile *17 km* long Fossdyke Canal between Lincoln and the River Trent at Torksey was built in about AD 65 and was scoured in 1122. Part of it is still in use today. Though the Exeter canal was cut as early as 1564–6, the first wholly artificial major navigation canal in the United Kingdom was the 18½ mile *29,7 km* long canal with 14 locks from Whitecoat Point to Newry, Northern Ireland opened on 28 Mar 1742. In Great Britain the Sankey Navigation Canal in Lancashire, 8 miles *12,8 km* in length, with 10 locks, was opened in November 1757.

Longest *World*

The longest canalised system in the world is the Volga–Baltic Canal opened in April 1965. It runs 1850 miles *2300 km* from Astrakhan up the Volga, *via* Kuybyshev, Gor'kiy and Lake Ladoga, to Leningrad, USSR. The longest canal of the ancient world has been the Grand Canal of China from Peking to Hangchou. It was begun in 540 BC and not completed until 1327 by which time it extended (including canalised river sections) for 1107 miles *1781 km*. The estimated work force *c.* AD 600 reached 5,000,000 on the Pien section. Having been allowed by 1950 to silt up to the point that it was, in no place, more than 6 ft *1,8 m* deep, it is now, however, plied by ships of up to 2000 tons/*tonnes*.

The Beloye More (White Sea) Baltic Canal from Belomorsk to Povenets, in the USSR, is 141 miles *227 km* long with 19 locks. It was completed with the use of forced labour in 1933. It cannot accommodate ships of more than 16 ft *5 m* in draught.

The world's longest big ship canal is the Suez Canal linking the Red and Mediterranean Seas, opened on 16 Nov 1869 but inoperative from June 1967 to June 1975. The canal was planned by the French diplomatist Count Ferdinand de Lesseps (1805–94) and work began on 25 Apr 1859. It is 100.6 miles *161,9 km* in length from Port Said lighthouse to Suez

Roads and 197 ft *60 m* wide. The construction work force was 8213 men and 368 camels. The largest vessel to transit has been SS *British Progress* a VLCC (Very Large Crude Carrier) of 228 589 tonnes dwt (length 329,66 m *1081.5 ft*; beam 48,68 m *159.7 ft* at a maximum draft of 25,60 m *84 ft*). This was southbound in ballast on 5 July 1976.

Busiest

The busiest big ship canal is the Panama, first transitted on 15 Aug 1914. In 1974 there were a record 14,304 ocean-going transits. The largest liner to transit is *Queen Elizabeth 2* (66,851 gross tons) on 25 Jan 1980 for a toll of $89,154.62 (*then* £38,760). The ships with the greatest beam to transit have been the *Acadia Forest* and the *Atlantic Forest* of 106.9 ft *32,58 m*. The lowest toll was 36 US cents by the swimmer Richard Halliburton in 1928. The fastest transit has been 2 hr 41 min by the US Navy hydrofoil *Pegasus* on 20 June 1979.

Longest *Great Britain*

Inland Waterways in Great Britain, normally defined as non-tidal (except for a few tidal 'links' on the Thames, Trent and Yorkshire Ouse) rivers and canals, consist of 2394 miles *3852 km* with 110 miles *177 km* being restored. Of this total 2125 miles *3420 km* are inter-linked.

The longest possible journey on the system would be one of 415¾ miles *669 km* and 157 locks from Bedford, on the Great Ouse to near Ripon, North Yorkshire.

Largest seaway

The world's longest artificial seaway is the St Lawrence Seaway (189 miles *304 km* long) along the New York State–Ontario border from Montreal to Lake Ontario, which enables 80 per cent of all ocean-going ships, and bulk carriers with a capacity of 26,000 tons *26 400 tonnes* to sail 2342 miles *3769 km* from the North Atlantic, up the St Lawrence estuary and across the Great Lakes to Duluth, Minnesota, USA, on Lake Superior (602 ft *183 m* above sea level). The project cost $470,000,000 (*then* £168 million) and was opened on 25 Apr 1959.

Irrigation canal

The longest irrigation canal in the world is the Karakumskiy Kanal, stretching 528 miles *850 km* from Haun-Khan to Ashkhabad, Turkmenistan, USSR. In September 1971 the 'navigable' length reached 280 miles *450 km*. The length of the £370 million project will reach 930 miles *1300 km*.

LOCKS

Largest *World*

The world's largest single lock is the sea lock at Zeebrugge, Belgium measuring 500 × 57 × 23 m *1640 × 187 × 75.4 ft* giving a volume of 655 300 m³ *857,066 yd³*. The Berendrecht Lock, Antwerp planned for completion in 1986 will have the same length but a width of 68 m *223 ft* at a depth of 21,5 m *70.5 ft* giving a volume of 731 000 m³ *956,000 yd³*.

Largest *Great Britain*

The largest and deepest lock in the United Kingdom is the Royal Portbury Entrance Lock, Bristol which measures 1200 × 140 ft *366 × 42,7 m* and has a depth of 66 ft *20,2 m*. It was opened in August 1977.

Deepest *World*

The world's deepest lock is the John Day dam lock on the Columbia river, Oregon and Washington, USA completed in 1963. It can raise or lower barges 113 ft *34,4 m* and is served by a 982 ton *998 tonne* gate.

Longest flight

The world's highest lock elevator overcomes a head of 68,58 m *225 ft* at Ronquières on the Charleroi-Brussels Canal, Belgium. The two 236 wheeled caissons each able to carry 1350 tons take 22 min to cover the 1432 m *4698 ft* long ramp. The highest rise of any boat-carrying plane in Britain was the 225 ft *68,6 m* of the 935 ft *285 m* long Hobbacott Down plane on the Bude Canal, Cornwall.

The longest flight of locks in the United Kingdom is on the Worcester and Birmingham Canal at Tardebigge, Hereford and Worcester, where in a 2½ mile *4 km* stretch there are the Tardebigge (30 locks) and Stoke (6 locks) flights which together drop the canal 259 ft *78,9 m*. The flight of locks on the Huddersfield Canal, closed in 1944, on the 7¼ mile *11,6 km* stretch to Marsden numbered 42.

Largest cut

The Gaillard Cut (known as 'the Ditch') on the Panama Canal is 270 ft *82 m* deep between Gold Hill and Contractor's Hill with a bottom width of 500 ft *152 m*. In one day in 1911 as many as 333 dirt trains each carrying 357 tons *363 tonnes* left this site. The total amount of earth excavated for the whole Panama Canal as of 1 Oct 1979 was 666,194,450 yd³ *509 338 960 m³* which total will be raised by the further widening of the Gaillard Cut.

7. DAMS

Earliest

The earliest known dams were those uncovered by the British School of Archaeology in Jerusalem in 1974 at Jawa in Jordan. These stone-faced earth dams are dated to *c.* 3200 BC.

Most massive

Measured by volume, the largest dam in the world is the 98 ft *29,8 m* high New Cornelia Tailings earth-fill dam, on the Ten Mile Wash, Arizona, USA with a volume of 274,015,735 yd³ *209 501 000 m³* completed in 1973 to a length of 6.74 miles *10,85 km*.

Largest concrete

The world's largest concrete dam, and the largest concrete structure in the world, is the Grand Coulee Dam on the Columbia River, Washington State, USA. Work on the dam was begun in 1933, it began working on 22 Mar 1941 and was completed in 1942 at a cost of $56 million. It has a crest length of 4173 ft *1272 m* and is 550 ft *167 m* high. It contains 10,585,000 yd³ *8 092 000 m³* of concrete and weighs about 19,285,000 tons *19 595 000 tonnes*. The hydro-electric power plant (now being extended) will have a capacity of 9,780,000 kW.

Highest

The highest dam in the world is the Grande Dixence in Switzerland, completed in September 1961 at a cost of 1600 million Swiss francs (*then £151,000,000*). It is 935 ft *285 m* from base to rim, 2296 ft *700 m* long and the total volume of concrete in the dam is 7,792,000 yd³ *5 957 000 m³*. The Rogunsky earth-fill dam will have a final height of 1066 ft *325 m* across the Vakhsh river, Tadzhikistan, USSR with a crest length of only 2165 ft *660 m*. Building since 1973, it may be completed in 1985.

Longest

The 41 m *134.5 ft* high Yacyreta–Apipe dam across the Paraná on the Paraguay–Argentina borders extends for 72 km *44.7 miles*. In the early 17th century an impounding dam of moderate height was built in Lake Hungtze, Kiangsu, China, to a reputed length of 100 km *62 miles*.

The longest sea dam in the world is the Afsluitdijk stretching 20.195 miles *32,5 km* across the mouth of the Zuider Zee in two sections of 1.553 miles *2,499 km* (mainland of North Holland to the Isle of Wieringen) and 18.641 miles *30 km* from Wieringen to Friesland. It has a sea-level width of 293 ft *89 m* and a height of 24 ft 7 in *7,5 m*.

Strongest

The world's strongest structure will be the 242 m *793 ft* high Sayano-Shusenskaya dam on the River Yenisey, USSR which is under construction and designed to bear a load of 18 000 000 tonnes/*tons* from a fully-filled reservoir of 31,300 million m³ *41,000 million yd³* capacity.

United Kingdom

The most massive dam in Britain is the Northumbrian Water Authority's Kielder Dam, 52 m *170 ft* high earth embankment measuring 1140 m *3740 ft* in length and 5 300 000 m³ *6,932,000 yd³*. There are longer low dams or barrages of the valley cut-off type, notably the Hanningfield Dam, Essex, built from July 1952 to August 1956 to a length of 6850 ft *2088 m* and a height of 64.5 ft *19,7 m*. The rock-fill Llyn Brianne Dam, Dyfed is Britain's highest dam reaching 298½ ft *91 m* in Nov 1971 and becoming operational on 20 July 1972.

Largest reservoir *World*

The most voluminous man-made reservoir is at Bratsk (River Angara) USSR, with a volume of 137,214,000 acre-ft

The world's longest dam—part of the Yacyreta-Apipe dam on the Parana river, which stretches 72 km *44.7 miles* along the borders of Paraguay and Argentina.

169,25 km³. The dam was completed in 1964. The world's largest artificial lake measured by surface area is Lake Volta, Ghana, formed by the Akosombo dam completed in 1965. By 1969 the lake had filled to an area of 3275 miles² *8482 km²* with a shoreline 4500 miles *7250 km* in length.

The completion in 1954 of the Owen Falls Dam near Jinja, Uganda, across the northern exit of the White Nile from the Victoria Nyanza marginally raised the level of that *natural* lake by adding 166,000,000 acre-ft *204,75 km³*, and technically turned it into a reservoir with a surface area of 17,169,920 acres *6,9 million ha* (26,828 miles² *69 484 km²*).

The $4 billion Tacurai Dam will, by 1984, convert the Tocantins river into a 1900 km *1180 mile* long chain of lakes.

Largest reservoir *Great Britain*

The most capacious reservoir in Britain is Kielder Water in the North Tyne valley, Northumberland, which filled to 44,000 million gallons *2000 million hl* from 15 Dec 1980 to mid-1982, and which acquired a surface area of 2684 acres *1086 ha* and a perimeter of 27 miles *43,4 km* to become England's second largest lake. Rutland Water has a lesser capacity (27,300 million gallons *124 106 million l*) and a lesser perimeter (24 miles *38,6 km*) but a greater surface area of 3100 acres *1254 ha*. The deepest reservoir in Europe is Loch Morar, Highland, Scotland, with a maximum depth of 1017 ft *310 m* (see also page 64).

The largest wholly artificial reservoir in Great Britain is the Queen Mary Reservoir, built from August 1914 to June 1925, at Littleton, near Staines, Surrey, with an available storage capacity of 8130 million gal *369,6 million hl* and a water area of 707 acres *286 ha*. The length of the perimeter embankment is 20,766 ft *6329 m* (3.93 miles *6,32 km*).

Largest polder

The largest of the five great polders in the old Zuider Zee, Netherlands, will be the 149,000 acre *60 300 ha* (232.8 miles² *602,9 km²*) Markerwaard. Work on the 66 mile *106 km* long surrounding dyke was begun in 1957. The water area remaining after the erection of the 1927–32 dam (20 miles *32 km* in length) is called IJssel Meer, which will have a final area of 487.5 miles² *1262,6 km²*.

Largest levees

The most massive levees ever built are the Mississippi levees begun in 1717 but vastly augmented by the US Federal Government after the disastrous floods of 1927. These extend for 1732 miles *2787 km* along the main river from Cape Girardeau, Missouri, to the Gulf of Mexico and comprise more than 1000 million yd³ *765 million m³* of earthworks. Levees on the tributaries comprise an additional 2000 miles *3200 km*. The Pine Bluff, Arkansas to Venice, Louisiana segment of 650 miles *1046 km* is continuous.

8. TUNNELS

LONGEST

Water supply *World*

The world's longest tunnel of any kind is the New York City West Delaware water supply tunnel, begun in 1937 and completed in 1944. It has a diameter of 13 ft 6 in *4,1 m* and runs for 105 miles *168,9 km* from the Rondout Reservoir into the Hillview Reservoir, on the border of Yonkers and New York City, NY, USA.

Water supply *Great Britain*

The longest water supply tunnel in the United Kingdom is the Kielder Water tunnel system. These tunnels have been driven through the rock to link the Tyne Valley with the Wear Valley. A pipe then passes under the river Wear and the tunnel then proceeds to link up with the Tees Valley. The system is 20.2 miles *32,18 km* in length.

Railway *World*

The world's longest main-line rail tunnel is the 22,2 km (*13 miles 1397 yd*) long Oshimizu Tunnel (Daishimizu) on the Tōkyō–Niigata Joetsu line in central Honshū under the Tanigawa mountain which was holed through on 25 Jan 1979. The cost of the whole project will by March 1981 reach £3150 million. Fatalities in 7 years have been 13.

Railway *Great Britain*

Great Britain's longest main-line railway tunnel is the Severn Tunnel (4 miles 628 yd *6 km*), linking Avon and Gwent completed with 76,400,000 bricks between 1873 and 1886.

Sub-aqueous

The 33.49 mile *53,9 km* long Seikan Rail Tunnel has been bored 240 m *787 ft* beneath sea level and 100 m *328 ft* below the sea bed of the Tsugaru Strait between Tappi Saki, Honshū, and Fukushima, Hokkaidō, Japan. Tests started on the sub-aqueous section (14.5 miles *23,3 km*) in 1963 and construction in June 1972. It was holed through on 27 Jan 1983 after a loss of 33 lives. The cost by completion in 1985 will be $2.25 billion.

Subway

The world's longest continuous vehicular tunnel is the Moscow Metro underground railway line from Belyaevo to Medvedkovo. It is *c.* 30,7 km *19.07 miles* long and was completed in 1978/9.

Road *World*

The longest road tunnel is the 10.14 mile *16,32 km* long two-lane St Gotthard Road Tunnel from Göschenen to Airolo, Switzerland, opened to traffic on 5 Sept 1980. Nineteen lives were lost during the construction which cost Sw Fr 686 million (*then £173.6 million*) since autumn 1969.

Great Britain

The longest road tunnel in the United Kingdom is the Mersey Tunnel, joining Liverpool and Birkenhead, Merseyside. It is 2.13 miles *3,43 km* long, or 2.87 miles *4,62 km* including branch tunnels. Work was begun in December 1925 and it was opened by HM King George V on 18 July 1934. The total cost was £7¾ million. The 36 ft *11 m* wide 4-lane roadway carries nearly 7½ million vehicles a year. The first tube of the second Mersey Tunnel was opened on 24 June 1971.

Largest

The largest diameter road tunnel in the world is that blasted through Yerba Buena Island, San Francisco, California, USA. It is 76 ft *23 m* wide, 58 ft *17 m* high and 540 ft *165 m* long. More than 35,000,000 vehicles pass through on its two decks every year.

Hydro-electric, irrigation or sewerage *World*

The longest irrigation tunnel in the world is the 51.5 mile *82,9 km* long Orange-Fish Rivers Tunnel, South Africa, begun in 1967 at an estimated cost of £60 million. The boring was completed in April 1973. The lining to a minimum thickness of 9 inches *23 cm* will give a completed diameter of 17 ft 6 in *5,33 m*. The Majes project in Peru involves 98 km *60.9 miles* of tunnels for hydroelectric and water supply purposes. The dam is at 4200 m *13,780 ft* altitude. The Chicago TARP (Tunnels and Reservoir Plan) in Illinois, USA involves 120 miles *193 km* of sewerage tunnelling.

Bridge-Tunnel

The world's longest bridge-tunnel system is the Chesapeake Bay Bridge-Tunnel, extending 17.65 miles *28,40 km* from Eastern Shore, Virginia Peninsula to Virginia Beach, Virginia, USA. It cost $200,000,000 (*then £71,4 million*) and was completed after 42 months and opened to traffic on 15 Apr 1964. The longest bridged section is Trestle C (4.56 miles *7,34 km* long) and the longest tunnel is the Thimble Shoal Channel Tunnel (1.09 miles *1,75 km*).

Canal tunnels *World*

The world's longest canal tunnel is that on the Rove canal between the port of Marseilles, France and the river Rhône, built in 1912–27. It is 4.53 miles *7,29 km* long, 72 ft *22 m* wide and 50 ft *15 m* high, involving 2¼ million yd³ *1,7 million m³* of excavation.

Great Britain

The longest canal tunnel in Great Britain is the Standedge (more properly Stanedge) Tunnel in West Yorkshire on the Huddersfield Narrow Canal built from 1794 to 4 Apr 1811. It measures 3 miles 418 yd *5,21 km* in length and was closed on 21 Dec 1944. The British canal system has contained 84 tunnels exceeding 30 yd *27,4 m* of which 48 are still open. The longest of these is the 3056 yd *2,79 km* long Blisworth Tunnel on the Grand Union in Northamptonshire. The now closed Huddersfield Narrow Canal is the highest in the United Kingdom, at 638 ft *194 m* above sea-level.

Tunnelling records

The longest unsupported example of a machine-bored tunnel is the Three Rivers Water Tunnel driven 30,769 linear feet *9,37 km* with a 10.5 ft *3,2 m* diameter for the City of Atlanta, Georgia, USA from April 1980 to February 1982. S & M Constructors Inc of Cleveland, Ohio achieved 179 ft *54,5 m* in a day through the granite, schist and gneiss.

The NCB record of 251,4 m *824.8 ft* for a 3,80 m *12½ ft* wide, 2 m *6½ ft* high roadway by a team of 35 pitmen in 5 days was set at West Cannock No 5 Colliery on 30 Mar–3 Apr 1981.

9. SPECIALISED STRUCTURES

Advertising sign Highest *World*

The highest advertising signs in the world are the four Bank of Montreal logos atop the 72 storey 935 ft *285 m* tall First Canadian Place, Toronto. Each sign, built by Claude Neon Industries Ltd, measures 20 × 22 ft *6,09 × 6,70 m* and was lifted by helicopter.

Advertising sign Largest

The most conspicuous sign ever erected was the electric Citroën sign on the Eiffel Tower, Paris. It was switched on on 4 July 1925, and could be seen 24 miles *38 km* away. In six colours with 250,000 lamps and 56 miles *90 km* of electric cables. The letter 'N' which terminated the name 'Citroën' between the second and third levels measured 68 ft 5 in *20,8 m* in height. The whole apparatus was taken down after 11 years in 1936. For the largest ground sign see Chapter 6, page 88—Largest letter.

The world's largest neon sign was that owned by the Atlantic Coast Line Railroad Company at Port Tampa, Florida, USA. It measured 387 ft 6 in *118 m* long and 76 ft *23 m* high, weighed 175 tons *178 tonnes* and contained about 4200 ft *1280 m* of red neon tubing. It was demolished on 19 Feb 1970. The world's largest reported hoarding is one 44,5 m *146 ft* long and 17,5 m *57 ft 5 in* tall erected by Propaganda Campanella on Route N9, Buenos Aires, Argentina. Britain's largest illuminated sign is the word PLAYHOUSE extending 90 ft *27 m* across the frontage of the new theatre in Leeds, West Yorkshire opened in 1970.

An interior lit fascia advertising sign in Clearwater, Florida, USA completed by Adco Sign Corp in April 1983 measures 1168 ft 6½ in *356,17 m* in length.

The world's most massive animated sign is reputed to be that outside the Circus Circus Hotel, Reno, Nevada named Topsy, the Clown. It is 127 ft *38,7 m* tall and weighs over 40 tons *40,8 tonnes* with 1.4 miles *2,25 km* of neon tubing. His smile measures 14 ft *4,26 m* across.

Barn Largest

The largest barn in Britain is one at Frindsbury, Kent. Its length is 219 ft *66,7 m* and is still wholly roofed. The Ipsden Barn, Oxfordshire, is 385½ ft *117 m* long but 30 ft *9 m* wide (11,565 ft² *1074 m²*). The longest tithe barn in Britain is one measuring 268 ft *81 m* long at Wyke Farm, near Sherborne, Dorset.

Bonfire Largest

The largest recorded bonfire constructed in Britain was the Coronation bonfire using 800 tons *812 tonnes* of timber, 1000 gal *4546 litres* each of petroleum and tar. It was octagonal in shape and built to a height of 120 ft *36,67 m* with a base circumference of 155 ft *47,2 m* tapering to 20 ft *6,1 m* at the summit, on Arrowthwaite Brows at Whitehaven, Cumbria in 1902.

Breakwater Longest *World and Great Britain*

The world's longest breakwater is that which protects the Port of Galveston, Texas, USA. The granite South Breakwater is 6.74 miles *10,85 km* in length.

The longest breakwater in Great Britain is the North Breakwater at Holyhead, Anglesey, Gwynedd which is 9860 ft (1.86 miles *3005 m*) in length and was completed in 1873.

Buildings demolished by Explosives *Largest*

The largest building demolished by explosives has been the 21 storey Traymore Hotel, Atlantic City, New Jersey, USA, on 26 May 1972 by Controlled Demolition Inc of Towson, Maryland. This 600 room hotel had a cubic capacity of 6,495,500 ft³ *181 340 m³*. The tallest chimney ever demolished by explosives was the Matla Power Station chimney, Kriel, South Africa on 19 July 1981. It stood 275 m *902 ft* and was brought down by The Santon (Steeplejack) Co. Ltd of Manchester, England.

The greatest recorded simultaneous smokestack demolition was when 18 were felled at the London Brick Co Coronation Works at Kempston Hardwick, Bedfordshire on 30 Nov 1980 when Mrs Wyn Witherall fired the 100 lb *45,3 kg* of explosives laid by T. W. Robinson & Co.

Cemetery Largest

The world's largest cemetery is that in Leningrad, USSR, which contains over 500,000 of the 1,300,000 victims of the German army's siege of 1941–3. The largest cemetery in the United Kingdom is Brookwood Cemetery, Brookwood, Surrey. It is owned by the London Necropolis Co. and is 500 acres *200 ha* in extent with more than 225,000 interments.

Column Tallest

The tallest columns (as opposed to obelisks) in the world are the 36 fluted pillars 90 ft *27,43 m* tall, of Vermont marble in the colonnade of the Education Building, Albany, New York. Their base diameter is 6½ ft *1,98 m*. The tallest load-bearing stone columns in the world are those measuring 69 ft *21 m* in the Hall of Columns of the Temple of Amun at Karnak, opposite Thebes on the Nile, the ancient capital of Upper Egypt. They were built in the 19th dynasty in the reign of Rameses II in *c.* 1270 BC.

Crematorium Earliest

The oldest crematorium in Britain is one built in 1879 at Woking, Surrey. The first cremation took place there on 26 Mar 1885, the practice having been found legal after the cremation of Iesu Grist Price on Caerlan fields on 13 Jan 1884. The total number of people cremated in Britain since, has been 9,445,210 (to 31 Dec 1982), and the percentage (now 65.69%) is the highest in the world for any country in which cremation is voluntary.

Crematorium Largest

The largest crematorium in the world is at the Nikolo-Arkhangelskoye Cemetery, East Moscow, with 7 twin cremators of British design, completed in March 1972. It has several Halls of Farewell for atheists. Currently, Britain's largest is the City of London Crematorium, E.12, which performed a record 5395 cremations in 1979 and extends over 165 acres *66,77 ha*. The all-time total of 257,914 at Golders Green Crematorium (since 1902) remains unsurpassed.

Dock Gate

The world's largest dock gate is that at Nigg Bay, Cromarty Firth, Highlands, Scotland, first operated in March 1974. It

Hadstock Church's door in Essex, England which has been awaiting replacement for 944 years and is the oldest surviving example in the world. (*David Roberts*)

measures 408 ft *124 m* long, 50 ft *15,2 m* high with a 4 ft *1,21 m* thick base, is made of reinforced concrete and weighs 16,000 tons *16 257 tonnes* together with its sill, quoins and roundheads. The builders were Brown and Root-Wimpey Highland Fabricators.

Dome Largest *World and Great Britain*

The world's largest dome is the Louisiana Superdome, New Orleans, USA. It has a diameter of 680 ft *207,26 m* (See page 117 for further details.) The largest dome of ancient architecture is that of the Pantheon, built in Rome in AD 112, with a diameter of 142½ ft *43 m*.

The largest dome in Britain is that of the Bell Sports Centre, Perth, Scotland, with a diameter of 222 ft *67 m* designed by D. B. Cockburn and constructed in Baltic whitewood by Muirhead & Sons Ltd of Grangemouth, Central, Scotland.

Door Largest *World*

The largest doors in the world are the four in the Vehicle Assembly Building near Cape Canaveral, Florida, with a height of 460 ft *140 m* (see page 113). The world's heaviest door is that leading to the laser target room at Lawrence Livermore National Laboratory, California. It weighs 321.4 tons *326,5 tonnes*, is up to 8 ft *2,43 m* thick and was installed by Overly.

Door Largest *Great Britain*

The largest doors in Great Britain are those to the Britannia Assembly Hall, at Filton airfield, Avon. The doors are 1035 ft *315 m* in length and 67 ft *20 m* high, divided into three bays each 345 ft *105 m* across. The largest simple hinged door in Britain is that of Ye Old Bull's Head, Beaumaris, Anglesey, Gwynedd, which is 11 ft *3,35 m* wide and 13 ft *3,96 m* high.

Door Oldest

The oldest doors in Britain are those of Hadstock Church,

Essex, which date from *c.* 1040 AD and exhibit evidence of Danish workmanship.

Dry dock Largest *World*

The largest dry dock in the world is that at Koyagi, Nagasaki, Japan completed in 1972. It measures 990 m *3248 ft* long; 100 m *328 ft* in width and has a maximum shipbuilding capacity of 1,000,000 tons deadweight.

The largest shipbuilding dry dock in the UK is the Belfast Harbour Commission and Harland and Wolff building dock at Belfast, Northern Ireland. It was excavated by Wimpey's to a length of 1825 ft *556 m* and a width of 305 ft *93 m* and could accommodate tankers of 1,000,000 tons deadweight. Work was begun on 26 Jan 1968 and completed on 30 Nov 1969 and involved the excavation of 400,000 yd³ *306 000 m³*. The dry dock under construction at Port Rashid, Dubai, Persian Gulf, opened in March 1979 measures 1722 by 328 ft *525 × 100 m*.

Earthworks Largest *World*

The largest earthworks in the world carried out prior to the mechanical era were the Linear Earth Boundaries of the Benin Empire in the Bendel state of Nigeria. These were first reported in 1900 and partially surveyed in 1967. In April 1973 it was estimated by Mr Patrick Darling that the total length of the earthworks was probably between 4000 and 8000 miles *6400– 12 800 km* with the total amount of earth moved estimated at from 500 to 600 million yd³ *380–460 million m³*.

Earthworks Largest *Great Britain*

The greatest prehistoric earthwork in Britain is Wansdyke, originally Woden's Dyke, which ran 86 miles *138 km* from Portishead, Avon to Inkpen Beacon and Ludgershall, south of Hungerford, Berkshire. It is believed to have been built by the pre-Roman Wessex culture. The most extensive single site earthwork is the Dorset Cursus near Gussage St. Michael, dating from *c.* 1900 BC. The workings are 6 miles *9,7 km* in length, involving an estimated 250,000 yd³ *191 000 m³* of excavations. The largest of the Celtic hill-forts is that known as Mew Dun, or Maiden Castle, 2 miles *3 km* SW of Dorchester, Dorset. It covers 115 acres *46,5 ha* and was abandoned shortly after AD 43.

Fence Longest and Highest

The longest fence in the world was the dingo-proof fence enclosing the main sheep areas of Australia. The wire fence is 6 ft *1,8 m* high, 1 ft *30 cm* underground and stretches for 3437 miles *5531 km*. The Queensland State Government discontinued full maintenance in 1982 but 500 km *310 miles* is now being repaired. The world's tallest fences are security screens 20 m *65.6 ft* high erected by Harrop-Allin of Pretoria in November 1981 to keep out Soviet RP67 rocket sabotage missiles from fuel depots and refineries at Sasolburg, South Africa.

Flagstaff Tallest *World*

The tallest flagstaff ever erected was that outside the Oregon

The kind of fence which can neither be leaned on or talked over—the world's highest 20 m *65.6 ft* tall security fencing at Saselborg, South Africa put up in November 1981. (*Harrop-Allin, Pretoria*)

Building at the 1915 Panama-Pacific International Exposition in San Francisco, California, USA. Trimmed from a Douglas fir, it stood 299 ft 7 in *91 m* in height and weighed 45 tons *47 tonnes*. The tallest unsupported flag pole in the world is a 190 ft *57,9 m* tall (plus 12½ ft *3,81 m* below ground) metal pole weighing 20,000 lb *9070 kg* erected on 27 June 1981 at Chula Vista, California, USA. The concept was carried through by Jerry Leaf Sales Inc.

Flagstaff Tallest *Great Britain*

The tallest flagstaff in Great Britain is a 225 ft *68 m* tall Douglas fir staff at Kew, Richmond upon Thames, Greater London. Cut in Canada, it was shipped across the Atlantic and towed up the River Thames on 7 May 1958, to replace the old 214 ft *65 m* tall staff of 1919.

Fountain Tallest *World and Great Britain*

The world's tallest fountain is the Fountain at Fountain Hills, Arizona built at a cost of $1,500,000 for McCulloch Properties Inc. At full pressure of 375 lb/in² *26,3 kg/cm²* and at a rate of 5828 Imp. gal/min *26 500 litres/min* the 560 ft *170 m* tall column of water weighs more than 8 tons/*tonnes*. The nozzle speed achieved by the three 600 hp pumps is 146.7 mph *236 km/h*.

The tallest fountain in Great Britain is the Emperor Fountain at Chatsworth, Bakewell, Derbyshire. When first tested on 1 June 1844, it attained the then unprecedented height of 260 ft *79 m*. Since the war it has not been played to more than 250 ft *76 m* and rarely beyond 180 ft *55 m*.

Garbage dump Biggest

Reclamation Plant No. 1, Fresh Kills, Staten Island, opened in March 1974, is the world's largest sanitary landfill. In its first 4 months 450,000 tons *457 000 tonnes* of refuse from New York City was dumped on the site by 700 barges.

Gasholder Largest *World*

The world's largest gasholder is that at Fontaine l'Eveque, Belgium, where disused mines have been adapted to store up to 500 million m³ *17,650 million ft³* of gas at ordinary pressure. Probably the largest conventional gasholder is that at Wien-Simmering, Vienna, Austria, completed in 1968, with a height of 274 ft 8 in *84 m* and a capacity of 10.59 million ft³ *300 000 m³*.

Gasholder Largest *Great Britain*

The largest gasholder ever constructed in Great Britain is the East Greenwich Gas Works No. 2 Holder built in 1891 with an original capacity for 12,200,000 ft³ *346 000 m³*. As constructed its capacity is 8.9 million ft³ *252 000 m³* with a water tank 303 ft *92 m* in diameter and a full inflated height of 148 ft *45 m*. The No. 1 holder (capacity 8.6 million ft³ *243 500 m³*) has a height of 200 ft *61 m*. The River Tees Northern Gas Board's 1186 ft *361 m* deep underground storage in use since January 1959 has a capacity of 330,000 ft³ *9300 m³*.

Globe Largest revolving

The world's largest revolving globe is the 21½ ton/*tonnes* 27 ft 11 in *8,50 m* diameter sphere in Babson College Wellesley, Massachusetts, USA completed at a cost of $200,000 (*then £71,425*) in 1956.

Jetty Longest

The longest deep water jetty in the world is the Quai Hermann du Pasquier at Le Havre, France, with a length of 5000 ft *1524 m*. Part of an enclosed basin, it has a constant depth of water of 32 ft *9,8 m* on both sides.

Kitchen *Largest*

The largest kitchen ever set up has been the Indian Government field kitchen set up in April 1973 at Ahmadnagar, Maharashtra in the famine area which daily provided 1.2 million subsistence meals.

Lamp Post *Tallest*

The tallest lighting columns ever erected are four of 63,5 m *208 ft 4 in* made by Petitjean & Cie of Troyes, France and installed by Taylor Woodrow at Bansher Sports Complex, Muscat, Oman.

Lighthouse Brightest and Earliest *World*

The lighthouse with the most powerful light in the world is Créac'h d'Ouessant lighthouse, established in 1638 and last altered in 1939 on l'Ile d'Ouessant, Finisterre, Brittany, France. It is 163 ft *50 m* tall and, in times of fog, has a luminous intensity of up to 500 million candelas. For earliest lighthouse, see Seven Wonders of the World, p. 128.

The £18½ million 100 m *328 ft* tall rock lighthouse being built (1983–85) 40 km *24.8 miles* SW of l'Ile d'Ouessant will be visible at 40 nautical miles *74 km*. The lights with the greatest visible range are those 1092 ft *332 m* above the ground on the Empire State Building, New York City, NY, USA. Each of the four-arc mercury bulbs has a rated candlepower of 450,000,000, visible 80 miles *130 km* away on the ground and 300 miles *490 km* away from aircraft. They were switched on on 31 Mar 1956.

Lighthouse Brightest *Great Britain*
The lighthouse in Great Britain with the most powerful light is the shorelight at Strumble Head, near Fishguard, Dyfed. It has an intensity of 6,000,000 candelas. The Irish light with the greatest intensity is Aranmore on Rinrawros Point, County Donegal.

Lighthouse Remotest *Great Britain*
The most remote Trinity House lighthouse is The Smalls, about 16 sea miles (18.4 statute miles *29,6 km*) off the Dyfed coast. The most remote Scottish lighthouse is Sule Skerry, 35 miles *56 km* off shore and 45 miles *72 km* northwest of Dunnet Head, Highland. The most remote Irish light is Blackrock, 9 miles *14 km* off the Mayo coast.

Lighthouse Tallest
The world's tallest lighthouse is the steel tower 348 ft *106 m* tall near Yamashita Park in Yokohama, Japan. It has a power of 600,000 candles and a visibility range of 20 miles *32 km*.

Bishop Rock, Isles of Scilly measures 47,8 m *156.8 ft* high to its helipad. The tallest Scottish lighthouse is the 139 ft *42,3 m* tall North Ronaldsay lighthouse, Orkney Islands.

Marquee Largest *World and Great Britain*
The largest tent ever erected was one covering an area of 188,368 ft² *17 500 m²* (4.32 acres *1,7 ha*) put up by the firm of Deuter from Augsburg, W. Germany, for the 1958 'Welcome Expo' in Brussels, Belgium.

The largest marquee in Britain is one made by Piggot Brothers in 1951 and used by the Royal Horticultural Society at their annual show (first held in 1913) in the grounds of the Royal Hospital, Kensington and Chelsea, Greater London. The marquee is 310 ft *94 m* long by 480 ft *146 m* wide and consists of 18¾ miles *30 km* of 36 in *91 cm* wide canvas covering a ground area of 148,800 ft² *13 820 m²*. A tent 435 ft *132,5 m* long was erected in one lift by thirty-five men of the Military Corrective Training Centre, Colchester on 23 July 1980.

Maypole
The tallest reported Maypole erected in England was one of Sitka spruce 105 ft 7 in *32,12 m* tall put up in Pelynt, Cornwall on 1 May 1974. The permanent pole at Paganhill, near Stroud, Gloucestershire is 90 ft *27,43 m* tall.

Maze Largest
The world's largest maze is that at Longleat, nr Warminster, Wilts, with 1.61 miles *2,59 km* of paths flanked by 16,180 yew trees. It was opened on 6 June 1978. 'Il Labirinto' at Villa Pisani, Stra, Italy in which Napoleon was 'lost' in 1807 had 4 miles *6,4 km* of pathways.

Menhir *tallest*
The tallest menhir found is the 380 ton Grand Menhir Brisé, now in 5 pieces, which originally stood 69 ft *21 m* high at Locmariaquer, Britanny, France.

Monument Prehistoric *Largest*
Britain's largest megalithic prehistoric monument and largest existing henge are the 28½ acre *11,5 ha* earthworks and stone circles of Avebury, Wiltshire, 'rediscovered' in 1646. The earliest calibrated date in the area of this neolithic site is *c.* 4200 BC. The whole work is 1200 ft *365 m* in diameter with a 40 ft *12 m* ditch around the perimeter and required an estimated 15 million man-hours of work. The henge of Durrington Walls, Wiltshire, obliterated by road building, had a diameter of 1550 ft *472 m*. It was built from *c.* 2500 BC and required some 900,000 man hours.

The largest trilithons exist at Stonehenge, to the south of Salisbury Plain, Wiltshire, with single sarsen blocks weighing over 45 tons/*tonnes* and requiring over 550 men to drag them up a 9° gradient. The earliest stage of the construction of the ditch has been dated to 2180 ± 105 BC. Whether Stonehenge, which required some 30 million man-years, was a lunar calendar, a temple or an eclipse-predictor is still debated.

Monument Tallest
The world's tallest monument is the stainless steel Gateway to the West Arch in St Louis, Missouri, USA, completed on 28 Oct 1965 to commemorate the westward expansion after the Louisiana Purchase of 1803. It is a sweeping arch spanning 630 ft *192 m* and rising to the same height of 630 ft *192 m* and costing $29,000,000 (*then £10.35 million*). It was designed in 1947 by Eero Saarinen (d. 1961).

The tallest monumental column in the world is that commemorating the battle of San Jacinto (21 Apr 1836), on the bank of the San Jacinto river near Houston, Texas, USA. General Sam Houston (1793–1863) and his force of 743 Texan troops killed 630 Mexicans (out of a total force of 1600) and captured 700 others, for the loss of nine men killed and 30 wounded. Constructed in 1936–9, at a cost of $1,500,000 (*then £372,000*), the tapering column is 570 ft *173 m* tall, 47 ft *14 m* square at the base, and 30 ft *9 m* square at the observation tower, which is surmounted by a star weighing 196.4 tons *199,6 tonnes*. It is built of concrete, faced with buff limestone, and weighs 31,384 tons *31 888 tonnes*.

Monument, Youngest ancient
The newest scheduled ancient monuments are a hexagonal pill box and 48 concrete tank traps south of Christchurch, Dorset built in World War II and protected since 1973.

Mound Largest *World*
The gravel mound built as a memorial to the Seleucid King Antiochus I (reigned 69–34 BC) on the summit of Nemrud Dagi (8205 ft *2494 m*) south east of Malatya, Eastern Turkey measures 197 ft *59,8 m* tall and covers 7.5 acres *3 ha*.

Mound Largest *United Kingdom*
The largest artificial mound in Europe is Silbury Hill, 6 miles *9,7 km* west of Marlborough, Wiltshire, which involved the moving of an estimated 670,000 tons *681,000 tonnes* of chalk, at a cost of 18 million man-hours to make a cone 130 ft *39 m* high with a base of 5½ acres *2 ha*. Prof. Richard Atkinson in charge of the 1968 excavations showed that it is based on an innermost central mound, similar to contemporary round barrows, and is now dated to 2745 ± 185 BC. The largest long barrow in England is that inside the hill-fort at Maiden Castle (see Earthworks largest GB). It originally had a length of 1800 ft *548 m* and had several enigmatic features such as a ritual pit with pottery, limpet shells, and animal bones, but the date of these is not certain. The longest long barrow containing a megalithic chamber is that at West Kennet (*c.* 2200 BC), near Silbury, measuring 385 ft *117 m* in length.

Naturist resorts
The oldest resort is Der Freilichtpark, Klingberg, W. Germany established in 1903. The largest in the world is the Beau Valley Country Club, Warmbaths, South Africa extending over 4 million m² *988 acres* with up to 20,000 visitors a year. However, 100,000 people visit the smaller centre Helio-Marin at Cap d'Agde, southern France, which covers 90 ha *222 acres*. The term 'nudist camp' is deplored by naturists.

Obelisk (Monolithic) Largest and Oldest
The largest standing obelisk (from the Gk *obeliskos*, skewer or spit) in the world is the Egyptian obelisk brought from Egypt to the hippodrome of Constantinople in Istanbul, Turkey in AD 390. It stands 58 m *190.2 ft* tall. The unfinished obelisk, probably commissioned by Queen Hatshepsut *c.* 1490 BC, at Aswan is 41,75 m *136.8 ft* in length and weighs 1168 tonnes/*tons*. The largest obelisk in the United Kingdom is Cleopatra's Needle on the Embankment, London, which is 68 ft 5½ in *20 m* tall and weighs 186.3 tons *189,35 tonnes*. It was towed up the Thames from Egypt on 21 Jan 1878 and positioned on 13 Sept. The longest an obelisk has remained *in situ* is that still at Heliopolis, near Cairo, Egypt, erected by Senusret I *c.* 1750 BC.

Pier Longest *World*
The world's longest pier is the Dammam Pier, Saudi Arabia, on the Persian Gulf. A rock-filled causeway 4.84 miles *7,79 km* long joins the steel trestle pier 1.80 miles *2,90 km* long, which joins the Main Pier (744 ft *226 m* long), giving an overall length of 6.79 miles *10,93 km*. The work was begun in July 1948 and completed on 15 Mar 1950.

The kind of scarecrow which would give a dinosaur a fright. Wayne Kunkelman dwarfed by his 20 ft *6,09 m* tall creation on his farm in Pennsylvania, USA. (*Snipes Farm and Nursery*)

Pier Longest *Great Britain*

The longest pier in Great Britain is the Bee Ness Jetty, completed in 1930, which stretches 8200 ft *2500 m* along the west bank of the River Medway, 5 to 6 miles *8 to 9,6 km* below Rochester, at Kingsnorth, Kent.

Pyramid Largest

The largest pyramid, and the largest monument ever constructed, is the Quetzacóatl at Cholula de Rivadabia, 63 miles *101 km* south-east of Mexico City, Mexico. It is 177 ft *54 m* tall and its base covers an area of nearly 45 acres *18,2 ha.* Its total volume has been estimated at 4,300,000 yd³ *3 300 000 m³* compared with 3,360,000 yd³ *2,5 million m³* for the Pyramid of Cheops (*see* Seven Wonders of the World). The pyramid-building era here was between the 2nd and 6th centuries AD.

Pyramid Oldest

The oldest known pyramid is the Djoser step pyramid at Saqqâra, Egypt constructed to a height of 204 ft *62 m* originally with a Tura limestone casing in *c.* 2650 BC. The largest known single block comes from the Third Pyramid (the pyramid of Mycerinus) and weighs 290 tonnes *285 tons.* The oldest New World pyramid is that on the island of La Venta in south-eastern Mexico built by the Olmec people *c.* 800 BC. It stands 100 ft *30 m* tall with a base diameter of 420 ft *128 m.*

Scarecrow

The world's largest scarecrow was built by Wayne and Jacqueline Kunkelman to a height of 20 ft *6,09 m* with a spread of 19 ft *5,79 m* at Snipes Farm and Nursery, Morrisville, Pennsylvania, USA in October 1983.

Snow Construction *Largest*

The world's largest snow construction is the Ice Palace built in the winter of 1980–81 using 1600 tons/*tonnes* of snow, at Tokamachi City, Niigata prefecture, Japan. The overall height was 23 m *75 ft 5 in* and a total of 800 people and 50 bulldozers were used in the construction.

Stairs Longest *World*

The world's longest stairway is the service staircase for the Niesenbahn funicular which rises to 2365 m *7759 ft* near Spiez, Switzerland. It has 11,674 steps and a bannister. The stone cut T'ai Chan temple stairs of 6600 steps in the Shantung Mountains, China ascend 4700 feet in 5 miles *1428 m in 8 km.* The longest spiral staircase is one 1103 ft *336,2 m* deep with 1520 steps installed in the Mapco–White County Coal Mine, Carmi, Illinois, USA by Systems Control Inc in May 1981.

Stairs Longest *Great Britain*

The longest stairs in Britain are those from the transformer gallery to the surface 1065 ft *324 m* in the Cruachan Power Station, Argyll, Scotland. They have 1420 steps and the Work Study Dept. allows 27 min 41.4 sec for the ascent.

Statue Longest

Near Bamiyan, Afghanistan there are the remains of the recumbent Sakya Buddha, built of plastered rubble, which was 'about 1000 ft *305 m*' long and is believed to date from the 3rd or 4th century AD.

Statue Tallest

The tallest full-figure statue in the world is that of 'Motherland', an enormous pre-stressed concrete female figure on Mamayev Hill, outside Volgograd, USSR, designed in 1967 by Yevgenyi Vuchetich, to commemorate victory in the Battle of Stalingrad (1942–3). The statue from its base to the tip of the sword clenched in her right hand measures 270 ft *82,30 m. The Indian Rope Trick* statue by Calle Ornemark near Jönköping, Sweden measures 103 m *337 ft* from the feet of the *fakir* to the top of the rope 25 cm *9.8 in* in diameter. Its total weight is 144 tonnes *141.6 tons.*

Tidal River Barrier

The largest tidal river barrier in the world is the Thames Barrier at Woolwich, London with 9 piers and 10 gates. There are 6 rising sector gates 61 m *200 ft 1½ in* wide and 4 falling radial gates 31,5 m *103 ft 4 in* wide. The site was chosen in 1971. Costs to the end of 1982 were £400 million.

Tomb Largest

The largest tomb yet discovered is that of Emperor Nintoku (died *c.* AD 428) south of Osaka, Japan. It measures 1594 ft *485 m* long by 1000 ft *305 m* wide by 150 ft *45 m* high.

Totem pole Tallest

A totem pole 173 ft *52,73 m* tall was raised on 6 June 1973 at Alert Bay, British Columbia, Canada. It tells the story of the Kwakiutl and took 36 man-weeks to carve.

SEVEN WONDERS OF THE WORLD

The Seven Wonders of the World were first designated by Antipater of Sidon in the 2nd century BC. They included the Pyramids of Giza, built by three Fourth Dynasty Egyptian Pharaohs, Khwfw (Khufu or Cheops), Kha-f-Ra (Khafre, Khefren or Chepren) and Menkaure (Mycerinus) near El Giza (El Gizeh), south-west of El Qâhira (Cairo) in Egypt. The Great Pyramid ('Horizon of Khufu') was finished *c.* 2580 BC. Its original height was 480 ft 11 in *146,5 m* (now, since the loss of its topmost stones and the pyramidion, reduced to 449 ft 6 in *137 m*) with a base line of 756 ft *230 m* and thus covering slightly more than 13 acres *5 ha.* It has been estimated that a permanent work force of 4000 required 30 years to manoeuvre into position the 2,300,000 limestone blocks averaging 2½ tons/*tonnes* each, totalling about 5,750,000 tons *5 840 000 tonnes* and a volume of 90,700,000 ft³ *2 568 000 m³.* A costing exercise published in December 1974, indicated that it would require 405 men 6 years at a cost of $1.13 billion (*then £500 million*).

Of the other six wonders only fragments remain of the Temple of Artemis (Diana) of the Ephesians, built in *c.* 350 BC. at Ephesus, Turkey (destroyed by the Goths in AD 262), and of the Tomb of King Mausolus of Caria, built at Halicarnassus, now Bodrum, Turkey, in *c.* 325 BC. No trace remains of the Hanging Gardens of Semiramis, at Babylon, Iraq (*c.* 600 BC; the 40 ft *12 m* tall marble, gold and ivory statue of Zeus (Jupiter), by Phidias (5th century BC at Olympia, Greece (lost in a fire at Istanbul); the 117 ft *35 m* tall statue by Chares of Lindus of the figure of the god Helios (Apollo) called the Colossus of Rhodes (sculptured 292–280 BC, destroyed by an earthquake in 224 BC); or the 400 ft *122 m* tall world's earliest lighthouse, built by Sostratus of Cnidus *c.* 270 BC as a pyramidically shaped tower of white marble, (destroyed by earthquake in AD 1375), on the island of Pharos (Greek, *pharos* = lighthouse), off the coast of El Iskandariya (Alexandria), Egypt.

Vats Largest

The largest vat in the world is named 'Strongbow', used by H.P. Bulmer Ltd., the cider makers of Hereford, England. It measures 64½ ft *19,65 m* in height and 75½ ft *23,0 m* in diameter with a capacity of 1,630,000 gallons *74 099 hectolitres.*

The largest wooden wine cask in the world is the Heidelberg Tun completed in 1751 in the cellar of the Friedrichsbau Heidelberg, West Germany. Its capacity is 1855 hectolitres *40,790 gal.*

Wall Longest *World*

The Great Wall of China, completed during the reign of Chhin Shih Huang-ti (246–210 BC), has a main line length of 2150 miles *3460 km* with a further 1780 miles *2860 km* of branches and spurs, with a height of from 15 to 39 ft *4,5 to 12 m* and up to 32 ft *9,8 m* thick. It runs from Shanhaikuan, on the Gulf of Pohai, to Yümēn-kuan and Yang-kuan and was kept in repair up to the 16th century. Some 32 miles *51,5 km* of the Wall have been destroyed since 1966. Part of the wall was blown up to make way for a dam in July 1979.

Wall Longest *Great Britain*

The longest of the Roman Walls built in Britain was the 15–20 ft *4,5–6 m* tall Hadrian's Wall, built in the period AD 122–126. It ran across the Tyne-Solway isthmus for 73½ miles *118 km* from Bowness-on-Solway, Cumbria, to Wallsend-on-Tyne, Tyne and War, and was abandoned in AD 383.

Water Tower

The world's tallest water tower is that at Elizabethtown, New York State, USA built in 1965 to a height of 210 ft *64 m* with a capacity of 250,000 gallons *9462 hl*

Waterwheel Largest *World and Great Britain*

The largest waterwheel in the world is the Mohammadieh Noria wheel at Hama, Syria with a diameter of 131 ft *40 m* dating from Roman times. The Lady Isabella wheel at Laxey, Isle of Man is the largest in the British Isles and was built for draining a lead mine and completed on 27 Sept 1854, and disused since 1929. It has a circumference of 228 ft *69 m*, a diameter of 72½ ft *22 m* and an axle weighing 9 tons/*tonnes*. The largest waterwheel in Britain is the 50 ft 5 in *15,36 m* diameter wheel built in 1870 at the Welsh Industrial and Maritime Museum, Cardiff. It worked until 1925 at Dinorwic, Gwynedd and is 5 ft *1,52 m* in width.

Window Largest

The largest sheet of glass ever manufactured was one of 50 m² *538.2 ft²*, or 20 m *65 ft 7 in* by 2,5 m *8 ft 2½ in*, exhibited by the Saint Gobian Company in France at the *Journées Internationales de Miroiterie* in March 1958. The largest single windows in the world are those in the Palace of Industry and Technology at Rondpoint de la Défense, Paris, with an extreme width of 218 m *715.2 ft* and a maximum height of 50 m *164 ft.*

Wine cellar

The largest wine cellars in the world are at Paarl, those of the Ko-operative Wijnbouwers Vereeniging, known as KWV, near Cape Town, in the centre of the wine-growing district of South Africa. They cover an area of 25 acres *10 ha* and have a capacity of 30 million gal *136 million litres*. The Cienega Winery of the Almaden Vineyards in Hollister, California, USA covers 4 acres *1,6 ha* and can house 37,300 oak barrels containing 1.83 million gallons of wine.

Ziggurat Largest

The largest ziggurat ever built was by the Elamite King Untash *c.* 1250 BC known as the Ziggurat of Choga Zanbil, 30 km *18.6 miles* from Haft Tepe, Iran. The outer base was 105 × 105 m *344 ft* and the fifth 'box' 28 × 28 m *91.8 ft* nearly 50 m *164 ft* above. The largest surviving ziggurat (from the verb *zaqaru*, to build high) or stage-tower is the Ziggurat of Ur (now Muquyyar, Iraq) with a base 61 × 45,7 m *200 × 150 ft* built to three storeys surmounted by a summit temple. The first and part of the second storeys now survive to a height of 60 ft *18 m*. It was built in the reign of Ur-nammu (*c.* 2113–2096 BC).

right: **Great Britain's largest ever waterwheel, the 50 ft 5 in diameter wheel now in the Welsh Industrial and Maritime Museum, Cardiff.** (*Amgueddfa Genedlaethol Cymru*)

Deepest *World*

Man's deepest penetration into the Earth's crust is a geological exploratory drilling near Zapolarny, Kola peninsula USSR which on 28 Dec 1983 reached 12 000 m *39,370 ft* or *7.45 miles.* Progress once averaging 11 m *36 ft* per day has understandably greatly slowed towards the eventual target of 15 000 m *49,212 ft*, in 1989–90. The temperature is already 200° C *392° F.*

Deepest *Ocean Drilling*

The deepest recorded drilling into the sea bed by the *Glomar Challenger* of the US Deep Sea Drilling Project is one of 5709 ft *1740 m* off N.W. Spain in 1976. The deepest site is now 7034 m *23,077 ft* below the surface on the western wall of the Marianas Trench (see pp. 58–9) in May 1978.

Oil fields

The largest oil field in the world is the Ghawar field, Saudi Arabia developed by ARAMCO which measures 150 miles by 22 miles *240 km by 35 km.*

The area of the designated parts of the UK Continental shelf as at 1 Apr 1975 was 223,550 miles² *579 000 km²* with total recoverable reserves of 3200 million tonnes of oil and 51,000,000 million ft³ *1 443 000 million m³* of gas. Gas was first discovered in the West Sole Field in October 1965 and oil in the Forties Field (Block 22/17) at 11,000 ft *3352 m* from the drilling barge *Sea Quest* on 18 Sept 1970, though a small gasfield was detected near Whitby, N. Yorkshire in 1937. The most productive oil field is expected to be Brent (found in July 1971) where the B platform was installed in August 1976. Production in 1979 reached 350,000 barrels a day and peaked to 850,000 bbd in 1983. The whole UK production in 1979 was 76,415,581 tonnes or 19,558 million Imperial gal. The deepest drilling in British waters is 2400 ft *731 m* in Block 206, west of Shetland by Shell using the drill ship *Petrel* in April 1980.

Gas Deposits

The largest gas deposit in the world is at Urengoi, USSR with an eventual production of 180,000 million m³ per year through 6 pipelines from a total estimated to be 7,000,000 million m³.

Oil platforms *Largest*

The world's most massive oil platform is the *Statfjord B* Concrete Gravity-base platform built at Stavanger, Norway

Lion Cavern, Hhohho, Swaziland (*see below:* Earliest Mine).
(*The Swaziland Archaeological Research Association*)

and operated by Mobil Exploration Norway Inc. Tow-out to its permanent field began on 1 Aug 1981 and it was the heaviest object ever moved—816,000 tonnes or 803,000 long tons ballasted weight. The £1.1 billion structure was towed by 8 tugs with a combined power of 115,000 hp. The height of the concrete structure is 204 m *670 ft* and the overall height 271 m *890 ft*. It thus weighs almost three times the weight of each of the towers of the World Trade Centre (290,000 long tons). The world's tallest production platform is the £1300 million 1024 ft *312 m* tall BP Magnus platform in the North Sea. Production started in July 1983. The 70 000 tonnes structure was built to withstand 100 ft *30,4 m* waves and deliver 120,000 barrels a day to the Sullom Voe Terminal, Shetland.

Gusher Greatest

The greatest wildcat ever recorded blew at Alborz No 5 well, near Qum, Iran on 26 Aug 1956. The uncontrolled oil gushed to a height of 170 ft *52 m* at 120,000 barrels per day at a pressure of 9000 lb/in² *60 055 kPa*. It was closed after 90 days work by B. Mostofi and Myron Kinley of Texas, USA.

Oil Spills Greatest

The slick from the Mexican marine blow-out beneath the drilling rig *Ixtoc I* in the Gulf of Campeche, Gulf of Mexico, on 3 June 1979 reached 400 miles *640 km* by 5 Aug 1979. It eventually was capped on 24 Mar 1980 after a loss of 3,000,000 barrels (535,000 tons).

The worst oil spill in history was of 236,000 tons/*tonnes* of oil from the super-tankers *Atlantic Empress* and *Aegean Captain* when they collided off Tobago on 19 July 1979. The worst oil spill in British waters was from the 118,285 dwt *Torrey Canyon* which struck the Pollard Rock off Land's End on 18 Mar 1967 resulting in a loss of 106,000 tons of oil.

Flare Greatest

The greatest gas fire was that which burnt at Gassi Touil in the Algerian Sahara from noon on 13 Nov 1961 to 9.30 a.m. on 28 Apr 1962. The pillar of flame rose 450 ft *137 m* and the smoke 600 ft *182 m*. It was eventually extinguished by Paul Neal ('Red') Adair (b. 1932), of Houston, Texas, USA, using 550 lb *245 kg* of dynamite. His fee was understood to be about $1,000,000 (*then* £357,000).

Water well Deepest *World*

The world's deepest water bore is the Stensvad Water Well 11-W1 of 7320 ft *2231 m* drilled by the Great Northern Drilling Co. Inc. in Rosebud County, Montana, USA in October–November 1961. The Thermal Power Co. geothermal steam well begun in Sonoma County, California in 1955 is now down to 9029 ft *2752 m*.

Water well Deepest *Great Britain*

The deepest well in Great Britain is a water table well 2842 ft *866 m* deep in the Staffordshire coal measures at Smestow. The deepest artesian well in Britain is that at the White Heather Laundry, Stonebridge Park, Brent, Greater London, bored in 1911 to a depth of 2225 ft *678 m*. The deepest known hand dug well is one dug to 1285 ft *391,6 m* in 1858 to March 1862 on the site of Fitzherbert School, Woodingdean, Brighton, East Sussex.

MINES

Earliest (*World*)	41,250 BC ± 1600	Lion Cavern, Haematite (red iron ore)	Ngwenya, Hhohho, Swaziland
Earliest (*GB*)	3390 BC ± 150	Flint	Church Hill, Findon, W. Sussex
Deepest (*World*)[1]	12,394 ft *3777 m* (2.34 miles)	Gold, Western Deep Levels (temp 131°F *55°C*)	Carletonville, South Africa
Deepest (*GB, all-time*)	4132 ft *1259 m*	Coal, Arley Seam, Parsonage Colliery (Feb 1949)	Leigh, Greater Manchester
(*GB, current*)	3690 ft *1127 m*	Coal, Bickershaw Colliery	Bickershaw, Greater Manchester
(*Cornwall*)	3600 ft *1097 m*	Tin, Williams Shaft, Dolcoath (1910)	Near Camborne, Cornwall
Copper (*deepest, open cast*)	2590 ft *789 m*	Bingham Canyon (began 1904) diameter 2.3 miles *3,7 km*	Utah, USA
Copper (*largest underground*)	356 miles *573 km* tunnels	San Manuel Mine, Magma Copper Co	Arizona, USA
Lead (*largest*)	> 10 per cent of world output	Viburnum Trend	Southeast Missouri, USA
Goldmining (*area*)	> 51 per cent of world output	38 mines of the Witwatersrand Discovery in 1886	South Africa
Gold Mine (*largest world*)[2]	12,100 acres *4900 ha*	East Rand Proprietary Mines Ltd	Boksburg, Transvaal, South Africa
Gold Mine (*largest, GB*)	120,000 fine oz (1854–1914)	Clogau, St David's (disc. 1836)	Gwynedd, Wales
Gold Mine (*richest*)	49.4 million fine oz	Crown Mines (all-time yield)	Transvaal, South Africa
Iron Mine (*largest*)	20 300 million tonnes rich ore	Lebedinsky (45–65% ore)	Kursk region, USSR
Platinum (*largest*)	1,000,000 oz *28 tonnes* per annum	Rustenberg Group, Impala plant	Springs, South Africa
Tungsten Mine (*largest*)	2000 tonnes per day	Union Carbide Mount Morgan mine	Near Bishop, California, USA
Uranium (*largest*)	5000 tons of uranium oxide	Rio Tinto Zinc open cast pit	Rössing, Namibia, SW Africa
Spoil Dump (*largest, world*)	275 million yd³ *210 million m³*	New Cornelia Tailings	Ten Mile Wash, Arizona, USA
Spoil Dump (*largest, GB*)[3]	114 acre *46 ha* 130 ft *40 m* high	Cutacre Clough Colliery tip (18 million tonnes)	Lancashire
Quarry (*largest, world*)	2.81 miles² *7,21 km²* 2540 ft *774 m* deep. 3700 million short tons *3355 million tonnes*	Bingham Canyon Copper Mine	Nr. Salt Lake City, Utah, USA
Quarry (*largest, GB*)	500 ft *150 m* deep, 1.6 mile *2,6 km* circumference	Old Delabole Slate Quarry (since *c.* 1570)	Cornwall
Open Cast Coal Mine	1130 ft *325 m* deep 21 km² *8 mile²* area	Fortuna-Garsdorf (lignite) (began 1955)	Nr. Bergheim, W. Germany
Coal Mine (*oldest, U.K.*)	*c.* 1822	founded by William Stobart	Wearmouth, near Sunderland, Durham

[1] Sinking began in June 1957. Scheduled to reach 3880 m *12 730 ft* by 1992 with 14 000 ft or 2.65 miles regarded as the limit. No 3 vertical ventilation shaft is the world's deepest shaft at 2948,9 m *9675 ft*. This mine requires 130,000 tons of ore per day and refrigeration which uses the energy it would take to make 35,000 tons of ice. The deepest exploratory coal mining shaft is one reaching 6700 ft *2042 m* near Thorez in the Ukranian Donbas field, USSR in Aug 1983.
[2] The world's most productive gold mine may be Muruntau, Kyzyl Kum, Uzbekistan, USSR. According to one western estimate it produces 80 tonnes of gold in a year. It has been estimated that South Africa has produced in 96 years (1886–1982) 36,400 tons or more than 31 per cent of all gold mined since 3900 BC.
[3] Reclamation plan announced 13 Sept 1982 for 1983–1996.

Chapter 8

THE MECHANICAL WORLD

The oldest square-rigged sailing vessel in the world, the S.V. *Ciudad de Inca* built in 1858 (see p. 132).

1. SHIPS

The Guinness Book of Ships and Shipping Facts and Feats by Tom Hartman was published in August 1983 priced £9.95

EARLIEST SEA-GOING BOATS

Aborigines are thought to have been able to cross the Torres Strait from New Guinea to Australia, then at least 70 km *43½ miles* across, as early as 40,000 BC. They are believed to have used double canoes. The earliest surviving 'vessel' is a pinewood dug-out found in Pesse, Netherlands and dated to *c.* 6315 BC, and now at Groningen University. The earliest representation of a boat is disputed between possible rock art outlines of mesolithic skin-boats in Høgnipen, Norway (10,000–7750 BC); Minateda, Spain (12,000–3000 BC) and Kobystan, USSR (8000–6000 BC). An 18 in *45 cm* long paddle was found at the Star Carr, North Yorkshire site, described in 1948. It has been dated to *c.* 7600 BC and is now in the Cambridge Museum of Archaeology.

The oldest surviving boat is the 142 ft *43,4 m* long 40 ton Nile boat or Royal Ship of King Cheops buried near the Great Pyramid of Khufu, Egypt *c.* 2515 BC. Its discovery was announced in May 1954 and it has been reassembled in Cairo.

The oldest shipwreck ever found is one of a Cycladic trading vessel located off the islet of Dhókós, near the Greek island of Hydra reported in May 1975 and dated to 2450 BC ± 250.

Earliest power

Propulsion by steam engine was first achieved when in 1783 the Marquis Jouffroy d'Abbans (1751–1832) ascended a reach of the river Saône near Lyon, France, in the 180 ton *182 tonnes* paddle steamer *Pyroscaphe*.

The tug *Charlotte Dundas* was the first successful power-driven vessel. She was a stern paddle-wheel steamer built for the Forth and Clyde Canal, Scotland in 1801–2 by William Symington (1763–1831), using a double-acting condensing engine constructed by James Watt (1736–1819). The screw propeller was invented and patented by the Kent farmer Sir Francis Pettit Smith (1808–71) in 1836.

Oldest vessels

The oldest mechanically propelled boat in the world of certain date is the 48 ton Bristol steam driven dredger or drag-boat *Bertha* of 50 ft *15,42 m*, designed by I. K. Brunel in 1844 and afloat in the custody of the Exeter Maritime Museum, Devon, England. Mr G. H. Pattinson's 40 ft *12,20 m* steam launch *Dolly*, which was raised after 67 years from Ullswater, Cumbria, in 1962 and now on Lake Windermere, also probably dates from the 1840s. The world's oldest active steam ship is the *Skibladner*, which has plied Lake Mjøsa, Norway since 1856. She has had two major refits and was built in Motala, Sweden. The oldest motor vessel afloat in British waters is the *Proven* on the run from the Clyde to the Inner Hebrides. She was built in Norway in 1866. The oldest vessel on *Lloyd's Yacht Register* is the twin screw steam yacht *Esperance* built on the Clyde in 1869 and salvaged from Windermere in 1941.

The oldest square-rigged sailing vessel in the world is the restored SV *Ciudad de Inca*, built near Barcelona, Spain in 1858. She is 125 ft *38,1 m* overall with a grt of 127 tons. She was restored in 1981–82 for operation by the China Clipper Society of Maidstone, Kent.

Earliest turbine

The first turbine ship was the *Turbinia*, built in 1894 at Wallsend-on-Tyne, Tyne and Wear, to the design of the Hon. Sir Charles Parsons, OM, KCB (1854–1931). The *Turbinia* was 100 ft *30,48 m* long and of 44½ tons *45,2 tonnes* displacement with machinery consisting of three steam turbines totalling about 2000 shaft horsepower. At her first public demonstration in 1897 she reached a speed of 34.5 knots (39.7 mph *63,9 km/h*).

PASSENGER LINERS

Largest active

The world's largest and the world's longest ever liner is the *Norway* of 70,202.19 grt and 315,66 m *1035 ft 7½ in* in overall length with a capacity of 2400 passengers. She was built as the *France* in 1961 and renamed after purchase in June 1979 by Knut Kloster of Norway. Her second maiden voyage was from Southampton on 7 May 1980. Britain's largest liner is RMS *Queen Elizabeth 2* of 67,140 gross tons and with an overall length of 963 ft *293 m* completed for the Cunard Line Ltd. in 1969. She set a 'turn round' record of 5 hr 47 min at New York on 21 Nov 1983. In her 1985 World Cruise, the price of the Penthouse suite was set at $309,000 (£216,000).

Largest ever

The RMS *Queen Elizabeth* (finally 82,998 but formerly 83,673 gross tons), of the Cunard fleet, was the largest passenger vessel ever built and had the largest displacement of any liner in the world. She had an overall length of 1031 ft *314 m* and was 118 ft 7 in *36 m* in breadth and was powered by steam turbines which developed 168,000 hp. Her last passenger voyage ended on 15 Nov 1968. In 1970 she was removed to Hong Kong to serve as a floating marine university and renamed *Seawise University*. On 9 Jan 1972 she was fired by 3 simultaneous outbreaks. Most of the gutted hull had been cut up and removed by December 1977. *Seawise* was a pun on the owner's initials—C. Y. Tung (1911–1982).

WARSHIPS

Battleships *Largest World*

The largest battleship in service in the world is the 887 ft 9 in *270,6 m* long USS *New Jersey* with a full load displacement of 58,000 tons *58 000 tonnes*. She was the last fire support ship on active service off the Lebanon coast from 14 Dec 1983 to 26 Feb 1984. The $405 million refit of USS *Iowa* was completed in May 1984. USS *Missouri* and USS *Wisconsin* are also being re-activated.

Largest all-time

The Japanese battleship *Yamato* (completed on 16 Dec 1941 and sunk south-west of Kyūshū, Japan, by US planes on 7 Apr 1945) and *Musashi* (sunk in the Philippine Sea by 11 bombs and 16 torpedoes on 24 Oct 1944) were the largest battleships ever commissioned, each with a full load displacement of 72,809 tons *73 977 tonnes*. With an overall length of 863 ft *263 m*, a beam of 127 ft *38,7 m* and a full load draught of 35½ ft *10,8 m* they mounted nine 460 mm *18.1 in* guns in three triple turrets. Each gun weighed 162 tons *164,6 tonnes* and was 75 ft *22,8 m* in length firing a 3200 lb *1451 kg* projectile.

Largest Great Britain

Britain's largest ever and last battleship was HMS *Vanguard* (1944–1960) with a full load displacement of 51,420 tons *52 245 tonnes* and an overall length of 814 ft *248,1 m*. She mounted eight 15 in *38 cm* guns.

Guns and Armour

The largest guns ever mounted in any of HM ships were the 18 in *45 cm* pieces in the light battle cruiser (later aircraft carrier) HMS *Furious* in 1917. In 1918 they were transferred to the monitors HMS *Lord Clive* and *General Wolfe*. The thickest armour ever carried was in HMS *Inflexible* (completed 1881), measuring 24 in *60 cm* backed by teak up to a maximum thickness of 42 in *106,6 cm*.

Fastest destroyer

The highest speed attained by a destroyer was 45.25 knots (51.84 mph *83,42 km/h*) by the 2830 ton/*tonne* French destroyer *Le Terrible* in 1935. She was built in Blainville and powered by four Yarrow small tube boilers and two Rateau geared turbines giving 100,000 shaft horse-power. She was removed from the active list at the end of 1957.

AIRCRAFT CARRIERS

Largest *World*

The warships with the largest full load displacement in the world are the US Navy aircraft carriers USS *Nimitz, Dwight D. Eisenhower* and *Carl Vinson* at 91,487 tons. They are 1092 ft *322,9 m* in length overall with 4½ acres *1,82 ha* of flight deck and have a speed well in excess of 30 knots *56 km/h* from their 4 nuclear-powered 260,000 shp reactors. They have to be refuelled after about 900,000 miles *1 450 000 km* steaming. Their complement is 6300 and the total cost of the *Eisenhower*, commissioned on 18 Oct 1977, exceeded $2 billion (*then £1052 million*), excluding the 90-plus aircraft carried. USS *Enterprise* is, however, 1102 ft *335,8 m* long and thus still the longest warship ever built.

The Royal Navy's newest aircraft is H.M. Anti-Submarine Cruiser *Illustrious* (19,500 tonnes), which became operational in 1982 at a cost of £175 million. She has a 550 ft *167,6 m* long flight deck and is 677 ft *206,3 m* long overall, and has a top speed of 28 knots being powered by 4 Rolls Royce Olympus TM3B gas turbines.

SUBMARINES

Largest *World*

The world's largest submarines are of the USSR Typhoon class code named Oscar. The launch of the first at the secret covered shipyard at Severodvinsk in the White Sea was announced by NATO on 23 Sept 1980. It is believed to have a dived displacement of 30,000 tonnes, measure *c.* 165 m *540 ft* overall and is armed with twenty SS NX 20 missiles with a 6250 miles *10 050 km* range, each with 12 warheads. By 1987 two others building in Leningrad will also be operational, each deploying 240 warheads.

Great Britain

The largest submarines ever built for the Royal Navy are the four atomic-powered nuclear missile R class boats with a surface displacement of 7500 tons *7620 tonnes* and 8400 tons *8534 tonnes* submerged, a length of 425 ft *129,5 m*, a beam of 33 ft *10 m* and a draught of 30 ft *9,1 m*. The longest submarine patrol ever spent dived and unsupported is 111 days by H.M. Submarine *Warspite* (Cdr. J. G. F. Cooke RN) in the South Atlantic from 25 Nov 1982 to 15 Mar 1983. She sailed 30,804 nautical miles *57 085 km.*

Fastest

The Russian Alfa-Class nuclear-powered submarines have a reported maximum speed of 42 knots *77,8 km/h* down to a depth of 2000 ft *610 m*. A US spy satelite over Leningrad's naval yard on 8 June 1983 showed they had been lengthened to *240 ft 73 m.*

Deepest

The two USN vessels able to descend 12,000 ft *3650 m* are the 3-man *Trieste II* (DSV I) of 303 tons recommissioned in November 1973 and the DSV 2 (deep submergence vessel) USS *Alvin*. The *Trieste II* was reconstructed from the record-breaking bathyscaphe *Trieste* but without the Krupp-built sphere, which enabled it to descend to 35,820 ft *10 917 m.* (See Chapter 10 Greatest ocean descent).

TANKERS

Largest

The world's largest tanker and ship of any kind is the 564,739 tonnes deadweight *Seawise Giant* completed for C. Y. Tung in 1979. She is 458,45 m *1504 ft* long with a beam of 68,86 m *225 ft 11 in* and has a draught of 24,61 m *80 ft 9 in*. She was lengthened by Nippon Kokan in 1980 by adding an 81 m *265 ft 8 in* midship section.

CARGO VESSELS

Largest

The largest vessel in the world capable of carrying dry cargo is the Liberian ore/oil carrier *World Gala* of 133,748 GT *282,462 dwt* with a length of 1109 ft *338 m* and a beam of 179 ft *54,5 m* owned by Liberian Trident Transports Inc. completed in 1973. The largest British ore/oil carrier is Lombard North Central Leasing's *Rimula* built in Sweden in 1974 of 121,165 GT, *227,412 dwt* with a length of 332,77 m *1091 ft 9 in.*

Largest whale factory

The largest whale factory ship is the USSR's *Sovietskaya Ukraina* (32,034 gross tons), with a summer deadweight of 46,000 tons *46 738 tonnes* completed in October 1959. She is 217,8 m *714 ft 6 in* in length and 25,8 m *84 ft 7 in* in the beam.

Largest barges

The world's largest RoRo (Roll-on, Roll-off) ships are the four *El Rey* class barges of 16,700 tons and 580 ft *176,78 m* in length. They were built by the FMC Corp of Portland, Oregon, USA, and are operated by Crowley Maritime Corp of San Francisco between Florida and Puerto Rico with tri-level lodging of up to 376 truck-trailers.

Most powerful tugs

The world's largest and most powerful tugs are the *Wolraad Waltemade* and her sister ship *John Ross* of 2822 grt rated at 19,200 shaft horse-power and with a bollard pull of 172.7 tons (90% of full power). They have an overall length of 94,623 m *310 ft 5 in* and a beam of 49 ft 10 in *15,2 m*. They were built to handle the largest tankers and were completed in April 1976 (Leith, Scotland) and in October 1976 (Durban, South Africa).

Largest car ferry

The world's largest car and passenger ferry is the 30.5 knot 24,600 grt GTS *Finnjet* which entered service across the Baltic between Helsinki and Travemünde, West Germany on 13 May 1977. She can carry 350 cars and 1532 passengers.

Largest propeller

The world's largest ship propeller is the triple bladed screw of 11,0 m *36 ft 1 in* diameter made by Kawasaki Heavy Industries Ltd on 17 Mar 1982 for the 208,000 ton bulk-ore tanker *Hoei Maru*.

Largest hydrofoil

The world's largest naval hydrofoil is the 212 ft *64,6 m* long

El Conquistador, the world's largest Ro-Ro, one of four barges each designed to carry up to 376 truck-trailers.

Plainview (310 tons *314 tonnes* full load), launched by the Lockheed Shipbuilding and Construction Co. at Seattle, Washington, USA on 28 June 1965. She has a service speed of 50 knots (57 mph *92 km/h*). Three 165 ton Supramar PTS 150 Mk III hydrofoils carrying 250 passengers at 40 knots *74 km/h* ply the Malmö-Copenhagen crossing. They were built by Westermoen Hydrofoil Ltd. of Mandal, Norway. A 500 ton wing ground effect vehicle capable of carrying 900 tons has been reported in the USSR.

Largest River Boat

The world's largest inland river-boat is the 378 ft *115,2 m* long SS *Admiral* now undergoing a 6 year $26.7 million renovation at St Louis, Missouri as a Mississippi river floating 'entertainment center'.

Most powerful icebreaker

A 61,000 ton/*tonne* nuclear powered barge-carrying merchantman designed for work along the USSR's Arctic coast was completed in early 1982 and is known to be designed to break ice. The longest purpose-built icebreaker is the 25 000 ton 460 ft *140 m* long *Rossiya*, powered by 75,000 h.p. nuclear engines launched at Leningrad in November 1983.

The largest *converted* icebreaker has been the 1007 ft *306,9 m* long SS *Manhattan* (43,000 shp), which was converted by the Humble Oil Co. into a 150,000 ton *152 407 tonnes* icebreaker with an armoured prow 69 ft 2 in long. She made a double voyage through the North-West Passage in arctic Canada from 24 Aug to 12 Nov 1969. The North-West Passage was first navigated by Roald Amundsen (Norway) in the sealing sloop *Gjöa* on 11 July 1906.

Yacht most expensive

King Khalid's Saudi Arabian 212 ft *64,6 m* Royal yacht was upstaged as the most expensive in 1979 by a five-deck 282 footer *85,95 m* built by the Benetti Shipyard, Viareggio, Italy for a reputed hull price of $24 million (*then £10.9 million*) to the order of Adnan Khashoggi. It has a helicopter and 5 speed boats.

Largest dredger

The world's most powerful dredger is the 468.4 ft *142,7 m* long *Prins der Nederlanden* of 10,586 grt. She can dredge 20,000 tonnes/*tons* of sand from a depth of 35 m *115 ft via* two suction tubes in less than an hour.

Wooden ship

The heaviest wooden ship ever built was the *Richelieu*, 333 ft 8 in *101,70 m* long and of 8534 tons launched in Toulon, France on 3 Dec 1873. HM Battleship *Lord Warden*, completed in 1869, displaced 7940 tons *8060 tonnes*. The longest modern wooden ship ever built was the New York built *Rochambeau* (1867–72) formerly *Dunderberg*. She measured 377 ft 4 in *115 m* overall. It should be noted that the biblical length of Noah's Ark was 300 cubits or, at 18 in *45,7 cm* to a cubit, 450 ft *137 m* (but see Junks p. 134).

Largest human powered

The largest human powered ship was the giant Tessarakonteres 3-banked catamaran galley with 4000 rowers built for Ptolemy IV *c.* 210 BC in Alexandria, Egypt. It measured 128 m *420 ft* with up to 8 men to an oar of 38 cubits (17,5 m *57 ft*) in length. The world's longest canoe is the 117 ft *35,7 m* long 20 ton Kauri wood Maori war canoe Nga Toki Matawhaorua built by adzes at Kerikeri Inlet, New Zealand in 1940 for a crew of 70 or more. A claim for a 'snake boat' 135 ft *41,1 m* long with 100 paddles from Kerala, Southern India is now being investigated.

Light vessels
The earliest station still marked by a light vessel is the Newarp in the North Sea, off Great Yarmouth in 1791. A Nore Lightvessel was first placed in the Thames estuary in 1732.

SAILING SHIPS

Largest
The largest sailing vessel ever built was the *France II* (5806 gross tons), launched at Bordeaux in 1911. The *France II* was a steel-hulled, five-masted barque (square-rigged on four masts and fore and aft rigged on the aftermost mast). Her hull measured 418 ft *127,4 m* overall. Although principally designed as a sailing vessel with a stump topgallant rig, she was also fitted with two steam engines. She was wrecked off New Caledonia on 13 July 1922. The only seven-masted sailing schooner ever built was the 375.6 ft *114,4 m* long *Thomas W. Lawson* (5218 gross tons) built at Quincy, Massachusetts, USA in 1902 and lost in the English Channel on 15 Dec 1907.

The world's only surviving First Rate Ship-of-the-Line is the Royal Navy's 104-gun battleship HMS *Victory* laid down at Chatham, Kent on 23 July 1759 constructed from the wood of some 2200 oak trees. She bore the body of Admiral Nelson from Gibraltar to Portsmouth arriving 44 days after serving as his victorious flagship at the Battle of Trafalgar on 21 Oct 1805. In 1922 she was moved to No. 2 dock, Portsmouth–site of the world's oldest graving dock. The length of her cordage (both standing and running rigging) is 100,962 ft (19.12 miles *30,77 km.*)

Largest junks
The largest junk on record was the sea-going *Cheng Ho*, flagship of Admiral Cheng Ho's 62 treasure ships, of *c.* 1420, with a displacement of 3100 tons *3150 tonnes* and a length variously estimated up to 538 ft *164 m* and believed to have had 9 masts. A river junk 361 ft *110 m* long, with treadmill-operated paddle-wheels, was recorded in AD 1161. In *c.* AD 280 a floating fortress 600 ft *182,8 m* square, built by Wang Chün on the Yangtze, took part in the Chin-Wu river war. Present-day junks do not, even in the case of the Chiangsu traders, exceed 170 ft *51,8 m* in length.

Longest day's run under sail
The longest day's run claimed by any sailing ship was one of 465 nautical miles (535.45 statute miles *861,72 km*) by the clipper *Champion of the Seas* (2722 registered tons) of the Liverpool Black Ball Line running before a north-westerly gale in the south Indian Ocean under the command of Capt. Alex. Newlands. The elapsed time between the fixes was 23 hr 17 min giving an average of 19.97 knots *37,00 km/h.*

Largest sails
Sails are known to have been used for marine propulsion since 3500 BC. The largest spars ever carried were those in HM Battleship *Temeraire*, completed at Chatham, Kent, on 31 Aug 1877. The fore and main yards measured 115 ft *35 m* in length. The mainsail contained 5100 ft *1555 m* of canvas, weighing 2 tons *2,03 tonnes* and the total sail area was 25,000 ft² *2322 m²*. This compares with an area of 18,000 ft² *1672 m²* for the parachute spinnaker on Vanderbilt's *Ranger* in 1937.

Largest wreck
The largest ship ever wrecked has been the 312,186 dwt VLCC (Very Large Crude Carrier) *Energy Determination* which blew up and broke in two in the Straits of Hormuz on 12 Dec 1979. Her full value was $58 million (*then £26.3 million*).

Most massive collision
The closest approach to an irresistible force striking an immovable object occurred on 16 Dec 1977, 22 miles *35 km* off the coast of Southern Africa when the tanker *Venoil* (330,954 dwt) struck her sister ship *Venpet* (330,869 dwt).

OCEAN CROSSINGS

Atlantic *Earliest*
The earliest crossing of the Atlantic by a power vessel, as opposed to an auxiliary engined sailing ship, was a 22-day voyage begun in April 1827, from Rotterdam, Netherlands, to the West Indies by the *Curaçao*. She was a 127 ft *38,7 m* wooden paddle boat of 438 tons, built as the *Calpe* in Dover in 1826 and purchased by the Dutch Government for the West Indian mail service. The earliest Atlantic crossing entirely under steam (with intervals for desalting the boilers) was by HMS *Rhadamanthus* from Plymouth to Barbados in 1832. The earliest crossing of the Atlantic under continuous steam power was by the condenser-fitted packet ship *Sirius* (703 tons *714 tonnes*) from Queenstown (now Cóbh), Ireland, to Sandy Hook, New Jersey, USA, in 18 days 10 hr on 4–22 Apr 1838.

Atlantic *Fastest World*
The fastest Atlantic crossing was made by the *United States* (then 51,988, now 38,216 gross tons), former flagship of the United States Lines. On her maiden voyage between 3 and 7 July 1952 from New York City, to Le Havre, France, and Southampton, England, she averaged 35.59 knots, or 40.98 mph *65,95 km/h* for 3 days 10 hr 40 min (6.36 p.m. GMT, 3 July to 5.16 a.m., 7 July) on a route of 2949 nautical miles *5465 km* from the Ambrose Light Vessel to the Bishop Rock Light, Isles of Scilly, Cornwall. During this run, on 6–7 July 1952, she steamed the greatest distance ever covered by any ship in a day's run (24 hr)—868 nautical miles *1609 km*, hence averaging 36.17 knots (41.65 mph *67,02 km/h*). The maximum speed attained from her 240,000 shp engines was 38.32 knots (44.12 mph *71,01 km/h*) on trials on 9–10 June 1952.

Pacific *Fastest*
The fastest crossing of the Pacific Ocean from Yokohama to Long Beach, California (4840 nautical miles *8960 km*) was 6 days 1 hr 27 min (30 June–6 July 1973) by the container ship *Sea-Land Commerce* (50,315 tons) at an average of 33.27 knots (38.31 mph *61,65 km/h*).

Channel Crossing *Fastest*
The fastest crossing of the English Channel by a commercial ferry is 52 min 49 sec from Dover to Calais by Townsend Thoresen's *Pride of Free Enterprise* in a Force 7 Gale on 9 Feb 1982.

HOVERCRAFT (skirted air cushion vehicles)

Earliest
The ACV (air-cushion vehicle) was first made a practical proposition by Sir Christopher Sydney Cockerell, CBE, FRS (b. 4 June 1910), a British engineer who had the idea in 1954, published his Ripplecraft report 1/55 on 25 Oct 1955 and patented it on 12 Dec 1955. The earliest patent relating to air-cushion craft was applied for in 1877 by John I. Thornycroft (1843–1928) of Chiswick, London and the Finn Toivo Kaario developed the idea in 1935. The first flight by a hovercraft was made by the 4 ton/*tonnes* Saunders-Roe SR-N1 at Cowes on 30 May 1959. With a 1500 lb *680 kg* thrust Viper turbojet engine, this craft reached 68 knots *126 km/h* in June 1961. The first hovercraft public service was run across the Dee Estuary by the 60 knot *111 km/h* 24-passenger Vickers-Armstrong VA-3 between July and September 1962.

Largest
The world's largest civil hovercraft is the 305 ton British-built SRN4 Mk III with a capacity of 418 passengers and 60 cars. It is 185 ft *56,38 m* in length, is powered by 4 Bristol Siddeley Marine Proteus engines giving a maximum speed in excess of the permitted operating speed of 65 knots.

Fastest warship
The world's fastest warship is the 78 ft *23,7 m* long 100 ton/*tonne* US Navy test vehicle SES-100B. She attained a world record 91.9 knots *103.9 mph* on 25 Jan 1980 on the Chesapeake Bay Test Range, Maryland, USA. The 3000 ton US Navy Large Surface Effect Ship (LSES) was built by Bell Aerospace under contract from the Department of Defense in 1977–81.

Longest flight
The longest hovercraft journey was one of 5000 miles *8047 km* through eight West African countries between 15 Oct 1969 and 3 Jan 1970 by the British Trans-African Hovercraft Expedition.

Highest
The greatest altitude at which a hovercraft is operating is on Lago Titicaca, Peru, where since 1975 an HM2 Hoverferry has been hovering 12,506 ft *3811 m* above sea level.

2. ROAD VEHICLES

Guinness Superlatives has now published automotive records in greater detail in the more specialist publication *Car Facts and Feats* (3rd edition price £6.95).

COACHING

Before the widespread use of tarred road surfaces from 1845 coaching was slow and hazardous. The zenith was reached on 13 July 1888 when J. Selby, Esq., drove the 'Old Times' coach 108 miles *173 km* from London to Brighton and back with 8 teams and 14 changes in 7 hr 50 min to average 13.79 mph *22,19 km/h*. Four-horse carriages could maintain a speed of 21⅓ mph *34 km/h* for nearly an hour. The *Border Union* stage coach, built *c.* 1825, ran 4 in hand from Edinburgh to London (393 miles *632 km*). When it ceased in 1842, due to competition from railways, the allowed schedule was 42 hr 23 min to average better than 9¼ mph *14,9 km/h*.

MOTOR CARS

Most cars

For 1980 it was estimated that the United States, with 155,890,000 vehicles, passed 37.9 per cent of the total world stock of 411,113,000.

Earliest automobiles *Model*

The earliest automobile of which there is record is a two-foot-long steam-powered model constructed by Ferdinand Verbiest (d. 1687) a Belgian Jesuit priest, and described in his *Astronomia Europaea*. His model of 1668 was possibly inspired either by Giovanni Branca's description of a steam turbine, published in his *La Macchina* in 1629, or by writings on 'fire carts' or *Nan Huai-Jen* during the Chu dynasty (*c.* 800 BC). The Swiss Isaac de Rivaz (d. 1828) built a carriage powered by his 'explosion engine' in 1805.

Earliest automobiles *Passenger-carrying*

The earliest mechanically propelled passenger vehicle was the first of two military steam tractors, completed at the Paris Arsenal in 1769 by Nicolas-Joseph Cugnot (1725–1804). This reached 2¼ mph *3,6 km/h*. Cugnot's second, larger tractor, completed in May 1771, today survives in the *Conservatoire nationale des arts et métiers* in Paris. Britain's first steam carriage carried eight passengers on 24 Dec 1801 in Camborne, Cornwall and was built by Richard Trevithick (1771–1833).

Earliest automobiles *Internal combustion*

The first true internal-combustion engined vehicle was that built by the Londoner Samuel Brown (Patent 5350, 25 Apr 1826) whose 4 hp *4,05 cv* two cylinder atmospheric gas 88 litre engined carriage climbed Shooters Hill, Blackheath, Kent in May 1826. Britain's continuous motoring history started in Nov 1894 when Henry Hewetson drove his imported Benz Velo in the south-eastern suburbs of London. The first successful petrol-driven car, the Motorwagen, built by Karl-Friedrich Benz (1844–1929) of Karlsruhe, ran at Mannheim, Germany, in late 1885. It was a 5 cwt *250 kg* 3-wheeler reaching 8–10 mph *13–16 km/h*. Its single cylinder 4-stroke chain-drive engine (bore 91,4 mm, stroke 160 mm) delivered 0.85 hp *0,86 cv* at 200 rpm. It was patented on 29 Jan 1886. Its first 1 km road test was reported in the local newspaper, the *Neue Badische Landeszeitung*, of 4 June 1886, under the news heading 'Miscellaneous'. Two were built in 1885 of which one has been preserved in 'running order' at the Deutsches Museum, Munich.

Registrations *Earliest and Most Expensive*

The world's first plates were probably introduced by the Parisian police in France in 1893. Registration plates were introduced in Britain in 1903. The original A1 plate was secured by the 2nd Earl Russell (1865–1931) for his 12 hp *12,1 cv* Napier. This plate, willed in September 1950 to Mr Trevor T. Laker of Leicester, was sold in August 1959 for £2500 in aid of charity. It was reported in April 1973 that a 'cherished' number plate changed hands for £14,000 in a private deal. Licence plate No 3 was reported in Jan 1984 to have been sold at a Hong Kong Government auction for £94,000.

FASTEST CARS (see also p. 136)

Diesel engined

The prototype 230 hp 3 litre Mercedes C 111/3 attained 327,3 km/h *203.3 mph* in tests on the Nardo Circuit, Southern Italy on 5–15 Oct 1978, and in April 1978 averaged 195.398 mph *314,462 km/h* for 12 hours, so covering a world record 2399.76 miles *3773,55 km*.

Rocket Powered Sleds

The highest speed recorded on ice is 247.93 mph *399,00 km/h* by *Oxygen* driven by Sammy Miller (b. 15 Apr 1945) on Lake George, NY, USA on 15 Feb 1981 (see also p. 142).

The 200 mph 320 *km/h* and 'street legal' Vector W2 Twin-Turbo HTME built by Vector Cars of Los Angeles, California.

FASTEST CARS

CATEGORY	MPH	KM/H	CAR	DRIVER	PLACE	DATE
Jet Engined (*official*)	633.468	*1019,4*	Thrust 2	Richard Noble (GB)	Black Rock Desert Nevada, USA	4 Oct 1983
Rocket Engined (*official*)	622.287	*1001,473*	Blue Flame	Gary Gabelich (US)	Bonneville, Utah, USA	23 Oct 1970
Wheel Driven (*turbine*)	429.311	*690,909*	Bluebird	Donald Campbell (UK)	Lake Eyre, Australia	17 July 1964
Wheel Driven (*multi piston engines*)	418.504	*673,516*	Goldenrod	Robert Summers (US)	Bonneville, Utah, USA	12 Nov 1965
Wheel Driven (*single piston engine*)	357.391	*575,149*	Herda-Knapp-Milodon	Bob Herda	Bonneville, Utah, USA	2 Nov 1967
Rocket Engined (*unofficial*)*	739.666	*1190,377*	Budweiser Rocket	Stan Barrett (US)	Edwards Air Force Base, California, USA	17 Dec 1979

* This published speed of Mach 1.0106 is *not* officially sanctioned by the USAF whose Digital Instrumented Radar was not calibrated or certified. The radar information was *not* generated by the vehicle directly but by an operator aiming the dish by means of a TV screen. A claim to 6 signigicant figures appears unjustifiable.

Road cars

Various detuned track cars have been licensed for road use but are not purchasable production models. Manufacturers of very fast and very expensive models are understandably reluctant to allow maximum speed tests to be carried out. The fastest current manufacturer's *claim* (as opposed to independently road-tested) for any road car is the Vector W2 Twin Turbo HTME custom order car from Vector Cars, Venice, California with a 'terminal velocity' in excess of 200 mph *321,8 km/h*. The highest claim for a production road car is 188 mph *302,5 km/h* for the Ferrari 512 BBi. The highest ever *tested* speed is 168 mph *270 km/h* for this same car despite its being 'detoxed' to meet US emission standards. The highest road-tested acceleration reported is 0–60 mph *0–96,5 km/h* in 4.1 sec for a Volkswagen double engined Scirocco prototype in 1983.

LARGEST CARS

World

Of cars produced for private road use, the largest has been the Bugatti 'Royale' type 41, known in Britain as the 'Golden Bugatti', of which only six (not seven) were made at Molsheim, France by the Italian Ettore Bugatti, and some survive. First built in 1927, this machine has an 8-cylinder engine of *12,7* litres capacity, and measures over 22 ft *6,7 m* in length. The bonnet is over 7 ft *2 m* long. Of custom built cars the longest is the stretched 1976 Cadillac owned by Gino Dentie of Studio City, California, USA. The finished result is 40 ft *12,19 m* overall and weighs 10,468 lb *4748 kg*. (For cars not intended for private use, see Largest engines).

Largest engines *All-time and current records*

The world's most powerful piston engine car is 'Quad Al.' It was designed and built in 1964 by Jim Lytle and was first shown in May 1965 at the Los Angeles Sports Arena. The car featured four Allison V12 aircraft engines with a total of 6840 in³ *112,087 cc* displacement and 12,000 hp. The car has 4-wheel drive, 8 wheels and tyres, and dual 6-disc clutch assemblies. The wheelbase is 160 in *406,4 cm*, and weighs 5860 lb *2658 kg*. It has 96 spark plugs and 96 exhaust pipes.

The largest car ever used was the 'White Triplex', sponsored by J. H. White of Philadelphia, Pennsylvania, USA. Completed early in 1928, after two years work, the car weighed about 4 tons *4,06 tonnes* and was powered by three Liberty V12 aircraft engines with a total capacity of 81,188 cc, developing 1500 bhp at 2000 rpm. It was used to break the world speed record but crashed at Daytona, Florida, USA on 13 Mar 1929.

Currently the most powerful car on the road is the 6-wheeled Jameson-Merlin, powered by a 27,000 cc 1760 hp Rolls Royce V12 Merlin aero-engine, governed down to a maximum speed of 185 mph *298 km/h*. It has a range of 300 miles *480 km* with tanks of 60 gal *272 litres* capacity. The vehicle weighs 2.65 tons *2,69 tonnes* overall.

Largest engines *Production car*

The highest engine capacity of a production car was 13½ litres *824 in³*, in the case of the US Pierce-Arrow 6–66 Raceabout of 1912–18, the US Peerless 6–60 of 1912–14 and the Fageol of 1918. The most powerful production car ever built was the V8 engine of 500.1 in³ *8194 cc*, developing 400 bhp, used in the 1970 Cadillac Fleetwood Eldorado.

Petrol consumption

The world record for fuel economy on a closed circuit course (one of 14.076 miles *22,00 km*) was set by Ben Visser (US) in a highly modified 1.5 litre *90.8 in³* 1959 Opel CarΛvan station wagon in the annual Shell Research Laboratory contest at Wood River, Illinois, driven by Ben and Carolyn Visser on 2 Oct 1973 with 451.90 ton miles per US gal and 376.59 miles *606,0 km* on one US gal, i.e. *3,78 litres*. These figures are equivalent to 542.70 ton miles and 452.26 miles *727,84 km* on an imperial gallon i.e. *4,54 litres*. The tyre pressure was 200 lb/in² and the maximum speed was 12 mph *19,3 km/h*. In Oct 1979 at the International Fuel Saving Competition for cars and special vehicles in Switzerland a 20 cc diesel engined 3-wheeler driven by Franz Maier of Stuttgart covered 1284.13 km on 1 litre of fuel—equivalent to 3627.26 miles to the Imperial gallon. Douglas Malewicki drove 263.6 miles *424,2 km* from Anaheim, California to Las Vegas, Nevada at an average speed of 56.3 mph *90,6 km/h* using only 1.684 US gallons of fuel for an mpg of 156.53 (US) 187.98 (Imperial) or *66,55 km* per-litre in his 3-wheeled 359 cc diesel powered *California Commuter* road car. The route involved ascents of 7993 ft *2436 m*.

Ultra built by the University of Saskatchewan, Canada set an amateur world record at 15 mph *24,1 km/h* driven by Bronie Ewenchuk at Marshall, Michigan, USA on 4 June 1983 with 1914 miles per Imperial gallon *677 km/litre*.

Most durable car

The highest recorded mileage for a car was 1,184,880 authenticated miles *1 906 879 km* by August 1978 for a 1957 Mercedes 180 D owned by Robert O'Reilly of Olympia, Washington State, USA. Its subsequent fate is unknown. R. L. Bender of Madison, Wisconsin claimed 1,020,000 miles *1 641 530 km* for his car in December 1983.

Taxis

The largest taxi fleet is that in Mexico City, Mexico of more than 30,000, compared with the New York City figure of 12,500 plus an equal number of 'gypsies'. London's most durable 'cabby' was F. Fuller, who drove from 26 Oct 1908 until he handed in his badge on 16 Sept 1966—57 years later. On 1 May 1984 there were 13,200 cabs and 18,000 drivers in London. The longest fare on record is one of 7533 miles *12 133 km* through 10 countries from Marble Arch, London on 19 Sept–18 Oct 1981. The trip was sponsored for charity. The driver was Stephen Tillyer.

MOST EXPENSIVE CARS

Special

The most expensive car to build has been the US Presidential 1969 Lincoln Continental Executive delivered to the US Secret Service on 14 Oct 1968. It has an overall length of 21 ft 6.3 in *6,56 m* with a 13 ft 4 in *4,06 m* wheel-base and with the addition of 2 tons *2,03 tonnes* of armour plate, weighs 5.35 tons *5,43 tonnes* (12,000 lb *5443 kg*). The estimated research, development and manufacture cost was $500,000 (*then £208,000*) but it is rented at $5000 (*now £2300*) per annum. Even if all four tyres were shot out it can travel at 50 mph *80 km/h* on inner rubber-edged steel discs. Carriage House Motor Cars Ltd of New York City in March 1978 completed 4 years work on converting a 1973 Rolls Royce including lengthening it by 30 in *76,2 cm*. The price tag was $500,000 (*then £263,157*).

LONG DISTANCE DRIVING

Round the world driving

The fastest circumnavigation embracing more than an equator's length of driving (24,901.47 road miles *40 075,0 km*) is one in 74 days 1 hr 11 min by Garry Sowerby (driver) and Ken Langley (navigator) of Canada from 6 Sept to 19 Nov 1980 in a Volvo 245 DL westwards from Toronto, Canada through 4 continents and 23 countries. The distance covered was 43 030 km *26,738 miles* (see below for their Cape to Cape record).

Cape to London

The record for the 11,674 mile *18 787 km* road route from Cape Town, South Africa to London is 14 days 19 hr 26 min set by husband and wife Brig John and Dr Lucy Hemsley on 8–22 Jan 1983 in a Range Rover.

Round Britain driving

The best recorded time for non-stop driving the 3644.3 miles *5864,7 km* Round Britain course on an Official Certified Trial under the surveillance of a motoring organisation and with Tachograph readings, is 78 hr 31 min to average 46.41 mph *74,68 km/h* in a Triumph Acclaim driven by David Gittins, Robert Morgan and Richard Neale on 10–14 May 1982. This charity trial by Hagley and District Round Table was sponsored by DIY Motor Stores, Austin Rover and Lex Mead (Stourbridge).

right: **Brig. John and Dr Lucy Hemsley who drove from Cape Town to London in 355 hours 26 minutes.**

below: **Ken Langley (left) and Garry Sowerby who drove 12,531 miles *20 166 km* from Cape to Cape in 28 days 13 hr 10 min on 4 Apr–2 May 1984.** (*Mats Liljedahl*)

bottom: **The Hagley and District Round Tablers who broke the Round Britain Driving record in May 1982.**

Standard

The most expensive British standard car is the Rolls-Royce 8 cylinder 6750 cc Camargue, quoted in May 1984 at £83,122 (incl. tax). More expensive are custom built models. Jack Barclay Ltd of Berkeley Square, London W1 quote £300,000 for an armour-plated Rolls-Royce Phantom VI (including tax).

The only owner of 25 new Rolls-Royces is believed to be Bhagwan Shri Rajneesh (b. 1931), the Indian mystic of Rajneeshpusam, Oregon, USA. His disciples have bestowed these upon him.

Used

The greatest price paid for any used car has been $421,040 (*then £210,520*), for a 1936 Mercedes-Benz Roadster from the M. L. Cohn collection, by a telephone bidder in Monaco, at Christie's sale on 25 Feb 1979 at the Los Angeles Convention Center. A Rolls-Royce Silver Ghost of 1907 exhibited in San Jose, California in August 1982 was insured for $2 million. The greatest collection of vintage cars is the William F. Harrah Collection of 1700, estimated to be worth more than $4 million (*£2.3 million*), at Reno, Nevada, USA. Mr Harrah was still looking for a Chalmer's Detroit 1909 Tourabout, an Owen car of 1910–12 and a Nevada Truck of 1915 at the time of his death in 1978.

Most inexpensive

The cheapest car of all-time was the 1922 Red Bug Buckboard, built by Briggs and Stratton Co of Milwaukee, Wisconsin, USA listed at $150–$125. It had a 62 in *1,57 m* wheel base and weighed 245 lb *111 kg*. The early models of the King Midget cars were sold in kit form for self-assembly for as little as $100 (*then £24 16s*) as late as 1948. By May 1984 the cheapest quoted new car price in Britain was £2098 for a Fiat 126, 652 cc 2 door car.

Longest production

The longest any car has been in mass production is 44 years (1938 to date), including wartime interruptions, in the case of the Volkswagen 'Beetle' series, originally designed by Ferdinand Porsche. The 20 millionth car came off the final production line in Mexico on 15 May 1981. Residual production continues in South America. Britain's all-time champion is the Morgan series 4/4 from 27 Dec 1935 from the Morgan Motor Car of Malvern (founded 1910). Britain's champion seller has been the Mini which originally sold for £496 19s 2d in August 1959. Sales reached 4,940,000 by May 1984.

Mountain driving

Cars have been driven up Ben Nevis, Highland, Scotland (4406 ft *1343 m*) on 4 occasions. The record times are 7 hr 23 min (ascent) and 1 hr 55 min (descent) by George F. Simpson in an Austin 7 on 6 Oct 1928. Henry Alexander accomplished the feat twice in May 1911 (Model T Ford) and on 13 Sept 1928 (Model A Ford).

Driving in reverse

Charles Creighton (1908–70) and James Hargis of Maplewood, Missouri, USA, drove their Ford Model A 1929 roadster in reverse from New York City 3340 miles *5375 km* to Los Angeles, California on 26 July–13 Aug 1930 without once stopping the engine. They arrived back in New York in reverse on 5 Sept so completing 7180 miles *11 555 km* in 42 days. The highest average speed attained in any non-stop reverse drive exceeding 500 miles *800 km* was achieved by Gerald Hoagland who drove a 1969 Chevrolet Impala 501 miles *806,2 km* in 17 hr 38 min at Chemung Speed Drome, New York, USA on 9–10 July 1976 to average 28.41 mph *45,72 km/h*.

Two Wheel Driving

The longest recorded distance for driving on 2 wheels by a professional stunt man is 5.6 miles *9,01 km* on a Chevrolet Chevelle by Joie Chitwood, Jr on the Indianapolis Speedway, USA on 13 May 1978.

Oldest driver

Roy M. Rawlins (b. 10 July 1870) of Stockton, California, USA, was warned for driving at 95 mph *152 km/h* in a 55 mph *88,5 km/h* zone in June 1974. On 25 Aug 1974 he was awarded a California State licence valid till 1978 by Mr John Burrafato, but Mr Rawlins died on 9 July 1975, one day short of his 105th birthday. Mrs Maude Tull of Inglewood, California, who took to driving aged 91 after her husband died, was issued a renewal on 5 Feb 1976 when aged 104. Britain's only recorded centenarian driver was Herbert Warren (1874–1975) of Whatlington, Norfolk, who drove a 1954 Standard 10. The oldest age at which a woman has passed the Department of Transport driving test has been 88 years 5 months by Mrs Harriet Emma Jack (*née* Morse) (b. 9 Dec 1887) on 18 May 1976 in Bognor Regis, West Sussex. She was still driving aged 96. The highest year number ever displayed on a Veteran Motorist's badge was '75' by Walter Herbert Weake, who started his accident free career in 1894 and drove daily until his death in 1969, aged 91. Major Geoffrey Chance CBE (b. 16 Dec 1893) of Braydon, Wiltshire who began driving in 1908 successfully took a driving test to re-qualify after a 'minor bump' aged 90 years 90 days at Swindon, Wiltshire on 15 March 1984.

Youngest driver

Instances of drivers have been recorded in HM Armed Forces much under 17 years. Mrs P. L. M. Williams (b. 3 Feb 1926), now of Risca, Gwent, as Private Patterson in the ATS drove a 5 ton truck in 1941 aged 15. Gordon John Graham of Clydebank, Strathclyde passed his advanced driving test aged 17 years 18 days on 20 November 1973. David Paul Barrow (b. 28 Mar 1966) of Ormskirk passed his test aged 16 years 114 days on 20 July 1982.

Driving tests

The record for persistence in taking the Ministry of Transport's Learner's Test is held by Mrs Miriam Hargrave (b. 3 Apr 1908) of Wakefield, West Yorkshire, who failed her 39th driving test in eight years on 29 Apr 1970 after 'crashing' a set of red lights. She triumphed at her 40th attempt after 212 lessons on 3 Aug 1970. The examiner was alleged not to have known about her previous 39 tests. In 1978 she was reported to still disdain right-hand turns. The world's easiest tests have been those in Egypt in which the ability to drive 6 m *19.64 ft* forward and the same in reverse has been deemed sufficient. In 1979 it was reported that accurate reversing had been added between two rubber traffic cones. 'High cone attrition' soon led to the substitution of white lines. Mrs Fannie Turner (b. 1903) of Little Rock, Arkansas, USA passed her *written* test for drivers on her 104th attempt in October 1978.

Between Feb 1938 and July 1983 driving instructor John W. Cole of Woolwich, London has submitted to and passed 61 varied driving tests.

Buses *Earliest*

The first municipal motor omnibus service in the world was inaugurated on 12 Apr 1903 between Eastbourne railway station and Meads, East Sussex, England. A steam-powered bus named *Royal Patent* ran between Gloucester and Cheltenham for 4 months in 1831.

Largest fleet

In 1983 the world's largest bus fleet is the 6580 single-deck buses in Rio de Janeiro, Brazil. Of London Transport's 5412 fleet, 4853 are double-deckers.

Longest

The longest buses in the world are the 10.72 ton *10 870 kg*, 76 ft *23,16 m* long articulated buses, with 121 passenger seats and room also for 66 'strap-hangers' built by the Wayne Corporation of Richmond, Indiana, USA for use in the Middle East.

Longest route

The longest regularly scheduled bus route is by 'Across Australia Coach Lines', who inaugurated a regular scheduled service between Perth and Brisbane on 9 Apr 1980. The route is 5455 km *3389 miles* taking 75 hr 55 min. The longest bus service in Great Britain is 654 miles *1052 km* between Perth and Eastbourne operated by Midland Scottish.

Trolleybuses

Having been the last local authority in Britain with trolleybuses, the West Yorkshire authority may reintroduce a fleet of 71 in the Bradford-Leeds area.

Caravans *Longest journey*

The longest continuous motor caravan journey is one of 143,716 miles *231 288 km* by Harry B. Coleman and Peggy Larson in a Volkswagen Camper from 20 Aug 1976 to 20 Apr 1978 through 113 countries. Saburo Ouchi (b. 7 Feb 1942) of Tokyo, Japan drove 270 000 km *167,770 miles* in 91 countries from 2 Dec 1969 to 10 Feb 1978.

Road Vehicles

Largest

The largest caravans built in Britain are the £300,000 'State Super Caravans', 18 m *59 ft 0½ in* in length and 3,5 m *11 ft 5¾ in* wide built by Coventry Steel Caravans Ltd of Newport Pagnell, Buckinghamshire since 1977.

Fastest

The world speed record for a caravan is 124.91 mph *201,02 km/h* by an Alpha 14 towed by a Le Mans Aston Martin V8 saloon driven by Robin Hamilton at RAF Elvington, North Yorkshire on 14 Oct 1980.

Vehicles *Most massive*

The most massive vehicle ever constructed is the Marion eight-caterpillar crawler used for conveying *Saturn V* rockets to their launching pads at Cape Canaveral, Florida, USA. (*see* Chapter 4, Most powerful rocket). It measures 131 ft 4 in *40 m* by 114 ft *34,7 m* and the two built cost $12,300,000 (*then £5,125,000*). The loaded train weight is 8036 tons *8165 tonnes*. Its windscreen wipers with 42 in *106 cm* blades are the world's largest.

The most massive automotive land vehicle is 'Big Muskie' the 10,700 ton *10 890 tonnes* mechanical shovel built by Bucyrus Erie for the Musk mine. It is 487 ft *148,43 m* long; 151 ft *46,02 m* wide and 222 ft *67,66 m* high with a grab capacity of 325 tons.

The longest vehicle ever built is the Arctic Snow Train owned by the world famous wire-walker Steve McPeak (US). This 54 wheeled 572 ft *174,3 m* long vehicle was built by R G Le Tourneau Inc of Longview, Texas for the US Army. Its gross train weight is 400 tons with a top speed of 20 mph *32 km/h* and it was driven by a crew of 6 when used as an 'Overland Train' for the military. McPeak repaired it and every punctured wheel lonehanded in often sub-zero temperatures in Alaska. It generates 4680 shp and has a capacity of 6522 Imperial gallons *29 648 litres*.

Wrecker *Most powerful*

The world's most powerful wrecker is the Vance Corporation 25 ton *25,4 tonne* 30 ft *9,14 m* long Monster No. 2 stationed at Hammond, Indiana, USA. It can lift in excess of 160 tons *163 tonnes* on its short boom.

Earth mover *Largest*

The world's largest earth mover is the Balderson 'Double Dude' plow (plough) harnessed to two Caterpillar D9H 820 flywheel horsepower tractors. It can cast 14,185 yd³ *10 845 m³* per hour. The largest single tractor is the 700 hp 114 in *2896 mm* gauge D10 of 95.55 short tons *86 683 kg* operating weight.

Dumper truck *Largest*

The world's largest dump truck is the Terex Titan 33–19 manufactured by the Terex Division of General Motors Corporation. It has a loaded weight of 539.9 tons *548,6 tonnes* and a capacity of 312½ tons *317,5 tonnes*. When tipping its height is 56 ft *17,06 m*. The 16 cylinder engine delivers 3300 hp. The fuel tank holds 1300 Imperial gallons *5904,6 litres*. It went into service in November 1974.

Tractor *Largest*

The world's largest tractor is the $459,000 (*then £285,000*) US Department of Agriculture Wide Tractive Frame Vehicle completed by Ag West of Sacramento, California in June 1982. It measures 33 ft *10,05 m* between its wheels which are designed to run on permanent paths and weighs 21.87 tons *22,22 tonnes*.

Fire engine *Most powerful*

The world's most powerful fire appliance is the 860 hp 8-wheel Oshkosh firetruck used for aircraft fires. It can discharge 41,600 gal *190 000 l* of foam through two turrets in just 150 sec. It weighs 59.0 tons *60 tonnes*. The fastest on record is the Jaguar XJ12 – 'Chubb Firefighter', which, in Nov 1982, attained a speed of 130.57 mph *210,13 km/h* in tests when servicing the *Thrust 2* land speed record trials (see pp. 136 & 177).

Ambulance Largest

The world's largest ambulances are the 18 m *59 ft 0½ in* long articulated Alligator Jumbulances Mark VI, VII and VIII, operated by The Across Trust to convey the sick and handicapped on holidays and pilgrimages to the Continent. They are built by Van Hool of Belgium with Fiat engines, cost £176,000 and convey 44 patients and staff.

Monster No. 2, the world's most powerful 'wrecker' which can lift over 160 tons. (*Vance Corporation*)

Tyres Largest

The world's largest tyres are manufactured in Topeka, Kansas by the Goodyear Co for giant dumper trucks. They measure 12 ft *3,65 m* in diameter, weigh 12,500 lb *5670 kg* and cost $74,000 (*£49,000*). A tyre 17 ft *5,18 m* in diameter is believed to be the limitation of what is practical.

Skid marks Longest

The longest recorded skid marks on a public road have been those 950 ft *290 m* long left by a Jaguar car involved in an accident on the M1 near Luton, Bedfordshire, on 30 June 1960. Evidence given in the High Court case *Hurlock* v. *Inglis and others* indicated a speed 'in excess of 100 mph *160 km/h* before the application of the brakes. The skid marks made by the jet-powered *Spirit of America*, driven by Norman Craig Breedlove, after the car went out of control at Bonneville Salt Flats, Utah, USA, on 15 Oct 1964, were nearly 6 miles *9,6 km* long.

Amphibious vehicle circumnavigation

The only circumnavigation by an amphibious vehicle was achieved by Ben Carlin (Australia) (d. 7 Mar 1981) in an amphibious jeep 'Half-Safe'. He completed the last leg of the Atlantic crossing (the English Channel) on 24 Aug 1951. He arrived back in Montreal, Canada on 8 May 1958 having completed a circumnavigation of 39,000 miles *62 765 km* over land and 9600 miles *15 450 km* by sea and river. He was accompanied on the trans Atlantic stage by his ex-wife Elinore (US) and on the long trans Pacific stage (Tokyo to Anchorage) by Broye Lafayette De-Mente (b. Missouri, 1928).

Snowmobiles

Richard and Raymond Moore and Loren Matthews drove their snowmobile 5876 miles *9456 km* from Fairbanks, Alaska to Fenton, Michigan, USA, in 39 days from 3 Feb–13 Mar 1980.

Rubber-Powered Vehicle

The greatest distance achieved by an elastic-powered car is 482,25 m *527.4 yd* by 'Olive-Goo' designed by a team from Japan on 24 Mar 1980. On 27 Mar 1981 she covered 100 m *328 ft* in 19.34 secs.

Tow Longest

The longest tow on record was one of 4759 miles *7658 km* from Halifax, Nova Scotia to Canada's Pacific Coast, when Frank J. Elliott and George A. Scott of Amherst, Massachusetts, persuaded 168 passing motorists in 89 days to tow their Model T Ford (in fact engineless) to win a $1000 bet on 15 Oct 1927.

Lawn mowers

The widest gang mower in the world is the 5 ton 60 ft *18,28 m* wide 27 unit Big Green Machine used by the sod farmer Jay Edgar Frick of Monroe, Ohio. It mows an acre in 60 sec. On 28 Mar–1 Apr 1959 a Ransome *Matador* motor mower was driven for 99 hr non-stop over 375 miles *603 km* Edinburgh to London. The greatest distance covered in the annual 12 hour Lawn

The longest item moved on British roads, the 221 ft *67,36 m* nitric acid column transported by Sunter Bros of Head-Wrightson Teesdale Ltd. on 25 Mar 1984.

Load heaviest *World*

The world's record road load is one of a 1540 ton *1564 tonne* methanol distillation unit at Madinat Al-Jubail Al-Sinaiyah, Saudi Arabia in March 1982 on a rig with a train weight of 1900 tons *1930 tonnes*. It measures 27 m wide × 28 m long × 40 m high *88.5 × 91.8 × 131.2 ft*.

Great Britain

The heaviest road load moved in the United Kingdom has been a 476 tonnes *468,4 tons* 194 ft *59,13 m* long Vacuum Distillation Column from Faw-

ley Power Station to the Esso Refinery at Fawley by Mammoet-Econofreight on 24 July 1981. The gross weight of the load plus bogies (excluding tractors) was 696 tonnes *685 tons* and the overall train length was 336 ft 3½ in *102,50 m*. The longest item moved on British roads has been a 221 ft *67,36 m* long 270 tonne nitric acid column transported by Sunter Bros. from Head Wrightson Teesdale Ltd. factory at Stockton-on-Tees to the I.C.I. complex at Billingham on 25 Mar 1984 (overall train length 96.58 m *316 ft 10 in*).

below: The deck of Britoil's Beatrice platform being moved by ITM (Offshore) Ltd as an integrated piece weighing 3576 tonnes—the heaviest load ever moved on wheels. The move on to a barge was at the Port Clarence yard of Cleveland Redpath on Teeside, England, on 15 Aug 1983.

(ITM (Offshore) Ltd)

left: Part of the assemblage of multi-wheeled trailers used by ITM (Offshore) Ltd for moving massive offshore modules for North Sea installations. On 3 Aug 1983 a record breaking trailer with 1120 wheels was used to move Mobil's Beryl B North Sea platform deck at the same time.

Mower Race (under the rules of the BLMRA, the British Lawn Mower Racing Association) is 276 miles *84,12 km* by Tony Hazelwood, Derek Bell, Tony Smith and Ray Kilminster at Wisborough Green, W. Sussex on 21–22 June 1980.

Go-Karting

The highest mileage recorded in 24 hours on a closed twisting circuit for go-karts driven by a 4 man team is 1018 laps of a mile *1638,3 km* at Erbsville Kartway, Waterloo, Ontario, Canada. The 5 h.p. 140 cc Honda engined kart was driven by Owen Nimmo, Gary Ruddock, Jim Timmins and Danny Upshaw on 4–5 Sept 1983.

MOTORCYCLES

Guinness Superlatives Ltd have published more specialist volumes entitled *The Guinness Book of Motor-Cycling Facts and Feats* by LJK Setright (£6.95) and *The Guinness Guide to Motorcycling* by Peter Carrick (£10.95).

Earliest (see also Chapter 12)

The earliest internal combustion-engined motorised bicycle was a wooden-framed machine built at Bad Cannstatt in Oct-Nov 1885 by Gottlieb Daimler (1834–1900) of Germany and first ridden by Wilhelm Maybach (1846–1929). It had a top speed of 12 mph *19 km/h* and developed one-half of one horsepower from its single-cylinder 264 cc four-stroke engine at 700 rpm. Known as the 'Einspur', it was lost in a fire in 1903. The first motorcycles of entirely British production were the 1046 cc Holden flat-four and the 2¾ hp Clyde single both produced in 1898. The earliest factory which made motorcycles in quantity was opened in 1894 by Heinrich and Wilhelm Hildebrand and Alois Wolfmüller at Munich, West Germany. In its first two years this factory produced over 1000 machines, each having a water-cooled 1488 cc twin-cylinder four-stroke engine developing about 2.5 bhp at 600 rpm—the highest capacity motor cycle engine ever put into production.

Fastest road machine

The 115 bhp Japanese Honda V65 Magna with a liquid-cooled, in line V-4, 16 valve DoHC engine of 1098 cc capacity has a design speed of 173 mph *278,4 km/h*.

Fastest racing machine

There is no satisfactory answer to the identity of the fastest track machine other than to say that the current Kawasaki, Suzuki and Yamaha machines have all been geared to attain speeds marginally in excess of 300 km/h *186.4 mph* under race conditions.

Duration record

The longest time a solo motorcycle has been kept in nonstop motion is 500 hr by Owen Fitzgerald, Richard Kennett and Don Mitchell who covered 8432 miles *13 570 km* in Western Australia on 10–31 July 1977.

Most on One Machine

On 5 Oct 1983, 30 members of the Police Traffic Branch, Brisbane, Qld, Australia travelled 600 m *656 yd* on a Yamaha 1100XS at Surfers Paradise track, Qld. In Nov 1983 a team of 31 French gendarmes, were reported to have ridden a single machine.

'Wheelie'

Capt Michael J. Brundage drove his Honda XL-250 on the Interstate 20 highway west of Fort Worth, Texas on its back wheel only for a 32.4 mile *52,1 km* 'wheelie' on 23 July 1982. The first recorded case of bettering 100 mph *160,9 km/h* on one wheel was by Ottis Lance at Penwell Raceway Park, Texas, USA on 21 May 1983 with 112 mph *180,2 km/h* over 440 yds *402 m* on a Suzuki GS-1000.

Most expensive

The most expensive road motorcycle available in Britain is the Suzuki GSX 1100, powered by an Italian made Bimota SB4 engine, priced at £7999. In June 1980 a 1912 Henderson Model A was auctioned in the US for $18,000 (*then £7825*).

Coast to Coast USA

Dwight B. Mitchell and Steve Kirkpatrick drove 2945 miles *4739 km* from New York City to San Francisco in 74 hr 37 min (av. 39.46 mph *63,5 km/h*) on Honda 400 cc motorcycles on 11–15 June 1983.

Round Britain

Michael T. Parry of Great Missenden, Buckinghamshire riding a BMW visited all the 62 mainland counties of Great Britain in 38 hours on 16–19 Aug 1980.

BICYCLES

Earliest

The first design for a machine propelled by cranks and pedals, with connecting rods has been attributed to Leonardo da Vinci (1452–1519), or one of his pupils, dated *c.* 1493. The earliest such design actually built was in 1839–40 by Kirkpatrick Macmillan (1810–78) of Dumfries, Scotland. It is now in the Science Museum, Kensington and Chelsea, Greater London.

Longest

The longest true tandem bicycle ever built (i.e. without a third stabilizing wheel) is one of 20,40 m *66 ft 11 in* for 35 riders built by the Pedaalstompers Westmalle of Belgium. They rode *c.* 60 m *195 ft* in practice on 20 Apr 1979. The machine weighs 1100 kg *2425 lb*.

Smallest

The world's smallest wheeled bicycle ridden by a professional circus performer is one with 4,5 cm *1.77 in* wheels weighing 1050 g *37 oz* built and ridden by Raino Frischknecht of West Germany in 1981. Its overall wheelbase measures 14,6 cm *5¾ in*.

Largest

A classic Ordinary bicycle with wheels of 64 in *162,5 cm* diameter front and 20 in *50,8 cm* back was built *c.* 1886 by the Pope Manufacturing Co of Massachusetts, USA. It is now owned by Paul Niquette of Connecticut.

A bicycle with an 8 ft 2½ in *2,50 m* front wheel with pedal extenders was built in 1878 for circus demonstrations.

Fastest *World and British*

The world speed records for human powered vehicles (HPV's) are 58.64 mph *94,37 km/h* (single rider) by Dave Grylls at the Ontario Speedway, California on 27 Oct 1980; and 62.92 mph *101,25 km/h* (multiple riders) by Dave Grylls and Leigh Barczewski at the Ontario Speedway on 4 May 1980. A British 200 m record was set by S. Poulter in 'Poppy Flyer', in 9.10 sec at Greenham Common, Berkshire on 2 Aug 1981.

Endurance

On 10–21 July 1983, 24 City and Guilds College, London students drove an HPV round Great Britain on a 3675 mile *5914 km* route to average 14.41 mph *23,19 km/h*.

Unicycle records

The tallest unicycle ever mastered is one 101 ft 9 in *31,01 m* tall ridden by Steve McPeak (with a safety wire or mechanic

Raino Frischknecht riding the world's smallest bicycle on wheels of 4,5 cm 1.77 in diameter. (David F Hoy)

suspended to an overhead crane) for a distance of 376 ft *114,6 m* in Las Vegas in October 1980. The freestyle riding of ever taller unicycles (that is without any safety harness) must inevitably lead to serious injury or fatality. Brock Allison of Red Deer, Alberta, Canada unicycled 5982,3 km *3717.3 miles* from Vancouver to Halifax in 56 days 10¾ hr on 1 May–26 June 1982. Brian Davis, 33 of Tillicoultry, Clackmannan, Scotland rode 901 miles *1450 km* from Land's End to John O'Groats on 16 May to 4 June 1980 in 19 days 1 hr 45 min. Johnnie Severin of Atwater, California, USA set a record for 100 miles *160,9 km* in 9 hr 20 min 53 sec on 10 Jan 1981. The sprint record from a standing start over 100 metres is 14.89 sec by Floyd Grandall of Pontiac, Michigan, USA, in Tokyo, Japan on 24 Mar 1980.

'Wheelie'

A world record duration record of 1 hr 16 min 54 sec was set by Craig Strong (GB) at Picketts Lock, Edmonton, north London on 7 Jan 1983.

Penny-farthing record

The record for riding from Land's End to John O'Groats on Ordinary bicycles, more commonly known in the 1870s as Penny-farthings, is 10 days 7 hr 12 min by James Richard Moir, 37 of St Leonards-on-Sea, East Sussex on 5–15 June 1977.

Underwater Cycling

Thirty-two certified Scuba divers in 60 hours on 27–29 Nov 1981 rode a submarine tricycle 64.96 miles *104,54 km* on the bottom of Amphi High School pool, Tucson, Arizona, USA, in a scheme devised by Lucian Spataro to raise money for the Casa De Los Ninos Nursery.

3. RAILWAYS

Guinness Superlatives publish railway records in much greater detail in the more specialist publication *Guinness Book of Rail Facts and Feats* 3rd edition (price £6.95).

TRAINS

Earliest

Wagons running on wooden rails were used for mining as early as 1550 at Leberthal, Alsace, and in Britain for conveying coal at Wollaton near Nottingham from 1603–15 and at Broseley colliery, Shropshire, in October 1605. The earliest commercially successful steam locomotives worked on the Middleton Colliery Railway to Leeds, Yorkshire, authorised by Britain's first Railway Act on 9 June 1758. Richard Trevithick (1771–1883) built his first steam locomotive for the 3 ft *914 mm* gauge iron plateway at Coalbrookdale, Shropshire, in 1803, but there is no evidence that it ran. His second and passenger-carrying locomotive did work at Penydarran, Mid Glamorgan, Wales, on 22 Feb 1804, but it broke the plate rails. The first permanent public railway to use steam traction was the Stockton & Darlington, from its opening on 27 Sept 1825 from Shildon to Stockton via Darlington, in Cleveland. The 7 ton/*tonne Locomotion* could pull 48 tons/*tonnes* at a speed of 15 mph *24 km/h*. It was designed and driven by George Stephenson (1781–1848). The first regular steam passenger service was inaugurated over a one mile section (between Bogshole Farm and South Street in Whitstable) on the 6¼ mile *10,05 km* Canterbury & Whitstable Railway in Kent on 3 May 1830, hauled by the engine *Invicta*. The first practical electric railway was Werner von Siemens' oval metre-gauge demonstration track about 300 m *328 yd* long at the Berlin Trades Exhibition on 31 May 1879.

Fastest

The highest speed attained by a railed vehicle is 6121 mph *9851 km/h* or Mach 8 by an unmanned rocket sled over the 9½ mile *15,2 km* long rail track at White Sands Missile Range, New Mexico, USA on 5 Oct 1982. The world's fastest rail speed with passengers is 517 km/h *321.2 mph* by a Maglev (magnetic levitation) test train over the 7 km *4.3 mile* long JNR experimental track at Miyazaki, Japan in December 1979. The highest speed recorded on any national rail system is 236 mph *380 km/h* by the French SNCF high speed train TGV-PSE on trial near Tonnerre on 26 Feb 1981. The TGV (Train à Grande Vitesse) inaugurated on 27 Sept 1981 by Sept 1983 reduced its scheduled time for the Paris–Lyon run of 425 km *264 miles* to 2 hr exactly, so averaging 212,5 km/h *132 mph. The peak speed attained is 270 km/h 168 mph.*

A progressive table of railway speed records since 1892 was published in the 23rd edition on page 141.

Steam

The highest speed ever ratified for a steam locomotive was

126 mph *202 km/h* over 440 yd *402 m* by the LNER 4–6–2 No. 4468 *Mallard* (later numbered 60022), which hauled seven coaches weighing 240 tons *243 tonnes* gross, down Stoke Bank, near Essendine, between Grantham, Lincolnshire, and Peterborough, Cambridgeshire, on 3 July 1938. Driver Joseph Duddington was at the controls with Fireman Thomas Bray. The engine suffered some damage. On 12 June 1905 a speed of 127.06 mph *204,48 km/h* was claimed for the 'Pennsylvania Special' near Elida, Ohio, USA but has never been accepted by leading experts.

United Kingdom

The fastest point-to-point schedule in Britain is that from Paddington to Bristol Parkway on British Rail's Western Region HST Service at 103.15 mph *166 km/h* in 65 min over 111.75 miles *179,8 km*.

Great Britain

British Rail inaugurated their HST (High Speed Train) daily services between London–Bristol and South Wales on 4 Oct 1976. On 10 Apr 1979 one covered the 94 miles *151,2 km* between Paddington, London, and Chippenham, Wiltshire, in 50 min 31 sec for a start-to-stop average of 111.64 mph *179,67 km/h*. The peak speed was 125 mph *201 km/h*. The electric British Rail APT-P (Advanced Passenger Train-Prototype) attained 162 mph *261 km/h,* between Glasgow and Carlisle on its first revenue-earning run on 7 Dec 1981. It covered the 400 miles *644 km* from Glasgow to London in 4¼ hr.

Longest Non-stop

The longest run on British Rail without any advertised stop is the Night Motorail Service from Inverness to Euston. The distance is 567.75 miles *913,7 km* and the time taken is 11 hr 4 min. The longest passenger journey without a stop is the re-inaugurated Flying Scotsman's 268.5 mile *432,1 km* run from Kings Cross to Newcastle en route to Edinburgh.

Most powerful World

The world's most powerful steam locomotive, measured by tractive effort, was No. 700, a triple articulated or triplex 2–8– 8–8–4, 6-cylinder engine built by the Baldwin Locomotive Co in 1916 for the Virginian Railroad. It had a tractive force of 166,300 lb *75 434 kg* working compound and 199,560 lb *90 520 kg* working simple.

Probably the heaviest train ever hauled by a single engine was one of 15,300 tons *15 545 tonnes* made up of 250 freight cars stretching 1.6 miles *2,5 km* by the *Matt H. Shay* (No. 5014), a 2–8–8–8–2 engine which ran on the Erie Railroad from May 1914 until 1929.

Longest freight train

The longest and heaviest freight train on record was about 4 miles *6 km* in length consisting of 500 coal cars with three 3600 hp diesels pulling and three more in the middle, on the Iaeger, West Virginia, to Portsmouth, Ohio, USA stretch of 157 miles *252 km* on the Norfolk and Western Railway on 15 Nov 1967. The total weight was nearly 42,000 tons *42 674 tonnes*. British Rail's heaviest freight train began its regular run on 16 Sept 1983 from Merehead Quarry Somerset to Acton, West London with 3300 tonnes of limestone in 43 wagons and 2 engines stretching nearly ½ mile *800 m*.

Greatest load

The heaviest single pieces of freight ever conveyed by rail are limited by the capacity of the rolling stock. The world's strongest rail carrier with a capacity of 807 tonnes is the 336 tonne 36 axle 92 m *301 ft 10 in* long 'Schnabel' built for a US railway by Krupp, W. Germany, in March 1981.

The heaviest load carried by British Rail was a 122 ft *37,1 m* long boiler drum, weighing 275 tons *279 tonnes* which was carried from Immingham Dock to Killingholme, Humberside, in September 1968. They also move their own rails in lengths of 300 feet *91,44 m*.

The heaviest load ever moved on rails is the 10,700 ton Church of the Virgin Mary built in 1548 in the village of Most, Czechoslovakia, in October–November 1975 because it was in the way of coal workings. It was moved 800 yd *730 m* at 0.0013 mph *0,002 km/h* over 4 weeks at a cost of £9 million.

right: The LNER 4-6-2 Mallard which in 1938 set a world record for a steam engine with 126 mph *202 km/h*. (*Pat Gibbon*) *below:* The French TGV which has recorded the highest ever speed on a national rail system. (*French Railways*)

TRACKS

Longest line

The world's longest run is one of 9438 km *5864½ miles* on the Trans Siberian line from Moscow to Nakhodka, USSR, in the Soviet Far East. There are 97 stops in the journey which takes 8 days 4 hr 25 min. The Baykal-Amur northern main line (BAM), begun with forced labour in 1938, was scheduled for completion on 29 Oct 1984. A total of 10,000 million ft³ *283 million m³* of earth had to be moved and 3700 bridges built in this £8000 million project.

Longest straight

The longest straight in the world is on the Commonwealth Railways Trans Australian line over the Nullarbor Plain from Mile 496 between Nurina and Loongana, Western Australia, to Mile 793 between Ooldea and Watson, South Australia, 297 miles *478 km* dead straight although not level. The longest straight on British Rail is the 18 miles *29 km* between Barlby and Staddlethorpe Junctions on the Selby, North Yorkshire, to Kingston-upon-Hull, Humberside, line.

Widest and Narrowest

The widest gauge in standard use is 5 ft 6 in *1,676 m*. This width is used in Spain, Portugal, India, Pakistan, Bangladesh, Sri Lanka, Argentina and Chile. In 1885 there was a lumber railway in Oregon, USA with a gauge of 8 ft *2,4 m*. The narrowest gauge in use on public railways is 1 ft 3 in *0,381 m* on the Ravenglass & Eskdale Railway, Cumbria (7 miles *11,2 km*) and the Romney, Hythe & Dymchurch line in Kent (14 miles *22,53 km*). 'Le Chemin de fer interet locale' between Muir de Bretagne and Caurel, Cote du Nord, France had a gauge of 31 cm *12.2 in* and ran for 5 km *3.1 miles*.

Highest *World*

The world's highest standard gauge (4 ft 8½ in *1,43 m*) track is on the Peruvian State Railways at La Cima, on the Morococha Branch at 15,806 ft *4817 m* above sea-level. The highest point on the main line is 15,688 ft *4781 m* in the Galera tunnel.

Great Britain

The highest point of the British Rail system is at the pass of Drumochter on the former Perth–Inverness border, where the track reaches an altitude of 1484 ft *452 m* above sea-level. The highest railway in Britain is the Snowdon Mountain Railway, which rises from Llanberis, Gwynedd to 3493 ft *1064 m* above sea-level, just below the summit of Snowdon (*Yr Wyddfa*). It has a gauge of 2 ft 7½ in *800 mm*.

Lowest

The lowest point on British Rail is in the Severn Tunnel—144 ft *43,8 m* below sea-level.

Steepest gradient *World*

The world's steepest standard gauge gradient by adhesion is 1:11 between Chedde and Servoz on the metre gauge SNCF Chamonix line, France.

Great Britain

The steepest sustained adhesion-worked gradient on main line in the United Kingdom is the 2 mile *3,2 km* Lickey incline of 1:37.7 just south west of Birmingham. From the tunnel bottom to James Street, Liverpool, on the former Mersey Railway, there is a stretch of 1:27; and between Folkestone Junction and Harbour a mile *1,6 km* of 1:30.

Slightest gradient

The slightest gradient posted on the British Rail system is one indicated as 1 in 14,400 between Pirbright Junction and Farnborough, Hampshire. This could be described alternatively as England's most obtuse summit.

Busiest rail system

The world's most crowded rail system is the Japanese National Railways, which by 1983 carried 18,472,000 passengers daily. Professional pushers are employed on the Tōkyō Service to squeeze in passengers before the doors can be closed. Among articles lost in 1982 were 555,368 umbrellas, 323,576 clothing items, 184,500 spectacles and 177,066 purses.

Calling All Stations

Alan M. Witton (b. 1943) of Chorlton, Manchester visited every open British Rail station (2362) in a continuous tour for charity of 16,592¾ miles *26 703 km* in 27,136 minutes on 13 July–28 Aug 1980.

John E. Ballenger of Dunedin, Florida, USA has logged 76,485 miles *123 090 km* of unduplicated rail routes in North and South America.

Most Countries in 24 hours

The record number of countries travelled through entirely by train in 24 hours is 10 by W. M. Elbers and R. G. Scholten on 29–30 July 1981. They started in West Germany *via* Netherlands, Belgium, Luxembourg, France, Switzerland, Liechtenstein, Austria, Italy arriving in Yugoslavia 23 hr 34 min later.

Handpumped Railcars

A speed of 20 mph was first surpassed at Port Moody, British Columbia, Canada over 300 m *985 ft* by the 5 man team (1 pusher, 4 pumpers) from Port Moody Motors with 33.54 sec on 27 June 1982.

Longest Journey

The longest journey on the British Rail system is from Penzance, Cornwall to Wick, Caithness, Scotland, *via* London, Glasgow, Aberdeen and Inverness, a round trip of 2229¼ miles *3587,6 km*. It was travelled by John Shaw of Huddersfield for charity on 22–24 Sept 1983 in 50 hr 20 mins.

STATIONS

Largest *World*

The world's largest railway station is Grand Central Terminal, Park Avenue and 43rd Street, New York City, NY, USA, built 1903–13. It covers 48 acres *19 ha* on two levels with 41 tracks on the upper level and 26 on the lower. On average more than 550 trains and 180,000 people per day use it, with a peak of 252,288 on 3 July 1947.

Great Britain

The largest railway station in extent on the British Rail system is the 17-platform Clapham Junction, London, covering 27¾ acres *11,22 ha* with a total face of 11,185 ft *3409 m*. The station with the largest number of platforms is Waterloo, London (24½ acres *9,9 ha*), with 21 main and two Waterloo and City Line platforms, with a total face of 15,352 ft *4679 m*. Victoria Station (21¼ acres *8,80 ha*) with 17 platforms has, however, a total face length of 18,412 ft *5611 m*.

Oldest

The oldest station in the world is Liverpool Road Station, Manchester, England first used on 15 Sept 1830. It is now part of a museum.

Busiest

The busiest railway junction in Great Britain is Clapham Junction, Wandsworth, Greater London, on the Southern Region of British Rail, with an average of 2200 trains passing through each 24 hr (May 1984).

Highest

The highest station in the world is Condor, Bolivia at 15,705 ft *4786 m* on the metre gauge Rio Mulato to Potosi line. The highest passenger station on British Rail is Corrour, Highland, at an altitude of 1347 ft *410,5 m* above sea-level.

Waiting rooms

The world's largest waiting rooms are the four in Peking Station, Chang'an Boulevard, Peking, China, opened in September 1959, with a total standing capacity of 14,000.

Longest platform

The longest railway platform in the world is the Khargpur platform, West Bengal, India, which measures 2733 ft *833 m* in length. The State Street Center subway platform staging on 'The Loop' in Chicago, Illinois, USA, measures 3500 ft *1066 m* in length.

The longest platform in the British Rail system is the 1977 ft 4 in *602,69 m* long platform at Gloucester.

UNDERGROUND RAILWAYS

Most extensive

The earliest (first section opened 10 Jan 1863) and one of the most extensive underground or rapid transit railway systems of the 67 in the world is that of the London Transport Executive, with 247 miles *398 km* of route, of which 82 miles *131 km* is bored tunnel and 20 miles *32 km* is 'cut and cover'. This whole system is operated by a staff of 11,000 serving 267 stations. The 450 trains comprising 3875 cars carried 563,000,000 passengers in 1983. The greatest depth is 221 ft *67,3 m* near Hampstead on the Northern Line. The longest journey without a change is Epping to West Ruislip—34.1 miles *54,8 km*. The record for touring the 277 stations is 17 hr 37 min by C. M. Mulvany of London on 3 Dec 1981.

The subway with most stations in the world is the New York City Transport Authority (first section opened on 27 Oct 1904) with a total of 231.73 route miles *372,93 km* and 1,096,006,529 passengers in 1979. The 458 stations are closer set than London's. The record for travelling the whole system was 21 hr 8½ min by Mayer Wiesen and Charles Emerson on 8 Oct 1973.

Busiest
The world's busiest metro system is that in Greater Moscow with as many as 6½ million passengers per day. It has 115 stations and 184 km *114.9 miles* of track. The record transit (with 18 changes) is 8 hr 10 min 22 sec by Eric Rudkin of Chuddesden, Derbyshire on 29 Sept 1982.

MODEL RAILWAYS
The non-stop duration record for a model train (loco plus 6 coaches, is 864 hr 30 min from 1 June–7 July 1978, covering 678 miles *1091 km,* organised by Roy Catton at 'Pastimes' Toy Store, Mexborough, S. Yorkshire. The longest recorded run by a model *steam* locomotive is 144 miles *231,7 km* in 27 hr 18 min by the 7¼ inch *18,4 cm* gauge 'Winifred' built in 1974 by Wilf Grove at Thames Ditton, Surrey on 8–9 Sept 1979. 'Winifred' works on 80 lb/in² *5,6 kg/cm²* pressure and is coal-fired with cylinders 2⅛ in *54 mm* in diameter and 3⅛ in *79 mm* stroke. The most miniature model railway ever built is one of 1:1000 scale by Jean Damery (b. 1923) of Paris. The engine ran on a 4½ volt battery and measures $\frac{5}{16}$ in *7,9 mm* overall.

TRAMS

Longest tram journey
The longest tramway journey now possible is from Krefeld St Tönis to Witten Annen Nord, W. Germany. With luck at the 8 inter-connections the 105,5 km *65.5 mile* trip can be achieved in 5½ hr. By late 1977 there were still some 315 tramway systems surviving of which the longest is that of Leningrad, USSR with 2500 cars on 53 routes. The last in Britain is at Blackpool, Lancashire.

Oldest
The oldest trams in revenue service in the world are Motor cars 1 and 2 of the Manx Electric Railway dating from 1893.

Orville (left) and Wilbur Wright who designed, and built, *Flyer I* (drawings above) in which Orville made the first controlled power-driven flight on 17 Dec 1903.

4. AIRCRAFT

Guinness Superlatives has published aircraft records in much greater detail in the specialist publication *Guinness Book of Air Facts and Feats* (4th edition) (price £8.95).

Note—The use of the Mach scale for aircraft speeds was introduced by Prof. Ackeret of Zürich, Switzerland. The Mach number is the ratio of the velocity of a moving body to the local velocity of sound. This ratio was first employed by Dr Ernst Mach (1838–1916) of Vienna, Austria in 1887. Thus Mach 1.0 equals 760.98 mph *1224,67 km/h* at sea-level at 15°C, and is assumed, for convenience, to fall to a constant 659.78 mph *1061,81 km/h* in the stratosphere, *i.e.* above 11 000 m *36,089 ft.*

EARLIEST FLIGHTS

World
The first controlled and sustained power-driven flight occurred near the Kill Devil Hill, Kitty Hawk, North Carolina, USA, at 10.35 a.m. on 17 Dec 1903, when Orville Wright (1871–1948) flew the 12 hp chain-driven *Flyer I* for a distance of 120 ft *36,5 m* at an airspeed of 30 mph *48 km/h*, a ground speed of 6.8 mph *10,9 km/h* and an altitude of 8–12 ft *2,5–3,5 m* for about 12 sec watched by his brother Wilbur (1867–1912) 4 men and a boy. Both brothers, from Dayton, Ohio, were bachelors because, as Orville put it, they had not the means to 'support a wife as well as an aeroplane'. The *Flyer* is now in the National Air and Space Museum at the Smithsonian Institution, Washington DC.

The first hop by a man-carrying aeroplane entirely under its own power was made when Clément Ader (1841–1925) of France flew in his *Eole* for about 50 m *164 ft* at Armainvilliers, France, on 9 Oct 1890. It was powered by a lightweight steam engine of his own design which developed about 20 hp (15 kW).

The earliest 'rational design' for a flying machine, according to the Royal Aeronautical Society, was that published by Emanuel Swedenborg (1688–1772) in Sweden in 1717.

Great Britain
The first officially recognised flight in the British Isles was made by the US citizen Samuel Franklin Cody (1861–1913) who flew 1390 ft *423 m* in his own biplane at Farnborough, Hampshire, on 16 Oct 1908. Horatio Frederick Phillips (1845–1924) almost certainly covered 500 ft *152 m* in his Phillips II 'Venetian blind' aeroplane at Streatham, in 1907. The first Briton to fly was George Pearson Dickin, a journalist from Southport, Lancashire as a passenger to Wilbur Wright at Auvóur, France on 3 Oct 1908. The first resident British citizen to fly in Britain was J. T. C. Moore-Brabazon (later Lord Brabazon of Tara PC, GBE, MC) (1884–1964) with 3 short but sustained flights on 30 Apr–2 May 1909.

Cross-Channel
The earliest cross-Channel flight by an aeroplane was made on Sunday, 25 July 1909 when Louis Blériot (1872–1936) of France flew his *Blériot XI* monoplane, powered by a 23 hp Anzani engine, 26 miles *41,8 km* from Les Baraques, France, to Northfall Meadow near Dover Castle, England, in 36½ min, after taking off at 4.41 a.m.

Jet-engined *World*
Proposals for jet propulsion date back to Captain Marconnet (1909) of France, and Henri Coanda (1886–1972) of Romania, and to the turbojet proposals of Maxime Guillaume in 1921. The earliest tested run was that of the British Power Jets Ltd's

above: David Boyce, with G-BOOM, the Hawker Hunter used during his 38 min 58 sec journey from Paris to London on 24 Sept 1983. *below:* Capt. Charles Lindbergh (USA) who made the first solo flight across the Atlantic in his 'Spirit of St Louis on 20–21 May 1927. (*Teledyne Ryan Aeronautical*)

experimental WU (Whittle Unit) on 12 Apr 1937, invented by Flying Officer (now Air Commodore Sir) Frank Whittle (b. Coventry, 1 June 1907), who had applied for a patent on jet propulsion in 1930. The first flight by an aeroplane powered by a turbojet engine was made by the Heinkel He 178, piloted by Flug Kapitan Erich Warsitz, at Marienehe, Germany, on 27 Aug 1939. It was powered by a Heinkel He S3b engine (834 lb *378 kg* as installed with long tailpipe) designed by Dr Hans 'Pabst' von Ohain and first tested in August 1937.

Great Britain

The first British jet flight occurred when Fl Lt P. E. G. 'Jerry' Sayer, OBE (k. 1942) flew the Gloster-Whittle E.28/39 (wing span 29 ft *8,84 m*, length 25 ft 3 in *7,70 m*) fitted with an 860 lb *390 kg* s. t. Whittle W-1 engine for 17 min at Cranwell, Lincolnshire, on 15 May 1941. The maximum speed was *c.* 350 mph *560 km/h*.

Supersonic flight

The first supersonic flight was achieved on 14 Oct 1947 by Capt. (later Brig.-Gen) Charles ('Chuck') Elwood Yeager, USAF retd (b. 13 Feb 1923), over Edwards Air Force Base, Muroc, California, USA, in a Bell XS-1 rocket plane ('Glamorous Glennis') with Mach 1.015 (670 mph *1078 km/h*) at an altitude of 42,000 ft *12 800 m*. The first British aircraft to attain Mach 1 in a dive was the de Havilland D. H. 108 tailless research aircraft on 6 Sept 1948, piloted by John Derry.

Trans-Atlantic

The first crossing of the North Atlantic by air was made by Lt-Cdr (later Rear Admiral) Albert Cushion Read (1887–1967) and his crew (Stone, Hinton, Rodd, Rhoads and Breese) in the 84 knot *155 km/h* US Navy/Curtiss flying-boat NC-4 from Trepassey Harbour, Newfoundland, *via* the Azores, to Lisbon, Portugal, on 16–27 May 1919. The whole flight of 4717 miles *7591 km* originating from Rockaway Air Station, Long Island, NY on 8 May, required 53 hr 58 min, terminating at Plymouth, England, on 31 May.

The Newfoundland–Azores flight of 1200 miles *1930 km* took 15 hr 18 min at 81.7 knots *151,4 km/h*.

Non-stop

The first non-stop trans-Atlantic flight was achieved 18 days later from 4.13 p.m. GMT on 14 June 1919, from Lester's Field, St John's, Newfoundland, 1960 miles *3154 km* to Derrygimla bog near Clifden, County Galway, Ireland, at 8.40 a.m. GMT, 15 June, when the pilot, Capt John William Alcock, DSC (1892–1919), and the navigator Lt Arthur Whitten Brown (1886–1948) flew across in a Vickers *Vimy*, powered by two 360 hp Rolls-Royce *Eagle VIII* engines. Both men were created civil KBE's on 21 June 1919 when Alcock was aged 26 years 227 days, and shared a *Daily Mail* prize of £10,000.

Solo

The 79th man to achieve a trans-Atlantic flight but the first to do so solo was Capt (later Brig) Charles Augustus Lindbergh (Hon AFC) (1902–74) who took off in his 220 hp Ryan monoplane 'Spirit of St. Louis' at 12.52 p.m. GMT on 20 May 1927 from Roosevelt Field, Long Island, NY, USA. He landed at 10.21 p.m. GMT on 21 May 1927 at Le Bourget airfield, Paris, France. His flight of 3610 miles *5810 km* lasted 33 hr 29½ min and he won a prize of $25,000 (*then £5300*).

Most Flights

John M. Winston, a senior British Airways Flight Engineer, flew 1277 trans-Atlantic flights from 10 May 1947 to 14 Dec 1978—a total of 20,100 hr.

Trans-Pacific

The first non-stop Pacific flight was by Major Clyde Pangborn and Hugh Herndon in the Bellanca cabin 'plane *Miss Veedol* from Sabishiro Beach, Japan 4558 miles *7335 km* to Wenatchee, Washington, USA in 41 hr 13 min on 3–5 Oct 1931. (For earliest crossing see 1924 flight below).

Circumnavigational flights

Strict circumnavigation requires passing through two antipodal points thus with a minimum distance of 24,859.75 miles *40 007,89 km*. The FAI permits flights which exceed the length of the Tropic of Cancer or Capricorn *viz* 22,858.754 miles *36 787,599 km*.

The earliest such flight of 26,345 miles *42 398 km* was by two

US Army Douglas DWC amphibians in 57 'hops'. The *Chicago* was piloted by Lt Lowell H. Smith and Lt Leslie P. Arnold and the *New Orleans* was piloted by Lt Erik H. Nelson and Lt John Harding between 6 Apr and 28 Sept 1924 beginning and ending at Seattle, Washington, USA.

The earliest solo claim was by Wiley Hardemann Post (1898–1935) (US) in the Lockheed Vega 'Winnie Mae' starting and finishing at Floyd Bennett Field, New York City on 15–22 July 1933 in 10 'hops'. The distance of 15,596 miles *25 099 km* with a flying time of 115 hr 36 min was however at too high a latitude to qualify.

The first non-stop round-the-world flight completed on 2 Mar 1949 was made by the USAF's Boeing B-50 Superfortress *Lucky Lady II* piloted by Capt James Gallagher from Carswell AFB, Texas in 94 hr 1 min. The aircraft was refuelled 4 times on its 23,452 mile *37 742 km* flight.

The fastest flight has been the non-stop eastabout flight of 45 hr 19 min by three flight-refuelled USAF B-52's led by Maj-Gen Archie J. Old Jr. They covered 24,325 miles *39 147 km* on 16–18 Jan 1957 finishing at March Air Force Base, Riverside, California, having averaged 525 mph *845 km/h* with four in-flight refuellings by KC-97 aerial tankers.

The first circum-polar flight was solo by Capt Elgen M. Long, 44, in a Piper Navajo on 5 Nov–3 Dec 1971. He covered 38,896 miles *62 597 km* in 215 flying hours. The cabin temperature sank to −40°C −40°F over Antarctica.

Circumnavigation *Smallest aircraft*
The smallest aircraft to complete a circumnavigation is the 20 ft 11 in *6,38 m* single-engined 180 hp Thorp T-18 built in his garage by its pilot Donald P. Taylor of Sage, California. His 26,190 mile *42 148 km* flight in 37 stages took 176 flying hours ending at Oshkosh, Wisconsin on 30 Sept 1976.

Largest wing span
The aircraft with the largest wing span ever constructed is the $40 million Hughes H.4 *Hercules* flying-boat ('Spruce Goose'), which was raised 70 ft *21,3 m* into the air in a test run of 1000 yd *914 m*, piloted by Howard Hughes (1905–76), off Long Beach Harbor, California, USA, on 2 Nov 1947. The eight-engined 190 ton *193 tonnes* aircraft had a wing span of 319 ft 11 in *97,51 m* and a length of 218 ft 8 in *66,64 m* and never flew again. In a brilliant engineering feat she was moved bodily by Goldcoast Corp aided by the US Navy barge crane YD-171 on 22 Feb 1982 to her final resting place 6 miles *9,6 km* across the harbour under a 700 ft *213,4 m* diameter dome.

Heaviest
The highest recorded gross take off weight of any aircraft has been 379.9 tons *386,0 tonnes* in the case of a Boeing 747-200B 'Jumbo' jet during certification tests of its Pratt & Whitney JT9D-7Q engines on 23 May 1979. Some versions are certified for standard airline operation at a maximum take-off weight of 371.9 tons *377,9 tonnes*.

A Boeing 747 (Capt. Eric Moody) became the 'worlds heaviest glider' when all 4 engines stopped at 37,000 ft *11 275 m* due to volcanic ash from Mt. Galunggung, Indonesia on 24 June 1982 on Flight BA.009 with 263 aboard. The crew got the engines restarted after 13 min and landed the plane at Jakarta.

The $40 million Piasecki Helistat, comprising 4 helicopters and a US Navy blimp was exhibited on 26 Jan 1984 at Lakehurst, New Jersey, USA. It has dimensions of more than 100 m *328 ft* and a designed ability to lift weights of 26 tons.

Solar Powered
The solar-powered *Solar Challenger*, designed by a team led by Dr Paul MacCready, was flown for the first time entirely under solar power on 20 Nov 1980. On 7 July 1981, piloted by Steve Ptacek (USA), the *Solar Challenger* became the first aircraft of this category to achieve a crossing of the English Channel. Taking off from Pontois-Cormeilles, Paris, the 163 mile *262,3 km* journey to Manston, Kent was completed in 5 hr 23 min at a maximum altitude of 3353 m *11,000 ft*. The aircraft has a wingspan of 47 ft *14,3 m*.

Smallest
The smallest aeroplane ever flown is the Stits *Skybaby* biplane, designed and built by Ray Stits at Riverside, California, USA, and first flown by Robert H. Starr on 26 May 1952. It was 9 ft 10 in *3 m* long, with a wing span of 7 ft 2 in *2,18 m*, and weighed 452 lb *205 kg* empty. It was powered by an 85 hp Continental C85 engine, giving a top speed of 185 mpg *297 km/h*. The smallest jet is the 280 mph *450 km/h Silver Bullet* weighing 432 lb *196 kg* with a 17 ft *5,18 m* wing span built by Bob Bishop (USA).

Bombers *Heaviest*
The world's heaviest bomber is the eight-jet swept-wing Boeing B-52H *Stratofortress*, which has a maximum take-off weight of 488,000 lb (217.86 tons *221,35 tonnes*). It has a wing span of 185 ft *56,38 m* and is 157 ft 6¾ in *48,02 m* in length, with a speed of over 650 mph *1046 km/h*. The B-52 can carry twelve SRAM thermonuclear short range attack missiles or twenty-four 750 lb *340 kg* bombs under its wings and eight more SRAM's or eighty-four 500 lb *226 kg* bombs in the fuselage. The ten-engined Convair B-36J, weighing 183 tons *185 tonnes*, had a greater wing span, at 230 ft *70,10 m* but it is no longer in service. It had a top speed of 435 mph *700 km/h*.

Fastest
The world's fastest operational bombers are the French Dassault *Mirage IV*, which can fly at Mach 2.2 (1450 mph *2333 km/h*) at 36,000 ft *11 000 m*; the American General Dynamics FB-111A, with a maximum speed of Mach 2.5; and the Soviet swing-wing Tupolev Tu-22M known to NATO as 'Backfire', which has an estimated over-target speed of Mach 2.0 but which may be as fast as Mach 2.5 and a combat radius of up to 3570 miles *5745 km*.

Airliner Largest *World*
The highest capacity jet airliner is the Boeing 747 'Jumbo Jet', first flown on 9 Feb 1969 (see Heaviest aircraft) and has a capacity of from 385 to more than 500 passengers with a maximum speed of 602 mph *969 km/h*. Its wing span is 195.7 ft *59,64 m* and its length 231.8 ft *70,7 m*. It entered service on 22 Jan 1970. The Boeing 747-300 with a lengthened upper deck, which allows an extra 37 passengers, entered service in March 1983.

The greatest passenger load on a commercial airliner was 610 on a Trans-America airline Boeing 747 flight from Hong Kong to Oakland, California on 27 Feb 1981.

Great Britain
The largest ever British aircraft was the experimental Bristol Type 167 *Brabazon*, which had a maximum take-off weight of 129.4 tons *131,4 tonnes*, a wing span of 230 ft *70,10 m* and a length of 177 ft *53,94 m*. This eight-engined aircraft first flew on 4 Sept 1949. The *Concorde* (see below) has a maximum take-off weight of 408,000 lb *185 065 kg* (182.14 tons).

Airliner Fastest
The supersonic BAC/Aerospatiale *Concorde*, first flown on 2 Mar 1969, with a capacity of 128 passengers, cruises at up to Mach 2.2 (1450 mph *2333 km/h*). It flew at Mach 1.05 on 10 Oct 1969, exceeded Mach 2 for the first time on 4 Nov 1970 and became the first supersonic airliner used on passenger services on 21 Jan 1976 when Air France and British Airways opened services simultaneously between, respectively, Paris–Rio de Janeiro and London–Bahrain. Services between London and New York and Paris and New York began on 22 Nov 1977. The New York–London record is 2 hr 56 min 35 sec set on 1 Jan 1983.

Most capacious
The Aero Spacelines Guppy-201 has a cargo hold with a usable volume of 39,000 ft³ *1104,4 m³* and a maximum take-off weight of 75.9 tons *77,1 tonnes*. Wing span is 156.2 ft *47,63 m*, length 143.8 ft *43,84 m* and overall height 48.5 ft *14,78 m*. The giant Lockheed C-5A Galaxy military transport has a main cargo hold with a usable volume of 34,795 ft³ *985,3 m³*, and a maximum take-off weight of 343.3 tons *348,8 tonnes*. Its wing span is 222.7 ft *67,88 m*, length 247.8 ft *75,54 m* and overall height 65.1 ft *19,85 m*. It has in addition forward and rear upper decks with a combined volume of 8030 ft³ *227,4 m³*, which accommodates the flight crew, and provides seating for a relief crew and others, totalling 15 forward and 75 troops on the rear deck. When full details become available it is almost certain that the Galaxy will be superseded by the Soviet

Antonov An-400 (NATO name *Condor*) which is estimated to have a wing span of 243.5 ft *74,2 m*.

Largest propeller

The largest aircraft propeller ever used was the 22 ft 7½ in *6,9 m* diameter Garuda propeller, fitted to the Linke-Hofmann R II built in Breslau, Germany (now Wroclaw, Poland), which flew in 1919. It was driven by four 260 hp Mercedes engines and turned at only 545 rpm.

Scheduled flights *Longest*

The longest distance scheduled non-stop flight is the weekly Pan-Am Sydney–San Francisco non-stop 13 hr 25 min Flight 816, in a Boeing 747 SP, opened in December 1976, over 7475 statute miles *12 030 km*. The longest delivery flight by a commercial jet is 8936 nautical miles or 10,290 statute miles *16 560 km* from Seattle, Washington, USA to Cape Town, South Africa by the South African Airway's Boeing 747 SP (Special performance) 'Matroosberg' with 178 400 kg *175.5 tons* of pre-cooled fuel in 17 hr 22½ min on 23–24 Mar 1976.

Shortest

The shortest scheduled flight in the world is that by Loganair between the Orkney Islands of Westray and Papa Westray which has been flown with Britten-Norman Islander twin-engined 10-seat transports since September 1967. Though scheduled for 2 min, in favourable wind conditions it has been accomplished in 58 sec by Capt Andrew D. Alsop.

Gary W. Rovetto of Island Air on 21 Mar 1980 flew on the scheduled flight from Center Island to Decatur Island, Washington, USA in 41 sec.

Paris–London

The fastest time to travel the 214 miles *344 km* from central Paris to central London (BBC TV centre) is 38 min 58 sec by David Boyce on 24 Sept 1983 by motorcycle–helicopter to Le Bourget; Hawker Hunter jet (pilot Michael Carlton) to Biggin Hill, Kent; helicopter to the TV centre car park.

London–New York

The record for central London to downtown New York City by helicopter and Concorde is 3 hr 59 min 44 sec and the return in 3 hr 40 min 40 sec both by David J. Springbett, 1981 Salesman of the Year, and David Boyce of Stewart Wrightson (Aviation) Ltd on 8 and 9 Feb 1982.

HIGHEST SPEED

Official record

The official air speed record is 2193.167 mph *3529,56 km/h* by Capt Eldon W. Joersz and Maj George T. Morgan, Jr, in a Lockheed SR-71A near Beale Air Force Base, California, USA over a 15 to 25 km course on 28 July 1976.

Air-launched record

The fastest fixed-wing aircraft in the world was the US North American Aviation X-15A-2, which flew for the first time (after modification from X-15A) on 28 June 1964 powered by a liquid oxygen and ammonia rocket propulsion system. Ablative materials on the airframe once enabled a temperature of 3000°F to be withstood. The landing speed was 210 knots (242 mph *389,1 km/h*) momentarily. The highest speed attained was 4534 mph *7297 km/h* (Mach 6.72) when piloted by Maj William J. Knight, USAF (b. 1930), on 3 Oct 1967. An earlier version piloted by Joseph A. Walker (1920–66), reached 354,200 ft *107 960 m* (67.08 miles) also over Edwards Air Force Base, California, USA, on 22 Aug 1963. The programme was suspended after the final flight of 24 Oct 1968.

The US NASA Rockwell International Space Shuttle Orbiter *Columbia* was launched from the Kennedy Space Center, Cape Canaveral, Florida commanded by Cdr John W. Young USN and piloted by Robert L. Crippen on 12 Apr 1981 after the expenditure of $9900 million since 1972. *Columbia* broke all records for space by a fixed wing craft with 16,600 mph *26 715 km/h* at main engine cut-off. After re-entry from 400,000 ft *122 km*, experiencing temperatures of 2160°C *3920°F*, she glided home weighing 97 tonnes/tons with the highest ever landing speed of 216 mph *347 km/h* on Rogers Dry Lake, California on 14 Apr 1981. Under a new FAI Category P for Aerospacecraft, the *Columbia* is holder of the current

absolute world record for duration of 8 days 00 hr 04 min 45 sec, with two astronauts, but *Challenger* (launched 18 June 1983) has since set a duration record of 6 days 02 hr 23 min 59 sec with five astronauts including Sally K. Ride, the first female Space Shuttle astronaut, and on a previous mission set a new record altitude of 206.36 miles *332,1 km*.

Fastest jet

The world's fastest jet aircraft is the USAF Lockheed SR-71 reconnaissance aircraft (see Official record) which was first flown on 22 Dec 1964 and is reportedly capable of attaining an altitude ceiling of close to 100,000 ft *30 480 m*. The SR-71 has a wing span of 55.6 ft *16,94 m* and a length of 107.4 ft *32,73 m* and weighs 170,000 lb (75.9 tons) (75.9 tons *77,1 tonnes*) at take-off. Its reported range is 2982 miles *4800 km* at Mach 3 at 78,750 ft *24 000 m*. At least 30 are believed to have been built. The fastest combat aircraft in the world is the USSR Mikoyan MiG-25 fighter (code name 'Foxbat'). The reconnaissance 'Foxbat-B' has been tracked by radar at about Mach 3.2 (2110 mph *3395 km/h*). When armed with four large underwing air-to-air missiles known to NATO as 'Acrid', the fighter 'Foxbat-A' is limited to Mach 2.8 (1845 mph *2969 km/h*). The single-seat 'Foxbat-A' spans 45 ft 9 in *13,95 m*, is 73 ft 2 in *22,3 m* long and has a maximum take-off weight of 79,800 lb *36 200 kg*.

Fastest biplane

The fastest recorded biplane was the Italian Fiat C.R.42B, with a 1010 hp Daimler-Benz DB601A engine, which attained 323 mph *520 km/h* in 1941. Only one was built.

Fastest piston-engined aircraft

The fastest speed at which a piston-engined aeroplane has ever been measured was for a cut-down privately owned Hawker *Sea Fury* which attained 520 mph *836 km/h* in level flight over Texas, USA, in August 1966 piloted by Mike Carroll (k. 1969) of Los Angeles. The FAI accredited record for a piston-engined aircraft is 517.055 mph *832,12 km/h* over Mojave, California by Frank Taylor (US) in a modified North American P-51D *Mustang* powered by a 3000 hp Packard Merlin, over a 15 to 25 km course, on 30 July 1983.

Fastest propeller-driven aircraft

The Soviet Tu-114 turboprop transport is the world's fastest propeller-driven aeroplane. It achieved a recorded speed 545.076 mph *877,212 km/h* carrying heavy payloads over measured circuits. It is developed from the Tupolev Tu-95 bomber, known in the West as the 'Bear', and has four 14,795 hp engines. The turboprop-powered Republic XF-84H prototype US Navy fighter which flew on 22 July 1955 had a top *design* speed of 670 mph *1078 km/h* but was abandoned.

Fastest trans-Atlantic flight

The trans-Atlantic flight record is 1 hr 54 min 56.4 sec by Maj James V. Sullivan, 37, and Maj Noel F. Widdifield, 33 flying a Lockheed SR-71A eastwards on 1 Sept 1974. The average speed, slowed by refuelling by a KC-135 tanker aircraft, for the New York–London stage of 3461.53 miles *5570,80 km* was 1806.963 mph *2908,026 km/h*. The solo record (Gander to Gatwick) is 8 hr 47 min 32 sec by Capt John J. A. Smith in a Rockwell 685 on 12 Mar 1978.

Altitude *Official record*

The official world altitude record by an aircraft taking off from the ground under its own power is 123,524 ft (23.39 miles *37 650 m*) by Aleksandr Fedotov (USSR) in a Mikoyan E.266M, (MiG-25) aircraft, powered by two 30,865 lb *14 000 kg* thrust turbojet engines, on 31 Aug 1977.

Duration

The flight duration record is 64 days 22 hr 19 min and 5 sec, set up by Robert Timm and John Cook in a Cessna 172 'Hacienda'. They took off from McCarran Airfield, Las Vegas, Nevada, USA, just before 3.53 p.m. local time on 4 Dec 1958, and landed at the same airfield just before 2.12 p.m. on 7 Feb 1959. They covered a distance equivalent to six times round the world with continued refuellings, without landing.

The record for duration without refuelling is 84 hr 32 min, set by Walter E. Lees and Frederic A. Brossy in a Bellanca monoplane with a 225 hp Packard Diesel engine, at Jacksonville, Florida, USA on 25–28 May 1931. The longest non-stop flight without refuelling was a 12,532 mile *20 169 km* flight from Okinawa to Madrid, Spain by a USAF B-52H on 10–11 Jan 1962.

Aircraft

AIRPORTS

Largest *World*

The world's largest airport is the £2100 million King Khalid International Airport outside Riyadh, Saudi Arabia covering an area of 86 miles² *221 km²*, opened on 14 Nov 1983. It has the world's largest control tower 243 ft *74 m* in height. The Hajj Terminal at the £2800 million King Abdul-Aziz airport near Jeddah is the world's largest roofed structure covering 1,5 km² *370 acres*. The present 6 runways and 5 terminal buildings of the Dallas/Fort Worth Airport, Texas, USA are planned to be extended to 9 runways and 13 terminals with 260 gates with an ultimate capacity for 150 million passengers. The world's largest airport terminal is Hartsfield Atlanta International Airport opened on 21 Sept 1980 with floor space covering 50.50 acres *20,43 ha*. It has 138 gates handling nearly 50 million passengers a year but has a capacity for 75 million.

Great Britain

Seventy-four airline companies from 68 countries operate scheduled services into Heathrow Airport—London (2957 acres *1197 ha*), and during 1983 there was a total of 260,100 air transport movements handled by a staff of 45,000 employed by the various companies and the British Airports Authority. The total number of passengers, both incoming and outgoing, was 26,749,200. The most flights yet handled by Heathrow in a day was 986 on 19 July 1974 and the largest number of passengers yet handled in a day was 112,880 on 31 Aug 1980. Aircraft fly to more than 90 countries.

Busiest

The world's busiest airport is the Chicago International Airport, O'Hare Field, Illinois, USA with a total of 671,724 movements and 42,873,953 passengers in the year 1983. This represents a take-off or landing every 46.9 sec round the clock. Heathrow Airport, London handles more *international* traffic than any other. The busiest landing area ever has been Bien Hoa Air Base, south Vietnam, which handled more than 1,000,000 take-offs and landings in 1970. The world's largest 'helipad' was An Khe, south Vietnam.

Highest and lowest

The highest airport in the world is La Sa (Lhasa) Airport, Tibet at 14,315 ft *4363 m*.

The highest landing ever made by a fixed-wing 'plane is 19,947 ft *6080 m* on Dhaulagiri, Himalaya by a Pilatus Porter, named 'Yeti', supplying the 1960 Swiss Expedition. The lowest landing field is El Lisan on the east shore of the Dead Sea, 1180 ft *360 m* below sea-level, but during World War II BOAC Short C-class flying boats operated from the surface of the Dead Sea 1292 ft *394 m* below sea level. The lowest international airport is Schiphol, Amsterdam, at 13 ft *3,9 m* below sea-level. Rotterdam's airport is fractionally lower at 15 ft *4,5 m*.

Farthest and Nearest to city or capital centres

The airport farthest from the city centre it allegedly serves is Viracopos, Brazil, which is 60 miles *96 km* from São Paulo. The Gibraltar airport is 880 yd *800 m* from the centre.

Longest runway *World*

The longest runway in the world is one of 7 miles *11 km* in length (of which 15,000 ft *4572 m* is concreted) at Edwards Air Force Base on the bed of Rogers Dry Lake at Muroc, California, USA. The whole test centre airfield extends over 65 miles² *168 km²*. In an emergency an auxiliary 12 mile *19 km* strip is available along the bed of the Dry Lake. The world's longest civil airport runway is one of 16,076 ft (3.04 miles *4,89 km*) at Pierre van Ryneveld Airport Upington, South Africa constructed in five months from August 1975 to January 1976. A paved runway 20,500 ft (3.88 miles *6,24 km*) long appears on maps of Jordan at Abu Husayn.

Great Britain

The longest runway available normally to civil aircraft in the United Kingdom is No. 1 at Heathrow Airport—London, measuring 12,800 ft (2.42 miles *3,90 km*).

HELICOPTERS

Fastest

The official world speed record for a pure helicopter is 228.9 mph *368,4 km/h* set by Gourguen Karapetyan in a Mil A-10 on a 15 to 25 km course near Moscow, USSR on 21 Sept

The US Space Shuttle Orbiter *Columbia* lifts off on mission STS4. (*NASA*)

1978. An average speed of 35.4 mph *56,97 km/h* was maintained in the first circumnavigation by H. Ross Perot and J. W. Coburn in a Bell 206 L-1 Long Ranger II on 1–30 Sept 1982.

Largest

The world's largest helicopter is the Soviet Mil *Mi-12* ('Homer'), also known as the V-12. It is powered by four 6500 hp turboshaft engines and has a span of 219 ft 10 in *67 m* over its rotor tips with a length of 121 ft 4½ in *37,00 m* and weighs 103.3 tons *105 tonnes*.

Greatest Load

On 3 Feb 1982 at Podmoscovnoé in the Soviet Union, a Mil Mi-26 heavy-lift helicopter, crewed by G. V. Alfeurov and L. A. Indeev (co-pilot), lifted a total mass of 125,153.8 lb *56 768,8 kg* (55.87 tons *56,77 tonnes*) to a height of 2000 m *6560 ft*.

Smallest

The Aerospace General Co one-man rocket assisted minicopter weighs about 160 lb *72,5 kg* and can cruise 250 miles *400 km* at 85 mph *137 km/h*.

Highest

The altitude record for helicopters is 40,820 ft *12 442 m* by an Aérospatiale SA315B *Lama*, over France on 21 June 1972. The highest recorded landing has been at 23,000 ft *7000 m* below the South-East face of Everest in a rescue sortie in May 1971. The World Trade Center helipad is 1385 ft *422 m* above street level in New York City on the South Tower.

Circumnavigation

H. Ross Perot, 23 and Jay Coburn both of Dallas, Texas made the first helicopter circumnavigation in 'Spirit of Texas' on 1–30 Sept 1982. The first solo round-the-world flight in a helicopter was completed by Dick Smith (Australia) on 22 July 1983. Flown from and to the Bell Helicopter facility at Fort Worth, Texas, in a Bell Model 206L Long Ranger III, his unhurried flight began on 5 Aug 1982 and covered a distance of 35,258 miles *56 742 km*.

AUTOGYROS

Earliest

The autogyro or gyroplane, a rotorcraft with an unpowered rotor turned by the airflow in flight, preceded the practical helicopter with engine-driven rotor. Juan de la Cierva (Spain), made the first successful autogyro flight with his model C.4 (commercially named an *Autogiro*) at Getafe, Spain, on 9 Jan 1923.

Speed, altitude and distance records

Wing Cdr Kenneth H. Wallis (GB) holds the straight-line distance record of 543.27 miles *874,32 km* set in his WA-116F autogyro on 28 Sept 1975 non-stop from Lydd, Kent to Wick, Highland. Wg Cdr Wallis flew his WA-116, with 72 hp McCulloch engine, to a record speed of 111.2 mph *179 km/h* over a 3 km *1.86 mile* straight course on 12 May 1969. On 20 July 1982, flying from Boscombe Down, Wiltshire, he established a new autogyro altitude record of 18,516 ft *5643,7 m* in his WA-121/Mc. This, the smallest and lightest Wallis autogyro to date, is powered by a 100 hp Wallis/McCulloch engine.

FLYING-BOAT

Fastest

The fastest flying-boat ever built has been the Martin XP6M-1 *Seamaster*, the US Navy 4 jet engined minelayer flown in 1955–9 with a top speed of 646 mph *1040 km/h*. In September 1946 the Martin JRM-2 *Mars* flying-boat set a payload record of 68,327 lb *30 992 kg*. The official flying-boat speed record is 566.69 mph *912 km/h*, set up by Nikolai Andrievsky and crew of two in a Soviet Beriev M-10, powered by two AL-7 turbojets, over a 15 to 25 km course on 7 Aug 1961. The M-10 holds all 12 records listed for jet-powered flying-boats, including an altitude of 49,088 ft *14 962 m* set by Georgiy Buryanov and crew over the Sea of Azov on 9 Sept 1961.

AIRSHIPS

Earliest

The earliest flight in an airship was by Henri Giffard from Paris in his steam-powered coal-gas 88,300 ft³ *2500 m³* 144 ft *43,8 m* long airship on 24 Sept 1852. The earliest British airship was a 20,000 ft³ *566 m³* 75 ft *22,8 m* long craft built by Stanley Spencer whose maiden flight was from Crystal Palace, Bromley, Greater London on 22 Sept 1902. The latest airship to be built in Britain is the 235,400 ft³ *6666 m³* 193.6 ft *59 m* long Skyship 600 designed and built by Airship Industries. This 20 passenger dirigible (G-SKSC) was flown for the first time at RAE Cardington, Bedfordshire on 6 Mar 1984.

Largest *Rigid*

The largest rigid airship ever built was the 210.5 ton *213,9 tonne* German *Graf Zeppelin II* (LZ 130), with a length of 245 m *803.8 ft* and a capacity of 7,062,100 ft³ *199 981 m³*. She made her maiden flight on 14 Sept 1938 and in May and August 1939 made radar spying missions in British air space. She was dismantled in April 1940. Her sister ship *Hindenburg* was 5.6 ft *1,70 m* longer.

British

The largest British airship was the R101 built by the Royal Airship Works, Cardington, Bedfordshire, which first flew on 14 Oct 1929. She was 777 ft *236,8 m* in length and had a capacity of 5,508,800 ft³ *155 995 m³*. She crashed near Beauvais, France, killing 48 aboard on 5 Oct 1930.

Non-Rigid

The largest non-rigid airship ever constructed was the US Navy ZPG 3-W which had a capacity of 1,516,300 ft³ *42 937 m³*, was 403.4 ft *122,9 m* long and 85.1 ft *25,93 m* in diameter, with a crew of 21. She first flew on 21 July 1958, but crashed into the sea in June 1960.

Hot-Air

The world altitude, duration and distance records, of 10,365 ft *3159 m*, 1 hr 26 min 52 sec, and 23.03 miles *37,07 km* respectively, are held by the Cameron D-38 hot-air airship flown at Cunderdin, W. Australia on 27 Aug 1982 by R. W. Taaffe (Australia).

Greatest passenger load

The most people ever carried in an airship was 207 in the US Navy *Akron* in 1931. The trans-Atlantic record is 117 by the German *Hindenburg* in 1937.

Distance records

The FAI accredited straight line distance record for airships is 3967.1 miles *6384,5 km*, set up by the German *Graf Zeppelin*, captained by Dr Hugo Eckener, between 29 Oct and 1 Nov 1928. The German Zeppelin L59 flew from Yambol, Bulgaria to south of Khartoum, Sudan and returned on 21–25 Nov 1917 to cover a minimum of 4500 miles *7250 km*.

The first crossing of the United States was by *Super Chicken III* (pilots Fred Gorell and John Shoecraft) from Costa Mesa, California, 2515 miles *4047 km* to Blackbeard's Island, Georgia on 9–12 Oct 1981.

Duration record

The longest recorded flight by a non-rigid airship (without refuelling) is 264 hr 12 min by a US Navy Goodyear-built ZPG-2 class ship (Cdr J. R. Hunt USN) from South Weymouth NAS, Massachusetts, USA on 4–15 Mar 1957 landing back at Key West, Florida, USA having flown 9448 miles *15 205 km*.

BALLOONING

Earliest

The earliest recorded ascent was by a model hot air balloon invented by Father Bartolomeu de Gusmão (*né* Lourenço) (b. Santos, Brazil, 1685), which was flown indoors at the Casa da India, Terreiro do Paço, Portugal on 8 Aug 1709.

Distance record (*Great-circle distance between take-off and first landing point*)

The record distance travelled by a balloon is 5208.68 miles *8382,54 km* by the Raven experimental helium-filled balloon *Double Eagle V* (capacity 11 300 m³ *399,053 ft³*) on 9–12 Nov 1981, from Nagashima, Japan to Covello, California. The crew for this first manned balloon crossing of the Pacific Ocean was Ben L. Abruzzo, 51, Rocky Aoki, 43 (Japan), Ron Clark, 41 and Larry M. Newman, 34.

Highest *Unmanned*

The highest altitude attained by an unmanned balloon was 170,000 ft *51 815 m* by a Winzen balloon of 47.8 million ft³ *1,35 million m³* launched at Chico, California in October 1972.

Manned

The greatest altitude reached in a manned balloon is the unofficial 123,800 ft (23.45 miles *37 735 m*) by Nicholas Piantanida (1933–66) of Bricktown, New Jersey, USA, from Sioux Falls, South Dakota, USA, on 1 Feb 1966. He landed in a cornfield in Iowa but did not survive. The official record is 113,740 ft *34 668 m* by Cdr Malcolm D. Ross, USNR and the late Lt-Cdr Victor A. Prother, USN in an ascent from the deck of USS *Antietam* on 4 May 1961, over the Gulf of Mexico.

Largest

The largest balloon built is one with an inflatable volume of 70 million ft³ *2 million m³* by Winzen Research Inc, Minnesota, USA.

Ballooning (*Hot-Air*)

(Modern revival began in USA in 1961. First World Championships 10–17 Feb 1973 at Albuquerque, New Mexico, USA.)

The world's distance record for hot-air balloons is 717.52 miles *1154,74 km*, set by French balloonists Michel Arnould and Hélène Dorigny on 25–26 Nov 1981 in the Cameron Type A-530 *Semiramis* from Ballina, County Mayo, Eire to St Christophe-en-Boucherie, France. This flight has also been homologated by the FAI as a new world duration record for hot-air balloons of 29 hr 5 min 48 sec, and in addition the *Semiramis* is now the largest hot-air balloon ever built with a volume of 530,000 ft³ *15 008 m³*. On 31 Oct 1980 Julian Nott (GB) attained an altitude, which has been ratified by the FAI, of 55,137 ft *16 805 m*, taking off from Longmont, near Denver, Colorado, USA, in the Cameron-built ICI balloon *Innovation*. The FAI endurance and distance record for a gas and hot-air balloon is 96 hr 24 min and 2074.817 miles *3339,086 km* by *Zanussi* crewed by Donald Allan Cameron (GB) and Major Christopher Davey which failed by only 103 miles *166 km* to achieve the first balloon crossing of the Atlantic on 30 July 1978.

The record altitude in an open basket is 53,000 ft *16 154,4 m* by Chauncey M. Dunn (US) on 1 Aug 1979. He wore a pressure suit.

PERSONAL AVIATION RECORDS

Oldest and Youngest Passengers

Airborne births are reported every year. The oldest person to fly has been Mrs Jessica S. Swift (b. Anna Stewart 17 Sept 1871) aged 110 yrs 3 months, from Vermont to Florida, USA in Dec 1981. The oldest Briton to fly was probably Mrs Julia Caroline Black (b. 24 Feb 1874 d. 12 May 1980) on a British Caledonian flight from Abbotsinch to Gatwick on 17 Nov 1978 when aged 104 years 8 months.

Youngest and Oldest pilots

The youngest age at which anyone has ever qualified as a military pilot is 15 yr 5 months in the case of Sgt Thomas Dobney (b. 6 May 1926) of the RAF. He had overstated his age (14 yr) on entry. The youngest solo pilot has been Cody A. Locke in a Cessna 150 aircraft near Mexiculi, Mexico on 24 Feb 1983, when aged 9 years 316 days. The wholly untutored James A. Stoodley aged 14 years 5 months took his 13 year old brother John on a 29 minute joy ride in an unattended US Piper Cub trainer aircraft near Ludgershall, Wiltshire in December 1942.

The world's oldest pilot is Ed McCarty (b. 18 Sept 1885) of Kimberly, Idaho, USA, who in 1979 was flying his rebuilt 30-year-old Ercoupe aged 94. The oldest British pilot is Air Commodore Harold 'Daddy' Probyn CB, CBE, DSO (b. 8 Dec 1891), who first flew with the RFC in 1916 and was flying in Kenya on his 92nd birthday 67 years later in 1983.

Most flying hours

Max Conrad (1903–79) (USA) between 1928 and mid-1974 totalled 52,929 hr 40 min logged flight—more than 6 years airborne. He completed 150 trans-Atlantic crossings in light aircraft. The record as a supersonic passenger is by Mr Fred Finn who made his 476th Concorde crossing in June 1984.

Most take-offs and landings from airports

Al Yates and Bob Phoenix of Texas, USA made 193 take-offs and daylight landings at unduplicated airfields in 14 hr 57 min in a Piper Seminole, on 15 June 1979.

Human-powered flight

The world distance record for human powered flight was set on 12 June 1979 by Dr Paul MacCready's man powered aircraft *Gossamer Albatross*, piloted and pedalled by Bryan Allen. The *Albatross* took off from Folkestone at 05.51 hrs and landed 22.26 miles *35,82 km* distant at Cap Gris Nez, France at 08.40 hrs. The duration was 2 hr 49 min, and this achievement won the £100,000 prize offered by Henry Kremer for the first man-powered crossing of the English Channel. The 70 lb *31,75 kg Gossamer Condor* (96 ft *29,26 m* wing-span) designed by Dr Paul MacCready, flew the figure-of-8 course between pylons 880 yd *804,6 m* apart, powered by the 9¾ stone *61,2 kg* Bryan Allen at Shafter Airport, California on 23 Aug 1977 to win the £50,000 Kremer prize. The flight lasted 7 min 27.5 sec.

MODEL AIRCRAFT

Altitude, speed and duration

Maynard L. Hill (US) flying radio-controlled models established the World record for altitude of 26,929 ft *8208 m* on 6 Sept 1970 and on 4 July 1983 set a closed circuit distance record of 1231 miles *765 km*. The free flight speed record is 213.70 mph *343,92 km/h* by V. Goukoune and V. Myakinin (both USSR) with a radio-controlled model at Klementyeva, USSR, on 21 Sept 1971. The record duration flight is one of 32 hr 7 min 40 sec by Eduard Svoboda (Czechoslovakia), flying a radio controlled glider on 23–24 Aug 1980. An indoor model powered by a rubber motor designed by J. Richmond (USA) set a duration record of 52 min 14 sec on 31 Aug 1979.

Cross-channel

The first cross-channel model helicopter flight was achieved

Cody Locke, who flew solo in a Cessna 150 aircraft when aged only 9 years 316 days.

by an 11 lb *5,00 kg* model Bell 212 radio-controlled by Dieter Zeigler for 32 miles *52 km* between Ashford, Kent and Ambleteuse, France on 17 July 1974.

Smallest

The smallest model aircraft to fly is one weighing 0.004 oz *0,1 g* powered by attaching a horsefly and designed by the insectonaut Don Emmick of Seattle, Washington, USA on 24 July 1979. One flew for 5 minutes at Kirkland, Washington, USA.

Paper aircraft

The flight duration record for a paper aircraft is 16.89 sec by Ken Blackburn in the Reynolds Coliseum, North Carolina State University, USA on 29 Nov 1983. The indoor record with a 12 ft *3,65 m* ceiling is 1 min 33 sec set in the Fuji TV studios, Tokyo, Japan on 21 Sept 1980. A paper plane was reported and witnessed to have flown 1¼ miles *2,0 km* by 'Chick' C. O. Reinhart from a 10th storey office window at 60 Beaver Street, New York City across the East River to Brooklyn in August 1933, helped by a thermal from a coffee-roasting plant. An indoor distance of 155 ft 7 in *47,42 m* was recorded by Eugene Sykes at the McChord Air Force Base, Washington, USA, on 4 Feb 1982.

5. POWER PRODUCERS

Steam engines

The oldest steam engine in working order is the 1812 Boulton & Watt 26 hp 42 in *1066 mm* bore beam engine on the Kennet & Avon Canal at Great Bedwyn, Wiltshire. It was restored by the Crofton Society in 1971 and still runs periodically.

The largest single cylinder steam engine ever built was that designed by Matthew Loam of Cornwall and made by the Hayle Foundry Co in 1849 for installation for land draining at Haarlem Netherlands. The cylinder was 12 ft *3,65 m* in diameter such that each stroke also of 12 ft *3,65 m* lifted 13,440 gallons *61 096 l* or 60 tons of water.

The most efficient steam engine recorded was Taylor's engine built by Michael Loam for the United Mines, Gwennap, Cornwall in 1840. It registered only 1.7 lb of coal per horsepower per hour.

Earliest atomic pile

The world's first atomic pile was built in a disused squash court at Stagg Field, University of Chicago, Illinois, USA. It went 'critical' at 3.25 pm on 2 Dec 1942.

Power plant Largest *World*

Currently, the world's most powerful installed power station is the Grand Coulee, Washington State, USA with 9.7 million kilowatt hours (ultimately 10,080 MW) which began operating in 1942.

The $11 billion Itaipu power station on the Paraña river by the Brazil-Paraguay border began generating power in 1983 and will by 1988/89 attain 12,600,000 kW from 18 turbines. Construction began in 1975 with a force reaching 28,000 workers. A 20,000 MW power station project on the Tunguska River, USSR was announced in February 1982.

The world's largest coal-fired power complex at Ekibastuz, Kazakhstan, USSR began generating in May 1982.

Great Britain

The power station with the greatest installed capacity in Great Britain is Longannet, Fife, Scotland which attained 2400 MW by December 1972. At Drax, North Yorkshire, 6 × 660 MW sets yielding 3960 MW are expected to be in commission by 1984. A 3300 MW oil-fired installation is under construction on the Isle of Grain, Kent.

The largest hydroelectric plant in the UK is the North of Scotland Hydroelectricity Board's Power Station at Loch Sloy, Strathclyde. The installed capacity of this station is 130 MW. The Ben Cruachan Pumped Storage scheme was opened on 15 Oct 1965 at Loch Awe, Strathclyde, Scotland. It has a capacity of 400 MW and cost £24,000,000. The 1880 MW underground pumped storage scheme at Dinorwig, Gwynedd is the largest built in Europe with a head of 1739 ft *530 m* and a capacity of 13,770 ft³/sec *390 m³/sec*. The £425 million plant was completed in 1984 and the capacity is 1681 MW.

Nuclear power station *Largest*

The world's largest atomic power station with 4 × 950 MW reactors giving 3800 MW is the station in Leningrad, USSR. Work began in 1974 and it attained full operation in October 1982.

Nuclear reactor *Largest*

The largest single nuclear reactor in the world is the 1500 MW reactor at the Ignalinskaya station, Lithuania, USSR, put on full power in Jan 1984. The largest in the US is the 1255 MW reactor installed at Grand Gulf I, Port Gibson, Mississippi in 1983.

Fusion power

Tokamak-7, the prototype thermonuclear reactor was declared in January 1982 by USSR academician Velikhov to be operating 'reliably for months on end'. The world's largest experimental station is the Joint European Torus at Culham, Oxfordshire built in 1979–84.

Solar power plant

The largest solar furnace in the world is the $141 million 10 megawatt 'Solar I', 12 miles *19,3 km* southeast of Barstow, California first tested in April 1982. It comprises 1818 mirrors in concentric circles focused on a boiler atop a 255 ft *77,7 m* high tower. Sunlight from 222 heliostats is concentrated on a target 114 ft *34,7 m* up in the power tower. The $30 million thermal solar energy system at Pakerland Packing Co, Bellevue Plant, Green Bay, Wisconsin, USA completed in Jan 1984 comprises 9750 4 × 8 ft *1,21 × 2,43 m* collectors covering 7.16 acres *or 28 985 m²*. It will yield up to 8000 million BTU's a month.

Tidal power station

The world's first major tidal power station is the *Usine marèmotrice de la Rance*, officially opened on 26 Nov 1966 at the Rance estuary in the Golfe de St Malo, Brittany, France. It was built in five years at a cost of 420,000,000 francs (£34,685,000), and has a net annual output of 544,000,000 kWh. The 880 yd *804 m* barrage contains 24 turbo alternators. The $1000 million (£540 million) Passamaquoddy project for the Bay of Fundy in Maine, USA, and New Brunswick, Canada, remains a project. A $46 million (*then* £25.5 million) pilot Annapolis River project for the Bay of Fundy was begun in 1981.

Boiler Largest

The largest boilers ever designed are those ordered in the United States from the Babcock & Wilcox Company (USA) with a capacity of 1330 MW so involving the evaporation of 9,330,000 lb *4 232 000 kg* of steam per hour. The largest boilers now being installed in the United Kingdom are the three 660 MW units for the Drax Power Station (see p. 152) designed and constructed by Babcock & Wilcox Ltd.

Generator Largest

Generators in the 2,000,000 kW (or 2000 MW) range are now in the planning stages both in the UK and the USA. The largest under construction is a Turbo-Generator of 1500 MW being installed at the Ignalina Atomic Power Station in Lithuania.

Turbines Largest

The largest hydraulic turbines are those rated at 815,000 kW (equivalent to 1.1 million hp), 32 ft *9,7 m* in diameter with a 401 ton *407 tonnes* runner and a 312½ ton *317,5 tonnes* shaft installed by Allis-Chalmers at the Grand Coulee 'Third Powerplant', Washington, USA.

Pump

The world's largest reversible pump-turbine is that made by Allis-Chalmers for the Bath County project, Virginia, USA. It has a maximum rating of 457 MW as a turbine and maximum operating head of 393 m *1289 ft*. The impeller/runner diameter is 6349 mm *20 ft 9 in* with a synchronous speed of 257.1 rpm.

Longest Lasting Battery

The zinc foil and sulfur dry pile batteries made by Watlin and Hill of London in 1840 have powered ceaseless tintinnabulation inside a bell jar at the Clarendon Laboratory, Oxford since 1840. The first 'perpetual motion' patent filed under the World Patent Cooperation Treaty was No 80/00866 by Edmund and Robert Kraus of California, USA.

Gasworks Largest

The flow of natural gas from the North Sea is diminishing the manufacture of gas by the carbonisation of coal and the reforming process using petroleum derivatives. Britain's largest ever gasworks, 300 acres *120 ha*, were at Beckton, Newham. Currently, the largest gasworks in the UK are the Breakwater Works at Oreston, Plymouth, Devon which opened in 1966–7 and cover an area of 19 acres *7,6 ha*. They convert complex hydrocarbons into methane and produce 50 million ft³ *1 415 850 m³* per day.

Biggest black-out

The greatest power failure in history struck seven north-eastern US States and Ontario, Canada, on 9–10 Nov 1965. About 30,000,000 people in 80,000 miles² *207 200 km²* were plunged into darkness. Only two were killed. In New York City the power failed at 5.27 pm and was not fully restored for 13½ hr. The total consequential losses in the 52 min New York City power failure of 13 July 1977 including looting was put at $1 billion (*then £580 million*).

Windmill Earliest

The earliest recorded windmills are those used for grinding corn in Iran (Persia) in the 7th century AD.

The earliest date attributed to a windmill in England is 1185 for one at Weedley, near Hull, Humberside. The oldest Dutch mill is the towermill at Zeddam, Gelderland built in *c*. 1450. The oldest working mill in England is the post-mill at Outwood, Surrey, built in 1665, though the Ivinghoe Mill in Pitstone Green Farm, Buckinghamshire, dating from 1627, has been restored. The postmill in North Ronaldsay, Orkney Islands operated until 1905.

Windmill Largest

The world's most powerful wind generator is the 3000 kW 150 m *492 ft* tall turbine, built by Grosse Wind energie–Anlage which was set up in 1982 on the Friesian coast of West Germany. A £5.6 million 3000 kW aerogenerator with 60 m *196 ft 10 in* blades on Burgar Hill, Evie, Orkney is planned for completion by Taylor Woodrow in 1985. It should yield 9 million kW/hours per annum. The $14.2 million GEC MOD-5A installation on the North shore of Oahu, Hawaii, USA will produce 7300 kW when the wind reaches 32 mph *51,5 km/h* with 400 ft *122 m* rotors. Installation started in March 1984.

Windmill *Largest conventional*

The largest Dutch windmill is the Dijkpolder in Maasland built in 1718. The sails measure 95¾ ft *29 m* from tip to tip. The tallest windmill in the Netherlands is De Walvisch in Schiedam built to a height of 108 ft *33 m* in 1794. The tallest windmill still standing in Britain is the 9 storey Sutton mill, Norfolk built in 1853 which before being struck by lightning in 1941 had sails 73 ft *22,2 m* in diameter with 216 shutters.

above: The COMILOG ropeway in Gabon, West Africa, which is the world's longest conveyor belt extending for 76 km *47.2 miles.*
right: The world's largest blast furnace at the Ōita works, Kyūshū, Japan, with an inner volume of 5070 m³ *179,040 ft³. below right:* The world's longest single flight conveyor belt in Western Australia which measures 18 miles *29 km.*

6. ENGINEERING

Blast furnace Largest

The world's largest blast furnace is one with an inner volume of 5070 m³ *179,040 ft³* and a 14,8 m *48 ft 6¼ in* diameter hearth at the Oita Works, Kyūshū, Japan completed in October 1976 with an annual capacity of 4,380,000 tons *4 451 500 tonnes.*

Cat cracker Largest

The world's largest catalyst cracker is the Exxon Co's Bayway Refinery plant at Linden, New Jersey, USA with a fresh feed rate of 5,040,000 US gal *19 077 000 litres* per day.

Conveyor belt Longest

The world's longest single flight conveyor belt is one of 18 miles *29 km* in Western Australia by Cable Belt Ltd of Camberley, Surrey. The longest installation in Great Britain is also by Cable Belt and of 5½ miles *8,9 km* underground at Longannet Power Station, Fife, Scotland. The world's longest multi-flight conveyor is one of 100 km *62 miles* between the phosphate mine near Bucraa and the port of El Aaiun, Morocco, built by Krupps and completed in 1972. It has 11 flights of between 9 and 11 km *5.6–6.8 miles* and was driven at 4,5 m/sec *10.06 mph* but has been closed down due to Polisario Front guerrilla activity.

The longest conveyor belt in the world is the Compagnie Minère de l'Ogooué or COMILOG installation built in 1959–62 for the Moanda manganese mine in Gabon which extends 76 km *47.2 miles.* It has 858 towers and 2800 buckets with 155 km *96.3 miles* of wire rope running over 6000 idler pulleys.

Crane Most Powerful *World*

The world's most powerful cranes are those aboard the semi-submersible vessel *Balder* (105,000 tonnes displacement) operated by Heerema Marine Contractors, Switzerland. Each has one 3000 and one 2000 tonne capacity crane which, working in tandem, could raise a 4000 tonne piece. The *Balder* set a record with a 3412 tonne lift in Aug 1983 and in March 1984 was refitted to raise her capacity to close to 6000 tonnes. The American company Brown & Root announced the building of a 140 000 tonne crane-ship with lifting capacity of 6500 tonnes in December 1983.

Gantry crane Most powerful

The 92.3 ft *28,14 m* wide Rahco (R. A. Hanson Disc. Ltd) gantry crane at the Grand Coulee Dam Third Powerplant was tested to lift a load of 2232 long tons *2268 tonnes* in 1975. It lowered a 3,944,000 lb *1789 tonne* generator rotor with an accuracy of $\frac{1}{32}$ in *0,8 mm*.

Crane Tallest mobile

The tallest mobile crane in the world is the 810 tonnes Rosenkranz K10001 with a lifting capacity of 1000 tonnes *984 tons*, a combined boom and jib height of 202 m *663 ft*. It is carried on 10 trucks each limited to 75 ft 8 in *23,06 m* and an axle weight of 118 tonnes *116 tons*. It can lift 30 tonnes *29.5 tons* to a height of 106 m *525 ft*.

Dragline Largest *World*

The Ural Engineering Works at Ordzhonikdze, USSR, completed in March 1962, has a dragline known as the ES-25(100) with a boom of 100 m *328 ft* and a bucket with a capacity of 31.5 yd³ *24 m³*. The world's largest walking dragline is the Bucyrus-Erie 4250W with an all-up weight of 12,000 tons *12 192 tonnes* and a bucket capacity of 220 yd³ *168 m³* on a 310 ft *94,4 m* boom. This machine, the world's largest mobile land machine, is now operating on the Central Ohio Coal Company's Muskingum site in Ohio, USA.

Great Britain

The largest dragline excavator in Britain is 'Big Geordie', the Bucyrus-Erie 1550W 6250 gross hp, weighing 3000 tons *3048 tonnes* with a forward mast 160 ft *48,7 m* high. On open-cast coal workings at Butterwell, Northumberland in September 1975, it proved able to strip 100 tons *101 tonnes* of overburden in 65 sec with its 65 yd³ *49,7 m³* bucket on a 265 ft *80,7 m* boom. It is owned by Derek Crouch (Contractors) Ltd of Peterborough, Cambridgeshire.

Escalator Longest

The term was registered in the US on 28 May 1900 but the earliest 'Inclined Escalator' was installed by Jesse W. Reno on the pier at Coney Island, New York in 1896. The first installation in Britain was at Harrods, Knightsbridge, London in November 1898. The escalators on the Leningrad Underground, USSR at Lenin Square have 729 steps and a vertical rise of 59,68 m *195 ft 9½ in*. The longest escalators in Britain are the four in the Tyne Tunnel, Tyne and Wear installed in 1951. They measure 192 ft 8 in *58,7 m* between combs with a vertical lift of 85 ft *25,9 m* and a step speed of up to 1.7 mph *2,7 km/h*. The world's longest 'moving sidewalks' are those installed in 1970 in the Neue Messe Centre, Dusseldorf, W. Germany which measure 225 m *738 ft* between comb plates. The longest in Great Britain is the 375 ft *114,3 m* long Dunlop Starglide at London Airport Terminal 3 installed in March-May 1970.

Excavator Largest

The world's largest excavator is the 13,000 tonne bucket wheel excavator being assembled at the open cast lignite-mine of Hambach, W. Germany with a rating of 200 000 m³ *260,000 yd³* per 20 hr working day. It is 210 m *690 ft* in length and 82 m *269 ft* tall. The wheel is 67,88 m *222 ft* in circumference with 5 m³ *6.5 yd³* buckets.

Forging Largest

The largest forging on record is one of a 450,600 lb *204,4 tonnes* 55 ft *16,76 m* long generator shaft for Japan, forged by the Bethlehem Steel Corp, Pennsylvania in October 1973.

Lathe Largest

The world's largest lathe is the 126 ft *38,4 m* long 416,2 tonne giant lathe built by Waldrich Siegen of Germany in 1973 for the South African Electricity Supply Commission at Rosherville. It has a capacity for 300 tonne work pieces and a swing-over bed of 5 m *16 ft 5 in* in diameter.

Greatest lift

The heaviest lifting operation in engineering history was the 41,000 short ton (36,607 long tons *37 194 tonnes*) roof of the Velodrome in Montreal, Canada in 1975. It was raised by jacks some 4 in *10 cm* to strike its centering.

Oldest machinery *World*

The earliest machinery still in use is the *dâlu*—a water-raising instrument known to have been in use in the Sumerian civilization which originated *c.* 3500 BC in Lower Iraq thus even earlier than the *Saqiyas* on the Nile.

Great Britain

The oldest piece of machinery (excluding clocks) operating in the United Kingdom is the snuff mill driven by a water wheel at Messrs Wilson & Co's Sharrow Mill in Sheffield, South Yorkshire. It is known to have been operating in 1797 and more probably since 1730.

Nut Largest

The largest nuts ever made weigh 5,3 tonnes *104.3 cwt* each and have an outside diameter of 52 in *132 cm* and a 25 in *63,5 cm* thread. Known as 'Pilgrim Nuts', they are manufactured by Doncasters Moorside Ltd of Oldham, Lancashire for use on the columns of a large forging press.

Oil tank Largest

The largest oil tanks ever constructed are the five Aramco 1½ million barrel storage tanks at Ju'aymah, Saudi Arabia. The tanks are 72 ft *21,94 m* tall with a diameter of 386 ft *117,6 m* and were completed in March 1980.

Passenger lift Fastest *World*

The fastest domestic passenger lifts in the world are the express lifts to the 60th floor of the 240 m *787.4 ft* tall 'Sunshine 60' building, Ikebukuro, Tōkyō, Japan completed 5 Apr 1978. They were built by Mitsubishi Corp and operate at a speed of 2000 ft/min *609,6 m/min* or 22.72 mph *36,56 km/h*. Much higher speeds are achieved in the winding cages of mine shafts. A hoisting shaft 6800 ft *2072 m* deep, owned by Western Deep Levels Ltd in South Africa, winds at speeds of up to 40.9 mph *65,8 km/h* (3595 ft *1095 m* per min). Otitis-media (popping of the ears) presents problems much above even 10 mph *16 km/h*.

Great Britain

The longest lift in the United Kingdom is one 930 ft long inside the B.B.C. T.V. tower at Bilsdale, West Moor, North Yorkshire, built by J. L. Eve Construction Co Ltd. It runs at 130 ft/min *39,6 m/min*. The longest fast lifts are the two 15-passenger cars in the Post Office Tower, Maple Street, London W1 which travel 540 ft *164 m* at up to 1000 ft/min *304 m/min*.

Michael Bracey established an involuntary duration record when trapped in a lift for 59 hr 55 min in Newcastle-upon-Tyne, England on 29 Feb 1980.

Pipelines *Oil*

The world's earliest pipeline of 2 in *5 cm* cast iron laid at Oil Creek, Pennsylvania, USA in 1863 was torn up by trade unionists.

The longest crude oil pipeline in the world is the Interprovincial Pipe Line Company's installation from Edmonton, Alberta, Canada to Buffalo, New York State, USA, a distance of 1775 miles *2856 km*. Along the length of the pipe 13 pumping stations maintain a flow of 6,900,000 gal *31 367 145 litres* of oil per day. The eventual length of the Trans-Siberian Pipeline will be 2319 miles *3732 km*, running from Tuimazy through Omsk and Novosibirsk to Irkutsk. The first 30 mile *48 km* section was opened in July 1957.

Submarine pipelines

The world's longest submarine pipeline is that of 425 km *264 miles* for natural gas from the Union Oil Platform to Rayong, Thailand opened on 12 Sept 1981. The longest North Sea pipeline is the Ekofisk–Emden line stretching 260 miles *418 km* and completed in July 1975. The deepest North Sea pipeline is that from the Cormorant Field to Firths Voe, Shetland at 530 ft *162 m*.

Natural gas

The longest natural gas pipeline in the world is the Trans-Canada Pipeline which by 1974 had 5654 miles *9099 km* of pipe up to 42 in *106,6 cm* in diameter. The Tyumen–Chelyabinsk–Moscow–Brandenburg gasline stretches 4330 km *2690 miles*.

The large calibre Urengoi-Uzhgorod line to Western Europe began in November 1982 stretches 4451 km *2765 miles* and was completed on 25 July 1983. It has a capacity of 32,000 million m³ *42,000 million yd³* per annum.

Water

The world's longest water pipeline runs from the Jubail desalination plant to Riyadh, Saudi Arabia over 470 km *292 miles* and was opened in April 1983.

Pipeline Most expensive

The world's most expensive pipeline is the Alaska pipeline running 798 miles *1284 km* from Prudhoe Bay to Valdez. By completion of the first phase in 1977 it had cost at least $6000 million (£3250 million). The pipe is 48 in *1,21 m* diameter and will eventually carry up to 2 million barrels of crude oil per day.

Press Largest

The world's two most powerful production machines are forging presses in the USA. The Loewy closed-die forging press, in a plant leased from the US Air Force by the Wyman-Gordon Company at North Grafton, Massachusetts, USA weighs 9469 tons *9620 tonnes* and stands 114 ft 2 in *34,79 m* high, of which 66 ft *20,1 m* is sunk below the operating floor. It has a rated capacity of 44,600 tons *45 315 tonnes*, and went into operation in October 1955. The other similar press is at the plant of the Aluminium Company of America at Cleveland, Ohio. There has been a report of a press in the USSR with a capacity of 75 000 tonnes *73,800 tons* at Novo Kramatorsk. The Bêché and Grohs counter-blow forging hammer, manufactured in W. Germany are rated at 60,000 tonnes/*tons*. The most powerful press in Great Britain is the closed-die forging and extruding press installed in 1967 at the Cameron Iron Works, Livingston, Lothian. The press is 92 ft *28 m* tall (27 ft *8,2 m* below ground) and exerts a force of 30,000 tons *30 481 tonnes*.

Printer Fastest

The world's fastest printer is the Radiation Inc electro-sensitive system at the Lawrence Radiation Laboratory, Livermore, California. High speed recording of up to 30,000 lines each containing 120 alphanumeric characters per minute is attained by controlling electronic pulses through chemically impregnated recording paper which is rapidly moving under closely spaced fixed styli. It can thus print the wordage of the whole Bible (773,692 words) in 65 sec—3333 times as fast as the world's fastest typist.

Radar installation *Largest*

The largest of the three installations in the US Ballistic Missile Early Warning System (BMEWS) is that near Thule, in Greenland, 931 miles *1498 km* from the North Pole, completed in 1960 at a cost of $500,000,000 (then £178.5 million). Its sister stations are one at Cape Clear, Alaska, USA, completed in 1961, and a $115,000,000 (then £41.07 million) installation at Fylingdales Moor, North Yorkshire, completed in June 1963. The largest scientific radar installation is the 21 acre *84 000 m²* ground array at Jicamarca, Peru.

Ropeway or telepherique Highest *World*

The highest and longest aerial ropeway in the world is the Teleférico Mérida (Mérida téléphérique) in Venezuela, from Mérida City (5379 ft *1639,5 m*) to the summit of Pico Espejo (15,629 ft *4763,7 m*), a rise of 10,250 ft *3124 m*. The ropeway is in four sections, involving 3 car changes in the 8 mile ascent in 1 hr. The fourth span is 10,070 ft *3069 m* in length. The two cars work on the pendulum system—the carrier rope is locked and the cars are hauled by means of three pull ropes powered by a 230 hp *233 cv* motor. They have a maximum capacity of 45 persons and travel at 32 ft *9,7 m* per sec (21.8 mph *35,08 km/h*). The longest single span ropeway is the 13,500 ft *4114 m* span from the Coachella Valley to Mt San Jacinto (10,821 ft *3298 m*), California, USA, inaugurated on 12 Sept 1963.

The world's longest wire ropes being coiled onto a transfer barge by a Honda motorcycle for eventual use by the CEGB cross-Channel power cable. Each of these 4 ropes measures 14.9 miles *24 km* long. (*Northern Photographic Service*)

Great Britain

Britain's longest cabin lift is that at Llandudno, Gwynedd, opened in June 1969. It has 42 cabins with a capacity of 1000 people per hour and is 5320 ft *1621 m* in length.

Transformer Largest

The world's largest single phase transformers are rated at 1,500,000 kV of which eight are in service with the American Electric Power Corporation. Of these five stepdown from 765 to 345 kV. Britain's largest transformers are those rated at 1,000,000 kVa 400/275 kV built by Hackbridge & Hewittic Co Ltd, Walton-on-Thames, Surrey first commissioned for the CEGB in October 1968.

Transmission lines *Longest*

The longest span between pylons of any power line in the world is that across the Sogne Fjord, Norway, between Rabnaberg and Fatlaberg. Supplied in 1955 by the Whitecross Co Ltd of Warrington, Cheshire, and projected and erected by A. S. Betonmast of Oslo as part of the high-tension power cable from Refsdal power station at Vik, it has a span of 16,040 ft *4888 m* and a weight of 12 tons/*tonnes*. In 1967 two further high tensile steel/aluminium lines 16,006 ft *4878 m* long, and weighing 33 tons *33,5 tonnes*, manufactured by Whitecross and BICC were erected here. The longest in Britain are the 5310 ft *1618 m* lines built by J. L. Eve Co across the Severn with main towers each 488 ft *148 m* high.

Highest

The world's highest are those across the Straits of Messina, with towers of 675 ft *205 m* (Sicily side) and 735 ft *224 m* (Calabria) and 11,900 ft *3627 m* apart. The highest lines in Britain are those made by BICC at West Thurrock, Essex, which cross the Thames estuary suspended from 630 ft *192 m* tall towers at a minimum height of 250 ft *76 m*, with a 130 ton *132 tonnes* breaking load. They are 4500 ft *1371 m* in length.

Highest voltages

The highest voltages now carried are 1,330,000 volts 1224 miles *1970 km* on the DC Pacific Inter-tie in the United States. The Ekibastuz DC transmission lines in Kazakhstan, USSR are planned to be 2400 km *1490 miles* long with 1,500,000 volt capacity.

Valve Largest

The world's largest valve is the 32 ft *9,75 m* diameter, 170 ton/*tonne* butterfly valve designed by Boving & Co Ltd of London

for use at the Arnold Airforce Base engine test facility in Tennessee, USA.

Wire ropes *Longest, Strongest and Heaviest*

The longest wire ropes in the world are the 4 made at British Ropes Ltd, Wallsend, Tyneside each measuring 24 000 m *14.9 miles*. The ropes are 35 mm *1.3 in* in diameter, weigh 108,5 tonnes *106.8 tons* each and were ordered by the CEGB for use in the construction of the 2000 MW cross-Channel power cable. The thickest ever made are spliced crane strops from wire ropes 28,2 cm *11¼ in* thick made of 2392 individual wires in March 1979 by British Ropes Ltd of Doncaster at Willington Quay, Tyneside, designed to lift loads of up to 3000 tons/*tonnes*. The heaviest ever wire ropes (4 in number) are each of 130 tonnes/*tons*, made for the twin shaft system of Western Deep Levels Gold Mine, South Africa, by Haggie Rand Ltd of Johannesburg.

TIME PIECES

Clock *Oldest*

The earliest mechanical clock, that is one with an escapement, was completed in China in AD 725 by I Hsing and Liang Lingtsan.

The oldest surviving working clock in the world is the faceless clock dating from 1386, or possibly earlier, at Salisbury Cathedral, Wiltshire, which was restored in 1956 having struck the hours for 498 years and ticked more than 500 million times. Earlier dates, ranging back to *c.* 1335, have been attributed to the weight-driven clock in Wells Cathedral, Somerset, but only the iron frame is original. A model of Giovanni de Dondi's heptagonal astronomical clock of 1348–64 was completed in 1962.

Clock Largest *World*

The world's most massive clock is the Astronomical Clock in the Cathedral of St Pierre, Beauvais, France, constructed between 1865 and 1868. It contains 90,000 parts and measures 40 ft *12,1 m* high, 20 ft *6,09 m* wide and 9 ft *2,7 m* deep. The Su Sung clock, built in China at K'aifeng in 1088–92, had a 20 ton *20,3 tonnes* bronze armillary sphere for 1½ tons, *1,52 tonnes* of water. It was removed to Peking in 1126 and was last known to be working in its 40 ft *12,1 m* high tower in 1136.

The world's largest clock face is that of the floral clock at Tokachigaoka Park, Otofuke, Hokkaido, Japan, completed on 1 Aug 1982 with a diameter of 18 m *59 ft 0⅝ in*.

The world's largest clock face—the floral clock at Tokachigaoka Park, Otofuke, Japan. It measures 18 m *59 ft 0⅝ in* in diameter.

Public

The largest four-faced clock in the world is that on the building of the Allen-Bradley Company of Milwaukee, Wisconsin, USA. Each face has a diameter of 40 ft 3½ in *12,28 m* with a minute hand 20 ft *6,09 m* in overall length. The tallest four-faced clock in the world is that of the Williamsburgh Savings Bank in Brooklyn, New York City, NY, USA. It is 430 ft *131 m* above street level.

Great Britain

The largest clock in the United Kingdom is that on the Royal Liver Building (built 1908–11) with dials 25 ft *7,62 m* in diameter and the 4 minute hands each 14 ft *4,26 m* long. The mechanism and dials weigh 22 tons and are 220 ft *67 m* above street level.

Longest stoppage 'Big Ben'

The longest stoppage of the clock in the House of Commons clock tower, London since the first tick on 31 May 1859 has been 13 days from noon 4 Apr to noon 17 Apr 1977. In 1945 a host of starlings slowed the minute hand by 5 min.

Clock Most accurate

The most accurate and complicated clockwork in the world is the Olsen clock, installed in the Copenhagen Town Hall, Denmark. The clock, which has more than 14,000 units, took 10 years to make and the mechanism of the clock functions in 570,000 different ways. The celestial pole motion of the clock will take 25,753 years to complete a full circle and is the slowest moving designed mechanism in the world. The clock is accurate to 0.5 sec in 300 years—50 times more accurate than the previous record.

Clock Most expensive

The highest price paid for any English-made clock is £500,000 for a Thomas Tompion (1639–1713) bracket clock bought by the British Museum by private treaty on 15 July 1982.

Pendulum longest

The longest pendulum in the world is 22,5 m *73 ft 9¾ in* on the water-mill clock installed by Hattori Tokeiten Co. in the Shinjuku NS Building, Tokyo, Japan in 1983.

Watch Oldest

The oldest watch (portable clockwork time-keeper) is one made of iron by Peter Henlein in Nürnberg (Nüremberg), Bavaria, Germany, in *c.* 1504 and now in the Memorial Hall, Philadelphia, Pennsylvania, USA. The earliest wrist watches were those of Jacquet-Droz and Leschot of Geneva, Switzerland, dating from 1790.

Watch Smallest

The smallest watches in the world are produced by Jaeger Le Coultre of Switzerland. Equipped with a 15-jewelled movement they measure just over ½ in *1,2 cm* long and ³⁄₁₆ in, *0,476 cm* in width. The movement, with its case, weighs under 0,25 oz *7 g*.

Watch Thinnest

The world's thinnest wrist watch is the Swiss Concord Delirium IV. It measures 0,98 mm *0.0385 in* thick and retailed for $16,000 *£6800* (including 18 carat gold strap) in June 1980.

Watch Most expensive

Excluding watches with jewelled cases, the most expensive standard men's pocket watch is the Swiss *Grande Complication* by Audemars-Piguet which retailed for £72,000 in March 1984. The *Kallista* watch with 130 carats of precious stones by Vacheron et Constantin of Geneva was valued in Apr 1981 at $5 million (*then £2,272,000*). The record price for an antique watch is $166,300 (*then £75,600*) paid to Capt. Peter Belin USN by L. C. Mannheimer of Zurich at Sotheby Parke Bernet, New York on 29 Nov 1979 for a gold studded case watch of *c.* 1810 by William Anthony of London.

Time measurer Most accurate *World*

The most accurate time-keeping devices are the twin atomic hydrogen masers installed in 1964 in the US Naval Research Laboratory, Washington, DC. They are based on the frequency of the hydrogen atom's transition period of 1,420,450,751,694 cycles/sec. This enables an accuracy to within 1 sec in 1,700,000 years.

Sundial Largest

The world's largest sundial is one with a 25 ft *7,62 m* gnomon and a readable shadow of 125 ft *38,1 m* installed by Walter R. T. Witschey at the Science Museum of Virginia at Richmond, Va on 12 Mar–3 May 1981. The sun's shadow travels 7 in *17,7 cm* per minute at the equinox.

A sundial with a diameter of 26 ft *7,92 m* was built at Hilton Head Island, South Carolina, USA in Aug 1983.

COMPUTERS

A geared calculator date *c.* 80 BC was found in the sea by Antikythera Island off northwest Crete.

The earliest programmable electronic computer was the 1500 valve Colossus formulated by Prof Max H. A. Newman FRS (b. 1897) and built by T. H. Flowers MBE. It was run in December 1943 at Bletchley Park, Buckinghamshire to break the German coding machine Enigma. It arose from the concept published in 1936 by Dr Alan Mathison Turing OBE, FRS (1912–54) in his paper *On Computable Numbers with an Application to the Entscheidungsproblem.* Colossus was declassified on 25 Oct 1975. The world's first stored-programme computer was the Manchester University Mark I which incorporated the Williams storage cathode ray tube (pat. 11 Dec 1946). It ran its first programme, written by Prof Tom Kilburn CBE FRS (b. 1921) for 52 min on 21 June 1948.

Computers were greatly advanced by the invention of the point-contact transistor by John Bardeen and Walter Brattain announced in July 1948, and the junction transistor by R. L. Wallace, Morgan Sparks and Dr William Bradford Shockley (b. 1910) in early 1951. The concept of the integrated circuit, which has enabled micro-miniaturization, was first published on 7 May 1952 by Geoffrey W. A. Dummer MBE (b. 1909) in Washington DC. The Microcomputer was achieved in 1969–73 by M. E. Hoff Jr of Intel Corporation with the production of the microprocessor silicon chip '4004'.

The computer planned to be the world's biggest by a factor of 40 is the $50 million NASF (Numerical Aerodynamic Simulation Facility) at NASA's Ames Research Center, Palo Alto, California. The tenders from CDC and Burroughs called for a capacity of 12.8 gigaflops (12,800 million complex calculations per second).

Most powerful and Fastest *World*

The world's most powerful and fastest computer is the CRAY-1, designed by Seymour R. Cray of Cray Research, Inc, Minneapolis, Minnesota USA. The clock period is 12.5 nanoseconds and memory ranges up to 1,048,576 64-bit words, resulting in a capacity of 8,388,608 bytes of main memory. (N.B. a 'byte' is a unit of storage compressing 8 'bits' collectively equivalent to one alphabetic symbol or two numericals.) It attains speeds of 200 million floating point operations per second. With 32 CRAY DD-19 disk storage units, it has a storage capacity of 7.7568×10^{10} bits. The cost of a mid-range system was quoted in mid-1979 as about $8.8 million (*then £4 million*). The most powerful British computer is the International Computer's Distribution Array Processor—the ICL DAP.

Control Data Corporation announced the CYBER Model 205-444 system from Arden Hills, Minnesota, USA on 2 June 1980 which has a memory of 4 million 64-Bit words and cost $16.5 million (*£7 million*) at delivery in January 1981. In a test on 19 Nov 1982 the CYBER model 205-424 achieved 791,860,000 calculations in a second.

The CRAY-1/S system, introduced in 1981, has an additional 8 million words of buffer memory and a storage capacity of 19 gigabytes or 1.55136×10^{11} bits with a system cost of up to $17 million for the maximum configuration.

Megabits

The megabit barrier was broken in February 1984, with the manufacture of a 1024K bit integrated circuit, the size of a drawing pin head and as thin as a human hair, by 4 Japanese companies, Hitachi, NEC, NTT Atsugi Electrical Communications and Toshiba. Toshiba announced that manufacture of an 80 picosecond LSI (large scale integration) chip of gallium arsenide would start in 1985/86.

IBM had announced the first 512K bit 120 nanosecond dynamic access memory chip ⅜ in *9,5 mm* square from Essex Junction, Vermont, USA, on 15 Sept 1983.

Chapter 9

THE
BUSINESS
WORLD

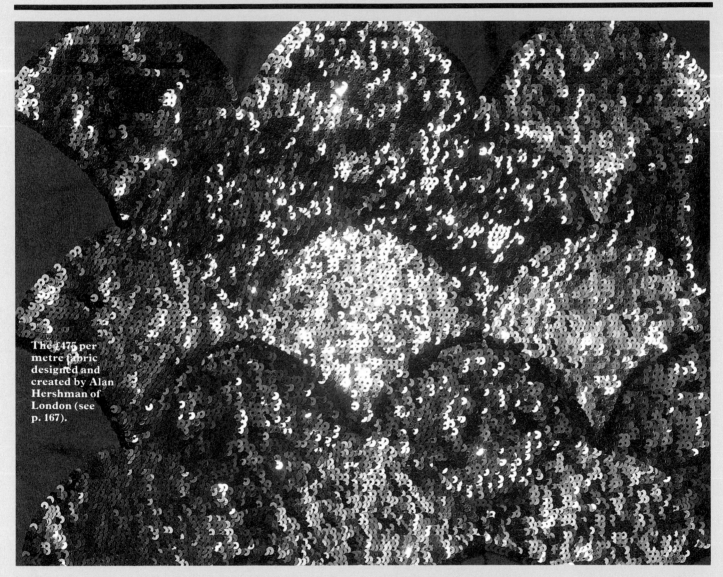

The £475 per metre fabric designed and created by Alan Hershman of London (see p. 167).

1. COMMERCE

The $ (US) has in this chapter been converted at a fixed mean rate of $1.4 to the £ Sterling and at the relevant rates for other dates.

Oldest industry

The oldest known industry is flint knapping, involving the production of chopping tools and hand axes, dating from at least 3 million years ago. The earliest evidence of trading dates from 28000 BC in Central Europe. Agriculture is often described as 'the oldest industry in the world', whereas in fact there is no evidence yet that it was practised before *c.* 11,000 BC.

Oldest company *World*

The oldest company in the world is the Faversham Oyster Fishery Co, referred to in the Faversham Oyster Fishing Act 1930, as existing 'from time immemorial', *i.e.* in English law from before 1189. The Shore Porters' Society of Aberdeen, a haulier, shipping and warehouse partnership, is known to have been established before 4 June 1498.

Great Britain

The Royal Mint has origins going back to AD 287. The Oxford University Press celebrated a 500th anniversary of the earliest origin of printing in Oxford in 1478 in 1978. The Whitechapel Bell Foundry of Whitechapel Road, London, E1, has been in

business since 1570. The retail business in Britain with the oldest history is the Cambridge bookshop, which, though under various ownership, has traded from the site of 1 Trinity Street since 1581 and since 1907 under its present title Bowes & Bowes. R. Durtnell & Sons, builders, of Brasted, Kent, has been run by the same family since 1591. Mr Richard Durtnell is of the 12th generation. The first bill of adventure signed by the English East India Co, was dated 21 Mar 1601.

Greatest assets *World all-time*

The business with the greatest amount in physical assets has been the Bell System, which comprised the American Telephone and Telegraph Company, and its subsidiaries. The Bell System's total assets on the consolidated balance sheet at the time of its divestiture and break-up into 8 companies on 31 Dec 1983 reached $149,529 million *£106,800 m.* The plant involved included more than 142 million telephones. The number of employees was 1,036,000. The company's market value of $47,989 million (*then £30,960 million*) was held among 3,055,000 share-holders. A total of 20,109 shareholders had attended the Annual Meeting in April 1961, thereby setting a world record.

Currently the largest assets of any corporation are $62,962,990,000 (*£44,974 million*) by the Exxon Corporation, the world's largest oil company, on 1 Jan 1984. They have 156,000 employees. The first company to have assets in excess of $1 billion was the United States Steel Corporation with $1400 million (*then £287.73 million*) at the time of its creation by merger in 1917.

Great Britain

The biggest British industrial company is Imperial Chemical Industries plc with assets employed of £7600 million as at 1 Jan 1984. Its staff and payroll averaged 117,900 during the year. The company, which has more than 300 UK and overseas subsidiaries, was formed on 7 Dec 1926 by the merger of four concerns—British Dyestuffs Corporation Ltd; Brunner, Mond & Co Ltd; Nobel Industries Ltd and United Alkali Co Ltd. The first chairman was Sir Alfred Moritz Mond (1868–1930), later the 1st Lord Melchett.

The net assets of The 'Shell' Transport and Trading Company, plc, at 31 Dec 1983 were £7,855,200,000, comprising mainly its 40 per cent share in the net assets of the Royal Dutch/Shell Group of Companies which stood at £19,566 million. Group companies employ 156,000. 'Shell' Transport was formed in 1897 by Marcus Samuel (1853–1927), later the 1st Viscount Bearsted.

Greatest profit and loss

The greatest net profit ever made by any corporation in 12 months is $7647 million (*£4933 million*) by American Telephone and Telegraph Co from 1 Oct 1981 to 30 Sept 1982.

The Argentine petroleum company YPF (Yacimientos Petroliferos) (Government owned) lost a trading record US $3,820,963,000 in 1981. The greatest loss ever recorded by private enterprise has been $4900 million (*£3500 million*) for the 4th quarter of 1983 by American Telephone & Telegraph Co due to extraordinary charges relating to its divestiture (see above). The 1982–83 Annual Report of British Steel published on 12 July 1983 showed losses of £869 million for the year ended 2 Apr 1983. The projected loss for the National Coal Board in the tax year ending on 31 Mar 1984 was £875 million.

Greatest sales

The first company to surpass the $1 billion (US) mark in annual sales was the United States Steel Corporation in 1917. Now there are 543 corporations with sales exceeding £1000 million including 243 from the United States. The *Fortune 500 List* of April 1984 is headed by the Exxon Corporation of New York with $88,561,134,000 (*£63,260 million*) for 1983.

The top gross profits in the United Kingdom in *The Times 1000 1982–83* was British Petroleum with £6586 million. The biggest loss maker was Vauxhall Motors with £53,542,000.

Largest take-over

The largest corporate take-over agreement in commercial history is by Standard Oil Co. of California who agreed on 5 Mar 1984 to buy Gulf Corporation for $13,200 million (*£9428 million*).

The biggest takeover in Britain took place when BAT Industries won control of Eagle Star Insurance on 18 Jan 1984 with a record bid of £968 million.

Biggest write off

The largest reduction of assets in the history of private enterprise was the $800 million (*£347 million*) write-off of Tristar aircraft development costs announced on 23 Nov 1974.

Greatest Bankruptcy

William G. Stern (b. Hungary, 1936) of Golders Green, north London, a US citizen since 1957, who set up Wilstar Group Holding Co in the London property market in 1971 was declared bankrupt for £104,390,248 in February 1979. This figure rose to £142,978,413 by Feb 1983. He was discharged for £500,000 suspended for 2½ years on 28 Mar 1983.

Companies

The number of companies on the register in Great Britain at 31 Dec 1983 was 956,411 of which 6508 were public and the balance private companies.

Most directorships

The record for directorships was set in 1961 by Hugh T. Nicholson, formerly senior partner of Harmood Banner & Co, London who, as a liquidating chartered accountant, became director of all 451 companies of the Jasper group in 1961 and had 7 other directorships.

Advertising agency

The largest advertising agency in 1983, as listed in *Advertising Age*, is Dentsu Incorporated of Japan with estimated billings of $3214 million (*£2295 million*). *Advertising Age* ranks Saatchi and Saatchi Compton Ltd No 1 in Britain with 1983 billings of $492,693,300 (*£352,000,000*).

Biggest advertiser

The world's biggest advertiser is Sears, Roebuck and Co, with $898,800,000 (*£642 million*) in 1982 excluding its catalogue.

Aircraft manufacturer

The world's largest aircraft manufacturer is The Boeing Company of Seattle, Washington, USA. The corporation's sales totalled $11,130,000,000 (*£7950 million*) in 1983 and it had 82,000 employees and assets valued at $7,471,000,000 (*then £5336 million*) at 1 Jan 1984. Cessna Aircraft Company of Wichita, Kansas, USA, in the year 1983, had a total sales of $524,395,000 (*then £374.5 million*). The company has produced more than 174,600 aircraft since Clyde Cessna's first was built in 1911.

Airline *Largest*

The largest airline in the world is the USSR State airline 'Aeroflot', so named since 1932. This was instituted on 9 Feb 1923, with the title of Civil Air Fleet of the Council of Ministers of the USSR, abbreviated to 'Dobrolet'. It operates 1300 aircraft over about 620,000 miles *1,000,000 km* of routes, employs 500,000 people and carried 109 million passengers to 102 countries in 1983. Most luggage is 'self-handled'. Smoking is allowed only after 4 hours flying. The commercial airline carrying the greatest number of passengers (April 1983) was Eastern Airlines of Miami, Florida, USA (formed 1928) with 35,032,000 passengers. The company had 39,200 employees and a fleet of 268 jet planes. On 1 Apr 1984 British Airways were operating a fleet of 150 aircraft (including 35 helicopters). Staff employed on airline activities totalled 36,500 and 14.6 million passengers were carried in 1982/3 on 358,976 miles *577,718 km* of unduplicated routes.

Oldest

The oldest existing national airline is Koninklijke-Luchtvaart-Maatschappij NV (KLM) of the Netherlands, which opened its first scheduled service (Amsterdam–London) on 17 May 1920, having been established on 7 Oct 1919. One of the original constituents of BOAC, Handley-Page Transport Ltd, was founded in May 1919 and merged into Imperial Airways in 1924. Delag (Deutsche Luftschiffahrt AG) was founded at Frankfurt am Main on 16 Nov 1909 and started a scheduled airship service in June 1910. Chalk's International Airline has been flying amphibians between Miami, Florida and the Bahamas since July 1919. Albert 'Pappy' Chalk flew from 1911 to 1975.

Aluminium producer

The world's largest producer of primary aluminium is the Aluminum Company of America (Alcoa) of Pittsburgh, USA with its affiliated companies. The company had an output of 1 919 000 tonnes *1 888 692 tons* in 1983. The Aluminum Company of Canada Ltd owns the largest aluminium smelter in the western world, at Arvida, Quebec, with a capacity of 475,000 short tons *431 000 tonnes* per annum. The parent company Alcan's total sales for the year 1983 were $5208 million (*then £3720 million*).

Art auctioneering

The largest and oldest firm of art auctioneers in the world is the Sotheby Parke Bernet Group of London and New York, founded in 1744. The turnover in 1982–83 was $417,321,270 (*£298,086,620*). The highest total for any house sale auction was theirs on 18–27 May 1977 at the 6th Earl of Rosebery's home at Mentmore, Buckinghamshire which reached £6,389,933 or *$10.9 million*. HM Government had turned down an offer of £2 million. The total realized at the art sale at Sotheby Parke, Bernet, New York on 18 May 1983 was $37 million (*then £23.87 million*). It included the sale of 16 paintings from the H. O. Havemeyer collection.

Bank

The International Bank for Reconstruction and Development (founded 27 Dec 1945), the 'World Bank', a United Nations specialised agency, at 1818 H Street NW, Washington, DC, USA, has an authorized share capital of $80 billion (*£52,322 million*). There were 144 members with a subscribed capital of $49,000 million (*£35,000 million*) at 30 June 1982. The International Monetary Fund in Washington, DC, USA has 146 members with total quotas of SDR 88,998.5 million (*$94,349.9 million or £67,392 million*) at 1 Mar 1984.

The USSR State Bank was claimed by Tass to be the world's largest on 15 Jan 1983 incorporating 'nearly 4500 banking institutions within its single system'. No asset figures were disclosed. The commercial bank with the greatest assets is Citicorp of New York with $129,900 million (*£83,800 million*) at 31 Dec 1982. Its operating income was $747 million (*£482 million*). Barclays Bank (with Barclays Bank International and other subsidiary companies) had some 5200 branches and offices in over 80 countries (2900 in the United Kingdom) in December 1983. Deposits totalled £57,029 million and assets £64,904 million. The bank with the largest network in the United Kingdom is the National Westminster with consolidated total assets of £60,017,000,000 and 3836 branches (3400 in UK) as at 31 Dec 1983. The bank with most branches is The State Bank of India with 9695 on 1 Jan 1984 with assets of £17,468 million.

Bank building

The world's tallest bank building is the Bank of Montreal's First Bank Tower, Toronto, Canada which has 72 storeys and stands 935 ft *284,98 m*. The largest bank vault in the world, measuring 350 × 100 × 8 ft *106,7 × 30,4 × 2,4 m* and weighing 879 tons *893 tonnes* is in the Chase Manhattan Building, New York City, completed in May 1961. Its six doors weigh up to 40 tons *40,6 tonnes* apiece but each can be closed by the pressure of a forefinger.

Banquet Greatest *Outdoors*

It was estimated that some 30,000 attended a military feast at Radewitz, Poland on 25 June 1730 thrown by King August II (1709–33).

Indoors

The greatest number of people served indoors at a single sitting was 18,000 municipal leaders at the Palais de l'Industrie, Paris on 18 Aug 1889.

Most expensive

The menu for the main 5½ hr banquet at the Imperial Iranian 2500th Anniversary gathering at Persepolis in October 1971 was probably the most expensive ever compiled. It comprised quail eggs stuffed with Iranian caviar, a mousse of crayfish tails in Nantua sauce, stuffed rack of roast lamb, with a main course of roast peacock stuffed with *foie gras,* fig rings and raspberry sweet champagne sherbet, with wines including *Château Lafite-Rothschild* 1945 at £40 per bottle from Maxime's, Paris.

Book shop

The book shop with most titles and the longest shelving (30 miles *48 km*) in the world is W. & G. Foyle Ltd, City of Westminster, Greater London. First established in 1904 in a small shop in Islington, the company is now at 113–119 Charing Cross Road. The area on one site is 75,825 ft² *7044 m²*. The most capacious individual bookstore in the world measured by square footage is Barnes & Noble Bookstore of Fifth Ave at 18th Street, New York City, USA with 154,250 ft² *14 330 m²* and with 12.87 miles *20,71 km* of shelving.

Brewer *Oldest*

The oldest brewery in the world is the Weihenstephan Brewery, Freising, near Munich, W. Germany, founded in AD 1040.

Largest World

The largest single brewing organisation in the world is Anheuser-Busch, Inc based in St Louis, Missouri, USA, with 11 breweries in the US. In 1983 the company sold 60,500,000 US barrels, equivalent to *12,492 million Imp. pints*, the greatest annual volume ever produced by a brewing company. The company's St Louis plant covers 100 acres *40,5 ha* and after completion of current modernization projects will have an annual capacity in excess of 13,000,000 US barrels *2684 million Imp. pints*. The largest brewery on a single site is Adolph Coors Co of Golden, Colorado, USA where 13.7 million barrels *2828 million Imp. pints* were sold in 1983.

Europe

The largest brewery in Europe is the Guinness Brewery at St James's Gate, Dublin, Ireland, which extends over 56.15 acres *22,72 ha*. The business was founded in 1759.

Great Britain

The largest brewing company in the United Kingdom based on its 7616 public houses, 1007 off-licences and over 100 hotels, is Bass plc. The company has net assets of £1,414,900,000, controls 13 breweries and has 71,207 employees. Their sales figure for the year ending 30 Sept 1983 was £1,988,400,000. The company has substantial leisure and betting interests.

Greatest exports

The largest exporter of beer, ale and stout in the world is Arthur Guinness & Sons plc, of Dublin, Ireland. Exports of Guinness from the Republic of Ireland in the 52 weeks ending 31 Mar 1984 were 777,689 bulk barrels (bulk barrel = 36 Imperial gallons), which is equivalent to 1,227,257 half pint glasses (*1,162,337 30-centilitre glasses*) per day.

Brickworks

The largest brickworks in the world is the London Brick Products Limited plant at Stewartby, Bedfordshire. The works, established in 1898, now cover 221 acres *90 ha* and have a production capacity of 13,000,000 bricks and brick equivalent each week.

Building contractors

The largest construction company in the United Kingdom is George Wimpey plc (founded 1880), of London, who undertake building, civil, mechanical, electrical and chemical, offshore and marine engineering work worldwide employing 26,000 staff. The turnover of work was £1480 million in over 30 countries in 1983.

Building societies

The biggest building society in the world is the Halifax Building Society of Halifax, West Yorkshire. It was established in 1853 and has total assets exceeding £17,000,000,000. It has 11,081 employees and over 2400 offices.

Chemist shop chain

The largest chain of chemist shops in the world is Boots The Chemists, which has 1025 retail branches. The firm was founded by Jesse Boot (b. Nottingham, 1850), later the 1st Baron Trent, who died in 1931.

Chocolate factory

The world's largest chocolate and confectionery factory is that built by Hershey Chocolate Company in Hershey, Pennsylvania, USA in 1903–5. It has 2,000,000 ft² *185,800 m²* of floor space.

Clothiers

The world's largest clothiers are the Brenninkmeyer family whose business was founded in the Netherlands in 1841 and whose annual sales are now estimated to be some $6000 million *£4285 million*.

Computer company

The world's largest computer firm is International Business Machines (IBM) Corporation of New York which resisted from 1969 the Justice Department's largest anti-trust suit. This was withdrawn on 8 Jan 1982 as 'without merit'. In 1983 assets were $37,243,000,000 (*£26,602 million*) and sales were $40,180,000,000 (*28,700 million*). In Oct 1979 it made the largest borrowing in corporate history with $1 billion.

Department stores *World*

F. W. Woolworth, who celebrated their centenary year in 1979, now operate a total of 5124 stores world wide. Frank W. Woolworth opened his first Five and Ten Cent Store in Utica, New York State on 22 Feb 1879. The 1982 income from continuing operations was $82 million (*£53,000,000*).

Great Britain

The largest department store in the United Kingdom is Harrods Ltd of Knightsbridge, Royal Borough of Kensington and Chelsea, Greater London named after Henry Charles Harrod, who opened a grocery in Knightsbridge Village in 1849. It has a total selling floor space of *60 729 m²*, employs 4000 people and achieved record sales of £220 million for the year ending 29 Jan 1984.

Highest sales per unit area

The department store with the fastest-moving stock in the world is the Marks & Spencer premier branch, known as 'Marble Arch' at 458 Oxford Street, City of Westminster, Greater London. The figure of £1400 worth of goods per square foot of selling space per year is believed to be an understatement. The selling area is 92,400 ft² *8584 m²*. The company has 263 branches in the UK and operates on over 6 million ft² *558 000 m²* of selling space and now has stores on the Continent and Canada.

Longest wait for a sale

Shaun Carter of Eastbourne, East Sussex began camping outside Selfridges, Oxford Street, London W1 at 6.20 p.m. on 16 Dec to be first in the queue for the 9 a.m. Sale on 29 Dec 1982—302 hr 40 min later.

Distillery

The world's largest distilling company is The Seagram Company Ltd, of Canada. Its sales in the year ending 31 Jan 1984 totalled US $2,647,552,000 (*£1891 million*). The group employs about 14,200 people, including about 11,000 in the United States.

The largest establishment for blending and bottling Scotch whisky is owned by John Walker & Sons Limited at Kilmarnock, Strathclyde, where there is a capacity to fill over 3 million bottles each week. 'Johnnie Walker' is the world's largest-selling brand of Scotch whisky. The largest malt Scotch whisky distillery is the Tomatin Distillery, Highland, established at 1028 ft *313 m* above sea level in 1897, with an annual capacity of 5.0 million proof gallons. The world's largest-selling brand of gin is Gordon's.

Fisheries

The greatest catch ever recorded with a single throw is 2471 tonnes by the purse seine-net boat M/S 'Flømann' from Hareide, Norway in the Barents Sea on 28 Aug 1983. It was estimated that more than 120 million fish were caught in this shoal.

Grocery stores

The largest grocery chain in the world is Safeway Stores, Incorporated of Oakland, California, USA with sales in 1983 of $18,585,217,000 (*£13,275 million*) and total current assets valued at $1,729,146,000 (*£12,351 million*) as at 1 Jan 1984. The company has 2507 stores totalling 69,694,600 ft² *6 474 628 m²*. The total number of employees is 162,088.

Hotelier

The top revenue-earning hotel business is the Holiday Inn Hotel System, with an estimated 1983 revenue of $4600 million (*£3285 million*), from 1707 hotels (310,337 rooms) at 31 Dec 1983 in 53 countries. The business was founded by Charles Kemmons Wilson with his first Holiday Inn Hotel on Summer Avenue, Memphis, Tennessee, USA in 1952.

Insurance

It was estimated in 1978 that the total premiums paid in the

The coat of arms and supporters from Aberdeen, Scotland of the only surviving 15th century company still active (see page 161).

United States first surpassed $100 billion (*then £52,600 million*) or $1400 *£736* per household. The company with the highest volume of insurance in force in the world is the Prudential Insurance Company of America of Newark, New Jersey, USA with $509,964 million (*£364,260 million*) at 31 Dec 1983, which is more than 2½ times the UK National Debt figure. The admitted assets are $72,249 million (*£51,606 million*).

Great Britain

The largest life assurance company in the United Kingdom is the Prudential Corporation plc. At 1 Jan 1984 the tangible assets were £16,713,800,000 and the total amount assured was £72,445,300,000.

Life policies Largest

The largest life assurance policy ever written was one for $44 million (*£244 million*) for a Calgary land developer Victor T. Uy in February 1982 by Transamerica Occidental Life Assurance Co. The salesman was local manager Lorenzo F. Reyes. The highest pay-out on a single life has been some $18 million (*then £7.5 million*) to Mrs Linda Mullendore, wife of an Oklahoma rancher, reported on 14 Nov 1970. Her murdered husband had paid $300,000 in premiums in 1969.

Marine

The largest ever marine insurance loss was £46 million for the self-propelled semi-submersible drilling platform Ocean Ranger (14,914 tons gross) built for Ocean Drilling & Exploration Co of New Orleans in 1976. On 15 Feb 1982 she was lost with 84 lives in the Hibernia Field, off Newfoundland. The 83,000 grt LNG (Liquid Natural Gas) Carrier *Aquarius* built in 1977 by General Dynamics Corporation, Massachusetts, USA is currently insured for $175 million *£103 million*. This vessel is owned by Wilmington Trust Company, Delaware, USA, and chartered to the Burmah Oil Co, Ltd.

The largest sum claimed for consequential losses is $1700 million (*£890 million*) against owning, operating and building corporations, and Claude Phillips resulting from the 66 million gallon oil spill from M. T. *Amoco Cadiz* on the Brittany Coast on 16 Mar 1978.

A claim for $300 million (*then £127.6 million*) was provisionally agreed by Lloyd's on 31 July 1980 in connection with alleged structural defects in three liquefied natural gas carriers being built for El Paso Natural Gas at Avondale Shipyards, New Orleans, Louisiana, USA.

Land *Owner*

The world's largest landowner is the United States Government, with a holding of 769,863,000 acres (1,203,000 miles² *3 116 000 km²*) which is more than the area of the world's 8th largest country Argentina and 12.8 times larger than the United Kingdom. The world's largest *private* landowner is

LONDON STOCK EXCHANGE 1935 – 1984.

The highest number of markings received in one day on the London Stock Exchange was 32,665 on 14 Oct 1959 following the 1959 General Election. The record for a year is 4,397,138 'marks' in the year ending 31 Mar 1960. There were 7213 securities (*cf.* 9749 peak in June 1973) listed at 31 Dec 1982. Their total nominal value was £196,179 million (gilt-edged £96,279 million) and their market value was £608,743 million (gilt-edged £97,391 million).

Bank rate continues at 4%

1935 | 1936 | 1937 | 1938 | 1939 | 1941 | 1942 | 1943 | 1944 | 1945 | 1946 | 1947 | 1948 | 1949 | 1950 | 1951 | 1952 | 1953 | 1954 | 1955 | 1956 | 1957 | 1958

Lowest closing figure
49.4 on 26 June 1940.

Most markings
Highest number of markings received in one day 32,665 on 14 Oct 1959.

reputed to be International Paper Co with 9 million acres *3,64 million ha*. The United Kingdom's greatest ever private landowner was the 3rd Duke of Sutherland, George Granville Sutherland-Leveson-Gower, KG (1828–92), who owned 1,358,000 acres *549 560 ha* in 1883. Currently the largest landholder in Great Britain is the Forestry Commission (instituted 1919) with 3,090,973 acres *1 250 900 ha*. Currently the landowner with the largest known acreage is the 9th Duke of Buccleuch (b. 1923) with 336,000 acres *136,035 ha*. The longest tenure is that by St Paul's Cathedral of land at Tillingham, Essex, given by King Ethelbert before AD 616.

Value Highest

The world's most expensive land is in central Hong Kong. In May 1982 freehold land for highrise building reportedly realized up to £11,000 per square foot. The freehold price for a grave site with excellent *Fung Shui* in Hong Kong may cost HK$200,000 for 4 ft × 10 ft *1,21 × 3,04 m* or £19,400 per ft². The real estate value per square metre of the two topmost French vineyards, Grande and Petite Cognac vineyards in Bordeaux, has not been recently estimated. The China Square Inch Land Ltd at a charity auction on 2 Dec 1977 sold 1 cm² *0.155 in²* of land at Sha Tau Kok for HK$2000 (the equivalent of US$17,405,833,737 per acre). The purchasers were Stephen and Tony Nicholson. The most expensive land in Britain is that in the City of London. The freehold price on small prime sites reached £1950/ft² (*£21,230/m²*) in mid 1973.

Greatest auction

The greatest auction was that at Anchorage, Alaska on 11 Sept 1969 for 179 tracts comprising 450,858 acres *182 455 ha* of the oil-bearing North Slope, Alaska. An all-time record bid of $72,277,133 for a 2560 acre *1036 ha* lease was made by the Amerada Hess Corporation—Getty Oil consortium. This £30,115,472 bid indicated a price of $28,233 (*then £11,763*) per acre.

Highest rent

The highest rentals in the world in Jan 1984 for prime sites, according to *World Rental Levels* by Richard Ellis of London, are on Manhattan, New York at £37.54 and London £31.00 per square foot. With added service charges and rates London is top at £52.70.

Mineral water

The world's largest mineral water firm is Source Perrier, near Nîmes, France with an annual production of more than 2,100,000,000 bottles, of which 1,200,000,000 now come from Perrier and Contrexeville. The French drink about 60 litres *105½ pt* of mineral water per person per year.

Motor car manufacturer *Largest World*

In 1980 Japan with 11,043,000 vehicles overtook the USA as the world's No 1 motor manufacturer. The largest manufacturing company in the world is General Motors Corporation of Detroit, Michigan, USA. During 1983 worldwide sales totalled $74,581,600,000 (*£53,272 million*). Its assets at 31 Dec 1983 were valued at $20,799,800,000 (*£14,857 million*). Its total 1983 payroll was $19,605,300,000 (*£14,004 million*) to an average of 691,000 employees. Dividends paid in 1983 were $892,200,000 (*£637,285,000*).

Great Britain

The largest British manufacturer was BL PLC with 576,000 vehicles produced and a sales turnover of £3421 million of which £1486 million was overseas sales in 1983. Direct exports were £917 million.

Largest plant

The largest single automobile plant in the world is the Volkswagenwerk, Wolfsburg, West Germany, with 56,298 employees and a capacity for 4056 vehicles daily. The surface area of the factory buildings is 385 acres *156 ha* and that of the whole plant 4999 acres *2022 ha* with 43.5 miles *70 km* of rail sidings.

Salesmanship

The all-time record for automobile salesmanship in units sold individually is 1425 in 1973 by Joe Girard of Michigan, USA, author of *How to Sell Anything to Anybody*, winner of the No. 1 Car Salesman title each year in 1966–77. His lifetime total of one-at-a-time 'belly to belly' selling was 13,001 sales, all retail with a record 174 in a month. He retired on 1 Jan 1978 to teach others his art and has now had published *How to Sell Yourself*.

Oil refineries *Largest*

The world's largest refinery has been the Amerada Hess refinery in St Croix, Virgin Islands with an annual capacity of 28 million tonnes *27.55 million tons*. The largest oil refinery in the United Kingdom is the Esso Refinery at Fawley, Hampshire. Opened in 1921 and much expanded in 1951, it has a capacity of *15,6 million tonnes* per year. The total investment together with the associated chemical plant, on the 1300 acre *526 ha* site is £369 million. The area occupied by the Shell Stanlow Refinery at Ellesmere Port, Cheshire, founded in 1922, and now with a capacity of 18 million tonnes per year, is 2000 acres *810 ha*.

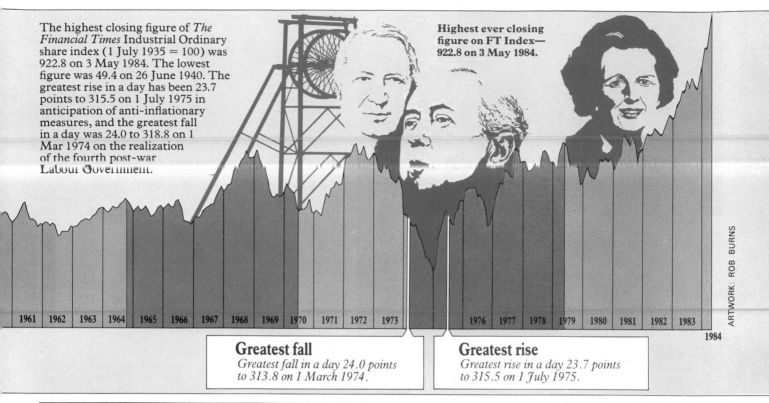

The highest closing figure of *The Financial Times* Industrial Ordinary share index (1 July 1935 = 100) was 922.8 on 3 May 1984. The lowest figure was 49.4 on 26 June 1940. The greatest rise in a day has been 23.7 points to 315.5 on 1 July 1975 in anticipation of anti-inflationary measures, and the greatest fall in a day was 24.0 to 318.8 on 1 Mar 1974 on the realization of the fourth post-war Labour Government.

Highest ever closing figure on FT Index— 922.8 on 3 May 1984.

ARTWORK: ROB BURNS

| 1961 | 1962 | 1963 | 1964 | 1965 | 1966 | 1967 | 1968 | 1969 | 1970 | 1971 | 1972 | 1973 | | 1976 | 1977 | 1978 | 1979 | 1980 | 1981 | 1982 | 1983 |

1984

Greatest fall
Greatest fall in a day 24.0 points to 313.8 on 1 March 1974.

Greatest rise
Greatest rise in a day 23.7 points to 315.5 on 1 July 1975.

STOCK EXCHANGES

The oldest Stock Exchange of the 138 listed throughout the world is that of Amsterdam, in the Netherlands, founded in 1602.

Most highly valued UK Co
The General Electric Company stock valuation was £6,104,267,000 on 26 July 1982.

Highest par value
The highest denomination of any share quoted in the world is a single share in F. Hoffmann-La Roche of Basel worth Sw. Fr 101,000 (£21,992) on 23 Apr 1976. The record for the London Stock Echange is £100 for preference shares in Baring Brothers & Co Ltd, the bankers.

U.S. records
The highest index figure on the Dow Jones average (instituted 8 Oct 1896) of selected industrial stocks at the close of a day's trading was 1287.2 on 29 Nov 1983. The record day's trading was 159,999,031 shares on 5 Jan 1984. The old, record trading volume in a day on the New York Stock Exchange of 16,410,030 shares on 29 Oct 1929, the 'Black Tuesday' of the famous 'crash' was unsurpassed until April 1968. The Dow Jones industrial average, which reached 381.71 on 3 Sept 1929, plunged 30.57 points on 29 Oct 1929, on its way to the Depression's lowest point of 41.22 on 8 July 1932. The largest decline in a day, 38.33 points, occurred on 28 Oct 1929. The total lost in security values from 1 Sept 1929 to 30 June 1932 was $74,000 million (*then £23,000 million*). The greatest paper loss in a year was $209,957 million (*then £87,500 million*) in 1974. The record daily increase of 28.40 on 30 Oct 1929 was most recently bettered on 3 Nov 1982 with 43.41 points to 1065.49. The largest transaction on record 'share-wise' was on 25 May 1983 for 7,000,000 shares of Ramada Inns Inc. The largest stock trade in the history of the New York Exchange was a 7,000,000 share block of Occidental Petroleum PrI stock at $111.125 in a $333,375,000 (*then £238 million*) transaction

on 2 Mar 1984. The highest price paid for a seat on the NY Stock Exchange was $515,000 (*then £214,580*) in 1969. The lowest 20th century price was $17,000 in 1942. The market value of stocks listed on the New York Stock Exchange reached an all-time high at the end of November 1983— $1,605,557,593,419.

Largest and smallest equity
The greatest aggregate market value of any corporation at year end was $74.0 billion (*then £52,860 million*) for IBM on 31 Dec 1983.

Britain's smallest public listed company is Dura Mill Ltd of Whitworth, Lancashire, producers of very high quality yarn with a capitalization of £85,000 in 30 p shares.

Greatest personal loss
The highest recorded personal paper losses on stock values have been those of Ray A. Kroc, Chairman of McDonald's Corporation with $64,901,718 (*then £27 million*) on 8 July 1974 and Edwin H. Land, President of Polaroid Corporation with $59,397,355 on 28–29 May 1974, when Polaroid stock closed $12.12 down at $43\frac{1}{4}$ on that day.

Largest new issue
The American Telegraph & Telephone Company offered $1375 million's worth of shares in a rights offer on 27,500,000 shares of convertible preferred stock on the New York market on 2 June 1971. The largest offering on the London Stock Exchange by a United Kingdom company was the £624 million rights offer of British Petroleum Co plc on 23 June 1981.

Largest investment house
The largest securities company in the world, and once the world's largest partnership with 124 partners, before becoming a corporation in 1959, is Merrill, Lynch, Pierce, Fenner & Smith Inc (founded 6 Jan 1914) of New York City, USA. Its parent, Merrill, Lynch and Co, has assets of $26 billion, 44,000 employees, 1000 offices and 4.8 million customer accounts. The firm is referred to in the United States stock exchange circles as 'The Thundering Herd' or a 'Breed Apart'.

For details of most markings and other facts relating to the London Stock Exchange, see diagram above

The Bowater plant near Sittingbourne, Kent, the largest paper mill in the UK.

Paper mills

The world's largest paper mill is that established in 1936 by the Union Camp Corporation at Savannah, Georgia, USA, with an all-time record output in 1980 of 1,038,656 short tons *942 246 tonnes*. The largest paper mill in the United Kingdom is the Bowaters Kemsley Mill near Sittingbourne, Kent with a complex covering an area of 260 acres *105 ha* and a capacity in excess of 300,000 tons/*tonnes* a year.

Pharmaceuticals

The world's largest pharmaceutical company is American Home Products of New York with sales of $4,856,501,000 (*£3468 million*). Britain's largest drug *and* food turnover in 1982–83 was by Glaxo with £1027.5 million.

Photographic store

The photographic store with the largest selling area is Jessop of Leicester Ltd's Photo Centre, Hinckley Road, Leicester opened in June 1979 with an area now of 27,000 ft² *2508 m²*.

Public relations

The world's largest public relations firm is Hill and Knowlton, Inc with headquarters at 420 Lexington Avenue, New York City, NY, USA and with fifty other offices throughout the world. The firm employs a full-time staff of more than 1200.

The world's pioneer public relations publication is *Public Relations News*, founded by Mrs Denny Griswold in 1944 and which now circulates in 89 countries.

Publishing

The publishing company generating most net revenue is Time Inc of New York City with $2717 million (*£1940 million*) in 1983. The largest educational book publishing concern in the world is the Book Division of McGraw-Hill Inc of New York with sales of $406,492,000 (*£290.3 million*) in 1983 with 2244 new books and educational products.

Restaurateurs

The largest restaurant chain in the world is that operated by McDonald's Corporation of Oak Brook, Illinois, USA, founded on 15 April 1955 in Des Plaines, Chicago by Ray A. Kroc BH (Bachelor of Hamburgerology). By 1 March 1984 the number of McDonald's restaurants licensed and owned in 31 countries and 3 US territories reached 7778, with an aggregate throughput of 48 billion 100 per cent beef hamburgers under the motto 'Q.S.C. & V.'—for quality, (fast) service, cleanliness and value. Sales systemwide in 1983 were $8,686,575,000 million (*£6205 million*). Britain's largest hotel and catering group is Trusthouse Forte who employ up to 47,000 full and part-time staff in the UK, 13,000 overseas, and who had a turnover of £1,012,000,000 in 1982–83. They have 800 hotels world-wide.

San Francisco had, in 1983, 4293 dining establishments or 92.6 per square mile.

Fish and chip restaurant

The world's largest fish and chip shop is Harry Ramsden's, White Cross, Guiseley, West Yorkshire with 180 staff serving 1,600,000 customers per annum, who consumed 290 tons of fish and 450 tons of potatoes.

Retailer

The largest retailing firm in the world is Sears, Roebuck and Co (founded by Richard Warren Sears in North Redwood railway station, Minnesota in 1886) of Chicago, Illinois, USA. World-wide revenues were $30,019,800,000 (*£19.368 million*) in the year ending 31 Dec 1982 when Sears Merchandise Group had 831 retail stores, 1204 catalogue, retail and telephone sales offices and 1551 independent catalogue merchants in the USA and total assets valued at $36,643,100,000 (*23,641 million*).

Ship-building

In 1983 there was 15,911,143 gross tonnage of ships, excluding sailing ships, non-propelled vessels and vessels of less than 100 gross tonnage, completed throughout the world. The figures for Romania and People's Republic of China are incomplete. Japan completed 6,670,317 gross tonnage (41.92 per cent of the world total). The United Kingdom ranked sixth with 496,835 gross tonnage. The world's leading shipbuilding firm in 1983 was Hyundai of Korea (South), which completed 39 vessels of 1,038,188 gross tonnage. Physically the largest ship yard in the United Kingdom is Harland and Wolff Ltd of Queen's Island, Belfast, which covers some 300 acres *120 ha*.

Shipping line

The largest shipping owners and operators are Exxon Corporation (see p. 159) whose fleets of owned/managed and chartered tankers in 1983 totalled a daily average of 15,730,000 deadweight tons.

Shopping centre

The world's first shopping centre was Roland Park Shopping Center, Baltimore, Maryland, USA built in 1896. The world's largest shopping centre is the Del Amo Fashion Center, Torrance, California with 2,542,199 ft² *236 170m²* or 58.36 acres under one roof. It was opened in Oct 1981. The world's largest wholesale merchandise mart is the Dallas Market Center, located on Stemmons Freeway, Dallas, Texas, USA with nearly 9.3 million ft² *864 000 m²* in 8 buildings. The complex covers 150 acres *60 ha* with some 3400 permanent showrooms displaying merchandise of more than 26,000 manufacturers. The Center attracts 600,000 buyers each year to its 38 annual markets and trade shows. The largest shopping centre in Britain is the Manchester Arndale Centre which has a floor area of 2,246,200 ft² *208 672 m²* including the 481,300 ft² *44 713 m²* car park for 1800 cars. It was built in 1976–79 and has a gross shopping area of 1,187,000 ft² *110 270 m²*. The £40 million centre at Milton Keynes, Buckinghamshire opened in August 1979 has the longest mall in the world—650 m *2132 ft*.

Soft drinks

The world's most profitable soft drink is Coca-Cola with over 280,000,000 drinks sold per day by early 1984 in more than 155 countries. Coke was launched as a tonic by Dr John S. Pemberton of Atlanta, Georgia in 1886. The Coca-Cola Company was formed in 1892 and the famous bottle was patented in 1915.

Steel company *World*

The world's largest producer of steel has been Nippon Steel of Tōkyō, Japan which produced 26,85 million tonnes *26.42 million tons* of crude steel in 1983. The Fukuyama Works of Nippon Kokan has a capacity of more than 16 000 000 tonnes/*tons* per annum. Its work force is 76,000.

Largest store

The world's largest store is R. H. Macy & Co Inc at Broadway and 34th Street, New York City, NY, USA. It covers 50.5 acres *20,3 ha* and employs 13,600 who handle 400,000 items. The sales of the company and its subsidiaries in 1983 were $3,468,144,000 (*£2477 million*). Mr Rowland Hussey Macy's sales on his first day at his fancy goods store on 6th Avenue, on 27 Oct 1858, were recorded as $11,06 (*then £2.20*).

Sugar Mill

The highest recorded output for any sugar mill was set in 1966–67 by Ingenio de San Cristobal y Anexas, S.A., Veracruz, Mexico with 247,900 tonnes refined from 2,886,074 tonnes of cane ground. The world's largest cane sugar plant is the California & Hawaii Sugar Co plant founded in 1906 at Crokett, California with an output of 8 million lb per day.

Largest supermarket

The world's largest supermarkets (self-service with check-

outs) were the Piggly Wiggly chain started in 1916 by Clarence Saunders (1881–1953) in Memphis, Tennessee, USA. Above 25,000 ft² or *2500 m²* net shopping area, stores are usually termed superstores or hypermarkets. The largest such in Britain is the 104,000 ft² *9660 m²* Tesco hypermarket at Weston Favell, Northampton opened in Nov 1978 with a parking capacity for 1300 cars.

Tobacco company

Subsidiary and affiliates of B.A.T. Industries (founded in London in 1902 as British-American Tobacco Co.) comprise the world's largest tobacco concern. They operate 119 tobacco factories in 52 countries: consolidated turnover in 1983 was £11,046 million and total assets were £6094 million at 31 Dec 1983. The Group's sales in 1983 topped 546,000 million cigarettes.

The world's largest cigarette plant is the $300 million Philip Morris plant at Richmond, Virginia, USA opened in October 1974. Employing 5500 people the facility produces more than 530 million cigarettes a day.

Toy manufacturer

The world's largest single manufacturer of toys is Mattel Inc of Hawthorne, Los Angeles, USA founded in 1945. Its total net sales for the year ending 28 Jan 1984 were $633,413,000 (*£460 million*) for 3 divisions of which Mattel Toys is the largest.

Toy shop

The world's biggest toy shop is Hamleys of Regent Street Ltd, founded in 1760 in Holborn and removed to Regent Street, London, W1 in 1901. It has selling space of 45,000 ft² *4180 m²* on 6 floors with over 300 employees during the Christmas season. It was taken over by Debenhams on 12 May 1976.

Undertaker (or Mortician)

The world's largest undertaking business is the SCI (Service Corporation International) with 279 funeral homes and 40 flower shops with associated limousine fleets and cemeteries. Their annual revenue in the most recession-proof of industries in the year ending 30 Apr 1983 was $208,536,000 (*£1,345,400*).

Vintners

The oldest champagne firm is Ruinart Père et Fils founded in 1729. The oldest cognac firm is Augier Frères & Co, established in 1643.

2. MANUFACTURED ARTICLES

Antique *Largest*

The largest antique ever sold has been London Bridge in March 1968. The sale was made by Mr Ivan F. Luckin of the Court of Common Council of the Corporation of London to the McCulloch Oil Corporation of Los Angeles, California, USA for $2,460,000 (*then £1,029,000*). The 10,000 tons/*tonnes* of façade stonework were re-assembled at a cost of £3 million, at Lake Havasu City, Arizona and 're-dedicated' on 10 Oct 1971.

Armour *Most Expensive*

The highest auction price paid for a suit of armour is £1,925,000 by B. H. Trupin (US) on 5 May 1983 at Sotheby's, London for the suit made in Milan by Giovanni Negroli in 1545 for Henri II, King of France from the Hever Castle Collection in Kent, England.

Heaviest

The armour of William Somerset, 3rd Earl of Worcester made at the Royal Workshop, Greenwich *c.* 1570 weighed 81 lb 9 oz *37,0 kg*. If his five bullet-proof exchange elements were substituted the total weight reaches 133 lb 13 oz *60,7 kg*.

Beds *Largest functional*

In Bruges, Belgium, Philip, Duke of Burgundy had a bed 12½ ft wide and 19 ft long *3,81 × 5,79 m* erected for the perfunctory *coucher officiel* ceremony with Princess Isabella of Portugal in 1430. The largest bed in Great Britain is the Great Bed of Ware, dating from *c.* 1580, from the Crown Inn, Ware, Hertfordshire, now preserved in the Victoria and Albert Museum, London. It is 10 ft 8½ in wide, 11 ft 1 in long and 8 ft 9 in tall *3,26 × 3,37 × 2,66 m*. The largest bed currently

The most expensive suit of armour. This royal suit was auctioned for £1,925,000 at Sotheby's on 5 May 1983, and was made for Henri II of France (1547–1559) by Giovanni Negroli.

marketed in the United Kingdom is a Super Size Diplomat bed, 9 ft wide by 9 ft long, *2,74 m²* from The London Bedding Centre, Sloane Street, SW1 which would cost more than £4000.

Heaviest

The heaviest bed is a water bed 9 ft 7 in × 9 ft 10 in *2,92 × 2,99 m* owned by Milan Vacek of Canyon County, California since 1977. The thermostatically heated water alone weighs 4205 lb *1907 kg*.

Beer cans

Beer cans date from a test marketing by Krueger Beer of Newark, New Jersey at Richmond, Virginia in 1935. The largest collection is claimed by Paul W. and Tom E. Bates of Goodlettsville, Tennessee, USA with 5584 beer and 14,256 soda cans as at Jan 1984. A Rosalie Pilsner can sold for $6000 (*then £2700*) in the US in April 1981.

Beer mat collections (*Tegestology*)

The world's largest collection of beer mats is owned by Leo Pisker of Vienna, who had collected over 100,000 different mats from 147 countries by April 1984. The largest collection of purely British mats is 28,400 by Tim J. Stannard of Birmingham by April 1984.

Blanket

The largest blanket ever made measured 68 × 100 ft *20,7 × 30,48 m* weighing 600 lb *272 kg*. It was knitted in 20,160 squares in 10 months (October 1977–July 1978) by *Woman's Weekly* readers for Action Research for The Crippled Child. It was shown on BBC TV *Record Breakers* in October 1978.

Just part of the world's greatest collection of 25,640 different bottle caps amassed by Helge Friholm.

Bottle caps

Since 1950 Helge Friholm (b. 1910) of Søborg, Denmark has amassed 25,640 different bottle caps (to Feb 1984).

Candle

A candle 80 ft *24,38 m* high and 8½ ft *2,59 m* in diameter was exhibited at the 1897 Stockholm Exhibition by the firm of Lindahls. The overall height was 127 ft *38,70 m*.

Carpets and rugs *Earliest*

The earliest carpet known is a woollen pile-knotted carpet, red on white ground excavated at Pazyryk, USSR in 1947, dated to the 5th century BC and now preserved in Leningrad.

Largest

Of ancient carpets the largest on record was the gold-enriched silk carpet of Hashim (dated AD 743) of the Abbasid caliphate in Baghdad, Iraq. It is reputed to have measured 180 by 300 ft *54,86 × 91,44 m*. A 52,225 ft² *4851 m²* or 1.23 acre 28 ton red carpet was laid on 13 Feb 1982, by the Allied Corporation, from Radio City Music Hall to the New York Hilton along the Avenue of the Americas.

Most finely woven

The most finely woven carpet known is one with more than 2490 knots per in² *980 per cm²* from a fragment of an Imperial Mughal prayer carpet of the 17th century now in the Altman collections in the Metropolitan Museum of Art, New York City, NY, USA. The most magnificent carpet ever made was the Spring carpet of Khusraw made for the audience hall of the Sassanian palace at Ctesiphon, Iraq. It was about 7000 ft² *650 m²* of silk, gold thread and encrusted with emeralds. It was cut up as booty by military looters in AD 635 and from the known realization value of the pieces must have had an original value of some £100,000,000.

Chair *Largest*

The world's largest chair is the 2000 lb *907 kg* 33 ft 1 in *10,08 m* tall, 19 ft 7 in *5,96 m* wide chair constructed by Anniston Steel & Plumbing Co. Inc for Miller Office Furniture in Anniston, Alabama, USA and completed in May 1981.

Chandelier *Largest*

The world's largest chandelier was built in Murano, Italy in 1953 for the Casino Knokke, Belgium. It measures 8 m *26 ft 3 in* in circumference and 7 m *23 ft* in height and weighs 37 tons/*tonnes* with 1896 electric lights. Britain's largest is in the Chinese Room at the Pavilion, Brighton.

Chocolates

The most expensive chocolates are by Charbonel et Walker at $35 (*then £21.88*) per pound *453 g* box.

Christmas cracker

The largest functional cracker ever constructed was one 56 ft 7 in *17,24 m* in length and 9½ ft *2,9 m* in diameter built for British Rail Hull Paragon Station and pulled on 21 Nov 1980.

Cigars *largest*

The largest cigar ever made measures 5,095 m *16 ft 8¼ in* in length and weighs 262 kg *577 lb 9 oz* (over ¼ ton) taking 243 hours and using 3330 full tobacco leaves. It was made by Tinus Vinke and Jan Weijmer in Feb 1983 and is in the Tobacco Museum in Kampen, Holland. The largest marketed cigar in the world is the 14 in *35,5 cm* Valdez Emperado by San Andres Cigars.

Most expensive

The most expensive standard cigar in the world is the 11½ in *29,2 cm* long Don Miguel 'Cervantes', which retails in Britain at £15.00.

Cigar bands

Joseph Hruby of Lyndhurst, Ohio has the largest known collection of cigar bands with 175,391 different examples dating from *c.* 1895.

Most voracious smokers

Jim Purol and Mike Papa each smoked 135 cigarettes simultaneously for 5 min on 5 Oct 1978 at Rameys Lounge, Detroit, Michigan, USA. On 3 Sept 1979 at the same venue, they each smoked 27 cigars simultaneously for 5 min and in 1983 Purol smoked 38 pipes. Simon Argevitch of Oakland, California, USA raised his old record to 17 standard size cigars, whilst simultaneously emitting bird calls or singing, on Fishermans Wharf, San Francisco on 3 July 1982.

Cigarettes *Consumption*

The heaviest smokers in the world are the people of the United States, where 640,000 million cigarettes (an average of 3750 per adult) were consumed at a cost of some $21,200 million (*£11,700 million*) in 1981. The people of China, however, were estimated to consume 725,000 million in 1977. In Senegal 80% of urban males smoke. The peak consumption in the United Kingdom was 3230 cigarettes per adult in 1973. The peak volume was 243,100,000 lb *110,2 million kg* in 1961, compared with 83.0 million kg *183 million lb* in 1983 when 101,600 million cigarettes were sold.

In the United Kingdom 47 per cent of adult men and 36 per cent of adult women smoked in 1983.

Tar/Nicotine content

Of the 141 brands most recently analysed for the Dept of Health and Social Security, the one with highest tar/nicotine content is *Capstan Full Strength* with 25/2.4 mg per cigarette. *Silk Cut Ultra Low King Size, Embassy Ultra Mild King Size*

A carpet upon which even angels might fear to tread—the 17th century 'Polonaise' silk and metal thread carpet auctioned at Sotheby's for a world record £210,000 on 13 Oct 1982 (see p. 168).

and *John Player King Size Ultra Mild* with <4/0.3 are at the lower risk end of the league table. In the Philippines there is a brand with 71 mg nicotine per cigarette.

Most popular
The world's most popular cigarette is 'Marlboro', a filter cigarette made by Phillip Morris, which sold 237,000 million units in 1982. The largest selling British cigarette in 1983 was *Benson and Hedges Special Filter*. The Wills brand 'The Three Castles' was introduced in 1878.

Longest and shortest
The longest cigarettes ever marketed were 'Head Plays', each 11 in *27,9 cm* long and sold in packets of 5 in the United States in about 1930, to save tax. The shortest were 'Lilliput' cigarettes, each 1¼ in *31,7 mm* long, and ⅛ in *3 mm* in diameter, made in Great Britain in 1956.

Largest collection
The world's largest collection of cigarettes is that of Robert E. Kaufman, MD, of 950 Park Avenue, New York City 10028, NY, USA. In April 1984 he had 7780 different cigarettes with kinds of tips made in 172 countries. The oldest brand represented is 'Lone Jack', made in the USA in *c.* 1885. Both the longest and shortest (see above) are represented.

Cigarette cards
The earliest known tobacco card is 'Vanity Fair' dated 1876 issued by Wm S. Kimball & Co., Rochester, New York. The earliest British example appeared *c.* 1883 in the form of a calendar issued by Allen & Ginter, of Richmond, Virginia, trading from Holborn Viaduct, City of London. The largest known collection is that of Mr Edward Wharton-Tigar, MBE (b. 1913) of London with a collection of more than 1,000,000 cigarette and trade cards in about 45,000 sets.

Cigarette lighter *Most expensive*
The most expensive cigarette pocket lighter in the world is the 18 carat white gold Dunhill Gemline lighter set with a 2.57 ct VSG colour emerald-cut diamond, with an additional 8.37 ct worth of brilliant-cut diamonds of VSH colour, and selling for £32,500 at Dunhill in St. James's, London in 1984.

Cigarette packets
The earliest surviving cigarette packet is the Finnish 'Petit Canon' packet for 25, made by Tollander & Klärich in 1860, from the Ventegodt Collection. The rarest is the Latvian 700-year anniversary (1201–1901) Riga packet, believed to be unique, from the same collection. The largest verified private collection is one of 60,955 from over 150 countries owned by Vernon Young of Farnham, England.

Credit card collection
The largest collection of valid credit cards at 8 May 1984 is one of 1167 (all different) by Walter Cavanagh (b. 1943) of Santa Clara, California, USA. The cost of acquisition to 'Mr. Plastic Fantastick' was nil, and he keeps them in the world's longest wallet—250 ft *76,2 m* long weighing 35 lb *15,87 kg* worth more than $1.25 million in credit.

Curtain
The largest curtain ever built has been the bright orange-red 4 ton *4064 kg* 185 ft *56 m* high curtain suspended 1350 ft *411 m* across the Rifle Gap, Grand Hogback, Colorado, USA by the Bulgarian-born sculptor Christo, (*né* Javacheff) on 10 Aug 1971. It blew apart in a 50 mph *80 km/h* gust 27 hr later. The total cost involved in displaying this work of art was $750,000 (*then £312,500*).

The world's largest functional curtain is one 550 ft long × 65 ft high *167,6 × 19,8 m* in the Brabazon hanger at British Aerospace Filton, Bristol used to enclose aircraft in the paint spraying bay. It is electrically drawn.

Dolls *Largest*
The most outsize 'doll' ever paraded was made by the Belgian student body KSA on 15 May 1983 in Ostend. It measured 51,07 m *167 ft 6 in* overall. The most massive 'guy' built was one 62 ft 4 in *19 m* high by the Fermain Youth Club, Macclesfield on 5 Nov 1983.

Dress *Most expensive*
The EVA suits for extra-vehicular activity worn by space shuttle crews from 1982 had a unit cost of $2.3 million (*then £1,437,000*). The dress with the highest price tag ever exhibited by a Paris fashion house was one in the Schiaparelli spring/summer collection on 23 Jan 1977. 'The Birth of Venus' designed by Serge Lepage with 512 diamonds was priced at Fr. 7,500,000 (*then £880,000*).

The coronation robe for Emperor Field Marshall Jean-Bédel Bokassa with a 39 ft *11,8 m* long train was encrusted with 785,000 pearls and 1,220,000 crystal beads by Guiselin of Paris for £77,125. It was used at Bangui, Central African Empire (now Republic) on 4 Dec 1977.

Fabrics *Earliest and Most expensive*
The oldest surviving fabric discovered from Level VI A at Çatal Hüyük, Turkey has been radio-carbon dated to 5900 BC.

The most expensive fabric obtainable is Vicuña cloth manufactured by Fuji Keori Ltd of Osaka, Japan at US$3235 (*£2087*) per metre in July 1983. The most expensive evening wear

RECORDS FOR ANTIQUES

left: A sum of £990,000 was paid for this world's most expensive piece of furniture. It is the French royal family's black and gold lacquer secretaire.

above: The world's most expensive toy— the £25,500 tin-plate model of Stephenson's *Rocket* made in Germany in 1909. (*Sotheby's, London*)

ART NOUVEAU
The highest auction price for any piece of art nouveau is $360,000 (*then £163,600*) for a spider-web leaded glass mosaic and bronze table lamp by L. C. Tiffany at Christie's, New York on 8 Apr. 1980.

BED
A 1930 black lacquer kingsize bed made by Jean Durand was auctioned at Christie's, New York City on 2 Oct 1983 for £49,668.

BLANKET
The most expensive blanket was a Navajo Churro handspun serape of *c.* 1852 sold for $115,500 (*then £79,500*) at Sotheby's, New York City on 22 Oct 1983.

CARPET
In 1946 the Metropolitan Museum, New York, privately paid $1 million (*then £248,138*) for the 26.5 × 13.6 ft *807 × 414 cm* Anhalt Medallion carpet made in Tabriz or Kashan, Persia *c.* 1590. The highest price ever paid at auction for a carpet is £231,000 for a 17th century 'Polonaise' silk and metal thread carpet at Sotheby's, London on 13 Oct 1982.

CERAMICS
The Greek urn painted by Euphronios and thrown by Euxitheos in *c.* 530 was bought by private treaty by the Metropolitan Museum of Art, New York, for $1.3 million (*then £541,666*) in August 1972.

CHAIR
The highest price ever paid for a single chair is $275,000 (*then £177,500*) on 23 Oct 1982 at Sotheby's in Manhattan, for the Chippendale side chair attributed to Thomas Affleck of Philadelphia, USA and made in *c.* 1770.

CIGARETTE CARD
The most valuable card is one of the 6 known baseball series cards of Honus Wagner, who was a non-smoker, which was sold in New York in December 1981 for $25,000 (*then £13,900*).

DOLLS
The highest price paid at auction for a doll is £16,000 for a William and Mary English wooden doll *c.* 1690 at Sotheby's, London on 29 May 1984.

FURNITURE
The highest price ever paid for a single piece of furniture is £990,000 at Sotheby's, London on 8 July 1983 by Mrs Seward Johnson for a black and gold lacquer secrétaire à abbant attributed to Adam Weisweiler for the Cabinet du Roi, Versailles in 1784.

The English furniture record was set by a black-japanned bureau-bookcase of *c.* 1705. Formerly owned by Queen Mary, it made $860,000 (*then £463,366*) at Christie's, New York on 18 Oct 1981.

GLASS
The auction record is £520,000 for a Roman glass cage-cup of *c.* AD 300 measuring 7 in *17,78 cm* in diameter and 4 in *10,16 cm* in height, sold at Sotheby's, London, on 4 June 1979 to Robin Symes.

GOLD PLATE
The world's highest auction price for a single piece of gold plate is £66,000 (*then $122,000*) for an English George III salver, known as 'The Rutland Salver', made by Paul Storr of London, 1801. The salver, which is 12 in *30,5 cm* in diameter, is engraved with the arms of Manners, Dukes of Rutland and of the 16 towns and cities, the gold Freedom boxes of which were melted down to make the salver. It was sold by Sotheby Parke Bernet, London, on 4 May 1978.

GUNS
The highest price ever paid for a single gun is £125,000 given by the London dealers F. Partridge for a French flintlock fowling piece made for Louis XIII, King of France in *c.* 1615 and attributed to Pierre le Bourgeoys of Lisieux, France (d. 1627). This piece was included in the collection of the late William Goodwin Renwick of the United States sold by Sotheby's, London on 21 Nov 1972 (see

also Pistols). It is now in the Metropolitan Museum, New York, USA.

HAT
The highest price ever paid for a hat is $66,000 (*then £34,750*) by the Alaska State Museum at a New York City auction in Nov 1981 for a Tlingit Kiksadi ceremonial frog helmet from *c.* 1600.

ICON
The record auction price for an icon is $150,000 (*then £67,500*) paid at Christie's, New York on 17 Apr 1980 for the *Last Judgement* (from the George R. Hann collection, Pittsburgh, USA) made in Novgorod in the 16th century.

JADE
The highest price ever paid for an item in jade is $396,000 (£270,307) at Sotheby's, New York on 6 Dec 1983 for a mottled brownish-yellow belt-hook and pendant mask of the Warring States Period of Chinese history.

JEWELS
The highest auction price for any jewels is £2,825,000 (or £3.1 million with the buyer's premium) for two pear-shaped diamond drop earings of 58.6 and 61 carats at Sotheby's, Geneva on 14 Nov 1980. Neither the buyer nor seller was disclosed.

PAPERWEIGHT
The highest price ever paid for a glass paperweight is $143,000 (*£97,278*) at Sotheby's, New York City, USA on 2 Dec 1983 for a blue glass weight made at Pantin, Paris *post* 1850.

PISTOL
The highest price paid at auction for a pistol is £110,000 at Christie's London on 8 July 1980 for a Sadeler wheel-lock holster pistol from Munich dated *c.* 1600.

PLAYING CARDS
The highest price paid for a deck of playing cards is $143,352 (*£98,850*) by the New York Metropolitan Museum at Sotheby's, London on 6 Dec 1983.

PORCELAIN AND POTTERY
The highest auction price for any ceramic or any Chinese work of art is £792,000 for a blue and white Ming vase of 1426–35 bought by Hirano of Japan at Sotheby's, London on 15 Dec 1981.

POT LID
The highest price paid for a pot lid is £3300 for a seaweed patterned 'Spanish Lady' lid sold at Phillips, London on 19 May 1982.

SILVER
The highest price ever paid for silver is £612,500 for the pair of Duke of Kingston tureens made in 1735 by Meissonnier and sold by Christie's, Geneva on 8 Nov 1977. The English silver record is £484,000 at Sotheby's, London on 3 May 1984 for the Duke of Northumberland's Shield of Achilles, made in 1822 by Rundell, Bridge and Rundell.

SNUFF BOX
The highest price ever paid for a snuff box is Sw. Fr. 1,540,000 (*then £435,028*) in a sale at Christie's, Geneva on 11 May 1982 for a gold snuff box dating from 1760–65 and once owned by Frederick the Great of Prussia. It was purchased by S. J. Phillips, the London dealers, for stock.

SPOONS

A Wiener werkstaffe spoon by Josef Hoffmann, Austria *c.* 1905, was sold at Sotheby's, London for £17,600 on 28 Apr 1983. A set of 13 Henry VIII Apostle spoons owned by Lord Astor of Hever were sold for £120,000 on 24 June 1981 at Christie's, London.

STUFFED BIRD

The highest price ever paid for a stuffed bird is £9000. This was given on 4 Mar 1971 at Sotheby's, London, by the Iceland Natural History Museum for a specimen of the Great Auk (*Alca impennis*) in summer plumage, which was taken in Iceland *c.* 1821; this particular specimen stood 22½ in *57 cm* high. The Great Auk was a flightless North Atlantic seabird, which was finally exterminated on Eldey, Iceland in 1844, becoming extinct through hunting. The last British sightings were at Co. Waterford in 1834 and St Kilda, Western Isles *c.* 1840.

SWORD

The highest price paid for a sword is the $145,000 (*then £85,800*) paid for the gold sword of honour, presented by the Continental Congress of 1779 to General Marie Jean Joseph Lafayette, at Sotheby Parke Bernet, New York City, USA on 20 Nov 1976.

TAPESTRY

The highest price paid for a tapestry is £550,000 for a Swiss Medieval tapestry frieze in two parts dated 1468–1476 at Sotheby's, Geneva, on 10 Apr 1981 by the Basle Historische Museum.

THIMBLE

The record auction price for a thimble is £8000 paid by the London dealer Winifred Williams at Christie's, London on 3 Dec 1979 for a Meissen dentil-shaped porcelain piece of *c.* 1740.

TOY

The auction record for a toy is £25,500 for a model train set of Stephenson's *Rocket* made by Marklin of Germany in tin plate in 1909 at Sotheby's, London on 29 May 1984.

TYPEWRITER

The highest price paid for an antique machine is £3000 for an 1886 Daw and Tait machine auctioned at Sotheby's, London on 12 Dec 1980.

WALKING STICK

The highest auction price for a walking stick has been $24,200 (*then £17,285*) at Sotheby Parke Bernet, New York in 1983 for an octagonal whale ivory nobbed stick decorated by Scrimshanders in 1845.

fabric was that designed by Alan Hershman of Duke Street, London at £475 per metre. Each square metre, despite 155,000 hand sewn sequins, weighs less than 7 oz *198 g*.

Finest cloth

The most expensive cloth, the brown-grey throat hair of Indian goats, is Shatoosh (or Shatusa), finer, and more expensive than Vicuña. It was sold by Neiman-Marcus of Dallas, Texas, USA, at $1000 (£555) per yard but supplies have now dried up.

Firework

The largest firework ever produced has been *Universe I* exploded for the Lake Toya Festival, Hokkaido, Japan on 20 Aug 1983. The 421 kg *928 lb* shell was 108 cm *42.5 in* in diameter and burst to a diameter of 860 m *2830 ft*, with a 5 colour display. The longest firework 'waterfall' set off in Britain was one of 313 ft *94,45 m* by Swindon Town F.C. on 5 Nov 1983.

Flags *Oldest*

The oldest known flag is one dating to *c.* 500 BC found in the excavation of the princesses graves in Hunan, Changsha, China. The Friesian flag still flown in the Netherlands dates from the 9th century AD.

Largest

The largest flag in the world, the 'Great American Flag', was displayed at Evansville, Indiana on 22 Mar 1980 measuring 411 ft *125 m* by 210 ft *64 m* with a weight of 7 tons/*tonnes* in readiness for its eventual hoisting on the Verrazano Narrows Bridge, New York, USA on 4 July 1981. It was the brainchild of Len Silverfine. The largest Union Flag (or Union Jack) was one 240 × 108 ft *73,15 × 32,91 m* displayed at the Royal Tournament, Earl's Court, London in July 1976. It weighed more than a ton and was made by Form 4Y at Bradley Rowe School, Exeter, Devon. The largest flag *flown* from a flagstaff is a US flag 50 × 100 ft *15,24 × 30,48 m* first raised on 25 Nov 1983 at Outlet Malls of America, Plano, Texas, USA. The study of flags is known as vexillology.

Float

The largest float is the 150 ft *45,7 m* long, 22 ft *6,7 m* wide 'Agree' Float bearing 51 All-American Homecoming 'Queens' used at the Orange Bowl parade, Miami, Florida, USA on 29 Dec 1977.

Furniture *Oldest British*

The oldest surviving piece of British furniture is a three-footed tub with metal bands found at Glastonbury, Somerset, and dating from between 300 and 150 BC.

Largest Piece

The largest item of furniture in the world is the wooden bench in Green Park, Obihiro, Hokkaido, Japan which seats 1282 people and measures 400 m *1312 ft 4 in* long. It was completed by a team of 770 on 19 July 1981.

Glass

The most priceless example of the art of glass-making is usually regarded as the glass Portland Vase which dates from late in the 1st century BC or 1st century AD. It was made in Italy, and was in the possession of the Barberini family in Rome from at least 1642. It was eventually bought by the Duchess of Portland in 1792 but smashed while in the British Museum in 1847. The thinnest glass made is 0,3 mm $\frac{1}{85}$*th of an inch* thick for digital displays by Nippon glass Corp.

Gold plate

The gold coffin of the 14th century BC Pharaoh Tutankhamun discovered by Howard Carter on 16 Feb 1923 in the Valley of the Kings, western Thebes, Egypt weighed 110,4 kg *243 lb*. The exhibition at the British Museum attracted 1,656,151 people (of whom 45.7 per cent bought catalogues) from 30 Mar to 30 Dec 1972, resulting in a profit of £657,731.22.

Jig-saw *Earliest and largest*

The earliest jig-saws were made as 'dissected maps' by John Spilsbury (1739–69) in Russell Court off Drury Lane, London *c.* 1762. The largest jig-saw ever made is *Popeye and Friends* measuring 72 × 44 ft *21,94 × 13,41 m* with 13,296 pieces at Macy's World's Largest Games Festival at Herald Square, New York City, on 21 Aug 1983. Gimbels of New York City sold in 1933 a Ringling Barnum Circus Puzzle 8½ × 13 ft *2,59 × 3,96 m* weighing 597 lb *270 kg* with 50,000 pieces made by Eureka Jig Saw Puzzle Co. of Philadelphia, Pennsylvania, USA.

Custom-made Stave puzzles made by Steve Richardson of Vermont, USA of 2300 pieces cost $3700 (*then £2430*) in Jan 1983. The most difficult are those manufactured by Förlaget Kärnan AB of Helsingborg, Sweden with a density of 40,000 unique pieces to the square metre or 25.8 to the square inch.

Matchbox labels

The oldest match label of accepted provenance is that of Samuel Jones *c.* 1830. The finest collection of trade mark labels (excluding any bar or other advertising labels) is some 280,000 pieces collected by the phillumenist Robert Jones of Indianapolis, USA. The greatest British prize is a Lucifer & Congreve label of *c.* 1835.

Nylon *Sheerest*

The lowest denier nylon yarn ever produced is the 6 denier used for stockings exhibited at the Nylon Fair in London in February 1956. The sheerest stockings normally available are 9 denier. An indication of the thinness is that a hair from the average human head is about 50 denier.

Penknife

The penknife with the greatest number of blades is the Year Knife made by the cutlers, Joseph Rodgers & Sons Ltd, of Sheffield, England, whose trade mark was granted in 1682. The knife was built in 1822 with 1822 blades but had to halt at 1973 because there was no further space. It was acquired by Britain's largest hand tool manufacturers, Stanley Works (Great Britain) Ltd of Sheffield, South Yorkshire in 1970.

Pens *Most expensive*

The most expensive writing pens are the 18 carat pair of pens (one fibre-tipped and one ballpoint) capped by diamonds of 3.88 carats sold by Alfred Dunhill (see Cigarette lighter) for £9943 the pair (incl. VAT). The most expensive fountain pen is the Mont Blanc 18 carat gold and platinum nibbed Meisterstück made by Dunhill in Hamburg, West Germany and retailing in April 1984 for $4250 (*then £3035*).

Pistol

In December 1983 it was reported that Mr Ray Bily (US) owned an initialled gold pistol made for Hitler which was valued for insurance purposes at $375,000 (*£267,850*).

Post cards

Deltiology is claimed to be the third largest collecting hobby next only to stamps and coins. Austria issued the first cards in 1869 followed by Britain in 1872. Values tend to be obscured by the philatelic element.

Quilting

The world's largest quilt, designed by A. Platteau, was made by the people of Kortrijk-Rollegem, Belgium. It comprises 16,240 squares measuring 21,24 × 30,35 m *69.6 × 99.5 ft*. On 28 Aug 1982 it was hoisted by two cranes.

Ropes *Largest and Longest*

The largest rope ever made was a coir fibre launching rope with a circumference of 47 in *119 cm* made in 1858 for the British liner *Great Eastern* by John and Edwin Wright of Birmingham. It consisted of four strands, each of 3780 yarns. The longest fibre rope ever made without a splice was one of 10,000 fathoms or 11.36 miles *18 288 m* of 6½ in *16,5 cm* circumference manila by Frost Brothers (now British Ropes Ltd) in London in 1874.

The strongest cable-laid wire rope strop made is one 282 mm *11.1 in* in diameter with a breaking strain of 3250 tonnes.

Shoes

James Smith, founder of James Southall & Co of Norwich, England introduced sized shoes in 1792. The firm began making 'Start-rite' children's shoes in 1923.

Emperor Bokassa of the Central African Republic commissioned pearl-studded shoes from the House of Berluti, Paris for his self-coronation in Dec 1977 at a cost of $85,000 (*then £38,800*).

The most expensive standard shoes obtainable are mink-lined golf shoes with 18 carat gold embellishments and ruby-tipped spikes made by Stylo Matchmakers International Ltd, of Northampton, England which retail for £6250, or $8750 per pair in the USA.

Largest

Excluding cases of elephantiasis, the largest shoes ever sold are a pair size 42 built for the giant Harley Davidson of Avon Park, Florida, USA. The normal limit is size 14. For advertising and display purposes facsimiles of shoes weighing up to 1,5 tonnes have been constructed.

Silver

The largest single pieces of silver are the pair of water jugs of 10,408 troy oz 4.77 cwt *242,7 kg* made in 1902 for the Maharaja of Jaipur (1861–1922). They are 160 cm *5 ft 3 in* tall, with a circumference of 2,48 m *8 ft 1½ in*, and have a capacity of 1800 gallons *8182 litres*. They are now in the City Palace, Jaipur. The silversmith was Gorind Narain.

Snuff *Most expensive*

The most expensive snuff obtainable in Britain is 'Café Royale' sold by G. Smith and Sons (est. 1869) of 74, Charing Cross Road, City of Westminster, Greater London. It sells at £1.94 per oz. as at 1 Apr 1984.

Sofa *Longest*

The longest standard sofa manufactured for market is the King Talmage Sofa, 12 ft 2 in *3,7 m* in length made by the Talmageville Furniture Manufacturers, California, USA.

Table *Longest*

A buffet table 1007,3 m *3304 ft 10 in* long was set up for the 400th anniversary of Hudiksvall, Sweden on 19 June 1982. Some 4000 people including HM The King of Sweden were seated.

Table cloth

The world's largest table cloth is one 219 yd *200 m* long by 2 yd *1,8 m* wide double damask made by John S. Brown & Sons Ltd of Belfast in 1972 and shipped to a royal palace in the Middle East. There was also an order for matching napkins for 450 places.

Tapestry *Earliest*

The earliest known examples of tapestry woven linen are three pieces from the tomb of Thutmose IV, the Egyptian pharaoh and dated to 1483–1411 BC.

Largest

The largest single piece of tapestry ever woven is 'Christ in His Majesty', measuring 72 ft by 39 ft *21,94 × 11,88 m* designed by Graham Vivian Sutherland OM (1903–80) for an altar hanging in Coventry Cathedral, West Midlands. It cost £10,500, weighs ¾ ton *760 kg* and was delivered from Pinton Frères of Felletin, France, on 1 Mar 1962.

Longest embroidery

The famous Bayeux *Telle du Conquest, dite tapisserie de la reine Mathilde*, a hanging 19½ in *49,5 cm* wide by 231 ft *70,40 m* in length depicts events of the period 1064–6 in 72 scenes and was probably worked in Canterbury, Kent, in *c.* 1086. It was 'lost' for 2½ centuries from 1476 until 1724. The Overlord Embroidery of 34 panels each 8 × 3 ft *2,43 × 0,91 m*, commissioned by Lord Dulverton CBE, TD (b. 1915) from the Royal School of Needlework, London, was completed in 1979 after 100 man years of work and is 41 ft *12,49 m* longer than the Bayeux and has the largest area of any embroidery with 816 ft² *75,8 m²*. An uncompleted 8 in *20,3 cm* deep 1280 ft *390,14 m* embroidery of scenes from C. S. Lewis's Narnia children's stories has been worked by Mrs Margaret S. Pollard of Truro, Cornwall to the order of Mr Michael Maine.

Tartan *Earliest*

The earliest evidence of tartan is the so-called Falkirk tartan, found stuffed in a jar of coins in Bells Meadow, Falkirk, Scotland. It is of a dark and light brown pattern and dates from *c.* AD 245. The earliest reference to a specific named tartan has been to a Murray tartan in 1618 although Mackay tartan was probably worn earlier. There are 1300 tartans known to the Museums of Scottish Tartans at Cumrie, Perthshire. HRH Prince of Wales is eligible to wear 11 including the Balmoral which has been exclusive to the Royal Family since 1852.

Tea Towels

The largest reported collection of unduplicated tea towels is 500 by Mr Tony Judkin of Luton, Bedfordshire.

Time capsule

The world's largest time capsule is the Tropico Time Tunnel of 10,000 ft³ *283 m³* in a cave in Rosamond, California, USA, sealed by the Kern Antelope Historical Society on 20 Nov 1966 and intended for opening in AD 2866.

Typewriters

The first patent for a typewriter was by Henry Mill in 1714 but the earliest known working machine was made by Pellegrine Turri (Italy) in 1808.

Vase *Largest*

The largest vase on record is one 8 ft *2,78 m*, in height, weighing 650 lb *294,8 kg*, thown by Sebastiano Maglio at Haeger Potteries of Dundee, Illinois, USA (founded 1872) during August 1976.

The Chinese ceramic authority Chingwah Lee of San Francisco was reported in Aug 1978 to have appraised a unique 39 in *99 cm* K'ang Hsi 4-sided vase then in a bank vault in Phoenix, Arizona, USA at '$60 million' (*then £30 million*).

Wreath *Most expensive*

The most expensive wreath on record was that presented to Sri Chinmoy in New York City, USA on 11 July 1983 by Ashrita Furman and Pahar Meltzer. It was handled by the Garland of Divinity's Love Florist, contained 10,000 flowers, and cost $3500 (*£2260*).

3. AGRICULTURE

Origins

It has been estimated that only 21 per cent of the world's land surface is cultivable and that only 7.6 per cent is actually under cultivation. Evidence adduced in 1971 from Nok Nok Tha and Spirit Cave, Thailand tends to confirm plant cultivation and animal domestication was part of the Hoabinhian culture *c.* 11,000 BC. Reindeer may have been domesticated as early as *c.* 18,000 BC but definite evidence is still lacking.

Goat was domesticated at Asiab, Iran by *c.* 8050 BC and dog at Star Carr, North Yorkshire by *c.* 7700 BC: the earliest definite date for sheep is *c.* 7200 BC at Argissa-Magula, Thessaly, Greece and for pig and cattle *c.* 7000 BC at the same site. The earliest date for horse is *c.* 4350 BC from Dereivka, Ukraine, USSR. Ancient trackings sighted by a US space shuttle in 1982 indicate perhaps an even earlier domestication of draft animals.

FARMS

Earliest

The earliest dated British farming site is a neolithic one, enclosed within the Iron Age hill-fort at Hembury, Devon, excavated during 1934–5 and now dated to 4210–3990 BC. Pollen analysis from two sites Oakhanger, Hampshire, and Winfrith Heath, Dorset (Mesolithic *c.* 5000 BC) indicates that Mesolithic man may have had herds which were fed on ivy during the winter months.

Largest *World*

The largest farms in the world are collective farms (*sovkhozes*) in the USSR. These have been reduced in number from 235,500 in 1940 to only 18,000 in 1980 and have been increased in size so that units of over 60,000 acres *25 000 ha* are not uncommon. The pioneer farm owned by Laucidio Coelho near Campo Grande, Mato Grosso, Brazil in *c.* 1901 was 3358 miles² *8700 km² 2.15 million* acres with 250,000 head of cattle at the time of his death in 1975.

Great Britain

The largest farms in the British Isles are Scottish hill farms in the Grampians. The largest arable farm is that of Elvedon, Suffolk, farmed by the Earl of Iveagh. Here 11,246 acres *4553 ha* are farmed on an estate of 22,918 acres *9278 ha*, the greater part of which was formerly derelict land. The 1983 production included 9821 tonnes *9665 tons* of grain and 47 375 tonnes *46,626 tons* of sugar beet. The livestock includes 505 beef cattle, 1021 ewes and 5500 pigs.

Cattle station

The world's largest cattle station is Strangeray Springs, South Australia extending over 11,594 miles² 7,420,160 acres *3 002 790 ha*—more than the area of England's four largest counties of North Yorkshire, Cumbria, Devon and Lincolnshire with Nottinghamshire 'thrown in'. Until 1915 the Victoria River Downs Station, Northern Territory had an area of 22,400,000 acres (35,000 miles² *90 650 km²*), the same as England's 20 largest counties put together.

Rice Farming

The largest continuous wild rice (*Zizania aquatica*) farm in the world is Clearwater Rice Inc. at Clearbrook, Minnesota, USA with 2000 acres *809 ha*. In 1983 it yielded 386,148 lb *175,15 tonnes* per acre.

Sheep station

The largest sheep station in the world is Commonwealth Hill, in the north-west of South Australia. It grazes between 70,000 and 90,000 sheep, *c.* 700 cattle and 54,000 uninvited kangaroos in an area of 4080 miles² *10 567 km²*, i.e. larger than the combined area of Norfolk and Suffolk. The head count on Sir William Stevenson's 30,000 acre *12 140 ha* Lochinver Station in New

Part of the world's largest rice 'paddy' which is to be found not in Asia but in the United States.

Zealand was 117,500 on 1 Jan 1983 on 21,000 acres *8500 ha*. The largest sheep move on record occurred when 27 horsemen moved a mob of 43,000 sheep 40 miles *64 km* from Barcaldine to Beaconsfield Station, Queensland, Australia, in 1886.

Turkey farm

The world's largest turkey farm is that of Bernard Matthews plc, centred at Gt Witchingham, Norfolk, with 2300 workers tending 7,500,000 turkeys.

Chicken ranch

The world's largest chicken ranch is the 345 acre *140 ha* 'Egg City' Moorpark, California established by Julius Goldman in 1961. Some 2,220,000 eggs are laid daily by 3.0 million hens.

Piggery

The world's largest piggery is the Sljeme pig unit in Yugoslavia which is able to process 300,000 pigs in a year. Even larger units may exist in Romania but details are at present lacking.

Cow shed

The longest cow shed in Britain is that of the Yorkshire Agricultural Society at Harrogate, North Yorkshire. It is 456 ft *139 m* in length with a capacity of 686 cows. The National Agricultural Centre, Kenilworth, Warwickshire, completed in 1967, has, however, capacity for 782 animals.

Foot-and-mouth disease

The worst outbreak of foot-and-mouth disease in Great Britain was that from Salop on 25 Oct 1967 to 25 June 1968 in which there were 2364 outbreaks and 429,632 animals slaughtered at a direct and consequential loss of £150,000,000. The outbreak of 1871, when farms were much smaller, affected 42,531 farms. The disease first appeared in Great Britain at Stratford, East London in August 1839.

Sheep shearing

The highest recorded speed for sheep shearing in a working day was that of John Fagan who machine-sheared 804 lambs (average 89.3 per hour) in 9 hr at Hautora Rd, Pio Pio, New Zealand on 8 Dec 1980. Peter Casserly of Christchurch, New Zealand, achieved a solo blade (i.e. hand-shearing) record of 353 lambs in 9 hours on 13 Feb 1976. In a shearing marathon, four men machine-shore 2519 sheep in 29 hr at Stewarts Trust, Waikia, Southland, New Zealand on 11 Feb 1982.

Mr Lavor Taylor (b. 27 Feb 1896) of Ephraim, Utah claims to have sheared 515,000 sheep to May 1984.

Great Britain

British records for 9 hr have been set at 555 by Roger Poyntz-Roberts (300) and John Savery (255) on 9 June 1971 (sheep caught *by* shearers), and 610 by the same pair (sheep caught *for* shearers) in July 1970.

Sheep *Survival*

On 2 Mar 1978, Peter Boa of Sciberscross, Strath Brora, Sutherland, Scotland dug out 9 sheep buried in snow for 33 days. Two ewes were alive.

Mushroom farm

The largest mushroom farm in the world is the Butler County Mushroom Farm, Inc, founded in 1937 in a disused limestone mine near West Winfield, Pennsylvania, USA. It employs over 1000 in a maze of underground galleries 110 miles *177 km* long, producing over 24,000 short tons *21 770 tonnes* of mushrooms per year.

Largest wheat field

The largest single fenced field sown with wheat was one of 35,000 acres *14 160 ha* sown in 1951 south west of Lethbridge, Alberta, Canada.

Largest vineyard

The world's largest vineyard is that extending over the Mediterranean façade between the Rhône and the Pyrenees in the *départements* Hérault, Gard, Aude, and Pyrénées-Orientales in an area of 840 000 ha *2,075 685 acres* of which 52.3 per cent is *monoculture viticole.*

Largest hop field

The largest hop field in the world is one of 1836 acres *743 ha* near Toppenish, Washington State, USA. It is owned by John I. Haas, Inc, the world's largest hop growers, with hop farms in California, Idaho, Oregon and Washington State, with a total net area of 4112 acres *1664 ha.*

Community garden *Largest*

The largest recorded community garden project is that operated by the City Beautiful Council, and the Benjamin Wegerzyn Garden Center, Dayton. Ohio, USA. It comprises 1173 allotments each of $812\frac{1}{4}$ ft² *74,45 m².*

CROP YIELDS

Wheat

Crop yields for highly tended small areas are of little significance. The British record is 111.4 cwt/acre *13,99 tonnes/ha* at 15.5% moisture on a field of 43.24 acres *17,49 ha* by Gordon Rennie of Clifton Mains, Newbridge, Lothian, Scotland.

Barley

A yield of 84.6 cwt/acre *10 620 kg/ha* of Ingri Winter Barley was achieved in 1982 by Mr John Parsons and his son Nick at Claypits Farm, Goodnestone, Kent from a 42 acre *17,0 ha* field.

Corn

A yield of 352.64 US bushels ($15\frac{1}{2}$ per cent moisture) from an acre, using De Kalb XL-54, was achieved by Roy Lynn, Jr near Kalamazoo, Michigan, USA on 30 Sept 1977.

Sugar beet

The highest recorded yield for sugar beet is 62.4 short tons (55.71 long tons) per acre *139,9 tonnes/ha* by Andy Christensen and Jon Giannini in the Salinas Valley, California, USA.

Potato picking

The greatest number of US barrels picked in a $9\frac{1}{4}$ hr day is 235 by Walter Sirois (b. 1917) of Caribou, Maine, USA on 30 Sept 1950.

Field to Loaf Record

The fastest time for producing loaves from growing wheat is 46 min 8 sec at St Nicholas Mill, Thanet, Kent on 30 Aug 1983.

Ploughing

The world championship (instituted 1953) has been staged in 17 countries and won by ploughmen of ten nationalities of which the United Kingdom has been most successful with 7 championships. The only man to take the title three times has been Hugh Barr of Northern Ireland in 1954–5–6.

The fastest recorded time for ploughing an acre *0,404 ha* (minimum 32 right-hand turns and depth 9 in *22 cm*) is 11 min 33.5 sec by John Binning using a Fiskars 5 furrow 14 in *35,5 cm* plough towed by a Same Hercules 160 hp tractor on land belonging to Mr E. W. Morgan & Son of Easton Court Farm, Little Hereford, Shropshire on 24 Sept 1981.

The greatest recorded acreage ploughed with a 6 furrow plough to a depth of 7 in *17,7 cm* in 24 hr is 123.4 acres *49,9 ha* by David Griffiths and Pat Neylan using a Lamborghini R-1056 DT tractor in the Nakuru District, Kenya on 6–7 July 1978. Frank Allinson of Leyburn, N Yorks, ploughed for 250 hr 9 min 50 sec on 14–24 Nov 1981. DMI Inc. of Goodfield, Illinois, USA marketed a 'Hydrawide' plough with 21 furrows in 1978.

Largest rick

A rick of 40,400 bales of straw was completed from 22 July to 3 Sept 1982 by Nick and Tom Parsons with a gang of 8 at Cuckoo-pen Barn Farm, Birdlip, Gloucestershire. It measured 150 × 30 × 60 ft high *45,7 × 9,1 × 18,2 m high* and weighed some 700 tons *711 tonnes.* They baled, hauled and ricked 24,200 bales in 7 consecutive days on 22–29 July.

LIVESTOCK

Note: Some exceptionally high livestock auction sales are believed to result from collusion between buyer and seller to raise the ostensible price levels of the breed concerned. Others are marketing and publicity exercises with little relation to true market prices.

Highest Priced *Bull*

The highest price ever paid for a bull is $2,500,000 (then £1,087,000) for the beefalo (a $\frac{3}{8}$ bison, $\frac{3}{8}$ charolais, $\frac{1}{4}$ Hereford) 'Joe's Pride' sold by D. C. Basalo of Burlingame, California to the Beefalo Cattle Co of Canada, of Calgary, Alberta, Canada on 9 Sept 1974. The young 14 month old Canadian Holstein bull 'Pickland Elevation B. ET' was bought by Premier Breeders of Stamfordham, Northumberland for £233,000.

The biggest bovine reunion—Isabelle the Limousin cow at St Ives, Cambridgeshire, inspecting her 19 calves.
When they were embryos they were implanted into host mothers.

The highest price ever paid for a bull in Britain is 60,000 guineas (£63,000), paid on 5 Feb 1963 at Perth, Scotland, by James R. Dick (1928–74) co-manager of Black Watch Farms, for 'Lindertis Evulse', an Aberdeen-Angus owned by Sir Torquil and Lady Munro of Lindertis, Kirriemuir, Tayside, Scotland. This bull failed a fertility test in August 1963, thus becoming the world's most expensive piece of beef.

Cow

The highest price ever paid for a cow is $300,000 (*then* £136,360) for the Holstein-Friesian 'Pammies Citation Paula' by Dreamstreet Holsteins Inc., Walton, NY, USA at the Hilltop Hanover Farm sale on 21 Nov 1980. The British record is £33,600 for 'Ullswater Beatexus 8th', a British Friesian sold to The British Livestock Embryo Syndicate of Royston, Hertfordshire by Sir Keith and Lady Showering of West Horrington, Wells, Somerset on 9 May 1981 (auctioneers: Hobsons).

Sheep

The highest price ever paid for a ram is $A79,000 (£49,500) by the Gnowangerup Animal Breeding Centre, Western Australia for a Merino ram from the Colinsvale Stud, South Australia at the Royal Adelaide Show on 10 Sept 1981.

The British auction record is £21,000 paid by Mr W. Sheddon of Brighouse, Balmaclellan, Kirkcudbright, Scotland for A. W. Carswell & Son's Blackface ram on 4 Oct 1978.

The highest price ever paid for wool is $A125,000 per kg greasy (£31.50 per lb) for a bale of extra superfine combing Merino fleece from the Launceston, Tasmania sales on 4 Mar 1982. It was sold by E. J. Dowling & Sons of Ross, Tasmania to Fujii Keori Ltd of Osaka. This Japanese firm has been top bidders each year from 1972 to 1983 inclusive.

Pig

The highest price ever paid for a pig is $42,500 (£21,500) for a Duroc boar named 'Glacier', owned by Baize Durocs of Stamford, Texas, USA, by Wilbert & Myron Meinhart of Hudson, Iowa, on 24 Feb 1979. The UK record is 3300 guineas (£3465), paid by Malvern Farms for the Swedish Landrace gilt 'Bluegate Ally 33rd' owned by Davidson Trust in a draft sale at Reading, Berkshire on 2 Mar 1955.

Horse

The highest price for a draught horse is $47,500 (£9970) paid for the 7-year-old Belgian stallion 'Farceur' by E. G. Good at Cedar Falls, Iowa, USA on 16 Oct 1917. A Welsh mountain pony stallion 'Coed Cock Bari' was sold to an Australian builder in Wales in September 1978 for 21,000 guineas (*then* £22,050).

Donkey

Perhaps the lowest ever price for livestock was at a sale at Kuruman, Cape Province, South Africa in 1934 where donkeys were sold for less than 2p each.

Heaviest *Cattle*

Of heavyweight cattle the heaviest on record was a Holstein-Durham cross named 'Mount Katahdin' exhibited by A. S. Rand of Maine, USA in 1906–10 and frequently weighed at an even 5000 lb *2267 kg*. He was 6 ft 2 in *1,88 m* at the shoulder with a 13 ft *3,96 m* girth and died in a barn fire *c.* 1923. The British record is the 4480 lb *2032 kg* of 'The Bradwell Ox' owned by William Spurgin of Bradwell, Essex. He was 15 ft *4,57 m* from nose to tail and had a girth of 11 ft *3,35 m* when 6 years old in 1830. The largest breed of heavyweight cattle is the Chianini, brought to Italy from the Middle East in pre-Roman times. Mature bulls average 5 ft 8 in *1,73 m* at the forequarters and weigh 2865 lb *1300 kg*. The Airedale Heifer of East Riddlesdon, nr. Keighley, South Yorkshire *c.* 1820 was 11 ft 10.6 in *3,62 m* long and weighed 2640 lb *1197,5 kg*.

The highest recorded birthweight for a calf is 225 lb *102 kg* from a British Friesian cow at Rockhouse Farm, Bishopston, Swansea, West Glamorgan, in 1961.

Pigs

The heaviest hog recorded was the Poland-China hog 'Big Bill' of 2552 lb *22¾ cwt 1157,5 kg* measuring 9 ft *2,75 m* long with a belly on the ground, owned by Burford Butler of Jackson, Tennessee, USA and chloroformed in 1933. Raised by W. J. Chappall he was mounted and displayed in Weekly County, Tennessee until 1946. The British record is a hog of 12 cwt 66 lb *639,5 kg* bred by Joseph Lawton of Astbury, Cheshire. In 1774 it stood 4 ft 8½ in *1,43 m* in height and was 9 ft 8 in *2,94 m* long. The highest recorded weight for a piglet at weaning (8 weeks) is 81 lb *36,7 kg* for a boar, one of nine piglets farrowed on 6 July 1962 by the Landrace gilt 'Manorport Ballerina 53rd', *alias* 'Mary', and sired by a Large White named 'Johnny' at Kettle Lane Farm, West Ashton, Trowbridge, Wiltshire.

Sheep

The highest recorded birthweight for a lamb in the world is 38 lb *17,2 kg* at Clearwater, Sedgwick County, Kansas, USA in 1975, but neither this lamb nor the ewe survived.

Broiler growth

The record for growth for flocks of at least 2400 at 56 days is 2,901 kg *6.396 lb* with a conversion rate of 2.17 by D. B. Marshall (Newbridge) Ltd of Newbridge, Midlothian, Scotland reported in October 1981.

Prolificacy *Cattle*

On 25 Apr 1964 it was reported that a cow named 'Lyubik' had given birth to seven calves at Mogilev, USSR. Five live and one dead calf were recorded from a Fresian at Te Puke, North Island, New Zealand on 27 July 1980 but none survived. A case of five live calves at one birth was reported in 1928 by T. G. Yarwood of Manchester. The life-time prolificacy record is 30 in the case of a cross-bred cow owned by G. Page of Warren Farm, Wilmington, East Sussex, which died in November

1957, aged 32. A cross-Hereford calved in 1916 and owned by A. J. Thomas of West Hook Farm, Marloes, Dyfed, Wales, produced her 30th calf in May 1955 and died in May 1956, aged 40.

'Soender Jylland's Jens' a Danish black and white bull left 220,000 surviving progeny by artificial insemination when he was put down aged 11 in Copenhagen in September 1978. 'Bendalls Adema', a Friesian bull, died aged 14 at Clondalkin, County Dublin, Ireland on 8 Nov 1978 having sired an estimated 212,000 progeny by artificial insemination.

Pigs

The highest recorded number of piglets in one litter is 34, thrown on 25–26 June 1961 by a sow owned by Aksel Egedee of Denmark. In February 1955 a Wessex sow owned by Mrs E. C. Goodwin of Paul's Farm, Leigh, near Tonbridge, Kent, had a litter of 34, of which 30 were born dead. The highest reported number of live births in Britain is 30 by W. Ives of Dane End Fruit Farm, near Ware, Hertfordshire from a white Welsh sow in September 1979. A sow, 'Bessie' owned by Mr L. Witt of Bath, Avon farrowed litters of 19 on 12 Nov 1975, 19 (3 still-born) on 5 Apr 1976 and 21 (3 still-born) on 16 Sept 1976 making 59 in a 12 month period (53 reared).

Sheep

A case of eight lambs at a birth was reported by D. T. Jones of Priory Farm, Gwent, in June 1956 and by Ken Towse of Buckton near Bridlington in March 1981 but none lived. A case of a sheep living to 26 years was recorded in flock book records by H. Poole, Wexford, Ireland. Many cases of sextuplet lambs have been reported.

Egg-laying

The highest authenticated rate of egg-laying is by a white leghorn chicken hen, no. 2988 at the College of Agriculture, University of Missouri, USA, with 371 eggs in 364 days in an official test conducted by Professor Harold V. Biellier ending on 29 Aug 1979. The UK record is 353 eggs in 365 days in a National Laying Test at Milford, Surrey in 1957 by a Rhode Island Red owned by W. Lawson of Welham Grange, Retford, Nottinghamshire.

The heaviest egg reported is one of 16 oz *454 g*, with double yolk and double shell, laid by a white Leghorn at Vineland, New Jersey, USA, on 25 Feb 1956. The largest recorded was one of 'nearly 12 oz' for a 5 yolked egg 12¼ in *31 cm* around the long axis and 9 in *22,8 cm* around the shorter axis laid by a Black Minorca at Mr Stafford's Damsteads Farm, Mellor, Lancashire in 1896.

The highest recorded annual average for a flock is 313 eggs in 52 weeks from a flock of 1000 Warren-Stadler SSL layers (from 21 weeks of age) by Eric Savage, White Lane Farm, Albury, Surrey, England in 1974–5.

Most yolks

The highest claim for the number of yolks in a chicken's egg is 9 reported by Mrs Diane Hainsworth of Hainsworth Poultry Farms, Mount Morris, New York, USA in July 1971 and also from a hen in Kirghizia, USSR in August 1977.

Goose egg

The white goose 'Speckle' owned by Donny Brandenberg, of Goshen, Ohio, USA, on 3 May 1977 laid a 24 oz *680 g* egg measuring 13½ × 9½ in *34 × 24 cm* in circumferences.

Duck

An Indian Runner Duck, owned by Mrs M. Atkinson of Burnham-on-Sea, Somerset, repeatedly laid 362 eggs in 365 days from 1 Aug 1981.

Milk yields *Cows*

The highest recorded world lifetime yield of milk is 403,439 lb (180.10 tons *182 990 kg*) by the US Holstein cow 'Breezewood Patsy Bar Pontiac' (b. 11 June 1964) owned by Gelbke Bros. of Vienna, Ohio to 22 June 1981. The greatest yield of any British cow was that given by the British Friesian 'Guillyhill Janna 2nd', owned by S. H. West. This cow yielded 330,939 lb *150 111 kg* up to 1973. The greatest recorded yield for one lactation (maximum 365 days) is 55,661 lb *25 247 kg* by the Holstein 'Beecher Arlinda Ellen' owned by Mr and Mrs Harold L. Beecher of Rochester, Indiana, USA in 1975. The British lactation record (305 days) was set by 'Queenie' (b. 5 May

1974), a Friesian–Ayrshire cross, owned by Peter Healey of Street Farm, Eggington, Bedfordshire at 19 195 kg *42,317 lb* in 1980–81. The highest reported milk yield in a day is 241 lb *109,3 kg* by 'Urbe Blanca' in Cuba on or about 23 June 1982.

Hand milking

Andy Faust at Collinsville, Oklahoma, USA in 1937 achieved 120 US gal *99.92 UK gal* in 12 hr.

Goats

The highest recorded milk yield for any goat is 7714 lb *3499 kg* in 365 days by 'Osory Snow-Goose' owned by Mr and Mrs G. Jameson of Leppington, N.S.W., Australia in 1977. The part Nubian milk goat 'Lou' owned by Mrs Jonnie Stinson of Springtown, Texas, USA was lactating for the 5 years up to her death on 15 Nov 1980.

Butter fat yield

The world record lifetime yield is 16,370 lb *7425 kg* by the US Holstein 'Breezewood Patsy Bar Pontiac' in 3979 days (see left also for yield record). Her lactation record for 365 days of 2230 lb *1011 kg* was reported on 8 Oct 1976. The British record butter fat yield in a lifetime is 12,166 lb *5518 kg* by the Ayrshire cow 'Craighead Welma' owned by W. Watson Steele from 273,072 lb at 4.45 per cent. The British record for 365 days is 761 kg *1677.7 lb* by 'Crookgate Aylwinia 7' a Friesian, owned by J. V. Machin of Hill Farm, Penley near Wrexham, Clwyd, set on 5 May 1973. The United Kingdom record for butter fat in one day is 9.30 lb *4,218 kg* (79 lb *35,8 kg* milk at 11.8 per cent) by Queens Letch Farms' Guernsey Cow 'Thisbe's Bronwen of Trewollack'.

Cheese

The most active cheese-eaters are the people of France, with an annual average in 1982 of 18,9 kg *41.6 lb* per person. The world's biggest producer is the United States with a factory production of 4,773,500,000 lbs (2,165,000 tons *2 200 000 tonnes*) in 1980. The UK cheese consumption in 1982 was 6,4 kg *14.1 lb* per head.

Oldest

The oldest and most primitive cheeses are the Arabian *kishk*, made of dried curd of goats' milk. There are today 450 named cheeses in 18 major varieties, but many are merely named after different towns and differ only in shape or the method of packing. France has 240 varieties.

Most expensive

The world's most expensive cheese in its home market is Le Leruns made from Ewes milk at 90 francs per kilo (*now £3.40 per lb*). Cheese made to the Liederkranz formula in Van Wert, Ohio, USA retails for $2.25 per 4 oz; equivalent to $9.00 (*£6.40*) per lb. Britain's most costly traditional cheese is Blue Wensleydale which has no fixed price but is obtainable from some shops for between £2.50 and £3.00 per lb. The unlawfully made English Blue Vinney 'changes hands' for c. £4.00 per lb.

Largest

The largest cheese ever made was a cheddar of 34,591 lb *15 190 kg* made in 43 hr on 20–22 Jan 1964 by the Wisconsin Cheese Foundation for exhibition at the New York World's Fair, USA. It was transported in a specially designed refrigerated tractor trailer 'Cheese Mobile' 45 ft *13,71 m* long.

CHICKEN PLUCKING

Ernest Hausen (1877–1955) of Fort Atkinson, Wisconsin, USA, died undefeated after 33 years as a champion. On 19 Jan 1939 he was timed at 4.4 sec and reputedly twice did 3.5 sec a few years later.

The record time for plucking 12 chickens clean by a team of 4 women at the annual Chicken Plucking Championship at Masaryktown, Florida, USA is 32.9 sec set on 9 Oct 1976 by Doreena Cary, Diane Grieb, Kathy Roads and Dorothy McCarthy.

TURKEY PLUCKING

Vincent Pilkington of Cootehill, County Cavan, Ireland killed and plucked 100 turkeys in 7 hr 32 min on 15 Dec 1978. His record for a single turkey is 1 min 30 sec on RTE Television in Dublin on 17 Nov 1980.

On 23 May 1983 Joe Glaub (USA) killed 7300 turkeys in a 'working' day.

Chapter 10

HUMAN ACHIEVEMENTS

1. ENDURANCE AND ENDEAVOUR

North Pole conquest

The claims of neither of the two US Arctic explorers, Dr Frederick Albert Cook (1865–1940) nor Cdr (later Rear Ad.) Robert Edwin Peary (1856–1920), of the US Naval Civil Engineering branch in reaching the North Pole are subject to positive proof. Cook accompanied by the Eskimos, Ah-pellah and Etukishook, two sledges and 26 dogs, struck north from a point 60 miles *96,5 km* north of Svartevoeg, on Axel Heiberg I., Canada, 460 miles *740 km* from the Pole on 21 Mar 1908, allegedly reaching Lat. 89° 31′ N on 19 Apr and the Pole on 21 Apr. Peary, accompanied by his Negro assistant, Matthew Alexander Henson (1866–1955) and the four Eskimos, Ooqueah, Eginwah, Seegloo and Ootah (1875–1955), struck north from his Camp Bartlett (Lat. 87° 44′ N.) at 5 a.m. on 2 Apr 1909. After travelling another 134 miles *215 km*, he

Polar Circumnavigation (First)

Sir Ranulph Fiennes, Bt and Charles Burton of the British Trans-Globe Expedition travelled South from Greenwich (2 Sept 1979), via the South Pole (17 Dec 1980) and the North Pole (11 Apr 1982), and back to Greenwich arriving after a 35,000 mile *56 325 km* trek on 29 Aug 1982.

NORTH POLE

Greenwich
START 1979
FINISH 1982

Barcelona

Timbuktu

Cape Town

Cape Town

SOUTH POLE

Sydney

ARTWORK: ROB BURNS

'Ice Group' Trans-Globe Expedition. Left to right; Charles Burton (Mechanic) Sir Ranulph Fiennes (Navigator and Expedition Leader) and Oliver Shepard (Radio Operator).

allegedly established his final camp, Camp Jessup, in the proximity of the Pole at 10 a.m. on 6 Apr and marched a further 42 miles *67,5 km* quartering the sea-ice before turning south at 4 p.m. on 7 Apr. On excellent pack ice and modern sledges Wally Herbert's 1968–9 Expedition (see below) attained a best day's route mileage of 23 miles *37 km* in 15 hr. Cook claimed 26 miles *41,8 km* twice while Peary claimed a surely unsustainable average of 38 miles *61 km* for 8 consecutive days.

The earliest indisputable attainment of the North Pole over the sea-ice was at 3 p.m. (Central Standard Time) on 19 Apr 1968 by Ralph Plaisted (US) and three companions after a 42-day trek in four Skidoos (snow-mobiles). Their arrival was independently verified 18 hr later by a US Air Force weather aircraft. The sea bed is 13,410 ft *4087 m* below the North Pole.

Naomi Uemura (1941–1984) the Japanese explorer and mountaineer became the first person to reach the North Pole in a solo trek across the Arctic Ice Cap at 4.45 a.m., GMT on 1 May 1978. He had travelled 450 miles *725 km* setting out on 7 Mar from Cape Edward, Ellesmere Island in northern Canada. He averaged nearly 8 miles *13 km* per day with his sled 'Aurora' drawn by 17 huskies.

The first women to set foot on the North Pole was Mrs Fran Phipps, wife of the Canadian bush pilot Weldy Phipps on 5 Apr 1971. Galina Aleksandrovna Lastovskaya (b. 1941) and Lilia Vladislavovna Minina (b. 1959) were crew members of the USSR atomic icebreaker *Arktika* which reached the Pole on 17 Aug 1977.

The soviet scientist Dr Pavel A. Gordienko and 3 companions were arguably the first ever to stand on the exact point Lat. 90° 00′ 00″ N (+300 metres) on 23 Apr 1948.

South Pole conquest

The first men to cross the Antarctic circle (Lat. 66° 30′ S.) were the 193 crew of the *Resolution* (462 tons/tonnes) (Capt James Cook RN (1728–79) and *Adventure* (336 tons/tonnes) (Lt T. Furneaux) on 17 Jan 1773 in 39° E. The first person known to have sighted the Antarctic ice shelf was Capt. F. F. Bellinghausen (Russian) (1778–1852) on 27 Jan 1820 from the vessels *Vostock* and *Mirnyi*. The first known to have sighted the mainland of the continent was Capt William Smith (1790–1847) and Master Edward Bransfield, RN, in the brig *Williams*. They saw the peaks of Trinity Land 3 days later on 30 Jan 1820.

The South Pole (alt. 9186 ft *2779 m* on ice and 336 ft *102 m* bed rock) was first reached at 11 a.m. on 16 Dec 1911 by a Norwegian party led by Capt. Roald Engebereth Gravning Amundsen (1872–1928), after a 53-day march with dog sledges from the Bay of Whales, to which he had penetrated in the *Fram*. Subsequent calculations showed that Olav Olavson Bjaaland (the last survivor, dying in June 1961, aged 88) and Helmer Hanssen probably passed within 400–600 m of the exact pole. The other two members were Sverre H. Hassell (d. 1928) and Oskar Wisting (d. 1936).

Women

The first woman to set foot on Antarctica was Mrs Karoline Mikkelsen on 20 Feb 1935. No woman stood on the South Pole until 11 Nov 1969. On that day Lois Jones, Eileen McSaveney, Jean Pearson, Terry Lee Tickhill (all US), Kay Lindsay (Australia) and Pam Young (NZ) arrived by air.

First on both Poles

Dr Albert P. Crary (USA) reached the North Pole in a Dakota aircraft on 3 May 1952. On 12 Feb 1961 he arrived at the South Pole by Sno Cat on a scientific traverse party from the McMurdo Station. He thus pre-empted David Porter by 18 years.

Arctic crossing

The first crossing of the Arctic sea-ice was achieved by the British Trans-Arctic Expedition which left Point Barrow, Alaska on 21 Feb 1968 and arrived at the Seven Island Archipelago north-east of Spitzbergen 464 days later on 29 May 1969 after a haul of 2920 statute miles *4699 km* and a drift of 700 miles *1126 km* compared with the straight line distance of 1662 miles *2674 km*. The team was Wally Herbert (leader), 34, Major Ken Hedges, 34, RAMC, Allan Gill, 38, and Dr Roy Koerner, 36 (glaciologist), and 40 huskies. The only crossing achieved in a single season was that by Fiennes and Burton

(see below) from Alert via the North Pole to the Greenland Sea in open snowmobiles.

Antarctic crossing

The first surface crossing of the Antarctic continent was completed at 1.47 p.m. on 2 Mar 1958, after a trek of 2158 miles *3473 km* lasting 99 days from 24 Nov 1957, from Shackleton Base to Scott Base *via* the Pole. The crossing party of twelve was led by Dr (now Sir) Vivian Ernest Fuchs (born 11 Feb 1908). The 2600 mile *4185 km* trans-Antarctic leg from Sanae to Scott Base of the 1980–82 Trans-Globe Expedition was achieved in 66 days from 26 Oct 1980 to 11 Jan 1981 having passed through the South Pole on 23 Dec 1980. The 3 man party on snowmobiles comprised Sir Ranulph Fiennes (b. 1944), Oliver Shepard and Charles Burton.

Polar Circumnavigation *(First)* see p. 175.

Longest sledge journeys

The longest totally self-supporting Polar sledge journey ever made was one of 1080 miles *1738 km* from West to East across Greenland on 18 June to 5 Sept 1934 by Capt M. Lindsay (1905–1981) (later Sir Martin Lindsay of Dowhill, Bt, CBE, DSO), Lt Arthur S. T. Godfrey, RE, (later Lt Col, k. 1942), Andrew N. C. Croft (later Col, DSO) and 49 dogs. The first ice-cap crossing was that of Nansen who in 1888 travelled from South-east Greenland with man-hauled sledges to the West Coast.

Lunar conquest

Neil Alden Armstrong (b. Wapakoneta, Ohio, USA of Scottish (*via* Ireland) and German ancestry, on 5 Aug 1930), command pilot of the Apollo XI mission, became the first man to set foot on the Moon on the Sea of Tranquility at 02.56 and 15 sec GMT on 21 July 1969. He was followed out of the Lunar Module *Eagle* by Col. Edwin Eugene Aldren, Jr, USAF (b. Glen Ridge, New Jersey, USA of Swedish, Dutch and British ancestry, on 20 Jan 1930), while the Command Module *Columbia* piloted by Lt Col Michael Collins, USAF (b. Rome, Italy, of Irish and pre-Revolutionary American ancestry, on 31 Oct 1930) orbited above.

Eagle landed at 20.17 and 42 sec GMT on 20 July and lifted off at 17.54 GMT on 21 July, after a stay of 21 hr 36 min. The Apollo XI had blasted off from Cape Canaveral, Florida at 13.32 GMT on 16 July and was a culmination of the US space programme which, at its peak, employed 376,600 people and attained in the year 1966–7 a peak budget of $5,900,000,000 (*then £2460 million*).

There is evidence that Pavel Belyayev was the cosmonaut selected by the USSR for a manned circumlunar flight in *Zond 7* on 9 Dec 1968, 12 days before the Apollo VIII flight but no launch took place.

Altitude *Man*

The greatest altitude attained by man was when the crew of the ill-fated Apollo XIII were at apocynthion (*i.e.* their furthest point) 158 miles *254 km* above the lunar surface and 248,655 miles *400 187 km* above the Earth's surface at 1.21 a.m. BST on 15 Apr 1970. The crew were Capt. James Arthur Lovell, Jr USN (b. Cleveland, Ohio, 25 Mar 1928), Fred Wallace Haise Jr (b. Biloxi, Miss., USA, 14 Nov 1933) and the late John L. Swigert (1931–82).

Altitude *Woman*

The greatest altitude attained by a woman is 340 km *211 miles* by Pilot-Cosmonaut of the USSR Svetlana Savitskaya (b. 1948) during her flight in *Soyuz T7* on 19–27 Aug 1982. The record in an aircraft is 24 336 m *79,842 ft* by Natalia Prokhanova (USSR) (b. 1940) in an E-33 jet, on 22 May 1965.

Speed *Man*

The fastest speed at which humans have travelled is 24,791 mph *39 897 km/h* when the Command Module of Apollo X carrying Col (*now* Brig Gen) Thomas Patten Stafford, USAF (b. Weatherford, Okla. 17 Sept 1930), and Cdr Eugene Andrew Cernan (b. Chicago, 14 Mar 1934) and Cdr (*now* Capt) John Watts Young, USN (b. San Francisco, 24 Sept 1930), reached this maximum value at the 400,000 ft *121,9 km* altitude interface on its trans-Earth return flight on 26 May 1969.

Speed *Woman*

The highest speed ever attained by a woman is 28 115 km/h

MILESTONES IN THE LAND SPEED RECORDS 1935–1984

Sir Malcolm Campbell's *Bluebird* which first bettered 300 mph *482 km/h* in 1935 at Bonneville Salt Flats, Utah, USA.

The late Gary Gabelich's *Blue Flame* which first exceeded 1000 km/h *621.37 mph* in 1970 at Bonneville.

The first penetration of the sound barrier by a wheeled vehicle—the *Budweiser Rocket* an unofficial 739 mph *1190 km/h* at Edwards Air Base, California in 1979.

Richard Noble (G.B.) alongside his Rolls Royce Avon Jet *Thrust 2*—official holder of the world land speed record since October 1983. (*Chris Marks*)

PAT GIBBON/EDDIE BOTCHWAY

17,470 mph by Jnr Lt (now Lt Col) Valentina Vladimirovna Tereshkova-Nikolayev (b. 6 Mar 1937) of the USSR in *Vostok 6* on 16 June 1963. The highest speed ever achieved by a woman aircraft pilot is 2687,42 km/h *1669.89 mph* by Svetlana Savitskaya (USSR) reported on 2 June 1975.

Land speed *Man*

The highest reputed speed on land is 739.666 mph *1190,377 km/h* or Mach 1.0106 by Stan Barrett (US) in *The Budweiser Rocket*, a rocket engined 3 wheeled car at Edwards Air Force Base, California on 17 Dec 1979 (*but see also p. 136*).

The *official* one mile land speed record is 633.468 mph *1019,467 km/h* set by Richard Noble OBE (b. 1946) on 4 Oct 1983 over the Black Rock Desert, north Nevada, USA in his 17 000 lb thrust Rolls Royce Avon 302 jet powered *Thrust 2*, designed by John Ackroyd.

The highest land speed attained in Britain is 263.92 mph *424,74 km/h* by Richard Noble in *Thrust 2* at Greenham Common, Berkshire on 25 Sept 1980.

Land speed *Women*

The highest land speed recorded by a woman is 524.016 mph *843,323 km/h* by Mrs Kitty Hambleton *née* O'Neil (US) in the 48,000 hp rocket-powered 3-wheeled S.M.1 *Motivator* over the Alvard Desert, Oregon, USA on 6 Dec 1976. Her official two-way record was 512.710 mph *825,126 km/h* and she probably touched 600 mph *965 km/h* momentarily.

MILESTONES IN ABSOLUTE HUMAN ALTITUDE RECORDS

Altitude Ft	m	Pilot	Vehicle	Place	Date	
80*	24	Jean François Pilâtre de Rozier (1757–1785) (France)	Hot Air Balloon (tethered)	Fauxbourg, Paris	15 & 17 Oct	1783
c.330	c.100	de Rozier and the Marquis d'Arlandes (1742–1809) (France)	Hot Air Balloon (free flight)	LaMuette, Paris[1]	21 Nov	1783
c.3000	c.900	Dr Jacques-Alexander-Cesar Charles (1746–1823) and Ainé Robert (France)	Charliere Hydrogen Balloon	Tuileries, Paris	1 Dec	1783
c.9000	c.2750	Dr J.-A.-C. Charles (France)	Hydrogen Balloon	Nesles, France	1 Dec	1783
c.13,000	c.4000	James Sadler (GB)	Hydrogen Balloon	Manchester	May	1785
25,400[2]	7740	James Glaisher (1809–1903) (UK)	Hydrogen Balloon	Wolverhampton	17 July	1862
31,500	9615	Prof. A. Berson (Germany)	Hydrogen Balloon Phoenix	Strasbourg, France	4 Dec	1894
36,565	11 145	Sadi Lecointe (France)	Nieuport Aircraft	Issy-les-Moulineaux, France	30 Oct	1923
51,961	15 837	Prof. Auguste Piccard and Paul Kipfer (Switzerland)	FNRS 1 Balloon	Augsburg, Germany	27 May	1931
72,395	22 066	Capts Orvill A. Anderson and Albert W. Stevens (US Army Air Corps)	US Explorer II Helium Balloon	Rapid City, South Dakota, USA	11 Nov	1935
79,600	24 262	William Barton Bridgeman (USA)	US Douglas D558–11 Skyrocket	California, USA	15 Aug	1951
126,200	38 465	Capt Iven C. Kincheloe, Jr (USAF)	US Bell X-2 Rocket 'plane	California, USA	7 Sept	1956
169,600	51 694	Joseph A. Walker (USA)	US X-15 Rocket 'plane	California, USA	30 Mar	1961
Statute miles 203.2	Km 327	Flt-Major Yuriy A. Gagarin (USSR) (1934–68)	USSR Vostok I Capsule	Orbital flight	12 Apr	1961
234,672	377 268,9	Col Frank Borman, USAF, Capt James Arthur Lovell, Jr, USN and Major William A. Anders, USAF	US Apollo VIII Command Module	Circum-lunar flight	25 Dec	1968
248,655	400 187	Capt James Arthur Lovell Jr, USN, Frederick Wallace Haise Jr and John L. Swigert Jr (1931–82)	US Apollo XIII	Abortive lunar landing mission	15 Apr	1970

* There is some evidence that Father Bartolomeu de Gusmao flew in his hot-air balloon in his 4th experiment post August 1709 in Portugal.
[1] Duration c.1.54 to 2.16 pm from Château de LaMuette to Butte aux Cailles, Paris 13°. Volume of the 70 ft 21,3 m high balloon was 60 000 'piedcubes' c.1700 m³.
[2] Glaisher, with Henry Tracey Coxwell (1819–1900) claimed 37,000 ft 11 275 m from Wolverhampton on 5 Sept 1862. Some writers accept 30,000 ft 9145 m.
Note: A complete progressive table comprising entries from 1783 to date was published in the 23rd edition of 1977.

PROGRESSIVE SPEED RECORDS

Speed m.p.h.	Km/h	Person and Vehicle	Place	Date	
25	40	Sledging	Heinola, Finland	c.6500 BC	
35	55	Horse-riding	Anatolia, Turkey	c.1400 BC	
45	70	Mountain Sledging	Island of Hawaii (now USA)	ante AD 1500	
50	80	Ice Yachts (earliest patent)	Netherlands	AD 1600	
56.75	95	Grand Junction Railway 2-2-2: Lucifer	Madeley Banks, Staffs, England	13 Nov	1830
87.8	141,3	Tommy Todd, downhill skier	La Porte, California, USA	Mar	1873
90.0	144,8	Midland Railway 4-2-2 7 ft 9 in 2,36 m single	Ampthill, Bedford, England	Mar	1897
130.61	210,2	Siemens and Halske electric engine	Marienfeld-Zossen, near Berlin	27 Oct	1903
c.150	c.257,5	Frederick H. Marriott (fl. 1957) Stanley Steamer Wogglebug	Ormond Beach, Florida, USA	26 Jan	1907
210.64	339	Sadi Lecointe (France) Nieuport-Delage 29	Villesauvage, France	25 Sept	1921
415.2	668,2	Flt Lt (Later Wing Cdr) George Hedley Stainforth AFC Supermarine S.6B	Lee-on-Solent, England	29 Sept	1931
623.85	1004	Flugkapitan Heinz Dittmar Me. 163V–1	Peenemunde, Germany	2 Oct	1941
967	1556	Capt Charles Elwood Yeager, USAF Bell XS–1	Muroc Dry Lake, California, USA	26 Mar	1948
2905	4675,1	Major Robert M. White, North American X–15	Muroc Dry Lake, California, USA	7 Mar	1961
c.17,560	c.28 260	Flt Maj Yuriy Alekseyevich Gagarin, Vostok 1	Earth orbit	12 Apr	1961
24,226	38 988	Col Frank Borman, USAF, Capt James Arthur Lovell, Jr, USN, Major William A. Anders, USAF Apollo VIII	Trans-lunar injection	21 Dec	1968
24,790.8	39 897,0	Cdrs Eugene Andrew Cernan and John Watts Young, USN and Col Thomas P. Stafford, USAF Apollo X	Re-entry after lunar orbit	26 May	1969

Note: A complete progressive table comprising entries from pre-historic times to date was published in the 23rd edition of 1977.

Water speed *Man*

The highest speed ever achieved on water is an estimated 300 knots (345 mph *556 km/h*) by Kenneth Peter Warby, MBE, (b. 9 May 1939) on the Blowering Dam Lake, NSW, Australia on 20 Nov 1977 in his unlimited hydroplane *Spirit of Australia*. The official world water speed record is 514,389 km/h *319.627 mph 277.57 knots* set on 8 Oct 1978 by Warby on Blowering Dam Lake.

Woman

The fastest woman on water is Mary Rife (USA), who has driven her drag boat *Proud Mary* at more than 190 mph *305 km/h*.

Water speed *Propeller driven*

The highest officially recorded speed for propeller-driven craft is 215.33 mph *346,54 km/h* by Eddie Hill in his supercharged hydroplane *The Texan* on Lake Irvine, California on 5 June 1983. On a one-way run *Climax* recorded 205.19 mph *330,22 km/h*.

Most travelled *Man*

The man who had visited more countries than anyone was Jesse Hart Rosdail (1914–77) of Elmhurst, Illinois, USA, a 5th grade teacher. Of all the separately administered countries and territories listed in the *UN Population Report*, he had visited all excepting only North Korea and French Antarctic Territories. He estimated his mileage to visit 215 countries was 1,626,605 statute miles *2 617 766 km*.

Fred Jurgen Specovius (b. 1943) (West Germany) has visited all 170 sovereign countries except the impenetrable North Korea and all the non-sovereign territories except 6. He speaks 6 languages and has used up 14 passports.

Horseback

The most travelled man in the horseback era was probably the Methodist preacher Francis Asbury (b. Birmingham, England), who travelled 264,000 miles *424 850 km* in North America from 1771 to 1815 preaching 16,000 sermons.

Most isolated *Man*

The farthest any human has been removed from his nearest living fellow man is 2233.2 miles *3596,4 km* in the case of the Command Service Module pilot Alfred M. Worden on the US Apollo XV lunar mission of 30 July–1 Aug 1971.

Passport Records

The world's most expensive passports are those from the USSR. In Feb 1982 an emigration permit was 220 roubles (£172) or up to 3500 roubles (over £2700) on the black market. If applications involved a whole family or travel to the West, the necessary accompanying visa was refused 996 times in each 1000 applications.

Round the World

The fastest time for a round the world trip on scheduled flights for a circumnavigation is 44 hr 6 min by David J. Springbett (b. 2 May 1938) of Taplow, Buckinghamshire, from Los Angeles eastabout *via* London, Bahrain, Singapore, Bangkok, Manila, Tokyo and Honolulu on 8–10 Jan 1980 over a 23,068 mile *37 124 km* route.

The FAI rates any flight taking off and landing at the same point, which is as long as the Tropic of Cancer (viz 22,858.754 miles 36 787,599 km) as a circumnavigational flight.

Greatest ocean descent

The record ocean descent was achieved in the Challenger Deep

The world's greatest globe-trotter—Fred J. Specovius of West Germany for whom North Korea is the 'last frontier' (see page 178). Left to right, Fred in the High Andes, in the Opium Triangle, with the penguins in South Georgia and in the desert of Western Australia.

of the Marianas Trench, 250 miles *400 km* south-west of Guam, in the Pacific Ocean, when the Swiss-built US Navy bathyscaphe *Trieste*, manned by Dr Jacques Piccard (b. 1914) (Switzerland) and Lt Donald Walsh, USN, reached the ocean bed 35,820 ft (6.78 miles *10 917 m*) down, at 1.10 p.m. on 23 Jan 1960 (see page 63). The pressure of the water was 16,883 lbf/in² *1183 kgf/cm²* and the temperature 37.4° F *3° C*. The descent required 4 hr 48 min and the ascent 3 hr 17 min.

Deep diving records
The record depth for the extremely dangerous activity of breath-held diving is 105 m *344 ft* by Jacques Mayol (France) off Elba, Italy, in December 1983 for men and 147½ ft *45 m* by Giuliana Treleani (Italy) off Cuba in September 1967 for women. Mayol descended on a sled in 104 sec and ascended in 90 sec. The record dive with Scuba (self-contained underwater breathing apparatus) is 437 ft *133 m* by John J. Gruener and R. Neal Watson (USA) off Freeport, Grand Bahama on 14 Oct 1968. The record dive utilizing gas mixtures (nitrogen, oxygen and helium) is a simulated dive of 2250 ft *685,8 m* in a dry chamber by Stephen Porter, Len Whitlock and Erik Kramer at the Duke University Medical Center in Durham, North Carolina on 3 Feb 1981 in a 43 day trial in a sphere of 8 ft *2,43 m*. Patrick Raude and 5 Comex divers left and returned to the bell 'Petrel' at 501 m *1643 ft*, off Cavalaire, France, in 1982.

Deepest underwater escapes
The deepest underwater rescue achieved was of the *Pisces III* in which Roger R. Chapman, 28 and Roger Mallinson, 35 were trapped for 76 hr when it sank to 1575 ft *480 m* 150 miles *240 km* south-east of Cork, Ireland on 29 Aug 1973. She was hauled to the surface by the cable ship *John Cabot* after work by Pisces V, Pisces II and the remote control recovery vessel US CURV on 1 Sept. The greatest depth of an actual escape without any equipment has been from 225 ft *68,58 m* by Richard A. Slater from the rammed submersible *Nekton Beta* off Catalina Island, California, USA on 28 Sept 1970.

Deepest salvage
The greatest depth at which salvage has been achieved is 16,500 ft *5029 m* by the bathyscaph *Trieste II* (Lt Cdr Mel Bartels, USN) to attach cables to an 'electronic package' on the sea bed 400 miles *645 km* north of Hawaii on 20 May 1972. Project Jennifer by USS *Glomar Explorer* in June/July 1974 to recover a Golf class USSR submarine, 750 miles *1200 km* NW of Hawaii, cost $550 million but was not successful.

Flexible dress divers
The deepest salvage operation ever achieved with divers was on the wreck of HM Cruiser *Edinburgh* sunk on 2 May 1942 in the Barents Sea off Northern Norway inside the Arctic Circle in 803 ft *244,7 m* of water. Twelve divers dived on the wreck in pairs using a bell from the *Stephaniturm* (1423 tons) over 32 days under the direction of former RN officer and project director Michael Stewart from 17 Sept to 7 Oct 1981.

The 431 gold ingots were divided; £14.6 million to the USSR, £7.3 million to HM Government and some £18 million to the salvage contractors, Jessop Marine Recoveries Ltd (10%) and Wharton Williams Ltd (90%). John Rossier, 28 was the first to touch the gold. The longest decompression time was 7 days 10 hr 27 min. The £39.9 million is an all-time record but 34 bars worth £4 million were believed unrecovered.

Greatest penetration into the earth
The deepest penetration made into the ground by man is in the Western Deep Levels Mine at Carletonville, Transvaal, South Africa where a record depth of 3777 m *12,500 ft* (2.36 miles) has been attained. The rock temperature at this depth is 131° F *55° C*.

Shaft sinking record
The one month (31 days) world record is 1251 ft *381,3 m* for a standard shaft 26 ft *7,92 m* in diameter at Buffelsfontein Mine, Transvaal, South Africa, in March 1962. The British record of 131,2 m *430 ft* of 7,92 m *26 ft* diameter shaft was set in No 2 Shaft of the NCB's Whitemoor Mine near Selby, North Yorkshire in 31 days (15 Nov–16 Dec 1982).

Longest on a raft
The longest recorded survival alone on a raft is 133 days (4½ months) by Second Steward Poon Lim BEM (b. Hong Kong) of the UK Merchant Navy, whose ship, the SS *Ben Lomond*, was torpedoed in the Atlantic 565 miles *910 km* west of St Paul's Rocks in Lat. 00° 30′ N Long. 38° 45′ W at 11.45 a.m. on 23 Nov 1942. He was picked up by a Brazilian fishing boat off Salinópolis, Brazil, on 5 Apr 1943 and was able to walk ashore. In July 1943, he was awarded the BEM and now lives in New York City.

Maurice and Maralyn Bailey survived 118⅓ days in an inflatable dinghy 4½ ft *1,37 m* in diameter in the north-east Pacific from 4 Mar to 30 June 1973.

Most marriages *World*
The greatest number of marriages accumulated in the monogamous world is 26 by the former Baptist minister Glynn 'Scotty' Wolfe (b. 25 July 1908) of Blythe, California, who first married in 1927. His latest wife was the tattooed Cristine Sue Camacho, 38, married on 28 Jan 1984 but who left in May. His previous oldest wife was 22. His total number of children is, he says, 41. He has additionally suffered 24 mothers-in-law.

Mrs Beverly Nina Avery, then aged 48, a bar-maid from Los Angeles, California, USA, set a monogamous world record in October 1957 by obtaining her sixteenth divorce from her fourteenth husband, Gabriel Avery. She alleged outside the court that five of the 14 had broken her nose.

The record for bigamous marriages is 104 by Giovanni Vigliotto, one of some 50 aliases used by either Fred Jipp (b. New York City, 3 Apr 1936) or Nikolai Peruskov (b. Siracusa,

Sicily, 3 Apr 1929) over the span 1949–1981 in 27 US States and 14 other countries. Four victims were aboard one ship in 1968 and two in London. On 28 Mar 1983 in Phoenix, Arizona he was sentenced to 28 years for fraud, 6 years for bigamy and fined $336,000.

Great Britain

The only monogamous citizen married eight times is Olive Joyce Wilson of Marston Green, Birmingham. She has consecutively been Mrs John Bickley; Mrs Don Trethowan; Mrs George Hundley; Mrs Raymond Ward; Mrs Harry Latrobe; Mrs Leslie Harris; Mrs Ray Richards and now Mrs John Grassick. All were divorced except Mr Hundley, who died.

Oldest bride and bridegroom

Dyura Avramovich reportedly aged 101, married Yula Zhivich, admitting to 95, in Belgrade, Yugoslavia in November 1963.

The British record was set by Sir Robert Mayer CH, KCVO (b. 1879) who married Jacqueline Noble, 51 in London on 10 Nov 1980 when aged 101 years.

Mrs Winifred Clark (b. 13 Nov 1871) became Britain's oldest recorded bride when she married Albert Smith, 80, at St. Hugh's Church, Cantley, South Yorkshire the day before her 100th birthday.

Longest engagements

The longest engagement on record was between Octavio Guillen, and Adriana Martinez. They finally took the plunge after 67 years in June 1969 in Mexico City, Mexico. Both were then 82.

Longest marriage *World*

The longest recorded marriages are of 86 years between Sir Temulji Bhicaji Nariman and Lady Nariman from 1853 to 1940 resulting from a cousin marriage when both were five. Sir Temulji (b. 3 Sept 1848) died, aged 91 years 11 months, in August 1940 at Bombay. Lazurus Rowe (b. Greenland, New

MARINE CIRCUMNAVIGATION RECORDS

(Compiled by Sq Ldr D. H. Clarke, DFC, AFC)

A true circumnavigation entails passing through two antipodal points (which are at least 12,429 statute miles *20 000 km* apart).

CATEGORY	VESSEL	NAME	START PLACE AND DATE	FINISH DATE AND DURATION
Earliest	*Vittoria* Expedition of Fernão de Magalhães, c. 1480–k. 1521	Juan Sebastian de Elcano or Del Cano (d. 1526) and 17 crew	Seville, Spain 20 Sept 1519	San Lucar, 6 Sept 1522 30,700 miles *49 400 km*
Earliest British	*Golden Hind* (ex *Pelican*) 100 tons/*tonnes*	Francis Drake (c. 1540–96) (Knighted 4 April 1581)	Plymouth, 13 Dec 1577	26 Sept. 1580
Earliest Woman	*Etoile*	Crypto-female valet of M. de Commerson, named Baré	St Malo, 1766	1769
Earliest fore-and-aft rigged vessel	*Union* 98 tons (Sloop)	John Boit Junior, 19–21, (US) and 22 crew	Newport, RI 1794 (via Cape Horn westabout)	Newport, RI 1796
Earliest Yacht	*Sunbeam* 170 ft *51,8 m* 3 Mast Topsail schooner	Lord and Lady Brassey (GB) passengers and crew	Cowes, Isle of Wight 1876	Cowes, Isle of Wight 1877
Earliest Solo	*Spray* 36¾ ft *11,20 m* gaff yawl	Capt Joshua Slocum, 51, (US) (a non-swimmer) (No 1 solo circum)	Newport, RI, *via* Magellan Straits, 24 Apr 1895	3 July 1898 46,000 miles *74 000 km*
Earliest Motor Boat	*Speejacks* 98 ft *29,87 m*	Albert Y. Gowen (US) wife and crew	New York City 1921	New York City 1922
Earliest Woman Solo	*Mazurek* 31 ft 2 in *9,5 m* Bermudan Sloop	Krystyna Chojnowska-Liskiewicz (Poland) (No 58 solo circum)	Las Palmas 28 Mar 1976 westabout *via* Panama	Tied knot 21 Mar 1978
Earliest Woman Solo (*via* Cape Horn)	*Express Crusador* 53 ft *16,15 m* Bermuda Sloop	Naomi James (NZ/GB) (later DBE) (No 59 solo circum)	Dartmouth 9 Sept 1977 (Cape Horn 19 Mar 1978)	Dartmouth 8 June 1978 (266 days 19 hr)
Smallest Boat	*Super Shrimp* 18 ft 4 in *5,58 m* Bermuda Sloop	Shane Acton (GB) Iris Derungs (Swiss)	Cambridge, England August 1972	Cambridge, England August 1980 (E–W *via* Panama Canal)
Earliest Submerged	*US Submarine Triton*	Capt Edward L. Beach USN plus 182 crew	New London, Connecticut 16 Feb 1960	10 May 1960 39,708 miles *49 422 km*
Earliest non-stop Solo (Port to Port)	*Suhaili* 32.4 ft *9,87 m* Bermudan Ketch	Robin Knox Johnston CBE (b. 1939) (No 25 solo circum)	Falmouth, 14 June 1968	22 Apr 1969 (312 days)
Longest non-stop alone at sea	*Dar Przemysla* 46 ft 7 in *14,2 m* Ketch	Henryk Jaskula (Poland) (No 68 solo circum)	Gdynia 1979 (W–E via Cape Horn)	Gdynia 1980 (344 days)
Fastest Solo (speed)	*Manureva* (ex *Pen Duick IV*) 70 ft *21,33 m* Trimaran	Alain Colas (France) (No 40 solo circum)	Saint Malo *via* Sydney	29 Mar 1974 (169 days) (av speed 178.5 mpd)
Earliest solo in both directions	*Solitaire* 34 ft *10,36 m* Bermudan Sloop	Lew Powles (GB) (No 62 & 71 solo circum)	Falmouth 1975 (E–W) Lymington 1980 (W–E)	(*via* Panama) Lymington 1978 (*via* Horn) Lymington 1981
Earliest solo in both directions (*via* Horn)	*Ocean Bound* 41 ft 1 in *12,52 m* Bermudan Sloop	David Scott Cowper (GB) (No 66 & 78 solo circum)	Plymouth 1979 (W–E) Plymouth 1981 (E–W)	Plymouth 1980 Plymouth 1982 (see below)
Fastest Solo (Time)	*Credit Agricole* 56 ft *17,07 m* Bermudan Cutter	Philippe Jeantot (Fr) (No 84 solo circum)	Newport 1982 (W–E *via* Cape Horn)	Newport, 1983 159 days 2 hr 26 min 25,560 miles at av speed 166,94 mpd
Fastest Time (non-stop solo)	*De Zeeuwse Stromen* 35 ft 1 in *10,7 m* Bermudan Ketch	Pieun Van Der Lugt (Dutch) (No 76 solo circum)	Zierikzee, Holland 1981 (W–E *via* Horn)	Zierikzee, 1982 285 days 23 hr 57 min
Fastest time and fastest speed (yacht)	*Flyer* 76 ft *23,1 m* Bermudan Sloop	Cornelis von Rietschoten (Dutch) (and 15 crew)	Portsmouth 29 Aug 1981 (W–E *via* Cape Horn)	29 Mar 1982 120 days 6 hr 35 min (220.7 mpd)
Fastest (clipper)	*James Baines* 266 ft *81,07 m*	Capt C. McDonald (GB) and crew	Liverpool to Melbourne (58 days) 1854	Melbourne to Liverpool (69 days) 1855
Fastest Solo Westabout (*via* Cape Horn)	*Ocean Bound* 41 ft 1 in *12,52 m* Bermudan sloop	David Scott Cowper (GB) (No 78 solo circum)	Plymouth 22 Sept 1981 (south of 5 capes)	Plymouth 17 May 1982 (221 sailing days) 31,350 miles *50 451 km* av 141.85 mpd
Fastest-ever time (yacht)	*Awahnee II* 53 ft *16,15 m* Bermuda Cutter	Bob Griffith (US) (5 crew)	Bluff, NZ. 1970 (W–E *via* Horn)	Bluff, NZ. 1971 (88 sailing days plus 23 days stopovers)
Fastest-ever time (clipper)	*Red Jacket* 260 ft *79,24 m*	Capt S. Reid (GB) and crew	From/to Lat 26° 25' W (*via* Horn)	62 days 22 hr 1854
Earliest Solo Double circumnavigation	*Perie Banou* 33 ft 7 in *10,24 m* Bermudan Sloop	Jon Sanders (Australia) (No 75 & 81 solo circum)	Freemantle 1981 (W–E) (continuously at sea)	(*via* Horn) Freemantle 1982 (*via* Plymouth) 420 days 1982

* Eduard Roditi, author of *Magellan of the Pacific*, advances the view that Magellan's slave, Enrique, was the first circumnavigator. He had been purchased in Malacca and it was shown that he already understood the Filipino dialect Vizayan, when he reached the Philippines from the east. He 'tied the knot' off Limasawa on 28 Mar 1521. The first to circumnavigate in both directions was Capt Tobias Furneaux, RN (1735–81) as second lieutenant aboard the *Dolphin* from/to Plymouth east to west *via* the Magellan Straits in 1766–68 and as captain of the *Adventure* from/to Plymouth west to east *via* Cape Horn in 1772–4.

TRANS-ATLANTIC AND PACIFIC MARINE RECORDS
(Compiled by Sq Ldr D. H. Clarke, DFC, AFC)

TRANS-ATLANTIC MARINE RECORDS

CATEGORY	NAME	VESSEL	START	FINISH	DURATION	DATE
Earliest Canoe	'Finn-Man' (Eskimo)	Kayak 11 ft 10 in *3,6 m*	Greenland	Humber, England	Time not known	1613
Earliest Rowing	John Brown + 5 British deserters from garrison	Ship's boat *c.* 20 ft *6,1 m*	St Helena (10 June)	Belmonte, Brazil (fastest ever row)	28 days (83 mpd)	1799
Earliest Crossing (2 men)	C. R. Webb + 1 crew (US)	*Charter Oak* 43 ft *13,1 m*	New York	Liverpool	35 days 15 hr	1857
Earliest Trimaran (Raft)	John Mikes + 2 crew (US)	*Non Pareil,* 25 ft *7,62 m*	New York	Southampton	51 days	1868
Earliest Solo Sailing (E–W)	Josiah Shackford (US)	15 ton gaff sloop	Bordeaux, France	Surinam (Dutch Guiana)	35 days	1786
Earliest Solo Sailing (W–E)	Alfred Johnson (US)	*Centennial* 20 ft *6,09 m*	Glos., Mass	Wales	46 days	1876
Earliest Woman (with US husband)	Mrs Joanna Crapo (b. Scotland)	*New Bedford* 20 ft *6,09 m* (Bermudan ketch)	Chatham, Mass.	Newlyn, Cornwall	51 days (Earliest with Bermudan rig)	1877
Earliest Single-handed race	J. W. Lawlor (US) (winner)	*Sea Serpent* 15 ft *4,57 m*	Boston (21 June)	Coverack, Cornwall	45 days	1891
Earliest Rowing by 2 men	Georg Harboe and Frank Samuelsen (Nor)	*Fox* 18½ ft *5,58 m*	New York City (6 June)	Isles of Scilly (1 Aug)	55 days (56 mpd)	1897
Fastest Solo Sailing (W–E)	J. V. T. McDonald (GB)	*Inverarity* 38 ft *11,58 m*	Nova Scotia	Ireland	16 days (147 mpd)	1922
Earliest Canoe (with sail)	Franz Romer (Germany)	*Deutscher Sport* 21½ ft *6,55 m*	Las Palmas	St Thomas	58 days (47 mpd)	1928
Earliest Woman Solo (East–West)	Ann Davison (GB)	*Felicity Ann* 23 ft *7,01 m*	Portsmouth Las Palmas (20 Nov 1952)	Dominica	65 days	1952–3
Earliest Woman Solo (W–E)	Gladys Gradley (US)	*Lugger* 18 ft *5,5 m*	Nova Scotia	Hope Cove, Devon	60 days	1903
Earliest Woman Solo (across 2 oceans)	Anna Woolf (SA)	*Zama Zulu* 43 ft *13,1 m* (Ferroconcrete)	Cape Town	Bowling, Scotland	8920 miles in 109 days	1976
Fastest Woman solo	Naomi James DBE	*Kriter Lady* 53 ft *16,15 m*	Plymouth	Newport, R.I.	25 days 19 hr 12 min	1980
Fastest 2-woman crew	Annick Martin (Fr) Annie Cordelle (Fr)	*Super Marches Bravo* 45 ft *13,7 m*	Plymouth	Newport, R.I.	21 days 4 hr 28 min	1981
Smallest (Across two oceans)	Gerry Spiess (US) (see also Trans-Pac)	*Yankee Girl* 10 ft *3,05 m*	Norfolk Virginia (1 June)	Falmouth (24 July)	54 days	1979
Smallest West–East	Wayne Dickinson (US)	*God's Tear* 8 ft 11 in *2,71 m*	Allerton, Mass (30 Oct)	Aranmore NW Eire (22 Mar)	142 days	1982–3
Smallest (East–West) (Southern)	Eric Peters (GB)	*Toniky-Nou* 5 ft 10½ in *1,79 m* barrel	Las Palmas (25 Dec)	St Francoise, Guadaloupe (8 Feb)	46 days	1982–3
Fastest Crossing Sailing (multihull) (East–West)	Eric Tabarly (France) + 2 crew	*Pen Duick IV* 67 ft *20,42 m*	Tenerife	Martinique	251.4 miles *404,5 km*/ day (10 days 12 hours)	1968
Fastest Crossing Sailing (monohull) (East–West)	Wilhelm Hirte & crew (Ger)	*Kriter II* 80 ft *24,38 m*	Canary Is.	Barbados	13 days 8 hr	1977
Fastest Crossing (multihull) (West–East)	Marc Pajôt (Fr) plus 3 crew	*Elf Aquitaine* 18,6 m *61 ft* Catamaran	Sandy Hook, NJ 4 July	Lizard, Cornwall 14 July	9 days 10 hr 6 min av 13.3 kts	1981
Fastest Crossing monohull (West–East)	Wilson Marshall (US) & crew	*Atlantic* 185 ft *56,38 m*	Sandy Hook, NJ	Lizard, Cornwall (3054 miles)	12 days 4 hr (fastest noon to noon 341 miles)	1905
Fastest Crossing Sail (West–East)	A. Eldridge (US) and crew	*Red Jacket* (Clipper) 260 ft *79,24 m*	Sandy Hook, NJ	Liverpool Bar	12 days 00 hr 00 min 277.7 mpd	1854
Fastest Solo East–West (Northern) (monohull)	Kazimierz Jaworski (Poland)	*Spaniel II* 56 ft *17,06 m*	Plymouth	Newport, R.I.	19 days 13 hr 25 min	1980
Fastest East–West (Northern) monohull	Bruno Bacilieri (It) Marc Vallin	*Faram Serenissima* 66½ ft *20,27 m*	Plymouth	Newport, R.I.	16 days 1 hr 25 min	1981
Fastest Solo East–West (Northern) (multihull)	Philip Weld (US)	*Moxie* 51 ft *15,54 m* (Tri)	Plymouth	Newport, R.I.	17 days 23 hr 12 min	1980
Fastest Solo East–West (Southern) (monohull)	Sir Francis Chichester KBE (GB)	*Gipsy Moth V* 57 ft *17,37 m*	Portuguese Guinea	Nicaragua	179.1 miles *288,2 km*/ day (22.4 days)	1970
Fastest Ever Yacht Sail (N. route) (East–West)	Chay Blyth (GB) Rob James (GB), (the late)	*Brittany Ferries GB* 65½ ft *20 m* (Tri)	Plymouth	Newport, R.I.	14 days 13 hr 54 min 212.1 mpd	1981
Fastest Solo Rowing East–West	Sidney Genders, (51 years) (GB)	*Khaggavisana* 19¾ ft *6,02 m*	Penzance, Cornwall	Miami, Florida *via* Antigua	37.8 miles *60,8 km*/day 160 days 8 hr	1970
Fastest Solo Rowing West–East	Gérard d'Aboville (Fr)	*Captaine Cook* 5,60 m *18 ft 4 in*	Chatham, Mass 10 July	Ushant, France 20 Sept	71 days 23 hr 72 km *44.8 mpd*	1980
Earliest Solo Rowing East–West	John Fairfax (GB)	*Britannia* 22 ft *6,70 m*	Las Palmas (20 Jan)	Ft Lauderdale, Florida (19 July)	180 days	1969
Earliest Solo Rowing West–East	Tom McClean (Ireland)	*Super Silver* 20 ft *6,90 m*	St John's, Newfoundland (17 May)	Black Sod Bay, Ireland (27 July)	70.7 days	1969
Youngest Solo Sailing	David Sandeman (17½ years) (GB)	*Sea Raider* 35 ft *10,67 m*	Jersey, C.I.	Newport, R.I.	43 days	1976
Oldest Solo Sailing	Monk Farnham (72 years 270 days)	*Seven Bells* 28 ft *8,53 m*	Hampton, Virginia	Falmouth	40 days (from Bermuda)	1981
Earliest by Sailboard	Christian Marty (Fr) (Escorted by yacht *Assiduous*)	*Sodim* (type)	Dakar Senegal	Kourou Fr Guiana	37 days 16 hr 4 min (slept on board)	1981–2

TRANS-PACIFIC MARINE RECORDS

CATEGORY	NAME	VESSEL	START	FINISH	DURATION	DATE
Fastest (Trans Pac)	Bill Lee (US)	*Merlin* 67 ft *20,42 m*	Los Angeles, Cal	Honolulu, Hawaii	8 days 11 hr 1 min	1977
Fastest Yacht (Australia–Horn)	O. K. Pennendreft (Fr) + 13 crew	*Kriter II* 80 ft *24,38 m*	Sydney	Cape Horn	21 days (275 mpd)	1975–6
Fastest Clipper (Australia–Horn)	Capt J. N. Forbes (GB) + crew	*Lightning* 244 ft *74,36 m*	Melbourne	Cape Horn	19 days 1 hr (315 mpd)	1854
Fastest Solo Monohull (Australia–Horn)	Philippe Jeantot (Fr)	*Credit Agricole* 56 ft *17,07 m*	Sydney	Cape Horn	29 days 23 hr (5709 miles, av 190.6 mpd)	1982–3
Fastest seven days solo run	Philippe Jeantot (Fr)	*Credit Agricole* 56 ft *17,07 m*	As above 8 Feb	On passage 15 Feb	Covered 1552 miles (Fastest noon to noon 240 miles)	1983
Earliest Solo (Woman)	Sharon Sites Adams (US)	*Sea Sharp II* 31 ft *9,45 m*	Yokohama, Japan	San Diego, Cal	75 days (5911 miles)	1969
Earliest Rowing	John Fairfax (GB) Sylvia Cook (GB)	*Britannia II* 35 ft *10,66 m*	San Francisco, Cal. 26 Apr 1971	Hayman I., Australia 22 Apr 1972	362 days	1971–2
Earliest Rowing Solo	Peter Bird, 36 (GB)	*Hele-on-Britannia* 32 ft *9,75 m*	San Francisco 23 Aug 1982	Gt. Barrier Reef Australia 14 June 1983	294 days 9000 miles *14 480 km*	1982–3
Smallest Sailing	Gerry Spiess (US)	*Yankee Girl* 10 ft *3,05 m*	Long Beach, Cal	Sydney	105 days	1981
Earliest raft (shore to shore)	Vital Alsar (Sp) and 3 crew	*La Balsa* (Balsa logs) 42 ft *12,8 m*	Guayaquil Ecuador	Mooloolaba Australia	160 days	1970

N.B.—The earliest single-handed Pacific crossings were achieved East–West by Bernard Gilboy (US) in 1882 in the 18 ft *5,48 m* double-ender *Pacific* to Australia and West–East by Fred Rebel (Latvia) in the 18 ft *5,48 m Elaine,* (from Australia) and Edward Miles (US) in the 36¾ ft *11,2 m Sturdy II* (from Japan) both in 1932, the latter *via* Hawaii.

Hampshire, 1725) and Molly Webber were recorded as marrying in 1743. He died first in 1829 after 86 years of marriage.

Great Britain

James Frederick Burgess (born 3 March 1861, died 27 Nov 1966) and his wife Sarah Ann, *née* Gregory (born 11 July 1865, died 22 June 1965) were married on 21 June 1883 at St James's, Bermondsey, London, and celebrated their 82nd anniversary.

Golden Weddings

Despite the advent of the computer, records on golden (or 50 year long) weddings remain still largely uncollated. Unusual cases reported include that of Mrs Agnes Mary Amy Mynott (b. 25 May 1887) who attended the golden wedding of her daughter Mrs Violet Bangs of St Albans on 20 Dec 1980, 23 years after her own. The 3 sons and 4 daughters of Mr and Mrs J. Stredwick of East Sussex *all* celebrated golden weddings between May 1971 and April 1981. Triplets Lucille (Mrs Vogel), Marie (Mrs McNamara) and Alma (Mrs Prom) Pufpaff all celebrated their golden weddings on 12 Apr 1982 having all married in Cleveland, Minnesota in 1932.

Most married

Jack V. and Edna Moran of Seattle, Washington, USA have married each other 40 times since the original and only really necessary occasion on 27 July 1937 in Seaside, Oregon. Subsequent ceremonies have included those at Banff, Canada (1952), Cairo, Egypt (1966) and Westminster Abbey, London (1975).

Mass ceremony

The largest mass wedding ceremony was one of 5837 couples from 83 countries officiated over by Sun Myung Moon (b. 1920) of the Holy Spirit Association for the Unification of World Christianity in the Chamsil Gymnasium, Seoul, South Korea on 14 Oct 1982. The response to the question 'Will you swear to love your spouse for ever?' is 'Ye'.

Most Expensive Wedding

The wedding of Mohammed, son of Shaik Zayid ibn Sa'id al-Makhtum, to Princess Salama in Abu Dhabi in May 1981 lasted 7 days and cost an estimated £22 million in a purpose built stadium for 20,000.

Latest Divorce

In March 1980 a divorce was reported in the Los Angeles Superior Court, California between Bernardine and Leopold Delpes in which both parties were aged 88. The British record age is 101 years by Harry Bidwell at Brighton, Sussex on 21 Nov 1980.

Dining out

The world champion for eating out is Fred E. Magel of Chicago, Illinois, USA who since 1928 has dined out 46,000 times in 60 nations as a restaurant grader (to 21 June 1983). He asserts the one which served largest helpings was Zehnder's Hotel, Frankenmuth, Michigan, USA. Mr Magel's favourite dishes are South African rock lobster and mousse of fresh English strawberries.

Party giving

The 'International Year of the Child' children's party in Hyde Park, London was attended by Royal Family and 160,000 children on 30–31 May 1979. The longest street party ever staged was for 5500 children by the Oxford Street Association to celebrate the Royal Wedding of TRH The Prince and Princess of Wales on 25 July 1981 along the entire length from Park Street to St. Giles Circus, London.

The largest Christmas Party ever staged was that thrown by

Fred Magel (right) the champion diner out before taking his 46,000th restaurant meal. He chose Zehnder's in Frankenmuth, Michigan, where second helpings are unknown.

The Boeing Company in the 65,000 seat Kingdome, Seattle, Washington, USA, in two shows totalling 103,152 people on 15 Dec 1979, managed by general chairman John Mathiasen and produced by Greg Thompson with a cast of 2500. The floor was decorated with 1000 Christmas trees each with 100 lights; 150,000 snow white balloons and three ice ponds.

Toastmasters

The Guild of Professional Toastmasters (founded 1962) has only 12 members. Its founder and President, Ivor Spencer, once had to listen to a speech in excess of 2 hr by the maudlin guest of honour of a retirement luncheon. The Guild also elects the most boring speaker of the year, but for professional reasons, will not publicize the winners' names until a decent interval has elapsed. Red coats were introduced by the pioneer professional, William Knight-Smith (d. 1932) *c.* 1900.

Lecture agency

In 1980 Bob Jones of Wellington, New Zealand addressed a seminar of 1048 people in Auckland on property. He received $NZ200,000 or $NZ16,666 per hour. In March 1981 it was reported that both Johnny Carson and Bob Hope commanded fees of $40,000 (*then £18,000*).

Working week

A case of a working week of 142 hours was recorded in June 1980 by Dr Paul Ashton, 32 the anaesthetics registrar at Birkenhead General Hospital, Merseyside. This left an average each day of 3 hr 42 min 51 sec for sleep. Some non-consultant doctors are actually contracted to work 110 hours a week or be available for 148 hours. Some contracts for fully salaried University lecturers call for a 3 hr week or a 72 hr year spread over 24 weeks.

Working career

The longest working life has been that of 98 years by Mr Izumi (see Chapter 1, pp. 10), who began work goading draft animals at a sugar mill at Isen, Tokunashima, Japan in 1872. He retired as a sugar cane farmer in 1970 aged 105.

The longest working life recorded in the UK was that of Susan O'Hagan (1802–1909) who was in domestic service with 3 generations of the Hall family of Lisburn, near Belfast, Northern Ireland for 97 years from the age of 10 to light duties at 107.

The longest recorded industrial career in one job in Britain was that of Miss Polly Gadsby who started work with Archibald Turner & Co of Leicester aged 9. In 1932, after 86 years service, she was still at her bench wrapping elastic, at the age of 95. Mr Theodore C. Taylor (1850–1952) served 86 years with J. T. & T. Taylor of Batley, West Yorkshire including 56 years as chairman. Currently the longest serving and the oldest chairman (appointed July 1926) of any board of directors is Mrs Mary Henrietta Anne Moody (b. 7 Apr 1881) of Mark & Moody Ltd, printers and booksellers of Stourbridge, West Midlands. Edward William Beard (1878–1982), a builder of Swindon, Wiltshire retired in October 1981 from the firm he founded in 1896 after 85 years. Commissioner Catherine Bramwell-Booth (b. 1883) has been serving the Salvation Army since 1903.

Most durable coal miner

George Stephenson (b. 21 Apr 1833) worked at William Pit, a Whitehaven Colliery, Cumbria from 1840 (aged 7) for 82 years until his retirement in 1922. He died on 18 Mar 1926 aged 92 years 10 months having received a testimonial of £54 12s.

Longest pension

Miss Millicent Barclay, daughter of Col William Barclay was born posthumously on 10 July 1872 and became eligible for a Madras Military Fund pension to continue until her marriage. She died unmarried on 26 Oct 1969 having drawn the pension for every day of her life of 97 years 3 months.

Medical families

The 4 sons and 5 daughters of Dr Antonio B. Vicencio of Los Angeles all qualified in 1964–82. Eight sons of John Robertson of Benview, Dumbarton, Scotland graduated as medical doctors between 1892 and 1914. Henry Lewis Lutterloh and Elizabeth Grantham of Chatham County, North Carolina, USA were the grandparents of 19 medical doctors. From 1850 to 1962 they practiced a total of 704 man-years. The Maurice family of Marlborough, Wiltshire have had the same practice for 6 generations since 1792.

MISCELLANEOUS ENDEAVOURS

Accordion playing

Tom Luxton of Oldbury, West Midlands, played an accordion for 84 hr on 4–7 Aug. 1982.

Apple peeling

The longest single unbroken apple peel on record is one of 172 ft 4 in *52,51 m* peeled by Kathy Wafler, of Wolcott, NY, USA in 11 hr 30 min at Long Ridge Mall, Rochester, NY on 16 Oct 1976. The apple weighed 20 oz *567 g*.

Apple picking

The greatest recorded performance is 365½ US bushels (354.1 Imperial bushels *128,80 hectolitres*) picked in 8 hr by George Adrian, 32 of Indianapolis, Indiana, USA, on 23 Sept 1980.

Auctioneering

The longest one man auction on record is for 36 hours by Reg Coates in Gosport, Hampshire on 11–12 Dec 1982.

Bag-carrying

The greatest non-stop bag-carrying feat carrying 1 cwt *50,8 kg* of household coal in an open bag is 32 miles *51,5 km* by Brian Newton in 10 hr 18 min from Leicester to the Nottingham border on 27 May 1983.

The record for the 1012,5 m *1107.2 yd* course annual Gawthorpe, West Yorkshire race is 4 min 19 sec by Terry Lyons, 36 on 16 Apr 1979.

Bag-pipes

The longest duration pipe has been one of 100 hr by Neville Workman, Clive Higgins, Patrick Forth and Paul Harris, playing two at a time in shifts, of Churchill School Pipe Band, Harare, Zimbabwe on 9–13 July 1976.

Balancing on one foot

The longest recorded duration for balancing on one foot is 33 hr by V. S. Kumar Anandan of Colombo, Sri Lanka on 15–17 May 1980. The disengaged foot may not be rested on the standing foot nor may any object be used for support or balance.

Balloon flights

The longest reported toy balloon flight is one of 9000 miles *14 500 km* from Atherton, California, USA, (released by Jane Dorst on 21 May 1972) and found on 10 June at Pietermaritzburg, South Africa. The longest recorded hydrogen-filled balloon flight from the geographical British Isles is one of 5880 miles *9460 km* from Jersey which was returned from Camps Bay, Cape Province, South Africa on 28 Apr 1974, 43 days after release by Gerard Wankling.

Balloon release

The largest mass balloon release ever attempted was 300,424 balloons to form a 'flag' measuring 552 × 338 ft *168 × 103 m* at Itasca, Illinois, USA on 4 July 1983. A sudden wind caused premature lift-off of 210,000 balloons.

Band marathons

The longest recorded 'blow-in' is 100 hr 2 min by the Du Val Senior High School, Lanham, Maryland, USA on 13–17 May 1977. The minimum number of musicians is 10.

Band One-man

Dave Sheriff of Rugby, Warwickshire played

simultaneously 12 instruments (4 melody, 8 percussion) at the Mainos TV Studios, Helsinki, Finland on 10 Nov 1983. Dave Sheriff (see above) played his one-man band (which must include at least 3 instruments played simultaneously) for 70 hr 1 min on 5–8 Mar 1984 at Chappell's Music Store, Milton Keynes, Bucks. The greatest number of instruments played in a single rendition is 157 in 2 min 47 sec by Guy Marchi, 33, at The Sheraton Hotel, Edmonton, Alberta, Canada on 17 May 1983.

Barrel jumping *on Ice Skates*

The official distance record is 29 ft 5 in *8,99 m* over 18 barrels by Yvon Jolin at Terrebonne, Quebec, Canada on 25 Jan 1981. The feminine record is 20 ft 4½ in *6,21 m* over 11 barrels by Janet Hainstock in Michigan, USA, on 15 Mar 1980.

Barrel rolling

The record for rolling a full 36 gallon metal beer barrel over a measured mile is 8 min 7.2 sec by Phillip Randle, Steve Hewitt, John Round, Trevor Bradley, Colin Barnes and Ray Glover of Haunchwood Collieries Institute and Social Club, Nuneaton, Warwickshire on 15 Aug 1982. A team of 10 rolled a 63½ kg *140 lb* barrel 240,35 km *150 miles* in 30 hr 31 min in Chlumcany, Czechoslovakia on 27–28 Oct 1982.

Barrow pushing

The heaviest loaded barrow pushed for a minimum 50 level feet *15,24 m* is one loaded with bricks weighing a gross 1.08 tons (1103,1 kg *2432 lb*) by Gary Windebank at Romsey Fête, Hampshire on 18 June 1983.

Barrow Racing

The fastest time attained in a 1 mile *1,609 km* wheelbarrow race is 4 min 52.04 sec by John Coates and Brian Roades of Richmond, BC, Canada on 6 July 1980 at the Ladner Sports Festival, Delta, B.C. Brothers-in-law Malcolm Shipley and Adrian Freeburg pushed each other from John O'Groats to Land's End for charity in 30 days from 28 July–26 Aug 1981.

Bath tub racing

The record for the annual international 36 miles *57,9 km* Nanaimo to Vancouver, British Columbia bath tub race is 1 hr 29 min 40 sec by Gary Deathbridge (Australia) on 30 July 1978. Tubs are limited to 75 in *1,90 m* and 6 hp motors. The greatest distance for paddling a hand propelled bath tub in 24 hr is 90.5 miles *145,6 km* by 13 members of Aldington Prison Officers Social Club, nr. Ashford, Kent on 28–29 May 1983.

Baton twirling

The Apple Core Baton Twirling Corps of Bridgeview, Illinois, USA twirled for 92½ hr on 4–8 Apr 1983.

Beard of bees

All records for beards of bees were eclipsed in Oct 1983 when a pyramid of six cheer leaders from the University of California were smothered by bees having been sprayed by a chemical attractant. This category will now be retired.

Bed making

The record time set under the rigorous rules of the Australian Bedmaking Championships is 28.2 sec solo by Wendy Wall, 34, of Hebersham, Sydney, NSW on 30 Nov 1978. The British pair record with 1 blanket, 2 sheets, an undersheet, an uncased pillow, 1 counterpane and 'hospital' corners is 24.0 sec by Judith Strange and Catheryn Marsden of High Peak College, Buxton,, Derbyshire on 11 Mar 1978.

Bed of nails

The duration record for lying on a bed of nails (sharp 6-inch *15,2 cm*; 2 in 5 *cm* apart) is 273 hr by Alan Andrew, 26 at Barry, Wales on 5–14 Dec 1983. His fiancée Katherine Weston accompanied him for the last 34 hr. Much longer durations are claimed by uninvigilated *fakirs*— the most extreme case being *Silki* who claimed 111 days in São Paulo, Brazil ending on 24 Aug 1969.

Bed pushing

The longest recorded push of a normally sessile object is of 3233 miles 1150 yd *5204 km* in the case of a wheeled hospital bed by a team of 9 employees of Bruntsfield Bedding centre, Edinburgh on 21 June–26 July 1979.

Bed race

The record time for the annual Knaresborough Bed Race (established 1966) in North Yorkshire is 13 min 08 sec for the 2 mile 63 yd *3,27 km* course crossing the River Nidd by the Long Distance Walkers Association on 11 June 1983.

Beer label collecting

The greatest collection of different British Beer labels is 27,845 (to 1 Jan 1984) by Keith Osborne, Hon Sec of The Labologists Society (founded by Guinness Exports Ltd in 1958). His oldest is one from D. B. Walker & Co, Warrington of *c.* 1846.

Beer mat flipping

Lack of standardisation of the size and weight of beer mats has bedevilled the chronicling of records in this international pursuit.

A figure of 102 was reported from Stephen Thornton, 22, of Romsey, Hants on 16 Jan 1980.

Beer Stein Carrying

Barmaid Rosie Schedelbauer covered 15 m

49 ft 2½ in in 4.0 sec with 5 full steins in each hand in a televised contest at Königssee, West Germany on 29 June 1981.

Best man

The world's champion 'best man' is Mr Wally Gant, a bachelor fishmonger from Wakefield, West Yorkshire, who officiated for the 50th time since 1931 in December 1964.

Bicycle *Most mounting simultaneously*

On 6 Aug 1981 at Fuchu, Tokyo, Japan thirteen members of the Mito-Itomi Unicycle Club mounted and rode a single bicycle a distance of 10 m *32.8 ft*.

Billiard table jumping

Joe Darby (1861–1937) cleared a full-sized 12 ft *3,65 m* billiard table lengthwise, taking off from a 4 in *10 cm* high solid wooden block, at Wolverhampton, West Midlands on 5 Feb 1892.

Bomb defusing

The highest reported number of unexploded bombs defused by any individual is 8000 by Werner Stephan in West Berlin, Germany, in the 12 years from 1945 to 1957. He was killed by a small grenade on the Grunewald blasting site on 17 Aug 1957. Britain's two most highly decorated bomb disposal officers were the late Cdr H. Syme GC GM★ and Lt-Cdr J. Bridge GC GM★.

Bond signing

The greatest feat of bond signing was that performed by Arne Aaaser of Den Norske Creditbank, Oslo who signed 20,000 bonds in 16 hr 2 min 50 sec on 4–5 Mar 1982.

Boomerang throwing

The earliest mention of a word similar to *boomerang* is *wo-murrang* in Collins *Acct. N.S. Wales Vocab.* published in 1798. The earliest certain Australian account of a returning boomerang (term established, 1827) was in 1831 by Major (later Sir Thomas) Mitchell. Curved throwing sticks for wild fowl hunting were found in the tomb of Tutankhamun dating from the mid 14th century BC.

World championships and codified rules were not established until 1970. The Boomerang Association of Australia's championship record for distance reached from the thrower before the boomerang returns is 111 m *364.1 ft* diameter by Bob Burwell in November 1981 at Albury. The longest unofficial out and return record on record is one of 375 ft *114,3 m* by Peter Ruhf (US) at Randwick, Sydney, NSW, Australia on 28 June 1982. David Schummy (GB) kept a boomerang aloft for 31.31 sec at Dulwich, London on 24 Apr 1983. The greatest number of consecutive two handed catches on record is 146 by Bernard 'Bunny' Read of Albury at Melbourne, Victoria on 3 Apr 1981.

Brick carrying

The greatest distance achieved for carrying a brick 8 lb 15 oz *4,053 kg* in a nominated ungloved hand in an uncradled downward pincher grip is 45 miles *72,4 km* by David and Kym Barger of Lamar, Missouri, USA on 21 May 1977.

The feminine record for a 9 lb 12 oz *4,422 kg* brick is 19.2 miles *30,89 km* by Cynthia Ann Smolko of Denville, New Jersey, USA on 14 May 1977. The British record for a 6 lb *2,72 kg* smooth-sided brick is 3 miles *4,82 km* by Karen Stevenson of Wallasey, Merseyside on 24 Jan 1981.

Bricklaying

Ralph Charnock of Benfleet, Essex set The

Brick Development Association Bricklaying Championship record at Colindale, north-west London on 30 Sept 1981. He laid 711 bricks in 60 minutes, according to the strict rules of the Guild of Bricklayers. He broke his record with 725 in 60 min on 17 June 1983 at Wiggins Construct, Thundersley, Essex.

Bricklifting

Fred Burton (b. 1944) of Cheadle, Staffs, lifted twenty-four 8 × 4 × 2½ in *20,3 × 10,1 × 6,3 cm* bricks horizontally at Wolstanton Social Club, Newcastle, Staffs on 20 Nov 1982. The span was 62 in *157,5 cm* and the weight 112½ lb *51,03 kg*. He weighed only 167 lb *75,7 kg*.

Brick racing

The record times recorded at the Annual NFBTE Young Builders Dry-brick championship in Leicester are 100 metres: 1 min 7.0 sec + 11 penalty points giving a gross 1 min 18.0 sec by Ian Jones on 3 June 1979, and 1 mile (team): 21 min 25 sec + 118 penalties giving an overall time of 23 min 23 sec by William Davis & Company (Leicester) Ltd, on 15 June 1980.

Brick throwing

The greatest reported distance for throwing a standard 5 lb *2,268 kg* building brick is 44,54 m *146 ft 1 in* by Geoff Capes at Braybrook School, Orton Goldhay, Cambridgeshire on 19 July 1978.

Bubble gum blowing

The greatest reported diameter for a bubble gum bubble is 19¼ in *48,9 cm* by Susan Montgomery, 18 of Fresno, Calif, USA in April 1979. The British record also using 'Bubble Yum' is 16½ in *42 cm* by Nigel Fell, 13 from Derriaghy, N. Ireland in November 1979. This was equalled by John Smith of Willingham, Cambridgeshire on 25 Sept 1983.

Burial alive

Voluntary burial alive (for which claims up to 217 days have been published) are inadmissible unless the depth of the coffin is a minimum 2 m *6 ft 6¾ in* below ground; the coffin has a maximum cubic capacity of 1,5 million cc or *54 ft³* and the single aperture for communication and feeding has a maximum dimension of 10 cm or *4 inches*. 'Country' Bill White, 50, was so buried from 31 July to 19 Dec 1981 (141 days) in Killeen, Texas, USA.

Camping Out

The silent Indian *fakir* Mastram Bapu 'contented father' has remained on the same spot by the roadside in the village of Chitra for 22 years 1960–82.

Canal Jumping

In the 1979 Fierljeppen Championship at Winsam, Friesland, Netherlands, Catharinus Hoekstra leapt 17,39 m *57 ft* across the water with a pole. A distance of 18,40 m *60 ft 4 in* has been attributed to Aarth de Wit.

Can top collecting

The longest recorded one-man chain of can tops is one of 11.2 miles *18,02 km* collected since 4 July 1969 by Arthur J. Jordan Sr of Yorkstown, Virginia, USA to the estimated number of 710,000 as of 14 May 1979.

Card throwing

Kevin St Onge threw a standard playing card 185 ft 1 in *56,41 m* at the Henry Ford Community College Campus, Dearborn, Michigan, USA on 12 June 1979.

Carriage Driving

The only man to drive 48 horses in a single

hitch is Dick Sparrow of Zearing, Iowa, USA in 1972–77. The lead horses were on reins 135 ft *41 m* long.

Car wrecking

The greatest number of cars wrecked in a stunting career is 1839 to 1 June 1984 by Dick Sheppard of Gloucester, England.

Catapulting

The greatest recorded distance for a catapult shot is 1362 ft *415 m* by James M. Pfotenhauer using a patented 16½ ft *5,02 m* 'Monarch IV Supershot' and a 53 calibre lead musket ball on Ski Hill Road, Escanaba, Michigan, USA on 10 Sept 1977.

Champagne fountain

The tallest successfully filled column of champagne glasses is one 23 high filled from the top by Carl Groves and Peter Sellars on the 'Daryl Somers show', Channel 9 TV, Richmond, Vic, Australia on 19 Apr 1983.

Clapping

The duration record for continuous clapping (sustaining an average of 140 claps per min audible at 100 yd *91 m*) is 50 hr 17 min by Ashrita Furman of Jamaica, New York, USA on 10–12 Aug 1981.

Club swinging

Albert Rayner set a world record of 17,512 revolutions (4.9 per sec) in 60 min at Wakefield, W Yorkshire on 27 July 1981. M. Dobrilla swung continuously for 144 hr at Cobar, NSW finishing on 15 Sept 1913.

Coal cutting

The most productive coal mine in Britain has been Bagworth Colliery, Leicestershire with 5.8 tonnes per man shift in the 41 weeks from April to 31 Dec 1980. The colliery dates from 1829. The individual record for filling is 218 tons in a week of 5 shifts by Jim Marley (b. 1914) at East Walbottle Colliery, Tyne and Wear, England in 1949. This included 47½ tons in 6 hr. The NCB record for a week's production by a 48 man team is 32,333 tonnes at their biggest pit at Kellingley Colliery, Castleford, North Yorkshire in the pre-Christmas 'Bull Week' in December 1982.

Coal shovelling

The record for filling a ½-ton *508 kg* hopper with coal is 31.0 sec by Piet Groot at the Inangahua A. and P. Show, New Zealand on 5 Feb 1983.

Coin balancing

The greatest recorded feat of coin-balancing is the stacking of 175 Canadian coins on top of a Canadian Commemorative penny which was freestanding vertically on another coin by Bruce McConachy (b. 1963) of West Vancouver, BC, at Faak am Se, Austria on 14 Sept 1982.

Coin snatching

The greatest number of 10p pieces clean caught from being flipped from the back of a forearm into the same palm is 62 by Andrew Gleed at the *Evening Star* offices, Ipswich on 22 Sept 1978. Claims beyond 100 coins (using US 25 cent pieces) are disproved by the fact that this is beyond the capacity even of the *upturned* human hand.

Competition winnings

The largest individual competition prize win on record is $307,500 (*then £109,821*) by Herbert J. Idle, 55, of Chicago in an encyclopaedia contest run by Unicorn Press Inc on 20 Aug 1953. The highest value first prize offered in Britain has been a £32,000 Magirus 232D 26Fk tipper in a competition run by Iveco UK Ltd in April 1982, and won by Neil Gardiner of Gossops Green, West Sussex.

Cow chip tossing

The record distances in the country sport of throwing dried cow chips depends on whether or not the projectile may or may not be 'moulded into a spherical shape'. The greatest distance achieved under the 'non-sphericalization and 100% organic' rule (established in 1970) is 266 ft *81,07 m* by Steve Urner at the Mountain Festival, Tehachapi, California, USA on 14 Aug 1981.

Crawling

The longest continuous voluntary crawl (progression with one or other knee in unbroken contact with the ground) on record is 26.5 miles *42,64 km* by Rod Mahon and Ken Mackenzie of Newton Abbot, Devon on 18 Jan 1982.

Crochet

Mrs Barbara Jean Sonntag (b. 1938) of Craig, Colorado, USA crocheted 330 shells plus 5 stitches (equivalent to 4412 stitches) in 30 min at a rate of 147 stitches a minute on 13 Jan 1981 She also set a record for a crochet chain on 31 Oct 1981 with a strand measuring 34.9 miles *56,16 km*. Mrs Sybille Anthony bettered all knitting marathons in a 120 hr crochet marathon at Toombul Shopping-town, Queensland, Australia on 3–7 Oct 1977.

Cubism

Minh Thai, 16, a Vietnamese refugee won the World Rubik Cube Championship held in Budapest, Hungary on 5 June 1982. His winning time after standardized dislocations was 22,95 sec. Ernö Rubik (Hungary) patented the device in 1975 with 43,252,003,274,489, 856,856,000 possible combinations.

Cucumber slicing

Norman Johnson of Blackpool College of Art and Technology set a record of 13.4 sec for slicing a 12 in *30,48 cm* cucumber 1½ in *3,81 cm* diameter at 22 slices to the inch (total 244 slices) on West Deutscher Rundfunk in Cologne on 3 Apr 1983.

Custard pie throwing

The most times champion in the annual World Custard Pie Championships at Coxheath, Kent (instituted 1968) have been the 'The Birds', ('The Bashers') and the 'Coxheath Men' ('Custard Kings') each with 3 wins. The target (face) must be 8 ft 3⅞ in *2,53 m* from the thrower who must throw a pie no more than 10¼ in *26,03 cm* in diameter. Six points are scored for a square hit full in the face.

Demolition work

Fifteen members of the Black Leopard Karate Club demolished a 7-room wooden farmhouse west of Elnora, Alberta, Canada in 3 hr 18 min by foot and empty hand on 13 June 1982.

Debating *Most protracted*

A mixed team (limited to 13) debated the motion 'That this House Believes in Britain' for 50 hr 19 min 24 sec at Caterham School, Surrey on 10–12 July 1982.

Domino toppling

The greatest number of dominoes (set up singlehanded) toppled is 281,581 out of 320,236 set up, by Klaus Friedrich, 22, in Bayern, West Germany on 27 Jan 1984. The dominoes fell within 12 min 57.3 sec having taken 31 days (10 hours daily) to set up.

The record for a team (maximum 4 people) is 295,000 by Klaus Friedrich at Furth, West Germany on 28 Jan 1984.

Drumming

The world's duration drumming record is 1009 hr 6 min 20 sec by Laurent Rebboah of Cupertino, California, USA, on 22 Sept–3 Nov 1983.

DANCING

Largest and longest dances

The largest dance ever staged was that put on by the Houston Livestock show at the Astro Hall, Houston, Texas, USA on 8 Feb 1969. The attendance was more than 16,500 with 4000 turned away. An estimated total of 20,000 dancers took part in the National Square Dance Convention at Louisville, Kentucky, USA on 26 June 1983.

Marathon dancing must be distinguished from dancing mania, or tarantism, which is a pathological condition. The worst outbreak of this was at Aachen, Germany, in July 1374, when hordes of men and women broke into a frenzied and compulsive choreomania in the streets. It lasted for hours till injury or complete exhaustion ensued.

The most severe marathon dance staged as a public spectacle was one by Mike Ritof and Edith Boudreaux who logged 5148 hr 28½ min to win $2000 at Chicago's Merry Garden Ballroom, Belmont and Sheffield, Illinois, USA from 29 Aug 1930 to 1 Apr 1931. Rest periods were progressively cut from 20 to 10 to 5 to nil minutes per hour with 10 inch steps and a maximum of 15 seconds for closure of eyes.

Ballet. In the *entrechat* (a vertical spring from the fifth position with the legs extended crisscrossing at the lower calf), the starting and finishing position each count as one such that in an *entrechat douze* there are *five* crossings and uncrossings. This was performed by Wayne Sleep for the BBC *Record Breakers* programme on 7 Jan 1973. He was in the air for 0.71 sec.

Ballet *Most turns.* The greatest number of spins called for in classical ballet choreography is the 32 *fouettés rond de jambe en tournant* in 'Swan Lake' by Pyotr Ilyich Chaykovskiy (Tschaikovsky) (1840–93). Miss Rowena Jackson (later Chatfield), MBE (b. Invercargill, NZ, 1925) achieved 121 such turns at her class in Melbourne, Victoria, Australia, in 1940.

Ballet *Most Curtain Calls.* The greatest recorded number of curtain calls ever received by ballet dancers is 89 by Dame Margaret Evelyn Arias, DBE *née* Hookham (born Reigate, Surrey, 18 May 1919) *alias* Margot Fonteyn, and Rudolf Hametovich Nureyev (born on a train near Irkutsk, USSR, 17 Mar 1938) after a performance of 'Swan Lake' at the Vienna Staatsoper, Austria, in October 1964.

Ballet *Largest Cast.* The largest number of ballet dancers used in a production in Britain has been 2000 in the London Coster Ballet of 1962, directed by Lillian Rowley, at the Royal Albert Hall, London.

Ballroom *Marathon.* The indivual continuous world record for ballroom dancing is 120 hr 30 min by Alain Dumas on 28 June–3 July 1983 at the Disco-Shop, Granby, Quebec, Canada. Nine girls worked shifts as his partner.

Ballroom *Champions.* The world's most successful professional ballroom dancing champions have been Bill Irvine, MBE and Bobbie Irvine, MBE, who won 13 world titles between 1960 and 1972. The oldest competitive ballroom dancer is Albert J. Sylvester CBE, JP (b. 24 Nov 1889) of Corsham, Wiltshire. In 1977 he won the topmost amateur Alex Moore award for a 10 dance test with his partner Paula Smith in Bath on 26 Apr 1977. By 1981 he had won nearly 50 medals and trophies since he began dancing in 1964.

Belly dancing. The longest recorded belly dance was one of 100 hr by Sabra Starr at Teplitzki's Hotel, Atlantic City, New Jersey, USA on 4–8 July 1977.

Charleston. The Charleston duration record is 110 hr 58 min by Sabra Starr of Lansdowne, Pennsylvania, USA on 15–20 Jan 1979.

Conga. The longest recorded conga was one comprising a 'snake' of 8659 people from the South Eastern Region of the Camping and Caravanning Club of Great Britain and Ireland on 4 Sept 1982.

Disco. The longest recorded disco dancing marathon is one of 371 hr by John Sharples of Preston, Lancashire on 18 Jan–3 Feb 1982.

Flamenco. The fastest flamenco dancer ever measured is Solero de Jerez aged 17 who in Brisbane, Australia in September 1967 in an electrifying routine attained 16 heel taps per second or a rate of 1000 a minute.

High kicking. The world record for high kicks is 9100 in 6 hr 51 min by V. S. Kumar Anandan at Galle Face, Colombo, Sri Lanka on 31 Dec 1980–1 Jan 1981. Veronica Evans set a speed record of 50 kicks in 25.0 sec in Manchester on 24 Dec 1931.

Jiving. The duration record for non-stop jiving is 97 hr 42 min by Richard Rimmer (with a relay of partners) of Caterham, Surrey on 11–16 Nov 1979. Under the strict rules of the European Rock n' Roll Association the duration pair record is 22 hr by Mirco and Manuela Catalono at the Olympia Shopping Centre, Munich on 6–7 Feb 1981.

Limbo. The lowest height for a bar (flaming) under which a limbo dancer has passed is 6⅛ in *15,5 cm* off the floor by Marlene Raymond, 15 at the Port of Spain Pavilion, Toronto, Canada on 24 June 1973. Strictly no part of the body other than the sole or side of the foot should touch the ground though the brushing of a shoulder blade does not in practice usually result in disqualification.

Tap. The fastest *rate* ever measured for any tap dancer has been 1440 taps per min (24 per sec) by Roy Castle on the BBC TV *Record Breakers* programme on 14 Jan 1973. The greatest ever assemblage of tap dancers in a single routine is 2647 organised by Brian Smith of TVW7, in aid of the annual Telethon, at the Concert Hall, Perth, Western Australia on 16 Oct 1982.

The house which got the chop from the Black Leopard karate team of Alberta, Canada (see page 185).

(see page 185).

Faux pas

If measuring by financial consequence, the greatest *faux pas* on record was that of the young multi-millionaire, James Gordon Bennett, committed on 1 Jan 1877 at the family mansion of his demure fiancée one Caroline May, in Fifth Avenue, New York City. Bennett arrived in a two-horse cutter late and obviously in wine. By dint of intricate footwork, he gained the portals to enter the withdrawing room where he was the cynosure of all eyes. He mistook the fireplace for a plumbing fixture more usually reserved for another purpose. The May family broke the engagement and Bennett (1841–1918) was obliged to spend the rest of his foot-loose and fancy-free life based in Paris with the resultant non-collection of millions of tax dollars by the US Treasury.

Feminine beauty

Female pulchritude being qualitative rather than quantitative does not lend itself to records. It has been suggested that, if the face of Helen of Troy (*c.* 1200 BC) was capable of launching 1000 ships, a unit of beauty sufficient to launch one ship should be a millihelen. The earliest national beauty contest was staged at Atlantic City, New Jersey, USA in 1921 and was won by a thin blue-eyed blonde with a 30 in *76,2 cm* chest, Margaret Gorman. The Miss World contest began in London in July 1951. The maximum dimensions of any winner were those of Miss Egypt, Antigone Costanda, in 1954 whose junoesque characteristics were at 40–26–38 in *101–66–96 cm* and thus in advance of the classic Western idea of allure. The United Kingdom is the only country to have produced five winners. They were Rosemarie Frankland (1961); Ann Sidney (1964); Lesley Langley (1965); Helen Morgan (1974), who resigned and Sarah-Jane Hutt (1983). The maximum number of contestants was 68 in November 1975. The shortest reign was that of 18 hours by Miss Germany (Gabriella Brum) in 1980.

The world's largest beauty pageant is the annual Miss Universe contest inaugurated in Long Beach, California, USA, in 1952. The most successful country has been the USA with winners in 1954–56–60–67. The number of countries represented has reached 80 with Miss New Zealand, 19 year-old Lorraine Elizabeth Downes, reigning in 1983–4.

The record-breaking cat-walk team in Dublin (see Fashion Show, longest, above left).

(see Fashion Show, longest, above left).

Ducks and drakes

The best accepted ducks and drakes (stone-skipping) record is 24 skips (10 plinkers and 14 pitty-pats) by Warren Klope, 20 of Troy, Michigan being the best score of 6 flat, 4 in *10 cm* limestones, skipped in the annual Mackinac Island, Michigan, USA stone skipping tournament on 5 July 1975. This was equalled by John S. Kolar of Birmingham, Michigan and Glenn Loy Jr of Flint, Michigan on 4 July 1977.

Egg dropping

The greatest height from which fresh eggs have been dropped (to earth) and remained intact is 198 m *650 ft* by David S. Donoghue from a helicopter on 2 Oct 1979 on a Tokyo Golf Course.

Egg Hunt

The greatest egg hunt on record involved 30,600 hard-boiled eggs hidden in Stone Mountain Park, Georgia, USA for a hunt on 11 Apr 1982 organised by Stone Mountain Memorial Association.

Egg and spoon racing

Chris Riggio of San Francisco, California, USA completed a 28.5 mile *45,86 km* fresh egg and dessert spoon marathon in 4 hr 34 min on 7 Oct 1979.

Egg shelling

Two kitchen hands, Harold Witcomb and Gerald Harding, shelled 1050 dozen eggs in a 7¼ hr shift at Bowyers, Trowbridge, Wiltshire on 23 Apr 1971. Both were blind.

Egg throwing

The longest authenticated distance for throwing a fresh hen's egg without breaking is 96,90 m *317 ft 10 in* by Risto Antikainen to Jyrki Korhonen at Siilinjarvi, Finland on 6 Sept 1982.

Escapology

The most renowned of all escape artists has been Ehrich Weiss *alias* Harry Houdini (1874–1926), who pioneered underwater escapes from locked, roped and weighted containers while handcuffed and shackled with irons.

One of the major manufacturers of strait-jackets acknowledges that an escapologist 'skilled in the art of bone and muscle manipulation' could escape from a standard jacket in seconds. There are however methods by which such circumvention can itself be circumvented. Nick Janson of Benfleet, Essex has demonstrated his ability to escape from handcuffs locked on him by more than 1000 different police officers.

Family tree *Longest*

The farthest back the lineage of any family has been traced is that of K'ung Ch'iu or Confucius (551–479 BC). His 4 greats' grandfather K'ung Chia is known from the eighth century BC. This man's 85th lineal descendants Wei-yi (b. 1939) and Wei-ning (b. 1947) live today in Taiwan (Formosa).

Fashion show *Longest*

The longest distance covered by girl models is 71.1 miles *114,4 km* on 19–21 Sept 1983 by Roberta Brown and Lorraine McCourt at Parke's Hotel, Dublin, Ireland. The male model Eddie Warke covered a further 11.9 miles *19,1 km* on the catwalk.

Fire pumping

The greatest gallonage stirrup-pumped by a team of 8 in an 80 hr charity pump is 13,901 gal *63 192 litres* by the White Watch team of the London Salvage Corps in Battersea Park on 2–5 May 1980.

Fire pump manhandling

The longest unaided tow of a fire appliance in excess of 10 cwt *508 kg* in 24 hr on a closed circuit is 211 miles *339,5 km* by a 32 man team of the Dublin Fire Brigade with an 11 cwt *558,8 kg* fire pump on 18–19 June 1983.

Flute marathon

The longest recorded marathon by a flautist is 48 hr by Joe Silmon in HMS *Grampus* in Gosport, Hampshire on 19–20 Feb 1977.

Flying Disc throwing

The World Flying Disc Federation indoor records are Men: 121,6 m *399 ft* by Van Miller at Flagstaff, Arizona on 18 Sept 1982; and Women: 229.6 ft *69,9 m* by Suzanne Fields at Cedar Falls, Iowa on 26 Apr 1981. The outdoor records are: Men: 166,42 m *546 ft* by Morten Sandorff, 21 May 1983, Farum, Denmark; and Women: 401.5 ft *122,3 m* by Liz Reeves, 14 June 1980, Surrey, England. The throw, run and catch record is 83,10 m *272 ft 7 in* by Steve Bentley on 8 Apr 1982 at Sacramento, California. The group marathon record is 1198 hr by Prince George's Community College Flying High Club on 1 June–22 July 1983.

Gladiatorial combat

Emperor Trajan of Rome (AD 98–117) staged a display involving 4941 pairs of gladiators over 117 days. Publius Ostorius, a freed-man, survived 51 combats in Pompeii.

Gold panning

The fastest time recorded for 'panning' 8 planted gold nuggets in a 10 in *25,4 cm* diameter pan is 9.23 sec by Bob Box (*above*) of Ahwahnee, California, and the female record is 10.03 sec by Susan Bryeans (*below*) of Fullerton, California both in the 23rd World Gold Panning Championship on 6 Mar 1983 at Knotts Berry Farm, Buena Park, California, USA.

Golf ball balancing

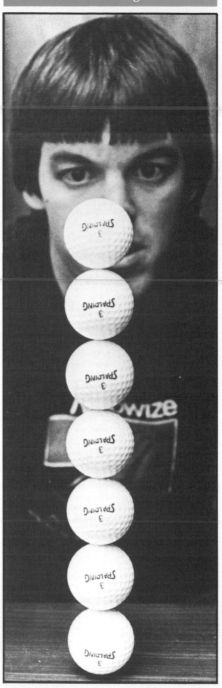

Lang Martin balanced 7 golf balls vertically without adhesive at Charlotte, North Carolina, USA on 9 Feb 1980.

Grape catching

The greatest distance at which a grape thrown from level ground has been caught in the mouth is 270 ft 4 in *82,4 m* by Paul J. Tavilla at Dedham, Massachusetts on 9 Aug 1979. On 16 May 1982 he caught a grape thrown 321 ft 5 in *97,9 m* off a 31 storey building in Fort Lauderdale, Florida. A claim for 354 ft *107,9 m* is now under investigation from Denver, Colorado.

Grave digging

It is recorded that Johann Heinrich Karl Thieme, sexton of Aldenburg, Germany, dug 23,311 graves during a 50-year career. In 1826 *his* understudy dug his grave.

Guitar playing

The longest recorded solo guitar playing marathon is one of 253 hr 20 min by Ray Rogers on 16–27 July 1979 in Mansfield, Ohio, USA in aid of The March of Dimes.

Gum boot throwing

The longest recorded distance (a Size 8 Challenger Dunlop Boot) for 'Wellie wanging' is 173 ft *52,73 m* by Tony Rodgers of Warminster, Wilts on 9 Sept 1978. Rosemary Payne established the feminine record at Cannon Hill Park, Birmingham on 21 June 1975 with 129 ft 11 in *39,60 m*.

Gun running

The record for the Royal Tournament Naval Field Gun competition (instituted 1907, with present rules since 1913) is 2 min 41.1 sec by the Devonport Field Gun crew at Earl's Court, Kensington & Chelsea, London on 16 July 1983. The barrel alone weighs 8 cwt *406 kg*. The wall is 5 ft *1,52 m* high and the chasm 28 ft *8,53 m* across. The Portsmouth crew returned 2 min 40.7 sec in a training practice run at Whale Island, Portsmouth, Hampshire in 1972.

Haggis hurling

The longest recorded distance for throwing a haggis (min. weight 1 lb 8 oz *680 g* is 163 ft 9½ in *49,92 m* by Alan Pettigrew at the Ardrossan Highland Games on 14 June 1981.

Hair-dressing

Pierre Ortiz cut, set and styled hair continuously for 342 hr on 10–26 May 1981 in his 'New York New York' salon, Huntingdon Beach, California, USA.

Hair splitting

The greatest reported achievement in hair splitting has been that of the former champion cyclist and craftsman Alfred West (b. London, 14 Apr 1901) who has succeeded in splitting a human hair 17 times into 18 parts on eight occasions.

Handbell ringing

The longest recorded handbell ringing recital has been one of 52 hr 9 min by the 12 Handbell Ringers of Esslesfield School, Sheffield on 17–19 July 1982.

Handshaking

A world record for handshaking was set up by Theodore Roosevelt (1858–1919), President of the USA, when he shook hands with 8513 people at a New Year's Day, White House Presentation in Washington, DC, USA on 1 Jan 1907. The radio personality Gary Craig reported he had made 15,000 consecutive handshakes among his listeners in Hartford, Connecticut in 1982. Many record claims have been rendered meaningless because aspirants merely tend to arrange circular queues or wittingly or unwittingly shake the same hands repetitively.

High diving

The highest regularly performed head first dives are those of professional divers from La Quebrada ('the break in the rocks') at Acapulco, Mexico, a height of 87½ ft *26,7 m*. The leader of the 27 divers in the exclusive Club de Clavadistas is Raul Garcia (b. 1928) with more than 35,000 dives. The first feminine accomplishment was by Mrs Barbara Winters (b. 12 Nov 1953), *née* Mayer, on 7 Dec 1976. The base rocks, 21 ft *6,40 m* out from the take-off, necessitate a leap of 27 ft *8,22 m* out. The water is 12 ft *3,65 m* deep. The world record high dive is 171 ft

52,1 m by Bruce Boccia, Randy Dickison, Dana Kunze, David Lindsay and Rick Winters (all USA) at Orlando, Florida on 13 Mar 1982. The feminine record is 109 ft 4 in *33,3 m* by Debi Beachel (USA) in Rome on 28 Oct 1982. The highest witnessed in Britain is one of 108 ft *32,9 m* into 8 ft *2,43 m* of water at the Aqua show at Earl's Court, London on 22 Feb 1946 by Roy Fransen, 32.

On 8 May 1885, Sarah Ann Henley, aged 24, jumped from the Clifton Suspension Bridge, which crosses the Avon, England. Her 250 ft *76 m* fall was slightly cushioned by her voluminous dress and petticoat acting as a parachute. She landed, bruised and bedraggled, in the mud on the north bank and was carried to hospital by four policemen. On 11 Feb 1968 Jeffrey Kramer, 24, leapt off the George Washington Bridge 250 ft *76 m* above the Hudson River, New York City, NY and survived. Of the 696 (to 1 Jan 1980) identified people who have made 240 ft *73 m* suicide dives from the Golden Gate Bridge, San Francisco, California, USA since 1937, twelve survived of whom Todd Sharratt, 17, was the only one who managed to swim ashore unaided.

Col Harry A. Froboess (Switzerland) jumped 110 m *360 ft* into the Bodensee from the airship *Graf Hindenburg* on 22 June 1936.

The greatest height reported for a dive into a flaming tank is one of 100 ft *20,4 m* into 7½ ft *2,28 m* by Bill McGuire, 48 at the Holiday Inn, Chicago City Center, Illinois, USA on 14 Aug 1975. Kitty O'Neill dived 180 ft *54,8 m* from a helicopter over Northridge, California on 9 Sept 1979 onto an air cushion measuring 30 × 60 ft *9,14 × 18,28 m* for a TV film stunt.

Highest shallow dive

Henri La Mothe (b. 1904) set a record diving 28 ft *8,53 m* into 12⅜ in *31,43 cm* of water in a child's paddling pool in Northridge, California, on 7 Apr 1979. He struck the water chest first at a speed of 28.4 mph *45,7 km/h*.

High-wire act

The greatest height above street level of any high wire performance has been from a 140 ft *42,6 m* wire between the 1350 ft *411 m* twin towers of the World Trade Center, New York City by Philippe Petit, 24 of Nemours, France on 7 Aug 1974. He was charged with criminal trespass after a 75 min display of at least 7 crossings. The police psychiatrist opined 'Anyone who does this 110 storeys up can't be entirely right'.

Hitch-hiking

The title of world champion hitch-hiker is claimed by Devon Smith who from 1947 to 1971 thumbed lifts totalling 291,000 miles *468 300 km*. In 1957 he covered all the then 48 US States in 33 days. It was not till his 6013th 'hitch' that he got a ride in a Rolls-Royce. The hitch-hiking record for the 874 miles *1406 km* from Land's End, Cornwall, to John o'Groats, Highland, Scotland, is 17 hr 50 min by Andrew Markham of Brigg, S Humbs. on 3–4 Sept 1979. The time before the first 'hitch' on the first day is excluded. The fastest time recorded for the round trip is 42 hr 15 min by Charlotte Allard and Fay Gillanders of Sherborne, Dorset on 30 Aug–1 Sept 1982.

Hod carrying

Jim Ford of Bury, Lancs carried bricks totalling 158,5 kg *349 lb 7 oz* up the minimum 12 foot *3,65 m* ladder (17 rungs) on 12 Sept 1983 at the BBC TV Studios in London for *Record Breakers*. Eric Stenman of Jakobstad, Finland carried 74 bricks of 4 kg *8.8 lb* each so totalling 296 kg *65¼ lb* in a 4 kg *8.8 lb* hod 5 metres *16.4 ft* on the flat before ascending up a runged ramp to a height of 7 ft *2,13 m* on 25 July 1939.

Hoop rolling

In 1968 it was reported that Zolilio Diaz (Spain) had rolled a hoop 600 miles *965 km* from Mieres to Madrid and back in 18 days.

Hop scotch

The longest recorded hop scotch marathon is one of 100 hr by Joellen Glass and Lesa Young of Seattle, Washington, USA on 1–5 Sept 1982.

House of cards

The greatest number of storeys achieved in building freestanding houses of standard playing cards is 61 in the case of a tower using 3650 cards to a height of 11 ft 7 in *3,53 m* built by James Warnock at Cantley, Quebec, Canada, on 8 Sept 1978.

Hula hooping

The highest claim for sustaining gyrating hoops between shoulders and hips is 81 by William Kleeman 'Chico' Johnson (b. 8 July 1939) on BBC TV 'Record Breakers' on 18 Sept 1983. Three complete gyrations are mandatory. The longest recorded marathon for a single hoop is 54 hr by Kym Coberly of Denton, Texas, USA on 7–9 Oct 1978.

Human cannonball

The record distance for firing a human from a cannon is 175 ft *53,3 m* in the case of Emanuel Zacchini in the Ringling Bros and Barnum & Bailey Circus, Madison Square Gardens, New York City, USA, in 1940. His muzzle velocity has been estimated at 54 mph *86,9 km/h*. On his retirement the management were fortunate in finding that his daughter Florinda was of the same calibre. An experiment on Yorkshire TV on 17 Aug 1978 showed that when Miss Sue Evans, 17 was fired she was ⅜ in *9,5 mm* shorter on landing.

In the Halifax explosion of 6 Dec 1917 (*see* Accidents & Disasters Table, Chap. 11) A. B. William Becker, AM (d. 1969) was blown some 1600 yd *1,46 km* but was found breathing but deaf in a tree.

Human fly

The longest climb achieved on the vertical face of a building occurred on 25 May 1981 when Daniel Goodwin, 25, scaled the outside of the 1454 ft *443 m* Sears Tower, Chicago in 7 hr 25 min at the rate of 3.2 ft/min *99 cm/min* using 'T' clamps and suction cups. The name of the masked 'human fly', who has ridden at 380 km/h *240 mph* atop a DC-8 jetliner in April 1977 has not been disclosed. It is however believed unlikely that he is a member of the jet set. Lead climber Jean-Claude Droyer (b. 8 May 1946) of Paris and Pierre Puiseux (b. 2 Dec 1953) of Pau, France climbed up the outside of the Eiffel Tower to a height of 300 m *984 ft* with no dynamic mechanical assistance on 21 July 1980. Jean-Claude took 2 hr 18 min 15 sec to complete the climb.

Jaromir Wagner (b. Czechoslovakia 1941) became the first man to fly the Atlantic standing on the wing of an aircraft. He took off from Aberdeen, Scotland on 28 Sept 1980.

Joke cracking

Felipe Carbonell joked for 40 hr on 9–11 Sept 1983 in the Circus tent of the Hotel Crillon Convention Centre, Lima, Peru. The duo record is 52 hr by Wayne Malton and Mike Hamilton at the Howard Johnson Motor Hotel, Toronto airport, Ontario, Canada on 13–16 Nov 1975.

Jumble Sale

Britain's largest Jumble Sale was 'Jumbly '79' sponsored by *Woman's Own* at Alexandra Palace, London on 5–7 May 1979 in aid of Save The Children Fund. The attendance was 60,000 and the gross takings in excess of £60,000. The Winnetka Congregational Church, Illinois, USA raised $134,098.23 (then £95,784) in their 52nd one-day rummage sale on 10 May 1984.

The Cleveland Convention Center, Ohio, White Elephant Sale (inst. 1933) of 28–29 Oct 1981 raised $382,270.19 (then £212,370). The 2500 volunteers took $120,000 (then £66,660) from more than 10,000 rummagers in the first 2 hours from 208,000 ft² *19 323 m²* of stalls.

Karate Chop

Karatekas have been measured to exert a force of 3000 newtons *675 lb f* and can develop a

Jane Wyman (the one-time Mrs Ronald Reagan) with Regis Toomey whose 185 second screen kiss was a war-time sensation (see p. 189). (*Ronald Grant*)

The world's largest ever kite prior to ascent.

downward chopping speed of 14,4 m/sec *32.2 mph*.

Claims for breaking bricks and wooden slats etc. are unsatisfactory because of the lack of any agreed standards upon which comparisons can be made of friability and the spacing of fulcrums.

Kiss of life

Five members of the St John Ambulance Clifton Combined Division, York, N Yorkshire maintained a 'Kiss of Life' for 240 hr with 224,029 inflations on 26 July–5 Aug 1981. The 'patient' was a dummy.

Kissing

The most prolonged osculatory marathon in cinematic history is one of 185 sec by Regis Toomey and Jane Wyman (later Mrs Ronald Reagan) in *You're In the Army Now* released in 1940. Patricia Hougan and Brad Spacy of Southern California kissed for 17 days 9 hours ending on 2 July 1983. Jonathan Hook kissed 4106 women in 8 hr in Community Action fund raising at Newcastle University on 10 Mar 1983, a rate of 1 per 7.01 sec.

Underwater

The most protracted kiss underwater was one of 2 min 18 sec by Toshiaki Shirai and Yukiko Nagata on Channel 8, Fuji TV in Tokyo, Japan on 2 Apr 1980.

Kite flying *Largest*

At Long Beach, Washington State, USA on 24 Sept 1983 a 1600 lb *725,7 kg* parafoil kite measuring 115 × 124 ft *35 × 37,8 m* was flown.

Kite flying *Greatest number*

The most kites flown on a single line is 4128 by Kazuhiko Asaba, 55 at Kamakura, Japan on 21 Sept 1978.

Kite flying *Altitude*

A claim for 37,908 ft *11 544 m* (by triangulation) by Steven W. Flack over Boonville, New York, USA, on 9 Sept 1978 is not unreservedly accepted by *Kite Lines* magazine of Baltimore, Maryland, USA. The kite was not recovered. The classic record is 9470 m *31,955 ft* by a chain of 8 kites over Lindenberg, East Germany on 1 Aug 1919.

Kite flying *Duration*

The longest recorded flight is one of 180 hr 17 min by the Edmonds Community College team at Long Beach, Washington, USA on 21–29 Aug 1982. Managing the flight of the J-5 parafoil was Harry N. Osborne.

Knitting

The world's most prolific hand-knitter of all time has been Mrs Gwen Matthewman of Featherstone, West Yorkshire. She had attained a speed of 111 stitches per min in a test at Phildar's Wool Shop, Central Street, Leeds on 29 Sept 1980. Her technique has been filmed by the world's only Professor of Knitting—a Japanese.

Knot-tying

The fastest recorded time for tying the six Boy Scout Handbook Knots (square knot, sheet bend, sheep shank, clove hitch, round turn and two half hitches and bowline) on individual ropes is 8.1 sec by Clinton R. Bailey Sr, 52, of Pacific City, Oregon, USA, on 13 Apr 1977.

Leap frogging

Fourteen members of the Phi Gamma Delta Club at the University of Washington, Seattle, USA, covered 602 miles *968,8 km* in 114 hr 46 min on 20–25 Mar 1983. (Total leaps 108,463—one every 9.77 yd.)

Life saving

In November 1974 the City of Galveston, Texas and the Noon Optimist Club unveiled a plaque to the deaf-mute lifeguard Leroy Colombo (1905–74) who saved 907 people from drowning in the waters around Galveston Island from 1917 to his death.

Lightning most times struck

The only man in the world to be struck by lightning 7 times is ex-Park Ranger Roy C. Sullivan (US) the human lightning conductor of Virginia. His attraction for lightning began in 1942 (lost big toe nail), and was resumed in July 1969 (lost eyebrows), in July 1970 (left shoulder seared), on 16 Apr 1972 (hair set on fire), on 7 Aug 1973 (new hair refired and legs seared), on 5 June 1976 ankle injured, and sent to Waynesboro Hospital with chest and stomach burns on 25 June 1977 after being struck while fishing. In Sept 1983 he was reported to have died by his own hand.

Lion-taming

The greatest number of lions mastered and fed in a cage by an unaided lion-tamer was 40, by 'Captain' Alfred Schneider in 1925. Clyde Raymond Beatty handled more than 40 'cats' (mixed lions and tigers) simultaneously. Beatty (b. Bainbridge, Ohio, 10 June 1903, d. Ventura, California, USA, 19 July 1965) was the featured attraction at every show he appeared with for more than 40 years. He insisted upon being called a lion-trainer. More than 20 lion-tamers have died of injuries since 1900.

Log rolling

The record number of International Championships is 10 by Jubiel Wickheim (of Shawnigan Lake, British Columbia, Canada) between 1956 and 1969. At Albany, Oregon on 4 July 1956 Wickheim rolled on a 14 in. *35,5 cm* log against Chuck Harris of Kelso, Washington USA for 2 hr 40 min before losing.

Magician Most Versatile

Under the surveillance of the President of the Magic Circle, Paul Daniels (b. 6 Apr 1938) performed 47 separate tricks in 4 min on his TV magic show on 27 May 1983.

Merry go round

The longest merry go round marathon on record is one of 312 hr 43 min by Gary Mandau, Chris Lyons and Dana Dover in Portland, Oregon, USA on 20 Aug–2 Sept 1976.

Message in a bottle

The longest recorded interval between drop and pick-up is 72 years in the case of a message thrown from the *SS Arawatta* out of Cairns, Queensland on 9 June 1910 in a lotion bottle and reported to be found on Moreton Island on 6 June 1983.

Meteorological balloon inflation

Contests involving the bursting of hot water bottles by sheer lung power is regarded as medically most inadvisable and the category has been discontinued. Substituted for this activity will be the inflation of standardized 1000 gramme meteorological balloons to a diameter of 8 ft *2,43 m* against time. Mel Robson, 40 of Newcastle-upon-Tyne, England achieved a time of 1 hr 46 min on television in Tokyo, Japan on 11 Mar 1982.

Milk bottle balancing

The greatest distance walked by a person continuously balancing a full pint milk bottle on the head is 24 miles *38,6 km* by Ashrita Furman of Jamaica, NY, USA on 10 July 1983.

Morse

The highest recorded speed at which anyone has received morse code is 75.2 words per minute—over 17 symbols per second. This was achieved by Ted R. McElroy of the United States in a tournament at Asheville, North Carolina, USA on 2 July 1939. The highest speed recorded for hand key transmitting is 475 symbols a minute by Harry A. Turner of the US Army Signal Corps at Camp Crowder, Missouri on 9 Nov 1942. Thomas Morris, a GPO operator, is reputed to have been able to send at 39–40 wpm in *c.* 1919 but this is not verifiable.

Musical chairs

The largest game on record was one starting with 4514 participants and ending with Scott Ritter, 18, on the last chair at Ohio State University, Ohio, USA on 25 Apr 1982.

Needle threading

The record number of times a strand of cotton can be threaded through a number 13 needle (eye $\frac{1}{2}$ in, by $\frac{1}{16}$ in, *12,7 mm × 1,6 mm*) in 2 hr is 3795 by Miss Brenda Robinson of the College of Further Education, Chippenham, Wiltshire on 20 Mar 1971.

Noodle making

Mark Pi of the China Gate Restaurant, Columbus, Ohio, USA made 2048 noodle strings (over 5 ft *1,52 m*) in 34.5 sec on 12 Feb 1983.

Omelette making

The greatest number of two-egg omelettes made in 30 min is 217 by Howard Helmer of New York City, USA, at Disneyland, Anaheim, California, USA, on 14 July 1978.

Onion peeling

The record for peeling 50 lb *22,67 kg* of onions is 3 min 18 sec by Alain St. John in Plainfield, Conn., USA, on 6 July 1980. Under revised rules stipulating a minimum of 50 onions, Alfonso Salvo of York, Pennsylvania, USA peeled 50 lb *22,67 kg* of onions (52 onions) in 5 min 23 sec on 28 Oct 1980.

Organ

The longest recorded electric organ marathon is one of 411 hr by Vince Bull at the Comet Hotel, Scunthorpe, South Humberside on 2–19 June 1977. The longest church organ recital ever sustained has been 92 hr by Robert A. Hawkins of New Longton, Preston, Lancs on 15–19 June 1981.

Paddle Boating

The longest recorded voyage in a paddle boat is 2226 miles *3582 km* in 103 days by the foot power of Mick Sigrist and Brad Rud down the Mississippi River from the headwaters in Minnesota to the Gulf of Mexico on 4 Aug–11 Nov 1979.

Parachuting *Longest fall without*

It is estimated that the human body reaches 99 per cent of its low level terminal velocity after falling 1880 ft *573 m* which takes 13–14 secs. This is 117–125 mph *188–201 km/h* at normal atmospheric pressure in a random posture, but up to 185 mph *298 km/h* in a head down position.

Vesna Vulovic, 23, a Jugoslavenski Aerotransport hostess, survived when her DC–9 blew up at 33,330 ft *10 160 m* over the Czechoslovak village of Serbska Kamenice on 26 Jan 1972. She was in hospital for 16 months after emerging from a 27 day coma and having many bones broken. She is now Mrs Breka.

The British record is 18,000 ft *5485 m* by Flt-Sgt Nicholas Stephen Alkemade, aged 21, who jumped from a blazing RAF *Lancaster* bomber over Germany on 23 Mar 1944. His headlong fall was broken by a fir tree near Oberkürchen and he landed without a broken bone in a snow bank 18 in *45 cm* deep.

Piano-playing

The longest piano-playing marathon has been one of 1218 hr (50 days 18 hr) playing 22 hr every day (with 5 min intervals each playing hour) from 7 May to 27 June 1982 by David

Scott at Wagga Wagga Leagues Football Club, NSW, Australia.

In the now discontinued non-stop category the longest on record was 176$\frac{3}{4}$ hr (7 days 8$\frac{3}{4}$ hr) by Jim Montecino in the Trocadero Ball Room, Auckland, New Zealand in 1951.

Piano smashing

The record time for demolishing an upright piano and passing the entire wreckage through a circle 9 in *22,8 cm* in diameter is 1 min 37 sec by six members of the Tinwald Rugby Football Club, Ashburton, New Zealand led by David Young on 6 Nov 1977. Messrs Anthony Fukes, Mike Newman and Terry Cullington smashed a piano with bare hands and feet in 2 min 53 sec in Nottingham on 25 Aug 1979. (All wreckage was passed through the circle.)

Piano tuning

The record time for pitch raising (one semitone or 100 cents) and then returning a piano to a musically acceptable quality is 4 min 20 sec by Steve Fairchild at the Piano Technicians Guild contest at the Dante Piano Co factory, NY, USA on 5 Feb 1980.

Pillar box standing

The record number of people to pile on top of a pillar box (oval top of 6 ft² *0,55 m²*) is 29, all students of the City of London College, Moorgate, in Finsbury Circus, City of London on 21 Oct 1971.

Pipe smoking

The duration record for keeping a pipe (3,3 g *0.1 oz* of tobacco) continuously alight with only an initial match under IAPSC (International Association of Pipe Smokers Clubs) rules is 126 min 39 sec by the five-time champion William Vargo of Swartz Creek, Michigan at the 27th World Championships in 1975. The only other 5-time champion is Paul T. Spaniola (USA) (1951–66–70–73–77). Longer durations have been recorded in less rigorously invigilated contests in which the foul practices of 'tamping' and 'gardening' are not unknown.

Plate spinning

The greatest number of plates spun simultaneously is 72 by Shukuni Sasaki of Takamatsu, Japan at Nio Town Taiyo Exhibition, Kagawa, on 16 July 1981. The British record is 54 set by Holley Gray set during BBC *Record Breakers* on 6 May 1980.

Pogo stick jumping

The greatest number of jumps achieved is 122,171 by Michael Barban of St Louis, Missouri, USA in 15 hr 26 min on 13 Feb 1982.

Pole-squatting

Modern records do not, in fact, compare with that of St Simeon the Younger, (*c.* 521–597 AD) called Stylites (Greek, *stylos* = pillar) a monk who spent his last 45 years up a stone pillar on The Hill of Wonders, near Antioch, Syria. This is probably the longest lasting example of record setting.

There being no international rules, the 'standards of living' atop poles vary widely. The record squat is 440 days by H. David Werder in Clearwater, Florida, USA from 7 Nov 1982 until removed by police on 21 Jan 1984.

The British record is 32 days 14 hr by John Stokes, aged 32, of Moseley, West Midlands in a barrel on a 45 ft *13,70 m* pole in Birmingham, ending on 27 June 1966. This is claimed as a world record for a barrel.

Pop group

The duration record for a 4-man pop-playing

PARACHUTING RECORDS

Category	Name		Place		Date
First from Tower	Louis-Sébastian Lenormand (1757–1839)	quasi-parachute	Montpellier France		1783
First from Balloon	André-Jacques Garnerin (1769–1823)	2230 ft *680 m*	Monceau Park, Paris	22 Oct	1797
Earliest Mid-air Rescue	Miss Dolly Shepherd brought down Miss Louie May on her single 'chute	from balloon at 11,000 ft *3350 m*	Longton, Staffordshire	9 June	1908
First from Aircraft (man)	'Captain' Albert Berry	Aerial exhibitionist	St. Louis, Missouri	1 Mar	1912
(woman)	Mrs Georgina 'Tiny' Broadwick (b. 1893)		Griffith Park, Los Angeles	21 June	1913
First Free Fall	Mrs Georgina 'Tiny' Broadwick	Pilot Glenn L. Martin	North Island, San Diego, California	13 Sept	1914
Lowest Escape	S/Ldr Terence Spencer, DFC, RAF	30–40 ft *9–12 m*	Wismar Bay, Baltic	19 April	1945
Longest Duration Fall	Lt Col Wm H. Rankin, USMC	40 min due to thermals	North Carolina	26 July	1956
Highest Escape	Flt Lt J. de Salis and Fg Off P. Lowe, RAF	56,000 ft *17 068 m*	Monyash, Derby	9 April	1958
Longest Delayed Drop (man)	Capt Joseph W. Kittinger	84,700 ft 16.04 miles *25 816 m* from balloon at 102,800 ft *31 333 m*	Tularosa, New Mexico	16 Aug	1960
(woman)	O. Kommissarova (USSR)	14 100 m *46,250 ft*	over USSR	21 Sept	1965
(civilian, over UK)	P. Halfacre, R. O'Brien, R. James	27,300 ft *8321 m* from 30,000 ft *9144 m*	Sibson, Peterborough	27 Aug	1983
(civilian, world)	R. W. K. Beckett (GB) Harry Ferguson (GB)	30,000 ft *9144 m* from 32,000 ft *9754 m*	D. F. Malan Airport, Capetown	23 Nov	1969
(group, U.K.)	S/Ldr J. Thirtle, AFC; Fl Sgt. A. K. Kidd, AFM; Sgts L. Hicks (d. 1971), P. P. Keane, AFM BEM, K. J. Teesdale, AFM	39,183 ft *11 943 m* from 41,383 ft *12 613 m*	Boscombe Down, Wiltshire	16 June	1967
Most Southerly	T/Sgt Richard J. Patton (d. 1973)	Operation Deep Freeze	South Pole	25 Nov	1956
Most Northerly	Dr Jack Wheeler (US); pilot Capt. Rocky Parsons − 25° F (− 31,6° C)		In Lat. 90° 00' N	15 Apr	1981
Cross Channel (Lateral fall)	Sgt. Bob Walters with 3 soldiers and 2 Royal Marines	22 miles *35,4 km* from 25,000 ft *7600 m*	Dover to Sangatte, France	31 Aug	1980
Career total (man)	Yuri Baranov and Anatolyi Osipov (USSR)	10,000	over USSR	to Sept	1980
(woman)	Valentina Zakoretskaya (USSR)	8000	over USSR	1964–Sept	1980
Highest Landing	Ten USSR parachutists[3]	23,405 ft *7133 m*	Lenina Peak	May	1969
Heaviest Load	US Space Shuttle *Columbia* external rocket retrieval	80 ton capacity, triple array, each 120 ft *36,5 m* diameter	Atlantic off Cape Canaveral, Florida	12 Apr	1981
Highest from Bridge	Donald R. Boyles	1053 ft *320 m*	Royal Gorge, Colorado	7 Sept	1970
Highest Tower Jump	Herbert Leo Schmidtz (US)	KTUL-TV Mast 1984 ft *604 m*	Tulsa, Oklahoma	4 Oct	1970
Biggest Star (3.4 sec hold)	72 man team	Formation held 3.4 sec (US Parachuting Assc. rules)	De Land, Florida	3 Apr	1983
Highest column (world)	22 Chinese team		China	March	1984
(Great Britain)	17 Royal Marine Team		Netheravon, Wilts	18 Apr	1984
Lowest Indoor Jump	Andy Smith and Phil Smith	192 ft *58,5 m*	Houston Astrodome, Texas	16–17 Jan	1982
Most travelled	Kevin Seaman from a Cessna Skylane (pilot Charles E. Merritt)	12,186 miles *19 611 km*	Jumps in all 50 US States	26 July–15 Oct	1972
Oldest Man	Edwin C. Townsend	85 years 1 day	Riverview, Florida, USA	6 Feb	1982
Woman	Mrs. Stella Davenport (GB)	75 years 8 months	Bridlington Aerodrome, Humberside	27 June	1981
24 Hr Total	D. Bruce MacLaughlin (US)	235 (120 at night)	East Taunton, Mass, USA	17–18 Sept	1981

[1] *The king of Ayutthaya, Siam in 1687 was reported to have been diverted by an ingenious athlete parachuting with two large umbrellas. Faustus Verancsis is reputed to have descended in Hungary with a framed canopy in 1617.*

[2] *Maximum speed in rarefied air was 625.2 mph 1006 km/h. at 90,000 ft 27 430 m—marginally supersonic.*

[3] *Four were killed.*

group is 144 hr by 'Rocking Ricky and the Velvet Collars' at The Talardy Hotel, St Asaph, Clwyd, N. Wales on 12–18 Nov 1976.

Potato peeling

The greatest amount of potatoes peeled by 5 people to an institutional cookery standard with standard kitchen knives in 45 min is 266,5 kg *587 lb 8 oz* by J. Mills, M. McDonald, P. Jennings, E. Gardiner and V. McNulty at Bourke Street Hall, Melbourne, Vic, Australia on 17 Mar 1981.

Pram pushing

The greatest distance covered in pushing a pram in 24 hr is 345.25 miles *555,62 km* by Runner's Factory of Los Gatos, California, USA with an All-Star team of 57 California runners on 23–24 June 1979. A team of 10 students from Sir Joseph Banks and East Hills High Schools, Chipping Norton, NSW, Australia, with an adult 'Baby', covered 388 ,408 km *241,34 miles* in 24 hr on 16–17 Nov 1979.

'Psychiatrist' fastest

The world's fastest 'psychiatrist' was Dr Albert L. Weiner of Erlton, New Jersey, USA, who was trained solely in osteopathy but who dealt with up to 50 psychiatric patients a day in four treatment rooms. He relied heavily on narco-analysis, muscle relaxants and electro-shock treatments. In December 1961 he was found guilty on 12 counts of manslaughter from using unsterilized needles.

Quoit throwing

The world's record for rope quoit throwing is

Pole Squatter Kornelius Gerrit, waving from atop his 16 metre high perch after 414 days in Scheffers, Netherlands on 11 June 1983. Even his record has now been surpassed—**see p. 190.**

The record human pyramid of 29 forming on the pedestal of a single London postbox (see page 190). (*Sunday Times*)

an unbroken sequence of 4002 pegs by Bill Irby, Snr of Australia in 1968.

Ramp jumping

The longest distance ever achieved for motor cycle long jumping is *64,60 m* 212 ft by Alain Jean Prieur (b. 4 July 1939) of France at Montlhéry near Paris over 16 buses on 6 Feb 1977. The pioneer of this form of exhibition—Evel Knievel (b. Robert Craig Knievel, 17 Oct 1938 at Butte, Montana, USA) had suffered 433 bone fractures by his 1975 season. His abortive attempt to cross the 1600 ft *485 m* wide and 600 ft *180 m* deep Snake River Canyon, Idaho on 8 Sept 1974 in a rocket reputedly increased his life-time earnings by $6 million (*then £2½ million*). The longest jump in Britain is 208 ft *63,30 m* by Chris Bromham at Bromley Common, South London on 29 Aug 1983.

Riding in armour

The longest recorded ride in full armour (8 stone *50,8 kg*) is one of 167 miles *268,7 km* from Edinburgh to Dumfries in 3 days (riding time 28 hr 30 min) by Dick Brown, 48, on 13–15 June 1979.

Rocking chair

The longest recorded 'Rockathon' is 444 hr by Linda Kennedy at the IKEA store, Calgary, Alberta, Canada on 16 Jan–3 Feb 1984.

Roller Limbo

Denise Culp of Rock Hill, South Carolina, USA went under a 5¼ in *13,33 cm* bar on roller skates on 22 Jan 1984.

Rolling pin

The record distance for a woman to throw a 2 lb *907 g* rolling pin is 175 ft 5 in *53,4 m* by Lori La Deane Adams, 21 at Iowa State Fair, Iowa, USA, on 21 Aug 1979.

Sand Sculpturing

The largest sand sculpture on record was an 8498 ft *2590 m* long representation of a 19th century train along Virginia Beach, Virginia, USA on 2 Oct 1983 organized by Louise Lowenthal.

Scooter riding

The greatest distance covered by a team of 25 in 24 hr is 336.11 miles *540,93 km* by Wimmera Young Farmers, Victoria, Australia on 22–23 Mar 1980.

Search *Longest*

Walter Edwin Percy Zillwood (b. Deptford, London SE8, Dec 1900) traced his missing sister Lena (Mrs Elizabeth Eleanor Allen, b. Nov 1897, d. Jan 1982) after 79 years through the agency of the Salvation Army on 3 May 1980.

See-saw

George Partridge and Tamara Marquez of Auburn High School, Washington, USA on a suspension see-saw completed 1101 hr 40 min (indoor) on 28 Mar–13 May 1977. Georgia Chaffin and Tammy Adams of Goodhope Jr. High School, Cullman, Alabama, USA completed 730 hr 30 min (outdoor) on 25 June–25 July 1975.

Sermon

The longest sermon on record was delivered by the Rev. Ronald Gallagher at the Baptist Temple, Lynchburg, Virginia, USA for 120 hr on 26 June–1 July 1983. From 31 May to 10 June 1969 the 14th Dalai Lama (b. 6 July 1934 as Tenzin Gyalto) the exiled ruler of Tibet, completed a sermon on Tantric Buddhism for 5–7 hr per day to total 60 hr in India.

Shaving

The fastest demon barber on record is Gerry Harley, who shaved 987 men in 60 min with a safety razor in Gillingham, Kent on 28 Apr 1983 taking a perfunctory 3.64 sec per volunteer.

Sheaf tossing

The world's best performance for tossing a 3,63 kg *8 lb* sheaf for height is 19,77 m *64.86 ft* by Trond Ulleberg of Skolleborg, Norway on 11 Nov 1978. Such pitchfork contests date from 1914.

Shoeshine boys

In this category (limited to a team of 4 teenagers; duration of 8 hr; shoes 'on the hoof') the record is 6780 pairs by the Sheffield Citadel Band of Salvation Army, S. Yorkshire, on 27 Feb 1982.

Shorthand fastest

The highest recorded speeds ever attained under championship conditions are: 300 words per min (99.64 per cent accuracy) for 5 min and 350 wpm (99.72 per cent accuracy, that is, two insignificant errors) for 2 min by Nathan Behrin (USA) in tests in New York in December 1922. Behrin (b. 1887) used the Pitman system invented in 1837. Morris I. Kligman, official court reporter of the US Court House, New York has taken 50,000 words in 5 hr (a sustained rate of 166.6 wpm). Rates are much dependent upon the nature, complexity and syllabic density of the material. Mr. G. W. Bunbury of Dublin, Ireland held the unique distinction of writing at 250 wpm for 10 min on 23 Jan 1984.

Mr Arnold Bradley achieved a speed of 309 words per minute without error using the Sloan-Duployan system with 1545 words in 5 minutes in a test in Walsall, West Midlands on 9 Nov 1920.

Shouting

The greatest number of wins in the national town criers' contest is 11 by Ben Johnson of Fowey, Cornwall, who won in 1939, 1949–55, 1966, 1969 and 1973. The first national feminine champion has been Mrs Henrietta Sargent, town-crier, of The Three Horse Shoes, Cricklade, Wiltshire in 1980. On being told she had beaten the other 31 contestants she said 'I'm speechless'. (See also Longest-ranged voice, Chapter 1 page 17.)

Showering

The most prolonged continuous shower bath on record is one of 336 hr by Arron Marshall of Rockingham Park, Western Australia on 29 July–12 Aug 1978. The feminine record is 121 hr 1 min by Lisa D'Amato on 5–10 Nov 1981 at Harper College, Binghamton, New York, USA. Desquamation can be a positive danger.

Singing

The longest recorded solo singing marathon is one of 180 hr by Robert Sim at The Waterfront Hotel, Kingston-upon-Hull, Humberside on 18–25 Mar 1983. The marathon record for a choir has been 72 hr 2 min by the combined choir of Girl's High School and Prince Edward School, Salisbury, Zimbabwe on 7–10 Sept 1979. Acharya Prem Bhikuji started chanting the Akhand Ram Dhum in 1964 and devotees took this up in rotation completing their devotions 13 years later on 31 July 1977 at Jamnagar, India.

Skate boarding

'World' championships have been staged intermittently since 1966. David Frank, 22 covered 238.36 miles *383.6 km* in 31 hr 1 min in Toronto, Canada on 9–10 July 1983.

The highest speed recorded on a skate board

under USSA rules is 71.79 mph *115,53 km/h* on a course at Mt Baldy, California in a prone position by Richard K. Brown, 33, on 17 June 1979. The stand-up record is 53.45 mph *86,01 km/h* by John Hutson, 23 at Signal Hill, Long Beach, California on 11 June 1978. The high jump record is 5 ft 5.7 in *1,67 m* by Trevor Baxter (b. 1 Oct 1962) of Burgess Hill, Sussex at Grendole, France on 14 Sept 1982. At the 4th US Skateboard Association championship, at Signal Hill on 25 Sept 1977, Tony Alva, 19, jumped 17 barrels (17 ft *5,18m*).

Slinging

The greatest distance recorded for a sling-shot is 1434 ft 2 in *437,13 m* using a 51 in *129,5 cm* long sling and a 2 oz *56,5 g* stone by Lawrence L. Bray at Loa, Utah, USA on 21 Aug 1981.

Smoke ring blowing

The highest recorded number of smoke rings formed from the lips from a single pull of a cigarette (cheek-tapping is disallowed) is 355 by Jan van Deurs Formann of Copenhagen achieved in Switzerland in August 1979.

Snakes and Ladders

The longest recorded game of Snakes and Ladders has been one of 260 hr by a team of six (four always in play) from Essex Young Farmers Club, West Mersea, Essex, on 29 Jan to 9 Feb 1982.

Snow shoeing

The fastest officially recorded time for covering a mile *1609,34 m* is 6 min 23.8 sec by Richard Lemay (Frontenac Club, Quebec, Canada) at Manchester, New Hampshire, USA in 1973.

Spear Throwing

The greatest distance achieved throwing a spear with the air of a woomera is 326 ft 6 in *99,51 m* (or 9 ft 2 in *2,79 m* beyond the Javelin record) by Bailey Bush on 27 June 1982 at Camden, NSW, Australia.

Spinning

The duration record for spinning a metal top by hand is 12 min 44 sec by Peter Hodgson of Southend-on-Sea, Essex on 28 May 1984.

Spitting

The greatest distance achieved at the annual tobacco spitting classic (instituted 1955) at Raleigh, Mississippi, USA, is 33 ft 7½ in *10,24 m* by Jeff Barber on 25 July 1981. (In 1980 he reached 45 ft *13,71 m* at Fulton, Miss.). In the 3rd International Spittin', Belchin' and Cussin' Triathlon, Harold Fielden reached 34 ft 0¼ in *10,36 m* at Central City, Colorado, USA, on 13 July 1973. Distance is dependent on the quality of salivation, absence of cross wind, the two finger pucker and coordination of the back arch and neck snap. Sprays or wads smaller than a dime are not measured. Randy Ober of Bentonville, Arkansas, USA spat a tobacco wad 47 ft 7 in *14,50 m* at the Calico 5th Annual Tobacco Chewing and Spitting Championships north of Barstow, California, USA on 4 Apr 1982. The record for projecting a melon seed under WCWSSCA rules is 65 ft 4 in *19,91 m* by John Wilkinson in Luling, Texas, USA, on 28 June 1980. The furthest reported distance for a cherry stone is 65 ft 2 in *19,86 m* by Rick Krause, at Eau Claire, Michigan, USA on 5 July 1980. Spitters who care about their image wear 12 in *30,4 cm* block-ended boots so practice spits can be measured without a tape.

Stair climbing

The 100 storey record for stair climbing was set by Dennis W. Martz in the Detroit Plaza Hotel,

SKIPPING

Albert Rayner of Wakefield, the fastest skipper or rope jumper in action.

The longest recorded non-stop skipping marathon was one of 12 hr 8 min by Frank P. Oliveri (est. 120,744 turns) at Great Lakes Training Center, North Chicago, Illinois, USA on 13 June 1981.

Other records made without a break:

MOST QUINTUPLE TURNS 5 by Katsumi Suzuki, Saitama, Japan, 29 May 1975

MOST TURNS IN 1 MIN 330 by Brian D. Christensen, Ridgewood Shopping Center, Tennessee, 1 Sept 1979

MOST TURNS IN 10 SEC 128 by Albert Rayner, Stanford Sports, Birmingham, 19 Nov 1982

MOST DOUBLES (WITH CROSS) 830 by Mark W. de C. Baker at Paradise Gardens, Cattai, NSW, Australia, 20 Feb 1983

DOUBLE TURNS 10 133 by Katsumi Suzuki, Saitama, Japan, 27 Sept 1979

TREBLE TURNS 381 by Katsumi Suzuki, Saitama, Japan, 29 May 1975

QUADRUPLE TURNS 51 by Katsumi Suzuki, Saitama, Japan, 29 May 1975

QUINTUPLE TURNS 6 by Hidemasa Tateda (b. 1968), Aomori, Japan, 19 June 1982

DURATION 1264 miles *2034 km* by Tom Morris, Brisbane-Cairns, Queensland, 1963

MOST ON SINGLE ROPE (MINIMUM 12 TURNS OBLIGATORY) 160 (50 m rope) by Shimizu Iida Junior High School, Shizuoka-ken, Japan, 10 Dec 1982

MOST TURNS ON SINGLE ROPE (TEAM OF 90) 97 by Erimomisaki School, Hokkaido, Japan, 28 May 1983

ON A TIGHTROPE 58 (consecutive) by Bryan Andro (*né* Dewhurst) TROS TV, Holland, 6 Aug 1981

Detroit, Michigan, USA, on 26 June 1978 at 11 min 23.8 sec. Richard Black, 44, President of the Maremont Corporation ran a vertical mile on the stairs of Lake Point Tower, Chicago on 13 July 1978 in continuous action with 1 hr 25 min 6 sec ascent time and 44 min 39 sec descent time. *These records can only be attempted in buildings with a minimum of 70 storeys.*

The record for the 1760 steps in the world's tallest free-standing structure, Toronto's CN Tower, is 10 min 10 sec by Michael Round on 9 Aug 1980. Robert C. Jezequel ran 7 round trips in 6 hr 23 min in 1982 without use of the elevator for a vertical height of 15 708 ft *4787 m*.

Pete Squires raced up the 1575 steps of the Empire State Building, New York City on 12 Feb 1981 in 10 min 59 sec.

In the line of duty Bill Stevenson has mounted 334 of the 364 steps of the tower in the Houses of Parliament, 4000 times in 15 years (1968–83)—equivalent to 24.9 ascents of Everest.

Standing

The longest period on record that anyone has continuously stood is for more than 17 years in the case of Swami Maujgiri Maharij when performing the *Tapasya* or penance from 1955 to November 1973 in Shahjahanpur, Uttar Pradesh, India. When sleeping he would lean against a plank. He died aged 85 in Sept 1980.

Stamp licking

The Post Office staged a contest for tearing from sheets and individually affixing stamps to envelopes in 4 mins. The inaugural winner at St Martin's le Grand, London EC1 on 12 Feb 1984 was the comedian Frankie Howerd with 72.

Stilt-walking

Hop stringers use stilts up to 15 ft *4.57 m*. In 1892 M. Garisoain of Bayonne stilt-walked 8 km *4.97 miles* into Biarritz in 42 min to average 11,42 km/h *7.10 mph*. In 1891 Sylvain Dornon stilt-walked from Paris to Moscow *via* Vilno in 50 stages for the 1830 miles *2945 km*. Another source gives his time as 58 days. Even with a safety or Kirby wire very high stilts are *extremely* dangerous—25 steps are deemed to constitute 'mastery'. Eddy Wolf (also known as Steady Eddy) of Loyal, Wisconsin, USA mastered stilts measuring 40 ft 2 in *12,24 m* from ground to ankle over a distance of 31 steps without touching his safety handrail wires, in Hollywood, California on 4 Dec 1981. His aluminium stilts weighed 40 lb *18,1 kg* each. Joe Long (b. Kenneth Caesar), who has suffered 5 fractures, mastered 56 lb *25,4 kg* 24 ft *7,31 m* stilts at the BBC TV Centre, London on 8 Dec 1978. The endurance record is 3008 miles *4804 km* from Los Angeles, California to Bowen, Kentucky, USA, from 20 Feb to 26 July 1980 by Joe Bowen. Masaharu Tatsushiro, 28, (Japan) ran 100 m *328 ft* on 1 ft *30,48 cm* high stilts in 14.15 sec in Tōkyō on 30 Mar 1980.

Stowaway

The most rugged stowaway was Socarras Ramirez who escaped from Cuba on 4 June 1969 by stowing away in an unpressurized wheel well in the starboard wing of a Douglas DC8 from Havana to Madrid in a 5600 mile *9010 km* Iberian Airlines flight. He survived 8 hr at 30,000 ft *9145 m* where temperatures were −8° F −*22° C*.

Stretcher bearing

The longest recorded carry of a stretcher case with a 10 st *63,5 kg* 'body' is 127 miles *204,34 km* in 45 hr 45 min by two four man teams from the Sri Chinmoy marathon team of Jamaica, NY, USA, on 17–19 Apr 1981.

The record limited to Youth Organizations (under 20 years of age) and 8 hr carrying is 42.02 miles *67,62 km* by 8 members of the Henry Meoles School, Moreton, Wirral, Cheshire on 13 July 1980.

String ball largest

The largest ball of string on record is one of 12 ft 9 in *3,88 m* in diameter, 40 ft *12,19 m* in circumference and weighing 10 tons/*tonnes* amassed by Francis A. Johnson of Darwin, Minnesota, USA, between 1950–78.

Submergence

The most protracted underwater endurance record (excluding the use of diving bells) is 147 hr 15 min established by Robert Ingolia in tests in which the US Navy was the beneficiary of all data in 1961.

The *continuous* duration record (i.e. no rest breaks) for 'Scuba' (i.e. self-contained and without surface air hoses) is 78 hr 2 min by Michael Moore (above) of the Viking Sub-Aqua Club in the St. Mary's Hospital pool, Baldoyle, County Dublin, Ireland, on 26–29 Dec. 1982. Measures have to be taken to reduce the risk of severe desquamation in such endurance trails. The pre-existing record was 69 hr 1 min by Valmore E. Willhite of Athol, Maryland, USA on 16–19 Sept 1981.

Suggestion boxes

The most prolific example on record of the use of any suggestion box scheme is that of John Drayton (b. 18 Sept 1907) of Newport, Gwent who has plied British Rail and the companies from which it was formed with a total of 31,028 suggestions from 1924 to 18 Apr 1984 of which one in seven were accepted. In 1979–80 Ford Motor Co received 5,376 suggestions in 365 days.

Swinging

The record duration for continuous swinging is 185 hr by Mollie Jackson of Tarrytown, New York, USA on 25 Mar–1 Apr 1979.

Switchback riding

The endurance record for rides on a roller coaster is 368 hr by Jim King at the Miracle Strip Amusement Park, Panama City, Florida, USA, on 22 June–7 July 1980. He covered a distance of 10,425 miles *16 780 km* to average 28.3 mph *45,59 km/h.* The minimum qualifying average speed required is 25 mph *40 km/h.*

Tailoring

The highest speed in which the manufacture of a 3 piece suit has been made from sheep to finished article is 1 hr 34 min 33.42 sec by 65 members of the Melbourne College of Textiles, Pascoe Vale, Victoria, Australia on 24 June 1982. The catching and fleecing took 2 min 21 sec, the carding, spinning, weaving and tailored occupied the remaining time.

Talking

The world record for non-stop talking has been 159 hr by Kapila Kumarasinghe, 16 in a lecture on Buddhist culture in Colombo, Sri Lanka on 18–24 June 1981. A feminine non-stop talking record was set by Mrs Mary E. Davis, who on 2–7 Sept 1958 started at a radio station in Buffalo, New York, USA and did not draw breath until 110 hr 30 min 5 sec later in Tulsa, Oklahoma, USA. For longest continuous political speeches (see Filibusters, Chap XI).

Historically the longest recorded after-dinner speech with unsuspecting victims was one of 3 hr by the Rev. Henry Whitehead (d. March 1896) at the Rainbow Tavern, Fleet Street, London on 16 Jan 1874. Gyles Brandreth spoke for 12½ hours at the National Playing Fields Association dinner at the London Embassy Hotel, W.2 on 3–4 Apr 1982 until after breakfast.

T-bone dive

The so-called T-bone dives or Dive Bomber crash by cars off ramps over and on to parked cars are often measured by the number of cars, but owing to their variable size and that their purpose is purely to cashion the shock, distance is more significant. The longest recorded distance in this highly dangerous activity is 232 ft 1 in *70,73 m* by Jacquie De Creed, 26, in a 17 year old Ford Mustang at Santa Pod Raceway, Bedfordshire on 3 Apr 1983.

Teeth-pulling

The man with 'the strongest teeth in the world' is 'Hercules' John Massis (b. Wilfried Oscar Morbée, 4 June 1940) of Oostakker, Belgium, who raised a weight of 233 kg *513⅔ lb* 15 cm *6 in* from the ground with a teeth bit at Evrey, France on 19 Mar 1977. Massis prevented a helicopter from taking off using only a tooth-bit harness in Los Angeles, California, USA on 7 Apr 1979 for a *Guinness Spectacular* TV Show.

Throwing

The greatest distance any inert object heavier than air has been thrown is 857 ft 8 in *261,42 m,* in the case of a plastic 'Skyro' by Tom McRann, 30, in Golden Gate Park, San Francisco, Calif, USA, on 9 June 1980.

Tightrope walking

The greatest 19th century tightrope walker was Jean François Gravelet, *alias* Charles Blondin (1824–97), of France, who made the earliest crossing of the Niagara Falls on a 3 in *76 mm* rope, 110 ft *335 m* long, 160 ft *48,75 m* above the Falls on 30 June 1859. He also made a crossing

with Harry Colcord, pick-a-back on 15 Sept 1860. Though other artists still find it difficult to believe, Colcord was his agent. The oldest wirewalker was 'Professor' William Ivy Baldwin (1866–1953), who crossed the South Boulder Canyon, Colorado, USA on a 320 ft *97,5 m* wire with a 125 ft *38,1 m* drop on his 82nd birthday on 31 July 1948.

Tightrope walking *Endurance*

The world tightrope endurance record is 185 days by Henri Rochetain (b. 1926) of France on a wire 394 ft *120 m* long, 82 ft *25 m* above a supermarket in Saint Etienne, France, on 28 Mar–29 Sept 1973. His ability to sleep on the wire has left doctors puzzled. Steven G. Wallenda, 33, walked 2.36 miles *3,81 km* on a wire 250 ft *76,2 m* long 32 ft *9,75 m* high at North Port, Florida, USA on 26 Mar 1983 in 3 hr 31 min.

Tightrope walking *Highest and Steepest*

Steve McPeak (b. 21 April 1945) of Las Vegas, Nevada, USA ascended the 46,6 mm *1.83 in* diameter Zugspitzbahn cable for a vertical height of 705 m *2313 ft* in 3 stints aggregating 5 hr 4 min on 24/25/28 June 1981. The maximum gradient over the stretch of 2282 m *7485 ft* was above 30 degrees. Earlier on 28 June 1981 he had walked on a thinner stayed cable 181 steps across a gorge at the top of the 2963 m *9721 ft* mountain with a sheer drop of 960 m *3150 ft* below him.

The first crossing of the River Thames was achieved by Charles Elleano (b. 1911) of Strasbourg, France on a 1050 ft *320 m* wire 60 ft *18,2 m* above the river in 25 min on 22 Sept 1951.

Tree-climbing

The fastest speed climb up a 100 ft *30,4 m* fir spar pole and return to the ground is one of 27.16 sec by Ed Johnson of Victoria, BC, Canada in July 1982 at the Lumberjack World Championships in Hayward, Wisconsin.

The fastest time up a 9 m *29.5 ft* coconut tree barefoot is 4.88 sec by Fuatai Solo, 17, in Sukuna Park, Fiji on 22 Aug 1980.

Tree-sitting

The duration record for sitting in a tree is 431 days by Timothy Roy at Golf N'Stuff Amusement Park, Norwalk, Calif., USA from 4 July 1982–8 Sept 1983.

Typewriting *fastest*

The highest recorded speeds attained with a ten-word penalty per error on a manual machine are:

One Min: 170 words, Margaret Owen (US) (Underwood Standard), New York, 21 Oct 1918. One Hour: 147 words (net rate per min) Albert Tangora (US) (Underwood Standard), 22 Oct 1923.

The official hour record on an electric machine is 9316 words (40 errors) on an IBM machine, giving a net rate of 149 words per min, by Margaret Hamma, now Mrs Dilmore (US), in Brooklyn, New York City, NY, USA on 20 June 1941. Mrs Barbara Blackburn of Everett, Washington State, can maintain 150 wpm for 50 min (37,500 key strokes) and attain speeds of 170 wpm using the Dvorak Simplified Keyboard (DSK) system.

In an official test in 1946 Stella Pajunas, now Mrs Garnaid, attained a rate of 216 words in a minute on an IBM machine.

Typewriting *Longest*

The world duration record for typewriting on an electric machine is 214 hr by Violet Gibson Burns at Cremorne, Sydney, Australia on 18–27 Feb 1980.

The longest duration typing marathon on a manual machine is 120 hr 15 min by Mike Howell, a 23-year-old blind office worker from Greenfield, Oldham, Greater Manchester on 25–30 Nov 1969 on an Olympia manual typewriter in Liverpool. In aggregating 561,006 strokes he performed a weight movement of 2482 tons *2521 tonnes* plus a further 155 tons *157 tonnes* on moving the carriage for line spacing. Mrs Aletta Fourie (South Africa) set a numerical record at the BEXA championship in Johannesburg in Sept 1983 by typing spaced numbers from 1 to 642 in 5 mins without error on an Olivetti ET 121. Les Stewart of Mudjimba Beach, Qld, Australia has typed the numbers 1 to 309,000 in words on 6,070 quarto sheets as of 13 Feb 1984. His target is to become a "millionaire".

Tyre supporting

The greatest number of motor tyres supported in a free-standing 'lift' is 96 by Gary Windebank of Romsey, Hants on Feb 1984. The total weight was 1440 lb *653 kg*. The tyres used were Michelin XZX 155 × 13.

Unsupported circle

The highest recorded number of people who have demonstrated the physical paradox of all being seated without a chair is an unsupported circle of 10,323 employees of the Nissan Motor Company at Komazawa Stadium, Tokyo, Japan on 23 Oct 1982.

Waiters marathon

Beverly Hills restaurateur Roger Bourban, Switzerland, *Le garçon rapide*, ran a full marathon in full uniform in London on 9 May 1982 carrying a free standing open bottle of mineral water on a tray in the same hand (gross weight 3 lb 2 oz *1,42 kg*) in 2 hr 47 min.

Walking on hands

The duration record for walking on hands is 1400 km *871 miles* by Johann Hurlinger, of Austria, who in 55 daily 10 hr stints, averaged 1.58 mph *2,54 km/h* from Vienna to Paris in 1900. Thomas P. Hunt of USAF Academy, Colorado Springs, completed a 50 m *54.68 yd* inverted sprint in 18.4 sec in Tokyo on 22 Sept 1979. Four men (Bob Sutton, Danny Scannell, Phil Johnson and John Hawkins) relayed a mile in Oak Ridge, Tennessee, USA on 13 Mar 1983 in 31 min 15.8 sec.

Walking on Water

Using outsize shoes-cum-floats Fritz Weber walking on the Main from Beyreuth over 300 km *185 miles* to Mainz on 1 Sept to 15 Oct 1983.

Wall of death

The greatest endurance feat on a wall of death was 6 hr 7 min 38 sec by Hugo Dabbert (b. Hildesheim, 24 Sept 1938) at Rüsselsheim, West Germany on 14 Aug 1980. He rode 6841 laps on the 10 m *32.8 ft* diameter wall on a Honda CM 400T averaging 35,2 km/h *21.8 mph* for the 214,8 km *133.4 miles*.

Whip cracking

The longest stock whip ever 'cracked' (*i.e.* the end made to travel above the speed of sound— 760 mph *1223 km/h*) is one of 104 ft 5 in *31,82 m* (excluding the handle) wielded by Noel Harris at Melbourne, Australia on 24 June 1982.

Whistling *Loudest and Longest*

Roy Lomas (see above) achieved 122.5 decibels at 2½ metres in the Deadroom at the BBC Manchester Studios on 19 Dec 1983. The whistling marathon record is by David 'Harpo' Hall of Berkeley, California, USA, who completed 25 hr non-stop on the AM San Francisco TV Show on 1 Apr 1983.

Window cleaning

On 6 Aug 1984 at the Pine Rivers Annual Show, Lawnton, Queensland, Australia Barry Nuttall achieved 26.27 sec without a smear. 3 standard 1040 × 1153 mm *40.94 × 45.39 in* office windows with a 300 mm *11.8 in* long squeegee and 9 litres *15.83 pts* of water.

Wire Slide

The greatest distance recorded in a wire slide is from a height of 175 ft *53,3 m* over a distance of 300 ft *91,44 m* by Grant Page with Bob Woodham over his shoulder across the Australian landmark known as 'The Gap' for the filmed episode in 'The Stunt Men' in 1972.

Wood-cutting

The earliest competitions date from Tasmania in 1874. The records set at the Lumberjack World Championships at Hayward, Wisconsin, USA, (founded 1960) are:

Power Saw	9.74 sec
Sven Johnson (US)	1982
One-Man Bucking	21.70 sec
Merv Jensen (NZ) (d. Apr 1983)	1982
Standing Block Chop	25.38 sec
Mel Lentz (US)	1982
Underhand Block Chop	18.66 sec
Mel Lentz (US)	1982
Two-Man Bucking	9.44 sec
Merv Jensen (NZ) Cliff Hughes (NZ)	1982
Hand Splitting a cord into quarters*	53 min 40 sec
Richard Sawyer (US)	1982

White pine logs 14 in *25,6 cm* diameter are used for chopping and 20 in *50,8 cm* for sawing.

* Hardwood (white ash) cord of 128 ft *3,62 m* using a quartering wedge at Sag Harbour, NY, on 2 July 1982.

Writing minuscule

In 1926 an account was published of Alfred McEwen's pantograph record in which the 56 word version of the Lord's Prayer was written by diamond point on glass in the space of 0.0016 × 0.0008 in *0,04 × 0,02 mm*. Frank C. Watts of Felmingham, Norfolk demonstrated for photographers on 24 Jan 1968, his ability, without mechanical or optical aid, to write the Lord's Prayer 34 times (9452 letters) within the size of a definitive UK postage stamp (viz.) 0.84 × 0.71 in *21,33 × 18,03 mm*. Tsutomu Ishii of Tokyo demonstrated the ability to write the names of 184 countries on a single grain of rice and the words TOKYO JAPAN in Japanese on a human hair in April 1983. In Dec 1980 Michael Isaacson, Associate Professor of the School of Applied and Engineering Physics, Cornell University, Ithaca, New York, succeeded in etching the 16 letters in 'molecular devices' on a sodium chloride crystal with a 100,000 volt electron beam. The 'writing' was 2 nanometers wide.

Writing under handicap

The ultimate feat in 'funny writing' would appear to be the ability to write extemporaneously and decipherably backwards, upside down, laterally inverted (mirror-style) while blindfolded with both hands simultaneously. Three claims to this ability with both hands and feet simultaneously, by Mrs Carolyn Webb of Thirlmere, NSW, Australia, Mrs Judy Hall of Chesterfield, Virginia, USA, and Robert Gray of Toronto, Ontario, Canada are outstanding but have not been witnessed in the act by our staff.

Yodelling

The most protracted yodel on record was that of Errol Bird for 10 hr 15 min in Lisburn, Northern Ireland on 6 Oct 1979. It has been defined as 'repeated rapid changes from the chest-voice to falsetto and back again'.

Yo-yo

The yo-yo originates from a Filipino jungle fighting weapon recorded in the 16th century weighing 4 lb *1,81 kg* with a 20 ft *6 m* thong. The word means 'come-come'. Though illustrated in a book in 1891 as a bandalore the craze did not begin until it was started by Donald F. Duncan of Chicago, USA in 1926. The most difficult modern yo-yo trick is the 'Whirlwind' incorporating both inside and outside horizontal loop-the-loops. The individual continuous endurance record is 120 hr by John Winslow of Gloucester, Virginia, USA on 23–28 Nov 1977. Dr Allen Bussey in Waco, Texas, USA on 23 Apr 1977 completed 20,302 loops in 3 hr (including 6886 in a single 60 min period). He used a Duncan Imperial with a 34½ in *87,6 cm* nylon string.

The largest yo-yo ever constructed was one by Dr Tom Kuhn weighing 256 lb *116,11 kg* test launched from a 150 ft *52,2 m* crane in San Francisco, California, USA, on 13 Oct 1979.

CIRCUS RECORDS

A table of historic circus records from 1859 to date was published in the 26th Edition at p. 233. New records set since 1975 see below

The world's largest permanent circus is Circus Circus, Las Vegas, Nevada, USA opened on 18 Oct 1968 at a cost of $15,000,000 (*then £6,250,000*). It covers an area of 129,000 ft² *11 984 m²* capped by a tent-shaped flexiglass roof 90 ft *27,43 m* high. The largest travelling circus is the Circus Vargas in the USA which can accommodate 5000 people under its Big Top.

Flying Trapeze: Downward circles or 'Muscle grinding'—1350 by Sarah Denu (age 14) (US) Madison, Wisconsin, USA, 21 May 1983. Single heel hang on swinging bar, Angela Revelle (Angelique), Australia, 1977.

Highest Aerial Act: Celeste Starr performed a trapeze act suspended from a cable car on the Teleférico Mérida, Venezuela (15,629 ft *4763 m*) in July 1981.

Triple Twisting Double Somersault: Tom Robin Edelston to catcher John Zimmerman, Circus World, Florida, 20 Jan 1981.

Full Twisting Triple and the Quadruple Somersault: Vasquez Troupe. Miguel Vasquez to catcher Juan Vasquez at Ringling Bros, Amphitheatre, Chicago, USA in Nov 1981.

Triple Back Somersault with 1½ Twists: Terry Cavaretta Lemus (now Mrs. St Jules).

Teeter Board: Six man high perch pyramid, Emilia Ivanova (Bulgaria) of the Kehaiovi Troupe at Inglewood, California, USA, 21 July 1976.

Trampoline: Septuple twisting back somersault to bed and quintuple twisting back somersault to shoulders by Marco Canestrelli to Belmonte Canestrelli at Madison Square, NY, USA on 5 Jan and 28 Mar 1979. Richard Tison (France) performed a triple twisting triple back somersault for television near Berchtesgarden, West Germany on 30 June 1981.

Flexible Pole: Double full twisting somersault to a 2 in *5,08 cm* diameter pole by Roberto Tabak (aged 11) in Sarasota, Florida, USA in 1977.

Human Pyramid (or Tuckle): Twelve (3 high) supported by a single understander. Weight 771 kg *1700 lb* or 121.4 stone by Tahar Davis of the Hassani Troupe at BBC TV Pebble Mill Studio, Birmingham, England, on 17 Dec 1979.

9 high by top-mounter Josep-Joan Martínez Lozano, 10, of the Colla Vella dels Xiquets 12 m *39 ft* tall on 25 Oct 1981 in Valls, Spain.

Clown, Oldest: Charlie Revel (b. Andrea Lassere in Spain 24 Apr 1896) performed for 82 years (1899–1981).

Sara Denu, 14, (*left*), setting her unrivalled record of 1350 muscle grinds in a gym in Wisconsin, USA, in 1983.

JUGGLING RECORDS

7 clubs: Albert Petrovski (USSR), 1963; Sorin Munteanu (Romania), 1975; Jack Bremlov (Czech), currently
8 plates: Enrico Rastelli (Italy), 1896–1931
10 balls: Enrico Rastelli (Italy), 1896–1931
11 rings: Albert Petrovski (USSR), 1963–66; Eugene Belaur (USSR), 1968; Sergei Ignatov (USSR), 1973
Pirouettes with 5 cigar boxes: Kris Kremo (Swiss) (quadruple turn with 3 boxes in mid-air), 1977
Duration 5 clubs: 16 min 20 sec, Ignatov in USSR, 1977
3 clubs while running: Brad Heffler (USA) 100 yd *91,44 m* in 13.6 sec (this is termed 'Joggling')
5 Ping-Pong balls with mouth: Gran Picaso (Spain), 1971
5 balls inverted: Bobby May (USA), since 1953

WEALTH AND POVERTY

The comparison and estimations of extreme personal wealth are beset with intractable difficulties. Quite apart from reticence and the element of approximation in the valuation of assets, as Jean Paul Getty (1892–1976) once said 'if you can count your millions you are not a billionaire'. The term millionaire was invented *c.* 1740 and billionaire in 1861. The earliest dollar centi-millionaire was Cornelius Vanderbilt (1794–1877) who left $100 million in 1877. The earliest billionaires were John Davison Rockefeller (1839–1937); Henry Ford (1863–1947) and Andrew William Mellon (1855–1937). In 1937, the last year in which all 3 were alive, a billion US dollars were worth £205 million but that amount of sterling would today have a purchasing power nearing £3000 million.

Richest men *World*

Many of the riches of most of the world's 29 remaining monarchs are national rather than personal assets. The least fettered and most monarchical is H.H. the Sultan of Brunei, Sir Hassanal Bolkiah Mu'izzaddin Waddaulah Hon GCMG (b. 15 July 1946). Brunei's annual oil revenue is £2,700 million and its foreign reserves are £10,000 million all of which is effectually at his personal disposal. The personal assets of Sulaiman Abdel-Aziz al-Rahji (b. Bukhariyah, Arabian Desert) were reported to be $2940 million (*£1876 million*) in May 1983. The richest

US billionaire is now probably David Packard (b. 1912) founder with Bill Hewlett of the electronics firm of Hewlett-Packard in a garage in Palo Alto, California in 1938. As Chairman of the Board his stock was, by March 1983, already valued at $1800 million.

Richest man *Great Britain*

The richest man in Great Britain is reputed to be Sir John Moores, CBE the co-founder of Littlewoods football pools in 1924. In 1973 he was estimated to be worth about £400 million (hence £1460 million in 1984 £'s). His first job after leaving school at 14 was as a telephone operator. He was born in Eccles, Lancashire on 25 Jan 1896. He reassumed the chairmanship of Littlewoods on 17 Oct 1980 and finally retired in February 1982.

Highest incomes

The greatest incomes derive from the collection of royalties per barrel by rulers of oil-rich sheikhdoms, who have not abrogated personal entitlement. Shaikh Zayid ibn Sultan an-Nuhayan (b. 1918) head of state of the United Arab Emirates arguably has title to some $9000 million of the country's annual gross national product.

The highest gross income ever achieved in a single year by a private citizen is an estimated $105,000,000 (*then £21½ now*

£325 million) in 1927 by the Neopolitan born Chicago gangster Alphonse ('Scarface Al') Capone (1889–1947). This was derived from illegal liquor trading and alky-cookers (illicit stills), gambling establishments, dog tracks, dance halls, 'protection' rackets and vice. On his business card Capone described himself as a 'Second hand Furniture Dealer'. The highest gross earned income in a year by a UK subject is reputedly in excess of £25 million earned by Paul McCartney MBE in years since 1979.

Proved wills and death duties
Sir John Reeves Ellerman, 2nd Bt, (1909–73) left £53,238,370 on which all-time record death duties were payable. This is the largest will ever proved in the United Kingdom. The greatest will proved in Ireland was that of the 1st Earl of Iveagh (1847–1927), who left £13,486,146).

Millionairesses
The world's wealthiest woman was probably Princess Wilhelmina Helena Pauline Maria of Orange-Nassau (1880–1962), formerly Queen of the Netherlands from 1890 to her abdication, 4 Sept 1948, with a fortune which was estimated at over £200 million. The largest amount proved in the will of a woman in the United Kingdom has been the £7,607,168 of the Rt. Hon Countess of Sefton in 1981. Mrs. Anna Dodge (later Mrs. Hugh Dillman) who was born in Dundee, Scotland, died on 3 June 1970 in the United States, aged 103, and left an estate of £40,000,000.

The cosmetician Madame Charles Joseph Walker *née* Sarah Breedlove (b. Louisiana Delta, USA 23 Dec 1867) is reputed to have become the first self-made millionairess. She was an uneducated Negro orphan scrub-woman whose fortune was founded on a hair straightener.

Millionaire and millionairess *Youngest*
The youngest person ever to accumulate a million dollars was the child film actor Jackie Coogan (b. Los Angeles, 26 Oct 1914) co-star with Sir Charles Chaplin (1889–1977) in 'The Kid' made in 1920. Shirley Temple (b. Santa Monica, California 23 Apr 1928), formerly Mrs John Agar, Jr, now Mrs Charles Black, accumulated wealth exceeding $1,000,000 (*then £209,000*) before she was 10. Her child actress career spanned the years 1934–9.

Richest families
It has been tentatively estimated that the combined value of the assets nominally controlled by the Du Pont family of some 1600 members may be of the order of $150,000 million. The family arrived in the USA from France on 1 Jan 1800. Capital from Pierre Du Pont (1730–1817) enabled his son Eleuthère Irénée Du Pont to start his explosives company in the United States. It was estimated in 1984 that both sons and both daughters of Haroldson Lafayette Hunt, the former Texan oilman possessed fortunes in excess of $1,000 million each.

Largest dowry
The largest recorded dowry was that of Elena Patiño, daughter of Don Simón Iturbi Patiño (1861–1947), the Bolivian tin millionaire, who in 1929 bestowed £8,000,000 from a fortune at one time estimated to be worth £125,000,000.

Greatest miser
If meanness is measurable as a ratio between expendable assets and expenditure then Henrietta (Hetty) Howland Green (*née* Robinson) (1835–1916), who kept a balance of over $31,400,000 (*then £6.2 million*) in one bank alone, was the all-time world champion. Her son had to have his leg amputated because of her delays in finding a *free* medical clinic. She herself ate cold porridge because she was too thrifty to heat it. Her estate proved to be of $95 million (*then £19 million [and now worth £270 million]*).

Return of cash
The largest amount of *cash* ever found and returned to its owners was $500,000 (US) found by Lowell Elliott, 61 on his farm at Peru, Indiana, USA. It had been dropped in June 1972 by a parachuting hi-jacker.

Jim Priceman, 44, assistant cashier at Doft & Co Inc returned an envelope containing $37.1 million (*then £20.6 million*) in *negotiable* bearer certificates found outside 110 Wall Street to A G Becker Inc of New York City on 6 April 1982. In announcing a reward of $250 (*then £140*) Beckers were acclaimed as 'being all heart'.

Greatest bequests
The greatest bequests in a life-time of a millionaire were those of the late John Davison Rockefeller (1839–1937), who gave away sums totalling $750,000,000 (now £350 million). The greatest benefactions of a British millionaire were those of William Richard Morris, later the Viscount Nuffield, GBE, CH (1877–1963), which totalled more than £30,000,000 between 1926 and his death on 22 Aug 1963. The Scottish-born US citizen Andrew Carnegie (1835–1919) is estimated to have made benefactions totalling £70 million during the last 18 years of his life. These included 7689 church organs and 2811 libraries. He had started life in a bobbin factory at $1.20 per week.

The largest bequest made in the history of philanthropy was the $500,000,000 (*then £178,570,000*) gift, announced on 12 Dec 1955, to 4157 educational and other institutions by the Ford Foundation (established 1936) of New York City, NY, USA.

Salary Highest *World*
The highest reported remuneration of any US businessman was $51,544,000 (£33¼ million) in salary, bonus and stock options received by Mr Frederick W. Smith, board chairman of Federal Express in 1982. The highest amount in salary and bonuses was $2 million (£1,290,000) to George L. Shinn, chairman of First Boston Corporation.

Highest Fees
The highest paid investment consultant in the world is Dr Harry D. Schultz, who operates from Western Europe. His standard consultation fee for 60 minutes is $2000 on weekdays and $3000 at weekends. His quarterly retainer permitting companies to call him on a daily basis is $28,125. He writes and edits an information packed International Newsletter instituted in 1964 now sold at $25 or £11 per copy.

Salary Highest *Great Britain*
The highest salary paid by any public company in 1982–83 was £521,500 to Mr Richard V. Giordano (b. New York, 1931), chief executive of BOC (British Oxygen) International.

Golden handshake
The highest carat handshake reported was one of 'nearly £700,000' attributed to Mr Bill Fieldhouse CBE (b. 1 Jan 1932) from Letraset of which he had been a director since 1969.

Lowest incomes
The poorest people in the world are the Tasaday tribe of cave-dwellers of central Mindanao, Philippines, who were 'discovered' in 1971 without any domesticated animals, agriculture, pottery, wheels or clothes.

2. HONOURS, DECORATIONS AND AWARDS

Oldest Order
The earliest honour known was the 'Gold of Honour' for extraordinary valour awarded in the 18th dynasty *c.* 1440–1400 BC. A statuette was found at Qan-el-Kebri, Egypt. The order which can trace its origins furthest back is the Military Hospitaller Order of St Lazarus of Jerusalem founded by St Basil the Great in the 4th Century AD. The prototype of the princely Orders of Chivalry is the Most Noble Order of the Garter founded by King Edward III in *c.* 1348. A date as early as AD 809 has been attributed to the Most Ancient Order of the Thistle but is of doubtful provenance.

Eponymous record
The largest object to which a human name is attached is the universe itself—in the case of the 'standard' cosmological model devised in 1922 by the Russian mathematician Aleksandr Aleksandrovitch Friedman (1888–1925) and has been known as Friedman's Universe.

Most titles
The most titled person in the world is the 18th Duchess of Alba (Alba de Tormes), Doña Maria del Rosario Cayetana Fitz-

GLUTTONY RECORDS

Records for eating and drinking by trenchermen do not match those suffering from the rare disease of bulimia (morbid desire to eat) and polydipsia (pathological thirst). Some bulimia patients have to spend 15 hr a day eating, with an extreme consumption of 384 lb 2 oz *174,236 kg* of food in six days by Matthew Daking, aged 12, in 1743 (known as Mortimer's case). Fannie Meyer of Johannesburg, after a skull fracture, was stated in 1974 to be unsatisfied by less than 160 pints of water a day. By October 1978 he was down to 52 pints. Miss Helge Andersson (b. 1908) of Lindesberg, Sweden was reported in January 1971 to have been drinking 40 pints *22,73 litres* of water a day since 1922—a total of 87,600 gal *3982 hectolitres*.

The world's greatest trencherman has been Edward Abraham ('Bozo') Miller (b. 1909) of Oakland, California, USA. He consumes up to 25,000 calories per day or more than 11 times that recommended. He stands 5 ft 7½ in *1,71 m* tall but weighs from 20 to 21½ st *127–139 kg* with a 57 in *144 cm* waist. He had been undefeated in eating contests since 1931 (see below). He ate 27 (2 lb *907 g*) pullets at a sitting in Trader Vic's, San Francisco in 1963. Phillip Yadzik (b. 1912) of Chicago in 1955 ate 77 large hamburgers in 2 hours and in 1957 101 bananas in 15 min. The bargees on the Rhine are reputed to be the world's heaviest eaters with 5200 calories a day. However the New Zealand Sports Federation of Medicine reported in December 1972 that a long-distance road runner consumed 14,321 calories in 24 hr.

While no healthy person has been reported to have succumbed in any contest for eating non-toxic food or drinking non-alcoholic drinks, such attempts, from a medical point of view, must be regarded as *extremely* inadvisable, particularly among young people. Gluttony record attempts should aim at improving the *rate* of consumption rather than the volume. Guinness Superlatives will not list any records involving the consumption of more than 2 litres *3.52 Imperial pints* of beer nor any at all involving spirits. Nor will records for such potentially dangerous categories as live ants, chewing gum, marsh mallow or raw eggs with shells be published. The ultimate in stupidity—the eating of a bicycle—has however been recorded since it is unlikely to attract competition.

Specific records have been claimed as follows:

Liquidising, processing or puréeing foodstuffs is not permitted. However drinking during attempts is permissible.

BAKED BEANS
2780 cold baked beans one by one with a cocktail stick in 30 min by Karen Stevenson, of Wallasey, Merseyside on 4 Apr 1981.

BANANAS
17 (edible weight minimum 4½ oz *128 g* each) in 2 min by Dr Ronald L. Alkana at the University of California, Irvine on 7 Dec 1973.

BEER
Steven Petrosino drank one litre of beer in 1.3 sec on 22 June 1977 at 'The Gingerbreadman', Carlisle, Pennsylvania.
Peter G. Dowdeswell (b. London 29 July 1940) of Earls Barton, Northants holds the following records:
2 pints—2.3 sec Zetters Social Club, Wolverton, Bucks, 11 June 1975.
2 litres—6.0 sec Carriage Horse Hotel, Higham Ferrers, Northants, 7 Feb 1975.

Yards of Ale
2½ pints—5.0 sec RAF Upper Heyford, Oxfordshire, 4 May 1975.
3 pints—5.4 sec Corby Town S.C., Northamptonshire, 23 Jan 1976.

Upsidedown
2 pints—6.4 sec Top Rank Club, Northants, 25 May 1975.

CHAMPAGNE
1000 bottles per annum by Bobby Acland of the 'Black Raven', Bishopsgate, City of London.

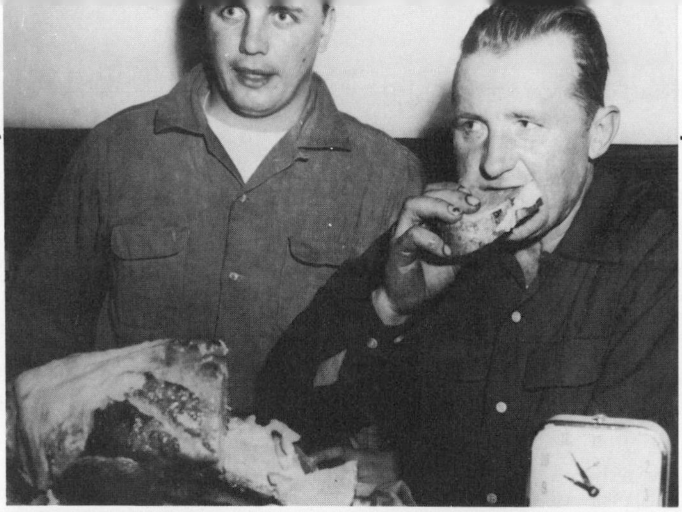

Hamburger King, Philip Yazdzik, the famous Chicago trencherman from the 'bad old days'. On 25 Apr 1955, he demolished 77 hamburgers 'at a sitting'. Today's 'Gluttony Records' are sensibly recorded only over much more abbreviated times.

CHEESE
16 oz *453 g* of Cheddar in 1 min 13 sec by Peter Dowdeswell (see above) in Earls Barton, Northants on 14 July 1978.

CHICKEN
1.701 kg *3 lb 12 oz* in 12 min 37 sec by Shaun Barry at the Cardinal Wolsey Hotel, East Molesey, Surrey on 26 Jan 1984.

CLAMS
424 (Littlenecks) in 8 min by Dave Barnes at Port Townsend Bay, Washington, USA on 3 May 1975.

COCKLES
2 pints *113,5 centilitres* in 2 min 35 sec by Steve Roberts at Leigh-on-Sea, Essex on 12 Sept 1981.

DOUGHNUTS
12¾ (51 oz *1,445 kg*) in 5 min 46 sec by James Wirth, and 13 (52 oz *1,474 kg*) in 6 min 1.5 sec by John Haight, both at the Sheraton Inn, Canandaigua, New York on 3 Mar 1981.

EELS
1 lb *453 g* of elvers in 13.7 sec by Peter Dowdeswell at Reeves Club, Bristol on 20 Oct 1978.

EGGS
(Hard Boiled) 14 in 58 sec by Peter Dowdeswell (see above) at the Stardust Social Club, Corby, Northants on 18 Feb 1977.
(Soft Boiled) 32 in 78 sec by Peter Dowdeswell in Northampton, on 8 Apr 1978.
(Raw) 13 in 2.2 sec by Peter Dowdeswell at BBC, Norwich on 26 Jan 1978.

FRANKFURTERS
23 (2 oz *56,6 g*) in 3 min 10 sec by Lynda Kuerth, 21, at the Veterans Stadium, Philadelphia, on 12 July 1977.

GHERKINS
1 lb *453 g* in 43.6 sec by Rex Barker of Elkhorn, Nebraska, USA on 30 Oct 1975.
1 lb *453 g* (liquidized) in 35.2 sec by Peter L. Citron on TV in San Francisco, USA on 1 Apr 1983. *This category has now been retired.*

GRAPES
3 lb 1 oz of grapes in 34.6 sec by Jim Ellis of Montrose, Michigan, USA on 30 May 1976.

HAGGIS
26 oz *737 g* in 49 sec by Peter Dowdeswell at The Grand Hotel, Hartlepool on 21 Feb 1983.

HAMBURGERS
20¾ hamburgers (each weighing 3½ oz *100 g* totalling *2,07 kg* of meat) and buns in 30 min by Alan Peterson at Longview, Washington, USA on 8 Feb 1979.

ICE CREAM
3 lb 6 oz *1,530 kg* in 50.04 sec by Tony Dowdeswell at the Cardinal Wolsey Hotel, East Molesey, Surrey on 26 Jan 1984. The ice cream must be unmelted.

JELLY
1.1 lb *500 g* in 28.57 sec by Peter Dowdeswell at the Stardust Centre, Corby, Northamptonshire on 15 Nov 1983.

KIPPERS
27 (self-filleted) in 60 min by Karen Stevenson of Wallasey, Merseyside on 5 Mar 1982.

LEMONS
12 quarters (3 lemons) whole (including skin and pips) in 15.3 sec by Bobby Kempf of Roanoke, Virginia, USA on 2 May 1979.

MEAT
One whole roast ox in 42 days by Johann Ketzler of Munich, Germany in 1880.

MEAT PIES
22 (each weighing 5½ oz *156 g*) in 18 min 13 sec by Peter Dowdeswell of Earls Barton, Northants on 5 Oct 1978.

MILK
2 pt (1 Imperial quart or *113,5 centilitres*) in 3.2 sec by Peter Dowdeswell (see above) at Dudley Top Rank Club, West Midlands on 31 May 1975.

OYSTERS (*Eating, Opening*)
4 lb 13 oz *2,18 kg* (edible mass of 250) in 2 min 52.33 sec by Ron Hansen at the Packer's Arms, Queenstown, South Island, New Zealand on 30 June 1982. The record for opening oysters is 100 in 3 min 1 sec by Douglas Brown, (b. 1944) at Christchurch, New Zealand on 29 Apr 1975.

PANCAKES
(6 inch *15,2 cm* diameter buttered and with syrup) 62 in 6 min 58.5 sec by Peter Dowdeswell (see above) at The Drapery, Northampton on 9 Feb 1977.

PEANUTS
100 (whole unshelled) singly in 46 sec by Jim Kornitzer, 21 at Brighton, Sussex on 1 Aug 1979.

PICKLED ONIONS
91 pickled onions (total weight 30 oz *850 g*) in 1 min 8 sec by Pat Donahue in Victoria, British Columbia on 9 Mar 1978.

POTATOES
3 lb *1,36 kg* in 1 min 22 sec by Peter Dowdeswell in Earls Barton, Northants on 25 Aug 1978.

POTATO CRISPS
Thirty 2 oz *56,6 g* bags in 24 min 33.6 sec, without a drink, by Paul G. Tully of Brisbane University in May 1969. Charles Chip Inc of Mountville, Pennsylvania produced crisps 4 × 7 in *10 × 17,5 cm* from outsize potatoes in February 1977.

PRUNES
144 in 35 sec by Peter Dowdeswell at Pleasurewood Hills American Theme Park, Lowestoft, Suffolk on 25 Sept 1983.

RAVIOLI
5 lb *2,25 kg* (170 squares) in 5 min 34 sec by Peter Dowdeswell at Pleasurewood Hills American Theme Park, Lowestoft, Suffolk on 25 Sept 1983.

SANDWICHES
40 in 17 min 53.9 sec (jam 'butties' 6 × 3¾ × ½ in *15,2 × 9,5 × 1,2 cm*) by Peter Dowdeswell on 17 Oct 1977 at The Donut Shop, Reedley, California, USA.

SAUSAGE MEAT
96 sausages each 1 oz *28,3 g*, in 6 min by Steve Meltzer of Brooklyn, New York at Roosevelt Raceway, Westbury, NY, USA, on 14 Oct 1974. No 'Hot Dog' contest results have been remotely comparable.

SHRIMPS
3 lb *1,36 kg* in 4 min 8 sec by Peter Dowdeswell of Earls Barton, Northants on 25 May 1978.

SNAILS
350 in 8 min 29 sec by Thomas Greene of La Plata, Maryland in Dominique's Restaurant, Washington DC, on 14 July 1981.

SPAGHETTI
100 yd *91,44 m* in 21.7 sec by Peter Dowdeswell at The Globe Hotel, Weedon, Northants on 25 Feb 1983.

STRAWBERRIES
2 lb 8 oz *1,13 kg* in 27.19 sec by Peter Dowdeswell at the Stardust Centre, Corby, Northamptonshire on 15 Nov 1983.

TORTILLA
74 (total weight 4 lb 1½ oz *1,85 kg*) in 30 min by Tom Nall in the 2nd World Championship at Mariano's Mexican Restaurant, Dallas, Texas, USA on 16 Oct 1973.

TREE
11 ft *3,35 m* Birch (4.7 in *12 cm* diameter trunk) in 89 hrs by Jay Gwaltney, 19 on WKQX's 'Outrageous Contest', Chicago, 11–15 Sept 1980.

WHELKS
100 (unshelled) in 5 min 17 sec by John Fletcher at The Apples and Pears Public House, Liverpool Street Station, London on 18 Aug 1983.

WINKLING
50 shells picked (with a straight pin) in 3 min 15 sec by Mrs B. Charles at Eastbourne, East Sussex on 4 Aug 1982.

GREATEST OMNIVORE
Michel Lotito (b. 1950) of Grenoble, France, known as Monsieur Mangetout, has been eating metal and glass since 1959. Gastroenterologists have X-rayed his stomach but remain mystified. His diet since 1966 has included seven bicycles, a supermarket trolley in 4½ days, 7 TV sets and a low calorie Cessna light aircraft which he ate in Caracas, Venezuela.

James Stuart y Silva. She is 8 times a duchess, 15 times a marchioness, 21 times a countess and is 19 times a Spanish grandee.

Versatility

The only person to win a Victoria Cross and an Olympic Gold Medal has been Lt Gen Sir Philip Neame, VC, KBE, CB, DSO (1888–1978). He won the VC in 1914 and was an Olympic gold medallist for Britain for rifle shooting in 1924 though under the illusion at the time that he was shooting for the British Empire. The only George Cross holder who is also a Fellow of the Royal Society is Prof Peter Victor Danckwerts, GC, MBE, FRS F Eng (b. 1916) who diffused 16 parachute mines in under 48 hr in the London docks during the Battle of Britain as a Sub Lt RNVR.

Victoria Cross *Double awards*

The only three men ever to have been awarded a bar to the Victoria Cross (instituted 29 Jan 1856) are:

Surg-Capt (later Lt-Col) Arthur Martin-Leake, VC*, VD, RAMC (1874–1953) (1902 and bar 1915).
Capt Noel Godfrey Chavasse, VC*, MC, RAMC (1884–1917) (1916 and bar posthumously 14 Sept 1917).
Second Lieut (later Capt) Charles Hazlitt Upham, VC*, NZMF (b. 21 Sept 1908) (1941 and bar 1942).

The most VC's awarded in a war were the 634 in World War I (1914–18). The greatest number won in a single action was 11 at Rorke's Drift in the Zulu War on 22–23 Jan 1879. The school with most recipients is Eton College, Col H. H. Jones being the 36th in the Falklands Campaign.

Victoria Cross *Youngest*

The lowest established age for a VC is 15 years 100 days for Hospital Apprentice Andrew (wrongly gazetted as Arthur) Fitzgibbon (born at Peteragurh, northern India, 13 May 1845) of the Indian Medical Services for bravery at the Taku Forts in northern China on 21 Aug 1860. The youngest living VC is Lieutenant Rambahadur Limbu (b. Nepal, 1939) of the 10th Princess Mary's Own Gurkha Rifles. The award was for his courage as a L/Cpl while fighting in the Bau district of Sarawak, East Malaysia, on 21 Nov 1965.

Victoria Cross *Longest lived*

The longest lived of all the 1351 winners of the Victoria Cross has been Lt Col Harcus Strachan VC. He was born in Bo'ness, Scotland on 7 Nov 1884 and died in Vancouver, Canada on 1 May 1982 aged 97 years 175 days.

Most highly decorated

The six living persons to have been twice decorated with any of the United Kingdom's topmost decorations are Capt C. H. Upham VC and bar; the Viscount De L'Isle VC, KG; HRH the Queen Mother CI, GCVO, GBE, who is a Lady of the Garter and a Lady of the Thistle; HRH the Duke of Edinburgh KG, KT; HRH Prince Charles KG, KT and HM King Olaf V of Norway KG, KT, GCB, GCVO. Lord De L'Isle is the only person who has both the highest military and highest civil honour. Britain's most highly decorated woman is the World War II British agent Mrs Odette Hallowes GC, MBE, Légion d'Honneur, Ordre St George (Belge), who survived imprisonment and torture at the hands of the Gestapo in 1943–45. Violette Reine Elizabeth Szabo (*née* Bushnell) GC (1921–45) lost her husband in the French Legion at El Alamein in 1942. He was Etienne Szabo, Medaille Militaire, Legion d'Honneur and Croix de Guerre.

Youngest Award

The youngest age at which an official gallantry award has ever been won is 8 years in the case of Anthony Farrer who was given the Albert Medal on 23 Sept 1916 for fighting off a cougar at Cowichan Lake, Vancouver Island, Canada to save Doreen Ashburnham. She was also awarded the AM which in 1971 was exchanged for the George Cross.

Record Price

The highest ever paid for a VC group has been £110,000 for the medals of the Battle of Britain fighter pilot Wing Cdr J. B. Nicholson VC, DFC, AFC (k. 1944), one of the only 3 men ever to win the VC actually defending Britain. The auction was at Christie's, London on 8 May 1983.

Order of Merit

The Order of Merit (instituted on 23 June 1902) is limited to 24 members. The longest lived holder has been the Rt Hon. Bertrand Arthur William Russell, 3rd Earl Russell, who died on 2 Feb 1970 aged 97 years 260 days. The oldest recipient was Admiral of the Fleet the Hon. Sir Henry Keppel, GCB, OM, (1809–1904), who received the Order aged 93 years 56 days on 9 Aug 1902. The youngest recipient has been HRH the Duke of Edinburgh, KG, KT, OM, GBE, who was appointed on his 47th birthday on 10 June 1968.

Most mentions in despatches

The record number of 'mentions' is 24 by Field Marshal the Rt Hon Sir Frederick Sleigh Roberts Bt, the Earl Roberts, VC, KG, KP, PC, GCB, OM, GCSI, GCIE, VD (1832–1914).

Most post-nominal letters

Lord Roberts (see above) who was also a privy counsellor, was the only non-royal holder of 8 sets of *official* post-nominal letters. Currently the record number is seven by Marshal of the RAF the Rt Hon Lord Elworthy KG, GCB, CBE, DSO, MVO, DFC, AFC (b. 23 Mar 1911) of New Zealand. HRH the Duke of Windsor (1894–1972) when Prince of Wales had 10 sets and was also a privy counsellor *viz.* KG, KT, KP, PC, GCB, GCSI, GCMG, GCIE, GCVO, GBE, MC. He later added the ISO but never used the OM or DSO of which orders he had also been sovereign.

USSR

The USSR's highest award for valour is the Gold Star of a Hero of the Soviet Union. Over 10,000 were awarded in World War II. Among the 109 awards of a second star were those to Marshal Iosif Vissarionovich Dzhugashvili, *alias* Stalin (1879–1953) and Lt-General Nikita Sergeyevich Khrushchyov (1894–1971). The only war-time triple awards were to Marshal Georgiy Konstantinovich Zhukov, Hon GCB (1896–1974) (subsequently awarded a fourth Gold Star) and to the leading air aces Guards' Colonel (now Marshal of Aviation Aleksandr Ivanovich Pokryshkin) and Aviation Maj Gen Ivan Nikitovich Kozhedub. Zhukov also uniquely had the Order of Victory, twice, the Order of Lenin (6 times) and the Order of the Red Banner, (thrice). Leonid Brezhnev (1907–1982) was 4 times Hero of the Soviet Union; Hero of Socialist Labour, Order of Victory, Order of Lenin (8 times) and Order of the Red Banner (twice).

Germany

The Knight's Cross of the Iron Cross with swords, diamonds and golden oak-leaves was uniquely awarded to Col Hans Ulrich Rudel (1916–1982) for 2530 operational flying missions on the Eastern Front in 1941–5. He destroyed 519 Soviet armoured vehicles.

The Gurkha Lieutenant R Limbu VC, 44, the youngest of all living holders of the Victoria Cross. He had won this highest of all gallantry decorations as a 26 year old Lance Corporal in Sarawak in 1965.

Chapter 11

THE HUMAN WORLD

The worlds' ultimate ice cream sundae—a 12 ton monster under construction by a team of over 50 confectioners in Vermont, USA (see page 229).

1. POLITICAL AND SOCIAL

Detailed information on all the sovereign and non-sovereign countries of the world is contained in *The Guinness Book of Answers* (4th Edition) (Price £6.95).

Largest political division

The British Commonwealth of Nations, a free association of 49 sovereign independent states together with 25 non-sovereign states and dependencies administered by them covers an area of 13,095,000 miles² *33 915 000 km²* with a population which in 1980 surpassed 1,000,000,000. The British Empire began to expand when Henry VII patented trade monopolies to John Cabot in March 1496 and the East India Co. was incorporated on 31 Dec 1600.

COUNTRIES

The world comprises 170 sovereign countries and 57 separately administered non-sovereign territories making a total of 227. The United Nations additionally still list the *de jure* territories of East Timor (now incorporated into Indonesia), Western Sahara (now in Morocco) and the uninhabited Canton Island (now in Kiribati) but do not list the three Baltic States of Estonia, Latvia and Lithuania though their forcible incorporation into the USSR in 1940 is not internationally recognized. Neither do they list the *de facto* territories of Taiwan, Mayotte or Spanish North Africa.

Largest

The country with the greatest area is the Union of Soviet Socialist Republics (the Soviet Union), comprising 15 Union (constituent) Republics with a total area of 22 402 200 km² *8,648,500 miles²*, or 15.0 per cent of the world's total land area, and a total coastline (including islands) of 106 360 km *66,090 miles*. The country measures 8980 km *5580 miles* from east to west and 4490 km *2790 miles* from north to south and is 91.8 times the size of the United Kingdom. Its population on 1 Jan 1982 was 268.8 million.

The United Kingdom covers 94,221 miles² *244 030 km²* (including 1197 miles² *3100 km²* of inland water), or 0.16 per cent of the total land area of the world. Great Britain is the world's eighth largest island, with an area of 84,186 miles² *218 040 km²* and a coastline 4928 miles *7930 km* long, of which Scotland accounts for 2573 miles *4141 km*, Wales 426 miles *685 km* and England 1929 miles *3104 km*.

Smallest

The smallest independent country in the world is the State of the Vatican City or Holy See (Stato della Città del Vaticano), which was made an enclave within the city of Rome, Italy on 11 Feb 1929. The enclave has an area of 44 hectares *108.7 acres*. The maritime sovereign country with the shortest coastline is Monaco with 3.49 miles *5,61 km* excluding piers and break-waters. The world's smallest republic is Nauru, less than 1 degree south of the equator in the Western Pacific, which became independent on 31 Jan 1968, has an area of 5263 acres *2129 ha* and a population of 7000 (latest estimate mid-1981).

The smallest colony in the world is Gibraltar (since 1969, the City of Gibraltar) with an area of 2½ miles² *5,8 km²*. However, Pitcairn Island, the only inhabited (54 people, 1981) island of a group of 4 (total area 18½ miles² *48 km²*) has an area of 1½ miles² or 960 acres *388 ha*.

The official residence, since 1834, of the Grand Master of the Order of the Knights of Malta totalling 3 acres *1,2 ha* and comprising the Villa del Priorato di Malta on the lowest of Rome's seven hills, the 151 ft *46 m* Aventine, retains certain diplomatic privileges as does 68 Via Condotti. The Order has accredited representatives to foreign governments and is hence sometimes cited as the smallest 'state' in the world.

Flattest and Most Elevated

The country with the lowest highest point is the Republic of the Maldives which attains 8 ft *2,4 m*. The country with the highest lowest point is Lesotho. The egress of the Senqu (Orange) river-bed is 4530 ft *1381 m* above sea level.

Most impenetrable boundary

The 'Iron Curtain' (858 miles *1380 km*) dividing the Federal Republican (West) and the Democratic Republican (East) parts of Germany, utilizes 2,230,000 land mines and 50,000 miles *80 500 km* of barbed wire, much of it of British manufacture, in addition to many watch-towers containing detection devices. The whole strip of 270 yd *246 m* wide occupies 133 miles² *344 km²* of East German territory and cost an estimated $7000 million to build and maintain. It reduced the westward flow from more than 200,000 in 1961 to 186,000 escapees from 1962–83 and to only 18 a month in 1980 including the 106th fatality. Construction of a second wall began in East Berlin in March 1984.

Longest and Shortest frontier

The longest *continuous* frontier in the world is that between Canada and the United States, which (including the Great Lakes boundaries) extends for 3987 miles *6416 km* (excluding 1538 miles *2547 km* with Alaska). The frontier which is crossed most frequently is that between the United States and Mexico. It extends for 1933 miles *3110 km* and there are more than 120,000,000 crossings every year. The Sino-Soviet frontier, broken by the Sino-Mongolian border, extends for 4500 miles *7240 km* with no reported figure of crossings. The 'frontier' of the Holy See in Rome measures 2.53 miles *4,07 km*. The land frontier between Gibraltar and Spain at La Linea, closed since 1969, measures 1672 yd *1,53 km*. Zambia, Zimbabwe, Botswana and Namibia (South West Africa) almost merge.

Most frontiers

The country with the most land frontiers is China, with 13— Mongolia, USSR, North Korea, Hong Kong, Macau, Vietnam, Laos, Burma, India, Bhutan, Nepal, Pakistan and Afghanistan. These extend for 24 000 km *14,900 miles*. France, if all her *Départements d'outre-mer* are included, may, on extended territorial waters, have 20 frontiers. The United Kingdom's frontier with the Republic of Ireland measures 223 miles *358 km*.

POPULATIONS

World

The daily increase in the world's population is 216,400, or 150 per minute. For past, present and future estimates (see table).

Most populous country

The largest population of any country is that of China, which in *pinyin* is written Zhongguo (meaning central land). The census of July 1982 was 1,008,175,288. The rate of natural

WORLD POPULATION *Progressive estimates*

Date	Millions	Date	Millions
10 000 BC	c. 5	1950	2513
AD 1	c. 200	1960	3049
1000	c. 275	1970	3704
1250	375	1975	4033
1500	420	1976	4107
1650	550–600	1977	4182
1700	615	1978	4284
1750	720	1979	4357
1800	900	1980	4432
1900	1625	1981	4608
1920	1862	1982	4686
1930	2070	1983*	4665
1940	2295	2000	6100

* *Provisional Estimate for mid-year.*

† *The UN publication 'State of World Population, 1984' forecast that the world population will not stabilize until 2095 at c. 10,500 million and will reach 6100 million by 31 Dec 2000.*

Note The all-time peak annual increase of 2.0% c. 1958–1962 had declined to 1.73% by 1975–1980. By 1990 this should decline to 1.5%. This, however, produces an annual increment of 80 million to even higher figures in the 1990s. In 1981 the UN population projections forecast that the world's population would stabilize at 10,500 million by AD 2110.

increase in the People's Republic of China is now estimated to be 38,700 a day or 14.1 million per year. The census required 5,100,000 enumerators to work for 10 days. India is set to overtake China during the next century.

Least populous

The independent state with the smallest population is the Vatican City or the Holy See (see Smallest country, above), with 1008 inhabitants in 1984 and a nil return for births.

Most densely populated

The most densely populated territory in the world is the Portuguese province of Macau (or Macao), on the southern coast of China. It has an estimated population of 350,000 (mid-1982) in an area of 6.2 miles² *16,05 km²* giving a density of 56,450 per mile² *21 805 per km²*.

The Principality of Monaco, on the south coast of France, has a population of 26,000 (mid-1982) in an area of 473 acres *189 ha* giving a density of 36,765/mile² *14 195/km²*. The above acreage is inclusive of marine infilling which has increased the land area by some 20 per cent. Singapore has 2,472,000 (mid-1982) people in an inhabited area of 73 miles² *189 km²*.

Of territories with an area of more than 1000 km², Hong Kong (405 miles² *1049 km²*) contains 5,233,000 (estimated mid-1982), giving the territory a density of 12,920/mile² *4988/km²*. Hong Kong is now the most populous of all colonies. The

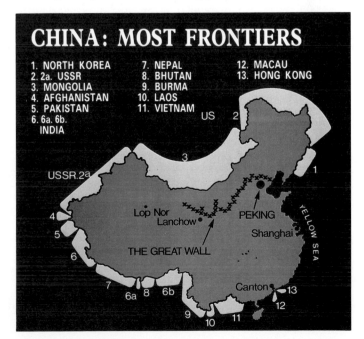

CHINA: MOST FRONTIERS

1. NORTH KOREA
2. 2a. USSR
3. MONGOLIA
4. AFGHANISTAN
5. PAKISTAN
6. 6a. 6b. INDIA
7. NEPAL
8. BHUTAN
9. BURMA
10. LAOS
11. VIETNAM
12. MACAU
13. HONG KONG

US

USSR. 2a

Lop Nor
Lanchow
THE GREAT WALL
PEKING
Shanghai
YELLOW SEA
Canton

After waiting 18 years for a visa to leave the Soviet Union, Benjamin Bogomolny checks his entry, as the world's most patient 'refusenik', in one of the rarest books in the USSR.

transcription of the name is from a local pronunciation of the Peking dialect version of Xiang gang (a port for incense). The 1976 by-census showed that the West Area of the urban district of Mong Kok on the Kowloon Peninsula had a density of 252,090/km² *652,910/mile²*. In 1959, at the peak of the housing crisis, it was reported that in one house designed for 12 people the number of occupants was 459, including 104 in one room and 4 living on the roof.

Of countries over 1000 miles² *2589 km²* the most densely populated is Bangladesh with a population of 92,619,000 (mid-1982 estimate) living in 55,126 miles² *142 775 km²* at a density of 1680/mile² *648/km²*. The Indonesian island of Java (with an area of 48,763 miles² *126 295 km²*) had a population of 94,693,000 (1981 estimate), giving a density of 1941/mile² *750/km²*.

The United Kingdom (94,221 miles² *244 030 km²*) had an estimated population of 56,376,800 at mid-1983, giving a density of 598 persons/mile² *231/km²*. The population density for the Greater London Borough of Kensington and Chelsea is 11,222/km² *29,064/mile²*.

Most sparsely populated

Antarctica became permanently occupied by relays of scientists from October 1956. The population varies seasonally and reaches 2000 at times.

The least populated territory, apart from Antarctica, is Kalaatllit Nunaat (formerly Greenland), with a population of 52,000 (estimated mid-1982) in an area of 840,000 miles² *2 175 000 km²* giving a density of one person to every 16.15 miles² *41,83 km²*. Some 84.3 per cent of the island comprises an ice-cap.

The lowest population densities in the United Kingdom are in the Scottish Highlands and Islands with 13,1/km² *33.9/mile²*. The most sparsely populated county in England is Northumberland with 154.15/mile² *59,51/km²*.

Emigration

More people emigrate from Mexico than from any other country. An estimated 800,000 emigrated illegally into the USA in 1976 alone. A total of 233,000 emigrated from the UK in 1981. Her largest number of emigrants in any one year was 360,000 in 1852, mainly from Ireland.

Immigration

The country which regularly receives the most legal immigrants is the United States, with an annual limit of 425,000. It has been estimated that in the period 1820–1980, the USA has received 49,655,952 *official* immigrants. One in 24 of the US population is however an *illegal* immigrant to which another 700,000 were added in 1980. The peak year for immigration into the United Kingdom was the 12 months from 1 July 1961 to 30 June 1962, when about 430,000 Commonwealth citizens arrived. The number of new Commonwealth and Pakistani immigrants in 1983 was 27,600 added to an estimated total of 2,200,000 or 4.0% of the population by mid 1982.

Most patient 'Refusenik'

The USSR citizen who has waited longest for an exit visa is Benjamin Bogomolny (b. 7 Apr 1946) who first applied in 1966.

Tourism

In 1983 the United Kingdom received 12,499,000 visitors who spent an estimated £3655 million excluding fares to British carriers.

Birth rate *Highest and Lowest*

The rate for the whole world was 27.5 per 1000 in 1982. The highest estimated by the UN is 54.6 per 1000 for Kenya in 1980. A world wide survey published in 1981 showed only Nepal (48.9) with a still rising birth rate.

Excluding Vatican City, where the rate is negligible, the lowest recorded rate is 10.1 for the Federal Republic of Germany and San Marino (1982). The fastest falling is in Thailand where the 3.3 average number of children per family has fallen to 1.8 in 10 years.

The 1983 rate in the United Kingdom was 12.8/1000 (12.7 in England and Wales, 12.6 in Scotland and 17.4 in Northern Ireland), while the 1981 rate for the Republic of Ireland was 21.0 registered births per 1000. The highest number of births in England and Wales (since the first full year of 463,787 in 1838) has been 957,782 in 1920 and the lowest this century 569,259 in 1977. After falling each year since 1964 (875,972) the figure started rising again at the end of 1977 with the 1983 figure being 629,100 or 1723 per day or 1.19 per minute.

Death rate *Highest and Lowest.*

The death rate for the whole world was 10.7 per 1000 in 1982. The highest of the latest available estimated death rates is 29.4 deaths per 1000 of the population in Kampuchea in 1975–80.

The lowest of the latest available recorded rates is 3.1 deaths/1000 in Samoa in 1980.

The 1983 rate in the United Kingdom was 11.7/1000 (11.6 in England and Wales, 12.5 in Scotland and 10.2 in Northern Ireland). The highest SMI (Standard Mortality Index where the national average is 100) is in Salford, Greater Manchester with a figure of 133. The 1981 rate for the Republic of Ireland was 9.4 registered deaths per 1000.

Natural increase

The rate of natural increase for the whole world is estimated to be 27.5–10.7 = 16.8 per 1000 in 1982 compared with a peak 22 per 1000 in 1965. The highest of the latest available recorded rates is 40.4 (54.6 – 14.2) in Kenya in 1980.

The 1983 rate for the United Kingdom was 1.1 (0.9 in England and Wales, 0.1 in Scotland and 7.2 in Northern Ireland). The rate for the first time in the first quarter of 1975 became one of natural decrease. The figure for the Republic of Ireland was 10.9/1000 in 1982.

The lowest rate of natural increase in any major independent country is in W. Germany with a negative figure of −1.5 per 1000 (10.1 births and 11.6 deaths) for 1982. Only 11 other countries have declining populations.

Marriage ages

The country with the lowest average ages for marriage is India, with 20.0 years for males and 14.5 years for females. At the other extreme is Ireland, with 31.4 for males and 26.5 for females. In the People's Republic of China the *recommended* age for marriage for men has been 28 and for women 25. In England and Wales the peak ages for marriage are 22.8 years (male) and 19.6 years (female).

Divorces

The country with most divorces is the United States with a total of 1,180,000 in 1982—a rate of 47.29 per cent on the then current annual total of marriages (*cf* 50.65% in 1979).

Sex ratio

There were estimated to be 1003.5 men in the world for every 1000 women (1975). The country with the largest recorded shortage of males is the USSR, with 1145.9 females to every 1000 males (1981 census). The country with the largest recorded woman shortage is Pakistan, with 885 to every 1000 males in 1972. The figures are, however, probably under-enumerated due to *purdah*. The ratio in the United Kingdom was 1056 females to every 1000 males at mid-1982, and is expected to be 1014.2/1,000 by AD 2000.

Infant mortality

The world rate in 1978 was 91 per 1000 live births. Based on deaths before one year of age, the lowest of the latest available recorded rates is 6.5 in Finland in 1981.

The highest recorded infant mortality rate reported has been 195 to 300 for Burma in 1952 and 259 for Zaïre in 1950. In Ethiopia the infant mortality rate was unofficially estimated to be nearly 550/1000 live births in 1969. Many Third World countries have ceased to make returns.

The United Kingdom figure for 1983 was 10.1/1000 live births (England and Wales 10.0, Scotland 11.5, Northern Ireland 12.8). The Republic of Ireland figure for 1975–80 was 11.2.

Life expectation

World expectation of life is rising from 47.4 years (1950–55) towards 64.5 years (1995–2000). There is evidence that life expectation in Britain in the 5th century AD was 33 years for males and 27 years for females. In the decade 1890–1900 the expectation of life among the population of India was 23.7 years.

Based on the latest available data, the highest recorded expectation of life at age 12 months is 73.7 years for males and 79.7 years for females in Iceland (1979–80).

The lowest recorded expectation of life at birth is 27 years for both sexes in the Vallée du Niger area of Mali in 1957 (sample survey, 1957–8). The figure for males in Gabon was 25 years in 1960–1 but 45 for females.

The latest available figures for England and Wales (1978–80) are 70.2 years for males and 76.2 years for females. Scotland and Northern Ireland are both 68.4 years for males and 74.6 years for females, and for the Republic of Ireland (1980) 70.0 years for males and 75.0 for females. The British figure for 1901–10 was 48.53 years for males and 52.83 years for females.

Housing

For comparison, dwelling units are defined as a structurally separated room or rooms occupied by private households of one or more people and having separate access or a common passageway to the street.

The country with the greatest recorded number of private housing units is India, with 100,251,000 occupied in 1972.

Great Britain had a stock of 21,328,000 dwellings as at 1 Jan 1984, of which 59.0% was owner-occupied. The record number of permanent houses built in a year has been 413,715 in 1968.

Physicians

The country with the most physicians is the USSR, with 831,300, or one to every 307 persons. China had an estimated 1.4 million para-medical personnel known as 'bare foot doctors' by 1981. In the United Kingdom there were 154,318 doctors qualified to work as specialists, in general practice or in industry as at 1 Jan 1984.

The country with the lowest recorded proportion is Upper Volta, with 58 physicians (one for every 92,759 people) in 1970.

Dentists

The country with the most dentists is the United States, where 145,000 were registered members of the American Dental Association in 1983.

Psychiatrists

The country with the most psychiatrists is the United States. The registered membership of the American Psychiatric Association (inst. 1894) was 27,000 in 1983. The membership of the American Psychological Association (inst. 1892) was 65,000 in 1983.

Hospital Largest *World*

The largest mental hospital in the world is the Pilgrim State Hospital, West Brentwood, Long Island, NY, USA, with 3618 beds. It formerly contained 14,200 beds.

The busiest maternity hospital in the world is the Mama Yemo Hospital, Kinshasa, Zaïre with 41,930 deliveries in 1976. The record 'birthquake' occurred on a day in May 1976 with 175 babies born. It has 599 beds.

Great Britain

The largest hospitals of any kind in Great Britain are Hartwood Hospital near Shotts, Lanarkshire with 1700 staffed beds for mentally ill patients and Winwick Hospital near Warrington, which has 1567 staffed beds.

The largest general hospital in Great Britain is the St James Hospital, Leeds, West Yorkshire, with 1430 staffed beds.

The largest maternity hospital in Great Britain is the Simpson Memorial Maternity Pavilion, Edinburgh with 225 staffed beds.

The largest children's hospital in Great Britain is Queen Mary's Hospital for Children, at Carshalton, Sutton, Greater London, with 151 staffed beds.

Longest stay in hospital

Miss Martha Nelson was admitted to the Columbus State Institute for the Feeble-Minded in Ohio, USA in 1875. She died in January 1975 aged 103 years 6 months in the Orient State Institution, Ohio after spending more than 99 years in institutions.

Most expensive

In mid 1983 the average daily cost of a day's stay in a California hospital was $755 (*then* £530) or $5134 (£3615) for average stay. Boston City Hospital, Massachusetts were reported on 1 Dec 1982 to have sent a bill to Michael Saltwick for a 37 day stay and for cancer surgery on his wife for $238,000 (£153,500).

CITIES

Oldest *World*

The oldest known walled town in the world is Arīhā (Jericho). The latest radio-carbon dating on specimens from the lowest levels reached by archaeologists indicate habitation there by perhaps 3000 people as early as 7800 BC. The settlement of Dolní Věstonice, Czechoslovakia, has been dated to the Gravettian culture *c.* 27000 BC. The oldest capital city in the world is Dimashq (Damascus), the capital of Syria. It has been continuously inhabited since *c.* 2500 BC.

Great Britain

The oldest town in Great Britain is often cited as Colchester, the old British Camulodunum, headquarters of Belgic chiefs in the 1st century BC. However, the name of the tin trading post Salakee, St Mary's, Isles of Scilly, is derived from pre-Celtic roots and hence *ante* 550 BC. The oldest borough in Britain is reputed to be Barnstaple, Devon whose charter was granted by King Athelstan (927–939) in AD 930.

Most populous *World*

The most populous 'urban agglomeration' in the world is the 'Keihin Metropolitan Area' (Tōkyō.Yokohama Metropolitan Area) of 1081 miles² *2800 km²* containing an estimated 28,043,000 people in 1978. The municipal population of Tōkyō in 1983 was 11,736,214. The population of the metropolitan area of Greater Mexico City in 1979 was published as 13,950,364.

Great Britain

The largest conurbation in Britain is Greater London (estab-

WORLD'S MOST POPULOUS *Urban Settlements* *Progressive List*

Population	Name		Date
> 100	Dolní Věstonice	Czechoslovakia	c.27000 BC
c. 150	Chemi Shanidar	Iraq	8900 BC
3,000	Jericho (Arīhā)	Occupied Jordan	7800 BC
50,000	Uruk (Erech) (now Warka)	Iraq	3000 BC
250,000	Greater Ur (now Tell Muqayyar)	Iraq	2200 BC
350,000	Babylon (now al-Hillah)	Iraq	600 BC
500,000	Pataliputra (Patna) Bihār	India	400–185 BC
600,000	Seleukia (near Baghdad)	Iraq	300 BC– 165 AD
1,100,000	Rome (founded c. 510 BC)	Italy	133 BC
1,500,000	Angkor	Cambodia	900 AD
1.0–1.5 million	Hangchow (now Hangzhou)	China	1279
707,000	Peking (Cambaluc), (now Beijing)	China	1578
1,117,290	Greater London	United Kingdom	1801
8,615,050	Greater London (peak)	United Kingdom	1939
11,736,214	**Tokyo**	Japan	1983

Note: The UN projections for AD 2000 for Greater Mexico City and Tōkyō-Yokohama are 31,616,000 and 26,128,000.

lished on 1 Apr 1965), with a population of 6,765,100 (1982 estimate). The residential population of the City of London (677.3 acres *274 ha* plus 61.7 acres *24,9 ha* foreshore) is 5200 (1982 estimate) compared with 128,000 in 1801. The peak figure for Greater London was 8,615,050 in 1939.

Largest in area

The world's largest town, in area, is Mount Isa, Queensland, Australia. The area administered by the City Council is 15,822 miles² *40 978 km²*. The largest conurbation in the United Kingdom is the county of Greater London with an area of 609.8 miles² *1579,5 km²*.

Towns, villages and hamlets *Great Britain*

The smallest place with a town council is Caerwys, Clwyd, Wales with a population of 801. The town has a charter dated 1290. Llanwrtyd Wells, Powys (pop 614 in 1979) has had a town mayor and council since 1974. The strongest claimant to be Britain's oldest village is Thatcham, Berkshire. The earliest Mesolithic settlement there has been dated to 7720 BC.

Highest *World*

The highest capital in the world, before the domination of Tibet by China, was Lhasa, at an elevation of 12,087 ft *3684 m* above sea-level. La Paz, the administrative and *de facto* capital of Bolivia, stands at an altitude of 11,916 ft *3631 m* above sea-level. El Alto airport is at 4080 m *13,385 ft*. The city was founded in 1548 by Capt Alonso de Mendoza on the site of an Indian village named Chuquiapu. It was originally called Ciudad de Nuestra Señora de La Paz (City of Our Lady of Peace), but in 1825 was renamed La Paz de Ayacucho, its present official name. Sucre, the legal capital of Bolivia, stands at 9301 ft *2834 m* above sea-level. The new town of Wenchuan, founded in 1955 on the Chinghai–Tibet road, north of the Tangla range, is the highest in the world at 5100 m *16,732 ft* above sea-level. The highest dwellings in the world are those at Bāsisi, India near the Tibet border at *c.* 19,700 ft *5988 m*.

Great Britain

The highest village in Britain is Flash, in northern Staffordshire, at 1518 ft *462 m* above sea-level. The highest in Scotland is Wanlockhead, in Dumfries and Galloway at 1380 ft *420 m* above sea-level.

Lowest

The settlement of Ein Bokek, which has a synagogue, on the shores of the Dead Sea is the lowest in the world at 1291 ft *393,5 m* below sea-level.

Northernmost

The world's most northerly town with a population of more than 10,000 is the Arctic port of Dikson, USSR in 73° 32′ N. The northernmost village is Ny Ålesund (78° 55′ N.), a coalmining settlement on King's Bay, Vest Spitsbergen, in the Norwegian territory of Svalbard, inhabited only during the winter season. The northernmost capital is Reykjavik, the capital of Iceland, in 64° 08′ N. Its population was estimated to be 83,500 (1980 est.). The northernmost permanent human occupation is the base at Alert (82° 31′ N.), on Dumb Bell Bay, on the north-east coast of Ellesmere Island, northern Canada.

Southernmost

The world's southernmost village is Puerto Williams (population about 350), on the north coast of Isla Navarino, in Tierra del Fuego, Chile, 680 miles *1090 km* north of Antarctica. Wellington, the North Island, New Zealand is the southernmost capital city on 41° 17′ S. The world's southernmost administrative centre is Port Stanley (51° 43′ S.), in the Falkland Islands, off South America.

Most remote from the sea

The largest town most remote from the sea is Ürümqi in Xinjiang (formerly Tihwa, Sinkiang), capital of the Uighur Autonomous Region of China, at a distance of about 1400 miles *2250 km* from the nearest coastline. Its population was estimated to be 320,000 in 1974.

Thatcham, Britain's oldest village as it appeared in 1902. Bone, and flint implements (see left) found there date from *c.* 7720 BC—1200 years before England became an island. (*Postcard from the collection of Sue Hopson, artifacts: Newbury District Museum*)

2. ROYALTY & HEADS OF STATE

Oldest ruling house and Longest Reign

The Emperor of Japan, Hirohito (born 29 Apr 1901), is the 124th in line from the first Emperor, Jimmu Tenno or Zinmu, whose reign was traditionally from 660 to 581 BC, but more probably from *c.* 40 BC to *c.* 10 BC. The present Emperor, who succeeded on 25 Dec 1926 is currently the world's longest reigning monarch.

Her Majesty Queen Elizabeth II (b. 21 Apr 1926) represents dynasties historically traceable at least back until the 4th century AD; in the case Tegid, great grandfather of Cunedda, founder of the House of Gwynedd in Wales; she is 54th in line. If the historicity of some early Scoto-Irish and Pictish kings were acceptable, the lineage could be extended to about 70 generations.

Reigns *Longest All Time*

The longest recorded reign of any monarch is that of Phiops II or Neferkare, a Sixth Dynasty Pharaoh of ancient Egypt. His reign began in *c.* 2281 BC, when he was aged 6, and is believed to have lasted *c.* 94 years. Musoma Kanijo, chief of the Nzega district of western Tanganyika (now part of Tanzania), reputedly reigned for more than 98 years from 1864, when aged 8, until his death on 2 Feb 1963. The longest reign of any major European monarch was that of King Louis XIV of France, who ascended the throne on 14 May 1643, aged 4 years 231 days, and reigned for 72 years 110 days until his death on 1 Sept 1715, four days before his 77th birthday. Afonso I Henriques of Portugal reigned first as a Count and then as the first King for 73 years 220 days from 30 Apr 1112 to 6 Dec 1185.

Roman Occupation

During the 369 year long Roman occupation of England, Wales and parts of southern Scotland there were 40 sole and 27 co-Emperors of Rome. Of these the longest reigning was Constantinus I (The Great) from 31 Mar 307 to 22 May 337– 30 years 2 months.

Shortest

King Virabahu of the Kalinga Kshatriya dynasty of Ceylon (Sri Lanka) was assassinated a few hours after he was crowned at Polonnaruwa in 1196.

left: Britain's longest-lived head of state Richard Cromwell (1626–1712), son of Oliver. He was Lord Protector for 9 months in 1658–59 (see below). *right:* His even longer lived grandmother Elizabeth Steward, mother of Oliver, who died in 1654 at an age variously estimated to be 89 to 94.

Highest post-nominal numbers

The highest post-nominal number ever used to designate a member of a Royal House was 75 briefly enjoyed by Count Heinrich LXXV Reuss (1800–1). All male members of this branch of this German family are called Heinrich and are successively numbered from I upwards *each* century.

British regnal numbers date from the Norman conquest. The highest is 8, used by Henry VIII (1509–1547) and by Edward VIII (1936) who died as HRH the Duke of Windsor, on 28 May 1972. Jacobites liked to style Henry Benedict, Cardinal York (b. 1725), the grandson of James II, as Henry IX in respect of his 'reign' from 1788 to 1807 when he died as last survivor in the male line of the House of Stuart.

Longest lived 'Royals'

The longest life among the Blood Royal of Europe has been that of the late HRH Princess Alicia of Bourbon who was born

MONARCHY RECORDS

	Kings	Queens Regnant	Queens Consort
LONGEST REIGN OR TENURE	59 years 96 days[1] George III 1760–1820	63 years 216 days Victoria 1837–1901	57 years 70 days Charlotte 1761–1818 (Consort of George III)
SHORTEST REIGN OR TENURE	77 days[2] Edward V 1483	13 days[3] Jane, 6–19 July 1553	154 days Yoleta (1285–6) (second consort of Alexander III)
LONGEST LIVED	81 years 239 days George III (b. 1738–d. 1820)	81 years 243 days Victoria (b. 1819–d. 1901)	85 years 303 days Mary of Teck (b. 1867–d. 1953) (Consort of George V)
MOST CHILDREN (LEGITIMATE)[5]	18 Edward I 1272–1307	9[6] Victoria (b. 1819–d. 1901)	15 Eleanor (*c.* 1244–90) and Charlotte (b. 1744–d. 1818)
OLDEST TO START REIGN OR CONSORTSHIP	64 years 10 months William IV 1830–7	37 years 5 months Mary I 1553–8	56 years 53 days Alexandra (b. 1844–d. 1925) (Consort of Edward VII)
YOUNGEST TO START REIGN OR CONSORTSHIP	269 days Henry VI in 1422	6 or 7 days Mary, Queen of Scots in 1542	6 years 11 months Isabella (second consort of Richard II in 1396)
MOST MARRIED	6 times Henry VIII 1509–47	3 times Mary, Queen of Scots 1542–67 (executed 1587)	4 times Catherine Parr (b. *c.* 1512–d. 1548) (sixth consort of Henry VIII)
MOST ALIVE SIMULTANEOUSLY	Between 30 Oct 1683 (birth of George Augustus of Hanover, later George II) and 6 Feb 1685 (death of Charles II) there were 7 monarchs living simultaneously (Charles II, James II, William and Mary, Anne, George I and II) and also Richard Cromwell (d. 1712) the 2nd Lord Protector and *de facto* Head of State in 1658–59.		

Notes (Dates are dates of reigns or tenures unless otherwise indicated).

[1] *James Francis Edward, the Old Pretender, known to his supporters as James III, styled his reign from 16 Sept 1701 until his death 1 Jan 1766 (i.e. 64 years 109 days).*
[2] *There is the probability that in pre-Conquest times Sweyn 'Forkbeard', the Danish King of England, reigned for only 40 days in 1013–14.*
[3] *She accepted the allegiance of the Lords of the Council (9 July) and was proclaimed on 10 July so is often referred to as the '9 (or 10) day Queen'.*
[4] *Richard Cromwell (b. 4 Oct 1626), the 2nd Lord Protector from 3 Sept 1658 until his abdication on 24 May 1659, lived under the alias John Clarke until 12 July 1712 aged 85 years 9 months and was thus the longest lived Head of State.*
[5] *Henry I (b. 1068–d. 1135) in addition to one (possibly two) legitimate sons and a daughter had at least 20 bastard children (9 sons, 11 daughters), and possibly 22, by six mistresses.*
[6] *Queen Anne (b. 1665–d. 1714) had 17 pregnancies, which produced only 5 live births.*

on 29 June 1876 and died on 20 Jan 1975 aged 98 years 206 days. The greatest age among European Royal Consorts is the 101 years 268 days of HSH Princess Leonilla Bariatinsky (b. Moscow, 9 July 1816), who married HSH Prince Louis of Sayn-Wittgenstein-Sayn and died in Ouchy, Switzerland on 1 Feb 1918. The longest-lived Queen on record has been the Queen Grandmother of Siam, Queen Sawang (b. 10 Sept 1862), 27th daughter of King Mongkut (Rama IV); she died on 17 Dec 1955 aged 93 years 3 months.

HRH Princess Alice Mary, VA, GCVO, GBE, Countess of Athlone (b. 25 Feb 1883) became the longest ever lived British 'royal' on 15 July 1977 and died aged 97 years 313 days on 3 Jan 1981. She fulfilled 20,000 engagements, including the funerals of five British monarchs.

Youngest King and Queen

Forty-five of the world's 170 sovereign states are not republics. They are lead by 1 Emperor, 12 Kings, 4 Queens, 3 princely rulers, 2 Sultans, 3 Amirs, the Pope, a Shaik, a Ruler and one elected monarch. Queen Elizabeth II is Head of State of 16 other Commonwealth countries. That with the youngest King is Bhutan where King Jigme Singye Wangchuk was born 11 Nov 1955, succeeded on 24 July 1972 when aged 16 years and 8 months. That with youngest Queen is Denmark with Queen Margrethe II (b. 16 Apr 1940). Obi Keagboekuzi I of Agbor in Nigeria, the 18th obi since 1270, was born on 29 June 1977 and succeeded his father, the 17th obi, on 31 Oct 1979 aged 2 years 4 months.

Heaviest monarch

The world's heaviest monarch is the 6 ft 3 in *1,90 m* tall King Taufa'ahau of Tonga who in Sept 1976 was weighed on the only adequate scales in the country at the airport recording 33 st (462 lb) *209,5 kg*.

Most prolific

The most prolific monogamous 'royals' have been Prince Hartmann of Liechtenstein (1613–86) who had 24 children, of whom 21 were live born, by Countess Elisabeth zu Salm-Reifferscheidt (1623–88). HRH Duke Roberto I of Parma (1848–1907) also had 24 children but by two wives. One of his daughters HIM Empress Zita of Austria (b. 9 May 1892) was exiled on 23 Mar 1919 but visited Vienna, her titles intact on 17 Nov 1982 reminding republicans that her father succeeded to the throne of Parma in 1854.

Head of State *Oldest and Youngest*

The oldest head of state in the world is the President of Italy, Alessandro Pertini (b. 27 Sept 1896). Master Sgt Samuel Kanyon Doe, head of state of Liberia was born on 6 May 1952. He became Chairman of the People's Redemption Council in April 1980 aged 27.

Earliest Elected Female

President Vigdis Finnbogadottir (b. 1930) of Iceland became the first democratically elected female head of state on 30 June 1980 and took office on 1 Aug 1980.

3. LEGISLATURES

PARLIAMENTS—WORLD

Earliest and Oldest

The earliest known legislative assembly was a bicameral one in Erech, Iraq *c.* 2800 BC. The oldest legislative body is the *Althing* of Iceland founded in AD 930. This body, which originally comprised 39 local chieftains at Thingvellir, was abolished in 1800, but restored by Denmark to a consultative status in 1843 and a legislative status in 1874. The legislative assembly with the oldest continuous history is the Tynwald Court in the Isle of Man, which is believed to have originated more than 1000 years ago.

Largest

The largest legislative assembly in the world is the National People's Congress of the People's Republic of China. The fifth Congress, when convened in 1978, had 3497 members. Its standing committee has 197 members.

Smallest quorum

The House of Lords has the smallest quorum, expressed as a percentage of eligible voters, of any legislative body in the world, namely less than one-third of 1 per cent. To transact business there must be three peers present, including the Lord Chancellor or his deputy. The House of Commons quorum of 40 MPs, including the Speaker or his deputy, is 20 times as exacting.

Highest paid legislators

The most highly paid of all the world's legislators are Members of the US Congress whose basic annual salary was raised on 1 Jan 1984 to $69,800 (*then £42,820*) and limited honoraria to $20,940 (*then £12,850*). In addition up to $1,021,167 (*£658,817*) per annum is allowed for office help, with a salary limit of $49,491 (*now £32,220*) for any one staff member (limited to 16 in number). Senators are allowed up to $143,000 (*£92,258*) per annum for an official office expense account from which official travel, telegram, long distance telephone, air mail, postage, stationery, subscriptions to newspapers, and office expenses in home state are paid. They also command very low rates for filming, speech and radio transcriptions and, in the case of women senators, beauty treatment. When abroad they have access to 'counterpart funds'. A retiring President electing to take also his congressional pension would enjoy a combined pension of $103,500 (*£66,774*) per annum.

Longest membership

The longest span as a legislator was 83 years by József Madarász (1814–1915). He first attended the Hungarian Parliament in 1832–6 as *oblegatus absentium* (*i.e.* on behalf of an absent deputy). He was a full member in 1848–50 and from 1861 until his death on 31 Jan 1915.

UN Speech *Longest*

The longest speech made in the United Nations has been one of 4 hr 29 min by President Dr Fidel Castro Ruz (b. 13 Aug 1927) of Cuba on 26 Sept 1960.

Filibusters

The longest continuous speech in the history of the United States Senate was that of Senator Wayne Morse (1900–74) of Oregon on 24–25 Apr 1953, when he spoke on the Tidelands Oil Bill for 22 hr 26 min without resuming his seat. Interrupted only briefly by the swearing-in of a new senator, Senator Strom Thurmond (b. 1902) (South Carolina, Democrat) spoke against the Civil Rights Bill for 24 hr 19 min on 28–29 Aug 1957. The United States national record duration for a filibuster is 43 hr by Texas State senator Bill Meier against nondisclosure of industrial accidents in May 1977.

Greatest Lobbyist

M. C. Ford of Chicago lobbied the US Congress for 39 years before being invested with the US Marine Corps Medal. He had been tortured by the Japanese in occupied China in 1938–39.

Treaty *Oldest*

The world's oldest treaty is the Anglo-Portuguese Treaty of Alliance signed in London over 600 years ago on 16 June 1373. The text was confirmed 'with my usual flourish' by John de Banketre, Clerk.

Constitutions

The world's oldest constitution is that of the United States of America ratified by the necessary Ninth State (New Hampshire) on 21 June 1788 and declared to be in effect on 4 Mar 1789. The only countries without one document constitutions are Israel, Libya, New Zealand, Oman, Saudi Arabia and the United Kingdom.

PARLIAMENTS—UNITED KINGDOM

Earliest

The earliest known use of the term 'parliament' is an official English royal document, in the meaning of a summons to the King's (Henry III's) council, dates from 19 Dec 1241.

The Houses of Parliament of the United Kingdom in the Palace of Westminster, London, had 1838 members (House of Lords 1188, House of Commons 650) in June 1984.

Longest

The longest English Parliament was the 'Pensioners' Parliament of Charles II, which lasted from 8 May 1661 to 24 Jan 1679, a period of 17 years 8 months and 16 days. The longest United Kingdom Parliament was that of George V, Edward VIII and George VI, lasting from 26 Nov 1935 to 15 June 1945, a span of 9 years 6 months and 20 days.

Shortest

The parliament of Edward I, summoned to Westminster for 30 May 1306, lasted only 1 day. The parliament of Charles II at Oxford from 21–28 Mar 1681 lasted 7 days. The shortest United Kingdom Parliament was that of George III, lasting from 15 Dec 1806 to 29 Apr 1807, a period of only 4 months and 14 days.

Longest sittings

The longest sitting in the House of Commons was one of 41½ hr from 4 p.m. on 31 Jan 1881 to 9.30 a.m. on 2 Feb 1881, on the question of better Protection of Person and Property in Ireland. The longest sitting of the Lords has been 19 hr 16 min from 2.30 p.m. on 29 Feb to 9.46 a.m on 1 Mar 1968 on the Commonwealth Immigrants Bill (Committee stage). The longest sitting of a Standing Committee occurred from 10.30 a.m. 11 May to 12.08 p.m. 13 May 1948 when Standing Committee D considered the Gas Bill through two nights for 49 hr 38 min.

Longest speech

The longest recorded continuous speech in the Chamber of the House of Commons was that of Henry Peter Brougham (1778–1868) on 7 Feb 1828, when he spoke for 6 hr on Law Reform. He ended at 10.40 p.m. and the report of this speech occupied 12 columns of the next day's edition of *The Times*. Brougham, created the 1st Lord Brougham and Vaux on 22 Nov 1830, then set the House of Lords record, also with 6 hours on 7 Oct 1831, when speaking on the second reading of the Reform Bill. The longest back bench speech under present, much stricter, Standing Orders has been one of 3 hr 16 min by Sir Bernard Braine (b. 1914) the Conservative member for Essex, South East concerning Canvey Island on 23–24 July 1974. John Golding (Labour, Newcastle-under-Lyme) spoke for 11 hr 15 min in committee on 8–9 Feb 1983.

The longest speech in Stormont, Northern Ireland was one of 9½ hr by Tommy Henderson MP on the Appropriations Bill on 26–27 May 1936.

Greatest parliamentary petition

The greatest petition has been supposed to be the Great Chartist Petition of 1848 but of the 5,706,000 'signatures' only 1,975,496 were valid. The largest of all time was for the abolition of Entertainment Duty with 3,107,080 signatures presented on 5 June 1951.

Most time consuming legislation

The most profligate use of parliamentary time was on the Government of Ireland Bill of 1893–4, which required 82 days in the House of Commons of which 46 days was in Committee. The record for a standing committee is 59 sessions for the Police and Criminal Evidence Bill from 17 Nov 1983 to 29 Mar 1984.

Divisions

The record number of divisions in the House of Commons is 64 on 23–24 Mar 1971 including 57 in succession between midnight and noon. The largest division was one of 350–310 on the vote of no confidence on 11 Aug 1892.

ELECTIONS—WORLD

Largest

The largest elections in the world were those of January 1980 for the Indian *Lok Sabha* (Lower House) which has 542 elective seats. The in-coming Prime Minister Mrs Indira Gandhi was better known by her symbol (a raised hand palm outwards) than by name among the 363,945,873 voters from 22 states and 9 union territories.

Closest

The ultimate in close general elections occurred in Zanzibar (now part of Tanzania) on 18 Jan 1961, when the Afro-Shirazi Party won by a single seat, after the seat of Chake-Chake on Pemba Island had been gained by a single vote.

The narrowest recorded percentage win in an election would seem to be for the office of Southern District highway commissioner in Mississippi State, USA on 7 Aug 1979. Robert E. Joiner was declared the winner over W. H. Pyron with 133,587 votes to 133,582. The loser got more than 49.9999 per cent of the votes.

Most decisive

North Korea recorded a 100 per cent turn-out of electors and a 100 per cent vote for the Worker's Party of Korea in the general election of 8 Oct 1962. The next closest approach was in Albania on 14 Nov 1982 when a single voter spoiled national unanimity for the official (and only) Communist candidates, who thus obtained only 99.99993 per cent of the poll in a 100 per cent turn out of 1,627,968.

Most bent

In the Liberian presidential election of 1927 President Charles D. B. King (1875–1961) was returned with a majority over his opponent, Mr Thomas J. R. Faulkner of the People's Party, officially announced as 234,000. President King thus claimed a 'majority' more than 15½ times greater than the entire electorate.

Highest personal majority

The highest ever personal majority by any politician has been 424,545 by Ram Bilas Paswan, 30, the Janata candidate for Hajipur in Bihar, India in March 1977. The electorate was 625,179.

Communist parties

The largest national Communist party outside the Soviet Union (17,000,000 members in 1981) and Communist states has been the Partito Comunista Italiano (Italian Communist Party), with a membership of 2,300,000 in 1946. The total was 1,700,000 in 1976. The membership in mainland China was estimated to be 39,000,000 in 1984.

The Communist Party of Great Britain, formed on 31 July 1920 in Cannon Street Station Hotel, London, attained its peak membership of 56,000 in December 1942, compared with 15,691 in July 1983 of whom 8,270 paid their dues.

Voting age Extremes

The eligibility for voting is 15 years of age in the Philippines and 25 years in Andorra.

Most Coups

Statisticians contend Bolivia, since it became a sovereign country in 1825, has had 189 *coups*.

PRIME MINISTERS AND STATESMEN—WORLD

Oldest

The longest lived Prime Minister of any country is Christopher Hornsrud, Prime Minister of Norway from 28 Jan to 15 Feb 1928. He was born on 15 Nov 1859 and died on 13 Dec 1960, aged 101 years 28 days. The Hon. Richard Gavin Reid (b. Glasgow 17 Jan 1879), Premier of Alberta, Canada in 1934–35 died on 17 Oct 1980 aged 101 years 274 days.

BRITISH AND IRISH LARGEST AND SMALLEST PRIMARY LOCAL GOVERNMENT AREAS

By Size and Population				By Area (in acres/hectares)				By Home/Population				
	Largest			**Smallest**				**Most Populous**			**Least Populous**	
England[1]	North Yorkshire	2,053,067	*830 865*	Isle of Wight	94,064	*38 067*		Greater London	6,754,500		Isle of Wight	119,800
Wales	Dyfed	1,425,226	*576 781*	South Glamorgan	102,868	*41 630*		Mid Glamorgan	536,400		Powys	110,600
Scotland[2]	Highland[3]	6,274,171	*2 539 122*	Orkney	241,123	*97 581*		Strathclyde	2,383,077		Orkney	19,239
Northern Ireland[4]	Fermanagh	419,951	*169 952*	North Down	17,893	*7 241*		Belfast City[5]	324,900		Moyle[5]	14,400
Republic of Ireland	Cork County	1,834,155	*742 257*	Louth	203,447	*82 334*		Dublin County & City[6]	1,003,164		Leitrim[6]	27,609

[1] The most populous city in England outside Greater London is Birmingham (pop. 1,012,900). The most populous cities in Wales and Scotland are, respectively, Cardiff, South Glamorgan (pop. 279,800) and Glasgow, Strathclyde (pop. 751,014).
[2] Scotland's 33 Counties were replaced on 16 May 1975 by nine regions and three Island Areas.
[3] The inclusion by Act of Parliament on 10 Feb 1972 of Rockall in the District of Harris in Western Isles put the extremities of that Authority at the record distance apart of 302 miles 486 km.
[4] The largest of the 6 geographical counties is Tyrone 806,618 acres 326 548 ha.
[5] 1982 estimate.
[6] 1981 census figure.

PRIME MINISTERIAL RECORDS: *Left to right* H. H. Asquith (Longest serving this century) Duke of Wellington (shortest ministry) Stanley Baldwin (most times) Harold Macmillan (longest lived) William Pitt (youngest) Margaret Thatcher (first woman P.M.) Sir Robert Walpole (longest term) Winston Churchill (oldest in office) Earl of Bath (shortest term)
ARTWORK: DON ROBERTS AND PETER HARRIS

El Hadji Muhammad el Mokri, Grand Vizier of Morocco, died on 16 Sept 1957, at a reputed age of 116 Muslim (*Hijri*) years, equivalent to 112.5 Gegorian years. The oldest age of first appointment has been 81 years in the case of Morarji Ranchhodji Desai of India (b. 29 Feb 1896) in March 1977.

Longest term of office

Prof. Dr António de Oliveira Salazar, GCMG (Hon.) (1889–1970) was the President of the Council of Ministers (*i.e.* Prime Minister) of Portugal from 5 July 1932 until 27 Sept 1968—36 years 84 days. He was superseded 11 days after going into coma. The longest serving democratically elected premier was Tage Erlander of Sweden for 22 years 357 days from 10 Oct 1946 to 1 Oct 1969.

Andrei Andreevich Gromyko (b. 6 July 1909) has been Minister of Foreign Affairs of the USSR since 15 Feb 1957 having been Deputy Foreign Minister since 1946.

EUROPEAN ASSEMBLY ELECTION RECORDS

In the European Assembly elections of 14 June 1984 the highest majority in the 81 U.K. constituencies was 95,557 (L. Smith, Lab) in Wales South-East. Lowest was 2,625 (Sir Peter Vanneck, Con) in Cleveland and Yorkshire North. Largest and smallest electorates were 574,022 in Essex North-East and

PRIME MINISTERIAL RECORDS

Though given legal warrant in the instrument of the Congress of Berlin in 1878 and an established place in the orders of Precedence in England and Scotland in 1904, the office of Prime Minister was not statutorily recognised until 1917. All previous acknowledged First Ministers had tenure as First Lords of the Treasury with the exception of No. 12, William Pitt, Earl of Chatham, who controlled his ministers as Secretary of State of the Southern Department or as Lord Privy Seal. The first to preside over his fellow King's ministers was Walpole from 1721.

LONGEST SERVING	20 years 326 days	1st	Sir Robert Walpole KG (1676–1745)	3 Apr 1721–12 Feb 1742
LONGEST SERVING (*20th century*)	8 years 243 days	38th	Earl of Oxford and Asquith, KG (1852–1928)	8 Apr 1908–7 Dec 1916
MOST MINISTRIES	5 times	41st	Earl Baldwin, KG (1867–1947)	22 May 1923–28 May 1937
SHORTEST SERVING IN OFFICE	120 days	22nd	George Canning (1770–1827)	10 Apr–8 Aug 1827
YOUNGEST TO ASSUME OFFICE	24 years 205 days	17th	Hon. William Pitt (1759–1806)	19 Dec 1783 (declined when 23 yr 275 days)
OLDEST TO FIRST ASSUME OFFICE	70 years 109 days	31st	Viscount Palmerston, KG, GCB (1784–1865)	6 Feb 1855
GREATEST AGE IN OFFICE	84 years 64 days	33rd	William Gladstone (1809–1898)	3 Mar 1894 (elected at 82 yr 171 days)
LONGEST LIVED	90+ years	47th	Earl of Stockton, OM (b. 10 Feb 1894)	from 6 Apr 1984 (so surpassing No 44)
LONGEST SURVIVAL AFTER OFFICE	41 years 45 days	13th	Duke of Grafton, KG (1735–1811)	from 28 Jan 1770
SHORTEST LIVED	44 years	7th	Duke of Devonshire, KG (1720–1764)	d. 2 Oct 1764 (exact birth date unknown)
SHORTEST MINISTRY	22 days	24th	Duke of Wellington, KG, GCB, GCH (1769–1852)	17 Nov–9 Dec 1834
SHORTEST POSSESSION OF SEALS	c. 48 hours	4th	Earl of Bath (1684–1764)	10–12 Feb 1746
SHORTEST PRIOR SERVICE AS MP	2 years 11 months	17th	Hon. William Pitt (1759–1806)	–19 Dec 1783
LONGEST PRIOR SERVICE AS MP	47 years	31st	Viscount Palmerston, KG, GCB (1784–1865)	1807–6 Feb 1855
LONGEST SUBSEQUENT SERVICE AS MP	22 years 156 days	39th	Earl Lloyd George, OM (1863–1945)	22 Oct 1922–26 Mar 1945
LONGEST SPAN AS MP	63 years 360 days	44th	Sir Winston Churchill, KG, OM, CH (1874–1965)	1 Oct 1900–25 Sep 1964
RICHEST	£7¼ million (now say £190 million)	29th	Earl of Derby, KG, GCMG (1799–1869)	Annual rent roll in 1869 £170,000
POOREST	£40,000 (now > £1 million) in debt	17th	Hon. William Pitt (1759–1806)	Level of personal debt by 1800
TALLEST	6 ft 1½ in *1,83 m*	51st	James Callaghan (b. 27 Mar 1912)	
SHORTEST	5 ft 4¾ in *1,64 m*	28th	Lord John Russell, KG, GCMG (1792–1878)	Seven month baby: max. wt. 8 stone *50,7 kg*
MOST CHILDREN (*fathered*)	15 or 16	13th	Duke of Grafton, KG (1735–1811)	Twice married
MOST CHILDREN (*uniquely mothered*)	2	52nd	Mrs Margaret Thatcher (b. 13 Oct 1925)	Twins born, 21 Aug 1953
MOST LIVING SIMULTANEOUSLY	18	9th–27th	Peel (b. 5 Feb 1788) to death of 9th Earl of Bute (d. 10 Mar 1792)	1788–1792
MOST LIVING EX PRIME MINISTERS	5	9th, 13–16th	Bute, Grafton, North, Shelburne, Portland (Pitt) till Bute died	19 Dec 1783–10 Mar 1792
	5	46–50th	Eden, Macmillan, Home, Wilson, Heath (Callaghan) till Eden died	5 Apr 1976–14 Jan 1977
	5	47–51st	Macmillan, Home, Wilson, Heath, Callaghan (Mrs Thatcher)	from 4 May 1979

307,265 in Highlands and Islands. Highest turnout was 42.4 per cent in Wales North. Lowest was 25.2 per cent in London North-East. Northern Ireland voted under a system of proportional representation.

MAJORITIES—UNITED KINGDOM

Party

The largest party majorities were those of the Liberals, with 307 seats and a record of 66.7% of the vote in 1832. In 1931 the Coalition of Conservatives, Liberals and National Labour candidates had a majority of 491 seats and 60.5% of the vote. The narrowest party majority was that of the Whigs in 1847, with a single seat. The highest popular vote for a single party was 13,948,883 for Labour in 1951.

The largest majority on a division was one of 463 (464 votes to 1), on a vote of confidence in the conduct of World War II, on 29 Jan 1942. Since the war the largest has been one of 461 (487 votes to 26) on 10 May 1967, during the debate on the government's application for Britain to join the European Economic Community (the 'Common Market').

HOUSE OF LORDS

Oldest member

The oldest member ever was the Rt Hon the 5th Baron Penrhyn, who was born on 21 Nov 1865 and died on 3 Feb 1967, aged 101 years 74 days. The oldest now is the Rt Hon Lord Shinwell PC CH (b. 18 Oct 1884) who first sat in the Lower House in Nov 1922. The oldest peer to make a maiden speech was Lord Maenan (1854–1951) aged 94 years 123 days (see Oldest creation, p. 200).

Youngest member

The youngest present member of the House of Lords has been HRH the Prince Charles Philip Arthur George, KG, KT, GCB, the Prince of Wales (b. 14 Nov 1948). All Dukes of Cornwall, of whom Prince Charles is the 24th, are technically eligible to sit, regardless of age—in his case from his succession on 6 Feb 1952, aged 3. The 20th and 21st holders, later King George IV (b. 1762) and King Edward VII (b. 1841), were technically entitled to sit from birth. The youngest creation of a life peer or peeress under the Peerage Act 1958 has been that of Lady Masham (b. 14 Apr 1935) who was created Baroness Masham of Ilton at the age of 34 years 262 days.

POLITICAL OFFICE HOLDERS

Chancellorship *Longest and shortest tenures*

The Rt Hon Sir Robert Walpole, KG, later the 1st Earl of Orford (1676–1745), served 22 years 5 months as Chancellor of the Exchequer, holding office continuously from 12 Oct 1715 to 12 Feb 1742, except for the period from 16 Apr 1717 to 2 Apr 1721. The briefest tenure of this office was 26 days in the case of the Baron (later the 1st Earl of) Mansfield (1705–93), from 11 Sept to 6 Oct 1767. The only man with four terms in this office was the Rt Hon William Ewart Gladstone (1809–98).

Foreign Secretaryship *Longest tenures*

The longest continuous term of office of any Foreign Secretary has been the 10 years 360 days of Sir Edward Grey, KG, MP (later Viscount Grey of Fallodon) from 10 Dec 1905 to 5 Dec 1916. The Most Hon Robert Arthur Talbot Gascoyne-Cecil, Marquis of Salisbury, KG, GCVO, in two spells in 1887–92 and 1895–1900 aggregated 11 years 87 days in this office.

Colonial Secretaryship *Longest tenures*

The longest term of office has been 19 years 324 days by the Rt Hon Henry Bathurst, Earl Bathurst (1762–1834), who was Secretary of State for the Colonial and War Department from 11 June 1812 to 1 May 1827. The longest tenure this century has been the 5 years 78 days of the Rt Hon Alan Tindal Lennox-Boyd, Viscount Boyd of Merton, PC CH (1904–82) from 28 July 1954 to 13 Oct 1959.

Speakership *Longest*

Arthur Onslow (1691–1768) was elected Mr Speaker on 23 Jan 1728, at the age of 36. He held the position for 33 years 43 days, until 18 Mar 1761 allowing for the 'lost' 11 days (3–13 Sept 1752).

MPs *Youngest (see also p 212)*

The youngest ever women M.P. has been Josephine Bernadette Devlin now Mrs Michael McAliskey (b. 23 Apr 1947) elected for Mid Ulster (Ind. Unity) aged 21 yr 359 days on 17 Apr 1969. Henry Long (1420–90) was returned for an Old Sarum seat also at the age of 15. His precise date of birth is unknown. Minors were debarred in law in 1695 and in fact in 1832.

Oldest

The oldest of all members was Samuel Young (b. 14 Feb 1822), Nationalist MP for East Cavan (1892–1918), who died on 18 Apr 1918, aged 96 years 63 days. The oldest 'Father of the House' in Parliamentary history was the Rt Hon Charles Pelham Villiers (b. 3 Jan 1802), who was the member for Wolverhampton South when he died on 16 Jan 1898, aged 96 years 13 days. He was a Member of Parliament for 63 years 6 days, having been returned at 17 elections. The oldest member is Robert Edwards MP (Lab) for Wolverhampton South East (b. 16 Jan 1905).

far left: Lord Shinwell, the only M.P. in 743 years to have spoken in his 100th year. *left:* The Countess of Iveagh, who won the highest ever majority for any woman MP.

Longest span

The longest span of service of any MP is 63 years 11 months (1 Oct 1900 to 25 Sept 1964) by the Rt Hon Sir Winston Leonard Spencer-Churchill, KG, OM, CH, TD (1874–1965), with breaks only in 1908 and 1922–24. The longest continuous span was that of C. P. Villiers (see above). The longest span in the Palace of Westminster (both Houses of Parliament) has been 73 years by the 10th Earl of Wemyss and March GCVO, who, as Sir Francis Wemyss-Charteris-Douglas, served as MP for East Gloucestershire (1841–6) and Haddingtonshire (1847–83) and then took his seat in the House of Lords, dying on 30 June 1914, aged 95 years 330 days.

1 **Lowest Electorate 1983** Western Isles : 22,822

2 **Largest Constituency by Area** Ross, Cromarty & Skye 2,359,772 acres *955,000 ha*

2 **Youngest Current MP** Charles Kennedy (SDP/All) (b. 25 Nov 1959) Ross, Cromarty & Skye

3 **Least votes since Universal Franchise** 5 Lt Cdr W. Boaks DSC RN (Public Safety Democratic Monarchist White Resident) Glasgow (Hillhead) 25 Mar 1982

3 **Lowest Expenses** £54 James Maxton Glasgow (Bridgeton) 1935

4 **Longest Serving Woman MP** Dame Irene Ward 1931–1974 Wallsend-Tynemouth

5 & **21** **Narrowest Majority** 1 vote by H. E. Duke (Unionist) Dec 1910 Exeter, Devon and 1 vote Matthew Fowler (Lib) 1895 Durham

6 **Lowest Vote** Nil in 1860 for F. R. Lees (Temperance) Ripon

7 **Heaviest Ever Poll (GB)** Darwen (Lancs) 92.7% in 1924

8 **Dead-Heat** Returning Officer declared dead heat (1886) and gave casting vote to J. E. W. Addison (Con) Ashton-Under-Lyne (now Greater Manchester). Dead heat at Cirencester, Gloucester 13 Oct 1892 by-election. New by-election 23 Feb 1893 won by H. L. W. Lawson (Lib)

9 **Narrowest Majority Since Universal Franchise** A. J. Flint (National Labour) Ilkeston (Derbyshire) by 2 votes 1931

10 **Oldest Father of the House** C. P. Villiers (Con) in 1898, 96 years of age, Wolverhampton South

11 **Narrowest Majority 1983** 7 votes Derek Spencer (Con) Leicester South

12 & **18** **Most Recounts** 7 Peterborough 1966 and 7 Brighton (Kemptown) 1964

13 **Youngest Ever MP** Aged 15/16 Edmund Waller (1606–87) in 1621 Amersham (Bucks)

14 **Greatest Swing : By-Election** 44.4% Bermondsey 24 Feb 1983

14 **Largest Ever Electorate** 217,900 Hendon (Barnet) 1941

14 **Smallest Electorate** 10,851 City of London 1945

14 **Lowest By-Election Poll** 9.3% South Poplar (London) Aug 1942

14 **Lowest Ever General Election Poll** 29.7% 1918 Kennington (London)

14 **Lowest General Election Vote** 13 B. C. Wedmore (Belgrano) Finchley 9 June 1983

14 **Lowest 1983 Poll** City of London and Westminster South : 51.8%

14 **Most General Election Candidates** 11 Finchley 9 June 1983 in which the total 2579 candidates was a record

15 **Fastest ever result** 57 min Billericay (Essex) 1959

16 **Highest Majority by a Woman** 38,823 Countess of Iveagh (Con) 1931 Southend (Essex)

17 **Youngest MP for GB seat since 1832** 21 years 183 days Hon Esmond Harmsworth Isle of Thanet (Kent)

18 **Highest Ever Majority** 62,253 Sir Cooper Rawson (Con) Brighton (Sussex) 1931 and **Most Votes** 75,205

18 & **12** **Most Recounts** 7 Peterborough 1966 and 7 Brighton (Kemptown) 1964

19 **Highest Electorate 1983** Isle of Wight : 94,226

19 **Most Votes 1983** 38,407 Stephen Ross (Lib/All) Isle of Wight

20 **Most Rotten Borough** (8 Electors for 2 unopposed members) 1821 Old Sarum (Wiltshire) No elections contested 1295–1831

21 & **5** **Narrowest Majority** 1 vote H. E. Duke (Unionist) Dec 1910 Exeter, Devon and 1 vote Matthew Fowler (Lib) 1895 Durham

22 **Fastest 1983 result** 69 min Torbay (Devon)

23 **First Woman MP to take seat** Nancy Astor 1919 Plymouth

24 **Current Father of the House** L. J. Callaghan (Lab) Elected 1945 (Cardiff South & Penarth)

25 **Largest UK Majority 1983** Michael M. Foot (Lab) Blaenau Gwent 23,705

26 **Heaviest Ever Poll (UK)** Fermanagh & S Tyrone : 93.42% 1951

26 **Heaviest Poll 1983 (UK)** Fermanagh & S Tyrone : 88.6%

26 **Youngest Member UK (since 1832)** James Dickson (Liberal) (1859–1941) returned for Dungannon Tyrone on 25 June 1880 aged 21 years 67 days

27 **Most By-Election Candidates** 17 Chesterfield 1 Mar 1984. Rt Hon A. N. Wedgwood-Benn contested for a current record 14th time (12 times returned)

28 **Highest Poll 1983 (GB)** Cornwall North 86.08%

Map of UK ELECTORAL RECORDS

ARTWORK: EDDIE BOTCHWAY

Briefest span

There are two 18th century examples of posthumous elections. Capt the Hon Edward Legge RN (1710–47) was returned unopposed for Portsmouth on 15 Dec 1747. News came later that he had died in the West Indies 87 days before polling. In 1780 John Kirkman standing for the City of London expired before polling had ended but was nonetheless duly returned. A. J. Dobbs (Lab, Smethwick) elected on 5 July 1945 was killed on the way to take his seat at Westminster.

Women MPs *Earliest*

The first woman to be elected to the House of Commons was Mme. Constance Georgine Markievicz (*née* Gore Booth). She was elected as member (Sinn Fein) for St Patrick's Dublin, in December 1918. The first woman to take her seat was the Viscountess Astor, CH (1879–1964) (b. Nancy Witcher Langhorne at Danville, Virginia, USA; formerly Mrs Robert Gould Shaw), who was elected Unionist member for the Sutton Division of Plymouth, Devon, on 28 Nov 1919, and took her seat three days later. The first woman to take her seat from the island of Ireland was Lady Fisher *née* Patricia Smiles as unopposed Ulster Unionist for North Down on 15 Apr 1953 as Mrs Patricia Ford.

Heaviest and Tallest

The heaviest MP of all-time is believed to have been Cyril Smith MBE, Liberal member for Rochdale since October 1972, when in January 1976 his peak reported weight was 29 st 12 lb *189,60 kg*. Sir Louis Gluckstein GBE, TD, QC (1897–1979), who served for East Nottingham (1931–45), was an unrivalled 6 ft 7½ in *2,02 m*. Currently the tallest is the Hon. Archie Hamilton member for Epsom and Ewell at 6 ft 6 in *1,98 m*.

Mayoralties

The longest recorded mayoralty was that of Edmond Mathis (1852–1953) *maire* of Ehuns, Haute-Saône, France for 75 years (1878–1953). The mayoralty of the City of London dates from 1192 with the 20 year term of Henry Fitz Ailwyn till 1212. The most elections, since these became annual in 1215, has been 8 by Gregory de Rokesley (1274/5 to 1280/1). The earliest recorded mayor of the City of York, Nigel, dates from 1142. Alderman G. T. Paine served as Mayor of Lydd, Kent for 29 consecutive years in 1931 to 1961. The first recorded all-female mayoral team was the Mayor, Mayoress and Deputy Mayor of Lancaster city council in May 1972. In Hyndburn Borough Council in May 1981 there was a fourth lady with the appointment of a Deputy Mayoress.

Local Government Service Duration Records

Major Sir Philip Barber Bt, DSO, TD, DL (1876–1961) served as county councillor for Nottinghamshire for 63 years 41 days from 8 Mar 1898 to 18 Apr 1961. Henry Winn (1816–1914) served as parish clerk for Fulletby near Horncastle, Lincolnshire for 76 years.

The office of reeve was first mentioned in AD 787 and evolved to that of shire reeve hence sheriff.

Weight of Legislation

The greatest amount of legislation in a year has been 11,453 pages (83 Public general acts and 2251 Statutory Instruments) in 1975. This compares with 46 Acts and 1130 Instruments of 1998 pages in 1928. Most Acts were 123 in 1939 and fewest 39 in 1929 and 1942. The peak for Statutory Instruments was 2916 in 1947.

4. MILITARY AND DEFENCE

Note Guinness Superlatives Ltd. has published a specialist volume entitled *The Guinness Book of Tank Facts and Feats* (3rd edition) by Kenneth Macksey (£7.95). This work deals with all the aspects of the development and history of the tank and other armoured fighting vehicles in greater detail.

WAR

Earliest Conflict

The oldest known weapon is a broken wooden spear found in April 1911 at Clacton-on-Sea, Essex by S. Hazzledine Warren. This is much beyond the limit of carbon-dating and is estimated to have been fashioned before 200,000 BC.

The longest of history's countless wars was the 'Hundred Years War' between England and France, which lasted from 1338 to 1453 (115 years), although it may be said that the nine Crusades from the First (1096–1104) to the Ninth (1270–91), extending over 195 years comprised a single Holy War. The Swiss Jean Jacques Babel estimated that since *c.* 3500 BC there have only been 292 years without recorded warfare.

Shortest

The shortest war on record was that between the United Kingdom and Zanzibar (now part of Tanzania) from 9.02 to 9.40 a.m. on 27 Aug 1896. The UK battle fleet under Rear-Admiral (later Admiral Sir) Harry Holdsworth Rawson (1843–1910) delivered an ultimatum to the self-appointed Sultan Sa'īd Khalid to evacuate his palace and surrender. This was not forthcoming until after 38 minutes of bombardment. Admiral Rawson received the Brilliant Star of Zanzibar (first class) from the new Sultan Hamud ibn Muhammad. It was proposed at one time that elements of the local populace should be compelled to defray the cost of the ammunition used.

Bloodiest

By far the most costly war in terms of human life was World War II (1939–45), in which the total number of fatalities, including battle deaths and civilians of all countries, is estimated to have been 54,800,000 assuming 25 million USSR fatalities and 7,800,000 Chinese civilians killed. The country which suffered most was Poland with 6,028,000 of 22.2 per cent of her population of 27,007,000 killed. The total combatant death roll from World War I was 9,700,000 compared with the 15,600,000 of World War II.

In the case of the United Kingdom, however, the heaviest armed forces fatalities occurred in World War I (1914–18), with 765,399 killed out of 5,500,000 engaged (13.9 per cent), compared with 265,000 out of 5,896,000 engaged (4.49 per cent) in World War II.

In the Paraguayan war of 1864–70 against Brazil, Argentina and Uruguay, their population was reduced from 1,400,000 to 220,000 of whom only 30,000 were adult males.

Surgeon Major William Brydon CB (1811–1873) was the sole survivor of the 7 day retreat of 16,000 soldiers and camp followers from Kabul, Afghanistan. His horse died two days after his arrival at Jellalabad, India on 13 Jan 1842.

Bloodiest civil

The bloodiest civil war in history was the T'ai-p'ing ('Great Peace') rebellion, in which peasant sympathizers of the Southern Ming dynasty fought the Manchu Government troops in China from 1851 to 1864. The rebellion was led by the deranged Hung Hsiu-ch'üan (executed) who imagined himself to be a younger brother of Jesus Christ. His force was named *T'ai-p'ing T'ien Kuo* (Heavenly Kingdom of Great Peace). According to the best estimates, the loss of life was between 20,000,000 and 30,000,000 including more than 100,000 killed by Government forces in the sack of Nanking on 19–21 July 1864.

Most costly

The material cost of World War II far transcended that of the rest of history's wars put together and has been estimated at $1.5 million million. The total cost to the Soviet Union was estimated in May 1959 at 2,500,000,000,000 roubles (*£100,000 million*) while a figure of $530,000 million has been estimated for the USA. In the case of the United Kingdom the cost of £34,423 million was over five times as great as that of World War I (£6700 million) and 158.6 times that of the Boer War of 1899–1902 (£217 million).

Last battle on British soil

The last pitched land battle in Britain was at Culloden Field, Drummossie Moor, near Inverness, Highland, on 16 Apr 1746. The last Clan battle in Scotland was between Clan Mackintosh and Clan MacDonald at Mulroy, Highland in 1689. The last battle on English soil was the Battle of Sedgemoor, Somerset, on 6 July 1685, when the forces of James II defeated the supporters of Charles II's illegitimate son, James Scott (formerly called Fitzroy or Crofts), the Duke of Monmouth (1649–85). During the Jacobite rising of 1745–6, there was a skirmish at Clifton Moor, Cumbria, on 18 Dec 1745, when the British forces under Prince William, the Duke of Cumberland (1721–65), brushed with the rebels of Prince Charles Edward

The climax of the War of the Roses at the Battle of Towton, North Yorkshire. It was here on 29 Mar 1461 that 36,000 Yorkists defeated 46,000 Lancastrians leaving at least 28,000 dead on the battlefield. (Radio Times Hulton Picture Library)

Stuart (1720–88) with about 12 killed on the King's side and 5 Highlanders. This was a tactical victory for the Scots under Lord George Murray.

Bloodiest battle *Modern*

The battle with the greatest recorded number of *military* casualties was the First Battle of the Somme, France from 1 July to 19 Nov 1916, with 1,043,896—Allied 623,907 (of which 419,654 were British) and 419,989 German. The published German figure of *c.* 670,000 is not now accepted. The gunfire was heard on Hampstead Heath, London. The greatest death roll in a battle has been estimated at *c.* 2,100,000 in the Battle of Stalingrad ending with the German surrender on 2 Feb 1943 by Field Marshal Friedrich von Paulus (d. 1957). The Soviet garrison commander was Gen Vassilyi Chuikov. Additionally 1,515 civilians from a pre-war population of more than 500,000 were found alive after the battle. The final investment of Berlin by the Red Army on 16 Apr–2 May 1945 involved 3,500,000 men; 52,000 guns and mortars; 7750 tanks and 11,000 aircraft on both sides.

Ancient

Modern historians give no credence, on logistic grounds, to the casualty figures attached to ancient battles, such as the 250,000 reputedly killed at Plataea (Greeks *v* Persians) in 479 BC or the 200,000 allegedly killed in a single day.

British

The bloodiest battle fought on British soil was the Battle of Towton, in North Yorkshire, on 29 Mar 1461, when 36,000 Yorkists defeated 40,000 Lancastrians. The total loss has been estimated at between 28,000 and 38,000 killed. A figure of 80,000 British dead was attributed by Tacitus to the battle of AD 61 between Queen Boudicca (Boadicea) of the Iceni and the Roman Governor of Britain Suetonius Paulinus, for the reputed loss of only 400 Romans in an army of 10,000. The site of the battle is unknown but may have been near Borough Hill, Daventry, Northamptonshire, or more probably near Hampstead Heath, Greater London. Prior to this battle the Romans had lost up to 70,000 in Colchester and London.

Greatest naval battle

The greatest number of ships and aircraft ever involved in a sea–air action was 231 ships and 1996 aircraft in the Battle of Leyte Gulf, in the Philippines. It raged from 22 to 27 Oct 1944, with 166 Allied and 65 Japanese warships engaged, of which 26 Japanese and 6 US ships were sunk. In addition 1280 US and 716 Japanese aircraft were engaged. The greatest purely naval battle of modern times was the Battle of Jutland on 31 May 1916, in which 151 Royal Navy warships were involved against 101 German warships. The Royal Navy lost 14 ships and 6097 men and the German fleet 11 ships and 2545 men. The greatest of ancient naval battles was the Battle of Salamis, Greece on 23 Sept 480 BC. There were an estimated 800 vessels in the defeated Persian fleet and 310 in the victorious Greek fleet with a possible involvement of 190,000 men. The death roll at the Battle of Lepanto on 7 Oct 1571 has been estimated at 33,000.

Invasion Greatest *Seaborne*

The greatest invasion in military history was the Allied land, air and sea operation against the Normandy coasts of France on D-day, 6 June 1944. Thirty-eight convoys of 745 ships moved in on the first three days, supported by 4066 landing craft, carrying 185,000 men and 20,000 vehicles, and 347 minesweepers. The air assault comprised 18,000 paratroopers from 1087 aircraft. The 42 available divisions possessed an air support from 13,175 aircraft. Within a month 1,100,000 troops, 200,000 vehicles and 750,000 tons of stores were landed. The Allied invasion of Sicily on 10–12 July 1943 involved the landing of 181,000 men in 3 days.

Airborne

The largest airborne invasion was the Anglo-American assault of three divisions (34,000 men), with 2800 aircraft and 1600 gliders, near Arnhem, in the Netherlands, on 17 Sept 1944.

Last on the soil of Great Britain

The last invasion of Great Britain occurred on 12 Feb 1797, when the Irish-American adventurer General Tate landed at Carreg Gwastad with 1400 French troops. They surrendered near Fishguard, Dyfed, to Lord Cawdor's force of the Castlemartin Yeomanry and some local inhabitants armed with pitchforks. The UK Crown Dependency of the Falkland Islands were occupied by Argentine troops on 2 Apr 1982. British troops re-landed at San Carlos on 21 May and accepted the surrender of Brig Gen Mario Menéndez on 14 June 1982.

Greatest evacuation

The greatest evacuation in military history was that carried out by 1200 Allied naval and civil craft from the beach-head at Dunkerque (Dunkirk), France, between 27 May and 4 June 1940. A total of 338,226 British and French troops were taken off.

Worst sieges

The worst siege in history was the 880-day siege of Leningrad, USSR by the German Army from 30 Aug 1941 until 27 Jan 1944. The best estimate is that between 1.3 and 1.5 million defenders and citizens died. The longest recorded siege was that of Azotus (now Ashdod), Israel which according to Herodotus was invested by Psamtik I of Egypt for 29 years in the period 664–610 BC.

Longest Range Attack

The longest range attack in aviation history was from Ascension Island to Port Stanley, Falkland Is. by a refuelled RAF Vulcan bomber in a round trip of more than 8000 miles *12 875 km.*

DEFENCE

The estimated level of spending on **armaments** throughout the world in 1983 was in excess of $700,000 million *£500,000 million.* This represents £107 per person per annum, or 10 per cent of the world's total production of goods and services. It was estimated in 1983 that there were 26 million full-time armed force regulars or conscripts.

The budgeted expenditure on defence by the US government for the fiscal year 1984 was $249,800 million (*£178,400 million*). The first budget resolution for 1985 was $297,000 million.

The defence burden on the USSR has been variously estimated as a percentage of GNP to be >15% (by China), up to 14% by Britain and up to 13% by the CIA and thus may be nearly treble that of the US.

ARMED FORCES

Largest

Numerically the largest regular armed force in the world is that of the USSR with 5,050,000 (1983). China however has a People's Liberation Army of 3,988,000 and para-military forces of armed and unarmed militias estimated by the International Institute of Strategic Studies at 12 million. The USA's military manpower is 2,136,400 (1983).

Navies *Largest*

The largest navy in the world in terms of manpower is the United States Navy, with a manpower of 569,000 and 194,600 Marines in mid-1983. The active strength in 1983 included 4 nuclear powered aircraft carriers, with 10 others, 2 battleships, 90 attack nuclear submarines and 5 diesel attack submarines, 28 cruisers, 68 destroyers, 90 frigates and 65 amphibious warfare ships. The USSR navy has a larger submarine fleet of 276 vessels (119 nuclear, 157 diesel). It has 5 aircraft carriers, 35 cruisers, 40 nuclear armed and 25 gun destroyers.

The strength of the Royal Navy in mid-1983 included 4 nuclear submarines with strategic atomic missiles, 12 other nuclear and 15 diesel attack submarines and 3 anti-submarine commando carriers, a helicopter cruiser, 13 guided weapon destroyers, and 45 frigates. The uniformed strength was 71,727 including Fleet Air Arm and Royal Marines in mid-1983. In 1914 the Royal Navy had 542 warships including 72 capital ships with 16 building thus being the largest navy in the world.

Admiral *Longest serving*

Admiral of the Fleet Sir Provo Wallis GCB (1791–1892) first served on *HMS Cleopatra* in Oct 1804. Because of his service on *HMS Cleopatra* in 1805 against the French he was kept on the active list in 1870 for life. He thus was 87 years 4 months on paid active service though he was earlier on the books as a volunteer from 1795–1804 for a further 9 years—a system by which even infants could gain seniority on joining.

Armies *Oldest*

The oldest army in the world is the 83-strong Swiss Guard in the Vatican City, with a regular foundation dating back to 21 Jan 1506. Its origins, however, extend back before 1400.

Largest

Numerically, the world's largest army is that of the People's Republic of China, with a total strength of some 3,600,000 in mid-1983. The total size of the USSR's army in mid-1983 was estimated by the International Institute of Strategic Studies at 1,800,000 men, believed to be organised into 184 divisions. The strength of the British Army was 162,036 at 31 Jan 1984. The NATO agreement requires not less than 55,000 in West Germany. The basic strength maintained in Northern Ireland is in excess of 10,000. Between 1969 and 1 Jan 1984 2365 people have been killed.

The beaches of Normandy, northern France 40 years on. The Allied flags of the Netherlands, Norway, United Kingdom, France, the USA, Canada and Belgium fly to mark the anniversary of the greatest invasion by sea in military history on D.Day on 6 June 1944. (*Fox/Keystone*)

Oldest soldiers

The oldest old soldier of all time was probably John B. Salling of the army of the Confederate States of America and the last accepted survivor of the US Civil War (1861–5). He died in Kingsport, Tennessee, USA on 16 Mar 1959, aged 113 years 1 day. The oldest Chelsea pensioner, based *only* on the evidence of his tombstone, was the 111-year-old William Hiseland (b. 6 Aug 1620, d. 7 Feb 1732). The longest serving British soldier has been Field Marshal Sir William Maynard Gomm GCB (1784–1875), who was an ensign in 1794 and the Constable of the Tower at his death aged 91.

Youngest soldiers

Dr Kenneth Vernon Bailey MC (b. 14 Dec 1897) served as a 2nd Lieutenant in the 2/8th Btn Manchester Regt. for some 6 weeks before his 17th birthday. Probably the youngest enlistment in the 20th century was of William Frederick Price, (b. 1 June 1891), who was enlisted into the Army at Aldershot on 23 May 1903, aged 11 years 356 days.

Youngest conscripts

President Francisco Macias Nguema of Equatorial Guinea decreed in March 1976 compulsory military service for all boys between 7 and 14. Any parent refusing to hand over his or her son 'will be imprisoned or shot'.

Tallest soldiers

The tallest soldier of all time was Väinö Myllyrinne (1909–63) who was inducted into the Finnish Army when he was 7 ft 3 in *2,21 m* and later grew to 8 ft 1¼ in *2,47 m.* The British Army's tallest soldier was Benjamin Crow who was signed on at Lichfield in November 1947 when he was 7 ft 1 in *2,15 m* tall. Edward Evans (1924–58), who later grew to 7 ft 8½ in *235 cm,* was in the Army when he was 6 ft 10 in *2,08 m.*

British regimental records

The oldest regular regiment in the British Army is the Royal Scots, raised in French service in 1633, though the Buffs (Royal East Kent Regiment) can trace back their origin to independent companies in Dutch pay as early as 1572. The Coldstream Guards, raised in 1650, were, however, placed on the establishment of the British Army before the Royal Scots and the Buffs. The oldest armed body in the United Kingdom is the Queen's Bodyguard of the Yeomen of the Guard formed in 1485. The Honourable Artillery Company, formed from the Fraternity of St. George, Southwark, received its charter from Henry VIII in 1537 but this lapsed until re-formed in 1610. The infantry regiment with most battle honours is The Queen's Lancashire Regiment with 188.

The most senior regiment of the Reserve Army is The Royal Monmouthshire Royal Engineers (Militia) formed on 21 Mar 1577 and never disbanded, with battle honours at Dunkirk, 1940 and Normandy, 1944.

Greatest mutiny

In the 1914–18 War 56 French divisions comprising some 650,000 men and their officers refused orders on the Western Front sector of General Nivelle in April 1917 after the failure of his offensive.

Longest march

The longest march in military history was the famous Long March by the Chinese Communists in 1934–5. In 368 days, of which 268 days were of movement, from October to October, their force of 90,000 covered 6000 miles *9650 km* from Kiangsi to Yenan in Shensi *via* Yünnan. They crossed 18 mountain ranges and six major rivers and lost all but 22,000 of their force in continual rear-guard actions against Nationalist Kuo-min-tang (KMT) forces.

On the night of 12–13 Sept 1944 a team of nine from B Company 4th Infantry Battalion of the Irish Army made a night march of 42 miles *67,59 km* in full battle order carrying 40 lb *18,1 kg* in 11 hr 49 min.

Air Forces *Oldest*

The earliest autonomous air force is the Royal Air Force whose origin began with the Royal Flying Corps (created 13 May 1912); the Air Battalion of the Royal Engineers (1 Apr 1911) and the Corps of Royal Engineers Balloon Section (1878) which was first operational in Botswana (then Bechuanaland) in 1884. The Prussian Army used a balloon near Strasbourg, France as early as 24 Sept 1870.

Largest

The greatest Air Force of all time was the United States Army Air Force (now called the US Air Force), which had 79,908 aircraft in July 1944 and 2,411,294 personnel in March 1944. The US Air Force including strategic air forces had 592,000 personnel and 3700 combat aircraft in mid-1983. The USSR Air Force is undergoing massive reorganisation but best estimates indicate 465,000 men in mid-1984. It had 5950 combat aircraft and 2300 armed helicopters. In addition, the USSR's Offensive Strategic Rocket Forces had about 325,000 operational personnel in mid-1983. The strength of the Royal Air Force was 89,827 with 620 combat aircraft in mid-1983.

BOMBS

Heaviest

The heaviest conventional bomb ever used operationally was the Royal Air Force's 'Grand Slam', weighing 22,000 lb *9975 kg* and measuring 25 ft 5 in *7,74 m* long, dropped on Bielefeld railway viaduct, Germany, on 14 Mar 1945. In 1949 the United States Air Force tested a bomb weighing 42,000 lb *19 050 kg* at Muroc Dry Lake, California, USA. The heaviest known nuclear bomb has been the 4 tonne 9 megatonne carried by US B-53 bombers. These bombs 3,67 m *12 ft 0½ in* in length were phased out by Jan 1984.

Atomic

The first atom bomb dropped on Japan by the United States in 1945 had an explosive power equivalent to that of 12,500 short tons *12.5 kilotons* of trinitrotoluene ($C_7H_5O_6N_3$), called TNT. Code-named 'Little Boy' it was 10 ft *3,04 m* long and weighed 9000 lb *4080 kg* and burst 1670 ft *509 m* above Hiroshima. The most powerful thermo-nuclear device so far tested is one with a power equivalent of 57,000,000 short tons of TNT, or 57 megatons, detonated by the USSR in the Novaya Zemlya area at 8.33 a.m. GMT on 30 Oct 1961. The shock wave was detected to have circled the world three times, taking 36 hr 27 min for the first circuit. Some estimates put the power of this device at between 62 and 90 megatons. The largest US H-Bomb tested was the 18–22 megaton 'Bravo' at Bikini Atoll, Marshall Islands on 1 Mar 1954. On 9 Aug 1961, Nikita Khrushchyov, then the Chairman of the Council of Ministers of the USSR, declared that the Soviet Union was capable of constructing a 100-megaton bomb, and announced the possession of one in East Berlin, Germany, on 16 Jan 1963. Such a device could make a crater in rock 355 ft *107 m* deep and 1.8 miles *2,9 km* wide and a fireball 46,000 ft or 8.7 miles *13,9 km* in diameter.

Atom bomb theory began with Einstein's publication of the $E = mc^2$ formula in *Annalen der Physik* in Leipzig on 14 May 1907. This postulated that the latent energy of 1 gram of matter was 89,875,517,873.781 dynes. It became a practicality with the mesothorium experiments of Otto Hahn, Fritz Strassman and Lise Meitner on 17 Dec 1938. Work started in the USSR on atomic bombs in June 1942 although their first chain reaction was not achieved until December 1945 by Dr Igor Vasilyevich Kurchatov. The concept of a thermo-nuclear fusion bomb was that of Edward Teller in 1942. Development was ordered by President Truman on 30 Jan 1950 and code-named 'Super'. The bomb only became practical as a result of a calculation by Stanislaw Ulam.

Largest nuclear weapons

The most powerful ICBM are the USSR's SS–18s (Model 4) with 10 half-megaton MIRVs (multiple independently-targetable re-entry vehicles). Models 1 and 3 have a single 20 megaton warhead. The US Minuteman III has 3 MIRVs each of 335 kiloton force.

No official estimate has been published of the potential power of the device known as Doomsday, but this far surpasses any tested weapon. If it were practicable to construct, it is mooted that a 50,000 megaton cobalt-salted device could wipe out the entire human race except people deep underground and who did not emerge for at least five years.

Largest 'conventional' explosion

The largest use of conventional explosive was for the demolition of the fortifications and U Boat pens at Heligoland on 18 Apr 1947. A net charge of 3797 tons *4061 tonnes* (7122 tonnes gross) was detonated by Commissioned Gunner E. C. Jellis of the RN team headed by Lt F. T. Woosnam RN aboard *HMS Lasso* lying 9 miles *14,5 km* out to sea.

Most bombed country

The most heavily bombed country in the world has been Laos. It has been estimated that between May 1964 and 26 Feb 1973 some 2½ million tons of bombs of all kinds were dropped along the North to South Ho Chi Minh Trail supply route to South Vietnam.

TANKS

Earliest

The first tank was 'No 1 Lincoln' modified to become '*Little Willie*' built by William Foster & Co Ltd of Lincoln. It first ran on 6 Sept 1915. Tanks were first taken into action by the Heavy Section, Machine-Gun Corps, which later became the Royal Tank Corps, at the battle of Flers-Courcelette in France, on 15 Sept 1916. The Mark I Male tank, which was armed with a pair of 6-pounder guns and 4 machine-guns, weighed 28 tons *28,4 tonnes* and was driven by a motor developing 105 hp which gave it a maximum road speed of 3 to 4 mph *4,8–6,4 km/h*.

Heaviest and fastest

The heaviest tank ever constructed was the German Panzer Kampfwagen Maus II, which weighed 189 tons *192 tonnes*. By 1945 it had reached only the experimental stage and was not proceeded with.

The heaviest operational tank used by any army was the 74 ton *75,2 tonnes* 13-man French Char de Rupture 2C bis of 1922. It carried a 155 mm howitzer and had two 250 hp engines giving a maximum speed of 8 mph *12 km/h*. The world's most heavily armed tank is the Soviet T-72 with a 125 mm *4.92 in* high velocity gun. The British AVRE 'Centurion' has a 165 mm *6.5 in* low velocity demolition gun. The world's fastest tank is the British Scorpion AFV which can touch 50 mph *80,5 km/h* with 75% payload.

The heaviest British armoured vehicle ever built was the 78-ton *79 tonnes* prototype 'Tortoise'. With a crew of seven and a designed speed of 12 mph *19 km/h*, this tank had a width 2 in *5 cm* less than that of the one-time operational 65-ton *66 tonnes* 'Conqueror'. The most heavily armed is the 52-ton *52,8 tonnes* 'Chieftain', put into service in November 1966, with a 120 mm gun.

GUNS

Earliest

Although it cannot be accepted as proved, the best opinion is that the earliest guns were constructed in North Africa, possibly by Arabs, in *c.* 1250. The earliest representation of an English gun is contained in an illustrated manuscript dated 1326 at Oxford. The earliest anti-aircraft gun was an artillery piece on a high angle mounting used in the Franco-Prussian War of 1870 by the Prussians against French balloons.

Largest

The two most massive guns ever constructed were used by the Germans in the siege of Sevastopol on the Eastern Front. They were of a calibre of 800 mm *31.5 in* with barrels 28,87 m *94 ft 8¼ in* long and named *Dore* and *Gustav*. Their remains were discovered, one near Metzenhof, Bavaria in Aug 1945 and the other in the Soviet zone. They were built by Krupp as railway guns carried on 24 cars two of which had 40 wheels each. The whole assembly of the gun was 42,9 m *141 ft* long and weighed 1323 tons *1344 tonnes* with a crew of 1500. The range for an 8¼ ton projectile was 29 miles *46,67 km*.

During the 1914–18 war the British Army used a gun of 18 in *457 mm* calibre. The barrel alone weighed 125 tons *127 tonnes*. In World War II the 'Bochebuster', a train-mounted howitzer with a calibre of 18 in *457 mm* firing a 2500 lb *1133 kg* shell to a maximum range of 22,800 yd *20 850 m*, was used from 1940 onwards as part of the Kent coast defences.

Greatest range

The greatest range ever attained by a gun was achieved by the HARP (High Altitude Research Project) gun consisting of two 16.5 in *419 mm* calibre barrels in tandem 36,4 m *119.4 ft* long weighing 150 tonnes/tons at Yuma, Arizona, USA. On 19 Nov 1966 an 84 kg *185 lb* projectile was fired to an altitude of 180 km *111.8 miles* or *590,550 ft*. The static V3 underground firing tubes built in 50 degree shafts near Mimoyecques, near Calais, France to bombard London were never operative.

The famous long range gun, which shelled Paris in World War I, was the *Kaiser Wilhelm geschütz* with a calibre of 220 mm *8.66 in*, a designed range of 79.5 miles *127,9 km* and an achieved range of 76 miles *122 km* from the Forest of Cérpy in March 1918. The Big Berthas were mortars of 420 mm *16.53 in* calibre and with a range of less than 9 miles *14 500 m*.

Mortars

The largest mortars ever constructed were Mallets mortar (Woolwich Arsenal, London, 1857), and the 'Little David' of World War II, made in the USA. Each had a calibre of 36¼ in *920 mm*, but neither was ever used in action. The heaviest mortar used was the tracked German 600 mm *23.6 in* siege piece known as 'Karl' before Stalingrad, USSR.

Largest cannon

The highest calibre cannon ever constructed is the *Tsar Puchka* (King of Cannons), now housed in the Kremlin, Moscow, USSR. It was built in the 16th century with a bore of 920 mm *36.2 in* and a barrel 10 ft 5 in *3,18 m* long. It weighs 2400 *pouds* (*sic*) or 40 tonnes. The Turks fired up to seven shots per day from a bombard 26 ft *7,92 m* long, with an internal calibre of 42 in *1066 mm* against the walls of Constantinople (now Istanbul) from 12 Apr to 29 May 1453. It was dragged by 60 oxen and 200 men and fired a 1200 lb *543 kg* stone cannon ball.

Military engines

The largest military catapults, or onagers, could throw a missile weighing 60 lb *27 kg* a distance of 500 yd *457 m*.

Conscientious Objector *Most Obdurate*

The only Conscientious Objector to be 6 times court martialled in World War II was Gilbert Lane of Wallington, Surrey. He served 31 months detention and 183 days imprisonment.

Nuclear Delivery Vehicles

As of 1 Jan 1984 the USSR deployed 2524 strategic nuclear delivery vehicles or 274 above the SALT II contractual ceiling. The USA on the same date deployed 1896 vehicles or 354 below the 2250 SALT II limit.

5. JUDICIAL

LEGISLATION AND LITIGATION

Statutes *Oldest*

The earliest known judicial code was that of King Ur-Hammu during the third dynasty of Ur, Iraq, in *c.* 2110 BC. The oldest

English statute in the Statute Book is a section of the Statute of Marlborough of 1267, retitled in 1948 'The Distress Act, 1267'. Some statutes enacted by Henry II (d. 1189) and earlier kings are even more durable as they have been assimilated into the Common Law. An extreme example is Ine's Law concerning the administration of shires. Ine reigned 689–726 AD.

Longest in the United Kingdom

Measured in bulk the longest statute of the United Kingdom, is the Income Corporation Taxes Act, 1970, which ran to 540 sections, 15 schedules and 670 pages. It is 1½ in *37 mm* thick and costs £8.00. However, its 540 sections are surpassed in number by the 748 of the Merchant Shipping Act, 1894. Of old statutes, 31 George III xiv, the Land Tax Act of 1791, written on parchment, consists of 780 skins forming a roll 1170 ft *360 m* long.

Shortest

The shortest statute is the Parliament (Qualification of Women) Act, 1918, which runs to 27 operative words—'A woman shall not be disqualified by sex or marriage from being elected to or sitting or voting as a Member of the Commons House of Parliament'. Section 2 contains a further 14 words giving the short title.

Most inexplicable

Certain passages in several Acts have always defied interpretation and the most inexplicable must be a matter of opinion. A Judge of the Court of Session of Scotland once sent the Editor his candidate which reads, 'In the Nuts (unground), (other than ground nuts) Order, the expression nuts shall have reference to such nuts, other than ground nuts, as would but for this amending Order not qualify as nuts (unground) (other than ground nuts) by reason of their being nuts (unground).'

Earliest English patent

The earliest of all known English patents was that granted by Henry VI in 1449 to Flemish-born John of Utyman for making the coloured glass required for the windows of Eton College. The peak number of applications for patents filed in the United Kingdom in any one year was 63,614 in 1969. The shortest, concerning a harrow attachment, of 48 words was filed on 14 May 1956 while the longest, comprising 2318 pages of text and 495 pages of drawings, was filed on 31 Mar 1965 by IBM to cover a computer.

Most protracted litigation

The longest contested law suit ever recorded ended in Poona, India on 28 Apr 1966, when Balasaheb Patloji Thorat received a favourable judgement on a suit filed by his ancestor Maloji Thorat 761 years earlier in 1205. The points at issue were rights of presiding over public functions and precedences at religious festivals.

The dispute over the claim of the Prior and Convent (now the Dean and Chapter) of Durham Cathedral to administer the spiritualities of the diocese during a vacancy in the See grew fierce in 1283. It flared up again in 1672 and 1890; an attempt in November 1975 to settle the issue, then 692 years old, was unsuccessful. Neither side admit the legitimacy of writs of appointment issued by the other even though identical persons are named.

Fastest trial

The law's shortest delay occurred in Duport Steel and Others *v.* Sirs and Others heard in the High Court on 25 Jan 1980; the appeal was heard on 26 Jan and the appeal heard in the House of Lords on 1 Feb (am) with the decision given pm.

Longest trial

The longest trial in criminal history was *People of the State of California v Angelo Buono, Jr.* involving 10 charges of the Hillside murders of young women from 18 Oct 1977 to Feb 1978. The jury trial took 345 trial days over 2 years 2 days (16 Nov 1981–18 Nov 1983) with a 57,079 page transcript, 400 witnesses and 2000 exhibits. Judge Ronald M. George imposed nine sentences of life without parole on 9 Jan 1984.

Longest British trials

The longest trial in the annals of British justice was the Tichborne personation case. The civil trial began on 11 May 1871, lasted 103 days and collapsed on 6 Mar 1872. The criminal trial went on for 188 days, resulting in a sentence on 28 Feb 1874 for two counts of perjury (two 7 year consecutive terms of imprisonment with hard labour) on the London-born Arthur Orton, *alias* Thomas Castro (1834–98), who claimed to be Roger Charles Tichborne (1829–54), the elder brother of Sir Alfred Joseph Doughty-Tichborne, 11th Bt (1839–66). The whole case thus spanned 1025 days. The jury were out for only 30 minutes.

The impeachment of Warren Hastings (1732–1818), which began in 1788, dragged on for seven years until 23 Apr 1795, but the trial lasted only 149 days. He was appointed a member of the Privy Council in 1814.

The fraud case *R v Bouzaglo and others* ended before Judge Brian Gibbens on 1 May 1981 having lasted 274 days. They appealed on 10 Dec 1981. Trial costs were estimated at £2.5 million.

The fluoridation case *McColl v Strathclyde Regional Council* before Lord Jauncey lasted 204 days ending on 27 JULY 1982.

Murder

The longest murder trial in Britain was that at the Old Bailey, London of Reginald Dudley, 51, and Robert Maynard, 46 in the Torso Murder of Billy Moseley and Micky Cornwall which ran before Mr Justice Swanwick from 11 Nov 1976 to 17 June 1977 with 136 trial days. Both men were sentenced to life (minimum 15 years) imprisonment. The costs were estimated to exceed £500,000 and the evidence 3,500,000 words.

Divorce

The longest trial of a divorce case in Britain was *Gibbons v. Gibbons and Roman and Halperin*. On 19 Mar 1962, after 28 days, Mr Alfred George Boyd Gibbons was granted a decree *nisi* against his wife Dorothy for adultery with Mr John Halperin of New York City, NY, USA.

Shortest trials

The shortest recorded British murder hearings were *R. v. Murray* on 28 Feb 1957 and *R. v. Cawley* at Winchester assizes on 14 Dec 1959. The proceedings occupied only 30 sec on each occasion.

Litigants in Person

Since the Union of Parliament in 1707 the only Scot to win an appeal in person before the House of Lords has been Mr Jack Malloch, an Aberdeen Schoolmaster in 1971. He was restored to his employment under the dormant but operative Teachers Act, 1882 with costs.

Dr Mark Feldman, a podiatric surgeon, of Lauderhill, Florida became the first litigant in person to secure 7 figures ($1 million) before a jury in compensatory and punitive damages in Sept 1980. The case concerned conspiracy and fraud alleged against 6 other doctors.

Longest address

The longest address in a British court was in *Globe and Phoenix Gold Mining Co. Ltd. v. Amalgamated Properties of Rhodesia*. Mr William Henry Upjohn, KC (1853–1941) concluded his speech on 22 Sept 1916, having addressed the court for 45 days.

Highest bail *World*

The highest amount ever demanded as bail was $46,500,000 (then *£16,608,333*) against Antonio De Angelis in a civil damages suit by the Harbor Tank Storage Co. filed in the Superior Court, Jersey City, New Jersey, USA on 16 Jan 1964 in the Salad Oil Swindle. He was released on 4 June 1973. Hassen Ebtehaj, later Chairman of the Iranian Bank in Teheran, was in 1967 granted bail in excess of $50 million.

Great Britain

The highest bail figure in a British court is £325,000 each, granted to Roy Garner and Kenneth Howard of North London by the High Court on 31 Mar 1983. They had been in custody after arrest at Gatwick Airport in connection with trading in Krugerrands.

Longest arbitration

The longest arbitration (under the 1950 Act) on record has been the Royce Arbitration. It lasted 239 days and concerned the Milchell Construction Co. and the East Anglian Regional Hospital Board over the building of Peterborough Hospital.

The longest case before an Industrial Tribunal has been 44 days during more than 13 months (2 May 1977–29 June 1978) when the columnist C. Gordon Tether contested the fairness of his dismissal by *The Financial Times* in person.

Best attended trial

The greatest attendance at any trial was that of Major Jesús Sosa Blanco, aged 51, for an alleged 108 murders. At one point in the 12½ hr trial (5.30 p.m. to 6 a.m., 22–23 Jan 1959), 17,000 people were present in the Havana Sports Palace, Cuba. He was executed on 18 Feb 1959.

Greatest damages *Personal injury World*

The greatest personal injury damages ever awarded were to a male child of undisclosed identity born in 1979 at the US Army's Le Herman General Hospital in a medical malpractice suit. If the child which had 'total cerebral palsy' lives out his expectation of life the potential US federal government payment will reach $70 million. Reports of 30 Sept 1983 did not disclose the name of the US Army doctor.

On 24 Nov 1983 a jury in Corpus Christi, Texas, USA awarded punitive damages of $106 million *£75 million* against the Ford Motor Co for alleged design faults in the Ford Mustang II in which Bevary Durrill, 20, died in 1974. An appeal is pending.

Great Britain

The record damages in the High Court are £414,563 awarded by Mr Justice Taylor in December 1981 to Mrs Carol Brown, of Morden, Surrey, against Merton, Sutton and Wandsworth Area Health Authority for injuries resulting from the administration of epidural anaesthesia during the birth of her first child in January 1979.

Breach of contract

The greatest damages ever awarded for a breach of contract were £610,392, awarded on 16 July 1930 to the Bank of Portugal against the printers Waterlow & Sons Ltd, of London, arising from their unauthorized printing of 580,000 five-hundred escudo notes in 1925. This award was upheld in the House of Lords on 28 Apr 1932. One of the perpetrators, Arthur Virgilio Alves Reis, served 16 years (1930–46) in gaol.

Breach of promise

The largest sum involved in a breach of promise suit in the United Kingdom was £50,000, accepted in 1913 by Miss Daisy Markham, *alias* Mrs Annie Moss (d. 20 Aug 1962, aged 76), in settlement against the 6th Marquess of Northampton DSO (1885–1978).

Defamation *World*

A sum of $16,800,000 (*£6,720,000*) was awarded to Dr John J. Wild, 58, at the Hennepin District Court, Minnesota, USA, on 30 Nov 1972 against The Minnesota Foundation and others for defamation, bad-faith termination of a contract, interference with professional business relationship and $10.8 million in punitive damages. The Supreme Court of Minnesota granted an option of a new trial or a $1.5 million *remittitur* to Dr Wild on 10 Jan 1975. The $39.6 million awarded in Columbus, Ohio on 1 Mar 1980 to Robert Guccione, publisher of *Penthouse*, for defamation against Lowry Flynt, publisher of *Hustler* was reduced by Judge Craig Wright to $4 million on 17 Apr 1980. The hearing ended in May 1982 with *Penthouse* being cleared of libel.

The greatest damages for defamation ever awarded in the United Kingdom have been £327,000 in the Courts in Edinburgh in favour of Capital Life Assurance Co against the *Scottish Daily Record* and the *Sunday Mail* for articles published in the latter in 1975.

The most expensive and longest defamation trial was *Orme v. Associated Newspapers Ltd.*, known as the Moonies case before Mr Justice Comyn from 6 Oct 1980 to 31 Mar 1981. The *Daily Mail*'s article of May 1978 was found not to be defamatory of the Unification Church. Costs had reached £800,000 when leave to appeal to the House of Lords was refused on 10 Feb 1983.

A $640 million libel suit was brought by the California resort La Costa against *Penthouse* and its publisher in March 1975. In May 1982 a jury found for the magazine. In July their verdict was set aside by a California judge, who was then removed from the case. Costs exceed $10 million to date.

Greatest compensation for Wrongful Imprisonment

William De Palma (b. 1938) of Whittier, California, agreed to a $750,000 (*then £340,000*) settlement for 16 months wrongful imprisonment in McNeil Island Federal Prison, on 12 Aug 1975 after a 15 year sentence for armed robbery in Buena Park on forged fingerprint evidence in 1968.

The greatest Crown compensation in Britain for wrongful imprisonment has been £17,500 paid to Laszlo Virag, 35, who had been sentenced to 10 years imprisonment at Gloucester assizes in 1969 for theft and shooting and wounding a police officer. His acceptance of this sum was announced on 23 Dec 1974 after his having been released in April 1974 on grounds of mistaken identification.

Greatest Alimony

The highest alimony awarded by a court has been $2,261,000 (*then £983,000*) against George Storer Sr, 74, in favour of his third wife Dorothy, 73, in Miami, Florida on 29 Oct 1974. Mr Storer, a broadcasting executive, was also ordered to pay his ex-wife's attorney $200,000 (*then £86,950*) in fees.

Greatest Alimony Suit

Belgian born Sheika Dena Al-Fassi, 23, filed the highest ever alimony claim of $3000 million (*then £1666 million*) against her former husband Sheik Mohammed Al-Fassi, 28, of the Saudi Arabia royal family in Los Angeles, California in February 1982. Mr Marvin Mitchelson explaining the size of the settlement claim alluded to the Sheik's wealth which included 14 homes in Florida alone and numerous private aircraft. On 14 June 1983 she was awarded $81 million (*then £52 million*) and declared she would be 'very very happy' if she was able to collect.

Greatest divorce settlement

The highest High Court divorce award received was £700,000 on 13 Nov 1980 for 'Mrs P' after 23 years of marriage against her former husband from Jersey from whom she had been receiving £6000 per annum. In *Edgar v Edgar* in 1980, £750,000 was awarded but this was set aside on appeal when Mrs Edgar accepted a much lesser figure.

Patent case

The greatest settlement ever made in a patent infringement suit is $55.8 million (*£37.2 million*) in Pfizer Inc v International Rectifier Corp. and Rochelle Laboratories over the antibiotic dioxycycline on 5 July 1983.

Largest suit

The highest amount of damages ever sought to date is $675,000,000,000,000,000 (then equivalent to 10 times the US national wealth) in a suit by Mr I. Walton Bader brought in the US District Court, New York City on 14 Apr 1971 against General Motors and others for polluting all 50 states.

Largest Law firm

The world's largest law firm is Baker & McKenzie with 600 lawyers in 29 countries. It was founded in Chicago in 1949.

Highest costs

The trial judge in *R v. Sinclair and others* (the handless corpse murder) ordered the international drug trafficker Alexander James Sinclair, 36 of N.Z. (sentenced to a minimum term of 20 years for the murder of Marty Johnstone found in a quarry at Chorley, Lancashire) to pay £1 million for the Crown's costs.

The most expensive man-hunt in police history was one costing £4 million terminated on 13 June 1981 with the arrest of Peter William Sutcliffe, known as the Yorkshire Ripper, in Sheffield, South Yorkshire. His trial at the Old Bailey, London, cost £250,000 and resulted in his being sentenced to a minimum of 30 years for 13 murders and 7 attempted murders which orphaned 25 children.

Longest lease

Part of the Cattle Market, Dublin, Ireland was leased by John Jameson to the city's corporation on a lease for 100,000 years expiring on 21 January AD 101,863.

Greatest lien

The greatest lien ever imposed by a court is 40,000 million lire (*then £27 million*) on 9 Apr 1974 upon Vittorio and Ida Riva in Milan for back taxes allegedly due on a chain of cotton mills around Turin, Italy.

Wills *Shortest*

The shortest valid will in the world is 'Vše zene', the Czech for 'All to wife', written and dated 19 Jan 1967 by Herr Karl

Britain's most loquacious ever lawyer W. H. Upjohn KC. His concluding speech in the Globe and Phoenix Gold Mining case of 1916 went on for 45 days.

Tausch of Langen, Hesse, Germany. The shortest will contested but subsequently admitted to probate in English law was the case of *Thorn v. Dickens* in 1906. It consisted of the three words 'All for Mother'.

Longest

The longest will on record was that of Mrs Frederica Cook (USA), in the early part of the century. It consisted of four bound volumes containing 95,940 words. The will of Thomas Cubitt (1788–1855), the London builder, ran to 34,740 words.

Judges *Most Durable*

The oldest recorded active judge was Judge Albert R. Alexander (1859–1966) of Plattsburg, Missouri, USA. He was the magistrate and probate judge of Clinton County until his retirement aged 105 years 8 months on 9 July 1965.

United Kingdom

The greatest recorded age at which any British judge has sat on a bench was 93 years 9 months in the case of Sir William Francis Kyffin Taylor, GBE, KC (*later* Lord Maenan), who was born on 9 July 1854 and retired as presiding judge of the Liverpool Court of Passage in April 1948, having held that position since 1903. Sir Salathiel Lovell (1619–1713) was, however, still sitting when he died on 3 May 1713 in his 94th or 95th year. The greatest age at which a House of Lords judgement has been given is 92 in the case of the 1st Earl of Halsbury (b. 3 Sept 1823) in 1916. Lord Chief Baron of Exchequer in Ireland, the Rt. Hon. Christopher Palles (1831–1920) served for 42 years from 17 Feb 1874 till 1916.

Master of the Rolls

The longest tenure of the Mastership of the Rolls since the office was inaugurated in 1286 has been 24 years 7 months by David de Wollore from 2 July 1346 to 27 March 1371. The longest tenure since the Supreme Court Judicature Act, 1881 has been that of 20 years by Lord Denning (b. 23 Jan 1899) from 1962 to 30 Sept 1982. He had been first appointed a high court judge in 1944. William Morland held the office for 77 days while in 1629 Sir Humphrey May died 'soon after' his appointment on 10 April.

Judge Youngest

No collated records on the ages of judicial appointments exist.

However David Elmer Ward had to await the legal age of 21 before taking office after nomination in 1932 as Judge of the County Court at Fort Myers, Florida, USA.

The youngest certain age at which any English judge has been appointed is 31, in the case of Sir Francis Buller (b. 17 Mar 1746), who was appointed Second Judge of the County Palatine of Chester on 27 Nov 1777, and Puisne Judge of the King's Bench on 6 May 1778, aged 32 years 1 month. The lowest age of appointment this century has been 42 years 2 months of Lord Hodson in 1937.

Most Judges
Lord Balmerino was found guilty of treason by 137 of his peers on 28 July 1746. In *R* v. *Canning* at the Old Bailey in 1754 Elizabeth Canning was deported to Connecticut for wilful perjury by 19 judges voting 10 to 9. In *Young, James and Webster* v. *United Kingdom*, the British Rail 'Closed Shop' case, before the European Court of Human Rights in Strasbourg on 3–4 Mar 1981, Mr David Calcutt QC won a judgement for the railwaymen by 18 to 3.

Youngest English QC
The earliest age at which a barrister has taken silk this century is 33 years 8 months in the case of Mr (later the Rt Hon Sir) Francis Raymond Evershed (1899–1966) in April 1933. He was later Lord Evershed, Master of the Rolls. Buller (see above) was nepotistically given silk aged 31, being a nephew of the then Lord Chancellor, Lord Bathurst.

Most successful
Sir Lionel Luckhoo KCMG CBE, senior partner of Luckhoo and Luckhoo of Georgetown, Guyana succeeded in getting his 245th successive murder charge acquittal by 12 Aug 1982.

Most Durable Solicitors
William George (1865–1967), brother of David Lloyd George, passed his preliminary law examination in May 1880 and was practising until December 1966 aged 101 years 9 months. The most durable firm is Thomson, Snell & Passmore of Tonbridge, Kent begun by the Rev Nicholas Hooper, a part-time scrivener in 1570.

CRIME

Mass Killings *China*
The greatest massacre ever imputed by the government of one sovereign nation against the government of another is that of 26,300,000 Chinese during the regime of Mao Tse-tung between 1949 and May 1965. This accusation was made by an agency of the USSR Government in a radio broadcast on 7 Apr 1969. The broadcast broke down the figure into four periods:—2.8 million (1949–52); 3.5 million (1953–7); 6.7 million (1958–60); and 13.3 million (1961–May 1965). The highest reported death figures in single monthly announcements on Peking radio were 1,176,000 in the provinces of Anhwei, Chekiang, Kiangsu, and Shantung, and 1,150,000 in the Central South Provinces. Po I-po, Minister of Finance, is alleged to have stated in the organ *For a lasting peace, for a people's democracy* 'in the past three years (1950–2) we have liquidated more than 2 million bandits'. General Jacques Guillermaz, a French diplomat estimated the total executions between February 1951 and May 1952 at between 1 million and 3 million. In April 1971 the Executive cabinet or *Yuan* of the implacably hostile government of The Republic of China in Taipei, Taiwan announced its official estimate of the mainland death roll in the period 1949–69 as 'at least 39,940,000'. This figure, however, excluded 'tens of thousands' killed in the Great Proletarian Cultural Revolution, which began in late 1966. The Walker Report published by the US Senate Committee of the Judiciary in July 1971 placed the parameters of the total death roll within China since 1949 between 32.25 and 61.7 million. An estimate of 63.7 million was published by Jean-Pierre Dujardin in *Figaro* magazine of 19–25 Nov 1978.

USSR
The total death roll in the Great Purge, or *Yezhovshchina*, in the USSR, in 1936–8 has, not surprisingly, never been published. Evidence of its magnitude may be found in population statistics which show a deficiency of males from *before* the outbreak of the 1941–5 war. The reign of terror was administered by the *Narodny Kommissariat Vnutrennykh Del*

(NKVD), or People's Commissariat of Internal Affairs, the Soviet security service headed by Nikolay Ivanovich Yezhov (1895–1939), described by Nikita Khrushchyov in 1956 as a 'degenerate'. S. V. Utechin, regarded estimates of 8,000,000 or 10,000,000 victims as 'probably not exaggerations'. On 17 Aug 1942 Stalin indicated to Churchill in Moscow that 10 million *kulaks* had been liquidated for resisting the collectivization of their farms. Nobel Prize winner Alexander Solzhenitsyn estimated the loss of life from State repression and terrorism from October 1917 to December 1959 under Lenin, Stalin and Khrushchev at 66,700,000.

Nazi Germany
Obersturmbannführer (Lt-Col) Karl Adolf Eichmann (b. Solingen, W. Germany 19 Mar 1906) of the SS was hanged in a small room inside Ramleh Prison, near Tel Aviv, Israel, at just before midnight (local time) on 31 May 1962, for his complicity in the deaths of an indeterminably massive number of Jews during World War II, under the instruction given in April 1941 by Adolf Hitler (1889–1945) for 'the Final Solution' (*Endlösung*). The best estimate is that 5.8 million Jews were killed in Europe in 1939–45.

At the SS (*Schutzstaffel*) extermination camp (*Vernichtungslager*) known as Auschwitz-Birkenau (Oświęcim-Brzezinka), near Oświęcim (Auschwitz), in southern Poland, where a minimum of 920,000 people (Soviet estimate is 4,000,000) were exterminated from 14 June 1940 to 18 Jan 1945, the greatest number killed in a day was 6000. The man who operated the release of the 'Zyklon B' cyanide pellets into the gas chambers there during this time was Sgt Major Moll (variously Mold). The Nazi (*Nationalsozialistische Deutsche Arbeiterpartei*) Commandant during the period 1940–3 was Rudolph Franz Höss who was tried in Warsaw from 11 Mar to 2 Apr 1947 and hanged, aged 47, at Oświęcim on 15 Apr 1947.

Forced labour
No official figures have been published of the death roll in Corrective Labour Camps in the USSR, first established in 1918. The total number of such camps was known to be more than 200 in 1946 but in 1956 many were converted to less severe Corrective Labour Colonies. An estimate published in the Netherlands puts the death roll between 1921 and 1960 at 19,000,000. The camps were administered by the *Cheka* until 1922, the OGPU (1922–34), the NKVD (1934–46), the MVD (1946–53) and the KGB (Komitet Gosudarstvennoi Bezopasnostc) since 1953. Solzhenitsyn's aggregate best estimate is that the number of inmates has been 66 million. The study by S. Grossu published 1975 stated there were then 2 million political prisoners in 96 camps. In China there are no published official statistics on the numbers undergoing *Lao Jiao* (Education through Labour) nor *Lao Dong Gai Zao* (Reform through manual labour). An estimate published by Bao Ruo-wang, who were released in 1964 due to his father having been a Corsican, was 16,000,000 which then approached 3 per cent of the population.

Genocide
In the genocide in Kampuchea, formerly Cambodia, according to the Khmer Rouge foreign minister Ieng Sarg, more than a third of the 8 million Khmers were killed between 17 Apr 1975 and January 1979. The highest 'class' ideals induced indifference to individual suffering to the point of serving as a warrant for massacre. Under the rule of Saloth Sar *alias* Pol Pot, a founder member of the CPK (Communist Party of Kampuchea, formed in September 1960) towns, money and property were abolished and economical execution by bayonet and club introduced for such offences as falling asleep during the day, asking too many questions, playing non-Communist music, being old and feeble, being the offspring of an 'undesirable' or being too well educated. Deaths at the Tuol Sleng interrogation centre reached 582 in a day. It has been estimated that 35 million Chinese were wiped out in the Mongolian invasion of 1210–19.

Saving of Life
The greatest number of people saved from extinction by one man is an estimated 90,000 Jews in Budapest, Hungary from July 1944 to January 1945 by the Swedish diplomat Raoul Wallenberg (b. 4 Aug 1912). After escaping an assassination attempt by the Nazis, he was imprisoned without trial by the

Soviet Union. On 6 Feb 1957 Mr Gromyko said Prisoner 'Walenberg' had died in a cell in Lubyanka Jail, Moscow on 16 July 1947. Sighting reports within the Gulag system have persisted for 35 years after his disappearance. He was made an Honorary Citizen of the USA on 5 Oct 1981 and in March 1984 there was an agitation in Hungary to restore his removed statue to St Stephan's Park, in Budapest.

Largest criminal organization

The largest syndicate of organized crime is the Mafia or La Cosa Nostra, which has infiltrated the executive, judiciary and legislature of the United States. It consists of some 3000 to 5000 individuals in 25 'families' federated under 'The Commission' with an annual turnover in vice, gambling, protection rackets, cigarettes, bootlegging, hijacking, narcotics, loan-sharking and prostitution estimated in a US News & World Report of Dec 1982 at $200 billion. The origin in the US dates from 1869 in New Orleans. The biggest Mafia (derived from an arabic expression connoting beauty, excellence allied with bravery) killing was on 11–13 Sept 1931 when 40 mafiosi were liquidated following the murder in New York of Salvatore Maranzano, *Il Capo di Tutti Capi*, on 10 Sept.

Murder rate *Highest*

The country with the highest recorded murder rate is Brazil, with 104 homicides for each 100,000 of the population in 1983, or 370 per day. A total of 592 deaths was attributed to one Colombian bandit leader, Teófilo ('Sparks') Rojas, aged 27, between 1948 and his death in an ambush near Armenia on 22 Jan 1963. Some sources attribute 3500 slayings to him during La Violencia of 1945–62.

The highest homicide rates recorded in New York City have been 58 in a week in July 1972 and 13 in a day in August 1972. In 1973 the total for Detroit, Michigan (pop. then 1.5 million) was 751. The Chicago Crime Commission published in March 1983 a list of 1081 unsolved gang slayings since 1919.

Lowest

The country with the lowest officially recorded rate in the world is The Maldives with a nil rate among its naturals since its independence in July 1965. In the Indian state of Sikkim, in the Himalayas, murder is, however, practically unknown, while in the Hunza area of Kashmir, in the Karakoram, only one definite case by a Hunzarwal has been recorded since 1900.

Great Britain

In Great Britain the total number of homicides and deaths from injuries purposely inflicted by other persons in the year 1981 was 612. This figure compares with a murder total of 124 in 1937 and 125 in 1958.

Terrorist Outrages

The greatest civilian death toll from a terrorist bomb was 85 killed and 200 injured at the central railway station, Bologna, Italy on 2 Aug 1980. Pierluigi Pagliai, 28, described as a suspect, was arrested in a shoot-out in Bolivia on 10 Oct 1982.

Most prolific murderers *World*

It was established at the trial of Behram, the Indian thug, that he had strangled at least 931 victims with his yellow and white cloth strip or *ruhmal* in the Oudh district between 1790 and 1840. It has been estimated that at least 2,000,000 Indians were strangled by Thugs (*burtotes*) during the reign of the Thugee (pronounced tugee) cult from 1550 until its final suppression by the British *raj* in 1853. The greatest number of victims ascribed to a murderess has been 650 in the case of Countess Elizabet Bathory (1560–1614) of Hungary. At her trial which began on 2 Jan 1611 a witness testified to seeing a list of her victims in her own handwriting totalling this number. All were alleged to be young girls from the neighbourhood of her castle at Csejthe where she died on 21 Aug 1614. She had been walled up in her room for the 3½ years after being found guilty.

20th century

Pedro Alonso López (b. Columbia, 1949) known as the 'Columbian Monster', was reported captured by the villagers of Ambato, Ecuador in early March 1980. He admitted to more than 300 murders of pre-teen girls in Colombia, Peru and Ecuador since 1973. The remains of 53 victims of the 110 admitted to in Ecuador were rapidly detected after his confession.

In drunken rampage lasting 8 hours on 26–27 Apr 1982 Policeman Wou Bom-Kon, 27, killed 57 people and wounded 35 with 176 rounds of rifle ammunition and hand grenades in the Kyong Sang-Namdo province of South Korea. He blew himself up with a grenade.

United Kingdom

Six men were each charged with 21 murders at Lancaster Crown Court on 9 June 1975 concerning the bombing of the two Birmingham public houses Mulberry Bush and Tavern in the Town on 21 Nov 1974. They were John Walker, Patrick Hill, Robert Hunter, Noel McIlkenny, William Power and Hugh Callaghan. The Home Office began, in February 1981, to investigate the attribution of 26 deaths between 1973 and 1979 to the self-confessed arsonist Bruce Lee. In January 1981 he was sent to a mental hospital by Leeds Crown Court, but on 14 Mar 1982 he retracted his confessions and on 2 Dec 1983 the Court of Appeal quashed charges of causing 11 of the deaths.

Judith Minna Ward, 25, of Stockport, Cheshire was convicted on 11 separate murder charges on 4 Nov 1974 making 12 in all arising from the explosion in an army coach on the M.62 near Drighlington, West Yorkshire on 4 Feb 1974. Mary Ann Cotton (*née* Robson) (b. 1832, East Rainton, County Durham),

left: George Blake (*né* Behar), whose treachery attracted a term of 42 years' imprisonment in 1961. This was the longest ever in British penal history. *centre:* Ruth Ellis, 28, the 14th and last woman executed in Britain this century. She was hanged for murder in 1955. *right:* S S Colonel Karl Adolf Eichmann hanged in Tel Aviv, Israel, in 1962. He was tried and found guilty of being the foremost organiser of Hitler's genocide of European Jewry in 1941–45.

CENTRAL PRESS

MIRRORPIC

PLANET NEWS

hanged in Durham Jail on 24 Mar 1873 is believed to have poisoned 14, possibly 20, people.

Dennis Andrew Nilsen, 37 of 23 Cranley Gardens, Muswell Hill, north London admitted to 15 one at a time murders between Dec 1978 and Feb 1983 and was sentenced to life with a 25 year minimum on 4 Nov 1983.

Dominic McGlinchey was reported in November 1983 to have admitted to 30 killings in Northern Ireland before his arrest in and extradition from the Republic. On 7 May 1981 John Thompson of Hackney, London was found guilty at the Old Bailey of the 'specimen' murder by arson of Archibald Campbell and jailed for life. There were 36 other victims at the Spanish Club, Denmark St, London.

'Smelling out'
The greatest 'smelling out' recorded in African history occurred before Shaka (1787–1828) and 30,000 Nguni subjects near the River Umhlatuzana, Zululand (now Natal, South Africa) in March 1824. After 9 hr, over 300 were 'smelt out' as guilty of smearing the Royal *Kraal* with blood, by 150 witch-finders led by the hideous female *isangoma* Nobela. The victims were declared innocent when Shaka admitted to having done the smearing himself to expose the falsity of the power of his diviners. Nobela poisoned herself with atropine ($C_{17}H_{23}NO_3$), but the other 149 witch-finders were thereupon skewered or clubbed to death.

Suicide
The estimated daily rate of suicides throughout the world surpassed 1000 in 1965. The country with the highest suicide rate is Hungary, with 42.6 per 100,000 of the population in 1977. The country with the lowest recorded rate is Jordan with a single case in 1970 and hence a rate of 0.04 per 100,000. In England and Wales there were 4419 suicides in 1981, or an average of 12.1 per day. In the northern hemisphere April and May tend to be peak months.

Mass Suicide
The final total of the mass cyanide poisoning of the People's Temple cult near Port Kaituma, Guyana on 18 Nov 1978 was 913. The leader was the paranoid 'Rev.' Jim Jones of San Francisco, who had deposited 'millions of dollars' overseas.

Mass Poisonings
On 1 May 1981 the first victim of the Spanish cooking oil scandal fell ill. On 12 June it was discovered that his cause of death was the use of 'denatured' industrial colza from rape seed. By May 1984 the death toll was over 350 dead with thousands maimed. The manufacturers Ramon and Elias Ferrero await trial in Carabanchel Jail, Madrid.

Robbery
The greatest robbery on record was that of the Reichsbank following Germany's collapse in April/May 1945. The Pentagon in Washington described the event first published in the *Guinness* Book in 1957 as 'an unverified allegation'. *Nazi Gold* by Ian Sayer and Douglas Botting published in 1984 revealed full details and estimated the total haul at current values as £2,500 million.

On 26 Nov 1983 six masked men removed 6,800 bars of gold in 76 boxes worth £25 million from the Brinks-Mat Ltd vault at the Heathrow Trading Estate.

Art
The greatest recorded art robbery by market valuation was the removal of 19 paintings, valued at £8,000,000 taken from Russborough House, Blessington, County Wicklow, Ireland, the home of Sir Alfred and Lady Beit by 4 men and a woman on 26 Apr 1974. They included the £3 million Vermeer 'Lady Writing a Letter with her maid'. The paintings were recovered on 4 May near Glandore, County Cork. Dr Rose Bridgit Dugdale (b. 1941) was convicted. It is arguable that the value of the *Mona Lisa* at the time of its theft from The Louvre, Paris on 21 Aug 1911 was greater than this figure. It was recovered in Italy in 1913 when Vincenzo Perruggia was charged with its theft. On 1 Sept 1964 antiquities reputedly worth £10,000,000 were recovered from 3 warehouses near the Pyramids, Egypt.

Bank
During the extreme civil disorder prior to 22 Jan 1976 in Beirut, Lebanon, a guerilla force blasted the vaults of the British Bank of the Middle East in Bab Idriss and cleared out safe deposit boxes with contents valued by former Finance Minister, Lucien Dahadah, at $50 million and by another source as an 'absolute minimum' of $20 million.

Britain's greatest ever robbery was of 9 certificates of deposit worth more than £10 million from the Bank of Sepah-Iran, Eastcheap, London on 4–5 Dec 1982. A thermic lance was used.

Train
The greatest recorded train robbery occurred between about 3.03 a.m. and 3.27 a.m. on 8 Aug 1963, when a General Post Office mail train from Glasgow, Scotland, was ambushed at Sears Crossing and robbed at Bridego Bridge near Mentmore, Buckinghamshire. The gang escaped with about 120 mailbags containing £2,631,784 worth of bank notes being taken to London for destruction. Only £343,448 was recovered.

Jewels
The greatest recorded theft of jewels was from the bedroom of the 'well-guarded' villa of Prince Abdel Aziz Bin Ahmed Al-Thani near Cannes, France on 24 July 1980 valued at $16,000,000 (*then £7¼ million*). The haul from Bond Jewellers, Conduit St, London W1 on 20 June 1983 was estimated to be £6 million.

Greatest kidnapping ransom
Historically the greatest ransom paid was that for Atahualpa by the Incas to Francisco Pizarro in 1532–3 at Cajamarca, Peru which constituted a hall full of gold and silver worth in modern money some $170 million (*£95 million*).

The greatest ransom ever reported is 1500 million pesos (*£25,300,000*) for the release of the brothers Jorge Born, 40 and Juan Born, 39, of Bunge and Born, paid to the left wing urban guerilla group Montoneros in Buenos Aires, Argentina on 20 June 1975.

The youngest person kidnapped has been Carolyn Wharton born at 12.46 p.m. on 19 Mar 1955 in the Baptist Hospital, Texas, USA and kidnapped, by a woman disguised as a nurse, at 1.15 p.m. aged 29 min.

Greatest hijack ransom
The highest amount ever paid to aircraft hijackers has been $6 million (*then £3.42 million*) by the Japanese government in the case of a JAL DC-8 at Dacca Airport on 2 Oct 1977 with 38 hostages. Six convicted criminals were also exchanged. The Bangladesh government had refused to sanction any retaliatory action.

Largest narcotics haul
In Oct 1983 it was estimated that the narcotics crime in the USA was running at $80,000 million per annum with cocaine dealers turning a profit of $35,000 million and illegal domestic 'green collar' marijuana growers netting $13,900 million.

The greatest drug haul ever achieved was 12,500 kg *12.3 tons* of cocaine with a street value of $1,200 million (£860 million) taken in the Caqueta jungle province of Colombia on 10 Mar 1984 in 10 processing plants protected by the armed wing of the Colombian Communist Party FARC (Fuerzas Armadas Revolucionarias Columbias).

The bulkiest haul was 2850 long tons *2 903 000 kg* of Colombian marijuana in the 14 month long 'Operation Tiburon' concluded by the DEA with the arrest of 495 people and the seizure of 95 vessels announced on 5 Feb 1982.

The Home Office disclosed on 23 Dec 1977 that 13 million LSD tablets with a street value approaching £100 million had been destroyed on the conclusion of 'Operation Julie'.

Greatest banknote forgery
The greatest forgery was the German Third Reich government's forging operation, code name 'Bernhard', engineered by SS Sturmbannfuhrer Alfred Naujocks of the Technical Dept of the German Secret Service Amt VI F in Berlin in 1940–1. It involved £150,000,000 worth of £5 notes.

Biggest bank fraud
The largest amount of money named in a defalcation case has

been a gross £33,000,000 at the Lugano branch of Lloyd's Bank International Ltd in Switzerland on 2 Sept 1974. Mr Mark Colombo was arrested pending charges including falsification of foreign currency accounts and suppression of evidence.

Computer fraud

Between 1964 and 1973, 64,000 fake insurance policies were created on the computer of the Equity Funding Corporation involving $2000 million.

Stanley Mark Rifkin (b. 1946) was arrested in Carlsbad, California by the FBI on 6 Nov 1978 charged with defrauding a Los Angeles bank of $10.2 million (*then £4.85 million*) by manipulation of a computer system. He was sentenced to 8 years in June 1980.

Theft

It was estimated in Nov 1983 that the greatest theft in the world is running at $160,000 million per annum. This is the value of 'bosses time' paid for but not worked in the United States in 1983/84.

Welfare swindle

The greatest welfare swindle yet worked was that of the gypsy Anthony Moreno on the French Social Security in Marseille. By forging birth certificates and school registration forms, he invented 197 fictitious families and 3000 children on which he claimed benefits from 1960 to mid-1968. Moreno, nicknamed 'El Chorro' (the fountain), was later reported free of extradition worries and living in luxury in his native Spain having absquatulated with an estimated £2,300,000.

Largest object ever stolen by a single man

On a moonless night at dead calm high water on 5 June 1966 armed with only a sharp axe, N William Kennedy slashed free the mooring lines at Wolfe's Cove, St Lawrence Seaway, Quebec, Canada, of the 10,639 dwt S S *Orient Trader* owned by Steel Factors Ltd of Ontario. The vessel drifted to a waiting blacked out tug thus escaping a ban on any shipping movements during a violent wild-cat waterfront strike. She sailed for Spain.

Maritime fraud

A cargo of 180 000 tonnes of Kuwaiti crude oil on the supertanker *Salem* at Durban was sold without title to the South African government in Dec 1979. The ship mysteriously sank off Senegal on 17 Jan 1980 leaving the government to pay £148 million ($305 million) to Shell International who owned the shipment.

CAPITAL PUNISHMENT

Capital punishment is known to have dated at least from neolithic times as evidenced by the finding of Tollsneed man in Denmark. The countries in which capital punishment is still prevalent include China (perhaps 500 shootings per annum); South Africa (about 100 hangings for rape, robbery and murder); Turkey; Iran; USA (re-introduced in 38 States for the most heinous murders); USSR (23 capital offences including profiteering and speculation for which some 400 businessmen are shot annually).

Capital punishment was first abolished *de facto* in 1798 in Liechtenstein. The death penalty for murder was formally abolished in Britain on 18 Dec 1969. Between the 5–4 Supreme Court decision against capital punishment in June 1972 and January 1983, 38 of the 50 States of the USA voted to restore it.

Capital punishment in the British Isles dates from AD 450, but was abolished by William I and re-imposed by Henry I, reaching a peak in the reign of Edward VI (1547–53), when an average of 560 persons were executed annually at Tyburn alone. Even into the 19th century, there were 223 capital crimes, though people were, in practice, hanged for not more than 25 of these. Between 1830 and 1964 the most murderers hanged in a year was 27 (24 men, 3 women) in 1903. While in 1956 there were no executions.

Largest hanging

The most people hanged from one gallows was 38 Sioux Indians by William J. Duly outside Mankato, Minnesota, USA for the murder of unarmed citizens on 26 Dec 1862. The Nazi

Feldkommandant simultaneously hanged 50 Greek resistance men as a reprisal in Athens on 22 July 1944.

Last hangings

The last public execution in England took place outside Newgate Prison, London at 8 a.m. on 26 May 1868, when Michael Barrett was hanged for his part in the Fenian bomb outrage on 13 Dec 1867, when 12 were killed outside the Clerkenwell House of Detention, London. The earliest non-public execution was of the murderer Thomas Wells on 13 Aug 1868. The last public hanging in Scotland was that of the murderer Joe Bell in Perth in 1866. The last in the United States occurred at Owensboro, Kentucky in 1936. The last hangings in the United Kingdom were those of Peter Anthony Allen (b. 4 Apr 1943) at Walton Prison, Liverpool, and John Robson Walby (b. 1 Apr 1940), *alias* Gwynne Owen Evans, at Strangeways Gaol, Manchester both on 13 Aug 1964. They had been found guilty of the capital murder of John Alan West, on 7 Apr 1964. The 14th, youngest and last woman executed this century was Mrs Ruth Ellis (*née* Neilson), 28, for the murder of David Blakely, 25, shot outside the Magdala, Hampstead, on 10 Apr 1955. She was executed on 13 July at Holloway. The last hanging in the Republic of Ireland was in 1954.

Last from yard-arm

The last naval execution at the yard-arm was the hanging of Private John Dalliger, Royal Marines, aboard HMS *Leven* in Victoria Bay near Lu-ta, China, on 13 July 1860. Dalliger had been found guilty of two attempted murders.

Youngest

Although the hanging of persons under 18 was expressly excluded only in the Children's and Young Person's Act, 1933 (Sec. 33), no person under that age was, in fact, executed more recently than 1887. The lowest satisfactorily recorded age was of a boy aged 8 'who had malice, cunning and revenge' in firing two barns and who was hanged at Abingdon, Oxfordshire in the 17th century. The youngest persons hanged since 1900 have been six 18 year olds, the most recent of whom was Francis Robert George ('Flossie') Forsyth on 10 Nov 1960.

Oldest

The oldest person hanged in the United Kingdom since 1900 was a man of 71 named Charles Frembd (*sic*) at Chelmsford Gaol on 4 Nov 1914, for the murder of his wife at Leytonstone, Waltham Forest, Greater London. In 1822 John Smith, said to be 80, of Greenwich, Greater London, was hanged for the murder of a woman.

Last public guillotining

The last person to be publicly guillotined in France was the murderer Eugen Weidmann before a large crowd at Versailles, near Paris, at 4.50 a.m. on 17 June 1939. In January 1978 Marcel Chevalier was nominated to succeed his uncle Andre Obrecht as executioner who had in turn succeeded his uncle Henri Desfourneaux. Dr Joseph Ignace Guillotin (1738–1812) died a natural death. He had advocated the use of the machine designed by Dr Antoine Louis in 1789 in the French constituent assembly. The last use before abolition in 1981 was on 10 Sept 1977 at Baumettes Prison, Marseilles for the torturer and murderer Hamida Djandoubi, 28.

Death row

In January 1983 there were 1137 prisoners in 38 of the 50 US states on 'Death Row'. Caryl Whittier Chessman, aged 38 and convicted of 17 felonies, was executed on 2 May 1960 in the gas chamber at the California State Prison, San Quentin, California, USA. In 11 years 10 months and one week on 'death row', Chessman had won eight stays. Charlie Brooks became the sixth US citizen to be executed since 1967 on 14 Dec 1982 at Huntsville, Texas. He received a lethal injection of sodium thiopental, pancuronium bromide and potassium chloride.

Executioners

The longest period of office of a Public Executioner was that of William Calcraft (1800–79), who was in action from 1828 to 25 May 1874 and officiated at nearly every hanging outside and later inside Newgate Prison, London. On 2 Apr 1868 he hanged the murderess Mrs Frances Kidder, 25, outside Maidstone Jail, Kent—the last public execution of a woman.

For 56 years from 1900 to the retirement of Albert in February

National Debt

The largest national debt of any country in the world is that of the United States, where the gross federal public debt of the Federal Government supassed the 'trillion' (10^{12}) dollar mark on 30 Sept 1981. By February 1984 it had reached $1,457.5 billion. This amount in dollar bills would make a pile 79,083 miles *127 273 km* high, weighing 1,107,962 tons *1 021 946 tonnes.*

The National Debt in Great Britain was less than £1 million during the reign of James II in 1687. It was £142,545 million or £2527 per person at 31 Mar 1984. This amount placed in a pile of brand new £1 notes would be 8685.8 miles *13 978 km* in height.

Most Foreign Debt

The country most heavily in overseas debt is Brazil with $93,000 million by March 1984. The highest *per caput* is that of Chile with $17,000 million for a population of 11.5 million in mid-1983 or $1478 per person.

Gross National Product

The country with the largest Gross National Product is the United States reaching $3 trillion ($3 \times 10^{12}$) in 1981. By 1 Jan 1984 this was running at $3,432.0 billion. The GNP of the United Kingdom at factor cost was £257,509 million for 1983.

National wealth

The richest nation, measured by average per caput, is the United Arab Emirates with $30,070 in 1980. The USA which had taken the lead in 1910 was 14th behind 3 Arab, 9 West European countries and Brunei in 1980. The United Kingdom stood 25th with $7920 (*then £4400*) per head. It has been estimated that the value of all physical assets in the USA on 1 Jan 1983 was $12.5 trillion ($10^{12}$) or $53,800 per caput. The figure for private wealth in the United Kingdom was £325,000 million (1976) or £5811 per head.

Poorest country

The lowest published annual income per caput of any country in the world is Bhutan with a tentative $80 (1980) but the World Bank has no data for Kampuchea, Laos, Somalia or Vietnam.

Gold reserves *World*

The country with the greatest monetary gold reserve is the United States, whose Treasury had 263.37 million fine oz of the world's 946.91 million fine oz on hand in February 1984. Valued at $400 per fine oz, these amounts translate to $105,348.0 million and $378,764.0 million respectively. The United States Bullion Depository at Fort Knox, 30 Miles *48 km* south-west of Louisville, Kentucky, USA has been the principal Federal depository of US gold since Dec 1936. Gold is stored in 446,000 standard mint bars of 400 troy ounces *12,4414 kg* measuring $7 \times 3\frac{5}{8} \times 1\frac{5}{8}$ in, *17,7 × 9,2 × 4,1 cm.*

Gold and foreign currency reserves *Great Britain*

The lowest published figure for the sterling area's gold and convertible currency reserves was $298,000,000 (*then £74 million*) on 31 Dec 1940. The valuation on 1 Apr 1981 was a peak $28,212 million and the peak figure for gold was $7334 million on 31 Dec 1981. The figure for 1 Jan 1984 was $17,817 million of which $5,914 million was in gold.

Minimum Lending Rate

The highest ever figure for the British bank rate (since 13 Oct 1972, the Minimum Lending Rate) has been 17 per cent from 15 Nov 1979 to 3rd July 1980. The longest period without a change was the 12 years 13 days from 26 Oct 1939 to 7 Nov 1951, during which time the rate stayed at 2 per cent. This lowest ever rate had been first attained on 22 Apr 1852.

Balance of Payments

The most favourable current balance of payments figure for the United Kingdom has been a surplus of £7,272 million in 1981 (best quarter Jan–Mar £2,698 million). The worst figure was a deficit of £3,591 million in 1974. Monthly figures are regarded as too erratic to be of great significance.

Worst inflation *World*

The world's worst inflation occurred in Hungary in June 1946, when the 1931 gold pengő was valued at 130 trillion (1.3×10^{20}) paper pengős. Notes were issued for 'Egymillard billion' (one milliard billion or 10^{21}) pengős on 3 June and withdrawn on 11 July 1946. Vouchers for 1000 billion billion

(10^{27}) pengős were issued for taxation payment only. On 6 Nov 1923 the circulation of Reichsbank marks reached 400,338,326,350,700,000,000 and inflation was 755,700 million fold on 1913 levels. The country with the highest current rate of inflation is Argentina with 567% in mid-1984.

Worst inflation *Great Britain*

The United Kingdom's worst rate in a year has been for August 1974 to August 1975 when inflation ran at a rate of 26.9 per cent compared with 3.7 per cent for May 1982 to May 1983 and 5.1 per cent for May 1983 to May 1984. The Tax and Price Index (allowing for tax reliefs) was 3.0 per cent in June 1983. The peak TPI extrapolated figure was 31.9 per cent in August 1975.

PAPER MONEY

Earliest

Paper money is an invention of the Chinese first tried in AD 910 and prevalent by AD 970. The world's earliest bank notes (*banco-sedler*) were issued in Stockholm, Sweden, in July 1661. The oldest surviving banknote is one of 5 dalers dated 6 Dec 1662. The oldest surviving printed Bank of England note is one for £555 to bearer, dated 19 Dec 1699 ($4\frac{1}{2} \times 7\frac{1}{2}$ in, *11,4 × 19,6 cm*).

Largest and smallest

The largest paper money ever issued was the one kwan note of the Chinese Ming dynasty issue of 1368–99, which measured 9×13 in *22,8 × 33,0 cm*. In Oct 1983 one sold for £340. The smallest national note ever issued was the 10 bani note of the Ministry of Finance of Romania, in 1917. It measured (printed are) $27,5 \times 38$ mm *1.09 × 1.49 in*. Of German *notgeld* the smallest are the 1–3 pfg of Passau (1920–21) measuring $18 \times 18,5$ mm *0.70 × 0.72 in*.

Highest denominations *World*

The highest denomination notes in circulation are US Federal Reserve Bank notes for $10,000 (£5260). They bear the head of Salmon Portland Chase (1808–73). None has been printed since July 1944 and the US Treasury announced in 1969 that no further notes higher than $100 would be issued. Only 350 $10,000 bills remain in circulation or unretired.

Great Britain

Two Bank of England notes for £1,000,000 still exist, dated before 1812 but these were used only for internal accounting. In November 1977 the existence of a Treasury £1 million note dated 30 Aug 1948 came to light and was sold by private treaty for $A18,500 (*then £11,300*) in Australia.

The highest issued denominations have been £1000 notes, first printed in 1725, discontinued on 22 Apr 1943 and withdrawn on 30 Apr 1945. At least 16 of these notes were still unretired up to Nov 1979 (last data to be published). Of these perhaps 10 are in the hands of collectors or dealers.

Lowest denomination *World*

The lowest denomination legal tender bank note is the 1 sen (or 1/100th of a rupiah) Indonesian note. Its exchange value in mid-1984 was 140 to the new penny.

Great Britain

The lowest denomination Bank of England notes ever printed were the black on pale blue half-crown (now $12\frac{1}{2}$p) notes in 1941, signed by the late Sir Kenneth Peppiatt. Very few examples have survived and they are now valued at from £750.

Highest circulation

The highest ever Bank of England note circulation in the United Kingdom was £12,152,000,000 on 14 Dec 1983—equivalent to a pile of £1 notes 603.95 miles *971,97 km* high.

CHEQUES AND COINS

Largest *World*

The greatest amount paid by a single cheque in the history of banking has been one for Rs. 16,640,000,000 equivalent to £852,791,660 handed over by Hon. Daniel P. Moynihan, Ambassador of the USA to India in New Delhi on 18 Feb 1974. An internal US Treasury cheque for $4,176,969,623.57 was drawn on 30 June 1954.

Largest *Great Britain*

The largest cheque drawn in Britain was one for £604,604,115 drawn on 1 Sept 1982 by British Petroleum Oil Development

Ltd, payable to the Inland Revenue covering part of BP's North Sea Oil tax bill. If converted to pound notes this would comprise a stack 36.84 miles *59,28 km* high.

Greatest collection

The highest price paid for a coin collection has been $7,300,000 (*then £3,550,000*) for a hoard of 407,000 US silver dollars from the La Vere Redfield estate in a courtroom auction in Reno, Nevada on 27 Jan 1976 by Steven C. Markoff of A-Mark Coin Co. Inc. of Beverley Hills, California.

Largest hoards

The largest hoard ever found was one of about 80,000 aurei in Brescello near Modena, Italy in 1914 believed to have been deposited *c.* 37 BC. The numerically largest hoard ever found was the Brussels hoard of 1908 containing *c.* 150,000 coins. A hoard of 56,000 Roman coins was found at Cunetio near Marlborough, Wiltshire on 15 Oct 1978.

The greatest discovery of treasure is the estimated $2000 million of gold coins and platinum ingots from the sunken Tsarist battleship *Admiral Nakhimov* 8524 tons/*tonnes* 200 ft *60 m* down off the Japanese island of Tsushima. She sank on 27 May 1905.

Largest mint

The largest mint in the world is the US Treasury's mint built in 1965–9 on Independence Mall, Philadelphia, covering 11½ acres *4,65 ha* with an annual capacity on a 3 shift 7-day week production of 8000 million coins. A single stamping machine can produce coins at a rate of 10,000 per hour.

Charity Fund Raising

The greatest recorded amount raised by a charity walk or run is (Can)$24.7 million by Terry Fox (1958–81) of Canada who ran from St John's, Newfoundland to Thunder Bay, Ontario with an artificial leg in 143 days from 12 Apr–2 Sept 1980. He covered 5373 km *3339 miles*.

Largest charity collection

The most valuable column of coins amassed for charity was one of 50p pieces worth £8,380.50p created by Whitehaven Round Table and knocked over on 17 Dec 1983. The longest and highest value line of coins in Britain was 4.26 miles *6,86 km* in length (£5,296) laid by pupils and staff at Marlwood School, Alveston, Bristol and by Clifton Rugby Club on 13 Sept 1981. (*For details of the overseas record see Stop Press.*)

LABOUR

Trade union Oldest *Great Britain*

The oldest of the 105 trade unions affiliated to the Trades Union Congress (founded 1868) is the National Society of Brushmakers and General Workers (current membership 725) founded in 1747.

Trade union Largest *World*

The world's largest union has been Solidarność (Solidarity) in Poland which by October 1980 was reported to have 8,000,000 members. The union with the longest name is the International Association of Marble, Slate and Stone Polishers, Rubbers and Sawyers, Tile and Marble Setters' Helpers and Marble Mosaic and Terrazzo Workers Helpers or IAMSSPRSTMSHMMTWH of Washington DC, USA.

Trade union Largest *Great Britain*

The largest union in the United Kingdom is the Transport and General Workers' Union, with 1,632,957 members at April 1984. Their peak membership was 2,086,281 in 1979.

Trade union Smallest

The smallest TUC affiliated unions are the Wool Shear Workers' Trade Union of Sheffield and the Cloth Pressers Society with a membership of 28 and 16 respectively. The unaffiliated London Handforged Spoon and Fork Makers' Society instituted in July 1874, has a last reported membership of 6.

Labour dispute *Earliest*

A labour dispute concerning monotony of diet and working conditions was recorded in 1153 BC in Thebes, Egypt. The earliest recorded strike was one by an orchestra leader from Greece named Aristos in Rome *c.* 309 BC. The cause was meal breaks.

COINS

Oldest

World: c. 670 BC electrum staters of King Gyges of Lydia, Turkey[1]

British: c. 95 BC Westerham type gold stater (51 known)[2]

Earliest Dated

Samian silver tetradrachm struck in Zankle (now Messina), Sicily dated year 1 *viz* 494 BC—shown as 'A'

Christian Era: MCCXXXIIII (1234) Bishop of Roskilde coins, Denmark (6 known)

British: 1539 James V of Scotland silver 'bonnet piece'

Heaviest

World: 19,71 kg *43 lb 7¼ oz* Swedish 10 daler copper plate 1644[3]

British: 39,94 g *1.4066 oz* Gold £5 piece. The latest mintages are dated 1980, 1981 and 1982. (Legal tender record)[4]

Lightest and Smallest

World: 0.002 g or 14,000 to the oz Nepalese silver ¼ Jawa *c.* 1740

British: 7.27 grains or 61 to the oz Maundy silver one penny piece since 1822

Most Expensive

World: Agrigentum decadrahm sold by private treaty to Nelson Bunker Hunt (US) for $900,000 in Oct 1980

British: £36,000 bid for Henry VII sovereign of 1492 at Spink's, London on 2 June 1983

Rarest

World: Many 'singletons' known e.g. Only 700 Axumite coins known of which only one of bronze and gold of Kaleb I *c.* AD 500

British: Unique: 1952 George VI half-crown; 1954 Elizabeth II 1d sold in March 1978 for £23,000

[1] Chinese uninscribed 'spade' money of the Chou dynasty has been dated to *c.* 770 BC.
[2] Bellovaci type gold staters circulated as early as *c.* 130 BC but were struck in Northern France and not in Britain.
[3] The largest coin-shaped coin was the 200 Mohur Indian gold coin of 1654 5⅜ in *136 mm* in diameter weighing 70 troy oz *2177 g* of which no known example now survives.
[4] The George III 'Cartwheel' Copper 2d coin of 1797 weighed 2.04 oz *58,0 g*. The 5 guinea gold pieces.

The year 494 BC the Sicilian silver tetradrachms was designated as Year A and thus became the earliest ever example of a coin being dated.

The most valuable column of coins for charity about to be toppled at Whitehaven Hospital by the former Lord-Lieutenant of Cumbria, the late J. C. Wade OBE. (*Guy Brian*)

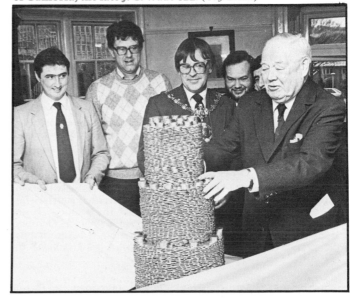

WORLD'S GREATEST CONSUMERS

Of all the countries in the world, based on the latest available data, Belgium–Luxembourg has the largest available total of calories per person. The net supply averaged 3645 per day in 1974. The United Kingdom average was 3349 per day in 1974. The lowest *reported* supply figures are 1728 calories per day in Upper Volta in 1974. It has been estimated that Britons eat 7¼ times their own weight in food per annum or 70,000 tons/*tonnes* per day. The highest calorific value of any foodstuff is that of pure animal fat with 930 calories per 100 g *3.5 oz*. Pure alcohol provides 710 calories per 100 g.

***Below*. The World's greatest consumers per head, per day. Figures in square brackets refer to UK consumption.**

PROTEIN Australia and New Zealand 106 g *3.79 oz* (1969) [88 g *3.1 oz* (*1968–9*)]	COFEE[3] Finland—36,52 g *1.28 oz* (1980) [*5,75 g* 0.20 oz (*1980*)]
CEREALS[1] Egypt—600 g *21.95 oz* (1966–7) [*7.14 oz* 202 g (*1977*)]	WATER USA—1544 gal 70211 (1974) 1982 Czech. 48 gall/p.p.a. UK 1983 5027000 hectolitres
SUGARS Bulgaria—177 g *6.26 oz* (1977) [*4.1 oz* 116 g (*1977*)] in 1982 46 kg/caput/p.a.	BEER W. Germany—40,2 cl *0.708 pints* (1981) [*0.537 pints* 30,5 cl (*1981*)]
MEAT USA—308 g *10.89 oz* (1977) [*193 g* 6.8 oz (*1977*)]	WINE France—25,1 cl *0.44 pints* (1980) [*0.030 pints* 1,7 cl (*1978*)]
SWEETS Britain—1.20 oz *4,01 g* (1979)	SPIRITS Poland—1,53 cl *0.026 pints* (1978) [*0.008 pints* 0,47 cl (1978)]
TEA[2] Ireland—0.36 oz *10,2 g* (1977) [*0.285 oz* 8,09 g (*1981*)]	

[1] Figures for 1977 from China suggest a possible consumption (including rice) of 890 g *31.3 oz.*

[2] The most expensive tea marketed in the UK is 'Oolong Peach Blossom', specially imported for Fortnum & Mason of Piccadilly, City of Westminster, London. In June 1983 it retailed for £4.95 per 125 g or *£17.96 per lb*. Tea-bags were invented by Thomas Sullivan of New York in 1904.

[3] The most expensive coffee in the US is Jamaican Blue Mountain which retails for up to $20 per lb (*£12.90 per lb £28.45 per kg*).

Labour dispute *Largest*

The most serious single labour dispute in the United Kingdom was the General Strike of 4–12 May 1926, called by the Trades Union Congress in support of the Miners' Federation. During the nine days of the strike 1,580,000 people were involved and 14,500,000 working days were lost.

During the year 1926 a total of 2,750,000 people were involved in 323 different labour disputes and the working days lost during the year amounted to 162,300,000, the highest figure ever recorded. The provisional figures for 1983 were 3,593,000 working days involving 1255 stoppages with 540,000 workers involved.

Labour dispute *Longest*

The world's longest recorded strike ended on 4 Jan 1961, after 33 years. It concerned the employment of barbers' assistants in Copenhagen, Denmark. The longest recorded major strike was that at the plumbing fixtures factory of the Kohler Co. in Sheboygan, Wisconsin, USA, between April 1954 and October 1962. The strike is alleged to have cost the United Automobile Workers' Union about $12,000,000 (*then £4.8 million*) to sustain.

Unemployment *Highest*

The highest recorded percentage unemployment in Great Britain was on 23 Jan 1933, when the total of unemployed persons on the Employment Exchange registers was 2,903,065, representing 22.8% of the insured working population. The peak figure for the post-war period has been 13.5% (3,225,200) on 13 Jan 1983.

Unemployment *Lowest*

In Switzerland in December 1973 (pop. 6.6 million), the total number of unemployed was reported to be 81. The lowest recorded peace-time level of unemployment in Britain was 0.9 per cent on 11 July 1955, when 184,929 persons were registered. The peak figure for the Employed labour force in the United Kingdom has been 25,520,000 in December 1979.

ASSOCIATION *Largest*

The largest single association in the world is the Blue Cross and Blue Shield Association, the US-based hospital insurance organization with a membership of 79,662,452 on 1 Jan 1984. Benefits paid out in 1983 totalled $34,602,745,060 (*£24,715 million*). The largest association in the United Kingdom is the Automobile Association (formed 1905) with a membership which reached 5,600,754 in March 1984.

Oldest Club

Britain's oldest gentleman's club is White's, St James', London, opened *c.* 1697 by Francis White (d. 1711), as a Chocolate House, and moved to its present site in 37 St. James's in 1755. This has been described as an 'oasis in a desert of democracy'. Britain's oldest known dining club is the 'Corporation of St Pancras' of Chichester, West Sussex, known as The Wheelbarrow Club. It was formed on 4 Aug 1689 and is still in being.

CONSUMPTION

Prohibition

The longest lasting imposition of prohibition has been 26 years in Iceland (1908–34). Other prohibitions have been Russia, later USSR (1914–24) and USA (1920–33). The Faeroe Islands have had a public (as opposed to private licensed) prohibition since 1918. By way of contrast the Northern Territory of Australia's annual intake has been estimated to be as high as 416 pints *236 litres* per person. A society for the prevention of alcoholism in Darwin had to disband in June 1966 for lack of support. It is perhaps noteworthy that the only parliamentary candidate on record in Britain ever to receive a nil vote was in 1860 at Ripon, North Yorkshire by Mr F. R. Lees, who described himself as a Temperance Chartist.

Biggest round

The largest round of drinks ever recorded was one for 1501 people stood by Paul Deer at U-Zoo & Co., Atlanta, Georgia, USA on 14 July 1982.

Largest dish

The largest menu item in the world is roasted camel, prepared occasionally for Bedouin wedding feasts. Cooked eggs are stuffed in fish, the fish stuffed in cooked chickens, the chickens stuffed into a roasted sheep carcass and the sheep stuffed into a whole camel.

Most expensive food

The most expensively priced food (as opposed to spice) is First Choice Black Périgord truffle (*Tuber melanosporum*) retailed at £8.50 per 12.5 g *0.44 oz* tin.

Longest banana split

The longest banana split ever made was one of 8510 ft *2594 m* (over 1.6 miles) in length embracing 15,912 bananas, 950 gal *4319 litres* of ice cream, 919 lb *416,8 kg* chocolate syrup, 297¾ gal *1353,5 litres* of topping, 276 lb *125 kg* of nuts and 8910 cherries by the Junior Class of Millburn High School, Millburn, New Jersey on 22 May 1983.

Largest barbecue

On 31 Jan 1981, 46,386 chicken halves supplied by Ernie Morgado were barbecued for 15,000 people at Iolani School, Honolulu, Hawaii. At the 1982 holding of the annual Fancy Farm Picnic, Kentucky (est. 1880) on 6 August the consumption of mutton, pork and chicken meat reached 15,000 lb *6,80 tonnes*. The cook was Harold Carrico.

Largest beefburger

The largest beefburger on record is one of 2001 kg *4411.41 lb* made on 26 Mar 1983 by the 'Slager 2001' butchers of Ukkel, Brussels, Belgium. The burger had a surface area of 36 m² *387.5 ft²* and was cut into 7440 portions after grilling.

Largest cake
The largest cake ever created was a Stars and Stripes cake of 81,982 lb *37,18 tonnes* including 30,786 lb *13,96 tonnes* of icing baked in 14½ hours by Chef Franz Eichenauer at the Convention Hall, Atlantic City, New Jersey, USA on 4 July 1982. The tallest recorded free-standing wedding cake is one of over 40 tiers, 58 ft *11,38 m* tall. It was made by Roy Butterworth and M. Olaizola on 7 May 1983 in Québec, Canada.

Heaviest and Largest Easter eggs
The heaviest Easter egg ever made was one weighing 3430 kg *7561 lb 13½ oz*, measuring 10 ft *3,04 m* high, by Siegfried Berndt at 'Macopa' Patisserie, Leicester, England and completed on 7 Apr 1982. An egg 5,42 m *17 ft 9⅜ in* tall weighing 2323 kg *5121 lb* was exhibited by Patisserie Eueen Lauwers at Schelle, Belgium on 19 Mar 1983.

Largest haggis
The largest haggis (encased in 7 ox stomach linings) on record was one weighing 541½ lb *245,6 kg* made for the CWS Hypermarket of Glasgow, Scotland by David A. Hall Ltd. of Broxburn Lothian, Scotland in January 1980. The cooking time was 12 hr.

Longest loaf
The longest one-piece loaf ever baked was one of 428,29 m *1405 ft 1¾ in* baked by the First Bellair School Scout Group, South Africa on 10–12 June 1983.

Largest apple pie
The largest apple pie ever baked was that by the ITV Chef Glynn Christian in a 40 ft × 23 ft *12 m × 7 m* dish at Hewitts Farm, Chelsfield, Kent on 25–27 Aug 1982. Over 600 bushels of apples were included in the pie which weighed 30,115 lb *13,66 tonnes*. It was cut by Rear Admiral Sir John Woodward.

Largest cherry pie
The largest cherry pie ever made was one weighing a total of 6¼ tons *6350 kg* and containing 4950 lb *2245 kg* of cherries. It measured 14 ft 4 in *4,36 m* in diameter, 24 in *60,96 cm* in depth, and was baked in the grounds of the Medusa Cement Corporation, Charlevoix, Michigan on 15 May 1976, as part of the town's contribution to America's Bicentennial celebrations.

Largest meat pie
The largest meat pie ever baked weighed 5¾ tons, measuring 18 × 6 ft 18 in deep *5,48 × 1,83 × 0,45 m*, the eighth in the series of Denby Dale, West Yorkshire pies, to mark four royal births, baked on 5 Sept 1964. The first was in 1788 to celebrate King George III's return to sanity, but the fourth (Queen Victoria's Jubilee, 1887) went a bit 'off' and had to buried in quick-lime.

Largest mince pie
The largest mince pie recorded was one of 2260 lb *1025 kg* 20 × 5 ft *6,09 × 1,52 m*, baked at Ashby-de-la-Zouch, Leicestershire on 15 Oct 1932.

Largest omelette
The largest omelette in the world was one made of 20,117 eggs on a pan measuring 30 × 10 ft *9,1 × 3,04 m* cooked by CHQR Radio, Calgary, and the Alberta Egg and Fowl Marketing Board on 27 June 1981 at Calgary's Southcentre Mall, Alberta, Canada.

Longest pastry
The longest pastry in the world is the 'record' pastry 489,87 m *1607 ft 2 in* in length made by the Gothenburg Patissiers Association of Sweden (organiser Sven Gustavsson) at The Liseberg Amusement Park on 15 June 1983.

Largest pizza pie
The largest pizza ever baked was one measuring 80 ft 1 in *24,4 m* in diameter, hence 5037 ft² *468 m²* in area and 18,664 lb *8465 kg* in weight at the Oma Pizza Restaurant, Glen Falls, New York, USA owned by Lorenzo Amato on 8 Oct 1978. It was cut into 60,318 slices.

Potato mash
A single serving of 18,260 lb *8,26 tonnes* of potato mash was prepared in a concrete mixer for the 17th Annual Potato Bowl at Grand Forks, North Dakota, USA on 4 Sept 1982.

The finishing touches being put to the lowest storey of the world's ultimate in wedding cakes. The top 24 storeys protruded through the ceiling.

Largest iced lollipop
The world's largest iced lollipop was one of 5750 lb *2608 kg* constructed for the Westside Assembly of God Church, Davenport, Iowa, USA on 7 Sept 1975. The largest 'regular' lollipop was one of 400 lb *181,4 kg* (220 lb of sugar and 180 lb of corn syrup) made by American Candy Co, Selma, Alabama for the World's Fair, Knoxville, Tennessee, USA on 28 Apr 1982.

Blackpool rock
The mightiest piece of Blackpool lettered rock ever produced was a piece weighing more than 3 cwt *152 kg* delivered on 16 Apr 1975 to the Royal Variety Club of Great Britain in London by Ashton Candy Co. Ltd. of Blackpool.

Largest salami
The largest salami on record was one 8,91 m *29 ft 2¾ in* long with a circumference of 71 cm *28 in*, weighing 333 kg *734.13 lb* made by Don Smallgoods for Australian Safeway Stores at Broadmeadows, Vic on 23 Apr 1982.

Longest sausage
The longest continuous sausage ever made was one of 5.54 miles *8,91 km* weighing 2.38 tons *2418 kg* by Rex's Sausage Manufacturing Co of Stirchley, Birmingham, on 22 June 1983.

Strawberry Bowl
The largest bowl of strawberries with a net weight of 451 lb *204,57 kg* was weighed on 25 June 1983 at Guildhall, Worcester.

Largest sundae
The largest ice cream sundae ever concocted is one of 27,102 lb *12,293 kg* with strawberries, nuts and whipped topping constructed at St. Albans, Vermont, USA on 15 Apr 1983.

Largest Yorkshire pudding
The largest Yorkshire pudding on record is one measuring 18 ft 6 in × 3 ft 11 in *5,63 × 1,19 m* baked for 4¾ hr at the Swan's Nest Hotel, Stratford-upon-Avon, Warwickshire by Bob Wyatt and Kevin Fernley on 28 Nov 1981.

Top selling sweet
The world's top selling sweets (candies) are Life Savers with 29,651,840,000 rolls between 1913 and 30 June 1980. A tunnel formed by the holes in the middle placed end to end would stretch to the moon and back 3 times. Thomas Syta of Van Nuys, California, USA made one last 7 hr 10 min (with hole intact) on 15 Jan 1983.

The world's largest port at New York. This can accommodate the berthing of 391 ships simultaneously.

Spice *Most expensive*

Prices for wild gingseng (root of *Panax quinquefolius*), from the Chan Pak Mountain area of China thought to have aphrodisiac qualities were reported in November 1977 to be as high as $23,000 (*then £10,454*) per ounce in Hong Kong. Total annual shipments from Jilin Province do not exceed 4 kg *140 oz* a year. A leading medical journal in the USA has likened its effects to 'corticosteroid poisoning'.

Spice *'Hottest'*

The hottest of all spices is claimed to be Siling labuyo from the Philippines.

Most Expensive fruit

On 5 Apr 1977 John Synnott of Ashford, Co. Wicklow, Ireland sold 1 lb *453 g* of strawberries (a punnet of 30 berries) to the restaurateur, Mr Leslie Cooke, at auction by Walter L. Cole Ltd. in the Dublin Fruit Market for £530 or £17.70 a berry.

Rarest condiment

The world's most prized condiment is Cà Cuong, a secretion recovered in minute amounts from beetles in northern Vietnam. Owing to war conditions, the price had risen to $100 (*now £57*) per ounce *28 g* before supplies virtually ceased in 1975.

ENERGY CONSUMPTION

To express the various forms of available energy (coal, liquid fuels and water power, etc., but omitting vegetable fuels and peat), it is the practice to convert them all into terms of coal.

The highest consumption in the world is in the United States, with an average of 13 240 kg *260.1 cwt* per person. With only 5.3 per cent of the world's population the US consumes 28.6 per cent of the world's gasoline and 32.9 per cent of the world's electric power. The United Kingdom average was 6365 kg *125.2 cwt* per person in 1979. The lowest recorded average for 1974 was 13 kg *28.6 lb* per person in Rwanda.

MASS COMMUNICATIONS

Airline

The country with the busiest airlines system is the United States of America where 231,514,402,000 revenue passenger miles were flown on scheduled domestic and local services in 1983. This was equivalent to an annual trip of 985 miles *1585 km* for every one of the inhabitants of the USA. The United Kingdom airlines flew 559 568 927 km *347,699,430 miles* and carried 36,261,927 passengers on all services excluding Air Taxi operations in 1983.

Merchant shipping

The world total of merchant shipping, excluding vessels of less than 100 tons gross, sailing vessels and barges, was 76,106 vessels of 422,590,317 tons gross on 1 July 1983. The largest merchant fleet in the world as at mid-1983 was that under the flag of Liberia with 2062 ships of 67,564,000 tons gross. The UK figure for mid-1983 was 2570 ships of 19,121,457 tons gross.

Largest and busiest ports

Physically, the largest port in the world is the Port of New York and New Jersey, USA. The port has a navigable waterfront of 755 miles *1215 km* (295 miles *474 km* in New Jersey) stretching over 92 miles^2 *238 km^2*. A total of 261 general cargo berths and 130 other piers give a total berthing capacity of 391 ships at one time. The total warehousing floor space is 422.4 acres *170,9 ha*. The world's busiest port and largest artificial harbour is Rotterdam-Europoort in the Netherlands which covers 38 miles^2 *100 km^2*. It handled 30,820 sea-going vessels carrying a total of 233 million tonnes of sea-going cargo, and about 180,000 barges in 1983. It is able to handle 310 sea-going vessels simultaneously of up to 318,000 tonnes and 70 ft *21,34 m* draught.

Railways

The country with the greatest length of railway is the United States, with 198,963 miles *320 000 km* of track at 1 Jan 1980. The farthest anyone can get from a railway on the mainland island of Great Britain is 110 miles *177 km* by road in the case of Southend, Mull of Kintyre.

The number of journeys made on British Rail in 1983 was 695,200,000 (average 27 miles *43,5 km*) compared with the peak year of 1957, when 1101 million journeys (average 20.51 miles *33 km*) were made.

Road *Mileages*

The country with the greatest length of road is the United States (all 50 States), with 3,851,880 miles *6 199 000 km* of graded roads at 1 Jan 1982. Regular driving licences are issuable at 15, without a driver education course only in Hawaii and Mississippi. Thirteen US States issue restricted juvenile licences at 14.

Great Britain has 213,555 miles *343 685 km* of road including 1659 miles *2671 km* of motorway at April 1983 and 20,226,000 vehicles in 1983.

The first sod on Britain's first motorway, the M6 Preston By-Pass, was cut by bulldozer driver Fred Hackett on 12 June 1956 on the section between junctions 29 and 32 opened in December 1958. Britain's longest uninterrupted dual carriageway is from Plymouth to Exeter (A38) and thence by the M5 and M6 for 515 miles *829 km* terminating at Dunblane Fourways Restaurant, Stirling, Scotland.

Economic

Traffic volume *Highest*

The highest traffic volume of any point in the world is at the East Los Angeles interchange (Santa Ana, Pomona, Golden State and Santa Monica Freeways), California, USA with a 24-hr average on weekdays of 458,060 vehicles in 1983—318 per minute. The most heavily travelled stretch of road is between 43rd and 47th Street on the Dan Ryan Expressway, Chicago with an average daily volume of 254,700 vehicles.

The territory with the highest traffic density in the world is Hong Kong. By 1 Jan 1981 there were 278,952 motor vehicles on 734.4 miles *1182 km* of serviceable roads giving a density of 4.63 yd *4,23 m* per vehicle. The comparative figure for Great Britain in 1981 was 22.78 yd *20,83 m*. The world's busiest bridge is the Howrah Bridge across the river Hooghly in Calcutta. In addition to 57,000 vehicles a day it carries an incalculable number of pedestrians across its 1500 ft *457 m* long 72 ft *21,9 m* wide span.

The greatest traffic density at any one point in Great Britain is at Hyde Park Corner, London. The flow (including the underpass) for 24 hours in 1982 was 214,000 vehicles. The busiest Thames bridge in 1982 was Putney Bridge, with a 24-hr average of 57,700 vehicles compared with 72,500 for the Blackwall Tunnel. Britain's busiest section of motorway is between junctions 3 and 4 of the M4 registering 92,800 vehicles per 24 hours by 1980.

Traffic jams *Largest*

The longest traffic jam ever reported was that of 16 Feb 1980 which stretched northwards from Lyon 176 km *109.3 miles* towards Paris. The longest traffic jam reported in Britain was one of 35 miles *56 km* out of 42.5 miles *75,6 km* road length between Torquay and Yarcombe, Devon, on 25 July 1964 and 35 miles *56 km* on the A30 between Egham, Surrey and Micheldever, Hampshire on 23 May 1970. The traffic jam on the M5 in Avon on 24 July 1982 stretched 18 miles *28,96 km* from Falfield to Naish Hill in 3 lanes.

Road *Widest*

The widest street in the world is the Monumental Axis running for 1½ miles *2,4 km* from the Municipal Plaza to the Plaza of the Three Powers in Brasilia, the capital of Brazil. The six-lane Boulevard was opened in April 1960 and is 250 m *273.4 yd* wide. The San Francisco–Oakland Bay Bridge Toll Plaza has 23 lanes (17 west bound) serving the Bridge in Oakland, California.

The only instance of 17 carriageway lanes side by side in Britain occurs on the M61 at Linnyshaw Moss, Worsley, Greater Manchester.

Road *Narrowest*

The world's narrowest street is in Port Isaac, Cornwall at the junction of Temple Bar and Dolphin Street. It is popularly known as 'Squeeze-belly alley' and in 19$\frac{5}{16}$ in *49 cm* wide at its narrowest point.

Road *Longest*

The longest motorable road in the world is the Pan-American Highway, from North West Alaska to Santiago, Chile, thence eastward to Buenos Aires, Argentina and terminating in Brasilia, Brazil. There remains a gap known as the Tapon del Darién, in Panama and the Atrato Swamp, Colombia. This was first traversed by the land rover La Cucaracha Carinosa (The Affectionate Cockroach) of the Trans-Darien Expedition 1959–60 crewed by former SAS man Richard E Bevir (UK) and engineer Terence John Whitfield (Australia). They left Chepo, Panama on 3 Feb 1960 and reached Quibdó, Colombia on 17 June averaging 220 yd *201 m* per hour of indescribable difficulty. The Range Rover VXC 868K of the British Trans-Americas Expedition was the first vehicle to traverse the American continent end-to-end, leaving Alaska on 3 Dec 1971 and arriving in Tierra del Fuego on 9 June 1972 after a journey of 17,018 miles *27 387 km.*

Most complex interchange

The most complex interchange on the British road system is that at Gravelly Hill, north of Birmingham on the Midland Link Motorway section of the M6 opened on 24 May 1972. There are 18 routes on 6 levels together with a diverted canal and river, which consumed 26,000 tons/*tonnes* of steel, 250,000 tons/*tonnes* of concrete, 300,000 tons/*tonnes* of earth and cost £8,200,000.

A model of what in 1983 is certain to become Britain's busiest motorway interchange. The M4 to the west of London Airport intersects the circum. London motorway the M25

Street *Longest World*

The longest designated street in the world is Yonge Street running north and west from Toronto, Canada. The first stretch completed on 16 Feb 1796 ran 34 miles 53 chains *55,783 km*. Its official length now extended to Rainy River at the Ontario–Minnesota border is 1178.3 miles *1896,2 km*.

Longest Great Britain and Commonest Name

The longest designated road in Great Britain is the A1 from London to Edinburgh of 404 miles *650 km*. The longest Roman roads were Watling Street, from Dubrae (Dover) 215 miles *346 km* through Londinium (London) to Viroconium (Wroxeter), and Fosse Way, which ran 218 miles *350 km* from Lindum (Lincoln) through Aquae Sulis (Bath) to Isca Dumnoniorum (Exeter). However, a 10 mile *16 km* section of Fosse Way between Ilchester and Seaton remains indistinct. The commonest street name in Greater London is High Street (122) followed by Station Road (100).

Shortest

The title of 'The Shortest Street in the World' has been claimed since 1907 by McKinley Street in Bellefontaine, Ohio, USA built of 'vitrified brick' and measuring 30 ft *9,14 m* in length. The shortest reported measurement of a street in Britain is the 51 ft 10 in *15,79 m* of Queen Charlotte Street, Windsor, Berkshire.

Steepest

The steepest streets in the world are Filbert Street, Russian Hill and 22nd Street, Dolores Heights, San Francisco with gradients of 31.5 per cent or 1 in 3.17. Lombard Street between Leavenworth and Hyde with 8 consecutive 90 degree turns of 20 ft *6,1 m* radius is described as the 'Crookedest street in the world'. It was so made in 1922 to reduce the gradient to 18.2%. Britain's steepest motorable road is the unclassified Chimney Bank which is signposted '1 in 3' at Rosedale Abbey, North Yorkshire. The County Surveyor states it is 'not quite' a 33 per cent gradient. Of the five unclassified roads with 1 in 3 gradients the most severe is Hard Knott Pass between Boot and Ambleside, Cumbria.

Longest hill

The longest steep hill on any road in the United Kingdom is on the road westwards from Lochcarron towards Applecross in Highland, Scotland. In 6 miles *9,6 km* this road rises from sea-level to 2054 ft *626 m* with an average gradient of 1 in 15.4, the steepest part being 1 in 4.

Road *Highest World*

The highest trail in the world is an 8 mile *13 km* stretch of the Kang-ti-suu between Khaleb and Hsin-chi-fu, Tibet which in two places exceeds 20,000 ft *6080 m*. The highest carriageable road in the world is one 1180 km *733.2 miles* long between Tibet and south western Sinkiang, completed in October 1957, which takes in passes of an altitude up to 18,480 ft *5632 m* above sea-level. Europe's highest pass (excluding the Caucasian passes) is the Col de Restefond (9193 ft *2802 m*) completed in 1962 with 21 hairpins between Jausiers and Saint Etienne-de-Tinée, France. It is usually closed between early October and early June. The highest motor road in Europe is the Pico de Veleta in the Sierra Nevada, southern Spain. The shadeless climb of 36 km *22.4 miles* brings the motorist to 11,384 ft *3469 m* above sea-level and became, on completion of a road on its southern side in Summer 1974, arguably Europe's highest 'pass'.

Highest Great Britain

The highest road in the United Kingdom is the A6293 unclassified tarmac, private extension at Great Dun Fell,

made Professor of Mathematics at Edinburgh University on the recommendation of Sir Isaac Newton.

Professors *Most durable*

Dr Joel Hildebrand (1881–1983), Professor Emeritus of Physical Chemistry at the University of California, Berkeley, became first an Assistant Professor in 1913 and published his 275th research paper 68 years later in 1981. The longest period of which any professorship has been held in Britain is 63 years in the case of Thomas Martyn (1735–1825), Professor of Botany at Cambridge University from 1762 until his death. The last professor-for-life was the pathologist Professor Henry Roy Dean (1879–1961) for his last 39 years at Cambridge.

Senior Wranglers

Since 1910 the Wranglers (first class honours students in the Cambridge University mathematical Tripos, part 2) have been placed in alphabetical order only. In 1890 Miss Philippa Garrett Fawcett (d. 1948) in Newnham was placed 'above the Senior Wrangler'.

Youngest undergraduate and graduate

The most extreme recorded case of undergraduate juvenility was that of William Thomson (1824–1907), later Lord Kelvin, OM, GCVO, who entered Glasgow University aged 10 years 4 months in October 1834 and matriculated on 14 Nov 1834. Dr Merrill Kenneth Wolf (b. 28 Aug 1931) of Cleveland, Ohio took his B.A. in music from Yale University in September 1945 in the month of his 14th birthday. Ruth Lawrence (b. 1971) of Huddersfield, North Yorkshire passed Pure Mathematics O level at the age of 9 and Pure Mathematics A level and Grade 1 S level in June 1981 aged 10. She was accepted for entrance to Oxford at the age of 12.

Schools *Oldest in Britain*

The title of the oldest existing school in Britain is contested. It is claimed that King's School in Canterbury, Kent, was a foundation of Saint Augustine, some time between his arrival in Kent in AD 597 and his death in *c.* 604. Cor Tewdws (College of Theodosius) at Llantwit Major, South Glamorgan, reputedly burnt down in AD 446, was refounded, after an elapse of 62 years, by St Illtyd in 508 and flourished into the 13th century. Winchester College, Hampshire was founded in 1382. The Pedagogue's House, King Edward VI School, Stratford-upon-Avon, Warwickshire was built in 1427.

School Largest *World*

In 1983/84 South Point High School, Calcutta, India (founded 1954) had an enrolment of 12,350 regular students.

Great Britain

The school with the most pupils in Great Britain was Exmouth Comprehensive, Devon with 2599 (1983–84). The highest enrolment in Scotland has been at Our Lady's Roman Catholic High School, Motherwell, Strathclyde with a peak of 2325 in August 1977. The total in Holy Child School, Belfast, Northern Ireland reached 2752 in 1973 before being split up. The highest enrolment in 1983/84 is 2,329 at the Methodist College, Belfast.

School Most Expensive *World*

The annual cost of keeping a pupil at Le Rosey, Gstaad, Switzerland in 1983/84 was reputed to be $20,000.

Great Britain

In the academic year 1983–84 St. Andrew's Private Tutorial Centre, Cambridge, England (principals W. A. Duncombe and C. T. Easterbrook) charged £10,352 for full-time science students (tuition and accommodation). The most expensive school in Great Britain is Millfield (founded 1935) in Street, Somerset (headmaster C. R. M. Atkinson). The annual fee for boarding entries in 1983–4 is £5970. The most expensive girls' school in 1983 was Benenden, Kent (founded 1923) with annual fees of £4050.

Earliest Comprehensive School

Lakes School, Cumbria, formerly Windermere Grammar School (closed in 1865), Westmorland, became comprehensive in 1945. Calder High School was established after formal rejection of the 11 plus examinations from two West Riding schools in 1950. The earliest purpose-built was Kidbrooke Comprehensive for Girls, London SE opened in 1954.

Oldest old school tie

The practice of wearing distinctive neckties bearing the colours of registered designs of schools, universities, sports clubs, regiments, etc., appears to date from *c.* 1880. The practice originated in Oxford University, where boater bands were converted into use as 'ribbon ties'. The earliest definitive evidence stems from an order from Exeter College for college ties, dated 25 June 1880.

PTA Oldest

The Parent-Teacher Association with the earliest foundation date in Britain is St. Christopher School, Letchworth, Parents' Circle formed in 1919.

Most schools

The greatest documented number of schools attended by a pupil is 265 by Wilma Williams, now Mrs R. J. Horton, from 1933–43 when her parents were in show business in the USA.

Most 'O' and 'A' levels

Dr Francis L. Thomason of Tottenham, London had by January 1984 accumulated 45 O and O/A, 8 A and 1 S levels making a total of 54 of which 22 were in the top grade. A. F. Prime, a prisoner in HM Open Prison Sudbury, accumulated a total of 1 S, 14 A's and 34 O's between 1968 and 1982. Environmental difficulties tend to make study harder in prison than elsewhere.

Stephen Murrell of Crown Woods School, Eltham passed 8 A levels at one sitting in June 1978 achieving 7 at grade A. Robert Pidgeon (b. 7 Feb 1959) of St Peter's School, Bournemouth, secured 13 O level passes at grade A at one sitting in the summer of 1975. Subsequently he passed 3 A levels at grade A and 2 S levels with firsts. Andrew Maclaren (b. 1963) of Chelmsford, Essex passed 14 O levels, 5 A levels all at grade A and 3 S levels at grade one—making 22 top grades. At Queens' College, Cambridge he got first class honours in 1983.

Youngest headmaster

The youngest headmaster of a major public school was Henry Montagu Butler (b. 2 July 1833), appointed Headmaster of Harrow School on 16 Nov 1859, when aged 26 years 137 days. His first term in office began in January 1860.

Most durable don

Dr Martin Joseph Routh (b. Sept 1755) was President of Magdalen College, Oxford, from April 1791 for 63 years 8 months, until his death in his 100th year on 22 Dec 1854. He had previously been a fellow for 16 years and was thus a don for a span of 79 years.

Most durable teachers

David Rhys Davies (1835–1928) taught as a pupil teacher and latterly as teacher and headmaster of Dame Anna Child's School, Whitton, Powys (1879–1928) for a total of 76 years 2 months. Col Ernest Achey Loftus CBE, TD, DL (b. 11 Jan 1884) served as a teacher over a span of 73 years from May 1901 in York, England until 18 Feb 1975 in Zambia retiring as the world's oldest civil servant aged 91 years 38 days. His father William was born in Hull in the reign of William IV in 1832.

Elsie Marguerite Touzel (b. 1889) of Jersey began her teaching career aged 16 in 1905 and was teaching at Les Alpes School, Faldonet until her retirement on 30 Sept 1980.

Highest Endowment

The greatest single gift in the history of higher education has been $125 million to Louisiana State University by C. B. Pennington in 1983.

8. RELIGIONS

Oldest

Human burial, which has religious connotations, is known from *c.* 100,000 BC among *Homo sapiens neanderthalensis*. The Judaic way of life was formulated as early as 2000 BC.

Largest

Religious statistics are necessarily only approximate. The test of adherence to a religion varies widely in rigour, while many individuals, particularly in the East, belong to two or more religions.

Christianity is the world's prevailing religion, with some 1,070,000,000 adherents in 1983. The Vatican statistics office reported that in 1982 there were 783,660,000 Roman Catholics. The largest non-Christian religion is Islam (Muslim) with some 600,000,000 followers.

In the United Kingdom the Anglicans comprise members of the Established Church of England, the Dis-established Church in Wales, the Episcopal Church in Scotland and the Church of Ireland. The Church of England has two provinces (Canterbury and York), 44 dioceses, 10,805 full time diocesan clergymen and 13,530 parishes (1 Jan 1984).

In Scotland the most numerous group is the Church of Scotland (12 Synods, 47 Presbyteries), which had 902,714 members as at 31 Dec 1983.

Largest clergies

The world's largest religious organization is the Roman Catholic Church, with 138 Cardinals, 424 archbishops, 2420 bishops, 413,600 priests and 960,991 nuns in 1983. There are about 420,000 churches.

Jews

The total of world Jewry was estimated to be 16.8 million in 1983. The highest concentration is in North America, with 7.3 million, of whom 2.0 million are in the New York area. The total in Israel is 3,255,000. The total of British Jewry is 410,000 of whom 280,000 are in Greater London, and 13,000 in Glasgow. The total in Tōkyō, Japan, is only 400.

PLACES OF WORSHIP

Earliest *World*

A sculpted stone face, half primate/half feline, discovered by Dr Leslie Freeman of the University of Chicago in the El Juyo cave shrine, Northern Spain, is the oldest known religious shrine and is dated to *c.* 12,000 BC. The oldest surviving Christian church in the world is a converted house in Douro-Europos now Qal'at es Salihiye in eastern Syria, dating from AD 232.

Oldest *Great Britain*

The oldest ecclesiastical building in the United Kingdom is a 6th century cell built by St Brendan in AD 542 on Eileachan Naoimh (pronounced Noo), Garvelloch Islands, Strathclyde. The Church in Great Britain with the oldest origins is St Martin's Church in Canterbury, Kent. It was built in AD 560 on the foundations of a 1st century Roman church. The chapel of St Peter on the Wall, Bradwell-on-Sea, Essex was built in AD 654–660. The oldest church in Ireland is the Gallerus Oratory, built in *c.* 750 at Ballyferriter, near Kilmalkedar, County Kerry. Britain's oldest nunnery is St Peter and Paul Minster, on the Isle of Thanet, Kent. It was founded in *c.* 748 by the Abbess Eadburga of Bugga. The oldest catholic church is St Etheldreda, Holborn, London founded in 1251. The oldest non-conformist chapel is the thatched chapel at Horningsham, Wiltshire dated 1566.

Temple Largest

The largest religious structure ever built is Angkor Wat (City Temple), enclosing 402 acres *162,6 ha* in Kampuchea, southeast Asia. It was built to the Hindu god Vishnu by the Khmer King Suryavarman II in the period 1113–50. Its curtain wall measures 1400 × 1400 yd *1280 × 1280 m* and its population, before it was abandoned in 1432, was 80,000. The whole complex of 72 major monuments begun *c.* AD 900 extends over 15 × 5 miles *24 × 8 km*. The largest Buddhist temple in the world is Borobudur, near Jogjakarta, Indonesia built in the 8th century. It is 103 ft *31,5 m* tall and 403 ft *123 m* square.

The largest Mormon temple is the Salt Lake Temple, Utah, USA completed in April 1983 and with a floor area of 253,015 ft^2 or 5.80 acres *23 505 m^2*.

Cathedral Largest *World*

The world's largest cathedral is the cathedral church of the Diocese of New York, St John the Divine, with a floor area of 121,000 ft^2 *11 240 m^2* and a volume of 16,822,000 ft^3 *476 350 m^3*. The cornerstone was laid on 27 Dec 1892, and work on the Gothic building was stopped in 1941. Work re-started in earnest in July 1979. In New York it is referred to as 'Saint John the Unfinished'. The nave is the longest in the world, 601 ft *183,18 m* in length, with a vaulting 124 ft *37,79 m* in height.

The cathedral covering the largest area is that of Santa Mariá de la Sede in Sevilla (Seville), Spain. It was built in Spanish Gothic style between 1402 and 1519 and is 414 ft *126,18 m* long, 271 ft *82,60 m* wide and 100 ft *30,48 m* high to the vault of the nave.

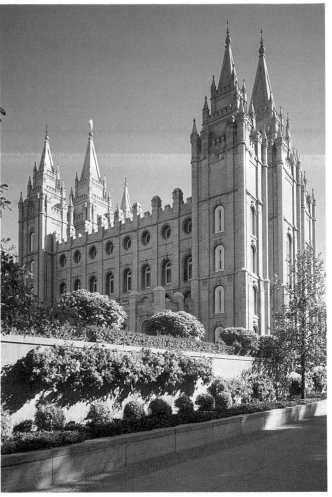

The world's largest Mormon Temple. This covers 5.8 acres *23,505 m^2* in Salt Lake City, Utah, USA.

Cathedral Largest *Great Britain*

The largest cathedral in the British Isles is the Cathedral Church of Christ in Liverpool. Built in modernized Gothic style, work was begun on 18 July 1904, and it was finally consecrated on 25 Oct 1978 after 74 years (*cf.* Exeter 95 years) using ½ million stone blocks and 12 million bricks at an actual cost of some £6 million. The building encloses 104,275 ft^2 *9687 m^2* and has an overall length of 636 ft *193,85 m*. The Vestey Tower is 331 ft *100,88 m* high. It contains the highest vaulting in the world—175 ft *53,34 m* maximum at undertower and the highest Gothic arches ever built being 107 ft *32,61 m* at apices.

Cathedral Smallest

The smallest church in the world designated as a cathedral is that of the Christ Catholic Church, Highlandville, Missouri, USA. Consecrated in July 1983 it measures 14 × 17 ft *4,26 × 5,18 m* and has seating for 18 people. The smallest cathedral in use in the United Kingdom (of old foundation) is St Asaph in Clwyd, Wales, it is 182 ft *55,47 m* long, 68 ft *20,72 m* wide and has a tower 100 ft *30,48 m* high. Oxford Cathedral in Christ Church (College) is 155 ft *47,24 m* long. The nave of the Cathedral of the Isles on the Isle of Cumbrae, Strathclyde measures only 40 × 20 ft *12,19 × 6,09 m*. The total floor area is 2,124 ft^2 *197,3 m^2*.

Church Largest *World*

The largest church in the world is the basilica of St Peter, built between 1492 and 1612 in the Vatican City, Rome. The length of the church, measured from the apse, is 611 ft 4 in *186,33 m*. The area is 162,990 ft^2 *15 142 m^2*. The inner diameter of the famous dome is 137 ft 9 in *41,98 m* and its centre is 119 m *390 ft 5 in* high. The external height is 457 ft 9 in *139,52 m*.

The elliptical Basilique of St Pie X at Lourdes, France, completed in 1957 at a cost of £2,000,000 has a capacity of 20,000 under its giant span arches and a length of 200 m *656 ft*.

The crypt of the underground Civil War Memorial Church in the Guadarrama Mountains, 45 km *28 miles* from Madrid, Spain, is 260 m *853 ft* in length. It took 21 years (1937–58) to build, at a reported cost of £140,000,000, and is surmounted by a cross 150 m *492 ft* tall.

Church Largest *Great Britain*

The largest Church in the United Kingdom is the Collegiate Church of St Peter at Westminster built AD 1050–1745. Its maximum dimensions are overall: length 530 ft *161,5 m*; breadth across transept 203 ft *61,87 m* and internal height 101 ft 8 in *30,98 m*. The largest parish church is the Parish Church of the Most Holy and Undivided Trinity at Kingston-upon-Hull covering 27,235 ft² *2530 m²* and with an external length and width of 288 ft × 124 ft *87,7 × 37,7 m*. It is also believed to be the country's oldest brick building serving its original purpose, dating from *c.* 1285. Both the former Cathedral of St Mungo, Glasgow and Beverley Minster, Humberside are now used as parish churches. The largest school chapel is that of the 150 ft *45,7 m* high Lancing College, West Sussex.

Church Smallest *World*

The world's smallest church is the Union Church at Wiscasset, Maine, USA, with a floor area of 31½ ft² *2,92 m²* (7 × 4½ ft *2,13 × 1,37 m*). St. Gobban's Church, Portbradden, County Antrim, Northern Ireland measures 12 ft 1½ in by 6 ft 6 in *3,7 × 2,0 m*.

Church Smallest *Great Britain*

The smallest church in use in England is Bremilham Church, Cowage Farm, Foxley near Malmesbury, Wiltshire which measures 12 × 12 ft *3,65 × 3,65 m* and is used for service once a year. The smallest completed medieval English church in regular use is that at Culbone, Somerset, which measures 35 × 12 ft *10,66 × 3,65 m*. The smallest Welsh chapel is St Trillo's Chapel, Rhôs-on-Sea (Llandrillo-yn-Rhos), Clwyd, measuring only 12 × 6 ft *3,65 × 1,83 m*. The smallest chapel in Scotland is St Margaret's, Edinburgh, measuring 16½ × 10½ ft *5,02 × 3,20 m*, giving a floor area of 173¼ ft² *16,09 m²*.

Synagogue Largest *World*

The largest synagogue in the world is the Temple Emanu-El on Fifth Avenue at 65th Street, New York City, NY, USA. The temple, completed in September 1929, has a frontage of 150 ft *45,72 m* on Fifth Avenue and 253 ft *77,11 m* on 65th Street. The Sanctuary proper can accommodate 2500 people, and the adjoining Beth-El Chapel seats 350. When all the facilities are in use, more than 6000 people can be accommodated.

Synagogue Largest *Great Britain*

The largest synagogue in Great Britain is the Edgware Synagogue, Barnet, Greater London, completed in 1959, with a capacity of 1630 seats. That with highest registered membership is Ilford Synagogue with 2492 at 1 Jan 1983.

Mosque Largest

The largest mosque ever built was the now ruinous al-Malawiya mosque of al-Mutawakil in Samarra, Iraq built in AD 842–52 and measuring 9.21 acres *3,72 ha* with dimensions of 784 × 512 ft *238,9 × 156,0 m*. The world's largest mosque in use is the Umayyad Mosque in Damascus, Syria built on a 2000-year-old religious site measuring 157 × 97 m *515 × 318 ft* thus covering an area of 3.76 acres *1,52 ha*. The largest mosque will be the Merdeka Mosque in Djakarta, Indonesia, which was begun in 1962. The cupola will be 45 m *147.6 ft* in diameter and the capacity in excess of 50,000 people.

Minaret *Tallest*

The tallest minarets in the world are the 4 of 105 m *344 ft 5 in* being built for a new mosque in Malaysia. The Qutb Minar, south of New Delhi, India, built in 1194 is 238 ft *72,54 m* tall.

Pagoda *Tallest and Oldest*

The world's tallest pagoda is the Phra Pathom Chedi at Nakhon Pathom, Thailand, which was built for King Mongkut in 1853–70. It rises to 115 m *377 ft*. The oldest pagoda in China is Sung-Yo Ssu in Honan built with 15 12-sided storeys, in AD 523 though the 326 ft *99,3 m* tall Shwedagon Pagoda, Rangoon, Burma is built on the site of a 27 ft *8,2 m* tall pagoda dating to 585 BC.

Sacred Object *Most Valuable*

The sacred object with the highest intrinsic value is the 15th century gold Buddah in Wat Trimitr Temple in Bangkok, Thailand. It is 10 ft *3,04 m* tall and weighs an estimated 5½ tonnes. At $500 per fine ounce its intrinsic worth has been calculated to be £28½ million. The gold under the plaster exterior was only found in 1954.

Nave *Longest*

The longest nave in the United Kingdom is that of St Albans Cathedral, Hertfordshire, which is 285 ft *86,86 m* long. The central tower of Liverpool's Anglican Cathedral (internal overall length 636 ft *193,85 m*) interrupts the nave with an undertower space.

Spire Tallest *World*

The tallest cathedral spire in the world is that of the Protestant Cathedral of Ulm in Germany. The building is early Gothic and was begun in 1377. The tower, in the centre of the west façade, was not finally completed until 1890 and is 160,90 m *528 ft* high. The world's tallest church spire is that of the Chicago Temple of the First Methodist Church on Clark Street, Chicago, Illinois, USA. The building consists of a 22-storey skyscraper (erected in 1924) surmounted by a parsonage at 330 ft *100,5 m*, a 'Sky Chapel' at 400 ft *121,92 m* and a steeple cross at 568 ft *173,12 m* above street level.

Great Britain

The highest spire in Great Britain is that of the church of St Mary, called Salisbury Cathedral, Wiltshire. The Lady Chapel was built in the years 1220–5 and the main fabric of the cathedral was finished and consecrated in 1258. The spire was added later, *ante* 1305, and reaches a height of 404 ft *123,13 m*. The central spire of Lincoln Cathedral completed in *c.* 1307 and which fell in 1548 was 525 ft *160,02 m* tall.

Stained glass *Oldest*

The oldest stained glass in the world represents the Prophets in a window of the cathedral of Augsberg, Bavaria, Germany, dating from *c.* 1050. The oldest datable stained glass in the United Kingdom is represented by 12th century fragments in the Tree of Jesse in the north aisle of the nave of York Minster, dated *c.* 1150, and medallions in Rivenhall Church, Essex which appear to date from the first half of that century. Dates late in the previous century have been attributed to glass in a window of the church at Compton, Surrey, and a complete window in St Mary the Virgin, Brabourne, Kent.

Stained glass *Largest*

The largest stained glass window is the complete mural of The Resurrection Mausoleum in Justice, Illinois, measuring 22,381 ft² *2079 m²* in 2448 panels completed in 1971. The largest single stained glass window in Great Britain is the East window in Gloucester Cathedral measuring 72 × 38 ft *21,94 × 11,58 m*, set up to commemorate the Battle of Crécy (1346), while the largest area of stained glass is 128 windows, totalling 25,000 ft² *2 322 m²* in York Minster.

Brasses

The world's oldest monumental brass is that commemorating Bishop Yso von Wölpe in Andreaskirche, Verden, near Hanover, W. Germany, dating from 1231. An engraved coffin plate of St Ulrich (d. 973), laid in 1187, was found buried in the Church of SS Ulrich and Afra, Augsburg, W. Germany in 1979. The oldest brass in Great Britain is of Sir John D'Abernon (d. 1277) at Stoke D'Abernon, near Leatherhead, Surrey, dating from *c.* 1320.

A dedication brass dated 24 Apr 1241 in Ashbourne church, Derbyshire has been cited as the earliest arabic writing extant in Britain.

CHURCH PERSONNEL

Saints

There are 1848 'registered' saints (including 60 St Johns) of whom 628 are Italians, 576 French and 271 from the United Kingdom and Ireland. Of these 8 came from Cambridge and 7 from Oxford between 1535 and 1645 but none from the House of Commons. Britain's first Christian martyr was St Alban executed *c.* AD 209. The first US born saint is Mother Elizabeth Ann Bayley Seton (1774–1821) canonized 14 Sept 1975. The total includes 76 Popes.

Most rapidly canonized

The shortest interval that has elapsed between the death of a

ROMAN CATHOLIC RECORDS—POPES AND CARDINALS

Longest Papal Reign	Pius IX—Giovanni Maria Mastai-Ferretti (1846–1878)	31 years 236 days
Shortest Papal Reign	Stephan II (752)	2 days
Longest Lived Pope	St. Agatho (d. 681) (probably exaggerated)	?106 years
	Leo XIII—Gioacchino Pecci (1810–1903)	93 years 140 days
Youngest Elected	Benedict IX—Theophylact (c. 1020–1056) in 1032	11 or 12 years
Last Married	Adrian II (pre-celibacy rule)	elected 867
Last with Children	Alexander VI—Rodrigo Borgia (1431–1503) father of six	elected 1492
Last non-Cardinal	Urban VI—Bartolomeo Prignano (1318–89), Archbishop of Bari	8 Apr 1378
Last Briton	Adrian IV—Nicholas Breakspear (c. 1100–59), b. Abbots Langley, Hertfordshire	4 Dec 1154
Last previous non-Italian	Adrian VI—Adrian Florenz Boeyens (Netherlands)	elected 31 Aug 1522
Slowest Election	Gregory X—Teobaldi Visconti, 31 months	Feb 1269–1 Sept 1271
Fastest Election	Julius II—on first ballot	21 Oct 1503
Slowest Canonization	St. Leo III—over span of 857 years	816–1673
Oldest Cardinal (*all-time*)	Georgio da Costa (b. Portugal, 1406) d. Rome aged 102 years	18 Sept 1508
Oldest Cardinal (*current*)	Pietro Parente (b. 16 Feb 1891) 93rd birthday	fl. 16 Feb 1984
Youngest Cardinal (*all-time*)	Luis Antonio de Bourbon (b. 25 July 1727) aged 8 years 147 days	elected 19 Dec 1735
Youngest Cardinal (*current*)	Jaime L. Sin, Archbishop of Manila (b. 31 Aug 1928)	in 57th year
Longest Serving	Cardinal Duke of York, grandson of James VII of Scotland and II of England, 60 years 10 days	1747–1807

Saint and his canonization was in the case of St Anthony of Padua, Italy, who died on 13 June 1231 and was canonized 352 days later on 30 May 1232. For the other extreme of 857 years see Papal table.

Bishopric *Longest tenure*
The longest tenure of any Church of England bishopric is 57 years in the case of the Rt Rev. Thomas Wilson, who was consecrated Bishop of Sodar and Man on 16 Jan 1698 and died in office on 7 Mar 1755. Of English bishoprics the longest tenures, if one excludes the unsubstantiated case of Aethelwulf, reputedly Bishop of Hereford from 937 to 1012, are those of 47 years by Jocelin de Bohun (Salisbury) 1142–89 and Nathaniel Crew or Crewe (Durham) 1674–1721.

Bishop *Oldest*
The oldest serving bishop (excluding Suffragans and Assistants) in the Church of England as at mid 1984 was the Right Reverend Douglas Feaver, Bishop of Peterborough, who was born on 22 May 1914.

The oldest Roman Catholic bishop in recent years has been Bishop Angelo Teutonico, formerly Bishop of Aversa (b. 28 Aug 1874), who died aged 103 years 276 days on 31 May 1978. He had celebrated Mass about 24,800 times. Bishop Herbert Welch of the United Methodist Church, who was elected a bishop for Japan and Korea in 1916, died on 4 Apr 1969 aged 106.

Bishop *Youngest*
The youngest bishop of all time was HRH The Duke of York and Albany, KG, GCB, GCH, the second son of George III, who was elected Bishop of Osnabrück, through his father's influence as Elector of Hanover, at the age of 196 days on 27 Feb 1764. He resigned after 39 years' enjoyment.

The youngest serving bishop (excluding Suffragans and Assistants) in the Church of England as at mid 1984 is the Rt Rev Robert Williamson (b. 18 Dec 1932), Bishop of Bradford.

Oldest parish priest
Father Alvaro Fernandez (b. 8 Dec 1880) has been parish priest at Santiago de Abres, Spain since 1919.

Longest incumbency
The longest Church of England incumbency on record is one of 75 years 357 days by the Rev. Bartholomew Edwards, Rector of St Nicholas, Ashill, Norfolk from 1813 to 1889. There appears to be some doubt as to whether the Rev. Richard Sherinton was installed at Folkestone from 1524 or 1529 to 1601. If the former is correct it would surpass the Norfolk record. The parish of Farrington, Hampshire had only two incumbents in a 122 year period viz Rev. J. Benn (28 Mar 1797 to 1857) and Rev. T. H. Massey (1857 to 5 Apr 1919). From 1675 to 1948 the incumbents of Rose Ash, Devon were from 8 generations of the family of Southcomb.

Longest serving chorister
Harry Phillips (1884–1983) joined the choir of St Michael and All Angels West Felton, Shropshire in 1893 aged 8. He was still serving as a chorister 90 years later in April 1983. Having become a chorister in 1876 at the age of 9, Thomas Rogers was appointed vicar's warden in 1966 at Montacute, Somerset.

Parishes *Largest and Smallest*
The smallest parish in the United Kingdom is The Scares which consists of rocky islets in Luce Bay with an area of 1.10 acres *0.44 ha* and included in Wigtown, Dumfries and Galloway. In 1982 the parish of Dallinghoo Wield, Suffolk boasted a population of nil and an area of 38 acres *14,6 ha*. The largest parish is Kilmonivaig in Inverness, Highland with an area of 267,233.03 acres *108 145,46 ha*.

Oldest parish register
The oldest part of any parish register surviving in England is a sheet from that of Alfriston, East Sussex recording a marriage on 10 July 1504. Scotland's oldest surviving register is that for Anstruther-Wester, Fife, with burial entries from 1549.

Crowds *Largest*
The greatest recorded number of human beings assembled with a common purpose was an estimated 12,700,000 at the Hindu festival of Kumbh-Mela, which was held at the confluence of the Yamuna (formerly called the Jumna), the Ganges and the invisible 'Sarasvati' at Allahabad, Uttar Pradesh, India, on 19 Jan 1977. The holiest time during this holiest day since 1833 was during the planetary alignment between 9.28 and 9.40 a.m. during which only 200,000 achieved immersion to wash away the sins of a lifetime. The queue at the grave of the chansonier and guitarist Vladimir Visotsky (died 28 July 1980), stretched 10 km *6.2 miles*.

Largest funerals
The funeral of the charismatic C. N. Annadurai (died 3 Feb 1969) Madras Chief Minister was, according to a police estimate attended by 15 million. The longest funeral in Britain was probably that of Vice Admiral Viscount Nelson on 9 Jan 1806. Ticket-holders were seated in St Paul's Cathedral by 8.30 a.m. Many were unable to leave until after 9 p.m.

Biggest demonstrations
A figure of 2.7 million was published from China for the demonstration against the USSR in Shanghai on 3–4 Apr 1969 following the border clashes, and one of 10 million for the May Day celebrations of 1963 in Peking.

9. ACCIDENTS AND DISASTERS

WORST IN THE WORLD

DATE	LOCATION	NUMBER KILLED	DISASTER
1347-51	Eurasia: The Black Death (bubonic, pneumonia and septicaemic plague)	75,000,000	Pandemic
1311-40	Mongol extermination of Chinese Peasantry	35,000,000	Genocide
1918	Worldwide: Influenza	21,640,000	Influenza
1969-71	Northern China (revealed May 1981)	c. 20,000,000[1]	Famine
April-Nov 1970	Ganges Delta Islands, Bangladesh	1,000,000	Circular Storm[2]
Oct 1887	Hwang-ho River, China	900,000	Flood
23 Jan 1556	Shensi Province, China (duration 2 hours)	830,000	Earthquake
16 Dec 1920	Kansu Province, China	180,000	Landslide
6 Aug 1945	Hiroshima, Japan	141,000	Atomic Bomb
5-7 Apr 1815	Tambora Sumbawa, Indonesia	92,000	Volcanic Eruption
13-15 Feb 1945	Dresden, Germany	c. 50,000	Conventional bombing[3]
31 May 1970	Yungay, Huascarán, Peru	c. 18,000[4]	Avalanches
30 Jan 1945	Wilhelm Gustloff (25,484 tons) German liner torpedoed off Danzig by USSR submarine S-13	c. 7700	Marine (single ship)
11 Aug 1979	Manchhu River Dam, Morvi, Gujarat, India	c. 5000	Dam Burst
c. 8 June 1941	Chungking (Zhong qing) China air raid shelter	c. 4000[5]	Panic
5-13 Dec 1952	London fog, England	2,850	Smog
1931-35	Hawk's Nest hydroelectric tunnel, W. Virginia, USA	c. 2000	Tunnelling (Silicosis)
6 Dec 1917	Halifax, Nova Scotia, Canada	1963[6]	Explosion
May 1845	The Theatre, Canton, China	1670	Fire[7] (single building)
26 April 1942	Honkeiko Colliery, China (coal dust explosion)	1572	Mining[8]
13-16 July 1863	New York City anti-conscription riots	c. 1200	Riot
2 or 3 Nov 1982	Petrol tanker explosion inside Salang Tunnel, Afghanistan	c. 1100	Road[9]
18 Nov 1978	People's Temple cult by cyanide, Jonestown, Guyana	913	Mass Suicide
19-20 Feb 1945	Japanese soldiers, Ramree I., Burma (disputed)	c. 900	Crocodiles
6 June 1981	Bagmati River, Bihar state, India	>800	Railway
16 May 1770	Daupine's Wedding, Seine, Paris	>800	Fireworks
18 Mar 1925	South Central States, USA (3 hours)	689	Tornado
27 Mar 1977	KLM-Pan Am Boeing 747 ground crash, Tenerife	583	Aircraft (Civil)
April-May 1979	Novosibirsk B & CW plant, USSR	c. 300	Bacteriological & Chemical
20 April 1888	Moradabad, Uttar Pradesh, India	246	Hail
23 Oct 1983	Lorry bomb, US Marine barracks, Beirut, Lebanon	243	Terrorism
27 Mar 1980	Alexander L. Kielland 'Flotel' (10,105 tons), North Sea	123	Off-Shore Oil Plant
18 Feb 1942	Le Surcouf rammed by US merchantman Thomas Lykes in Caribbean	130	Submarine
10 May 1977	Israeli military 'Sea Stallion', West Bank	54	Helicopter
9 Mar 1976	Cavalese resort, Northern Italy	42	Ski Lift (Cable car)
Dec 1952	USSR Expedition on Mount Everest	40[10]	Mountaineering
27 Mar 1980	Vaal Reefs Gold mine lift fell 1.2 miles 1.93 km	23	Elevator (Lift)
23 Dec 1975	Hut in Chinamasa Kraal nr. Umtali, Zimbabwe (single bolt)	21	Lightning
13-15 Aug 1979	28th Fastnet Race — 23 boats sank or abandoned in Force 11 gale	19	Yacht Racing
27 Jan 1967	Apollo oxygen fire, Cape Kennedy, Fla, USA	3	Space Exploration
29 June 1971	Soyuz II re-entry over USSR		
c. Dec 1957	Venting of plutonium extraction wastes, Kyshtym, USSR	high but undisclosed[18]	Nuclear Waste Accident

WORST IN THE UNITED KINGDOM

DISASTER	NUMBER KILLED	LOCATION	DATE
Pandemic	800,000	The Black Death (bubonic, pneumonic and septicaemic plague)	1347-50
Genocide			
Influenza	225,000	Influenza	Sept-Nov 1918
Famine	1,500,000[11]	Ireland (famine and typhus)	1846-51
Circular Storm[2]	c. 8000	The Channel Storm	26 nov 1703
Flood	c. 2000[12]	Severn Estuary	20 Jan 1606
Earthquake	4	East Anglian Earthquake	22 April 1884
Landslide	144	Pantglas coal tip No 7, Aberfan, Mid Glamorgan	21 Oct 1966
Atomic Bomb			
Volcanic Eruption			
Conventional bombing[3]	1436	London	10-11 May 1941
Avalanches	8	Lewes, East Sussex	27 Dec 1836
Marine (single ship)	c. 800[13]	HMS Royal George, off Spithead	29 Aug 1782
Dam Burst	250	Bradfield Reservoir, Dale Dyke, near Sheffield, South Yorkshire (embankment burst)	12 Mar 1864
Panic	183	Victoria Hall, Sunderland, Tyne and Wear	16 June 1883
Smog	2,850	Excess deaths	5-13 Dec 1952
Tunnelling (Silicosis)			
Explosion	134[14]	Chilwell, Notts. (explosive factory)	1 July 1918
Fire[7] (single building)	188[15]	Theatre Royal, Exeter	5 Sept 1887
Mining[8]	439	Universal Colliery, Senghenydd, Mid Glamorgan	14 Oct 1913
Riot	565 (min)	London anti-Catholic Gordon riots	2-13 June 1780
Road[9]	33	Coach crash, River Dibb, nr Grassington, North Yorks	27 May 1975
Mass Suicide			
Crocodiles			
Railway	227[16]	Triple collision, Quintins Hill, Dumfries & Galloway	22 May 1915
Fireworks			
Tornado	75	Tay Bridge collapsed under impact of two tornadic vortices	28 Dec 1879
Aircraft (Civil)	118[17]	BEA Trident 1C, Staines, Surrey	18 June 1972
Bacteriological & Chemical			
Hail			
Terrorism	21	Birmingham Pub bombs (IRA)	21 Nov 1974
Off-Shore Oil Plant	24	Aboard North Sea pentagonal semi-submersible (see left)	27 Mar 1980
Submarine	99	HMS Thetis, during trials, Liverpool Bay	1 June 1939
Helicopter			
Ski Lift (Cable car)			
Mountaineering	6	On Cairngorm, Scotland (4084 ft)	21 Nov 1971
Elevator (Lift)			
Lightning	31	(Annual total) Worst year on record (annual av. 12)	1914
Yacht Racing	19	(See left) Of 316 starters only 128 finished	13-15 Aug 1979
Space Exploration			
Nuclear Waste Accident			

1 In 1770 the great Indian famine carried away a proportion of the population estimated as high as one third, hence a figure of tens of millions. The figure for Bengal alone was also probably about 10 million. The figure for the Northern China famine of Feb 1877–Sept 1878 was 9,500,000. It has been estimated that more than 5 million died in the post-World War I famine of 1920–1 in the USSR. The USSR government in July 1923 informed Mr (later President) Herbert Hoover that the ARA (American Relief Administration) had since August 1921 saved 20 million lives from famine and famine diseases.

2 This figure published in 1972 for the Bangladeshi disaster was from Dr Afzal, Principal Scientific Officer of the Atomic Energy Authority Centre, Dacca. One report asserted that less than half of the population of the 4 islands of Bhola, Charjabbar, Hatia and Ramagati (1961 Census 1.4 million) survived. The most damaging hurricane recorded was the billion dollar Betsy (name now retired) in 1965 with an insurance pay-out of $715 million. Hurricane Frederic (Sept 1979) cost insurers $752 million in inflated dollars.

3 The number of civilians killed by the bombing of Germany has been put variously as 593,000 and 'over 635,000': A figure of c. 140,000 deaths in the USAF fire raids on Tōkyō of 13 Mar 1945 has been attributed. Total Japanese fatalities were 600,000.

4 A total of 18,000 Austrian and Italian troops were reported to have been lost in the Dolomite valleys of Northern Italy on 13 Dec 1916 in more than 100 snow avalanches. Some of the avalanches were triggered by gun-fire.

5 It was estimated that some 5000 people were trampled to death in the stampede for free beer at the coronation celebration of Czar Nicholas II in Moscow in May 1896.

6 Some sources maintain that the final death roll was over 3000 on 6–7 Dec. Published estimates of the 11,000 killed at the BASF chemical plant explosion at Oppau, W. German on 21 Sept 1921 were exaggerated. The best estimate is 561 killed.

7 >200,000 killed in the sack of Moscow, freed by the Tartars in May 1571. Worst ever hotel fire 162 killed, Hotel Daeyungak, Seoul, South Korea 25 Dec 1971. Worst Circus fire 168 killed Hartford, Conn. USA 6 July 1944.

8 The worst gold mining disaster in South Africa was 152 killed due to flooding in the Witwatersrand Gold Mining Co. Gold Mine in 1909.

9 Some estimates ran as high as 2700 victims from carbon monoxide asphyxiation after Soviet military sealed both ends of the 1.7 mile 2.7 km long tunnel. The worst ever years for road deaths in the USA and the UK have been respectively 1969 (56,400) and 1941 (9169). The global aggregate death roll was put at 25 million by September 1975. The world's highest death rate is 29 per 100,000 in 1978 in Luxembourg and Portugal. The greatest pile-up on British roads was on the M6 near Lymm Interchange, near Thelwall, involving 200 vehicles on 13 Sept 1971 with 11 dead and 60 injured.

10 According to Polish sources, not confirmed by the USSR. Also 23 died on Mount Fuji, Japan, in blizzard and avalanche on 20 Mar 1972.

11 Based on the net rate of natural increase between 1841 and 1851, a supportable case for a loss of population of 3 million can be made out if rates of enumeration of 25 per cent (1841) and 10 per cent (1851) are accepted. Potato rot (Phytophthora infestans) was first reported on 13 Sept 1845.

12 Death rolls of 100,000 were reputed in England and Holland in the floods of 1099, 1421 and 1446.

13 c. 2800 were lost on HM Troopship Lancastria 16,243 tons off St. Nazaire on 17 June 1940. The Princess Alice collision on the Thames with the Bywell Castle off Woolwich on 3 Sept 1878 killed 786.

14 HM Armed Cruiser Natal blew up off Invergordon killing 428 on 30 Dec 1915.

15 In July 1212, 3000 were killed in the crush, burned or drowned when London Bridge caught fire at both ends. The death roll in the Great Fire of London of 1666 was only 8. History's first 'fire storm' occurred in the Quebec Yard, Surrey Docks, Southwark, London during the 300-pump fire in the Blitz on 7–8 Sept 1940. Dockland casualties were 306 killed. Britain's most destructive fire was the £165 million loss at the Army Ordnance depot, Donnington, Shropshire in June 1982.

16 The 213 yd 194.7 m long troop train was telescoped to 67 yd 61.2 m. Signalmen Meakin and Tinsley were sentenced for manslaughter. Britain's worst underground train disaster was the Moorgate Tube disaster of 28 Feb 1975 when 43 were killed.

17 The worst crash by a UK operated aircraft was that of the Dan-Air Boeing 727 from Manchester which crashed into a mountain on the Canary Islands on 25 Apr 1980 killing 146 people. There were no survivors.

18 More than 30 small communities in a 1200 km² 460 mile² area eliminated from USSR maps since 1958. Possibly an ammonium nitrate-hexone explosion.

Chapter 12

SPORTS GAMES & PASTIMES

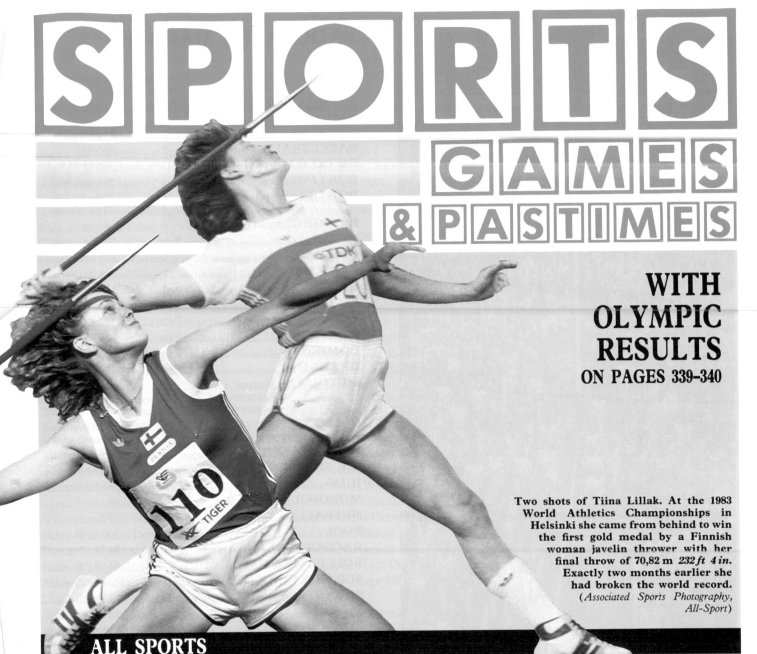

WITH OLYMPIC RESULTS ON PAGES 339–340

Two shots of Tiina Lillak. At the 1983 World Athletics Championships in Helsinki she came from behind to win the first gold medal by a Finnish woman javelin thrower with her final throw of 70,82 m *232 ft 4 in*. Exactly two months earlier she had broken the world record. (*Associated Sports Photography, All-Sport*)

ALL SPORTS

See also The Guinness Book of Sports Facts *by Stan Greenberg, published at £6.95 in 1984.*

Earliest
The origins of sport stem from the time when self-preservation ceased to be the all-consuming human preoccupation. Archery was a hunting skill in mesolithic times (by *c.* 8000 BC), but did not become an organised sport until later, certainly *c.* AD 300, among the Genoese and possibly as early as the 12th century BC, as an archery competition is described in Homer's Iliad. The earliest dated evidence for sport is *c.* 2750–2600 BC for wrestling. Ball games by girls depicted on Middle Kingdom murals at Beni Hasan, Egypt have been dated to *c.* 2050 BC.

Fastest
The highest speed reached in a non-mechanical sport is in sky-diving, in which a speed of 185 mph *298 km/h* is attained in a head-down free falling position, even in the lower atmosphere. In delayed drops speeds of 625 mph *1005 km/h* have been recorded at high rarefied altitudes. The highest projectile speed in any moving ball game is *c.* 188 mph *302 km/h* in pelota. This compares with 170 mph *273 km/h* (electronically-timed) for a golf ball driven off a tee.

Slowest
In wrestling, before the rules were modified towards 'brighter wrestling', contestants could be locked in holds for so long that a single bout once lasted for 11 hr 40 min. In the extreme case of the 2 hr 41 min pull in the regimental tug o' war in Jubbulpore, India, on 12 Aug 1889, the winning team moved a net distance of 12 ft *3,6 m* at an average speed of 0.00084 mph *0,00135 km/h*.

Longest
The most protracted sporting contest was an automobile duration test of 222,621 miles *358 273 km* (equivalent to 8.93 times around the equator) by Appaurchaux and others in a Ford Taunus at Miranas, France. This was contested over 142 days in July–Nov 1963.

The most protracted non-mechanical sporting event is the *Tour de France* cycling race. In 1926 this was over 3569 miles *5743 km* lasting 29 days but is now reduced to 23 days.

Largest pitch
The largest pitch of any ball game is that of polo, with 12.4 acres *5,0 ha*, or a maximum length of 300 yd *274 m* and a width, without side boards, of 200 yd *182 m*. With boards the width is 160 yd *146 m*. Twice a year in the Parish of St Columb Major, Cornwall, a game called Hurling (not to be confused with the Irish game) is played on a 'pitch' which consists of the entire Parish, approximately 25 square miles *64,7 km²*.

Youngest and oldest internationals

The youngest age at which any person has won international honours is eight years in the case of Joy Foster, the Jamaican singles and mixed doubles table tennis champion in 1958. The youngest British international has been diver Beverley Williams (b. 5 Jan 1957), who was 10 yr 268 days old when she competed against the USA at Crystal Palace, London, on 30 Sept 1967. It would appear that the greatest age at which anyone has actively competed for his country was 72 yr 280 days in the case of Oscar Swahn (see above) who won a silver medal for shooting in the Olympic Games at Antwerp on 26 July 1920. He qualified for the 1924 Games but was unable to participate due to illness. Britain's oldest international was Hilda Lorna Johnstone (b. 4 Sept 1902) who was 70 yr 5 days when she was placed twelfth in the Dressage competition at the 1972 Games.

Most versatile

Charlotte 'Lottie' Dod (1871–1960) won the Wimbledon Singles tennis title five times between 1887 and 1893, the British Ladies Golf Championship in 1904, an Olympic silver medal for archery in 1908, and represented England at hockey in 1899. She also excelled at skating and tobogganing. Mildred 'Babe' Zaharias (*née* Didrikson) (1914–56) (USA) won two gold medals (80 m hurdles and javelin) and a silver (high jump) at the 1932 Olympic Games. She set world records at those three events in 1930–32. She was an All-American basketball player for three years and set the world record for throwing the baseball 296 ft *90,22 m*. Switching to golf she won the US women's Amateur title in 1946 and the US Women's Open in 1948, 1950 and 1954. She also excelled at several other sports. Charles Burgess Fry (GB) (1872–1956) was probably the most versatile male sportsman at the highest level. On 4 Mar 1893 he equalled the world long jump record of 23 ft 6½ in *7,17 m*. He represented England *v.* Ireland at soccer (1901) and played first-class rugby for the Barbarians. His greatest achievements were at cricket, where he headed the English batting averages in six seasons and captained England in 1912. He was an excellent angler and tennis player.

Most prolific record breaker

Between 24 Jan 1970 and 1 Nov 1977 Vasili Alexeyev (USSR) (b. 7 Jan 1942) broke 80 official world records in weightlifting.

Longest reign

The longest reign as a world champion is 33 years (1829–62) by Jacques Edmond Barre (France) (1802–73) at real tennis. The longest reign as a British champion is 41 years by the archer Alice Blanche Legh (1855–1948) who first won the Championship in 1881 and for the 23rd and final time in 1922 aged 67.

Shortest reign

Olga Rukavishnikova (USSR) (b. 13 Mar 1955) held the pentathlon world record for 0.4 sec at Moscow on 24 July 1980. That is the difference between her second place time of 2 min 04.8 sec in the final 800 m event of the Olympic five-event competition, and that of third-placed Nadyezhda Tkachenko (USSR), whose overall points were better, 5083 to 4937.

Heaviest sportsman

The heaviest sportsman of all-time was the professional wrestler William J. Cobb of Macon, Georgia, USA, who in 1962 was billed as the 802 lb (57 st 4 lb *363 kg*) 'Happy Humphrey'. The heaviest player of a ball-game was the 487 lb *221 kg* Bob Pointer, the US Football tackle formerly on the 1967 Santa Barbara High School Team, California, USA.

Greatest earnings

The greatest fortune amassed by an individual in sport is an estimated $69 million by the boxer Muhammad Ali Haj (USA) in 1960–81. The highest paid woman athlete in the world is tennis player Martina Navratilova (b. Prague, Czechoslovakia, 18 Oct 1956) whose official career earnings passed $8 million in 1984 (*see p. 321*).

Biggest sports contract

In March 1982, the National Football League concluded a deal worth $2000 million for five years coverage of American Football by the three major TV networks, ABC, CBS and NBC. This represents $14.2 million for each league team.

Largest crowd

The greatest number of live spectators for any sporting spectacle is the estimated 2,500,000 who annually line the route of the New York Marathon. However, spread over 23 days, it is estimated that more than 10,000,000 see the annual *Tour de France* cycling race along the route.

The largest crowd travelling to any single sporting venue is 'more than 400,000' for the annual *Grand Prix d'Endurance* motor race on the Sarthe circuit near Le Mans, France. The record stadium crowd was one of 199,854 for the Brazil *v.* Uruguay soccer match in the Maracaña Municipal Stadium, Rio de Janeiro, Brazil, on 16 July 1950.

Most participants

The *Round the Bays*, 6.5 mile *10,5 km* run in Auckland, New Zealand attracted an estimated 80,000 runners on 27 Mar 1982. The 1983 Women's International Bowling Congress Championship tournament attracted 75,480 bowlers for the 83-day event held 7 Apr—1 July at Showboat Lanes, Las Vegas, Nevada, USA. The most runners in a marathon were the 18,469 in the London marathon on 13 May 1984, of whom 16,580 finished. The biggest mass run in Great Britain is the half-marathon Great North Run, from Newcastle to South Shields, with about 21,500 starters on 19 June 1983.

Largest television audience

The largest television audience for a single sporting event, excluding Olympic events, was an estimated 1500 million who saw the final of the 1982 soccer World Cup.

Most sportsmen

According to a report in 1978, 55 million people are active in sports in the USSR. The country has 3282 stadiums, 1435 swimming pools and over 66,000 indoor gymnasia. It is estimated that some 29 per cent of the population of E. Germany participate in sport regularly.

Worst disasters

The worst sports disaster in recent history was when an estimated 604 were killed after some stands at the Hong Kong Jockey Club racecourse collapsed and caught fire on 26 Feb 1918. During the reign of Antoninus Pius (AD 138–161) the upper wooden tiers in the Circus Maximus, Rome, collapsed during a gladiatorial combat killing some 1112 spectators. Britain's worst sports disaster was when 66 were killed and 145 injured at the Rangers *v.* Celtic football match at Exit 13 of Ibrox Park stadium, Glasgow on 2 Jan 1971.

AEROBATICS

Earliest

The first aerobatic 'manoeuvre' is generally considered to be the sustained inverted flight in a Bleriot of Célestin-Adolphe Pégoud (1889–1915), at Buc, France on 21 Sept 1913, but Lieut. Peter Nikolayevich Nesterov (1887–1914), of the Imperial Russian Air Service, performed a loop in a Nieuport Type IV monoplane at Kiev, USSR on 27 Aug 1913.

World Championships

Held biennially since 1960 (excepting 1974), scoring is based on the system devised by Col José Aresti of Spain. The competitions consist of two compulsory and two free programmes. The team competition has been won on five occasions by the USSR. No individual has won more than one title. Igor Egorov (USSR) who won in 1970, was also second in 1976. The most successful in the women's competition has been Lidia Leonova (USSR) with first place in 1976, second in 1978 and third in 1972. The only medal achieved by Britain has been a bronze in the team event at Kiev, USSR in 1976. The highest individual placing by a Briton is fourth by Neil Williams (1935–77) in 1976.

Inverted flight

The duration record for inverted flight is 4 hr 9 min 5 sec by John 'Hal' McClain in a Swick Taylorcraft on 23 Aug 1980 over Houston International Raceways, Texas, USA.

Loops

On 21 June 1980, R. Steven Powell performed 2315⅚ inside loops in a Bellanca Decathalon over Almont, Michigan, USA. John McClain achieved 180 outside loops in a Bellanca Super Decathalon on 2 Sept 1978 over Houston, Texas, USA.

Ken Ballinger completed 155 consecutive loops in a Bellanca Citabria on 6 Aug 1983 over Staverton Airport, Cheltenham, Gloucestershire.

ANGLING

For further information on fishing see The Guinness Guides to Salt Water Angling *by Brian Harris,* to Game Fishing *by Dr William Currie, and to Coarse Fishing by Michael Prichard and Michael Shepley, published by Guinness Superlatives at £10.95, £9.95 and £10.95 respectively.*

Catch *Largest Single*

The largest officially ratified fish ever caught on a rod is a man-eating great white shark (*Carcharodon carcharias*) weighing 2664 lb *1208 kg* and measuring 16 ft 10 in *5,13 m* long, caught on a 130 lb *58 kg* test line by Alf Dean at Denial Bay, near Ceduna, South Australia, on 21 Apr 1959. A great white shark weighing 3388 lb *1537 kg* was caught by Clive Green off Albany, Western Australia, on 26 Apr 1976 but will remain unratified as whale meat was used as bait. The biggest ever rod-caught fish by a British angler is a 1260 lb *571,5 kg* black marlin, by Edward A. Crutch off Cairns, Queensland, Australia on 19 Oct 1973.

In June 1978 a great white shark measuring 29 ft 6 in *9,00 m* in length and weighing over 10,000 lb *4536 kg* was harpooned and landed by fishermen in the harbour of San Miguel, Azores.

The largest marine animal ever killed by *hand* harpoon was a blue whale 97 ft *29,56 m* in length, by Archer Davidson in Twofold Bay, New South Wales, Australia, in 1910. Its tail flukes measured 20 ft *6,09 m* across and its jaw bone 23 ft 4 in *7,11 m*.

The largest fish ever caught in a British river was a 388 lb *175,99 kg* sturgeon (9 ft 2 in *2,79 m* long) landed by Alec Allen (1895–1972), helped by David Price, from the River Towy, between Llandilo and Carmarthen, S. Wales, on 25 July 1933.

Catch *Smallest*

The smallest fish to win a competition is a smelt, weighing $\frac{1}{16}$ oz *1 dram*, caught by Peter Christian at Buckenham Ferry, Norfolk, England on 9 Jan 1977, in defeating 107 other competitors. For the smallest full-grown fish *see p. 39.*

Spear fishing

The largest fish ever taken underwater was an 804 lb *364 kg* giant black grouper or jewfish by Don Pinder of the Miami Triton Club, Florida, USA, in 1955. The British spear-fishing record is 89 lb *40,36 kg* for an angler fish by James Brown (Weymouth Association Divers) in 1969.

Championship records *World*

The *Confédération Internationale de la Pêche Sportive* championships were inaugurated as European championships in 1953. They were recognised as World Championships in 1957. France won twelve times between 1956 and 1981 and Robert Tesse (France) took the individual title uniquely three times, in 1959–60, 1965. The record weight (team) is 76 lb 8 oz 8 dr *34,71 kg* in 3 hr by West Germany on the Neckar at Mannheim, West Germany on 21 Sept 1980. The individual record is 37 lb 7 oz 3 dr *16,99 kg* by Wolf-Rüdiger Kremkus (West Germany) at Mannheim on 20 Sept 1980. The most fish caught is 652 by Jacques Isenbaert (Belgium) at Dunajvaros, Yugoslavia on 27 Aug 1967.

Championship records *British*

The National Angling Championship (instituted 1906) has been won seven times by Leeds (1909–10, 1914, 1928, 1948–9, 1952). Only James H. R. Bazley (Leeds) has ever won the individual title twice (1909, 1927). The record catch is 76 lb 9 oz *34 kg 720* by David Burr (Rugby) in the Huntspill, Somerset in 1965. The largest single fish caught in the Championships is a carp of 14 lb 2 oz *6 kg 406* by John C. Essex on 13 Sept 1975 on the River Nene, Peterborough. The team championship is determined on points earned by team members in each section. The points record in Division 1, where there are 80 teams of 12 anglers, is 883 by Nottingham Federation in 1980 on the lower Trent. The winning team in 1983, Nottingham Federation, produced a team weight of 63,99 kg *141.07 lbs* of fish.

Match fishing

In a sweepstake on the Sillees River, a tributary of the Erne, Co. Fermanagh, Ulster, on 14 May 1981, Peter Burrell weighed in 258 lb 9½ oz *117,29 kg* of fish in the five hour open event.

Casting records

The longest freshwater cast ratified under ICF (International Casting Federation) rules is 175,01 m *574 ft 2 in* by Walter

Neil Mackellow from Crawley, West Sussex sets the UK Surfcasting record to win the 1983 UKSF final at Norwich. (*Angler's Mail*)

Kummerow (W. Germany), for the Bait Distance Double-Handed 30 g event held at Lenzerheide, Switzerland in the 1968 Championships. The British National record is 148,78 m *488 ft 1 in* by Andy Dickison on the same occasion. The longest Fly Distance Double-Handed cast is 78,38 m *257 ft 2 in* by Sverne Scheen (Norway), also at Lenzerheide in September 1968. Peter Anderson set a British National professional record of 70,50 m *231 ft 3 in* on water at Scarborough on 11 Sept 1977, and Hugh Newton cast 80,47 m *264 ft* on land at Stockholm, Sweden on 20 Sept 1978. The UK Surfcasting Federation record (150 gr *5¼ oz* weight) is 815 ft *248 m* by Neil Mackellow on 4 Sept 1983 at Norwich.

Longest fight

The longest recorded individual fight with a fish is 32 hr 5 min by Donal Heatley (b. 1938) (New Zealand) with a black marlin (estimated length 20 ft *6,09 m* and weight 1500 lb *680 kg*) off Mayor Island off Tauranga, North Island on 21–22 Jan 1968. It towed the 12 ton/*tonnes* launch 50 miles *80 km* before breaking the line.

IGFA WORLD RECORDS

The International Game Fish Association (IGFA) recognise world records for game fish—both Freshwater and Saltwater—for a large number of species of fish. Their thousands of categories include all-tackle, various line classes and tippet classes for fly fishing.

Freshwater All-Tackle records

The heaviest category recognised by the IGFA is for the sturgeon—468 lb *212,28 kg* by Joey Pallotta on 9 July 1983 off Benicia, California, USA.

An 834 lb *378,30 kg* sturgeon was landed (not by rod) by Garry Oling on 11 Aug 1981 from the Fraser River at Albion, British Columbia, Canada.

Saltwater All-Tackle records

The heaviest category recognised by the IGFA is for the White Shark—2664 lb *1208,38 kg* by Alfred Dean on 21 Apr 1959 off Ceduna, Australia.

ARCHERY

Earliest references

Though the earliest evidence of the existence of bows is seen in the Mesolithic cave paintings in Spain, archery as an organized sport appears to have developed in the 3rd century AD. Competitive archery may however date back to the 12th century BC. The oldest archery body in the British Isles is the Royal Company of Archers, the Sovereign's bodyguard for

Scotland, dating from 1676, though the Society of Kilwinning Archers, in Scotland, have contested the Papingo Shoot since 1488. The world governing body is the *Fédération Internationale de Tir à l'Arc* (FITA), founded in 1931.

World Records *Single FITA rounds*

Event	Points	Name and Country	possible	Year
MEN				
FITA	1341	Darrell Pace (USA)	1440	1979
90 m	322	Vladimir Yesheyev (USSR)	360	1980
70 m	339	Tomi Poikolainen (Finland)	360	1983
50 m	345	Richard McKinney (USA)	360	1982
30 m	356	Darrell Pace (USA)	360	1978
Team	3908	USA (Darrell Pace, Richard McKinney, Jerry Pylpchuk)	4320	1983
WOMEN				
FITA	1325	Lyudmila Arshanikova (USSR)	1440	1984
70 m	328	Natalia Butuzova (USSR)	360	1979
60 m	338	Lyudmila Arshanikova (USSR)	360	1984
50 m	331	Paivi Meriluoto (Fin)	360	1982
30 m	353	Valentina Radionova (USSR)	360	1981
Team	3925	USSR (Lyudmila Arshanikova, Natalia Butuzova, Sebinsio Rustamova)	4320	1983

Highest Championship scores

The highest scores achieved in either a world or Olympic championship for Double FITA rounds are: men, 2617 points (possible 2880) by Darrell Pace (b. 23 Oct 1956) (USA) and Richard McKinney (b. 20 Oct 1963) (USA); and women, 2616 points by Kim Jin Ho (N. Korea), both at Long Beach, California, USA on 21–22 Oct 1983.

British records

York Round—possible 1296 pts: Single Round, 1160 Steven Hallard at Meriden on 26 June 1983. Double Round, 2240 Steven Hallard at Stoneleigh on 14 Aug 1983.

Hereford (Women)—possible 1296 pts: Single Round, 1182 Elaine Tomkinson at Bingley on 10 Aug 1980. Double Round, 2331 Sue Willcox at Oxford on 27–28 June 1979.

FITA Round (Men): Steven Hallard, 1300 Single Round and 2566 Double Round, both at Castle Ashby, Nottinghamshire on 20 May 1983.

FITA Round (Women's): Single Round, 1273 Pauline Edwards at Worcester on 23 July 1983. Double Round, 2520 Rachel Fenwick at Brussels, Belgium on 12–13 Aug 1978.

Most titles *World*

The greatest number of world titles (instituted 1931) ever won by a man is four by Hans Deutgen (b. 28 Feb 1917) (Sweden) in 1947–50. The greatest number won by a woman is seven by Janina Spychajowa-Kurkowska (b. 8 Feb 1901) (Poland) in 1931–4, 1936, 1939 and 1947. Oscar Kessels (Belgium) (1904–68) participated in 21 world championships.

Most titles *Olympic*

Hubert van Innis (1866–1961) (Belgium) won six gold and three silver medals at the 1900 and 1920 Olympic Games.

Most titles *British*

The greatest number of British Championships is 12 by Horace Alfred Ford (1822–80) in 1849–59 and 1867, and 23 by Alice Blanche Legh (1855–1948) in 1881, 1886–92, 1895, 1898–1900, 1902–9, 1913 and 1921–2. Miss Legh was inhibited from winning from 1882 to 1885—because her mother Piers Legh was Champion—and for four further years 1915–8 because there were no Championships owing to the First World War.

Flight shooting

The longest recorded distance ever shot is 1 mile 268 yd *1854,40 m* in the unlimited footbow class by Harry Drake (b. 7 May 1915) (USA) at Ivanpah Dry Lake, California, USA on 24 Oct 1971. The female footbow record is 1113 yd 2 ft 6 in *1018,48 m* by Arlyne Rhode (b. 4 May 1936) at Wendover, Utah, USA on 10 Sept 1978. Alan Webster (England) set the flight record for the handbow with 1231 yd 1 ft 10 in *1126,19 m* on 2 Oct 1982 and April Moon (USA) set a women's record of 1039 yd 1 ft 1 in *950,39 m* on 13 Sept 1981, both at Ivanpah Dry Lake. Drake holds the crossbow flight record with 1359 yd 2 ft 5 in in *1243,4 m* on 14 Oct 1967 and the regular footbow record with 1542 yd 2 ft 10 ins *1410,87 m* on 6 Oct 1979 both at Ivanpah Dry Lake.

Greatest draw

Gary Sentman, of Roseberg, Oregon, USA drew a longbow

weighing a record 176 lb *79,83 kg* to the maximum draw on the arrow of 28¼ in in *72 cm* at Forksville, Penn., on 20 Sept 1975.

24 Hours—target archery

The highest recorded score over 24 hours by a pair of archers is 51,633 during 48 Portsmouth Rounds by Jimmy Watt and Gordon Danby at the Epsom Showgrounds, Auckland NZ, on 18–19 Nov 1977.

24 Hours—field archery

The highest recorded score at field archery is 123,724 by six members of the Holland Moss Field Archery Club at Holland Moss Field, Pimbo, Lancashire on 28–29 Apr 1983. Bill Chambers set an individual record score of 30,506.

BADMINTON

See also The Guinness Book of Badminton *by Pat Davis, published in 1983 at £7.95.*

Origins

A similar game was played in China in the 2nd millennium BC. The modern game may have evolved *c* 1870 at Badminton Hall in Avon, the seat of the Dukes of Beaufort or from a game played in India. The first modern rules were codified in Poona in 1876. The oldest club is the Newcastle Badminton Club formed as the Armstrong College Club on 24 Jan 1900.

Thomas Cup

The International Championship or Thomas Cup (instituted 1948) has been won eight times by Indonesia in 1958, 1961, 1964, 1970, 1973, 1976, 1979 and 1984.

Uber Cup

The Ladies International Championship or Uber Cup (instituted 1956) has been won five times by Japan (1966, 1969, 1972, 1978 and 1981).

Inter County Championship

The championships were instituted on 30 Oct 1930 and Surrey have most wins with 22 between 1955 and 1984.

Most titles

The men's singles in the All-England Championships (instituted 1899) have been won a record eight times by Rudy Hartono Kurniawan (Indonesia) (b. 18 Aug 1948) in 1968–74 and 1976. The greatest number of championships won was (incl. doubles) is 21 by G. A. Thomas (later Sir George Alan Thomas, Bt.) (1881–1972) between 1903 and 1928. The women's title has been won ten times by Judy Hashman (*née* Devlin) (USA) (b. 22 Oct 1935) in 1954, 1957–8, 1960–4, 1966–7. She also equalled the greatest number of championships won of 17 by Muriel Lucas (later Mrs King Adams) from 1899 to 1910.

MOST INTERNATIONAL APPEARANCES

	Times	Men	
England	133	Michael G. Tredgett	1970–84
Scotland	67	Robert S. McCoig	1956–76
Ireland	64	Bill Thompson	1975–84
Wales	51	David Colmer	1964–80
	Times	**Women**	
England	96	Gillian Gilks (*née* Perrin)	1966–84
Wales	63	Sue Brimble	1969–84
Ireland	60	Barbara Beckett	1971–84
Scotland	54	Pamela Hamilton	1975–84

Shortest game

In the 1969 Uber Cup in Jakarta, Indonesia, Noriko Takagi (later Mrs Nakayama) (Japan) beat Poppy Tumengkol (Indonesia) in 9 min.

Longest hit

Frank Rugani drove a shuttlecock 79 ft 8½ in *24,29 m* in indoor tests at San José, California, USA, on 29 Feb 1964.

BASEBALL

Earliest game

The Rev Thomas Wilson, of Maidstone, Kent, England, wrote disapprovingly, in 1700, of baseball being played on Sundays.

The earliest baseball game under the Cartwright (Alexander Joy Cartwright Jr 1820–92) rules was at Hoboken, New Jersey, USA, on 19 June 1846, with the New York Nine beating the Knickerbockers 23–1 in four innings.

Home runs *Most*

Henry Louis 'Hank' Aaron (Milwaukee and Atlanta Braves) (b. 5 Feb 1934) holds the major league career home run record of 755, from 1954 to 1976. Joshua Gibson (1911–47) of Homestead Grays and Pittsburgh Crawfords, Negro League clubs, achieved a career total of nearly 800 homers including an unofficial total of 75 in 1931. The US major league record for home runs in a season is 61 by Roger Eugene Maris (b. 10 Sept 1934) for New York Yankees in 162 games in 1961. George Herman 'Babe' Ruth (1895–1948) hit 60 in 154 games in 1927. The most official home runs in minor leagues is 72 by Joe Bauman of Rosewell, New Mexico in 1954.

Longest home run

The longest home run ever measured was one of 618 ft *188,4 m* by Roy Edward 'Dizzy' Carlyle (1900–56) in a minor league game at Emeryville Ball Park, California, USA, on 4 July 1929. In 1919 Babe Ruth hit a 587 ft *178,9 m* homer in a Boston Red Sox *v.* New York Giants exhibition match at Tampa, Florida.

Longest throw

The longest throw (ball weighs 5–5¼ oz *141–148 g*) is 445 ft 10 in *135,88 m* by Glen Edward Gorbous (b. Canada 8 July 1930) on 1 Aug 1957. The longest throw by a woman is 296 ft *90,2 m* by Mildred Ella 'Babe' Didrikson (later Mrs George Zaharias) (US) (1914–56) at Jersey City, New Jersey, USA on 25 July 1931.

US MAJOR LEAGUE RECORDS

(AL American League, NL National League)

BATTING

Batting av., career	.367	Tyrus Raymond Cobb (AL)	1905–28
Batting av., season	.438	Hugh Duffy (Boston, NL)	1894
" "	.422	Napoleon Lajoie (Philadelphia, AL)	1901
Runs, career	2244	Tyrus Raymond Cobb	1905–28
RBIs, career	2297	Henry 'Hank' Aaron	1954–76
" season	190	Lewis Rober 'Hack' Wilson (Chicago, NL)	1930
" game	12	James LeRoy Bottomley (St Louis, NL)	16 Sept 1924
" innings	7	Edward Cartwright (St Louis, AA)	23 Sept 1890
Base hits, career	4191	Tyrus Raymond Cobb	1905–28
" season	257	George Harold Sisler (St Louis, AL)	1920
Hits, consecutive	12	Michael Franklin 'Pinky' Higgins	19–21 June 1938
" "	12	Walter 'Moose' Dropo	14–15 July 1952
Consecutive games batted safely	56	Joseph Paul DiMaggio (New York, AL)	15 May–16 July 1941
Stolen bases, career	938	Louis Clark Brock	1961–79
" " season	130	Rickey Henderson (Oakland, AL)	1982
Consecutive games played	2130	Henry Louis 'Lou' Gehrig	1 June 1925–30 April 1939

PITCHING

Games won, career	511	Denton True 'Cy' Young	1890–1911
" " season	60	Charles Gardner Radbourne (Providence, NL)	1884
Consecutive games won	24	Carl Owen Hubbell (New York, NL)	1936–37
Shutouts, career	113	Walter Perry Johnson	1907–27
" season	16	George W. Bradley (St Louis, NL)	1876
	16	Grover Cleveland Alexander (Philadelphia, NL)	1916
Strikeouts, career	3709	Steven Carlton (St Louis, Philadelphia, NL)	1965–83
" season	383	Lynn Nolan Ryan (California, AL)	1973
No-hit games, career	5	Lynn Nolan Ryan	1966–81
Earned run av., season	0.90	Ferdinand Schupp (140 inn) (New York, NL)	1916
" "	1.01	Hubert 'Dutch' Leonard (222 inn) (Boston, AL)	1914
" "	1.12	Robert Gibson (305 inn) (St Louis, NL)	1968
Complete games, career	751	Denton True 'Cy' Young	1890–1911

BASEBALL WORLD SERIES RECORDS

(AL American League, NL National League)

Most wins	22	New York Yankees (AL)	1923–78
Most series played	14	Lawrence P. 'Yogi' Berra (New York, AL)	1947–63
Most home runs in a game	3	George H. 'Babe' Ruth (New York, AL)	6 Oct 1926
	3	Reginald M. Jackson (New York, AL)	18 Oct 1977
Only perfect pitch (in 9 innings)		Donald J. Larson (New York, AL) *v* Brooklyn	8 Oct 1956

Japanese league records Superior to those in US major leagues:

Home runs, career	868	Sadaharu Oh (Yomuiri)	1959–80
Stolen bases, career	939	Yutaka Fukumoto (Hankyu)	1969–83

Fastest base runner

The fastest time for circling bases is 13.3 sec by Ernest Evar Swanson (1902–73) at Columbus, Ohio, in 1932, at an average speed of 18.45 mph *29,70 km/h.*

Fastest pitcher

The fastest recorded pitcher was Lynn Nolan Ryan (then of the California Angels) (b. 31 Jan 1947) who, on 20 Aug 1974 at Anaheim Stadium, California, USA, was measured to pitch at 100.9 mph *162,3 km/h.*

Youngest player

The youngest major league player of all time was the Cincinnati pitcher, Joseph Henry Nuxhall (b. 30 July 1928) who started his career in June 1944, aged 15 yr 314 days.

Record attendances and receipts

The World Series record attendance is 420,784 (six games) when the Los Angeles Dodgers beat the Chicago White Sox 4–2 on 1–8 Oct 1959. The single game record is 92,706 for the fifth game at the Memorial Coliseum, Los Angeles, California, on 6 Oct 1959. The highest seating capacity in a baseball stadium is now 74,208 in the Cleveland Municipal Stadium, Ohio, USA. The all-time season record for attendances for both leagues has been 45,540,338 in 1983.

An estimated 114,000 spectators watched a game between Australia and an American Services team in a 'demonstration' event during the Olympic Games at Melbourne, 1 Dec 1956.

BASKETBALL

Origins

The game of 'Pok-ta-Pok' was played in the 10th century BC, by the Olmecs in Mexico, and closely resembled basketball in its concept. 'Ollamalitzli' was a variation of this game played by the Aztecs in Mexico as late as the 16th century. If the solid

Kareem Abdul-Jabbar, the highest points scorer ever in the NBA. *(All-sport/Alvin Chung)*

rubber ball was put through a fixed stone ring the player was entitled to the clothing of all the spectators. Modern basketball (which may have been based on the German game *Korbball*) was devised by the Canadian-born Dr James A. Naismith (1861–1939) at the Training School of the International YMCA College at Springfield, Massachusetts, USA, in mid-December 1891. The first game played under modified rules was on 20 Jan 1892. The International Amateur Basketball Federation (FIBA) was founded in 1932, and the English Basket Ball Association in 1936.

Most titles *Olympic*

The USA won all seven Olympic titles from the time the sport was introduced to the Games in 1936 until 1968, without losing a single match. In 1972 in Munich their run of 63 consecutive victories in matches in the Olympic Games was broken when they lost 50–51 to the USSR in the disputed Final match. They won their eighth title in 1976.

Most titles *World*

The USSR have won most titles at both the men's World Championships (inst. 1950) with three (1967, 1974 and 1982) and Women's (inst. 1953) with six (1959, 1964, 1967, 1971, 1975 and 1983).

Most titles *European*

The most European Champions Cup (instituted 1957) wins is seven by Real Madrid, Spain. The women's title has been won 18 times by Daugawa, Riga, Latvia, USSR. The most wins in the European Nations Championships for men is 13 by the USSR, and in the women's event 17 also by the USSR.

Most titles *American Professional*

The most National Basketball Association (NBA) titles (instituted 1947), played for between the leading professional teams in the United States, have been won by the Boston Celtics with 15 victories between 1957 and 1984.

Most titles *English*

The most English National championship wins (instituted 1936) have been by London Central YMCA, with eight wins in 1957–8, 1960, 1962–4, 1967 and 1969. The English National League title has been won seven times by Crystal Palace 1974, 1976–8, 1980 and 1982–3. Most English Women's cups (instituted 1965) have been won by Tigers with eight wins, 1972–3, 1976–80 and 1982.

Highest score *International*

The highest score recorded in a senior international match is 251 by Iraq against Yemen (33) at New Delhi in November 1982 at the Asian Games. The highest in a British Championship is 125 by England when beating Wales (54) on 1 Sept 1978. England beat Gibraltar 130–45 on 31 Aug 1978.

Highest score *Match*

The highest aggregate score in an NBA match is 370 when the Detroit Pistons (186) beat the Seattle Nuggets (184) in Denver on 13 Dec 1983. Overtime was played after a 145–145 tie in regulation time.

Highest score *United Kingdom*

The highest score recorded in a match is 250 by the Nottingham YMCA Falcons v. Mansfield Pirates at Nottingham, on 18 June 1974. It was a handicap competition and Mansfield received 120 points towards their total of 145. The highest score in a senior National League match is 167 by West Bromwich Kestrels v. Milton Keynes (69) on 13 Feb 1983. The highest in the National Cup is 146 by Doncaster v. Cleveland (109) on 11 Feb 1976.

Highest score *Individual*

Mats Wermelin, 13, (Sweden) scored all 272 points in a 272–0 win in a regional boys' tournament in Stockholm, Sweden on 5 Feb 1974. The highest single game score in an NBA game is 100 points by Wilton Norman Chamberlain (b. 21 Aug 1936) for Philadelphia v. New York on 2 Mar 1962. The most in a college game is 113 points by Clarence 'Bevo' Francis, for Rio Grande College, Ohio v. Hillsdale at Jackson, Ohio on 2 Feb 1954. The record score by a woman is 156 points by Marie Boyd (now Eichler) of Central HS, Lonaconing, Maryland, USA in a 163–3 defeat of Ursaline Academy, Cumberland on 25 Feb 1924.

The highest score by a British player is 124 points by Paul Ogden for St Albans School, Oldham (226) v. South Chadder-

ton (82) on 9 Mar 1982. The highest individual score in an English National League (Div. One) or Cup match is 68 points by Bobby Cooper of London Central YMCA v. Exeter on 2 Mar 1979.

Most points

Kareem Abdul-Jabbar (formerly Lewis Ferdinand Alcindor) (b. 16 Apr 1947) has scored a career record points total in NBA matches since his debut in 1969. Playing for Los Angeles Lakers on 4 Apr 1984 he passed the total of 31,419 scored by Wilt Chamberlain in 1960–73. Chamberlain set a season's record 4029 for Philadelphia in 1962. The record for the most points scored in a college career is (women): 4061, Pearl Moore of Francis Marion College, Florence, S. Carolina, 1975–9, (men): 4045 by Travis Grant for Kentucky State in 1969–72. In the English National League, Ian Day (b. 16 May 1953) has scored 3456 points in 203 games, 1973–84.

Tallest players

The tallest player of all time is reputed to be Suleiman Ali Nashnush (b. 1943) who played for the Libyan team in 1962 when measuring 2,45 m *8 ft*. Aleksandr Sizonenko of Kuibyshev Stroitel and USSR is 2,39 m *7 ft 10 in* tall. The tallest woman player was Iuliana Semenova (USSR) (b. 9 Mar 1952) at a reported 7 ft 2 in *2,18 m* and weighing 281 lb *127,4 kg*. The tallest British player has been the 7 ft 6¼ in *2,29 m* tall Christopher Greener of London Latvians whose International debut for England was v. France on 17 Dec 1969.

Most accurate

The greatest goal shooting demonstration has been by Ted St Martin of Jacksonville, Florida, who, on 25 June 1977, scored 2036 consecutive free throws. In a 24-hr period, 31 May–1 June 1975 Fred L. Newman of San José, California, USA scored 12,874 baskets out of 13,116 throws (98.15 per cent accuracy).

Longest recorded goal

The longest recorded field goal in a match is a measured 89 ft 3 in *27,20 m* by Les Henson for Virginia Tech v. Florida State on 21 Jan 1980. A British record of 75 ft 9½ in *23,10 m* is claimed by David Tarbatt (b. 23 Jan 1949) of Altofts Aces v. Harrogate Demons at Featherstone, West Yorkshire on 27 Jan 1980.

Largest ever gate

The Harlem Globetrotters (USA) played an exhibition in front of 75,000 in the Olympic Stadium, West Berlin, Germany, in 1951. The largest indoor basketball attendance was at the Superdome, New Orleans, Louisiana, USA, where admissions of 61,612 were recorded for both the semi-finals (27 Mar 1982) and final (29 Mar 1982, University of North Carolina v. Georgetown University) of the 1982 NCAA Division One tournament.

BILLIARDS AND SNOOKER

Further information is available in the Guinness Book of Snooker *by Clive Everton (£7.50 hardback, 1981 or £5.95 limp-back, 1982) published by Guinness Superlatives Ltd.*

BILLIARDS

Earliest mention

The earliest recorded mention of billiards was in France in 1429, while Louis XI, King of France 1461–83, is reported to have had a billiard table. The first recorded public billiards room in England was the Piazza, Covent Garden, London, in the early part of the 19th century. Rubber cushions were introduced in 1835 and slate beds in 1836.

Most titles *Professional*

The greatest number of world championship titles (instituted 1870) won by one player is eight by John Roberts, Jnr (1847–1919) (England) in 1870 (twice), 1871, 1875 (twice), 1877 and 1885 (twice). The greatest number of United Kingdom titles (instituted 1934) won by any player is seven (1934–39 and 1947) by Joe Davis (1901–78) (England), who also won four world titles (1928–30 and 1932). William F. Hoppe (USA) (1887–1959) won 51 'world' titles in the United States variant of the game between 1906 and 1952.

Most titles *Amateur*

The record for world amateur titles is four by Robert James Percival Marshall (Australia) (b. 10 Apr 1910) in 1936, 1938,

1951 and 1962. The greatest number of English Amateur Championships (instituted 1888) ever won is 15 by Norman Dagley (b. 27 June 1930) in 1965–66, 1970–75, 1978–84. The record number of women's titles is eight by Vera Selby (b. 13 Mar 1930) 1970–8.

Highest breaks

Tom Reece (1873–1953) made an unfinished break of 449,135, including 249,152 cradle cannons (two points each) in 85 hr 49 min against Joe Chapman at Burroughes' Hall, Soho Square, London, between 3 June and 6 July 1907. This was not recognized because press and public were not continuously present. The highest certified break made by the anchor cannon is 42,746 by William Cook (England) from 29 May to 7 June 1907. The official world record under the then baulk-line rule is 1784 by Joe Davis in the United Kingdom Championship on 29 May 1936. Walter Albert Lindrum (Australia) (1898–1960) made an official break of 4137 in 2 hr 55 min against Joe Davis at Thurston's on 19–20 Jan 1932, before the baulk-line rule was in force. Davis has an unofficial personal best of 2502 (mostly pendulum cannons) in a match against Tom Newman (1894–1943) (England) in Manchester in 1930. The highest break recorded in amateur competition is 1149 by Michael Ferreira (India) at Calcutta, India on 15 Dec 1978. On 1 Jan 1983 the more stringent 'two pot' rule under which Robert Marshall (Aus) made a break of 702 at Brisbane on 17 Sept 1953 was restored. No higher break has since been made with this rule in force.

Fastest century

Walter Lindrum made an unofficial 100 break in 27.5 sec in Australia on 10 Oct 1952. His official record is 100 in 46.0 sec set in Sydney in 1941.

3 CUSHION

This pocketless variation dates back to 1878. The world governing body, the *Union Mondiale de Billiard* (UMB) was formed in 1928. The most successful exponent spanning the pre and post international era from 1906 to 1952 was Willie Hoppe who won 51 billiards championships in all forms. Most UMB titles have been won by Raymond Ceulemans (Belgium) (b. 1937) with 16 (1963–6, 1968–73, 1975–80), with a peak average of 1.679 in 1978.

SNOOKER

Origins

Research shows that snooker was originated by Colonel Sir Neville Francis Fitzgerald Chamberlain (1856–1944) as a hybrid of 'black pool', 'pyramids' and billiards, in Jubbulpore, India in 1875. It did not reach England until 1885, where the modern scoring system was adopted in 1891. Championships were not instituted until 1916. The World Professional Championship was instituted in 1927.

Most titles *World*

The world professional title (inst 1927) was won a record 15 times by Joe Davis, 1927–40 and 1946. The most wins in the amateur championships (inst 1963) have been two by Gary Owen (England) in 1963 and 1966, and Ray Edmonds (England) 1972 and 1974.

Most titles *Women*

Maureen Baynton (*née* Barrett) won a record eight women's amateur championships between 1954 and 1968, as well as seven at billiards.

World Championships *Youngest*

The youngest player to win a world title is Jimmy White (GB) (b. 2 May 1962) who was 18 yr 191 days when he won the World Amateur Snooker championship in Launceston, Tasmania, Australia on 9 Nov 1980.

Highest breaks

Over 100 players have achieved the 'maximum' break of 147. The first to do so was E. J. 'Murt' O'Donoghue (b. New Zealand 1901) at Griffiths, NSW, Australia on 26 Sept 1934. The first officially ratified 147 was by Joe Davis against Willie Smith at Leicester Square Hall, London on 22 Jan 1955. The first maximum achieved in a major tournament was by John Spencer (b. 18 Sept 1935) at Slough, Berkshire on 13 Jan 1979, but the table had oversized pockets. Steve Davis (b. 22 Aug 1957) had a ratified break of 147 against John Spencer in the

(*left*) Cliff Thorburn celebrates as befits the man who scored the first maximum 147 break in snooker's world championships (*All-Sport*)

(*below*) Ross McInnes (*l*) and Mick McGoldrick (*r*) current and previous world record holders for speed potting at pool.

Lada Classic at Oldham on 11 Jan 1982. The first 147 scored in the World Championships was by Cliff Thorburn (Canada) (b. 16 Jan 1948) against Terry Griffiths at the Crucible Theatre, Sheffield on 23 April 1983, thereby winning a £10,000 jackpot prize.

The official world amateur record break is 140 set by Joe Johnson (England) (b. 29 July 1952) in the TUC Club, Middlesbrough, Cleveland in 1978. David Taylor (b. 29 July 1943) made three consecutive frame clearances of 130, 140, and 139 (total 409) at Minehead, Somerset, on 1 June 1978. Jim Meadowcroft (b. 15 Dec 1946) made four consecutive frame clearances of 105, 115, 117 and 125 at Connaught Leisure Centre, Worthing on 27 Jan 1982.

POOL

Pool or championship pocket billiards with numbered balls began to become standardized *c.* 1890. The greatest exponents were Ralph Greenleaf (USA) (1899–1950) who won the 'world' professional title 19 times (1919–37) and William Mosconi (USA) (b. 27 June 1913) who dominated the game from 1941 to 1957.

The longest consecutive run in an American straight pool match is 625 balls by Michael Eufemia at Logan's Billiard Academy, Brooklyn, NY, on 2 Feb 1960. The greatest number of balls pocketed in 24 hr is 13,437 by Patrick Young at the Lord Stanley, Plaistow, London on 20–21 July 1981.

The record time for potting all 15 balls in a speed competition

(possible 900) is 886 by Albert 'Allie' Brandt of Lockport, New York, USA, on 25 Oct 1939. The record by a woman is 853 by Sherrie Langford at Clearwater, Florida, USA, on 19 Feb 1982. The record for consecutive strikes in sanctioned match play is 33, first achieved by John Pezzin (b. 1930) at Toledo, Ohio, USA on 4 Mar 1976. The highest number of sanctioned 300 games is 27 (till 1982) by Elvin Mesger of Sullivan, Missouri, USA. The maximum 900 for a three-game series was achieved by Glenn Allison (b. 1930) at the La Habra Bowl in Los Angeles, California on 1 July 1982, but this was not recognised by the ABC due to the oiling patterns on the boards. It has been recorded four times in unsanctioned games—by Leon Bentley at Lorain, Ohio, USA, on 26 Mar 1931; by Joe Sargent at Rochester, New York State, USA, in 1934; by Jim Margie in Philadelphia, Pennsylvania, USA, on 4 Feb 1937 and by Bob Brown at Roseville Bowl, California, USA on 12 Apr 1980. Such series must have consisted of 36 consecutive strikes (*i.e.* all pins down with one ball).

The highest average for a season attained in sanctioned competition is 242 by John Rogard of Susquehanna, Pa., USA for 66 games in 1981–82.

Highest scores *Great Britain*
The United Kingdom record for a three-game series is 785 by Daniel John Smith (b. 15 June 1955) at the Charrington Bowl, Tolworth, Surrey on 18 Dec 1980. The record score for a single game is 300, first achieved by Albert Kirkham (b. 1931) of Burslem, Staffordshire, on 5 Dec 1965, which has since been equalled on several occasions. The best by a woman is 299, first achieved by Carole Cuthbert at the Airport Bowl, Hayes, Middlesex on 16 Mar 1972. The three-game series record for a woman player is 740 by Elizabeth Cullen at the Astra Bowl, RAF Brize Norton, Oxfordshire on 15 Mar 1983.

Highest earnings
Earl Anthony (b. 1938) has won a record $1,257,021 in Professional Bowlers Association (PBA) competition to May 1984. He has won a lifetime record 41 PBA titles.

SKITTLES

24 Hours
Eight players from Torquay United Social Club Blues knocked down 82,421 West Country skittles on 14–15 Oct 1983 at the T.U.S.C., Torquay, Devon. The highest hood skittle score in 24 hr is 107,487 pins by 12 players from the Plume of Feathers, Daventry, Northamptonshire, on 19–20 Mar 1976. The highest long alley score is 20,473 by eight players from the Thorntree Inn, Waingroves, Derbyshire on 12–13 May 1984. The highest table skittle score in 24 hr is 90,446 skittles by 12 players at the Finney Gardens Hotel, Hanley, Staffs on 27–28 Dec 1980.

BOWLS

OUTDOOR

Origins
Bowls can be traced back to at least the 13th century in England. The Southampton Town Bowling was formed in 1299. A green dating back to 1294 is claimed by the Chesterfield Bowling Club. After falling into disrepute, the game was rescued by the bowlers of Scotland who, headed by William W. Mitchell (1803–84), framed the modern rules in 1848–9.

Most titles *World*
The only man to win two singles titles is David John Bryant (b. 27 Oct 1931) (England) in 1966 and 1980. Australia has won the doubles event on two occasions, 1966 and 1980. At Johannesburg, South Africa, in February 1976, the South African team achieved an unprecedented clean sweep of all four titles and the team competition (Leonard Trophy).

Most titles *International Championship*
In the annual International Championships (instituted 1903) Scotland have won a record 34 times including 11 consecutive wins from 1965 to 1975.

Most titles *English & British*
The record number of English Bowls Association (founded 8 June 1903) championships is 15 won or shared by David Bryant, including six singles (1960, 1966, 1971–3, 1975), three pairs (1965, 1969, 1974), two triples (1966, 1977) and four fours championships (1957, 1968, 1969 and 1971). He has also won six British Isles titles (four singles, one pairs, one fours) in the period 1957–74.

Highest score
The highest score achieved in an international bowls match is the 63–1 victory by Swaziland v Japan during the World Championships at Melbourne, Australia on 16 Jan 1980.

Most eights
Freda Ehlers and Linda Bertram uniquely scored three consecutive eights in the Southern Transvaal pairs event at Johannesburg, South Africa on 30 Jan 1978.

International appearances
The greatest number of international appearances outdoors by any bowler is 78 reached by Syd Thompson (b. 29 Aug 1912) for Ireland 1947–73. He also has had 50 indoor caps. The youngest bowler to represent England was Gerard Anthony Smyth (b. 29 Dec 1960) at 20 yr 196 days on 13 July 1981. The youngest ever EBA singles champion was David J. Cutler (b. 1 Aug 1954) at 25 yr 16 days in 1979. He had been a member of the winning triples team at 18 yr 18 days in 1972.

INDOOR

The English Indoor Bowling Association became an autonomous body in 1971. Prior to that it was part of the English Bowling Association.

Most titles
The four-corner international championship was first held in 1936. England have won most titles with 20 wins. The National Singles title (inst. 1960) has been won most often by David Bryant with nine wins (1960, 1966, 1971–3, 1975, 1978–9, 1983). David Bryant has won the World Indoor Championship (inst 1979) three times, 1979–81.

The youngest EIBA singles champion, John Dunn (b. 6 Oct 1963) was 17 yr 117 days when he won in 1981.

Highest score
The highest score in a British International match is 52 by Scotland v. Wales (3) at Teeside in March 1972.

C. Hammond and B. Funnell of The Angel, Tonbridge beat A. Wise and C. Lock 55–0 over 21 ends in the second round of the EIBA National Pairs Championships on 17 Oct 1983 at The Angel, Tonbridge, Kent.

BOXING

Earliest references
Boxing with gloves was depicted on a fresco from the Isle of Thera, Greece which has been dated 1520 BC. The earliest prize-ring code of rules was formulated in England on 16 Aug 1743 by the champion pugilist Jack Broughton (1704–89), who reigned from 1734 to 1750. Boxing, which had, in 1867, come under the Queensberry Rules formulated for John Sholto Douglas, 9th Marquess of Queensberry (1844–1900), was not established as a legal sport in Britain until after the ruling, R. v. Roberts and Others, of Mr Justice Grantham, following the death of Billy Smith (Murray Livingstone) due to a fight on 24 Apr 1901.

Longest fights
The longest recorded fight with gloves was between Andy Bowen of New Orleans (1867–94) and Jack Burke in New Orleans, Louisiana, USA, on 6–7 Apr 1893. The fight lasted 110 rounds and 7 hr 19 min (9.15 p.m.–4.34 a.m.), and was declared no contest (later changed to a draw). Bowen won an 85 round bout on 31 May 1893. The longest bare knuckle fight was 6 hr 15 min between James Kelly and Jack Smith at Fiery Creek, Dalesford, Victoria, Australia on 3 Dec 1855. The longest bare knuckle fight in Britain was 6 hr 3 min (185 rounds) between Bill Hayes and Mike Madden at Edenbridge, Kent, on 17 July 1849. The greatest number of rounds was 276 in 4 hr 30 min when Jack Jones beat Patsy Tunney in Cheshire in 1825.

Shortest fights
There is a distinction between the quickest knock-out and the shortest fight. A knock-out in 10½ sec (including a 10 sec count)

occurred on 23 Sept 1946, when Al Couture struck Ralph Walton while the latter was adjusting a gum shield in his corner at Lewiston, Maine, USA. If the time was accurately taken it is clear that Couture must have been more than half-way across the ring from his own corner at the opening bell. The shortest fight on record appears to be one in a Golden Gloves tournament at Minneapolis, Minnesota, USA, on 4 Nov 1947 when Mike Collins floored Pat Brownson with the first punch and the contest was stopped, without a count, 4 sec after the bell.

The fastest officially timed knock-out in British boxing is 11 sec (including a doubtless fast 10 sec count) when Jack Cain beat Harry Deamor, both of Notting Hill, London, at the National Sporting Club on 20 Feb 1922.

The shortest world heavyweight title fight was when the referee stopped the fight after 63 sec when Michael Dokes (USA) (b. 10 Aug 1958) beat Mike Weaver (USA) for the WBA title on 10 Dec 1982. The shortest world title fight was when Al McCoy knocked out George Chip in 45 sec for the middleweight crown in New York on 7 Apr 1914. The shortest ever British title fight was one of 40 sec (including the count), when Dave Charnley knocked out David 'Darkie' Hughes in a lightweight championship defence in Nottingham on 20 Nov 1961.

Most British titles
The most defences of a British heavyweight title is 14 by 'Bombardier' Billy Wells (1889–1967) from 1911 to 1919. The only British boxer to win three Lonsdale Belts outright was Henry William Cooper (b. 3 May 1934), heavyweight champion (1959–69, 1970–1). He retired after losing to Joe Bugner (b. Hungary, 13 Mar 1950), having held the British heavyweight title from 12 Jan 1959 to 28 May 1969 and from 24 Mar 1970 to 16 Mar 1971.

Tallest
The tallest boxer to fight professionally was Gogea Mitu (b. 1914) of Romania in 1935. He was 7 ft 4 in *233 cm* and weighed 23 st 5 lb (327 lb) *148 kg*. John Rankin, who won a fight in New Orleans, Louisiana, USA, in November 1967, was reputedly also 7 ft 4 in *233 cm*.

Longest career
The heavyweight Jem Mace (GB) (1831–1910), known as 'the gypsy', had a career lasting 35 years from 1855 to 1890, but there were several years in which he had only one fight. Bobby Dobbs (USA) (1858–1930) is reported to have had a 39 year career from 1875 to 1914. Walter Edgerton, the 'Kentucky Rosebud', knocked out John Henry Johnson aged 45 in four rounds at the Broadway AC, New York City, USA, on 4 Feb 1916, when aged 63.

Most fights
The greatest recorded number of fights in a career is 1024 by Bobby Dobbs (USA) (see above). Abraham Hollandersky, *alias* Abe the Newsboy (USA), is reputed to have had up to 1039 fights from 1905 to 1918, but many of them were exhibition bouts.

Most fights without loss
Edward Henry (Harry) Greb (USA) (1894–1926) was unbeaten in 178 bouts, including 117 'No Decision', in 1916–23. Of boxers with complete records Packey McFarland (USA) (1888–1936) had 97 fights (five draws) in 1905–15 without a defeat. Pedro Carrasco (Spain) (b. 7 Nov 1943) won 83 consecutive fights from 22 April 1964 to 3 Sept 1970, drew once and had a further nine wins before his loss to Armando Ramos in a WBC lightweight contest on 18 Feb 1972.

Most knock-outs
The greatest number of finishes classed as 'knock-outs' in a career (1936–63) is 145 by Archie Moore (USA) (b. Archibald Lee Wright, 13 Dec 1913 or 1916). The record for consecutive KO's is 44 by Lamar Clark (b. 1 Dec 1934) (USA) from 1958 to 11 Jan 1960. He knocked out six in one night (five in the first round) at Bingham, Utah, on 1 Dec 1958.

Largest purse
The greatest purse received is a reported $11,000,000 by Ray Charles 'Sugar Ray' Leonard (USA) (b. 17 May 1956) when he beat Thomas Hearns (USA) (b. 18 Oct 1958) for the undisputed world welterweight title at Las Vegas on 16 Sept 1981. The total purse was an estimated $17.1 million.

Larry Holmes (*l*) retained his WBC heavyweight title with a technical KO in the 13th round against Gerry Cooney (*r*) in 1982 in a fight which had record receipts. (*All-Sport*)

Highest earnings in career
The largest fortune made in a fighting career is an estimated $69 million (including exhibitions) by Muhammad Ali from October 1960 to December 1981 in 61 fights comprising 549 rounds.

Attendances *Highest*
The greatest paid attendance at any boxing fight has been 120,757 (with a ringside price of $27.50) for the Tunney v. Dempsey world heavyweight title fight at the Sesquicentennial Stadium, Philadelphia, Pennsylvania, USA, on 23 Sept 1926. The indoor record is 63,350 at the Ali v. Leon Spinks fight in the Superdrome, New Orleans, Louisiana, USA, on 15 Sept 1978. Record receipts of $7,293,600 were reported for the WBC world heavyweight title fight at Las Vegas on 11 June 1982 when Larry Holmes (USA) (b. 3 Nov 1949) beat Gerry Cooney (USA) (b. 24 Aug 1956). The British attendance record is 82,000 at the Len Harvey v. Jock McAvoy fight at White City, London, on 10 July 1939.

The highest non-paying attendance is 135,132 at the Tony Zale v. Billy Pryor fight at Juneau Park, Milwaukee, Wisconsin, USA, on 16 Aug 1941.

Attendances *Lowest*
The smallest attendance at a world heavyweight title fight was 2434 at the Clay v. Liston fight at Lewiston, Maine, USA, on 25 May 1965.

WORLD HEAVYWEIGHT CHAMPIONS
Earliest title fight
The first world heavyweight title fight, with gloves and 3 min rounds, was that between John Lawrence Sullivan (1858–1918) and 'Gentleman' James John Corbett (1866–1933) in

New Orleans, Louisiana, USA, on 7 Sept 1892. Corbett won in 21 rounds.

Longest and shortest reigns

The longest reign of any world heavyweight champion is 11 years 8 months and 7 days by Joe Louis (USA) (b. Joseph Louis Barrow, 1914–81), from 22 June 1937, when he knocked out James Joseph Braddock in the eighth round at Chicago, Illinois, USA, until announcing his retirement on 1 Mar 1949. During his reign Louis made a record 25 defences of his title. The shortest reign was by Leon Spinks (USA) (b. 11 July 1953) for 212 days from 15 Feb to 15 Sept 1978. Ken Norton (USA) (b. 9 Aug 1945) was recognised by the WBC as champion for 72 days from 29 Mar–9 June 1978. The longest lived world heavyweight champion was Jack Dempsey who died on 31 May 1983 aged 87 yr 341 days.

Most recaptures

Muhammad Ali (b. Cassius Marcellus Clay Jr. 17 Jan 1942) is the only man to regain the heavyweight championship twice. Ali first won the title on 25 Feb 1964 defeating Sonny Liston. He defeated George Foreman on 30 Oct 1974 having been stripped of the title by the world boxing authorities on 28 Apr 1967. He won the WBA title from Leon Spinks on 15 Sept 1978 having previously lost to him on 15 Feb 1978.

Undefeated

Rocky Marciano (b. Rocco Francis Marchegiano) (1923–69) is the only world heavyweight champion to have been undefeated during his entire professional career (1947–56). He won all his 49 fights, 43 by knockouts or stoppages.

Oldest and Youngest

The oldest man to win the heavyweight crown was Jersey Joe Walcott (USA) (b. Arnold Raymond Cream, 31 Jan 1914) who knocked out Ezzard Mack Charles (1921–75) on 18 July 1951 in Pittsburgh, Pennsylvania, when aged 37 yr 168 days. Walcott was the oldest holder at 38 yr 236 days, losing his title to Rocky Marciano (1923–69) on 23 Sept 1952. The youngest age at which the world title has been won is 21 yr 331 days by Floyd Patterson (USA) (b. 4 Jan 1935), when he won the vacant title by beating Archie Moore in Chicago, Illinois, USA, on 30 Nov 1956.

Heaviest and lightest

The heaviest world champion was Primo Carnera (Italy) (1906–67), the 'Ambling Alp', who won the title from Jack Sharkey in six rounds in New York City, NY, USA, on 29 June 1933. He scaled 267 lb *121 kg* for this fight but his peak weight was 270 lb *122 kg*. He had an expanded chest measurement of 53 in *134 cm* and the longest reach at 85½ in *217 cm* (finger tip to finger tip). The lightest champion was Robert James 'Bob' Fitzsimmons (1863–1917), from Helston, Cornwall, who at a weight of 167 lb *75 kg*, won the title by knocking out James Corbett in 14 rounds at Carson City, Nevada, USA, on 17 Mar 1897.

The greatest differential in a world title fight was 86 lb *39 kg* between Carnera (270 lb *122 kg*) and Tommy Loughran (184 lb *83 kg*) of the USA, when the former won on points at Miami, Florida, USA, on 1 Mar 1934.

Tallest and shortest

The tallest world champion according to measurements by the Physical Education Director of the Hemingway Gymnasium, Harvard University, was Carnera at 6 ft 5.4 in *196,6 cm* although he was widely reported and believed to be up to 6 ft 8½ in *204 cm*. Jess Willard (1881–1968), who won the title in 1915, often stated to be 6 ft 6¼ in *199 cm* was in fact 6 ft 5¼ in *196 cm*. The shortest was Tommy Burns, world champion from 23 Feb 1906 to 26 Dec 1908, who stood 5 ft 7 in *170 cm* and weighed between 168 and 180 lb *76–81 kg*.

WORLD CHAMPIONS (any weight)

Longest and shortest reign

Joe Louis's heavyweight duration record of 11 years 252 days stands for all divisions. The shortest reign has been 33 days by Tony Canzeroni (USA) (1908–59) who was Junior Welterweight champion from 21 May to 23 June 1933.

Youngest and oldest

The youngest age at which any world championship has been won is 17 yr 176 days by Wilfred Benitez (b. New York, 12 Sept 1958) of Puerto Rico, who won the WBA light

welterweight title in San Juan, PR, on 6 Mar 1976. The oldest world champion was Archie Moore who was recognised as a light heavyweight champion up to 10 Feb 1962 when his title was removed. He was then believed to be between 45 and 48. Bob Fitzsimmons had the longest career of any official world titleholder with over 32 years from 1882 to 1914. He won his last world title aged 40 yr 183 days in San Francisco, California on 25 Nov 1903.

Longest fight

The longest world title fight (under Queensberry Rules) was that between the lightweights Joe Gans (1874–1910), of the USA, and Oscar Matthew 'Battling' Nelson (1882–1954), the 'Durable Dane', at Goldfield, Nevada, USA, on 3 Sept 1906. It was terminated in the 42nd round when Gans was declared the winner on a foul.

Most recaptures

The only boxer to win a world title five times at one weight is 'Sugar' Ray Robinson (USA) (b. Walker Smith, Jr, 3 May 1921), who beat Carmen Basilio (USA) in the Chicago Stadium on 25 Mar 1958, to regain the world middleweight title for the fourth time. The record number of title bouts in a career is 33 or 34, at bantam and featherweight, by George Dixon (1870–1909), *alias* 'Little Chocolate', of Canada, between 1890 and 1901.

Greatest weight span

The only man to hold world titles at three weights *simultaneously* was Henry 'Homicide Hank' Armstrong (b. 12 Dec 1912), now the Rev Henry Jackson, of the USA, at featherweight, lightweight and welterweight from August to December 1938.

Greatest 'tonnage'

The greatest 'tonnage' recorded in any fight is 700 lb *317 kg* when Claude 'Humphrey' McBride (Oklahoma) 340 lb *154 kg* knocked out Jimmy Black (Houston), who weighed 360 lb *163 kg* in the third round at Oklahoma City on 1 June 1971. The greatest 'tonnage' in a world title fight was 488¾ lb *221½ kg*, when Carnera, then 259¼ lb *117½ kg* fought Paolino Uzcudun 229½ lb *104 kg* of Spain in Rome on 22 Oct 1933.

Most knock-downs in Title fights

Vic Toweel (South Africa) (b. 12 Jan 1929) knocked down Danny O'Sullivan of London 14 times in ten rounds in their world bantamweight fight at Johannesburg on 2 Dec 1950, before the latter retired.

AMATEUR

Most Olympic titles

Only two boxers have won three Olympic gold medals: southpaw László Papp (b. 25 Mar 1926) (Hungary), middleweight 1948, light-middleweight 1952 and 1956; Teofilo Stevenson (b. 23 Mar 1952) (Cuba), heavyweight 1972, 1976 and 1980. The only man to win two titles in one celebration was Oliver L. Kirk (USA), who won both bantam and featherweight titles in St Louis, Missouri, USA, in 1904, when the US won all the titles. In 1908 Great Britain won all five titles.

Oldest gold medallist

Richard Kenneth Gunn (1871–1961) (GB) won the Olympic featherweight gold medal on 27 Oct 1908 in London aged 37 yr 254 days.

World Championships

Two boxers have won two world championships (inst. 1974): Teofilo Stevenson (Cuba), heavyweight 1974 and 1978, and Angel Herrera (b. 2 Aug 1952) (Cuba), featherweight 1978 and lightweight 1982.

Most titles *Great Britain*

The greatest number of ABA titles won by any boxer is six by Joseph Steers at middleweight and heavyweight between 1890 and 1893. Alex 'Bud' Watson (b. 27 May 1914) of Leith, Scotland won the Scottish heavyweight title in 1938, 1942–3, and the light-heavyweight championship 1937–9, 1943–5 and 1947, making ten in all. He also won the ABA light-heavyweight title in 1945 and 1947.

Longest span

The greatest span of ABA title-winning performances is that of the heavyweight Hugh 'Pat' Floyd (b. 23 Aug 1910), who won in 1929 and gained his fourth title 17 years later in 1946.

CANOEING

Origins
The acknowledged pioneer of canoeing as a modern sport was John Macgregor (1825–92), a British barrister, in 1865. The Canoe Club was formed on 26 July 1866.

Most titles *Olympic*
Gert Fredriksson (b. 21 Nov 1919) of Sweden has won most Olympic gold medals with six in 1948, 1952, 1956 and 1960. The most by a woman is three by Ludmila Pinayeva (*née* Khvedosyuk) (b. 14 Jan 1936) (USSR), in 1964, 1968 and 1972. The most gold medals at one Games is three by Vladimir Parfenovich (b. 2 Dec 1958) (USSR) in 1980.

Most titles *World*
12 titles have been won by Vladimir Parfenovich, 1979–83. Birgit Fischer (GDR) (b. 25 Feb 1962) won all three gold medals in the world championships of 1981–3 and one at the 1980 Olympics for a women's record of ten. The most individual titles by a British canoeist is three by Alan Emus, canoe sailing 1961, 1965 and 1969.

Most titles *British*
The most British Open titles (instituted 1936) ever won is 32 by John Laurence Oliver (Lincoln Canoe Club) (b. 12 Jan 1943) from 1966 to 1976 including 12 individual events. David Mitchell (Chester S&CC) won eight British slalom titles in 1963–8, 1970–1.

Highest speed
The Olympic 1000 m best performance of 3 min 02.70 sec set in a heat by the USSR K4 at Moscow on 31 July 1980, represents an average speed of 12.24 mph *19,70 km/h*. They achieved 13.14 mph *21,15 km/h* for the first 250 m.

Longest journey
The longest journey ever made by canoe is one of 8880 miles *14 290 km* from New Orleans by paddle and portage via the Mississippi River, Prescott, Minnesota, Grand Portage, Lake Superior and across Canada to the Bering Sea and Nome, Alaska by Jerry Robert Pushcar (b. 26 Nov 1949), accompanied only by a Samoyed dog, from 10 Jan 1975 to 12 Nov 1977.

The longest journey without portages or aid of any kind is one of 6102 miles *9820 km* by Richard H. Grant and Ernest 'Moose' Lassy circumnavigating the eastern USA via Chicago, New Orleans, Miami, New York and the Great Lakes from 22 Sept 1930 to 15 Aug 1931.

Longest open sea voyage
Beatrice and John Dowd, Ken Beard and Steve Benson (Richard Gillett replaced him mid-journey) paddled 2170 miles *3491 km* (of a total 2192 miles *3527 km*) from Venezuela to Miami, Florida, USA, via the West Indies, 11 Aug 1977–29 Apr 1978 in two Klepper Aerius 20 kayaks.

Cross-Channel
The singles record across the English Channel is 3 hr 33 min 47 sec by Andrew William Dougall Samuel (b. 12 July 1937) of Glasgow, from Shakespeare Bay, Dover, to Wissant, France, on 5 Sept 1976. The doubles record is 2 hr 54 min 54 sec by Andrew Samuel and Sgt John David Anderson (RAF) (b. 18 Mar 1957) in a K2 *Accord*, from Shakespeare Bay, Dover to Cap Gris Nez, France on 22 Aug 1980.

Charles Elliott canoeing on the Swan River in Western Australia at the 220 km point when he passed the previous record distance in 24 hours.

The record for a double crossing is 12 hr 47 min in K1s by nine members of the Canoe Camping Club, GB, on 7 May 1976.

North Sea
On 4–5 June 1976 Derek Hutchison, Tom Caskey and Dave Hellawell paddled K1s from Felixstowe, Suffolk to Ostend, Belgium, over 100 miles *160 km* across open sea, in 31 hr.

Loch Ness
The fastest time for a K1 from Fort Augustus to Lochend (22.7 miles *36,5 km*) is 3 hr 33 min 4 sec by Andrew Samuel (Trossachs Canoe and Boat Club) on 19 Oct 1975.

Highest altitude
In September 1976 Dr Michael Leslie Jones (1951–78) and Michael Hopkinson of the British Everest Canoe Expedition canoed down the River Dudh Kosi, Nepal from an altitude of 17,500 ft *5334 m*.

Longest race
The longest regularly held canoe race in the USA is the Texas Water Safari (inst. 1963), 419 miles *674 km* from San Marcos to Seadrift on the San Marcos and Guadalupe rivers. Butch Hodges and Robert Chatham set a record of 37 hr 18 min on 5–6 June 1976.

24 Hours
The solo 24-hour canoe record is 225,4 km *140.1 miles* by Charles Frederick Elliott (b. 30 Jan 1940) in a WW.K1 in the annual Western Australia Canoe Marathon on the Swan River, on 13–14 Nov 1982. The women's record was set at 156,4 km *97.2 miles* by Lydia Formentin in 1979.

Greatest lifetime distance
Fritz Lindner of Berlin, W. Germany, totalled 91 486 km *56,847 miles* from 1928 to 1983.

Eskimo Rolls
Bruce Jeffery Parry (Australia) (b. 25 Sept 1960) achieved 1000 eskimo rolls in 52 min 37.7 sec at Carrara, Queensland, Australia on 2 Oct 1983. Julian Dean achieved 1555 continuous rolls at Casterton Swimming Pool, Cumbria, taking 1 hr 49 min 45 sec on 6 Dec 1983. A 'hand-rolling' record of 100 rolls in 3 min 23 sec was set by John Bouteloup at Crystal Palace, London on 25 Feb 1980.

DOWNSTREAM CANOEING

River	Miles	Km	Name and Country	Route	Date	Duration
RHINE	714	*1149*	Sgt Charles Kavanagh (GB)	Chur, Switzerland to Willemstad, Neth.	13 Feb–2 Apr 1961	17½ days
	714	*1149*	Four RAF canoeists (GB)	Chur to Willemstad	28 Apr–7 May 1981	8 days 16 hr
MURRAY-DARLING	1980	*3186*	Six students of St Albert's College, UNE (Australia)	Gunnedah, NSW to Lake Alexandrina, SA	Dec 1975	—
MISSISSIPPI	2552	*4107*	Valerie Fons and Verlen Kruger (USA)	Lake Itasca, Minnesota to Gulf of Mexico	27 Apr–20 May 1984	23 days 10 hr 20 min
ZAIRE (CONGO)	2600	*4185*	John and Julie Batchelor (GB)	Moasampanga to Banana	8 May–12 Sept 1974	128 days
AMAZON	3800	*6115*	Alan Trevor Holman (GB/Aus) (b. 21 Feb 1944)	Quitani, Peru to Cabo Maguavi, Brazil	9 Aug–3 Dec 1982	116 days
MISSISSIPPI-MISSOURI	3810	*6132*	Nicholas Francis (GB)	Three Forks, Montana to New Orleans, La.	13 July–25 Nov 1977	135 days
NILE	4000	*6500*	John Goddard (US), Jean Laporte and André Davy (France)	Kagera to the Delta	Nov 1953–July 1954	9 months

CARD GAMES

CONTRACT BRIDGE

Bridge (a corruption of Biritch, a now-obsolete Russian word whose meanings include 'declarer') is thought to be either of Levantine origin, similar games having been played there in the early 1870s, or to have come from India.

Auction Bridge (highest bidder names trump) was invented *c.* 1902. The contract principle, present in several games (notably the French game *Plafond, c.* 1917) was introduced to Bridge by Harold Sterling Vanderbilt (USA) on 1 Nov 1925 during a Caribbean voyage aboard the SS *Finland*. It became a world-wide craze after the USA *v.* Great Britain challenge match between Romanian-born Ely Culbertson (1891–1955) and Lt-Col Walter Thomas More Buller (1887–1938) at Almack's Club, London, in September 1930. The USA won the 200-hand match by 4845 points.

Most World titles

The World Championship (Bermuda Bowl) has been won most often by Italy's Blue Team (*Squadra Azzura*), 1957–9, 1961–3, 1965–7, 1969, 1973–5. Italy also won the Olympiad in 1964, 1968 and 1972. Giorgio Belladonna (b. 7 June 1923) was in all these winning teams.

Most master points

In the latest ranking list based on Master Points awarded by the World Bridge Federation, the leading male player in the world was Giorgio Belladonna (Italy) with $1766\frac{1}{4}$ points. The leading Briton is Boris Schapiro (b. 22 Aug 1909) in 19th place with 353 points. The world's leading woman player is Dorothy Hayden Truscott (USA) with 331 points, and third Rika 'Rixi' Markus (Austria, later GB) with 281 points.

Barry Crane of Los Angeles has led the American Contract Bridge League rankings since 1968 and by April 1984 had a record total of 31,989 master points. The most master points scored in a year is 2725 by Ronald Anderson (USA) in 1980.

The first man to win 10,000 master points was Oswald Jacoby (USA) (b. 8 Dec 1902) in October 1967. He had been a member of the winning World Championship team in 1935 and on 4 Dec 1983 became the oldest member of a winning team of a major open team championship in the Curtis Reisinger Trophy.

Youngest Life Master

Dougie Hsieh (b. 23 Nov 1969) of New York City became the world's youngest ever Life Master in 1981 at 11 yr 306 days. The youngest ever female Master is Patricia Thomas (b. 10 Oct 1968) at 14 yr 28 days in 1982.

Giorgio Belladonna, the ace Italian bridge player of the famous Squadra Azzura. (*Associated Press*)

Perfect deals

The mathematical odds against dealing 13 cards of one suit are 158,753,389,899 to 1, while the odds against receiving a 'perfect hand' consisting of all 13 spades are 635,013,559,596 to 1. The odds against each of the four players receiving a complete suit (a 'perfect deal') are 2,235,197,406,895,366,368,301,559,999 to 1.

CRIBBAGE

The invention of the game (once called Cribbidge) is credited to the English dramatist Sir John Suckling (1609–42).

Rare hands

Edward Morawski, Greenfield, Mass, USA, Eleanor Jonsson, Saskatoon, Canada, and F. Art Skinner, Alberta, Canada are reported to have had three maximum 29 point hands. Paul Nault of Athol, Mass, USA had two such hands within eight games in a tournament on 19 Mar 1977. At Blackpool, Lancashire, Derek Hearne dealt two hands of six clubs with the turn-up the remaining club on 8 Feb 1976. Bill Rogers of Burnaby, BC, Canada scored 29 in the crib in 1975.

WHIST

Whist, first referred to in 1529 (*as trump*), was the world's premier card game until 1930. The rules were standardised in 1742.

Highest score

The highest score claimed for 24 hands is 209 by Mrs E. Heslop at Teignmouth, Devon on 5 Jan 1973, by Mrs A. Lulham at Hurstmonceux, East Sussex, on 21 Jan 1978, and by Walter Booth at Wyaston, Ashbourne, Derby on 31 July 1982.

CAVING—*(see also pp. 61–62)*

PROGRESSIVE WORLD DEPTH RECORDS Compiled by Dr A. C. Waltham, Trent Polytechnic, Nottingham.

ft	m	Cave	Country	Cavers	Date
453	138	Macocha	Czechoslovakia	J. Nagel *et al.*	1748
741	226	Grotta di Padriciano	Italy	A. Lindner *et al.*	1839
1076	328	Grotta di Trebiciano	Italy	A. Lindner *et al.*	1841
1509	460	Geldloch	Austria	—	1923
1574	480	Antro di Corchia	Italy	E. Fiorentino Club	1934
1978	603	Trou du Glaz	France	P. Chevalier *et al.*	1947
2418	737	Reseau de la Pierre St Martin	France	G. Lepineux *et al.*	July 1953
2962	903	Gouffre Berger	France	F. Petzl *et al.*	Sept 1954
3123	952	Gouffre Berger	France	L. Potié *et al.*	Aug 1955
3681	1122	Gouffre Berger	France	F. Petzl *et al.*	July 1956
3715	1133	Gouffre Berger	France	K. Pearce	Aug 1963
3842	1171	Reseau de la Pierre St Martin	France	A.R.S.I.P.	Aug 1966
4335	1321	Reseau de la Pierre St Martin	France	A.R.S.I.P.	Aug 1975
4457	1358	Gouffre Jean Bernard	France	Groupe Vulcain	July 1979
4600	1402	Gouffre Jean Bernard	France	P. Penez	Mar 1980
4773	1455	Gouffre Jean Bernard	France	P. Penez & F. Vergier	Feb 1981
4888	1490	Gouffre Jean Bernard	France	P. Penez & J. Fantoli	Feb 1982
5035	1535	Gouffre Jean Bernard	France	Groupe Vulcain	Oct 1983

N.B. The Gouffre Jean Bernard and the Reseau de la Pierre St Martin have both been explored via multiple entrances. The Jean Bernard has never been entirely descended, and the Pierre St Martin was only completely descended in one visit in 1978; consequently after August 1963 the 'sporting' records for the greatest descent into a cave should read:

ft	m	Cave	Country	Cavers	Date
3743	1141	Gouffre Berger	France	Spéléo Club de Seine	July 1968
4335	1321	Reseau de la Pierre St Martin	France	P. Courbon *et al.*	Sept 1978
4457	1358	Gouffre Jean Bernard	France	A. Ciezewski *et al.*	Feb 1980

The deepest cave explored through a single entrance is:

ft	m	Cave	Country	Cavers	Date
4391	1338	Sima de la Puerta de Illamina	Spain	F. Vergier	Aug 1981

CRICKET

See also The Guinness Book of Cricket Facts and Feats *by Bill Frindall, published at £8.95 in 1983.*

Origins

The earliest evidence of the game of cricket is from a drawing depicting two men playing with a bat and ball dated *c.* 1250. The game was played in Guildford, Surrey, at least as early as 1550. The earliest major match of which the full score survives was one in which a team representing England (40 and 70) was beaten by Kent (53 and 58 for 9) by one wicket at the Artillery Ground in Finsbury, London, on 18 June 1744. Cricket was played in Australia as early as 1803. The first international match was played between Canada and USA in 1844. Fifteen years later those countries were host to the first English touring team. The first touring team to visit England was an Australian Aborigine XI in 1868.

FIRST-CLASS CRICKET (1815 to 1982)

A substantial reduction in the English first-class cricket programme since 1968 has rendered many of the record aggregates for a season unassailable.

BATTING RECORDS—TEAMS

Highest innings

The highest recorded innings by any team was one of 1107 runs in 10 hr 30 min by Victoria against New South Wales in an Australian Sheffield Shield match at Melbourne on 27–28 Dec 1926.

The highest innings in Test cricket and the highest made in England is 903 runs for 7 wickets declared in 15 hr 17 min, by England against Australia at Kennington Oval, London, on 20, 22 and 23 Aug 1938. The highest innings in a county championship match is 887 in 10 hr 50 min by Yorkshire *v.* Warwickshire at Edgbaston, Birmingham on 7–8 May 1896.

Lowest innings

The lowest recorded innings is 12 made by Oxford University *v.* the Marylebone Cricket Club (MCC) at Cowley Marsh, Oxford on 24 May 1877, and 12 by Northamptonshire *v.* Gloucestershire at Gloucester on 11 June 1907. On the occasion of the Oxford match, however, the University batted a man short. The lowest in modern times is 14 by Surrey *v.* Essex at Chelmsford on 30 May 1983. The lowest score in a Test innings is 26 by New Zealand *v.* England in the second innings at Auckland on 28 Mar 1955.

Bob Taylor played his first Test in 1971, but kept out by Alan Knott, did not reappear until the age of 36 in 1977. Long regarded as the best 'keeper in the world he totalled 174 dismissals in 57 Tests to June 1984. (*All-Sport*)

The lowest aggregate for two innings is 34 (16 in first and 18 in second) by Border *v.* Natal in the South African Currie Cup at East London on 19 and 21 Dec 1959.

Greatest victory

The greatest recorded margin of victory is an innings and 851 runs, when Pakistan Railways (910 for 6 wickets declared) beat Dera Ismail Khan (32 and 27) at Lahore on 2–4 Dec 1964. The largest margin in England is an innings and 579 runs by England over Australia at The Oval on 20–24 Aug 1938 when Australia scored 201 and 123 with two men short in both innings. The most one-sided county match was when Surrey (698) defeated Sussex (114 and 99) by an innings and 485 runs at The Oval on 9–11 Aug 1888.

INDIVIDUAL CAREER RECORDS—All First-Class Cricket (FC) and Test Cricket (Test)

			Name	Team	Year
BATTING					
Most runs	FC	61,237	Sir John Berry 'Jack' Hobbs (1882–1963) (av 50.65)	Surrey/England	1905–34
	Test	8394	Sunil Manohar Gavaskar (b. 10 July 1949) (av 52.46)	India (99 Tests)	1971–83
Most centuries	FC	197	Sir Jack Hobbs (in 1315 innings)	Surrey/England	1905–34
	Test	30	Sunil Gavaskar	India	1971–83
Highest average	FC	95.14	Sir Donald George Bradman (b. 27 Aug 1908) (28,067 runs in 338 innings)	NSW/South Australia/Australia	1927–49
	Test	99.94	Sir Don Bradman (6996 runs in 80 innings)	Australia	1928–48
BOWLING					
Most wickets	FC	4187	Wilfred Rhodes (1877–1973) (av 16.70)	Yorkshire/England	1898–1930
	Test	355	Dennis Keith Lillee (b. 18 July 1949) (av 23.92)	Australia (70 Tests)	1971–84
Most hat-tricks	FC	7	Douglas Vivian Parson Wright (b. 21 Aug 1914)	Kent	1932–57
	Test	2	Hugh Trumble (1867–1938)	Australia	1890–1904
		2	Thomas James Matthews (1884–1943) (in same match)	Australia	1912
Lowest average	Test (min 15 wkts)	10.75	George Alfred Lohmann (1865–1901) (112 wkts)	England (18 Tests)	1886–96
WICKET-KEEPING					
Most dismissals	FC	1614†	Robert William Taylor (b. 17 July 1941)	Derbyshire/England	1960–83
	Test	355	Rodney William Marsh (b. 4 Nov 1947)	Australia (96 Tests)	1970–84
Most catches	FC	1444†	Robert Taylor	Derbyshire/England	1960–83
	Test	343	Rodney Marsh	Australia	1970–84
Most stumpings	FC	415	Leslie Ethelbert George Ames (b. 3 Dec 1905)	Kent/England	1926–51
	Test	52	William Albert Stanley Oldfield (1894–1976)	Australia (54 Tests)	1920–37
FIELDING					
Most catches	FC	1018	Frank Edward Woolley (1887–1978)	Kent/England	1906–38
	Test	122	Gregory Stephen Chappell (b. 7 Aug 1948)	Australia (87 Tests)	1970–84
MOST MATCHES					
First class		1107	Wilfred Rhodes	Yorkshire/England	1898–1930
Test		114	Michael Colin Cowdrey (b. 24 Dec 1932)	England	1954–75

† To start 1984 season.

INDIVIDUAL SEASON'S RECORDS—All First-Class Cricket in England

		Name	Team	Year
BATTING				
Most runs	3816 (av 90.85)	Denis Charles Scott Compton (b. 23 May 1918)	Middlesex/England	1947
Most centuries	18	Denis Compton (in 50 innings with 8 not outs)	Middlesex/England	1947
Highest average	115.66	Sir Donald Bradman (2429 runs in 26 innings, with 5 not outs)	Australians	1938
BOWLING				
Most wickets	304 (av 18.05)	Alfred Percy 'Tich' Freeman (1888–1965) (1976.1 overs)	Kent	1928
Lowest average	8.54 (min 100 wkts)	Alfred Shaw (1842–1907) (186 wkts)	Nottinghamshire	1880
WICKET-KEEPING				
Most dismissals	127	Leslie Ames (79 caught, 48 stumped)	Kent	1929
Most catches	96	James Graham Binks (b. 5 Oct 1935)	Yorkshire	1960
Most stumpings	64	Leslie Ames	Kent	1932
FIELDING				
Most catches	78	Water Reginald Hammond (1903–65)	Gloucestershire	1928

INDIVIDUAL RECORDS IN A TEST SERIES

		Name	Team	Year
BATTING				
Most runs	974 (av 139.14)	Sir Donald Bradman	Australia v. England (5 Tests)	1930
Most centuries	5	Clyde Leopold Walcott (b. 17 Jan 1926)	West Indies v. Australia (5 Tests)	1954–55
Highest average	563.00	Walter Reginald Hammond (563 runs in 2 innings, 1 not out)	England v. New Zealand (2 Tests)	1932–33
BOWLING				
Most wickets	49 (av 10.93)	Sydney Francis Barnes (1873–1967)	England v. South Africa (4 Tests)	1913–14
Lowest average	5.80 (min 20 wkts)	George Alfred Lohmann (35 wkts)	England v. South Africa (3 Tests)	1895–96
WICKET-KEEPING				
Most dismissals	28 (all caught)	Rodney Marsh	Australia v. England (5 Tests)	1982–83
Most stumpings	9	Percy William Sherwell (1880–1948)	South Africa v. Australia (5 Tests)	1910–11
FIELDING				
Most catches	15	John Morrison 'Jack' Gregory (1895–1973)	Australia v. England (5 tests)	1920–21
ALL-ROUND				
400 runs/30 wickets	475/34	George Giffen (1859–1927)	Australia v. England (5 Tests)	1894–95

During the winter of 1983/4 Sunil Gavaskar passed first Geoff Boycott's record number of runs and then Don Bradman's record number of centuries in Test cricket. (*All-Sport*)

Most runs in a day

The greatest number of runs scored in a day is 721 all out (ten wickets) in 5 hr 48 min by the Australians *v.* Essex at Southchurch Park, Southend-on-Sea on 15 May 1948. The Test record for runs in a day is 588 at Old Trafford, Manchester, on 27 July 1936 when England added 398 and India were 190 for 0 in their second innings by the close.

BATTING RECORDS—INDIVIDUALS

Highest innings

The highest individual innings recorded is 499 in 10 hr 35 min by Hanif Mohammad (b. 21 Dec 1934) for Karachi *v.* Bahawalpur at Karachi, Pakistan, on 8, 9 and 11 Jan 1959. The highest score in England is 424 in 7 hr 50 min by Archibald Campbell MacLaren (1871–1944) for Lancashire *v.* Somerset at Taunton on 15–16 July 1895. The record for a Test match is 365 not out in 10 hr 14 min by Sir Garfield St Aubrun Sobers (b. 28 July 1936) playing for West Indies against Pakistan at Sabina Park, Kingston, Jamaica, on 27 Feb–1 Mar 1958. The England Test record is 364 by Sir Leonard Hutton (b. 23 June 1916) *v.* Australia at The Oval on 20, 22 and 23 Aug 1938.

Longest innings

The longest innings on record is one of 16 hr 10 min for 337 runs by Hanif Mohammad (Pakistan) *v.* West Indies at Bridgetown, Barbados, on 20–23 Jan 1958. The English record is 13 hr 17 min by Len Hutton in his record Test score of 364.

Most runs *Off an over*

The only batsman to score 36 runs off a six-ball over was Sir Garfield Sobers (Nottinghamshire) off Malcolm Andrew Nash (b. 9 May 1945) (Glamorgan) at Swansea on 31 Aug 1968. The ball (recovered from the last hit from the road by a small boy) was duly presented to Sobers.

Most runs *Off a ball*

The most runs scored off a single hit is ten by Albert Neilson Hornby (1847–1925) off James Street (1839–1906) for Lancashire *v.* Surrey at The Oval on 14 July 1873, and ten by Samuel Hill Wood (later Sir Samuel Hill Hill-Wood) (1872–1949) off Cuthbert James Burnup (1875–1960) in the Derbyshire *v.* MCC match at Lord's, London, on 26 May 1900.

Most sixes *In an innings*

The highest number of sixes hit in an innings is 15 by John Richard Reid (b. 3 June 1928), in an innings of 296, lasting 3 hr 40 min, for Wellington v. Northern Districts in the Plunket Shield Tournament at Wellington, New Zealand, on 14–15 Jan 1963. The Test record is ten by Walter Hammond in an innings of 336 not out for England v. New Zealand at Auckland on 3 Mar and 1 Apr 1933.

Most sixes *In a match*

The highest number of sixes in a match is 17 (ten in the first and seven in the second innings) by William James Stewart (b. 31 Oct 1934) for Warwickshire v. Lancashire at Blackpool on 29–31 July 1959. His two innings were of 155 and 125.

Most boundaries in an innings

The highest number of boundaries was 68 (all in fours) by Percival Albert Perrin (1876–1945) in an innings of 343 not out for Essex v. Derbyshire at Chesterfield on 18–19 July 1904.

Double hundreds

The only batsman to score double hundreds in both innings is Arthur Edward Fagg (1915–77), who made 244 and 202 not out for Kent v. Essex at Colchester on 13–15 July 1938. Sir Donald Bradman scored a career record 37 double hundreds 1927–49.

'Carrying bat'

Cecil John Burditt Wood (1875–1960), of Leicestershire, is the only batsman to carry his bat through both completed innings of a match, and score a hundred in both innings, (107 not out, 117 not out) on 12–14 June 1911 v Yorkshire at Bradford.

Fastest scoring

The fastest 50 was completed off 13 balls in 8 min (1.22 to 1.30 p.m.) and in 11 scoring strokes by Clive Clay Inman (b. 29 Jan 1936) in an innings of 57 not out for Leicestershire v. Nottinghamshire at Trent Bridge, Nottingham on 20 Aug 1965. Full tosses were bowled to expedite a declaration.

The fastest hundred was completed in 35 min off between 40 and 46 balls by Percy George Herbert Fender (b. 22 Aug 1892), when scoring 113 not out for Surrey v. Northamptonshire at Northampton on 26 Aug 1920. Steven Joseph O'Shaughnessy (b. 9 Sept 1961) also scored a hundred in 35 minutes for Lancashire v. Leicestershire at Old Trafford, Manchester off 54 balls on 13 Sept 1983. In all he scored 105 and with Graham Fowler put on 201 runs for the 1st wicket in 45 mins. The match was 'dead' and irregular bowlers were used.

The hundred in fewest recorded deliveries was by David William Hookes (b. 3 May 1955) in 34 balls, in 43 min, for South Australia v. Victoria at Adelaide on 25 Oct 1982. In all he scored 107 from 40 balls in this the second innings, following 137 in the first innings. The most prolific scorer of hundreds in an hour or less was Gilbert Laird Jessop (1874–1955), with 11 between 1897 and 1913. The fastest Test hundred was one in 70 min off 67 balls by John Morrison 'Jack' Gregory (1895–1973) for Australia v. South Africa at Johannesburg on 12 Nov 1921. Edwin Boaler Alletson (1884–1963) scored 189 runs in 90 min for Nottinghamshire v. Sussex at Hove on 20 May 1911.

A double hundred in 120 min was achieved by Gilbert Jessop (286) for Gloucestershire v. Sussex at Hove on 1 June 1903 and equalled by Clive Hubert Lloyd (West Indians) (b. 31 Aug 1944) v. Glamorgan at Swansea, on 9 Aug 1976.

The fastest treble hundred was completed in 181 min by Denis Compton, who scored 300 for the MCC v. North-Eastern Transvaal at Benoni on 3–4 Dec 1948.

Slowest scoring

The longest time a batsman has ever taken to score his first run is 1 hr 37 min by Thomas Godfrey Evans (b. 18 Aug 1920), who scored 10 not out for England v. Australia at Adelaide on 5–6 Feb 1947. The longest innings without scoring is 87 minutes by Vincent Richard Hogg (b. 3 July 1952) for Zimbabwe–Rhodesia 'B' v. Natal 'B' at Pietermaritzburg in the South African Castle Bowl competition on 20 Jan 1980.

The slowest hundred on record is by Mudassar Nazar (b. 6 Apr 1956) of Pakistan v. England at Lahore on 14–15 Dec 1977. He required 9 hr 51 min for 114, reaching the 100 in 9 hr 17 min. The slowest double hundred recorded is one of 10 hr 22 min by The Nawab Mansur Ali of Pataudi (b. 5 Jan 1941),

during an innings of 200 for South Zone v. West Zone in the Duleep Trophy Final at Bombay on 29–31 October 1967.

Highest partnership

The record partnership for any wicket is the fourth wicket stand of 577 by Gul Mahomed (b. 15 Oct 1921), who scored 319, and Vijay Samuel Hazare (b. 11 Mar 1915) 288 in the Baroda v. Holkar match at Baroda, India, on 8–10 Mar 1947. The highest stand in English cricket is the first-wicket partnership of 555 by Percy Holmes (1886–1971) (224 not out) and Herbert Sutcliffe (1894–1978) (313) for Yorkshire v. Essex at Leyton on 15–16 June 1932.

The highest Test partnership is 451 for the second wicket by William Harold Ponsford (b. 19 Oct 1900) (266) and Sir Donald Bradman (244) for Australia v. England at the Oval on 18 Aug 1934, and 451 for the third wicket by Mudassar Nazar (231) and Javed Miandad (b. 12 Jun 1957) (280 not out) for Pakistan v. India at Hyderabad, Pakistan on 14–15 Jan 1983.

BOWLING

Most wickets *In an innings*

The taking of all ten wickets by a single bowler has been recorded many times but only one bowler has achieved this feat on three occasions—Alfred Freeman of Kent, against Lancashire at Maidstone on 24 July 1929, against Essex at Southend on 13–14 Aug 1930 and against Lancashire at Old Trafford on 27 May 1931. The fewest runs scored off a bowler taking all ten wickets is ten, when Hedley Verity (1905–43) of Yorkshire dismissed (eight caught, one lbw, one stumped) Nottinghamshire at Leeds on 12 July 1932. The only bowler to bowl out all ten was John Wisden (1826–84) of Sussex, playing for North v. South at Lord's in 1850.

Most wickets *Match*

James Charles Laker (b. 9 Feb 1922) of Surrey took 19 wickets for 90 runs (9–37 and 10–53) for England v. Australia in the Fourth Test at Old Trafford, on 27–31 July 1956. No other bowler has taken more than 17 wickets in a first-class match.

Most wickets *In a day*

The greatest number of wickets taken in a day's play is 17 (for 48 runs) by Colin Blythe (1879–1917), for Kent v. Northamptonshire at Northampton on 1 June 1907; by Hedley Verity for 91 runs, for Yorkshire v. Essex at Leyton on 14 July 1933; and by Thomas William John Goddard (1900–66) for 106 runs, for Gloucestershire v. Kent at Bristol on 3 July 1939.

Most consecutive wickets

No bowler in first-class cricket has yet achieved five wickets with five consecutive balls. The nearest approach was that of Charles Warrington Leonard Parker (1882–1959) (Gloucestershire) in his own benefit match against Yorkshire at Bristol on 10 Aug 1922, when he struck the stumps with five successive balls but the second was called as a no-ball. The only man to have taken four wickets with consecutive balls more than once is Robert James Crisp (b. 28 May 1911) for Western Province v. Griqualand West at Johannesburg on 24 Dec 1931 and against Natal at Durban on 3 Mar 1934.

Patrick Ian Pocock (b. 24 Sep 1946) took five wickets in six balls, six wickets in nine balls and seven wickets in eleven balls for Surrey v. Sussex at Eastbourne on 15 Aug 1972. In his own benefit match at Lord's on 22 May 1907, Albert Edwin Trott (1873–1914) of Middlesex took four Somerset wickets with four consecutive balls and then later in the same innings achieved a 'hat trick'.

Most consecutive maidens

Hugh Joseph Tayfield (b. 30 Jan 1929) bowled 16 consecutive eight-ball maiden overs (137 balls without conceding a run) for South Africa v. England at Durban on 25–26 Jan 1957. The greatest number of consecutive six-ball maiden overs bowled is 21 (131 balls) by Rameshchandra Gangaram 'Bapu' Nadkarni (b. 4 Apr 1932) for India v. England at Madras on 12 Jan 1964. The English record is 17 overs (105 balls) by Horace Leslie Hazell (b. 30 Sept 1909) for Somerset v. Gloucestershire at Taunton on 4 June 1949. Alfred Shaw (1842–1907) of Nottinghamshire bowled 23 consecutive four-ball maiden overs (92 balls) for North v. South at Trent Bridge on 17 July 1876.

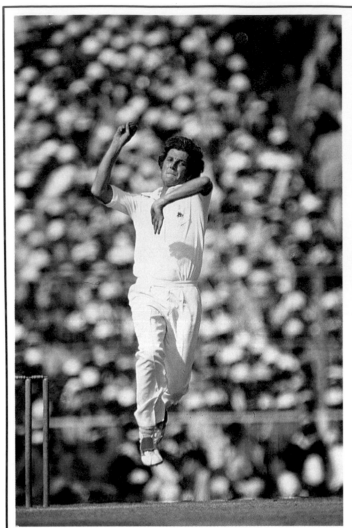

(left) Bob Willis first played for England in 1971. To the start of the 1984 season he had taken 319 wickets in Test cricket, having passed Fred Trueman's English record of 307 in January 1984. *(right)* Imran Khan achieved prodigious all-round success in 1982–3. In eleven months he played in 13 Tests scoring 562 runs (av. 56.20) and taking 88 wickets (av. 13.94). He passed 2000 runs in Tests in December 1983, and has now taken 232 wickets in 51 Tests. *(All-Sport)*

Most balls

The most balls bowled in a match is 917 by Cottari Subhann Nayudu (b. 18 Apr 1914), 6–153 and 5–275, for Holkar v. Bombay at Bombay on 4–9 Mar 1945. The most balls bowled in a Test match is 774 by Sonny Ramadhin (b. 1 May 1929) for West Indies v. England, 7–49 and 2–179, at Edgbaston on 29 May–4 June 1957. In the second innings he bowled a world record 588 balls (98 overs).

Most expensive bowling

The greatest number of runs hit off one bowler in one innings is 362, scored off Arthur Alfred Mailey (1886–1967) in the New South Wales v. Victoria match at Melbourne on 24–28 Dec 1926. The greatest number of runs ever conceded by a bowler in one match is 428 by Cottari Subhann Nayudu in the Holkar v. Bombay match above. The most runs conceded in a Test innings is 298 by Leslie O'Brien 'Chuck' Fleetwood-Smith (1910–71) for Australia v. England at the Oval on 20–23 Aug 1938.

Fastest

The highest electronically measured speed for a ball bowled by any bowler is 99.7 mph *160,45 km/h* by Jeffrey Robert Thomson (b. 16 Aug 1950) (Australia) during the Second Test v. the West Indies in December 1975. Albert Cotter (1883–1917) of New South Wales, Australia, is reputed to have broken a stump on more than 20 occasions.

WICKET-KEEPING

Most dismissals *Innings*

The most dismissals by a wicket-keeper in an innings is eight (all caught) by Arthur Theodore Wallace 'Wally' Grout (1927–68) for Queensland against Western Australia at Brisbane on 15 Feb 1960. The most stumpings in an innings is six by Henry 'Hugo' Yarnold (1917–74) for Worcestershire v. Scotland at Broughty Ferry, Tayside, on 2 July 1951. The Test record is seven (all caught) by Wasim Bari (b. 23 Mar 1948) for Pakistan v. New Zealand at Auckland on 23 Feb 1979, and by Robert Taylor for England v. India at Bombay on 15 Feb 1980.

Most dismissals *Match*

The greatest number of dismissals by a wicket-keeper in a match is 12 by Edward Pooley (1838–1907), eight caught, four stumped, for Surrey v. Sussex at The Oval on 6–7 July 1868; nine caught, three stumped by Donald Tallon (b. 17 Feb 1916) of Australia for Queensland v. New South Wales at Sydney on 2–4 Jan 1939; and also nine caught, three stumped by Hedley Brian Taber (b. 29 Apr 1940) for New South Wales v. South Australia at Adelaide 13–17 Dec 1968. The record for catches is 11 by Arnold Long (b. 18 Dec 1940), for Surrey v. Sussex at Hove on 18 and 21 July 1964, by Rodney Marsh for Western Australia v. Victoria at Perth on 15–17 Nov 1975 and by David Leslie Bairstow (b. 1 Sept 1951) for Yorkshire v. Derbyshire at Scarborough on 8–10 Sept 1982. The most stumpings in a match is nine by Frederick Henry Huish (1869–1957) for Kent v. Surrey at The Oval on 21–23 Aug 1911. The Test record for dismissals is ten, all caught, by Robert Taylor for England v. India at Bombay, 15–19 Feb 1980.

FIELDING

Most catches *Innings and Match*

The greatest number of catches in an innings is seven, by Michael James Stewart (b. 16 Sept 1932) for Surrey v. Northamptonshire at Northampton on 7 June 1957, and by Anthony Stephen Brown (b. 24 June 1936) for Gloucestershire v. Nottinghamshire at Trent Bridge on 26 July 1966.

The most catches in a Test match is seven by Gregory Stephen Chappell (b. 7 Aug 1948) for Australia *v.* England at Perth on 13–17 Dec 1974, and by Yajurvindra Singh (b. 1 Aug 1952) for India *v.* England at Bangalore on 28 Jan–2 Feb 1977.

Walter Hammond held a match record total of ten catches (four in the first innings, six in the second) for Gloucestershire *v.* Surrey at Cheltenham on 16–17 Aug 1928. The record for a wicket-keeper is 11 (see wicket-keeping).

Longest throw

A cricket ball (5½ oz *155 g*) was reputedly thrown 140 yd 2 ft *128,6 m* by Robert Percival, a left-hander, on Durham Sands racecourse on Easter Monday, 18 Apr 1881.

OTHER TEST RECORDS

Test appearances

The highest number of Test captaincies is 64 by Clive Lloyd of West Indies from 1974 to May 1984. The most innings batted in Test matches is 193 in 108 Tests by Geoffrey Boycott. Gundappa Ranganath Viswanath (India) (b. 12 Feb 1949) holds the record for consecutive Tests, with 87 from 19 Mar 1971 to 4 Feb 1983. In all Viswanath played in 91 Tests. The English record for consecutive Tests is 65 by Alan Philip Eric Knott (b. 9 Apr 1946), 1971–7 and by Ian Botham, 1978–84.

Longest match

The lengthiest recorded cricket match was the 'timeless' Test between England and South Africa at Durban on 3–14 Mar 1939. It was abandoned after ten days (eighth day rained off) because the boat taking the England team home was due to leave. The total playing time was 43 hr 16 min and a record Test match aggregate of 1981 runs were scored.

Largest crowds

The greatest attendance at a cricket match is about 394,000 for the Test between India and England at Eden Gardens, Calcutta on 1–6 Jan 1982. The record for a Test series is 933,513 for Australia and England (5 matches) in 1936–37. The greatest recorded attendance at a cricket match on one day was 90,800 on the second day of the Test between Australia and West Indies at Melbourne on 11 Feb 1961. The English record is 159,000 for the Test between England and Australia at Headingley, Leeds, on 22–27 July 1948, and the record for one day probably a capacity of 46,000 for a match between Lancashire and Yorkshire at Old Trafford on 2 Aug 1926. The English record for a Test series is 549,650 for the series against Australia in 1953.

Ian Botham, England's ace all-rounder, returned to his best form in the second Test against the West Indies at Lord's in 1984. He took eight wickets in a Test innings for the second time in his career and during his innings of 81 passed 4000 runs in Test cricket. (*All-Sport*)

THE DOUBLE

The 'double' of 1000 runs and 100 wickets in the same season was performed a record number of 16 times by Wilfred Rhodes between 1903 and 1926. The greatest number of consecutive seasons in which a player has performed the 'double' is 11 (1903–13) by George Herbert Hirst (1871–1954), of Yorkshire and England. Hirst is also the only player to score 2000 runs (2385) and take 200 wickets (208) in the same season (1906).

TEST CRICKET

The first player to achieve 2500 runs and 250 wickets in a Test career was Ian Terrence Botham (b. 24 Nov 1955) with 3805 runs and 286 wickets in 67 matches to 1 June 1984. Botham is the only player to score a hundred and take eight wickets in a single innings in the same Test, with 108 and eight for 34 for England *v.* Pakistan at Lord's on 15–19 June 1978. He scored a hundred (114) and took more than ten wickets (6–58 and 7–48) in a Test, for England *v.* India in the Golden Jubilee Test at Bombay on 15–19 Feb 1980. This feat was emulated by Imran Khan (b. 25 Nov 1952) with 117, 6–98 and 5–82 for Pakistan *v.* India at Faisalabad on 3–8 Jan 1983. Botham also completed the double of 1000 runs and 100 wickets in the fewest Test matches (21) on 30 Aug 1979. Kapil Dev Nikhanj (b. 6 Jan 1959) of India achieved this double in the shortest time span, 1 year 107 days and at the youngest age, 21 yr 27 days, in his 25th Test. The double of 2000 runs and 200 wickets was achieved in fewest matches (42) by Botham and at the youngest age by Kapil Dev at 24 yr 68 days.

Greatest receipts

The world record for receipts from a match is £389,297 at the Test between England and Australia at Lords on 2–7 July 1981. The Test series record is £1,533,205 for the England v. Australia Tests of June–Sept 1981.

WORLD CUP

The Prudential World Cup has been held at four-yearly intervals from 1975. It was won in 1975 and 1979 by West Indies and in 1983 by India. The highest team score was 338 for 5 by Pakistan v. Sri Lanka at Swansea on 9 June 1983, and the lowest 45 by Canada v. England at Old Trafford on 14 June 1979. A higher team score, 348 for 9, was achieved by Bermuda v. Malaysia, in the preceding ICC Trophy matches, at Wednesbury, W. Midlands on 16 June 1982. The highest individual score was 175 not out by Kapil Dev for India v. Zimbabwe at Tunbridge Wells on 18 June 1983. The best bowling was seven wickets for 51 runs by Winston Walter Davis (b. 18 Sept 1958) for West Indies v. Australia at Headingley on 12 June 1983.

ENGLISH COUNTY CHAMPIONSHIP

The greatest number of victories since 1890, when the championship was officially constituted, has been secured by Yorkshire with 29 outright wins, and one shared with Nottinghamshire and Middlesex in 1949. The most 'wooden spoons' have been won by Northamptonshire, with eleven since 1923. They did not win a single match between May 1935 and May 1939. The record number of consecutive title wins is seven by Surrey from 1952 to 1958. The greatest number of appearances in county championship matches is 763 by Wilfred Rhodes for Yorkshire between 1898 and 1930, and the greatest number of consecutive appearances is 423 by Kenneth George Suttle (b. 25 Aug 1928) of Sussex between 1954 and 1969. James Graham Binks (b. 15 Oct 1935) played in every county championship match for Yorkshire between his debut in 1955 and his retirement in 1969—412 matches. The seven sons of the Rev Henry Foster, of Malvern, uniquely all played county cricket for Worcestershire between 1899 and 1934.

OLDEST AND YOUNGEST

The oldest man to play in a Test match was Wilfred Rhodes, aged 52 yr 165 days, when he played for England v. West Indies at Kingston, Jamaica on 12 April 1930. Rhodes made his Test debut in the last Test of W. G. Grace, who at 50 yr 320 days at Nottingham on 3 June 1899 was the oldest ever Test Captain. The youngest Test captain was the Nawab of Pataudi (later Mansur Ali Khan) at 21 yr 77 days on 23 Mar 1962 for India v. West Indies at Bridgetown, Barbados. The youngest Test player was Mushtaq Mohammad (b. 22 Nov 1943), aged 15 yr 124 days, when he played for Pakistan v. West Indies at Lahore on 26 March 1959. England's youngest player was Dennis Brian Close (b. 24 Feb 1931) aged 18 yr 149 days v. New Zealand at Old Trafford on 23 July 1949.

The oldest player in first-class cricket was Col Cottari Kanakaiya Nayudu (1895–1967) (India), aged 68 yr 4 days, when he played for the Maharashtra Governor's XI v. Chief Minister's XI at Nagpur, India on 4 Nov 1963. The youngest is reputed to be Qasim Feroze (Pakistan) (b. 21 Jan 1958) who played for Bahawalpur v. Karachi Whites on 19 Jan 1971 aged 12 yr 363 days. The oldest Englishman was George Robert Canning, the 4th Lord Harris (1851–1932) who played for Kent v. All India at Catford on 4 July 1911 aged 60 yr 151 days. The youngest English first-class player was Charles Robertson Young when he played for Hampshire against Kent at Gravesend on 13 June 1867, aged 15 yr 131 days.

WOMEN'S CRICKET

Earliest

The first recorded women's match took place at Gosden Common, Surrey, England on 26 July 1745. *Circa* 1807 Christina Willes is said to have introduced the roundarm bowling style. The first Test match was Australia v. England at Brisbane on 28–31 Dec 1934. The International Women's Cricket Council was formed in 1958.

Batting *Individual*

The highest individual innings recorded is 224 not out by Mabel Bryant for Visitors v. Residents at Eastbourne, East Sussex, in August 1901. The highest innings in a Test match is 189 by Elizabeth Alexandra 'Betty' Snowball for England v. New Zealand at Christchurch, NZ on 16 Feb 1935. The highest Test innings in England is 179 by Rachel Flint (*née* Heyhoe) (b. 11 June 1939) for England v. Australia at The Oval, London on 27–28 July 1976. Rachel Flint also has scored the most runs in Test cricket with 1594 (av. 63.76) in 25 matches from December 1960 to July 1979.

Batting *Team*

The highest innings score by any team is 567 by Tarana v. Rockley, at Rockley, NSW Australia in 1896. The highest Test innings is 503 for five wickets declared by England v. New Zealand at Christchurch, NZ on 16 and 18 Feb 1935. The most in a Test in England is 379 by Australia v. England at The Oval, London on 26–27 July 1976. The highest innings total by any team in England is 410 for two wickets declared by the South v. East at Oakham, Leicestershire on 29 May 1982.

The lowest innings in a Test is 35 by England v. Australia at St Kilda, Melbourne, Australia on 22 Feb 1958. The lowest in a Test in England is 63 by New Zealand at Worcester on 5 July 1954.

Bowling

The greatest number of wickets taken in Test matches is 77 (av. 13.49) by Mary Beatrice Duggan (England) (1925–73) in 17 Tests from 1949 to 1963. She recorded the best Test analysis with seven wickets for six runs for England v. Australia at St Kilda, Melbourne on 22 Feb 1958.

On 26 June 1931 Rubina Winifred Humphries (b. 19 Aug 1915), for Dalton Ladies v. Woodfield SC, took all ten wickets for no runs. (She also scored all her team's runs.) This bowling feat was equalled by Rosemary White (b. 22 Jan 1938) for Wallington LCC v. Beaconsfield LCC in July 1962.

World Cup

Three women's World Cups have been staged. Australia won in 1978 and 1982 and England in 1973. The highest individual score in this series is 138 not out by Janette Ann Brittin (b. 4 July 1959) for England v. International XI at Hamilton, New Zealand on 14 Jan 1982.

MINOR CRICKET RECORDS
(where excelling those in First Class Cricket)

Highest individual innings

In a Junior House match between Clarke's House (now Poole's) and North Town, at Clifton College, Bristol, 22–23, 26–28 June 1899, Arthur Edward Jeune Collins (1885–1914) scored an unprecedented 628 not out in 6 hr 50 min, over five afternoons' batting, carrying his bat through the innings of 836. The scorer, E. W. Pegler, gave the score as '628—plus or minus 20, shall we say'.

Fastest individual scoring

Stanley Keppel 'Shunter' Coen (South Africa) (1902–67) scored 50 runs (11 fours and one six) in 7 min for Gezira v. the RAF in 1942. The fastest hundred by a prominent player in a minor match was by Vivian Frank Shergold Crawford (1879–1922) in 19 min at Cane Hill, Surrey on 16 Sept 1899. David Whatmore scored 210 (including 25 sixes and 12 fours) off 61 balls for Alderney v. Sun Alliance at Alderney on 19 June 1983. His first 100 came off 33 balls and his second off 25 balls.

Successive sixes

Cedric Ivan James Smith hit nine successive sixes for a Middlesex XI v. Harrow and District at Rayner's Lane, Harrow in 1935. This feat was repeated by Arthur Dudley Nourse (1910–81) in a South African XI v. Military Police match at Cairo, Egypt in 1942–3. Nourse's feat included six sixes in one over.

Fastest and Slowest scoring rates

In the match Royal Naval College, Dartmouth v. Seale Hayne Agricultural College in 1923, Kenneth Anderson Sellar (now Cdr 'Monkey' Sellar, DSO, DSC, RN) (b. 11 Aug 1906) and Leslie Kenneth Allen Block (later Judge Block, DSC) (1906–80) were set to score 174 runs in 105 min but achieved this total in 33 min, so averaging 5.27 runs per min. Playing for Gentlemen of Leicestershire CC v. Free Foresters, at Oakham, Rutland, on 19 Aug 1963, Ian H. S. Balfour batted for 100 min without adding to his score of five. He went on to make 39.

Consecutive not out hundreds

Gerald Vivian William Lukehurst (b. 5 Oct 1917), hit six consecutive not out hundreds for Gore Court and F. Day's XI between 3 July and 20 July 1955.

Most runs off a ball

A scoring stroke of 11 (all run, with no overthrows) was achieved by Lt (later Lt-Col) Philip Mitford (1879–1946), QO Cameron Highlanders, in a Malta Governor's Cup match on 28 May 1903.

Most runs off an over

H. Morely scored 62, nine sixes and two fours, off an eight-ball over from R. Grubb which had four no balls in a Queensland country match in 1968–9.

Greatest stand

T. Patten and N. Rippon made 641 for the third wicket for Buffalo v. Whorouly at Gapsted, Victoria, Australia, on 19 Mar 1914.

Bowling

Stephen Fleming, bowling for Marlborough College 'A' XI, New Zealand v. Bohally Intermediate at Blenheim, New Zealand in December 1967 took nine wickets in consecutive balls. In February 1931 in South Africa, Paul Hugo also took nine wickets with nine consecutive balls for Smithfield School v. Aliwal North. In the Inter-Divisional Ships Shield at Purfleet, Essex, on 17 May 1924, Joseph William Brockley (b. 9 Apr 1907) took all ten wickets, clean bowled, for two runs in 11 balls—including a triple hat trick. Jennings Tune took all ten wickets, all bowled, for 0 runs in five overs for Cliffe v. Eastrington in the Howden and District League at Cliffe, Yorkshire on 6 May 1922.

In 1881 Frederick Robert Spofforth (1835–1926) at Bendigo, NSW, Australia clean bowled all ten wickets in *both* innings. J. Bryant for Erskine v. Deaf Mutes in Melbourne on 15 and 22 Oct 1887, and Albert Rimmer for Linwood School v. Cathedral GS at Canterbury, New Zealand in December 1925 repeated the feat. In 1910, H. Hopkinson, of Mildmay CC London, took 99 wickets for 147 runs.

Maurice Hanes bowled 107 consecutive balls (17 overs and five balls) for Bedworth II v. A P Leamington II at Bedworth, Warwickshire on 16 June 1979, without conceding a run.

Wicket-keeping

In Ceylon, playing for Mahinda College v. Galle CC, at the Galle Esplanade, Welihinda Badalge Bennett (b. 25 Jan 1933) caught four and stumped six batsmen in one innings, on 1 March 1953.

Fielding

In a Wellington, New Zealand secondary schools 11-a-side match on 16 Mar 1974, Stephen Lane, 13, held 14 catches in the field (seven in each innings) for St Patrick's College, Silverstream v. St Bernard's College, Lower Hutt.

ENGLISH ONE-DAY CRICKET RECORDS

GC/NWB—Gillette Cup (inst. 1963)/Nat West Bank Trophy (from 1981)—60 overs matches
JPL—John Player League (inst. 1969)—40 overs matches   B & H—Benson & Hedges Cup (inst. 1972)—55 overs matches

MOST WINS
GC/NWB—4 Lancashire 1970–2, 1975
JPL —3 Kent 1972–3, 1976
B & H —3 Kent 1973, 1976, 1978

HIGHEST INDIVIDUAL INNINGS
GC/NWB—206 Alvin Isaac Kallicharan (b. 21 Mar 1949) Warwickshire v. Oxfordshire, 1984
JPL —176 Graham Alan Gooch (b. 23 July 1953) Essex v. Glamorgan, Southend, 1983
B & H —198* Graham Gooch, Essex v. Sussex, Hove, 1982

BEST INDIVIDUAL BOWLING
GC/NWB—7–15 Alan Leonard Dixon (b. 27 Nov 1933) Kent v. Surrey, The Oval, 1967
JPL —8–26 Keith David Boyce (b. 11 Oct 1943) Essex v. Lancashire, Old Trafford, 1971
Alan Ward (b. 10 Aug 1947) took 4 wickets in 4 balls, Derbyshire v. Sussex, Derby, 1970
B & H —7–12 Wayne Wendell Daniel (b. 16 Jan 1956) Middlesex v. Minor Counties (East), Ipswich, 1978

MOST DISMISSALS IN INNINGS
GC/NWB—6 Robert William Taylor (b. 17 July 1941) Derbyshire v. Essex, Derby, 1981
JPL —7 Bob Taylor, Derbyshire v. Lancashire, Old Trafford, 1975
B & H —8 Derek John Somerset Taylor (b. 12 Nov 1942) Somerset v. Cambridge University, Taunton, 1982

HIGHEST INNINGS TOTAL
GC/NWB—392–5 Warwickshire v. Oxfordshire, Edgbaston, 1984
JPL —310–5 Essex v. Glamorgan, Southend, 1983
B & H —350–3 Essex v. Oxford & Cambridge Universities, Chelmsford, 1979

LOWEST COMPLETED INNINGS TOTAL
GC/NWB—41 Cambridgeshire v. Buckinghamshire, Cambridge, 1972; 41 Middlesex v. Essex, Westcliff, 1972; 41 Shropshire v. Essex, Wellington, 1974
JPL —23 Middlesex v. Yorkshire, Headingley, 1974
B & H —56 Leicestershire v. Minor Counties, Wellington, 1982

HIGHEST PARTNERSHIP
GC/NWB—234*—4th wkt David Lloyd (b. 18 Mar 1947) & Clive Hubert Lloyd (b. 31 Aug 1944) Lancashire v. Gloucestershire, Old Trafford, 1978
JPL —273—2nd wicket Graham Gooch & Kenneth Scott McEwan (b. 16 July 1952) Essex v. Nottinghamshire, Trent Bridge, 1983
B & H —285*—2nd wicket Gordon Greenidge & David Roy Turner (b. 5 Feb 1949) Hampshire v. Minor Counties (South), Amersham, 1973

* Not out

With his majestic innings of 189 not out for the West Indies v. England at Old Trafford on 31 May 1984 Isaac Vivian Richards (b. 7 Mar 1952) made the highest score ever in a one-day International match. *(Varley Picture Agency)*

CROQUET

Earliest references

Croquet was probably derived from the French game *Jeu de Mail* first mentioned in the 12th century. In its present-day form, it originated as a country-house lawn game in Ireland in the 1830s when it was called 'crokey' and was introduced to Hampshire 20 years later. The first club was formed in the Steyne Gardens, Worthing, West Sussex in 1865.

Most championships

The greatest number of victories in the Open Croquet Championships (instituted at Evesham, Hereford & Worcester, 1867) is ten by John William Solomon (b. 1932) (1953, 1956, 1959, 1961, 1963–8). He also won ten Men's Championships (1951, 1953, 1958–60, 1962, 1964–5, 1971 and 1972), ten Open Doubles (with Edmond Patrick Charles Cotter) (1954–5, 1958–9, 1961–5 and 1969) and one Mixed Doubles (with Freda Oddie) in 1954, making a total of 31 titles. Solomon has also won the President's Silver Cup (inst. 1934) on nine occasions (1955, 1957–9, 1962–4, 1968 and 1971), and was Champion of Champions on all four occasions that this competition has been run (1967–70).

Dorothy Dyne Steel (1884–1965), fifteen times winner of the Women's Championship (1919–39), won the Open Croquet Championship four times (1925, 1933, 1935–36). She had also five Doubles and seven Mixed Doubles for a total of 31 titles.

International trophy

The MacRobertson International Shield (instituted 1925) has been played for eleven times. Great Britain have a record seven wins (in 1925, 1937, 1956, 1963, 1969, 1974 and 1983). Five international appearances were made by J. C. Windsor (Australia) in 1925, 1928, 1930, 1935 and 1937 and John Solomon (GB) in 1951, 1956, 1963, 1969 and 1974.

Lowest handicap

Historically the lowest playing handicap has been that of Humphrey Osmond Hicks (Devon) (b. 1904) with minus 5½. In 1974 the limit was however fixed at minus 5. The player holding the lowest handicap is G. Nigel Aspinall with minus 5.

Grete Waitz finishing third in the 1984 world cross-country championships, after five previous victories in the event. She was unbeaten for 12 years in cross-country and road races and set four women's world bests for the marathon. (All-Sport)

CROSS-COUNTRY RUNNING

WORLD (FORMERLY INTERNATIONAL) CHAMPIONSHIPS

The earliest recorded international cross-country race took place over 14,5 km *9 miles 18 yd* from Ville d'Avray, outside Paris, on 20 Mar 1898 between England and France (England won by 21 points to 69). The inaugural International Cross-Country Championships took place at the Hamilton Park Racecourse, Scotland, on 28 Mar 1903. The greatest margin of victory is 56 sec or 390 yd *356 m* by John 'Jack' Thomas Holden (England) (b. 13 Mar 1907) at Ayr Racecourse, Scotland, on 24 Mar 1934. Since 1973 the race has been run under the auspices of the International Amateur Athletic Federation.

The greatest men's team wins have been those of England, with a minimum of 21 points (the first six runners to finish) on two occasions, at Gosforth Park, Newcastle, Tyne and Wear, on 22 Mar 1924, and at the Hippodrome de Stockel, Brussels, Belgium, on 20 Mar 1932.

Most appearances

Marcel Van de Wattyne (Belgium) (b. 7 July 1924) ran in a record 20 races, 1946–65. The women's record is 16 by Jean Lochhead (Wales) (b. 24 Dec 1946), 1967–79, 1981, 1983–4.

Most wins

The greatest number of team victories have been by England with 45 for men, 11 for junior men and 6 for women.

The greatest number of men's individual victories is four by Jack Holden (England) in 1933–5 and 1939, by Alain Mimoun-o-Kacha (France) (b. 1 Jan 1921) in 1949, 1952, 1954 and 1956 and by Gaston Roelants (Belgium) (b. 5 Feb 1937) in 1962, 1967, 1969 and 1972. The women's race has been won five times by Doris Brown-Heritage (USA) (b. 17 Sept 1942) 1967–71, and by Grete Waitz (*née* Andersen) (Norway) (b. 1 Oct 1953), 1976–81 and 1983.

English championship

The English Cross-Country Championship was inaugurated at Roehampton, Wandsworth, London, in 1877. The most individual titles won is four by Percy H. Stenning (1854–92) (Thames Hare and Hounds) in 1877–80 and Alfred E. Shrubb (1878–1964) (South London Harriers) in 1901–4. The most successful club in the team race has been Birchfield Harriers from Birmingham with 27 wins and one tie between 1880 and 1953. The largest field was the 1862 starters and 1723 finishers in the senior race in 1984 at Newark, Nottinghamshire.

Largest field

The largest recorded field in any cross-country race was 11,763 starters (10,810 finished) in the 30 km *18.6 miles* Lidingöloppet, near Stockholm, Sweden, on 3 Oct 1982.

CURLING

Origins

Although a 15th century bronze figure in the Florence Museum appears to be holding a curling stone, the earliest illustration of the sport was in one of the Flemish painter Pieter Bruegel's winter scenes *c.* 1560. The game was probably introduced into Scotland by Flemings in the 15th century. The earliest documented club is Muthill, Tayside, Scotland, formed in 1739. Organized administration began in 1838 with the formation in Edinburgh of the Grand (later Royal) Caledonian Curling Club, the international legislative body until the foundation of the International Curling Federation in 1966. The first indoor ice rink to introduce curling was in Montreal, Canada in 1807, and the first in Britain was at Southport, Merseyside in 1878.

The USA won the first Gordon International Medal series of matches, between Canada and the USA, at Montreal in 1884. Curling is to be added to the programme of the 1988 Olympic Games, having been a demonstration sport at the Games of 1924, 1932 and 1964.

Most titles

The record for World championships (inst. 1959) for the Air Canada Silver Broom is 15 wins by Canada, in 1959–64, 1966,

1968–72, 1980, 1982–3. The most Strathcona Cup (inst. 1903) wins is seven by Canada (1903, 1909, 1912, 1923, 1938, 1957, 1965) against Scotland. Switzerland have won most Women's World Championships (inst. 1979) with two titles (1979 and 1983).

'Perfect' games

Stu Beagle, of Calgary, Alberta, Canada, played a perfect game (48 points) against Nova Scotia in the Canadian championships (Brier) at Fort William (now Thunder Bay), Ontario, on 8 Mar 1960. Dernice Fokuto, of Edmonton, Alberta, Canada, skipped her rink to two consecutive eight-enders on the same ice at the Derrick Club, Edmonton, on 10 Jan and 6 Feb 1973. Two eight-enders in one bonspiel were scored at the Parry Sound Curling Club, Ontario, Canada on 6–8 Jan 1983. Andrew McQuistin, of Stranraer, skipped a Scotland rink to a 1–0 win over Switzerland, scoring in the tenth end after nine consecutive blank ends, in the Uniroyal World Junior Championships at Kitchener-Waterloo, Ontario, Canada on 16 Mar 1980.

Largest bonspiel

The largest bonspiel in the world is the Manitoba Bonspiel held annually in Winnipeg, Canada. There were 768 teams, or rinks, of four, a total of 3072 curlers, in the 1984 tournament.

Largest rink

The world's largest curling rink is the Big Four Curling Rink, Calgary, Alberta, Canada opened in 1959. 96 teams and 384 players are accommodated on two floors each with 24 sheets of ice.

CYCLING

Earliest race

The earliest recorded bicycle race was a velocipede race over 2 km *1.24 miles* at the Parc de St Cloud, Paris, on 31 May 1868, won by Dr James Moore (GB) (1847–1935) (later Chevalier de la Legion d'Honneur).

Highest speed

The highest speed ever achieved on a bicycle is 140.5 mph *226,1 km/h* by Dr Allan V. Abbott, 29, of San Bernadino, California, USA, behind a wind-shield mounted on a 1955 Chevrolet over ¾ mile *1,2 km* at Bonneville Salt Flats, Utah, USA on 25 Aug 1973. His speed over a mile *1,6 km* was 138.674 mph *223,174 km/h*. It should be noted that considerable help is provided by the slipstreaming effect of the lead vehicle. Fred Markham recorded an official unpaced 8.80 sec for 200 m (50.84 mph *81,81 km/h*) on a streamlined bicycle at Ontario, California, USA, on 6 May 1979.

The greatest distance ever covered in one hour is 122,771 km *76 miles 504 yd* by Leon Vanderstuyft (Belgium) (1890–1964) on the Montlhery Motor Circuit, France, on 30 Sept 1928, achieved from a standing start paced by a motorcycle. The 24 hr record behind pace is 860 miles 367 yd *1384,367 km* by Hubert Ferdinand Opperman (later Hon Sir) (b. 29 May 1904) in Melbourne, Australia on 23 May 1932.

Most titles *Olympic*

The most gold medals won is three by Paul Masson (France) (1874–1945) in 1896, Francisco Verri (Italy) (1885–1945) in 1906 and Robert Charpentier (France) (1916–66) in 1936. Daniel Morelon (France) won two in 1968, and a third in 1972. He also won a bronze medal in 1964. In the 'unofficial' 1904 cycling programme, Marcus Hurley (USA) (1884–1950) won four events.

Most titles *British*

Beryl Burton (b. 12 May 1937), 25 times British all-round time trial champion (1959–84), has won 70 individual road TT titles, 14 track pursuit titles and 12 road race titles. Mrs Burton's career overshadows all male achievements. Ian Hallam (b. 24 Nov 1948) won a record 25 men's titles, 1969–82.

Tour de France

The greatest number of wins in the Tour de France (inaugurated 1903) is five by Jacques Anquetil (France) (b. 8 Jan 1934), 1957, 1961–4 and by Eddy Merckx (Belgium) (b. 17 June 1945), 1969–72 and 1974. The closest race ever was in 1968 when after 4665 km *2898.7 miles* over 25 days (27 June–21 July) Jan Janssen (Netherlands) (b. 19 May 1940) beat Herman van Springel (Belgium) in Paris by 38 sec. The fastest average speed was 37,84 km/h *23.51 mph* by Bernard Hinault (France) (b. 14 Nov 1954) in 1981. The longest race was 5745 km *3569 miles* in 1926, and most participants were 170 starters in 1982 and 1984. The longest ever stage was the 486 km from Les Sables d'Olonne to Bayonne in 1919. The longest in 1984 was 338 km from Nantes to Bordeaux.

Tour of Britain (Milk Race)

Four riders have won the Tour of Britain twice each—Bill Bradley (1959–60), Les West (1965, 1967), Fedor den Hertog (Netherlands) (1969, 1971) and Yuri Kashurin (USSR) (1979, 1982). The closest race ever was in 1976 when after 1035 miles *1665,07 km* over 14 days (30 May–12 June) Bill Nickson (GB) (b. 30 Jan 1953) beat Joe Waugh (GB) by 5 sec. Den Hertog recorded the fastest average speed of 25.20 mph *40,55 km/h* in the 1971 race (1096 miles *1763,84 km*). Malcolm Elliott (b. 1 July 1961) won a record six stages in 1983. The longest Milk Race was in 1969 (1515 miles *2438,16 km*) although the longest ever Tour of Britain was in 1953 (1631 miles *2624,84 km* starting and finishing in London) under *Daily Express* sponsorship.

Six-day races

The most wins in 6-day races is 88 out of 233 events by Patrick Sercu (b. 27 June 1944), of Belgium, 1964–83.

Longest one-day race

The longest single-day 'massed start' road race is the 551–620 km *342–385 miles* Bordeaux–Paris, France, event. Paced over all or part of the route, the highest average speed was in 1981 with 47,186 km/h *29.32 mph* by Herman van Springel (Bel) (b. 14 Aug 1943) for 584,5 km in 13 hr 35 min 18 sec.

Land's End to John o' Groats

The 'end to end' record for the 847 miles *1363 km* is 1 day 21 hr 3 min 16 sec (average speed 18.80 mph *30,25 km/h*) by John Woodburn (b. 22 Dec 1936) on 14–15 Aug 1982. The feminine record is 2 days 11 hr 7 min by Eileen Sheridan (b. 18 Oct 1923) on 9–11 July 1954. She completed 1000 miles *1609 km* in 3 days 1 hr.

Francesco Moser took time off from the European circuit to make two record smashing rides in Mexico City in January 1984. He became the first man to cycle over 50 km in an hour without assistance, with first 50,809 km and then 51,151 km. *(All-Sport)*

INDOOR TRACKS

MEN
Professional unpaced standing start:
1 hour .... 46 847 km *29 miles 192 yd*.......... Siegfried Adler (West Germany) .... Zürich, Switzerland .... 2 Aug 1968

Professional unpaced flying start:
500 metres .... 28:48.6 .... Urs Freuler (Switzerland) .... Vienna, Austria .... 2 Oct 1981

Amateur unpaced standing start:
1 km .... 1:02.955.......... Lothar Thoms (GDR) (b. 18 May 1956) .... Moscow, USSR .... 22 July 1980
5 km .... 5:50.205.......... Aleksandr Krasnov (USSR) (b. 7 Apr 1960) .... Moscow, USSR .... 27 Apr 1983
10 km .... 12:06.29 .... Hans-Henrik Oersted (Denmark) (b. 13 Dec 1954) Copenhagen, Denmark .... 28 Nov 1978
20 km .... 24:52.83 .... Mikhail Sveshnikov (USSR) .... Moscow, USSR .... 28 Apr 1983

Amateur unpaced flying start:
200 metres .... 10.249 .... Sergei Kopylov (USSR) (b. 29 July 1960) .... Moscow, USSR .... 6 Aug 1982
500 metres .... 27.836.......... Otari Mchedlishvili (USSR) .... Moscow, USSR .... 12 Oct 1983
1 km .... 1:00.279.......... Sergei Kopylov (USSR) .... Moscow, USSR .... 30 July 1982

Amateur motor-paced:
50 km .... 34:59.962 .... Aleksandr Romanov (USSR) .... Moscow, USSR .... 31 Jan 1984
100 km .... 1 hr 15:04.490....... Aleksandr Romanov (USSR) .... Moscow, USSR .... 30 Jan 1983
1 hour .... 87,430 km *54 miles 575 yd*.......... Aleksandr Romanov (USSR) .... Moscow, USSR .... 28 Apr 1984

WOMEN
Unpaced standing start:
1 km .... 1:13.777.......... Erika Salumyae (USSR) .... Moscow, USSR .... 21 Sept 1983
5 km .... 6:42.237.......... Galina Tsareva (USSR) .... Moscow, USSR .... 27 Oct 1982
10 km .... 13:41.519......... Galina Tsareva (USSR) .... Moscow, USSR .... 18 Jan 1983
20 km .... 27:46.73 .... Galina Tsareva (USSR) .... Moscow, USSR .... 28 Apr 1983
100 km .... 2 hr 31:30.43 .... Mieke Havik (Netherlands) .... Rotterdam, Netherlands .... 19 Sept 1983

Unpaced flying start:
200 metres .... 11.547.......... Natalia Krushelnitskaya (USSR) .... Moscow, USSR .... 22 Apr 1982
500 m .... 31.112.......... Natalia Krushelnitskaya (USSR) .... Moscow, USSR .... 23 Apr 1982
1 km .... 1:09.077.......... Galina Tsareva (USSR) .... Moscow, USSR .... 10 June 1980

LONG DISTANCE BESTS
24 hr .... 830,1 km *515.8 miles*.......... Teuvo Louhivouri (Finland) .... Tampere to Kolari, Finland .... 9–10 Sept 1974
1 000 km .... 32 hr 4 min.......... Herman de Munck (Belgium) .... Keerbergen, Belgium .... 23–24 Sept 1983
1 000 miles .... 51 hr 12 min 32 sec.......... Herman de Munck (Belgium) .... Keerbergen, Belgium .... 23–25 Sept 1983

ROLLER CYCLING

Paul Swinnerton (GB) achieved a record 102 mph *164 km/h* for 200 m on rollers on 12 Feb 1982 at Stoke-on-Trent. The four-man 12 hr record is 717.9 miles *1155,5 km* by a Northampton team at the Guildhall, Northampton, on 28 Jan 1978. The 24 hr solo record is 792.7 miles *1275,7 km* by Bruce W. Hall at San Diego University, Calif., USA on 22–23 Jan 1977.

STATIONARY CYCLING

Rudi Jan Jozef De Greef (b. 28 Dec 1955) stayed stationary without support for 10 hr at Meensel-Kiezegem, Belgium on 19 Nov 1982.

DARTS

Further information can be obtained from the Guinness Book of Darts by Derek Brown, published by Guinness Superlatives Ltd at £7.50 (hard-back) and £5.95 (paperback, 1982 edition).

Origins

The origins of darts date from the use by archers of heavily weighted ten-inch throwing arrows for self-defence in close quarters fighting. The 'dartes' were used in Ireland in the 16th century and darts was played on the *Mayflower* by the Plymouth pilgrims in 1620. The modern game dates from at least 1896 when Brian Gamlin of Bury, Lancashire, is credited with inventing the present numbering system on the board. The first recorded score of 180 was by John Reader at the Highbury Tavern in Sussex in 1902. Today there are an estimated 6,000,000 darts players in the British Isles.

Most titles

Eric Bristow (b. 25 Apr 1957) has most wins in the World Masters Championship (inst. 1974) with four, in 1977, 1979, 1981 and 1983, and in the World Professional Championship (inst. 1978) with three, in 1980, 1981 and 1983. Bristow completed a unique treble in 1983 by also winning the World Cup singles. The only men to win the annual *News of the World* individual Championship twice are Tommy Gibbons (Ivanhoe Working Men's Club) of Conisbrough, South Yorkshire, in 1952 and 1958; Tom Reddington (b. 1922) of New Inn, Stonebroom, Derbyshire in 1955 and of George Hotel, Alfreton, Derbyshire 1960; Tom M. Barrett (1909–81) (Odco Sports Club, London) in 1964 and 1965; Stefan Lord (b. 4

Dec 1954) of the Stockholm Super Darts Club, Sweden in 1978 and 1980, and Eric Bristow in 1983 and 1984. John Lowe (b. 21 July 1945) is the only other man to have won each of the four major world titles: World Masters, 1976 and 1980; World Professional, 1979; World Cup Singles, 1981; and *News of the World*, 1981.

The National Darts Association of Great Britain individual title was won by Tom O'Regan (b. 28 Feb 1939) of the Northern Star, New Southgate, Greater London in 1970–2. Maureen Flowers (b. 6 Dec 1946), in 1979 and 1980, is the only double winner of the NDA women's individual title.

World Cup

The first World Cup was held at the Wembley Conference Centre, London in 1977. Wales were the inaugural champions and England won in 1979, 1981 and 1983.

Longest unbeaten run

Mike Bowell (b. 31 May 1947) of Paulton Darts League, Avon, won 152 consecutive competition games from 9 Feb 1971 to 29 Nov 1974. The White Horse Inn, Ashton-under-Lyne, Manchester, were undefeated in a total of 169 matches from 31 May 1979 to 9 Feb 1981.

Fastest match

The fastest time taken for a match of three games of 301 is 1 min 58 sec by Ricky Fusco (GB) at the Perivale Residents Association Club, Middlesex, on 30 Dec 1976.

Fastest 'Round the board'

The record time for going round the board clockwise in 'doubles' at arm's length is 9.2 sec by Dennis Gower at the Millers Arms, Hastings, East Sussex on 12 Oct 1975 and 14.5 sec in numerical order by Jim Pike (1903–60) at the Craven Club, Newmarket in March 1944. The record for this feat at the 9 ft *2,7 m* throwing distance, retrieving own darts, is 2 min 13 sec by Bill Duddy (b. 29 Sept 1932) at The Plough, Haringey, London on 29 Oct 1972.

Least darts

Scores of 201 in four darts, 301 in six darts, 401 in seven darts and 501 in nine darts, have been achieved on various occasions. The lowest number of darts thrown for a score of 1001 is 19 by Cliff Inglis (b. 27 May 1935) (160, 180, 140, 180, 121, 180, 40) at the Bromfield Men's Club, Devon on 11 Nov 1975. A score of 2001 in 52 darts was achieved by Alan Evans (b. 14 June 1949) at Ferndale, Glamorgan on 3 Sept 1976. 3001 in 79 darts was thrown by Charlie Ellix (b. 18 Oct 1941) at The Victoria Hotel, Tottenham, London on 29 April 1977.

Ten hour scores

The record number of trebles scored in 10 hr is 2787 by David Broad (b. 11 Feb 1939) from 9984 darts thrown on 26 Feb 1983 at Blantyre Sports Club, Malawi. David Broad scored a record 3085 doubles (out of 9945 darts) in 10 hr at Blantyre on 17 Mar 1984. The greatest score amassed in 10 hr is 487,588 by Bruce Campbell and Peter Dawson at the Waikiki Hotel, Safety Bay, Western Australia, on 14 Oct 1978.

24 hr scores

Eight players from the Royal Hotel, Newsome, Huddersfield scored 1,358,731 in 24 hr on one board on 26–27 May 1981.

Million and one up

Eight players from The Grapevine, South Oxhey, Hertfordshire scored 1,000,001 with 38,925 darts in one session on 26–28 Aug 1983.

(right) Eric Bristow, the 'Crafty Cockney', began playing darts at the age of eleven and made his England debut seven years later. Since then he has won almost every major prize. *(All-Sport)* *(below)* Team members and supporters from the Grapevine, South Oxhey, celebrate their record million and one at darts.

EQUESTRIAN SPORTS

See also The Guinness Guide to Equestrianism *by Dorian Williams, published by Guinness Superlatives Ltd. (price £8.95).*

Origins
Evidence of horse-riding dates from a Persian engraving dated *c.* 3,000 BC. Pignatelli's academy of horsemanship at Naples dates from the 16th century. The earliest jumping competition was at the Agricultural Hall, Islington, London, in 1869. Equestrian events have been included in the Olympic Games since 1912.

Most Olympic medals
The greatest number of Olympic gold medals is five by Hans-Günter Winkler (b. 24 July 1926) (W. Germany) who won four team gold medals as captain in 1956, 1960, 1964 and 1972 and won the individual Grand Prix in 1956. The most team wins in the Prix des Nations is five by Germany in 1936, 1956, 1960, 1964 and 1972. The lowest score obtained by a winner is no faults by Frantisek Ventura (1895–1969) (Czechoslovakia) on *Eliot*, 1928 and Alwin Schockemöhle (b. 29 May 1937) (W. Germany) on *Warwick Rex*, 1976. Pierre Jonqueres d'Oriola (b. 1 Feb 1920) (France) uniquely won the individual gold medal twice, 1952 and 1964. Richard John Hannay Meade (b. 4 Dec 1938) (Great Britain) is the only British rider to win three gold medals—as an individual in 1972 and team titles in 1968 and 1972, all in the 3-day event.

Most titles *World*
The men's world championships (inst. 1953) have been won twice by Hans-Günter Winkler (W. Germany) (1954–5) and Raimondo d'Inzeo (Italy) (1956 and 1960). The women's title (1965–74) was won twice by Jane 'Janou' Tissot (*née* Lefebvre) (France) (b. Saigon, 14 May 1945) on *Rocket* (1970 and 1974).

Most titles *BSJA*
The most BSJA championships won is five by Alan Oliver (b. 8 Sept 1931) (1951, 1954, 1959, 1969–70). The only horses to have won twice are *Maguire* (Lt-Col Nathaniel Kindersley) (1900–80) in 1945 and 1947, *Sheila* (Seamus Hayes) in 1949–50, *Red Admiral* (Oliver) in 1951 and 1954 and *Stroller* (Marion Mould) in 1968 and 1971. The record for the Ladies' Championship is eight by Patricia Smythe (b. 22 Nov 1928), now Mrs Koechlin. She won on *Flanagan* in 1955, 1958 and 1962—the only three-time winner and also in 1952–3, 1957, 1959 and 1961.

Lucinda Green on Beagle Bay whom she rode to her record sixth Badminton success. She was also World champion in 1982 and European champion in 1975 and 1977. *(All-Sport)*

King George V Gold Cup and Queen Elizabeth II Cup
David Broome (b. 1 Mar 1940) has won the King George V Gold Cup (first held 1911) a record five times, 1960 on *Sunsalve*, 1966 on *Mister Softee*, 1972 on *Sportsman*, 1977 on *Philco* and 1981 on *Mr Ross*. The Queen Elizabeth II Cup (first held 1949), for women, has been won four times by Elizabeth Edgar (b. 28 Apr 1943), 1977 on *Everest Wallaby*, 1979 on *Forever*, 1981 and 1982 on *Everest Forever*. The only horse to win both these trophies is *Sunsalve* in 1957 (with Elisabeth Anderson) and 1960.

President's Trophy (World Team Championship)
Instituted in 1965, the Trophy has been won most times by Great Britain with ten in 1965, 1967, 1970, 1972–4, 1977–9 and 1983.

Three-day event
The Badminton Three-Day Event (inst. 1949) has been won six times by Lucinda Green (*née* Prior-Palmer) (b. 7 Nov 1953) in 1973 (on *Be Fair*), 1976 (*Wide Awake*), 1977 (*George*), 1979 (*Killaire*), 1983 (*Regal Realm*) and 1984 (*Beagle Bay*)

Jumping records
The official *Fédération Equestre Internationale* high jump record is 8 ft $1\frac{1}{4}$ in *2,47 m* by *Huasó*, ridden by Capt Alberto Larraguibel Morales (Chile) at Vina del Mar, Santiago, Chile, on 5 Feb 1949, and 27 ft $6\frac{3}{4}$ in *8,40 m* for a long jump over water by *Something*, ridden by André Ferreira (S. Africa) at Johannesburg on 26 Apr 1975.

The British record is 7 ft $7\frac{5}{16}$ in *2,32 m* by the 16.2 hands *167 cm* grey gelding *Lastic* ridden by Nick Skelton (b. 30 Dec 1957) at Olympia, London, on 16 Dec 1978. On 25 June 1937, at Olympia, the Lady Wright (*née* Margery Avis Bullows) set the best recorded height for a British equestrienne on her liver chestnut *Jimmy Brown* at 7 ft 4 in *2,23 m*.

The greatest recorded height reached bareback is 7 ft *2,13 m* by Michael Whitaker (b. 17 Mar 1960) on *Red Flight* at Dublin on 14 Nov 1982.

Driving
The biennial World Driving Championships have been held five times since 1972. Great Britain have most team wins with three, 1972, 1974 and 1980. The best individual performance by Britons have been silver medals won by Col Sir John Miller in 1972, and George Bowman in 1980.

Longest ride
Thomas L. Gaddie (USA) rode 11,217.2 miles *18 052 km* from Dallas, Texas to Fairbanks, Alaska and back in 295 days, 12 Feb to 2 Dec 1980, with seven horses.

FENCING

Origins

'Fencing' (fighting with single sticks) was practised as a sport, or as a part of a religious ceremony, in Egypt as early as *c.* 1360 BC. The first governing body for fencing in Britain was the Corporation of Masters of Defence founded by Henry VIII before 1540 and fencing has been practised as sport, notably in prize fights, since that time. The foil was the practice weapon for the short court sword from the 17th century. The épée was established in the mid-19th century and the light sabre was introduced by the Italians in the late 19th century.

Most titles *World*

The greatest number of individual world titles won is five by Aleksandr Romankov (USSR) (see table), but Christian d'Oriola (France) won four world foil titles, 1947, 1949, 1953–4 as well as two individual Olympic titles. Of the three women foilists with three world titles, only Ilona Schacherer-Elek won two individual Olympic titles (1936 and 1948).

Most titles *Olympic*

The most individual Olympic gold medals won is three by Ramón Fonst (Cuba) (1883–1959) in 1900 and 1904 (two) and by Nedo Nadi (Italy) (1894–1952) in 1912 and 1920 (two). Nadi also won three team gold medals in 1920 making a then unprecedented total of five gold medals at one celebration. Edoardo Mangiarotti (Italy) (b. 7 Apr 1919) with six gold, five silver and two bronze, holds the record of 13 Olympic medals. He won them for foil and épée from 1936 to 1960. The most gold medals by a woman is four (one individual, three team) by Elena Novikova-Belova (USSR) (b. 28 July 1947) from 1968 to 1976, and the record for all medals is seven (two gold, three silver, two bronze) by Ildikó Sagi-Retjö (formerly Ujlaki-Retjö) (Hungary) (b. 11 May 1937) from 1960 to 1976.

British Olympic records

The only British fencer to win a gold medal is Gillian Mary Sheen (b. 21 Aug 1928) in the 1956 foil. A record three Olympic medals were won by Edgar Seligman (1867–1958) with silver medals in the épée team event in 1906, 1908 and 1912. Henry William Furse Hoskyns (b. 19 Mar 1931) has competed most often for Great Britain with six Olympic appearances, 1956–76.

FIELD SPORTS

FOXHUNTING

Earliest references

Hunting the fox in Britain became popular from the second half of the 18th century though it is mentioned very much earlier. Prior to that time hunting was confined principally to the deer and the hare.

Pack *Oldest*

The Old Charlton Hunt (later the Goodwood) in West Sussex, now extinct, the Duke of Monmouth and Lord Grey of Werke at Charlton, Sussex, and the Duke of Buckingham in north Yorkshire, owned packs which were entered to fox only during the reign (1660–85) of Charles II.

Pack *Largest*

The pack with the greatest number of hounds has been the Duke of Beaufort's hounds maintained at Badminton, Avon, since 1786. At times hunting six days a week, this pack once had 120 couples at hounds. It now meets four days a week.

Longest span

Jean Bethel 'Betty' McKeever (*née* Dawes) (b. 26 Feb 1901) has been Master of the Blean Beagles in Kent since 1909. The 10th Duke of Beaufort (1900–84) was Master of Foxhounds from 1924 to 1983 and hunted on 3895 days from 1920–67.

Longest hunt

The longest recorded hunt was one held by Squire Sandys which ran from Holmbank, northern Lancashire to Ulpha, Cumbria, a total of nearly 80 miles *128 km* in reputedly only 6 hr, in January or February 1743. The longest duration hunt was one of 10 hr 5 min by Charlton Hunt of West Sussex, which ran from East Dean Wood at 7.45 am to a kill over 57¼ miles *92 km* away at 5.50 pm on 26 Jan 1738.

Most Days Hunting

Between 1968 and 1984, J. N. P. Watson, Hunting Correspondent to Country Life, hunted with 168 different packs of foxhounds, staghounds and harehounds in Britain, Ireland, USA and Europe.

GAME SHOOTING

LARGEST BRITISH BAGS

Hare	1,215	*11 guns*	Holkham, Norfolk, 19 Dec 1877
Rabbit	6,943	*5 guns*	Blenheim, Oxfordshire, 17 Oct 1898
Geese (Brent)	704[1]	*32 punt-guns*	Colonel Russell i/c, River Blackwater, Essex, c. 1860
Grouse	1,070	*1 gun*	Thomas, 6th Baron Walsingham in Yorkshire, 30 Aug 1888
Grouse	2,929	*8 guns*	Littledale and Abbeystead, Lancashire, 12 Aug 1915
Partridge (Wild)	2,015[2]	*6 guns*	Rothwell, Lincolnshire, 3 Oct 1952
Pheasant	3,937	*7 guns*[3]	Hall Barn, Beaconsfield, Buckinghamshire, 18 Dec 1913
Pigeon	561	*1 gun*	K. Ransford, Salop-Powys, 22 July 1970
Snipe	1,108	*2 guns*	Tiree, Inner Hebrides, 25 Oct–3 Nov 1906
Woodcock	228	*6 guns*	Ashford, County Galway, Ireland, 28 Jan 1910
Woodpigeon	550	*1 gun*	Major A. J. Coates, near Winchester, Hampshire, 10 Jan 1962

[1] *Plus about 250 later picked up.*   [2] *Plus 104 later picked up.*
[3] *Including H.M. King George V.*

MOST OLYMPIC AND WORLD FENCING TITLES

Event		Olympic Gold Medals		World Championships (not held in Olympic years)
Men's Foil, Individual	2	Christian d'Oriola (France) (b. 3 Oct 1928) 1952, 56	5	Aleksandr Romankov (USSR) (b. 7 Nov 1953) 1974, 77, 79, 82, 83
	2	Nedo Nadi (Italy) (1894–1952) 1912, 20		
Men's Foil, Team	6	France 1924, 32, 48, 52, 68, 80	13	USSR 1959, 61–3, 65–6, 69–70, 73–4, 79, 81–2
Men's Epée, Individual	2	Ramón Fonst (Cuba) (1883–1959) 1900, 04	3	Georges Buchard[2] (France) (b. 21 Dec 1893) 1927, 31, 33
			3	Aleksey Nikanchikov (USSR) (1940–72) 1966–7, 70
Men's Epée, Team	6	Italy 1920, 28, 36, 52, 56, 60	10	Italy 1931, 33, 37, 49–50, 53–5, 57–8
Men's Sabre, Individual	2	Dr Jenö Fuchs (Hungary) (b. 29 Oct 1882) 1908, 12	3	Aladár Gerevich (Hungary) (b. 16 Mar 1910) 1935, 51, 55
	2	Rudolf Kárpáti (Hungary) (b. 17 July 1920) 1956, 60	3	Jerzy Pawlowski (Poland) (b. 25 Oct 1932) 1957, 65–6
	2	Jean Georgiadis (Greece) (b. 1874) 1896, 1906	3	Yakov Rylsky (USSR) (b. 25 Oct 1928) 1958, 61, 63
	2	Viktor Krovopouskov (USSR) (b. 29 Sept 1948) 1976, 80		
Men's Sabre, Team	9	Hungary 1908, 12, 28, 32, 36, 48, 52, 56, 60	17	Hungary 1930–1, 33–5, 37, 51, 53–5, 57–8, 66, 73, 78, 81, 82
Women's Foil, Individual	2	Ilona Schacherer-Elek (Hungary) (b. 17 May 1907) 1936, 48	3	Helène Mayer (Germany) (1910–53) 1929, 31, 37
			3	Ilona Schacherer-Elek (Hungary) 1934–5, 51
			3	Ellen Müller-Preis (Austria) (b. 6 May 1912) 1947, 49, 50 (shared)
Women's Foil, Team	4	USSR 1960, 68, 72, 76	14	USSR 1956, 58, 61, 63, 65–6, 70–1, 74–5, 77–9, 82

MOST AMATEUR FENCING ASSOCIATION TITLES

Foil	(Instituted 1898)	7	John Emrys Lloyd (b. 8 Sept 1905)	1928, 1930–3, 1937–8
Epée	(Instituted 1904)	6	Edward O. 'Teddy' Bourne (b. 30 Sept 1948)	1966, 1972, 1974, 1976–8
Sabre	(Instituted 1898)	6	Dr Roger F. Tredgold (1912–75)	1937, 1939, 1947–9, 1955
Foil (Ladies)	(Instituted 1907)	10	Gillian M. Sheen (now Mrs Donaldson)	1949, 1951–8, 1960

Record heads

The world's finest head is the 23-pointer stag in the Maritzburg collection, E. Germany. The outside span is 75½ in *191 cm*, the length 47½ in *120 cm* and the weight 41½ lb *18,824 kg*. The greatest number of points is probably 33 (plus 29) on the stag shot in 1696 by Frederick III (1657–1713), the Elector of Brandenburg, later King Frederick I of Prussia.

Largest tally to a single sportsman

556,813 head of game fell to the guns of the 2nd Marquess of Ripon between 1867 and when he dropped dead on a grouse moor after shooting his 52nd bird on the morning of 22 Sept 1923. This figure included 241,234 pheasants, 124,193 partridge and 31,900 hares. (His game books are held by the gunmakers, James Purdey and Sons.)

FIVES

ETON FIVES

A handball game against the buttress of Eton College Chapel was first recorded in 1825. New courts were built at Eton in 1840, the rules were codified in 1877, rewritten laws were introduced three times and last amended in 1981. There are courts in several countries besides England, with more than a dozen in northern Nigeria.

America's greatest sporting occasion is the Superbowl. In 1984 the Los Angeles Raiders scored a record 38 points aided by a record 74 yd touchdown by No. 32 Marcus Allen. (All-Sport)

Most titles

One pair has won the Amateur Championship (Kinnaird Cup) eight times—Anthony Hughes and Arthur James Gordon Campbell (1958, 1965–8, 1971, 1973 and 1975). Hughes was also in the winning pair in 1963 and has played in 19 finals. The Clubs' championship (the Alan Barber Cup) has been won a record eleven times by Old Cholmeleians (1969–70, 1975, 1977–84). The Douglas Keeble Cup for the National League has been won a record seven times by Old Edwardians (1975–7, 1981–4).

RUGBY FIVES

As now known, this game dates from *c.* 1850 with the first inter-public school matches recorded in the early 1870s. The Oxford v. Cambridge contest was inaugurated in 1925 and the Rugby Fives Association was founded in the home of Dr Edgar Cyriax (1874–1954), in Welbeck Street, London, on 29 Oct 1927. The dimensions of the Standard Rugby Fives court were approved by the Association in 1931.

Most titles

The greatest number of Amateur Singles Championships (instituted 1932) ever won is eleven by Wayne Enstone in 1973–8 and 1980–4. The record for the Amateur Doubles Championship (instituted 1925) is seven shared by John Frederick Pretlove (1952, 1954, 1956–9, 1961) and David E. Gardner (1960, 1965–6, 1970–2, 1974).

FOOTBALL (AMERICAN)

Origins

American Football, a direct descendant of the British games of soccer and rugby, evolved at American Universities in the 19th century. The first match under the Harvard Rules was played by Harvard against McGill University of Montreal at Cambridge, Mass., in 1874. The Intercollegiate Football Association was founded in 1876. The professional game dates from August 1895 when Latrobe played Jeanette at Latrobe, Pennsylvania. The American Professional Football Association was formed in 1919. This became the National Football League (NFL) in 1922 and the American Football League (AFL) in 1960; they merged in 1970. The USFL was formed in 1982.

Super Bowl

First held in 1967 between the winners of the NFL and the AFL. Since 1970 it has been contested by the winners of the National and American Conferences of the NFL. Pittsburgh Steelers have most wins, four, 1975–6 and 1979–80. The highest aggregate score was in 1979 when Pittsburgh beat Dallas Cowboys 35–31. The highest team score and record victory margin was set when the Los Angeles Raiders beat Washington Redskins 38–9 in 1984. The Green Bay Packers won a record 11 NFL titles between 1929 and 1967.

College Football *Highest team score*

Georgia Tech, Atlanta, Georgia scored 222 points, including a record 32 touchdowns, against Cumberland University, Lebanon, Tennessee (nil) on 7 Oct 1916.

PROFESSIONAL RECORDS—AMERICAN FOOTBALL

Most points	career	2002	George Blanda	1949–75
	season	176	Paul Hornung (Green Bay)	1960
	game	40	Ernie Nevers (Chicago Cardinals)	1929
Most touchdowns	career	126	Jim Brown (Cleveland)	1957–65
	season	23	O. J. Simpson (Buffalo)	1975
	game	6	Ernie Nevers (Chicago Cardinals)	1929
		6	William 'Dub' Jones (Cleveland)	1951
		6	Gale Sayers (Chicago)	1965
Most yards gained rushing	career	12,312	Jim Brown (Cleveland)	1957–65
	season	2003	O. J. Simpson (Buffalo)	1975
	game	275	Walter Payton (Chicago Bears)	1977
Most passes completed	career	3686	Fran Tarkenton (Minnesota, NY Giants)	1961–78
	season	360	Dan Fouts (San Diego)	1981
	game	42	Richard Todd (New York Jets)	1980

FOOTBALL (ASSOCIATION)

See also The Guinness Book of Soccer Facts and Feats (*5th ed.*) by *Jack Rollin published by Guinness Superlatives Ltd. at £7.95 in 1983.*

Origins

A game with some similarities termed *Tsu-chu* was played in China in the 4th and 3rd centuries BC. One of the earliest references to the game in England is a Royal Proclamation by Edward II in 1314 banning the game in the City of London. The earliest clear representation of the game is an Edinburgh print dated 1672–3. The game was standardised with the formation of the Football Association in England on 26 Oct 1863. The oldest club is Sheffield FC, formed on 24 Oct 1857. Eleven per side became standard in 1870.

PROFESSIONAL

Longest match

The duration record for first class fixtures was set in the Copa Libertadores in Santos, Brazil, on 2–3 Aug 1962, when Santos drew 3–3 with Penarol FC of Montevideo, Uruguay. The game lasted 3 hr 30 min (with interruptions), from 9.30 pm to 1 am.

The longest British match on record was one of 3 hr 23 min between Stockport County and Doncaster Rovers in the second leg of the Third Division (North) Cup at Edgeley Park, Stockport, Greater Manchester on 30 Mar 1946.

Longest unbeaten streak

Nottingham Forest were undefeated in 42 consecutive Division I matches from 20 Nov 1977 to 9 Dec 1978. In Scottish Football Glasgow Celtic were undefeated in 62 matches (49 won, 13 drawn), 13 Nov 1915–21 April 1917.

Most postponements

The Scottish Cup tie between Inverness Thistle and Falkirk during the winter of 1978–9 was postponed a record 29 times due to weather conditions. Finally Falkirk won the game 4–0.

GOAL SCORING

Teams

The highest score recorded in a first-class match is 36. This occurred in the Scottish Cup match between Arbroath and Bon Accord on 5 Sept 1885, when Arbroath won 36–0 on their home ground. But for the lack of nets and the consequent waste of retrieval time the score must have been even higher.

The highest margin recorded in an international match is 17, when England beat Australia 17–0 at Sydney on 30 June 1951. This match is not listed by England as a *full* international. The highest in the British Isles was when England beat Ireland 13–0 at Belfast on 18 Feb 1882.

The highest score between English clubs in any major competition is 26, when Preston North End beat Hyde 26–0 in an FA Cup tie at Deepdale, Lancashire on 15 Oct 1887. The biggest victory in an FA Cup Final is six when Bury beat Derby County 6–0 at Crystal Palace on 18 Apr 1903, in which year Bury did not concede a single goal in the five Cup matches.

The highest score by one side in a Football League (Division I) match is 12 goals when West Bromwich Albion beat Darwen 12–0 at West Bromwich, West Midlands on 4 Apr 1892; when Nottingham Forest beat Leicester Fosse by the same score at Nottingham on 21 Apr 1909; and when Aston Villa beat Accrington 12–2 at Perry Barr, W. Midlands on 12 Mar 1892.

The highest aggregate in League Football was 17 goals when Tranmere Rovers beat Oldham Athletic 13–4 in a Third Division (North) match at Prenton Park, Merseyside, on Boxing Day, 1935. The record margin in a League match has been 13 in the Newcastle United 13, Newport County 0 (Division II) match on 5 Oct 1946 and in the Stockport County 13, Halifax 0 (Division III (North)) match on 6 Jan 1934.

The highest number of goals by any British team in a professional league in a season is 142 in 34 matches by Raith Rovers (Scottish Division II) in the 1937–8 season. The English League record is 134 in 46 matches by Peterborough United (Division IV) in 1960–1.

Individual

The most scored by one player in a first-class match is 16 by

Stephan Stanis (*né* Stanikowski, b. Poland, 15 July 1913) for Racing Club de Lens *v.* Aubry-Asturies, in Lens, France, in a wartime French Cup game on 13 Dec 1942.

The record number of goals scored by one player in an international match is ten by Sofus Nielsen (1888–1963) for Denmark *v.* France (17–1) in the 1908 Olympics and by Gottfried Fuchs (1889–1972) for Germany who beat Russia 16–0 in the 1912 Olympic tournament (consolation event) in Sweden.

BRITISH GOAL SCORING RECORDS

SCOTTISH CUP ...	13	John Petrie for Arbroath v Bon Accord on 5 Sept 1885
FOOTBALL LEAGUE	10	Joe Payne (1914–77) for Luton Town v Bristol Rovers (Div 3S) at Luton on 13 Apr 1936
F. LEAGUE DIV I	7	Ted Drake (b. 16 Aug 1912) for Arsenal v Aston Villa at Birmingham on 14 Dec 1935 James David Ross for Preston NE v Stoke at Preston on 6 Oct 1888
FA CUP (PRELIM)	10	Chris Marron for South Shields v Radcliffe at South Shields on 20 Sept 1947
FA CUP....................	9	Edward 'Ted' McDougall (b. 8 Jan 1947) for Bournemouth v Margate at Bournemouth on 20 Nov 1971
SCOTTISH DIV I	8	James Edward McGrory (1904–82) Celtic v Dunfermline at Celtic Park, Glasgow on 14 Jan 1928
HOME INTERNATIONAL...	6	Joe Bambrick (b. 3 Nov 1905) for Ireland v Wales at Belfast on 1 Feb 1930
AMATEUR INTERNATIONAL...	6	William Charles Jordan (1885–1949) for England v France at Park Royal, London on 23 Mar 1908; Vivian John Woodward (1879–1954) for England v Holland at Stamford Bridge, London on 11 Dec 1909; Harold A. Walden for Great Britain v Hungary at Stockholm, Sweden on 1 July 1912

Season

The best season League records are 60 goals in 39 League games by William Ralph 'Dixie' Dean (1907–80) for Everton (Division I) in 1927–8 and 66 goals in 38 games by James Smith (1902–76) for Ayr United (Scottish Division II) in the same season. With three more in Cup ties and 19 in representative matches Dean's total was 82.

Career

Artur Friedenreich (1892–1969) (Brazil) scored an undocumented 1329 goals in a 43 year first class football career. The most goals scored in a specified period is 1216 by Edson Arantes do Nascimento (Brazil) (b. 23 Oct 1940), known as Pelé, from 7 Sept 1956 to 2 Oct 1974 in 1254 games. His best year was 1959 with 126 and the *milesimo* (1000th) came in a penalty for his club Santos in the Maracaña Stadium, Rio de Janeiro on 19 Nov 1969 when playing his 909th first-class match. He later played for New York Cosmos and on his retirement on 1 Oct 1977 his total had reached 1281 in 1363 games. He added two more goals later in special appearances. Franz 'Bimbo' Binder (b. 1 Dec 1911) scored 1006 goals in 756 games in Austria and Germany between 1930 and 1950.

The international career record for England is 49 goals by Robert 'Bobby' Charlton (b. 11 Oct 1937). His first was *v.* Scotland on 19 Apr 1958 and his last on 20 May 1970 *v.* Colombia.

The greatest number of goals scored in British first-class football is 550 (410 in Scottish League matches) by James McGrory of Glasgow Celtic (1922–38). The most scored in League matches is 434, for West Bromwich Albion, Fulham, Leicester City and Shrewsbury Town, by George Arthur Rowley (b. 21 Apr 1926) between 1946 and April 1965. Rowley also scored 32 goals in the F.A. Cup and one for England 'B'.

Fastest goals

The fastest Football League goals on record were scored in 6 sec by Albert E. Mundy (b. 12 May 1926) (Aldershot) in a Division IV match *v.* Hartlepool United at Victoria Ground,

Hartlepool, Cleveland on 25 Oct 1958, by Barrie Jones (b. 31 Oct 1938) (Notts Co) in a Division III match *v.* Torquay United on 31 Mar 1962, by Keith Smith (b. 15 Sept 1940) (Crystal Palace) in a Division II match *v.* Derby County at the Baseball Ground, Derby on 12 Dec 1964 and by Tommy W. Langley (b. 8 Feb 1958) (Queen's Park Rangers) in a Division II match *v.* Bolton Wanderers on 11 Oct 1980.

The fastest confirmed hat-trick is in 2½ minutes by Ephraim 'Jock' Dodds (b. 7 Sept 1915) for Blackpool *v* Tranmere Rovers on 28 Feb 1943, and by Jimmy Scarth (b. 26 Aug 1920) for Gillingham *v* Leyton Orient in Div III (Southern) on 1 Nov 1952. A hat-trick in 1 min 50 sec is claimed for Maglioni of Independiente *v.* Gimnasia y Escrima de la Plata in Argentina on 18 Mar 1973. John McIntyre (Blackburn Rovers) scored four goals in 5 min *v.* Everton at Ewood Park, Blackburn, Lancashire on 16 Sept 1922. William 'Ginger' Richardson (West Bromwich Albion) scored four goals in 5 min from the kick-off against West Ham United at Upton Park on 7 Nov 1931. Frank Keetley scored six goals in 21 min in the 2nd half of the Lincoln City *v.* Halifax Town league match on 16 Jan 1932. The international record is three goals in 3½ min by Willie Hall (Tottenham Hotspur) for England against Ireland on 16 Nov 1938 at Old Trafford, Greater Manchester.

Fastest own goal

Torquay United's Pat Kruse (b. 30 Nov 1953) equalled the fastest goal on record when he headed the ball into his own net only 6 sec after kick-off *v.* Cambridge United on 3 Jan 1977.

GOALKEEPING

Individual record

The longest that any goalkeeper has succeeded in preventing any goals being scored past him in international matches is 1142 min for Dino Zoff (Italy), from September 1972 to June 1974. The Football League record is 1103 min by Steve Death (b. 19 Sept 1949) for Reading in Division IV from 24 March to 18 Aug 1979.

FA CHALLENGE CUP AND SCOTTISH FA CUP

Most wins

The greatest number of FA Cup wins is seven by Aston Villa, 1887, 1895, 1897, 1905, 1913, 1920 and 1957 (nine final appearances) and by Tottenham Hotspur, 1901, 1921, 1961, 1962, 1967, 1981 and 1982 (seven appearances). Newcastle United and Arsenal have been in the final 11 times. The highest aggregate scores have been 6–1 in 1890 and 4–3 in 1953.

The greatest number of Scottish FA Cup wins is 26 by Celtic in 1892, 1899, 1900, 1904, 1907–8, 1911–12, 1914, 1923, 1925, 1927, 1931, 1933, 1937, 1951, 1954, 1965, 1967, 1969, 1971, 1972, 1974, 1975, 1977 and 1980.

Youngest player

The youngest player in a FA Cup Final was Paul Allen (b. 28 Aug 1962) of West Ham United, who played against Arsenal on 10 May 1980 aged 17 years 256 days. Derek Johnstone (Rangers) (b. 4 Nov 1953) was 16 years 11 months old when he played in the Scottish League Cup Final against Celtic on 24 Oct 1970. The youngest goal scorer in the FA Cup Final was Norman Whiteside (b. 7 May 1965) for Manchester United *v.* Brighton at 18 yr 19 days on 26 May 1983. The youngest player ever in the FA Cup competition was Scott Endersby (b. 20 Feb 1962) who was only 15 years 288 days old when he played in goal for Kettering *v.* Tilbury on 26 Nov. 1977.

Most medals

Three players have won five FA Cup winner's medals: James Forrest (Blackburn Rovers) (1884–6, 1890–1); the Hon Sir Arthur Fitzgerald Kinnaird, KT (Wanderers) (1873, 1877–8) and Old Etonians (1879, 1882) and Charles H. R. Wollaston (Wanderers) (1872–3, 1876–8).

The most Scottish Cup winners' medals won is eight by Charles Campbell (Queen's Park) in 1874–6, 1880–2, 1884 and 1886.

Longest tie

The most protracted FA Cup tie in the competition proper was that between Stoke City and Bury in the third round with Stoke winning 3–2 in the fifth meeting after 9 hr 22 min of play in January 1955. The matches were at Bury (1–1) on 8 Jan; Stoke on Trent on 12 Jan (abandoned after 22 min of extra time with the score 1–1); Goodison Park (3–3) on 17 Jan; Anfield (2–2) on 19 Jan; and finally at Old Trafford on 24 Jan. In the 1972 final qualifying round Alvechurch beat Oxford City after five previous drawn games (total playing time 11 hours).

FOOTBALL LEAGUE CUP (inst. 1960–1, now Milk Cup)

The most wins is four by Liverpool, 1981–4.

The teams in the all-Merseyside Milk Cup final of 1984, which Liverpool won 1–0 in the replay after 0–0 in the first game. To the end of the 1984 season in all their derby matches Liverpool had won 46 to Everton's 44, with 40 drawn. *(All-Sport)*

BRITISH INTERNATIONAL CHAMPIONSHIP

The British International Championship began in 1883–84 when all four home countries: England, Scotland, Ireland and Wales started playing against each other. England were the most successful with 34 outright wins, Scotland second with 24, Wales seven and Ireland three. England were also concerned with all 20 shared titles, Scotland 17, Wales and Ireland five each as goal average or goal difference did not count in determining the winner until 1978–79.
The two highest scoring victories were Wales 11 Ireland 0 in 1888 and Scotland 11 Ireland 0 in 1901. The highest aggregate of goals saw England beat Scotland 9–3 in 1961.

Arthur Albiston *(left)* challenges Tony Woodcock *(right)* for England v Scotland in 1984. Woodcock scored the equalising goal for England in what may be the final match of the British International Championship. *(Associated Sports Photography)*

SCOTTISH LEAGUE CUP (inst. 1946–7)
The most wins is 11 by Rangers between 1947 and 1984.

LEAGUE CHAMPIONSHIPS

World
The record number of successive national League championships is nine by Celtic (Scotland) 1966–74, CSKA, Sofia (Bulgaria) 1954–62 and MTK Budapest (Hungary) 1917–25. The Sofia club hold a European postwar record of 23 league titles.

English
The greatest number of League Championships (Division I) is 15 by Liverpool in 1901, 1906, 1922, 1923, 1947, 1964, 1966, 1973, 1976–7, 1979–80 and 1982–84. The record number of wins in a season is 33 from 42 matches by Doncaster Rovers in Division III (North) in 1946–7. The Division I record is 31 wins from 42 matches by Tottenham Hotspur in 1960–1. In 1893–4 Liverpool won 22 and drew 6 in 28 Division II games. They also won the promotion match.

'Double'
The only FA Cup and League Championship 'doubles' are those of Preston North End in 1889, Aston Villa in 1897, Tottenham Hotspur in 1961 and Arsenal in 1971. Preston won the League without losing a match and the Cup without having a goal scored against them throughout the whole competition.

Scottish
Glasgow Rangers have won the Scottish League Championship 36 times between 1899 and 1978 and were joint champions on another occasion. Their 76 points in the Scottish Division I in 1920–1 represents a record in any division.

Closest win
In 1923–4 Huddersfield won the Division I championship over Cardiff by 0.02 of a goal with a goal average of 1.81.

TOURNAMENT RECORDS

World Cup
The *Fédération Internationale de Football Association* (FIFA) was founded in Paris on 21 May 1904 and instituted the World Cup Competition on 13 July 1930, in Montevideo, Uruguay.

Countries to win three times have been Brazil in 1958, 1962 and 1970 and Italy in 1934, 1938 and 1982. Brazil was also second in 1950 and third in 1938 and 1978, and is the only one of the 47 participating countries to have played in all twelve competitions. Antonio Carbajal (b. 1923) played for Mexico in goal in the five competitions from 1950 to 1966.

The record goal scorer has been Just Fontaine (b. Marrakesh, Morocco, 18 Aug 1933) (France) with 13 goals in six games in the final stages of the 1958 competition in Sweden. The most goals scored in a final is three by Geoffrey Charles Hurst (b. 8 Dec 1941) (West Ham United) for England *v.* W. Germany on 30 July 1966. Gerd Müller (W. Germany) (b. 3 Nov 1945) holds the aggregate record for goals scored in the World Cup Finals with 14 in 1970 and 1974.

The highest score in a World Cup match is New Zealand's 13–0 defeat of Fiji in a qualifying match at Auckland on 15 Aug 1981. The highest score in the Finals Tournament is Hungary's 10–1 win over El Salvador at Elche, Spain on 15 June 1982. The fastest goal in World Cup competition was one in 27 sec by Bryan Robson (b. 11 Jan 1957) for England *v.* France in Bilbao on 16 June 1982.

World Club Championship

This club tournament was started in 1960 between the winners of the European Cup and the Copa Libertadores, the South American equivalent. The most wins is three by Penarol, Uruguay in 1961, 1966 and 1982.

European Championship (*formerly Nations Cup*)

The European equivalent of the World Cup started in 1958 and is staged every four years. Each tournament takes two years to run with the semi-finals and final in the same country. W. Germany have won twice in 1972 and 1980.

European Champion Clubs Cup

The European Cup for the League champions of the respective nations was approved by FIFA on 8 May 1955 and was run by the European governing body UEFA (Union of European Football Associations) which came into being in the previous year. Real Madrid won the first final, and have won a record six times, including five times consecutively, 1956–60, 1966. The highest score in a final was Real Madrid's 7–3 win over Eintracht Frankfurt at Hampden Park, Glasgow on 18 May 1960.

Glasgow Celtic became the first British club to win the Cup beating Inter-Milan 2–1 in Lisbon, Portugal, on 25 May 1967. They also became the only British club to win the European Cup and the two senior domestic tournaments (League and Cup) in the same season. Liverpool, winners in 1977, 1978, 1981 and 1984, have been the most successful British club.

European Cup Winners Cup

A tournament for the national Cup winners started in 1960–1. Clubs to win twice have been AC Milan 1968 and 1973, Anderlecht 1976 and 1978, and Barcelona 1979 and 1982. Tottenham Hotspur were the first British club to win the trophy, beating Atletico Madrid 5–1 in Rotterdam in 1963.

UEFA Cup

Originally known as the International Inter-City Industrial Fairs Cup, this club tournament began in 1955. The first competition lasted three years, the second two years. In 1960–1 it became an annual tournament and since 1971–2 has been replaced by the UEFA Cup. The first British club to win the trophy was Leeds United in 1968. The most wins is three by Barcelona in 1958, 1960 and 1966.

The Real Madrid team which won their fifth successive European Cup Final in 1960. Back (*l-r*) Dominguez, Marquitos, Santamaria, Pachin, Vidal, Zarraga. Front (*l-r*) Canario, Del Sol, Di Stefano, Puskas, Gento. (*Reportajes Graficos*)

PLAYERS

Most durable player

The most durable player in League history has been Terence Lionel Paine (b. 23 Mar 1939) who made 824 league appearances from 1957 to 1977 playing for Southampton and Hereford Utd. Norman John Trollope (b. 14 June 1943) made 770 League appearances for one club, Swindon Town, between 1960 and 1980.

Transfer fees

The greatest transfer fee quoted for a player is 15,895 million lire (£6.9 million) by Napoli in 1984 for Diego Maradona (Argentina) (b. 30 Oct 1960) from Barcelona. This exceeded the *c.* £5 million that Barcelona paid for Maradona in 1982.

The record fee between British clubs was £1,500,000 (incl VAT and other levies) paid by Manchester United to West Bromwich Albion for Bryan Robson on 3 Oct 1981.

Heaviest goalkeeper

The biggest goalkeeper in representative football was the England international Willie J. 'Fatty' Foulke (1874–1916), who stood 6 ft 3 in *1,90 m* and weighed 22 st 3 lb *141 kg*. His

Michel Platini dives over Pfaff of Belgium *(left)* in the European Championships match of 1984. Platini scored a record nine goals in the five match finals series, which culminated in France's first victory in an international soccer championship. Platini scored hat-tricks against both Belgium and Yugoslavia.
(All-Sport/Trevor Jones)

last games were for Bradford City, by which time he was 26 st *165 kg*. He once stopped a game by snapping the cross bar.

Oldest and youngest caps

The oldest cap has been William Henry 'Billy' Meredith (1874–1958) (Manchester City and United) who played outside right for Wales *v.* England at Highbury, London, on 15 Mar 1920 when aged 45 yr 229 days. He played internationally for a record span of 26 years (1895–1920).

Norman Whiteside played for Northern Ireland *v.* Yugoslavia, at 17 yr 42 days on 17 June 1982, the youngest ever to play in the World Cup.

The youngest cap in the four home countries internationals has been Norman Kernaghan (Belfast Celtic) who played for Ireland *v.* Wales in 1936 aged 17 yr 80 days. It is possible, however, that W. K. Gibson (Cliftonville) who played for Ireland *v.* Wales on 24 Feb 1894 at 17 was slightly younger. England's youngest home international was Duncan Edwards (1936–58) the Manchester United left half, against Scotland at Wembley on 2 Apr 1955, aged 18 yr 183 days. The youngest Welsh cap was John Charles (b. 27 Dec 1931), the Leeds United centre half, against Ireland at Wrexham on 8 Mar

MOST INTERNATIONAL APPEARANCES *British Isles*

England	108	Robert Frederick 'Bobby' Moore (b. 12 Apr 1941)	West Ham U/Fulham		1962–73
Northern Ireland	105	Patrick A. Jennings (b. 12 June 1945)	Watford/Tottenham H/Arsenal		1964–84
Scotland	90	Kenneth M. Dalglish (b. 4 Mar 1951)	Celtic/Liverpool		1971–83
Wales	68	Ivor Allchurch (b. 29 Dec 1929)	Swansea C/Newcastle/Cardiff C/Worcester C		1950–68
Rep. of Ireland	60	Michael J. 'Johnny' Giles (b. 6 Jan 1940)	Manchester U/Leeds U/West Bromwich A		1960–79

1950, aged 18 yr 71 days. Scotland's youngest international has been Johnny Lambie, Queen's Park inside-forward, at 17 yr 92 days v. Ireland on 20 Mar 1886.

Most international appearances

The greatest number of appearances for a national team is 150 by Hector Chumpitaz (b. 12 Apr 1943) (Peru) from 1963 to 1982. This includes all matches played by the national team. The record for full internationals against other national teams is 115 by Bjorn Nordqvist (Sweden) (b. 6 Oct 1942) from 1963 to 1978.

ATTENDANCES

Greatest crowds

The greatest recorded crowd at any football match was 205,000 (199,854 paid) for the Brazil v. Uruguay World Cup match in the Maracaña Municipal Stadium, Rio de Janeiro, Brazil on 16 July 1950. The record attendance for a European Cup match is 136,505 at the semi-final between Glasgow Celtic and Leeds United at Hampden Park, Glasgow on 15 Apr 1970.

The British record paid attendance is 149,547 at the Scotland v. England international at Hampden Park, Glasgow, on 17 Apr 1937. It is, however, probable that this total was exceeded (estimated 160,000) on the occasion of the FA Cup Final between Bolton Wanderers and West Ham United at Wembley Stadium on 28 Apr 1923, when the crowd broke in on the pitch and the start was delayed 40 min until the pitch was cleared. The counted admissions were 126,047.

The Scottish Cup record attendance is 146,433 when Celtic played Aberdeen at Hampden Park on 24 Apr 1937. The record attendance for a League match in Britain is 118,567 for Rangers v. Celtic at Ibrox Park, Glasgow on 2 Jan 1939.

The highest attendance at an amateur match has been 120,000 in Senayan Stadium, Jakarta, Indonesia, on 26 Feb 1976 for the Pre-Olympic Group II final, North Korea v. Indonesia.

Smallest crowd

The smallest crowd at a full home international was 2315 for the Wales v. Northern Ireland match of 27 May 1982 at the Racecourse Ground, Wrexham, Clwyd. The smallest paying attendance at a Football League fixture was for the Stockport County v. Leicester City match at Old Trafford, Greater Manchester, on 7 May 1921. Stockport's own ground was under suspension and the 'crowd' numbered 13 but an estimated 2000 gained free admission. When West Ham beat Castilla of Spain (5–1) in the European Cup Winners Cup at Upton Park, Greater London, on 1 Oct 1980 and when Aston Villa beat Besiktas of Turkey (3–1) in the European Cup at Villa Park on 15 Sept 1982, there were no paying spectators due to disciplinary action by the European Football Union.

Greatest receipts

The record gross FA Cup receipts at Wembley, London, is £918,000 (excluding radio and television fees) for the final on 22 May 1982. The 'gate' at the first FA Cup Final at Kensington Oval, London on 16 Mar 1872 was £100.

The greatest receipts at any World Cup final were 2,664,925.60 Deutsche Marks (then c. £442,000) for W. Germany v. Netherlands at Munich on 7 July 1974.

The record for a British international match is £671,000 for the England v. Hungary match at Wembley on 18 Nov 1981.

OLYMPIC GAMES

The only country to have won the Olympic football title three times is Hungary in 1952, 1964 and 1968. The United Kingdom won the unofficial tournament in 1900 and the official tournaments of 1908 and 1912. The highest Olympic score is Denmark (17) v. France 'A' (1) in 1908.

OTHER MATCHES

Highest scores *Teams*

In 1975, in a Scottish ladies league match, Edinburgh Dynamos FC beat Lochend Thistle 42–0.

In an under-14 league match between Midas FC and Courage Colts, in Kent, on 11 Apr 1976, the full time score after 70 min play was 59–1. Top scorer for Midas was Kevin Graham with 17 goals. Courage had scored the first goal.

Needing to improve their goal 'difference' to gain promotion in 1979, Ilinden FC of Yugoslavia, with the collusion of the opposition, Mladost, and the referee, won their final game of the season by 134–1. Their rivals in the promotion race won their match, under similar circumstances by 88–0.

Highest scores *Individual*

Linda Curl of Norwich Ladies scored 22 goals in a 40–0 league victory over Milton Keynes Reserves at Norwich on 25 Sept 1983.

Highest scores *Season*

The greatest number of goals in a season reported for an individual player in junior professional league football is 96 by Tom Duffy (b. 7 Jan 1937), who played centre forward for Ardeer Thistle FC, Strathclyde in the 1960–1 season. Paul Anthony Moulden (b. 6 Sept 1967) scored 289 goals in 40 games for Bolton Lads Club in Bolton Boys Federation intermediate league and cup matches in 1981–2. An additional 51 goals scored in other tournaments brought his total to 340, the highest season figure reported in any class of competitive football for an individual.

Fastest goals

Wind-aided goals in 3 sec after kick-off have been scored by a number of players. Tony Bacon, of Schalmont HS scored three goals v. Icabod Crane HS in 63 sec at Schenectady, New York, USA on 8 Oct 1975.

Fastest own goal

The fastest own goal on record was one in 5 sec 'scored' by Peter Johnson of Chesham United in a match against Wycombe Wanderers on 21 Feb 1976.

Longest match

A match between Saint Ignatius College Preparatory of San Francisco and Bellarmine College Preparatory of San Jose lasted 4 hr 56 min (230 min playing time) at San Francisco, California, USA on 6 Feb 1982.

Longest ties

The aggregate duration of ties in amateur soccer have not been collated but it is recorded that in the London FA Intermediate Cup first qualifying round Highfield FC Reserves had to meet Mansfield House FC on 19 and 26 Sept and 3, 10 and 14 Oct 1970 to get a decision after 9 hr 50 min play with scores of 0–0, 1–1, 1–1, 3–3, and 0–2. In the Hertfordshire Intermediate Cup, London Colney beat Leavesden Hospital after 12 hr 41 min play and seven ties from 6 Nov to 17 Dec 1971.

Largest tournament

The Metropolitan Police 5-a-side Youth Competition in 1981 attracted an entry of 7008 teams, a record for an FA sanctioned competition.

Most and Least successful teams

The Home Farm FC, Dublin, Ireland, between 12 Oct 1968 and 10 Oct 1970 won 79 consecutive matches. Winlaton West End FC, Tyne and Wear, completed a run of 95 league games without defeat between 1976 and 1980. In six successive years the Larkswood County Junior School team of 1959–60 was unbeaten, winning 118 games and drawing three. Stockport United FC, of the Stockport Football League, lost 39 consecutive League and Cup matches, September 1976 to 18 Feb 1978.

In 5-a-side football, Hebburn Argyle Juniors won 253 successive games from 17 Oct 1977 to 12 Mar 1984.

Most indisciplined

In the local Cup match between Tongham Youth Club, Surrey and Hawley, Hampshire, on 3 Nov 1969 the referee booked all 22 players including one who went to hospital, and one of the linesmen. The match, won by Tongham 2–0, was described by a player as 'A good, hard game'.

In a Gancia Cup match at Waltham Abbey, Essex on 23 Dec 1973, the referee, Michael J. Woodhams, sent off the entire Juventus-Cross team and some club officials. Glencraig United, Faifley, nr Clydebank, had all 11 team members and two substitutes for their match against Goldenhill Boys' Club on 2 Feb 1975 booked in the dressing room before a ball was kicked. The referee, Mr Tarbet of Bearsden, took exception to the chant which greeted his arrival. It was not his first meeting with Glencraig. The teams drew 2–2.

Ball control

Mikael Palmqvist (Sweden) juggled a regulation soccer ball for 12 hr 15 min non-stop with feet, legs and head without the ball ever touching the ground at Zürich, Switzerland on 7–8 Oct 1983. He also headed a regulation football non-stop for $4\frac{1}{2}$ hr at Göteborg, Sweden in 1984.

FOOTBALL (GAELIC)

Earliest references

The game developed from inter-parish 'free for all' with no time-limit, no defined playing area nor specific rules. The earliest reported match was Meath v. Louth, at Slane in 1712. Standardisation came with the formation of the Gaelic Athletic Association in Thurles, Ireland, on 1 Nov 1884.

Most titles

The greatest number of All Ireland Championships won by one team is 27 by Ciarraidhe (Kerry) between 1903 and 1981. The greatest number of successive wins is four by Wexford (1915–18) and Kerry twice (1929–32, 1978–81). Leinster has won most Inter-provincial championships (Railway Cup) with 18 between 1928 and 1974. Sean O'Neill (Down) holds the record of eight medals with Ulster (1960–71).

Highest scores

The highest team score in an All-Ireland final was when Dublin, 27 (5 goals, 12 points) beat Armagh, 15 (3 goals, 6 points) on 25 Sept 1977. The highest combined score was 45 points when Cork (26) beat Galway (19) in 1973. A goal equals three points. The highest individual score in an All-Ireland final has been 2 goals, 6 points by Jimmy Keaveney (Dublin) v. Armagh in 1977, and by Michael Sheehy (Kerry) v. Dublin in 1979.

Lowest scores

In four All-Ireland finals the combined totals have been 7 points; 1893 Wexford (1 goal, till 1894 worth 5 points, 1 point) v. Cork (1 point); 1895 Tipperary (4 points) v. Meath (3 points); 1904 Kerry (5 points) v. Dublin (2 points); 1924 Kerry (4 points) v. Dublin (3 points).

Most appearances

The most All-Ireland finals contested is ten by Dan O'Keeffe (Kerry) of which seven (a record) were on the winning side.

Largest crowd

The record crowd is 90,556 for the Down v. Offaly final at Croke Park, Dublin, in 1961.

FOOTBALL (RUGBY LEAGUE)

There have been four different scoring systems in rugby league football. For the purpose of these records all points totals remain as they were under the system in operation at the time they were made.

Origins

The Rugby League was formed on 29 Aug 1895 at the George Hotel, Huddersfield, W. Yorks. Twenty one clubs from Yorkshire and Lancashire were present and all but one agreed

Joe Lydon won the Lance Todd Trophy for the man of the match in the Rugby League Challenge Cup in 1984, when his team Widnes beat Wigan 19–6 in a game which brought in record receipts. (*Sporting Pictures*)

to resign from the Rugby Union and form the 'Northern Rugby Football Union'. Though payment for loss of wages was the major cause of the breakaway the 'Northern Union' did not embrace full professionalism until 1898. A reduction in the number of players per team from 15 to 13 took place in 1906 and the present title of 'Rugby League' was adopted in 1922. The word 'Northern' was dropped in 1980.

Most titles

There have been seven World Cup Competitions. Australia have most wins, with four, 1957, 1968, 1970 and 1977 as well as a win in the International Championship of 1975.

The Northern Rugby League was formed in 1901. Wigan have won the League Championship a record nine times (1909, 1922, 1926, 1934, 1946, 1947, 1950, 1952 and 1960).

In the Rugby League Challenge Cup (inaugurated 1896–7) Leeds have most wins with ten, 1910, 1923, 1932, 1936, 1941–2 (wartime), 1957, 1968, 1977–8. Oldham is the only club to appear in four consecutive Cup Finals (1924–7).

Since 1974–75 there have been five major competitions for RL clubs: Challenge Cup, League Championship, Premiership, John Player Trophy and County Cup. Over this period only Widnes have won three in one season (Challenge Cup, John Player Trophy and Lancashire Cup) in 1978–79. Leeds and Wigan both have a record 33 wins in these five competitions.

Three clubs have won all possible major Rugby League trophies in one season: Hunslet, 1907–8, Huddersfield, 1914–15 and Swinton, 1927–8, all won the Challenge Cup, League Championship, County Cup and County League (now defunct).

HIGHEST SCORES

Senior match

The highest aggregate score in a game where a senior club has been concerned, was 121 points, when Huddersfield beat Swinton Park Rangers by 119 (19 goals, 27 tries) to 2 (one goal) in the first round of the Northern Union Cup on 28 Feb 1914. The highest score in League football is 112 points by Leeds v. Coventry (nil) on 12 Apr 1913.

Challenge Cup Final

The highest score in a Challenge Cup Final is 38 points (8 tries, 7 goals) by Wakefield Trinity v. Hull (5) at Wembley on 14 May 1960. The record aggregate is 47 points when Featherstone Rovers beat Bradford Northern 33–14 at Wembley on 12 May 1973. The greatest winning margin was 34 points when Huddersfield beat St Helens 37–3 at Oldham on 1 May 1915.

International match

The highest score in an international match is Australia's 63–13 defeat of England at Paris, France on 31 Dec 1933. The

Jim Sullivan displays the form which brought him the rugby league goal kicking record.
(Radio Times Hulton)

highest score in a World Cup match is the 53–19 win by Great Britain over New Zealand at Hameau, Paris on 4 Nov 1972.

Touring teams

The record score for a British team touring Australasia is 101 points by England v. South Australia (nil) at Adelaide in May 1914. The record for a touring team in Britain is 92 (10 goals, 24 tries) by Australia against Bramley's 7 (2 goals, 1 try) at the Barley Mow Ground, Bramley, near Leeds, on 9 Nov 1921.

Most points *Season*

Barrow scored a record 1230 points (209 tries, 185 goals, 24 drop goals) in the 1983–4 season, playing in 41 Cup and League games.

HIGHEST INDIVIDUAL SCORES

Most points, goals and tries in a game

George Henry 'Tich' West (1882–1927) of Hull Kingston Rovers scored 53 points (10 goals and a record 11 tries) in a First Round Challenge Cup-tie v. Brookland Rovers on 4 Mar 1905.

The most goals in a Cup match is 22 kicked by Jim Sullivan (1903–77) for Wigan v. Flimby and Fothergill on 14 Feb 1925. The most goals in a League match is 15 by Mick Stacey for Leigh v. Doncaster on 28 Mar 1976. The most tries in a League match is 10 by Lionel Cooper (b. Australia 1922) for Huddersfield v. Keighley on 17 Nov 1951.

Most points *League*

Jimmy Lomas (Salford) scored a record 39 points (5 tries, 12 goals) against Liverpool City (78–0) on 2 Feb 1907.
Season
The record number of points in a season was scored by Benjamin Lewis Jones (Leeds) (b. 11 Apr 1931) with 496 (194 goals, 36 tries) in 1956–7.
Career
Neil Fox scored 6220 points (2575 goals, 358 tries, 4 drop goals) in a senior Rugby League career from 10 Apr 1956 to the end of the 1979–80 season.

Most tries *Season*

Albert Aaron Rosenfeld (1885–1970) (Huddersfield), an Australian-born wing-threequarter, scored 80 tries in 42 matches in the 1913–14 season.
Career
Brian Bevan (b. Australia, 24 Apr 1924), a wing-threequarter, scored 796 tries in 18 seasons (16 with Warrington, two with Blackpool Borough) from 1946 to 1964. He scored 740 for Warrington, 17 for Blackpool and 39 in representative matches.

Most goals *Season*

The record number of goals in a season is 221 by David Watkins (b. 5 Mar 1942) (Salford) in the 1972–3 season. His total was made up in League, Cup, other competitions, and a Salford v. New Zealand match.
Career
Jim Sullivan (Wigan) kicked 2859 goals in his club and representative career, 1921–46.

Most consecutive scores

David Watkins (Salford) played and scored in every club game during seasons 1972–3 and 1973–4; contributing 41 tries and 403 goals—a total of 929 points, in 92 games.

Individual international records

Jim Sullivan (Wigan) played in most internationals (60 for Wales and Great Britain) kicked most goals (160) and scored most points (329).

Mick Sullivan (no kin) (b. 12 Jan 1934) of Huddersfield, Wigan, St Helens and York played in 51 international games for England and Great Britain and scored a record 45 tries.

Most Challenge Cup Finals

Eric Batten (Leeds, Bradford Northern and Featherstone Rovers) played in a record eight Challenge Cup Finals including war-time guest appearances between 1941 and 1952 and was on four winning sides.

Seven players have been in four Challenge Cup winning sides—Alan Edwards, Eric Batten, Alex Murphy, Brian Lockwood, Mick Adams, Keith Elwell and Eric Hughes. Alan Edwards was the only one to do so with four different clubs, Salford 1938, Leeds 1942, Dewsbury 1943, Bradford Northern 1949.

Youngest player

Harold Wagstaff (1891–1939) played his first League game for Huddersfield at 15 yr 175 days, for Yorkshire at 17 yr 141 days, and for England at 17 yr 228 days.

The youngest player in a Cup Final was Shaun Edwards (b. 17 Oct 1966) at 17 yr 201 days for Wigan when they lost 6–19 to Widnes at Wembley on 5 May 1984.

Most durable player

The most appearances for one club is 769 by Jim Sullivan for Wigan, 1921–46. He played a record 921 first class games in all. The longest continuous playing career is that of Augustus John 'Gus' Risman (b. Cardiff 21 Mar 1911) who played his first game for Salford on 31 August 1929 and his last for Batley on 27 December 1954.

Keith Elwell (Widnes) played in 239 consecutive games for his club from May 1977 to September 1982. In his Wigan career, 1972–84, he received a record 28 winners' or runners-up medals in the major competitions.

Most and least successful teams

Wigan won 31 consecutive league games from February 1970 to February 1971. Hull won all 26 League Division II matches in the 1978–9 season. Doncaster hold the record of losing 40 consecutive League games from 16 Nov 1975 to 21 Apr 1977.

Record transfer fees

The highest RL transfer fee is £72,500 paid to Wigan for fullback George H. Fairbairn (b. 27 July 1954) by Hull Kingston Rovers on 7 June 1981.

Greatest crowds

The greatest attendance at any Rugby League match is 102,569 for the Warrington v. Halifax Challenge Cup Final replay at Odsal Stadium, Bradford, on 5 May 1954.

The record attendance for any international match is 70,204 for the Test between Australia and England on the Sydney Cricket Ground on 6 June 1932. The highest international attendance in Britain is 43,500 for the Test between Great Britain and Australia at Odsal Stadium, Bradford on 29 January 1949.

Greatest receipts

The highest receipts for a match in the world have been £686,171 for the Wigan v. Widnes Final at Wembley on 5 May 1984.

FOOTBALL (RUGBY UNION)

See also The Guinness Book of Rugby Facts and Feats (*2nd edition*) by Terry Godwin, *published in 1983 at £8.95.*

Records are determined in terms of present day scoring values, i.e. a try at 4 points; a dropped goal, penalty or goal from a mark at 3 points; and a conversion at 2 points. The actual score, in accordance with which ever of the eight earlier systems was in force at the time, is also given, in brackets.

Origins

Though there are records of a game with many similarities to Rugby dating back to the Roman occupation, the game is traditionally said to have originated from a breach of the rules of the football played in November 1823 at Rugby School by William Webb Ellis (later the Rev) (*c*. 1807–72). This handling code of football evolved gradually and was known to have been played at Cambridge University by 1839. The Rugby Football Union was founded on 26 Jan 1871.

INTERNATIONAL CHAMPIONSHIP

The International Championship was first contested by England, Ireland, Scotland and Wales in 1884. France first played in 1910.

Most wins

Wales have won a record 21 times outright and tied for first a further ten times. Since 1910 Wales have 15 wins and 9 ties and England 15 wins and 7 ties.

Highest team score

The highest score in an International Championship match was set at Swansea in 1910 when Wales beat France 49–14 or 59–16 on present day scoring values (8 goals, 1 penalty goal, 2 tries to 1 goal, 2 penalty goals, 1 try).

Season's scoring

Jean-Patrick Lescarboura (France) (b. 12 Mar 1961) scored a record 54 points (10 penalty goals, 6 conversions, 4 dropped goals) in 1984.

Individual match records

W. J. Bancroft kicked a record 9 goals (8 conversions and 1 penalty goal) for Wales *v.* France at Swansea on 1910.

HIGHEST TEAM SCORES

Internationals

The highest score in any full International was when France beat Spain by 92 points (including 19 tries) to nil at Oléron, France on 4 Mar 1979.

The highest aggregate score for any International match between the Four Home Unions is 69 when England beat Wales by 69 points (7 goals, 1 drop goal and 6 tries) to 0 at Blackheath, London in 1881. (Note: there was no point scoring in 1881).

The highest score by any Overseas side in an International in the British Isles is 53 points (7 goals, 1 drop goal and 2 tries) to 0 when South Africa beat Scotland at Murrayfield, Edinburgh, on 24 Nov 1951 (44–0).

Tour match

The record score for any international tour match is 125–0 (17 goals, 5 tries and 1 penalty goal) (103–0) when New Zealand beat Northern New South Wales at Quirindi, Australia, on 30 May 1962. The highest under scoring in use for the game is 117–6 for New Zealand's defeat of South Australia on 1 May 1974.

Match

In Denmark, Comet beat Lindo by 194–0 on 17 Nov 1973. The highest British score is 174–0 by 7th Signal Regiment *v.* 4 Armoured Workshop, REME, on 5 Nov 1980 at Herford, W. Germany. Scores of over 200 points have been recorded in school matches, for example Radford School beat Hills Court 214 points (31 goals and 7 tries) to 0 (200–0) on 20 Nov 1886.

Season

The highest number of points accumulated in a season by a rugby club is 1607 points by Pontypool, Gwent in 1983–4. The record number of tries is 269 by Bridgend, Dyfed in 1983–4.

HIGHEST INDIVIDUAL SCORES

Internationals

Colin Mair scored 30 points (9 conversions, 4 penalty goals) for Scotland *v.* Japan at Tokyo on 18 Sept 1977. The highest individual points score in any match between members of the International Board is 26 by Alan Hewson (b. 1953) (1 try, 2 conversions, 5 penalty goals and a drop goal) for New Zealand against Australia at Auckland on 11 Sept 1982.

Ian Scott Smith (Scotland) (1903–72) scored a record six consecutive international tries in 1925; comprised of the last three *v.* France and two weeks later, the first three *v.* Wales. His 24 tries, 1924–33, is the record for an international career.

Jean-Patrick Lescarboura, whose deadly accurate kicking brought him the points scoring record for the International Championship in 1984. (*All-Sport*)

The most points scored in an international career is 301 by Andrew Robertson Irvine (Heriots) (b. 16 Sept 1951), 273 for Scotland (including 12 *v.* Romania) and 28 for the British Lions from 1973 to 1982.

Season

The first class rugby scoring record for a season is 581 points by Samuel Arthur Doble (1944–77) of Moseley, in 52 matches in 1971–2. He also scored 47 points for England in South Africa out of season.

Career

William Henry 'Dusty' Hare (b. 29 Nov 1952) of Leicester, scored 5111 points in first class games from 1971–84, comprising 1800 for Nottingham, 2502 for Leicester, 219 for England, 88 for the British Lions and 502 in other representative matches.

Match

Jannie van der Westhuizen scored 80 points (14 tries, 9 conversions, 1 dropped goal, 1 penalty goal) for Carnarvon (88) *v.* Williston (12) at North West Cape, S. Africa on 11 March 1972.

In a junior house match in February 1967 at William Ellis School, Edgware, Greater London, between Cumberland and Nunn, Thanos Morphitis, 12, contributed 90 points (13 tries and 19 conversions) (77) to Cumberland's winning score.

All-rounder

Canadian international, Barrie Burnham, scored all possible ways—try, conversion, penalty goal, drop goal, goal from mark—for Meralomas *v.* Georgians (20–11) at Vancouver, BC, on 26 Feb 1966.

Most International Appearances

The following totals are limited to matches between the seven member countries of the 'International Rugby Football Board' and France. Including 12 appearances for the British Lions, Mike Gibson has played in 81 international matches, Willie John McBride (b. Co. Antrim, 6 June 1940) made a record 17 appearances for the British Lions, as well as 63 for Ireland.

Youngest International

Edinburgh Academy pupils Ninian Jamieson Finlay (1858–1936) and Charles Reid (1864–1909) were both 17 yr 36 days old when they played for Scotland *v.* England in 1875 and 1881 respectively.

However, as Finlay had one less leap year in his lifetime up to his first cap, the outright record must be credited to him. Daniel Brendan Carroll (b. 17 Feb 1892) was aged only 16 yr 149 days when he played for Australia in the 1908 Olympic Games Rugby tournament —not considered to be a 'full' international.

Bristol winger Alan Morley had his best ever try scoring season in 1983–4, adding 50 to his career record. *(Associated Sports Photography)*

MOST INTERNATIONAL APPEARANCES			
Ireland	69	Cameron Michael Henderson Gibson (b. 3 Dec 1942)	1964–79
New Zealand	55	Colin Earl Meads (b. 3 June 1936)	1957–71
Wales	55	John Peter Rhys 'JPR' Williams (b. 2 Mar 1949)	1969–81
France	52	Roland Bertranne (b. 6 Dec 1949) (in all—69)	1971–81
Scotland	51	Andrew R. Irvine (b. 16 Sept 1951)	1973–82
	51	James Menzies 'Jim' Renwick (b. 12 Feb 1952)	1972–83
England	43	Anthony Neary (b. 25 Nov 1948)	1971–80
Australia	39	Peter G. Johnson (b. 1938)	1958–72
	39	Gregory Victor Davis (b. 27 July 1939)	1963–72
South Africa	38	Frederick Christoffel Hendrick Du Preez (b. 28 Nov 1935)	1960–71
	38	Jan Hendrik Ellis (b. 5 Jan 1943)	1965–76

County Championships

The County Championships (inst. 1889) have been won most often by Gloucestershire with 15 titles (1910, 1913, 1920–2, 1930–2, 1937, 1972, 1974–6 and 1983–4). The most individual appearances is 104 by Richard Trickey (Sale) (b. 6 Mar 1945) for Lancashire between 1964 and 1978.

Club Championships

The most outright wins in the RFU Club Competition (John Player Cup, inst. 1971–2) is three by Leicester, 1979–81. Gloucester won in 1972 and 1978 and shared the Cup in 1982.

The most wins in the Welsh Rugby Union Challenge Cup (Schweppes Welsh Cup, inst. 1971–2) is four by Llanelli, 1973–6. The most wins in the Scottish League Division One (inst. 1973–4) is seven by Hawick, 1973–4 to 1977–8 , 1981–2 and 1983–4.

Seven-a-sides *Origins*

Seven-a-side rugby dates from 28 Apr 1883 when Melrose RFC Borders in order to alleviate the poverty of a club in such a small town staged a seven-a-side tournament. The idea was that of Ned Haig, the town's butcher.

Middlesex Seven-a-sides

The Middlesex Seven-a-sides were inaugurated in 1926. The most wins is nine by Richmond (inc. once by their second Seven) (1951, 1953, 1955, 1974–5, 1977, 1979–80, 1983).

Greatest crowd

The record paying attendance is 104,000 for Scotland's 12–10 win over Wales at Murrayfield, Edinburgh, on 1 Mar 1975.

Highest posts

The world's highest Rugby Union goal posts are 110 ft ½ in *33,54 m* high at the Roan Antelope Rugby Union Club, Luanshya, Zambia. The posts at Brixham RFC, Devonshire, are 57 ft *17,37 m* high with an additional 1 ft *0,30 m* spike.

Longest kicks

The longest recorded successful drop-goal is 90 yd *82 m* by Gerald Hamilton 'Gerry' Brand (b. 8 Oct 1906) for South Africa *v.* England at Twickenham, Greater London, on 2 Jan 1932. This was taken 7 yd *6 m* inside the England 'half' 55 yd *50 m* from the posts and dropped over the dead ball line.

The place kick record is reputed to be 100 yd *91 m* at Richmond Athletic Ground, Greater London, by Douglas Francis Theodore Morkel (b. 1886) in an unsuccessful penalty for South Africa *v.* Surrey on 19 Dec 1906. This was not measured until 1932. In the match Bridlington School 1st XV *v.* an Army XV at Bridlington, Humberside on 29 Jan 1944, Ernie Cooper (b. 21 May 1926), captaining the school, landed a penalty from a measured 81 yd *74 m* from the post with a kick which carried over the dead ball line.

Fastest try

The fastest try in an international game was when H. L. 'Bart' Price scored for England *v.* Wales at Twickenham on 20 Jan 1923 less than 10 sec after kick off.

Most tries

Alan Morely (b. 25 June 1950) has scored 417 tries in senior rugby in 1968–84 including 329 for Bristol, a record for one club. John Huins scored 85 tries in 1953–4, 73 for St Luke's College, Exeter and 12 more for Neath and in trial games.

Longest try

The longest 'try' ever executed is by a team of 15, from Power-House RUFC, Victoria, Australia, who ran a try of 1470.6 miles *2366,7 km* on 4–13 Mar 1983 around Albert Park Lake,

Victoria. There were no forward passes or knock-ons, and the ball was touched down between the posts in the prescribed manner (Law 12).

Most successful team

The Leamington Spa junior team played 92 successive games without defeat from 6 Oct 1980 to 13 Apr 1984.

GAMBLING

World's biggest win

The world's biggest individual gambling win is $8,800,000 by Nicholas Jarich in the Pennsylvania state lottery on 23 July 1983.

World's biggest loss

An unnamed Italian industrialist was reported to have lost £800,000 in 5 hr at roulette in Monte Carlo, Monaco on 6 Mar 1974. A Saudi Arabian prince was reported to have lost more than $1 million in a single session at the Metro Club, Las Vegas, USA in December 1974.

Largest casino

The largest casino in the world is the Resorts International Casino, Atlantic City, NJ, USA. It reported a record month in July 1983 with winnings of $29.3 million. The Casino comprises 60,000 ft² *5574 m²*, containing 127 gaming tables and 1640 slot machines. Attendances total over 35,000 daily at peak weekends.

BINGO

Bingo is a lottery game which, as keno, was developed in the 1880s from lotto, whose origin is thought to be the 17th century Italian game *tumbule*. It has long been known in the British Army (called Housey-Housey) and the Royal Navy (called Tombola). The winner was the first to complete a random selection of numbers from 1 to 90. The USA version called Bingo differs in that the selection is from 1 to 75. There are six million players in the United Kingdom.

Largest house

The largest 'house' in Bingo sessions was 15,756 at the Canadian National Exhibition, Toronto on 19 Aug 1983. Staged by the Variety Club of Ontario Tent #28, there was total prize money of $C250,000 with a record one-game payout of $C100,000.

Earliest and latest Full House

A 'Full House' call occurred on the 15th number by Norman A. Wilson at Guide Post Workingmen's Club, Bedlington, Northumberland on 22 June 1978, by Anne Wintle of Brynrethin, Mid Glamorgan, on a coach trip to Bath on 17 Aug 1982 and by Shirley Lord at Kahibah Bowling Club, New South Wales, Australia on 24 Oct 1983. 'House' was not called until the 86th number at the Hillsborough Working Men's Club, Sheffield, S. Yorkshire on 11 Jan 1982. There were 32 winners.

ELECTIONS

The highest ever individual bet was £90,000 to win £20,000 for the Conservative party to return the most MPs in the 1983 General Election, by an unnamed man. A bet of £5000 at 200–1 was placed by Frank Egerton in April 1975 that his political Centre Party would win the next General Election. It didn't.

FOOTBALL POOLS

Two unnamed punters won c. £1.5 million each in November 1972 on the state run Italian pools. The winning dividend paid out by Littlewoods Pools in their first week in February 1923 was £2 12s 0d (£2.60). In 1982–83 the three British Pools companies which comprise the Pool Promoters Association (Littlewoods, Vernons and Zetters) had a total record turnover of £454,433,000 of which Littlewoods contributed over 70%.

Biggest win

The greatest sum won from the British Pools is £953,874.10 by David Preston, 47, of Burton-on-Trent, Staffs, on 23 Feb 1980. This total comprised £804,573.35 from Littlewoods Pools and £149,300.75 from Vernons Pools. The record payout to two people is £1,260,349.96 by Littlewoods on 14 Apr 1984; £650,070.20 to Mr. Desmond Keogh and eight workmates

from St. Helens, Merseyside; £610,279.76 to Mrs Violet Stevens and her family of Canvey Island, Essex. Littlewood's record total payout in one week is £2,132,326 on 27 Feb 1982.

The odds for selecting 8 draws (if there are only 8 draws) from 55 matches for an all-correct line are 1,217,566.350 to 1 against. (In practice, the approximate odds of winning a dividend of any size on Littlewoods Pools are 80 to 1.)

HORSE RACING

Highest ever odds

The highest secured odds were 1,099,299 to 1 by a backer from Otley, West Yorkshire on a seven horse accumulator on 10 May 1975. He won £10,992.99 for a 1p bet out of a total stake of £1.76 which in all netted him £12,878.14. Edward Hodson of Wolverhampton landed a 3,956,748 to 1 bet for a 55p stake on 11 Feb 1984, but his bookmaker had a £3000 payout limit. The world record odds on a 'double' are 31,793 to 1 paid by the New Zealand Totalisator Agency Board on a five shilling tote ticket on *Red Emperor* and *Maida Dillon* at Addington, Christchurch, in 1951.

Greatest pay-out

Three punters each received $C735,403 for picking winners of six consecutive races at Exhibition Park, Vancouver, BC, Canada on 10 July 1982. The lowest price paid for a winning ticket was $4.

Biggest tote win

The best recorded tote win was one of £341 2s 6d to 2s (*£341.12½ to 10p*) representing odds of 3,410¼ to 1, by Catharine Unsworth of Blundellsands, Liverpool at Haydock Park on a race won by *Coole* on 30 Nov 1929. The highest odds in Irish tote history were £289.64 for 10p unit on *Gene's Rogue* at Limerick on 28 Dec 1981.

Largest bookmaker

The world's largest bookmaker is Ladbrokes of London with a turnover from gambling in 1983 of £637 million. The largest chain of betting shops is that of Ladbrokes with 1315 shops in the United Kingdom in 1983.

Topmost tipster

The only recorded instance of a racing correspondent forecasting ten out of ten winners on a race card was at Delaware Park, Wilmington, Delaware, USA on 28 July 1974 by Charles Lamb of the *Baltimore News American*.

JAI-ALAI

The highest parimutuel payout in the USA was for a group of punters who won $988,326 (less $197,664 paid to the Internal Revenue) for a $2 ticket naming six consecutive winning Jai-Alai players at Palm Beach, Florida on 1 Mar 1983.

ROULETTE

The longest run on an ungaffed (*i.e.* true) wheel reliably recorded is six successive coups (in No. 10) at El San Juan Hotel, Puerto Rico on 9 July 1959. The odds with a double zero were 1 in 38⁶ or 3,010,936,383 to 1.

The longest 'marathon' on record is one of 31 days from 10 Apr to 11 May 1970 at The Casino de Macao, to test the validity or invalidity of certain contentions in 20,000 spins.

SLOT MACHINES

The biggest beating handed to a 'one-armed bandit' was $2,478,716.15 by Rocco Dinubilo from Fresno, California at Harrah's Tahoe Casino, Nevada, USA on 31 Dec 1983.

GLIDING

Origins

Isadore William Deiches has researched evidence of the use of gliders in Ancient Egypt *c.* 2500–1500 BC. Emanuel Swedenborg (1688–1772) of Sweden made sketches of gliders *c.* 1714. The earliest man-carrying glider was designed by Sir George Cayley (1773–1857) and carried his coachman (possibly John Appleby) about 500 yd *457 m* across a valley in Brompton Dale, North Yorkshire in the summer of 1853.

GLIDING—SELECTED WORLD RECORDS
(Single-seaters)

DISTANCE	907.7 miles *1460,8 km*	Hans-Werner Grosse (W. Germany) in an ASW-12 on 25 Apr 1972 from Lübeck to Biarritz
DECLARED GOAL DISTANCE	779.4 miles *1254,26 km*	Bruce Drake, David Speight, S. H. 'Dick' Georgeson (all NZ) all in Nimbus 2s, Te Anau to Te Araroa, 14 Jan 1978
GOAL AND RETURN	1023.2 miles *1646,68 km*	Tom Knauff (USA) in a Nimbus 3 from Williamsport, Pennsylvania to Knoxville, Tennessee on 25 April 1983
ABSOLUTE ALTITUDE	46,266 ft *14 102 m*	Paul F. Bikle, Jr (USA) in a Schweizer SGS 1–23E over Mojave, California on 25 Feb 1961
ALTITUDE GAIN	42,303 ft *12 894 m*	Paul Bikle on 25 Feb 1961 (see above)

SPEED OVER TRIANGULAR COURSE		
100 km	121.28 mph *195,18 km/h*	Ingo Renner (Australia) in a Nimbus 3 on 14 Dec 1982
300 km	98,59 mph *158,67 km/h*	Hans-Werner Grosse (W. Germany) in an ASW-17 over Australia on 24 Dec 1980
500 km	99.20 mph *159,65 km/h*	Hans-Werner Grosse (W. Germany) in an ASW-22 on 20 Dec 1983
750 km	89.25 mph *143,63 km/h*	Hans-Werner Grosse (W. Germany) in an ASW-17 over Australia on 6 Jan 1982
1000 km	90.29 mph *145,32 km/h*	Hans-Werner Gross (W. Germany) in an ASW-17 over Australia on 3 Jan 1979
1250 km	82.79 mph *133,24 km/h*	Hans-Werner Grosse (W. Germany) in an ASW-17 over Australia on 9 Dec 1980

BRITISH NATIONAL RECORDS[1]
(Single-seaters)

589.9 miles *949,7 km*		Karla Karel in a LS-3 over Australia on 20 Jan 1980
360 miles *579,36 km*		H. C. N. Goodhart in a Skylark 3, Lasham, Hants, to Portmoak, Scotland on 10 May 1959
621.9 miles *1000,88 km*		William Malpas in a Mini-Nimbus, State College, Pa. to Bluefield, Va., USA on 28 Sept 1981
37,729 ft *11 500 m*		H. C. N. Goodhart in a Schweizer 1-23 over California, USA on 12 May 1955
33,022 ft *10 065 m*		D. Benton in a Nimbus 2 on 18 Apr 1980

88.99 mph *143,3 km/h*		E. Paul Hodge in a Standard Cirrus over Rhodesia on 30 Oct 1976
91.2 mph *146,8 km/h*		Edward Pearson in a Nimbus 2 over S.W. Africa on 30 Nov 1976
87.8 mph *141,3 km/h*		Bradley James Grant Pearson in an ASW-20 over South Africa on 28 Dec 1982
68.2 mph *109,8 km/h*		Michael R. Carlton in a Kestrel 19 over South Africa on 5 Jan 1975

[1] *British National Records may be set up by British pilots in any part of the world.*

Most titles World
The most World individual championships (inst. 1948) won is three by Helmut Reichmann (b. 1942) (W. Germany) in 1970, 1974, 1978 and Douglas George Lee (GB) (b. 7 Nov 1945) in 1976, 1978 and 1981.

Most titles British
The British national championship (inst. 1939) has been won five times by John Delafield (b. 31 Jan 1938) in 1968, 1972, 1976, 1978 and 1981. The first woman to win this title was Anne Burns (b. 23 Nov. 1915) of Farnham, Surrey on 30 May 1966.

HANG GLIDING

Origins
In the eleventh century the monk, Eilmer, is reported to have flown from the 60 ft *18,3 m* tower of Malmesbury Abbey, Wiltshire. The earliest modern pioneer was Otto Lilienthal (1848–96) (Germany) with about 2500 flights in gliders of his own construction between 1891 and 1896. In the 1950s Professor Francis Rogallo of the National Space Agency, USA, developed a flexible 'wing' from his space capsule re-entry researches.

Championships
The World Team Championships have been won most often by Great Britain (1978–9, 1981).

The official FAI record is 300,62 kms *186.80 miles* by John Pendry (GB) flying an Airwave Magic 3 from Horseshoe Meadows, Owens Valley, California to Summit Mtn., Monitop Range, Nevada, USA in July 83. The Womens official FAI record is 233,90 km *145.34 miles* by Judy Leden (GB) flying a Wills Wing Duck 160 from Horseshoe Meadows, Owens Valley, California to Luning, Nevada, USA. The British best is 209,20 km *130 miles* by John Pendry, flying a Magic 3 from Ditchling, West Sussex to Colyton near Seaton, Devon in April 84.

Greatest ascent
The official FAI height gain record is 4175 m *13,700 ft* by Ian Kibblewhite (New Zealand) in a Lightning 195 at Cerro Gordo, Owens Valley, California, USA on 22 July 1981. The British record is 3170 m *10,400 ft* by John Duncker at Wether Fell, North Yorkshire on 31 Aug 1982.

Greatest descent
Rory McCarthy (b. 25 June 1960) piloted a hang glider from a height of 34,500 ft *10 515 m* when he was released from a hot air balloon, to the ground, landing at Diss, Norfolk on 19 June 1984.

GOLF

See also The Guinness Book of Golf Facts and Feats (2nd edition) by Donald Steel, published at £8.95.

Origins
Although a stained glass window in Gloucester Cathedral, dating from 1350 portrays a golfer-like figure, the earliest mention of golf occurs in a prohibiting law passed by the Scottish Parliament in March 1457 under which 'goff be utterly cryit doune and not usit'. The Romans had a cognate game called *paganica* which may have been carried to Britain before AD 400. The Chinese Nationalist Golf Association claim the game is of Chinese origin ('*Ch'ui Wan*—the ball hitting game') in the 3rd or 2nd century BC. There were official ordinances prohibiting a ball game with clubs in Belgium and Holland from 1360. Gutta percha balls succeeded feather balls in 1848 and by 1902 were in turn succeeded by rubber-cored balls, invented in 1899 by Coburn Haskell (USA). Steel shafts were authorised in the USA in 1925 and in Britain in 1929.

Club Oldest
The oldest club of which there is written evidence is the Gentlemen Golfers (now the Honourable Company of Edinburgh Golfers) formed in March 1744—ten years prior to the institution of the Royal and Ancient Club of St Andrews, Fife. However the Royal Burgess Golfing Society of Edinburgh claim to have been founded in 1735.

Club Largest
The club with the highest membership in the British Isles is the Royal and Ancient Golf Club of St Andrews, Fife, Scotland with 1800 members. The largest in England is 1757 at the Moor Park GC, Rickmansworth, Herts.

Course Highest
The highest golf course in the world is the Tuctu Golf Club in Morococha, Peru, which is 4369 m *14,335 ft* above sea-level at its lowest point. Golf has, however, been played in Tibet at an altitude of over 4875 m *16,000 ft*.

The highest golf course in Great Britain is one of nine holes at Leadhills, Strathclyde, 1500 ft *457 m* above sea-level.

Longest hole
The longest hole in the world is the 7th hole (par-7) of the Sano Course, Satsuki GC, Japan, which measures 831 m *909 yd*. In August 1927 the sixth hole at Prescott Country Club in Arkansas, USA, measured 838 yd *766 m*. The longest hole on a championship course in Great Britain is the sixth at Troon, Strathclyde, which stretches 577 yd *528 m*.

Largest green
Probably the largest green in the world is that of the par-6

The USA have dominated the Ryder Cup and won again in 1983, but this was after an epic struggle before non-playing captain Jack Nicklaus could collect the trophy after a 14½–13½ victory at Palm Beach, Florida. *(All-Sport)*

695 yd *635 m* fifth hole at International GC, Bolton, Massachusetts, USA, with an area greater than 28,000 ft^2 *2600 m^2*.

Biggest bunker

The world's biggest bunker (called a trap in the USA) is Hell's Half Acre on the 585 yd *535 m* seventh hole of the Pine Valley course, Clementon, New Jersey, USA, built in 1912 and generally regarded as the world's most trying course.

Longest course

The world's longest course is the par-77 8325 yd *7612 m* International GC, (*see also above*), from the 'Tiger' tees, remodelled in 1969 by Robert Trent Jones. Floyd Satterlee Rood used the United States as a course, when he played from the Pacific surf to the Atlantic surf from 14 Sept 1963 to 3 Oct 1964 in 114,737 strokes. He lost 3511 balls on the 3397.7 mile *5468 km* trail.

Longest drives

In long-driving contests 330 yd *300 m* is rarely surpassed at sea-level. In officially regulated long driving contests over level ground the greatest distance recorded is 392 yd *358 m* by William Thomas 'Tommie' Campbell (b. 24 July 1927) (Foxrock Golf Club) at Dun Laoghaire, Co. Dublin, in July 1964.

On an airport runway Valentin Barrios (Spain) drove a Slazenger B51 ball 568½ yd *520 m* at Palma, Majorca on 7 Mar 1977. The greatest recorded drive on an ordinary course is one of 515 yd *471 m* by Michael Hoke Austin (b. 17 Feb 1910) of Los Angeles, California, USA, in the US National Seniors Open Championship at Las Vegas, Nevada, on 25 Sept 1974. Austin, 6 ft 2 in *1,88 m* tall and weighing 210 lb *92 kg* drove the ball to within a yard of the green on the par-4 450 yd *412 m* fifth hole of the Winterwood Course and it rolled 65 yd *59 m* past the flagstick. He was aided by an estimated 35 mph *56 km/h* tailwind.

A drive of 2640 yd (1½ miles) *2414 m* across ice was achieved by an Australian meteorologist named Nils Lied at Mawson Base, Antarctica, in 1962. Arthur Lynskey claimed a drive of 200 yd *182 m* horizontal and 2 miles *3200 m* vertical off Pikes Peak, Colorado (14,110 ft *4300 m*) on 28 June 1968. On the Moon the energy expended on a mundane 300 yd *274 m* drive would achieve, craters permitting, a distance of 1 mile *1,6 km*.

Longest putt

The longest recorded holed putt in a major tournament was one of 86 ft *26 m* on the vast 13th green at the Augusta National, Georgia by Cary Middlecoff (b. 6 Jan 1921) (USA) in the 1955 Masters' Tournament. Robert Tyre 'Bobby' Jones Jr (1902–71) was reputed to have holed a putt in excess of 100 ft *30 m* at the fifth green in the first round of the 1927 Open at St. Andrews.

SCORES

Lowest 9 holes and 18 holes *Men*

At least four players are recorded to have played a long course (over 6000 yd *5486 m*) in a score of 58, most recently Monte Carlo Money (USA) (b. 3 Dec 1954) the par-72, 6607 yd *6041 m* Las Vegas Municipal GC, Nevada, USA on 11 Mar 1981. The lowest recorded score on a long course in Britain is 58 by Harry Weetman (1920–72) the British Ryder Cup golfer, for the 6171 yd *5642 m* Croham Hurst Course, Croydon, Surrey, on 30 Jan 1956. Alfred Edward Smith (b. 1903) the Woolacombe professional, achieved an 18-hole score of 55 (15 under bogey 70) on his home course on 1 Jan 1936. The course measured 4248 yd *3884 m*. The detail was 4, 2, 3, 4, 2, 4, 3, 4, 3 = 29 out, and 2, 3, 3, 3, 3, 2, 5, 4, 1 = 26 in.

Nine holes in 25 (4, 3, 3, 2, 3, 3, 1, 4, 2) was recorded by A. J. 'Bill' Burke in a round in 57 (32 + 25) on the 6389 yd *5842 m* par-71 Normandie course St Louis, Missouri, USA on 20 May 1970. The tournament record is 27 by Mike Souchak (USA) (b. 10 May 1927) for the second nine (par-35) first round of the 1955 Texas Open (*see 72 holes*), Andy North (USA) (b. 9 Mar 1950) second nine (par-34), first round, 1975 BC Open at En-Joie GC, Endicott, NY and José Maria Canizares (Spain) (b. 18 Feb 1947), first nine, third round, in the 1978 Swiss Open on the 6811 yd *6228 m* Crans-Sur course.

The United States PGA tournament record for 18 holes is 59 (30 + 29) by Al Geiberger (b. 1 Sept 1937) in the second round of the Danny Thomas Classic, on the 72-par 7249 yd *6628 m* Colonial GC course, Memphis, Tennessee on 10 June 1977. Three golfers have recorded 59 over 18 holes in non-PGA tournaments; Samuel Jackson Snead (b. 27 May 1912) in the third round of the Sam Snead Festival at White Sulphur Springs, West Virginia, USA on 16 May 1959; Gary Player (South Africa) (b. 1 Nov 1935) in the second round of the Brazilian Open in Rio de Janeiro on 29 Nov 1974, and David Jagger (GB) (b. 9 June 1949) in a Pro-Am tournament prior to the 1973 Nigerian Open at Ikoyi Golf Club, Lagos.

Lowest 18 holes *Women*

The lowest recorded score on an 18-hole course (over 6000 yd *5486 m*) for a woman is 62 (30 + 32) by Mary 'Mickey' Kathryn Wright (b. 14 Feb 1935) (USA) on the Hogan Park Course (par-71, 6286 yd *5747 m*) at Midland, Texas, USA, in November 1964. Wanda Morgan (b. 22 Mar 1910) recorded a score of 60 (31 + 29) on the Westgate and Birchington Golf Club course, Kent, over 18 holes (5002 yd *4573 m*) on 11 July 1929.

Lowest 18 holes *Great Britain*

The lowest score recorded in a first class professional tournament on a course of more than 6000 yd *5486 m* in Great Britain is 61 (29 + 32), by Thomas Bruce Haliburton (1915–75) of Wentworth GC in the Spalding Tournament at Worthing, West Sussex, in June 1952, and 61 (32 + 29) by Peter J. Butler (b. 25 Mar 1932) in the Bowmaker Tournament on the Old Course at Sunningdale, Berkshire, on 4 July 1967.

Lowest 36 holes

The record for 36 holes is 122 (59 + 63) by Sam Snead in the 1959 Sam Snead Festival on 16–17 May 1959. Horton Smith (1908–1963), twice US Masters Champion, scored 121 (63 + 58) on a short course on 21 Dec 1928 (*see 72 holes*). The lowest score by a British golfer has been 124 (61 + 63) by Alexander Walter Barr 'Sandy' Lyle (b. 9 Feb 1958) in the Nigerian Open at the 6024 yd *5508 m* (par-71) Ikoyi Golf Club, Lagos in 1978.

Lowest 72 holes

The lowest recorded score on a first-class course is 255 (29 under par) by Leonard Peter Tupling (b. 6 Apr 1950) (GB) in the Nigerian Open at Ikoyi Golf Club, Lagos in February 1981, made up of 63, 66, 62 and 64 (average 63.75 per round).

The lowest 72 holes in a US professional event is 257 (60, 68, 64, 65) by Mike Souchak in the 1955 Texas Open at San Antonio.

The lowest 72 holes in an Open championship in Europe is 262 (67, 66, 66, 63) by Percy Alliss (GB) (1897–1975) in the 1932 Italian Open at San Remo, and by Lu Liang Huan (Taiwan) (b. 10 Dec 1935) in the 1971 French Open at Biarritz. Kelvin D. G. Nagle (b. 21 Dec 1920) of Australia shot 261 in the Hong Kong Open in 1961. The lowest for four rounds in a British first class tournament is 262 (66, 63, 66 and 67) by Bernard Hunt in the Piccadilly tournament on the par-68 6184 yd *5655 m* Wentworth East Course, Virginia Water, Surrey on 4–5 Oct 1966.

Horton Smith scored 245 (63, 58, 61 and 63) for 72 holes on the 4700 yd *4297 m* course (par-64) at Catalina Country Club, California, USA, to win the Catalina Open on 21–23 Dec 1928.

Highest score

The highest score for a single hole in the British Open is 21 by a player in the inaugural meeting at Prestwick in 1860. Double figures have been recorded on the card of the winner only once, when Willie Fernie (1851–1924) scored a ten at Musselburgh, Lothian, in 1883. Ray Ainsley of Ojai, California, took 19 strokes for the par-4 16th hole during the second round of the US Open at Cherry Hills Country Club, Denver, Colorado, on 10 June 1938. Most of the strokes were used in trying to extricate the ball from a brook. Hans Merell of Mogadore, Ohio, took 19 strokes on the par-3 16th (222 yd *203 m*) during the third round of the Bing Crosby National Tournament at Cypress Point Club, Del Monte, California, USA, on 17 Jan 1959. It is recorded that Chevalier von Cittern went round 18 holes in 316, averaging 17.55 per hole, at Biarritz, France in 1888. Steven Ward took 222 strokes for the 6212 yd *5680 m* Pecos Course, Reeves County, Texas, USA, on 18 June 1976—but he was only aged 3 years 286 days.

Most shots for one hole

A woman player in the qualifying round of the Shawnee Invitational for Ladies at Shawnee-on-Delaware, Pennsylvania, USA, in *c.* 1912, took 166 strokes for the short 130 yd *118 m* 16th hole. Her tee shot went into the Binniekill River and the ball floated. She put out in a boat with her exemplary, but statistically minded husband at the oars. She eventually beached the ball 1½ miles *2,4 km* downstream but was not yet out of the wood. She had to play through one on the home run. In a competition at Peacehaven, Sussex, England in 1890, A. J. Lewis had 156 putts on one green without holing out.

Rounds fastest *Individual*

With such variations in lengths of courses, speed records, even for rounds under par, are of little comparative value. Rick Baker completed 18 holes (6142 yd *5616 m*) in 25 min 48.47 sec at Surfer's Paradise, Queensland, Australia on 4 Sept 1982, but this test permitted the striking of the ball whilst still moving. The record for a still ball is 28.09 min by Gary Shane Wright (b. 27 Nov 1946) at Tewantin-Noosa Golf Club, Queensland (18 holes, 6039 yd *5522 m*) on 9 Dec 1980.

Rounds fastest *Team*

Seventy-six players completed the 18-hole 6040 yd *5327 m* course at Surfers Paradise, Queensland, Australia in 12 min 14.1 sec on 1 Mar 1981 using only one ball.

Rounds slowest

The slowest stroke play tournament round was one of 6 hr 45 min taken by South Africa in the first round of the 1972 World Cup at the Royal Melbourne GC, Australia. This was a four-ball medal round, everything holed out.

Most rounds

The greatest number of rounds played on foot in 24 hr is 22 rounds and five holes (401 holes) by Ian Colston, 35, at Bendigo GC, Victoria (par-73, 6061 yd *5542 m*) on 27–28 Nov 1971. The British record is 360 holes by Antony J. Clark at Childwall GC, Liverpool on 18 July 1983. The most holes played on foot in a week (168 hr) is 1128 by Steve Hylton at the Mason Rudolph Golf Club (6060 yd *5541m*), Clarkesville, Tennessee, USA, from 25–31 Aug 1980.

Throwing the golf ball

The lowest recorded score for throwing a golf ball round 18 holes (over 6000 yd or *5500 m*) is 82 by Joe Flynn (USA), 21, at the 6228 yd *5694 m* Port Royal Course, Bermuda, on 27 Mar 1975.

CHAMPIONSHIP RECORDS

The Open

The Open Championship was inaugurated in 1860 at Prestwick, Strathclyde, Scotland. The lowest score for 9 holes is 28 by Denis Durnian (b. 30 June 1950), at Royal Birkdale, Southport, Lancashire in the second round on 15 July 1983.

The lowest round in The Open is 63 by Mark Hayes (b. 12 July 1949) (USA) at Turnberry, Strathclyde, on 7 July 1977, and Isao Aoki (b. 31 Aug 1942) (Japan) at Muirfield, East Lothian, on 19 July 1980. Thomas Henry Cotton (b. 26 Jan 1907) at Royal St George's, Sandwich, Kent completed the first 36 holes in 132 (67 + 65) on 27 June 1934. The lowest 72-hole aggregate is 268 (68, 70, 65, 65) by Tom Watson (b. 4 Sept 1949) (USA) at Turnberry, ending on 9 July 1977.

US Open

The United States Open Championship was inaugurated in 1895. The lowest 72-hole aggregate is 272 (63, 71, 70, 68) by Jack Nicklaus (b. 21 Jan 1940) on the Lower Course (7015 yd *6414 m*) at Baltusrol Country Club, Springfield, New Jersey, on 12–15 June 1980. The lowest score for 18 holes is 63 by Johnny Miller (b. 29 Apr 1947) on the 6921 yd *6328 m* par-71 Oakmont Country Club course, Pennsylvania on 17 June 1973, Jack Nicklaus (*see above*) and Tom Weiskopf (USA) (b. 9 Nov 1942), both on 12 June 1980.

US Masters'

The lowest score in the US Masters' (instituted on the par-72 6980 yd *6382 m* Augusta National Golf Course, Georgia, in 1934) has been 271 by Jack Nicklaus in 1965 and Raymond Floyd (b. 4 Sept 1942) in 1976. The lowest rounds have been 64 by Lloyd Mangrum (1914–74) (first round, 1940), Jack Nicklaus (third round, 1965), Maurice Bembridge (GB) (b.

MOST TITLES *The most titles won in the world's major golf championships are as follows:*

Championship	Player	Titles	Years
The Open	Harry Vardon (1870–1937)	6	1896, 1898–9, 1903, 11, 14
The Amateur	John Ball (1861–1940)	8	1888, 90, 92, 94, 99, 1907, 10, 12
US Open	Willie Anderson (1880–1910)	4	1901, 03–5
	Robert Tyre Jones, Jr. (1902–71)	4	1923, 26, 29–30
	William Ben Hogan (b. 13 Aug 1912)	4	1948, 50–1, 53
	Jack William Nicklaus (b. 21 Jan 1940)	4	1962, 67, 72, 80
US Amateur	Robert Tyre Jones, Jr. (1902–71)	5	1924–25, 27–8, 30
PGA Championship (USA)	Walter Charles Hagen (1892–1969)	5	1921, 24–7
	Jack William Nicklaus (b. 21 Jan 1940)	5	1963, 71, 73, 75, 80
Masters' Championship (USA)	Jack William Nicklaus (b. 21 Jan 1940)	5	1963, 65–6, 72, 75
US Women's Open	Elizabeth 'Betsy' Earle-Rawls (b. 4 May 1928)	4	1951, 53, 57, 60
	'Mickey' Wright (b. 14 Feb 1935)	4	1958–59, 61, 64
US Women's Amateur	Glenna C. Vare (née Collett) (b. 20 June 1903)	6	1922, 25, 28, 30, 35
British Women's	Charlotte Cecilia Pitcairn Leitch (1891–1977)	4	1914, 20–1, 26
	Joyce Wethered (b. 17 Nov 1901) (Now Lady Heathcoat-Amory)	4	1922, 24–5, 29

Note: Nicklaus is the only golfer to have won five different major titles (The Open, US Open, Masters, PGA and US Amateur titles) twice and a record 19 all told (1959–80). His remarkable record in The US Open is four firsts, eight seconds and two thirds. In 1930 Bobby Jones achieved a unique 'Grand Slam' of the US and British Open and Amateur titles.

21 Feb 1945) (fourth round, 1974), Hale Irwin (b. 3 June 1945) (fourth round, 1975), Gary Player (S. Africa) (fourth round, 1978) and Miller Barber (b. 31 Mar 1931) (second round, 1979).

World Cup (formerly Canada Cup)
The World Cup (instituted as the Canada Cup in 1953) has been won most often by the USA with 16 victories between 1955 and 1983. The only men to have been on six winning teams have been Arnold Palmer (b. 10 Sept 1929) (1960, 1962–4, 1966–7) and Jack Nicklaus (1963–4, 1966–7, 1971 and 1973). Only Nicklaus has taken the individual title three times (1963–4, 1971). The lowest aggregate score for 144 holes is 544 by Australia, Bruce Devlin (b. 10 Oct 1937) and David Graham (b. 23 May 1946), at San Isidro, Buenos Aires, Argentina on 12–15 Nov 1970. The lowest individual score has been 269 by Roberto de Vicenzo (Argentina) (b. 14 Apr 1923), also in 1970.

Ryder Cup
The biennial Ryder Cup professional match between USA and the British Isles or Great Britain (Europe since 1979) was instituted in 1927. The USA have won 21½ to 3½ to date. William Earl 'Billy' Casper (b. San Diego, California, USA, 24 June 1931) has the record of winning most matches in the Trophy with 20 in 1961–75. Christy O'Connor Sr (b. 21 Dec 1924) (GB) played in ten matches up to 1973.

Walker Cup
The USA v. GB & Ireland series instituted in 1921 (for the Walker Cup since 1922 and now held biennially) has been won by the USA 25½–2½ to date. Joseph Boynton Carr (GB&I) (b. 18 Feb 1922) played in ten contests (1947–67).

Curtis Cup
The biennial ladies' Curtis Cup match between USA and Great Britain and Ireland was first held in 1932. The USA have won 19, GB&I 2 and two matches have been tied. Mary McKenna (GB&I) (b. 29 Apr 1949) played in a record eighth match in 1984.

Richest prizes
The greatest first place prize money was $500,000 (total purse $1,100,000) won by Johnny Miller in 1982 and Raymond Floyd in 1983, at Sun City, Bophuthatswana, S. Africa. Both won in play-offs, from Severiano Ballesteros and Craig Stadler respectively.

Highest earnings *US PGA and LPGA circuits*
The all time professional money-winner is Jack Nicklaus, with $4,490,817 to 17 July 1984. The record for a year is $530,808 by Tom Watson in 1980. The record career earnings for a woman is $1,690,441 from 1970 to 14 May 1984 by JoAnne Carner (*née* Gunderson) (b. 4 April 1939). She won a season's record $310,399 in 1982.

Highest earnings *European circuit*
Nicholas Alexander Faldo (b. 18 July 1957) won a European record £119,416 in 1983.

Most tournament wins
The record for winning tournaments in a single season is 18 (plus one unofficial), including a record 11 consecutively, by

John Byron Nelson (b. 4 Feb 1912) (USA), from 8 Mar–4 Aug 1945. Sam Snead won 84 official US PGA Tour events 1936–65, and has been credited with a total 134 tournament victories since 1934. The Ladies PGA record is 84 by Kathy Whitworth (b. 27 Sept 1939) from 1962 to June 1983.

Biggest winning margin
The greatest margin of victory in a major tournament is 21 strokes by Jerry Pate (b. 16 Sept 1953) (USA) in the Colombian Open with 262 on 10–13 Dec 1981.

Youngest and oldest champions
The youngest winner of The Open was Tom Morris, Jr. (1851–

Nick Faldo set a European money-winning record at golf in 1983. The following year he became the first British golfer to win an American tournament since Tony Jacklin 12 years earlier. *(All-Sport)*

75) at Prestwick, Strathclyde in 1868 aged 17 yr 249 days. The youngest winners of The Amateur title were John Charles Beharrell (b. 2 May 1938) at Troon, Strathclyde, on 2 June 1956, and Robert 'Bobby' E. Cole (b. 11 May 1948) (South Africa) at Carnoustie, Tayside, on 11 June 1966, both aged 18 yr 1 month. The oldest Open Champion was 'Old Tom' Morris (1821–1908), aged 46 yr 99 days when he won at Prestwick in 1867. In recent times the 1967 champion, Roberto de Vicenzo was aged 44 yr 93 days. The oldest winner of The Amateur was the Hon Michael Scott (1878–1959) at Hoylake, Merseyside in 1933, when 54 yr 297 days. The oldest United States Amateur Champion was Jack Westland (1904–82) at Seattle, Washington, on 23 Aug 1952, aged 47 yr 253 days.

Longest span
Jacqueline Ann Mercer (*née* Smith) (b. 5 Apr 1929) won her first South African title at Humewood GC, Port Elizabeth in 1948, and her fourth at Port Elizabeth GC on 4 May 1979, 31 years later.

Most club championships
Bernard Charles Cusack (b. 24 Jan 1920) has won a record total of 34 Club championships, including 33 consecutively, at the Narembeen GC, Western Australia, between 1943 and 1982. The women's record is 31 by Molly St John Pratt (b. 19 Oct 1912) at the Stanthorpe GC, Queensland, Australia from 1931 to 1979. The British record for amateur club championships is 30 wins between 1951 and 1984 by Helen Gray at Todmorden GC, Lancashire. The record for consecutive wins is 22 (1959–80) by Patricia Mary Shepherd (b. 7 Jan 1940) at Turriff GC, Aberdeenshire, Scotland.

Record tie
The longest delayed result in any National Open Championship occurred in the 1931 US Open at Toledo, Ohio. George von Elm (1901–61) and Billy Burke (1902–72) tied at 292, then tied the first replay at 149. Burke won the second replay by a single stroke after 72 extra holes.

Largest tournament
The Volkswagen Grand Prix Open Amateur Championship in the United Kingdom attracted a record 228,320 (172,640 men and 55,680 women) competitors in 1982.

HOLES IN ONE

Longest
The longest straight hole ever holed in one shot is the tenth (447 yd *408 m*) at Miracle Hills Golf Club, Omaha, Nebraska, USA by Robert Mitera (b. 1944) on 7 Oct 1965. Mitera stood 5 ft 6 in *1,68 m* tall and weighed 165 lb *75 kg* (11 st 11 lb). He was a two handicap player who normally drove 245 yd *224 m*. A 50 mph *80 km/h* gust carried his shot over a 290 yd *265 m* drop-off. The longest 'dog-leg' hole achieved in one is the 480 yd *439 m* fifth at Hope Country Club, Arkansas by L. Bruce on 15 Nov 1962. The feminine record is 393 yd *359 m* by Marie Robie on the first hole of the Furnace Brook Golf Club, Wollaston, Mass., USA, on 4 Sept 1949. The longest hole in one performed in the British Isles is the seventh (par-4, 393 yd *359 m*) at West Lancashire GC by Peter Richard Parkinson (b. 26 Aug 1947) on 6 June 1972.

Most
The greatest number of holes-in-one in a career is 66 by Harry Lee Bonner from 1967 to 1983, most at his home 9-hole course of Las Gallinas, San Rafael, California, USA. The British record is 31 by Charles T. Chevalier (1902–73) of Heaton Moor Golf Club, Stockport, Greater Manchester between 20 June 1918 and 1970.

Consecutive
There are at least 16 cases of 'aces' being achieved in two consecutive holes, of which the greatest was Norman L. Manley's unique 'double albatross' on the par-4 330 yd *301 m* seventh and par-4 290 yd *265 m* eighth holes on the Del Valle Country Club Course, Saugus, California, on 2 Sept 1964. The first woman to record consecutive 'aces' was Sue Prell, on the 13th and 14th holes at Chatswood Golf Club, Sydney, Australia on 29 May 1977.

The closest to achieving three consecutive holes in one was the late Dr Joseph Boydstone on the 3rd, 4th and 9th at Bakersfield GC, California, USA, on 10 Oct 1962 and the Rev Harold Snider (b. 4 July 1900) who aced the 8th, 13th and 14th holes of the par-3 Ironwood course, Arizona, USA on 9 June 1976.

Youngest and oldest
The youngest golfer recorded to have shot a hole-in-one was Coby Orr (5 years) of Littleton, Colorado on the 103 yd *94 m* fifth at the Riverside Golf Course, San Antonio, Texas in 1975. The oldest golfers to have performed the feat are (men): 94 yr 21 days, George William Augustin Anctil (b. 11 May 1889) on the 143 yd *131 m* 3rd at Enger Park GC, Duluth, Minnesota on 1 June 1983; (women): 86 yr 122 days, Maude Bridget Hutton (b. 7 Apr 1892) when she holed the 102 yd *93 m* 14th at Kings Inn Golf and Country Club, Sun City Center, Florida on 7 Aug 1978. The British record was set by Samuel Richard Walker (b. 6 Jan 1892) at the 156 yd *143 m* 8th at West Hove GC, Sussex at the age of 92 yr 169 days on 23 June 1984.

The oldest player to score his age is C. Arthur Thompson (1869–1975) of Victoria, British Columbia, Canada, who scored 103 on the Uplands course of 6215 yd *5682 m* aged 103 in 1973.

GREYHOUND RACING

Earliest meeting
In September 1876 a greyhound meeting was staged at Hendon, North London with a railed hare operated by a windlass. Modern greyhound racing originated with the perfecting of the mechanical hare by Owen Patrick Smith at Emeryville, California, USA, in 1919. St. Petersburg Kennel Club located in St. Petersburg, Florida, USA which opened on 3 Jan 1925, is the oldest greyhound track in the world still in operation on its original site. The earliest greyhound race behind a mechanical hare in the British Isles was at Belle Vue, Manchester, opened on 24 July 1926.

Derby
The only two greyhounds to have won the English Greyhound Derby twice (instituted 1927, now over 500 m *546 yd*) are *Mick the Miller* (whelped in Ireland, June 1926 and died 1939) on 25 July 1929, when owned by Albert H. Williams, and on 28 June 1930 (owned by Mrs Arundel H. Kempton), and *Patricia's Hope* on 24 June 1972 (when owned by Gordon and Basil Marks and Brian Stanley) and 23 June 1973 (when owned by G. & B. Marks and J. O'Connor). The highest prize was £35,000 to *Indian Joe* for the Derby on 28 June 1980. The only greyhounds to win the English, Scottish and Welsh Derby 'triple' are *Trev's Perfection*, owned by Fred Trevillion, in 1947, *Mile Bush Pride*, owned by Noel W. Purvis, in 1959, and *Patricia's Hope* in 1972. The only greyhound to win the American Derby, at Taunton, Mass., twice was *Real Huntsman* in 1950–51.

Grand National
The only greyhound to have won the Grand National (inst. 1927 over 525 yd *480 m*, now 500 m, and five flights) three times is *Sherry's Prince*, a 75 lb *32 kg* dog (whelped in April 1967, died July 1978) owned by Mrs Joyce Mathews of Sanderstead, Surrey, in 1970, 1971 and 1972.

Fastest greyhound
The highest speed at which any greyhound has been timed is 41.72 mph *67,14 km/h* (410 yd *374 m* in 20.1 sec) by *The Shoe* on the then straightaway track at Richmond, NSW, Australia on 25 Apr 1968. It is estimated that he covered the last 100 yd *91,44 m* in 4.5 sec or at 45.45 mph *73,14 km/h*. The highest speed recorded for a greyhound in Great Britain is 39.13 mph *62,97 km/h* by *Beef Cutlet*, when covering a straight course of 500 yd *457 m* in 26.13 sec at Blackpool, Lancashire, on 13 May 1933.

Fastest speeds for four-bend tracks
The fastest automatically timed speed recorded for a full 4-bend race is 38.89 mph *62,59 km/h* at Brighton, E. Sussex by *Glen Miner* on 4 May 1982 with a time of a 29.62 sec for 515 m *563 yd*. The fastest over hurdles is 37.64 mph *60.58 km/h* at Brighton by *Wotchit Buster* on 22 Aug 1978.

Most wins
The most career wins is 137 by the American greyhound, *Indy Ann*, who competed in 1955–56. The world record for consecutive victories is 31 by an American greyhound *Joe Dump* from 18 Nov 1978 to 1 June 1979. *Westpark Mustard,*

Dimitri Belozerchev became in 1983 at the age of 16 the youngest ever men's world champion at gymnastics. (*All-Sport*)

owned by Mr and Mrs Cyril Scotland, set a British record of 20 consecutive wins between 7 Jan and 28 Oct 1974.

Highest earnings

The career earnings record is held by *Marathon Hound* with over $225,000 in the USA, 1981–4. The richest first prize for a greyhound race is $100,000 won by *DD's Jackie* in the 1982 Greyhound Grand Prix at Hollywood, Florida, USA.

Longest odds

Apollo Prince won at odds of 250–1 at Sandown GRC, Springvale, Queensland, Australia on 14 Nov 1968.

GYMNASTICS

Earliest references

A primitive form of gymnastics was practised in ancient Greece and Rome during the period of the ancient Olympic Games (776 BC to AD 393) but Johann Friedrich Simon was the first teacher of modern gymnastics at Basedow's School, Dessau, Germany in 1776.

Most titles *World*

The greatest number of individual titles won by a man in the World Championships is ten by Boris Shakhlin (b. 27 Jan 1932) (USSR) between 1954 and 1964. He also won three team titles. The female record is ten individual wins and five team titles by Larissa Semyonovna Latynina (b. 27 Dec 1934) of the USSR, between 1956 and 1964. Japan has won the men's team title a record five times (1962, 1966, 1970, 1974, 1978) and the USSR the women's team title on eight occasions (1954, 1958, 1962, 1970, 1974, 1978, 1981 and 1983).

The most overall titles in Modern Rhythmic Gymnastics is three by Maria Gigova (Bulgaria) in 1969, 1971 and 1973 (shared). Galina Shugurova (USSR) (b. 1955) won eight apparatus titles from 1969–77.

Most titles *Olympic*

Japan (1960, 1964, 1968, 1972 and 1976) have won the men's team title most often. The USSR have won the women's title eight times (1952–80). The only men to win six individual gold medals are Boris Shakhlin (USSR), with one in 1956, four (two shared) in 1960 and one in 1964, and Nikolai Andrianov (USSR) (b. 14 Oct 1952), with one in 1972, four in 1976 and one in 1980.

Vera Caslavska-Odlozil (b. 3 May 1942) (Czechoslovakia), has won most individual gold medals with seven, three in 1964 and four (one shared) in 1968. Larissa Latynina won six individual gold medals and was in three winning teams in 1956–64 making nine gold medals. She also won five silver and four bronze making 18 in all—an Olympic record. The most medals for a male gymnast is 15 by Nikolai Andrianov (USSR), 7 gold, 5 silver and 3 bronze in 1972–80. Aleksander Ditiatin (USSR) (b. 7 Aug 1957) is the only man to win a medal in all eight categories in the same Games, with 3 gold, 4 silver and 1 bronze at Moscow in 1980.

Highest score *Olympics*

Nadia Comaneci (Romania) (b. 12 Nov 1961) was the first to achieve a perfect score, with seven of 10.00 at the Montreal Olympics in July 1976.

Youngest International and World Champion

Pasakevi 'Voula' Kouna (b. 6 Dec 1971) was aged 9 yr 299 days at the start of the Balkan Games at Serres, Greece on 1–4 Oct 1981, when she represented Greece. Olga Bicherova (USSR) (b. 26 Oct 1966) won the women's world title at 15 yr 33 days on 28 Nov 1981. The youngest male world champion was Dmitri Belozerchev (USSR) (b. 17 Dec 1966) at 16 years 315 days at Budapest, Hungary on 28 Oct 1983.

Most titles *British*

The British Gymnastic Championship was won ten times by Arthur John Whitford (b. 2 July 1908) in 1928–36 and 1939. He was also in four winning teams. Wray 'Nik' Stuart (b. 20 July 1927) equalled the record of nine successive wins, 1956–64. The women's record is eight by Mary Patricia Hirst (b. 18 Nov 1918) (1947, 1949–50 and 1952–6). The most overall titles in Modern Rhythmic Gymnastics is by Sharon Taylor with five successive 1977–81.

Most titles *World Cup*

In the first World Cup Competition, in London in 1975, Ludmilla Tourischeva (now Mrs Valeriy Borzov) (b. 7 Oct 1952) (USSR) won all five gold medals available.

Somersaults

Ashrita Furman performed 6,773 forward rolls over 10 miles *16,09 km* in Central Park, New York, USA on 19 Nov 1980. Corporal Wayne Wright of the Royal Engineers made a successful dive and tucked somersault over 37 men at Old Park

Barracks, Dover, Kent on 30 July 1980. Shigeru Iwasaki (b. 1960) backwards somersaulted over 50 m *54.68 yd* in 10.8 sec at Tokyo, Japan on 30 Mar 1980.

Largest gymnasium

The world's largest gymnasium is Yale University's nine-storey, Payne Whitney Gymnasium at New Haven, Connecticut, USA, completed in 1932 and valued at $18,000,000 £10,285,000.

CONSECUTIVE GYMNASTIC FEATS

Athletes are permitted to perform these endeavours in sets, but must remain in position throughout the activity.

Chins (from dead hang position) 170 Lee Chin Yong (b. 15 Aug 1925) at Backyon Gymnasium, Seoul, Korea on 10 May 1983.

Chins—One-arm (from a ring) 22 Robert Chisholm (b. 9 Dec 1952) at Queen's University, Kingston, Ontario, Canada on 3 Dec 1982. (Also 18 two-finger chins, 12 one-finger chins).

Parallel bar dips 718 Roger Perez (b. 11 July 1962) in 30 min 40 sec at Cosumnes River College, Sacramento, California, USA on 14 Dec 1983.

Press-ups (push-ups) 10,029 Colin Hewick at the South Holderness Sports Centre, Humberside on 18 July 1982.

Push-ups (One arm) 2754 Paul Lynch at Bedford Hotel, London on 15 July 1984.

Push-ups (Finger tip) 1753 Paul Lynch at Streatham London 19 July 1984.

Push-ups (One finger) 45 Mick Gooch at Crystal Palace, London on 26 May 1984.

Hand-stand push-ups 500 Danny Castoldi at the University of Southern California, Los Angeles, USA on 9 July 1983.

Leg raises 21,598 Louis Scripa Jr. in 6 hours at Fairfield, Cal., USA on 8 Dec 1983.

Jumping Jacks 40,014 August Hoffman Jr. at Van Nuys, Cal., USA on 4 Dec 1982.

HANDBALL

Origins

Handball, similar to association football, with hands substituted for feet, was first played *c.* 1895. It was introduced into the Olympic Games at Berlin in 1936 as an 11-a-side outdoor game with Germany winning, but when re-introduced in 1972 it was an indoor game with seven-a-side, the standard size of team since 1952.

By 1982 there were 80 countries affiliated to the International Handball Federation (founded 1946), and an estimated ten million participants. The earliest international match was when Sweden beat Denmark on 8 Mar 1935.

World and Olympic Champions

The most victories in Olympic competition have been those by the USSR in winning the men's and women's titles at Montreal, Canada in 1976, and the women's title at Moscow in 1980. The most victories won in World championship (inst. 1938) competition are by Romania with four men's and three women's titles from 1956 to 1974. The Super Cup is contested by men's Olympic and World Champions. First held in 1979, West Germany and the USSR have each won once.

Highest score

The highest score in an international match was recorded when the USSR beat Afghanistan 86–2 in the 'Friendly Army Tournament' at Miskolc, Hungary in August 1981.

HANDBALL (Court)

Origins

Handball played against walls or in a court is a game of ancient Celtic origin. In the early 19th century only a front wall was used but gradually side and back walls were added. The earliest international contest was in New York City, USA, in 1887 between the champions of the USA and Ireland. The court is now a standardised 60 ft *18 m* by 30 ft *9 m* in Ireland, Ghana and Australia, and 40 ft *12 m* by 20 ft *6 m* in Canada, Mexico and the USA. The game is played with both a hard and soft ball in Ireland and soft ball only in Australia, Canada, Ghana, Mexico and the USA.

Championship

World championships were inaugurated in New York in October 1964 with competitors from Australia, Canada,

Ireland, Mexico and the USA. The most wins have been two by the USA in 1964 and 1967 (shared with Canada).

Most titles

The US Championship 4-wall singles has been won six times by Jimmy Jacobs (b. 1931) in 1955–7, 1960, 1964–5. He also shared in six doubles titles, 1962–3, 1965, 1967–8, 1975. Fred Lewis also won six singles titles, 1972, 1974–6, 1978, 1981.

HARNESS RACING

Origins

Trotting races were held in Valkenburg, Netherlands in 1554. In England the trotting gait (the simultaneous use of the diagonally opposite legs) was known in the 16th century. The sulky first appeared in harness racing in 1829. Pacers thrust out their fore and hind legs simultaneously on one side.

Most successful driver

The most successful sulky driver in North American harness racing history has been Herve Filion (b. 1 Feb 1940) of Quebec, Canada with a record 8731 wins and $42.1 million in purse money to the end of the 1983 season. He won his twelfth North American championship in 1982. The most wins in a year is 637 by Herve Filion in 1974. The greatest earnings in a year is $6,104,082 by John Campbell in 1983.

Highest price

The highest price paid for a trotter is $5.25 million for *Mystic Park* by Lana Lobell Farms from Gerald & Irving Wechter of New York and Robert Lester of Florida, announced on 13 July 1982. The highest price ever paid for a pacer is $8.25 million for *Merger* by Finder/Guida of New York from John Campbell, David Morrissey and Peter Oud of Canada in 1982.

Greatest winnings

The greatest amount won by a trotting horse is $3,041,262 by *Ideal du Gazeau* (France) to July 1983. The record for a harness horse is $2,041,367 by *Cam Fella*, who also had 26 consecutive victories, 19 May–26 Nov 1983. *Niatross* (USA) won $2,019,213 in just two years 1979–80, including a season's record $1,414,313 in 1980.

The largest ever purse was £2,011,000 for the Woodrow Wilson Two-year-old race at Meadowlands, New Jersey on 6 Aug 1980, of which a record $1,005,000 went to the winner *Land Grant*, driven by Del Insko.

HARNESS RACING RECORDS AGAINST TIME

TROTTING

World (mile track)	1:54.0	*Arndon* (driver, Delvin Miller) (US) at Lexington, Kentucky, USA	6 Oct 1982
World race record (mile)	1:54.8	*Lindy's Crown* (driver, Howard Beissinger) (US) at Du Quoin, Illinois	30 Aug 1960
British record (mile)	2:06.8	*Ted Trot* (driver, John Blisset) at Chasewater, West Midlands	21 June 1975

PACING

World (mile track)	1:49.2	*Niatross* (driver, Clint Galbraith) (US) at Lexington, Kentucky, USA	1 Oct 1980
World race record (mile)	1:51.6	*Trenton* (driver, Tom Haughton) (US) at Springfield, Illinois, USA	21 Aug 1982
British record (mile)	2:02.1	*Lydia M* (driver, James Pickard) at York	10 July 1982

HOCKEY

Origins

A representation of two players with curved snagging sticks apparently in an orthodox 'bully' position was found in Tomb No. 17 at Beni Hasan, Egypt and has been dated to *c.* 2050 BC. There is a British reference to the game in Lincolnshire in 1277. The English Hockey Association was founded at Cannon Street Hotel, City of London on 16 Apr 1875. The Fédération Internationale de Hockey was formed on 7 Jan 1924.

The first organised club was the Blackheath Rugby and Hockey Club founded in 1861. The oldest club with a continuous history is Teddington HC formed in the autumn of 1871. They played Richmond on 24 Oct 1874 and used the first recorded circle *versus* Surbiton at Bushey Park on 9 Dec 1876. The first international match was the Wales *v.* Ireland match at Rhyl on 26 Jan 1895. Ireland won 3–0.

Most Olympic medals

The Indians were Olympic Champions from the re-inception of Olympic hockey in 1928 until 1960, when Pakistan beat them 1–0 at Rome. They had their eighth win in 1980. Of the seven Indians who have won three Olympic team gold medals two have also won a silver medal—Leslie Walter Claudius (b. 25 Mar 1927) in 1948, 1952, 1956 and 1960 (silver) and Udham Singh (b. 4 Aug 1928) in 1952, 1956, 1964 and 1960 (silver). A women's tournament was added to the Olympic Games in 1980, when the winners were Zimbabwe.

World Cup

Pakistan have won most men's World Cups (inst. 1971) with three, 1971, 1978 and 1982. The Netherlands have won most women's World Cups (inst. 1974) with three, 1974, 1978 and 1983.

MEN

Highest international score

The highest score in international hockey was when India defeated the United States 24–1 at Los Angeles, California, USA, in the 1932 Olympic Games. The greatest number of goals in a home international match was when England defeated France 16–0 at Beckenham on 25 Mar 1922.

Most international appearances

Avtar Singh Sohal (b. 22 Mar 1938) represented Kenya 167 times between 1957 and 1972. The most by a home countries player is 139 by H. David Judge (b. 19 Jan 1936) with 124 for Ireland and 15 for Great Britain from 1957 to 1978.

IRELAND	124	H. David Judge	1957–78
WALES	100	David Austin Savage (b. 15 Dec 1940)	1962–81
SCOTLAND	85	Christopher Sutherland (b. 6 Dec 1949)	1969–83
ENGLAND	81	Norman Hughes (b. 30 Sept 1952)	1977–84
GREAT BRITAIN	56	John W. Neill (England) (b. 15 May 1934)	1959–68

Greatest scoring feats

The greatest number of goals scored in international hockey is 150 by Paul Litjens (Netherlands) (b. 9 Nov 1947) in 112 games to April 1979. M. C. Marckx (Bowden 2nd XI) scored 19 goals against Brooklands 2nd XI (score 23–0) on 31 Dec 1910. He was selected for England in March 1912 but declined due to business priorities. Between 1923 and 1958, Fred H. Wagner scored 1832 goals for Beeston HC, Nottingham Casuals and the Nottinghamshire county side. David Ashman has scored 1373 goals for one club, Hamble Old Boys, Southampton, from 1958 to 1984.

The fastest goal in an international was in 7 sec by John French for England v. West Germany at Nottingham, on 25 Apr 1971.

Greatest goalkeeping

Richard James Allen (b. 4 June 1902) (India) did not concede a goal during the 1928 Olympic Tournament and only a total of three in the following two Olympics of 1932 and 1936. In these three Games India scored a total of 102 goals.

Longest game

The longest international game on record was one of 145 min (into the sixth period of extra time), when Netherlands beat Spain 1–0 in the Olympic tournament at Mexico City on 25 Oct 1968. Club matches of 205 min have twice been recorded: The Hong Kong Football Club beat Prison Sports Dept as the first to score in 'sudden death' play-off after 2–2 at full time on 11 Mar 1979 and Gore Court beat Hampstead in the first round of the English Club Championships in 1983.

WOMEN

Origins

The earliest women's club was East Molesey in Surrey, England formed in c. 1887. The Wimbledon Ladies Hockey Club, founded one year later, is still in existence. The first national association was the Irish Ladies' Hockey Union founded in 1894. The All England Women's Hockey Association held its first formal meeting in Westminster Town Hall, London, on 23 Nov 1895. The first international match was an England v. Ireland game in Dublin in 1896. Ireland won 2–0.

Highest scores

The highest score in a women's international match was when England beat France 23–0 at Merton, Greater London, on 3

Norman Hughes passed Roland Brookeman's record number of English hockey caps during the 1983–4 season.

Feb 1923. In club hockey, Ross Ladies beat Wyeside, at Ross-on-Wye, Herefordshire, 40–0 on 24 Jan 1929, when Edna Mary Blakelock (b. 22 Oct 1904) scored a record 21 goals.

Most international appearances

WALES	138	Ann Ellis (b. 21 Sept 1940)	1963–80
ENGLAND	142	Valerie Robinson	1963–84
SCOTLAND	73	Marietta Craigie (b. 9 Apr 1950)	1970–83
IRELAND	60	Marie Bartlett (b. 7 Aug 1945)	1969–82

Highest attendance

The highest attendance at a women's hockey match was 65,165 for the match between England and the USA at Wembley, London, on 11 Mar 1978.

HORSE RACING

Origins

Horsemanship was an important part of the Hittite culture of Anatolia, Turkey dating from 1400 BC. The 33rd ancient Olympic Games of 648 BC in Greece featured horse racing. The earliest races recorded in England were those held in about AD 200 at Netherby, Cumbria, between Arab horses imported by the Romans.

Racecourse *Largest*

The world's largest racecourse is at Newmarket. It now comprises the Rowley Mile Course and the July Course, whose grandstands are about a mile apart, although a portion of the course is common to both. The Beacon Course of 4 miles 397 yd *6,80 km*, is no longer in use. The course is situated in the middle of Newmarket Heath, c 2500 acres, the largest training area in the world.

Largest prizes

The richest race ever held is the All-American Futurity, a race for quarter-horses over 440 yd *402 m* at Ruidoso Downs, New Mexico, USA. The prizes in 1982 totalled $2 million, the winner *Mr Master Bug* taking $1 million. The richest first prize for any thoroughbred race was $600,000 for the Arlington Million, Chicago, USA, in 1981, 1982 and 1983.

Most runners

The most horses in a race is 66 in the Grand National on 22 Mar 1929. The record for the Flat is 58 in the Lincolnshire Handicap at Lincoln on 13 Mar 1948. The most runners at a meeting were 214 (Flat) in seven races at Newmarket on 15 June 1915 and 229 (National Hunt) in eight races at Worcester on 13 Jan 1965.

Dead-heats

There is no recorded case in turf history of a quintuple dead-heat. The nearest approach was in the Astley Stakes, at Lewes, Sussex, on 6 Aug 1880 when *Mazurka*, *Wandering Nun* and *Scobell* triple dead-heated for first place a head in front of *Cumberland* and *Thora*, who dead-heated for fourth place. Each of the five jockeys thought he had won. The only three known examples of a quadruple dead-heat were between *Honest Harry*, *Miss Decoy*, *Young Daffodil* and *Peteria* at Bogside, on 7 June 1808, between *Defaulter*, *The Squire of Malton*, *Reindeer* and *Pulcherrima* in the Omnibus Stakes at The Hoo, Hertfordshire, on 26 Apr 1851, and between *Overreach*, *Lady Golightly*, *Gamester* and *The Unexpected* at Newmarket on 22 Oct 1855. Since the introduction of the photo-finish, the highest number of horses dead-heating has been three, on several occasions.

Horse *Most successful*

The horse with the best win-loss record was *Kincsem*, a Hungarian mare foaled in 1874, who was unbeaten in 54 races (1876–9), including the Goodwood Cup of 1878. *Camarero*, foaled in 1951, won his first 56 races in Puerto Rico from 19 Apr 1953 to 17 Aug 1955. (In his career to 1956 he won 73 of 77 races). The most wins in a career is 137 from 159 starts by *Galgo Jr* in Puerto Rico between 1930 and 1936.

Triple Crown Winners

The English Triple Crown (2000 Guineas, Derby, St Leger) has been won 15 times, most recently by *Nijinsky* in 1970. The American Triple Crown (Kentucky Derby, Preakness Stakes, Belmont Stakes) has been achieved 11 times, most recently by *Affirmed* in 1978.

Horse *Highest price*

The most expensive horse ever is *Shareef Dancer* syndicated for $40 million in August 1983 by his owner Sheikh Maktoum al Maktoum. 40 shares were issued at $1 million each. The most paid for a yearling is $10.2 m for *Snaafi Dancer* on 20 July 1983 at Keeneland, Kentucky, by Sheikh Mohammed al Maktoum.

Horse *Greatest winnings*

The career earnings record is $4,652,997 by the gelding *John Henry* (foaled 1975) with 34 wins from 75 races, from 1977 to 28 May 1984. The leading money-winning mare is *Trinycarol* with $2,644,516 from 18 wins in 26 races in 1981–3 in Venezuela and the USA. The most won in a year is $2,126,380 by the 4-year-old *All Along* in France and the USA in 1983.

Horses *Heaviest burden*

The biggest weight ever carried is 30 stone *190 kg* by both Mr Maynard's mare and Mr Baker's horse in a match won by the former over a mile at York on 21 May 1788.

Jockey *Wins on one card*

The most winners ridden on one card is eight by Hubert S. Jones, 17, from 13 rides at Caliente, Cal., USA on 11 June 1944, by Oscar Barattuci, at Rosario City, Argentina, on 15 Dec 1957 and by Dave Gall, from ten rides at Cahokia Downs, East St Louis, Illinois, USA on 18 Oct 1978. The longest winning streak is 12 by Sir Gordon Richards (b. 5 May 1904) (one race at Nottingham on 3 Oct, six out of six at Chepstow on 4 Oct and the first five races next day at Chepstow) in 1933.

Jockey *Youngest and oldest*

The youngest jockey was Australian-born Frank Wootton (1893–1940) (English champion jockey 1909–12), who rode his first winner in South Africa aged 9 years 10 months. The oldest jockey was Harry Beasley, who rode his last race at Baldoyle, Co. Dublin, Ireland on 10 June 1935 aged 83.

Jockey *Lightest*

The lightest recorded jockey was Kitchener (d. 1872), who

All Along is driven home by Walter Swinburn to win the 1983 Prix de l'Arc de Triomphe and earn the greatest prize money in a year. (*All-Sport*)

won the Tradesmen's Plate (Chester Cup) on *Red Deer* in 1844 at 3 st 7 lb *22 kg*. He was said to have weighed only 2 st 7 lb *16 kg* in 1840.

Jockey *Most successful*
The most successful jockey of all time has been William Lee 'Bill' Shoemaker (USA) (b. weighing 2½ lb *1,1 kg*, 19 Aug 1931) now weighing 94 lb *43 kg* and standing 4 ft 11 in *1,50 m*. From March 1949 to the end of 1983 he has ridden 8319 winners from 36,593 mounts earning $94,782,006.

The greatest amount ever won by any jockey in a year is $10,116,697 by Angel Cordero in the USA in 1983. The most winners ridden in a year is 546, from a record 2199 mounts, by Chris McCarron (USA) (b. 1955) in 1974.

Trainers
Jack Van Berg (USA) has the greatest number of wins in a year, 494 in 1976, and in a career, over 4200 to 1984. The greatest amount won in a year is $4,588,897 by Charley Whittingham (USA) in 1982.

Owners
The most winners in a year by an owner is 494 by Dan R. Lasater (USA) in 1974 when he also won a record $3,022,960 in prize money.

BRITISH TURF RECORDS

Horses *Most successful*
Eclipse (foaled 1764) still has the longest winning sequence, being unbeaten in a career of 18 races between May 1769 and October 1770. As the 1000 Guineas and the Oaks are restricted to fillies, only they can possibly win all five Classics. *Sceptre* came closest in 1902 when she won the 2000 Guineas, 1000 Guineas, Oaks and St Leger. In 1868 *Formosa* won the same four but dead-heated in the 2000 Guineas. The most races won in a season is 23 by three-year-old *Fisherman* in 1856. *Catherina* (foaled 1830) won a career record 79 out of 176 races, 1832–41. The only horse to win the same race in seven successive years was *Doctor Syntax* (foaled 1811) in the Preston Gold Cup (1815–21). The most successful sire was *Stockwell* (foaled 1849) whose progeny won 1153 races (1858–76) and in 1866 set a record of 132 races won. The biggest winning margin in a Classic is 20 lengths by Mayonaise in the 1000 Guineas in 1859. The greatest amount ever won by an English-trained horse is £515,352 by the mare *Time Charter* (foaled 1979) from 1981 to 7 July 1984.

Horses *Oldest winners*
The oldest horses to win on the Flat have been the 18-year-olds *Revenge* at Shrewsbury in September 1790 and *Marksman* at Ashford, Kent in September 1826. At the same age *Wild Aster* won three hurdle races in six days in March 1919 and *Sonny Somers* won two steeplechases in February 1980.

(above) Birthday Girl is led in by her owner Dr M. A. M. Ramaswamy, who has owned a record 109 'classic' winners in India from 1965 to January 1984. Accompanying him are Dr K. T. B. Menon and Aris David who trained 94 of these winners. The jockey is John Lowe.
(left) Bill Shoemaker passed Johnny Longden's career winners record of 6032 in 1970. The 4 ft 11 in tall jockey has now ridden well over 8000 winners. *(All-Sport)*

Jockeys *Most successful*
Sir Gordon Richards won 4870 races from 21,834 mounts from his first mount at Lingfield on 16 Oct 1920 to his last at Sandown on 10 July 1954. His first win was on 31 Mar 1921. In 1953, at his 28th and final attempt, he won the Derby, six days after his knighthood. In 1947 he won a record 269 races. He was champion jockey a record 26 times between 1925 and 1953. The most Classic races won by a jockey is 27 (possibly 29) by Frank Buckle (1766–1832), between 1792 and 1827. Lester Piggott (b. 5 Nov 1935) equalled this record with his 27th Classic win, on *Circus Plume* in the Oaks on 9 June 1984. His first was on *Never Say Die*, in the 1954 Derby.

WORLD SPEED RECORDS

Distance	Time min sec	mph	km/h	Name	Age	Weight carried lb	kg	Course	Date	
¼ mile	20.8	43.26	69,62	*Big Racket* (Mexico)	4	114	51,7	Mexico City, Mexico	5 Feb	1945
½ mile	44.4	40.54	65,24	*Sonido* (Venezuela)	2	111	50,3	‡Caracas, Venezuela	28 June	1970
				Western Romance (Canada)	3	116	52,6	Stampede Park, Calgary, Alberta, Canada	19 April	1980
				Northern Spike (Canada)	5	119	54,0	Winnipeg, Canada	23 Apr	1982
⅝ mile	53.6†	41.98	67,56	*Indigenous* (GB)	4	131	59,4	‡*Epsom, Surrey	2 June	1960
	53.70††	41.90	67,43	*Spark Chief* (GB)	4	110	49,8	‡*Epsom, Surrey	30 Aug	1983
	55.2	40.76	65,60	*Chinook Pass* (USA)	3	113	51,1	Longacres, Seattle, Washington, USA	17 Sept	1982
¾ mile	1:06.2	40.78	65,62	*Gelding by Blink—Broken Tendril* (GB)	2	123	55,7	*Brighton, East Sussex	6 Aug	1929
	1:07.2	40.18	64,66	*Grey Papa* (USA)	6	112	59,8	Longacres, Seattle, Washington, USA	4 Sept	1972
				Petro D. Jay (USA)	6	120	54,4	Turf Paradise, Phoenix, Arizona, USA	9 May	1982
1 mile	1:31.8	39.21	63,10	*Soueida* (GB)	4	126	57,1	*Brighton, East Sussex	19 Sept	1963
				Loose Cover (GB)	3	110	49,8	*Brighton, East Sussex	9 June	1966
	1:32.2	39.04	62,82	*Dr Fager* (USA)	4	134	60,7	Arlington, Illinois, USA	24 Aug	1968
1¼ miles	1:57.4	38.33	61,68	*Double Discount* (USA)	4	116	52,6	Santa Anita, Arcadia, California, USA	6 Oct	1977
1½ miles	2:23.0	37.76	60,76	*Fiddle Isle* (USA)	5	124	56,2	Santa Anita, Arcadia, California, USA	21 Mar	1970
				John Henry (USA)	5	126	57,1	Santa Anita, Arcadia, California, USA	16 Mar	1980
2 miles	3:15.0	36.93	59,43	*Polazel* (GB)	3	142	64,4	Salisbury, Wiltshire	8 July	1924
2½ miles	4:14.6	35.35	56,90	*Miss Grillo* (USA)	6	118	53,5	Pimlico, Baltimore, Maryland, USA	12 Nov	1948
3 miles	5:15.0	34.29	55.18	*Farragut* (Mexico)	5	113	51.2	Agua Caliente. Mexico	9 Mar	1941

* Epsom and Brighton courses include a sharp descent of ¼ mile.
** A more reliable modern record is 3 min 16.75 sec by Il Tempo (NZ) (7 yr, 130 lb) at Trentham, Wellington, New Zealand on 17 Jan 1970.
† Hand timed.   †† Electronically timed.   ‡ Straight courses.

MAJOR RACE RECORDS

RACE	RECORD TIME / Jockey	MOST WINS			LARGEST FIELD
		Trainer	Owner		

FLAT

RACE	RECORD TIME / Jockey	Jockey (Most Wins)	Trainer	Owner	LARGEST FIELD
Derby (1780) 1½ miles *2414 m* Epsom	2 min 33.8 sec *Mahmoud* 1936	9—Lester Piggott 1954, 57, 60, 68, 70, 72, 76, 77, 83	7—Robert Robson 1793, 1802, 09, 10, 15, 17, 23 7—John Porter 1868, 82, 83, 86, 90, 91, 99 7—Fred Darling 1922, 25, 26, 31, 38, 40, 41	5—3rd Earl of Egremont 1782, 1804, 05, 07, 26 5—H. H. Aga Khan III 1930, 35, 36, 48, 52	34 (1862)
1000 Guineas (1814) 1 mile *1609 m* Newmarket	1 min 37 sec *Camarée* 1950	7—George Fordham 1859, 61, 65, 68, 69, 81, 83	8—Robert Robson 1819, 20, 21, 22, 23, 25, 26, 27	8—4th Duke of Grafton 1819, 20, 21, 22, 23, 25, 26, 27	29 (1926)
2000 Guineas (1809) 1 mile *1609 m* Newmarket	1 min 35.8 sec *My Babu* 1948	9—Jem Robinson 1825, 28, 31, 33, 34, 35, 36, 47, 48	5—Fred Darling 1925, 31, 38, 42, 47	5—4th Duke of Grafton 1820, 21, 22, 26, 27 5—5th Earl of Jersey 1831, 34, 35, 36, 37	28 (1930)
Oaks (1779) 1½ miles *2414 m* Epsom	2 min 34.21 sec *Time Charter* 1982	9—Frank Buckle 1797, 98, 99, 1802, 03, 05, 17, 18, 23	8—Alec Taylor 1910, 17, 18, 19, 21, 22, 25, 26	6—4th Duke of Grafton 1813, 15, 22, 23, 28, 31	26 (1848)
St Leger (1776) 1 m 6 f 127 yd *2932 m* Doncaster	3 min 01.6 sec *Coronach* 1926 *Windsor Lad* 1934	9—Bill Scott 1821, 25, 28, 29, 38, 39, 40, 41, 46	16—John Scott 1827, 28, 29, 32, 34, 38, 39, 40, 41, 45, 51, 53, 56, 57, 59, 62	7—9th Duke of Hamilton 1786, 87, 88, 92, 1808, 09, 14	30 (1825)
King George VI and Queen Elizabeth Stakes (1951) 1½ miles *2414 m* Ascot	2 min 26.98 sec *Grundy* 1975	6—Lester Piggott 1965, 66, 69, 70, 74, 77	3—Vincent O'Brien 1958, 70, 77 3—Noel Murless 1966, 67, 68 3—Dick Hern 1972, 79, 80	2—Nelson Bunker Hunt 1973, 74	19 (1951)
Prix de l'Arc de Triomphe (1920) 2400 metres *1 mile 864 yd* Longchamp, France	2 min 28 sec *Detroit* 1980	4—Jacques Doyasbère 1942, 44, 50, 51 4—Frédéric 'Freddie' Head 1966, 72, 76, 79	4—Charles Semblat 1942, 44, 46, 49 4—Francois Mathet 1950, 51, 70, 82 4—Alec Head 1952, 59, 76, 81	6—Marcel Boussac 1936, 37, 42, 44, 46, 49	30 (1967)
VRC Melbourne Cup (1861) 3200 metres *1 mile 1739 yd* Flemington, Victoria, Australia	3 min 19.1 sec *Rain Lover* 1968	4—Bobby Lewis 1902, 15, 19, 27 4—Harry White 1974, 75, 78, 79	7—Bart Cummings 1965, 66, 67, 74, 75, 77, 79	4—Etienne de Mestre 1861, 62, 67, 78	39 (1890)
Kentucky Derby (1875) 1¼ miles *2012 m* Churchill Downs, USA	1 min 59.4 sec *Secretariat* 1973	5—Eddie Arcaro 1938, 41, 45, 48, 52 5—Bill Hartack 1957, 60, 62, 64, 69	6—Ben Jones 1938, 41, 44, 48, 49, 52	8—Calumet Farm 1941, 44, 48, 49, 52, 57, 58, 68	23 (1974)
Irish Sweeps Derby (1866) 1½ miles *2414 m* The Curragh	2 min 28.8 sec *Tambourine* 1962	6—Morny Wing 1921, 23, 30, 38, 42, 46	4—James Dunne 1883, 85, 1905, 08 4—Michael Dawson 1902, 04, 06, 09 4—Frank Butters 1932, 40, 48, 49 4—Paddy Prendergast 1950, 52, 63, 65 4—Vincent O'Brien 1953, 57, 70, 77	5—H. H. Aga Khan III 1925, 32, 40, 48, 49	24 (1962)

NATIONAL HUNT

RACE	RECORD TIME / Jockey	Jockey (Most Wins)	Trainer	Owner	LARGEST FIELD
Grand National (1839) 4½ miles *7242 m* Liverpool	9 min 01.9 sec *Red Rum* 1973	5—George Stevens 1856, 63, 64, 69, 70	4—Aubrey Hastings 1906, 15, 17 (at Gatwick), 24 4—Fred Rimell 1956, 61, 70, 76	3—Capt James Machell 1873, 74, 76 3—Sir Charles Assheton-Smith 1893, 1912, 13 3—Noel Le Mare 1973, 74, 77	66 (1929)
Cheltenham Gold Cup (1924) 3¼ miles *5230 m* Cheltenham	—(1)	4—Pat Taaffe 1964, 65, 66, 68	5—Tom Dreaper 1946, 64, 65, 66, 68	7—Dorothy Paget 1932, 33, 34, 35, 36, 40, 52	22 (1982)
Champion Hurdle (1927) 2 miles *3218 m* Cheltenham	—(1)	4—Tim Molony 1951, 52, 53, 54	5—Peter Easterby 1967, 76, 77, 80, 81	4—Dorothy Paget 1932, 33, 40, 46	24 (1964)

(1) *It would be unrealistic to include time records for these two races because they have been run over a variety of distances and, although always held at Cheltenham, several different courses have been used.*

Trainers *Most successful*

The record first-prize money earned in a season is £872,614 by Henry Cecil in 1982. The most Classics won by a trainer is 41 by John Scott (1794–1871) of Malton, Yorkshire between 1827 and 1863. Alex Taylor of Manton, Wiltshire headed the trainers' list for a record 12 seasons between 1907 and 1925. In 1867 John Day of Danebury, Hampshire won 146 races.

Owners *Most successful*

H H Aga Khan III (1877–1957) was leading owner a record 13 times between 1924 and 1952. The record first-prize money won in a season is £461,488 by Robert Edmund Sangster (b. 23 May 1936) in 1983. The most wins in a season is 115 by David Robinson in 1973. The most English Classics won is 20 by the 4th Duke of Grafton (1760–1844) between 1813 and 1831.

THE DERBY

The greatest of England's five Classics is the Derby Stakes, inaugurated on 4 May 1780, and named after the 12th Earl of Derby (1752–1834). The distance was increased in 1784 from a mile to 1½ miles *2414 km*. The race has been run at Epsom Downs, Surrey, except for the two war periods, when it was run at Newmarket, and is for three-year-olds only. Since 1884 the weights have been: colts 9 st *57 kg*, fillies 8 st 9 lb *55 kg*. Geldings were eligible until 1904.

Largest and smallest winning margins

Shergar, ridden by Walter R. Swinburn, won the Derby by a record ten lengths in 1981. There have been two dead-heats: in 1828 when *Cadland* beat *The Colonel* in the run-off, and in 1884 between *St Gatien* and *Harvester* (stakes divided).

John Francome, the record winning National Hunt jockey with Jenny Pitman, the first woman to train winners of both the Grand National (*Corbière* in 1983) and the Cheltenham Gold Cup (*Burrough Hill Lad* in 1984). (*All-Sport*)

Longest and shortest odds

Three winners have been returned at odds of 100–1: *Jeddah* (1898), *Signorinetta* (1908) and *Aboyeur* (1913). The shortest priced winner was *Ladas* (1894) at 2–9 and the hottest losing favourite was *Surefoot*, fourth at 40–95 in 1890.

Largest prize

The richest prize on the British Turf was £227,680 in the 205th Derby on 6 June 1984, won by Luigi Miglitti's *Secreto*.

NATIONAL HUNT

For more details see The Guinness Guide to Steeplechasing *by Gerry Cranham, Richard Pitman and John Oaksey, published by Guinness Superlatives Ltd. (price £11.95).*

Horse *Greatest winnings*

The greatest amount earned by a British-trained jumper is £196,053 by the 1982 Cheltenham Gold Cup winner *Silver Buck* (foaled 1972) from 1977 to 1984.

Horses *Most successful*

Triple champion hurdler *Sir Ken* (foaled 1947) won a record 16 hurdle races in succession, April 1951 to March 1953. *Dudley* (foaled 1914) also won 16 races in succession under NH Rules, Jan–Nov 1925.

Jockeys *Most successful*

The first National Hunt jockey to reach 1000 wins was Stan Mellor, b. 10 Apr 1937) on *Ouzo* at Nottingham on 18 Dec 1971. He retired on 18 June 1972 after 1049 wins (incl. 14 abroad) in 20 years. He also won three flat races. His UK total of 1035 was passed by John Francome (b. 13 Dec 1952) at Fontwell on 28 May 1984. His first winner had been in December 1970, and he ended the 1983–4 season on 1037 (from 4698 mounts).

The record number of wins in a season in 149 by John 'Jonjo' O'Neill (b. 13 Apr 1952) in 1977–8. The record number of successive wins is ten by John Alnam 'Johnny' Gilbert (b. 26 July 1920), 8–30 Sept 1959. The record number of National Hunt championships is seven by Gerald Wilson (1903–68) from 1933 to 1938 and 1941.

Trainers *Most successful*

The most first-prize money earned in a season is £358,837 from a record 120 winners by Michael Dickinson in 1982–3. He also achieved the unique feat in a championship race of training the first five horses in the 1983 Cheltenham Gold Cup, and on 27 Dec 1982 he trained 12 winners (from 21 runners) at six meetings. Fred Winter won a record seven trainers' championships between 1971 and 1978.

GRAND NATIONAL

The first Grand National Steeplechase may be regarded as the Grand Liverpool Steeplechase of 26 Feb 1839 though the race was not given its present name until 1847. It became a handicap in 1843. Until 1930 five-year-olds were eligible, but since then is has been for six-year-olds and above. Except for the two war periods (1916–18 and 1941–5) the race has been run at Aintree, near Liverpool, over a course of 30 jumps.

Most wins

The only horse to win three times is *Red Rum* (foaled 1965) in 1973, 1974 and 1977 from five runs. He came second in 1975 and 1976. *Manifesto* ran a record eight times (1895–1904). He won twice, came third three times and fourth once.

Highest prize

The highest prize and the richest ever over jumps in Great Britain was £54,769 won by *Hallo Dandy*, ridden by Neale Doughty and trained by Gordon W. Richards on 31 Mar 1984.

Highest weight

The highest weight ever carried to victory is 12 st 7 lb *79,4 kg* by *Cloister* (1893), *Manifesto* (1899), *Jerry M* (1912) and *Poethlyn* (1919).

HURLING

Earliest reference

A game of very ancient origin, hurling was included in the Tailteann Games (inst 1829 BC). It only became standardised with the formation of the Gaelic Athletic Association in Thurles, Ireland, on 1 Nov 1884. The Irish Hurling Union was formed on 24 Jan 1879.

Most titles *All-Ireland*

The greatest number of All-Ireland Championships won by one team is 24 by Cork between 1890 and 1978. The greatest number of successive wins is four by Cork (1941–4).

Most titles *Inter-provincials*

Munster holds the greatest number of inter-provincial (Railway Cup) championships with 34 (1928–77).

Most appearances

The most appearances in All-Ireland finals is ten shared by Christy Ring (Cork and Munster) and John Doyle (Tipperary). They also share the record of All-Ireland medals won with eight each. Ring's appearances on the winning side were in 1941–4, 1946 and 1952–4, while Doyle's were in 1949–51, 1958, 1961–2 and 1964–5. Ring also played in a record 22 inter-provincial finals (1942–63) and was on the winning side 18 times.

Highest and lowest scores

The highest score in an All-Ireland final (60 min) was in 1896 when Tipperary (8 goals, 14 points) beat Dublin (no goals, 4 points). The record aggregate score was when Cork (6 goals, 21 points, defeated Wexford (5 goals, 10 points) in the 80 min final of 1970. A goal equals three points. The highest recorded individual score was by Nick Rackard (Wexford), who scored 7 goals and 7 points against Antrim in the 1954 All-Ireland semi-final. The lowest score in an All-Ireland final was when Tipperary (1 goal, 1 point) beat Galway (nil) in the first championship at Birr in 1887.

Longest stroke

The greatest distance for a 'lift and stroke' is one of 129 yd *117 m* credited to Tom Murphy of Three Castles, Kilkenny, in a 'long puck' contest in 1906. The record for the annual *An Poc Fada* (Long Puck) contest (instituted 1961) in the ravines of the Cooley Hills, north of Dundalk, County Louth, is 65 pucks (drives) plus 87 yd *79 m* over the course of 3 miles 320 yd *5120 km* by Fionnbar O'Neill (Cork) in 1966. This represents an average of 84.8 yd *77,5 m* per drive.

Largest crowd

The largest crowd was 84,865 for the final between Cork and Wexford at Croke Park, Dublin, in 1954.

Wayne Gretzky has set new standards of goal scoring for the Edmonton Oilers in recent years. His team triumphed too in winning the 1984 Stanley Cup 4–1 from the New York Islanders, who had won the previous four years. (All-Sport)

ICE HOCKEY

Origins

There is pictorial evidence that a hockey-like game (*Kalv*) was played on ice in the early 16th century in The Netherlands. The game was probably first played in North America on 25 Dec 1855 at Kingston, Ontario, Canada, but Halifax also lays claim to priority. The International Ice Hockey Federation was founded in 1908. The National Hockey League (NHL) of North America was inaugurated 1917. The World Hockey Association was formed in 1971 and disbanded in 1979.

World Championships and Olympic Games

World Championships were first held for amateurs in 1920 in conjunction with the Olympic Games, which were also considered as World Championships up to 1968. From 1977 World Championships have been open to professionals. The USSR have won 19 world titles between 1954 and 1983, including the Olympic titles of 1956, 1964 and 1968. They have won three further Olympic titles in 1972, 1976 and 1984. Canada have also won 19 titles, between 1920 and 1961, including 6 Olympic titles (1920, 1924, 1928, 1932, 1948 and 1952). The longest Olympic career is that of Richard Torriani (b. 1 Oct 1911) (Switzerland) from 1928 to 1948. The most gold medals won by any player is three achieved by USSR players Vitaliy Davidov, Anatoliy Firssov, Viktor Kuzkin and Aleksandr Ragulin in 1964, 1968 and 1972, and by Vladislav Tretyak in 1972, 1976 and 1984.

Stanley Cup

The Stanley Cup, presented by the Governor-General, Lord Stanley (original cost $48.67), became emblematic of National Hockey League supremacy 33 years after the first contest at Montreal in 1893. It has been won most often by the Montreal Canadiens with 22 wins in 1916, 1924, 1930–1, 1944, 1946, 1953, 1956–60, 1965–6, 1968–9, 1971, 1973, 1976–9.

British Competitions

The English (later British) League championship (inst. 1934) has been won by the Wembley Lions four times in 1936–7, 1952 and 1957 and by Streatham (now Redskins) in 1950, 1953, 1960 and 1982. Murrayfield Racers have won the Northern League (inst. 1966) six times, 1970–2, 1976, 1979 and 1980. The Icy Smith Cup (first held 1966), emblematic of British club supremacy until 1981, was won by Murrayfield Racers nine times, 1966, 1969–72, 1975 and 1979–81. The British club championship (inst. 1982) was won by Dundee Rockets in 1982, 1983 and 1984.

Most goals *Team*

The greatest number of goals recorded in a world championship match was when Canada beat Denmark 47–0 in Stockholm, Sweden on 12 Feb 1949. The NHL record is 21 goals when Montreal Canadiens beat Toronto St Patrick's, at Montreal, 14–7 on 10 Jan 1920.

Most goals and points *Individual*

The most goals scored in a season in the NHL is 92 in the 1981–2 season by Wayne Gretzky (b. 26 Jan 1961) (Edmonton Oilers). He also scored a record 212 points (including 120 assists). He scored an additional 12 points (5 goals, 7 assists) in the Stanley Cup playoffs and 14 points (6 goals, 8 assists) for Canada in the World Championships in April 1982. He scored a record 125 assists the following season, 1982–83. The North American career record for goals is 1071 (801 in the NHL) by Gordie Howe (b. 31 Mar 1928) (Detroit Red Wings, Houston Aeros, New England Whalers and Hartford Whalers) from 16 Oct 1946 in 32 seasons ending in 1979–80. He took 2204 games to achieve the 1000th goal, but Robert Marvin 'Bobby' Hull (b. 3 Jan 1939) (Chicago Black Hawks and Winnipeg Jets) scored his 1000th in 1600 games on 12 Mar 1978.

Most goals and points *British*

The highest score and aggregate in a League match was set when Cleveland Bombers beat Richmond Flyers 41–2 at Billingham Forum on 19 Feb 1983. Ted Phillips (b. 19 Oct 1957) scored a record 20 points (13 goals, 7 assists). The most individual goals scored in a senior game is 14 by Roy Halpin (Canada) (b. 18 Oct 1955) for Dundee Rockets

Vladeslav Tretyak, the great Soviet goal minder, at the 1984 Olympics, when he won his third gold medal. He competed at all World and European championships from 1970 to his retirement in 1984. (*All-Sport/Dave Cannon*)

in a 24–1 win over Durham Wasps at Dundee on 4 Apr 1982. Halpin set British senior records of 151 goals and 254 points in 48 games in the 1981–2 season.

Most points one game
The North American major league record for most points scored in one game is ten (3 goals, 7 assists) by Jim Harrison (b. 9 July 1947) (for Alberta, later Edmonton Oilers) in a WHA match at Edmonton on 30 Jan 1973, and by Darryl Sittler (b. 18 Sept 1950) (6 goals, 4 assists) for Toronto Maple Leafs in a NHL match at Toronto on 7 Feb 1976.

Fastest scoring *World*
In the NHL the fastest goal was after 4 sec in the second period by Joseph Antoine Claude Provost (b. 17 Sept 1933) (Montreal Canadiens) v. Boston Bruins at Montreal on 9 Nov 1957. Doug Smail of the Winnipeg Jets scored 5 sec from the opening whistle against St Louis on 20 Dec 1981. Canadian Bill Mosienko (Chicago Black Hawks) (b. 2 Nov 1921) scored three goals in 21 sec v. New York Rangers on 23 Mar 1952. Toronto scored eight goals in 4 min 52 sec v. New York Americans on 19 Mar 1938.

In minor leagues, Kim D. Miles scored in 3 sec for Univ of Guelph v. Univ of W Ontario on 11 Feb 1975. Three goals in 12 sec was achieved by Steve D'Innocenzo for Holliston v. Westwood in a high school match in Massachusetts, USA on 9 Jan 1982. The Skara Ishockeyclubb, Sweden, scored three goals in 11 sec against Örebro IK at Skara on 18 Oct 1981. The Vernon Cougars scored five goals in 56 sec against Salmon Arm Aces at Vernon, BC, Canada on 6 Aug 1982. The Kamloops Knights of Columbus scored seven goals in 2 min 22 sec v. Prince George Vikings on 25 Jan 1980.

Fastest scoring *Great Britain*
The fastest goal in the Heineken League was scored by Steve Johnson for Durham Wasps after four seconds v. Ayr Bruins at Ayr, Scotland on 6 Nov 1983. Kenny Westman (Nottingham Panthers) scored a hat trick in 30 sec v. Brighton Tigers on 3 Mar 1955.

Most successful goaltending
The most matches played by a goaltender in an NHL career without conceding a goal is 103 by Terrance 'Terry' Gordon Sawchuck (b. 28 Dec 1929) of Detroit, Boston, Toronto, Los Angeles and New York Rangers, between 1950 and 1967. Gerry Cheevers (b. 2 Dec 1940), Boston Bruins, went a record 33 successive games without a defeat in 1971–2.

Fastest player
The highest speed attributed to any player is 29.7 mph *47,7 km/h* for Bobby Hull. The highest puck speed is also attributed to Hull, whose left-handed slap shot has been timed at 118.3 mph *190,3 km/h.*

Longest match
The longest match was 2 hr 56 min 30 sec (playing time) when Detroit Red Wings beat Montreal Maroons 1–0 in the sixth period of overtime at the Forum, Montreal, at 2.25 a.m. on 25 Mar 1936. Norm Smith, the Red Wings goaltender, turned aside 92 shots for the NHL's longest single shutout.

ICE SKATING

Origins
The earliest reference to ice skating is in early Scandinavian literature referring to the 2nd century though its origins are believed, on archaeological evidence, to be ten centuries earlier still. The earliest English account of 1180 refers to skates made of bone. The earliest skating club was the Edinburgh Skating Club formed in about 1742. The first recorded race was from Wisbech to Whittlesea, East Anglia, in 1763. The earliest artificial rink in the world was opened at the Baker Street Bazaar, Portman Square, London, on 7 Dec 1842, although the surface was not of ice. The first artificial ice rink was opened in the King's Road, Chelsea, London on 7 Jan 1876. The National Skating Association of Great Britain was founded in 1879. The International Skating Union was founded at Scheveningen, Netherlands in 1892.

FIGURE SKATING

Most titles *Olympic*
The most Olympic gold medals won by a figure skater is three by Gillis Grafström (1893–1938) of Sweden in 1920, 1924, and 1928 (also silver medal in 1932); by Sonja Henie (1912–69) of Norway in 1928, 1932 and 1936; and by Irina Rodnina (b. USSR 12 Sept 1949) with two different partners in the Pairs event in 1972, 1976, and 1980.

Most titles *World*
The greatest number of individual world figure skating titles (instituted 1896) is ten by Ulrich Salchow (1877–1949) of Sweden, in 1901–5 and 1907–11. The women's record (inst. 1906) is also ten individual titles by Sonja Henie between 1927 and 1936. Irina Rodnina has won ten pairs titles (inst. 1908), four with Aleksey Ulanov (b. 4 Nov 1947) 1969–72, and six with her husband Aleksandr Zaitsev (b. 16 June 1952) 1973–8. The most ice dances titles (inst. 1952) won is six by Ludmila Pakhomova (b. 31 Dec 1946) and Aleksandr Gorshkov (b. 8 Oct 1946) (USSR) 1970–4 and 1976.

Most titles *British*
The most individual British titles is 11 by Jack Ferguson Page (1900–47) (Manchester SC) in 1922–31 and 1933, and six by Cecilia Colledge (b. 28 Nov 1920) (Park Lane FSC, London) in 1935–7 (two), 1938 and 1946. Page and Ethel M. Muckelt (1885–1953) won nine pairs titles, 1923–31. The most by an ice dance couple is six by Jayne Torvill (b. 7 Oct 1957) and Christopher Dean (b. 27 July 1958), 1978–83.

Triple Crown
The only British skaters to win the 'Grand Slam' of World, Olympic and European titles in the same year are John Anthony Curry (b. 9 Sept 1949) in 1976 and the ice dancers Jayne Torvill and Christopher Dean in 1984. Karl Schäfer (Austria) (1909–76) and Sonja Henie achieved double 'Grand Slams', both in the years 1932 and 1936.

Highest marks
The highest tally of maximum six marks awarded in an international championship was 29 to Jayne Torvill and Christopher Dean (GB) in the World ice dance championships at Ottawa, Canada on 22–24 Mar 1984. This comprised seven in the compulsory dances, a perfect set of nine for presentation in the set pattern dance and 13 in the free dance including another perfect set from all nine judges for artistic presentation. They previously gained a perfect set of nine sixes for artistic presentation in the free dance at the 1983 World Championships in Helsinki, Finland and at the 1984 Olympic Games in Sarajevo, Yugoslavia. In their career Torvill and Dean received a record total of 136 sixes.

The most by a soloist was seven to Donald Jackson (b. 2 Apr

(left) **World, Olympic and European champions Jayne Torvill and Christopher Dean ice dance to Ravel's** *Bolero*, **perfection in their final season as amateurs in 1984.** (*All-Sport*)

(above) **Robin Cousins, the 1980 Olympic champion, and now a professional, in the back flip at Richmond Ice Rink when he set a record and helped raise funds for the British Olympic Appeal.** (*All-Sport*)

1940) (Canada) in the world men's championship at Prague, Czechoslovakia, in 1962.

Distance

Robin Cousins (GB) (b. 17 Mar 1957) achieved 19 ft 1 in *5,81 m* in an Axel jump and 18 ft *5,48 m* with a back flip at Richmond Ice Rink, Surrey on 16 Nov 1983.

Largest rink

The world's largest indoor ice rink is in the Moscow Olympic arena which has an ice area of 8064 m² *86,800 ft²*. The five rinks at Fujikyu Highland Skating Centre, Japan total 26 500 m² *285,243 ft²*.

SPEED SKATING

Most titles *Olympic*

The most Olympic gold medals won in speed skating is six by Lidia Skoblikova (b. 8 Mar 1939) of Chelyabinsk, USSR, in 1960 (two) and 1964 (four). The male record is by Clas Thunberg (1893–1973) (Finland) with five gold (including one tied), and also one silver and one tied bronze in 1924 and 1928. Eric Heiden (USA) (b. 14 June 1958) also won five gold medals, all at Lake Placid, NY, USA, in 1980.

Most titles *World*

The greatest number of world overall titles (inst. 1893) won by

SPEED SKATING WORLD RECORDS

Distance	min sec	Name (Country)	Place	Date
MEN				
500 metres	36.57*	Pavel Pegov (USSR)	Medeo, USSR	26 Mar 1983
1000 metres	1:12.58	Pavel Pegov (USSR)	Medeo, USSR	25 Mar 1983
1500 metres	1:53.26	Oleg Bozhyev (USSR)	Medeo, USSR	24 Mar 1984
	1:53.22u	Andrei Bobrov (USSR)	Medeo, USSR	27 Dec 1983
3000 metres	4:04.06	Dmitriy Oglobin (USSR)	Medeo, USSR	28 Mar 1979
5000 metres	6:49.15	Viktor Shasherin (USSR)	Medeo, USSR	23 Mar 1984
10,000 metres	14:21.51	Igor Malkov (USSR)	Medeo, USSR	24 Mar 1984
	14:17.61u	Konstantin Kadhov (USSR)	Medeo, USSR	25 Dec 1982
WOMEN				
500 metres	39.69	Christa Rothenburger (GDR)	Medeo, USSR	25 Mar 1983
1000 metres	1:19.31	Natalia Petruseva (USSR)	Medeo, USSR	26 Mar 1983
1500 metres	2:03.34	Andrea Schöne (GDR)	Medeo, USSR	24 Mar 1984
3000 metres	4:20.91	Andrea Schöne (GDR)	Medeo, USSR	23 Mar 1984
5000 metres	7:34.52	Andrea Schöne (GDR)	Medeo, USSR	24 Mar 1984

* represents an average speed of 49,22 km/h *30.58 mph*. Note that Medeo, Alma Ata, USSR is situated at high altitude.
u unratified performance

BRITISH OUTDOOR RECORDS

Distance	min sec	Name	Place	Date
MEN				
500 metres	39.41	Archie Marshall	Davos, Switzerland	20 Jan 1980
1000 metres	1:19.23	Archie Marshall	Davos, Switzerland	20 Jan 1980
1500 metres	2:05.88	Derek Webber	Davos, Switzerland	23 Jan 1983
3000 metres	4:24.71	Derek Webber	Davos, Switzerland	22 Jan 1983
5000 metres	7:32.75	Brian Carvis	Inzell, W. Germany	7 Jan 1984
10,000 metres	15:35.74	Alan Luke	Inzell, W. Germany	7 Mar 1982
WOMEN				
500 metres	46.53	Kim Ferran	Inzell, W. Germany	5 Jan 1980
1000 metres	1:31.85	Kim Ferran	Madonna di Campiglio, Italy	10 Jan 1979
1500 metres	2:21.60	Amanda Horsepool	Inzell, W. Germany	07 Dec 1980
3000 metres	4:54.74	Kim Ferran	Inzell, W. Germany	6 Jan 1979

any skater is five by Oscar Mathisen (Norway) (1888–1954) in 1908–9 and 1912–14, and Clas Thunberg in 1923, 1925, 1928–9 and 1931. The most titles won in the women's events (inst. 1936) is four by Inga Voronina (*née* Artomonova) (1936–66) (USSR) in 1957, 1958, 1962 and 1964 and Atje Keulen–Deelstra (b. 31 Dec 1938) (Netherlands) 1970, 1972–4.

The record score achieved in the world overall title is 160.807 points by Viktor Shasherin (USSR) (b. 23 July 1962) at Medeo, USSR, 23–24 Mar 1984. The record women's score is 171.760 points by Andrea Schöne (GDR) (b. 1 Dec 1960) at Medeo, 23–24 Mar 1984.

Longest race

The 'Elfstedentocht' ('Tour of the Eleven Towns') was held in the Netherlands from the 1800s to 1963, covering 200 km *124 miles 483 yd*. It was transferred first to Lake Vesijärvi, near Lahti, Finland and in 1984 to Canada as the International Race of 11 Cities on the Ottawa River. The record time for 200 km is 6 hr 5 min 12 sec by Jan-Roelof Kruithof (Netherlands) on 25 Feb 1979 at Oulu, Finland.

24 hours

Hans Homma (Netherlands) skated 406 km in 24 hours in Ottawa, Canada in February 1984.

(right) **Karin Enke was the star of the 1984 Winter Olympics speed skating, winning two gold (1000 and 1500 metres) and two silver (500 and 3000 metres) medals. She has won four world sprint championships, a record she shares with Eric Heiden.** (*All-Sport*)

ICE AND SAND YACHTING

Origins

The sport originated in the Low Countries from the year 1600 (earliest patent granted) and along the Baltic coast. The earliest authentic record is Dutch, dating from 1768. Land or sand yachts of Dutch construction were first reported on beaches (now in Belgium) in 1595. The earliest International championship was staged in 1914.

Largest yacht

The largest ice yacht was *Icicle*, built for Commodore John E. Roosevelt for racing on the Hudson River, New York, in 1869. It was 68 ft 11 in *21 m* long and carried 1070 ft² *99 m²* of canvas.

Highest speeds *Ice*

The highest speed officially recorded is 143 mph *230 km/h* by John D. Buckstaff in a Class A stern-steerer on Lake Winnebago, Wisconsin, USA, in 1938. Such a speed is possible in a wind of 72 mph *115 km/h*.

Highest speeds *Sand*

The official world record for a sand yacht is 107 km/h *66.48 mph* set by Christian-Yves Nau (b. 1944) (France) in *Mobil* at Le Touquet, France on 22 Mar 1981, when the wind speed reached 120 km/h *75 mph*. A speed of 88.4 mph *142,26 km/h* was attained by Nord Embroden (USA) in *Midnight at the Oasis* at Superior Dry Lake, California, USA on 15 Apr 1976.

JUDO

Origins

Judo is a modern combat sport which developed out of an amalgam of several old Japanese fighting arts, the most popular of which was ju-jitsu (jiu-jitsu), which is thought to be of Chinese origin. Judo has greatly developed since 1882, when it was first devised by Dr Jigoro Kano (1860–1938). The International Judo Federation was founded in 1951.

Most titles *World and Olympic*

World championships were inaugurated in Tōkyō in 1956. Women's championships were first held in 1980 in New York. Yashiro Yamashito won seven consecutive Japanese titles 1977–83, and four world titles; Heavyweight 1979, 1981 and 1983 and Open 1981. He was undefeated in 188 successive fights in this period. Two other men have won four world titles, Wilhelm Ruska (b. 29 Aug 1940) (Netherlands), 1967, 1971 Heavyweight and the 1972 Olympic Heavyweight and Open titles, and Shozo Fujii (Japan) (b. 12 May 1950), the Middleweight title 1971, 1973, 1975, and 1979. Ingrid Berghmans (Belgium) with four, has won most medals by a woman in world championships, gold (Open) and bronze (72 kg) in 1980, gold (Open) and silver (72 kg) in 1982.

Most titles *British*

The greatest number of titles (inst. 1966) won is nine by David Colin Starbrook (b. 9 Aug 1945) (6th dan); Middleweight 1969–70, Light-heavyweight 1971–5 and the Open division 1970–1. A record six titles in the women's events (inst. 1971) were won by Christine Child (now Mrs Gallie) (b. 1946) (6th dan): Heavyweight in 1971–5 and the Open division in 1973.

Highest grades

The efficiency grades in Judo are divided into pupil (*kyu*) and master (*dan*) grades. The highest awarded is the extremely rare red belt *Judan* (10th dan), given only to seven men so far. The highest awarded to a woman is 6th dan, achieved by three Japanese women. The Judo protocol provides for an 11th dan (*Juichidan*) who also would wear a red belt, a 12th dan (*Junidan*) who would wear a white belt twice as wide as an

Heavyweight judo exponent Yashiro Yamashita was unbeaten from 1977 to 1983. (*All-Sport*)

Most titles *World*

The United States have won three of the four World Championships, in 1967, 1974 and 1982. Canada won the other in 1978 beating the USA 17–16 after extra time—this was the first drawn international match.

Most titles *English*

The English Club Championship (Iroquois Cup—inst. 1890), has been won most often by Stockport with 15 wins between 1897 and 1934. The record score in a final was set by Sheffield University, 30–5 *v.* Hampstead in 1982 and 30–1 *v.* Kenton in 1983.

Most international appearances

The record number of international representations is 33 for England by James Michael 'Mike' Roberts (Urmston) (b. 22 Feb 1946), to 1982. He is the only man to play in all four World Championships.

Highest scores

The highest score in an international match was the United States' 28–4 win over Canada at Stockport, Greater Manchester on 3 July 1978. England's highest score was their 19–11 win over Canada at Melbourne in 1974.

Fastest scoring

Rod Burns scored only 4 sec into the game for South Manchester and Wythenshawe *v.* Sheffield Univ. on 6 Dec 1975.

WOMEN'S LACROSSE

The first reported playing of lacrosse by women was in 1886. The All-England Women's Lacrosse Association was formed in 1912. The game has evolved from the men's game so that the rules now differ considerably.

World Championships

The first official championships, held in 1982 at Trent Bridge, Nottingham, England, were won by the USA.

Most international appearances

Caro Macintosh (b. 18 Feb 1932) made a record 52 appearances for Scotland, 1952–9. The record for Great Britain is eight by Celia Brackenridge (b. 22 Aug 1950), 1970–9.

Highest score

The highest score by an international team was by Great Britain and Ireland with their 40–0 defeat of Long Island during their 1967 tour of the USA.

ordinary belt and the highest of all, *Shihan*, but these have never been bestowed. The highest British native Judo grade is 8th dan by Charles Stuart Palmer (b. 1930).

KARATE

Origins

Based on techniques devised from the sixth century Chinese art of Shaolin boxing (Kempo), Karate was developed by an unarmed populace in Okinawa as a weapon against armed Japanese oppressors *c.* 1500. Transmitted to Japan in the 1920s by Funakoshi Gichin, this method of combat was refined into Karate and organised into a sport with competitive rules. The five major styles of Karate in Japan are: *Shotokan*, *Wado-ryu*, *Goju-ryu*, *Shito-ryu* and *Kyokushinkai*, each of which place different emphasis on speed and power, etc. Other styles include *Sankukai*, *Shotokai* and *Shukokai*. *Wu shu* is a comprehensive term embracing all Chinese martial arts. *Kung fu* is one aspect of these arts popularised by the cinema. (*See also p. 188*).

The Governing Body for the sport in Britain is the Martial Arts Commission upon which all the martial arts are represented.

Most titles

The only nation to have won two world karate championships is Great Britain, 1975 and 1982.

Top exponents

The leading exponents among karatekas are a number of 10th dans in Japan. The leading exponents in the United Kingdom are Tatsuo Suzuki (8th dan, *Wado-ryu*) (b. 27 Apr 1928) chief instructor to the European Karatedo Wadokai; Keinosuke Enoeda (8th dan, *Shotokan*), resident instructor to the Karate Union of Great Britain and Steve Arneil (7th dan, *Kyokushinkai*), British national born in South Africa.

LACROSSE

MEN'S LACROSSE

Origins

The game is of American Indian origin, derived from the inter-tribal game *baggataway*, and was played before 1492 by Iroquois Indians in lower Ontario, Canada and upper New York State, USA. The French named it after their game of *Chouler à la crosse*, known in 1381. It was introduced into Great Britain in 1867. The English Lacrosse Union was formed in 1892. Lacrosse was included in the Olympic Games of 1908 and featured as an exhibition sport in the 1928 and 1948 Games.

MARBLES

Origins

Marbles may have been a children's game in Ancient Egypt, and was introduced into Britain by the Romans in the 1st Century AD. It became a competitive sport under the British Marbles Board of Control at the Greyhound Hotel, Tinsley Green, Crawley, West Sussex in 1926.

Most championships

The British Championship (established 1926) has been won most often by the Toucan Terribles with 20 consecutive titles (1956–75). Three founder members, Len Smith, Jack and Charlie Dempsey played in every title win. They were finally beaten in 1976 by the Pernod Rams, captained by Len Smith's son, Paul. Len Smith (b. 13 oct 1917) has won the individual title 15 times (1957–64, 1966, 1968–73) but lost in 1974 to his son Alan.

Speed record

The record for clearing the ring (between 5¾ and 6¼ ft *1,75–1,90 m* in diameter) of 49 marbles is 2 min 57 sec by the Toucan Terribles at Worthing, West Sussex in 1971.

MODERN PENTATHLON and BIATHLON

Points scores in riding, fencing, cross country and hence overall scores have no comparative value between one competition and another. In shooting and swimming (300 m) the scores are of record significance and the best achievements are shown.

The Modern Pentathlon (Riding, Fencing, Swimming, Shooting and Running) was inaugurated into the Olympic Games at Stockholm in 1912. The Modern Pentathlon Association of Great Britain was formed in 1922. L'Union Internationale de Pentathlon Moderne et Biathlon (UIPMB) was founded in 1948. Originally the UIPM, the administration of Biathlon (cross-country skiing and shooting) was added in 1957, and the name modified accordingly.

MODERN PENTATHLON

Most titles World (Inst. 1949)

András Balczó (Hungary) (b. 16 Aug 1938) won the record number of world titles, six individual and seven team. He won the world individual title in 1963, 1965–7 and 1969 and the Olympic title in 1972. His seven team titles (1960–70) comprised five world and two Olympic.

Women's world championships were first held in 1981. Great Britain won the three team titles 1981–83, with Sarah Parker (b. 16 July 1956) a member of each of those teams. Wendy Johana Norman (b. 20 Feb 1965) won the individual title in 1982 and team golds in 1981–2. She also won the individual world cup title in 1980 and Great Britain won each of the three world cup team titles, 1978–80.

Most titles *Olympic*

The greatest number of Olympic gold medals won is three by András Balczó, a member of the winning team in 1960 and 1968 and the 1972 individual champion. Lars Hall (b. 30 Apr 1927) (Sweden) has uniquely won two individual Championships (1952 and 1956). Pavel Lednev (USSR) (b. 25 Mar 1943) won a record seven medals (two gold, two silver, three bronze), 1968–80. The best British performance is the team gold medal at Montreal, Canada 18–22 July 1976 by Jim Fox, Adrian Philip Parker and Daniel Nightingale. The best individual placing is fourth by Jeremy Robert 'Jim' Fox (b. 19 Sept 1941) at Munich in 1972.

Probably the greatest margin of victory was by William Oscar Guernsey Grut (b. 17 Sept 1914) (Sweden) in the 1948 Games in London, when he won three events and was placed fifth and eighth in the other two events.

Most titles *British*

The pentathlete with most British titles is Jim Fox, with ten (1963, 1965–8, 1970–4). Wendy Norman has won a record four women's titles, 1978–80 and 1982.

BIATHLON

The biathlon, which combines cross-country skiing and rifle shooting was first included in the Olympic Games in 1960, and world championships were first held in 1958.

Most titles *Olympic Games*

Magnar Solberg (Norway) (b. 4 Feb 1937), in 1968 and 1972, is the only man to have won two Olympic individual titles. The USSR have won all five 4 × 7,5 km relay titles, 1968–84. Aleksandr Tikhonov (b. 2 Jan 1947) who was a member of the first four teams also won a silver in the 1968 20 km.

Sarah Parker was a member of all three British modern pentathlon world championship teams. (*All-Sport*)

HIGHEST SCORES (In major competition)

	Performance	Points	Name and Place	Date and Venue
WORLD				
Shooting	200/200	—[1]	Charles Leonard (USA) (b. 23 Feb 1913)	3 Aug 1936 Berlin, Germany
	200/200	1132	Daniele Masala (Italy) (b. 12 Feb 1955)	21 Aug 1978 Jönkoping, Sweden
	200/200	1132	George Horvath (Sweden) (b. 14 Mar 1960)	22 July 1980 Moscow, USSR
Swimming	3 min 08.22 sec	1368	John Scott (USA) (b. 14 Apr 1962)	27 Aug 1982 London, England
BRITISH				
Shooting	198/200	1088	Timothy Kenealy (b. 3 Mar 1950)	Helsinki, Finland 4 June 1979
Swimming	3 min 18.1 sec	1288	Richard Lawson Phelps (b. 19 Apr 1961)	5 Aug 1983 Warendorf, W. Germany

[1] *points not given in 1936 Olympic Games.*

Most titles *World Championship*

Frank Ullrich (GDR) (b. 24 Jan 1958) has won a record six individual world titles, four at 10 km, 1978–81, including the 1980 Olympics, and two at 20 km 1982–3. Aleksandr Tikhonov was in ten winning USSR relay teams, 1968–80 and won four individual titles.

The biathlon world cup (inst 1979) was won three times by Frank Ullrich, 1980–2. He was 2nd in 1979 and 3rd in 1983.

The biathlon demands the endurance necessary to undertake cross-country skiing and the concentration and steadiness of shooting during the race. Frank Ullrich (GDR) has won most world titles. (All-Sport)

MOTORCYCLE RACING

See also The Guinness Book of Motorcycling Facts and Feats by L. J. K. Setright (price £7.95) and The Guinness Guide to Motorcycling by Peter Carrick (price £10.95).

Earliest race

The first motorcycle race was held over a mile *1,6 km* on an oval track at Sheen House, Richmond, Surrey, on 29 Nov 1897, won by Charles Jarrott (1877–1944) on a Fournier. The oldest motorcycle races in the world are the Auto-Cycle Union Tourist Trophy (TT) series, first held on the 15.81 mile *25,44 km* 'Peel' ('St John's') course in the Isle of Man on 28 May 1907, and still run in the island on the 'Mountain' circuit.

Fastest circuits *World*

The highest average lap speed attained on any closed circuit is 160.288 mph *257,958 km/h* by Yvon du Hamel (Canada) (b. 1941) on a modified 903 cc four-cylinder Kawasaki Z1 at the 31 degree banked 2.5 mile *4,02 km* Daytona International Speedway, Florida, USA, in March 1973. His lap time was 56.149 sec.

The fastest road circuit is the Francorchamps circuit near Spa, Belgium. It is 8.74 miles *14,12 km* in length and was lapped in 3 min 50.3 sec (average speed 137.150 mph *220,721 km/h*) by Barry Stephen Frank Sheene (GB) (b. 11 Sept 1950) on a 495 cc four-cylinder Suzuki during the Belgian Grand Prix on 3 July 1977.

Fastest circuits *United Kingdom*

The fastest circuit in the United Kingdom is the Portstewart-Coleraine-Portrush circuit in Londonderry, N. Ireland. The lap record (10.1 mile *16,26 km* lap) is 4 min 53.2 sec (average speed 124.060 mph *199,655 km/h*) by John Glyn Williams (1946–78) on a 747 cc four-cylinder Yamaha on lap five of the 750cc event of the North West 200, on 21 May 1977.

The lap record for the outer circuit (2.767 miles *4,453 km*) at the Brooklands Motor Course, near Weybridge, Surrey (open between 1907 and 1939) was 80.0 sec (average speed 124.51 mph *200,37 km/h*) by Noel Baddow 'Bill' Pope (later Major) (1909–71) of the United Kingdom on a Brough Superior powered by a supercharged 996 cc V-twin '8-80' JAP engine developing 110 bhp, on 4 July 1939.

Fastest race *World*

The fastest road race is the 500 cc Belgian Grand Prix held on the Francorchamps circuit (*see above*). The record time for this ten lap (87.74 mile *141,20 km*) race is 38 min 58.5 sec (average speed 135.068 mph *217,370 km/h*) by Barry Sheene, on a 495 cc four-cylinder Suzuki, on 3 July 1977.

Fastest race *United Kingdom*

The fastest race in the United Kingdom is the 750 cc event of the North-West 200 held on the Londonderry circuit (*see above*). The record lap speed is 127.63 mph *205,395 km/h* by Tom Herron (1949–79) on a 747 cc Yamaha in 1978.

Longest race

The longest race is the Liège 24 hr. The greatest distance ever covered is 2761.9 miles *4444,8 km* (average speed 115.08 mph *185,20 km/h*) by Jean-Claude Chemarin and Christian Leon, both of France, on a 941 cc four-cylinder Honda on the Francorchamps circuit on 14–15 Aug 1976.

Longest circuit

The 37.73 mile *60,72 km* 'Mountain' circuit, over which the principal TT races have been run since 1911 (with minor amendments in 1920), has 264 curves and corners and is the longest used for any motorcycle race.

Most successful riders *Tourist Trophy*

The record number of victories in the Isle of Man TT races is 14 by Stanley Michael Bailey Hailwood (1940–81) between 1961 and 1979. The first man to win three consecutive TT titles in two events was James A. Redman (Rhodesia) (b. 8 Nov 1931). He won the 250 cc and 350 cc events in 1963–5. Mike Hailwood is the only man to win three events in one year, in 1961 and 1967.

The TT circuit speed record is 118.47 mph *190,66 km/h* by Joey Dunlop on a Honda on 4 June 1984.

Most successful riders *World championships*

The most world championship titles (instituted by the *Fédération Internationale Motocycliste* in 1949) won are 15 by Giacomo Agostini (Italy) (b. 16 June 1942), the 350 cc in 1968–74, and 500 cc in 1966–72, 1975. He is the only man to win two world championships in five consecutive years (350 and 500 cc titles 1968–72).

Agostini won 122 races in the world championship series between 24 Apr 1965 and 29 Aug 1976, including a record 19 in 1970, also achieved by Mike Hailwood in 1966. Klaus Enders (W. Germany) (b. 1937) won six world side-car titles, 1967, 1969–70, 1972–4.

Most successful riders *Trials*

Yrjo Vesterinen (Finland) won a record three World trials championships, 1976–8. Samuel Hamilton Miller (b. 11 Nov 1935) won eleven A-CU Solo Trials Drivers' Stars in 1959–69.

Most successful riders *Moto-cross*

Joël Robert (Belgium) (b. 11 Nov 1943) won six 250 cc moto-cross world championships (1964, 1968–72). Between 25 Apr 1964 and 18 June 1972 he won a record fifty 250 cc Grands Prix. He became the youngest moto-cross world champion on 12 July 1964 when he won the 250 cc title aged 20 yr 244 days.

Most successful machines

Italian MV-Agusta machines won 37 world championships between 1952 and 1973, and 276 world championship races between 1952 and 1976. Japanese Honda machines won 29 world championship races and five world championships in 1966. In the seven years they contested the championship (1961–7) their annual average was 20 race wins.

Youngest and oldest world champions

Alberto 'Johnny' Cecotto (Venezuela) (b. 25 Jan 1956) is the youngest to win a world championship. He was 19 yr 211 days when he won the 350 cc title on 24 Aug 1975. The oldest was Hermann-Peter Müller (1909–76) of W. Germany, who won the 250 cc title in 1955 aged 46.

Highest speeds

Official world speed records must be set with two runs over a measured distance made in opposite directions within a time limit—1 hr for FIM records and 2 hr for AMA records.

Donald A. Vesco (USA) (b. 8 Apr 1939) riding his 21 ft *6,4 m* long *Lightning Bolt* streamliner, powered by two 1016 cc Kawasaki engines on Bonneville Salt Flats, Utah, USA on 28 Aug 1978 set AMA and FIM absolute records with an overall average of 318.598 mph *512,733 km/h* and had a fastest run at an average of 318.66 mph *513,165 km/h*.

The highest speed achieved over two runs in the UK is 191.897 mph *308.82 km/h* by Roy Francis Daniel (b. 7 Dec 1938) on his 998 cc supercharged twin-engined RDS Triumph at Elvington, N. Yorks on 29 July 1978. His average time for the flying 440 yd *402 m* was 4.69 sec.

The world record for 1 km *1,093.6 yd* from a standing start is 16.68 sec by Henk Vink (b. 24 July 1939) (Netherlands) on his supercharged 984 cc four-cylinder Kawasaki, at Elvington Airfield, North Yorkshire on 24 July 1977. The faster run was made in 16.09 sec.

The world record for 440 yd *402 m* from a standing start is 8.805 sec by Henk Vink on his supercharged 1132 cc four-cylinder Kawasaki at Elvington Airfield, North Yorkshire on 23 July 1977. The faster run was made in 8.55 sec.

The fastest time for a single run over 440 yd *402 m* from a standing start is 7.08 sec by Bo O'Brechta (USA) riding a supercharged 1200 cc Kawasaki-based machine at Ontario, California, in 1980. The highest terminal velocity recorded at the end of a 440 yd *402 m* run from a standing start is 199.55 mph *321,14 km/h* by Russ Collins (USA) at Ontario on 7 Oct 1978.

MOTOR RACING

See also The Guinness Guide to Grand Prix Motor Racing by Eric Dymock; revised edition published in 1983 at £11.95.

Earliest races

There are various conflicting claims, but the first automobile race was the 201 mile *323 km* Green Bay to Madison, Wisconsin, USA run in 1878 won by an Oshkosh steamer. In 1887 Count

Alain Prost set the early pace in the 1984 world drivers championship in a Marlboro McLaren. In 1983, driving a Renault he won the British Grand Prix at record speed and finished second, just two points behind Nelson Piquet for the world title. (*Sporting Pictures*)

Jules Felix Philippe Albert de Dion de Malfiance (1856–1946) won the *La Velocipede* 19.3 miles *31 km* race in Paris in a De Dion steam quadricycle in which he is reputed to have exceeded 37 mph *59 km/h*. The first 'real' race was from Paris to Bordeaux and back (732 miles *1178 km*) on 11–13 June 1895. The first to finish was Emile Levassor (1844–97) of France, in a Panhard-Levassor two-seater, with a 1.2 litre Daimler engine developing 3½ hp. His time was 48 hr 47 min (average speed 15.01 mph *24,15 km/h*). The first closed circuit race was held over five laps of a mile *1,6 km* dirt track at Narragansett Park, Cranston, Rhode Island, USA, on 7 Sept 1896, won by A. H. Whiting, driving a Riker electric.

The oldest race in the world, still regularly run, is the RAC Tourist Trophy, first staged on 14 Sept 1905, in the Isle of Man. The oldest continental race is the French Grand Prix first held on 26–27 June 1906. The Coppa Florio, in Sicily, has been irregularly held since 1900.

Fastest circuits

The highest average lap speed attained on any closed circuit is 250.958 mph *403,878 km/h* in a trial by Dr Hans Liebold (b. 12 Oct 1926) (Germany) who lapped the 7.85 mile *12,64 km* high-speed track at Nardo, Italy in 1 min 52.67 sec in a Mercedes-Benz C111-IV experimental coupé on 5 May 1979. It was powered by a V8 engine with two KKK turbochargers with an output of 500 hp at 6,200 rpm.

The highest average race lap speed for a closed circuit is 214.158 mph *344,654 km/h* by Mario Gabriele Andretti (USA) (b. Trieste, Italy, 28 Feb 1940) driving a 2.6 litre turbocharged Viceroy Parnelli-Offenhauser on the 2 mile *3,2 km*, 22 degree banked oval at Texas World Speedway, College Station, Texas, USA on 6 Oct 1973.

The fastest road circuit was the Francorchamps circuit near Spa, Belgium, then 8.761 miles *14,10 km* in length which was lapped in 3 min 13.4 sec (average speed 163.086 mph *262,461 km/h*) on 6 May 1973, by Henri Pescarolo (France) (b. 25 Sept 1942) driving a 2993 cc V12 Matra-Simca MS670 Group 5 sports car. The race lap average speed record at Berlin's AVUS track was 171.75 mph *276,38 km/h* by Bernd Rosemeyer (Germany) (1909–38) in a 6-litre V16 Auto Union in 1937.

The Motor Industry Research Association (MIRA) High Speed Circuit (2.82 mile *4,53 km* lap with 33-degree banking on the bends) at Lindley, Warwickshire, was lapped in 1 min 2.8 sec (average speed 161.655 mph *260,158 km/h*) by David Wishart Hobbs (b. 9 June 1939) driving a 4994 cc V12 Jaguar XJ13 Group 6 prototype sports car in April 1967.

Fastest pit stop

Robert William 'Bobby' Unser (USA) (b. 20 Feb 1934) took 4 sec to take on fuel on lap 10 of the Indianapolis 500 on 30 May 1976.

Fastest race

The fastest race is the Busch Clash at Daytona, Florida over 125 miles *201 km* on a 2½ miles 31 degree banked track. In 1979 Elzie Wylie 'Buddy' Baker (b. 25 Jan 1941) averaged 194.384 mph *312,831 km/h* in an Oldsmobile. Buddy Baker set the world record for a 500 mile *805 km* race in 1980 when he won the Daytona 500 at an average speed of 177.602 mph *285,823 km/h*. The NASCAR qualifying record was set in May 1983 at 202.650 mph *326,134 km/h* by Caleb 'Cale' Yarborough (b. 27 Mar 1939) at the Alabama International Motor Speedway.

Most race wins by driver

Richard Lee Petty (USA) (b. 2 July 1937) won 200 NASCAR

Grand National races in 946 starts, 1958–84. His best season was 1967 with 27 wins. His total earnings reached a record $5,504,977 on 25 July 1984. Geoff Bodine (b. 18 Apr 1949) won 55 races in 1978.

WORLD CHAMPIONSHIP GRAND PRIX MOTOR RACING

Drivers *Most successful*

The World Drivers' Championship, inaugurated in 1950, has been won a record five times by Juan-Manuel Fangio (Argentina) (b. 24 June 1911) in 1951, 1954–7. He retired in 1958, after having won 24 Grand Prix races (two shared).

The most Grand Prix victories is 27 by John Young 'Jackie' Stewart (GB) (b. 11 June 1939) between 12 Sept 1965 and 5 Aug 1973. James 'Jim' Clark (GB) (1936–68) holds the record for Grand Prix victories in one year with seven in 1963. He won a record 61 Formula One and Formula Libre races between 1959 and 1968. The most Grand Prix starts is 176 (out of a possible 184) between 18 May 1958 and 26 Jan 1975 by Norman Graham Hill (GB) (1929–75). Between 20 Nov 1960 and 5 Oct 1969 he took part in 90 consecutive Grands Prix.

Oldest and youngest

The youngest world champion was Emerson Fittipaldi (Brazil) (b. 12 Dec 1946) who won his first world championship on 10 Sept 1972 aged 25 yr 273 days. The oldest world champion was Juan-Manuel Fangio who won his last world championship on 18 Aug 1957 aged 46 yr 55 days.

The youngest Grand Prix winner was Bruce Leslie McLaren (1937–70) of New Zealand, who won the United States Grand Prix at Sebring, Florida, on 12 Dec 1959 aged 22 yr 104 days. The oldest Grand Prix winner (in pre-World Championship days) was Tazio Giorgio Nuvolari (Italy) (1892–1953), who won the Albi Grand Prix at Albi, France on 14 July 1946 aged 53 yr 240 days. The oldest Grand Prix driver was Louis Alexandre Chiron (Monaco) (1899–1979), who finished 6th in

Walter Röhrl, partnered by Christian Geistdorfer, drove an Audi Quattro to victory in the 1984 Monte Carlo Rally, to equal the drivers' record of wins. (*Sporting Pictures UK*)

the Monaco Grand Prix on 22 May 1955 aged 55 yr 292 days. The youngest Grand Prix driver was Michael Christopher Thackwell (New Zealand) (b. 30 Mar 1961) who took part in the Canadian GP on 28 Sept 1980, aged 19 yr 182 days).

Manufacturers

Ferrari have won a record eight manufacturers' world championships, 1961, 1964, 1975–7, 1979, 1982–3. Ferrari have 88 race wins in 359 Grands Prix, 1950–83.

Fastest race

The fastest average speed for a Grand Prix race for a circuit in current use is 224,050 km/h *139.218 mph* in the British Grand Prix (*see below*).

Toughest circuit

The most gruelling and slowest Grand Prix circuit is that for the Monaco Grand Prix (first run on 14 Apr 1929), round the streets and the harbour of Monte Carlo. It is 2.058 miles *3,312 km* in length and has eleven pronounced corners and several sharp changes of gradient. The race is run over 76 laps (156.4 miles *251,7 km*) and involves on average about 1600 gear changes. The record time for the race is 1 hr 54 min 11.259 sec (average speed 132,30 km/h *82.21 mph* by Riccardo Patrese (Italy) (b. 17 Apr 1954) in a Brabham–Ford on 23 May 1982. The race lap record is 1 min 26.35 sec (average speed 138,073 km/h *85.79 mph*) by Patrese in 1982. The practice lap record is 1 min 22.66 sec (average speed 144,242 km/h *89.63 mph*) by Alain Prost (France) (b. 24 Feb 1955) in a McLaren TAG Porsche on 2 June 1984.

Closest finish

The closest finish to a World Championship race was in the Italian Grand Prix at Monza on 5 Sept 1971. Just 0.61 sec separated winner Peter Gethin (GB) from the fifth placer.

BRITISH GRAND PRIX

First held in 1926 as the RAC Grand Prix, and held annually with the above name since 1949, the venue alternates between Brands Hatch, Kent and Silverstone, Northants.

Fastest speed

The fastest race time is 1 hr 24 min 39.78 sec, average speed 224,050 km/h *139.218 mph* by Alain Prost (France) in a Renault Elf Turbo RE30 on 16 July 1983 over 67 laps (316,14 km *196.44 miles*). The race lap record is 1 min 14.21 sec (av. speed 228,996 km/h *142,291 mph* also by Alain Prost in 1983. The practice lap record is 1 min 09.462 sec (244,549 km/h *151.956 mph*) by René Arnoux in a Ferrari 126C3 on 15 July 1983, all set at Silverstone.

Most wins

The most wins by a driver is five by Jim Clark, 1962–65 and 1967, all in Lotus cars. Ferrari have most wins with ten, 1951–4, 1956, 1958, 1961, 1976, 1978 and 1983.

LE MANS

The greatest distance ever covered in the 24 hour *Grand Prix d'Endurance* (first held on 26–27 May 1923) on the old Sarthe circuit at Le Mans, France is 5333,724 km *3314.222 miles* by Dr Helmut Marko (Austria) (b. 27 Apr 1943) and Jonkheer Gijs van Lennep (Netherlands) (b. 16 Mar 1942) in a 4907 cc flat-12 Porsche 917K Group 5 sports car, on 12–13 June 1971. The record for the current circuit is 5047,934 km *3136.64 miles* (av. speed 210,330 km/h *130.69 mph*) by Al Holbert (USA), Hurley Haywood (USA) and Vern Schuppan (Australia) in a Porsche 956 on 18–19 June 1983. The race lap record (8.475 mile *13,64 km* lap) is 3 min 34.2 sec (average speed 142.44 mph *229,244 km/h*) by Jean Pierre Jabouille (France) (b. 1 Oct 1942) driving an Alpine Renault on 11 June 1978. The practice lap record is 3 min 27.6 sec (av. speed 146.97 mph *236,53 km/h*) by Jacques-Bernard 'Jacky' Ickx (Belgium) (b. 1 Jan 1945) in a turbocharged 2.1 litre Porsche 936/78 on 7 June 1978.

Most wins

The race has been won by Ferrari cars nine times, in 1949, 1954, 1958 and 1960–5. The most wins by one man is six by Jacky Ickx, 1969, 1975–7 and 1981–2.

The race has been won 13 times by British cars: Bentley in 1924 and 1927–30, Lagonda in 1935, Jaguar in 1951, 1953 and 1955–7, Aston Martin in 1959 and a Gulf-Ford in 1975.

INDIANAPOLIS 500

The Indianapolis 500 mile *804 km* race (200 laps) was inaugurated in the USA on 30 May 1911. The most successful driver has been Anthony Joseph 'A.J.' Foyt, Jr (USA) (b. 16 Jan 1935) who won in 1961, 1964, 1967 and 1977. The record time is 3 hr 3 min 21 sec (average speed 163.612 mph *263,308 km/h*) by Rick Mears (USA) driving a Penske March-Cosworth on 26 May 1984. The race lap record is 46.41 sec (average speed 193.924 mph *312,090 km/h*) by Mario Andretti (b. Trieste, 28 Feb 1940) (USA), driving a Penske-Cosworth PC6 in 1978. The qualifying lap record speed is 210.689 mph *339,071 km/h* by Tom Sneva (USA) (b. 1 June 1948) driving a March-Cosworth on 18 May 1984.

The record prize fund was nearly $2,800,000 in 1984. The individual prize record is $434,060 by Rick Mears in 1984.

RALLIES

Earliest
The earliest long rally was promoted by the Parisian daily *Le Matin* in 1907 from Peking, China to Paris over about 7500 miles *12 000 km* on 10 June. The winner, Prince Scipione Borghese (1872–1927) of Italy, arrived in Paris on 10 Aug 1907 in his 40 hp Itala accompanied by his chauffeur, Ettore, and Luigi Barzini.

Longest
The longest ever rally was the *Singapore Airlines* London–Sydney Rally over 19,329 miles *31 107 km* from Covent Garden, London on 14 Aug 1977 to Sydney Opera House, won on 28 Sept 1977 by Andrew Cowan, Colin Malkin and Michael Broad in a Mercedes 280E. The longest held annually is the Safari Rally (first run 1953 through Kenya, Tanzania and Uganda) which is up to 3874 miles *6234 km* long, as in the 17th Safari held between 8 and 12 Apr 1971. It has been won a record five times by Shekhar Mehta (b. Uganda 1945) in 1973, 1979–82.

Monte Carlo
The Monte Carlo Rally (first run 1911) has been won a record four times by Sandro Munari (b. 1940) (Italy) in 1972, 1975, 1976 and 1977 and by Walter Röhrl (b. 7 Mar 1947) (with co-driver Christian Geistdorfer) in 1980, 1982–84, each time in a different car. The smallest car to win was an 851 cc Saab driven by Erik Carlsson (Sweden) (b. 5 Mar 1929) and Gunnar Häggbom (Sweden) on 25 Jan 1962, and by Carlsson and Gunnar Palm on 24 Jan 1963.

Britain
The RAC Rally (first held 1932) has been recognised by the FIA since 1957. Hannu Mikkola (Finland) (b. 24 May 1942) (with co-driver Arne Hertz) has a record four wins in a Ford Escort, 1978–9 and an Audi Quatro, 1981–2.

World Championship
Walter Röhrl is the only man to win two drivers' world championships (inst. 1979), 1980 and 1982.

DRAGGING

Piston engined
The lowest elapsed time recorded by a piston-engined dragster is 5.484 sec by Gary Beck (USA) at the 28th annual US Nationals at Indianapolis in 1982. The highest terminal velocity recorded is 257.14 mph *413,83 km/h* by Rocky Epperly (USA) at Irvine, California on 15 Oct 1983. Not accepted by the National Hot Rod Association, Donald Glenn Garlits (USA) (b. 1932) set an American Hot Rod Association record of 260.49 mph *419,21 km/h* on 11 July 1982 at Gary, Indiana in an AHRA approved top fuel dragster powered by a 480 cubic inch, supercharged, fuel injected Dodge V8 engine.

The world record for two runs in opposite directions over 440 yd *402 m* from a standing start is 6.70 sec by Dennis Victor Priddle (b. 1945) of Yeovil, Somerset, driving his 6424 cc supercharged Chrysler dragster developing 1700 bhp using nitromethane and methanol, at Elvington Airfield, North Yorkshire on 7 Oct 1972. The faster run was made in 6.65 sec.

Rocket or jet-engined
The highest terminal velocity recorded by any dragster is 392.54 mph *631,732 km/h* by Kitty O'Neil (USA) at El Mirage Dry Lake, California, USA on 7 July 1977. The lowest elapsed time was 3.72 sec also by Kitty O'Neil on the same occasion.

Terminal velocity is the speed attained at the end of a 440 yd 402 m run made from a standing start and elapsed time is the time taken for the run.

Highest speeds *See also pp. 136 and 177*
The world speed record for compression ignition engined cars is 190.344 mph *306,328 km/h* (average of two runs in opposite directions over a measured mile *1,6 km*) by Robert Havemann driving his *Corsair* streamliner, powered by a turbocharged 6981 cc 6-cylinder GMC 6–71 diesel engine developing 746 bhp, at Bonneville Salt Flats, Utah, USA, in August 1971. The faster run was made at 210 mph *337 km/h*.

The most successful land speed record breaker was Major Sir Malcolm Campbell (1885–1948) of the United Kingdom. He broke the official record nine times between 25 Sept 1924, with 146.157 mph *235,216 km/h* in a Sunbeam, and 3 Sept 1935, when he achieved 301.129 mph *480,620 km/h* in the Rolls-Royce engined *Bluebird*.

Duration record
The greatest distance ever covered in one year is 400 000 km *248,548.5 miles* by François Lecot (1879–1949), an innkeeper from Rochetaillée, near Lyon, France, in a 1900 cc 66 bhp Citroën 11 sedan, mainly between Paris and Monte Carlo, from 22 July 1935 to 26 July 1936. He drove on 363 of the 370 days allowed.

MOUNTAINEERING

See also The Guinness Book of Mountains and Mountaineering Facts and Feats by Edward Pyatt published at £8.95

Origins
Although bronze-age artifacts have been found on the summit of the Riffelhorn, Switzerland (9605 ft *2927 m*), mountaineering, as a sport, has a continuous history dating back only to 1854. Isolated instances of climbing for its own sake exist back to the 13th century. The Atacamenans built sacrificial platforms near the summit of Llullaillaco (22,058 ft *6723 m*) in late pre-Columbian times *c.* 1490. The earliest recorded rock climb in the British Isles was of Stac na Biorrach, St Kilda (236 ft *71,9 m*) by Sir Robert Moray in 1698.

Mount Everest
Mount Everest (29,028 ft *8848 m*) was first climbed at 11.30 a.m. on 29 May 1953, when the summit was reached by Edmund Percival Hillary (b. 20 July 1919), created KBE, of New Zealand, and the Sherpa, Tenzing Norgay (b., as Namgyal Wangdi, in 1914, formerly called Tenzing Khumjung Bhutia), who was awarded the GM. The successful expedition was led by Col (later Hon Brigadier) Henry Cecil John Hunt, CBE, DSO (b. 22 June 1910), who was created a Knight Bachelor in 1953, a life Baron on 11 June 1966 and KG on 23 Apr 1979.

The first climber to succeed three times was the Sherpa, Sundare (or Sungdare) on 5 Oct 1982. The first to succeed via three different routes was Yasuo Kato (Japan) (1949–82), who died shortly after his third ascent on 27 Dec 1982. Franz Oppurg (1948–81) (Austria) was the first to make the final ascent solo on 14 May 1978 while Reinhold Messner (Italy) was the first to make the entire climb solo on 20 Aug 1980. Messner and Peter Habeler (b. 22 July 1942) (Austria) made the first entirely oxygen-less ascent on 8 May 1978. The first Britons to reach the summit were Douglas Scott (b. 29 May 1941) and Dougal Haston (1940–77) on 24 Sept 1975. Five women have reached the summit, the first being Junko Tabei (b. 22 Sept 1939) (Japan) on 16 May 1975. The oldest person was Dr Gerhard Schmatz (W. Germany) (b. 5 June 1929) aged 50 yr 88 days on 1 Oct 1979.

Reinhold Messner (b. 17 Sept 1944), with his ascent of Kangchenjunga in 1982, became the first person to climb the world's three highest mountains, having earlier reached the summits of Everest and K2. He has successfully scaled a record ten of the world's 14 mountains of over 8 000 m *26,250 ft*.

Greatest walls
The highest final stage in any wall climb is that on the south face of Annapurna I (26,545 ft *8091 m*). It was climbed by the British expedition led by Christian John Storey Bonington (b.

celebration is eight by gymnast Aleksandr Ditiatin (USSR) (b. 7 Aug 1957) in 1980.

Most medals *National*

The total figures for medals for all Olympic events (including those now discontinued) for the Summer (1896–1980) and Winter Games (1924–80):

	GOLD	SILVER	BRONZE	TOTAL
1. USA[1]	660[2]	511	444	1615
2. USSR (formerly Russia)	402	330	296	1028
3. GB (including Ireland to 1920)[1]	169	205	186	560

[1] *Excludes medals won in Official Art competitions in 1912–48.*
[2] *The AAU (US) reinstated James Francis Thorpe (1888–1953) the disqualified highest scorer in the 1912 decathlon and pentathlon events on 12 Oct 1973 and the IOC presented medals to Thorpe's children in January 1983.*

Youngest and oldest gold medallists

The youngest ever winner was a French boy (whose name is not recorded) who coxed the Netherlands pair in 1900. He was 7–10 years old and he substituted for Dr Hermanus Brockmann, who coxed in the heats but proved too heavy. The youngest ever female champion is Marjorie Gestring (USA) (b. 18 Nov 1922, now Mrs Bowman), aged 13 yr 267 days, in the 1936 women's springboard event. Oscar Swahn (*see p. 240*) was in the winning Running Deer shooting team in 1912 aged 64 yr 258 days.

Youngest and oldest *Great Britain*

The youngest competitor to represent Britain in the Olympic Games was Magdalena Cecilia Colledge (b. 28 Nov 1920) aged 11 yr 73 days when she skated in the 1932 Games. The oldest was Hilda Lorna Johnstone (b. 4 Sept 1902) aged 70 yr 5 days in the Equestrian Dressage in the 1972 Games.

Longest span

The longest span of an Olympic competitor is 40 years by Dr Ivan Osiier (Denmark) (1888–1965) in fencing, 1908–32 and 1948, and Magnus Konow (Norway) (1887–1972) in yachting, 1908–20, and 1936–48. The longest feminine span is 24 years (1932–56) by the Austrian fencer Ellen Müller-Preis (b. 6 May 1912). Raimondo d'Inzeo (b. 8 Feb 1925) competed for Italy in equestrian events at a record eight celebrations from 1948 to 1976, gaining one gold, two silver and three bronze medals. Janice Lee York Romary (b. 6 Aug 1928) the US fencer, competed in all six Games from 1948 to 1968, and Lia Manoliu (Romania) (b. 25 Apr 1932) competed from 1952 to 1972 winning the discus in 1968.

The longest span of any British competitor is 28 years by Enoch Jenkins (b. 6 Nov 1892) who appeared in the 1924 and the 1952 Games in the clay pigeon shooting event, and the longest feminine span by Dorothy J. B. Tyler (*née* Odam) (b. 14 Mar 1920) who high-jumped from 1936 to 1956. The record number of appearances for Great Britain is six by fencer Bill Hoskyns from 1956 to 1976. Durward Randolph Knowles (b. 2 Nov 1917) competed in yachting for Britain in 1948 and in the following six Games for the Bahamas.

ORIENTEERING

Origins

Orienteering as now known was invented by Major Ernst Killander in Sweden in 1918. It was based on military exercises of the 1890s. The term was first used for an event at Oslo, Norway on 7 Oct 1900. World championships were instituted in 1966. Annual British championships were instituted in 1967 following the formation of the British Orienteering Federation.

Most titles *World*

Sweden has won the men's relay six times between 1966 and 1979 and the women's relay six times, 1966, 1970, 1974–6, 1981 and 1983. Two women's individual titles have been won by Ulla Lindkvist (Sweden), 1966 and 1968 and Annichen Kringstad-Svensson (Sweden), 1981 and 1983. The men's title has been won twice by Age Hadler (Norway) in 1966 and 1972, Egil Johansen (Norway) 1976 and 1978, and Ogvin Thon (Norway) in 1979 and 1981.

Most titles *British*

The men's relay has been won twice by Oxford University, 1975, 1979, and the women's relay three times by Derwent Valley Orienteers, 1975, 1979 and 1980. Geoffrey Peck (b. 27 Sept 1949) has won the men's individual title a record five times, 1971, 1973, 1976–7 and 1979. Carol McNeill (b. 20 Feb 1944) has won the women's title six times, 1967, 1969, 1972–76. She also won the over-35s title in 1984.

PARACHUTING (*See also p. 191*)

Origins

Parachuting became a regulated sport with the institution of world championships in 1951. A team title was introduced in 1954 and women's events were included in 1956.

Most titles *World*

The USSR won the men's team titles in 1954, 1958, 1960, 1966, 1972, 1976, and 1980, and the women's team title in 1956, 1958, 1966, 1968, 1972, and 1976. Nikolai Ushamyev (USSR) has won the individual title twice, 1974 and 1980.

Most titles *British*

Sgt Ronald Alan 'Scotty' Milne (b. 5 Mar 1952) of the Parachute Regiment has won the British title five times in 1976–7, 1979–81. Rob Colpus and Geoff Sanders have each shared ten British titles for Relative Work parachuting, the 4 Way and 8 Way titles won by their team 'Symbiosis' in 1976–7, 1979, 1981–2.

Greatest accuracy

Jacqueline Smith (GB) (b. 29 Mar 1951) scored ten consecutive dead centre strikes (10 cm *4 in* disc) in the World Championships at Zagreb, Yugoslavia, 1 Sept 1978. At Yuma, Arizona, USA, in March 1978, Dwight Reynolds scored a record 105 daytime dead centres, and Bill Wenger and Phil Munden tied with 43 nighttime DCs, competing as members of the US Army team, the Golden Knights. With electronic measuring the official FAI record is 50 DCs by Alexander Aasmiae (USSR) at Ferghana, USSR, Oct 1979.

The Men's Night Accuracy Landing Record on an electronic score pad is 27 consecutive dead centres by Cliff Jones (USA) in 1981.

PELOTA VASCA (*Jaï Alaï*)

Origins

The game, which originated in Italy as *longue paume* and was introduced into France in the 13 century, is said to be the fastest of all ball games. The glove or *gant* was introduced *c.* 1840 and the *chistera* was invented by Jean 'Gantchiki' Dithurbide of Ste Pée, France. The *grand chistera* was invented by Melchior Curuchague of Buenos Aires, Argentina in 1888.

The world's largest *frontón* (enclosed stadium) is the World Jaï Alaï at Miami, Florida, USA, which had a record attendance of 15,052 on 27 Dec 1975.

World Championships

The Federacion Internacional de Pelota Vasca stage world championships every four years (first in 1952). The most successful pair have been Roberto Elias and Juan Labat (Argentina), who won the *Trinquete Share* four times, 1952, 1958, 1962 and 1966. Labat won a record seven world titles in all. The most wins in the long court game *Cesta Punta* is three by Hamuy of Mexico, with two different partners, 1958, 1962 and 1966.

Highest speed

An electronically measured ball velocity of 188 mph *302 km/h* was recorded by José Ramon Areitio at the Newport Jai Alai, Rhode Island, USA on 3 Aug 1979.

Longest domination

The longest domination as the world's No. 1 player was enjoyed by Chiquito de Cambo (*né* Joseph Apesteguy) (France), (1881–1955) from the beginning of the century until succeeded in 1938 by Jean Urruty (France) (b. 19 Oct 1913).

PÉTANQUE

Origins

The origins of pétanque or boules can be traced back over 2000 years, but it was not until 1945 that the Fédération Français de Pétanque et Jeu Provençal was formed, and subsequently the Fédération Internationale (FIPJP). The first recognised British club was formed on 30 Mar 1966 as the Chingford Club de Pétanque and the British Pétanque Association was founded in 1974.

World Championships

Winners of the most world championships (inst. 1959) has been France with seven titles.

24-hour record

A three-man team from the Braintree and District Pétanque League scored a record 813 points in 65 games on 3–4 July 1982.

PIGEON RACING

Earliest references

Pigeon racing developed from the use of homing pigeons for carrying messages. The sport originated in Belgium from commercial services and the earliest long-distance race was from London to Antwerp in 1819, involving 36 pigeons.

Longest flights

The greatest recorded homing flight by a pigeon was made by one owned by the 1st Duke of Wellington (1769–1852). Released from a sailing ship off the Ichabo Islands, West Africa, on 8 April, it dropped dead a mile from its loft at Nine Elms, Wandsworth, London on 1 June 1845, 55 days later, having flown an airline route of 5400 miles *8700 km*, but an actual distance of possibly 7000 miles *11 250 km* to avoid the Sahara Desert. The official British duration record (into Great Britain) is 1173 miles *1887 km* in 15 days by C.S.O. (owned by Rosie and Bruce of Wick) in the 1976 Palamos Race. In the 1975 Palamos Race, *The Conqueror*, owned by Alan Raeside, homed to Irvine, Strathclyde, 1010 miles *1625 km*, in 43 hr 56 min. The greatest number of flights over 1000 miles flown by one pigeon is that of *Dunning Independence* owned by D. Smith which annually flew from Palamos to Dunning, Perthshire, Scotland 1039 miles *1662 km* between 1978 and 1981.

Highest speeds

In level flight in windless conditions it is very doubtful if any pigeon can exceed 60 mph *96 km/h*. The highest race speed recorded is one of 3229 yd *2952 m* per min (110.07 mph *177,14 km/h*) in the East Anglian Federation race from East Croydon on 8 May 1965 when the 1428 birds were backed by a powerful south south-west wind. The winner was owned by A. Vigeon & Son, Wickford, Essex.

The highest race speed recorded over a distance of more than 1000 km *621.37 miles* is 2432.7 yd *2224,5 m* per min (82.93 mph *133,46 km/h*) by a hen in the Central Cumberland Combine race over 683 miles 147 yd *1099,316 km* from Murray Bridge, South Australia to North Ryde, Sydney on 2 Oct 1971.

24 hr records

The world's longest reputed distance in 24 hr is 803 miles *1292 km* (velocity 1525 yd *1394 m* per min) by E. S. Petersen's winner of the 1941 San Antonio R.C. event in Texas, USA.

The best 24 hr performance into the United Kingdom is 724 miles 219 yd *1165,3 km* by E. Cardno's *Mormond Lad*, on 2 July 1977, from Nantes, France to Fraserburgh, Grampian. Average speed was 1648 yd *1507 m* per min (56.18 mph *90,41 km/h*).

Most first prizes

Owned by R. Green, of Walsall Wood, West Midlands, *Champion Breakaway* won 59 first prizes from 1972 to May 1979.

Highest priced bird

The highest recorded price paid for a pigeon is approximately £25,000 by a Japanese fancier for *De Wittslager* to Georges Desender (Belgium) in October 1978.

POLO

Earliest games

Polo is usually regarded as being of Persian origin having been played as *Pulu c.* 525 BC. Other claims have come from Tibet and the Tang Dynasty of China AD 250. The earliest polo club of modern times was the Kachar Club (founded in 1859) in Assam, India. The game was introduced into England from India in 1869 by the 10th Hussars at Aldershot, Hampshire and the earliest match was one between the 9th Lancers and the 10th Hussars on Hounslow Heath, Greater London, in

ELEPHANT POLO

Polo was first played on elephant-back in Jaipur, India in 1976. The World Elephant Polo Association was formed on 1 Apr 1982 and their first championships were staged at Tiger Tops, Nepal on 1 Apr 1983, when the winners were the Tiger Tops Tuskers captained by Mark Payne. The Hurlingham Polo Association 'takes no cognisance' of elephant polo.

July 1871. The earliest international match between England and the USA was in 1886.

Most titles

The British Open Championship for the Cowdray Park Gold Cup was first held in 1956. The most wins is five by Stowell Park, 1973–4, 1976, 1978 and 1980.

Highest handicap

The highest handicap based on eight 7½-min 'chukkas' is ten goals introduced in the USA in 1891 and in the United Kingdom and in Argentina in 1910. The latest of the 41 players ever to receive ten-goal handicaps are Thomas Wayman (USA) and Guillermo Gracida Jr (Mexico). The last (of six) ten-goal handicap players from Great Britain was Gerald Balding in 1939. A match of two 40-goal teams was staged for the first time ever, at Palermo, Buenos Aires, Argentina, in 1975.

The highest handicaps of the United Kingdom's current 600 players are nine by Julian Hipwood (b. 23 June 1946) and by Howard Hipwood. Claire J. Tomlinson of Gloucestershire has a handicap of four, the highest ever attained by a woman.

Highest score

The highest aggregate number of goals scored in an international match is 30, when Argentina beat the USA 21–9 at Meadow Brook, Long Island, New York, USA, in Sept 1936.

POWERBOAT RACING

See also The Guinness Book of Motorboating Facts and Feats *by Kevin Desmond, published by Guinness Superlatives Ltd (price £7.95).*

Origins

A petrol engine was first installed in a boat by Jean Joseph Etienne Lenoir (1822–1900) on the River Seine, Paris in 1865. Actual powerboat racing started in about 1900, the first prominent race being from Calais to Dover in 1903. International racing was largely established by the presentation of a Challenge Trophy by Sir Alfred Harmsworth in 1903. Thereafter racing developed mainly as a 'circuit' or short, sheltered course type competition. Offshore or sea passage races also developed, initially for displacement (non-planing) cruisers. Offshore events for fast (planing) cruisers began in 1958 with a 170 mile *273 km* passage race from Miami, USA to Nassau, Bahamas. Outboard motor, i.e. the combined motor/transmission detachable propulsion unit type racing began in the USA in about 1920. Both inboard and outboard motor boat engines are mainly petrol fuelled, but since 1950 diesel (compression ignition) engines have appeared and are widely used in offshore sport.

Highest Speeds (*For the world water speed record see page 178.*)

The highest speed recorded by a propeller-driven boat is 229.00 mph *368,54 km/h* by *The Texan*, a Kurtis Top Fuel Hydro Drag Boat, driven by Eddie Hill on 5 Sept 1982 at Chowchilla, California, USA. He also set a 440 yd *402 m*

Eddie Hill in his Kurtis Hydro *The Texan* pushed the Drag Boat speed record up to 229 mph in 1982 and the next year won the world series of drag boat racing and set the quarter-mile mark. (*Clyde Parkhurst*)

elapsed time record of 5.16 seconds in this boat at Firebird Lake, Arizona, USA on 13 Nov 1983.

The fastest speed recognised by the Union Internationale Motonautique for an outboard powered boat is in the Class OZ unlimited, circuit boat: 144.16 mph *232,00 km/h* by a Burgess catamaran powered by a 3.5 litre Johnson V8 engine, driven by Rick Frost on Lake Windermere, England on 11 Oct 1983.

The fastest speed recognised for an offshore boat was set by *Innovation*, a 35 ft *10,7 m* Maelstrom boat powered by three Johnson Evinrude outboard engines each of 214 cu in *3507 cc*, driven by Mike Drury at a mean speed for two runs of 131.088 mph *210,966 km/h* at New Orleans, Louisiana, USA on 31 March 1984.

The fastest speed recorded for a diesel (compression ignition) boat is 213,08 km/h *132.40 mph* by the 24 ft *7,3 m* BU221 hydroplane *Rothman's World Leader*, driven by Carlo Bonomi at Venice, Italy on 5 Dec 1982.

Highest race speeds

The highest speeds recorded in races are:
Offshore: 90.97 mph *146,4 km/h* by George Morales (USA) in a Mercruiser Special at Key West, Florida, USA in November 1983.
Circuit: 131.12 mph *211,02 km/h* by F. Forstei (Italy) in the R4 category.

Longest races

The longest offshore race has been the Port Richborough London to Monte Carlo Marathon Offshore International event. The race extended over 2947 miles *4742 km* in 14 stages on 10–25 June 1972. It was won by *H.T.S.* (*GB*) driven by Mike Bellamy, Eddie Chater and Jim Brooker in 71 hr 35 min 56 sec for an average of 41.15 mph *66,24 km/h*. The longest circuit race is the 24 hour race held annually since 1962 on the River Seine at Rouen, France. The 1983 winners Francois Greens, Jan van Brockels and Roger Robin of Belgium drove a Johnson outboard engined Piranha boat at an average speed of 75,02 km/h *46.63 mph*.

Longest Jetboat Jumps

The longest ramp jump achieved by a jetboat has been 120 ft *36,57 m* by Peter Horak (USA) in a Glastron Carlson CVX 20 Jet Deluxe with a 460 Ford V8 engine (take-off speed 55 mph *88 km/h*) for a documentary TV film, at Salton Sea, California, USA on 26 Apr 1980. The longest leap on to land is 172 ft *38,7 m* by Norm Bagrie (NZ) from the Shotover River on 1 July 1982 in the 1½ ton jetboat *Valvolene*.

RACKETS

Origins

There is record of the sale of a racket court at Southernhay, Exeter, Devon dated 12 Jan 1798. The game which is of 17th century origin was played by debtors in the Fleet Prison, London in the middle of the 18th century, and an inmate, Robert Mackay, claimed the first 'world' title in 1820. The first closed court champion was Francis Erwood at Woolwich in 1860. A new court was constructed at the Sea Court Club, Hayling Island, Hampshire in 1979.

Longest reign

Of the 20 world champions since 1820 the longest reign is by Geoffrey Willoughby Thomas Atkins (b. 20 Jan 1927) who held the title after beating the professional James Dear (1910–81) in 1954 and retired, after defending it four times, in April 1972.

Most Amateur titles

Since the Amateur singles championship was instituted in 1888 the most titles won by an individual is nine by Edgar Maximilian Baerlein (1879–1971) between 1903 and 1923. Since the institution of the Amateur doubles championship in 1890 the most shares in titles has been eleven by David Sumner Milford (b. 7 June 1905), between 1938 and 1959 and John Ross Thompson (b. 10 May 1918) between 1948 and 1966. Milford has also seven Amateur singles titles (1930–51), an Open title (1936) and held the World title from 1937 to 1946. Thompson has additionally won an Open singles title and five Amateur singles titles.

RACQUETBALL

Origins
Racquetball was invented in 1950 by Joe Sobek at the Greenwich YMCA, Connecticut, USA, originally as Paddle Rackets. The International Racquetball Association was founded in 1968 by Bob Kendler (USA). The British Racquetball Association was formed in 1981. John Trehearne has won three British titles, 1981–83.

RODEO

Origins
Rodeo which developed from 18th century *fiestas* came into being in the early days of the North American cattle industry. The sport originated in Mexico and spread from there into the cattle regions of the USA. Steer wrestling came in with Bill Pickett (1870–1932) of Texas, in 1900.

The largest rodeo in the world is the Calgary Exhibition and Stampede at Calgary, Alberta, Canada. The Stampede, as it is known, introduced a record prize of $500,000 in 1981. In that year the total paid attendance for the rodeo events over ten days was 122,268. The National Finals Rodeo, held annually in Oklahoma City, USA, had a record total prize money of $700,860 in December 1982.

Most world titles
The record number of all-round titles in the Association of Professional Rodeo Cowboys world championships is six by Larry Mahan (USA) (b. 21 Nov 1943) in 1966–70 and 1973 and, consecutively, 1974–9 by Tom Ferguson (b. 20 Dec 1950). Tom Ferguson had record career earnings of $909,089 to 21 May 1984. Jim Shoulders (b. 1928) of Henryetta, Oklahoma, USA has won a record 16 world championships between 1949 and 1959. The record figure for prize money in a single season is $153,391 by Roy Cooper (b. 13 Nov 1955) of Durant, Oklahoma, USA in 1983. The record for one rodeo is $29,268 by Jimmie Cooper at the National Finals Rodeo, Oklahoma City in December 1982.

Youngest champion
The youngest winner of a world title is Metha Brorsen, of Oklahoma, USA, who won the International Rodeo Association Cowgirls barrel-racing event in 1975 at 11 years old. The youngest champion in Professional Rodeo Cowboys Association/Women's Professional Rodeo Association competition is Jackie Jo Perrin of Antlers, Oklahoma, USA, who won the barrel-racing title in 1977 at age 13.

Time records
Records for timed events, such as calf-roping and steer-wrestling, are not always comparable, because of the widely varying conditions due to the size of arenas and amount of start given the stock. The fastest time recorded for roping a calf is 5.7 sec by Lee Phillips at Assiniboia, Saskatchewan, Canada in 1978, and the fastest time for overcoming a steer is 2.4 sec by James Bynum, at Marietta, Oklahoma, USA, in 1955, by Carl Deaton at Tulsa, Oklahoma, USA in 1976 and by Gene Melton at Pecatonica, Illinois, USA, in 1976.

The standard required time to stay on in bareback, saddle bronc and bull riding events is 8 sec. In the now discontinued ride-to-a-finish events, rodeo riders have been recorded to have survived 90 + min, until the mount had not a buck left in it.

The highest score in bull riding was 98 points out of a possible 100 by Denny Flynn on *Red Lightning* at Palestine, Illinois, USA in 1979.

Champion bull
The top bucking bull was probably *Honky Tonk*, an 11-year-old Brahma, who unseated 187 riders in an undefeated eight-year career to his retirement in September 1978.

Champion bronc
Traditionally a bronc called *Midnight* owned by Jim McNab of Alberta, Canada was never ridden in 12 appearances at the Calgary Stampede.

ROLLER SKATING

Origins
The first roller skate was devised by Jean Joseph Merlin (1735–1803) of Huy, Belgium, in 1760 and demonstrated by him in London but with disastrous results. James L. Plimpton of New York produced the present four-wheeled type and patented it in January 1863. The first indoor rink was opened in the Haymarket, London, in about 1824.

Most titles *Speed*
Most world speed titles have been won by Alberta Vianello (Italy) with 16 between 1953 and 1965. Most British national individual men's titles have been won by Michael Colin McGeogh (b. 30 Mar 1946) with 15 in 1966–83. Chloe Ronaldson (b. 30 Nov 1939) has won 40 individual and 13 team ladies' senior titles from 1958 to 1983.

Most titles *Figure*
The records for figure titles are five by Karl Heinz Losch in 1958–9, 1961–2 and 1966, and four by Astrid Bader, both of W. Germany, in 1965–8. Most world pair titles have been taken by Dieter Fingerle (W. Germany) with four in 1959, 1965–7 with two different partners.

Speed skating
The fastest speed put up in an official world record is 25.78 mph *41,48 km/h* when Giuseppe Cantarella (Italy) (b. 13 Aug 1944) recorded 34.9 sec for 440 yd *402 m* on a road at Catania, Sicily on 28 Sept 1963. The world mile record on a rink is 2 min 25.1 sec by Gianni Ferretti (Italy) (b. 11 May 1948) at Inzell, W. Germany on 28 Sept 1968. The greatest distance skated in 1 hr on a rink by a woman is 35,399 km *21.995 miles* by Marisa Anna Danesi (Italy) (b. 25 Nov 1935) at Inzell, W. Germany on 28 Sept 1968. The men's record on a track is 37,230 km *23.133 miles* by Alberto Civolani (Italy) (b. 16 Mar 1933) at Inzell, W. Germany on 28 Sept 1968. He went on to skate 50 miles *80,46 km* in 2 hr 20 min 33.1 sec.

Largest rink
The greatest indoor rink ever to operate was located in the Grand Hall, Olympia, London. Opened 1890 and closed in 1912 it had an actual skating area of 68,000 ft² *6 300 m²*. The current largest is the Fireside Roll-Arena, Hoffman Estates, Illinois, USA with a total skating surface of 29,859 ft² *2774 m²*.

Endurance
Theodore James Coombs (b. 1954) of Hermosa Beach, California, skated 5193 miles *8357 km* from Los Angeles to New York and back to Yates Center, Kansas from 30 May to 14 Sept 1979.

Land's End to John o'Groats
Steve Fagan, 20, roller skated the distance, 925 miles *1488 km*, in 9 days 10 hr 25 min on 1–10 May 1984.

ROLLER HOCKEY

Roller hockey (previously known as Rink Hockey in Europe) was introduced to Britain as Rink Polo, at the old Lava rink, Denmark Hill, London in the late 1870s. The Amateur Rink Hockey Association was formed in 1908, and in 1913 became the National Rink Hockey (now Roller Hockey) Association. Britain won the inaugural World Championship in 1936 since when Portugal has won most titles with 12 between 1947 and 1982. The European Championship (inst. 1926) was won by Portugal a record 15 times between 1947 and 1977.

ROWING

Oldest race
The Sphinx stela of Amenhotep II (1450–1425 BC) records that he *stroked* a boat for some three miles. The earliest established sculling race is the Doggett's Coat and Badge, which was first rowed on 1 Aug 1716 from London Bridge to Chelsea and is still contested annually. Although rowing regattas were held in Venice in 1300 the first English regatta probably took place on the Thames by the Ranelagh Gardens, near Putney in 1775.

MEN—Fastest times over 2 000 m course (still water)				
	min sec	Country	Place	Date
Single Sculls	6:49.68	Nikolai Dovgan, USSR	Amsterdam, Netherlands	26 Aug 1978
Double Sculls	6:12.48	Norway	Montreal, Canada	23 July 1976
Coxed Pairs	6:49.75	GDR	Duisberg, W Germany	4 Sept 1983
Coxless Pairs	6:32.63	GDR	Lucerne, Switzerland	23 Aug 1982
Coxed Fours	6:05.21	GDR	Lucerne, Switzerland	17 June 1984
Coxless Fours	5:53.65	GDR	Montreal, Canada	23 July 1976
Quadruple Sculls	5:45.97	GDR	Duisberg, W. Germany	4 Sept 1983
Eights	5:27.14	USA	Lucerne, Switzerland	17 June 1984

WOMEN—Fastest times over 1 000 m course (still water)				
Single Sculls	3:30.74	Cornelia Linse, GDR	Lucerne, Switzerland	18 June 1984
Double Sculls	3:09.97	GDR	Lucerne, Switzerland	18 June 1984
Coxless Pairs	3:26.32	GDR	Amsterdam, Netherlands	21 Aug 1977
Coxed Fours	3:11.18	GDR	Duisberg, W. Germany	4 Sept 1983
Quadruple Sculls	3:02.48	GDR	Duisberg, W. Germany	4 Sept 1983
Eights	2:54.05	USA	Lucerne, Switzerland	16 June 1984

Most Olympic medals

Five oarsmen have won three gold medals: John B. Kelly (USA) (1889–1960), father of the late HSH Princess Grace of Monaco, in the sculls (1920) and double sculls (1920 and 1924); his cousin Paul Vincent Costello (USA) (b. 27 Dec 1899) in the double sculls (1920, 1924 and 1928); Jack Beresford, Jr (GB) (1899–1977) in the sculls (1924), coxless fours (1932) and double sculls (1936), Vyacheslav Ivanov (USSR) (b. 30 July 1938) in the sculls (1956, 1960 and 1964) and Siegfried Brietzke (GDR) (b. 12 June 1952) in the coxless pairs (1972) and coxless fours (1976, 1980).

Boat Race

The earliest University Boat Race, which Oxford won, was from Hambledon Lock to Henley Bridge on 10 June 1829. Outrigged eights were first used in 1846. In the 130 races to 1984, Cambridge won 68 times, Oxford 61 times and there was a dead heat on 24 Mar 1877.

The race record time for the course of 4 miles 374 yd *6779 km* (Putney to Mortlake) is 16 min 45 sec by Oxford on 18 Mar 1984. This represents an average speed of 15.09 mph *24,28 km/h*. The smallest winning margin has been by a canvas by Oxford in 1952 and 1980. The greatest margin (apart from sinking) was Cambridge's win by 20 lengths in 1900.

The record to the Mile Post is 3 min 31 sec (Oxford 1978) an average speed of 17.06 mph *27,45 km/h*; Hammersmith Bridge 6 min 24 sec (Oxford 1978); Chiswick Steps 10 min 15 sec (Oxford 1984); and Barnes Bridge 13 min 57 sec (Oxford 1984).

Boris Rankov (Oxford, 1978–83) rowed in a record six winning boats. Susan Brown (b. 29 June 1958), the first woman to take part, coxed the winning Oxford boats in 1981 and 1982.

The heaviest man ever to row in a University boat has been Stephen G. H. Plunkett (Queen's) the No. 5 in the 1976 Oxford boat at 229 lb *104 kg*. The 1983 Oxford crew averaged a record 204.3 lb *92,5 kg*. The lightest oarsman was the 1882 Oxford Stroke, Alfred Herbert Higgins, at 9 st 6½ lb *60 kg*. The lightest coxes, Francis Henry Archer (Cambridge) (1843–89) in 1862 and Hart Parker Vincent Massey (Oxford) (b. Canada, 30 Mar 1918) in 1939, were both 5 st 2 lb *32,6 kg*.

Head of the River

A processional race for eights instituted in 1926, the Head has an entry limit of 420 crews (3780 competitors). The record for the course Mortlake–Putney (the reverse of the Boat race) is 17 min 10.42 sec by the ARA National Squad in 1982.

Henley Royal Regatta

The annual regatta at Henley-on-Thames, Oxfordshire, was inaugurated on 26 Mar 1839. Since then the course, except in 1923, has been about 1 mile 550 yd *2112 m* varying slightly according to the length of boat. In 1967 the shorter craft were 'drawn up' so all bows start level.

The most wins in the Diamond Challenge Sculls (inst. 1844) is six consecutively by Stuart A. Mackenzie (b. 5 Apr 1937) (Australia and GB) 1957–62. The record time is 7 min 40 sec by Sean Drea (Neptune RC, Ireland) on 5 July 1975. The Grand Challenge Cup (inst. 1839) for eights, has been won 27 times by Leander crews between 1840 and 1953. The record time for the event is 6 min 13 sec by Harvard Univ, USA, and a combined Leander/Thames Tradesmen crew, both on 5 July 1975.

Sculling

The record number of wins in the Wingfield Sculls (Putney to Mortlake) (instituted 1830) is seven by Jack Beresford, Jr. from 1920 to 1926. The fastest time has been 21 min 11 sec by Leslie Frank Southwood (b. 18 Jan 1906) on 12 Aug 1933. The most world professional sculling titles (instituted 1831) won is seven by William Beach (Australia) (1850–1935), 1884–87.

Oxford won the 1984 Boat race, for their ninth consecutive win, the longest domination since Cambridge's 13-year streak from 1924 to 1936. (*All-Sport*)

Highest speed

The highest recorded speed on non-tidal water for 2000 m *2187 yd* is by an East German eight in 5 min 27.14 sec (22,01 km/h *13.68 mph*) at Lucerne, Switzerland on 17 June 1984. A crew from Penn AC, USA, was timed in 5 min 18.8 sec (14.03 mph *22,58 km/h*) in the FISA Championships on the River Meuse, Liege, Belgium, on 17 Aug 1930.

Cross Channel

Ivor Lloyd sculled across the English Channel in a record 3 hr 35 min 1 sec on 4 May 1983. *For trans-Atlantic records see p. 181.*

River Thames

A crew of five from Poplar Fire Station, London Fire Brigade rowed the navigable length of the Thames, 185.88 miles *299,14 km*, from Lechlade Bridge, Gloucestershire to Southend Pier, Essex in 45 hr 32 min in a 22 ft 10 in *6,96 m* skiff on 16–18 Apr 1984. The fastest time from Folly Bridge, Oxford to Westminster Bridge, London (112 miles *180 km*) is 14 hr 35 min 46 sec by an eight from Guy's Hospital on 28 Apr 1974.

Longest race

The longest annual rowing race is the annual Tour du Lac Leman, Geneva, Switzerland for coxed fours (the five man crew taking turns as cox) over 160 km *99 miles*. The record winning time is 12 hr 52 min by LAGA Delft, Netherlands on 3 Oct 1982.

SHINTY

Origins

Shinty (from the Gaelic *sinteag*, a bound) has roots reaching back more than 2000 years to the ancient game of *camanachd*, the sport of the curved stick, the diversion of the heroes of Celtic history and legend. It was effective battle training, exercising speed and co-ordination of eye and arm along with aggression and cool self-control. In spite of the break up of the clan system in the Highlands of Scotland, the "ball plays", involving whole parishes, without limit in number or time except the fall of night, continued in areas such as Lochaber, Badenoch and Strathglass. Whisky and the inspiration of the bagpipes were important ingredients of these occasions. The ruling body of this apparently ungovernable game was established in 1893 when the Camanachd Association was set up at Kingussie, Highland.

Most titles

Newtonmore, Highland has won the Camanachd Association Challenge Cup (instituted 1896) a record 26 times (1896–1982). Johnnie Campbell of Newtonmore won a record 11 winners' medals. In 1923 the Furnace Club, Argyll won the cup without conceding a goal throughout the competition.

Highest scores

The highest Scottish Cup Final score was in 1909 when Newtonmore beat Furnace 11–3 at Glasgow, Dr Johnnie Cattanach scoring eight hails or goals. In 1938 John Macmillan Mactaggart scored ten hails for Mid-Argyll in a Camanachd Cup match.

SHOOTING

Earliest club

The Lucerne Shooting Guild (Switzerland) was formed *c.*1466 and the first recorded shooting match was at Zurich in 1472.

Most Olympic medals

The record number of medals won is 11 by Carl Townsend Osburn (USA) (1884–1966) in 1912, 1920 and 1924, consisting of five gold, four silver and two bronze. Six other marksmen have won five gold medals. The only marksman to win three individual gold medals has been Gudbrand Gudbrandsönn Skatteboe (Norway) (1875–1965), in 1906.

Bisley

The National Rifle Association was instituted in 1859. The Queen's (King's) Prize has been shot since 1860 and has only once been won by a woman—Marjorie Elaine Foster (1894–1974) (score 280) on 19 July 1930. Arthur George Fulton (1887–1972) won a record three times (1912, 1926, 1931). Both his father and his son also won the Prize.

The highest score (possible 300) for the final of the Queen's Prize is 295 by Lindsay Peden (Scotland) on 24 July 1982. The record for the Silver Medals is 150 (possible 150) by Martin John Brister (City Rifle Club) (b. 1951) and the Lord Swansea on 24 July 1971. This was equalled by John Henry Carmichael (WRA Bromsgrove RC) on 28 July 1979 and Robert Stafford on 26 July 1980, with the size of the bullseyes reduced.

Small-Bore

The National Small-Bore Rifle Association, of Britain, was formed in 1901. The British team record (1966 target) is 1988 × 2000 by Lancashire in 1968–9 and London in 1980–1. The British individual small-bore rifle record for 60 shots prone is 600 × 600, first achieved by John Palin (b. 16 July 1934) in Switzerland in 1972. Richard Hansen shot 5000 bullseyes in 24 hr at Fresno, Cal, USA on 13 June 1929.

Clay Pigeon

Most world titles have been won by Susan Nattrass (Canada) (b. 5 Nov 1950) with six in 1974–5, 1977–9, 1981. The record number of clay birds shot in an hour is 2215 by Joseph Kreckman at the Paradise Shooting Centre, Cresco, Pennsylvania, USA on 28 Aug 1983 (from 3176 shots from the hip). Graham Douglas Geater (b. 21 July 1947) shot 2264 targets in an hour on a Trapshooting range at the NILO Gun Club, Papamoa, New Zealand on 17 Jan 1981.

The maximum 200/200 was achieved by Ricardo Ruiz Rumoroso at the Spanish clay pigeon championships at Zaragoza on 12 June 1983.

Noel D. Townend achieved the maximum 200 consecutive Down the Line targets at Nottingham on 21 Aug 1983.

Bench rest shooting

The smallest group on record at 1000 yd *914 m* is 5.093 in *12,94 cm* by Rick Taylor with a 300 Weatherby at Williamsport, Penn., USA on 24 Aug 1980.

Highest score in 24 hr

The Easingwold Rifle and Pistol Club team of John Smith, Edward Kendall and Paul Duffield scored 120,242 points (averaging 95.66 per card) on 6–7 Aug 1983.

INDIVIDUAL WORLD RECORDS

Event			Possible—Score
FREE RIFLE	300 m	3 × 40 shots	1200—**1160**
Lones W. Wigger (USA)		Seoul, S. Korea	Oct 1978
Lones W. Wigger (USA)		Rio de Janeiro, Brazil	Nov 1981
		60 shots prone	600—**595**
K. Leskinen (Finland)		Oslo, Norway	1983
T. Müller (Switzerland)		Oslo, Norway	1983
STANDARD RIFLE	300 m	3 × 20 shots	600—**580**
Lones W. Wigger (USA)		Rio de Janeiro, Brazil	1 Nov 1981
SMALL-BORE RIFLE	50 m	3 × 40 shots	1200—**1180**
Kiril Ivanov (USSR)		Lvov, USSR	Dec 1982
		60 shots prone	600—**600**
Alistair Allan (GB)		Titograd, Yugoslavia	21 Sept 1981
Ernest Van de Zande (USA)		Rio de Janeiro, Brazil	1 Nov 1981
FREE PISTOL	50 ml	60 shots	600—**581**
Aleksandr Melentev (USSR)		Moscow, USSR	20 July 1980
RAPID FIRE PISTOL	25 m	60 shots	600—**599**
Igor Puzyrev (USSR)		Titograd, Yugoslavia	21 Sept 1981
CENTRE FIRE PISTOL	25 m	60 shots	600—**597**
Thomas D. Smith (USA)		São Paulo, Brazil	1963
STANDARD PISTOL	25 m	60 shots	600—**584**
Eric Buljong (USA)		Caracas, Venezuela	20 Aug 1983
RUNNING TARGET	50 m	60 shots 'normal runs'	600—**595**
Igor Sokolov (USSR)		Miskulc, Hungary	9 Aug 1981
TRAP	—	200 birds	200—**200**
Danny Carlisle (USA)		Caracas, Venezuela	20 Aug 1983
SKEET	—	200 birds	200—**200**
Matthew Dryke (USA)		São Paulo, Brazil	4 Nov 1981
AIR RIFLE	10 m	60 shots	600—**590**
Harald Stenvaag (Norway)		The Hague, Netherlands	19 Mar 1982
AIR PISTOL	10 m	60 shots	600—**591**
Vladas Tourla (USSR)		Caracas, Venezuela	20 Aug 1983

SKIING

See also The Guinness Book of Skiing *by Peter Lunn, published in 1983 at £8.95.*

Origins

The most ancient ski in existence was found well preserved in a peat bog at Hoting, Sweden, dating from *c.* 2500 BC. The earliest recorded military use of skiing was at the Battle of Isen, near Oslo, Norway in 1200. The Trysil Shooting and Skiing

Club, founded in Norway in 1861, claims it is the world's oldest. The oldest ski competitions are the Holmenkøllen Nordic events which were first held in 1866. The first downhill races were staged in Australia in the 1850s. The first Slalom event was run at Mürren, Switzerland, on 21 Jan 1922. The International Ski Federation (FIS) was founded on 2 Feb 1924, succeeding the International Skiing Commission, founded at Christiana (Oslo), Norway on 18 Feb 1910. The Ski Club of Great Britain was founded on 6 May 1903. The National Ski Federation of Great Britain was formed in 1964 and changed its name to the British Ski Federation in 1981.

Most titles *World Championships—Alpine*

The world Alpine championships were inaugurated at Mürren, Switzerland, in 1931. The greatest number of titles won has been by Christel Cranz (b. 1 July 1914) of Germany, with seven individual—four Slalom (1934, 1937–9) and three Downhill (1935, 1937, 1939), and five Combined (1934–5, 1937–9). She also won the gold medal for the Combined in the 1936 Olympics. The most won by a man is seven by Anton 'Toni' Sailer (b. 17 Nov 1935) (Austria) who won all four in 1956 (Giant Slalom, Slalom, Downhill and the non-Olympic Alpine Combination) and the Downhill, Giant Slalom and Combined in 1958.

Most titles *World Championships—Nordic*

The first world Nordic championships were those of the 1924 Winter Olympics in Chamonix, France. The greatest number of titles won is nine by Galina Kulakova (b. 29 Apr 1942) (USSR) in 1968–78. She also won four silver and four bronze medals for a record 17 in total. The most won by a man is eight, including relays, by Sixten Jernberg (b. 6 Feb 1929) (Sweden) in 1956–64. Johan Grøttumsbraaten (1899–1942) of Norway won six individual titles (two 18 km cross-country, four Nordic combined) in 1926–32. The record for a jumper is five by Birger Ruud (b. 23 Aug 1911) of Norway, in 1931–2 and 1935–7. Ruud is the only person to win Olympic events in each of the dissimilar Alpine and Nordic disciplines. In 1936 he won the ski-jumping and the Alpine downhill (which was not then a separate event, but only a segment of the combined event).

Marja-Liisa Hamaelaeinen won all three individual gold medals in the women's cross-country skiing events at the 1984 Winter Olympics. (*All-Sport*)

WORLD CUP

The World Cup was introduced for Alpine events in 1967 and for Nordic events in 1981. The most individual event wins is 79 by Ingemar Stenmark (Sweden) (b. 18 Mar 1956) in 1974–84, including a record 14 in one season in 1979. Annemarie Moser (nee Pröll) (Austria) (b. 27 Mar 1953) won a women's record 62 individual event wins, 1970–9. She had a record 11 consecutive downhill wins from Dec 1972 to Jan 1974.

Most World Cup titles: ALPINE
MEN

Overall	4	Gustavo Thoeni (Italy)	1971–3, 1975
Downhill	5	Franz Klammer (Austria)	1975–8, 1983
Slalom	9	Ingemar Stenmark (Sweden)	1975–81, 1983–4
Giant Slalom	7	Ingemar Stenmark	1975–6, 1978–81, 1984

Jean-Claude Killy (France) (b. 30 Aug 1943) is the only person to win all four titles—downhill, slalom, giant slalom and overall. He won them all in 1967.

WOMEN

Overall	6	Annemarie Moser (Austria)	1971–5, 1979
Downhill	7	Annemarie Moser	1971–5, 1978–9
Slalom	3	Lise-Marie Morerod (Switzerland)	1975–7
	3	Erika Hess (Switzerland)	1981–3
Giant Slalom	3	Annemarie Moser	1971–2, 1975

NORDIC
MEN

Jumping	2	Armin Kogler (Austria)	1981–2
Cross-country	2	Aleksandr Zavialov (USSR)	1981, 1983

WOMEN

Cross-country	2	Marja-Liisa Haemaelainen (Finland)	1983–4

Most titles *British*

The most British skiing overall titles won is four by Stuart Fitzsimmons (b. 28 Dec 1956) in 1973, 1975–6 and 1979. The most ladies' titles won is four by Isobel M. Roe (1938–9, 1948–9), Gina Hathorn (b. 6 July 1949) (1966, 1968–70), and Valentina Iliffe (b. 17 Feb 1956) (1975–6, 1979–80).

Ski-jumping

The longest ski-jump ever recorded is one of 185 m *607 ft* by Matti Nykaenen (b. 17 July 1963) (Finland) at Oberstdorf, W. Germany on 17 Mar 1984. The female record is 110 m *361 ft* by Tiina Lehtola (b. 3 Aug 1962) (Finland) at Ruka, Finland on 29 Mar 1981. The longest dry ski-jump is 92 m *302 ft* by Hubert Schwarz (W. Ger) at Berchtesgarten, W. Germany on 30 June 1981.

Highest speed—downhill

The highest speed claimed for a skier is 208,936 km/h *129.827 mph* by Franz Weber (Austria) and the fastest by a woman is 200,780 km/h *124.759 mph* by Melissa Dimino (USA) both at Les Arcs, France on 19 Apr 1984. The highest average speed in the Olympic downhill race was 104,53 km/h *64.95 mph* by William D. Johnson (USA) (b. 30 Mar 1960) at Sarajevo, Yugoslavia on 16 Feb 1984. The fastest in a World Cup downhill is 107,82 km/h *67.00 mph* by Harti Weirather (Austria) (b. 25 Jan 1958) at Kitzbühl, Austria on 15 Jan 1982.

Highest speed—cross country

Bill Koch (USA) (b. 13 Apr 1943) on 26 March 1981 skied ten times round a 5 km *3.11 miles* loop on Marlborough Pond, near Putney, Vermont, USA. He completed the 50 km in 1 hr 59 min 47 sec, an average speed of 25,045 km/h *15.57 mph*. A race includes uphill and downhill sections; the record time for a 50 km race is 2 hr 15 min 55.8 sec by Thomas Wassberg (Sweden) (b. 27 Mar 1956) in the 1984 Olympics, an average speed of 22,07 km/h *13.71 mph*. The record for a 15 km Olympic or World Championship race is 38 min 52.5 sec by Oddvar Braa (Norway) (b. 16 Mar 1951) at the 1982 World Championships, an average speed of 23,15 km/h *14.38 mph*.

Closest Verdict

The narrowest winning margin in a championship ski race was one hundredth of a second by Thomas Wassberg (Sweden) over Juha Mieto (Finland) (b. 20 Nov 1949) in the Olympic 15 km Cross-country race at Lake Placid, USA on 17 Feb 1980. His winning time was 41 min 57.63 sec.

Highest altitude

Jean Atanassilf and Nicolas Jaeger skied from 8200 m *26,900 ft* to 6200 m *20,340 ft* on the 1978 French Expedition on Mt Everest.

Steepest descent

The steepest descents in alpine skiing history have been by Sylvain Saudan. At the start of his descent from Mont Blanc on the north-east side down the Couloir Gervasutti from 4248 m *13,937 ft* on 17 Oct 1967 he skied to gradients of *c.* 60°.

Longest run

The longest all-downhill ski run in the world is the Weissfluhjoch-Küblis Parsenn course, near Davos, Switzerland, which measures 12,23 km *7.6 miles.* The run from the Aiguille du Midi top of the Chamonix lift (vertical lift 2759 m *9052 ft*) across the Vallée Blanche is 20,9 km *13 miles.*

Longest races

The world's longest ski races are the Grenader, run just North of Oslo, Norway and the König Ludwig Lauf in Oberammergau, W. Germany. Both are of 90 km *55.9 miles.* The Canadian Ski Marathon at 160 km *99 miles* from Lachute, Quebec to Ottawa, Ontario is longer, but is run in two parts on consecutive days.

The world's greatest Nordic ski race is the Vasaloppet, which commemorates an event of 1521 when Gustav Vasa (1496–1560), later King Gustavus Eriksson, fled 85,8 km *53.3 miles* from Mora to Sälen, Sweden. He was overtaken by loyal, speedy scouts on skis, who persuaded him to return eastwards to Mora to lead a rebellion and become the king of Sweden. The re-enactment of this return journey is now an annual event at 89 km *55.3 miles,* with a record 12,000 entrants (including 188 women) in 1981. The fastest time is 3 hr 58 min 8 sec by Konrad Hallenbarter (Switzerland) on 6 Mar 1983. The Vasaloppet is now the longest of ten long distance races in ten countries constituting the World loppet.

The longest downhill race is the *Inferno* in Switzerland, 14 km *8.7 miles* from the top of the Schilthorn to Lauterbrunnen. In 1981 there was a record entry of 1401, with Heinz Fringer (Switzerland) winning in a record 15 min 44.57 sec.

Long Distance Nordic skiing records

In 24 hr Alf Waaler covered 302,668 km *188 miles 122 yd* at Sanderstølen, Norway on 24–25 Mar 1984.

In 48 hr Bjørn Løkken (Norway) (b. 27 Nov 1937) covered 513,568 km *319 miles 205 yd* on 11–13 Mar 1982.

Ski-Parachuting

The greatest recorded vertical descent in parachute ski-jumping is 3300 ft *1006 m* by Rick Sylvester (b. 3 Apr 1942) (US) who on 28 July 1976 skied off the 6600 ft *2011 m* summit of Mt Asgard in Auyuittuq National Park, Baffin Island, Canada, landing on the Turner Glacier, the jump for a sequence in the James Bond film 'The Spy Who Loved Me'.

Ski-Bob *Origins*

The ski-bob was invented by J. C. Stevenson of Hartford, Connecticut, USA in 1891, and patented (No. 47334) on 19 Apr 1892 as a 'bicycle with ski-runners'. The Fédération Internationale de Skibob was founded on 14 Jan 1961 in Innsbruck, Austria and the first world championships were held at Bad Hofgastein, Austria in 1967. The Ski-Bob Association of Great Britain was registered on 23 Aug 1967. The highest speed attained is 166 km/h *103.4 mph* by Erich Brenter (b. 1940) (Austria) at Cervinia, Italy, in 1964.

Ski-Bob *World Championships*

The only ski-bobbers to retain a world championship are: men—Alois Fischbauer (Austria) (b. 6 Oct 1951), 1973 and 1975, Robert Mühlberger (W. Germany), 1979 and 1981; women—Gerhilde Schiffkorn (Austria) (b. 22 Mar 1950), 1967 and 1969, Gertrude Geberth (Austria) (b. 18 Oct 1951), 1971 and 1973.

Michela Figini of Switzerland became the youngest ever Olympic skiing champion when she won the downhill in 1984 at the age of 17 yr 315 days. (*All-Sport*)

Snowmobile

A record speed of 148.6 mph *239,1 km/h* was set by Tom Earhart (USA) in a Budweiser-Polaris snowmobile designed and owned by Bob Gaudreau at Lake Mille Lacs, Minnesota, USA on 25 Feb 1982. (*See also p. 139*).

Longest lift

The longest gondola ski lift is 6239 m *3.88 miles* long at Grindelwald-Männlichen, Switzerland (in two sections, but one gondola). The longest chair lift in the world is the Alpine Way to Kosciusko Châlet lift above Thredbo, near the Snowy Mountains, New South Wales, Australia. It takes from 45 to 75 min to ascend the 3.5 miles *5,6 km,* according to the weather. The highest is at Chacaltaya, Bolivia, rising to 5029 m *16,500 ft.*

GRASS SKIING

Grass skis were first manufactured by Josef Kaiser (W. Ger) in 1963. World Championships (awarded for giant slalom, slalom and combined) were first held in 1979. The most titles won is five by Ingrid Hirschhofer (Austria). The most by a man is four by Vincent Riewe (W. Germany), including all three in 1979.

The speed record is 86,88 km/h *53.99 mph* by Erwin Gansner (Switzerland); the British record is 79,11 km/h *49.16 mph* by Nigel Smith, both at Owen, West Germany on 5 Sept 1982.

SOFTBALL

Origins

Softball, the indoor derivative of baseball, was invented by George Hancock at the Farragut Boat Club of Chicago, Illinois in 1887. Rules were first codified in Minneapolis, Minnesota, USA in 1895 as Kitten Ball. The name Softball was introduced

MOST OLYMPIC TITLES—SKIING

Men Alpine	3	Anton 'Toni' Sailer (Austria) (b. 17 Nov 1935)	Downhill, slalom, giant slalom, 1956
	3	Jean-Claude Killy (France) (b. 30 Aug 1943)	Downhill, slalom, giant slalom, 1968
Men Nordic	4[1]	Sixten Jernberg (Sweden) (b. 6 Feb 1929)	50 km, 1956; 30 km, 1960; 50 km and 4 × 10 km, 1964
Women Alpine	2	Andrea Mead-Lawrence (USA) (b. 19 Apr 1932)	Slalom, giant slalom, 1952
	2	Marielle Goitschel (France) (b. 28 Sept 1945)	Giant slalom, 1964; slalom, 1968
	2	Marie-Therese Nadig (Switz) (b. 8 Mar 1954)	Downhill, giant slalom, 1972
	2[2]	Rosi Mittermaier (now Neureuther) (W. Germany) (b. 5 Aug 1950)	Downhill, slalom, 1976
	2[3]	Hanni Wenzel (Liechtenstein) (b. 14 Dec 1956)	Giant slalom, slalom 1980
Women Nordic	4[4]	Galina Kulakova (USSR) (b. 29 Apr 1942)	5 km, 10 km and 3 × 5 km relay, 1972; 4 × 5 km relay, 1976
	3 (individual)	Marja-Liisa Haemaelainen (Finland) (b. 10 Aug 1955)	5 km, 10 km and 20 km 1984

[1] *Jernberg also won three silver and two bronze for a record nine Olympic medals.*
[2] *Also won silver medal in Giant Slalom in 1976.*
[3] *Wenzel won a silver in the 1980 Downhill and a bronze in the 1976 Slalom.*
[4] *Kulakova also won two silver and two bronze medals in 1968, 1976 and 1980.*

The highly dangerous sport of Ice Speedway. 2½ inch *6 cm* spikes on the tyres are essential. This is Eric Stenlund of Sweden (b. 25 May 1962), the 1984 World Champion and the first non-Russian to win. (*Don Morley*)

by Walter Hakanson at a meeting of the National Recreation Congress in 1926. The name was adopted throughout the USA in 1930. Rules were formalised in 1933 by the International Joint Rules Committee for Softball and adopted by the Amateur Softball Association of America. The International Softball Federation was formed in 1950 as governing body for both fast pitch and slow pitch. It was re-organised in 1965.

Most titles

The USA has won the men's world championship (inst. 1966) four times, 1966, 1968, 1976 (shared), and 1980. The USA has twice won the women's title (inst. 1965) in 1974 and 1978.

WORLD CHAMPIONSHIP RECORDS

MEN

Most runs	12	Generoso Lopez (Venezuela)	1966
Most home runs	4	Robert 'Bob' Burrows (Canada)	1976
Most hits	17	Basil McLean (New Zealand)	1976
RBIs	14	Chuck Teuscher (USA)	1966
	14	Robert 'Bob' Burrows (Canada)	1976
Highest average	.556	Seiichi Tanaka (Japan)	1980
Most wins	6	Owen Walford (New Zealand)	1976
	6	Owen Walford (USA, formerly NZ)	1980
Most innings pitched	59	Ty Stofflet (USA)	1976
Most strikeouts	98	Ty Stofflet (USA)	1976
Most perfect games	1	Joe Lynch (USA); Chuck Richard (USA);	1976
		Dave Ruthowsky (Canada)	1968

WOMEN

Most runs	13	Kathy Elliott (USA)	1974
Most hits	17	Miyoko Naruse (Japan)	1974
Most doubles	4	Vicki Murray (New Zealand)	1982
	4	Suh-Chiung Ju (Taiwan)	1982
Most triples	6	Miyoko Naruse (Japan)	1974
	6	Yug-Feng Yang (Taiwan)	1982
RBIs	11	Miyoko Naruse (Japan); Keiko Usui (Japan);	
		Kathy Elliott (USA)	1974
Highest average	.550	Tamara Bryce (Panama)	1978
Most wins	6	Lorraine Wooley (Australia)	1965
	6	Nancy Welborn (USA)	1970
Most innings pitched	50	Nancy Welborn (USA)	1970
Most strikeouts	76	Joan Joyce (USA)	1974
Most perfect games	2	Joan Joyce (USA)	1974

SPEEDWAY

Origins

Motorcycle racing on large dirt track surfaces has been traced back to 1902 in the United States. The first organized 'short track' races were at the West Maitland (New South Wales, Australia) Agricultural Show in November 1923. The sport evolved in Great Britain with small diameter track racing at Droylsden, Greater Manchester on 25 June 1927 and a cinder track event at High Beech, Essex, on 19 Feb 1928.

British championships

The National League was contested from 1932 to 1964. The Wembley Lions who won in 1932, 1946–7, 1949–53, had a record eight victories. In 1965 it was replaced by the British League which Belle Vue have won four times, including three times in succession (1970–2). Wimbledon are the only club to have competed every year in National and British Leagues. Belle Vue (Manchester) had a record nine victories (1933–7, 1946–7, 1949 and 1958) in the National Trophy Knock-out Competition (held 1931–64). This was replaced in 1965 by the Knock Out Cup, which has been won three times by Cradley Heath, Belle Vue, Ipswich and Wimbledon.

World championships

The World Speedway Championship was inaugurated at Wembley, London in September 1936. The most wins have been six by Ivan Gerald Mauger (New Zealand) (b. 4 Oct 1939) in 1968–70, 1972, 1977 and 1979. Barry Briggs (New Zealand) (b. 30 Dec 1934) made a record 17 consecutive appearances in the finals (1954–70) and won the world title in 1957–8, 1964 and 1966. He also scored a record 201 points in world championship competition.

England have most wins in the World Team Cup (inst. 1960) with eight, and the World Pairs Championship (inst. 1968) with seven. Poland uniquely competed in 21 successive World Team Cup finals, 1960–80 and in a 22nd in 1984. The maximum 30 points were scored in the World Pairs Championship by Jerzy Szczakiel (b. 28 Jan 1949) and Andrzej Wyglenda (Poland) at Rybnik, Poland in 1971 and by Arthur Dennis Sigalos (b. 16 Aug 1959) and Robert Benjamin 'Bobby' Schwartz (b. 10 Aug 1956) (USA) at Liverpool, New South Wales, Australia on 11 Dec 1982.

Ove Fundin (Sweden) (b. 23 May 1933) won a record twelve world titles, five individual, one Pairs, and six World Team Cup medals in 1956–70.

Most points

In League racing the highest score recorded was when Crayford beat Milton Keynes 76–20 in the new 16-heat formula for the National League on 26 Oct 1982. A maximum possible score was achieved by Bristol when they defeated Glasgow (White City) 70–14 on 7 Oct 1949 in the National League Division Two. The highest number of League points scored by an individual in a season was 516 by Stephen Faulder Lawson (b. 11 Dec 1957) for Glasgow in the National League in 1982.

SQUASH RACKETS

See also The Guinness Book of Squash *by Michael Palmer, published in 1984 at £7.95.*

Earliest champion

Although rackets (US spelling racquets) with a soft ball was played in 1817 at Harrow School, Harrow, Greater London, there was no recognised champion of any country until John A. Miskey of Philadelphia won the American Amateur Singles Championship in 1907.

World Championships

Geoffrey B. Hunt (b. 11 Mar 1947) (Australia) won a record four World Open (inst. 1976) titles, 1976–7 and 1979–80, and three World Amateur (inst. 1967) titles. Australia have won a record four amateur team titles, 1967, 1969, 1971 and 1973.

Most titles *Open Championship*

The most wins in the Open Championship (amateurs or professionals), held annually in Britain, is eight by Geoffrey Hunt in 1969, 1974, 1976–81. Hashim Khan (Pakistan) (b.

1915) won seven times, 1950–5 and 1957, and has also won the Vintage title six times in 1978–83.

The most wins in the Women's Squash Rackets Championship is 16 by Heather Pamela McKay (*née* Blundell) (Australia) (b. 31 July 1941) from 1961 to 1977. She also won the World Open title in 1976 and 1979. In her career from 1959 to 1980 she only lost two games (one in 1960, one in 1962).

Most titles *Amateur Championship*
The most wins in the Amateur Championship is six by Abdel Fattah Amr Bey (Egypt) (b. 14 Feb 1910) later appointed Ambassador in London, who won in 1931–3 and 1935–7. Norman Francis Borrett (b. 1 Oct 1917) of England won in 1946–50.

Longest and shortest championship matches
The longest recorded competitive match was one of 2 hr 45 min when Jahangir Khan (Pakistan) (b. 10 Dec 1963) beat Gamal Awad (Egypt) (b. 8 Sept 1955) 9–10, 9–5, 9–7, 9–2, the first game lasting a record 1 hr 11 min, in the final of the Patrick International Festival at Chichester, West Sussex, England on 30 Mar 1983. Deanna Murray beat Christine Rees in only 9½ min in a Ladies Welsh title match at Rhos-on-Sea, Clwyd, on 21 Oct 1979.

Most international appearances

Men

Scotland	106	Christopher Wilson	1969–84
England	76	Philip Norman Ayton	1968–79
Wales	68	Robert Anthony Dolman	1960–80
N. Ireland	53	Robert Weir	1969–77

Women

Scotland	65	Dorothy Sharp (*née* McNeill)	1963–80
Wales	56	Deanna Murray	1974–83

Largest crowd
The finals of the British Open Squash Championships at Wembley Conference Centre, London had a record attendance for squash of 2,603 on 14 Apr 1984.

SURFING

Origins
The traditional Polynesian sport of surfing in a canoe (*ehorooe*) was first recorded by Captain James Cook, RN, FRS (1728–79) on his first voyage at Tahiti in December 1771. Surfing on a board (*Amo Amo iluna ka lau oka nalu*) was first described 'most perilous and extraordinary ... altogether astonishing and is scarcely to be credited' by Lt (later Capt) James King, RN, FRS in March 1779 at Kealakekua Bay, Hawaii Island. A surfer was first depicted by this voyage's official artist John Webber. The sport was revived at Waikiki by 1900. Hollow boards were introduced in 1929 and the light plastic foam type in 1956.

Most titles
World Amateur Championships were inaugurated in May 1964 at Sydney, Australia; the only surfer to win two titles has been Joyce Hoffman (US) in 1965 and 1966. A World Professional circuit was started in 1975 and Mark Richards (Australia) has won the men's title four times, 1979–82.

Highest waves ridden
Makaha Beach, Hawaii provides the reputedly highest consistently high waves often reaching the rideable limit of 30–35 ft *9–10 m*. The highest wave ever ridden was the *tsunami* of 'perhaps 50 ft *15,24 m*', which struck Minole, Hawaii on 3 Apr 1868, and was ridden to save his life by a Hawaiian named Holua.

Longest ride *Sea wave*
About four to six times each year rideable surfing waves break in Matanchen Bay near San Blas, Nayarit, Mexico which makes rides of *c.* 5700 ft *1700 m* possible.

Longest ride *River bore*
The longest recorded rides on a river bore have been set on the Severn bore, England. The official British Surfing Association record for riding a surfboard in a standing position is 0.7 mile *1,1 km* and for the longest ride on a surfboard standing or lying down is 2.94 miles *4,73 km* by Colin Kerr Wilson (b. 23 June 1954) on 23 May 1982.

SWIMMING

Earliest references
In Japan, swimming in schools was ordered by Imperial edict of Emperor Go-Yozei (1586–1611) in 1603 but competition was known from 36 BC. Sea water bathing was fashionable at Scarborough, North Yorkshire as early as 1660. In Great Britain competitive swimming originated from at least 1791. The earliest pool was Pearless Pool, North London, opened in 1743. Swimming races were particularly popular in the 1820s in Liverpool, where the earliest pool opened at St George's Pier Head, Liverpool in 1828.

Largest pools
The largest swimming pool in the world is the sea-water Orthlieb Pool in Casablanca, Morocco. It is 480 m *1574 ft* long and 75 m *246 ft* wide, and has an area of 3.6 ha *8.9 acres*. The largest land-locked swimming pool with heated water was the Fleishhacker Pool on Sloat Boulevard, near Great Highway, San Francisco, California, USA. It measured 1000 × 150 ft *304,8 × 45,7 m* and up to 14 ft *4,26 m* deep and contained 7,500,000 US gal *28 390 hectolitres* of heated water. It was opened on 2 May 1925 but has now been abandoned. The greatest spectator accommodation is 13,614 at Osaka, Japan. The largest in use in the United Kingdom is the Royal Commonwealth Pool, Edinburgh, completed in 1970 with 2000 permanent seats, but the covered over and unused pool at Earls Court, London (opened 1937) could seat some 12,000 spectators.

Fastest swimmer
The fastest 50 m in a 50 m pool is 22.54 sec by Robin Leamy (b. 1 Apr 1961) (USA), averaging 7,98 km/h *4.96 mph*, at Milwaukee, Wisconsin, USA on 15 Aug 1981. The fastest by a woman is 25.62 sec by Dara Torres (USA) (b. 15 Apr 1967), averaging 7,03 km/h *4.37 mph* at Clovis, California, USA on 6 Aug 1983.

Most world records
Men: 32, Arne Borg (Sweden) (b. 18 Aug 1901), 1921–9. Women: 42, Ragnhild Hveger (Denmark) (b. 10 Dec 1920), 1936–42. Under modern conditions (only metric distances in 50 m pools) the most is 26 by Mark Andrew Spitz (USA) (b. 10 Feb 1950), 1967–72, and 23 by Kornelia Ender (GDR) (b. 25 Oct 1958), 1973–6.

Most world titles
In the world championships (inst 1973) the most medals won is ten by Kornelia Ender with eight gold and two silver in 1973 and 1975. The most by a man is eight by Ambrose 'Rowdy' Gaines (USA) (b. 17 Feb 1959), five gold and three silver, in 1978 and 1982. The most gold medals is six by James Montgomery (USA) (b. 24 Jan 1955) in 1973 and 1975. The most medals in a single championship is six by Tracy Caulkins (USA) (b. 11 Jan 1963) in 1978 with five golds and a silver.

OLYMPIC RECORDS

Most gold medals *Men*
The greatest number of Olympic gold medals won is nine by Mark Spitz (USA): 100 m and 200 m freestyle 1972; 100 m and 200 m butterfly 1972; 4 × 100 m freestyle 1968 and 1972; 4 × 200 m freestyle 1968 and 1972; 4 × 100 m medley 1972. *All but one of these performances (the 4 × 200 m freestyle of 1968) were also new world records.*

Most gold medals *Women*
The record number of gold medals won by a woman is four shared by Patricia McCormick (*née* Keller) (USA) (b. 12 May 1930), the high and springboard diving double in 1952 and 1956 (also the female record for individual golds), Dawn Fraser (Australia) (b. 4 Sept 1937), the 100 m freestyle (1956, 1960 and 1964) and the 4 × 100 m freestyle (1956) and Kornelia Ender (GDR) the 100 and 200 m freestyle, 100 m butterfly and 4 × 100 m medley in 1976. Dawn Fraser is the only swimmer to win the same event on three successive occasions.

Most gold medals *British*
The record number of gold medals won by a British swimmer (excluding Water Polo, *q.v.*) is four by Henry Taylor (1885–1951) in the mile freestyle (1906), 400 m freestyle (1908), 1500 m freestyle (1908) and 4 × 200 m freestyle (1908).

Michael Gross, world 200 metres freestyle champion in 1982 and world record holder at that event and 200 metres butterfly. (*All-Sport/Tony Duffy*)

Most individual gold medals

The record number of individual gold medals won is four by Charles M. Daniels (USA) (1884–1973) (100 m freestyle 1906 and 1908, 220 yd freestyle 1904, 440 yd freestyle 1904); Roland Matthes (GDR) (b. 17 Nov 1950) with 100 m and 200 m backstroke 1968 and 1972; Mark Spitz and Pat McCormick. The most individual golds by a British swimmer is three by Henry Taylor.

Most medals *Men*

The most medals won is 11 by Mark Spitz who in addition to his nine golds won a silver (100 m butterfly) and a bronze (100 m freesyle) both in 1968.

Most medals *Women*

The most medals won by a woman is eight by Dawn Fraser, who in addition to her four golds won four silvers (400 m freestyle 1956, 4 × 100 m freestyle 1960 and 1964, 4 × 100 m medley 1960), Kornelia Ender who in addition to her four golds won four silvers (200 m individual medley 1972, 4 × 100 m medley 1972, 4 × 100 m freestyle 1972 and 1976) and Shirley Babashoff (USA) (b. 3 Jan 1957), who won two golds (4 × 100 m freestyle 1972 and 1976) and six silvers (100 m freestyle 1972, 200 m freestyle 1972 and 1976, 400 m and 800 m freestyle 1976, 4 × 100 m medley 1976).

Most medals *British*

The British record is eight by Henry Taylor who in addition to his four golds won a silver (400 m freestyle 1906) and three

SWIMMING—WORLD RECORDS (*set in 50m pools*)

(To 1 Aug 1984; see also pp. 339–40)

MEN

FREESTYLE	Min. Sec.	Name, Country and date of birth	Place	Date	
100 metres	49.36	Ambrose 'Rowdy' Gaines (USA) (b. 17 Feb 1959)	Austin, Texas, USA	3 Apr	1981
200 metres	1:47.44	Michael Gross (W. Germany) (b. 17 June 1964)	Los Angeles, USA	29 July	1984
400 metres	3:48.32	Vladimir Salnikov (USSR) (b. 21 May 1960)	Moscow, USSR	19 Feb	1983
800 metres	7:52.33	Vladimir Salnikov (USSR)	Los Angeles, USA	14 July	1983
1500 metres	14:54.76	Vladimir Salnikov (USSR)	Moscow, USSR	22 Feb	1983
4 × 100 metres relay	3:19.26	United States (Chris Cavanaugh, Robin Leamy, David McCagg, Ambrose 'Rowdy' Gaines)	Guayaquil, Ecuador	6 Aug	1982
4 × 200 metres relay	7:15.69	United States (Geoff Gaberino, David Larsen, Bruce Hayes, Richard Faeger)	Los Angeles, USA	30 July	1984
BREASTSTROKE					
100 metres	1:01.65	Steven Lundquist (USA)	Los Angeles, USA	29 July	1984
200 metres	2:14.58	Victor Davis (Canada) (b. 19 Feb 1964)	Toronto, Canada	19 June	1984
BUTTERFLY					
100 metres	53.08	Michael Gross (W. Germany)	Los Angeles, USA	30 July	1984
200 metres	1:57.05	Michael Gross	Rome, Italy	26 Aug	1983
BACKSTROKE					
100 metres	55.19	Richard Carey (USA) (b. 13 Mar 1963)	Caracas, Venezuela	21 Aug	1983
200 metres	1:58.86	Richard Carey	Indianapolis, Indiana, USA	27 June	1984
MEDLEY					
200 metres	2:02.25	Alex Baumann (Canada) (b. Prague 21 Apr 1964)	Brisbane, Australia	4 Oct	1982
400 metres	4:17.41	Alex Baumann	Los Angeles, USA	30 July	1984
4 × 100 metres relay	3:40.42	United States (Richard Carey, Steven Lundquist, Matthew Gribble, Ambrose 'Rowdy' Gaines)	Caracas, Venezuela	22 Aug	1983

WOMEN

FREESTYLE					
100 metres	54.79	Barbara Krause (GDR) (b. 7 July 1959)	Moscow, USSR	21 July	1980
200 metres	1:57.75	Kristin Otto (GDR) (b. 7 Feb 1965)	Magdeburg, GDR	23 May	1984
400 metres	4:06.28	Tracey Wickham (Australia) (b. 24 Nov 1962)	West Berlin, W. Germany	24 Aug	1978
800 metres	8:24.62	Tracey Wickham (Australia)	Edmonton, Canada	5 Aug	1978
1500 metres	16:04.49	Kim Lineham (USA) (b. 11 Dec 1962)	Fort Lauderdale, Florida, USA	19 July	1979
4 × 100 metres relay	3:42.71	GDR (Barbara Krause, Caren Metschuck, Ines Diers, Sarina Hulsenbeck)	Moscow, USSR	27 July	1980
4 × 200 metres relay	8:02.27	GDR (Kristin Otto, Astrid Strauss, Cornelia Sirch, Birgit Meineke)	Rome, Italy	23 Aug	1983
BREASTSTROKE					
100 metres	1:08.51	Ute Geweniger (GDR) (b. 24 Feb 1964)	Rome, Italy	25 Aug	1983
200 metres	2:28.36	Lina Kachushite (USSR) (b. 1 Jan 1963)	Potsdam, GDR	6 Apr	1979
BUTTERFLY					
100 metres	57.93	Mary Meagher (USA) (b. 27 Oct 1964)	Milwaukee, Wisconsin, USA	16 Aug	1981
200 metres	2:05.96	Mary Meagher	Milwaukee, Wisconsin, USA	13 Aug	1981
BACKSTROKE					
100 metres	1:00.86	Rica Reinisch (GDR) (b. 6 Apr 1965)	Moscow, USSR	23 July	1980
200 metres	2:09.91	Cornelia Sirch (GDR) (b. 23 Oct 1966)	Guayaquil, Ecuador	8 Aug	1982
MEDLEY					
200 metres	2:11.73	Ute Geweniger (GDR) (b. 24 Feb 1964)	East Berlin, GDR	4 July	1981
400 metres	4:36.10	Petra Schneider (GDR) (b. 11 Jan 1963)	Guayaquil, Ecuador	1 Aug	1982
4 × 100 metres relay	4:05.79	GDR (Ina Kleber, Ute Geweniger, Ines Geissler, Birgit Meineke)	Rome, Italy	26 Aug	1983

bronzes (4 × 200 m freestyle 1906, 1912, 1920). The most medals by a British woman is four by M. Joyce Cooper (now Badcock) (b. 18 Apr 1909) with one silver (4 × 100 m freestyle 1928) and three bronze (100 m freestyle 1928, 100 m backstroke 1928, 4 × 100 m freestyle 1932).

Closest verdict

The closest recorded win in the Olympic Games was in the Munich 400 m individual medley final of 30 Aug 1972 when Gunnar Larsson (Sweden) (b. 12 May 1951) got the verdict over Tim McKee (USA) (b. 14 Mar 1953) by 2/1000th of a second in 4 min 31.981 sec to 4 min 31.983 sec—a margin of 3 mm or the length grown by a finger nail in three weeks. This led to a change in international rules with timings and places decided only to hundredths.

DIVING

Most Olympic medals *World*

The most medals won by a diver are five (three gold, two silver) by Klaus Dibiasi (b. Austria, 6 Oct 1947) (Italy) in four Games from 1964 to 1976. He is also the only diver to win the same event (highboard) at three successive Games (1968, 1972 and 1976). Pat McCormick (*see p. 315*) won four gold medals.

Most Olympic medals *British*

The highest placing by a Briton has been the silver medal by Beatrice Eileen Armstrong (later Purdy) (1894–1981) in the 1920 highboard event. The best placings by male divers are the bronze medals by Harold Clarke (b. 1888) (plain high diving, 1924) and Brian Phelps (b. 21 Apr 1944) (highboard, 1960).

Most world titles

Phil Boggs (USA) (b. 29 Dec 1949) won three springboard gold medals, in 1973, 1975 and 1978 but Klaus Dibiasi (Italy) won four medals (two gold, two silver) in 1973 and 1975. Irina Kalinina (USSR) (b. 8 Feb 1959) has won five medals (three gold, one silver, one bronze) in 1973, 1975 and 1978. Greg Louganis (USA) (b. 29 Jan 1960), won one gold in 1978 and two in the 1982 world championships at Guayaquil, Ecuador, where he became the first to score over 700 points for the 11-dive springboard event with 752.67 on 1 Aug 1982. He went on to be awarded a score of 10.0 by all seven judges for his highboard inward 1½ somersault in the pike position.

Perfect dive

The first diver to be awarded a score of 10.0 by all seven judges was Michael Finneran (b. 21 Sept 1948) in the 1972 US Olympic Trials, in Chicago, Illinois, for a backward 1½ somersault, 2½ twist, from the 10 m board.

CHANNEL SWIMMING

Earliest

The first to swim the English Channel from shore to shore (without a life jacket) was the Merchant Navy captain Matthew Webb (1848–83) who swam breaststroke from Dover, England

---

BRITISH NATIONAL (long course) RECORDS　(To 1 Aug 1984)

MEN

Event	Time Min. Sec.	Name and date of birth	Place	Date
FREESTYLE				
100 metres	51.69	David Lowe (b. 28 Feb 1960)	Brisbane, Australia	2 Oct 1982
200 metres	1:51.52	Andrew Astbury (b. 29 Nov 1960)	Brisbane, Australia	2 Oct 1982
400 metres	3:53.29	Andrew Astbury	Brisbane, Australia	4 Oct 1982
800 metres	8:13.83	Simon Gray (b. 29 Apr 1959)	Blackpool, England	23 May 1980
1500 metres	15:31.42	Simon Gray	West Berlin, W. Germany	24 Aug 1978
4 × 100 metres relay	3:26.98	England (David Lowe, Philip Osborn, Philip Hubble, Richard Burrell)	Brisbane, Australia	1 Oct 1982
4 × 200 metres relay	7:24.78	U. Kingdom (Neil Cochran, Paul Easter, Paul Howe, Andrew Astbury)	Los Angeles, USA	30 July 1984
BREASTSTROKE				
100 metres	1:02.93	Adrian Moorhouse (b. 24 May 1964)	Brisbane, Australia	6 Oct 1982
200 metres	2:15.11	David Andrew Wilkie (b. 8 Mar 1954)	Montreal, Canada	24 July 1976
BUTTERFLY				
100 metres	54.28	Andrew Jameson (b. 19 Feb 1965)	Los Angeles, USA	30 July 1984
200 metres	2:00.21	Philip Hubble (b. 19 July 1960)	Split, Yugoslavia	11 Sept 1981
BACKSTROKE				
100 metres	57.72	Gary Abraham (b. 8 Jan 1959)	Moscow, USSR	24 July 1980
200 metres	2:04.23	Douglas Campbell (b. 30 Sept 1960)	Moscow, USSR	26 July 1980
INDIVIDUAL MEDLEY				
200 metres	2:04.99	Neil Cochran (b. 12 Apr 1965)	Coventry, England	28 May 1984
400 metres	4:25.38	Stephen Poulter (b. 18 Feb 1961)	Los Angeles, USA	30 July 1984
4 × 100 metres relay	3:47.71	United Kingdom (Gary Abraham, Duncan Goodhew, David Lowe, Martin Smith)	Moscow, USSR	24 July 1980

WOMEN

Event	Time Min. Sec.	Name and date of birth	Place	Date
FREESTYLE				
100 metres	56.60	June Croft (b. 17 June 1963)	Amersfoort, Netherlands	31 Jan 1982
200 metres	1:59.74	June Croft	Brisbane, Australia	4 Oct 1982
400 metres	4:10.27	Sarah Hardcastle (b. 9 April 1969)	Los Angeles, USA	31 July 1984
800 metres	8:32.61	Jacqueline 'Jackie' Willmott (b. 19 March 1965)	Guayaquil, Ecuador	7 Aug 1982
1500 metres	16:46.48	Jacqueline 'Jackie' Willmott	Edinburgh, Scotland	25 Apr 1980
4 × 100 metres relay	3:50.12	United Kingdom (Nicola Fibbens, June Croft, Annabelle Cripps, Deborah Gore)	Los Angeles, USA	31 July 1984
4 × 200 metres relay	8:15.21	United Kingdom (Annabelle Cripps, Sarah Hardcastle, Ruth Gilfillan, June Croft)	Crystal Palace, London	26 Feb 1984
BREASTSTROKE				
100 metres	1.11.05	Susannah 'Suki' Brownsdon (b. 16 Oct 1965)	Split, Yugoslavia	8 Sept 1981
200 metres	2:34.43	Susannah 'Suki' Brownsdon	Kiev, USSR	3 July 1981
BUTTERFLY				
100 metres	1:01.56	Ann Osgerby (b. 20 Jan 1963)	Rome, Italy	25 Aug 1983
200 metres	2:13.00	Ann Osgerby	Rome, Italy	27 Aug 1983
BACKSTROKE				
100 metres	1:03.61	Beverley Rose (b. 21 Jan 1964)	Los Angeles, USA	31 July 1984
200 metres	2:16.00	Katherine Read (b. 30 June 1969)	Coventry, England	28 May 1984
INDIVIDUAL MEDLEY				
200 metres	2:17.31	Sharron Davies (b. 1 Nov 1962)	Blackpool, England	20 Apr 1980
400 metres	4:46.83	Sharron Davies	Moscow, USSR	26 July 1980
4 × 100 metres relay	4:12.24	United Kingdom (Helen Jameson, Margaret Kelly, Ann Osgerby, June Croft)	Moscow, USSR	20 July 1980

Mary Meagher, born in Louisville, Kentucky, set her first world butterfly record in 1979 and won the world title in 1982 at 100 metres. (*All-Sport*)

to Calais Sands, France, in 21 hr 45 min from 12.56 p.m. to 10.41 a.m., 24–25 Aug 1875. He swam an estimated 38 miles *61 km* to make the 21-mile *33 km* crossing. Paul Boyton (USA) had swum from Cap Gris-Nez to the South Foreland in his patent life-saving suit in 23 hr 30 min on 28–29 May 1875. There is good evidence that Jean-Marie Saletti, a French soldier, escaped from a British prison hulk off Dover by swimming to Boulogne in July or August 1815. The first crossing from France to England was made by Enrico Tiraboschi, a wealthy Italian living in Argentina, in 16 hr 33 min on 12 Aug 1923, to win the *Daily Sketch* prize of £1000.

The first woman to succeed was Gertrude Caroline Ederle (b. 23 Oct 1906) (USA) (*see also p. 240*) who swam from Cap Gris-Nez, France to Deal, England on 6 Aug 1926, in the then overall record time of 14 hr 39 min. The first woman to swim from England to France was Florence Chadwick (b. 1918) (USA) in 16 hr 19 min on 11 Sept 1951. The first English-woman to succeed was Mercedes Gleitze (later Carey) (1900–81) who swam from France to England in 15 hr 15 min on 7 Oct 1927.

Fastest

The official Channel Swimming Association (founded 1927) record is 7 hr 40 min by Penny Dean (b. 21 Mar 1955) of California, USA, from Shakespeare Beach, Dover to Cap Gris-Nez, France, on 29 July 1978.

The fastest crossing by a relay team is 7 hr 17 min, by six Dover lifeguards, from England to France on 9 Aug 1981.

Earliest and latest

The earliest date in the year on which the Channel has been swum is 6 June by Dorothy Perkins (England) (b. 1942) in 1961, and the latest is 28 Oct by Michael Peter Read (GB) (b. 9 June 1941) in 1979.

Youngest and oldest

The youngest conqueror is Marcus Hooper (GB) (b. 14 June

1967) who swam from Dover to Sangatte, France in 14 hr 37 min on 5–6 Aug 1979, when he was aged 12 yr 53 days. The youngest girl is Samantha Claire Druce (GB) (b. 21 Apr 1971) who was 12 yr 119 days on 18 Aug 1983 when she swam from Dover to Cap Gris-Nez in 15 hr 27 min.

The oldest has been Ashby Harper (b. 1 Oct 1916) of Albuquerque, USA at 65 years 332 days when he swam from Dover to Cap Blanc Nez in 13 hr 52 min on 28 Aug 1982. The oldest woman was Stella Ada Rosina Taylor (b. Bristol, Avon, 20 Dec 1929) aged 45 yr 350 days when she did the swim in 18 hr 15 min on 26 Aug 1975.

Double crossing

Antonio Abertondo (b. Buenos Aires, Argentina, 1919), swam from England to France in 18 hr 50 min (8.35 a.m. on 20 Sept to 3.25 a.m. on 21 Sept 1961) and after about 4 min rest returned to England in 24 hr 16 min, landing at St Margaret's Bay at 3.45 a.m. on 22 Sept 1961, to complete the first 'double crossing' in 43 hr 10 min. Kevin Murphy (b. Bushey Heath, Herts, 1949) completed the first double crossing by a Briton in 35 hr 10 min on 6 Aug 1970. The first swimmer to achieve a crossing both ways was Edward Harry Temme (1904–78) on 5 Aug 1927 and 19 Aug 1934.

The fastest double crossing was in 18 hr 55 min by Cynthia 'Cindy' M. Nicholas (b. 20 Aug 1957) of Scarborough, Ont., Canada, on 28 Aug 1982. The first British woman to achieve the double crossing was Alison Streeter (b. 29 Aug 1964) in 21 hr 16 min on 4 Aug 1983. The fastest by a relay team is 16 hr 5½ min (including a 2 min rest) by six Saudi Arabian men on 11 Aug 1977.

Triple crossing

The first triple crossing was by Jon Erikson (USA) (b. 6 Sept 1954) in 38 hr 27 min on 11–12 Aug 1981.

Most conquests

The greatest number of Channel conquests is 30 by Michael

Read (GB) from 24 Aug 1969 to 8 July 1984, including a record six in one year. Cindy Nicholas made her first crossing on 29 July 1975 and her nineteenth (and fifth two-way) on 14 Sept 1982.

Underwater

The first underwater cross-Channel swim was achieved by Fred Baldasare (b. 1924) (USA), who completed a 42 mile *67,5 km* distance from France to England with Scuba equipment in 18 hr 1 min on 10–11 July 1962.

LONG DISTANCE SWIMMING

Longest swims

The greatest recorded distance ever swum is 1826 miles *2938 km* down the Mississippi, USA between Ford Dam near Minneapolis and Carrollton Ave, New Orleans, Louisiana, by Fred P. Newton, (b. 1903) of Clinton, Oklahoma from 6 July to 29 Dec 1930. He was 742 hr in the water.

The greatest distance covered in a continuous swim is 299 miles *481,5 km* by Ricardo Hoffmann (b. 5 Oct 1941) from Corrientes to Santa Elena, Argentina in the River Parana in 84 hr 37 min on 3–6 Mar 1981.

The longest ocean swim is one of 128.8 miles *207,3 km* by Walter Poenisch Snr (USA) (b. 1914) who started from Havana, Cuba, and arrived at Little Duck Key, Florida, USA (in a shark cage and wearing flippers) 34 hr 15 min later on 11–13 July 1978.

In 1966 Mihir Sen of Calcutta, India uniquely swam the Palk Strait from Sri Lanka to India (in 25 hr 36 min on 5–6 Apr); the Straits of Gibraltar (in 8 hr 1 min on 24 Aug); the length of the Dardanelles (in 13 hr 55 min on 12 Sept), the Bosphorus (in 4 hr on 21 Sept) and the length of the Panama Canal (in 34 hr 15 min on 29–31 Oct).

Irish Channel

The swimming of the 23 mile *37 km* wide North Channel from Donaghadee, Northern Ireland to Portpatrick, Scotland was first accomplished by Tom Blower of Nottingham in 15 hr 26 min in 1947. A record time of 11 hr 21 min was set by Kevin Murphy on 11 Sept 1970. The first Irish-born swimmer to achieve the crossing was Ted Keenan on 11 Aug 1973 in 52–56°F *11–13°C* water in 18 hr 27 min.

Bristol Channel

The first person to achieve a crossing of the Bristol Channel was Kathleen Thomas (now Mrs Day) (b. Apr 1906) who swam from Penarth, South Glamorgan to Weston-super-Mare, Avon in 7 hr 20 min on 5 Sept 1927. The record for the longer swim from Glenthorne Cove, Devon to Porthcawl, Mid-Glamorgan is 10 hr 46 min by Jane Luscombe (b. 13 Jan 1961) of Jersey, CI, on 19 Aug 1976.

Lake swims

The fastest time for swimming the 22.7 mile *36,5 km* long Loch Ness, is 9 hr 57 min by David Morgan (b. 25 Sept 1963) on 31 July 1983. The first successful swim was by Brenda Sherratt (b. 1948) of West Bollington, Cheshire on 26–27 July 1966. David Morgan achieved a unique double crossing of Loch Ness in 23 hr 4 min on 1 Aug 1983. The fastest time for swimming Lake Windermere, 10.5 miles *16,9 km* is 3 hr 49 min 56 sec by Karen Toole, 17, of Darlington on 5 Sept 1981. The fastest time for the Lake Windermere International Championship, 16.5 miles *26,5 km*, is 6 hr 10 min 33 sec by Mary Beth Colpo (USA) (b. 1961) on 5 Aug 1978.

Longest duration

The longest duration swim ever achieved was one of 168 continuous hours, ending on 24 Feb 1941, by the legless Charles Zibbelman, *alias* Zimmy (b. 1894) in a pool in Honolulu, Hawaii, USA. The longest duration swim by a woman was 87 hr 27 min in a salt-water pool by Myrtle Huddleston (USA) at Raven Hall, Coney Island, NY, USA, in 1931.

24 hours

J. Hestoy (Faroe Islands) was reported to have swum 89,174 km *55.41 miles* in a pool on 29–30 May 1982.

Greatest lifetime distance

Gustave Brickner (b. 10 Feb 1912) of Charleroi, Pennsylvania, USA in 56 years to November 1983 had recorded 37,426 miles *60 231 km*.

Long distance relays

The New Zealand national relay team of 20 swimmers swam a record 182,807 km *113.59 miles* in Lower Hutt, NZ in 24 hours, passing 160 km *100 miles* in 20 hr 47 min 13 sec on 9–10 Dec 1983. The most participants in a swim relay is 1900, 38 teams of 50, in Sao Paulo, Brazil on 1 Apr 1984. A team of four from Capalaba State Primary School—Kim Wilson, Tanya Obstoj, Paul Giles, Darren Sheldrick—set an endurance record of 168 hr with one of the team in the water at any time, covering 540,8 km *336 miles* on 12–19 Dec 1983 at Sheldon, Queensland, Australia.

Underwater relay

Peter Saville, John Mason, Robert Mortimer and Duncan Moulder, of Stratford upon Avon Sub Aqua Club, swam a relay of 279.099 miles *449,17 km* underwater in 168 hr at the Holiday Inn, Birmingham on 30 June–7 July 1979.

Sponsored swimming

The greatest amount of money collected in a charity swim was £49,083.74 by the Lions Club of Jersey, CI on 24–26 Feb 1984, at the Fort Regent Pool, St Helier.

TABLE TENNIS

Origins

The earliest evidence relating to a game resembling table tennis has been found in the catalogues of London sports goods manufacturers in the 1880s. The old Ping Pong Association was formed in 1902 but the game proved only a temporary craze until resuscitated in 1921. The English Table Tennis Association was formed on 24 Apr 1927.

Most English titles

The highest total of English men's titles (instituted 1921) is 20 by G. Viktor Barna (1911–72) (b. Hungary, Gyözö Braun). The women's record is 17 by Diane Rowe (b. 14 Apr 1933), now Mrs Eberhard Scholer. Her twin Rosalind (now Mrs Cornett) has won nine (two in singles).

The most titles won in the English Closed Championships is 18 by Desmond Douglas (b. 20 July 1955), a record seven

Desmond Douglas sharpened his play to top class in the Bundesliga in West Germany but has returned home regularly to win a record number of English Closed table tennis titles. (*All Sport*)

MOST WINS IN WORLD CHAMPIONSHIPS (Instituted 1926–7)

Event	Name and Nationality	Times	Years
Men's Singles (St Bride's Vase)	G. Viktor Barna (Hungary) (1911–72)	5	1930, 1932–5
Women's Singles (G. Geist Prize)	Angelica Rozeanu (Romania) (b. 15 Oct 1921)	6	1950–5
Men's Doubles	G. Viktor Barna (Hungary)	8	1929–35, 1939
Women's Doubles	Maria Mednyanszky (Hungary) (1901–79)	7	1928, 1930–5
Mixed Doubles (Men)	Ferenc Sido (Hungary) (b. 1923)	4	1949–50, 1952–3
(Women)	Maria Mednyanszky (Hungary)	6	1927–8, 1930–1, 1933–4

G. Viktor Barna gained a personal total of 15 world titles, while 18 have been won by Maria Mednyanszky.
Note: With the staging of championships biennially the breaking of the above records would now be virtually impossible.

MOST TEAM TITLES

Event	Team	Times	Years
Men's Team (Swaythling Cup)	Hungary	12	1927–31, 1933–5, 1938, 1949, 1952, 1979
Women's Team (Marcel Corbillon Cup)	Japan	8	1952, 1954, 1957, 1959, 1961, 1963, 1967, 1971

MOST WINS IN ENGLISH OPEN CHAMPIONSHIPS (Instituted 1921)

Event	Name and Nationality	Times	Years
Men's Singles	Richard Bergmann (Austria, then GB) (1920–70)	6	1939–40, 1948, 1950, 1952, 1954
Women's Singles	Maria Alexandru (Romania) (b. 1941)	6	1963–4, 1970–2, 1974
Men's Doubles	G. Viktor Barna (Hungary, then GB)	7	1931, 1933–5, 1938–9, 1949
Women's Doubles	Diane Rowe (GB) (now Scholer) (b. 14 Apr 1933)	12	1950–6, 1960, 1962–5
Mixed Doubles (Men)	G. Viktor Barna (Hungary, then GB)	8	1933–6, 1938, 1940, 1951, 1953
(Women)	Diane Rowe (GB) (now Scholer)	4	1952, 1954, 1956, 1960

men's singles, 1976 and 1979–84, seven men's doubles and four mixed doubles, and by Denis Neale (b. 12 Apr 1944) with six, seven and five respectively, 1966–77. A record seven women's singles were won by Jill Patricia Hammersley (now Parker *née* Shirley) (b. 6 Dec 1951) in 1973–6, 1978–9, 1981.

Internationals

The youngest ever international was Joy Foster, aged 8, when she represented Jamaica in the West Indies Championships at Port of Spain, Trinidad in Aug 1958. The youngest ever to play for England is Carl Prean (b. 20 Aug 1967), aged 14 yr 191 days, against Portugal at Lisbon on 27 Feb 1982.

Jill Parker played for England on a record 413 occasions, 1967–83.

Counter hitting

The record number of hits in 60 sec is 162 by English Internationals Nicky Jarvis (b. 7 Mar 1954) and Desmond Douglas at the Eccentric Club, London on 1 Dec 1976. This was equalled by Douglas and Paul Day (b. 20 Oct 1958) at Butlins, Blackpool, Lancs, on 21 Mar 1977. The most by women is 148 by Linda Howard and Melodi Ludi (now Hill) at Blackpool, Lancs, on 11 Oct 1977. With a bat in each hand, Gary D. Fisher of Olympia, Wash., USA, completed 5000 consecutive volleys over the net in 44 min 28 sec on 25 June 1979.

Highest speed

No conclusive measurements have been published but in a lecture M. Sklorz (W. Germany) stated that a smashed ball had been measured at speeds up to 170 km/h *105,6 mph.*

TAE KWON-DO

The founder and father of this martial art is General Choi Hong Hi 9th Dan, the highest Dan awarded. Tae Kwon-Do was officially recognised as part of Korean tradition and culture on 11 Apr 1955.

The highest Dan in Britain is Master Rhee Ki Ha 8th Dan, the Chief Instructor of the United Kingdom Tae Kwon-Do Association.

TENNIS (LAWN)

See also The Guinness Book of Tennis Facts and Feats by Lance Tingay, published in 1983 at £8.95.

Origins

The modern game is generally agreed to have evolved as an outdoor form of the indoor game of Tennis (see separate entry). 'Field Tennis' is mentioned in an English magazine—*Sporting Magazine*—of 29 Sept 1793. The earliest club for such a game, variously called Pelota or Lawn Rackets, was the Leamington Club founded in 1872 by Major Harry Gem. The earliest attempt to commercialise the game was by Major Walter Clopton Wingfield (1833–1912) who patented a form called 'sphairistike' on 23 Feb 1874. It soon became called Lawn Tennis. Amateur players were permitted to play with and against professionals in 'Open' tournaments in 1968.

Grand Slam

The grand slam is to hold at the same time all four of the world's major championship singles: Wimbledon, the United States, Australian and French championships. The first man to have won all four was Frederick John Perry (GB) (b. 18 May 1909) with the French title in 1935. The first man to hold all four championships simultaneously was John Donald Budge (USA) (b. 13 June 1915) with the French title in 1938. The first man to achieve the grand slam twice was Rodney George Laver (Australia) (b. 9 Aug 1938) having won in 1962 as an amateur and again in 1969 when the titles were 'open' to professionals.

Three women have achieved the grand slam: Maureen Catherine Connolly (USA) (1934–69), later Mrs Norman E. Brinker, in 1953; Margaret Jean Court (*née* Smith) (Australia) (b. 16 July 1942) in 1970 and Martina Navratilova (USA) (b. Prague, Czechoslovakia 18 Oct 1956) in 1983–4. Miss Navratilova also took all four women's double titles with Pamela Howard Shriver (USA) (b. 4 July 1962) in 1983–4.

The most singles championships in 'grand slam' tournaments is 24 by Margaret Court (eleven Australian, five French, five USA, three Wimbledon), 1960–73. The men's record is 12 by Roy Emerson (Australia) (b. 3 Nov 1936) (six Australian, two each French, USA, Wimbledon), 1961–7.

Fastest service

The fastest service timed with modern equipment is 137 mph *220 km/h* by Scott Carnahan (USA) at Los Angeles, California, USA, in Sept 1976. The fastest *ever* measured was one of 163.6 mph *263 km/h* by William Tatem Tilden (1893–1953) (USA) in 1931.

Longest game

The longest known singles game was one of 37 deuces (80 points) between Anthony Fawcett (Rhodesia) and Keith Glass (GB) in the first round of the Surrey championships at Surbiton, Surrey, on 26 May 1975. It lasted 31 min.

The longest tiebreaker was the 20–18 win to complete the third set by Bjorn Rune Borg (Sweden) (b. 6 June 1956) over Premjit Lall (India) in his 6–3, 6–4, 9–8 win in the first round of the 1973 Wimbledon Championships.

Greatest crowd

The greatest crowd at a tennis match was 30,472 at the Astrodome, Houston, Texas, on 20 Sept 1973, when Billie-Jean King (*née* Moffitt) (b. 22 Nov 1943) (USA) beat Robert Larimore Riggs (b. 25 Feb 1918) (USA). The record for an orthodox match is 25,578 at Sydney, NSW, Australia on 27 Dec 1954 in the Davis Cup Challenge Round (first day) Australia *v.* USA.

HIGHEST EARNINGS

Ivan Lendl (Czechoslovakia) (b. 7 Mar 1960) won a record $2,028,850 in 1982. The record for a woman is $1,772,956 in 1984 (to 24 July) by Martina Navratilova. Earnings from special restricted events and team tennis are not included. Miss Navratilova, in winning the French championships in June 1984, earned prize money of $98,146 for the singles, $19,591 for her share of the doubles plus a bonus of $1 million from the International Tennis Federation for taking the Grand Slam—a record $1,117,737 on the outcome of a tournament. Her lifetime earnings by 25 July 1984 reached $8,157,045.

The one match record is $500,000 by James Scott Connors (USA) (b. 2 Sept 1952) when he beat John David Newcombe (Australia) (b. 23 May 1944) in a challenge match at Caesar's Palace, Las Vegas, USA on 26 Apr 1975. The highest total prize money is $2,557,667 for the 1984 US Championships.

The greatest money-winners in tennis; Martina Navratilova (*below, left*) (*All-Sport/Steve Powell*), and Ivan Lendl, who won his first grand slam tournament, the French, in 1984. (*All-Sport/Vandystadt*)

Longest span as national champion

Walter Westbrook (b. June 1898) won the US National Clay Court men's doubles with Harvey Snodgrass in 1925. 58 years later he won the US National 85-and-over Clay Court men's singles championship. In the final he defeated Kirk Reid, whom he had first defeated to win the Western Clay Court Championships in 1925.

Dorothy May Bundy-Cheney (USA) (b. Sept 1916) won 116 US titles at various age groups from 1941 to 1982.

INTERNATIONAL TEAM COMPETITIONS

Davis Cup (inst. 1900)

The most wins in the Davis Cup, the men's international team championship, have been (to 1983) by the USA with 28. The most appearances for Cup winners is eight by Roy Emerson (Australia), 1959–62, 1964–7. The British Isles/Great Britain have won nine times in 1903–6, 1912, 1933–6.

Nicola Pietrangeli (b. 11 Sept 1933) (Italy) played a record 164 rubbers, 1954 to 1972, winning 120. He played 110 singles (winning 78) and 54 doubles (winning 42). He took part in 66 ties. The record number of rubbers by a British player is 65 (winning 43) by Michael J. Sangster (b. 9 Sept 1940), 1960–8;

the most wins is 45 from 52 rubbers by Fred Perry, including 34 of 38 singles, 1931–6.

Wightman Cup (inst. 1923)

The Wightman Cup has been won 45 times by the United States and 10 times by Great Britain. Virginia Wade (GB) (b. 10 July 1945) played in a record 19 ties and 54 rubbers, 1965–83. Christine Marie Lloyd (*née* Evert) (USA) (b. 21 Dec 1954) won all 22 of her singles matches, 1971 to 1982.

Federation Cup (inst. 1963)

The most wins in the Federation Cup, the women's international team championship, is 11 by the USA. Virginia Wade (GB) played each year from 1967 to 1983, in a record 55 ties, playing 100 rubbers, including 56 singles (winning 36) and 44 doubles (winning 30). Chris Lloyd won all her 28 singles matches and 14 of 15 doubles, 1977 to 1982.

WIMBLEDON CHAMPIONSHIPS

Most wins *Women*

Six times singles champion Billie-Jean King has won ten women's doubles and four mixed doubles during the period 1961 to 1979, to total a record 20 titles. Elizabeth Montague Ryan (USA) (1892–1979) won a record 19 doubles (12 women's, 7 mixed) titles from 1914 to 1934.

Laurie and Reggie Doherty dominated the Wimbledon championships at the turn of the century. (*BBC Hulton*)

Most wins *Men*

The greatest number of wins by a man has been 13 by Hugh Laurence Doherty (GB) (1875–1919) with five singles titles (1902–6) and a record eight men's doubles (1897–1901, 1903–5) partnered by his brother Reginald Frank (1872–1910).

Most wins *Singles*

The greatest number of singles wins was eight by Helen Newington Moody (*née* Wills) (USA) (b. 6 Oct 1905), who won in 1927–30, 1932–3, 1935 and 1938. The most men's singles wins since the Challenge Round was abolished in 1922 is five consecutively, by Bjorn Borg (Sweden) in 1976–80. William Charles Renshaw (GB) (1861–1904) won seven singles in 1881–6 and 1889.

Most wins *Mixed doubles*

The male record is four wins shared by Elias Victor Seixas (USA) (b. 30 Aug 1923) in 1953–6, Kenneth Norman Fletcher (Australia) (b. 15 June 1940) in 1963, 1965–6, 1968 and Owen Keir Davidson (Australia) (b. 4 Oct 1943) in 1967, 1971, 1973–4. The female record is seven by Elizabeth Ryan (USA) from 1919 to 1932.

Most appearances

Arthur William Charles 'Wentworth' Gore (1868–1928) (GB) made a record 36 appearances at Wimbledon between 1888 and 1927. In 1964, Jean Borotra (b. 13 Aug 1898) of France, made his 35th appearance since 1922. In 1977 he appeared in the Veterans' Doubles aged 78.

Youngest champions

The youngest champion was Charlotte 'Lottie' Dod (1871–1960), who was 15 yr 285 days when she won in 1887. Richard Dennis Ralston (USA) (b. 27 July 1942) was 17 yr 341 days when he won the men's doubles with Rafael Herrera Osuna (1938–69) of Mexico in 1960. The youngest male singles champion was Wilfred Baddeley (1872–1929) who won the Wimbledon title in 1891 aged 19 yr 175 days. The youngest ever player at Wimbledon is reputedly Mita Klima (Austria) who was 13 yr in the 1907 singles competition. The youngest player to win a match at Wimbledon is Kathy Rinaldi (b. 24 Mar 1967) (USA), at 14 yr 91 days on 23 June 1981.

Oldest champions

The oldest champion was Margaret Evelyn du Pont (*née* Osborne) (USA) (b. 4 Mar 1918) at 44 yr 125 days when she won the mixed doubles in 1962 with Neale Fraser (Aus). The oldest singles champion was Arthur Gore (GB) in 1909 at 41 yr 182 days.

Greatest crowd

The record crowd for one day is 38,291 on 27 July 1979. The record for the whole championship is 391,673 in 1984.

UNITED STATES CHAMPIONSHIPS

Most wins

Margaret Evelyn du Pont (*née* Osborne) won a record 24 titles between 1941 and 1960. She won a record 13 women's doubles (12 with Althea Louise Brough), eight mixed doubles and three singles. The men's record is 16 by William Tatem Tilden, including seven men's singles, 1920–25, 1929—a record for singles shared with Richard Dudley Sears (1861–1943), 1881–7; William A. Larned (1872–1926), 1901–2, 1907–11, and at women's singles by Molla Mallory (*née* Bjurstedt) (1892–

1959), 1915–6, 1918, 1920–2, 1926 and Helen Moody (*née* Wills), 1923–5, 1927–9, 1931.

Youngest and Oldest

The youngest champion was Vincent Richards (1903–59), who was 15 yr 139 days when he won the mixed doubles with Bill Tilden in 1918. The youngest singles champion was Tracy Ann Austin (b. 12 Dec 1962) who was 16 yr 271 days when she won the women's singles in 1979. The oldest champion was Margaret du Pont who won the mixed doubles at 42 yr 166 days in 1960. The oldest singles champion was William Larned at 38 yr 242 days in 1911.

FRENCH CHAMPIONSHIPS

Most wins (from International status 1925)

Margaret Court won a record 13 titles, five singles, four women's doubles and four mixed doubles, 1962–73. The men's record is nine by Henri Cochet (France) (b. 14 Dec 1901), four singles, three men's doubles and two mixed doubles, 1926–30. Bjorn Borg won a record six singles, 1974–81.

Youngest and oldest

The youngest male and female championships were the 1981 mixed doubles champions, Andrea Jaeger (b. 4 June 1965) at 15 yr 339 days and Jimmy Arias (b. 16 Aug 1964) at 16 yr 296 days. The youngest singles winner was Mats Wilander (Sweden) (b. 22 Aug 1964) at 17 yr 288 days in 1982.

The oldest champion was Elizabeth Ryan who won the 1934 women's doubles with Simone Mathieu (France) at 42 yr 88 days. The oldest singles champion was Andres Gimeno in 1972 at 34 yr 301 days.

TENNIS (REAL OR ROYAL)

Origins

The game originated as *jeu de paume* in French monasteries *c.* 1050. A tennis court is mentioned in the sale of the Hôtel de Nesle, Paris bought by King Philippe IV of France in 1308. The oldest of the surviving active Tennis Courts in Great Britain is that at Falkland Palace, Fife, Scotland, built by King James V of Scotland in 1539.

Most titles *World*

The first recorded World Tennis Champion was Clerge (France) *c.* 1740. Jacques Edmond Barre (France) (1802–73) held the title for a record 33 yr from 1829 to 1862. Pierre Etchebaster (1893–1980), a Basque, holds the record for the greatest number of successful defences of the title with eight between 1928 and 1952.

Most titles *British*

The Amateur Championship of the British Isles (instituted 1888) has been won 16 times by Howard Rea Angus (b. 25 June 1944) 1966–80 and 1982. Angus, a left-hander, is also the first British amateur to win a World title, in 1975.

TIDDLYWINKS

National Championships

Alan Dean (Edwinstowe, Notts) (b. 22 July 1949) has won the singles title a record five times, 1971–3, 1976, 1978. He has also won the pairs title five times. Jonathan Mapley (b. 1947) has won the pairs title a record six times, 1972, 1975, 1977, 1980 and 1983–4.

Guinness Trophy

England has been unbeaten against Scotland, Ireland and Wales since the Trophy's inception in 1960. The closest result has been their 59½–52½ win over Wales at Warwick on 7 Apr 1968.

Potting records

The record for potting 24 winks from 18 in *45 cm* is 21.8 sec by Stephen Williams (Altrincham Grammar School) in May 1966. Allen R. Astles (University of Wales) potted 10,000 winks in 3 hr 51 min 46 sec at Aberystwyth, Cardiganshire in February 1966. The greatest number of winks potted in 3 min by a relay of four is 29 by Paul Light, Paul Hoffman, Andrew James and Geoff Thorpe at 'The Castle', Cambridge on 6 Dec 1974.

TRACK AND FIELD ATHLETICS
See also The Guinness Book of Athletics Facts and Feats, *by Peter Matthews, published by Guinness Superlatives Ltd at £8.95.*

Both Mary Decker (*right*) and Jarmila Kratochvilova (*left*) were double gold medallists at the 1983 World Athletics Championships in Helsinki. Decker won at 1500 and 3000 metres. In 1973 she was the youngest ever US international athlete at 14 yr 224 days when she ran against the USSR. (*All-Sport*) Kratochvilova set world records at both 400 and 800 metres in 1983. She first ranked in the world's top ten at 400 metres in 1980 at the comparatively advanced age of 29. (*Associated Sports Photography*)

Origins

Track and field athletics date from the ancient Olympic Games. The earliest accurately known Olympiad dates from July 776 BC, at which celebration Coroibos won the foot race. The oldest surviving measurements are a long jump of 7,05 m *23 ft 1¼ in* by Chionis of Sparta in *c.* 656 BC and a discus throw of 100 cubits (about 46.30 m *152 ft*) by Protesilaus.

Earliest landmarks

The first time 10 sec ('even time') was bettered for 100 yd under championship conditions was when John Owen, then aged 30, recorded 9⅘ sec in the AAU Championship at Analostan Island, Washington, DC, USA, on 11 Oct 1890. The first recorded instance of 6 ft *1,83 m* being cleared in the high jump was when Marshall Jones Brooks (1855–1944) jumped 6 ft 0⅛ in *1,832 m* at Marston, near Oxford, on 17 Mar 1876. The breaking of the 'four-minute barrier' in the 1 mile *1609,34 m* was first achieved by Dr (now Sir) Roger Gilbert Bannister, CBE (b. Harrow, London, 23 Mar 1929), when he recorded 3 min 59.4 sec on the Iffley Road track, Oxford, at 6.10 p.m. on 6 May 1954.

Fastest speed

The fastest speed recorded in an individual world record is 36,51 km/h *22.69 mph*, but this does not allow for the effects of the delay in reaching peak speed from a standing start. Maximum speeds are likely to exceed 40 km/h *25 mph* for men and 36,5 km/h *22.5 mph* for women. Examination of video tapes for Frederick Carlton 'Carl' Lewis (b. 1 July 1961) on the last leg of the 4 × 100 metres sprint relay when the US team set a world record at Helsinki, Finland on 14 Aug 1983 showed his speed at 40,45 km/h *25.13 mph.*

Highest jumper above own head

The greatest height cleared above an athlete's own head is 23¼ in *59 cm* by Franklin Jacobs (USA) (b. 31 Dec 1957), who cleared 7 ft 7¼ in *2,32 m* at New York, USA, on 27 Jan 1978. He is only 5 ft 8 in *1,73 m* tall. The greatest height cleared by a woman above her own head is 30,5 cm *12 in* by Cindy John Holmes (USA) (b. 29 Aug 1960), 5 ft *1,525 m* tall, who jumped 6 ft *1,83 m* at Provo, Utah, USA on 1 June 1982.

Most Olympic titles *Men*

The most Olympic gold medals won is ten (an absolute Olympic record) by Ray C. Ewry (USA) (1874–1937) in the Standing High, Long and Triple Jumps in 1900, 1904, 1906 and 1908.

Most Olympic titles *Women*

The most gold medals won by a woman is four shared by Francina 'Fanny' E. Blankers-Koen (Netherlands) (b. 26 Apr 1918) with 100 m, 200 m, 80 m hurdles and 4 × 100 m relay, 1948; Betty Cuthbert (Australia) (b. 20 Apr 1938) with 100 m, 200 m, 4 × 100 m relay, 1956 and 400 m, 1964; and Bärbel Wöckel (*née* Eckert) (b. 21 Mar 1955) (GDR) with 200 m and 4 × 100 m relay in 1976 and 1980.

Most wins at one Games

The most gold medals at one celebration is five by Paavo Johannes Nurmi (Finland) (1897–1973) in 1924, and the most individual is four by Alvin C. Kraenzlein (USA) (1876–1928) in 1900, with 60 m, 110 m hurdles, 200 m hurdles and long jump.

Most Olympic titles *British*

The most gold medals won by a British athlete (excluding Tug of War and Walking, *q.v.*) is two by: Charles Bennett (1871–1949) (1500 m and 5000 m team, 1900); Alfred Tysoe (1874–1901) (800 m and 5000 m team, 1900); John Rimmer (1879–1962) (4000 m steeplechase and 5000 m team, 1900); Albert G. Hill (1889–1969) (800 m and 1500 m, 1920) and Douglas Gordon Arthur Lowe (1902–81) (800 m 1924 and 1928).

WORLD RECORDS *MEN*

World records for the 32 men's events (excluding the walking records—see under WALKING) scheduled by the International Amateur Athletic Federation. Fully automatic electric timing is mandatory for the six events up to the 400 metre distance.

RUNNING	Min Sec	Name and Country	Place	Date
100 metres	9.93A	Calvin Smith (USA) (b. 8 Jan 1961)	Colorado Springs, Colorado, USA	3 July 1983
200 metres	19.72A	Pietro Mennea (Italy) (b. 28 June 1952)	Mexico City, Mexico	12 Sept 1979
400 metres	43.86A	Lee Edward Evans (USA) (b. 25 Feb 1947)	Mexico City, Mexico	18 Oct 1968
800 metres	1:41.73	Sebastian Newbold Coe (GB) (b. 29 Sept 1956)	Florence, Italy	10 June 1981
1000 metres	2:12.18	Sebastian Newbold Coe (GB)	Oslo, Norway	11 July 1981
1500 metres	3:30.77	Steven Michael James Ovett (GB) (b. 9 Oct 1955)	Rieti, Italy	4 Sept 1983
1 mile	3:47.33	Sebastian Newbold Coe (GB)	Brussels, Belgium	28 Aug 1981
2000 metres	4:51.4	John George Walker (NZ) (b. 12 Jan 1952)	Oslo, Norway	30 June 1976
3000 metres	7:32.1	Henry Rono (Kenya) (b. 12 Feb 1952)	Oslo, Norway	27 June 1978
5000 metres	13:00.41	David Robert Moorcroft (GB) (b. 10 Apr 1953)	Oslo, Norway	7 July 1982
10,000 metres	27:13.81	Fernando Mamede (Portugal) (b. 1 Nov 1951)	Stockholm, Sweden	2 July 1984
20,000 metres	57:24.2	Josephus Hermens (Netherlands) (b. 8 Jan 1950)	Papendal, Netherlands	1 May 1976
25,000 metres	1 hr 13:55.8	Toshihiko Seko (Japan) (b. 15 July 1956)	Christchurch, New Zealand	22 Mar 1981
30,000 metres	1 hr 29:18.8	Toshihiko Seko (Japan)	Christchurch, New Zealand	22 Mar 1981
1 hour	20 944 m *13 miles 24 yd 2 ft*	Josephus Hermens (Netherlands)	Papendal, Netherlands	1 May 1976

HURDLING				
110 metres (3′ 6″ *106 cm*)	12.93	Renaldo Nehemiah (USA) (b. 24 Mar 1959)	Zürich, Switzerland	19 Aug 1981
400 metres (3′ 0″ *91,4 cm*)	47.02	Edwin Corley Moses (USA) (b. 31 Aug 1955)	Koblenz, W. Germany	31 Aug 1983
3000 metres steeplechase	8:05.4	Henry Rono (Kenya)	Seattle, Washington, USA	13 May 1978

RELAYS				
4 × 100 metres	37.86	United States National Team: Emmit King, William James Gault, Calvin Smith, Frederick Carlton Lewis	Helsinki, Finland	10 Aug 1983
4 × 200 metres	1:20.26†	University of Southern California, USA: Joel Andrews, James Sanford, William Mullins, Clancy Edwards	Tempe, Arizona, USA	27 May 1978
4 × 400 metres	2:56.16A	United States National Team: Vincent Edward Matthews, Ronald J. Freeman, George Lawrence James, Lee Edward Evans	Mexico City, Mexico	20 Oct 1968
4 × 800 metres	7:03.89	Great Britain: Peter Elliott, Gary Peter Cook, Steven Cram, Sebastian Newbold Coe	Crystal Palace, London	30 Aug 1982
4 × 1500 metres	14:38.8	West Germany: Thomas Wessinghage, Harald Hudak, Michael Lederer, Karl Fleschen	Cologne, W. Germany	17 Aug 1977

† *The time of 1:20.23 achieved by the Tobias Striders (Guy Abrahams, Mike Simmons, Donald O'Riley Quarrie, James Gilkes) at Tempe, Ariz., USA on 27 May 1978 was not ratified as the team was composed of varied nationalities.*

FIELD EVENTS	ft	in	m	Name and Country	Place	Date
High Jump	7	10	*2,39*	Zhu Jianhua (China) (b. 29 Mar 1963)	Eberstadt, W. Germany	10 June 1984
Pole Vault	19	4¼	*5,90*	Sergey Bubka (USSR) (b. 4 Dec 1963)	Crystal Palace, London	13 July 1984
Long Jump	29	2½	*8,90*A	Robert Beamon (USA) (b. 29 Aug 1946)	Mexico City, Mexico	18 Oct 1968
Triple Jump	58	8½	*17,89*A	João Carlos de Oliveira (Brazil) (b. 28 May 1954)	Mexico City, Mexico	15 Oct 1975
Shot 7.26 kg *16 lb*	72	10¾	*22,22*‡	Udo Beyer (GDR) (b. 9 Aug 1955)	Los Angeles, California, USA	25 June 1983
Discus 2 kg *4 lb 6.55 oz*	235	9	*71,86*†	Yuriy Dumchev (USSR) (b. 5 Aug 1958)	Moscow, USSR	29 May 1983
Hammer 7.26 kg *16 lb*	283	3	*86,34*	Yuri Sedykh (USSR) (b. 11 Jun 1955)	Cork, Ireland	3 July 1984
Javelin 800 g *28.22 oz*	343	10	*104,80*	Uwe Höhn (GDR) (b. 16 July 1962)	East Berlin, GDR	20 July 1984

DECATHLON

8798 points ... Jürgen Hingsen (W. Germany) (b. 25 Jan 1958) ... Mannheim, West Germany ... 8–9 June 1984
(1st day: 100 m 10.70 sec, Long Jump 7,76 m *25′ 5½″*, Shot Put 16,42 m *53′ 10½″*, High Jump 2,07 m *6′ 9½″*, 400 m 48,05 sec)
(2nd day: 110 m hurdles 14.07 sec, Discus 49,36 m *161′ 11″*, Pole Vault 4,90 m *16′ 0¾″*, Javelin 59,86 m *196′ 5″*, 1500 m 4:19.75 sec)

A *These records were set at high altitude—Mexico City 2240 m* 7349 ft*, Colorado Springs 2195 m* 7201 ft*. Best marks at low altitude have been: 100 m: 9.96 sec, Melvin Bernard Lattany (USA) (b. 10 Aug 1959), Athens, Georgia, USA, 5 May 1984. 200 m: 19.75 sec, Frederick Carlton 'Carl' Lewis (USA) (b. 1 July 1961), Indianapolis, Indiana, USA, 19 June 1983. 400 m: 44.26 sec, Alberto Juantorena (Cuba) (b. 21 Nov 1950), Montreal, Canada, 29 July 1976. Long Jump: 8.79 m* 28 ft 10¼ in*, Carl Lewis, Indianapolis, Indiana, USA, 19 June 1983. Triple Jump: 17,56 m* 57 ft 7½ in*, Willie Banks (USA) (b. 11 Mar 1956), Sacramento, California, USA, 21 June 1981. 4 × 400 m relay: USA (Herman Frazier, Benny Brown, Fred Newhouse, Maxie Parks) Montreal, Canada, 31 July 1976.*

‡ *Note: One professional performance is superior to the IAAF mark, but the same highly rigorous rules as to measuring and weighing were not necessarily applied.*
75 0 ... *22,86* ... *Brian Ray Oldfield (USA) (b. 1 Jan 1945)* ... *El Paso, Texas, USA* ... *10 May 1975*

† *Walter Ben Plucknett (USA) (b. 13 Apr 1954) threw 237 ft 4 in 72,34 m at Stockholm, Sweden on 7 July 1981 but was subsequently disqualified from competition.*

Most Olympic medals *Men*
The most medals won is 12 (nine gold and three silver) by Paavo Nurmi (Finland) in the Games of 1920, 1924 and 1928.

Most Olympic medals *Women*
The most medals won by a woman athlete is seven by Shirley de la Hunty (*née* Strickland) (Australia) (b. 18 July 1925) with three gold, one silver and three bronze in the 1948, 1952 and 1956 Games. A recently discovered photo-finish indicates that she finished third, not fourth, in the 1948 200 metres event, thus unofficially increasing her medal haul to eight. Irena Szewinska (*née* Kirszenstein) (Poland) (b. 24 May 1946) won three gold, two silver and two bronze in 1964, 1968, 1972 and 1976, and is the only woman athlete to win a medal in four successive games.

Most Olympic medals *British*
The most medals won by a British athlete is four by Guy M. Butler (1899–1981) with a gold medal for the 4 × 400 m relay and a silver in the 400 m in 1920 and a bronze medal for each of these events in 1924. Two British women athletes have won three medals: Dorothy Hyman (b. 9 May 1941) with a silver (100 m, 1960) and two bronze (200 m, 1960 and 4 × 100 m relay, 1964) and Mary Denise Rand (now Toomey, *née* Bignal), (b. 10 Feb 1940) with a gold (long jump), a silver (pentathlon) and a bronze (4 × 100 m relay), all in 1964.

Olympic champions *Oldest and youngest*
The oldest athlete to win an Olympic title was Irish-born Patrick J. 'Babe' McDonald (USA) (1878–1954) who was aged 42 yr 26 days when he won the 56 lb *25,4 kg* weight throw at Antwerp, Belgium on 21 Aug 1920. The oldest female champion was Lia Manoliu (Romania) (b. 25 Apr 1932) aged 36 yr 176 days when she won the discus at Mexico City on 18 Oct 1968. The youngest gold medallist was Barbara Jones (USA) (b. 26 Mar 1937) who was a member of the winning 4 × 100 m relay team, aged 15 yr 123 days, at Helsinki, Finland on 27 July 1952. The youngest male champion was Robert Bruce Mathias (USA) (b. 17 Nov 1930) aged 17 yr 263 days when he won the decathlon at London on 5–6 Aug 1948.

The oldest Olympic medallist was Tebbs Lloyd Johnson (b. 7 Apr 1900), aged 48 yr 115 days when he was third in the 1948 50,000 m walk. The oldest women's medallist was Dana Zátopkova aged 37 yr 248 days when she was second in the javelin in 1960.

World record breakers *Oldest and youngest*

For the greatest age at which anyone has broken a world record under IAAF jurisdiction *see p. 240.* The female record is 35 yr 255 days for Dana Zátopkova, *née* Ingrova (b. 19 Sept 1922) of Czechoslovakia, who broke the women's javelin record with 55,73 m *182 ft 10 in* at Prague, Czechoslovakia, on 1 June 1958. The youngest individual record breaker is Carolina Gisolf (b. 13 July 1913) (Netherlands) who set a women's high jump mark with 1.61 m *5 ft 3¾ in* at Maastricht, Netherlands on 18 July 1928, aged 15 yr 5 days. The male record is 17 yr 198 days by Thomas Ray (1862–1904) when he pole-vaulted 3.42 m *11 ft 2¾ in* on 19 Sept 1879 (both pre-IAAF records).

Most records in a day

Jesse Owens (1913–80) (USA) set six world records in 45 min at Ann Arbor, Michigan on 25 May 1935 with a 9.4 sec 100 yd at 3.15 p.m., a 26 ft 8¼ in *8,13 m* long jump at 3.25 p.m., a 20.3 sec *220 yd* (and 200 m) at 3.45 p.m. and a 22.6 sec 220 yd low hurdles (and 200 m) at 4.00 p.m.

Most national titles *Great Britain*

The greatest number of senior AAA titles (excluding those in tug of war events) won by one athlete is 14 individual and one

PROGRESSIVE HIGH JUMP RECORDS

The blue chart shows the improvement in the world high jump record from Michael Sweeney's 1,97 m in 1895 to the 2,39 m in 1984 by Zhu Jianhua (*right*), the first Chinese man to set a world record in athletics. (*Agence SAM*) The red chart shows how the women's record has risen to the 2,04 m cleared by Tamara Bykova (*below*) in 1983. She improved further to 2,05 m in June 1984. (*All-Sport*)

ARTWORK: EDDIE BOTCHWAY

relay title by Emmanuel McDonald Bailey (Trinidad) (b. 8 Dec 1920), between 1946 and 1952. The most won outdoors in a single event is 13 by Denis Horgan (Ireland) (1871–1922) in the shot put between 1893 and 1912. 13 senior titles were also won by Michael Anthony Bull (b. 11 Sept 1946) at pole vault, eight indoor and five out and by Geoffrey Lewis Capes (b. 23 Aug 1949) at shot, six indoor and seven out.

The greatest number of WAAA titles won by one athlete is 14 by Suzanne Allday (*née* Farmer) (b. 26 Nov 1934) with seven each at shot and discus between 1952 and 1962.

Most international appearances

The greatest number of international matches contested for any nation is 89 by Bjørn Bang Andersen (b. 14 Nov 1937) for Norway, 1960–81.

The greatest number of full Great Britain international appearances (outdoors and indoors) is 73 by Verona Marolin Elder (*née* Bernard) (b. 5 Apr 1953) from 1971 to 1983. The men's record is 67 by Geoff Capes, 1969–80. Mike Bull had 66 full internationals or 69 including the European Indoor Games, before these were official internationals. The most outdoors is 61 by Andrew Howard Payne (b. South Africa, 17 Apr 1931) from 1960 to 1974.

Oldest and youngest internationals

The oldest full Great Britain international was Hector Harold Whitlock (b. 16 Dec 1903) at the 1952 Olympic Games, aged 48 yr 218 days. The oldest woman was Christine Rosemary Payne (*née* Charters) (b. 19 May 1933) in the Great Britain *v.* Finland match on 26 Sept 1974, aged 41 yr 130 days. The youngest man was Ross Hepburn (b. 14 Oct 1961) *v.* the USSR on 26 Aug 1977, aged 15 yr 316 days, and the youngest woman was Janis Walsh (b. 28 Mar 1960) *v.* Belgium (indoor) at 60 m and 4 × 200 m relay on 15 Feb 1975, aged 14 yr 324 days.

Longest career

Duncan McLean (1884–1980) of Scotland set a world age—92

Carl Lewis (*left*), the greatest sprinter/long jumper since Jesse Owens. He first exceeded 28 ft *8,53 m* in the long jump in 1981 and is now challenging the 8,90 m *29 ft 2½ in* set by Bob Beamon in 1968 and once regarded as impregnable. Anisoara Cusmir (*above*) set four world long-jump records in 1982–3, culminating in 7,43 m *24 ft 4½ in* and improving the record by the biggest ever margin. (*All-Sport*)

record of 100 m in 21.7 sec in August 1977, over 73 years after his best ever sprint of 100 yd in 9.9 sec in South Africa in February 1904. At Athens, Greece, on 10 Oct 1976, Dimitrion Yordanidis, aged 98, completed a marathon race in 7 hr 33 min.

London to Brighton race

Ian Thompson (b. 16 Oct 1949) (Luton United H) won the 54.3 miles *87,4 km* race (inst. 1951) in 5 hr 15 min 15 sec on 28 Sept 1980, averaging 10.33 mph *16,62 km/h*. The most wins is four by Bernard Gomersall (b. 28 Aug 1932) in 1963–6.

'End to end'

The fastest run from John o'Groats to Land's End is 10 days 3 hr 30 min claimed by Fred Hicks (GB) for 876 miles *1410 km* on 20–30 May 1977.

Six-day races

The greatest distance covered by a man in six days (*i.e.* the 144 permissible hours between Sundays in Victorian times) was 623¾ miles *1003,828 km* by George Littlewood (1859–1912) (England), who required only 141 hr 57 min 30 sec for this feat on 27 Nov–2 Dec 1888 at the old Madison Square Garden, New York City, USA. The amateur records are: men— 927,600 km *576 miles 675 yd* by Thomas Patrick O'Reilly (b. 18 May 1945) at Nottingham on 22–28 Aug 1982; women— 676,981 km *420 miles 1155 yd* by Christine Barrett (b. 20 Aug 1948) at Stoke-on-Trent on 20–27 May 1984.

WORLD RECORDS *WOMEN*

World records for the 21 women's events scheduled by the International Amateur Athletic Federation. The same stipulation about automatically timed events applies in the six events up to 400 metres as in the men's list.

RUNNING

	Min sec	Name and Country	Place	Date
100 metres	10.79A	Evelyn Ashford (USA) (b. 15 Apr 1957)	Colorado Springs, Colorado, USA	3 July 1983
200 metres	21.71	Marita Koch (GDR) (b. 18 Feb 1957)	Karl Marx Stadt, GDR	10 June 1979
		Marita Koch	Potsdam, GDR	21 July 1984
400 metres	47.99	Jarmila Kratochvilova (Czechoslovakia) (b. 26 Jan 1951)	Helsinki, Finland	10 Aug 1983
800 metres	1:53.28	Jarmila Kratochvilova (Czechoslovakia)	Munich, W. Germany	26 July 1983
1500 metres	3:52.47	Tatyana Kazankina (USSR) (b. 17 Dec 1951)	Zürich, Switzerland	13 Aug 1980
1 mile	4:17.44	Maricica Puica (Romania) (b. 29 July 1950)	Rieti, Italy	16 Sept 1982
3000 metres	8:26.78	Svyetlana Ulmasova (USSR) (b. 4 Feb 1953)	Moscow, USSR	25 July 1982
5000 metres	14:58.89	Ingrid Kristiansen (née Christensen) (Norway) (b. 21 Mar 1956)	Oslo, Norway	28 June 1984
10000 metres	31:13.78	Olga Bondarenko (USSR) (b. 2 June 1964)	Kiev, USSR	23 June 1984

HURDLING

		Name and Country	Place	Date
100 metres (2' 9" *84 cm*)	12.36	Grazyna Rabsztyn (Poland) (b. 20 Sept 1952)	Warsaw, Poland	13 June 1980
400 metres (2' 6" *76 cm*)	53.58	Margarita Ponomaryeva [neé Navickaite] (USSR) (b. 10 Dec 1961)	Kiev, USSR	22 June 1984

RELAYS

		Name and Country	Place	Date
4 × 100 metres	41.53	GDR: Silke Gladisch, Marita Koch, Ingrid Auerswald, Marlies Göhr [*née* Oelsner]	E. Berlin, GDR	31 July 1983
4 × 200 metres	1:28.15	GDR: Marlies Göhr [*née* Oelsner], Romy Müller [*née* Schneider], Bärbel Wöckel [*née* Eckert], Marita Koch	Jena, GDR	9 Aug 1980
4 × 400 metres	3:15.92	GDR: Gesine Walther, Sabine Busch, Dagmar Rübsam, Marita Koch	Erfurt, GDR	3 June 1984
4 × 800 metres	7:50.17	USSR: Nadezha Olizarenko, Lyubov Gurina, Lyudmila Borisova, Irina Podyalovskaya	Moscow, USSR	4 Aug 1984

FIELD EVENTS

	ft	in	m	Name and Country	Place	Date
High Jump	6	9½	*2,07*	Lyudmila Andonova (Bulgaria) (b. 12 May 1960)	East Berlin, GDR	20 July 1984
Long Jump	24	4½	*7,43*	Anisoara Cusmir (Romania) (b. 28 June 1962)	Bucharest, Romania	4 June 1983
Shot 4 kg *8 lb 13 oz*	73	11	*22,53*	Natalia Lisovskaya (USSR) (b. 16 July 1962)	Sochi, USSR	26 May 1984
Discus 1 kg *2 lb 3.27 oz*	240	4	*73,26*	Galina Savinkova (USSR) (b. 15 Jul 1953)	Leselidze, USSR	22 May 1983
Javelin 600 g *21.16 oz*	245	3	*74,76*	Ilse Kristiina Lillak (Finland) (b. 15 Apr 1961)	Tampere, Finland	13 June 1983

HEPTATHLON

	Name and Country	Place	Date
6867 points	Sabine Paetz [*née* Mobius] (GDR) (b. 16 Oct 1957)	Potsdam, GDR	5-6 May 1984

(100 m hurdles 12.64 sec; High Jump 1,80 m *5 ft 10¾ in*; Shot 15.37 m *50 ft 5¼ in*; 200 m 23.37 sec; Long Jump 6,86 m *22 ft 6¼ in*; Javelin 44,62 m *146 ft 5 in*; 800 m 2 min 08.93 sec)

A *Set at 2200 m 7218 ft altitude. Best low altitude mark: 10.81 Marlies Göhr (née Oelsner) (GDR) (b. 21 Mar 1958), East Berlin, 8 June 1983.*

1000 miles

Siegfried 'Siggy' Bauer (New Zealand) ran 1000 miles *1609 km* in Australia in 12 days 12 hr 36 min 20 sec from Melbourne by road 92 miles *148 km* to Colac and then 2715 laps of a third of a mile track on 15–28 Nov 1983.

Longest non-stop run

The greatest non-stop run recorded is 352.9 miles *568 km* in 121 hr 54 min by Bertil Järlåker (Sweden) (b. 1936) at Norrköping, Sweden, 26–31 May 1980. He was moving for 95.04 per cent of the time.

Longest running race

The longest races ever staged were the 1928 (3422 miles *5507 km*) and 1929 (3665 miles *5898 km*) Trans-continental races from New York City, NY, to Los Angeles, California, USA. The Finnish-born Johnny Salo (1893–1931) was the winner in 1929 in 79 days, from 31 Mar to 18 June. His elapsed time of 525 hr 57 min 20 sec (averaging 6.97 mph *11,21 km/h*) left him only 2 min 47 sec ahead of Englishman Pietro 'Peter' Gavuzzi (1905–81).

Longest runs

The longest ever solo run is 10,608 miles *17,072 km* by Robert J. Sweetgall (USA) (b. 8 Dec 1947) around the perimeter of the USA starting and finishing in Washington, DC, 9 Oct 1982–15 July 1983. Ron Grant (Australia) (b. 15 Feb 1943) ran around Australia, 13,383 km *8316 miles* in 217 days 3 hr 45 min, running every day from 28 Mar to 31 Oct 1983. Max Telford (NZ) (b. Hawick, Scotland, 2 Feb 1935) ran 5110 miles *8224 km* from Anchorage, Alaska to Halifax, Nova Scotia, in 106 days 18 hr 45 min from 25 July to 9 Nov 1977. The fastest time reported for the cross-America run is 46 days 8 hr 36 min by Frank Giannino Jr (USA) (b. 1952) for the 3100 miles *4989 km* from San Francisco to New York on 1 Sept–17 Oct 1980.

Greatest mileage

Douglas Alistair Gordon Pirie (b. 10 Feb 1931) (GB), who set five world records in the 1950s, estimated that he had run a total distance of 216,000 miles *347,600 km* in 40 years to 1981.

The greatest distance run in one year is 15,472 miles *24,890 km* by Tina Maria Stone (b. Naples, Italy, 5 Apr 1934) of Irvine, California, USA in 1983.

Jay F. Helgerson (b. 3 Feb 1955) of Foster City, California, ran a certified marathon (26 miles 385 yd) or longer, each week for 52 weeks from 28 Jan 1979 to 19 Jan 1980, totalling 1418 racing miles *2282 km*.

Mass relay records

The record for 100 miles *160,9 km* by 100 runners belonging to one club is 7 hr 53 min 52.1 sec by Baltimore Road Runners Club, Towson, Maryland, USA, on 17 May 1981. The women's record is 10 hr 47 min 9.3 sec on 3 Apr 1977 by the San Francisco Dolphins Southend Running Club, USA. The best club time for a 100 × 400 metres relay is 1 hr 29 min

THE MARATHON

The marathon distance of 26 miles 385 yd *42,195 km* was standardised in 1924. There are no official records because of the varying severity of courses. The best recorded times are:

	Hr	min	sec			
MEN	2	8	13	Alberto Baudoy Salazar (USA) (b. 7 Aug 1958)	New York, USA	25 Oct 1981
WOMEN	2	22	43	Joan Benoit (USA) (b. 16 May 1957)	Boston, Mass, USA	18 Apr 1983

British records are:

	Hr	min	sec			
MEN	2	9	08	Geoff Smith (b. 24 Oct 1953)	New York, USA	23 Oct 1983
WOMEN	2	29	43	Joyce Esther Smith (b. 26 Oct 1937)	London	9 May 1982

RUNNING

	min sec	Name	Place	Date
100 metres	10.11	Allan Wipper Wells (b. 3 May 1952)	Moscow, USSR	24 July 1980
200 metres)	20.21	Allan Wipper Wells	Moscow, USSR	28 July 1980
400 metres	44.93	David Andrew Jenkins (b. 25 May 1952)	Eugene, Oregon, USA	21 June 1975
800 metres	1:41.73	Sebastian Newbold Coe (b. 29 Sept 1956)	Florence, Italy	10 June 1981
1000 metres	2:12.18	Sebastian Newbold Coe	Oslo, Norway	11 July 1981
1500 metres	3:30.77	Steven Michael James Ovett (b. 9 Oct 1955)	Rieti, Italy	4 Sept 1983
1 mile	3:47.33	Sebastian Newbold Coe	Brussels, Belgium	28 Aug 1981
2000 metres	4:57.71	Steven Michael James Ovett	Oslo, Norway	7 July 1982
3000 metres	7:32.79	David Robert Moorcroft (b. 10 Apr 1953)	London (Crystal Palace)	17 July 1982
5000 metres	13:00.41	David Robert Moorcroft	Oslo, Norway	7 July 1982
10,000 metres	27:30.3†	Brendan Foster (b. 12 Jan 1948)	London (Crystal Palace)	23 June 1978
20,000 metres	58:39.0	Ronald Hill (b. 25 Sept 1938)	Leicester	9 Nov 1968
25,000 metres	1 hr 15:22.6	Ronald Hill	Bolton, Lancashire	21 July 1965
30,000 metres	1 hr 31:30.4	James Noel Carroll Alder (b. 10 June 1940)	London (Crystal Palace)	5 Sept 1970
1 hour	12 miles 1268 yd *20 472m*	Ronald Hill	Leicester	9 Nov 1968

† *Ratified at 27:30.6*

HURDLING

		Name	Place	Date
110 metres	13.43	James Mark Holton (b. 6 Feb 1958)	Brisbane, Australia	4 Oct 1982
400 metres	48.12	David Peter Hemery (b. 18 July 1944)	Mexico City, Mexico	15 Oct 1968
3000 metres Steeplechase	8:13.78	Colin Robert Reitz (b. 5 April 1960)	Oslo, Norway	21 July 1984

RELAYS

		Name	Place	Date
4 × 100 metres	38.62	United Kingdom: Michael Anthony McFarlane, Allan Wipper Wells, Robert Cameron Sharp, Andrew Emlyn McMaster	Moscow, USSR	1 Aug 1980
4 × 200 metres	1:24.1	Great Britain: Brian William Green, Roger Wilfred Walters, Ralph Banthorpe, Martin Edward Reynolds	Paris, France	2 Oct 1971
4 × 400 metres	3:00.46	United Kingdom: Martin Edward Reynolds, Alan Peter Pascoe, David Peter Hemery, David Andrew Jenkins	Munich, W. Germany	10 Sept 1972
4 × 800 metres	7:03.89	United Kingdom: Peter Elliott, Gary Peter Cook, Steven Cram, Sebastian Newbold Coe	London (Crystal Palace)	30 Aug 1982
4 × 1500 metres	14:56.8	United Kingdom: Alan David Mottershead, Geoffrey Michael Cooper, Stephen John Emson, Roy Wood	Bourges, France	24 June 1979

FIELD EVENTS

	ft	in	m	Name	Place	Date
High Jump	7	4½	*2.25*	Geoffrey Peter Parsons (b. 14 Aug 1964)	Plymouth, Devon	9 July 1983
Pole Vault	18	6½	*5.65*	Keith Frank Stock (b. 18 Mar 1957)	Oslo, Norway	7 July 1981
Long Jump	27	0	*8.23*	Lynn Davies (b. 20 May 1942)	Bern, Switzerland	30 June 1968
Triple Jump	57	7¾	*17.57*	Keith Leroy Connor (b. 16 Sept 1957)	Provo, Utah, USA	5 June 1982
Shot 7.26 kg *16 lb*	71	1½	*21.68*	Geoffrey Lewis Capes (b. 23 Aug 1949)	Cwmbran, Gwent	18 May 1980
Discus 2 kg *4 lb 6.55 oz*	211	0	*64.32*†	William Raymond Tancred (b. 6 Aug 1942)	Woodford, Essex	10 Aug 1974
Hammer 7.26 kg *16 lb*	254	5	*77.54*	Martin Girvan (b. 17 Apr 1960)	Wolverhampton, Staffs	12 May 1984
Javelin 800 g *28.22 oz*	289	7	*88.26*	Arne-Roald Bradstock (b. 24 Apr 1962)	Arlington, Texas, USA	5 May 1984

† *William Raymond Tancred threw 64.94 m 213 ft 1in at Loughborough on 21 July 1974 and Richard Charles Slaney (b. 16 May 1956) threw 64,64 m 212 ft 1 in at San Diego, Cal, USA on 30 Apr 1982 but these were not ratified.*

DECATHLON (1962 Scoring Table)

8743 points	Francis Morgan 'Daley' Thompson (b. 30 July 1958)	Athens, Greece		7–8 Sept 1982

(1st day: 100 m 10.51 sec, Long Jump 7,80 m *25′ 7″*, Shot Put 15,44m *50′ 8″*, High Jump 2,03 m *6′ 8″*, 400 m 47.11 sec)

(2nd day: 110 m Hurdles 14.39 sec, Discus 47,48 m *149′ 2″*, Pole Vault 5,00 m *16′ 4¾″*, Javelin 63,56 m *208′ 6″*, 1500 m 4:23.81 sec)

UNITED KINGDOM (NATIONAL) RECORDS *WOMEN*

RUNNING

	Min sec	Name	Place	Date
100 metres	11.10	Kathryn Jane Smallwood [now Cook] (b. 3 May 1960)	Rome, Italy	5 Sept 1981
200 metres	22.13	Kathryn Jane Cook [*née* Smallwood]	Athens, Greece	9 Sept 1982
400 metres	50.46	Kathryn Jane Cook [*née* Smallwood]	London (Crystal Palace)	17 Sept 1982
800 metres	1:59.05	Christina Tracy Boxer (b. 25 Mar 1957)	Turin, Italy	4 Sept 1979
1500 metres	4:00.57	Christina Tracy Boxer	Gateshead, Tyne and Wear	6 July 1984
1 mile	4:30.20†	Christina Tracy Boxer	Gateshead, Tyne and Wear	8 July 1979
3000 metres	8:37.06	Wendy Sly [*née* Smith] (b. 5 Nov 1959]	Helsinki, Finland	10 Aug 1983
5000 metres	15:14.51	Paula Fudge [*née* Yeoman] (b. 30 Mar 1952)	Knarvik, Norway	13 Sept 1981
10000 metres	32:57.17†	Kathryn Mary Binns (b. 13 Jan 1958)	Sittard, Netherlands	14 Aug 1980

RELAYS

		Name	Place	Date
4 × 100 metres	42.43	United Kingdom: Heather Regina Hunte [now Oakes], Kathryn Jane Smallwood [now Cook], Beverley Lanita Goddard [now Callender], Sonia May Lannaman	Moscow, USSR	1 Aug 1980
4 × 200 metres	1:31.57	United Kingdom: Donna-Marie Louise Hartley [*née* Murray], Verona Marolin Elder [*née* Bernard], Sharon Colyear [now Danville], Sonia May Lannaman	London (Crystal Palace)	20 Aug 1977
4 × 400 metres	3:25.82	United Kingdom: Kathryn Jane Cook [*née* Smallwood], Linsey Tarrel Macdonald, Gladys Taylor, Joslyn Yvonne Hoyte-Smith	Athens, Greece	11 Sept 1982
4 × 800 metres	8:23.8	Great Britain: Joan Florence Allison [*née* Page], Sheila Janet Carey [*née* Taylor], Patricia Barbara Lowe [now Cropper], Rosemary Olivia Stirling [now Wright]	Paris, France	2 Oct 1971

HURDLING

		Name	Place	Date
100 metres	12.87	Shirley Elaine Strong (b. 18 Nov 1958)	Zürich, Switzerland	24 Aug 1983
400 metres	56.04	Susan Anita Jayne Morley (b. 6 Jan 1960)	Helsinki, Finland	10 Aug 1983

FIELD EVENTS

	ft	in	m	Name	Place	Date
High Jump	6	4¾	*1.95*	Diana Clare Elliot (b. 7 May 1961)	Oslo, Norway	26 June 1982
Long Jump	22	7¾	*6.90*	Beverley Kinch (b. 14 Jan 1964)	Helsinki, Finland	14 Aug 1983
Shot 4 kg *8 lb 13 oz*	62	3¾	*18,99**	Margaret Elizabeth Ritchie (b. 6 July 1952)	Tucson, Arizona, USA	7 May 1983
Discus 1 kg *2 lb 3.27 oz*	221	5	*67,48*	Margaret Elizabeth Ritchie	Walnut, California, USA	26 April 1981
Javelin 600 g *21.16 oz*	241	5	*73,58*	Theresa Ione Sanderson (b. 14 Mar 1956)	Edinburgh, Scotland	26 June 1983

Shirley Strong winning her fifth successive WAAA title with the second of four British records at 100 metres hurdles within a month in 1983. (*All-Sport*)

HEPTATHLON

6353 points .... Judith Earline Veronica Livermore (b. 14 Nov 1960) .... Sofia, Bulgaria .... 10–11 Sept 1983
(100 m hurdles 13.23 sec; High Jump 1,87 m *6' 1½"*; Shot 13,54 m
44' 5¼"; 200 m 24.75; Long Jump 6,10 m *20' 0¼"*; Javelin 38,60 m
126' 8"; 800 m 2 min 12.50 sec)

† Wendy Sly [*née* Smith) (b. 5 Nov 1959) ran 1 mile indoors in 4:30.09 in New York, USA on 28 Jan 1983.
* Venessa Anne Head (b. 1 Sept 1956) achieved 19,06 m *62 ft 6¾ in* indoors at St. Athan on 7 Apr 1984.

11.8 sec (average 53.5 sec) by the Physical Training Institute, Leuven, Belgium on 19 Apr 1978. The best women's club time for 100 × 100 metres is 23 min 28 sec by Amsterdamse dames athletiekvereniging, on 26 Sept 1981 in Amsterdam, Netherlands.

The longest relay ever run was 15,059 km *9357 miles* by 20 members of the Melbourne Fire Brigade around Australia on Highway No. 1 in 43 days 23 hr 58 min, 10 July–23 Aug 1983. The most participants is 4800, 192 teams of 25, in the Batavierenrace, 167,2 km *103.89 miles* from Nijmegan to Enschede, Netherlands, won in 9 hr 30 min 44 sec on 23 Apr 1983.

Ambidextrous shot put

The best recorded distance is 121 ft 6¾ in by Allan Feuerbach (b. 14 Jan 1948) (USA) (left 51 ft 5 in *15,67 m*, right 70 ft 1¼ in *21.38 m*) at Malmo, Sweden on 24 Aug 1974.

Highland Games

The weight and height of cabers (Gaelic *cabar*) vary considerably. Extreme values are 25 ft *7,62 m* and 280 lb *127 kg*. The Braemar caber (19 ft 3 in *5,86 m* and 120 lb *54,4 kg*) in Grampian, Scotland, was untossed from 1891 until 1951 when it was tossed by George Clark. The best authentic mark recorded for throwing the 56 lb weight for height, using one hand only is 17 ft 2 in *5,23 m* by Geoffrey Lewis Capes (GB) (b. 23 Aug 1949) at Lagos, Nigeria on 5 Dec 1982. The best throw recorded for the Scots hammer is 151 ft 2 in *46,08 m* by

William Anderson (b. 6 Oct 1938) at Lochearnhead on 26 July 1969.

Highest one-legged jump

One-legged Arnie Boldt (b. 1958), of Saskatchewan, Canada, cleared 2.04 m *6 ft 8¼ in* in Rome, Italy on 3 Apr 1981.

Oldest race

The oldest continuously held foot race is the 'Red Hose Race' held at Carnwath, Strathclyde, Scotland since 1508. The prize is a pair of hand-knitted knee length red hose. Michael Glen, of Bathgate, won a record 14 times, 1951–66.

Backwards running

Anthony 'Scott' Weiland, 27, ran the Detroit marathon, USA backwards in 4 hr 7 min 54 sec on 3 Oct 1982. Donald Davis (b. 10 Feb 1960) (USA) ran 1 mile backwards in 6 min 7.1 sec at the University of Hawaii on 21 Feb 1983. Ferdie Adoboe (USA) ran 100 yd backwards in 12.8 sec (100 m in 14.0 sec) at Amherst, Mass. on 28 July 1983.

Fastest blind sprinting

Graham Henry Salmon (GB) (b. 5 Sept 1952) ran 100 m *109 yd* in 11.4 sec at Grangemouth, Scotland on 2 Sept 1978.

Pancake racing

Dale R. Lyons (b. 26 Feb 1937) (GB) has run several marathons during which he tosses a 2 oz *57 g* pancake repeatedly en route in a 1½ lb *0,68 kg* pan. His fastest time is 2 hr 57 min 16 sec at Wolverhampton on 25 Mar 1984.

ULTRA LONG DISTANCE TRACK WORLD RECORDS *MEN*

Distance	Hr:min:sec	Name, country and date of birth	Place	Date
50 km	2:48:06	George Jeffrey Norman (GB) (b. 6 Feb 1945)	Timperley, Manchester, England	7 June 1980
40 miles	3:48:35	Donald Alexander Ritchie (GB) (b. 6 July 1944)	Hendon, London, England	16 Oct 1982
50 miles	4:51:49	Donald Alexander Ritchie	Hendon, London, England	12 Mar 1983
100km	6:10:20	Donald Alexander Ritchie	Crystal Palace, London	28 Oct 1978
100 miles	11:30:51	Donald Alexander Ritchie	Crystal Palace, London	15 Oct 1977
200 km	16:32:30	Donald Alexander Ritchie	Coatbridge, Scotland	29–30 Oct 1983
24 hours	274,480 km *170 ml 974 yd*	Dave Dowdle (GB) (b. 7 Nov 1954)	Gloucester, England	22–23 May 1982
48 hours	*420,000 km 260 ml 1717 yd*	Ramon Zabalo (France) (b. 1948)	Montauban, France	16–18 Mar 1984
	384,050 km *238 ml 1122 yd*	Dave Dowdle	Gloucester, England	13–15 May 1983

ULTRA LONG DISTANCE TRACK WORLD RECORDS *WOMEN*

20 km	1:06:55.5	Rosa Mota (Portugal) (b. 29 June 1958)	Lisbon, Portugal	14 May 1983
30 km	1:49:55.7	Chantal Langlacé (France) (b. 6 Jan 1955)	Amiens, France	3 Sept 1983
50 km	3:44:08*	Eleanor Adams (GB) (b. 20 Nov 1947)	Bingham, England	20 Nov 1982
40 miles	4:55:17*	Eleanor Adams	Bingham, England	20 Nov 1982
50 miles	6:20:42*	Leslie Watson (GB) (b. 4 Feb 1948)	Hendon, London, England	12 Mar 1983
	*6:17:30	Moniko Kuno (W. Germany) (on running watch at 50.2 ml)	Vogt, W. Germany	8–9 July 1983
100 km	8:39:10*	Lynn Fitzgerald (GB) (b. 9 Sept 1947)	Gloucester, England	22 May 1982
	*8:01:01	Moniko Kuno	Vogt, W. Germany	8–9 July 1983
100 miles	15:44:21	Lynn Fitzgerald	Nottingham, England	31 July–1 Aug 1983
200 km	21:38.40	Lynn Fitzgerald	Nottingham, England	31 July–1 Aug 1983
1 hour	18,084 km *11 ml 416 yd*	Silvana Cruciata (Italy) (b. 15 Feb 1953)	Rome, Italy	4 May 1981
24 hours	216,648 km *134 ml 1089 yd*	Rosalind Cox (née Paul) (GB) (b. 27 May 1959)	Nottingham, England	22–23 Aug 1982
48 hours	*299,908 km *186 ml 623 yd*	Rosalind Cox (née Paul) (GB)	Nottingham, England	22–24 Aug 1982
	325,158 km *202 ml 77 yd*	Eleanor Adams	Montauban, France	16–18 Mar 1984
* Significantly better road times:				
50 km	3:13:51	Janis Klecker (USA) (b. 18 July 1960)	Tallahassee, Florida, USA	17 Dec 1983
40 miles	4:43:22	Marcy Schwam (USA)	Chicago, USA	3 Oct 1982
50 miles	5:59:26	Marcy Schwam (USA)	Chicago, USA	3 Oct 1982
100 km	7:27:22	Chantal Langlacé (France)	Amiens, France	6 Sept 1980
100 miles	15:07.45	Christine Barrett (GB) (b. 20 Aug 1948)	Forthampton, Gloucester	14 Apr 1984

* yet to be confirmed

TRAMPOLINING

Origins

Trampolines were used in show business at least as early as 'The Walloons' of the period 1910–12. The sport of trampolining (from the Spanish word *trampolin*, a springboard) dates from 1936, when the prototype 'T' model trampoline was developed by George Nissen (USA).

Most titles

Four men have won a world title (instituted 1964) twice; Dave Jacobs (USA) in 1967–8, Wayne Miller (b. 1946) (USA), in 1966 and 1970, Richard Tison (b. 17 Aug 1956) (France) in 1974 and 1976 (shared), and Evgeni Janes (USSR), 1976 (shared) and 1978. Judy Wills (b. 1948) (USA) won the first five women's titles (1964–8). Two European titles (1969 and 1971) have been won by Paul Luxon (b. 1952) (GB), the 1972 world champion. A record seven United Kingdom titles have been won by Wendy Wright (1969–70, 1972–5, 1977). The most by a man have been five by Stewart Matthews (b. 19 Feb 1962) (1976–80).

Youngest international *Great Britain*

Andrea Holmes (b. 2 Jan 1970) competed for Britain at 12 years 131 days in the World Championships at Montana, USA on 13 May 1982.

TUG OF WAR

Origins

Though ancient China and Egypt have been suggested as the originators of the sport, it is known that neolithic flint miners in Norfolk, England practised 'rope-pulling'. The first rules were those framed by the New York AC in 1879. Tug of War was an Olympic sport from 1900 until 1920. In 1958 the Tug-of-War Association was formed to administer Britain's 600 clubs.

Most titles

The Wood Treatment team (formerly the Bosley Farmers) of Cheshire have represented England since 1964, winning two World and ten European Championships at 720 kg *1587 lb*. They also won 20 consecutive AAA Catchweight Championships 1959–78. Hilary Brown (b. 13 Apr 1934) was in every team. Trevor Brian Thomas (b. 1943) of British Aircraft Corporation Club is the only holder of three winner's medals in the European Open club competitions.

Longest pulls

The longest recorded pull (prior to the introduction of AAA rules) is one of 2 hr 41 min when 'H' Company beat 'E' Company of the 2nd Battalion of the Sherwood Foresters (Derbyshire Regiment) at Jubbulpore, India, on 12 Aug 1889. The longest recorded pull under AAA Rules (in which lying on the ground or entrenching the feet is not permitted) is one of 11 min 23 sec for the first pull between the Isle of Oxney and St Claret's at Chertsey, Surrey on 26 May 1979. The record time for 'The Pull' (inst. 1898), across the Black River,

between freshman and sophomore teams at Hope College, Holland, Mich, USA, is 3 hr 51 min on 23 Sept 1977, but the method of bracing the feet precludes the replacing of the preceding records.

VOLLEYBALL

Origins

The game was invented as *Minnonette* in 1895 by William G. Morgan at the YMCA gymansium at Holyoke, Massachusetts, USA. The International Volleyball Association was formed in Paris in April 1947. The Amateur (now English) Volleyball Association of Great Britain was formed in May 1955.

Most world titles

World Championships were instituted in 1949 for men and 1952 for women. The USSR has won six men's titles (1949, 1952, 1960, 1962, 1978, 1982) and four women's (1952, 1956, 1960 and 1970).

Most Olympic titles

The sport was introduced to the Olympic Games for both men and women in 1964. The USSR have won a record three men's (1964, 1968 and 1980) and three women's (1968, 1972 and 1980) titles. The only player to win four medals is Inna Ryskal (USSR) (b. 15 June 1944), who won silver medals in 1964 and 1976 and golds in 1968 and 1972. The record for men is held by Yuriy Poyarkov (USSR) (b. 10 Feb 1937) who won gold medals in 1964 and 1968 and a bronze in 1972.

Most internationals *Great Britain*

Nicholas Richard Keeley (b. 20 Dec 1947) made a record 124 international appearances for England from 1969 to April 1982. The women's record is 113 by Ann Jarvis (b. 3 June 1955) for England, 1974–83.

WALKING

Most Olympic medals

Walking races have been included in the Olympic events since 1906 but walking matches have been known since 1589. The only walker to win three gold medals has been Ugo Frigerio (Italy) (1901–68) with the 3000 m and 10,000 m in 1920 and 1924. He also holds the record of most medals with four (he won the bronze medal at 50,000 m in 1932) a total shared with Vladimir Golubnichiy (USSR) (b. 2 June 1936), who won gold medals for the 20,000 m in 1960 and 1968, the silver in 1972 and the bronze in 1964.

The best British performance has been two gold medals by George Edward Larner (1875–1949) for the 3500 m and the 10 miles in 1908, but Ernest J. Webb (1872–1937) won three medals being twice 'walker up' to Larner and finishing second in the 10,000 m in 1912.

Most titles

Four time Olympian, Ronald Owen Laird (b. 31 May 1938) of

TRACK WALKING—WORLD RECORDS

The International Amateur Athletic Federation recognises men's records at 20 km, 30 km, 50 km and 2 hours, and women's at 5 km and 10 km. This table also includes world bests for other standard distances.

Event	Time hr min sec	Name, country and date of birth	Place	Date
MEN				
3 km	10 54.6	Carlo Mattioli (Italy) (23 Oct 1954)	Milan, Italy (indoors)	6 Feb 1980
10 km	38 31.4	Werner Heyer (GDR) (14 Nov 1956)	East Berlin (indoors)	12 Jan 1980
20 km	1 18 39.9	Ernesto Canto (Mexico) (18 Oct 1959)	Fana, Norway	5 May 1984
30 km	*2 00 54.0	Ralf Kowalsky (GDR) (22 Mar 1962)	East Berlin, GDR	28 Mar 1982
	2 07 59.8	Jose Marin (Spain) (21 Jan 1950)	Barcelona, Spain	8 Apr 1979
50 km	3 41 38.4	Raul Gonzalez (Mexico) (29 Feb 1952)	Fana, Norway	25 May 1979
1 hour	15 156 metres	Ernesto Canto (Mexico)	Fana, Norway	5 May 1984
2 hours	*28 358 metres	Ralf Kowalsky (GDR)	East Berlin, GDR	28 Mar 1982
	28 165 metres	Jose Marin (Spain)	Barcelona, Spain	8 Apr 1979
WOMEN				
3 km	12 46.8	Olga Yarutkina (USSR) (indoors)	Moscow, USSR	4 Mar 1984
5 km	21 32.2	Olga Krishtop (USSR)	Penza, USSR	4 Aug 1984
10 km	44 56.1	Olga Krishtop (USSR)	Penza, USSR	4 Aug 1984

*Unratified

TRACK WALKING—BRITISH RECORDS

Event	Time hr min sec	Name and date of birth	Place	Date
MEN				
3 km	11 42.94	Philip John Vesty (5 Jan 1963)	London (Crystal Palace)	23 June 1984
10 km	40 53.60	Philip John Vesty	Cwmbran, Gwent	28 May 1984
20 km	1 26 22.0	Steven John Barry	Brighton, W. Sussex	28 June 1981
30 km	2 22 54.7	Dennis Jackson (29 June 1945)	Brighton, W. Sussex	28 June 1981
50 km	4 11 22	Robert William Dobson (4 Nov 1942)	Paris, France	10 Aug 1974
1 hour	13 987 metres	Steven John Barry	Brighton, W. Sussex	28 June 1981
2 hours	26 037 metres	Ronald Edward Wallwork (26 May 1941)	Stretford, Lancashire	31 July 1971
WOMEN				
3 km	13 25.2	Carol Joan Tyson (15 Dec 1957)	Östersund, Sweden	6 July 1979
5 km	23 11.2	Carol Joan Tyson	Östersund, Sweden	30 June 1979
10 km	48 11.4	Marion Fawkes (3 Dec 1948)	Gunnisfalt, Sweden	8 July 1979

ROAD WALKING—WORLD BEST PERFORMANCES

It should be noted that severity of road race courses and the accuracy of their measurement may vary, sometimes making comparisons of times unreliable.

Event	Time hr min sec	Name and date of birth	Place	Date
MEN				
20 km	*1 18 49	Daniel Bautista (Mexico) (4 Aug 1952)	Eschborn, W. Germany	29 Sept 1979
	1 19 29.6	Josef Pribilinec (Czechoslovakia) (6 July 1960)	Bergen, Norway	24 Sept 1983
30 km	2 03 06	Daniel Bautista (Mexico)	Cherkassy, USSR	27 Apr 1980
50 km	*3 37 36	Yevgeniy Ivchenko (USSR) (27 Jul 1938)	Moscow, USSR	24 May 1980
	3 40 46	Jose Marin (Spain)	Valencia, Spain	13 Mar 1983
WOMEN				
10 km	45 13.4	Xu Yongju (China)	Bergen, Norway	24 Sep 1983
20 km	1 36 35.7	Susan Cook (Australia)	Melbourne, Australia	19 Dec 1982
50 km	5 09 41	Lillian Millen (GB) (5 Mar 1945)	Sleaford, Lincs, GB	18 Jul 1981

*Possibly under distance

ROAD WALKING—BRITISH BEST PERFORMANCES

Event	Time hr min sec	Name	Place	Date
MEN				
20 km	1 22 51	Steven John Barry	Douglas, Isle of Man	26 Feb 1983
30 km	2 10 16	Steven John Barry	Brisbane, Australia	7 Oct 1982
50 km	4 02 00	Christopher Lloyd Maddocks (28 Mar 1957)	Vilanova, Spain	18 Mar 1984
WOMEN				
10 km	48 47	Irene Lillian Bateman (13 Nov 1947)	York	20 June 1981
20 km	1 40 45	Irene Lillian Bateman	Basildon, Essex	9 Apr 1983

LONGEST WALKS

The first person reported to have 'walked round the world' is George Matthew Schilling (USA) from 3 Aug 1897 to 1904, but the first verified achievement was by David Kunst (b. 1939) (USA) from 10 June 1970 to 5 Oct 1974. Tomas Carlos Pereira (b. Argentine, 16 Nov 1942) spent ten years, 6 Apr 1968–8 Apr 1978, walking 29,825 miles *48,000 km* around all five continents. George Meegan (*pictured top*) (b. 2 Oct 1952) from Rainham, Kent, England walked 19,019 miles *30 431 km* from Ushaia, the southern tip of South America to Prudhoe Bay in Northern Alaska, taking 2426 days from 26 Jan 1977 to 18 Sept 1983, and thus completed the first traverse of the Western Hemisphere. Sean Eugene Maguire (b. USA 15 Sept 1956) walked 7327 miles *11791 km* from the Yukon River, north of Livengood, Alaska, to Key West, Florida, USA, in 307 days, 6 June 1978–9 April 1979. The Trans-Canada (Halifax to Vancouver) record walk of 3764 miles *6057 km* is 96 days by Clyde McRae, 23, from 1 May to 4 Aug 1973. John Lees (b. 23 Feb 1945) of Brighton, East Sussex, England between 11 Apr and 3 June 1972, walked 2876 miles *4628 km* across the USA from City Hall, Los Angeles to City Hall, New York City in 53 days 12 hr 15 min (average 53.75 miles *86,49 km* a day). The longest continuous walk in Britain is one of 6824 miles *10 982 km*, around the British coast by John N. Merrill (b. 19 Aug 1943), from 3 Jan to 8 Nov 1978.

the New York AC, USA, won a total of 65 National titles from 1958 to 1976, plus four Canadian championships. The greatest number of UK National titles won by a British walker is 27 by Vincent Paul Nihill (b. 5 Sept 1939) from 1963 to 1975.

Longest race
The Paris–Colmar, until 1980 Strasbourg–Paris, event (inst. 1926 in the reverse direction), now about 518 km *322 miles* is the world's longest annual race walk. The fastest performance is by Robert Pietquin (Belgium) (b. 1938) who walked 507 km *315 miles* in the 1980 race in 60 hr 1 min 10 sec (deducting 4 hr compulsory stops). This represents an average speed of 8.45 km/h *5.25 mph.* Gilbert Roger (France) (b. 1914) won six times (1949, 1953–4, 1956–8). The first woman to complete the race was Annie van der Meer (Netherlands) (b. 24 Feb 1947), who was 10th in 1983 in 82 hr 10 min.

Dumitru Dan (1890–1978) of Romania was the only man of 200 entrants to succeed in a contest in walking 100,000 km *62,137 miles* organised by the Touring Club de France on 1 Apr 1910. He covered 96,000 km *59,651 miles* up to 24 Mar 1916 so averaging 43,85 km *27.24 miles* a day.

'End to end'
The fastest Land's End to John o'Groats walk is 12 days 21 hr 15 min for 851 miles *1370 km* by Norman Fox (b. 29 May 1947) on 1–13 Sept 1983. The women's record is 13 days 17 hr 42 min by Ann Sayer (b. 16 Oct 1936) on 20 Sept–3 Oct 1980. The Irish 'End to End' record over the 400.2 miles *644 km* from Malin Head, Donegal to Mizen Head, Cork is 5 days 22 hr 30 min, set by John 'Paddy' Dowling (b. 15 June 1929) on 18–24 Mar 1982.

London to Brighton
The record time for the 53 miles *85 km* walk is 7 hr 35 min 12 sec by Donald James Thompson (b. 20 Jan 1933) on 14 Sept 1957. Richard Esmond Green (b. 22 Apr 1924) completed the course a record 45 times from 1950 to 1980.

Longest non-stop walk
WO2 Norman Fox of the 7th Regiment, Royal Horse Artillery walked 646,019 km *401.436 miles* in 5 days 23 hr 29 min at Osnabrück, W. Germany on 1–7 Sept 1982. This was 586 laps of a 1102,412 m closed circuit. He was not permitted any stops for rest and was moving 98.07 per cent of the time.

24 hours

The best official performance for distance walked on a track in 24 hr is 133 miles 21 yd *214,06 km* by Huw Nielson (GB) at Walton-on-Thames, Surrey, on 14–15 Oct 1960. The best by a woman is 202,3 km *125.7 miles* by Annie van den Meer at Rouen, France, on 30 Apr–1 May 1984 over a 1,185 km lap road course.

Walking backwards

The greatest ever exponent of reverse pedestrianism has been Plennie L. Wingo (b. 24 Jan 1895) then of Abilene, Texas, who completed his 8000 mile *12 875 km* trans-continental walk from Santa Monica, California to Istanbul, Turkey, from 15 Apr 1931 to 24 Oct 1932. The longest distance recorded for walking backwards in 24 hr is 133,5 km *82.95 miles* by Donald A. Davis in Honolulu, Hawaii, USA on 22–23 Apr 1983.

WATER POLO

Origins

Water polo was developed in England as 'Water Soccer' in 1869 and first included in the Olympic Games in Paris in 1900.

Most Olympic titles

Hungary has won the Olympic tournament most often with six wins in 1932, 1936, 1952, 1956, 1964 and 1976. Great Britain won in 1900, 1908, 1912 and 1920.

Five players share the record of three gold medals; Britons, George Wilkinson (1879–1946) in 1900, 1908, 1912; Paulo 'Paul' Radmilovic (1886–1968), and Charles Sidney Smith (1879–1951) in 1908, 1912, 1920; and Hungarians Deszo Gyarmati (b. 23 Oct 1927) and György Kárpáti (b. 23 June 1935) in 1952, 1956, 1964. Gyarmati's wife (Eva Szekely) and daughter (Andrea) won gold and silver medals respectively in swimming. Paul Radmilovic also won a gold medal for the 4 × 200 m freestyle relay in 1908.

ASA championships

The greatest number of Amateur Swimming Association titles is 14 between 1956 and 1982, by London Polytechnic, who have also won a record ten National League (formed 1963) titles—1964, 1969–70, 1972–7, 1979.

Deena Brush set the world record for slalom water skiing at four buoys on an 11,25 m line in 1983. (All-Sport)

Most goals

The greatest number of goals scored by an individual in a home international is eleven by Terry Charles Miller (b. 2 Mar 1932) (Plaistow United), when England defeated Wales 13–3 at Newport, Gwent, in 1951.

Most international appearances

The greatest number of international appearances is 412 by Alexei Barkalov (USSR) (b. 18 Feb 1946), 1965–80. The British record is 126 by Martyn Thomas, of Cheltenham, 1964–78.

WATER SKIING

See also The Guinness Guide to Water Skiing by the late David Nations, OBE and Kevin Desmond (price £8.50).

Origins

The origins of water skiing lie in walking on planks and aquaplaning. A 19th century treatise on sorcerers refers to Eliseo of Tarentum who, in the 14th century, 'walks and dances' on the water. The first report of aquaplaning was on America's Pacific coast in the early 1900s. At Scarborough, Yorkshire, on 15 July 1914, a single plank-gliding contest was won by H. Storry.

The present day sport of water skiing was pioneered by Ralph W. Samuelson (1904–77) on Lake Pepin, Minnesota, USA, on two curved pine boards in the summer of 1922, though claims have been made for the birth of the sport on Lake Annecy (Haute Savoie), France at about the same time. The first world organisation, the United Internationale de Ski Nautique, was formed in Geneva on 27 July 1946. The British Water Ski Federation was founded in London in 1954.

Most titles

World Overall championships (inst. 1949) have been won twice by Alfredo Mendoza (USA) in 1953 and 1955, Mike Suyerhoud (USA) in 1967 and 1969, George Athans (Canada) in 1971 and 1973 and Sammy Duvall (USA) in 1981 and 1983, and three times by Willa McGuire (née Worthington) of the USA in 1949–50 and 1955 and Elizabeth 'Liz' Allan-Shetter (USA) in 1965, 1969 and 1975. Liz Allan-Shetter has won a record eight individual championship events and is the only person to win all four titles—slalom, jumping, tricks and overall in one year, at Copenhagen, Denmark in 1969. The USA has won the team championship on 14 successive occasions 1957–83. The most British Overall titles (instituted 1953) ever won by a man is seven by Michael Hazelwood (b. 14 Apr 1958) in 1974, 1976–9, 1981, 1983; the most by a woman is eight by Karen Jane Morse (b. 1956) in 1971–6, 1978, 1981.

Highest speed

The fastest water skiing speed recorded is 230,26 km/h *143.08 mph* by Christopher Michael Massey (Australia) on the Hawkesbury River, Windsor, New South Wales, Australia on 6 Mar 1983. His drag boat driver was Stanley Charles Sainty. Donna Patterson Brice (b. 1953) set a feminine record of 178,81 km/h *111.11 mph* at Long Beach, California on 21 Aug 1977. The fastest recorded speed by a British skier over a measured kilometre is 131,217 km/h *81.535 mph* (average) on Lake Windermere, Cumbria on 18 Oct 1973 by Billy Rixon. The fastest by a British woman is 122,187 km/h *75.92 mph* by Elizabeth Hobbs on Windermere, 14 Oct 1982.

Longest run

The greatest distance travelled is 2099,7 km *1304.6 miles* by Will Coughey on 18–19 Feb 1984 on Lake Tikitapu, New Zealand.

Barefoot

The first person to water ski barefoot is reported to be Dick Pope Jr at Lake Eloise, Florida, on 6 Mar 1947. The barefoot duration record is 2 hr 42 min 39 sec by Billy Nichols (USA) (b. 1964) on Lake Weir, Florida, on 19 Nov 1978. The backward barefoot record is 39 min by Paul McManus (Aust). The British duration record is 67 min 5 sec by John Doherty on 1 Oct 1974. The official barefoot speed record (two runs) is 177,06 km/h *110·02 mph* by Lee Kirk (USA) at Firebird Lake, Phoenix, Ariz, on 11 June 1977. His fastest run was 182,93 km/h *113.67 mph*. The fastest by a woman is 118,56 km/h *73.67 mph* by Karen Toms (Australia) on the Hawkesbury River, Windsor, New South Wales on 31 Mar 1984. Richard

WATER SKIING RECORDS

WORLD RECORDS—MEN

Slalom	4½ buoys on a 10,75 m line	Kris LaPoint (USA)	McCormick Lake, Seffner, Florida, USA	29 Apr 1984
Tricks	9940 points	Cory Pickos (USA) (b. 1964)	Callaway Gardens, Georgia, USA	10 July 1983
Jumping	61,5 m *202 ft*	Glenn Thurlow (Aus)	Moomba, Melbourne, Australia	14 Mar 1983

WORLD RECORDS—WOMEN

Slalom	4 buoys on a 11,25 m line	Deena Brush (USA)	Palm Beach, Florida, USA	2 Oct 1983
Tricks	7850 points	Natalia Ponomaryeva (née Rumyantseva) (USSR)	Montbéliard, France	24 June 1984
Jumping	45,8 m *150 ft 2 in*	Sue Lipplegoes (Australia)	Kirtons Farm, Reading, Berkshire	31 July 1983

BRITISH RECORDS—MEN

Slalom	4 buoys on a 10,75 m line	Andy Mapple (b. 3 Nov 1962)	McCormick Lake, Seffner, Florida, USA	29 Apr 1984
Tricks	7830 points	John Battleday (b. 1 Feb 1957)	Walton Hall	18 Sept 1983
Jumping	60,0 m *196 ft 10 in*	Michael Hazelwood (b. 14 Apr 1958)	Kirtons Farm, Reading, Berkshire	2 Aug 1981

BRITISH RECORDS—WOMEN

Slalom	2½ buoys at 12 m	Karen Jane Morse (b. 14 Aug 1956)	Austria	1980
Tricks	6350 points	Nicola Rasey (b. 6 June 1966)	Tallington, Stamford, Lincolnshire	22 May 1983
Jumping	44,9 m *147 ft*	Kathy Hulme (b. 11 Feb 1959)	Kirtons Farm, Reading, Berkshire	1 Aug 1982

Mainwaring (GB) reached 114,86 km/h *71.37 mph* at Holme Pierrepont, Nottinghamshire on 2 Dec 1978. The fastest official speed backward barefoot is 100 km/h *62 mph* by Robert Wing (Aus) on 3 Apr 1982.

The barefoot jump record is 18,70 m *61 ft 4 in* by Brett Wing (Australia) at Marine World in 1981. The British record is 15,80 m *51 ft 10 in* by Keith Donnelly in Ireland in 1978.

WEIGHTLIFTING

Origins

Competitions for lifting weights of stone were held in the ancient Olympic Games. The first championships entitled 'world' were staged at the Café Monico, Piccadilly, London, on 28 Mar 1891 and then in Vienna, Austria on 19–20 July 1898. Prior to that time, weightlifting consisted of professional exhibitions in which some of the advertised poundages were open to doubt.

The International Weightlifting Federation was established in 1920, and their first official championships were held in Tallinn, Estonia on 29–30 Apr 1922.

Most Olympic Medals

Norbert Schemansky (USA) (b. 30 May 1924) won a record four Olympic medals: Gold, middle-heavyweight 1952; Silver, heavyweight 1948; Bronze, heavyweight 1960 and 1964.

Most titles *World*

The most world title wins, including Olympic Games, is eight by John Davis (USA) (b. 12 Jan 1921) in 1938, 1946–52; by Tommy Kono (USA) (b. 27 June 1930) in 1952–9; and by Vasili Alexeyev (USSR) (b. 7 Jan 1942) 1970–7.

Youngest world record holder and champion

Naim Suleimanov (Bulgaria) (b. 23 Nov 1967) set 56 kg world records for clean and jerk (160 kg) and total (285 kg) at 15 yr 123 days at Allentown, New Jersey, USA on 26 Mar 1983. On 23 Oct 1983 in Moscow, USSR he became the youngest world champion at 15 yr 334 days.

Most successful British lifter

The only British lifter to win an Olympic title has been Launceston Elliot (1874–1930), the open one-handed lift champion in 1896 at Athens. Louis George Martin (b. Jamaica, 11 Nov 1936) won four World and European mid-heavyweight titles in 1959, 1962–3, 1965. He won an Olympic silver medal in 1964 and a bronze in 1960 and three Commonwealth gold medals in 1962, 1966, 1970. His total of British titles was 12.

Greatest lift

The greatest weight ever raised by a human being is 6270 lb *2844 kg* (2.80 tons *2,84 tonnes*) in a back lift (weight raised off trestles) by the 26 st *165 kg* Paul Anderson (USA) (b. 17 Oct 1932), the 1956 Olympic heavyweight champion, at Toccoa, Georgia, USA, on 12 June 1957. The greatest lift by a woman is 3564 lb *1616 kg* with a hip and harness lift by Josephine Blatt

Stefan Topurov (*right*) of Bulgaria became the first weightlifter to clean and jerk three times his bodyweight with this lift of 180 kg at the 1983 World Championships in Moscow. (*Bruce Klemens*)

(*née* Schauer) (1869–1923) at the Bijou Theatre, Hoboken, New Jersey, USA, on 15 Apr 1895.

Greatest overhead lifts

The greatest overhead lifts made from the ground are the clean and jerks achieved by super-heavyweights (see world record table). The greatest overhead lift ever made by a woman is 286 lb *129 kg* in a continental jerk by Katie Sandwina (*née* Brummbach, later Mrs Max Heymann) (1884–1952) of Germany, in *c.* 1911. She stood 5 ft 11 in *1,80 m* tall, weighed 210 lb *95 kg* (15 st) and is reputed to have unofficially lifted 312½ lb *141,747 kg* and to have shouldered a cannon, which allegedly weighed 1200 lb *544 kg*.

Greatest power lifts

Paul Anderson, as a professional, achieved 1200 lb *544 kg* in a squat so aggregating, with a 627 lb *284 kg* bench press and an 820 lb *371 kg* dead lift, a career total of 2647 lb *1200 kg*.

Hermann Görner (1891–1956) (Germany) performed a one-handed dead lift of 734½ lb *333,1 kg* in Dresden on 20 July 1920. Görner also raised 24 men weighing 4123 lb *1870 kg* on a plank on the soles of his feet in London on 12 Oct 1927 and carried on his back a 1444 lb *654 kg* piano for 52½ ft *16 m* at Leipzig on 3 June 1921. Willie Whoriskey achieved a British record one-handed deadlift of 670.9 lb *304,3 kg* at Bloxwich, W. Midlands on 26 Nov 1983. Clive Lloyd (b. 23 Aug 1961) achieved a one-handed straddle lift of 669 lb *303,5 kg* at Grosvenor House, London on 12 Aug 1983. This was a record 3.46 times his body weight of 87,8 kg *193.5 lb*.

The greatest power lift by a woman is a squat of 545½ lb *247,5 kg* by Jan Suffolk Todd (b. 22 May 1952) (USA) (weighing 88,5 kg *195 lb*) at Columbus, Georgia, USA in Jan 1981. Cammie Lynn Lusko (b. 5 Apr 1958) (USA) became the first woman to lift more than her body weight with one arm, with 59,5 kg *131 lbs* at a body weight of 58,3 kg *128.5 lb*, at Milwaukee, Wisconsin, USA on 21 May 1983.

A deadlifting record of 4,702,646.25 lb *2 133 084,85 kg* in 24 hr was set by a team of ten at the Darwen Weightlifting Club, Darwen, Lancs on 14–15 Aug 1981.

A team of nine from the Gymfit Sports Club, Leicester lifted 1 234 200 kg *2,720,942 lb* in 24 hr with bench presses at the Hogarth Club, Chiswick, London on 27–28 May 1984.

Cue Levering

Traffic warden Jim Mills (b. 24 May 1923) levered 24 16 oz *453 g* billiard cues simultaneously by their tips through 90 degrees to the horizontal, at Alfreton Park, Derbyshire, on 13 June 1982. Following this he levered a 22 oz *623 g* cue 1005 times consecutively, by the same method.

Strandpulling

The International Steel Strandpullers' Association was founded by Gavin Pearson (Scotland) in 1940. The greatest ratified poundage to date is a super-heavyweight right arm push of 815 lb *369,5 kg* by Malcolm Bartlett (b. 9 June 1955) of Oldham, Lancashire. He has also won a record 17 British Open titles. The record for the Back Press Anyhow is 645 lb *292,5 kg* by Barry Anderson, of Leeds, in 1975.

PROGRESSIVE WEIGHTLIFTING RECORDS

ARTWORK: EDDIE BOTCHWAY

This chart shows the improvement in the world heavyweight jerk record in each five-year period since 1925. The base figures show the record at the start of each period and the top figures the increase over the five years. Vasili Alexeyev depicted below was responsible for 31 improvements from 221,5 kg in 1970 to 256 kg in 1977. (*All-Sport*)

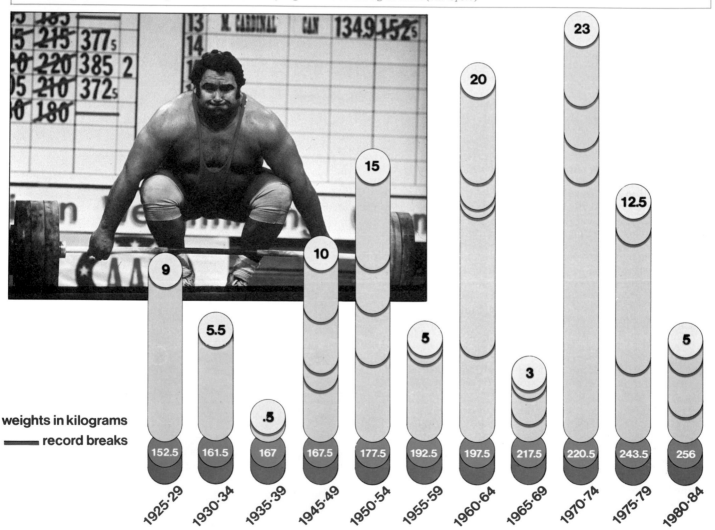

weights in kilograms
━━━ record breaks

Period	Base	Increase
1925-29	152.5	9
1930-34	161.5	5.5
1935-39	167	.5
1945-49	167.5	10
1950-54	177.5	15
1955-59	192.5	5
1960-64	197.5	20
1965-69	217.5	3
1970-74	220.5	23
1975-79	243.5	12.5
1980-84	256	5

WORLD WEIGHTLIFTING RECORDS

Bodyweight class	Lift	Lifted kg	Lifted lb	Name and Country	Place	Date
52 kg *114¾ lb* FLYWEIGHT	Snatch	115,5	254½	Neno Terziyski (Bulgaria)	San Marino	9 May 1983
	Jerk	152,5	336	Neno Terziyski (Bulgaria)	Vittoria, Spain	27 Apr 1984
	Total	262,5	578½	Neno Terziyski (Bulgaria)	Vittoria, Spain	27 Apr 1984
56 kg *123¼ lb* BANTAMWEIGHT	Snatch	131,5	289¾	Naim Suleimanov (Bulgaria)	Varna, Bulgaria	11 May 1984
	Jerk	170	374¾	Naim Suleimanov (Bulgaria)	Varna, Bulgaria	11 May 1984
	Total	300	661¼	Naim Suleimanov (Bulgaria)	Varna, Bulgaria	11 May 1984
60 kg *132¼ lb* FEATHERWEIGHT	Snatch	138,5	305¼	Amir Arizov (USSR)	Minsk, USSR	15 Mar 1984
	Jerk	180	396¾	Stefan Topurov (Bulgaria)	Moscow, USSR	24 Oct 1983
	Total	315	694¼	Stefan Topurov (Bulgaria)	Vittoria, Spain	28 Apr 1984
67.5 kg *148¾ lb* WELTERWEIGHT	Snatch	155,5	342¾	Vladimir Grachev (USSR)	Minsk, USSR	15 Mar 1984
	Jerk	196	432	Joachim Kunz (GDR)	Karl Marx Stadt, GDR	26 June 1981
	Total	345	760½	Joachim Kunz (GDR)	Karl Marx Stadt, GDR	26 June 1981
75 kg *165¼ lb* MIDDLEWEIGHT	Snatch	167,5	369¼	Vladimir Kuznyetsov (USSR)	Moscow, USSR	26 Oct 1983
	Jerk	210	462¾	Aleksandr Varbanov (Bulgaria)	Moscow, USSR	26 Oct 1983
		210,5	464	†Zdravko Stoichev (Bulgaria)	Vienna, Austria	4 Dec 1983
	Total	370	815½	Aleksandr Varbanov (Bulgaria)	Moscow, USSR	26 Oct 1983
				*Vladimir Kuznyetsov (USSR)	Moscow, USSR	26 Oct 1983
				*Zdravko Stoichev (Bulgaria)		1983
82.5 kg *181¾ lb* LIGHT-HEAVYWEIGHT	Snatch	180,5	397¾	Yurik Vardanyan (USSR)	Moscow, USSR	27 Oct 1983
	Jerk	223,5	492½	Aleksandr Pervi (USSR)	Frunze, USSR	5 Mar 1982
	Total	400	881¾	Yurik Vardanyan (USSR)	Moscow, USSR	25 July 1980
		400	881¾	*Asen Zlatev (Bulgaria)	Ljubljana, Yugoslavia	23 Sept 1982
90 kg *198¼ lb* MIDDLE-HEAVYWEIGHT	Snatch	195,5	431	Blagoi Blagoyev (Bulgaria)	Varna, Bulgaria	1 May 1983
	Jerk	232,5	512½	Viktor Solodov (USSR)	Vittoria, Spain	30 Apr 1984
	Total	420	925¼	Blagoi Blagoyev (Bulgaria)	Varna, Bulgaria	1 May 1983
100 kg *220½ lb*	Snatch	200	440¼	Yuri Zakharevich (USSR)	Odessa, USSR	4 Mar 1983
	Jerk	241	531¼	Pavel Kuznyetsov USSR)	Minsk, USSR	17 Mar 1984
	Total	440	970	Yuri Zakharevich (USSR)	Odessa, USSR	4 Mar 1983
110 kg *242½ lb* HEAVYWEIGHT	Snatch	196,5	433	Leonid Taranenko (USSR)	Odessa, USSR	5 Mar 1983
	Jerk	247,5	545½	Vyacheslav Klokov (USSR)	Moscow, USSR	30 Oct 1983
	Total	440	970	Vyacheslav Klokov (USSR)	Moscow, USSR	30 Oct 1983
Over 110 kg *242½ lb* SUPER-HEAVYWEIGHT	Snatch	211	465	Aleksandr Gunyashev (USSR)	Rheims, France	1 June 1984
	Jerk	261	575¼	Sergei Didyk (USSR)	Moscow, USSR	31 July 1983
	Total	465	1025	Aleksandr Gunyashev (USSR)	Rheims, France	1 June 1984

**IWF regulations do not permit tied records to be ratified.*

†Not ratified as meeting was not subject to full doping controls.

BRITISH WEIGHTLIFTING RECORDS (in kg)

Class	Snatch		Date		Jerk		Date		Total		Date	
52 kg	92,5	Precious McKenzie	25 Jan	1974	122,5	Precious McKenzie	25 Jan	1974	215	Precious McKenzie	25 Jan	1974
56 kg	105	Dean Willey	15 June	1981	132,5	Geoff Laws		1982	235	Geoff Laws		1982
60 kg	122,5	Dean Willey	20 Feb	1983	152,5	Dean Willey	26 Mar	1983	272,5	Dean Willey	26 Feb	1983
67,5 kg	137,5	Dean Willey	18 Dec	1983	167,5	Dean Willey	18 Feb	1984	300	Dean Willey	18 Feb	1984
75 kg	150	David Morgan	28 Jan	1984	185,5	David Morgan	24 Sept	1983	330	David Morgan	24 Sept	1983
82,5 kg	155	Newton Burrowes	3 Apr	1982	185	Newton Burrowes	27 Feb	1982	340	Newton Burrowes	3 Apr	1982
90 kg	160	Gary Langford	13 Apr	1980	201	David Mercer	26 May	1984	352,5	David Mercer	5 Aug	1984
100 kg	160,5	Gary Langford	7 Mar	1982	202,5	Peter Pinsent	17 Sept	1983	362,5	Peter Pinsent	17 Sept	1983
110 kg	175	Gary Taylor	29 Apr	1984	200	Brian Strange	28 Feb	1976	360	Gary Taylor	2 Apr	1984
Super	162,5	John Burns	5 Sept	1982	200	Andrew Kerr	9 Nov	1974	350	Brian Strange	4 Mar	1978

WORLD POWERLIFTING RECORDS (as at June 1984) (All weights in kilograms)

Class	Squat		Bench Press		Deadlift		Total	
MEN								
52 kg	242,5	Joe Cunha (USA) 1981	146,5	Joe Cunha 1982	233	Hideaki Inaba (Jap) 1983	567,5	Hideaki Inaba (Jap) 1980
56 kg	237,5	Hideaki Inaba (Jap) 1982	147,5	Hiroyaki Isagawa (Jap) 1981	289,5	Lamar Gant (USA) 1982	625	Lamar Gant 1982
60 kg	295	Joe Bradley (USA) 1980	180	Joe Bradley 1980	296,5	Lamar Gant 1983	707,5	Joe Bradley 1982
67,5 kg	297	Robert Wahl (USA) 1982	194	Kristoffer Hulecki (Swe) 1982	312,5	Raimo Valineva (Fin) 1981	732,5	Joe Bradley 1981
75 kg	327,5	Mike Bridges (USA) 1980	217,5	James Rouse (USA) 1980	325	Raimo Valineva 1982	850	Rick Gaugler (USA) 1982
					325u	Rick Crain (USA) 1983		
82,5 kg	379,5	Mike Bridges 1982	240	Mike Bridges 1981	357,5	Veli Kumpuniemi (Fin) 1980	952,5	Mike Bridges 1982
90 kg	375	Fred Hatfield (USA) 1980	255	Mike MacDonald (USA) 1980	372,5	Walter Thomas (USA) 1982	937,5	Mike Bridges 1980
100 kg	400	Fred Hatfield 1982	261,5	Mike MacDonald 1977	377,5	James Cash (USA) 1982	952,5	James Cash 1982
110 kg	393,5	Dan Wohleber (USA) 1981	270	Jeffrey Magruder (USA) 1982	395	John Kuc (USA) 1980	1000	John Kuc 1980
125 kg	412,5	David Waddington (USA) 1982	278,5	Tom Hardman (USA) 1982	385	Terry McCormick (USA) 1982	1005	Ernie Hackett (USA) 1980
							1030u	John Gamble (USA) 1983
125 + kg	445	Dwayne Fely (USA) 1982	300	Bill Kazmaier (USA) 1981	402	Bill Kazmaier 1981	1100	Bill Kazmaier 1981
WOMEN								
44 kg	133	Anna-Liisa Prinkkala (Fin) 1983	75	Teri Hoyt (USA) 1982	138?	D. Wicker (USA) 1983	317,5	Cheryl Jones 1983
48 kg	143	Diana Rowell (USA) 1983	82,5	Michelle Evris (USA) 1981	174,5	Majik Jones (USA) 1983	382,5	Majik Jones 1983
52 kg	155	Sisi Dolman-Gricar (Hol) 1983	84	Lynda Chicado-Shendow (USA) 1983	165	Vicki Steenrod (USA) 1982	390	Kali Bogias (Can) 1983
56 kg	161,5	Debbie Candelaria (USA) 1983	104,5	Juli Thomas (USA) 1982	183	Tina van Duyn-Woodley (Hol) 1983	440	Juli Thomas 1983
60 kg	200,5	Ruthi Shafer (USA) 1983	97,5	Eileen Todaro (USA) 1981	213	Ruthi Shafer 1983	500	Ruthi Shafer 1983
67,5 kg	189,5	Angie Ross (USA) 1983	105	Jennifer Weyland (USA) 1981	215	Jan Todd (USA) 1983	467,5	Jennifer Weyland 1981
75 kg	212,5	Beverley Francis (Aus) 1981	140	Beverley Francis 1981	212,5	L. Miller (Aus) 1983	550	Beverley Francis 1983
82,5 kg	218	Beverley Francis 1983	150	Beverley Francis 1981	227,5	Vicky Gagne (USA) 1981	577,5	Beverley Francis 1983
90 kg	213	Gael Martin (Aus) 1983	120,5	Gael Martin 1983	210	Rebecca Waibler (GFR) 1982	525	Gael Martin 1982
90 + kg	247,5	Jan Todd 1981	130	Gael Martin 1982	230	Wanda Sander (USA) 1981	567,5	Gael Martin 1982

u—not yet ratified.

BRITISH POWERLIFTING RECORDS

As at 29 May 1984. All weights in kilograms

Class	Squat		Bench Press		Deadlift		Total	
MEN								
52 kg	217,5	P. Stringer 1980	130	P. Stringer 1981	222,5	P. McKenzie 1975	530	P. Stringer 1982
56 kg	235	P. Stringer 1982	137,5	P. Stringer 1983	229	P. McKenzie 1973	567,5	N. Bhairo 1982
60 kg	247,5	A. Galvez 1981	140	P. Stringer 1984	275	E. Pengelly 1977	645	E. Pengelly 1979
67,5 kg	275	E. Pengelly 1981	165	H. Salih 1979	295	E. Pengelly 1982	710	E. Pengelly 1982
75 kg	302,5	J. Howells 1979	185	P. Fiore 1981	310	R. Limerick 1984	760	S. Alexander 1983
82,5 kg	335	M. Duffy 1981	210	M. Duffy 1981	355	R. Collins 1980	855	R. Collins 1980
90 kg	342,5	D. Caldwell 1982	222,5	J. Chandler 1983	350,5	R. Collins 1980	847,5	D. Caldwell 1982
100 kg	380	A. Stevens 1984	222,5	F. Nobile 1982	360	A. Stevens 1984	955	A. Stevens 1984
110 kg	370	A. Stevens 1984	230	P. Jordan 1979	380	A. White 1982	920	A. White 1982
125 kg	380	S. Zetolofsky 1984	227,5	A. Kerr 1982	362,5	D. Carter 1982	957,5	S. Zetolofsky 1984
125 + kg	380	S. Zetolofsky 1979	258	T. Purdoe 1971	377,5	A. Kerr 1982	982,5	A. Kerr 1983
WOMEN								
44 kg	105	J. White 1984	57,5	J. White 1983	130	A. Brown 1982	277,5	J. White 1984
48 kg	120	S. Smith 1983	72,5	S. Smith 1983	130	J. Hunter 1983	302,5	S. Smith 1983
52 kg	137,5	M. Green 1984	72,5	S. Smith 1982	155	J. Hunter 1984	345	J. Hunter 1984
56 kg	140	D. Mears 1983	65,5	M. Green 1983	155	D. Mears 1983	347,5	D. Mears 1983
60 kg	155	R. Bass 1983	77,5	R. Bass 1983	177,5	D. Webb 1984	402,5	R. Bass 1984
67,5 kg	165	D. Webb 1982	67,5	D. Webb 1981	175	D. Webb 1983	390	D. Webb 1982
75 kg	195	P. Morgan 1984	95	J. Oakes 1981	190	J. Oakes 1981	470	J. Oakes 1981
82,5 kg	207,5	J. Oakes 1983	112,5	J. Oakes 1983	205	J. Oakes 1984	510	J. Oakes 1984
90 kg	167,5	J. Jackson 1983	100	J. Kerr 1983	187,5	Y. Hanson-Nortey 1984	430	J. Kerr 1982
90 + kg	162,5	J. Kerr 1981	112,5	J. Kerr 1982	185	J. Kerr 1981	440	J. Kerr 1980

WRESTLING

(*above*) Wade Schalles in the East Coast Olympic Qualifying tournament. He defeated all eight opponents, pinning six. (*Steve Brown*) Sumo wrestler Kitanoumi, the master of Japan's national sport. (*All-Sport*)

Origins

The earliest depictions of wrestling holds and falls on wall plaques and a statue indicate that organised wrestling dates from *c.* 2750–2600 BC. It was the most popular sport in the ancient Olympic Games and victors were recorded from 708 BC. The Greco-Roman style is of French origin and arose about 1860. The International Amateur Wrestling Federation (FILA) was founded in 1912.

Most titles *Olympic*

Three Olympic titles have been won by: Carl Westergren (1895–1958) (Sweden) in 1920, 1924, 1932; Ivar Johansson (1903–79) (Sweden) in 1932 (two), 1936; and Aleksandr Medved (b. 16 Sept 1937) (USSR) in 1964, 1968, 1972. Imre Polyák (Hungary) (b. 16 Apr 1932) won four medals: silver for Greco-Roman featherweight class in 1952, 1956, 1960 and gold in 1964.

Most titles *World*

The freestyler Aleksandr Medved (USSR) (b. 16 Sept 1937) won a record ten world championships with the light-heavyweight titles in 1962–4 (Olympic) and 1966, heavyweight 1967–8 (Olympic), and super-heavyweight in 1969–72 (Olympic). The only wrestler to win the same title in seven successive years has been Valeriy Rezantsev (b. 2 Feb 1947) (USSR) in the Greco-Roman light-heavyweight class in 1970–6, including the Olympic Games of 1972 and 1976.

Most titles and longest span *British*

The most British titles won is ten by heavyweight Kenneth Alan Richmond (b. 10 July 1926) between 1949 and 1960. The longest span for BAWA titles is 24 years by George Mackenzie (1890–1957) between 1909 and 1933. He represented Great Britain in five successive Olympiads, 1908 to 1928.

Most wins

In international competition, Osamu Watanabe (b. 21 Oct 1940), of Japan, the 1964 Olympic freestyle featherweight champion, was unbeaten and unscored-upon in 187 consecutive matches. Wade Schalles (USA) won 821 bouts from 1964 to 1984, with 530 of these victories by pin.

Longest bout

The longest recorded bout was one of 11 hr 40 min when Martin Klein (1885–1947) (Estonia representing Russia) beat Alpo Asikáinen (1888–1942) (Finland) for the Greco-Roman middleweight 'A' event silver medal in the 1912 Olympic Games in Stockholm, Sweden.

Heaviest heavyweight

The heaviest wrestler in Olympic history is Chris Taylor (1950–79), bronze medallist in the super-heavyweight class in 1972, who stood 6 ft 5 in *1,96 m* and weighed over 420 lb *190 kg*. FILA are introducing an upper weight limit of 130 kg *286 lb* for international competition in 1985.

CUMBERLAND AND WESTMORLAND WRESTLING

J. Baddeley (middleweight in 1905–6, 1908–10, 1912) and Ernest Aubrey Bacon (b. 1893) (lightweight in 1919, 1921–3, 1928–9) both won six titles in the British amateur championships (inst. 1904).

PROFESSIONAL WRESTLING

Professional wrestling dates from 1874 in the USA. Georges Karl Julius Hackenschmidt (USSR) (1877–1968), Estonian-born, was undefeated at Greco-Roman contests from 1900 to his retirement in 1911. (*See also p. 104*).

SUMO WRESTLING

The sport's origins in Japan certainly date from *c.* 23 BC. The heaviest ever *sumotori* is Samoan-American Salevaa Fuali of Hawaii, *alias* Konishiki, who in 1984, at a height of 1,07 m *6 ft 1½ in*, attained 210,5 kg *464 lb*. Weight is amassed by over alimentation with a high protein stew called *chankonabe*. The most successful wrestlers have been Sadaji Akiyoshi (b. 1912) *alias* Futabayama, winner of 69 consecutive bouts in the 1930s, Koki Naya (b. 1940) *alias* Taiho ('Great Bird'), who won the Emperor's Cup 32 times up to his retirement in 1971 and the *ozeki* Torokichi *alias* Raiden who in 21 years (1789–1810) won 254 bouts and lost only ten for the highest ever winning percentage of 96.2. The youngest of the 59 men to attain the rank of *Yokozuna* (Grand Champion) was Toshimitsu Ogata (b. 16 May 1953) *alias* Kitanoumi, in July 1974 aged 21 years and two months. He set a record in 1978 winning 82 of the 90 bouts that top *rikishi* fight annually and has now won more individual contests than any other *rikishi*. Hawaiian born Jesse Kuhaulua (b. 16 June 1944), now a Japanese citizen named Daigoro Watanabe, *alias* Takamiyama was the first non-Japanese to win an official tournament in July 1972 and in 1981 set a record of 1231 consecutive top division bouts. He weighs at least 450 lb *204 kg*.

YACHTING

See also The Guinness Book of Yachting Facts and Feats (£4.95) *and* The Guinness Guide to Sailing (£11.95), *both by Peter Johnson, published by Guinness Superlatives Ltd.*

Origins

Yachting in England dates from the £100 stake race between Charles II and his brother James, Duke of York, on the Thames on 1 Sept 1661 over 23 miles from Greenwich to Gravesend. The oldest club in the world is the Royal Cork Yacht Club (formerly the Cork Harbour Water Club), established in Ireland in 1720. The oldest active club in Britain is the Starcross Yacht Club at Powderham Point, Devon. Its first regatta was held in 1772.

Olympic titles *World*

The first sportsman ever to win individual gold medals in four successive Olympic Games was Paul B. Elvström (b. 24 Feb 1928) (Denmark) in the Firefly class in 1948 and the Finn class in 1952, 1956 and 1960. He also won eight other world titles in a total of six classes. The lowest number of penalty points by the winner of any class in an Olympic regatta is three points (five wins, one disqualified and one second in seven starts) by *Superdocious* of the Flying Dutchman class (Lt. Rodney Stuart Pattisson RN (b. 5 Aug 1943) and Iain Somerled Macdonald-Smith (b. 3 July 1945)) at Acapulco Bay, Mexico in October 1968.

Olympic titles British

The only British yacht to win two titles was *Scotia* in the Open class and Half-One Ton class at the 1900 Regatta with Lorne Campbell Currie (1871–1926), and John H. Gretton (1867–1947). The only British yachtsman to win in two Olympic regattas is Rodney Pattisson in 1968 (*see above*) and again with *Superdoso* crewed by Christopher Davies (b. 29 June 1946) at Kiel, W. Germany in 1972. He gained a silver medal in 1976 with Julian Brooke Houghton (b. 16 Dec 1946).

Admiral's Cup

The ocean racing series with the most participating nations (three boats allowed to each nation) is the Admiral's Cup held by the Royal Ocean Racing Club. A record 19 nations competed in 1975, 1977 and 1979. Britain has a record eight wins.

America's Cup (*see p. 338*)

Longest race

The longest regular sailing race is the quadrennial Whitbread Round the World race (inst. Aug 1973) organized by the Royal Naval Sailing Association. The distance is 26,180 nautical miles from Portsmouth, and return with stops and re-starts at Cape Town, Auckland and Mar del Plata. The record (sailing) time is 120 days 6 hr 35 min by *Flyer* crewed by Cornelis van Rietschoten (Netherlands), finishing on 29 Mar 1982 (*see also p. 180–1*).

24 Hour Dinghy Race

The greatest distance covered in the West Lancashire Y.C. 24 hr race is 158.8 statute miles by an Enterprise from the Tynemouth Sailing Club on 13–14 Sept 1980. The Betio Boating Community sailed an Osprey, *Tamaroa*, 171.5 statute miles at Tarawa, Gilbert Islands, on 24–25 Sept 1977.

Highest speeds

The official world sailing speed record is 36.04 knots (*41.50 mph 66,78 km/h*) by the 73½ ft *22,40 m* proa *Crossbow II* over a 500 m *547 yd* course in Portland Harbour, Dorset, on 17 Nov 1980. The vessel (sail area 1400 ft² *130,06 m²*) was designed by Rod McAlpine-Downie and owned and steered by Timothy Colman. In an unsuccessful attempt on the record in October 1978, *Crossbow II* is reported to have momentarily attained a speed of 45 knots (51 mph *83 km/h*).

The fastest 24 hr single-handed run by a sailing yacht was recorded by Nick Keig (b. 13 June 1936), of the Isle of Man, who covered 340 nautical miles in a 37½ ft *11,43 m* trimaran *Three Logs of Mann I* during the Falmouth to Punta, Azores race on 9–10 June 1975, averaging 14.16 knots (16.30 mph *26,23 km/h*). The fastest bursts of speed reached were about 25 knots (28.78 mph *46,32 km/h*).

Marinas, *Largest*

The largest marina in the world is that of Marina Del Rey, Los Angeles, California, USA, which has 7500 berths. The largest in Britain is the Brighton Marina, East Sussex, with 2313 berths.

Most competitors

The most boats ever to start in a single race was 1947, of which 1767 finished in the Round Zealand (Denmark) race on 17–20 June 1983, over a course of 375 km *233 miles*. The greatest number to start in a race in Britain was 1187 keeled yachts and multihulls on 23 June 1984 from Cowes in the Annual Round-the-Island race. The fastest time achieved in this annual event is 4 hr 47 min 8 sec by the trimaran *Exmouth Challenger*, owned and sailed by Mark Gatehouse, on 19 June 1982.

Highest

The greatest altitude at which sailing has taken place is 16,109 ft *4910 m* on Laguna Huallatani, Bolivia, in Mirror Dinghy 55448, variously by Peter Williams, Gordon Siddeley, Keith Robinson and Brian Barrett, on 19 Nov 1977. The highest for boardsailing is 4970 m *16,300 ft* by Juan Felipe Marti, Juan Ojeda, Fermin Tarres and Philippe Levrel on Tilicho's Lake, Nepal on 20 Oct 1983.

BOARDSAILING

Origins

The High Court ruled on 7 Apr 1982 that Peter Chilvers (when aged 12) had devised a prototype of a boardsailer in 1958 in England. In 1968 Henry Hoyle Schweitzer and Jim Drake pioneered the sport, often termed windsurfing, in California, USA. World championships were first held in 1973 and the sport was added to the Olympic Games in 1984.

English Channel

The record time for boardsailing across the English Channel is 1 hr 4 min 33 sec by Baron Arnaud de Rosnay (France) on 4 July 1982 from Cap Gris Nez to Dover at an average speed of 16.9 knots (19.5 mph *31,3 km/h*). After 45 mins rest he returned to Wissant, France in 1 hr 4 min 37 sec.

Highest Speed

The record speed for boardsailing is 30.82 knots *57,08 km/h* by Fred Haywood (USA) at Weymouth, England on 15 Oct 1983 in a Force 7–8 wind. The British record is 28.97 knots *53,69 km/h* by Peter Bridgeman at Weymouth on 16 Oct 1983. The women's record is 24.20 knots *40,77 km/h* by Marie-Annick Mauss (France) at Sete in April 1984.

Endurance

Stéphane Peyron of France set an endurance record of 70 hr 3 min on 16–19 July 1984.

AMERICA'S CUP

The America's Cup was originally won as an outright prize by the schooner *America* on 22 Aug 1851 at Cowes and was later offered by the New York Yacht Club as a challenge trophy. On 8 Aug 1870 J. Ashbury's *Cambria* (GB) failed to capture the trophy from the *Magic*, owned by F. Osgood (USA). Since then the Cup has been challenged by Great Britain in 16 contests, in 2 contests by Canada, and by Australia 7 times, but the United States were undefeated winning 77 races and only losing eight until 1983 when **Australia II (*pictured*),** skippered by John Bertrand and owned by a Perth syndicate headed by Alan Bond beat *Liberty* 4–3, the narrowest series victory, at Newport, RI, USA. The closest race ever was the fourth race of the 1962 series, when the 12 metre sloop *Weatherly* beat her Australian challenger *Gretel* by about three and a half lengths, a margin of only 26 sec, on 22 Sept 1962. The fastest time ever recorded by a 12 metre boat for the triangular course of 24.3 sea miles is 2 hr 46 min 58 sec by *Gretel* in 1962.

The Games of the XXIII Olympiad were held in Los Angeles from 28 July to 12 August 1984. A record 140 countries and about 7400 athletes participated. Total spectator attendance was given as a record 5,767,923 including 1,421,627 for soccer and 1,129,465 for track and field events. The highest attendance for one event was 101,799 at the Rose Bowl, Pasadena for the soccer final in which France beat Brazil 2–0.

MEDALS

Leading nations were:

	Gold	Silver	Bronze	Total
USA	83	61	30	174
West Germany	17	19	23	59
Romania	20	16	17	53
Canada	10	18	16	44
Great Britain	5	11	21	37

Basketball: USA won a record ninth men's title and a first women's (USSR won in 1976 and 1980).

Boxing: US boxers won nine of the 12 gold medals.

Canoeing: Ian Ferguson (New Zealand) (b. 20 July 1952) won three gold medals to equal the record at one Games.

Gymnastics: A record 46 'perfect' marks of 10.00 were awarded. Ecaterina Szabo (Romania) won a total of four gold medals and a silver—the most in 1984 at any sport.

Handball: Yugoslavia won both men's and women's events, which with their men's win in 1972 ties the record number of Olympic wins.

Judo: Yashiro Yamashito (Japan) (b. 1 June 1957) added to his 7-year unbeaten record by winning the Open category.

Modern Pentathlon: Richard Phelps achieved a British best in swimming of 1304 points for his time of 3 min 16.224 sec.

Rowing: Pertti Karppinen (Finland) (b. 17 Feb 1953) won the single sculls, as in 1976 and 1980, to equal the record of three gold medals.

Diving (p. 317): Greg Louganis (USA) won two gold medals and set record totals of 754.41 for springboard and 710.91 for highboard.

Track and Field: Sebastian Coe set a British record of four Olympic medals in individual events. He won gold at 1500 m and silver at 800 m in both 1980 and 1984. Kathy Cook equalled the British women's record with three bronze medals—4 × 100 m 1980; 400 m and 4 × 100 m 1984.

British records set in Los Angeles

Swimming (in addition to those included on p. 317)

MEN

100 m freestyle	51.48	David Lowe.
1500 m freestyle	15:30.10	David Stacey.
4 × 100 m freestyle	3:23.61	UK (David Lowe, Roland Lee, Paul Easter, Richard Burrell).
200 m ind. med.	2:04.38	Neil Cochran.
4 × 100 m medley	3:47.39	UK (Neil Harper, Adrian Moorhouse, Andrew Jameson, Richard Burrell).

WOMEN

800 m freestyle	8:32.60	Sarah Hardcastle.
100 m butterfly	1:01.48	Nicola Fibbens.

Track and Field

MEN

4 × 400 m	2:59.13	UK (Kriss Akabusi, Garry Cook, Todd Bennett, Phil Brown).
Decathlon	8797	Daley Thompson (10.44, 8.01, 15.72, 2.03, 46.97; 14.34, 46.56, 5.00, 65.24, 4:35.00).

WOMEN

400 m	49.42	Kathy Cook
4 × 400 m	3:25.51	UK (Michelle Scott, Helen Barnett, Gladys Taylor, Joslyn Hoyte-Smith).
Marathon	2hr 28:24	Priscilla Welch.

Weightlifting

67.5 kg Dean Willey 140 Sn, 170 J, 310 total.

Olympic Champions 1984 for sports with measurable records

ARCHERY

Men

	points	
Darrell Pace (USA)	2616	OR

Women

Seo Hyang-Soon (S Kor)	2568	OR

ATHLETICS

Men

		min sec	
100 m	Carl Lewis (USA)	9.99	
200 m	Carl Lewis (USA)	19.80	OR
400 m	Alonzo Babers (USA)	44.27	

		min sec	
800 m	Joachim Cruz (Bra)	1 43.00	OR
1500 m	Sebastian Coe (GB)	3 32.53	OR
5000 m	Said Aouita (Mor)	13 05.59	OR
10000 m	Alberto Cova (Ita)	27 47.54	
Marathon	Carlos Lopes (Por)	2 hr 9.21	OR
110 m hurdles	Roger Kingdom (USA)	13.20	OR
400 m hurdles	Edwin Moses (USA)	47.75	
3000 m steeplechase	Julius Korir (Ken)	8 11.80	
4 × 100 m relay	USA	37.83	WR
4 × 400 m relay	USA	2 57.91	
20 km road walk	Ernesto Canto (Mex)	1 hr 23.13	OR
50 km road walk	Raul Gonzalez (Mex)	3 hr 47.26	OR

		metres	
High Jump	Dietmar Mögenburg (FRG)	2.35	
Pole Vault	Pierre Quinon (Fra)	5.75	
Long Jump	Carl Lewis (USA)	8.54	
Triple Jump	Al Joyner (USA)	17.26	
Shot	Alessandro Andrei (Ita)	21.26	
Discus	Rolf Danneberg (FRG)	66.60	
Hammer	Juha Tiainen (Fin)	78.08	
Javelin	Arto Härkönen (Fin)	86.76	
Decathlon	Daley Thompson (GB)	8797 points	OR, BR

Women

			min sec	
100 m	....	Evelyn Ashford (USA)	10.97	OR
200 m	....	Valerie Brisco-Hooks (USA)	21.81	OR
400 m	....	Valerie Brisco-Hooks (USA)	48.83	OR
800 m	....	Doina Melinte (Rom)	1 57.60	OR
1500 m	....	Gabriella Dorio (Ita)	4 03.25	
3000 m	....	Maricica Puica (Rom)	8 35.96	*
Marathon	....	Joan Benoit (USA)	2 hr 24.52	*
100 m hurdles	....	Benita Fitzgerald-Brown (USA)	12.84	
400 m hurdles	....	Nawal El Moutawakel (Mor)	54.61	*
4 × 100 m relay	....	USA	41.65	
4 × 400 m relay	....	USA	3 18.29	OR

			metres	
High Jump	....	Ulrike Meyfarth (FRG)	2.02	OR
Long Jump	....	Anisoara Stanciu (Rom)	6.96	
Shot	....	Claudia Losch (FRG)	20.48	
Discus	....	Ria Stalman (Neth)	65.36	
Javelin	....	Tessa Sanderson (GB)	69.56	OR
Heptathlon	....	Glynis Nunn (Aus)	6390 points	*

ROWING

Men

		Times over 2000 m course	min sec
Single Sculls	....	Pertti Karppinen (Fin)	7 00.24
Double Sculls	....	USA	6 36.87
Coxed Pairs	....	Italy	7 05.99
Coxless Pairs	....	Romania	6 45.39
Coxed Fours	....	Great Britain	6 18.64
Coxless Fours	....	New Zealand	6 03.48
Quadruple Sculls	....	West Germany	5 57.55
Eights	....	Canada	5 41.32

Women

		Times over 1000 m course	min sec	
Single Sculls	....	Valeria Racila (Rom)	3 40.68	OR
Double Sculls	....	Romania	3 26.75	
Coxless Pairs	....	Romania	3 32.60	
Coxed Fours	....	Romania	3 19.30	
Quadruple Sculls	....	Romania	3 14.11	
Eights	....	USA	2 59.80	OR

SHOOTING

Men

			score	
Free Pistol (50 m)	....	Xu Haifeng (Chn)	566	
Small-bore rifle (Prone)	....	Ed Etzel (USA)	599 =	OR
Small-bore (3 positions)	....	Malcolm Cooper (GB)	1173 =	WR
Rapid-fire Pistol	....	Takeo Kamachi (Jap)	595	
Running Game Target	....	Li Yuwei (Chn)	587	
Air Rifle	....	Philippe Heberle (Fra)	589	

Women

Standard Rifle	....	Wu Xiaoxuan (Chn)	581	*
Air Rifle	....	Pat Spurgin (USA)	393	*
Pistol Match	....	Linda Thom (Can)	585	*

Men or women

			score
Skeet	....	Matthew Dryke (USA)	198
Trap	....	Luciano Giovanetti (Ita)	192

SWIMMING

Men

			min sec	
100 m freestyle	....	Rowdy Gaines (USA)	49.80	OR
200 m freestyle	....	Michael Gross (FRG)	1 47.44	WR
400 m freestyle	....	George DiCarlo (USA)	3 51.23	OR
1500 m freestyle	....	Michael O'Brien (USA)	15 05.20	
100 m backstroke	....	Richard Carey (USA)	55.79	
200 m backstroke	....	Richard Carey (USA)	2 00.23	
100 m breaststroke	....	Steve Lundquist (USA)	1 01.65	WR
200 m breaststroke	....	Victor Davis (Can)	2 13.34	WR
100 m butterfly	....	Michael Gross (FRG)	53.08	WR
200 m butterfly	....	John Sieben (Aus)	1 57.04	WR
200 m ind. medley	....	Alex Baumann (Can)	2 01.42	WR
400 m ind. medley	....	Alex Baumann (Can)	4 17.41	WR
4 × 100 m freestyle	....	USA	3 19.03	WR
4 × 200 m freestyle	....	USA	7 15.69	WR
4 × 100 m medley	....	USA	3 39.30	WR

Women

			min sec	
100 m freestyle	....	Carrie Steinseifer & Nancy Hogshead (USA)	55.92	
200 m freestyle	....	Mary Wayte (USA)	1 59.23	
400 m freestyle	....	Tiffany Cohen (USA)	4 07.10	OR
800 m freestyle	....	Tiffany Cohen (USA)	8 24.95	OR
100 m backstroke	....	Theresa Andrews (USA)	1 02.55	
200 m backstroke	....	Jolanda De Rove (Neth)	2 12.38	
100 m breaststroke	....	Petra Van Staveren (Neth)	1 09.88	OR
200 m breaststroke	....	Anne Ottenbrite (Can)	2 30.38	
100 m butterfly	....	Mary Meagher (USA)	59.26	OR
200 m butterfly	....	Mary Meagher (USA)	2 06.90	OR
200 m ind. medley	....	Tracy Caulkins (USA)	2 12.64	OR
400 m ind. medley	....	Tracy Caulkins (USA)	4 39.24	
4 × 100 m freestyle	....	USA	3 43.43	
4 × 100 medley	....	USA	4 08.34	
Synchronised duet	....	Candy Costie & Tracie Ruiz (USA)	195.584 points	*
Synchronised solo	....	Tracie Ruiz (USA)	198.467 points	*

WEIGHTLIFTING

			Total in kg	
52 kg (Flyweight)	....	Zeng Guoqiang (Chn)	235.0	
56 kg (Bantamweight)	....	Wu Shude (Chn)	267.5	
60 kg (Featherweight)	....	Chen Weiqiang (Chn)	282.5	
67.5 kg (Lightweight)	....	Yao Jingyuan (Chn)	320.0	
75 kg (Middleweight)	....	Karl-Heinz Radschinsky (FRG)	340.0	
82.5 kg (Light heavyweight)	....	Petre Becheru (Rom)	355.0	
90 kg (Middle heavyweight)	....	Nicu Vlad (Rom)	392.5	OR
100 kg (First heavyweight)	....	Rolf Milser (FRG)	385.0	
110 kg (Second heavyweight)	....	Norberto Oberburger (Ita)	390.0	
110 kg + (Super heavyweight)	....	Dinko Lukin (Aus)	412.5	

m = metres   OR = Olympic Record   *not previously
WR = World Record   BR = British Record   held

(*above*) The largest flag ever flown in Australia—the 30 × 60 ft *9,14 × 18,59 m* Commonwealth flag—see p. 354.

THE HUMAN BEING

DIMENSIONS

Tallest humans

The only collated all-time list of *medically* measured giants between 7 ft 6 in *229 cm* and 8 ft 11 in *272 cm* does not include any Australians. On 26 June 1957 the death was reported in Melbourne, Vic, of Denis O'Duffy, who stood 7 ft 5¼ in *227 cm* in his prime. He was born in Cork, Ireland in 1905. Albert Fox of Port Campbell, Vic, stands 7 ft 3 in *221 cm*. He can hold a dozen hen's eggs in one hand. The University of Alabama basketball player Sue Geh (b. in Australia, 1960) was said in US press reports to be 8 ft 2 in *248,9 cm*. She was in fact 6 ft 9 in *205,7 cm*.

Heaviest human

The only collated all-time list of more than 60 examples of extreme obesity in excess of 40 st (560 lb *254 kg*) includes only two Australians, the heavier of whom was Barney Worth (b. Cooktown, Qld, March 1916), who stood 5 ft 10 in *177 cm* and weighed 42 st (588 lb *266 kg*) at his heaviest with an 80 in *203 cm* waist and a 72 in *183 cm* chest. He died in Bristol, England on 5 July 1955. His wife Joy (b. Cookstown, Qld, November 1914, d. Bristol, England, January 1955) weighed 37 st 8 lb *238,5 kg* at her peak.

ORIGINS

Earliest man

Hunter-gatherers are believed to have crossed open water, known to be at least 70 km *45 miles* wide, by 40,000 BC possibly in double canoes. Tasmania became enisled *c.* 10,000 BC but appears to have been populated at least 8000 years earlier.

Aboriginal population

The peak population of Aboriginals and Torres Strait Islanders is estimated at between 250,000 and 300,000 at the time of the earliest white occupation. In the 1981 Census, the number of people who identified themselves as Aboriginals or Torres Strait Islanders was 159,897. This compares with 72,000 in *c.* 1922.

Largest reserve

The largest of the 353 Aboriginal reserves is one of 44,800 miles² *116 030 km²* in the south-west of the Northern Territory. This reserve adjoins reserves in South Australia and Western Australia, which together cover 127,440 miles² *330 070 km²* under the Land Rights NT Act.

Tasmania

The distinctive Tasmanian Aboriginals became depleted in the first 30 years of settlement, as a result of disease and violent clashes with settlers, and the last full-blood was a woman who died on Kangaroo Island, SA, in 1888. The last Aboriginal on Tasmania itself was another woman named Truganini, who died on 8 May 1876 and was buried at Cascades, Hobart. Her skeleton was cremated in Hobart on 30 Apr 1976. The last male, William Lanney, had died in 1869.

LONGEVITY

The longest-lived Australian of whom there is satisfactory evidence was Mrs Jane Piercy of Bexley, NSW, (b. 2 Sept 1869) who died on 3 May 1981 aged 111 years 235 days. The longest male life in Australia is the 109 yrs 139 days of James Hull of Molong, NSW (b. London, England, 23 Apr 1852) who died on 9 Sept 1961. His parents emigrated when he was four. He attributed his long life partly to the fact he never learnt to dance. He fell out of a car and broke his leg when aged 100.

REPRODUCTIVITY

Nonuplets *First*

The world's only certain nonuplets were born to Mrs Geraldine Mary Broderick at the Royal Hospital for Women, Sydney, NSW, on 13 June 1971. None of the five boys (two stillborn) and four girls lived over 6 days when the last survivor, 12 oz *340 g* Richard succumbed.

Quintuplets *First*

The first Australian quintuplets were born at the Royal Women's Hospital, Brisbane, on 31 Dec 1967 to Mrs Roger Hardinge Braham of Tenterfield, NSW, and named Annabel (3 lb 15½ oz *1,799 kg*), Richard (3 lb 10½ oz *1,658 kg*), Faith (3 lb 10½ oz *1,658 kg*), Caroline (3 lb 5½ oz *1,515 kg*) and Geoffrey (3 lb 10½ oz *1,658 kg*) (d. 4 Jan 1968).

Triplets *Heaviest*

The heaviest triplets recorded in Australia were a boy and two girls born on 20 Nov 1965 to Mrs Valerie Burke of Horsham, Vic. Their individual weights were Campbell 8 lb 8½ oz *3,85 kg*, Jillian 8 lb 1 oz *3,65 kg* and Bronwyn 7 lb 2¼ oz *3,23 kg*, making a combined total of 23 lb 11¾ oz *10,76 kg*.

Most proximate births

Mrs Robert Stanley of Oakville, NSW, gave birth to a son Jason Robert on 19 Mar 1973 and a second son Troy Alexander on 28 Nov 1973, 254 days later.

Earliest Test Tube Baby

The world's first test tube twins, Stephen and Amanda, were delivered by Caesarian section of Mrs Radmila Mays, 31, at the Queen Victoria Medical Centre, Melbourne on 5 June 1981. Amanda weighed in at 5 lb 6 oz *2,43 kg*. The world's first test tube triplets (two girls and one boy) were also Australians, delivered at the Flinders Medical Centre, Adelaide on 8 June 1983. No names were released at the request of the parents.

Heaviest Baby

The heaviest weight recorded for a new-born baby in Australia is 16 lb 5 oz *7,4 kg* for Stephen John Lyttle at Kempsey Hospital on 26 Jan 1963.

Worst diseases

The most troublesome epidemic disease in Australia is deemed to be infective hepatitis. Plague, which reached Sydney from China at the end of the last century, was reported in 1200 cases in the decade 1900 to 1909. It was 37 per cent fatal.

Submergence

The longest recorded duration under water with survival is 'more than half an hour' by Reginald Ernest Daniels, 8, in Cudgen Creek, NSW on 26 Dec 1930. Dr M. J. Eatin injected arsenic into the inert body.

THE LIVING WORLD (*See also p. 31*)

MAMMALS

Largest World

The largest Blue whale killed in Australian waters was a 29,56 m *97 ft* long female harpooned by hand by Archer Davidson in Twofold Bay, NSW in 1910. It's jaw bone was 7,11 m *23 ft 4 in* long.

Largest and Heaviest land

The largest indigenous Australian land mammal, and the largest living marsupial, is the Red kangaroo (*Macropus rufus*). Adult males or 'boomers' stand 6–7 ft *83–213 cm* tall when fully erect (length along the curve of the body 7½–9 ft *229–274 cm*) and weigh 140–175 lb *63–79 kg*. The Eastern grey kangaroo (*Macropus giganteus*) is slightly smaller, but some Tasmanian 'foresters' rival the largest Reds for size.

The fastest speed recorded for a kangaroo is 40 mph *64,3 km/h* for a young female grey ('blue flyer') over a short distance. The longest measured bound is one of 42 ft *12,8 m* by a female Red kangaroo in January 1951. The high jump record is one by a kangaroo which, chased by dogs, cleared a pile of wood 10 ft *3,05 m* high and 27 ft *8,23 m* long.

Venomous

The only venomous mammals found in Australia are the semi-aquatic Platypus (*Ornithorhynchus anatinus*) with two venom glands and sharp spurs on the inside of its hind legs, and the Short-nosed echidna (*Tachyglossus aculeatus*) which has venomous spines covering most of its body. Both are found in eastern Australia and Tasmania.

Lowest blood temperature

For details of Australia's and the world's 'coldest' blooded mammal, see p. 23.

Heaviest ambergris

Details of the heaviest piece of ambergris recovered from an Australian Sperm whale are on p. 23.

PINNIPEDS

Largest and Smallest

Apart from an occasional Southern elephant seal (see p. 27) the largest pinniped regularly found in Australian waters is the Australian sea lion (*Neophoca cinerea*), which is found along the southern shores. Adult males measure up to 3,5 m *11 ft 6 in* in length and weigh up to 900 lb *408 kg*. The smallest is the Australian Fur Seal (*Arctocephalus pusillus doriferus*) which measures 2,01–2,27 m *6 ft 7 in–7 ft 5 in* in length and weighs 218–360 kg *480–794 lb*.

BATS

Largest and Smallest

The largest bat found in Australia is the Grey-headed flying fox (*Pteropus poliocephalus*) of Queensland and New South Wales, which has a wing expanse of up to 122 cm *4 ft* and weighs about 700 g *24.7 oz*. Australia's smallest bat is the Little bat (*Eptesicus pumilus*), found on both the mainland and Tasmania, which has a wing span of 203–228 mm *8–9 in* and weighs about 10 g *0.35 oz*.

MARSUPIALS

Longest lived

The greatest reliable age for a marsupial is 26 years 22 days recorded for a Common wombat (*Vombatus ursinus*) which died in London Zoo, England on 20 Apr 1906.

Smallest

For details on Australia's smallest mammal and the world's smallest marsupial, see p. 30.

Rarest

Australia's rarest marsupial is probably the Thylacine (*Thylacinus cynocephalus*), also known as the 'Tasmanian Wolf', the largest of the carnivorous marsupials (see p. 25). The Long-footed potoroo (*Potorous longipes*) of eastern Gippsland is known only from 9 wild specimens all collected since 1967.

DOMESTICATED ANIMALS

Horse *Oldest*

The greatest reliable age recorded for a horse in Australia is 52 for a 17 hand (5 ft 8 in *1,73 m*) light draught-horse named 'Monty', owned by Mrs Marjorie Cooper of Albury, NSW; the horse died on 25 Jan 1970. He was foaled in Wodonga, Vic, in 1917. The jaws of this horse are now preserved in the School of Veterinary Science at Melbourne University. For details of the oldest thoroughbred horse see p. 30.

Smallest

In March 1969 a measurement of 3.2 hands (14 in *36 cm*) was reported for a 'miniature' but probably not fully grown Shetland pony named 'Midnight', owned by Miss Susan Perry of Wirths Circus, Melbourne, Vic. The smallest foals born in Australia were two 12 in *30,5 cm* specimens, the first 'Quicksilver', b. 14 Nov 1975 and the second 'Tung Dynasty' b. 8 Feb 1978 both at Glenorie, NSW and bred by Norman J. Mitchell.

Dogs *Oldest*

For details of the oldest dog on record see p. 32. The death of an Australian cattle dog/Labrador cross named 'Chilla' occurred in Broadbeach, Queensland on 8 Mar 1983. Evidence that it was whelped on 5 Mar 1951 is not however fully substantiated since Chilla Porter (b. 11 Jan 1936), after whom he was named only became prominent in 1954.

Earliest

The oldest breed of Australian dog is the Dingo (*Canis familiaris dingo*) which may have been brought to Australia with aboriginal man from Asia *ante* 26,700 BC.

Tracking

'Whisky', an 8-year-old Jack Russell terrier, was lost by his master, truck driver Geoff Hancock at Hayes Creek, 120 miles *193 km* south of Darwin, NT, in October 1973. He turned up at Mambray Creek, 150 miles *240 km* north of Adelaide, SA on 13 June 1974 having covered 1700 miles *2720 km* across central Australia.

Cats *Heaviest*

On 23 June 1982 a weight of 20,7 kg *45 lb 10 oz* was recorded for a six-year-old neutered male tabby named 'Himmy' owned by Thomas Vyse of Redlynch, Cairns, Queensland.

Smallest

On 30 July 1979 a 20-month-old female named 'Kitu' owned by Wanda Mitka of Laverton, Vic, weighed in at 2 lb 10 oz *1,19 kg*.

Oldest

The oldest cat recorded in Australia was 'Fluffy' owned by Mrs Vera Hislop of Bicton, WA, which died on 14 Sept 1981 aged 33 years.

Largest kindle

On 13 Apr 1969 'Boccaccio Blue Danielle', a 1-year-old blue-pointed Siamese cat owned by Mrs Helen J. Coward of Klemzig, SA, gave birth to a live litter of 13 kittens.

Rabbits *Earliest*

A small number of common rabbits (*Oryctolagus curiculus*) were brought to Australia with the First Fleet in Jan 1788. Rabbits did not assume plague proportions until after the release of wild rabbits from Somerset, at Barwon Park, near Geelong, Vic, by Thomas Austin in 1859. The peak population, prior to the temporary reduction caused by the introduction of myxomatosis in 1951, has been estimated at 100,000,000,000 or 10,000 rabbits per human. (Rabbit, *oldest* see page 34.)

BIRDS

Earliest reference

The earliest reference to Australian birds was in a letter from Haevik Claeszoon van Hillegom on board the *Zeewolf* to the manager of the Dutch East India Company. He wrote of a 'few ternlets' being seen on 5 May 1618 off the west coast of Western Australia.

Australia's deadliest snake the taipan from Queensland (see pp. 37–38).

Largest and Heaviest

The largest bird found in Australia, and the second largest living bird after the Ostrich, is the Emu (*Dromaius (= Dromiceius) novaehollandiae*). Adult females (males are slightly smaller) stand 6–6¼ ft *1,83–1,93 m* in height and weigh 100–120 lb *45–54 kg*. It is also the fastest running flightless bird of Australia and can reach speeds up to 40 mph *64 km/h* over short distances. The first emu seen by Europeans was killed in what is now the area of Sydney, NSW, in 1788. Australia's heaviest flying bird is the Australian bustard (*Eupodotis australis*). The average adult cock bird weighs 13–16 lb *5,9–7,3 kg* but one outsized specimen weighed 32 lb *14,5 kg*.

Wing span

The Australian wedge-tailed eagle (*Aquila audax*) has the greatest expanse of wing of any living eagle. This species reaches its maximum size in Tasmania, and one female killed there in *c.* 1950 had a wing measurement of 9 ft 4 in *2,84 m*.

For size details of the Wandering albatross (*Diomedea exulans*) see p. 24.

Fastest flying

The fastest bird in Australian avifauna is the Fork-tailed swift (*Apus pacificus*) which may attain an air speed of 90 mph *144 km/h* in level flight.

Rarest

The strongest candidate for the title of Australia's rarest bird is the Eyrean grass wren (*Amytornis goyderi*) which reportedly became extinct in 1875. On 3 Sept 1961, however, it was rediscovered at Christmas Water Hole, near Lake Eyre, SA, but there have been no sightings since. The Australian night parrot (*Geopsittacus occidentalis*) of the deserts of Western and South Australia is only known from 15 specimens and none have been collected since 1897. Only 30 surviving examples of the Lord Howe Island wood rail (*Tricholimnas sylvestris*) were reported in May 1980.

Largest nest

The nesting site of the Mallee fowl (*Leipoa ocellata*) may involve the mounding of 300 yd³ *229 m³* of matter weighing 300 tons/*tonnes*.

Earliest exported

The earliest Australian bird to be taken abroad was the Black swan (*Cygnus atratus*), the emblem of Western Australia, in 1697.

Most popular

Since 1840 the Budgerigar (*Melopsittacus undulatus*), the commonest member of the parrot family in Australia, has become the world's most popular cage bird.

REPTILES

Largest and Heaviest

Despite reports from Queensland and Northern Territory of saltwater or estuarine crocodiles (*Crocodylus porosus*) measuring more than 30 ft *9,14 m* in length, the official record is held by Mr Keith Adams of Perth, WA, who harpooned a 20 ft 2 in *6,14 m* long bull in the MacArthur River near Borroloola, NT on 26 June 1960. Another claim which is also probably reliable but not so well substantiated is that of a 28 ft 4 in *8,63 m* bull shot by Mrs Kris Pawlowski on MacArthur Bank, Norman River, northwestern Queensland in July 1957.

Lizards *Largest*

Australia's largest lizard is the Perenty Goanna (*Varanus giganteus*) of the northern and central areas which grows up to 8 ft *2,4 m* in length.

Chelonians *Largest*

The largest chelonian found in Australian waters is the Pacific leatherback turtle (*Dermochelys coriacea schlegelii*) (see p. 37). In January 1951 a female measuring just over 8 ft *2,43 m* from head to tip of tail and 7 ft *2,13 m* across the flippers was caught in a fisherman's net at Bermagui, near Sydney. It weighed 1500 lb *680 kg*.

SNAKES

Longest

The longest snake found in Australia is the Amethystine python (*Liasis amethystinus*), which normally measures about 15 ft *4,57 m* in length when adult. One outsize individual shot at Green Hills, near Cairns, Queensland in 1948 measured 25 ft *7,62 m* and yielded a 28 ft *8,53 m* skin.

Fastest

The fastest Australian snakes are the racers (family *Elapidae*) which have been scientifically timed at speeds up to 3.5 mph *5,6 km/h*.

Most venomous

The deadliness of venomous snakes depends upon the toxicity of their venom (milligrammes per 100 grammes of the victim's bodyweight), the dosage deliverable at a bite and the total venom reservoir. For details of the world's and Australia's most venomous snakes see p. 37.

Sea snakes

The most venomous sea snake in the world is *Hydrophis melanocephalus* (maximum length 5 ft *152 cm*), which has a venom 100 times more toxic than any other known sea or land snake. It abounds around Ashmore Reef in the Timor Sea off north-west Australia. The longest known sea snake (50 species) is *Hydrophis spiralis*, which ranges from the Persian Gulf to the Malay Peninsula and Archipelago. The average adult length is *c.* 6 ft *1,83 m*, but specimens measuring 9–10 ft *2,74 –3,04 m* have been reliably reported.

AMPHIBIANS

Largest

Australia's largest indigenous amphibian is the Great barred river frog (*Myxophyes fasciolatus*) of the eastern coast, which measures 8 in *20 cm* from snout to extended hind feet.

The world's largest toad, the Marine toad (*Bufo marinus*) of tropical South America (see p. 38) was introduced into Queensland by sugar-cane growers in 1935.

FISHES

Largest

The world's largest fish, the rare Whale shark (*Rhinciodon typus*) (see p. 39) has been recorded in Australian waters. In April 1964 a 30 ft *9,22 m* individual weighing an estimated 7 tonnes was washed ashore in Anno Bay, NSW. In Nov 1883 a Basking shark (*Cetorhinus maximus*) measuring 30 ft 6 in *9,3 m* in length was stranded at Portland, Vic. A White pointer (*Carcharodon carcharias*) was caught by Peter and Robert Cunningham near Hobart, Tasmania in June 1981. It weighed 2 tonnes *4409 lb* and was 21 ft 4 in *6,5 m* long. At least 420 Australians have been killed by sharks this century.

The largest bony or 'true' fish found in Australian waters is the Ocean sunfish (*Mola mola*). On 18 Sept 1908 the steamer S.S. *Fiona* limped into Port Jackson, NSW with a huge sunfish stuck in the bracket of the port propeller. The carcase measured 14 ft *4,26 m* between the anal and dorsal fins and weighed 4928 lb *2235 kg* (2.24 tons *2,28 tonnes*).

Freshwater *Largest*

Australia's largest freshwater fish is the Murray cod (*Maccullaehella macquariensis*), which is really a giant perch. Weights of up to 150 lb *68 kg* have been reliably reported for this species, and in the 1902 drought a freakish example measuring over 6 ft *183 cm* in length and weighing 250 lb *113 kg* was reportedly caught on a line baited with kangaroo meat by bridge builders.

Most venomous

Australia's most venomous fish is the stonefish *Synanceja horrida*, which has been responsible for a number of deaths. In Jan 1950 a victim at Bundaberg, Queensland was saved by inhaling trilene (*trichlorethylene*) which served to numb the body and counteract the shock. An antivenin is now available.

ECHINODERMS

Most destructive

The 'Crown of Thorns' starfish (*Acanthaster planci*) of up to 24 in *60 cm* diameter, feeds on coral polyps and has since 1960 ravaged parts of the Great Barrier Reer.

ARACHNIDS

Largest spider

Australia's largest spider is the tarantula *Selenotypus plumipes*. A female with a leg span of 9.5 in *24 cm* and a body as big as a bantam's egg was reportedly collected in central NT in November 1938.

Smallest spider

Australia's smallest spider is the *Microlinypheus bryophilus* family (Argiopiedae) which was discovered in Lorne, Vic, in January 1928. Adult males have a body length of 0,6 mm *0.023 in* and adult females 0,8 mm *0.031 in*.

Most toxic spider

The most poisonous Australian spider is the male Sydney funnelweb spider (*Atrax robustus*), which has caused twelve known deaths since 1927. Half of the victims were children under the age of ten, all of whom died with 12 hr of being bitten. An antivenin for this species was developed in 1980.

Most poisonous tick

The world's most poisonous tick is the Bush tick (*Ixodes holocyelus*) which swells by a factor of 400 (1 mg to 400 mg) when feeding on a human. It has killed at least 20 people on the eastern coast this century.

CRUSTACEANS

Largest

The largest crustacean found in Australian waters is the Giant Spider Crab *Leptomithrax spinulosus*, which has been credited with claw spans of up to 7 ft *213 cm*. The heaviest Australian crustacean is the offshore xanthid *Pseudocarcinus gigas* of the Bass Strait. One individual caught off King Island measured 18 in *45 cm* across the shell and weighed 27 lb *12,25 kg*.

Largest freshwater

The largest freshwater crustacean in the world is the Giant freshwater crayfish *Astacopsis gouldi* weighing up to 9 lb *4 kg* and 2 ft *61 cm* in length, and found in streams in Tasmania.

INSECTS

Heaviest and Longest

The heaviest insect found in Australia is the spiny leaf insect *Extatosoma tirartum*, females of which probably scale at least 30 g *1.06 oz* in their egg-laying prime. The longest is *Acrophylla titan* which can measure 25 cm *9.84 in* in length.

Longest lived

Australia's longest lived insects are believed to be queen termites of the species *Nasutitermes troidiae*. One found in Queensland in 1872 was reportedly still breeding 63 years later but these insects do not normally survive more than 15 years. The tallest termite mounds are in Northern Australia and measure up to 24 ft *7 m*.

Fastest flying

In 1917 a speed of 61.3 mph *98,6 km/h* was recorded for an Australian dragonfly of the species *Austrophlebia costalis* over a distance of 80–90 yd *73–82 m*, but this was ground velocity. The maximum air speed attained by this dragonfly is *c.* 36 mph *57 km/h*, making it one of the swiftest flyers in the insect world.

Ants

The most dangerous ant in the world is the bulldog ant (*Myrmecia pyriformis*) of eastern Australia. Deaths were recorded in Mount Macedon, Vic, in November 1936, and in Launceston, Tas, in September 1963, the latter within 15 min of the bite. The most primitive species of ant in the world is the Australian *Nothomymecia macrops*.

LEPIDOPTERA

Largest and Smallest

For details of the world's and Australia's largest moth see p. 42. Australia's smallest moths are the minute and primitive moths of the family Mycroptergoidea.

SEGMENTED WORMS

Longest

The longest Australian species of earthworm is the Giant Gippsland earthworm or Karmai (*Megascolides australis*), first discovered in Brandy Creek, southern Gippsland, Vic, in 1868. An average-sized specimen measures 4 ft *121 cm* in length (2 ft *61 cm* when contracted) and nearly 7 ft *213 cm* when *naturally* extended. The longest accurately measured *Megascolides* on record was one collected before 1930 in southern Gippsland which measured 7 ft 2 in *218 cm* in length and over 13 ft *396 cm* when naturally extended. The eggs of this worm measure 2–3 in *50–75 mm* in length and 0.75 in *19 mm* in diameter.

MOLLUSCS

Largest

The largest mollusc ever recorded in Australian waters was a giant squid (*Architeuthis kirkii*) washed ashore at Wingan Inlet, Vic, in September 1948. It had a head and mantle length of 9 ft 2 in *2,79 m* and measured an estimated 28 ft *8,53 m* in overall length (the arms and tentacles had been torn off at a length of 4 ft *1,21 m*). Australia's largest shell is the Giant Clam (*Tridacna gigas*). One found in the Great Barrier Reef weighed 262,9 kg *579½ lb*.

Most venomous

The most venomous cephalopods in the world are the two closely related species of blue-ringed octopus *Hapalochlaena maculosa* and *H. lunulata* which have a combined range around the coasts of Australia. The neurotoxic venom carried by this small mollusc (radial spread 4–6 in *100–150 mm*) is so potent that scientists at the Commonwealth Serum Laboratories in Melbourne, Vic, say that one bite is sufficient to paralyse (or sometimes kill) seven people. The venom acts so quickly that an antivenin could only rarely, if ever, be used in time to save life.

CNIDARIANS

Most dangerous jellyfish

Australia's most dangerous jellyfish is the transparent Australian box-jelly *Chironex fleckeri*, also known as the 'sea-wasp', which is known to have been responsible for at least 60 deaths in the waters of Queensland since 1880. The cardiotoxic venom carried by this invisible killer works so rapidly that it can paralyse the heart in 30 sec. A toxoid for active immunisation is now available.

Largest sea-anemone

The largest known sea-anemone is *Discoma* sp. of the Great Barrier Reef, Qld, which has an expanded oral disc measuring up to 2 ft *61 cm* in diameter.

Largest structure

The largest structure ever built by living creatures is the 1260 mile *2027 km* long Great Barrier Reef, which covers an area of 80,000 miles² *128 000 km².* It consists of countless millions of dead and living stony corals (*Scleractinia*). It's accretion has taken 600 million years.

EXTINCT ANIMALS

Longest

The longest—and heaviest—land vertebrate so far recorded from Australia is a yet unnamed brachiosaurid found recently near Hughenden, Qld. Fossil remains of this dinosaur, which lived about 120,000,000 years ago, indicate it measured about 80 ft *24 m* in total length and weighed at least 50 tonnes.

Oldest vertebrate

Fossils of Australia's oldest dated vertebrate are the armoured jawless fishes (*Aranolaspis*), found in 1959 at South Alice Springs by D. J. Taylor and dated to 480 million years by Dr Alex Ritchie and J. Gilbert-Tomlinson in 1977.

Oldest tetrapod tracks

Three trackways—one of 38 footprints—were discovered in the Genoa River beds of eastern Victoria in 1971. The discoverers, Norman A. Wakefield and James W. Warren, after tests, concluded that the footprints were made about 355 million years ago by tetrapod vertebrates of 55–90 cm *21–35 in* long.

Largest marsupial

The largest known extinct marsupial was the giant wombat *Diprotodon optatum*, of the Nullarbor Plain, SA, which was 6 ft *183 cm* at the shoulder and 10 ft *305 cm* long. It is believed to have lived as recently as 13,000 BC and was therefore seen by the ancestors of aborigines. The gigantic kangaroo *Sthenurus*, also of the Pleistocene, reached a height of 10 ft *305 cm* and weighed up to 300 lb *136 kg*.

Largest bird

For details of the heaviest prehistoric bird see p. 46.

Largest marine reptile

Australia's largest marine reptile was *Kronosaurus queenslandicus*, a short-necked pliosaur which lived about 100,000,000 years ago. A skeleton excavated in 1931 at Army Downs, Queensland, measured 42 ft *12,8 cm* in length, with a 9 ft *2,7 m* long skull.

Largest chelonian

Australia's largest prehistoric marine turtle was allegedly *Cratochelone berneyi*, which swam in the shallow seas over what is now Queensland about 75,000,000 years ago.

PLANT KINGDOM

Oldest fossils

Microfossil remains of blue-green algae discovered in Marble Bar, WA announced on 31 Mar 1978 have been dated to 3500 million years ago.

Trees *Oldest*

A specimen of Huon pine (*Lagarostrobus franklinii*) endemic to Tasmania with an 8 m *26¼ ft* girth retrieved during salvage operations in southwest Tasmania was estimated to be 2200 years old.

Tallest

The tallest standing hardwood tree in the world is the mountain ash. Presently growing in the Andromeda Reserve in the Styx Valley in Tasmania are many specimens over 300 ft *91 m* with the tallest reaching 325 ft *99 m* when measured in 1962 (see

Australia's most lethal spider—the Sydney funnelweb spider (see p. 344). (*Commonwealth Serum Laboratories*)

FRUIT, VEGETABLE AND FLOWER RECORDS

	Dimensions	Grown by	Place	Date
Bananas (Bunch)	267 lb *121 kg*	Les & Ros Buglar	Tully, Qld	1 Mar 1981
Carrot	8 lb 13 oz *3,99 kg*	Thomas Argaet	Gundagai, NSW	1980
Garlic	732 g *25.82 oz*	Mark Saward	Mandurah, WA	Jan 1982
Lemon	24 in *60,9 cm* (girth)—5 lb 14 oz *2,65 kg*	Violet Phillips	Ingham, Qld	1974
Pear	3.09 lb *1,405 kg*	K & R Yeomans	Arding, Armidale, NSW	10 May 1979
Rockmelon	10,5 kg *23 lb 2 oz*	Ned Katich	Upper Swan, WA	Feb 1982
Sweet Potato	34 lb 8 oz *15,6 kg*	R. Gonchee	Belmont, Brisbane, Qld	1941
Tomato Plant (fruit)*	48 lb 8 oz *22 kg*	Reg & Cherrill McKay	Surfer's Paradise, Qld	1977–78
Dahlia	9 ft 10¾ in *3,01 m*	H. W. Deem	Cranbourne, Vic	1977
Rose	5470 blooms (*Cecile Bruner*)	Clifton W. Martin	Merrylands, NSW	13 Dec 1982

* An unsubstantiated claim has been received from Spearwood, WA for a yield of 79 lb 9 oz *36,08 kg*.

also p. 51). A Gum tree leaf from a Tasmanian Blue Gum (*E. globulus*) was reported in 1979 to measure 51 cm *20 in* from tip to tip at the end of the centre vein. The tallest natural fire lookout is 56 m *184 ft* up the Gloucester Tree at Pemberton, WA.

Hardest wood

Australia's hardest wood is *Acacia cambagei* which, using the Janka test, records a value of 4470 lb *2027 kg* for the tangential face. The tree can attain 40 ft *12,19 m* in height with a girth of 40 in *102 cm*.

Most pestilential

The introduced prickly pear (genus *Opuntia*) which covered 10 million acres *4 million ha* by 1900, had spread to 58 million acres *23 million ha* by 1920 and a peak 65 million acres *26 million ha* by 1925 to become a major menace. The *Cactoblastis cactorum* moth introduced in 1925 succeeded in controlling the pest and is gratefully commemorated by the Cactoblastis Memorial Hall at Boonarga, Qld.

Bush fire *Most widespread*

The most widespread bush fire on record was when the Moolah-Corinya (1 315 000 ha *3 250 000 acres*) and the Musheroo-Tundulya (285 000 ha *704 250 acres*) joined up in December 1974. The Ash Wednesday bush fires of 16 Feb 1983 over 853 500 ha *2,108 970 acres* killed 76 and did $390 million of damage.

Vine *Largest*

The largest vine in Australia is one at Chiltern, Vic, 158,5 cm *62.4 in* in circumference. It was planted in 1867 and in 1936 yielded its largest crop of 2½ tons/*tonnes*.

Ferns *Largest*

Details of the world's largest ferns on Norfolk Island are on page 50. The largest mainland fern is the tree fern *Cyathea australis* which grows to a height of 20 m *65.6 ft* with fronds to 3 m *9.8 ft*.

Orchid *Rarest*

The underground *Rhizanthella gardneri* has only been found four times since its discovery at Corrigan, WA by John Trott in 1928.

Moss *Tallest*

The world's tallest moss is the Australian species *Dawsonia superba*, which grows 12 in *30 cm* high.

PARKS, ZOOS

Largest

The largest true natural park is the Kosciusko National Park which covers 1,322,000 acres *535 000 ha* 2065 miles² *5348 km²*. A yet unnamed Conservation Park in South Australia covers 5,269,770 acres *2 132 602 ha*. The largest Wild Life Reserve in Australia is the Tamani Desert Sanctuary, which comprises 14,489 miles² *37 526 km²* of Northern Territory.

Botanic gardens

Australia's oldest botanic garden is Sydney's 66 acres *26 ha* at Farm Cove, instituted in 1816. The largest botanic garden is the 951 acre *385 ha* King's Park, Perth of which 647 acres *262 ha* is bushland.

Zoo *Oldest*

Australia's oldest extant zoo is the Melbourne Royal Park, founded in 1862, but a menagerie was established in Hyde Park, Sydney, in 1848.

Largest

Western Plains Zoo in Dubbo, NSW, opened in February 1977, is Australia's first open-range zoo and the largest zoo, covering an area of 300 ha *740 acres* and housing more than 700 specimens.

THE NATURAL WORLD

MAINLAND EXTREMITIES

Most northerly	Cape York, Qld	Lat. 10° 41′ S
Most southerly	Wilson's Promontory, Vic	Lat. 39° 08′ S
Most easterly	Cape Byron, NSW	Long. 153° 39′ E
Most westerly	Steep Point, WA	Long. 113° 09′ E

Earthquake *Greatest*

The largest earthquake known to have been felt in historic times in Australia was the submarine earthquake to the seaward of the Monte Bello Islands (epicentre lat. 19° 06′ S, Long. 111° 48′ E) at 0718 hours GMT on 19 Nov 1906. The magnitude of the surface wave scale was 7¾. The largest instrumentally measured earthquake with a land epicentre has been that at Lat. 31° 54′ S, Long. 117° 00′ E at 0258 hours GMT on 14 Oct 1968 which almost totally destroyed Meckering, WA. It was assigned a magnitude of 6.8 and caused an arcuate surface fault about 37 km *23 miles* long, with a maximum throw of 2 m *6½ ft*.

Volcanoes

Although there are no active volcanoes on the Australian continent, radio-carbon dating near the Mount Gambier crater, SA indicates that this last erupted *c.* AD 600.

Non-volcanic fire

Australia's (if not the world's) longest burning fire is that of a seam of coal under The Burning Mountain, nr Wingen, NSW, which is believed to have spontaneously combusted 'several thousand' years ago.

OCEANS

The deepest point in the waters of the Australian continental shelf is 420 ft *128 m* north of Port Side Three, WA. A sounding of 24,249 ft *7391 m* has been taken from the Diamantina Trench off Point D'Entrecasteaux, WA.

Highest waves

A stereo photograph of a wave calculated to be 24,9 m *81.7 ft* high was taken from the USSR's diesel-electric vessel *Ob'* in the South Pacific Ocean, about 600 km *370 miles* south of Macquarie Island, on 2 Apr 1956.

Highest tides

The greatest mean spring ranges on the coasts of continental Australia are 40 ft *12,19 m* in Collier Bay on the northwest coast.

Fastest currents

The most notorious 'tidal' races in Australian waters are at Hell's Gate, Macquarie Harbour, Tas, which exceed 8 knots *14,8 km/h* at times. The 'tidal' streams at the mouth of Port Phillip Bay, Vic, also reach 8 knots *14,8 km/h*. In parts of King Sound, near Derby, WA, true tidal streams exceed 8 knots *14,8 km/h* in the narrower passages.

AUSTRALIAN CONTINENT

The island continent of Australia has been variously described as the world's smallest continent or the world's largest island. It is the world's fourth largest (also the flattest and driest) land mass, behind Afro-Eurasia, The Americas and Antarctica, with a mainland area of 2,941,526 miles² *7 618 493 km²* and a circumnavigational length of 11,516 miles *18 533 km*. The coastline length at high water has been estimated at 36 735 km *22,826 miles*.

Highest points

State/territory	ft	m	Location
Australian Antarctic Territory	*c.* 14,010	4270	Spot 82° 30′ S 65° 30′ E
Heard Island	9005	2744	Big Ben
New South Wales	7316	2229	Mount Kosciusko
Victoria	6516	1986	Mount Bogong
Australian Capital Territory	6274	1912	Mount Bimberi
Tasmania	5305	1616	Mount Ossa
Queensland	5287	1611	Mount Bartle Frere
Northern Territory	4955	1510	Mount Zeil
South Australia	4723	1439	Mount Woodroffe
Western Australia	4104	1250	Mount Meharry
Lord Howe Island	2838	865	Mount Gower
Macquarie Island	1421	433	Mount Hamilton
Christmas Island	1170	356	Spot height
Norfolk Island (with Philip Island)	1036	315	Mount Pitt
Cocos (Keeling) Islands	20	6	Maximum height
Ashmore and Cartier Islands	8	2,4	Spot height

Rocks *Largest*

For details of the world's largest exposed rocky outcrop, Mount Augustus, WA, see page 60.

The Nullarbor Plain (Lat. *nulla arbor*—no tree) is strata of tertiary limestone and has been cited as the world's largest flat bed rock surface.

Land remotest from the sea

The nearest geographical feature to the central point of continental Australia is Central Mount Stuart (2770 ft *844 m*) in Northern Territory discovered in 1860. It is 465 miles *748 km* from the coast near Port MacArthur, NT.

Island *Largest*

Australia's largest island is the State of Tasmania which ranks 24th in the world, with an area of 26,215 miles² *67 896 km²*. The largest off-shore island is Melville Island, north of Darwin, with an area of 2240 miles² *5801 km²*.

Remotest

The remotest Australian island territory is Heard Island which is over 1000 miles *1600 km* from the nearest continental land.

Greatest range

Australia's longest mountain range is The Great Divide (formerly Great Dividing Range), which measures 2250 miles *3620 km* from the Iron Range in northern Queensland southward to Mount Gambier, SA. It is the fourth longest range in the world behind only the Andes, Rockies and Himalaya-Karakoram-Hindu Kush.

Extremities

The extremities of Australian land territory are:

		Lat.	Long.
Most northerly	Sae Island, Admiralty Islands 48 miles *77 km* south of the Equator	0 48 S	145° 16′ E
Most southerly	South Pole, Australian Antarctic Territory	90° 00′ S	—
Most easterly	Steels Point, Norfolk Island	29° S	167° E
Most westerly	The 45° East Meridian of Australian Antarctic Territory which crosses the coast through Enderbyland	67° 50′ S to 90° 00′ S	45° E

Largest Bay

Australia's largest bay is the Great Australian Bight. It measures 690 miles *1110 km* across between Capes Paisley and Catastrophe.

Sand dunes

Sand dunes are not stable. A height of 919 ft *280 m* has been surveyed on Moreton Island, Queensland.

The largest sand island in the world is Great Sandy (Fraser) Island (788 ft *240 m*) which is 77 miles *123 km* long and from 3 to 14 miles *4 to 22 km* across.

Greatest depression

The lowest point below sea level is in the southern part of Lake Eyre (North) which is 39 ft *11 m* below sea level.

RIVERS

Longest

The longest single-named river is the Darling (1702 miles *2739 km*) which can be regarded also as the longest tributary (of the Murray) which has a combined watercourse length of 2330 miles, *3250 km* to rank No 15 in the world.

The longest rivers in other states are the Gascoyne 475 miles *764 km* (wet season watercourse) in Western Australia and the Derwent (120 miles *193 km*) in Tasmania. In Northern Territory the Victoria has a watercourse of 400 miles *643 km*.

Largest river system

The Murray River and its tributaries drain 408,110 miles² *1 057 000 km²*.

Largest basin

The basin of the Murray-Darling is 369,000 miles² *955 700 km²*. The largest basin of a single named river is the 53,480 miles² *138 510 km²* of the Fitzroy River, Queensland.

Waterfall

Australia's highest major waterfall is the Wollomombi which descends a total of 240 m *787 ft* with a largest single leap of 626 ft *200 m* from the East Escarpment of the New England Plateau, NSW. The water reaches the Macleay River. The Wallaman Fall 48 km *30 miles* west of Ingham, Qld, descends 278 m *912 ft*.

LONGEST WATER-COURSE

The longest watercourse in Australia is the Spring Creek-Condamine-Balonne-Culgoa-Darling-Murray which, though intermittent, is 2376 miles *3824 km* long overall—the 15th longest watercourse in the world.

WEATHER RECORDS

Earliest record Capt. Cook on visibility—Point Hicks				20 Apr 1770
Highest shade temperature	127.5°F	*53,1°C*	Cloncurry, Qld	16 Jan 1889
Lowest temperature	−8°F	*−22,2°C*	Charlotte Pass, NSW	14 July 1945
				22 Aug 1947
Greatest rainfall (1 hr)	12.99 in	*330 mm*	Deeral, Qld	13 Mar 1936
(24 hr)	44.88 in	*1140 mm*	Bellenden Ker, Qld	4 Jan 1979
(1 yr)	442.91 in	*11 250 mm*	Bellenden Ker, Qld	1979
Highest surface wind speed	153 mph	*246 km/h*	Mardie, WA	19 Feb 1975
Hottest Place (av max)	96.3°F	*35,7°C*	Wyndham, WA	83 years to 1981
Hottest place	>100°F	*37,8°C*	Marble Bar, WA	161 days to 20 Apr 1924
Wettest Place (annual mean)	168.19 in	*4272 mm*	Tully, Qld	56 yrs to 1980
Driest Place (annual mean)'	4.10 in	*104 mm*	Troudaninna, S.A.	42 yrs to 1936

LAKES

The largest of Australia's salt lakes or *salinas* is Lake Eyre, SA, which covers an area of 3600 miles² *9300 km²* in two main basins. The greatest filling in living memory was in 1974 when the amount of water exceeded the 1951 surface figures of 3100 miles² *800 km²* by 35 per cent and water flowed from the north basin to the south *via* the Goyder Channel at an estimated rate of 55,000 gal/sec *250 000 litres/sec*.

Freshwater

Australia's largest freshwater lake was created when the dammed lakes Gordon and Pedder were joined by the McPartland Pass canal in Tasmania to give a total surface area of 510 km² *197 miles²*.

Deepest

Australia's deepest lake is St Clair, Tas, which is at least 700 ft *200 m* deep on its western side.

DESERT

Some 38 per cent of continental Australia, since it is receiving less than 250 mm *9.8 in* of rain per annum, can be classified as desert. The Australian Desert embraces the Great Sandy or Warburton (160,000 miles² *414 000 km²*), Great Victoria (125,000 miles² *323 000 km²*), Simpson or Arunta (120,000 miles² *310 000 km²*), Tanami, Gibson (85,000 miles² *220 000 km²*) and Sturt Deserts aggregating some 600,000 miles² *1 544 000 km²*.

GORGE

The Standley (or Standly) Chasm, 40 miles *64 km* west of Alice Springs, NT, in the Macdonnell Range descends 500 ft *152 m*. The King Creek Canyon in the George Gills Range, NT, is claimed to be more spectacular.

CAVES

The longest and deepest caves in Australia are on Tasmania. Exit Cave, in the south of the island, has more than 10 miles *16 km* of passages, and is the longest in the country. The deepest cave in Australia is Khazad-Dum, in the Junee Region of Tasmania, where a depth of 1060 ft *323 m* was reached in 1976. The largest cave passages in the country exist under the Nullarbor Plain. The Abrakurrie Cave has a chamber measuring 1100 ft × 150 ft *335 × 45 m* and 50–100 ft *15–30 m* high.

CLIFFS

The longest range of sea cliffs in Australian territory is that edging the Great Australian Bight. The basaltic land cliffs of the Great Western Tiers, Tas, rise over 2000 ft *600 m* from the floor of the Mersey River bed.

THE UNIVERSE & SPACE

Meteorites

The total number of noteworthy finds of meteoric (excluding tektite) material in Australia is about 130.

Largest craters

The confirmation of a major astrobleme (star wound) in Australia occurred in 1966 at Gosses Bluff, central Australia when K. A. W. Crook and P. J. Cook confirmed an extra-terrestrial cause. The tell-tale 'shatter cones' lie for 12 miles *19 km* round the crater rim which rises 900 ft *274 m* above the surrounding terrain enclosing a 150 ft *45 m* deep pan. The impact is believed to be due either to a high-velocity low-density comet or to a high-density low-velocity meteor of about 600 m *656 yd* diameter because the energy released was so violent that it melted quartz 1732°C *3149°F*. Estimates of the date of the event have been put at 133 million years ago.

The Wolfe Creek, WA, crater found in 1947 is of disputed origin. It has been suggested that it is due to the subsidence of a volcanic cauldron rather than to extraterrestrial agencies.

Aurora

Aurorae Australis or Southern Lights are visible on a few nights per year in the extreme southern parts of the continent and Tasmania.

Eclipses

Of the three significant solar eclipses this century, in which the belt of totality crossed Australia, that of 21 Sept 1922 had the longer period of 6 min 12 sec and this will not be approached in this century. A total eclipse was telecast in Australia on 23 Oct 1976.

Nearest stars

The very faint *Proxima Centauri* and *Alpha Centauri* which, apart from the Sun, form the nearest star system to the Earth, are Southern Hemisphere objects. According to the most up-to-date measurements they are respectively 4.22 and 4.35 light years distant.

Most distant object

The most distant heavenly body ever measured is the Quasar PKS 2000–330 which was located from the Anglo–Australian Telescope by a team in March 1982 in the constellation Sagitarius. Its red-shift (indicating a high speed of recession) was found to be 3.78, and thus consistent with a distance of 14,900 million light years (87,500 trillion miles, $1,40 \times 10^{23} km$).

ROCKETRY

Largest range

The Woomera rocket range was established as an Australia-United Kingdom enterprise in the south central desert, South Australia, in 1946.

Space tracking

The first man-made satellite to be tracked by radio from Australia was tracked by the Minitrack interferometer system at Woomera, SA. The satellite, America's 'Explorer 1', was used to measure cosmic radiation, micrometeorites and was responsible for the discovery of the Van Allen radiation belts during its active lifetime between 31 Jan and 23 May 1958.

Space communication

The first communication between a space traveller and an Australian took place between Astronaut John Glenn aboard America's first manned orbiting spacecraft, 'Friendship 7' and Gerry O'Connor at the Muchea station in Western Australia. 'Friendship 7' was placed into orbit on 20 Feb 1962 and was successfully recovered after three orbits and an orbiting lifetime of 4.9 hr.

early in 1977 has been cut into a 16½ carat gem valued at $300,000. This field is probably the world's most extensive.

Pearl

The most notable gem pearl found in Australian waters has been the 'Star of the West' fished off Broome, WA, in 1917. Its size is said to be equal to that of a sparrow's egg.

Opals

Some 95 per cent of the world's opals are quarried in Australia. For details of the world's largest opal see page 80.

Nuggets

For details of Australia's and the world's largest nuggets see page 80. Edward Hammond Hargraves (1816–91) first panned gold at Summerhill Creek, a left-bank Macquarie River tributary below Bathurst, NSW, on 12 Feb 1851. The $1 million Hand of Faith nugget was found near Wedderburn, Vic in Oct 1980.

Telescopes *Largest optical*

Australia's largest optical telescope is the 3,9 m *153 in* Anglo-Australian telescope installed at Siding Spring Observatory, nr Coonabarabran, NSW, at a cost of $16,000,000. HRH The Prince of Wales attended the inauguration ceremony on 16 Oct 1974. In 1976 the faintest then measured optical star, a pulsar in Vela (mag. 24) was discovered.

Most powerful

Australia's most powerful radio telescope is the 210 ft *64 m* diameter steerable dish which began operations in 1961 at Parkes, NSW. It can now operate at wavelengths as short as 3 mm *0.118 in*. The Parkes telescope relayed to the world the first television pictures of the historic 'Apollo XI' first moon landing on 21 July 1969. The unique Culgoora radio-heliograph involving 96 dishes of 40 ft *12 m* diameter arranged in a circle 5.84 miles *9,4 km* in circumference was completed in 1967.

Photography *Earliest*

The earliest photograph known to have been taken in Australia is dated 1841. It was a view of Sydney taken on a visit by a French photographer.

Largest particle accelerator

Australia's largest particle accelerator is the 14UD Pelletron Tandem at the Department of Nuclear Physics, Australian National University. This is also the world's highest energy Tandem Accelerator, reaching terminal voltages in excess of 14 million volts.

Wind tunnel

Australia's fastest wind tunnel is the Shock Tunnel installed in October 1969 at the Australian National University, Canberra which can produce velocities of up to 27,000 mph *43 452 km/h* for a millisecond.

The largest wind tunnel is the Subsonic 230 mph *370 km/h* 9 ft × 7 ft *2,7 m × 2,1 m* installation at the Aeronautical Research Laboratories, Melbourne, Vic, built by Kelly and Lewis and completed in 1941.

THE SCIENTIFIC WORLD

Gems and Minerals *Rarest*

An early claimant to the title of Australia's rarest mineral is Maldonite (Au_2Bi) a pinkish white stone of gold and bismuth found at Maldon, Vic, and reported by Ulrich in 1870. It has a specific gravity of 15.7 and it tarnishes to copper red and then to black. Other minerals are known from microscopic grains only.

Hardest

Diamonds have been found in every State and territory. The Ellendale-Argyle field, Western Australia yielded 11,385 carats in 1978–80. One stone exceeded 8¾ carats.

Diamond *Largest*

The largest diamond reported in Australia was one of 28 carats found in 1905 near Mount Werong, NSW by Williams and Donaldson. Some characteristics resembled those of Southern African stones.

Sapphire

Australia produces 75 per cent of the world's supply of rough sapphire. A rare orange-red stone found in Central Queensland

ARTS & ENTERTAINMENTS

Paintings and Drawings *Earliest*

The earliest cave rock paintings are of Aborigine creation and several sites have been discovered since Sir George Grey came upon the Kimberley rock paintings in northern Western Australia in 1837. Some discoveries by an expedition, sponsored by *The Australian* and largely staffed from Adelaide Museum, made in 1972, may however ante-date the Mootwingie art since the symbolism is not tribal aboriginal but possibly belonging to the 'Old People'. Faceted pigments discovered at Lake Mungo, NSW have been dated to 30,000 BC but the purpose may not have been artistic. The earliest European drawing is one of a kangaroo with two young in its pouch by an unknown artist and reproduced on the title page of *Speculum Orbis Terrae* by Cornelis De Jode published in Antwerp in 1593.

The oldest Australian oil painting extant is *A View of Sydney Cove* painted in 1794 by the convict Thomas Watling.

The earliest Australian engravings appear in the book by John William Lewin (1770–1819) called *Prodromus Entomology,*

Australia's biggest bark picture (see below).

Natural History of Lepidopterous Insects of New South Wales published in 1805.

Largest

Australia's biggest bark picture is one of 40 × 8 ft *12,19 × 2,43 m* completed by the Art in Bark Association, Brisbane, Qld on 30 Jan 1984.

Most expensive

The highest auction price for an Australian painting sold in Australia is $176,000 for *Mt. Zero and Lake Taylor* by Nicholas Chevalier sold by Sotheby's Australia on 23 Mar 1983. The highest auction price for an Australian painting by a living artist is $115,000 for *The Jacaranda Tree* by Brett Whitely on 8 Mar 1982 at Geoff Gray Pty Ltd by Robert Holmes a'Court. In September 1973 the Australian National Gallery paid $A1,300,000 for 'Blue Poles' by Jackson Pollock (1912–1956), an American painter.

The record auction price in Australia is $506,000 for a portrait of *Captain James Cook RN* by John Webber RA at the same sale.

Earliest RA

The first Australian to be elected a member of the Royal Academy was Sir Bertram MacKennal (1863–1931) in 1909. He was the engraver of the head of King George V, which appeared on the Imperial coinage from 1911 to 1936.

Galleries

Australia's first public art gallery was the Melbourne Gallery opened in 1861. Now renamed the National Gallery of Victoria, Melbourne, it is also the largest.

Museums

The earliest museum and that with the largest collection in Australia is the Australian Museum, Sydney, opened in 1827. It was moved to its present site in College Street, Sydney in 1846. The largest museum building is the National Gallery of Victoria and the largest natural history museum is The Australian Museum, Sydney.

LANGUAGE

Most languages

The former Australian territory of Papua New Guinea has, owing to so many isolated valleys, the greatest concentration of separate languages in the world with more than 10 per cent of the world's total of 5000.

Longest place name

The longest place name in Australia is the 19-letter name of a salina (salt lake) 60 miles *96 km* west of Lake Eyre in South Australia names Lake Cadibarrawirricanna. The longest palindromic name is Paraparap, a suburb of Darwin.

Longest personal name

The longest English surname in normal use in Australia is Featherstonehaugh (see page 89), of 17 letters.

Longest sentence

The longest sentence to have been printed in an Australian newspaper, with the editor's cooperation, is one of 5256 words in the *North Shore Times* of 18 Apr 1981 by Mark Virtue of Turramurra, NSW.

BOOKS

Earliest

The earliest book printed in Australia was *New South Wales General Standing Orders* published by George Howe in 1802. The earliest illustrated book printed in Australia is *Birds of New South Wales* by John William Lewin (1770–1819) which appeared in 1813. The earliest novel published in Australia is *Quintus Servinton* by Henry Savery (1791–1842) published in Hobart in 1830–1. There is evidence that the three-volume *Women's Love* by Mary Grimstone was begun before this date.

Rarest

Only three copies have survived of *Michael Howe*, the story of the last of the bush rangers by Thomas Wells published by Andrew Bent in 1818.

Most expensive

The most expensive book published in Australia is *The Birds of Paradise and Bower Birds* by William T. Cooper in a *de luxe* folio edition limited to 25 copies and published by William Collins, Sydney, in 1977 at a recommended price of $A6,000.

Longest novel

The longest novel published in Australia is *Poor Fellow My Country* by Xavier Herbert, a story of the life of Aborigines in the late 1930s and early 1940s. It was published by William Collins, Sydney, in an edition of 1463 pages and an estimated 850,000 words.

Most Durable Diarist

Cyril Goode of Newport, Vic began his diary on 1 Jan 1927 and passed the 6,000,000 word total in 1981.

Most Rejected Author

William A. Gold (b. 29 June 1922), who wrote 3 million unpublished words in 1956–74, received his 59th rejection for his eighth novel *One Best Seller* in November 1982.

Map

A map of Sydney cove, 15 × 30 cm *5.9 × 11.8 in*, drawn in 1791 by a convict was sold for $6500 at a Sydney auction in 1980.

Poetry

The earliest published Australian verse was written by the English-born Michael Massey Robinson (1744–1826) in 1810, twelve years after he had been transported. The earliest Australian poetry to be published in book form was that wrotten by Judge Barron Field (1786–1846) entitled *First Fruits of Australian Poetry* (Sydney, 1819). The earliest Australian-born poet was Charles Tompson (b. Sydney 1807—died 1883) whose *Wild Notes from the Lyre of a Native Minstrel* appeared in 1826.

Poet's corner

The only Australian commemorated in Poet's Corner, Westminster Abbey, London, is Adam Lindsay Gordon (1833–70). He committed suicide aged 37 after a "financial disappointment" and the publication of his *Bush Ballads and Galloping Rhymes*, and was buried in Melbourne.

Publisher

Angus and Robertson, founded in Sydney in January 1886, is the oldest and largest Australian publishing house.

Literary society

Australia's premier Literary Society is the Yorick Club, founded in Melbourne in 1868.

Oldest libraries

No private libraries are recorded in Australia before 1821. A Reading Room with subscribers was established in Sydney in 1827. The oldest State Public Library is that of Victoria, founded in 1853 and opened in 1856.

Largest libraries

The library with the greatest number of bound volumes in Australia is The University of Sydney Library, with 2,345,000 at 1 Jan 1984. In the field of film, pictures and maps the most comprehensive collection is in the National Library of Australia, Canberra. The largest collection of Australiana is at the Mitchell Library, Sydney.

NEWSPAPERS

Earliest *and* Oldest

Australia's earliest newspaper was the *Sydney Gazette and New South Wales Advertiser* published single-handed by the Government Printer, George Howe (1769–1821) on 5 Mar 1803. The oldest newspaper extant is the *Sydney Morning Herald*, so named in 1842 but originating from the little four-page weekly *Sydney Herald* which had appeared in 1831.

Highest circulation

The Australian daily newspaper with the highest circulation is *The Sun News Pictorial*, of Melbourne, currently with 591,684 (Sept 1983–Mar 1984). The highest circulation for a weekend paper is 646,045 (Oct 1983–Mar 1984) copies of *The Sun-Herald* of Sydney. The highest ever figure was 776,537 (Sept 1969).

Most advertising

The *Sydney Morning Herald* in 1973 carried a record 31,397,115 lines of classified advertising, which is more than that claimed by any other newspaper in the world.

Periodical

The Australian periodical with the highest circulation is *The Australian Women's Weekly* which sells 1,235,000 copies a week (Sept 1983). It also has the highest readership of any periodical—5,340,000 in 1983.

Longest editorship

The longest editorship has been 63 years 11 months by John Watson (b. 1834) who was editor of the South Australian newspaper *The Border Watch* from 1 Jan 1862 to 9 Dec 1925.

MUSIC

The oldest Australian musical instrument is the Aborigine didgeridoo—a hollow wooden blow tube 4–5 ft *1,2–1,5 m* in length. The earliest record of a piano in Australia was one unloaded from HMS *Sirius* in 1790. The earliest music school was one established in Sydney in 1836 and the earliest music festival was staged in St Mary's Cathedral, Sydney in 1838.

Organ *Oldest*

The oldest church organ installed in Australia was a London-built organ in St David's Church, Hobart in 1825.

Largest

The largest organ in Australia is the 50 ft *15,2 m* high organ in the concert hall of the $1.2 million Sydney Opera House. The organ, built by Ronald Sharp, has 127 stops and 10,500 pipes and was constructed between May 1969 and 30 May 1979.

Organist most durable

Henry Moore (1878–1970) was the voluntary organist at St John The Baptist Church, Reedy Creek, Singleton Parish, NSW for 75 years from 1891 to 1967.

Bells

The largest peal of bells in Australia is one of 13 bells in St Paul's Cathedral, Melbourne of which the tenor weighs 29 cwt 1 qr 4 lb *1487,7 kg*. The heaviest peal is the eight-bell peal in Adelaide Cathedral of which the tenor weighs 41 cwt 1 qr *2095,5 kg*.

Orchestras

Australia's earliest professional symphony orchestra was that organised by Dr Frederick Cowen in Melbourne in 1888. No over-seas orchestra visited Australia until the tour of the Czech Philharmonic Orchestra in 1959.

Opera Earliest

The first classical opera to be performed in Australia was Rossini's *Barber of Seville* in 1843. The first opera to be both written and performed in Australia was *Don Juan of Austria* by the English born Isaac Nathan (1790–1864) in 1847.

Largest opera house

Australia's largest opera house is the Sydney Opera House at Bennelong Point with a total capacity of 5200, built to a prize-winning design of the Danish architect Utzon at an ultimate cost of $A102 million and opened by HM The Queen on 20 Oct 1973.

THEATRE

The first purpose-built theatre in Australia was built in 1795 and opened on 16 Jan 1796 on a site of what is now Bligh Street, Sydney. The oldest existing theatre in Australia is the Theatre Royal, Hobart, built to a capacity of 1000 in 1837 and extensively renovated in 1952.

Largest

(See p. 102)

Earliest ballet

The first noted ballerina to visit Australia was Lola Montez in 1855. National interest was not aroused until the visits of Pavlova in 1926.

GRAMOPHONE RECORDS

Earliest million

I'll Never Find Another You by the Seekers, Judith Durham (b. Melbourne 3 July 1943); Athol Guy (b. Victoria 5 Jan 1940); Keith Potger (arrived Australia in 1946); and Bruce Woodley (b. Melbourne 25 July 1942) was the first of a number of million sellers by this group with 1¾ million. The highest sales for an Australian singles record is over 3,000,000 attributed to *Georgy Girl* composed by Tom Springfield and lyric by Jim Dale, which became No. 1 on the United States charts and The Seekers' fourth million seller.

Highest sales

Although accurate figures are not published, it can be safely assumed that the Seekers' aggregate 'singles equivalent' sales have surpassed the 13½ million attributed to Peter Dawson (b. Adelaide 1882, died 26 Sept 1961) who started making records in batches of 12 in 1904.

The record sales for any Australian-originated 'single' recording is 317,000 since its release in October 1980 for *Shaddup you face* by the Joe Dolce Music Theatre on the Astor Label.

Fastest selling

Rolf Harris's version of *Two Little Boys*, a sentimental song about the American Civil War, written in 1903, sold over 900,000 copies in its first 15 weeks (ending February 1970) in the United Kingdom alone. Harris was first attracted to this ballad at a sing-song at an Eldo Tracking Station in Northern Territory.

Largest crowd

An audience over-estimated at 200,000 for a concert by the Seekers at the Myer Music Bowl, Melbourne gathered in 1967. This then would have represented about 1 in 60 of the then population of the country.

Rock Concert Largest

A crowd of 160,000 assembled for the Radio 2SM Concert outside the Sydney Opera House on 1 Nov 1979 to hear 27 bands, including Stevie Wright, Sherbet and Max Merritt.

CINEMA

Earliest cinema

Australia's first cinema was the Salon Lumière, Sydney, opened on 28 Sept 1896 by Maurice Lestier. The first moving pictures were shown in Australia by Carl Hertz in August 1896. They were scenes of London shown in the Melbourne Opera House, now the Tivoli. The first moving pictures made in Australia were Sydney scenes shot in September 1896 by Maurice Lestier.

The first Australian-made dramatic film was *Soldiers of the Cross* made by the Salvation Army under Major Joseph Perry. It was shown on 13 Sept 1900 with a narration by Commandant Herbert Booth. It was more of an illustrated lecture. The first Australian-made feature film was *The Story of the Kelly Gang* which opened at the Melbourne Town Hall on 26 Dec 1906 and ran for about 1¼ hr. It was produced by J. & N. Tait.

RADIO

Earliest

The earliest antipodal reception of radio in Australia was on 22 Sept 1918 of a Marconi Company broadcast from Caernarvon, Wales, which was picked up by Ernest T. (later Sir Ernest) Fisk (1886–1965) at Wahroonga, Sydney. The earliest radio transmission was on 13 Aug 1919 of inter-room messages by Fisk, which were demonstrated to members of the Royal Society of New South Wales in Sydney.

The official start of radio was at 8 p.m. on 23 Nov 1923 with a concert from Sydney by Station 2SB (later 2BL) which had received the first licence ten days earlier on 13 Nov 1923. Radio 2UE is the oldest existing commercial station, having been started in the living room of C. V. Stevenson of Maroubra, NSW, on 26 Jan 1925. The Sydney station 2UW was given permission to broadcast continuously and has never been off the air since 22 Feb 1935.

Most Funds Raised by Appeal

Radio 3AW in their Bushfire appeal of 18 and 21 Feb 1983 raised $1,021,213 rising to $2,808,958 by Jan 1984.

Longest Broadcasts

The longest continuous broadcast has been 106 hr 10 min by John Gardner, 19, of Radio 2KA, Penrith, NSW on 9–14 May 1982. Station 2MBS-FM broadcast classical music for 23 hours non-stop ending at noon on 28 Oct 1979 with 'Opus 1 to 100'.

Longest running radio show compère

The longest running show, with the same compère, broadcast in Australia was the weekly ABC Radio 1 'Wilfrid Thomas Show' which started on 13 Mar 1941 as 'Wilfrid Thomas' Dinner Show'. The final broadcast went out in 1980. The longest running national show (with changed format and compères) was 'The Hospital Hour' last heard on ABC Radio 3 on 3 May 1977. It began as 'The Hospital Half Hour' on 10 Jan 1938.

TELEVISION

Earliest

The earliest public demonstration of television was on 10 Jan 1929 from the studios of Station 3UZ, Melbourne. This programme, produced by mechanical scanning, included silhouettes and animated cartoons. The earliest cathode ray transmissions were made in April 1934 in Brisbane of a Janet Gaynor film.

The pioneers Tom Elliott and Dr Val McDowall were given the earliest TV transmitting licences in 1935. The first public service television station—TCN of Sydney, started in September 1956.

Longest transmission

The longest TV transmission is 163 hr 18 min ending at 1.48 a.m. on 26 July 1969 given by GTV9 Melbourne, covering the period of the 'Apollo XI' mission to the moon from 19 July.

Biggest TV Prize

Hayword Mabberley of Chapel Hill, Queensland won $206,000 in cash and $137,536 in prizes on Channel 9's *Sale of the Century* on 3–12 Oct 1983.

STRUCTURES

Earliest

The earliest Aborigines had no structures of a permanence which have left datable traces. The earliest European buildings were palm-thatched hutments with walls of clay between timber supports built from the time of arrival of the First Fleet on 26 Jan 1788.

The oldest building extant is the brick-built Elizabeth Farm House, Parramatta, built in 1794, named after his wife by the owner, Capt John MacArthur (1767–1834). It was bought by a preservation trust for $50,000 in June 1969. The public building of earliest origin is the Old Government House, Parramatta on the Rose Hill site of the house of Governor Arthur Phillip in 1790 from which some surviving bricks derive.

First architect

Australia's first architect was Francis Howard Greenway (c. 1777–1837) who established his practice in Sydney as a civil architect in 1816 before being pardoned. His Hyde Park Barracks and St Matthews Church in Windsor, both completed in 1817, are in the Georgian style.

Tallest structure

The tallest structure in Australia is the 1271 ft *387 m* 'Tower Zero', one of 13 VLF transmitter towers erected in 1967 for the US Navy Communication Station Harold E. Holt, near Exmouth, North West Cape, WA.

Tallest Observation Tower

Centrepoint Tower in Sydney completed in 1977–81 is 304,8 m *1000 ft* above street level. The 2239 tonne turret has a capacity of 960 persons served by 1400 ft/min *25,6 km/h* elevators.

Tallest and Largest inhabited building

Australia's tallest building is the 68-storey MLC Office Tower in Sydney, which rises to 244 m *800.5 ft*. The architects were Harry Seidler and Associates and completion was in October 1977. It is the world's tallest reinforced concrete office building.

Highest habitation

The highest habitation in Australia is Cabramurra, NSW, at 5286 ft *1611 m* above sea level.

Largest stadium

Melbourne Cricket Ground, venue of the 1956 Olympic Games, achieved a capacity of 138,000 after the latest alterations.

Hotels *Oldest and Largest*

The Bush Hotel, New Norfolk, in Tasmania has held a licence continually since 1825. The largest hotel in Australia is the Sydney-Hilton, opened in October 1974, with 619 rooms.

Longest bar

Australia's longest bar is that of the 298 ft *90,8 m* long bar with 27 pumps at Mildura, Vic. It was built in 1938 and re-built in 1970 at the Working Men's Club.

Longest fence

For details of the world and Australian record see p. 126. This is 3437 miles *5531 km* in length.

BRIDGES

Earliest *and* Oldest

The first bridge in Australia was a timber bridge, built by convicts, over the Tank Stream, Sydney, NSW in October 1788 at the instigation of Governor Arthur Phillip (1738–1814). Australia's oldest extant bridge is the 210 ft *64 m* Richmond Bridge over the Coal River, Tas, built in 1823–5 to the design of Major Bell. The oldest on the mainland is the now by-passed Lennox Bridge over Lapstone Creek on the Western Road to Bathurst, NSW, built by David Lennox and completed on 28 June 1833. The by-pass was built in 1926.

Largest
Australia's largest bridge is the 51,900 ton *52 732 tonnes* Sydney Harbour Bridge linking Milson's Point with Dawes Point opened on 19 Mar 1932 nearly 9 years after the first sod was turned on 28 July 1923. It was designed by Mr (later Sir) Ralph Freeman (1880–1950) and built by Dorman Long Co. Ltd of Middlesbrough, England. The main span now carrying an eight-lane roadway, two sets of railway tracks, a footway and a cycleway is 1670 ft *509 m*—5 ft *1,5 m* less than the Bayonne Bridge, Staten Island, New York, which was completed 4 months earlier.

Longest
Australia's longest bridge is the $220 million West Gate Bridge, Melbourne opened on 15 Nov 1978. The river span is 1102 ft 6 in *336 m* and the overall length is 1.6 miles *2582,57 m.* The death toll in the 13 years of building was 36.

Concrete arch *Longest*
Australia's longest concrete arch bridge is the Gladesville Bridge over the Parramatta River, Sydney, NSW with a main span of 305 m *1000 ft*, completed in 1964.

Deepest pile
One of the piles supporting the Hawkesbury River Bridge, NSW was driven to a world's record depth of 283 ft *86,25 m* below the water level in 1970 by John Holland (Constructions) Pty Ltd.

Jetty *Longest*
The Lucinda sugar terminal jetty in Queensland is 5.76 km *3.58 miles* long.

DAMS

Highest
Australia's highest dam is the Dartmouth Dam on the Mitta Mitta River, Vic, opened on 9 Nov 1979, which is 180 m *590 ft* high. It cost $140 million and took six years to build. It is designed to hold back 4.5 million megalitres of water.

Longest
Australia's longest dam is the Ross River Dam, near Townsville, Qld, with an embankment length of 8168 m *26,798 ft.* It was completed in 1976.

Greatest reservoir capacity
The greatest storage capacity in an Australian man-made lake is 14 276 million m³ *19,262 million yd³* in the Gordon River Power Development, southwest Tasmania, completed in 1976.

Pre-stressed concrete
Australia's largest pre-stressed concrete dam is the Catagunya Dam on the River Derwent, in Tasmania. It is 49 m *160 ft* high with a crest of 925 ft *282 m.*

TUNNELS

Longest
The longest single tunnel in Australia is the 14.6 mile *23,4 km* long Eucumbene-Snowy (hydro-electric) Tunnel, but this is linked with the Snowy-Geehi (9.0 miles *14,4 km*) and the Murray 1 Pressure (7.3 miles *11,7 km*) tunnels to produce a system of an overall 30.9 miles *49,7 km.* This was completed in 1966.

LIGHTHOUSES

Earliest
A lighthouse was erected on South Head, Port Jackson, NSW, in 1816–18 and was replaced after 66 years' service.

Earliest laser beam
The world's first laser-beam lighthouse operates from the top of the 200th anniversary (1970) memorial to Captain Cook's discovery of the east coast at Point Danger.

Most northerly/southerly
Australia's most northerly lighthouse is on Bramble Cay Torres Strait. Australia's most southerly lighthouse is on Maatsuyker Island off southern Tasmania.

BORINGS

Uranium mine
The Jabiluka site, NT is Australia's largest deposit with some 705 000 tonnes of ore. The country's known resources were valued at $A67 000 million at March 1984.

Deepest
Australia's deepest on-shore bore is Wonnerup No. 1, WA, drilled in 1972 to 15,500 ft *4724 m* and plugged after only a gas show. The deepest offshore drilling has been the 15,520 ft *4730 m* Scott Reef No. 1 drilled in 1971 as a capped gas well.

Australia's deepest bore for water is the Springleigh Bore of 7009 ft *2136 m* in the Blackall district of Queensland begun in October 1913 and completed in July 1921. The Great Artesian Basin, extending over parts of three States and Northern Territory, measures 655,000 miles² *1 700 000 km².*

THE MECHANICAL WORLD

SHIPS

Earliest
The most primitive but conjectural craft used by the Aborigines in their migrations from South East Asia before the 40th millennium BC may have been double canoes and were the earliest sea-going craft known to man.

The earliest European ship incontrovertibly known to have come inshore to the Australian mainland was the Dutch *Duyfken* under Captain Willem Jansz (or Janssen) in 1606. There is, however, some evidence from a wreck, known as the 'Mahogany Ship', that a European vessel, possibly Portuguese, visited Australia in the 16th century.

The first British ship to reach Australia was *Tryal* which became wrecked on a reef near the Monte Bello Islands in 1622. The earliest Australian-built boat was reputedly by some Dutch survivors of a wreck on the Western Australian coast in 1728.

Earliest steam
The earliest steam vessel in Australian waters was the *Sophia Jane*, built in Great Britain, which ran out of Sydney in June 1831.

Earliest clippers
The first clipper to arrive in Australia was the barque *Phoenician* (478 tons) at Port Jackson, 91 days out of England. The fastest run has been credited to the *Thermophylae*, which made pilot-to-pilot runs in 60 days in both 1868–69 and 1870–1.

Largest
The largest ship ever built in Australia is the 85 130 tonnes dwt (48,947 grt) oil/bulk ore carrier *Clutha Capricorn* completed on 25 Oct 1972 at Whyalla Shipyard, South Australia.

Longest pilotage
The most extended single man pilotage service in the world is The Queensland Coast and Torres Strait Pilot Service (est. 1880) which extends over a traverse of 3000 miles *4825 km* with 33 boarding or landing points. The first major ship to traverse the Great Barrier Reef passage was HM Aircraft Carrier *Implacable* (Capt C. C. Hughes Hallett, CBE, RN) in November 1945.

ROAD VEHICLES

Coaching
The acme of the coaching era was attained in the 1870's when Cobb and Company, established in Melbourne in 1853, were harnessing 6000 horses a day and covering daily a mileage 'greater than the Earth's circumference' (24,902 miles *40 075 km*). Their largest coach was *The Leviathan* which was drawn by 22 horses and operated in Victoria. Their last coach ran in Queensland at Surat in August 1924.

Cars
The earliest Australian-built car was a steam-powered phaeton made by Herbert Thomson in Armadale, Vic, in 1896. The first petrol-engined car was the four-seater Daimler-like 'Pioneer' built in Victoria with a top speed of 10 mph *16 km/h.*

Mass production of 120,402 of the first (48/215) model Holden in Australia was begun on 29 Nov 1948 by General Motors-Holdens Ltd, founded by Sir Edward Holden (1885–1947) in 1931. Total Holden production to 2 June 1981 including Toaranas and Geminis was 4,000,000. The first all-Australian car produced was the 'Buckingham' launched in 1933 but never mass-produced.

Fastest
The highest speed attained in Australia was 429.311 mph *690,909 km/h over a flying 666 yd 608 m* by Donald Campbell, CBE (1921–67) in his 4400 shp gas turbine Bluebird-Proteus at Lake Eyre on 17 July 1964.

Oldest driver
Herbert Henry Klingberg (b. 24 Sept 1885) of Cleve, SA, passed his test on 24 Sept 1917 and last drove in Sept 1982 aged 97 years.

Longest Road Train
The longest triple road train is that hauled by a Scania 142 driven by Graham Le Monier and Bob Morrison. The 62 wheel rig weighs 115 tonnes and plys between Perth and Darwin.

Driving in Reverse
Barry Stewart, 35, drove non-stop in reverse, a 1968 Holden Kingswood 570.5 miles *918,1 km* in 24 hr 17 min at Pacific Fair, Broadbeach, Qld, on 25 Apr 1980 to average 23.77 mph *38,25 km/h*.

Slowest speed limit
The lowest speed limit over Australian administered territory is 15 mph *24 km/h* on Lord Howe Island, which is the responsibility of New South Wales.

Circuit of Australia *Car*
The first men to drive round Australia were Nevill Reid Westwood and G. L. Davies in their 5 cv Citroën. They left Perth on 25 Aug 1925 and returned from the opposite direction on 30 Dec—127 days later. A claim to be the first to do so, solo, was made by Mrs Mitchiko Teshima of Osaka, Japan from 17 June–10 Sept 1980 over 18 637 km *11 580 miles*.

Motorcycles
35 members of the Queensland Police Department rode a single machine on 23 June 1984.

The earliest motor cycle circuit was by Jack L. Bowers and Frank Smith in a 7 hp Harley-Davidson side-car combination in 78 days 20 hr from Sydney (11 July) to Sydney (29 Sept) 1929 with their speedometer showing 9687 miles *15 589 km*.

The first ever crossing of the Simpson Desert east to west (over 1100 sand ridges) was achieved on a 185 cc Honda trailbike by Robert Murray Crawford from Birdsville to Finke, NT on 5–7 July 1979 in 55 hours.

Sydney–London
Colin Payter covered the 11,000 landmiles *17 700 km* from Sydney to London on a motor cycle in 23 days in August–September 1974. His best stretch in Western Australia was 300 miles *530 km* in 3 hr.

Petrol station
The largest gallonage sold through a single pump in the world in 24 hr is 39 054,5 litres *8588,08 gal* at the Cinema Centre Service Station, Canberra, ACT on 25–26 Sept 1981.

Tyre Changing Speed Record
At the Sydney Motor Show on 28 Aug 1982 John Thompson of Stockton changed all 4 tyres of a car in 5 min 43 sec.

RAILWAYS

Earliest
Australia's first steam train ran 2½ miles *4 km* from Flinders Street, Melbourne, to Port Melbourne (Sandridge) on 12 Sept 1854. It was the 5 ft 3 in *1,60 m* gauge Melbourne & Hobson's Bay Railway. The first electric train ran between Newmarket and Flemington racecourse, Melbourne on 6 Oct 1918.

Highest
The highest altitude reached on the Australian Railway system is 4514 ft *1376 km* above sea level on the shoulder of Ben Lomond (4,987 ft *1520 m*), NSW.

Longest platform
The longest platform in Australia is No. 1 at Flinders Street Station, Melbourne which extends 707,7 m *2322 ft*.

Longest straight
For details of Australia's and the world's longest railway straight (297 miles *477 km*) across the Nullarbor Plain, see page 144. The Trans-Australian line was completed in 1917.

Most powerful engine
Australia's most powerful steam engine was the 260 ton 92 ft 5¾ in *28,18 m* long 'Heavy Harry' built in 1941 and retired in 1954.

Fastest speed
The SRA of NSW took delivery of its British built Inter-City XPT diesel train in 1982. It touched 113 mph *181,8 km/h* on trials but will be limited to working at 140 km/h *87 mph*.

Longest train
In June 1975 the first 230 car 5 loco iron ore train ran from Mount Newman to Port Hedland, WA. It had a gross train weight of 28 000 tonnes and a length of 2,5 km *8200 ft*.

State Capital Rail Networks
The fastest time for travelling the entire Sydney-Metropolitan rail network of 362 km *224.9 miles* is 17 hr 41 min by 13 boys from St. Aloysius College, Milsons Point, Sydney on 22 Dec 1983.

Greatest ticket collection
Dr E. N. Eadie, of Adelaide, Australia, has amassed a collection of 80,000 rail tickets from 140 countries, dating back to 1853.

AVIATION

Earliest flights
Australia's pioneer aeronaut was Lawrence Hargrave (1850–1915) who experimented with man-lifting box-kites. At Stanwell Park, NSW on 12 Nov 1894 he was hoisted 16 ft *4,87 m* off the ground by four large kites.

The earliest powered flight in Australia was in January 1910 by Colin Defries in an imported Wright biplane over Sydney racecourse. The first flight above 100 ft *30 m* was by Ehrich Weiss *alias* Houdini (1874–1926), the great escapologist, in a Voisin biplane at Digger's Rest, Vic, on 18 Mar 1910.

The first flight in Australia by an Australian in a home-built aircraft was by John R. Duigan of Melbourne at Mia Mia, Vic, on 16 July 1910 in a plane styled on Wright's Flyer. He flew only 24 ft *7,30 m* but on 7 Oct 1910 covered 196 yd *179 m* at a height of 12 ft *3,65 m*. The holder of Pilot's Licence No. 1 was W. E. Hart who flew from Penrith to Parramatta, NSW in 1911.

First London–Australia flight
The pioneer London to Australia flight of 11,294 miles *18 175 km* was made by Capt Sir Ross Macpherson Smith, and his brother Lt. Sir Keith Macpherson Smith, with Sgt J. M. Bennett, and Sgt W. H. Shiers, from Hounslow, Middlesex, to Darwin, Australia, from 12 Nov to 10 Dec 1919 in a Vickers Vimy Bomber.

The first woman to fly from England to Australia was Amy Johnson CBE (k. 1941) who took off unheralded in her de Havilland D.H.60G Gipsy Moth *Jason* from Croydon, England, on 5 May 1930 and landed to an idolising reception at Darwin on 24 May 1930. Judith Chisholm flew solo from London to Port Hedland in a Cessna in 83 hr in Nov 1980. The first solo flight by a man was by Sqn Ldr H. J. L. 'Bert' Hinkler in an Avro S81 from Croydon to Darwin *via* Rome, Calcutta and Bandung on 7–22 Feb 1928. The first United Kingdom to Australia non-stop flight was by a flight refuelled RAF Vulcan in 1961.

First trans-Australia
The first trans-Australia flight was in a B.E.2e flown by Capt H. N. Wrigley, DFC, and Lt A. W. Murphy, DFC, from Melbourne to Darwin in 46 hr flying time on 16 Nov–12 Dec 1919. The first all-Australian aircraft to be built was the Warrigal produced in 1928 for military purposes.

Earliest trans-Pacific
The earliest trans-Pacific flight was completed by Charles Edward Kingsford-Smith, MC (1897–1935), who was awarded

Tasmanian ploughman Tony Richardson in action (see p. 355.)

the AFC and knighted in 1932. His crew was Charles T. P. Ulm, Harry Lyon and James Warner. He left Oakland, California on 31 May 1928 and flew *via* Honolulu, Hawaii and Suva, Fiji, arriving in Brisbane on 9 June. The plane was a Fokker F. VII B–3M called *Southern Cross*.

Oldest airline

Australia's (and the English-speaking world's) oldest airline is the Queensland and Northern Territory Aerial Services Ltd (QANTAS) which was registered on 16 Nov 1920 as an air ferry service into the Queensland outback. The first regular service was between Charleville and Cloncurry (577 miles *928 km*) inaugurated on 2/3 Nov 1922 using an Armstrong-Whitworth FK-8.

The Flying Doctor Service, largely founded by the Rev John Flynn, had begun in 1925, but was more formally inaugurated at Cloncurry, Qld on 15 May 1928. The first flying doctor was Dr K. St Vincent Welch.

Ballooning

The largest balloon to be flown in the southern hemisphere was successfully launched from Alice Springs by the Department of Science, Balloon Launching Station crew on 4 Apr 1972. The balloon of 1 300 000 m³ *1,700,000 yd³* was launched for the Massachusetts Institute of Technology. It reached a height of 42 000 m *137,700 ft*; carried a payload weighing 832 kg *1834 lb*, and had a float duration of 26 hr 53 min. The Bass Strait, from Winchelsea, Vic, to Smithton, Tasmania (355 km *220 miles*) was first crossed on 1 May 1981.

POWER PRODUCERS AND ENGINEERING

Hydro-electric power station

Australia's largest hydro-electric power station is the Tumut 3 Power Station, which is part of the Snowy Mountains Scheme. The installed capacity is 1,500,000 kW.

Conveyor belt

The longest conveyor belt in Australia is one of 16 miles *25,75 km* running from a bauxite mine to a refinery at Gove, NT, on the Gulf of Carpentaria coast.

Pipelines

Australia's earliest major water pipeline was engineered as early as 1903 from near Perth a distance of 350 miles *563 km* to the Kalgoorlie gold fields. The system has since been extended five-fold by branches.

The longest gas pipeline in Australia is that running from the Moomba gas field, SA to Sydney, 1300 km *807 miles* distant. The longest petroleum pipeline is the $61 million 198 km *123 mile* Sydney–Newcastle line opened in 1981.

Most powerful computer

The most powerful computer in Australia is the CDC Cyber 205-622, installed in May 1984 at the CSIRO Division of Computing Research in Canberra. It was built in Minneapolis, USA.

THE BUSINESS WORLD *(Money in $A)*

Largest Merger

Australia's largest ever company merger was a $200 million deal between Australian Consolidated Industries and Acmil Ltd announced on 19 Jan 1981.

Australia's largest company

Australia's largest company is The Broken Hill Proprietary Co. Ltd (BHP), with total assets employed of $7,737,900,000 and a net profit after tax for year ending 31 May 1983 of $227,880,000. There are 56,000 people on the company payroll and 177,000 shareholders.

Life Assurance Company

Australia's largest life assurance company is the Australian Mutual Provident Society (AMP) (founded 1849) which had total assets of $10,286 million and a total amount assured of $62,036 million on 1 Jan 1984.

Largest Employer

Australia's largest single employer is the Australian Telecommunications Commission with more than 88,500 employees.

Winery *Largest*

The Berri Co-operative Winery and Distillery Ltd, which crushes 30,000 tons *30 480 tonnes* of grapes in a year, is Australia's largest.

Highest sales

G. J. Coles & Co. Ltd. of Melbourne became the first Australian retailer to top annual sales of $1000 million in 1974–5. Sales for the period ending July 1983 were $4,734,673,000. In July 1983 Coles and subsidiary companies had 885 stores throughout Australia and employed more than 72,000 people.

Shopping centre *Largest*

Westfield Shoppingtown built on 11.5 acres *4,6 ha* to five storeys in Parramatta, NSW is the largest in the southern hemisphere. The retail and mall area is 1,311,150 ft² *121 810 m²*.

Banks *Earliest*

The oldest of Australia's banks is the Bank of New South Wales set up in 1817 by a group of Sydney merchants and converted to a company in 1828.

Oldest 'antique'

Australia's oldest European artifact is a pewter plate inscribed with a date 25 Oct 1616 found nailed to a post and carried off in February 1697 at the northern end of Dirk Hartog Island (now Cape Inscription). It is now in the Rijks Museum, Amsterdam. The plate left in place of Dirk Hartog's Plate, called the 'Vlamingh Plate', is now in the Western Australia Museum at Perth.

Most valuable silver

The highest price made for a piece of Australian silver has been $12,000 for a claret jug 16¼ in *41,2 cm* tall by Hippolyte Felix Delarue at Ellenden's of Sydney on 22 Feb 1979.

Australian national flag

The design for the Flag of Australia was approved by King Edward VII in 1903 with a six pointed large Star, amended to seven points in 1908. The outer diameter of this Star was corrected in 1954. The largest national flag ever flown is one of 30 × 60 ft *9,14 × 18,59 m* raised on the Truckstops of Australia flagpole in Campbellfield, Victoria on 3 Feb 1984.

Toy *Most Massive*

The world's most massive toy is the 25 tonne 18,3 m *60 ft* tall rocking horse at Gumerachua, SA.

AGRICULTURE

Cattle station

Australia's largest cattle station is Strangeray Springs, SA, with an area of 11,594 miles² or 7,420,160 acres *3 002 790 ha*.

Sheep station

The largest sheep station is 'Commonwealth Hill', SA with an area of 4080 miles² *10 567 km²* carrying 70,000–90,000 sheep. The most sheep ever on one station was 356,000 at Wellshot, Qld. Currently the largest is Thylungra, Qld, which grazes about 125,000.

Ox Team *Largest*

The largest team of oxen on record is one of 72 bullocks harnessed 6 abreast by Bell Freeman, to pull a 27 ton load of mining machinery on the Burra Road, SA on 23 Jan 1852.

Rice

The highest rice yields in the world are achieved from the Riverina Irrigation Area in New South Wales, with yields of 9–11 tons per hectare.

Wool Sale Records

For world record see p. 173. The world record for lambswool was set in Western Victoria by Mr Merv Mibus of Dunkeld for a bale of superfine Merino at $32 per kg on 17 Feb 1982.

Draught Animals

In 1923 a wagon built by James Bennett of St Mary's, NSW, drawn by 15 horses carried 407 bags or 32 tons of wheat in a single load. At Riana, Tasmania on 15 Oct 1983 a team of 105 bullocks was coupled and driven as a single team.

Shearing records

The Australian record time for shearing a single ewe is 54.5 sec by Kevin Sarre. The Australian record for a day's blade shearing (i.e. by hand) of 7 hr 40 min is 321 Merinos by Jack Howe at Alice Downs, near Blackall, Qld in 1892. This was not beaten by mechanical shearing for 58 years. The current record for a 8 hr day is 500 Merinos by David James Ryan, at Spring Valley, Harrow, Victoria on 23 Aug 1979.

Ploughing

The fastest recorded time in Australia for ploughing an acre *0,404 ha* is 11 min 40.5 sec by Tony Richardson on 16 June 1982 at 'Mt Ireh', Longford, Tasmania.

HUMAN ACHIEVEMENTS

ENDURANCE AND ENDEAVOUR

Discovery and coastal exploration

The earliest incontrovertible recorded sighting of Australia by a European was in 1606 by the Dutch vessel *Duyfken* under Captain Willem Jansz (or Janssen). He discovered what is now known to be the west coast of Cape York, Qld. He doubled back at Cabo Keer-Weer (Cape Turn Again). The earliest European sighting of the west coast of Tasmania (Van Diemen's Land) was in 1642 by Abel Janszoon Tasman (b. Groningen, Holland *c.* 1603, d. 1659).

The earliest European landfall in Western Australia was in 1616 by Dirk Hartog, also a Dutch sea captain, who left behind a pewter plate dated 25 Oct 1616 at what is now Cape Inscription, Dirk Hartog Island, WA. The earliest European landfall on the east coast of the Australian mainland was on 20 Apr 1770 by Captain James Cook (b. Marton, Yorkshire, England 1728) in the British barque *Endeavour* at Cape Everard, Vic. The first landing was at Stringray Harbour (later Botany Bay) by Cook on 28 Apr 1770. The earliest circumnavigation was by Capt Matthew Flinders in 1802–3.

Polar exploration

The first men to reach the South Magnetic Pole were Sir Edgeworth David, KBE, CMG, DSO (1858–1934), who came to Australia from Wales in 1882, and Dr Sir Douglas Mawson, OBE (1882–1958), who came to Sydney aged 4 from Yorkshire, England. This they reached on 16 Jan 1909. Sir Douglas won the Polar medal three times for expeditions in 1908–9, 1911–14, and 1929–31. The first man to go under the Arctic Ice was Sir Hubert Wilkins (1888–1958) who in 1930, in the submarine *Nautilus*, got to within 400 miles *640 km* of the North Pole.

Water speed record (see p. 178)

Deep diving

The only Australian to have been credited with a world best performance for deep diving was Katherine Troutt, who reached a women's world record depth of 320 ft *97,5 m* in a Scuba dive off Sydney Heads, NSW, on 7 Sept 1964.

High diving

A height of 205 ft 9 in *62,71 m* has traditionally been ascribed to the sensational dive for a £100 fee by Alick Wickham of the Solomon Islands at Deep Rock into the Yarra River, Melbourne before a crowd estimated to be 60,000 in 1918. In 1956 Sir Frank Beaurepaire (1891–1956) published evidence that the promoter's height was highly exaggerated and that the height was in reality 96 ft 5 in *29,38 m*.

Longest marriage

Ernest Edward Dennett (b. 23 Aug 1884) and Clara Elizabeth Lapham (b. 28 June 1887) were married at St Barnabas Church, Sydney on 8 Aug 1904 and celebrated their 77th anniversary in 1981. She died on 27 Feb 1982.

HONOURS, DECORATIONS AND AWARDS

(An asterisk indicates a bar or second award of a decoration.)

The first list of awards of Australian decorations was announced on 14 June 1975. The highest civilian award for distinguished service is the Dame or Knight of the Order of Australia (AC) and the highest bravery award is the Cross of Valour (CV). The first to receive the Knighthood of the Order of Australia was Sir John Kerr AK, GCMG, GCVO on 24 May 1976.

KNIGHTHOOD

Earliest

The earliest conferment of a Knighthood on an Australian was in 1858 on Sir Richard Dry (b. Tasmania 1815–1869).

Youngest

Australia's youngest knight was Sir Ross Macpherson Smith, KBE, MC*, DFC**, AFC (b. Adelaide, 1892–1922) who was only 26 years of age when he was created KBE in 1919 for his flying services.

GREAT ORDERS OF CHIVALRY

The only Australians to have been invested with the Great Orders of Chivalry are Sir Richard Gardiner Casey, Baron Casey KG, PC, GCMG, CH, DSO, MC (1890–1977) and Rt Hon Sir Paul Hasluck KG, PC, GCMG, GCVO who were created Knights of the Order of the Garter in 1979. Rt Hon Sir Robert Menzies, KT, PC, AK, CH, QC, FRS (1894–1978), was created a Knight of the Order of the Thistle in 1963.

PEERAGE RECORDS

The first Australian-born person upon whom a peerage was conferred was Sir John Forrest (b. Bunbury, WA, 1847–1918), the explorer-statesman. He was created Baron Forrest of Bunbury in the year of his death.

The first Australian to take his seat in the House of Lords was the Rt Hon Stanley Melbourne Bruce, CH, MC (b. Melbourne, 1883–1967) as 'Viscount Bruce of Melbourne of Westminster Gardens in the City of Westminster.' He was introduced on 26 Mar 1947.

ORDER OF MERIT

The earliest appointment of an Australian resident to the Order of Merit was that of Sir (Frank) Macfarlane Burnet, OM, KBE on 12 June 1958. He was followed by the Rt Hon Sir Owen Dixon, OM, GCMG (b. 1886) in 1963. Professor George Gilbert Aimé Murray, OM (awarded 1941) was born in Sydney on 2 Jan 1866 but had left Australia aged 11. He died in Oxford, England in 1957.

OLDEST TITLE HOLDER

Australia's oldest titled person was Sir Charles Bickerton Blackburn, KCMG (b. 22 Apr 1874), former Chancellor of Sydney University, who died 16 July 1972 in his 99th year.

Eponymous record

The Australian with his name attached to more geographical features than any other is Sir Ferdinand von Mueller (1825–96), the botanist explorer, with the Mueller Range and Mount Mueller in Western Australia; a non-perennial river, The Mueller; and another Mount Mueller in Northern Territory; Muellers Range in Queensland and Mount von Mueller in Western Australia. His total of published scientific papers exceeded 1000.

Air aces

The most enemy aircraft ever destroyed by an Australian is 47 by Capt. R. A. Little, DSO*, DSC*, RNAS (1895–1918). In World War II Group Capt R. Caldwell, DSO, DFC*, was credited with 28½ kills.

NOBEL PRIZE WINNERS

Earliest and Youngest

Australia's earliest Nobel Prize winner was Sir William Lawrence Bragg, CH, OBE, MC (b. Adelaide, 1890–1971) who won the 1915 Physics Prize for his work (with his father Sir

MISCELLANEOUS ENDEAVOURS

Numerous miscellaneous endurance achievements by Australians or in Australia are recorded in the main section on pp. 183–195.

Banana eating

Michael Gallen of Cairns, Qld, ate 63 bananas in 10 min on 11 Oct 1972.

Bath tub pushing

The greatest distance covered in Australia in 24 hours pushing a wheeled bath tub with a passenger is 411,12 km *255,46 miles* by 25 members of ASIAC on 12–13 Sept 1981 at High Point West Shopping Centre, Maribyrnong, Vic.

Baton Twirling

Sharon Griffiths at Mount Pleasant Shopping Centre, North Mackay, Qld twirled for 86 hr 35 min on 11–15 Jan 1983.

Brick carrying

The record for the annual Narrogin Brick carrying contest in Western Australia (inst. 1960) is 40.0 miles *64,37 km* by Ronald D. Hamilton on 10 Oct 1970. The 8 lb 12 oz *3,968 kg* wire-cut semi-pressed brick has to be carried in a downward pincer position with a nominated ungloved hand.

Dancing

The greatest number of dancers in a single dance is 2,421 to Paul Jabara's disc 'Dance' at the Sydney Entertainment Centre on 14 Aug 1983.

Ballroom

Greg Smith and Marion Alleyne were the first Australians to win a World Amateur Championship in modern ballroom dancing at the Royal Albert Hall, London, on 26 May 1977.

Conga

On 14 Jan at the 1984 Amway Conference in Haymarket, Sydney 3,726 people formed the longest conga line in Australia.

Domino Toppling (Human)

A total of 2761 sub-teenage children (aged 5–12) at Metton Recreation Reserve, Vic on 15 Oct 1982 achieved a kneeling to lying nine pins record in 8 min 0.0 sec without injury or interruption.

Egg throwing

Ian Morris threw a fresh hen's egg 86,3 m *283 ft 1½ in* to catcher John Watts at Dubbo, NSW on 29 Nov 1983.

Gumboot throwing

Roland Doom set the Australian record of 44,2 m *145 ft* at the Pakenham Agricultural and Horticultural Show, Vic, on 11 Mar 1978.

Australia's world champion bedmaker Wendy Wall (see p. 183). (*David F Hoy*)

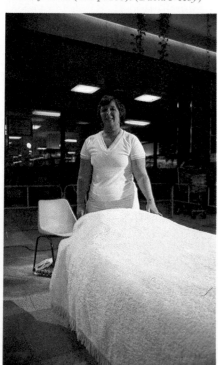

Hair-dressing

Albert di Lallo of Midland, WA, cut, set, and styled hair for 256 hr 35 min on 4–15 June 1978.

Ironing

The longest recorded ironing marathon is one of 127 hr by Michael Speed, at Roselands Shopping Centre, NSW, on 9–14 June 1979.

Kiss of Life

Five members of the Gymea Combined Division of the St John Ambulance Brigade of Oyster Bay, NSW maintained a Kiss of Life for 174 hr on 27 Aug–3 Sept 1980. The patient was a dummy.

Meteorological balloon inflation

David Sparke, a police officer, inflated a meteorological balloon to a diameter of 8 ft *2,43 m* in 2 hr 29 mins on Channel 9 TV on 12 May 1984.

Organ marathon

The longest electric organ-playing marathon in Australia is one of 100 hr by Peter Mason at Heberton, Qld, on 10–14 Sept 1980.

Parachuting

Bill Johnson of Sydney completed 1636 parachute linkups in freefall in Australia to July 1984.

Ramp Jumping

The professional Johnny Fogwell cleared 208 ft 9 in *63,62 m* at Calder Raceway, Melbourne on 13 Apr 1980. The front wheel collapsed on impact.

Rolling pin

The record distance for a woman to throw a 2 lb *907 g* rolling pin is 31,49 m *103 ft 3½ in* by Wendy Graham, 17 at the Moomba Festival, Flinders Park, Melbourne, Vic, on 13 Mar 1983.

Sign Language

The marathon record for maintaining sign language at or above 45 words/min is 35 hr 5 min by George Krams of Randwick on 1–2 Oct 1982.

Skipping

Double Turns	2089	Kevin Brooks, Southport, Qld, Dec 1977
Most Triples (with cross)	37	Mark W. de C. Baker, Sydney, NSW, 12 Aug 1980

Talking *Political speech*

The longest political speech is one of 31 hr 43 min by Rodney Gibson of Brisbane, Qld, on 19–20 Oct 1978.

Walking Underwater

A team of Pamela Dilworth and 5 men walked 82,9 km *51.5 miles* underwater in Sydney Harbour in 48 hrs on 2–4 Sept 1983.

Wheat lumping

The fastest time for carrying a 90 kg *198.4 lb* bag of wheat over 100 m *328 ft* (flying start) is 20.63 sec by Selwyn Neilson of Toowoomba, Qld, on 14 Mar 1981.

Wheelbarrow Pushing

The longest wheelbarrow push was one of some 14 500 km *9000 miles*, from 24 Apr 1975 to 6 May 1978 by Bob Hanley (b. 1913) starting and finishing at Sydney and pushing through Townsville, Qld; Mt Isa, Tennant Creek, Alice Springs, Nullarbor Plain, Perth, Adelaide and Melbourne.

Wool Bale Rolling

The fastest time for rolling a bale of wool (160–170 kg in weight) over a 200 m *656 ft* course is 2 min 23.9 sec by Garry Jackson at Bourke, NSW, on 20 Apr 1984.

Gary Brophy (centre) the champion whip cracker. At the Camden Show, N.S.W. on 6 Apr 1984 he succeeded with a whip 42,27 m *138 ft 8 in* long.

William Bragg, OM, KBE) on X-rays and crystal structures. He is the youngest ever Nobel laureate. Australians who have won Nobel Prizes, all shared for Medicine, are Sir Howard (Walter) (later Lord) Florey, OM (b. Adelaide 1898–1968) for penicillin in 1945; Sir (Frank) Macfarlane Burnet, OM, KBE (b. Traralgon, Vic, 3 Sept 1899) for immunology in 1960; and Sir John (Carew) Eccles (b. Melbourne, 27 Jan 1903) for work on brain nerves in 1963. Patrick Victor Martingdale White (b. 28 May 1912) was awarded the Literature prize in 1973 and Professor John Warcup Cornforth, CBE, FRS, D.Phil. (b. 7 Sept 1917) shared the Chemistry award in 1975.

AUSTRALIAN DECORATIONS

First VC	Sir Neville Reginald Howse (1863–1930)	4 June 1900 Boer War
Youngest living VC	W. O. Keith Payne (b. 30 Aug 1933)	1969 Vietnam
Most Decorations	Capt Sir Ross MacPherson-Smith, KBE, MC*, DFC**, AFC (1892–1922)	Word War I pilot and Aviator
Most initials	Air Com Sir Hughie Edwards, VC, KCMG, CB, DSO, OBE, DFC (1914–1982)	World War II pilot
MM (4 times)	Cpl Ernest A, Corey, MM*** (unique award in 1919) (1888–1972)	World War I stretcher-bearer

THE HUMAN WORLD

POLITICAL AND SOCIAL

The Commonwealth of Australia is the sixth largest country in the world with an area (including Tasmania) of 2,967,900 miles² *7 686 800 km²* and with a total coastline of 22,870 miles *36 800 km.* The population estimate for 1 Jan 1983 was 15,276,100. The UN projections for the population are 16,490,000 in 1985 and 20,245,000 in 2000. Australia ranks 46th in population (one below Sri Lanka) and 54th out of 170 in achieving sovereignty.

States *Largest*
The largest of the six states is Western Australia with an area of 975,924 miles² *2 527 631 km²* but historically New South Wales, although now only the fourth largest State, was, with its western boundary at 135°E, the only political unit until Van Diemen's Land (now Tasmania) was detached from it in 1825. From 1825, when the western boundary of New South Wales was extended for jurisdictional reasons to 129°E, until 1836 when South Australia was carved out of New South Wales, that colony occupied 2,076,300 miles² *5 377 600 km²*. Western Australia is larger than 151 of the 170 entire sovereign countries of the world.

Smallest
The smallest of the six States is Tasmania with 26,383 miles² *68 331 km²*. Tasmania is the world's 24th largest island.

The secession of the 'Hutt River Province' on 21 Apr 1970 is not recognised by the Commonwealth government. This 18,500 acre *7500 ha* holding of 'Prince' Leonard George Casley is 600 km *370 miles* north of Perth.

External territories *Largest*
The largest of the eight external Territories is Australian Antarctic Territory, which is formed from two sectors of the Antarctic continent, and covers 2,500,000 miles² *6 475 000 km²* (excluding ice shelf).

Smallest
The smallest of the eight external Territories are the Coral Sea Islands, a group of scattered reefs and islands spread over a sea area of 4,000,000 miles² *10 000 000 km²* with an actual land area of a few square miles.

Boundaries
South Australia, uniquely of the mainland States, has boundaries with all four of the others, as well as the internal territory of Northern Territory. The longest Great Circle boundary in the world is the 1161 miles *1868 km* division between Western Australia and Northern Territory and South Australia.

States *Most populous*
The most populous of the six States is New South Wales with 5,365,100 (1 Jan 1984). But Victoria is the most densely populated state with 46 persons per mile² *18 person per km²*.

Australia ranks equal eleventh in the world in national life expectancy at 74 years.

Least populous
The least populous of the six States is Tasmania with 433,300 (1 Oct 1983). But the least densely populated state is Western Australia with 1.4 persons per mile² *0,5 person per km²*. Northern Territory has a density of only 0.26 persons per mile² *0,10 persons per km²*.

State capitals
Sydney (NSW) has the highest population of the State capitals with 3,310,500 (June 1982). Adelaide, SA, at 72 per cent has the highest proportion of population of any State capital compared with the total State population closely followed by Melbourne and Perth, both at 71%.

Hospital *Largest and Earliest*
Australia's largest general hospital is the Royal Prince Alfred in Sydney, NSW, which has 1196 beds. The earliest hospital was started by John White at Sydney Cove within a month of the arrival of the First Fleet in 1788.

SOVEREIGNS, ROYALTY AND GOVERNORS-GENERAL

Kings and Queens of Australia
A *de facto* consequence of the enactment of the Statute of Westminister of 1931 was that the Sovereign of the United Kingdom of Great Britain and Northern Ireland became the sovereign of the independent Commonwealth of Australia. The style became *de jure* following the Royal Titles Act, 1953. HM Queen Elizabeth became the longest reigning of Australia's four sovereigns on 6 Apr 1967 by exceeding the length of her father's (George VI) reign of 15 years 57 days.

Earliest visits *By Sovereigns*
The earliest visit of a Sovereign of Australia (as Sovereign) to the Continent was by HM Queen Elizabeth on 3 Feb to 1 Apr 1954, during which time all States were visited. Her eleventh visit was in 1981. However, HRH Prince George of Wales (1865–1936), (later as HM King George V the first *de facto* King of Australia) landed (with his elder brother Prince Albert Victor, 1864–1892) in Australia on 15 May 1881 when HMS *Bacchante* put into King George Sound, Albany, WA with a storm-damaged rudder.

Governors General *Oldest*
The longest lived of Australia's Governors General was HE The Rt Hon. Sir Isaac Alfred Isaacs, GCB, GCMG, who died 11 Feb 1948 aged 92 years and 6 months. The oldest serving Governor General was also Sir Isaac who was 80 years and 5 months when he left office on 23 Jan 1936. He was also the first native-born holder of the office.

Youngest
The youngest Governor General was the 5th HE the Rt Hon Sir Thomas Denman, GCMG, KCVO, 3rd Baron Denman, who was 36 years 8 months old on assuming office on 31 July 1911.

Longest span
The longest span of years of service is the 9 years 7 days of HE Brigadier-General the Rt Hon the Hon Sir Alexander Gore Arkwright Hore-Ruthven, VC, GCMG, CB, DSO,* 1st Earl of Gowrie, ending 30 Jan 1945.

LEGISLATURES

Oldest building and legislature
Australia's oldest legislative building is Parliament House, Sydney, NSW which was originally built in 1829. The earliest fully elected (as opposed to partially nominated) legislative assembly was Tasmania's (then Van Diemen's Land) in 1854.

Largest
The largest in membership of the State legislatures is New South Wales' Legislative Assembly which has 99 members. The Federal Parliament's lower house, the House of Representatives, has 127 members.

Smallest
The smallest State legislature is Tasmania's House of Assembly with 35 members. The smallest legislative assembly is that of the Australian Capital Territory with 18 members.

Earliest secret ballot

The earliest popular secret ballot for any legislature in the British Empire was introduced in March 1856 in Victoria. The first State to introduce votes for women was South Australia in 1894 and the first to make voting compulsory was Queensland in 1915.

Smallest majority

The smallest majority in a Commonwealth election was for the Ballarat seat where in 1919 a Federal member was returned with a majority of one.

Referenda *Records*

A Referendum, being required by the Constitution to approve a constitutional change, or used for a controversial issue such as conscription in 1916 or 1917, has been held on 21 occasions, seeking consent to a total of 34 proposals since 1901. Only eight proposals have achieved an affirmative vote, of which the largest majority has been 4,656,106 on 27 May 1967 in favour of the interpretation that the Constitution could not be construed to authorise any discrimination against the Aboriginals.

Prime Ministers *Oldest*

The longest lived of Australia's Prime Ministers was the Rt Hon William Morris (Billy) Hughes, CH, who was born in Pimlico, London on 25 Sept 1862 and died on 28 Oct 1952 aged 90 years 33 days.

Youngest

The youngest Prime Minister was Hon John Christian Watson (1867–1941) who was 37 years and 18 days old when he took office on 27 Apr 1904.

Longest span

The longest span of years of service (not continuous) as Prime Minister is the 26 years 9 months by the Rt Hon Sir Robert Gordon Menzies, KT, AK, CH, QC, FRS (b. Victoria 20 Dec 1894 d. 15 May 1978) from 26 Apr 1939 to 26 Jan 1966. During the period he was continuously in office for a record period of 16 years 1 month from 19 Dec 1949 to the end of his 8th ministry on 26 Jan 1966.

Shortest span

Rt Hon Francis, Michael Forde (b. Mitchell, Qld, 1890) was Prime Minister of Australia for only 8 days from 6 to 13 July 1945.

Most times

Sir Robert Menzies was sworn Prime Minister eight times. (See *Longest span*).

State Premiers *Longest span*

Hon Sir Thomas Playford, GCMG (1896–1981) was Premier of South Australia from 5 Nov 1938 to 10 Mar 1965, a continuous period of over 26 years which is a British Commonwealth record. His grandfather was also State Premier of South Australia twice between 1887 and 1893.

Oldest

John Thomas 'Jack' Lang (b. 21 Dec 1876), Premier of New South Wales 1925–7 and 1930–2, died in Sydney on 27 Sept 1975 aged 98.

Legislators *Youngest*

William Arthur Neilson (b. 27 Aug 1925), later Tasmanian Premier, was first elected on 23 Nov 1946 aged 21 years 3 months.

MILITARY AND DEFENCE

War *Costliest*

Of the eight wars in which Australia has been involved since the Sudan Expedition of 1885, the country lost most in World War I (1914–18). A total of 59,342 were killed which was the highest proportion to population of any part of the British Empire. The World War II (1939–45) figure was 27,073 killed or died of wounds or as prisoners of the Japanese. The highest enlistment was 993,000 in World War II. The total armed strength in mid-1984 was 72,473 (Army 32,850; Air Force, 22,477 and Navy 17,146). The peak expenditure was attained on the 1942–3 Defence vote of £499,420,000 (*$998.84 million*).

Battle of Britain

Twenty-two Australian pilots took part in the Battle of Britain in 1940. Fourteen were killed, giving a casualty rate of over 63 per cent which was higher than any of the other 13 participating nations on the side of the Allies.

Attacks on Australia *Most severe*

Japanese aircraft attacked Darwin, NT, on twelve occasions from 19 Feb 1942 to 21 Aug 1943. The opening raid cost 240 killed and 11 ships sunk.

Navy warship *Largest*

The Royal Australian Navy's largest ship is HMAS *Supply* (26,500 tonnes) built in Belfast. The largest built in Australia is the fleet flagship and destroyer tender HMAS *Stalwart* (15,500 tonnes).

Fastest

The Navy's fastest ships are the 35 knot Perth class Guided-Missile Armed Destroyers HMAS *Brisbane*, HMAS *Hobart* and HMAS *Perth*.

Earliest action

Three Australian-manned warships took part in the Boxer campaign in China in 1900. The RAN's (instituted October 1911) first victory was the sinking of the German light cruiser *Emden* near the Cocos (Keeling) Islands by HMAS *Sydney* in November 1914.

Army *Earliest action*

The earliest occasion when Australian troops were in action was in 1885 when 750 men participated in the Sudan campaign. The peak enlistment was 691,400 men and 35,800 women for World War II (1939–45).

Highest rank

The highest rank attained by any Australian-born serviceman was the promotion to Field Marshal in 1950 of General Sir Thomas Albert Blamey, GBE, KCB, CMG, DSO (b. Wagga, NSW, 1884, d. 1951).

Most famous war hero

Australia's most renowned war hero was the legendary 'man with the donkey' who for 25 days of charmed life rescued numerous wounded at Gallipoli, Turkey, in 1915 and was then inevitably killed. He was established to be Private John Simpson Kirkpatrick (b. Durham, England, 1893) who had emigrated to Australia in 1910.

Air Force *Earliest*

Although the Royal Australian Air Force was established by proclamation on 31 Mar 1921 it was preceded by the Australian Flying Corps, a small élite force raised in 1915.

Largest explosion

Australia's greatest explosion resulted from the testing of United Kingdom atomic devices at the Monte Bello Islands off North West Cape, WA, in 1952.

War memorial *Largest*

The war memorial bearing most Australian names is The Villers–Bretonneux Memorial, east of Amiens, France, with 10,800 names of those without known graves who were killed in 1914–18.

War cemetery *Largest*

The cemetery containing the largest number of Australian war graves is The Port Moresby (Bomana) War Cemetery with 3347 graves and a memorial to 707 other Australians who died in 1939–45 without known graves.

JUDICIAL

Bush rangers

The earliest bush rangers were escaped convicts or 'bolters' who used the 'bush' as a base for their robbing activities. The earliest recorded was Black Caesar (*fl.* 1790–6), a Negro convict from the First Fleet, who was shot in 1796. Matthew Brady (1799–1826) terrorised areas of Tasmania in the period 1824–6 after escaping from Port Macquarie. He was arraigned on 300 charges, including numerous murder charges, after capture by John Batman (1801–39). The most chronicled of all bush rangers was Edward (Ned) Kelly (1855–80), who killed three policemen at Stringybark Creek and made two daring bank robberies in 1878–9. He was hanged in Melbourne on 11 Nov 1880.

Executions

Two septuple hangings were recorded in Australian criminal history. In 1838 Sir George Gipps (1791–1847) had 11 men retried for the massacre of Aborigines. Seven were later hanged. In 1857 seven men were hanged for the murder of John Giles Price (1808–57) aboard a prison hulk at Williamstown, Melbourne. Before the existence of an effective civil judiciary nine men of the Castle Hill Irish convict rebellion near Parramatta, NSW, were hanged by the Military, commanded by Major George Johnston.

Most Murder Charges

Arthur Hatton, 88 was charged in Sydney with 16 murders following a fire at Sylvania Nursing Home on 29 Apr 1981.

Last hanging

Ronald Ryan was the last murderer to be hanged. He was executed in Melbourne at 8 am on 3 Feb 1967. The last woman hanged in Australia was the murderess Mrs Jean Lee, 30, in Melbourne in 1951. Hanging was abolished in Apr 1975. The first state to abolish capital punishment was Queensland, in 1922.

Longest Criminal Trial

Six Jugoslav males were found guilty of conspiring to make and ignite explosives in Sydney on 9 Feb 1981 after a trial lasting 10 months.

Highest damages

In July 1980 Miss Debbie Snow, 24, was awarded $2,500,000 in the Supreme Court, Sydney for injuries received in the Granville, NSW rail disaster of 18 Jan 1977 which left her paraplegic and an amputee.

Greatest robbery

Australia's greatest robbery was at the Bank of New South Wales branch at Murwillumbah, NSW on 22 Nov 1978 when $1,763,000 was removed from their vault.

Most successful policeman

Australia's most successful enforcer of the law has been Sgt Jack 'Dead-Eye' Murphy of Melbourne, who between 1923 and his retirement in June 1948 shot below the waist eight criminals on the run. He also so outwitted *cockatoos* (sentries for illegal two-up gambling schools) that he secured 10,000 convictions in the period 1943–8.

ECONOMIC

Highest GNP

Australia's highest published figure for Gross National Product was $163,815 million for the year 1982–83. Australia ranks 12th in the latest World Bank rankings of the richest nations with US$11,140 per head in 1982.

Greatest Deficit

The estimated 1983–4 budget deficit was $8361 million. The actual deficit, announced in June 1984, was $7961 million.

Trade unions

Currently Australia's largest trade union is the Amalgamated Metals Foundry and Shipwrights Union. Total union membership on 30 April 1984 was 159,382.

Largest organisation

The largest membership of any Australian organisation is the Returned Services League of Australia whose membership at 31 Dec 1983 was 270,215 plus 25,107 Women Auxiliaries. The longest enjoyment of the Office of the Federal President of 'RSL' was 27 years by Sir Gilbert Dyett, CMG (1891–1965) from 1919 to 1946.

Beer consumption

The highest beer consumption in the world is attributed to Northern Territory, Australia, where peak consumption has been estimated as high as 52 gallons *236,31* per person per annum. The national average was 128.8 litres *226.8 pints* per head in 1981—second only to West Germany. A Society for the Prevention of Alcoholism in Darwin had to be disbanded in June 1966 for lack of support.

Biggest Breakfast on the Beach

An estimated 8,000 attended the beach breakfast at North Beach, Wollongong, NSW on 8 Feb 1983 thrown by Radio 2WL.

Largest Jelly

The world's largest jelly, a 35 000 litre *7700 gal* water melon flavoured pink jelly made by Paul Squires and Geoff Ross worth $14,000 was set at Roma Street Forum, Brisbane, Qld on 5 Feb 1981 in a tank by Pool Fab.

Roads *Earliest*

The first proper road in Australia was made in the first year of settlement 1788 on the order of Governor Arthur Phillip (1738–1814) who wanted to connect his house with the Dawes Battery.

Straightest

The 145 km *90 mile* stretch from Balladonia to Caiguna, WA, on Eyre Highway is dead straight.

Street *Widest*

The widest street planned for Australia was the main street of Sydney at 200 ft *60,96 m* as drafted by Augustus Theodore Henry Alt (1731–1815) the Surveyor General with the First Fleet. Unfortunately his plan was never adopted.

Longest

The longest sealed highway in Australia is the Stuart Highway, NT which connects Darwin to Alice Springs, 954 miles *1535 km* to the south. It was completed in 1943 for military reasons as a consequence of the Japanese air attacks on Darwin. The longest designated highway is Highway No 1 of 7700 miles *12 390 km* from north of Cairns clockwise to Darwin NT.

Banknotes *Earliest and Highest Denominations*

The earliest Commonwealth of Australia banknotes were those of 15 private banks and the Queensland Government superscribed in black, signed by Jas R. Collins and Geo. T. Allen and dated '1st Dec. 1910'. Private notes had been issued since 1817 by the Bank of New South Wales in denominations of 2s 6d.,

---

ACCIDENTS & DISASTERS (*Worst on record by categories in Australia*)

	Death Roll	
Influenza pandemic	10,000	Mainly in New South Wales—January-December 1919.
Bubonic plague	550	From Jan 1900 to 1910 there were 1200 reported cases—mainly from Erskine St Wharf, Sydney—of which 550 were fatal.
Marine	406	*Cataraqui*, a migrant ship foundered off King Island Bass Strait, 4 Aug 1835 (the worst location for wrecks—57 recorded).
Military insurrection	237	Cowra, NSW breakout from Japanese No. 12 Prisoner of War Camp (234 Japanese killed, 3 Australian Guards including Pte B. G. Hardy, GC and Pte R. Jones, GC 5 Aug 1944.
Mining	96	Mt Kembla, NSW underground explosion, 31 July 1902.
Flood	89	Gundagai, NSW, June 1852.
Railway	82	Granville Station, NSW Bridge stuck, then collapsed (also 83 injured) 18 Jan 1977.
Naval	82	HMAS *Voyager* collision with HMAS *Melbourne* off Jervis Bay, NSW on 10 Feb 1964.
Bushfire	76	Victoria and South Australia, 16 Feb 1983.
Tropical cyclone	65	Cyclone Tracy, Darwin, NT, 24–25 Dec 1974. Wind reached 134.8 mph *217 km/h*. Insurance pay-out $350 million but much property was underinsured. 140 were seriously injured, 55,000 were airlifted out.
Aircraft	37	Lae, New Guinea, Lockheed crashed 18 Apr 1948.
Bridge collapse	35	Westgate Bridge, Lower Yarra, Melbourne, 15 Oct 1970.
Riot	28–31	Eureka Stockade, near Ballarat, 3 Dec 1854.

In financial terms Australia's greatest natural disaster has been declared to be the floods of 29 Mar 1974. In the State of Queensland alone, rehabilitation payments have been estimated at a minimum of $50,000,000.

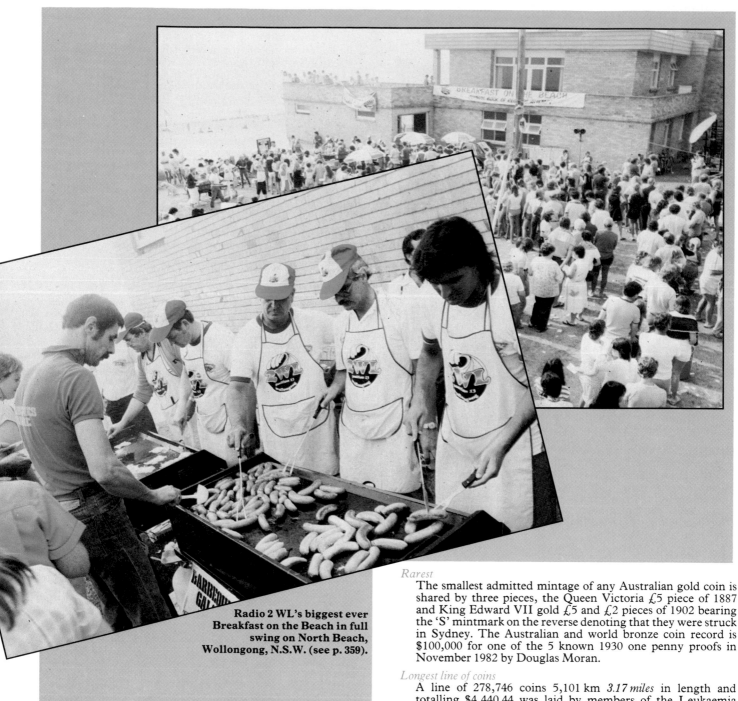

Radio 2 WL's biggest ever Breakfast on the Beach in full swing on North Beach, Wollongong, N.S.W. (see p. 359).

Rarest

The smallest admitted mintage of any Australian gold coin is shared by three pieces, the Queen Victoria £5 piece of 1887 and King Edward VII gold £5 and £2 pieces of 1902 bearing the 'S' mintmark on the reverse denoting that they were struck in Sydney. The Australian and world bronze coin record is $100,000 for one of the 5 known 1930 one penny proofs in November 1982 by Douglas Moran.

Longest line of coins

A line of 278,746 coins 5,101 km *3.17 miles* in length and totalling $4,440.44 was laid by members of the Leukaemia Foundation of Queensland at Evandale, Qld on 4 Dec 1982.

Telephone

The telephone was introduced to Australia in 1878. By June 1983 there were 8,266,600 telephones (538 per 1000 people) in Australia, of which 3,091,600 were in NSW. The total number of calls made in 1982–83 was 6,451,700,000.

Postage stamps *Earliest*

The earliest adhesive stamp of any kind to be issued in Australia was the New South Wales 1d. crimson lake 'Sydney view' on 1 Jan 1850. The first uniform series of stamps of the Commonwealth of Australia were 15 denominations of the Kangaroo and Map issue of January 1913. On 26 Sept 1975 six 1913 halfpenny kangaroo stamps were sold for $3300.

Highest catalogued value and Rarest

The highest value for any Australian stamp is $22,000 for one of the 15 known used specimens of the 4d. deep dull blue Western Australian black swan issue of 1854 with the error of an inverted frame. This was auctioned in Melbourne on 1 July 1977. A *tête bech* pair of George V 2d reds was sold at the same

5s., 10s., £1 and for £5. The first distinctive Commonwealth of Australia note was the blue ten-shilling note issued in May 1913. The highest denominations issued for currency were the £100 private banknotes superscribed in 1910 and the blue £100 Commonwealth note in 1914; a blue £1000 was issued for inter-bank settlements in 1914.

Coins *Gold*

The Adelaide Assay Office Type 1 gold pound was minted in 1852. An example was sold for US$82,000 in Sydney on 20 Nov 1980. The last Imperial gold coins minted in Australia were at Perth and Melbourne in 1931. The proof Gold $200 22 carat piece sale price was fixed at £310 in August 1980.

sale for $26,000. A unique perforate 11 × 11 Die 2 Two-penny Postage Due was discovered in 1972 by Mr Trevor Ross in Melbourne.

Highest price

The highest price quoted for a regular issue is $1819 for an unused specimen of the South Australian £20 claret of 1886.

EDUCATION

University Oldest

The oldest of Australia's 19 Universities is the University of Sydney founded in 1850.

Schools Oldest

Australia's first schools of any sort were Sunday Schools set up by the Rev Richard Johnson (1753–1827), chaplain to the First Fleet (1788). The first school teacher was Isabella Rosson, one of the 188 convict women.

Australia's earliest state-assisted schools were on Norfolk Island in December 1793. The first public school was founded by William Cape (1773–1847) at Sydney in 1824. Compulsory education was first introduced in Victoria in 1872.

Most Expensive

The most expensive public school in membership with the Headmasters conference is Geelong C. of E. Grammar School, Corio (founded 1855), with annual fees of $6930.

Longest teaching career

Christopher Carroll, BEM (b. 19 June 1902) began teaching on 1 Mar 1920 and died in his classroom at St Thomas' Christian Brothers' College, Melbourne, Vic, on 17 Oct 1975 after a continuous career of 55 years, of which 50 years 7 months was at one school.

Youngest headmaster

Alfred Carson was appointed headmaster of Geraldton School, WA, in 1878 at the age of 19.

Schools in the air

The earliest of the two-way radio schools devised to educate children in very remote districts, was established at Alice Springs, NT in 1951.

RELIGION

Earliest *Anglican*

The earliest Christian religious service held in Australia was on the second Sunday after the arrival of the First Fleet conducted under a tree by the Rev Richard Johnson on 3 Feb 1788. His text was 'What shall I render unto the Lord for all his benefits towards me.' The earliest church was built under his direction and opened on 25 Aug 1793. It burned down on 10 Oct 1798. The first Bishop of Australia was William Grant Broughton (1788–1853), appointed in 1836.

Roman Catholic

The first Mass was celebrated by the pardoned prisoner Rev James Dixon on 15 May 1803. The earliest Roman Catholic church established in Australia, at the instigation of the Rev John Joseph Therry, was St Mary's Cathedral, Sydney, in 1829. The first Roman Catholic Bishop was John Bede Polding (1794–1877) who was created Metropolitan of Australia on the detaching of Australia from the see of Mauritius in 1842. Australia's first cardinal was Patrick Frances Moran (1830–1911) who was nominated in 1885.

Tallest church

The greatest height of any Australian church is at St Patrick's Cathedral, Melbourne, at 340 ft *103,63 m*.

SPORTS, GAMES AND PASTIMES

ALL SPORTS

Largest crowd

Australia's largest sporting crowd to pass through turnstiles was the 121,696 at the 1970 Rules Grand Final—about one person to every 100 in the entire continent.

Most participants

The greatest number of participants in an Australian sporting event was the 33,708 entries in the City-to-Surf 14 km run in Sydney on 7 Aug 1983, of which *c.* 28,000 finished.

Youngest international

Brooke Dixon (b. 8 Dec. 1967) was 12 yr 22 days when she crewed for Max Barcham in the World Mirror Dinghy Championships at Perth, WA on 20 Dec 1979. Bronwyn McCaskill (b. 30 June 1966) was 12 yr 123 days when she was placed second for Australia in the World Barefoot Ski championship in Canberra on 31 Oct 1978.

Oldest champion

William Herbert Northam (now Sir) (skipper) (b. 28 Sept 1905) won an Olympic gold medal at the Tokyo Games on 21 Oct 1964 in the 5.5 m sailing event when aged 59 yr 23 days.

BADMINTON

Australia's first Badminton club was formed in Perth in 1900. The Australian Badminton Association was founded in 1935.

Most international appearances

George Robotham (NSW) (b. 1938) holds the men's record

with 15 caps up to 1969. The record for women is 15 by Audrey Swaby (WA) (b. 31 May 1958), 1976–83.

Marathon

Will Nayar (28) and Gary Miles (27) played badminton singles for 72 hr 30 min at Sorrento/Duncraig Community Centre, WA, from 1–4 June 1979.

BASEBALL

Baseball was first played in Australia by American immigrant miners in 1856. It was not played by Australians until 1885. The Australian Baseball Council (now Federation) was formed in 1933.

The record number of wins in the Claxton Shield (inst. 1934) inter-state competition is 15 by South Australia to 1980.

Ian Butcher hit five consecutive home runs for Fremantle Braves *v.* South Perth in a West Australian League match on 24 Jan 1982.

BASKETBALL

The national men's team championship (inst. 1946) has been won 18 times by Victoria (1948–82). The women's title (inst. 1955) has been won 13 times by South Australia (1955–83).

National league records

Reginald Leonardo Biddings (b. 23 Feb 1957) scored a record 63 points for Forestville Eagles (98) *v.* Bankstown Bruins (90) on 12 Apr 1981.

The most points scored in a career is 2,307 in 114 games, 1979–83, by Herb McEachen (b. 29 Nov 1954) for Canberra Mazda Cannons. The highest scoring average is 33.3 by Rocky Smith with 734 points in 22 games for St Kilda in 1980.

The most points scored by a team is 160 by Coburg Giants *v.* Frankston Bears (118) on 17 Mar 1984 and by Adelaide 36ers *v.* Hobart Devils (127) on 18 Mar 1984. The latter, at 287, is the aggregate score record.

The biggest winning margin is 88 for the 154–66 win by Coburg Giants over Sydney Supersonics on 6 May 1984.

Most wins in the Australian Championships (instituted 1935)			
Event	Times	Holder	Year
Men's Singles	6	Alan S. McCabe	1938–9, 1948–50, 1952
		Ong Eng Hong	1955–9, 1960–2
Women's Singles	6	Judy A. Nyirati	1969–73, 1975
Most titles including doubles:			
Men	17	Peter Cooper	between 1971 and 1980
Women	14	Kay Terry	between 1964 and 1977

BILLIARDS AND SNOOKER

Billiards

The first billiards match played in Australia was a grand challenge match for £100 in Sydney in 1836 between six gentlemen.

The Australian Amateur Billiards Championship (inst. 1920) has been won most often by Robert Marshall with 19 titles between 1936 and 1970. He also won a record four world amateur titles in 1936, 1938, 1951 and 1962. Walter Lindrum, (1898–1960), world champion in 1933 and 1934, was Australia's most successful professional.

Snooker

In 1978 Edward 'Eddie' Charlton (b. 31 Oct 1929) won the Australian Professional snooker championship for a record 18th time. The Amateur title (inst. 1953) has been won a record eight times by Max Williams between 1961 and 1973.

BOWLS (LAWN)

The most championships (inst. 1912–13) is six by Glynn de Villiers Bosisto (b. 15 Feb 1899) (Vic) with four singles (1949, 1951–3) and two fours (1951, 1957).

Keith Frank Poole (b. 24 Apr 1927) (Qld) represented Australia on a record ten occasions including the 1982 Commonwealth Games.

BOXING

The first fight recorded in Australia was when John Berringer (Parton) beat Charles Lifton (Sefton) over 56 rounds at Sydney Racecourse on 7 Jan 1814.

Largest crowd

The largest boxing crowd was 32,500 when Jimmy Carruthers (b. 5 July 1929) successfully defended his World Bantamweight title against Henry 'Pappy' Gault (USA) at Sydney Sports Ground on 13 Nov 1953.

Olympic Games

Australia's best Olympic performance is the silver medal won by Reginald Leslie 'Snowy' Baker (1884–1953) in the middle-weight final against John William Henry Tyler Douglas (GB) (1882–1930) on 27 Oct. 1908.

Most titles

Kerry Wayne Devlin (Tas.) (b. 17 July 1944) has won eight national amateur titles at welterweight and light-middleweight between 1970 and 1977. Three Australian professional titles have been held simultaneously by Billy Grime (1902–52),

Jim Webb of Wyoming, NSW, achieved the world record for the tenpin bowling marathon, playing for 195 hr 1 min. He bowled solidly for the first 36 hours before taking only a five minute break. (See main section).

feather, light and welter in 1927, and by Dave Sands (1926–52), middle, light-heavy and heavy in 1950.

Longest unbeaten run

Albert Griffiths 'Young Griffo' (1869–1927) won 115 fights before losing his 116th to Jack McAuliffe on 27 Aug 1894.

Shortest fight

The fastest knockout in an Australian title fight was 25 sec from bell to count out, when Herb Narvo (1913–58) won the heavyweight title from Billy Britt on 3 Apr 1943 at Newcastle, NSW. At Brisbane on 2 Nov 1951 Ian Gordon beat Frank Brooks, the referee stopping the fight at seven seconds.

Longest and shortest reigns as Australian Champions

Jack Carroll (1906–76) held the welterweight title for 9 yr 11 months, 1928–38. Tiger Payne held the heavyweight title for only eight days (18–26 Dec 1926).

Youngest and Oldest champions

Jackie Green (b. 12 Nov 1901) won a disputed Australian flyweight title in 1916 aged only 15. The oldest champion was Jerry Jerome (1874–1950) who won the middleweight title on 1 Feb 1913, aged 38 yr 264 days.

Heaviest and Tallest

Les McNabb weighed 22 st 3 lb *141 kg* when he fought his first fight in 1943. He was weighed on a railway weighbridge. The tallest Australian boxer was the late Jules Brancourt, the 1922 amateur heavyweight champion at 6 ft 11 in *2,11 m* who weighed 17 st *107,9 kg* and had a reach of 86 in *2,18 m*.

Greatest weight difference

The greatest difference in an Australian title fight was 83 lb *37,6 kg* when Herb Narvo (196 lb *88,9 kg*) knocked out Les McNabb (279 lb *126,5 kg*) on 8 Apr 1944 at Newcastle, NSW.

CANOEING

Most titles

Dennis Allan Green (b. 26 May 1931) won 64 Australian canoeing titles from 1955 to 1971 and secured, with Walter 'Wally' William Brown, the Olympic bronze medal for the Kayak Pairs at Melbourne in 1956.

Long distance

Ray Fisher and Ray Asmus canoed 2290 miles *3678 km* from Warwick, Qld via the Condamine, Balonne, Darling and Murray rivers to Goolwa, SA from 1 April to 20 June 1979. David L. McManus of the RAAF canoed 2225 km *1382 miles* down the Murray River from Hume Weir, Albury, NSW to Goolwa, SA in 16 days 16 hr 53 min from 15 Nov–1 Dec 1981.

CHESS

The most wins in the Australian Championships, since the Australian Chess Foundation was formed in 1922, is four by Cecil J. S. Purdy (NSW) (b. Egypt, 27 Mar 1907) (1935, 1937, 1949 and 1951) and Lajos Steiner (NSW) (b. Hungary, 14 June 1903) (1945, 1947, 1953 and 1959). Stanislas Christodoulou, at the Chevron Hotel, Melbourne, played 314 opponents in 24 hours on 29–30 Jan 1978. He lost only 16 games.

CRICKET—FIRST-CLASS

(*Records in this section apart from career records apply to those set by Australians in Australia*)

BATTING

Innings *Highest and Lowest*

See main entry for highest innings. The lowest recorded innings is 15 made by Victoria v. the Marylebone Cricket Club (MCC) at Melbourne on 9 Feb 1904. One man was absent ill.

Greatest victory

The greatest recorded margin of victory is an innings and 666 runs, when Victoria (1059) beat Tasmania at Melbourne on 2–3 Feb 1923. The greatest margin in a Sheffield Shield match is an innings and 656 runs, Victoria (1107) beat New South Wales at Melbourne on 24–29 Dec 1926.

Fastest scoring

In a Tasmania v. New South Wales match at Hobart on 26 Feb 1910, New South Wales scored a total of 448 at the rate of 110.61 runs for each 100 balls bowled.

See main section for fastest hundred by David Hookes, when having scored 137 in the first innings he became the first to score two centuries in a match three times in Sheffield Shield matches.

Highest individual innings

The highest individual innings is 452 not out in 6 hr 55 min by Sir Donald George Bradman (b. 27 Aug 1908) for New South Wales v. Queensland at Sydney on 4 and 6 Jan 1930. The record for a Test match in Australia is 307 in 12 hr 7 min by Robert Maskew Cowper (b. 5 Oct 1940) for Australia v. England at Melbourne on 12, 14 and 16 Feb 1966.

Most runs

Sir Donald Bradman (NSW and SA) holds the records for most runs in a career—28,067 from 1927—8 to 1948-9 and most runs in a season—1690 in 24 innings (six not out) at an average of 93.88 in 1928-9. He scored 6996 runs in 52 Tests (av. 99.94), including 29 centuries from 1928 to 1948. Most runs in Tests were scored by Gregory Stephen Chappell (b. 7 Aug 1948) with 7110 (av. 53.86) in 87 Tests from 1970 to 1984. Graham Neil Yallop (Vic) (b. 7 Oct 1952) scored a record 1834 runs (av. 107.88), including 8 centuries in Australia in a calendar year—1983.

The highest season's average by a batsman scoring 1000 runs is 152.12 by William Harold Ponsford (b. 19 Oct 1900) for 1217 runs in eight innings in 1927-8.

Most hundreds

The most hundreds in a season by an Australian is eight by Sir Donald Bradman in only 12 innings in the 1947-8 season and the most in a career is 117 also by Bradman between 1927 and 1949.

Record stand

The record stand for any partnership is 456 for the first wicket by William Ponsford (248) and Edgar Richard Mayne (1883–1961) (209) for Victoria v. Queensland at Melbourne in December 1923.

BOWLING

Most wickets

The most wickets taken in a season is 106 at an average of 13.59 by Charles Thomas Biass Turner (1862–1944) of New South Wales, in 1887-8. The record for a career is by Clarence Victor Grimmett (1891–1980) of Victoria and South Australia, who took 1424 wickets at an average of 22.28 between 1911–12 and 1940–1. The most wickets in Test matches have been taken by Dennis Lillee (see main section).

The taking of all ten wickets *in an innings* by a single bowler has been recorded four times in first-class cricket in Australia, the least expensive analysis being by Thomas Welbourn 'Tim' Wall (1904–81) of South Australia, who took all ten wickets for 36 runs against New South Wales at Sydney on 3 Feb 1933.

The most wickets in a match is 17 by George Giffen (1859–1927) of South Australia for 201 runs (9–91 and 8–110) for South Australia v. Victoria at Adelaide on 11–15 Mar 1886.

Wicket-keeping

Rodney Marsh holds the record for dismissals by wicket keeper in Test cricket (see main section) and in career—868, 1968-84.

FIELDING

Most catches

The greatest number of catches in an innings is six by James Francis Sheppard (c. 1889–1944) for Queensland v. New South Wales at Brisbane on 7 Nov 1914. Seven catches in a match have been held by Hugh Trumble (1867–1938) for Victoria v. South Australia at Melbourne in Dec–Jan 1900-1, by James Archibald Atkinson (1896–1956) for Tasmania v. Victoria at Melbourne in February 1929, by Eric Walter Freeman (b. 13 July 1944) for South Australia v. Western Australia at Adelaide in January 1972, and by Greg Chappell for Australia v. England at Perth in Dec 1974.

Sheffield Shield

The trophy for the inter-state championship (inst. 1892) has been won a record 37 times by New South Wales between 1896 and 1983. In 1978 Western Australia won with a record total of 147 points.

Youngest and Oldest

The youngest Australian to play in a Test match is Ian Davis Craig (b. 12 June 1935) who was aged 17 yr 239 days v. South Africa at Melbourne in February 1953. The youngest to play first-class cricket is Leonard John Junor (b. 28 Apr 1914) who was only 15 yr 266 days when he represented Victoria v. Western Australia at Melbourne on 18 Jan 1930. Robert Cameron (b. 6 Sept 1935) played for the South Australian country team v. the South African touring team aged 14 yr 167 days in February 1953. John Marshall (c. 1795–1876) played for Tasmania v. Victoria on 8 Mar 1854 when aged about 59 yr, but the oldest whose date of birth has been confirmed is George Moore (1000 1916) aged 51 yr 0 days when he played for New South Wales v. Victoria at Sydney on 8 Mar 1873.

CRICKET—MINOR

Batting

The highest score ever compiled by an Australian batsman is 566 runs in a minor match between Break o' Day and Wellington by Charles John Eady (1870–1945) at Hobart on 15, 21 March and 2 April 1902 in 7 hr 53 min or 71.79 runs per hour. Don Bradman scored a century off 22 balls in three overs at Blackheath, NSW, in 1931-2.

A record partnership of 641 was set by T. Patton and N. Rippon for Buffalo v. Whorouley at Gapsted, Vic. in 1913–14.

Wicket-keeping

Lee Andrews made nine catches in an innings for Bankstown-Canterbury v. Sydney University on 27 Nov 1982. Seven stumpings in an innings were made by Rex P. Blundell for West Torrens District CC v. Woodville District CC on 18 Oct 1969 at Thebarton Oval, SA, and by E. J. Long for North Sydney v. Burwood at Sydney in 1909–10.

CROQUET

Croquet was first played in Australia by English migrants in the 19th century. The Australian Croquet Council was formed in 1949 and the first national championships held in 1950.

The greatest number of Australian singles titles won is nine by Thomas William Howat (b. 18 Mar 1912) (Vic) between 1955 and 1968. In addition, with his wife, he won two doubles titles in 1959 and 1965. Spencer Buck (b. 13 Oct 1955), in 1980, is the only man to win all five events at the annual Australian Croquet Carnival.

In March 1984 Australia won for the first time the American International Challenge Cup, beating the USA 16–8.

CYCLING

The Boneshakers Club organised the first cycle race in 1869.

World Championships

The most world titles won by an Australian is four by Sid Patterson (b. 1927), two amateur (one sprint, one pursuit) and two professional pursuit, from 1949 to 1953.

Olympic titles

Australia's most successful Olympic cyclist was Russell Mockridge (1929–58) who won two gold medals (1000 m time trial and 2000 m tandem) at Helsinki in 1952.

Most National titles

Edgar Laurence 'Duncan' Gray (b. 17 July 1906) won most Australian Amateur Track Cycling Championships (inst. 1888) with 20 from 1928 to 1940. The most won at one meeting is five by Russell Mockridge (Vic) at Bundaberg in 1950 and at Adelaide in 1952 and by Richard Ploog (b. 1936) at Brisbane in 1957. Mac Sloane (Tas) won 13 Professional titles 1947–57. Bob Ryan (NSW) won five professional sprint titles in 1967–73.

Warrnambool Road Race

The race from Melbourne to Warrnambool (or in the reverse direction) (inst. 1895) is the oldest existing race in the world. The fastest time off scratch for the 161 miles *259,1 km* is 5 hr 37 min 10 sec by Wayne Hildred on 11 Oct 1980.

Trans-continental record

The record from Perth to Sydney (2798 miles *4502 km*) is 11 days 29 min by Bruce Hunt of Bayswater, WA in Nov 1974.

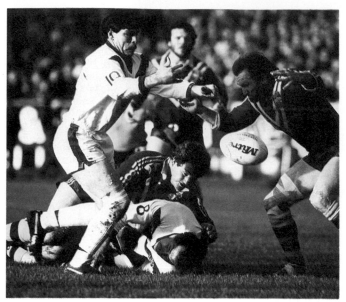

The unbeaten Australian 1982 touring team convincingly beat Great Britain in all three Tests, 40–4, 27–6 and 32–8. (*All-Sport*)

DARTS

Australasian Championships were first held in 1964, women's singles were introduced in 1972 and men's doubles in 1976. The most singles wins have been achieved by: men—4 Matt Bunovich, WA 1965–66, 1968 and 1971; women—3 Dawn Aitken, NZ 1975–6, 1978.

EQUESTRIAN SPORTS

Olympic titles

Australia's best Olympic performance was two gold and one silver medal at the 1960 Games at Rome. Lawrence Morgan (b. 5 Feb 1918) won the individual three-day event on *Salad Days* from Neale Lavis (b. 11 June 1930) (Australia) on *Mirrabooka*. Both shared with James William 'Bill' Roycroft (b. 17 Mar 1915) on *Our Solo* the team gold medal.

Long distance

Wally Eaglesham rode *Ben Hall* 1463 miles *2354 km* from Rockhampton, Queensland to Melbourne, Vic, between 24 Dec 1975 and 21 Feb 1976.

FENCING

Australia's oldest fencing club is the Sydney Swords Club founded in 1913.

Gregory Laurie Benkö (Vic) (b. 9 Oct 1952) won 16 National Championships (inst. 1949) from 1969 to 1981. John Fethers (b. 4 Dec 1929) the Victorian left-hander, and Benkö are the only two fencers to win all three weapons (foil, epée and sabre) in the 1951 and 1974 Championships respectively. Benkö attained Australia's highest ever placing in the Olympic Games with sixth in the foil at Montreal, 1976. Helen L. Smith has won a record six women's foil titles.

FOOTBALL (Australian Rules)

Most league premierships

The greatest number of League Premierships in the Victorian Football League (VFL) (inst. 1897) is 14 by Carlton between 1906 and 1982.

The record in the Western Australian NFL (inst. 1885) is 25 by East Fremantle from 1900 to 1979 and the record in the South Australian NFL (inst. 1877) is 27 by Port Adelaide between 1884 and 1981. A record ten in succession were won by Fremantle (WA) in 1887–96.

The player to have participated in most Premiership wins is A. E. 'Topsy' Waldron with ten for Norwood, SA between 1878 and 1891.

Most Carnival wins

Of the 19 triennial inter-state Carnival Series played (inst. 1908) Victoria have won all but those in 1911, 1921 and 1961.

Team scores *Highest*

The highest recorded score is the win by Western Suburbs, NSW over Balmain 370 to 25, scoring 57 goals and 28 behinds against 3 goals and 7 behinds on 26 Aug 1973. The VFL aggregate record is 345 points when St Kilda beat Melbourne 204–141 on 6 May 1978. The SANFL record is 396 points when Glenelg beat Central Districts 317–79 on 23 Aug 1975.

The record margin of victory in a VFL final is 83 points. Hawthorn beat Essendon 140–57 at the Melbourne CG on 26 Sept 1983.

The highest recorded score in junior football was set in 1981 when Brunswick under-19 beat Geelong West under-19 by 506 (77, 44) to nil.

Individual Scoring Records

The most goals scored in a match is 28 by Bill Wood of South Sydney, NSW against Sydney on 21 Aug 1943. Peter Hudson (b. 1946) holds the senior career goal scoring record with 2191 from 1963 to 1981 in the VFL and in Tasmania. He scored a season record 202 goals for Glenorchy, Tasmania in 1979. The VFL season's record is 150 by Bob Pratt (South Melbourne) in 1934 and by Peter Hudson (Hawthorn) in 1971. The career record in one state is 1419 goals by Ken Farmer (b. 1910) (North Adelaide, SA) between 1929 and 1941, with an additional 81 goals in inter-state games.

The goal scoring record in a junior match was set by Doug Ensor with 60 goals and 8 behinds for Noble Park, Victoria in June 1967. William Pearson of the Melbourne Amateur FA kicked 220 goals in the 1934 season.

Kicking Records

The longest recorded place kick is 98.45 m *107 yd 2 ft* by Albert Thurgood (Essendon, VFA) in practice with slight wind assistance, at East Melbourne on 22 June 1899. Thurgood also holds the record for the longest place kick recorded in a match at 95.71 m *104 yd 2 ft* against Carlton at East Melbourne in August 1893.

Most Senior Games

Harry Coventry played about 500 Senior Games between 1898 and 1927 in Tasmania. The record confirmed total is 448 by Kevin Murray (b. 18 June 1938) from 1955 to 1976 in Victoria and Western Australia. The VFL record is 384 by Kevin Bartlett (Richmond) 1955–82. The WANFL record is 371 by Mal Whinnen (West Perth) 1960–77, the SANFL record is 360 by Paul Bagshaw (Sturt) 1963–80.

Highest Attendance

The attendance record is 121,696 for the VFL Grand Final when Carlton beat Collingwood at Melbourne Cricket Ground on 26 Sept 1970.

FOOTBALL (Rugby League)

The Rugby League was formed in Sydney on 12 Aug 1907. The first club, Newtown, formed on 8 Jan 1908. The Australian Board of Control was formed in 1924.

Most points *Team*

The highest score by Australia in an international is 63 *v.* England (13) in Paris on 31 Dec 1933. The highest score by an Australian touring team is 92 *v.* Bramley (7) in 1921. The English touring team beat South Australia 101–0 at Adelaide in 1914. The most points scored by a club in one season is 673 by Parramatta, Sydney, NSW, in 1978.

Most successful team

The 1982 Australian team won every match on its tour of Great Britain and France, including five Tests.

Most points *Individual*

The greatest number of points scored for an Australian club in a season is 282 by Michael Cronin for Parramatta in 1978. Dave Brown (b. 1943) (Eastern Suburbs) scored 385 points in all games in the 1935 season. The greatest number of points scored in one game at senior level is 61 by Alf Fairhall, when Northern Suburbs, Newcastle, NSW, beat Morpeth-East Maitland 127–16 in 1940.

Australia *v.* Great Britain

The most appearances *v.* Britain is 14 by Keith Holman (b. 1929), 1950–61. The top Australian scorer is Graeme Langlands (b. 1942) with 6 tries and 43 goals for a total of 104 points.

SELECTED AUSTRALIAN GLIDING RECORDS

(Single seaters)

Distance	1095,05 km	680.43 *miles*	Ingo Renner in a Nimbus 3	30 Sept 1982
Declared Goal Flight	1095,05 km	680.43 *miles*	Ingo Renner in a Nimbus 3	30 Sept 1982
Goal and Return	1000,86 km	621.91 *miles*	George Vakkur in an Astir CS	8 Apr 1977
Absolute Altitude	9662 m	31,700 *ft*	Bert Persson in a Blanik (solo)	7 Feb 1970

Speed over Triangular Course

Men

100 km	195,3 km/h	121.35 *mph*	Ingo Renner in a Nimbus 3	14 Dec 1982
300 km	143,32 km/h	89.05 *mph*	Terrence Cubley in a Cirrus 75	10 Dec 1980
500 km	102,03 km/h	34.30 *mph*	Ingo Renner in a Nimbus 3	?? Jan 1983
750 km	134,00 km/h	83.26 *mph*	Robert J. Rowe in a Nimbus 2	15 Jan 1977
1000 km	129,68 km/h	80.58 *mph*	Ingo Renner in a Nimbus 3	6 Nov 1982

Women

100 km	139,45 km/h	86.65 *mph*	Susan Martin in a LS3	2 Feb 1979
300 km	129,25 km/h	80.47 *mph*	Susan Martin in a Ventus A	8 Feb 1981
500 km	133,14 km/h	82.73 *mph*	Susan Martin in a LS3	29 Jan 1979

Youngest International

The youngest Australian Test player is Kerry Boustead (Q), aged 18 yr 310 days when he played v. New Zealand at the Sydney Cricket Ground in 1978. Geoff Starling played v. New Zealand at 18 yr 178 days in 1971 but this was not a Test match.

Gate record

The greatest attendance at a League match in Australia was an official total (not including gate-crashers) of 78,056 who watched St. George and South Sydney at the Sydney Cricket Ground on 18 Sept 1965.

FOOTBALL (Rugby Union)

The first Rugby organisation was the Southern Union formed in 1874 (renamed the NSW Rugby Union in 1892) which was prior to the formation of any national Union except the Rugby Football Union (England) (1871) and the Scottish Rugby Union (1873). Sydney University formed a club in 1864. Rugby had been played in Sydney from 1829. The first overseas tour was by NSW to New Zealand in 1882 and the first tour received from the British Isles was in 1888. The first tour to Britain was in 1908.

Most international appearances

Peter G. Johnson (b. 1938) (Randwick, Sydney) has represented Australia internationally on 42 occasions including three matches v. Fiji, between 1958 and 1971.

Most team points

The highest score by Australia in any international match is 50 v. Japan (25) at Brisbane in 1975. The highest against an International Rugby Football Board country is 33 v. Scotland (9) at Sydney Cricket Ground on 10 July 1982. The most points scored against Australia is 38–13 by New Zealand at Dunedin in 1936 and 38–3 also by New Zealand at Auckland in 1972. The most points by an individual is 21 (3 goals, 5 penalties) by Paul McLean v. Scotland at Sydney on 10 July 1982. Australia's highest ever score in a tour match was when the Sixth Wallabies beat Glamorgan 51–18 at Neath, 16 Dec 1975. NSW Country beat Japan 97–20 at Morce, NSW on 6 Aug 1975 which is the greatest ever defeat of a National side.

Penrith beat Sydney–New Zealand 164–0 in a Sydney RU 1st Grade Third Division match at Penrith on 15 May 1982, with Brian Wood contributing a record 72 points (7 tries, 22 goals).

GAMBLING

Mick Bartley ('Melbourne Mick') (b. 1916) backed 36 winners in succession in 1960. He held the winning combination on a record jackpot tote of $356,535 on the Canberra Jackpot Tote on 26 June 1971. Before the 15% commission was deducted the gross amount was $419,453. On 28 Dec 1970 'Melbourne Mick' won a record $178,000 on a daily double at Randwick racecourse, Sydney. An unknown punter won $A348,849 for a $1 Trifecta combination bet on the Oakleigh Plate at Caulfield Vic. on 26 Feb 1983.

Bingo

John Joseph Griinke achieved a 'full house' when only 28 numbers had been called at Strathpine, Queensland on 17 July 1978.

GLIDING

The first flights were by George Taylor and Edward (later Sir Edward) Hallstrom at Narrabeen Beach, Sydney, NSW in 1909.

The most National Gliding Championship (inst. 1957) titles won is by Malcolm Jinks (South Australia) (b. 8 June 1944) of the Waikerie Club with 11 wins in the Open Class (1965–7, 1970–1, 1975–8, 1980 tied) and one win in the Standard Class. Ingo Renner (b. 1 June 1940) is the only Australian to win a world title at Räyskälä, Finland in 1976.

Hang Gliding

Official Australian records: rigid wing hang glider distance— 162 km *100.6 miles* Ron Grey in the Great Australian Bight in November 1980. Flex wing hang glider distance—159 km *98.8 miles* and height gain—2347 m *7700 ft* Denis Cummings from Mt Buffalo, Victoria in December 1983. Goal distance 67 km *41 miles* Wesley Hill from Ben Nevis, Victoria in January 1982.

Ray Chatfield set an unofficial distance record of 290 km *180 miles* from Mt. Bakewell, WA in February 1984.

GOLF

Earliest

Golf was reported to have been played on cleared farmland at Ratho, Bothwell, Tasmania before 1830 by a Scot, Alex Reid. Bothwell GC (9 holes) occupies the area today.

The earliest national championship was unusually the Australian Women's Amateur Championship played at Geelong, Victoria on 29–30 Aug 1894. This was shortly followed by the first men's Amateur Championship at Caulfield, on 9 Nov 1894.

Most titles

The most wins in the Australian Open Championship (inst. 1904) is seven by Gary Player (South Africa) in 1958, 1962–3, 1965, 1969–70 and 1974. The lowest score is by Player in 1965 with 264 (62, 71, 62, 69). The most wins by an Australian is five by Ivo Whitton (1893–1967), 1912–13, 1926, 1929, 1931.

The most wins in the Australian Amateur (inst. 1894) is four by Harry A. Howden, 1896–8 and 1901, the Hon. Michael Scott 1905, 1907, 1909–10, and Jim Ferrier (b 1915) 1935–6, 1938–9. The Australian Professional title (inst. 1906) has been won six times by Kel Nagle in 1949, 1954, 1958–9, 1965, 1968. The Women's Amateur title (inst. 1894) has been won four times by C. B. Mackenzie 1894–6, 1898, Mona Macleod 1921, 1926–7, 1932, and Pat Borthwick (b. 1926) 1948–9, 1953, 1956.

Youngest champion

Harry Llewellyn Williams (b. 12 July 1915) was 16 when he won the 1931 Australian Amateur Championship.

Low scoring in major tournaments

The lowest score for nine holes is 28 by David Good (Tas) at Yarra Yarra, Vic, on 9 Nov 1977. The lowest for 18 holes is 60 by Billy Dunk (b. 1938) at Merewether, NSW, in November 1970.

Holes in one

The youngest Australian to hole in one is Peter A. Toogood (b. 11 Apr 1930) (later Australian Amateur Champion), aged eight, at the 110 yd *100 m* 7th hole at Kingston Beach, Tasmania in 1938. The oldest Australian to hole in one is Cyril Legh Winser (1884–1983), at the 146 yd *133 m* 8th at Barwon Heads, Vic, in 1975, one week before his 91st birthday. The oldest Australian women to hole in one is Kaye Kearney at North Adelaide on 16 Apr 1982 at the age of 81.

GREYHOUND RACING

The earliest Greyhound meeting was staged at the Epping Racecourse, now Harold Park, Sydney on 28 May 1927.

Fastest greyhounds

The fastest ever Australian dog has been *The Shoe*, son of *Black Top*, timed to cover 410 yd *374,90 m* in 20.1 sec (av. 41.72 mph *67,14 km/h*) at Richmond, NSW, on 25 Nov 1968. On 25 Mar 1978 *Satan's Legend* ran 457 m *499.6 yd* in 25.95 sec (av. 39.39 mph *63,39 km/h*) at Harold Park, Sydney, NSW.

Largest prize

The greatest individual prize won by a greyhound in Australia is $52,310 by *Windfire* who won the Triple Crown series—the President's Cup, Summer Gift and Mandurah Cup—at Mandurah Raceway, Perth, WA. His final victory on 23 Mar 1984 won him $2,310 plus a bonus of $50,000. The greatest overall prize money for one event is $100,000 for the 1984 Australian Cup.

GYMNASTICS

Most National Championships (inst. 1950) have been won by Graham F. Bond (Qld) (b. 1937) with five titles in 1955, 1957, 1959–61. The record for women gymnasts is four jointly held by Jan Bedford and Valerie Norris (*née* Buffham) (b. 28 June 1943) (both WA) in 1961–4 and 1965–6, 1968–9 respectively. The youngest national champion has been Marina Sulicich (b. 18 Feb 1964) who was 13 yr 196 days when she won on 2 Sept 1977. The most titles won at Rhythmic Gymnastics is four by Karen Ho (b. 16 July 1963) (WA), 1978–80 and 1983.

The first Australian to win a medal in International competition was Lindsay Nylund (WA) (b. 30 Apr 1958) with a silver at the 1978 Commonwealth Games.

HARNESS RACING

Popular Alm achieved the fastest mile against time by an Australian pacer, 1:53.2 at Moonee Valley, Melbourne on 13 May 1983, and the fastest race mile, 1:54.5 at Albion Park, Brisbane on 29 Oct 1983.

The Inter-Dominion Championship (inst. 1936) has been won twice by *Captain Sandy* (1950 and 1953), by *Hondo Grattan* (1973–4) and by *Gammalite* (1983–4). The race return time for 2700 m *2952.75 yd* is 2:02.0 by *Gammalite* in Auckland, New Zealand in 1983.

HOCKEY

Olympics

Australian teams won silver medals in 1968 and 1976.

Most titles

The most National men's championships (inst. 1925) won is 26 by Western Australia to 1983. They have also won a record 30 women's titles (inst. 1946).

International Appearances

Greg Browning (Qld) (b. 14 Feb 1953) was only 16 years 176 days when he represented Australia *v.* New Zealand on 9 Aug 1969. Dr Richard Charlesworth (WA) (b. 6 Dec 1952) has represented Australia on a record 160 occasions to end 1983.

HORSE RACING

Earliest

The earliest race meeting in Australia was staged at Parramatta, NSW on 30 Apr 1810. Australian horse racing's continuous history dates from the opening of the Bellevue Hill course Sydney on 17 March 1825. The earliest steeplechase was run over 5 miles at Botany and Coogee in 1832. The totalisator was introduced on 8 Sept 1917 at the Randwick course.

Repeat dead heats

In the Australian Cup race of 1872 *Saladin* and *Flying Dutchman* dead-heated and again in the re-run. In the third running *Saladin* won by a neck. There was a double triple dead-heat at the Moorefield Course, Sydney in October 1903 when *Barindi, Highflyer* and *Loch Lochie* dead-heated over 1¼ miles and allegedly repeated this difficult feat on the re-run. A photo-finish triple dead-head occurred for the Victoria Racing Club's Hotham 1½ mile handicap on 3 Nov 1956 when *Ark Royal, Pandie Sun* and *Fighting Force* could not be separated.

Most successful horses

The unbeaten horse with the most impressive career has been *Grand Flaneur* in 1880–1. He won nine races in nine starts including the Australian Jockey Club Derby, the Victoria Racing Club Derby, the Champion Stakes, the St Leger and the Melbourne Cup in 1880. The most prize money has been won by *Kingston Town* with $1,605,790 in 41 starts (30 firsts, 5 seconds, 2 thirds, 2 fourths) to 27 May 1983.

Most successful trainer

Colin Hayes trained a record 200 winners in the 1979–80 season.

Seven winners in a day

Geoffrey Prouse rode all seven winners at the Elwick racecourse, Hobart on 22 Jan 1972. Noel Thompson also rode seven winners, all trained by Charles Eaton, at Cunnamulla, Queensland in May 1961.

Melbourne Cup

Australia's most famous (inst. 1861) and richest ($525,000, including trophies, in 1984) flat race is held on the first Tuesday in November by the Victoria Racing Club at Flemington Racecourse. Only *Archer* 1861 and 1862, *Peter Pan* 1932 and 1934, *Rain Lover* 1968 and 1969 and *Think Big* 1974 and 1975 have won twice. The record for the race, since 1972 held over 3200 m *1 mile 1739 yd* is 3 min 18.4 sec by *Gold and Black* on 1 Nov 1977. The time of *Rain Lover* in 1968, 3 min 19.1 sec for 2 miles *3218 m* is intrinsically faster. Robert Lewis (1878–1947) rode a record four winners in 1902, 1915, 1919 and 1927. He was second four times and third once. Harry White has also won four times, in 1974–5, 1978–9. J. Bart Cummings (b. 14 Nov 1927) has trained seven winners (1965–7, 1974–5, 1977, 1979) and four second place horses.

Grand National Steeplechase

The VRC Grand National (inst. 1866) now run over 3 miles 1 furlong *5000 m* at Flemington has been won five times by Tom McGinley (1965–6, 1968, 1970–1). The trainer Harold Myers won in 1958–9 and 1961.

MODERN PENTATHLON

The Amateur Modern Pentathlon Union of Australia was formed in 1954. The most Australian Championships (inst. 1956) won is six by Peter Neville Macken (b. 10 Nov 1938) (1961, 1964, 1967–8, 1971, 1974). The best international performance was by Peter Macken, fourth in the Olympic Games at Tōkyō in 1964 when the Australian team placed fifth. Macken took part in his fifth Olympic Games in Montreal in 1976.

MOTORCYCLE RACING

The Pioneer Motor Cycle Club was formed in Sydney, NSW in March/April 1903. The first major organised road races in the world were those of the Victorian Motor Cycle Club on 23 Apr 1906.

World Champions

The first Australian motorcycling world champion was Keith Campbell (1931–58) on a 350 cc Moto Guzzi in 1957.

Fastest

John Vevers set a ¼ mile flying start record for Class F solo motor cycles at Richmond Airfield, NSW on 11 Mar 1984 with a mean time of 5.776 sec for 155.817 mph *250,763 km/h* riding a Yoshimura Suzuki Bimota.

MOTOR RACING

Earliest

The earliest official event in Australia was on 12 Mar 1904 round the Sandown Park horse racing track when J. R. Crooke in a 4½ hp steam voiturette won an Automobile Club of Victoria event at an average speed of 19.6 mph *31,5 km/h.*

Fastest lap

At Sandown, Vic., on 13 Sept 1981, A. Costanzo in a McLaren M26 achieved a lap speed of 187,56 km/h *116.54 mph* on a 3,1 km *1.93 mile* circuit.

World Drivers' Championship

The most successful Australian in terms of the World Drivers' Championship (inst. 1950) has been Sir John Arthur 'Jack' Brabham (b. 2 Apr 1926) who won the title in 1959–60 and 1966.

Major Records

Flying kilometre	Austin Miller	263,7 km/h *163.9 mph*
Standing kilometre	Andrew Mustard	142,8 km/h *88.78 mph*
24 hours	R. Johnson, J. Laing-Peach,	4240,71 km *2635.06 miles*
	W. Cantell in a Ford Falcon XE	176,7 km/h *109.79 mph*

Australian Grand Prix

The most victories in the Australian Grand Prix (inst. 1928) is four by the late Alexander 'Lex' Davison (Vic) (1923–65) in 1954, 1957–8 and 1961.

National Championships

The most Championships won is nine (in three different categories) by Ian Geoghegan (b. 1939) (NSW) between 1963 and 1977. Most successive wins for an Australian Championship is six by Bruce Walton for the Hill Climb 1958–63.

Bathurst 1000 km

Australia's longest distance race (inst. 1960 over 500 miles) has been won seven times by Peter Brock (b. 26 Feb 1945) in 1972, 1975, 1978–80 and 1982–3.

Drag racing

The lowest elapsed time for a standing 440 yd recorded by an Australian is 5.816 sec by James Arthur 'Jim' Read (b. 29 Jan 1944) on 20 Nov 1982 and the record terminal velocity is 249.98 mph *402,303 km/h* on 12 Mar 1983, both at Castlereagh, NSW. Jim Read has won a record eleven national drag racing championships.

MOUNTAINEERING

Earliest

The first known ascent of Australia's highest peak, the 7316 ft *2229 m* Mount Kosciusko in the Snowy Range, NSW was in 1840 when Polish-born Sir Paul de Strezlecki (1797–1873) climbed to the summit with James Macarthur and named the mountain (without the 'z') after the Polish patriot Tadeusz Kosciuszko (1746–1817).

The greatest Australian first ascent was that of Mt Erebus (12,450 ft *3794 m*) the world's most southerly and Antarctica's only active volcano on 10 Mar 1908 by Sir Edgworth David, Sir Douglas Mawson and three other members of Shackleton's Expedition.

Ayers Rock

The record time for scaling Australia's most famous (but not largest) rock, Ayers Rock, Northern Territory is 12 min by Graham Anderson of New Zealand on 13 Apr 1973. It stands 1143 ft *348 m* above the surrounding plain, but is actually 2845 ft *867 m* above sea level.

OLYMPIC GAMES (See also p. 339)

Australia has been represented at all 21 celebrations (including those of 1906) of the modern summer Games.

Medal total

The total number of Olympic medals won by Australia since the inception of the Games prior to 1984 is 64 gold, 53 silver and 70 bronze, including three bronze medals in the 1906 Celebration. This total of 187 places Australia fourteenth in the all-time totals by nations. The most successful Games were those of 1956 with 35 medals.

Gold Medals *Earliest*

Australia's earliest gold medallist was Edwin H. Flack (London Athletic Club) (1874–1936) who won the 800 m and 1500 m but had to drop out of the 1896 Marathon—despite being attended by the British Ambassador's bowler hatted butler on a bicycle. The first woman champion was Fanny Durack (1892–1956) who won the 100 m freestyle swim at Stockholm in 1912.

Medals *Most*

Three Australians have won four Olympic gold medals: Murray Rose (Swimming)—400 m and 1500 m freestyle and 4 × 200 m Relay 1956, 400 m freestyle 1960; Betty Cuthbert (Athletics)—100 m, 200 m and 4 × 100 m Relay 1956, 400 m 1964; Dawn Fraser (b. 4 Sept 1937) (later Mrs Gary Ware) (Swimming)—100 m freestyle, 1956, 1960 and 1964, 4 × 100 m Relay 1956. Dawn Fraser holds the record for all medals with eight, as she also won four Silvers: 400 m freestyle 1956, and 4 × 100 m relay 1960, 1964 and the 4 × 100 m medley relay 1960.

Most appearances

Dennis Allan Green (Canoeing) (1956–72), Peter Macken (Modern Pentathlon) (1960–76), James Roycroft (Equestrianism) (1960–76) and Adrian Francis Powell (1960–76) (Canoeing) have all competed in five Games. Roycroft was selected as captain of the 1980 team, which withdrew from the Games at Moscow.

Youngest and Oldest

The youngest person to represent Australia in the Olympic Games is Ian David Johnston (b. 18 June 1947) cox of the Coxed Pairs at Rome on 31 Aug 1960 aged 13 yr 74 days. The youngest Australian gold medallist was Shane Elizabeth Gould (b. 23 Nov 1956) at 15 yr 279 days when she won the 200 metres individual medley, the first of her three gold medals, at Munich on 28 Aug 1972. The oldest Olympian is James William Roycroft (b. 17 Mar 1915) at 61 yr 129 days in the 3-Day Event at Montreal on 24 July 1976.

PARACHUTING

The first parachute jump in Australia was by J. T. Williams (b. Birmingham, England, 1855) from a balloon on 8 Dec 1888. The most overall championship (inst. 1960) wins is three by Kerry Tucker, 1973–4 and 1976. William (Bill) Johnson (b. 27 Nov 1937) had a record 3968 descents from 1958 to the end of 1981.

POWERBOAT RACING

The earliest competitions were in Sydney in 1905. The Australian Power Boating Association was formed in 1927.

The E. C. Griffith Cup for the National Unlimited Unrestricted Class Championship was instituted in 1910. The record number of wins is ten by Len Southward of Christchurch, New Zealand in *Redhead* from 1949 to 1958.

ROWING

The first recorded race was in Sydney Harbour on 15 May 1818 between three ships' crews and a local crew. The first regatta was on the Derwent at Hobart, Tasmania on 5 Jan 1827. Melbourne University Boat Club, formed 3 Sept 1859, is the oldest extant club.

Most titles

The record number of wins in the Amateur Sculling Championship of Australia (inst. 1868) is eight by Mervyn Thomas Wood (NSW) (b. 30 Apr 1917) in 1946–52 and 1955. The inter-Colonial, later inter-state, eight-oared championship of Australia was started in 1878 in Melbourne. Since 1920 the event has been for the King's Cup (donated by King George V) which has been won 20 times each by NSW and Victoria.

Olympic titles

Australians have won nine Olympic medals. Henry Robert Pearce (NSW) (1905–76) has won most golds with single sculls championships in 1928 and 1932. The sculler Mervyn Wood won most medals, three (one gold, one silver and one bronze) in the 1948, 1952 and 1956 Games respectively.

World Championships—most medals

Simon Gillett (b. 13 June 1958) stroked the Australian lightweight coxless four that won world titles in 1980 and 1981. He was also in the coxless four that won silver in 1977 and bronze in 1978.

SHOOTING

Rifle shooting was first organised in Australia in 1842 with the formation of the Sydney Rifle Club. In 1882 the first clay target shooting club, the Williamson and Melbourne Gun Club, was formed. Pistol shooting was not an organised sport until 1947.

Most titles

The greatest number of titles won in All Australian Shooting Championships is ten by Michael Papps (SA) (b. 1933) in Pistol Shooting (inst. 1958) between 1959 and 1970. In women's Pistol Shooting (inst. 1964) Gloria Vause (SA) won a record eight titles from 1964 to 1971.

Queen's Prize

Libby Felton (b. 1945) of Perth, WA became the first woman to win the Queen's Prize in Australia with a score of 348 out of a possible 355 in October 1974.

SPEEDWAY

Australian riders have won the world championship on four occasions; Lionel 'Les' Van Praag (b. 17 Dec 1908) in 1936, Arthur 'Bluey' Wilkinson (1911–40) in 1938 and Jack Ellis Young (b. 31 Jan 1925) in 1951 and 1952.

Australia's first Test match was against England in 1930. Aub Lawson (1913–77) competed in a record 84 Tests, gaining a record 680 points.

SQUASH

Australia's first court was completed at the Melbourne Club, Collins Street, Melbourne in July 1913 by adapting a rackets court into two squash courts.

Australian titles

National Championships were inaugurated in 1931 for men and in 1932 for women. Ken Hiscoe (b. 21 Feb 1938) won most titles for men with seven (1960–4, 1966, 1967) and Heather McKay (*née* Blundell) won 14, every year from 1960 to 1973 when she turned professional. The Australian Open Championship was first held in 1939, and has been an annual event from 1970. Geoff Hunt has won a record seven titles, 1971, 1973, 1976–80.

SURFING

The first Surf Club in Australia was the Bondi Surf Bathers' Lifesaving Club formed in February 1906.

Surf Life Saving Association of Australia

Formed in Sydney in 1907, the organisation has recorded rescues totalling 273,631 to the end of the 1982/3 season. Their Australian Championship annually attracts entries of over 3,000.

Ken Vidler (WA) has won a record 19 gold medals and Peter Lacey (Vic) with 14 gold, 14 silver and 10 bronze has won a medal at every championship, 1962–84.

Most titles

Open Surf Race (inst. 1914)	5	Robert Newbiggin (NSW)	1939–48
Open Surf Belt (1919)	4	Don Morrison (WA)	1947–53
	4	Peter Tibbitts (NSW)	1974–81
Beach Relay (1919)	7	Manly (NSW)	1926–72
	7	North Narrabeen (NSW)	1952–82
Long Surf Board (1938)	6	Denis Heussner (NSW)	1961–71
Rescue and Resuscitation (1914)	12	Bondi (NSW)	1914–72
March Past (1913)	13	Bundaberg (Qld)	1958—83
Open Surf Teams Race (1919)	15	Manly (NSW)	1919–60
Beach Sprint (1919)	5	John Bliss (NSW)	1940–53
Open Iron Man (1965)	4	Grant Kenny (Qld)	1979–83

Surfriding titles

The Australian Surfriding Championships were instituted in 1964. Robert 'Nat' Young (b. 1950) has won a record three men's open titles (1966–7 and 1969) and Gail Couper (b. 1948) five women's open titles (1966–7, 1971–2 and 1975).

SWIMMING

Most titles

Winner of most individual Australian championships (inst. 1894 as Australasian championships for men, and 1930 for women) has been Frank (later Sir Frank) Beaurepaire (1891–1956) (Vic) with 25 from 1908 to 1924, in which period he also competed in a record four Olympic Games. Winner of most women's titles has been Dawn Fraser (SA) with 23 individual championships and seven relays from 1955 to 1964. Two

SWIMMING

National Open Records, ratified best times recorded by Australians anywhere in the world as at July 1984

MEN

	Distance	Time min sec	Name	Place	Date
Freestyle	50 metres	22.97	Gregory Fasala (Vic) (b. 10 May 1965)	Darwin	10 Sept 1983
	100 metres	50.55	Mark William Stockwell (Qld) (b. 5 July 1963)	Brisbane	26 Feb 1984
	200 metres	1:51.48	Justin William Lemberg (Qld) (b. 23 Aug 1963)	Brisbane	23 Feb 1984
	400 metres	3:53.22	Justin William Lemberg	Brisbane	24 Feb 1984
	800 metres	8:02.91	Stephen Roy Holland (Qld) (b. 21 May 1958)	Sydney	29 Feb 1976
	1,500 metres	15:04.66	Stephen Roy Holland (Qld)	Montreal, Canada	20 July 1976
Backstroke	100 metres	56.50	Mark Anthony Kerry (NSW) (b. 4 Aug 1959)	Ft. Lauderdale, Fla., USA	17 Aug 1979
	200 metres	2:02.61	Mark Anthony Kerry (NSW)	Ft. Lauderdale, Fla., USA	16 Aug 1979
Butterfly	100 metres	55.17	Glenn Robert Buchanan (Qld) (b. 19 Nov 1962)	Tokyo, Japan	29 Aug 1983
	200 metres	2:01.17	Jon Sieben (Qld) (b. 24 Aug 1966)	Brisbane	24 Feb 1984
Breaststroke	100 metres	1:03.26	Peter Maxwell Evans (WA) (b. 1 Aug 1961)	Tokyo, Japan	29 Aug 1981
	200 metres	2:16.55	Glenn Stuart Beringen (SA) (b. 16 Sept 1964)	Brisbane	24 Feb 1984
Individual Medley	200 metres	2:06.72	Robert Andrew Woodhouse (Vic) (b. 23 June 1966)	Brisbane	25 Feb 1984
	400 metres	4:26.22	Robert Andrew Woodhouse	Brisbane	26 Feb 1984
Freestyle Relay	4 × 100 metres	3:23.37	Australian Team: Greg Fasala, Michael William Delany, Mark William Stockwell, Neil Brooks	Hamilton, New Zealand	9 Mar 1983
	4 × 200 metres	7:28.81	Australian Team: Graeme Neal McGufficke, Ronald John McKeon, Paul Colin Rowe, Graeme Thomas Brewer	Brisbane	4 Oct 1982
Medley Relay	4 × 100 metres	3:45.70	Australian Team: Mark Anthony Kerry, Peter Maxwell Evans, Mark Lyndon Tonelli, Neil Brooks	Moscow, USSR	24 July 1980

WOMEN

	Distance	Time	Name	Place	Date
Freestyle	50 metres	26.59	Angela Mary Russell (Qld) (b. 2 Mar 1967)	Brisbane	25 Feb 1984
	100 metres	57.15	Angela Mary Russell (Qld)	Brisbane	2 Oct 1982
	200 metres	2:00.60	Tracey Lee Wickham (Qld) (b. 24 Nov 1962)	Brisbane	4 Oct 1982
	400 metres	4:06.28	Tracey Lee Wickham (Qld)	Berlin, W. Germany	24 Aug 1978
	800 metres	8:24.62	Tracey Lee Wickham (Qld)	Edmonton, Canada	5 Aug 1978
	1,500 metres	16:06.63	Tracey Lee Wickham (Qld)	Perth	25 Feb 1979
Backstroke	100 metres	1:03.48	Lisa Marie Forrest (NSW) (b. 9 Mar 1964)	Brisbane	4 Oct 1982
	200 metres	2:13.46	Lisa Marie Forrest (NSW)	Brisbane	6 Oct 1982
Breaststroke	100 metres	1:12.73	Dimity Jean Douglas (NSW) (b. 3 July 1970)	Brisbane	23 Feb 1984
	200 metres	2:36.77	Sharon Maree Kellett (Qld) (b. 24 Feb 1968)	Brisbane	24 Feb 1984
Butterfly	100 metres	1:01.22	Lisa Gaye Curry (Qld)	Brisbane	3 Oct 1982
	200 metres	2:11.29	Michelle Jan Ford (NSW) b. 15 July 1962)	Edmonton, Canada	8 Aug 1978
Individual Medley	200 metres	2:16.94	Lisa Gaye Curry (Qld)	Brisbane	2 Oct 1982
	400 metres	4:48.56	Suzanne Ciscele Landells (Qld) (b. 12 Dec 1964)	Los Angeles	15 July 1983
Freestyle Relay	4 × 100 metres	3:54.11	Australian Team: Rosemary Edith Brown, Lisa Burnes, Michelle Jan Ford, Tracey Lee Wickham	Edmonton, Canada	5 Aug 1978
	4 × 200 metres	8:21.24	Queensland Team: Tracey Lee Wickham, Fiona Moore, Karen Van de Graaf, Rosemary Edith Brown	Melbourne	22 Mar 1980
Medley Relay	4 × 100 metres	4:16.75	Australian Team: Debra Lynn Forster, Lisa Gaye Curry, Tracey Lee Wickham, Rosemary Edith Brown	Edmonton, Canada	8 Aug 1978

swimmers have won a championship seven years in succession: Terry Gathercole (NSW) (b. 25 Nov 1935), 200 m breaststroke 1954–1960 and Judy-Joy Davies (b. 5 June 1928) (Vic), 100 m backstroke 1946–1952. Most diving titles won is 30 by Donald Douglas Wagstaff (Vic) (b. 12 Oct 1949) from 1966 to 1978.

Most world records

Dawn Fraser set 27 individual world records. The highest total for an Australian man has been John Konrads (NSW) (b. 21 May 1942) with 26. His sister Ilsa (b. 24 Mar 1944) also achieved 12 world records making 38 for the family.

English Channel

Linda McGill (NSW) (b. 1946) was the first Australian to swim the English Channel on 7 Aug 1965. On 30 Sept 1967 she crossed from France to England in 9 hr 59 min 57 sec, the fastest Australian crossing. John Koorey (NSW) was the first Australian man to swim it. He swam from France to England in September 1969 in 10 hr 32 min. Des Renford (NSW) (b. Aug 1927) has swum the English Channel 19 times 1970–1980.

TABLE TENNIS

Most titles

Australian championships were inaugurated in 1933 (and for women in 1936), since when the record number of single titles won is ten by Hungarian born Suzi Javor (b. 28 Dec 1933) in 1958–60, 1962–4, 1966–8 and 1970. She also won nine doubles for a total of 19. The record for the men's singles championship is five by Chayanond 'Charlie' Wuvanich in 1969–70 and 1972–4. Stephen Knapp won a total of 14 titles in 1973–8.

Youngest champion

The youngest ever Australian champion is Leanne Morrow (b. 3 Apr 1959) who won the 1973 Women's Open Singles title at the age of 14 yr 157 days.

TENNIS

The game was introduced from England during the 1870s. The earliest State championship was Victoria's at Melbourne in January 1880. The first National Championships were in 1905.

Australian Championships *Most titles*

Margaret Jean Court (*née* Smith) (b. 16 July 1942) won the women's singles 11 times (1960–6, 1969–71 and 1973) as well as eight women's doubles and two mixed doubles, for a record total of 21 titles. The men's singles record is six wins by Roy Stanley Emerson (Qld) (b. 3 Nov 1936), 1961 and 1963–7. Thelma Dorothy Long (*née* Coyne) (b. 30 May 1918) won a record 12 women's doubles and four mixed doubles for a record total of 16 doubles titles. Adrian Karl Quist (b. 4 Aug 1913) won ten consecutive men's doubles from 1936 to 1950 (the last eight with John Bromwich) and three men's singles.

Australian Championships *Longest span, oldest and youngest*

Thelma Long won her first (1936) and last (1958) titles 22 years apart. Kenneth Robert Rosewall (b. Sydney, 2 Nov 1934) won the singles in 1953 and in 1972—19 years later, at 37 yr 62 days the oldest singles winner. The oldest champion was (Sir) Norman Everard Brookes (1877–1968), who was 46 yr 2 months when he won the 1924 men's doubles. The youngest champions were Rodney W. Heath, aged 17, when he won the men's singles in 1905 and Margaret Smith, who won the women's singles at 17 yr 5 months in 1960.

Wimbledon

Australia's first Wimbledon champion was Norman Everard Brookes, in 1907. The first Australian winner of the women's singles was Margaret Court in 1963. She won ten Wimbledon titles (three singles, two women's and five mixed doubles) between 1963 and 1975. The best male record is nine by John David Newcombe (b. 23 May 1944), with three singles and six men's doubles from 1965 to 1974, but Rodney George Laver (b. 9 Aug 1938) won the singles four times in 1961–2, 1968–9.

Davis Cup

Australia have won the Davis Cup on 25 occasions, including six by Australasia during 1907–19, most recently in 1983. The greatest number of rubbers played by an Australian is 58 in 23 ties by John Herbert Crawford (b. 22 Mar 1908), winning 36, in 1928–37. Adrian Karl Quist has a record 42 wins in 55 rubbers, playing in a record 28 ties between 1933 and 1948.

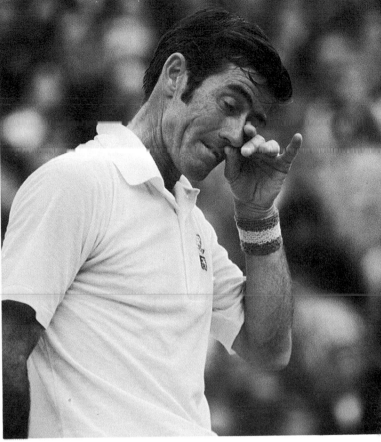

Ken Rosewall won the Australian singles title in 1953 and 1955 and with the advent of open competition, again in 1971 and 1972. Rosewall won eight Grand Slam singles titles in all, although never Wimbledon.

Roy Emerson appeared in a world record nine *consecutive* Challenge Rounds, won 15 out of 18 rubbers and was only once on the losing side.

Federation Cup

Australia have won the Federation Cup seven times from 1964 to 1974. Margaret Court won 35 of her 40 rubbers from 1963 to 1971, including all 20 singles. Kerry Reid (*née* Melville) (b. 7 Aug 1947) won 35 of 45 rubbers 1967–79.

Most major titles

Margaret Court won more titles in the 'big four' than any other player, male or female. Starting in 1960 she has won ten Wimbledon, 18 US (as well as four 'National' titles), 21 Australian and 13 French championships for a grand total of 62 (24 singles, 38 doubles).

Cliff Young set the Melbourne to Sydney running record at the age of 61.

Most games

William W. Bowrey (b. Sydney, 25 Dec 1943) was involved in the longest championship singles for any Australian when he lost in the 94th game to Vic Seixas (USA) in the third round of the Pennsylvania Grass Championship in 1966. Roy Emerson (partnered by Ron Barnes, Brazil) lost in the 105th game to the South Africans Ray Moore and Cliff Drysdale in the quarter-finals of the US Doubles Championship at Boston in 1967.

TRACK AND FIELD ATHLETICS—MEN

(as at July 1984) Best performances by Australians (for sprint races only automatically timed performances included)

Event	Time min sec	Name	Place	Date	
100 metres	10.26	Paul Andrew Narracott (ACT) (b. 8 Oct 1959)	Melbourne	6 Mar	1984
200 metres	20.06	Peter George Norman (Vic) (b. 15 June 1942)	Mexico City	16 Oct	1968
400 metres	44.84	Richard Charles Mitchell (Vic) (b. 24 Mar 1955)	Moscow, USSR	30 July	1980
800 metres	1:44.40	Ralph D. Doubell (Vic) (b. 11 Feb 1945)	Mexico City	15 Oct	1968
1000 metres	2:18.0	Michael Howard Hillardt (Qld) (b. 24 Jan 1961)	Melbourne	10 Dec	1983
1500 metres	3:34.20	Michael Howard Hillardt (Qld)	Sydney	11 Mar	1984
1 mile	3:53.33	Michael Howard Hillardt (Qld)	Adelaide	13 Mar	1982
2000 metres	5:01.3	Stephen John Foley (Vic) (b. 21 Nov 1957)	Adelaide	22 Dec	1979
3000 metres	7:47.2	Ronald William Clarke (Vic) (b. 21 Feb 1937)	Vasteras, Sweden	27 June	1967
5000 metres	13:16.6	Ronald William Clarke (Vic)	Stockholm, Sweden	7 May	1966
10,000 metres	27:39.89	Ronald William Clarke (Vic)	Oslo, Norway	14 July	1965
20,000 metres	58:37.2	Francois Robert de Castella (Vic) (b. 22 Feb 1957)	Rome, Italy	17 Apr	1982
25,000 metres	1 hr 20:31.4	Brian Morgan (NSW) (b. 15 Nov 1955)	Newcastle	24 May	1980
30,000 metres	1 hr 38:33.5	Brian Morgan (NSW)	Newcastle	24 May	1980
1 hour	20 516 m.	Francois Robert de Castella (Vic)	Rome, Italy	17 Apr	1982
	12 miles 1316 yd				
Marathon	2 hr 08:18	Francois Robert de Castella (Vic)	Fukuoka, Japan	6 Dec	1981

HURDLING

110 metres	13.58	Donald Ernest Wright (Qld) (b. 26 Apr 1959)	Brisbane	4 Oct	1982
400 metres	49.32	Bruce William Field (Vic) (b. 22 Jan 1947)	Christchurch, NZ	29 Jan	1974
3000 metres steeplechase	8:21.98	Kerry Dennis O'Brien (SA) (b. 17 Apr 1946)	Berlin, W. Germany	4 July	1970

RELAYS

4 × 100 metres	39.31	Australian Team:	Christchurch, NZ	2 Feb	1974
		Gregory D. Lewis, Laurence D'Arcy, Andrew Ratcliffe, Graham Haskell			
4 × 200 metres	1:23.8	E. Melbourne H. (Vic):	Melbourne	9 Mar	1975
		Laurence D'Arcy, Greg Lewis, Paul Soanes, Don Hanly			
4 × 400 metres	3:02.1	Victoria:	Melbourne	25 Feb	1984
		Peter van Miltenberg, Gary John Minihan, Michael Bruce Frayne, Richard Charles Mitchell			
4 × 800 metres	7:19.0	Australian Team:	Dublin, Ireland	22 Aug	1966
		Ken Roche, Ralph Doubell, Keith Wheeler, Noel Clough			
4 × 1500 metres	15:26.4	Box Hill AAC:	Melbourne	7 Mar	1976
		Paul Grinsted, John Bermingham, Peter Larkins, Graeme Crouch			

FIELD EVENTS

	ft	in	m	Name	Place	Date	
High Jump	7	5¾	2,28	John David Atkinson (Qld) (b. 29 Oct 1963)	Melbourne	31 Mar	1984
Pole Vault	18	2*	5,53	Donald George Baird (Vic) (b. 29 May 1951)	Long Beach, USA	16 Apr	1977
Long Jump	26	9	8,15	Gary Ronald Honey (Vic) (b. 26 July 1959)	Melbourne	31 Mar	1984
Triple Jump	57	3½	17,46	Kenneth John Lorraway (NSW) (b. 6 Feb 1956)	London, England	7 Aug	1982
Shot Putt	60	9¼	18,52	Philip Douglas Nettle (SA) (b. 24 Aug 1954)	Sydney	12 Feb	1984
Discus Throw	213	6	65,06	Wayne Ernest Martin (Qld) (b. 26 Feb 1955)	Newcastle	3 Jan	1979
Hammer Throw	249	0	75,90	Peter John Farmer (NSW) (b. 25 June 1952)	Vanves, France	14 Aug	1979
Javelin Throw	271	9	82,84	Manfred Rohkamper (Vic) (b. 18 May 1954)	Sydney	2 Mar	1980

DECATHLON	8,090 points	Peter Robert Hadfield (NSW) (b. 21 Jan 1955)	Adelaide	7–8 Apr	1984

TRACK AND FIELD ATHLETICS—WOMEN

(as at July 1984) Best performances by Australians (for sprint races only automatically timed performances included).

Event	min sec	Name	Place	Date	
100 metres	11.20	Raelene Ann Boyle (Vic) (b. 24 June 1951)	Mexico City	15 Oct	1968
200 metres	22.35	Denise Margaret Boyd [*née* Robertson] (Qld/Vic) (b. 15 Dec 1952)	Sydney	23 Mar	1980
400 metres	51.08	Raelene Ann Boyle (Vic)	Brisbane	5 Sept	1982
800 metres	1:59.0	Charlene Louise Rendina (Vic) (b. 18 Oct 1947)	Melbourne	28 Feb	1976
1500 metres	4:08.06	Jennifer Louise Orr (Vic) (b. 21 Jan 1953)	Munich, W. Germany	4 Sept	1972
1 mile	4:41.91	Terri-Ann Cater [*née* Wangman] (Vic) (b. 25 Sept 1956)	Melbourne	15 Dec	1983
3000 metres	8:53.7	Donna Gould (SA) (b. 10 June 1966)	Adelaide	30 May	1984
5000 metres	15:40.6	Donna Gould (SA)	Adelaide	15 Feb	1984
10000 metres	32:50.6	Lisa Frances Martin [*née* O'Dea] (SA) (b. 12 May 1960)	Melbourne	14 Feb	1984
Marathon	2 hr 32:22	Lisa Frances Martin (SA)	Rocket City, Alabama, USA	10 Dec	1983

HURDLING

100 metres	12.93	Pamela Ryan [*née* Kilborn] (Vic) (b. 12 Aug 1939)	Munich, W. Germany	4 Sept	1972
400 metres	55.89	Debbie Lee Flintoff (Vic) (b. 20 Apr 1960)	Brisbane	7 Oct	1982

RELAYS

4 × 100 metres	43.18	Australian Olympic Team:	Montreal, Canada	31 July	1976
		Barbara Wilson, Deborah Wells, Denise Margaret Robertson, Raelene Ann Boyle			
4 × 400 metres	3:25.56	Australian Olympic Team:	Montreal, Canada	31 July	1976
		Judith Canty, Verna Jaye Burnard, Charlene Louise Rendina, Bethanie Anne Nail			

FIELD EVENTS

	ft	in	m	Name	Place	Date	
High Jump	6	4¾	1,95	Christine Stanton [*née* Annison] (WA) (b. 12 Dec 1959)	Perth	22 Apr	1984
Long Jump	22	1½	6,74	Robyn Eona Lorraway [*née* Strong] (ACT) (b. 20 July 1961)	London	30 July	1983
Shot Putt	64	9¼	19,74	Gael Patricia Martin [*née* Mulhall] (Vic) (b. 27 Aug 1956)	Berkeley, Cal, USA	14 July	1984
Discus Throw	206	8	63,00	Gael Patricia Martin [*née* Mulhall] (Vic)	Melbourne	11 Jan	1979
Javelin Throw	227	3	69,28	Petra Janina Rivers (Vic) (b. 11 Dec 1952)	Brisbane	20 Mar	1982

HEPTATHLON	6282 points	Glynis Leanne Nunn [*née* Saunders] (SA) (b. 4 Dec 1960)	Brisbane	3–4 Oct	1982

TRACK AND FIELD ATHLETICS

Most titles

From 1960 to 1973 Warwick Selvey (NSW) won a record 18 individual national championships in the shot and discus events. The most by a woman is 17 by Pam Ryan (*née* Kilborn) in six different events from 1963 to 1972. She also was in seven winning relay teams, totalling 23 titles in all. The most titles at one event is 12 by Richard Leffler (b. 27 Mar 1932) at hammer between 1959 and 1973 and by Raymond Malcolm Boyd (b. 28 June 1951) at pole vault between 1970 and 1983.

Stawell Gift Record

The oldest professional race is the Stawell Gift instituted in 1878 as a handicap over 130 yd *118,8 m* till 1973 when it became 120 m *131 yd 8 in*. The record time is 12.0 sec by Jean-Louis Ravelomanantsoa (b. 30 Apr 1943) (Madagascar) the only ever winner off scratch in March 1975. The longest handicap for a winner is off 14½ yd *13,25 m* by N. C. Clarke in 1899. Only Bill Howard (1966, 1967) and Barry Foley (1970, 1972) have won twice.

24 hours

The greatest distance run on a standard track is 142 miles 1615 yd *230,003 km* by Joe Record at Crystal Palace, England, on 27–28 Oct 1979.

Long runs

William Francis King, the 'Flying Pieman' covered 192 miles *308 km* non-stop in 46 hr 30 min in New South Wales in 1848. George Perdon, 49, ran from North Mole, Fremantle to Circular Quay, Sydney, 2897 miles *4662 km* in 47 days 1 hr 54 min in August–September 1973. Cliff Young, 61, ran 875 km *543 miles* from Melbourne to Sydney in 5 days 15 hr 4 min on 23–27 Apr 1983.

WALKING

The earliest Australian walking championships were the 1 and 3 mile events in 1893.

Long Distance

On 25 Jan 1976 Tom Hayllar of Sydney completed a round-Australia walk of 7456 miles *12 000 km* begun on 1 Mar 1975. He also walked from Cape Byron, NSW to Steep Point, WA, 3524 miles *5672 km*, from 3 Mar–25 June 1978.

WALKING—MEN

The best track performances by Australians are:

Metres	hrs min sec	Name	Place	Date	
3000	11:11.5	David Gregory Smith (Vic) (b. 24 June 1955)	Sydney	8 Mar	1981
5000	19:31.53	David Smith (Vic)	Melbourne	31 Mar	1984
10,000	39:41.7	David Smith (Vic)	Melbourne	15 Feb	1984
20,000	1 26:07.8	David Smith (Vic)	Melbourne	27 June	1981
30,000	2 23:09.2	Noel Frederick Freeman (Vic) (b. 25 Dec 1938)	Melbourne	26 July	1969
50,000	4 06:39.0	Willi Alfred Sawall (Vic) (b. 7 Nov 1941)	Melbourne	14 Aug	1976
1 hour	14 103,65 m	Willi Sawall (Vic)	Collingwood	18 July	1981
2 hours	27 123,3 m	Willi Sawall (Vic)	Melbourne	24 May	1980

The best Australian performances for road walk distances are:

20,000	1 20:22.7	David Smith (Vic)	Melbourne	18 Dec	1983
30,000	2 08:00.4	Willi Sawall (Vic)	Melbourne	16 May	1982
50,000	3 46:34.0	Willi Sawall (Vic)	Adelaide	6 Apr	1980

WALKING—WOMEN

The best track performances by Australians include:

Metres	min sec	Name	Place	Date	
1500	6:10.8	Susan Cook [*née* Orr] (Vic) (b. 23 Apr 1958)	Canberra	21 Jan	1984
3000	12:56.5	Susan Cook (Vic)	Canberra	29 May	1982
5000	22:04.42	Susan Cook (Vic)	Melbourne	1 Apr	1984
10,000	45:47.0	Susan Cook (Vic)	Leicester	14 Sept	1983

WATER SKIING

World Championships

The only Australian to win a world title is Bruce Cockburn, who won the Tricks event at Copenhagen, Denmark in 1969. Australia have dominated the three world barefoot championships (inst. 1978), winning the team event each time. Brett Wing won the men's overall title three times.

Moomba Masters

The most overall titles at Moomba, Victoria is five by Mike Hazelwood (GB) in 1977–81.

Jumping

The record is held by Glenn Thurlow with 61.60 m *202 ft* at Moomba on 14 Mar 1983. The women's record is 41,20 m *135 ft 2 in* by Sue Lipplegoes (*née* Wright) at Kirtons Farm, Reading, England on 2 Aug 1961.

Brett Wing (NSW), champion barefoot water-skier. At the last World Championship in Acapulco, November 1982, Wing won the tricks event scoring a maximum 620 points in both rounds.

The architects of Australia's historic America's Cup victory. From left to right, the skipper John Bertrand, multi-millionaire Alan Bond who headed *Australia II's* syndicate, and Ben Lexcen, designer of the controversial keel.

WEIGHTLIFTING

Greatest single lift

Super heavyweight Dinko 'Dean' Lukin (SA) (b. 20 May 1960) (body weight 130 kg *287 lb*) clean and jerked 221 kg *487 lb* on 5 Oct 1982. Basilios 'Bill' Stellios (NSW) (b. 16 Apr 1959) lifted over 2½ times his body-weight with a jerk of 170 kg *374 lb* on 4 Oct 1980. He scaled 67,5 kg *148.75 lb*.

Most titles

Charles Henderson (NSW) won a record 12 national titles; 56 kg class 1951–60; 60 kg class 1962 and 1968.

WRESTLING

Most successful amateur

Richard Edward Garrard (b. 28 July 1910) won 516 of his 525 bouts in a career in which he won national titles from 1930 to 1955, three Commonwealth Games gold medals, lightweight 1934, 1938 and 1950 and an Olympic silver medal as a welter-weight in 1948, the best ever placing by an Australian.

Most titles

Arthur Tooby (Vic and later WA) won a record ten Australian Amateur titles at bantamweight between 1961 and 1971.

YACHTING

The first organised sailing races for prizes were at Hobart on 5 Jan 1827. The first Anniversary Regatta was at Sydney Harbour on 26 Jan 1828. The Victoria Yacht Club (now Royal Yacht Club of Victoria) was founded in 1856.

Olympic titles

Australia have won seven Olympic medals (three gold, one silver and three bronze) with the 1972 Regatta at Kiel, West Germany being the most successful with gold medals by David John Forbes (b. 26 Jan 1934) in the *Star Class* and John Bruce Cuneo (b. 16 June 1928) in the *Dragon*.

America's Cup

Australia ended the American superiority in the America's Cup in 1983 (see main section).

Sydney to Hobart

Australia's most famous race is the 630 nautical miles annual event from Sydney to Hobart which was instituted on 26 Dec 1945 with the smallest ever entry of nine yachts. The largest entry was 173 in 1983. Trygve Halvorsen and Magnus Halvorsen won the race in 1954 (*Solveig*), 1957 (*Anitra V*), 1963, 1964 and 1965 all in their *Freya*. The yacht with the best finishing record (before time corrections) is the *Morna*, later renamed *Kurrewa IV*, which was first home seven times from 1946 to 1960, but her best final placing was only third in 1946. The elapsed time course record is 2 days 14 hr 36 min 56 sec by John B. 'Jim' Kilroy's *Kialoa* (USA) in 1975.

AUSTRALIAN WEIGHTLIFTING RECORDS

National Senior Records as at 1 July 1983

Bodyweight Class	Lift	Lifted kg	Lifted lb	Name and State	Date
52 kg (*8 st 2 lb*)	Snatch	95	*209¼*	Nick Voukelatos (NSW)	24 Apr 1982
	Jerk	120	*264¼*	Nick Voukelatos (NSW)	24 Apr 1982
	Total	215	*473¾*	Nick Voukelatos (NSW)	24 Apr 1982
56 kg (*8 st 11 lb*)	Snatch	110	*242½*	Nick Voukelatos (NSW)	7 Apr 1984
	Jerk	137,5	*303*	George Vasiliades (NSW)	28 Aug 1972
	Total	242,5	*534½*	Nick Voukelatos (NSW)	7 Apr 1984
60 kg (*9 st 6 lb*)	Snatch	117,5	*259*	Daniel Mudd (NSW)	7 Apr 1984
	Jerk	142,5	*314*	George Vasiliades (NSW)	21 Oct 1973
	Total	252,5	*556½*	Daniel Mudd (NSW)	18 Mar 1984
67,5 kg (*10 st 8 lb*)	Snatch	138	*304*	Basilios Stellios (Vic)	10 Mar 1984
	Jerk	170,5	*375¾*	Basilios Stellios (Vic)	14 Aug 1982
	Total	305	*672¼*	Basilios Stellios (Vic)	10 Mar 1984
75 kg (*11 st 11 lb*)	Snatch	145	*319½*	Tony Pignone (NSW)	7 Apr 1984
	Jerk	177,5	*391¼*	Salvatore Castiglione (NSW)	9 Apr 1978
	Total	315	*694¼*	Tony Pignone (NSW)	18 Mar 1984
82,5 kg (*13 st*)	Snatch	152,5	*336*	Robert Kabbas (Vic)	25 Nov 1978
	Jerk	191	*421*	Robert Kabbas (Vic)	2 Dec 1978
	Total	337,5	*744*	Robert Kabbas (Vic)	25 Nov 1978
90 kg (*14 st 2 lb*)	Snatch	157,5	*347*	Nicolo Ciancio (Vic)	2 Aug 1975
	Jerk	200	*440¾*	Robert Kabbas (Vic)	29 May 1983
	Total	350	*771½*	Robert Kabbas (Vic)	29 May 1983
100 kg (*15 st 10 lb*)	Snatch	161	*354¾*	Gino Fratangelo (Tas)	16 May 1982
	Jerk	197,5	*435¼*	Gino Fratangelo (Tas)	27 May 1983
	Total	352,5	*777*	Gino Fratangelo (Tas)	16 May 1982
110 kg (*17 st 4 lb*)	Snatch	165	*363¾*	Donald Mitchell (NSW)	22 June 1980
	Jerk	207,5	*457¼*	Tony Hills (Tas)	7 Apr 1984
	Total	357,5	*788*	Joseph Kabalan (Vic)	29 May 1983
over 110 kg	Snatch	175	*385¾*	Dean Lukin (SA)	8 July 1984
(*17 st 4 lb*)	Jerk	235	*518*	Dean Lukin (SA)	8 July 1984
	Total	410	*903¾*	Dean Lukin (SA)	8 July 1984

AUSTRALIAN POWERLIFTING RECORDS

As ratified by the Australian Amateur Power Lifting Federation at 1 January 1984. All weights in kilograms

Class	Squat		Bench Press		Deadlift		Total	
MEN								
52 kg	157,5	J. Madsen (Qld) 1979	100	L. Skeen (Vic) 1980	212,5	L. Skeen 1980	452,5	L. Skeen 1980
56 kg	192,5	T. Dominguez (WA) 1980	117,5	L. Skeen (Vic) 1982	225	L. Skeen 1983	517,5	T. Zappia (SA) 1979
60 kg	232,5	G. Waszkiel (Qld) 1979	127,5	T. Zappia (WA) 1982	245	T. Koykka (WA) 1982	585	T. Koykka 1982
67,5 kg	277,5	C. Coliero (Vic) 1983	155	L. Andrews (WA) 1979	277	B. White (WA) 1962	675	C. Coliero (Vic) 1983
75 kg	292,5	G. Waszkiel (Qld) 1983	170	L. Andrews (WA) 1980	292,5	B. Waddell 1980	726	B. Waddell 1980
82,5 kg	312,5	B. Waddell (WA) 1983	185	C. Dean (NSW) 1982	302,5	B. Callaghan (WA) 1983	777,5	B. Waddell 1982
90 kg	320	J. Cappola (Vic) 1980	195	R. Sylvia (Vic) 1982	340	J. Cappola 1980	822,5	J. Cappola 1980
100 kg	310	J. MacGowan (WA) 1980	202,5	S. Blood (WA) 1983	330	J. MacGowan 1980	827,5	S. Blood (WA) 1983
110 kg	327,5	J. MacGowan (WA) 1981	217,5	M. Burnett (NT) 1982	340	J. MacGowan 1980	845	J. MacGowan 1981
125 kg	345	K. Falle (NSW) 1983	215	M. Barber 1981	330	N. Marriott (Vic) 1983	880	T. Lonsdale (WA) 1983
125 + kg	380	R. Rigby (Vic) 1983	230	A. Kapica (WA) 1979	357,5	R. Rigby (Vic) 1983	947,5	R. Rigby 1983
WOMEN								
44 kg	105	G. Botica (NSW) 1983	52,5	G. Botica (NSW) 1982	137,5	G. Botica 1983	295	G. Botica 1983
48 kg	125	S. Jordan (WA) 1980	60	S. Jordan 1980	145	S. Jordan 1980	330	S. Jordan 1980
52 kg	152,5	S. Jordan (WA) 1983	72,5	S. Jordan 1981	165	S. Jordan 1981	387,5	S. Jordan 1982
56 kg	140	A. Rountree (SA) 1982	75	L. Bird (SA) 1983	165,5	C. Evans (NSW) 1983	372,5	S. Jordan 1983
60 kg	157,5	H. Wittesch (SA) 1982	88	H. Wittesch 1982	167,5	H. Wittesch 1982	410	H. Wittesch 1982
67,5 kg	177,5	H. Wittesch (SA) 1983	95	H. Wittesch 1983	190	L. Miller (WA) 1983	455	L. Miller 1983
75 kg	212,5	B. Francis (Vic) 1981	140	B. Francis 1981	212,5	L. Miller 1983	550	B. Francis 1982
82,5 kg	217,5	B. Francis (Vic) 1983	150	B. Francis 1981	215	B. Francis 1983	577,5	B. Francis 1983
90 kg	212,5	G. Martin (Vic) 1982	122,5	G. Martin 1982	210	G. Martin 1982	542,5	G. Martin 1982
90 + kg	222,5	G. Martin (Vic) 1982	130	G. Martin 1982	215	G. Martin 1982	567,5	G. Martin 1982

CHAPTER 1 Human Being

Most Disparate Couple (p. 6) Nigel Wilks (6 ft 6 in *200 cm*) of Kingston upon Hull, England married Beverly Russell (4 ft *118,5 cm*) 30 June 1984.

Oldest Dwarf (p. 7) Miss Bokoyni reached her 105th birthday on 6 Apr 1984

Heaviest Living Human (p. 8) Pernitsch was measured in Gratkorn, near Graz and found to have a girth of 79 in *200,6 cm* in July 1984. A tattoo on his left arm proclaims 'Nobody is Perfect.'

Champion Irish Mother (p. 12) Mrs Catherine Scott (b. 4 July 1914) bore an authenticated total of 24 children.

Most voracious fire eater (p. 19) Gerry Mawdsley achieved 10,150 extinctions in 2 hours at Lostock, Greater Manchester on 4 Aug 1984.

Human Computer (p. 16) Creighton Carvello at the Speedway Hotel, Middlesbrough on 12 June 1984 memorized the correct sequence of 5 packs of cards on a single sighting with only 4 errors including a straight all correct run of 173 cards.

Motionlessness (p. 19) Willie Nugent, 36, stood motionless for charity for 12 hr 48 mins outside Tower Hill Hospital, Armagh, Northern Ireland on 20 June 1984.

Most Operations (p. 21) In July 1984 Joseph Ascough (b. 1935) of Nottingham faced an operation for the removal of pappillomas from his wind pipe which is believed to be his 324th since 1936.

Heart Transplant (p. 21) The youngest patient to undergo the operation was Hollie Roffey (b 20 July 1984) aged 10 days in a 5½ hour operation by Mr Magdi Yacoub at the National Heart Hospital, London on 30 July. The baby lived for 18 days after the operation but died aged 28 days on 17 August.

CHAPTER 2 Living World

Horse Tallest (p. 30) Britain's tallest living horse is the 19.1½ hand Shire gelding 'Goliath' (foaled 1977) owned by Young & Company's Brewery of Wandsworth, London.

Rabbit Longevity (p. 34) 18 yr 328 days by 'Flopsy' owned by Mrs L B Walker of Longford, Tasmania, caught on 6 Aug 1964 and died 29 June 1983.

Top Show Dog (p. 35) The Scottish Terrier 'Ch. Braeburn's Close Encounter' (whelped 22 Oct 1978) owned by Sonnie and Alan Novick of Plantation Acres, Florida, USA achieved her 141st Best-in-Show on 30 June 1984.

Rarest British Butterfly (p. 42) Large Blues were re-introduced from continental stocks in the 'West Country' in June 1984.

Locust Swarms (p. 42) In 1958 in the Somali Republic a swarm, actually measured, covered 400 miles² *1000 km²* and was estimated to contain *c* 60,000 million locusts which devoured *c.* 120 000 tons of biomass daily.

Worm Charming (p. 43) The record for attracting (by vibrations) earthworms to the surface of a 9 square metre plot in 30 minutes is 511 by Tom Shufflebotham in 1980 at Willaston CP School, Northwich, Cheshire

CHAPTER 3 Natural World

Earthquakes (p. 55) An earthquake measuring between 5 and 5.5 on the Richter Scale, with an epicentre in North Wales, struck at 8.02 am on 19 July 1984. There were two injured in Avon and Somerset and the shock dislocated traffic lights in Dublin.

Rainfall Most Intense (p. 58) Wisbech: for 28 June 1970 read 27 June.

CHAPTER 4 Universe and Space

Largest Object in the Universe (p. 72) A bent filament of galaxies in the constellations Pisces and Cetus announced by Burns and Batuski of the University of New Mexico in May 1984 measures 730 million light years in length.

First Feminine Space Walk (p. 74) Svetlana Savitskaya performed 3 hr 35 mins of EVA (extra vehicular activity) cutting, welding and spraying the USSR Salyut 7 space station on 25 July 1984.

CHAPTER 5 Scientific World

Newest Element (p. 75) With the discovery of Element 108 or anniloctium (Uno) by G Munzenberg *et al* (West Germany) in April 1984, there are now 109 elements.

Newest Particle (p. 75–76) A sub-atomic particle named Zeta was announced from West Germany on 2 Aug 1984.

Most Expensive Wine (p. 76) A jeroboam (equivalent to 6 bottles of Bordeaux) of Mouton Rothschild, 1870, was bought for resale by Bill Burford of Dallas, Texas, from Whitwham Wines, Altrincham for £26,500 on 16 July 1984.

Shortest Pulse of Light (p. 81) Massachusetts Institute of Technology (MIT) reported on 1 May 1984 that Erich P Ippen and coworkers had achieved a pulse of 8 wavelengths lasting 15 femtoseconds (15×10^{-15}s).

Lowest Equilibrium Temperature (p. 81) In June 1984 Prof. Lounasmaa (b. 1930) attained 30 namokelvins (3×10^{-8}K) above absolute zero at Espoo, Finland.

Most expensive bottle of wine

Microscope, Most Powerful (p. 82) Hitachi of Tokyo, Japan, announced on 27 June 1984 an electron microscope capable of resolving a single hydrogen atom 1×10^{-8} cm in diameter.

CHAPTER 6 Arts and Entertainments

Most Expensive Painting (p. 84) £7,470,500 (incl. V.A.T.) for Turner's *Seascape: Folkestone* from the estate of Lord Clark (1903–1983), bid by London dealer Charles Leggatt of Leggatt Bros at Sotheby's on 5 July 1984. It had been bought in 1951 for about £5,000.

Most Expensive Drawing (p. 85) £3,546,000 for Raphael's study of an apostle's head and hand for the Transfiguration in the Vatican for the Duke of Devonshire. The bid was believed to be by Mrs Seward Johnson (US) at Christies on 3 July 1984.

Longest Mural (p. 85) A mural 864 ft 11 in *263,6 m* long and 14 ft 8 in *4,47 m* high was painted on the walls of Pudu Prison, Kuala Lumpur, Malaysia, by 4 prisoners from 3 Feb 1983 to 11 June 1984.

Shortest Letter to *The Times* (p. 93) In a correspondence on the correct form of recording a plurality of academic doctorates *The Times* on 30 July 1984 published a letter from R. S. Cookson of London NW11 comprising the single abbreviated symbol 'Dr²?' in the interrogative. David Green's 103rd letter in *The Times* appeared on 3 Aug 1984.

Longest Play (p. 104) 'The Acting Life' requiring 19 hours 15 mins was staged in the Tom Mann Theatre, Sydney, Australia, on 17–18 Mar 1984 by a cast of 10. With intervals the production totalled 21 hours.

above: **Richard Parkhouse, all-Counties Motorcyclist** (*see text right*)
below: **One Motorcycle—35 Policemen** (*see text right*)

Highest Box Office (p. 107) *Indiana Jones and the Temple of Doom* by George Lucas and Steven Spielberg, starring Harrison Ford, broke all records for one day with $9.3 million on 27 May 1984 and $42.3 for its first 6 days in 1,685 theatres.

Top Selling Video (p. 110) Michael Jackson's 'The Making of Thriller' has been the No. 1 of all-time. In July 1984 it became the first video to surpass 100,000 sales in Britain.

CHAPTER 7 World's Structures

Canal Longest (p. 122) Volga-Baltic Canal for *2300 km* read *2975 km.*

CHAPTER 8 Mechanical World

Yacht (p. 133) The refit of the £20 million 470 foot *143,2 m* the Saudi Arabian Royal yacht *Abdul Aziz* was completed on 22 June 1984 at Vospers Yard, Southampton at a cost of £9 million.

Largest Sail Area (p. 134) H.M.Ss *Minotaur* (1863) and *Agincourt* (1865) with 5 masts and stunsails carried 32,377 yards^2 of canvas—the most of any warship.

Coaching (p. 135) John Parker (b. July 1939) drove a mail coach and four 136 miles *218,8 km* from Bristol to London in 17 hr 30 mins on 1–2 Aug 1984. Norwich Union's six teams of greys were changed 11 times, including a change by a team of 12 girl ostlers at Chiswick Green, in a record 41 seconds. An estimated 1 million people lined the route.

Most Durable Car (p. 136) R. L. Bender's car reached 1,021,041 miles *1643 206 km* on 9 June 1984. He has been driving it since 1958.

Fastest Production Car (p. 136) The Porsche 911 Turbo (£36,000) driven by John Morrison won a 'World's Fastest Car' contest at North Weald, Essex, on 30 June 1984 over the standing kilometre in 23.98 sec—terminal speed 135 mph *217 rm/h* beating a Lamborghini Countach LP 500, Aston Martin Vantage and a Aston Martin V8 Vantage.

Fuel Economy (p. 136) Ford's 15 cc UFO (Ultimate Fuel Optimiser) piloted by Dianne Harrwell recorded 3,803 mpg *1346 km/litre* at Silverstone, Northants on 4 July 1984.

Round Britain Driving (p. 137) A Marlow Round Table (No. 575) team of Trevor Bownass, Robert Clark, Richard Scott, with photographer Richard Thomson, covered 3644 miles *5864 km* in 65 hr 14 min to average 55.86 mph *89,89 km/h* in a Saab 900 on 17–20 May 1984.

Youngest Drivers (p. 138) Steve Brewster of Redcar, Cleveland passed the advanced test, 5 days after his standard test, on 30 July 1984 aged 17 years 10 days.

Heaviest Load (p. 140) On 14–15 July 1984 John Brown Engineers & Contractors BV moved the Conoco Kotter Field production deck with a roll out weight of 3805 tonnes for the Continental Netherlands Oil Company of Leidsenhage, Netherlands.

Round Britain (p. 141) Richard Parkhouse of Gwynedd covered all 62 mainland counties of Great Britain by motor cycle (Suzuki 6SX 750 EFE) on a 1634 mile *2629 km* route on 11–12 June 1984 in 28 hours 52 mins, averaging 56.6 mph *91,0 km/h.*

Most on one Motor Cycle (p. 141) At Montlery autodrome Paris, on 25 June 1984, 32 gendarmes mounted a single Harley Davidson. Unknown to them 35 members of the Brisbane Police Traffic Branch travelled 506 metres *553 yards* at 25 km/h *15,5 mph* at Surfer's Paradise, Queensland, Australia, on a Yamaha 1100 cc on 22 June 1984.

Motor Cycling (p. 141) Terry McGauran motor-cycled up the 1760 steps of the CN Tower, Toronto, Canada, on 26 June 1984.

Penny-Farthing Record (p. 142) G. P. Mills (Anfield BC) rode this course in 5 days 1 hr 45 min on a 53 inch Humber on 4–10 July 1886.

Underwater Cycling (p. 142) A team of 32 in 72 underwater hours achieved 87.81 miles *141,322 km* in Norvik, Norway on 28–31 Mar 1984.

Calling All Stations (p. 144) Colin M. Mulvany and Seth N. Vafiadis of London W12, visited every British Rail station (2,378) embracing also the Tyne and Wear, Strathclyde and London Underground systems (333 stations) for charity in 31 days 5 hr 8 min 58 sec over 15,527⅔ miles *24 989 km* to average 38.05 mph *61,2 km/h* on 4 June–5 July 1984.

Round Britain Flying (p. 151) E. K. Coventry (pilot) and D. Bullen (navigator) made full stop landings in a Piper Arrow in all England's 45 counties between dawn and dusk on 24 July 1984.

CHAPTER 9 *Business World*

Greatest Loss (p. 159) YPF excelled itself with an all-time record loss in 1983 of $4,643,995,000.

Greatest Barter Deal (p. 159) The greatest barter deal in trading history was 36 millon barrels of oil valued at £900 million in exchange for 10 Boeing 747's for the Royal Saudi Airline in July 1984.

Fine Art Auction Largest (p. 160) The record for any fine art auction in the United Kingdom was set by the Chatsworth House sale of £21,179,800 at Christie's on 3 July 1984.

Longest Wait for a Sale (p. 161) Philip Illsley camped in Oxford Street, London, outside Selfridge's from 4.40 p.m. on 13 Dec 1983 until admitted as 1st in the queue 352 hours 20 mins later at 9 a.m. on 28 Dec 1983.

Longest Cracker (p. 166) The longest functional cracker yet made was one 60 ft *18,28 m* long and 10 ft *3,04 m* in diameter made by Marks & Sparks Ltd for Christmas visitors to Pier One, Sydney, Australia, on 23 Dec 1983.

Longest Cracker (*see left*)

Earliest Jig Saw (p. 169) Spilsbury's 'Europe Divided into its Kingdoms' of 1766 was sold at Sotheby's, London on 27 July 1974 for £1,650.

Barley Crop Yield (p. 172) 93.7 cwt/acre *11,762 kg/ha* of Gerbel Winter set by Alex Brewster & Sons in 1984 on 20.48 acres *8,29 ha* at Kirknewton, Midlothian, Scotland.

CHAPTER 10 *Human Achievements*

Most Married Man (p. 179) Wife Number 24 (two previous wives were re-married) Cristine Sue Camacho was divorced on 25 July 1984 by Glynn Wolfe in his 26th divorce.

Auctioneering (p. 183) Lars 'Tusen Ting' Hansson auctioned solo for 38 hours 6 mins at Hillerstorp, Sweden on 28–30 Apr 1984.

Balancing on one Foot (p. 183) V. S. Kumar (Vivekanandan Selva Kumar Anandan) died attempting to swim the English Channel on 6 Aug 1984.

Bed of Nails (p. 183) for Andrew read Andrews—273 hr 5 mins.

Barrow Pushing (p. 183) Ben Read, 51, at Park Gate, Fareham, Hampshire, pushed a load of 3,415 lb *1549 kg* of bricks in a 308 lb *139,7 kg* barrow over 131 ft 5 in *40 m* on 24 Mar 1984.

Champagne Fountain (p. 184) The largest pyramid was one of 3,654 glasses, filled by Dan Westerdahl and his team with 1000 litres of champagne, in Stockholm on 28 May 1984.

Coin Balancing (p. 185) Bruce McConachy raised the record to 200 Canadian 25-cent coins, balanced on a vertical freestanding commemorative $10.00 coin, at West Vancouver, Canada on 8 Feb 1984.

Boomerang Throwing (p. 184) Consecutive Catching 653 by Bob Croll (Victoria) at Alburg N.S.W. on 7 Apr 1984. Flight Duration (with catch) 28.9 sec. by Bob Burwell

(Queensland) at Alburg N.S.W. on 7 Apr 1984. Accuracy 42 ex 50 by Brian Thomas (N.S.W.) at Valley Heights, N.S.W. on 26 Mar 1983.

Breathing Apparatus Marathon (p. 184) Firemen Paul Greenwood, Steve Perks, Nick Smith and Pete Cresswell from Chertsey Fire Station, Surrey, wore self-contained breathing apparatus continuously for 342 hr 10 min on 4–18 Aug 1984.

Debating (p. 185) University College Dublin Law Society debated the motion "That This House Would Adjourn" for 108 hr 26 min on 13–17 Feb 1984. No one spoke more than once and 219 participated.

Roller Limbo (p. 185) 5¼ ins *13,33 cm* by Tracey O'Callaghan, 9, at Bexley North, N.S.W., Australia on 2 June 1984.

Hair-dressing (p. 187) Hugo Vanpe raised the record to 366 hours in Kensington, South Africa, on 8–23 June 1984.

Hod Carrying (p. 188) Jim Ford achieved 355 lb *161 kg* at Hever Castle, Kent, on 28 June 1984 in the International Guinness TV Show presented by David Frost.

House of Cards (p. 188) Anthony de Bruxelles achieved 62 storeys in Weinheim, West Germany, on 4–6 May 1984.

Kiss of Life (p. 189) Five members of the St John's Ambulance of Casuarina, in Darwin, Northern Territory, Australia, inflated a dummy with 270,516 inflations for 295 hours on 10–23 Dec 1983. Four students (Fiona Thompson, Paul Lethebee, Katherine Dyke and Keith Hadman) from Pinderfields College, Wakefield, W. Yorkshire, sustained CPR (Cardio pulmonary resuscitation) for 55 hours on 5–7 July 1984.

Meteorological Balloon Blowing (p. 190) Nick Mason attained the stipulated diameter in 70 mins 2 secs at Heaton Moor RFC, Cheshire on 14 July 1984.

Pole-Squatting (p. 190) Reg Morris stayed in a barrel for 33 days 25 mins atop a 30 ft

9,14 m steel pole outside The Spring College, Shelfield, West Midlands, on 29 May–1 July 1984.

Parachuting (p. 191) The longest ever 'base' jump was made by Carl Ronald and Jean Katherine Campbell Boenische on 4 July 1984 from the 5784 ft *1763 m* high vertical cliff face of the Trollveggan Spire, Romsdal, western Norway. Carl was killed 3 days later. **Most Jumps in 24 hours** (p. 191) Alan Jones, 37 (former Capt. USMC) with 236 at Issaquah, Washington, USA on 13–14 July 1984.

Skipping (p. 193) Most Doubles with Cross 1,664 by Sean Birch at Tralee, Co. Kerry, Ireland on 27 Apr 1984.

Spinning (p. 193) Roger Wood spun by hand a brass top at NESCUT, Epsom, Surrey on 25 May 1984 for 36 mins 52 sec.

Stair Climbing (p. 193) A vertical mile record of 2 hr 1 min 25 sec was set by Dale Neil, 22, of Toronto, Canada in the Peachtree Plaza Hotel, Atlanta, Georgia, USA on 9 Mar 1984.

Switchback Riding (p. 194) M. M. Daniel Gladu and Normand St-Pierre rode Le Cyclone in Parc Belmont, Montreal for 503 hours on 18 July–10 Aug 1983.

Highest Fees (p. 197) The International Newsletter edited by Harry D. Schultz is now sold for $50 or £38 per copy.

Gluttony Records—Set by Peter Dowdeswell (p. 198) **Beer** 3½ pints Yard of Ale 6.20 sec at The Britannia, Halesowen St. Dudley, on 26 June 1984. **Cockles** 2 pints *113,5 centilitres* in 60.8 sec (by Tony Dowdeswell) at Kilmarnock Karnival, Ayrshire, on 1 June 1984. **Eggs** (*Soft Boiled*) 38 in 75 sec by Peter Dowdeswell at Kilmarnock Karnival, on 28 May 1984. (*Raw Eggs*) 13 in a single gulp (1.0 sec) by Peter Dowdeswell at Kilmarnock Karnival, on 16 May 1984. **Hamburgers** 21 (3½ oz) in 9 mins 42 sec in Yardley, Birmingham on 30 June 1984. **Jelly** 20 fluid oz in 13.11 sec at Stoke Mandeville, Buckinghamshire on 27 June 1984. **Snails** 1 kg (*35.27 oz*) in 3 m 45.78 sec at Hever Castle, Kent on 27 June 1984.

CHAPTER 11 Human World

Greatest Damages (p. 218) On 15 June 1984 Mrs David Foot, 40, received £424,648 in damages for the loss of her husband, a US airline pilot in a road accident near Symington, Strathclyde in April 1980. The family received £666,468 in all from Petrofina UK and SMT Sales and Services.

Last Hangings (p. 223) The subject of the last public hanging in Scotland was the murderer Robert Smith who was hanged outside Dumfries Jail in May 1868.

Longest and Most Valuable Line of Coins (p. 227) 15,6 km *9,69 miles* of pfennig pieces (worth DM 74,205.80) organised by soldiers of 21 Engineer Regt. in the town centre of Nienberg/Weser, West Germany, on 23–24 Sept 1983.

Largest Barbecue (p. 228) At the Sertoma Club Barbecue, New Port Richey, Florida, USA 16,143 lb *7322 kg* of beef was sold on 24 Mar 1984.

Largest Omlette (p. 229) Two thousand people ate a 25,000 egg omlette cooked on a pan measuring 10 × 5 m *32 ft 9⅜ in × 16 ft 4¾ in* at Beersel, Belgium on 30 June 1984.

Smörgåsbord Largest (p. 229) On 31 May 1984 in Kungsgaten, Stockholm a *smör-*(butter)-*gås*(goose)-*bord*(table) 1,208 ft *368,22 m* long was set up for 35,000 people.

Strawberry Bowl (p. 229) A 'bowl' of an estimated 18,000 strawberries weighing 481 lb *218 kg* was weighed at Great Ormond Street Hospital, London on 28 June 1984.

CHAPTER 12 Sports, Games and Pastimes

Endurance Marathons (p. 240) **Chess** 200 hrs; Roger Long and Gordon Croft at Dingles, Bristol, 11–19 May 1984. **Darts** 127 hrs 9 mins; Trevor Blair and David Howe at the Bingham Leisure Centre, Notts, 6–11 Aug 1984. **Horsemanship** 100 hrs 10 min; Paulette Stoudt rode at all paces (including jumping) at Shartlesville, Penn, USA, 13–17 June 1984. **Snooker** 200 hrs 7 min; Barry Turner and Chris Parker, and Pete Gardner and Sean Smith at Bournemouth, 14–22 July 1984. **Softball** (*slowpitch*) 95 hrs by two teams from the crew of USS Willamette (A0180) at US Naval Station, Pearl Harbor, Hawaii, 26–30 Apr 1984.

Aerobatics—World Championships (p. 242) The most successful in the women's competition has been Betty Stewart (USA) who has won twice, 1980 and 1982.

Billiards and Snooker *Pool* (p. 247) Stephen Sanders potted 88 consecutive balls under the rules of 14–1 at New Elm Park, Essex on 13 May 1984. *Speed Pool:* Ross McInnes broke 40 secs in practice before setting a T.V. record of 42.85 sec at Hever Castle, Kent on 27 June 1984.

Canoeing *Downstream Canoeing, River Rhine* (p. 253) 1140 kms *708 miles* Chur to Willemstad in 12 days 8½ hrs by David Montgomery.

Cricket (p. 259) With the completion of the England v West Indies Test series 1984: Clive Lloyd's Test captaincies number 69, and Ian Botham's Test career record is 4153 runs and 305 wickets in 72 matches. He achieved his 300th wicket in his 72nd Test.

Cycling *Most World Titles* (p. 264) Amateur Pursuit—also 3 Detlef Macha (GDR) (b. 13 Dec 1958), 1978, 1981–82.

Gambling (p. 281) Venero Pagano won $20 million on New York State's Lotto jackpot from a $5 bet on 26 July 1984. He would be paid about $952,000 a year for 21 years, minus taxes.

Golf (p. 285) Kathy Whitworth won her 85th LPGA tournament on 22 July 1984.

Motor Racing (p. 302) Le Mans race lap record 3 min 28.9 sec Bob Wollek (av. speed 145.16 mph *234,82 km/h*) in a Lancia C2-84 in 1984.

Mountaineering *Fell Running, Three Peaks* (p. 305) A team of 3 from the Greater Manchester Police Tactical Aid Group covered the distance in 8 hrs 22 min, being transported between the peaks by helicopter. Their running time was 5 hrs 4 min.

Parascending *Distance* Andrew Wakelin flew a measured distance in free flight after release of 2.19 miles *3,52 kms* in Artesia, New Mexico on 9 July 1984. *Duration* Lee Clements sustained free flight for 16 min 1 sec on a Harley Paramount 11 at RAF Elvington, England. *Accuracy* Nigel Horder scored four successive dead centres on 22 May 1983 at the Dutch Open, Flevhof, Holland.

Powerboating (p. 308) *Highest race speed*: Offshore—103.29 mph *166,229 km/h* Tony Garcia (USA) at Key West, Florida, USA in November 1983.

Rowing (p. 310)—*24 Hrs.* The greatest distance rowed in 24 hrs by a crew of eight is 130 miles *209 kms* by members of the Renmark Rowing Club, South Australia, on 20–1 Apr 1984.

Skiing (p. 312) *Highest speed—downhill*. John Clark set a British record of 121.05 mph *194,80 km/h* at Les Arcs, France on 18 Apr 1984.

Swimming (p. 315) *24 Hr Underwater* Paul Cryne swam 44.79 miles *72,08 kms* in a 24 hr period at Doha, Qatar on 26–7 July 1984 using sub-aqua equipment. He was swimming underwater for 89.1% of the time.

Tennis *Longest Game* (p. 320) 52 mins (9 deuces) between Nöelle Van Lottum and Sandra Begijn in the semi-finals of the under 13 Dutch National Indoor Championships in Ede, Gederland, on 12 Feb 1984. Dorothy Cheney's (p. 321) total of US titles is now 141.

Tennis Serve (p. 320) Steve Denton (Australia) (b. 5 Sept 1956) timed at 138 mph *222 km/h* at Beaver Creek, Colorado, USA on 29 July 1984.

Track and Field Athletics—Mass Relay Records (p. 327) The greatest distance covered in 24 hrs is 419,15 kms *260.45 miles* by a team of 10 from Capricornia Institute of Advanced Education, Queensland, Australia on 28–9 April 1984. *Correction* (p. 328) 110 m hurdles—spelling—Holtom.

Track and Field Records World women's discus (p. 327) 73,36 m *240 ft 8 in* Irina Meszynski (GDR) at Prague on 17 Aug 1984; British women's 1 mile (p. 328) 4:28.07 Wendy Sly at London (Crystal Palace) on 18 Aug 1984.

Trampolining (p. 330) *Somersaults* Richard Cobbing of Gateshead Metro Trampoline Club performed 1610 consecutive somersaults at Gateshead, Tyne and Wear, on 22 July 1984.

Yachting *Board Sailing* (p. 337) The longest wind surf ever made was by Timothy John Batstone (b. 22 Apr 1959) in circumnavigating 1770 miles *2849 kms* round Great Britain on 2 May–10 July 1984. He did 60.8 miles *97,8 kms* in a single stretch, made 140 sail changes and had zero falls on eight days. The longest 'snake' of boardsails was set by 51 windsurfers in tandem across Pembroke Bay, Guernsey on 22 July 1984.

An asterisk indicates a further reference in the Stop Press

GO FROM ONE EXTREME TO THE OTHER.

You've read the book. Now visit the show: The Guinness World of Records.

This extraordinary exhibition brings the pages of this all-time best-selling book to life.

It's a fascinating 3-dimensional presentation of facts, feats and fun for all the family.

You can rub shoulders with the world's tallest man (well almost) and marvel at a whole world of amazing achievement and fantastic phenomena.

Set in the heart of London, at the glittering new Trocadero Centre close to Piccadilly Circus, it's easy to get to by bus or tube.

So, visit us soon and we'll take you to extremes.

The Guinness World of Records. The fascinating exhibiton that goes to extremes.

THE GUINNESS WORLD OF RECORDS, THE TROCADERO, PICCADILLY CIRCUS, LONDON, ENGLAND.

Guinness Exhibitions are already established in:
USA New York City; Myrtle Beach, South Carolina; Gatlinburg and Nashville, Tennessee; San Francisco, California.
CANADA Niagara Falls, Ontario; SWEDEN Stockholm; JAPAN Mount Fuji.